Congressional
Investigations and Oversight

Congressional Investigations and Oversight

Case Studies and Analysis

SECOND EDITION

Lance Cole

PROFESSOR OF LAW,
PENN STATE DICKINSON SCHOOL OF LAW

Stanley M. Brand

DISTINGUISHED FELLOW IN LAW AND GOVERNMENT,
PENN STATE DICKINSON SCHOOL OF LAW
PRINCIPAL, BRANDWOODWARD LAW

Michael R. Dimino

PROFESSOR OF LAW,
WIDENER UNIVERSITY COMMONWEALTH LAW SCHOOL

CAROLINA ACADEMIC PRESS

Durham, North Carolina

Library of Congress Cataloging-in-Publication Data

Names: Cole, Lance (Law teacher), author. | Brand, Stanley M., author. |
  Dimino, Michael, author.
Title: Congressional investigations and oversight : case studies and
  analysis / Lance Cole, Stanley M. Brand, Michael R. Dimino, Sr.
Description: Second edition. | Durham, North Carolina : Carolina Academic
  Press, LLC, [2023] | Includes bibliographical references and index.
Identifiers: LCCN 2023013786 | ISBN 9781531023454 (paperback) | ISBN
  9781531023461 (ebook)
Subjects: LCSH: Governmental investigations--United States. | Legislative
  oversight--United States.
Classification: LCC KF4942 .C65 2023 | DDC 342.73/052--dc23/eng/20230410
LC record available at https://lccn.loc.gov/2023013786

Carolina Academic Press
700 Kent Street
Durham, NC 27701
(919) 489-7486
www.cap-press.com

Printed in the United States of America

For my wife Kim and daughter Carina, and for my grandmother,
Grace Seymour Cole, who taught me to love books and learning.

l.c.

Dedicated to my dear wife and partner, Ellen—
and the wisest counsel I've ever had.

s.m.b.

For Jennifer, my favorite person. And for Richard Nixon—
congressional investigator and target of congressional investigation.

m.r.d.

Contents

Table of Cases

Principal cases shown in **bold**.

Preface

This Book addresses a topic that is not included, or is addressed only in passing, in the typical law school curriculum, and that also does not receive substantial attention in many graduate school government and political science programs. This relative lack of academic attention notwithstanding, the congressional investigative and oversight process has played a vital role in our national history and has helped shape our legal and political systems. McCarthyism, Watergate, and Iran-Contra—to name just three examples—are chapters in our national history that are simply too important to let slip between the cracks separating the various academic fields. This Book seeks to bridge the gaps between the academic disciplines by providing an up-to-date, concise, and accessible analysis of the most important congressional investigations of the past century. We believe that students of law, government, and political science all will benefit from a deeper understanding of the events and legal issues that are analyzed in this Book.

A challenge in writing about congressional investigations and oversight is that the topic defies easy categorization. The subject matter can perhaps best be described as one part law, one part history, and one part politics. In writing this Book, however, we found the breadth and variety of the subject matter to be an advantage so long as we resisted any temptation to narrow our analytical perspective. Any effort to view the congressional investigative and oversight process through the lens of a single discipline—whether law, history, or government and political science—inevitably distorts the analysis and fails to capture the full depth of the issues presented. The case studies that are included in this Book take a more holistic approach, and seek to interweave law, history, and politics to paint an accurate and complete picture of these fascinating events. Students of all disciplines should find this Book both useful in attaining a deeper understanding of their own field and helpful in appreciating important intersections and overlaps with other fields of study.

A final reason to study the events that are included in this Book is for practicing lawyers, government officials, and private citizens who are caught up in the congressional investigative and oversight process to learn from history and avoid the mistakes of the past. Many of the tactical errors and missed opportunities that are described in this Book, from Alger Hiss's ill-advised attempt to clear his name by voluntarily appearing before the House Committee on Un-American Activities to the Iran-Contra Committee's failure to foresee the consequences of granting immunity to Oliver North and John Poindexter, provide valuable lessons for legislators and their staffs, attorneys representing clients in congressional investigations, and government officials or private citizens who may come under congressional scrutiny. We hope this Book will both contribute to the academic literature and provide a useful resource for those on the front lines in the real world of law, government, and politics.

Congressional
Investigations and Oversight

Chapter One

Background and History

Congressional Investigations at the Beginning of the Twentieth Century—Broad Investigative Powers

> *The taint of oil and corruption was eventually to stain both parties, causing at least three cabinet-level resignations, inspiring several Supreme Court decisions, and making the name Teapot Dome synonymous with the seamy side of American politics. This scandal also caused political thinkers, constitutional theorists, and government officials to discuss the proper role of Congress in the investigatory procedure.*
>
> Professor Hasia Diner, 1975

Introduction

This book is about the uniquely American institution known as the congressional investigation. Congressional investigations occupy a special place in our collective national experience. In important respects they serve as the "pressure valve" and response mechanism for our national crises and political scandals. The Teapot Dome scandal early in the twentieth century, the stock market crash of 1929, the Cold War communist threat, Watergate and the Nixon resignation, the Iran-Contra scandal, Whitewater and the Clinton impeachment, the 9/11 terrorist attacks, and the recent insurrection at the U.S. Capitol on January 6, 2021, all have, to varying degrees, been exposed and defined through congressional investigations.

The twentieth century was the era of congressional investigations. This is not to say that the nineteenth century did not witness some notable investigative forays by Congress, in terms of both intense public attention and important public policy accomplishments. For example, after the Civil War, the Joint Committee on Reconstruction held hearings that culminated with the passage of the Fourteenth Amendment. During the Grant administration, the congressional investigation of the Credit Mobilier scandal exposed efforts to bribe members of Congress and ended the political career of President Ulysses S. Grant's first Vice President and former Speaker of the House of Representatives Schuyler Colfax. Despite the importance of these and other historically significant nineteenth century congressional investigations, it was not until the Senate's Teapot Dome investigation of 1923 and 1924 that the institution of the congressional investigation, supported by the twentieth century's increasingly pervasive and technologically advanced national news media, attained its present status in our national consciousness.

The Teapot Dome investigation is also distinguished from its nineteenth century predecessors by its generation of two landmark Supreme Court cases that defined the scope of the congressional investigative power for almost half a century thereafter and laid the foundation for the great investigative forays and legislative accomplishments of the New Deal era. For that reason alone, it is accurate to say that, from a legal perspective at least, the modern era of congressional investigations begins with Teapot Dome.

The Teapot Dome Scandal

The Teapot Dome scandal began with reports that the administration of President Warren G. Harding was secretly selling off oil leases for federal naval oil reserve lands in California and Wyoming. The Wyoming reserve was known as "Teapot Dome" because of the distinctive teapot-like shape of a rock formation on the land. President Harding's Interior Secretary was former New Mexico Senator Albert B. Fall. Prior to his appointment by Harding to head the Interior Department, Fall had established a record in the Senate of opposing conservationists' efforts to preserve natural resources and strongly supporting private exploitation of public lands in the West.

In 1921, just a few months into the Harding administration, Secretary Fall arranged to have control of the naval oil reserves transferred to the Interior Department from the Department of the Navy and then promptly presided over the granting of drilling leases on the reserve properties. Two California reserves were leased to companies controlled by oil magnate Edward L. Doheny. Doheny had amassed great wealth in the oil business and also had a long association with Secretary Fall dating back to Fall's early days as a New Mexico lawyer, miner, and prospector. Doheny later testified that he expected the California leases to generate a profit of some $100 million. The Senate's investigation of the leases also revealed that, at the same time negotiations were underway for the first California lease, Fall had received $100,000 in cash from Doheny. When the payment was revealed during the Senate hearings, Fall and Doheny claimed the $100,000 was a loan and had no connection to the contemporaneous lease of the naval reserves. Fall had previously resigned as Interior Secretary (to go to work for Doheny) and subsequently was convicted of accepting a bribe from Doheny based upon acceptance of the $100,000 payment. Fall was the first presidential cabinet member in U.S. history to be convicted of a felony committed while in office.

In addition to investigating the circumstances of Interior Secretary Fall's leases of the naval oil reserves, the Senate was investigating the conduct of the Harding Justice Department under Attorney General Harry Daugherty. Daugherty was under attack both for failing to investigate and prosecute the naval oil lease cases and for other alleged serious improprieties at the Justice Department. As part of that investigation, the Senate committee that was investigating the Justice Department subpoenaed Attorney General Daugherty's brother, Ohio banker Mally Daugherty. Mally Daugherty refused to comply with the Senate subpoena, and the case eventually reached the Supreme Court:

McGrain v. Daugherty

273 U.S. 135 (1927)

Mr. Justice Van Devanter delivered the opinion of the court.

This is an appeal from the final order in a proceeding in *habeas corpus* discharging a recusant witness held in custody under process of attachment issued from the United States Senate in the course of an investigation which it was making of the administration of the Department of Justice. A full statement of the case is necessary.

The Department of Justice is one of the great executive departments established by congressional enactment and has charge, among other things, of the initiation and prosecution of all suits, civil and criminal, which may be brought in the right and name of the United States to compel obedience or punish disobedience to its laws, to recover property obtained from it by unlawful or fraudulent means, or to safeguard its rights in other respects; and also of the assertion and protection of its interests when it or its officers are sued by others. The Attorney General is the head of the department, and its functions are all to be exercised under his supervision and direction.

Harry M. Daugherty became the Attorney General March 5, 1921, and held that office until March 28, 1924, when he resigned. Late in that period various charges of misfeasance and nonfeasance in the Department of Justice after he became its supervising head were brought to the attention of the Senate by individual senators and made the basis of an insistent demand that the Department be investigated to the end that the practices and deficiencies which, according to the charges, were operating to prevent or impair its right administration might be definitely ascertained and that appropriate and effective measures might be taken to remedy or eliminate the evil. The Senate regarded the charges as grave and requiring legislative attention and action. Accordingly it formulated, passed and invited the House of Representatives to pass (and that body did pass) two measures taking important litigation then in immediate contemplation [*Ed. Note: lawsuits by the government to cancel the oil leases that Fall had approved*] out of the control of the Department of Justice and placing the same in charge of special counsel to be appointed by the President; and also adopted a resolution authorizing and directing a select committee of five senators—

> to investigate circumstances and facts, and report the same to the Senate, concerning the alleged failure of Harry M. Daugherty, Attorney General of the United States, to prosecute properly violators of the Sherman Anti-trust Act and the Clayton Act against monopolies and unlawful restraint of trade; the alleged neglect and failure of the said Harry M. Daugherty, Attorney General of the United States, to arrest and prosecute Albert B. Fall, Harry F. Sinclair, E.L. Doheny, C.R. Forbes, and their co-conspirators in defrauding the Government, as well as the alleged neglect and failure of the said Attorney General to arrest and prosecute many others for violations of Federal statutes, and his alleged failure to prosecute properly, efficiently, and promptly, and to defend, all manner of civil and criminal actions wherein the Government of the United States is interested as a party plaintiff or defendant. And said commit-

tee is further directed to inquire into, investigate and report to the Senate the activities of the said Harry M. Daugherty, Attorney General, and any of his assistants in the Department of Justice which would in any manner tend to impair their efficiency or influence as representatives of the Government of the United States.

The resolution also authorized the committee to send for books and papers, to subpoena witnesses, to administer oaths, and to sit at such times and places as it might deem advisable.

In the course of the investigation the committee issued and caused to be duly served on Mally S. Daugherty—who was a brother of Harry M. Daugherty and president of the Midland National Bank of Washington Court House, Ohio—a subpoena commanding him to appear before the committee for the purpose of giving testimony bearing on the subject under investigation, and to bring with him the "deposit ledgers of the Midland National Bank since November 1, 1920; also note files and transcript of owners of every safety vault; also records of income drafts; also records of any individual account or accounts showing withdrawals of amounts of $25,000 or over during above period." The witness failed to appear.

A little later in the course of the investigation the committee issued and caused to be duly served on the same witness another subpoena commanding him to appear before it for the purpose of giving testimony relating to the subject under consideration— nothing being said in this subpoena about bringing records, books or papers. The witness again failed to appear; and no excuse was offered by him for either failure.

The committee then made a report to the Senate stating that the subpoenas had been issued, that according to the officer's returns—copies of which accompanied the report—the witness was personally served; and that he had failed and refused to appear. After a reading of the report, the Senate adopted a resolution reciting these facts and proceeding as follows.

Whereas the appearance and testimony of the said M.S. Daugherty is material and necessary in order that the committee may properly execute the functions imposed upon it and may obtain information necessary as a basis for such legislative and other action as the Senate may deem necessary and proper: Therefore be it

Resolved, That the President of the Senate pro tempore issue his warrant commanding the Sergeant at Arms or his deputy to take into custody the body of the said M.S. Daugherty wherever found, and to bring the said M.S. Daugherty before the bar of the Senate, then and there to answer such questions pertinent to the matter under inquiry as the Senate may order the President of the Senate pro tempore to propound; and to keep the said M.S. Daugherty in custody to await the further order of the Senate.

It will be observed from the terms of the resolution that the warrant was to be issued in furtherance of the effort to obtain the personal testimony of the witness and, like the second subpoena, was not intended to exact from him the production of the various records, books and papers named in the first subpoena.

The warrant was issued agreeably to the resolution and was addressed simply to the Sergeant at Arms. That officer on receiving the warrant endorsed thereon a direction that it be executed by John J. McGrain, already his deputy, and delivered it to him for execution.

The deputy, proceeding under the warrant, took the witness into custody at Cincinnati, Ohio, with the purpose of bringing him before the bar of the Senate as commanded; whereupon the witness petitioned the federal district court in Cincinnati for a writ of *habeas corpus*. The writ was granted and the deputy made due return setting forth the warrant and the cause of the detention. After a hearing the court held the attachment and detention unlawful and discharged the witness, the decision being put on the ground that the Senate in directing the investigation and in ordering the attachment exceeded its powers under the Constitution, 299 Fed. 620. The deputy prayed and was allowed a direct appeal to this Court under §238 of the Judicial Code as then existing.

We have given the case earnest and prolonged consideration because the principal questions involved are of unusual importance and delicacy. They are (a) whether the Senate—or the House of Representatives, both being on the same plane in this regard—has power, through its own process, to compel a private individual to appear before it or one of its committees and give testimony needed to enable it efficiently to exercise a legislative function belonging to it under the Constitution, and (b) whether it sufficiently appears that the process was being employed in this instance to obtain testimony for that purpose.

Other questions are presented which in regular course should be taken up first.
[*Ed. Note: The Court concludes that it was lawful for the Deputy Sergeant-at-Arms to execute the warrant and take Daugherty into custody, and that a legislative arrest warrant based upon a committee report did not violate the Fourth Amendment probable cause requirement.*]

* * *

The Constitution provides for a Congress consisting of a Senate and House of Representatives and invests it with "all legislative powers" granted to the United States, and with power "to make all laws which shall be necessary and proper" for carrying into execution these powers and "all other powers" vested by the Constitution in the

United States or in any department or officer thereof. Art. I, secs. 1, 8. Other provisions show that, while bills can become laws only after being considered and passed by both houses of Congress, each house is to be distinct from the other, to have its own officers and rules, and to exercise its legislative function independently. Art. I, secs. 2, 3, 5, 7. But there is no provision expressly investing either house with power to make investigations and exact testimony to the end that it may exercise its legislative function advisedly and effectively. So the question arises whether this power is so far incidental to the legislative function as to be implied.

In actual legislative practice power to secure needed information by such means has long been treated as an attribute of the power to legislate. It was so regarded in the British Parliament and in the Colonial legislatures before the American Revolution; and a like view has prevailed and been carried into effect in both houses of Congress and in most of the state legislatures.

This power was both asserted and exerted by the House of Representatives in 1792, when it appointed a select committee to inquire into the St. Clair expedition and authorized the committee to send for necessary persons, papers and records. Mr. Madison, who had taken an important part in framing the Constitution only five years before, and four of his associates in that work, were members of the House of Representatives at the time, and all voted for the inquiry. 3 Cong. Ann. 494. Other exertions of the power by the House of Representatives, as also by the Senate, are shown in the citations already made. Among those by the Senate, the inquiry ordered in 1859 respecting the raid by John Brown and his adherents on the armory and arsenal of the United States at Harper's Ferry is of special significance. The resolution directing the inquiry authorized the committee to send for persons and papers, to inquire into the facts pertaining to the raid and the means by which it was organized and supported, and to report what legislation, if any, was necessary to preserve the peace of the country and protect the public property. The resolution was briefly discussed and adopted without opposition. Cong. Globe, 36th Cong., 1st Sess., pp. 141, 152. Later on the committee reported that Thaddeus Hyatt, although subpoenaed to appear as a witness, had refused to do so; whereupon the Senate ordered that he be attached and brought before it to answer for his refusal. When he was brought in he answered by challenging the power of the Senate to direct the inquiry and exact testimony to aid it in exercising its legislative function. The question of power thus presented was thoroughly discussed by several senators—Mr. Sumner of Massachusetts taking the lead in denying the power and Mr. Fessenden of Maine in supporting it. Sectional and party lines were put aside and the question was debated and determined with special regard to principle and precedent. The vote was taken on a resolution pronouncing the witness's answer insufficient and directing that he be committed until he should signify that he was ready and willing to testify. The resolution was adopted—44 senators voting for it and 10 against. The arguments advanced in support of the power are fairly reflected by the following excerpts from the debate:

> Mr. Fessenden of Maine. "Where will you stop? Stop, I say, just at that point where we have gone far enough to accomplish the purposes for which we were

created; and these purposes are defined in the Constitution. What are they? The great purpose is legislation. There are some other things, but I speak of legislation as the principal purpose. Now, what do we propose to do here? We propose to legislate upon a given state of facts, perhaps, or under a given necessity. Well, sir, proposing to legislate, we want information. We have it not ourselves. It is not to be presumed that we know everything; and if any body does presume it, it is a very great mistake, as we know by experience. We want information on certain subjects. How are we to get it? The Senator says, ask for it. I am ready to ask for it; but suppose the person whom we ask will not give it to us? Is this power, which has been exercised by Parliament, and by all legislative bodies down to the present day without dispute—the power to inquire into subjects upon which they are disposed to legislate—lost to us? Are we not in the possession of it? Are we deprived of it simply because we hold our power here under a Constitution which defines what our duties are, and what we are called upon to do?

"Congress has appointed committees after committees, time after time, to make inquiries on subjects of legislation. Had we not power to do it? Nobody questioned our authority to do it. We have given them authority to send for persons and papers during the recess. Nobody questioned our authority. We appoint committees during the session, with power to send for persons and papers. Have we not that authority, if necessary to legislation?...

"Sir, with regard to myself, all I have to inquire into is: is this a legitimate and proper object, committed to me under the Constitution; and then, as to the mode of accomplishing it, I am ready to use judiciously, calmly, moderately, all the power which I believe is necessary and inherent, in order to do that which I am appointed to do; and, I take it, I violate no rights, either of the people generally or of the individual, by that course."

Mr. Crittenden of Kentucky. "I come now to a question where the cooperation of the two branches is not necessary. There are some things that the Senate may do. How? According to a mode of its own. Are we to ask the other branch of the Legislature to concede by law to us the power of making such an inquiry as we are now making? Has not each branch the right to make what inquiries and investigation it thinks proper to make for its own action? Undoubtedly. You say we must have a law for it. Can we have a law? Is it not, from the very nature of the case, incidental to you as a Senate, if you, as a Senate, have the power of instituting an inquiry and of proceeding with that inquiry? I have endeavored to show that we have that power. We have a right, in consequence of it, a necessary incidental power, to summon witnesses, if witnesses are necessary. Do we require the concurrence of the other House to that? It is a power of our own. If you have a right to do the thing of your own motion, you must have all powers that are necessary to do it.

"The means of carrying into effect by law all the granted powers, is given where legislation is applicable and necessary; but there are subordinate matters, not amounting to laws; there are inquiries of the one House or the other House, which each House has a right to conduct; which each has, from the beginning, exercised the power to conduct; and each has, from the beginning, summoned witnesses. This has been the practice of the Government from the beginning; and if we have a right to summon the witnesses, all the rest follows as a matter of course."

The deliberate solution of the question on that occasion has been accepted and followed on other occasions by both houses of Congress, and never has been rejected or questioned by either.

* * *

We have referred to the practice of the two houses of Congress; and we now shall notice some significant congressional enactments. May 3, 1798, c. 36, 1 Stat. 554, Congress provided that oaths or affirmations might be administered to witnesses by the President of the Senate, the Speaker of the House of Representatives, the chairman of a committee of the whole, or the chairman of a select committee, "in any case under their examination." February 8, 1817, c. 10, 3 Stat. 345, it enlarged that provision so as to include the chairman of a standing committee. January 24, 1857, c. 19, 11 Stat. 155, it passed "An Act more effectually to enforce the attendance of witnesses on the summons of either house of Congress, and to compel them to discover testimony." This act provided, first, that any person summoned as a witness to give testimony or produce papers in any matter under inquiry before either house of Congress, or any committee of either house, who should willfully make default, or, if appearing, should refuse to answer any question pertinent to the inquiry, should, in addition to the pains and penalties then existing, be deemed guilty of a misdemeanor and be subject to indictment and punishment as there prescribed; and secondly, that no person should be excused from giving evidence in such an inquiry on the ground that it might tend to incriminate or disgrace him, nor be held to answer criminally, or be subjected to any penalty or forfeiture, for any fact or act as to which he was required to testify, excepting that he might be subjected to prosecution for perjury committed while so testifying. January 24, 1862, c. 11, 12 Stat. 333, Congress modified the immunity provision in particulars not material here. These enactments are now embodied in §§ 101–104 and 859 of Revised Statutes. They show very plainly that Congress intended thereby (a) to recognize the power of either house to institute inquiries and exact evidence touching subjects within its jurisdiction and on which it was disposed to act; (b) to recognize that such inquiries may be conducted through committees; (c) to subject defaulting and contumacious witnesses to indictment and punishment in the courts, and thereby to enable either house to exert the power of inquiry "more effectually;" and (d) to open the way for obtaining evidence in such an inquiry, which otherwise could not be obtained, by exempting witnesses required to give evidence therein from criminal and penal prosecutions in respect of matters disclosed by their evidence.

Four decisions of this Court are cited and more or less relied on, and we now turn to them.

ONE · BACKGROUND AND HISTORY

The first decision was in *Anderson v. Dunn*, 6 Wheat. 204. The question there was whether, under the Constitution, the House of Representatives has power to attach and punish a person other than a member for contempt of its authority—in fact, an attempt to bribe one of its members. The Court regarded the power as essential to the effective exertion of other powers expressly granted, and therefore as implied.

* * *

The next decision was in *Kilbourn v. Thompson*, 103 U.S. 168. The question there was whether the House of Representatives had exceeded its power in directing one of its committees to make a particular investigation. The decision was that it had. The principles announced and applied in the case are—that neither house of Congress possesses a "general power of making inquiry into the private affairs of the citizen"; that the power actually possessed is limited to inquiries relating to matters of which the particular house "has jurisdiction" and in respect of which it rightfully may take other action; that if the inquiry relates to "a matter wherein relief or redress could be had only by a judicial proceeding" it is not within the range of this power, but must be left to the courts, conformably to the constitutional separation of governmental powers; and that for the purpose of determining the essential character of the inquiry recourse may be had to the resolution or order under which it is made. The court examined the resolution which was the basis of the particular inquiry, and ascertained therefrom that the inquiry related to a private real-estate pool or partnership in the District of Columbia.... The Court pointed out that the resolution contained no suggestion of contemplated legislation; that the matter was one in respect to which no valid legislation could be had; that the bankrupts' estate and the trustee's settlement were still pending in the bankruptcy court; and that the United States and other creditors were free to press their claims in that proceeding. And on these grounds the Court held that in undertaking the investigation "the House of Representatives not only exceeded the limit of its own authority, but assumed power which could only be properly exercised by another branch of the government, because it was in its nature clearly judicial."

The case has been cited at times, and is cited to us now, as strongly intimating, if not holding, that neither house of Congress has power to make inquiries and exact evidence in aid of contemplated legislation. There are expressions in the opinion which, separately considered, might bear such an interpretation; but that this was not intended is shown by the immediately succeeding statement (p. 189) that "This latter proposition is one which we do not propose to decide in the present case because we are able to decide the case without passing upon the existence or non-existence of such a power in aid of the legislative function."

Next in order is *In re Chapman*, 166 U.S. 661. The inquiry there in question was conducted under a resolution of the Senate and related to charges, published in the press, that senators were yielding to corrupt influences in considering a tariff bill then before the Senate and were speculating in stocks the value of which would be affected by pending amendments to the bill. Chapman appeared before the committee in response to a subpoena, but refused to answer questions pertinent to the inquiry, and was indicted and convicted under the act of 1857 for his refusal. The Court sustained the constitutional validity of the act of 1857, and, after referring to the constitutional provision empowering either house to punish its members for disorderly behavior and by a vote of two-thirds to expel a member, held that the inquiry related to the integrity and fidelity of senators in the discharge of their duties, and therefore to a matter "within the range of the constitutional powers of the Senate" and in respect of which it could compel witnesses to appear and testify. In overruling an objection that the inquiry was without any defined or admissible purpose, in that the preamble and resolution made no reference to any contemplated expulsion, censure, or other action by the Senate, the Court held that they adequately disclosed a subject-matter of which the Senate had jurisdiction, that it was not essential that the Senate declare in advance what it meditated doing, and that the assumption could not be indulged that the Senate was making the inquiry without a legitimate object.

* * *

The latest case is *Marshall v. Gordon*, 243 U.S. 521. The question there was whether the House of Representatives exceeded its power in punishing, as for a contempt of its authority, a person—not a member—who had written, published and sent to the chairman of one of its committees an ill-tempered and irritating letter respecting the action and purposes of the committee. Power to make inquiries and obtain evidence by compulsory process was not involved. The Court recognized distinctly that the House of Representatives has implied power to punish a person not a member for contempt, as was ruled in *Anderson v. Dunn, supra*, but held that its action in this instance was without constitutional justification. The decision was put on the ground that the letter, while offensive and vexatious, was not calculated or likely to affect the House in any of its proceedings or in the exercise of any of its functions—in short, that the act which was punished as a contempt was not of such a character as to bring it within the rule that an express power draws after it others which are necessary and appropriate to give effect to it.

While these cases are not decisive of the question we are considering, they definitely settle two propositions which we recognize as entirely sound and having a bearing on its solution: One, that the two houses of Congress, in their separate relations, possess not only such powers as are expressly granted to them by the Constitution, but such auxiliary powers as are necessary and appropriate to make the express powers effective; and, the other, that neither house is invested with "general" power to inquire into private affairs and compel disclosures, but only with such limited power of inquiry as is shown to exist when the rule of constitutional interpretation just stated is rightly applied....

With this review of the legislative practice, congressional enactments and court decisions, we proceed to a statement of our conclusions on the question.

We are of the opinion that the power of inquiry—with process to enforce it—is an essential and appropriate auxiliary to the legislative function. It was so regarded and employed in American legislatures before the Constitution was framed and ratified. Both houses of Congress took this view of it early in their history—the House of

Representatives with the approving votes of Mr. Madison and other members whose service in the convention which framed the constitution gives special significance to their action—and both houses have employed the power accordingly up to the present time. The acts of 1798 and 1857, judged by their comprehensive terms, were intended to recognize the existence of this power in both houses and to enable them to employ it "more effectually" than before. So, when their practice in the matter is appraised according to the circumstances in which it was begun and to those in which it has been continued, of the constitutional provisions respecting their powers, and therefore should be taken as fixing the meaning of those provisions, if otherwise doubtful.

We are further of opinion that the provisions are not of doubtful meaning, but, as was held by this Court in the cases we have reviewed, are intended to be effectively exercised, and therefore to carry with them such auxiliary powers as are necessary and appropriate to that end. While the power to exact information in aid of the legislative function was not involved in those cases, the rule of interpretation applied there is applicable here. A legislative body cannot legislate wisely or effectively in the absence of information respecting the conditions which the legislation is intended to affect or change; and where the legislative body does not itself possess the requisite informa-tion—which not infrequently is true—recourse must be had to others who do possess it. Experience has taught that mere requests for such information often are unavailing, and also that information which is volunteered is not always accurate or complete; so some means of compulsion are essential to obtain what is needed. All this was true before and when the Constitution was framed and adopted. In that period the power of inquiry—with enforcing process—was regarded and employed as a necessary and appropriate attribute of the power to legislate—indeed, was treated as inhering in it. Thus there is ample warrant for thinking, as we do, that the constitutional provisions which commit the legislative function to the two houses are intended to include this attribute to the end that the function may be effectively exercised.

The contention is earnestly made on behalf of the witness that this power of in-quiry, if sustained, may be abusively and oppressively exerted. If this be so, it affords no ground for denying the power. The same contention might be directed against the power to legislate, and of course would be unavailing. We must assume, for present purposes, that neither house will be disposed to exert the power beyond its prop-er bounds, or without due regard to the rights of witnesses. But if, contrary to this assumption, controlling limitations or restrictions are disregarded, the decisions in *Kilbourn v. Thompson* and *Marshall v. Gordon* point to admissible measures of relief. And it is a necessary deduction from the decisions in *Kilbourn v. Thompson* and *In re Chapman* that a witness rightfully may refuse to answer where the bounds of the power are exceeded or the questions are not pertinent to the matter under inquiry.

We come now to the question whether it sufficiently appears that the purpose for which the witness's testimony was sought was to obtain information in aid of the leg-islative function. The court below answered the question in the negative and put its decision largely on this ground, as is shown by the following excerpts from its opinion (299 Fed. 638, 639, 640):

It will be noted that in the second resolution the Senate has expressly avowed that the investigation is in aid of other action than legislation. Its purpose is to "obtain information necessary as a basis for such legislative and other action as the Senate may deem necessary and proper." This indicates that the Senate is contemplating the taking of action other than legislative, as the outcome of the investigation, as least the possibility of so doing. The extreme personal cast of the original resolutions; the spirit of hostility towards the then Attorney General which they breathe; that it was not avowed that that legislative action was had in view until after the action of the Senate had been challenged; and that the avowal then was coupled with an avowal that other action was had in view—are calculated to create the impression that the idea of legislative action being in contemplation was an afterthought.

That the senate has in contemplation the possibility of taking action other than legislation as an outcome of the investigation, as thus expressly avowed, would seem of itself to invalidate the entire proceeding. But, whether so or not, the Senate's action is invalid and absolutely void, in that, in ordering and conducting the investigation, it is exercising the judicial function, and power to exercise that function, in such a case as we have here, has not been conferred upon it expressly or by fair implication. What it is proposing to do is to determine the guilt of the Attorney General of the shortcomings and wrongdoings set forth in the resolutions. It is "to hear, adjudge, and condemn." In so doing it is exercising the judicial function.

What the Senate is engaged in doing is not investigating the Attorney General's office; it is investigating the former Attorney General. What it has done is to put him on trial before it. In so doing it is exercising the judicial function. This it has no power to do.

We are of opinion that the court's ruling on this question was wrong, and that it sufficiently appears, when the proceedings are rightly interpreted, that the object of the investigation and of the effort to secure the witness's testimony was to obtain information for legislative purposes.

It is quite true that the resolution directing the investigation does not in terms avow that it is intended to be in aid of legislation; but it does show that the subject to be investigated was the administration of the Department of Justice—whether its functions were being properly discharged or were being neglected or misdirected, and particularly whether the Attorney General and his assistants were performing or neglecting their duties in respect of the institution and prosecution of proceedings to punish crimes and enforce appropriate remedies against the wrongdoers—specific instances of alleged neglect being recited. Plainly the subject was one of which legislation could be had and would be materially aided by the information which the investigation was calculated to elicit. This becomes manifest when it is reflected that the functions of the Department of Justice, the powers and duties of the Attorney General and the duties of his assistants, are all subject to regulation by congressional legislation, and that the department is maintained and its activities are carried on under such appropriations as in the judgment of Congress are needed from year to year.

The only legitimate object the Senate could have in ordering the investigation was to aid in legislating; and we think the subject-matter was such that the presumption should be indulged that this was the real object. An express avowal of the object would have been better; but in view of the particular subject-matter was not indispensable....

Of course, our concern is with the substance of the resolution and not with any nice questions of propriety respecting its direct reference to the then Attorney General by name. The resolution, like the charges which prompted its adoption, related to the activities of the department while he was its supervising officer; and the reference to him by name served to designate the period to which the investigation was directed.

We think the resolution and proceedings give no warrant for thinking the Senate was attempting or intending to try the Attorney General at its bar or before its committee for any crime or wrongdoing. Nor do we think it is a valid objection to the investigation that it might possibly disclose crime or wrongdoing on his part.

The second resolution—the one directing that the witness be attached—declares that his testimony is sought with the purpose of obtaining "information necessary as a basis for such legislative and other action as the Senate may deem necessary and proper." This avowal of contemplated legislation is in accord with what we think is the right interpretation of the earlier resolution directing the investigation. The suggested possibility of "other action" if deemed "necessary or proper" is of course open to criticism in that there is no other action in the matter which would be within the power of the Senate. But we do not assent to the view that this indefinite and untenable suggestion invalidates the entire proceeding. The right view in our opinion is that it takes nothing from the lawful object avowed in the same resolution and rightly inferable from the earlier one. It is not as if an inadmissible or unlawful object were affirmatively and definitely avowed.

We conclude that the investigation was ordered for a legitimate object; that the witness wrongfully refused to appear and testify before the committee and was lawfully attached; that the Senate is entitled to have him give testimony pertinent to the inquiry, either at its bar or before the committee; and that the district court erred in discharging him from custody under the attachment.

Another question has arisen which should be noticed. It is whether the case has become moot. The investigation was ordered and the committee appointed during the Sixty-eighth Congress. That Congress expired March 4, 1925. The resolution ordering the investigation in terms limited the committee's authority to the period of the Sixty-eighth Congress; but this apparently was changed by a later and amendatory resolution authorizing the committee to sit at such times and places as it might deem advisable or necessary. It is said in Jefferson's Manual: "Neither House can continue any portion of itself in any parliamentary function beyond the end of the session without the consent of the other two branches. When done, it is by a bill constituting them commissioners for the particular purpose." But the context shows that the reference is to the two houses of Parliament when adjourned by prorogation or dissolution by the King. The rule may be the same with the House of Representatives whose members are all elected for the period of a single Congress; but it cannot well be the same with the Senate, which is a continuing body whose members are elected for a term of six years and so each Congress, two-thirds always continuing into the next Congress, save as vacancies may occur through death or resignation.

Mr. Hinds in his collection of precedents says: "The Senate, as a continuing body, may continue its committees through the recess following the expiration of a Congress"; and, after quoting the above statement from Jefferson's Manual, he says: "The Senate, however, being a continuing body, gives authority to its committees during the recess after the expiration of a Congress." So far as we are advised the select committee having this investigation in charge has neither made a final report nor been discharged; nor has it been continued by an affirmative order. Apparently its activities have been suspended pending the decision of this case. But, be this as it may, it is certain that the committee may be continued or revived now by motion to that effect, and, if continued or revived, will have all its original powers.

Notes and Questions

1. **Scope of the Congressional Investigative Power.** In a series of lectures on the United States Constitution delivered in Philadelphia in 1790 and 1791, James Wilson, a drafter of the Constitution and later a member of the Supreme Court, called the House of Representatives "the grand inquest of the state" (echoing William Pitt the Elder's use of that phrase a half-century earlier to describe the inquisitorial powers of the English Parliament). In the *McGrain v. Daugherty* case, Mally Daugherty, the former Attorney General's brother, argued that Congress had no power to compel a private citizen to testify about private matters. The Senate resolution authorizing the investigation directed the committee "to inquire into, investigate, and report to the Senate the activities" of Attorney General Daugherty and his subordinates "which would in any manner tend to impair their efficiency or influence as representatives of the Government of the United States." How did the *McGrain* Court respond to Mally Daugherty's private-citizen argument? Does the *McGrain* decision recognize any limits on the scope of the congressional investigative power?

2. **The Power of Public Opinion.** When the Teapot Dome investigations began, there was little public interest in what were expected to be dry and technical hearings on obscure oil leasing actions by the Department of the Interior. There was also considerable skepticism about the legitimacy of politically influenced congressional investigations, as is demonstrated by evidence scholar and law school dean John H. Wigmore's contemporaneous characterization of "the Senatorial debauch of investigation—poking into political garbage cans and dragging the sewers of political intrigue." Public opinion shifted, however, when the investigations revealed that Secretary Fall had received $100,000 from Doheny at the same time Fall was administering the California leases, and that those leases could be expected to yield Doheny profits of some $100 million. With the passage of time, the Teapot Dome investigation has been ven-

erated as a model of congressional exposure of executive branch misconduct. What role should considerations of public opinion and interest play in the congressional investigative process? Should congressional investigators take into account the level of public interest in their proceedings and tailor their actions to capture the public's interest? Are generating public attention and seeking "exposure for the sake of exposure" legitimate objectives for a congressional investigation? What about efforts to influence presidential elections or other political races? See Chapter 8 for discussion of the influence of political considerations on investigations and Chapter 9 for discussion of the importance of aggressive congressional oversight.

3. Investigating High Government Officials. A notable aspect of the Teapot Dome Scandal was a concern that the Harding administration and Attorney General Harry Daugherty had politicized the Department of Justice and failed to adequately investigate and prosecute crimes connected with the leasing of the naval oil reserves. Senator Burton Wheeler, a Montana Democrat, introduced Senate Resolution 157 calling for an investigation of the Justice Department. Two special counsels—one from each political party—were appointed by President Coolidge (who was Harding's vice president and became president when Harding died unexpectedly in August 1923) and confirmed by the Senate to investigate the oil lease scandal: former Democratic Senator Atlee Pomerene of Ohio and Philadelphia Republican attorney, and later Supreme Court Justice, Owen Roberts. Pomerene and Roberts initially declined to rely upon the support of the Department of Justice and the FBI in their investigation, and instead relied upon support from Treasury Department Secret Service agents. They ultimately sued to cancel the naval oil leases and prosecuted former Interior Secretary Albert Fall and other key actors in the scandal. Congress cannot itself prosecute crimes that are exposed in the course of a congressional investigation and can only refer evidence of criminal misconduct to the Department of Justice for prosecution. How should Congress proceed when the Department of Justice has an actual or potential conflict of interest, as in cases involving senior government officials, or is unwilling for political reasons to prosecute a crime, as in a case when Congress finds that an executive branch official has committed criminal contempt of Congress by failing to provide testimony under subpoena? These problems are discussed further in Chapter 3, on Watergate, and Chapter 4, on the congressional investigations of allegations of misconduct by senior executive branch officials.

4. Nothing New Under the (Washington) Sun—Politicization of the Department of Justice. Among allegations that made up the Teapot Dome scandal were charges of what the McGrain opinion refers to as "misfeasance and nonfeasance" in the Justice Department under Attorney General Daugherty. Daugherty was President Harding's long-time political adviser from Ohio and had served as campaign manager for Harding's successful 1920 presidential bid. Harding rewarded Daugherty by appointing him Attorney General. The suspected misconduct in the Daugherty Justice Department extended well beyond failure to investigate and prosecute the Teapot Dome cases to allegations of widespread corruption and influence-peddling. What should be the role of Congress when it receives reports of misconduct in an executive branch department?

Are there any parallels between the issues facing Congress with respect to the Harding administration's Justice Department under Attorney General Daugherty and more recent events involving the Bush administration's Justice Department under Attorney General Alberto Gonzales? See Chapter 4 for further discussion of the congressional investigations of the George W. Bush administration's Department of Justice.

Teapot Dome Continued:
A Criminal Prosecution for Contempt of Congress

Interior Secretary Albert Fall leased the Teapot Dome naval oil reserves in Wyoming to Mammoth Oil Company, which was owned by Harry F. Sinclair. Like Doheny, Sinclair was a Harding administration insider and a crony of Fall. Sinclair had something else in common with Doheny—like Doheny, Sinclair gave Fall a large sum of money in connection with the lease of naval oil reserves and, as was the case with the Doheny payment, Fall and Sinclair claimed the money was a loan. The similarities do not end there—also like Doheny, Sinclair testified during the Senate investigation that he expected to profit by some $100 million from the Teapot Dome lease. Not surprisingly, Senate investigators doggedly pursued the details of Fall's dealings with Sinclair. Sinclair provided testimony to the Senate committee on five occasions between January and December of 1923, but when he was called before the committee again in March 1924, Fall refused to answer further questions, claiming that the committee no longer had jurisdiction to compel information from him. He was charged with contempt of Congress, and his case eventually reached the Supreme Court:

Sinclair v. United States
279 U.S. 263 (1929)

Mr. Justice Butler delivered the opinion of the court.

Appellant was found guilty of violating R.S., § 102; U.S.C., Tit. 2, § 192. He was sentenced to jail for three months and to pay a fine of $500. The case was taken to the Court of Appeals of the District of Columbia; that court certified to this court certain questions of law upon which it desired instruction for the proper decision of the case. We directed the entire record to be sent up. Judicial Code, § 239, U.S.C., Tit. 28, § 346.

Section 102 follows: "Every person who having been summoned as a witness by the authority of either House of Congress, to give testimony or to produce papers upon any matter under inquiry before either House, or any committee of either House of Congress, willfully makes default, or who, having appeared, refuses to answer any question pertinent to the question under inquiry, shall be deemed guilty of a misdemeanor, punishable by a fine of not more than $1,000 nor less than $100, and imprisonment in a common jail for not less than one month nor more than twelve months."

By way of inducement the indictment set forth the circumstances leading up to the offense, which in brief substance are as follows:

For many years, there had been progressive diminution of petroleum necessary for the operation of naval vessels; consequently the Government was interested to conserve the supply and especially that in the public domain.

Pursuant to the Act of June 25, 1910, 36 Stat. 847, the President, by executive orders dated September 2, 1912, December 13, 1912, and April 30, 1915, ordered that certain oil and gas bearing lands in California and Wyoming be held for the exclusive use of the navy. These areas were designated Naval Petroleum Reserves 1, 2 and 3, respectively.

The Act of February 25, 1920, 41 Stat. 437, provided for the leasing of public lands containing oil and other minerals. And the Act of June 4, 1920, 41 Stat. 812, directed the Secretary of the Navy to take possession of all properties in the naval reserves "on which there are no pending claims or applications for permits or leases under the" Leasing Act of February 25, 1920, "or pending applications for United States patent under any law," to conserve, develop, use and operate the same by contract, lease or otherwise, and to use, store, exchange or sell the oil and gas products thereof for the benefit of the United States. And it was declared that the rights of any claimants under the Leasing Act were not thereby adversely affected.

May 31, 1921, the President promulgated an executive order purporting to give the administration and conservation of all oil and gas bearing lands in the naval reserves to the Secretary of the Interior subject to supervision by the President.

April 7, 1922, the Secretary of the Navy and the Secretary of the Interior made a lease of lands in Reserve No. 3 to the Mammoth Oil Company. This was done by the procurement of the appellant acting as the president of the company. [*Ed. Note: The Court summarized the lease terms.*]

* * *

The lease to the Mammoth Company and the contract with the Transport Company came to the attention of the Senate, and it was charged that there had been fraud and bad faith in the making of them. Questions arose as to their legality, the future policy of the Government as to them and similar leases and contracts, and as to the necessity and desirability of legislation upon the subject.

April 29, 1922, the Senate adopted Resolution 282, calling upon the Secretary of the Interior for information and containing the following: "That the Committee on Public Lands and Surveys be authorized to investigate this entire subject of leases upon naval oil reserves with particular reference to the protection of the rights and equities of the Government of the United States and the preservation of its natural resources, and to report its findings and recommendations to the Senate."

June 5, 1922, Resolution 282 was amended by Resolution 294 by adding a provision that the committee "is hereby authorized … to require the attendance of witnesses by subpoenas or otherwise; to require the production of books, papers and documents.… The chairman of the committee, or any member thereof, may administer oaths to witnesses and sign subpoenas for witnesses."

* * *

February 7, 1924, the Senate passed Resolution 147, directing in substance the same as it had theretofore done by the two resolutions first above mentioned and also that the committee "ascertain what, if any, other or additional legislation may be advisable, and to report its findings and recommendations to the Senate."

The committee proceeded to exercise the authority conferred upon it and for that purpose held hearings at which witnesses were examined and documents produced. Appellant was summoned, appeared and was sworn December 4, 1923.

And the indictment charges that, on March 22, 1924, the matters referred to in these resolutions being under inquiry, and appellant having been summoned to give testimony and having been sworn as aforesaid did appear before the committee as a witness. The first count alleges that Senator Walsh, a member of the committee, propounded to him a question which appellant knew was pertinent to the matters under inquiry: "Mr. Sinclair, I desire to interrogate you about a matter concerning which the committee had no knowledge or reliable information at any time when you had theretofore appeared before the committee and with respect to which you must then have had knowledge. I refer to the testimony given by Mr. Bonfils concerning a contract that you made with him touching the Teapot Dome. I wish you would tell us about that."

And, to explain that question, the indictment states: "said Hon. Thomas J. Walsh thereby meaning and intending, as said Harry F. Sinclair then and there well knew and understood, to elicit from him the said Harry F. Sinclair, facts, which then were within his knowledge, touching the execution and delivery of a certain contract bearing date September 25, 1922, made and executed by and between said Mammoth Oil Company, one F. G. Bonfils and one John Leo Stack, which was executed on behalf of said Mammoth Oil Company by said Harry F. Sinclair as President of said Mammoth Oil Company, unto said F. G. Bonfils and said John Leo Stack, of the sum of $250,000.00 on or before October 15, 1922, in consideration of the release by said F. G. Bonfils and said John Leo Stack, of rights to lands described in said Executive Order of April 30, 1915, and embraced in the aforesaid lease of April 7, 1922." And that count concluded: "and that said Harry F. Sinclair then and there unlawfully did refuse to answer said question ..."

Senate Joint Resolution 54 was approved February 8, 1924. 43 Stat. 5. It recited that the leases and contracts above mentioned were executed under circumstances indicating fraud and corruption, that they were without authority, contrary to law, and in defiance of the settled policy of the Government; and the resolution declared that the lands embraced therein should be recovered and held for the purposes to which they were dedicated. It directed the President to cause suit to be instituted for the cancellation of the leases and contracts, to prosecute such other actions or proceedings, civil and criminal, as were warranted by the facts, and authorized the appointment of special counsel to have charge of the matter.

Prior to March 22, 1924, appellant, at the request of the committee, appeared five times before it, and was sworn as alleged. March 19, 1924, a United States marshal at New York served upon him a telegram, which was in form a subpoena signed by the chairman of the committee, requiring him to appear as a witness; and he did appear on March 22. Before any questions were put, he submitted a statement.

He disclaimed any purpose to invoke protection against self-incrimination and asserted there was nothing in the transaction which could incriminate him. He emphasized his earlier appearances, testimony, production of papers and discharge from further attendance. He called attention to Joint Resolution 54, discussed its provisions, and stated that a suit charging conspiracy and fraud had been commenced against the Mammoth Company and others and that the Government's motion for injunction and receivers had been granted, and that application had been made for a special grand jury to investigate the making of the lease. He asserted that the committee could not then investigate the matters covered by the authorization because the Senate by the adoption of the joint resolution had exhausted its power and Congress and the President had made the whole matter a judicial question which was determinable only in the courts. The statement concluded: "I shall reserve any evidence I may be able to give for those courts to which you and your colleagues have deliberately referred all questions of which you had any jurisdiction and shall respectfully decline to answer any questions propounded by your committee."

After appellant's statement, his counsel asked the privilege of presenting to the committee reasons why it did not have authority further to take testimony of appellant. In the course of his remarks he said: "Mr. Sinclair is already under oath before the committee ... he is on the stand now in every sense of the word, and the objection really is to any further examination of him on the subjects involved in this resolution." Discussion followed, and a motion was made: "That in the examination the inquiry shall not relate to pending controversies before any of the Federal counts in which Mr. Sinclair is a defendant, and which questions would involve his defense." During a colloquy that followed, one of the members said: "Of course we will vote it [the motion] down.... If we do not examine Mr. Sinclair about those matters, there is not anything else to examine him about." The motion was voted down. Then the appellant was asked the question set forth in the first count, and he said: "I decline to answer on the advice of counsel on the same ground."

Appellant contends that his demurrer to the several counts of the indictment should have been sustained and that a verdict of not guilty should have been directed. To support that contention he argues that the questions related to his private affairs and to matters cognizable only in the courts wherein they were pending, and that the committee avowedly had departed from any inquiry in aid of legislation.

He maintains that there was no proof of any authorized inquiry by the committee or that he was legally summoned or sworn or that the questions propounded were pertinent to any inquiry it was authorized to make, and that because of such failure he was entitled to have a verdict directed in his favor.

He insists that the court erred in holding that the question of pertinency was one of law for the court and in not submitting it to the jury and also erred in excluding evidence offered to sustain his refusal to answer.

1. The Committee on Public Lands and Surveys is one of the standing committees of the Senate. No question is raised as to the validity of its organization and existence. Under §101 of the Revised Statutes, U.S.C., Tit. 2, §191, its chairman and any of its members are empowered to administer oaths to witnesses before it. Section 102 plainly extends to a case where a person voluntarily appears as a witness without being summoned as well as to the case of one required to attend.

By our opinion in *McGrain v. Daugherty*, 273 U.S. 135, 173, decided since the indictment now before us was found, two propositions are definitely laid down: "One, that the two houses of Congress, in their separate relations, possess not only such powers as are necessary and appropriate to make the express powers effective; and, the other, that neither house is invested with 'general' power to inquire into private affairs and compel disclosures, but only with such limited power of inquiry as is shown to exist when the rule of constitutional interpretation just stated is rightly applied." And that case shows that, while the power of inquiry is an essential and appropriate auxiliary to the legislative function, it must be exerted with due regard for the rights of witnesses, and that a witness rightfully may refuse to answer where the bounds of the power are exceeded or where the questions asked are not pertinent to the matter under inquiry.

It has always been recognized in this country, and it is well to remember, that few if any of the rights of the people guarded by fundamental law are of greater importance to their happiness and safety than the right to be exempt from all unauthorized, arbitrary or unreasonable inquiries and disclosures in respect of their personal and private affairs. In order to illustrate the purpose of the court's will to uphold the right of privacy, we quote from some of their decisions.

In *Kilbourn v. Thompson*, 103 U.S. 168, this court, speaking through Mr. Justice Miller, said (p. 190): "... we are sure that no person can be punished for contumacy as a witness before either House, unless his testimony is required in a matter into which that House has jurisdiction to inquire, and we feel equally sure that neither of these bodies possesses the general power of making inquiry into the private affairs of the citizen." And referring to the failure of the authorizing resolution there under consideration to state the purpose of the inquiry (p. 195): "Was it to be simply a fruitless investigation into the personal affairs of individuals? If so, the House of Representatives had no power or authority in the matter more than any other equal number of gentlemen interested for the government of their country. By 'fruitless' we mean that it could result in no valid legislation on the subject to which the inquiry referred."

In *In re Pacific Railway Commission*, (Circuit Court, N.D., California) 32 Fed. 241, Mr. Justice Field, announcing the opinion of the court, said (p. 250): "Of all the rights of the citizen, few are of greater importance or more essential to his peace and happiness than the right of personal security, and that involves, not merely protection of his person from assault, but exemption of his private affairs, books, and papers, from the inspection and scrutiny of others. Without the enjoyment of this right, all other rights would lose half their value." And the learned Justice, referring to *Kilbourn v. Thompson*, *supra*, said (p. 253): "The case will stand for all time as a bulwark against the invasion of the right of the citizen to protection in his private affairs against the unlimited scrutiny of investigation by a congressional committee." And see concurring opinions of Circuit Judge Sawyer, p. 259 at p. 263, and of District Judge Sabin, p. 268 at p. 269.

In *Interstate Commerce Commission v. Brimson*, 154 U.S. 447, Mr. Justice Harlan, speaking for the court said (p. 478): "We do not overlook these constitutional limitations which, for the protection of personal rights, must necessarily attend all investigations conducted under the authority of Congress. Neither branch of the legislative department, still less any merely administrative body, established by Congress, possesses, or can be invested with, a general power of making inquiry into the private affairs of the citizen.... We said in *Boyd v. United States*, 116 U.S. 616, 630—and it cannot be too often repeated,—that the principles that embody the essence of constitutional liberty and security forbid all invasions on the part of the government and its employées of the sanctity of a man's home and the privacies of his life."

Harriman v. Interstate Commerce Commission, 211 U.S. 407, illustrates the unwillingness of this court to construe an Act of Congress to authorize any examination of witnesses in respect of their personal affairs. And see *United States v. Louisville & Nashville R.R.*, 236 U.S. 318, 335.

* * *

2. But it is clear that neither the investigation authorized by the Senate resolutions above mentioned nor the question under the consideration related merely to appellant's private or personal affairs. Under the Constitution (Art. IV, §3) Congress has plenary power to dispose of and to make all needful rules and regulations respecting the naval oil reserves, other public lands and property of the United States. And undoubtedly the Senate had power to delegate authority to its committee to investigate and report what had been and was being done by executive departments under the Leasing Act, the Naval Oil Reserve Act, and the President's order in respect of the reserves, and to make any other inquiry concerning the public domain.

While appellant caused the Mammoth Oil Company to be organized and owned all its shares, the transaction purporting to lease to it the lands within the reserve cannot be said to be merely or principally the personal or private affair of appellant. It was a matter of concern to the United States. The title to valuable government lands was involved. The validity of the lease and the means by which it had been obtained under existing law were subjects that properly might be investigated in order to determine what if any legislation was necessary or desirable in order to recover the leased lands or to safeguard other parts of the public domain.

Neither Senate Joint Resolution 54 nor the action taken under it operated to divest the Senate, or the committee, of power further to investigate the actual administration of the land laws. It may be conceded that Congress is without authority to compel disclosures for the purpose of aiding the prosecution of pending suits; but the authority of that body, directly or through its committees, to require pertinent disclosures in aid of its own constitutional power is not abridged because the information sought to be elicited may also be of use in such suits.

The record does not sustain appellant's contention that the investigation was avowedly not in aid of legislation. He relies on the refusal of the committee to pass the motion directing that the inquiry should not relate to controversies pending in court, and the statement of one of the members that there was nothing else to examine appellant about. But these are not enough to show that the committee intended to depart from the purpose to ascertain whether additional legislation might be advisable. It is plain that investigation of the matters involved in suits brought or to be commenced under Senate Joint Resolution 54 might directly aid in respect of legislative action.

3. [*Ed. Note: The Court concludes that the Senate resolutions authorized the committee's inquiry.*]

Appellant earnestly maintains that the question was not shown to be pertinent to any inquiry the committee was authorized to make. The United States suggests that the presumption of regularity is sufficient without proof. But, without determining whether that presumption is applicable to such a matter, it is enough to say that the stronger presumption of innocence attended the accused at the trial. It was therefore incumbent upon the United States to plead and show that the question pertained to some matter under investigation. Appellant makes no claim that the evidence was not sufficient to establish the innuendo alleged in respect of the question; the record discloses that the proof on that point was ample.

Congress, in addition to its general legislative power over the public domain, had all the powers of a proprietor and was authorized to deal with it as a private individual may deal with lands owned by him. *United States v. Midwest Oil Co.*, 236 U.S. 459, 474. The committee's authority to investigate extended to matters affecting the interest of the United States as owner as well as to those having relation to the legislative function.

Before the hearing at which appellant refused to answer, the committee had discovered and reported facts tending to warrant the passage of Senate Joint Resolution 54 and the institution of suits for the cancellation of the naval oil reserve leases. Undoubtedly it had authority further to investigate concerning the validity of such leases, and to discover whether persons, other than those who had been made defendants in the suit against the Mammoth Oil Company, had or might assert a right or claim in respect of the lands covered by the lease to that company.

The contract and release made and given by Bonfils and Stack related directly to the title to the lands covered by the lease which had been reported by the committee as unauthorized and fraudulent. The United States proposed to recover and hold such lands as a source of supply of oil for the Navy. S.J. Res. 54. It is clear that the question so propounded to appellant was pertinent to the committee's investigation touching the rights and equities of the United States as owner.

Moreover, it was pertinent for the Senate to ascertain the practical effect of recent changes that had been made in the laws relating to oil and other mineral lands in the public domain. The leases and contracts charged to have been unauthorized and fraudulent were made soon after the executive order of May 31, 1921. The title to the lands in the reserves could not be cleared without ascertaining whether there were outstanding any claims or applications for permits, leases or patents under the Leasing Act or other laws. It was necessary for the Government to take into account the rights, if any there were, of such claimants. The reference in the testimony of Bonfils to the contract referred to in the question propounded was sufficient to put the committee on inquiry concerning outstanding claims possibly adverse and superior to the Mammoth Oil Company's lease. The question propounded was within the authorization of the committee and the legitimate scope of investigation to enable the Senate to determine whether the powers granted to or assumed by the Secretary of the Interior and the Secretary of the Navy should be withdrawn, limited, or allowed to remain unchanged.

The question of pertinency under §102 was rightly decided by the court as one of law. It did not depend upon the probative value of evidence. That question may be likened to those concerning relevancy at the trial of issues in court, and it is not essentially different from the question as to materiality of false testimony charged as perjury in prosecutions for that crime. Upon reasons so well known that their repetition is unnecessary it is uniformly held that relevancy is a question of law.... [*Ed. Note: Citations omitted.*]

The reasons for holding relevancy and materiality to be questions of law in cases such as those above referred to apply with equal force to the determination of pertinency arising under §102. The matter for determination in this case was whether the facts called for by the question were so related to the subjects covered by the Senate's resolutions that such facts reasonably could be said to be "pertinent to the question under inquiry." It would be incongruous and contrary to well-established principles to leave the determination of such a matter to a jury. *Interstate Commerce Commission v. Brimson, supra* at 489. *Horning v. District of Columbia*, 254 U.S. 135.

6. There is no merit in appellant's contention that he is entitled to a new trial because the court excluded evidence that in refusing to answer he acted in good faith on the advice of competent counsel. The gist of the offense is refusal to answer pertinent questions. No moral turpitude is involved. Intentional violation is sufficient to constitute guilt. There was no misapprehension as to what was called for. The refusal to answer was deliberate. The facts sought were pertinent as a matter of law, and §102 made it appellant's duty to answer. He was bound rightly to construe the statute. His mistaken view of the law is no defense. *Armour Packing Co. v. United States*, 209 U.S. 56, 85. *Standard Sanitary Mfg. Co. v. United States*, 226 U.S. 20, 49.

7. The conviction on the first count must be affirmed. There were ten counts, demurrer was sustained as to four, *nolle prosequi* was entered in respect of two, and conviction was had on the first, fourth, fifth and ninth counts. As the sentence does not exceed the maximum authorized as punishment for the offense charged in the first count, we need not consider any other count. *Abrams v. United States*, 250 U.S. 616, 619.

Judgment affirmed.

Notes and Questions

1. Constitutional and Evidentiary Privileges in Congressional Investigations. The *Sinclair* court emphasized at the outset of its opinion that in refusing to testify before the Senate committee Sinclair had "disclaimed any purpose to invoke protection against self-incrimination." Rights based on constitutional provisions, such as the Fifth Amendment privilege against providing self-incriminatory testimony, can be invoked in congressional proceedings and their invocation will be upheld by the courts. Evidentiary privileges that are not constitutionally based but are applicable to court proceedings in the judicial branch, such as the attorney-client privilege, present more complicated issues when asserted in the context of a legislative branch investigative proceeding. Why do you suppose Sinclair chose not to rely upon his constitutional privilege against self-incrimination? What could the Committee have done to obtain Sinclair's testimony if he had asserted his privilege against self-incrimination? See Chapters 5 and 6 for further discussion of constitutional and evidentiary privileges in congressional investigations.

2. Scope of the Congressional Investigative Power—Redux. The Court rejects the argument that the Senate investigation "related merely to [Sinclair's] private or personal affairs," and recognizes the broad power of Congress "to make any other inquiry concerning the public domain" when investigating the leasing of naval oil reserves owned by the federal government. To what extent, if any, does the *Sinclair* opinion's broad conception of the investigative power of Congress turn on the fact that the subject of the Senate investigation was action by public officials involving property of the United States? To what extent does *Sinclair* support the assertion that the investigative power of Congress is constrained only by the scope of Congress's power to legislate? With respect to the latter question, what are the limits to the modern federal legislative power? *See* Peter J. Henning, *Misguided Federalism*, 60 Mo. L. Rev. 389 (2003); *see generally* RICHARD E. LEVY, THE POWER TO LEGISLATE: A REFERENCE GUIDE TO THE UNITED STATES CONSTITUTION (Praeger Publishers 2006). Is it broad enough to encompass congressional investigations into any area of business or commercial activity? Are there any purely "private or personal affairs" that are outside the scope of congressional investigative power? See Chapter 2 for discussion of congressional investigative activities that infringe upon constitutionally guaranteed rights and liberties.

3. Judicial Respect, and Lack Thereof, for Congressional Investigative Power. Both *McGrain* and *Sinclair* demonstrate a healthy respect for the congressional investigative process, but this has not been the unanimous judicial verdict. Justice Samuel Miller, a Lincoln appointee to the Court and author of the critical *Kilbourn v. Thompson* opinion (cited in *McGrain*), expressed harsh private criticism of congressional investigative powers:

> I think the public has been much abused, the time of the legislative bodies uselessly consumed and rights of citizens ruthlessly invaded under the now familiar pretext of legislative investigation and that it is time that it was understood that courts and grand juries are the only inquisitions into crime in this

country. I do not recognize the doctrine that Congress is the grand inquest of the nation, or has any such function to perform, nor that it can by the name of a report slander the citizen so as to protect the newspaper which publishes such slander. If the whole body cannot do this much less can one house do it . . .

As regards needed information on subjects purely legislative no doubt committees can be raised to inquire and report, money can be used to pay for such information and laws may be made to compel reluctant witnesses to give it under proper guaranty of their personal rights. This is sufficient, without subjecting a witness to the unlimited power of a legislative committee or a single branch of the legislative body.

Charles Fairman, *Justice Samuel F. Miller: A Study of a Judicial Statesman*, 50 POL. SCI. Q. 15, 35–36 n.72 (1935), *quoting* Letter from Samuel F. Miller to William Pitt Ballinger (Mar. 20, 1881).

Other courts have found the task of balancing the interests of subpoenaed witnesses against the legislative interests of the Congress difficult, if not highly inappropriate, and one Court of Appeals even beseeched the Congress to "creat[e] a method of allowing these issues to be settled by declaratory judgment" for "[e]ven though it may be constitutional to put a man to guessing how a court will rule on difficult questions like those raised in good faith in this suit, what is constitutional is not necessarily most desirable." *United States v. Tobin*, 306 F. 2d 270, 276 (D.C. Cir. 1962) (quoting the court below, 195 F. Supp. 588, 617 (D.D.C. 1961)).

Courts have recognized limits on the scope of the criminal contempt of Congress statute, however, such as in cases arising out of the anti-communist investigations of the 1950s. In one of those cases, a congressional committee was inquiring into communist activities in "the Albany area." The Supreme Court reversed the contemnor's conviction of contempt of Congress for refusing to answer questions about his student years at Cornell University, finding that such questions were not "pertinent" to its inquiry because it could "hardly be seriously contended that Cornell University is in the Albany area." *Deutch v. United States*, 367 U.S. 456, 470 (1961). On the one hand, the Court has stated, as it did in *McGrain*, that the power of inquiry may be as broad as the power to legislate and, on the other hand, it has required the Congress, as it did in *Deutch*, to articulate its claim of authority "as if it were one of technical jurisdiction or venue." 367 U.S. at 474 (Harlan, J., joined by Frankfurter, J., dissenting). The response of the courts to the congressional investigative activities of the anti-communist McCarthy era is examined in Chapter 2.

4. Criminal Contempt of Congress Prosecutions, Intent, and "Mistake of Law." Sinclair was prosecuted under a criminal contempt statute intended to punish witnesses for failing to comply with lawful congressional process. Sinclair's argument was that he believed, "in good faith on the advice of competent counsel," that the Senate committee had exceeded its authority and he therefore was acting lawfully in refusing to answer the questions put to him. The Supreme Court dismissed that argument in summary fashion:

No moral turpitude is involved. Intentional violation is sufficient to constitute guilt. There was no misapprehension as to what was called for. The refusal to answer was deliberate. The facts sought were pertinent as a matter of law, and § 102 made it appellant's duty to answer. He was bound rightly to construe the statute. *His mistaken view of the law is no defense.* [Emphasis added and citations omitted.]

Where does this leave a witness—and his or her counsel—who believes that a congressional investigation has exceeded its lawful authority? Must a witness risk a prison term to test the legal bounds of a congressional committee's investigative power? How likely is it that a witness would take that risk?

In a recent case arising out of the January 6, 2021, attack on the U.S. Capitol, a federal district court in Washington, D.C., followed the holding of *Sinclair* in rejecting a "reliance on advice of counsel" defense asserted by Steve Bannon, an associate of President Donald Trump who had refused to appear and produce documents in response to subpoenas from the House Select Committee to Investigate the January 6th Attack on the United States Capitol. At a pretrial hearing, Bannon sought the court's permission to argue to the jury at his upcoming criminal contempt of Congress trial that he relied on his counsel's advice that President Trump's assertion of executive privilege permitted him to refuse to comply with the committee's subpoenas. The federal district court disagreed, relying on the Supreme Court's holding in *Sinclair* and a subsequent 1961 D.C. Circuit case applying *Sinclair*, *Licavoli v. United States*, and stating:

> In *Licavoli v. United States*, the Court of Appeals held:
>
> > Since, as we have remarked, it has been established since the *Sinclair* case, *supra*, that reliance upon advice of counsel is no defense to a charge of refusing to answer a question, *such reliance is not a defense to a charge of failure to respond [to a Congressional subpoena]. The elements of intent are the same in both cases. All that is needed in either event is a deliberate intention to do the act. Advice of counsel does not immunize that simple intention. It might immunize if evil motive or purpose were an element of the offense. But such motive or purpose is not an element of either of these offenses.* We are of opinion that the doctrine laid down in *Sinclair* applies also to a charge of willfully making default. *Advice of counsel cannot immunize a deliberate, intentional failure to appear pursuant to a lawful subpoena lawfully served.*
> >
> > In the case at bar there can be no serious dispute about the deliberate intention of Licavoli not to appear before the Committee pursuant to its subpoena. That he meant to stay away was made abundantly clear. That he did so upon the advice of a lawyer is no defense. The trial judge correctly instructed the jury.
>
> 294 F.2d 207, 209 (D.C. Cir. 1961) (emphasis added).

* * *

But at the hearing, Bannon also raised a new argument: that *Licavoli* is inapplicable because it did not involve a claim of executive privilege. Since this argument had not been briefed, the Court asked the parties for supplemental briefing. *See* Def.'s Supp, Br. in Opp. (Def.'s Supp."), ECF No. 41; United States' Resp. to Def.'s Supp. Br. ("Gov't Resp."), ECF No. 43.

In his supplemental brief, Bannon notes the differences between his reliance on a claimed invocation of executive privilege and *Licavoli*, which included no claim of privilege. *See* Def.'s Supp. at 1–7. And Bannon argues that, because this case involves an inter-branch dispute, while *Licavoli* did not, it is not binding here. *See id.* at 7–10. The government disagrees. It argues that *Licavoli*'s rejection of the advice of counsel defense turned on the *mens rea* element of 2 U.S.C. §192, which cannot be different depending on the specific circumstances of the case, and which requires proof only of a deliberate and intentional failure to appear or produce records. *See* Gov't Resp. at 2–4.[1] As the government puts it, "[b]y advocating to allow him to raise an advice-of-counsel defense in his case, even though it is not available to others charged with contempt of Congress, the Defendant necessarily is advocating that the intent element of the offense should change depending on the factual circumstances of the crime." *Id.* at 4. And, the government argues, the differences that Bannon points to do not relate to the *mens rea* element or an advice-of-counsel defense. *See id.* at 5–9.

The Court agrees with the government. As the Court noted at the March 16 hearing, "[i]f this were a matter of first impression, the Court might be inclined to agree with defendant and allow this evidence in." Trans. at 87:11–13. But for the reasons stated on the record during the March 16 hearing, *Licavoli* remains binding, and Bannon has failed to demonstrate that it is inapplicable here. After all, *Licavoli* involved a prosecution under the exact statute that Bannon is charged with violating, *see Licavoli*, 294 F.2d at 207, and the Court of Appeals expressly held that an advice-of-counsel defense is unavailable for that charge. *See id.* at 207–09. Just as important, the Court of Appeals rejected the availability of that defense because of the *mens rea* required for a violation of 2 U.S.C. §192, and Bannon has provided no reason to believe that the *mens rea* element can or should be different depending on the circumstances of specific cases.

United States v. Bannon, Crim. Action No. 1:21-cr-00670 (CJN), April 6, 2022 (footnote in original). On July 22, 2022, after a jury trial in which the defense presented no evidence, Bannon was convicted of two misdemeanor counts of contempt of Congress,

---

1. Other courts have held that 2 U.S.C. §192 requires only a deliberate and intentional failure to appear or produce records. *See, e.g., United States v. Bryan*, 339 U.S. 323 (1950); *United States v. Fleischman*, 339 U.S. 349 (1950); *Dennis v. United States*, 171 F.2d 986, 990–91 (D.C. Cir. 1948); *Fields v. United States*, 164 F.2d 97, 99–100 (D.C. Cir. 1947).

one for refusing to testify and one for refusing to produce documents to the January 6 Committee.

What is the impact of the *Bannon* case? One knowledgeable commentator summarized the state of the law after the *Bannon* case as follows:

> Pending any further action upon appeal, the state of the law on the mens rea required to prove a criminal violation of the Contempt of Congress [*sic*] remains that "willfully" means a deliberate act of withholding the information under congressional subpoena. The statute does not require proof of "evil motive or purpose." Rather, the statute merely requires a deliberate intention not to respond to the congressional command.

Andy Wright, *What Kind of Guilty Mind Is Needed for the Contempt of Congress Statute?*, JUST SECURITY, April 26, 2022 , at justsecurity.org/81191/what-kind-of-guilty-mind-is-needed-for-the-comfort-of-congress-statute/.

5. The Cornerstone of the New Deal? The broad congressional investigative powers recognized by the Supreme Court in the *Daugherty* and *Sinclair* cases were soon put to use by Congress. After the stock market crash of 1929 and the subsequent collapse of the national economy, Congress embarked upon a massive effort to find both legislative solutions to the nation's problems and culpable villains to blame for the country's economic woes. Those inquiries yielded the New Deal legislative initiatives that transformed the U.S. government in the pre-World War II years. Thus, although the Supreme Court could not have foreseen the swift and broad impact of its rulings, the *Daugherty* and *Sinclair* cases in no small measure made possible the legislative accomplishments of the New Deal era. Perhaps the greatest example of congressional investigations resulting in immensely important legislative accomplishments is the Pecora Wall Street hearings of the early 1930s and the subsequent enactment of the federal banking and securities laws. Those events are covered later in this Chapter, but one final issue relating to the *Daugherty* and *Sinclair* cases merits examination here.

Teapot Dome: Recent Developments — A Different Standard for Presidents

The *Daugherty* and *Sinclair* cases have been the leading precedents defining the scope of congressional investigative power for almost a century. Although subsequent cases discussed in later chapters of this book refined their application, the broad contours of congressional investigative power set out in *Daugherty* and *Sinclair* were not significantly disturbed by the Supreme Court until 2020, when a case involving congressional subpoenas seeking President Donald Trump's financial records reached the Court:

Trump v. Mazars USA, LLP

591 U.S. ___, 140 S. Ct. 2019 (2020)

CHIEF JUSTICE ROBERTS delivered the opinion of the Court.

Over the course of five days in April 2019, three committees of the U.S. House of Representatives issued four subpoenas seeking information about the finances of President Donald J. Trump, his children, and affiliated businesses. We have held that the House has authority under the Constitution to issue subpoenas to assist it in carrying out its legislative responsibilities. The House asserts that the financial information sought here—encompassing a decade's worth of transactions by the President and his family—will help guide legislative reform in areas ranging from money laundering and terrorism to foreign involvement in U.S. elections. The President contends that the House lacked a valid legislative aim and instead sought these records to harass him, expose personal matters, and conduct law enforcement activities beyond its authority. The question presented is whether the subpoenas exceed the authority of the House under the Constitution.

We have never addressed a congressional subpoena for the President's information. Two hundred years ago, it was established that Presidents may be subpoenaed during a federal criminal proceeding, *United States v. Burr*, 25 F. Cas. 30 (No. 14,692d) (CC Va. 1807) (Marshall, Cir. J.), and earlier today we extended that ruling to state criminal proceedings, *Trump v. Vance, ante,* p. ___, 140 S. Ct. 2412 (2020). Nearly fifty years ago, we held that a federal prosecutor could obtain information from a President despite assertions of executive privilege, *United States v. Nixon*, 418 U.S. 683 (1974), and more recently we ruled that a private litigant could subject a President to a damages suit and appropriate discovery obligations in federal court, *Clinton v. Jones*, 520 U.S. 681 (1997).

This case is different. Here the President's information is sought not by prosecutors or private parties in connection with a particular judicial proceeding, but by committees of Congress that have set forth broad legislative objectives. Congress and the President—the two political branches established by the Constitution—have an ongoing relationship that the Framers intended to feature both rivalry and reciprocity. See The Federalist No. 51, p. 349 (J. Cooke ed. 1961) (J. Madison); *Youngstown Sheet & Tube Co. v. Sawyer*, 343 U.S. 579, 635 (1952) (Jackson, J., concurring). That distinctive aspect necessarily informs our analysis of the question before us.

[*Ed. Note: The Court described the three separate subpoenas issued by committees of the House of Representatives to Deutsche Bank and Mazars seeking President Trump's personal financial and business records, and recounted the procedural history of the case before it reached the Supreme Court.*]

The question presented is whether the subpoenas exceed the authority of the House under the Constitution. Historically, disputes over congressional demands for presidential documents have not ended up in court. Instead, they have been hashed out in the "hurly-burly, the give-and-take of the political process between the legislative and the executive." Hearings on S. 2170 et al. before the Subcommittee on Intergovernmental Relations of the Senate Committee on Government Operations, 94th Cong., 1st Sess., 87 (1975) (A. Scalia, Assistant Attorney General, Office of Legal Counsel).

* * * The Reagan and Clinton presidencies provide two modern examples:

During the Reagan administration, a House subcommittee subpoenaed all documents related to the Department of the Interior's decision whether to designate Canada a reciprocal country for purposes of the Mineral Lands Leasing Act. President Reagan directed that certain documents be withheld because they implicated his confidential relationship with subordinates. While withholding those documents, the administration made "repeated efforts" at accommodation through limited disclosures and testimony over a period of several months. 6 Op. of Office of Legal Counsel 751, 780 (1982). Unsatisfied, the subcommittee and its parent committee eventually voted to hold the Secretary of the Interior in contempt, and an innovative compromise soon followed: All documents were made available, but only for one day with no photocopying, minimal notetaking, and no participation by non-Members of Congress. *Id.*, at 780–781; see H. R. Rep. No. 97-898, pp. 3–8 (1982). [*Ed. Note: The Reagan executive privilege dispute is discussed in Chapter 4.*]

In 1995, a Senate committee subpoenaed notes taken by a White House attorney at a meeting with President Clinton's personal lawyers concerning the Whitewater controversy. The President resisted the subpoena on the ground that the notes were protected by attorney-client privilege, leading to "long and protracted" negotiations and a Senate threat to seek judicial enforcement of the subpoena. S. Rep. No. 104-204, pp. 16–17 (1996). Eventually the parties reached an agreement, whereby President Clinton avoided the threatened suit, agreed to turn over the notes, and obtained the Senate's concession that he had not waived any privileges. *Ibid.*; see L. Fisher, Congressional Research Service, Congressional Investigations: Subpoenas and Contempt Power 16–18 (2003). [*Ed. Note: The Whitewater notes attorney-client privilege dispute is discussed in Chapter 6.*]

Congress and the President maintained this tradition of negotiation and compromise—without the involvement of this Court—until the present dispute. Indeed, from President Washington until now, we have never considered a dispute over a congressional subpoena for the President's records. And, according to the parties, the appellate courts have addressed such a subpoena only once, when a Senate committee subpoenaed President Nixon during the Watergate scandal. See *infra*, at 13 (discussing *Senate Select Committee on Presidential Campaign Activities v. Nixon*, 498 F.2d 725 (D.C. Cir. 1974) (en banc). In that case, the court refused to enforce the subpoena, and the Senate did not seek review by this Court. [*Ed. Note: The Nixon tapes executive privilege dispute is discussed in Chapters 3 and 7.*]

This dispute therefore represents a significant departure from historical practice. Although the parties agree that this particular controversy is justiciable, we recognize that it is the first of its kind to reach this Court; that disputes of this sort can raise important issues concerning relations between the branches; that related disputes involving congressional efforts to seek official Executive Branch information recur on a regular basis, including in the context of deeply partisan controversy; and that Congress and the Executive have nonetheless managed for over two centuries to resolve such disputes among themselves without the benefit of guidance from us. Such longstanding practice "'is a consideration of great weight'" in cases concerning "the allocation of power between [the] two elected branches of Government," and it imposes on us a duty of care to ensure that we not needlessly disturb "the compromises and working arrangements that [those] branches ... themselves have reached." *NLRB v. Noel Canning*, 573 U.S. 513, 524–526 (2014) (quoting *The Pocket Veto Case*, 279 U.S. 655, 689 (1929)). With that in mind, we turn to the question presented.

Congress has no enumerated constitutional power to conduct investigations or issue subpoenas, but we have held that each House has power "to secure needed information" in order to legislate. *McGrain v. Daugherty*, 273 U.S. 135, 161 (1927). This "power of inquiry—with process to enforce it—is an essential and appropriate auxiliary to the legislative function." *Id.*, at 174. Without information, Congress would be shooting in the dark, unable to legislate "wisely or effectively." *Id.*, at 175. The congressional power to obtain information is "broad" and "indispensable." *Watkins v. United States*, 354 U.S. 178, 187, 215 (1957). It encompasses inquiries into the administration of existing laws, studies of proposed laws, and "surveys of defects in our social, economic or political system for the purpose of enabling the Congress to remedy them." *Id.*, at 187.

Because this power is "justified solely as an adjunct to the legislative process," it is subject to several limitations. *Id.*, at 197. Most importantly, a congressional subpoena is valid only if it is "related to, and in furtherance of, a legitimate task of the Congress." *Id.*, at 187. The subpoena must serve a "valid legislative purpose," *Quinn v. United States*, 349 U.S. 155, 161 (1955); it must "concern [] a subject on which legislation 'could be had,'" *Eastland v. United States Servicemen's Fund*, 421 U.S. 491, 506 (1975) (quoting *McGrain*, 273 U.S., at 177). Furthermore, Congress may not issue a subpoena for the purpose of "law enforcement," because "those powers are assigned under our Constitution to the Executive and the Judiciary." *Quinn*, 349 U.S., at 161. Thus Congress may not use subpoenas to "try" someone "before [a] committee for any crime or wrongdoing." *McGrain*, 273 U.S., at 179. Congress has no "'general' power to inquire into private affairs and compel disclosures," *id.*, at 173–174, and "there is no congressional power to expose for the sake of exposure," *Watkins*, 354 U.S., at 200. "Investigations conducted solely for the personal aggrandizement of the investigators or to 'punish' those investigated are indefensible." *Id.*, at 187. Finally, recipients of legislative subpoenas retain their constitutional rights throughout the course of an investigation. *See id.*, at 188, 198. And recipients have long been understood to retain common law and constitutional privileges with respect to certain materials, such as attorney-client communications and governmental communications protected by executive privilege. See, *e.g.*, Congressional Research Service, *supra*, at 16–18 (attorney-client privilege); *Senate Select Committee*, 498 F.2d, at 727, 730–731 (executive privilege).

The President contends, as does the Solicitor General appearing on behalf of the United States, that the usual rules for congressional subpoenas do not govern here because the President's papers are at issue. They argue for a more demanding standard based in large part on cases involving the Nixon tapes—recordings of conversations between President Nixon and close advisers discussing the break-in at the Democratic National Committee's headquarters at the Watergate complex. The tapes were subpoenaed by a Senate committee and the Special Prosecutor investigating the break-in, prompting President Nixon to invoke executive privilege and leading to two cases addressing the showing necessary to require the President to comply with the subpoenas. See *Nixon*, 418 U.S. 683; *Senate Select Committee*, 498 F.2d 725.

Those cases, the President and the Solicitor General now contend, establish the standard that should govern the House subpoenas here. Quoting *Nixon*, the President asserts that the House must establish a "demonstrated, specific need" for the financial information, just as the Watergate special prosecutor was required to do in order to obtain the tapes. 418 U.S., at 713. And drawing on *Senate Select Committee*—the D.C. Circuit case refusing to enforce the Senate subpoena for the tapes—the President and the Solicitor General argue that the House must show that the financial information is "demonstrably critical" to its legislative purpose. 498 F.2d, at 731.

We disagree that these demanding standards apply here. Unlike the cases before us, *Nixon* and *Senate Select Committee* involved Oval Office communications over which the President asserted executive privilege. That privilege safeguards the public interest in candid, confidential deliberations within the Executive Branch; it is "fundamental to the operation of Government." *Nixon*, 418 U.S., at 708. As a result, information subject to executive privilege deserves "the greatest protection consistent with the fair administration of justice." *Id.*, at 715. We decline to transplant that protection root and branch to cases involving nonprivileged, private information, which by definition does not implicate sensitive Executive Branch deliberations.

The standards proposed by the President and the Solicitor General—if applied outside the context of privileged information—would risk seriously impeding Congress in carrying out its responsibilities. The President and the Solicitor General would apply the same exacting standards to all subpoenas for the President's information, without recognizing distinctions between privileged and nonprivileged information, between official and personal information, or between various legislative objectives. Such a categorical approach would represent a significant departure from the longstanding way of doing business between the branches, giving short shrift to Congress's important interests in conducting inquiries to obtain the information it needs to legislate effectively. Confounding the legislature in that effort would be contrary to the principle that:

> "It is the proper duty of a representative body to look diligently into every affair of government and to talk much about what it sees. It is meant to be the eyes and the voice, and to embody the wisdom and will of its constituents. Unless Congress have and use every means of acquainting itself with the acts and the disposition of the administrative agents of the government, the country must be helpless to learn how it is being served." *United States v. Rumely*, 345 U.S. 41, 43 (1953) (internal quotation marks omitted).

Legislative inquiries might involve the President in appropriate cases; as noted, Congress's responsibilities extend to "every affair of government." *Ibid.* (internal quotation marks omitted). Because the President's approach does not take adequate account of these significant congressional interests, we do not adopt it.

The House meanwhile would have us ignore that these suits involve the President. Invoking our precedents concerning investigations that did not target the President's papers, the House urges us to uphold its subpoenas because they "relate[] to a valid legislative purpose" or "concern[] a subject on which legislation could be had." Brief for Respondent 46 (*quoting Barenblatt v. United States*, 360 U.S. 109, 127 (1959), and *Eastland*, 421 U.S., at 506). That approach is appropriate, the House argues, because the cases before us are not "momentous separation-of-powers disputes." Brief for Respondent 1. * * *

Far from accounting for separation of powers concerns, the House's approach aggravates them by leaving essentially no limits on the congressional power to subpoena the President's personal records. Any personal paper possessed by a President could potentially "relate to" a conceivable subject of legislation, for Congress has broad legislative powers that touch a vast number of subjects. Brief for Respondent 46. The President's financial records could relate to economic reform, medical records to health reform, school transcripts to education reform, and so on. Indeed, at argument, the House was unable to identify any type of information that lacks some relation to potential legislation. See Tr. of Oral Arg. 52–53, 62–65.

Without limits on its subpoena powers, Congress could "exert an imperious controul" over the Executive Branch and aggrandize itself at the President's expense, just as the Framers feared. The Federalist No. 71, at 484 (A. Hamilton); see *id.*, No. 48, at 332–333 (J. Madison); *Bowsher v. Synar*, 478 U.S. 714, 721–722, 727 (1986). And a limitless subpoena power would transform the "established practice" of the political branches. *Noel Canning*, 573 U.S., at 524 (internal quotation marks omitted). Instead of negotiating over information requests, Congress could simply walk away from the bargaining table and compel compliance in court.

The House and the courts below suggest that these separation of powers concerns are not fully implicated by the particular subpoenas here, but we disagree. We would have to be "blind" not to see what "[a]ll others can see and understand": that the subpoenas do not represent a run-of-the-mill legislative effort but rather a clash between rival branches of government over records of intense political interest for all involved. *Rumely*, 345 U.S., at 44 (quoting *Child Labor Tax Case*, 259 U.S. 20, 37 (1922) (Taft, C.J.)).

The interbranch conflict here does not vanish simply because the subpoenas seek personal papers or because the President was sued in his personal capacity. The President is the only person who alone composes a branch of government. As a result, there is not always a clear line between his personal and official affairs. "The interest of the man" is often "connected with the constitutional rights of the place." The Federalist No. 51, at 349. Given the close connection between the Office of the President and its occupant, congressional demands for the President's papers can implicate the relationship between the branches regardless whether those papers are personal or official. Either way, a demand may aim to harass the President or render him "complaisan[t] to the humors of the Legislature." *Id.*, No. 71, at 483. In fact, a subpoena for personal papers may pose a heightened risk of such impermissible purposes, precisely because of the documents' personal nature and their less evident connection to a legislative task. No one can say that the controversy here is less significant to the relationship between the branches simply because it involves personal papers. Quite the opposite. That appears to be what makes the matter of such great consequence to the President and Congress.

In addition, separation of powers concerns are no less palpable here simply because the subpoenas were issued to third parties. Congressional demands for the President's information present an interbranch conflict no matter where the information is held—it is, after all, the President's information. Were it otherwise, Congress could sidestep constitutional requirements any time a President's information is entrusted to a third party—as occurs with rapidly increasing frequency. Cf. *Carpenter v. United States*, 585 U.S. ___, ___, ___, 138 S. Ct. 2206, 2230 (2018) (slip op., at 15, 17). Indeed, Congress could declare open season on the President's information held by schools, archives, internet service providers, e-mail clients, and financial institutions. The Constitution does not tolerate such ready evasion; it "deals with substance, not shadows." *Cummings v. Missouri*, 4 Wall. 277, 325 (1867).

Congressional subpoenas for the President's personal information implicate weighty concerns regarding the separation of powers. Neither side, however, identifies an approach that accounts for these concerns. For more than two centuries, the political branches have resolved information disputes using the wide variety of means that the Constitution puts at their disposal. The nature of such interactions would be transformed by judicial enforcement of either of the approaches suggested by the parties, eroding a "[d]eeply embedded traditional way[] of conducting government." *Youngstown Sheet & Tube Co.*, 343 U.S., at 610 (Frankfurter, J., concurring).

A balanced approach is necessary, one that takes a "considerable impression" from "the practice of the government," *McCulloch v. Maryland*, 4 Wheat. 316, 401 (1819); see *Noel Canning*, 573 U.S., at 524–526, and "resist[s]" the "pressure inherent within each of the separate Branches to exceed the outer limits of its power," *INS v. Chadha*, 462 U.S. 919, 951 (1983). We therefore conclude that, in assessing whether a subpoena directed at the President's personal information is "related to, and in furtherance of, a legitimate task of the Congress," *Watkins*, 354 U.S., at 187, courts must perform a careful analysis that takes adequate account of the separation of powers principles at stake, including both the significant legislative interests of Congress and the "unique position" of the President, *Clinton*, 520 U.S., at 698 (internal quotation marks omitted). Several special considerations inform this analysis.

First, courts should carefully assess whether the asserted legislative purpose warrants the significant step of involving the President and his papers. "'[O]ccasion[s] for constitutional confrontation between the two branches' should be avoided whenever possible." *Cheney v. United States Dist. Court for D.C.*, 542 U.S. 367, 389–390 (2004) (quoting *Nixon*, 418 U.S., at 692). Congress may not rely on the President's information if other sources could reasonably provide Congress the information it needs in light of its particular legislative objective. The President's unique constitutional position means that Congress may not look to him as a "case study" for general legislation. *Cf.* 943 F.3d, at 662–663, n. 67.

Unlike in criminal proceedings, where "[t]he very integrity of the judicial system" would be undermined without "full disclosure of all the facts," *Nixon*, 418 U.S., at 709, efforts to craft legislation involve predictive policy judgments that are "not hamper[ed] ... in quite the same way" when every scrap of potentially relevant evidence is not available, *Cheney*, 542 U.S., at 384; see *Senate Select Committee*, 498 F.2d, at 732. While we certainly recognize Congress's important interests in obtaining information through appropriate inquiries, those interests are not sufficiently powerful to justify access to the President's personal papers when other sources could provide Congress the information it needs.

Second, to narrow the scope of possible conflict between the branches, courts should insist on a subpoena no broader than reasonably necessary to support Congress's legislative objective. The specificity of the subpoena's request "serves as an important safeguard against unnecessary intrusion into the operation of the Office of the President." *Cheney*, 542 U.S., at 387.

Third, courts should be attentive to the nature of the evidence offered by Congress to establish that a subpoena advances a valid legislative purpose. The more detailed and substantial the evidence of Congress's legislative purpose, the better. See *Watkins*, 354 U.S., at 201, 205 (preferring such evidence over "vague" and "loosely worded" evidence of Congress's purpose). That is particularly true when Congress contemplates legislation that raises sensitive constitutional issues, such as legislation concerning the Presidency. In such cases, it is "impossible" to conclude that a subpoena is designed to advance a valid legislative purpose unless Congress adequately identifies its aims and explains why the President's information will advance its consideration of the possible legislation. *Id.*, at 205–206, 214–215.

Fourth, courts should be careful to assess the burdens imposed on the President by a subpoena. We have held that burdens on the President's time and attention stemming from judicial process and litigation, without more, generally do not cross constitutional lines. See *Vance, ante*, at 12–14; *Clinton*, 520 U.S., at 704–705. But burdens imposed by a congressional subpoena should be carefully scrutinized, for they stem from a rival political branch that has an ongoing relationship with the President and incentives to use subpoenas for institutional advantage.

Other considerations may be pertinent as well; one case every two centuries does not afford enough experience for an exhaustive list.

When Congress seeks information "needed for intelligent legislative action," it "unquestionably" remains "the duty of *all* citizens to cooperate." *Watkins*, 354 U.S., at 187 (emphasis added). Congressional subpoenas for information from the President, however, implicate special concerns regarding the separation of powers. The courts below did not take adequate account of those concerns. The judgments of the Courts of Appeals for the D.C. Circuit and the Second Circuit are vacated, and the cases are remanded for further proceedings consistent with this opinion.

[*Ed. Note: Dissenting opinions of Justices Thomas and Alito omitted.*]

Notes and Questions

1. Implications of *Mazars*. How important is the special test applicable to congressional subpoenas seeking presidential information that is set out in *Mazars*? The Court seems to be reaffirming the principles of *Daugherty* and *Sinclair* for congressional subpoenas that do not seek presidential information, while at the same time strongly admonishing that a different standard applies when Congress subpoenas presidential information, whatever the nature of the information (personal or official) and whoever possesses it (the President or a third party). What will be the impact of this holding on future congressional oversight of presidential activities? See Chapters 4 and 9 for further discussion of this important question.

2. How Workable Is the *Mazars* Four-Part Test? Review the four-part test the Supreme Court sets out in *Mazars*. How much guidance will this test provide to lower federal courts in evaluating and ruling on future congressional subpoenas for presidential materials? In August 2021, a federal district court judge applied the *Mazars* four-part test to the House of Representatives' subpoenas and concluded that "the Committee's asserted legislative purpose of bolstering financial disclosure laws for Presidents and presidential candidates does not warrant disclosure of President Trump's personal and corporate financial records, when balanced against the separation of powers concerns raised by the broad scope of its subpoena." The court went on to conclude that "the Committee's other stated justifications for demanding President Trump's personal and corporate financial records—to legislate on the topic of federal lease agreements and conduct oversight of the General Service Administration's lease with Old Trump Post Office LLC, [*sic.*] and to legislate pursuant to Congress's authority under the Foreign Emoluments Clause—do not implicate the same separation of powers concerns. The records corresponding to those justifications therefore must be disclosed." *Trump v. Mazars USA LLP*, 560 F. Supp. 3d 47, 51 (D.D.C. 2021). (The court's analysis was affected by the fact that President Trump was no longer the incumbent President, prompting the court to apply a "*Mazars* lite" test because of what the court concluded were "greatly diminished" separation of powers issues presented by a congressional subpoena for a former President's financial information.) Do you agree with the court's conclusions in balancing the stated legislative purposes against separation of powers concerns? As discussed in Note 6 below, a three-judge panel of the D.C. Circuit reached a slightly different conclusion on the issue of how *Mazars* applies to a former President.

3. Does It Matter That the *Mazars* Subpoena Was for Personal Documents and Records, Not Official Presidential Documents? In his *Mazars* dissenting opinion, Justice

Thomas drew a distinction between congressional subpoenas for personal documents of a President and subpoenas for governmental documents relating to the President's performance of official duties:

> Thomas then examines the evolution of congressional subpoenas beginning at the Founding, arguing that early investigations into generals and members of Congress did not look at personal documents. In fact, Thomas writes, the only instances in which Congress sought personal documents involved material from a federally chartered bank.
>
> And the practice of issuing legislative subpoenas for nonofficial information was controversial throughout the 19th century. Thomas writes that when the Supreme Court first considered legislative subpoenas in *Kilbourn*, in 1880, it "cast... doubt on legislative subpoenas generally" and "held that the subpoena at issue was unlawful." In *McGrain*, the Supreme Court later upheld Congress's power to issue subpoenas as derived from its power to legislate—but, Thomas argues, *McGrain* "lacks any foundation in text or history." Though the Supreme Court has rolled back Congress's authority to compel testimony or documents after *McGrain*, Thomas would instead decline to apply *McGrain* altogether. For "it is readily apparent," he writes, "that the Committees have no constitutional authority to subpoena private, nonofficial documents."
>
> Finally, Thomas writes that the only concrete example of Congress being able to subpoena personal documents has been through the impeachment process. If Congress seeks to obtain Trump's financial records, he argues, "it should proceed through the impeachment power."

Rachel Bercovitz & Todd Carney, *Summary: The Supreme Court Rules in Trump v. Vance*, LAWFARE BLOG (July 10, 2020). Should it make a difference that the Committee was seeking President Trump's personal business records? Are the separation of powers issues different when personal business records are sought, rather than official presidential documents? (Separation of powers issues are discussed further in Chapters 4 and 9.) Would Justice Thomas's approach have prevented Congress from obtaining President Clinton's Whitewater business records, except in an impeachment inquiry? The Whitewater investigation is discussed in Chapter 6, and impeachment is discussed in Chapter 7.

4. Congressional Oversight and Legislative Investigative Powers vs. Criminal Justice Proceedings. In *Trump v. Vance*, a companion case decided the same day as *Mazars*, the Court upheld a New York state grand jury subpoena *duces tecum* directed at the Mazars accounting firm and requiring production by Mazars of financial records of President Trump and his personal businesses. *See Trump v. Vance*, 591 U.S. ___, 140 S. Ct. 2412 (2020). As in *Mazars*, Chief Justice Roberts wrote the opinion for the Court and noted that *Vance* was also a case of first impression: "This case involves—so far as we and the parties can tell—the first *state* criminal subpoena directed to a President." President Trump sued in federal court to enjoin enforcement of a New York state grand jury subpoena, arguing that under Article II and the Supremacy Clause of the Constitution, a sitting President is absolutely immune from state criminal process. The Supreme Court rejected Trump's argument for absolute immunity, concluding that "two centuries of experience confirm that a properly tailored criminal subpoena will not normally hamper the performance of the President's official duties" and "the burden on a President will ordinarily be lighter than the burden of defending against a civil suit." The Court also rejected the Department of Justice's *amicus curiae* argument that a heightened standard of need should apply to a state grand jury subpoena for presidential information, concluding that "the public's interest in fair and effective law enforcement cuts in favor of comprehensive access to evidence." In reaching these conclusions, the Court relied heavily on its prior decisions in cases involving Presidents Nixon (enforcing a federal criminal trial subpoena) and Clinton (holding that a sitting President is subject to civil suit while in office). The *Trump v. Vance* case is discussed in greater detail in Chapter 3.

5. Do *Mazars* and *Vance* Strike the Right Balance for Effective Presidential Oversight? Congressional oversight scholar Victoria Nourse has criticized the holdings of *Mazars* and *Vance*: "Taken together, the cases raise powerful questions about the separation of powers that only the future will decide. Put bluntly, why should the citizens of New York (or any other state for that matter) have an easier time checking the President than the citizens of the entire nation (as reflected in the House of Representatives)?" *See The Dark Side of* Mazars: *Should a New York Prosecutor Have More Power to Check the President than the House of Representatives?*, AMERICAN CONSTITUTION SOCIETY EXPERT FORUM (July 13, 2020). Professor Nourse went on to observe:

> That brings me to the real winner in these cases, at least in terms of constitutional power—the judiciary. In *Vance,* where financial records were sought for a grand jury investigation, the court was quite deferential, rejecting all the President's arguments including the argument that the subpoena had to have a "higher" showing because its target was the President. In *Mazars,* Congress was not given that same deference: precisely because the President was involved, a "higher" standard was imposed, one to be administrated by the courts. When given a choice of investigators—courts or Congress—courts chose themselves. One rule applies to judicial investigations of Donald Trump, another to congressional investigations.

Do you agree with Professor Nourse's assertions? Do the *Mazars* and *Vance* cases, taken together, show a bias on the part of the Supreme Court in favor of the criminal justice system, to the detriment of congressional oversight powers? For more discussion of this issue and what the future may hold for congressional oversight after the Trump administration upheavals, see Chapter 9.

6. *Mazars* Applied—to a former President. In July 2022, a three-judge panel of the D.C. Circuit applied *Mazars* to the ongoing dispute over the House Oversight Committee's subpoena, reissued on February 25, 2021, for President Trump's financial records. After reviewing the procedural history of the litigation and determining that the case was not moot, the three-judge panel addressed the effect of President Trump having left office while the litigation continued:

> Having determined that we retain jurisdiction to consider President Trump's challenge to the Committee's subpoena, we next consider by which test we should assess whether the subpoena "is related to, and in furtherance of, a legitimate task of the Congress." *Mazars*, 140 S. Ct. at 2035 (quotations omitted). One might wonder why that is even a question—after all, the Supreme Court already set out the framework that should govern the inquiry in this case and directed us to apply it on remand.
>
> In the Committee's view, though, the test prescribed by the Supreme Court in this case should no longer govern our analysis. That test, to the Committee, rested on the heightened separation-of-powers concerns raised by a congressional subpoena issued to a *sitting* President. But because President Trump is now a former President, the Committee argues, a more relaxed standard should control. The Committee thus urges us to set aside the four-factor inquiry set forth by the Supreme Court in this case and instead weigh "the Committee's need for the subpoenaed materials for its legislative purposes against the limited intrusion on the Presidency when Congress seeks a former President's information." House Br. 62. The Committee derives that standard from *Nixon v. Administrator of General Services*, 433 U.S. 425 (1977), which rejected a former President's challenge to a statute enabling the General Services Administration to take custody of his presidential records. *Id.* at 430.
>
> We do not accept the Committee's invitation to abandon the Supreme Court's *Mazars* test in the *Mazars* case itself. Whatever may be the appropriate standard when Congress issues a subpoena to a former President, the subpoena in this case, when issued, sought a sitting President's information. President Trump then brought this challenge while still in office; that same challenge remains pending; and the subpoena remains unchanged in all respects. At least in these specific circumstances, we do not understand that the *Mazars* test instantly ceased to apply—and a different standard immediately took hold—on the day President Trump left office. The ongoing litigation otherwise remained the same.
>
> True, separation-of-powers interests on the President's side of the ledger may be "subject to erosion over time after an administration leaves office." *Nixon v. GSA*, 433 U.S. at 451. But as we recently explained, "if there were no limits to Congress's ability to drown a President in burdensome requests the minute he leaves office, Congress could perhaps use the threat of a post-Presidency pile-on to try and influence the President's conduct while in office." *Trump v. Thompson*, 20 F.4th 10, 44 (D.C. Cir. 2021). Congress thus could wield the threat of intrusive post-Presidency subpoenas to influence the actions of a sitting President "for institutional advantage." *Mazars*, 140 S. Ct. at 2036. And

here, the Committee specifically made known, while President Trump remained in office, that the Committee "fully intend[ed] to continue [its] investigation … in the next Congress, regardless of who holds the presidency."

We note, lastly, that the person "who holds the presidency," President Biden, has not opposed former President Trump's efforts to challenge the Committee's subpoena. Indeed, the last word of the Executive Branch in this case, filed in our court on remand from the Supreme Court, was to argue that the subpoena must be invalidated under the *Mazars* test. Brief for the United States as Amicus Curiae at 8–15, *Mazars*, 832 F. App'x 6 (No. 19-5142). The circumstances here thus are unlike those we recently faced in *Trump v. Thompson*. There, former President Trump's attempt to assert executive privilege to prevent a House Committee from obtaining presidential records relating to the events of January 6, 2021, conflicted with President Biden's considered judgment that "Congress has demonstrated a compelling need for [the] documents and that disclosure is in the best interests of the Nation." *Thompson*, 20 F.4th at 32.

In its order denying a stay application in that case, the Supreme Court specifically left open the question whether President Trump's status as a former President could make any difference to his ability to assert executive privilege. *See* Order Denying Application for Stay 1–2, *Trump v. Thompson*, No. 21A272 (Sup. Ct. Jan. 19, 2022). The possibility that President Trump's ability to assert executive privilege may be unaffected by his status as a former President—even in the face of the sitting President's opposition—gives us all the more reason to conclude here that the test governing President Trump's challenge is unaffected by his departure from office during the litigation.

In short, we will apply the *Mazars* test to the Mazars subpoena.

[*Ed. Note: The court then undertook a detailed application of the four-factor* Mazars *test to each of the three investigative tracks that had been identified by the Committee.*]

Having applied the first, second, and third *Mazars* factors to the Committee's subpoena, we now take up the fourth factor, which is the last one specifically enumerated by the Supreme Court. And because we already have considerably circumscribed the subpoena pursuant to our obligation to "insist on a subpoena no broader than reasonably necessary to support Congress's legislative objective," 140 S. Ct. at 2036, we apply the fourth *Mazars* factor to the subpoena as narrowed. Under that factor, we must "assess the burdens imposed on the President by [the] subpoena." *Id.* We conclude that the subpoena, as narrowed, does not impose any unwarranted burdens on President Trump, so it need not be quashed or further limited under the fourth *Mazars* factor.

Now that President Trump is out of office, any burdens the Committee's subpoena imposes on him will no longer distract the head of the Executive Branch. That is significant in view of the Supreme Court's emphasis on avoiding "unnecessary intrusion into the operation of *the Office of the President*." *Id.* (emphasis added) (quoting *Cheney*, 542 U.S. at 387). President Trump acknowledges the point, admitting that direct burdens on the President's time and attention "never mattered much to begin with" under the fourth *Mazars* factor, "since no President is going to compile documents himself." Trump Br. 31. What is more, the subpoena is directed to President Trump's accounting firm, not the former President himself. To be sure, the time required to litigate this lawsuit falls on him in some measure. But he chose to bring the lawsuit, and at any rate, the "time and attention stemming from judicial process and litigation, without more, generally do not cross constitutional lines." *Mazars*, 140 S. Ct. at 2036. That must be especially true in the case of a President no longer in office.

President Trump contends that the subpoena is overly burdensome because of the sheer volume of personal financial records it seeks. He characterizes a subpoena seeking a full accounting of his personal financial situation as unnecessarily intrusive in its lack of specificity. But we have now narrowed that subpoena to ensure it is no broader than reasonably necessary to support the Committee's specific legislative objectives under each of its three investigative tracks. Compliance with the subpoena as narrowed, in our view, does not impose an undue burden on President Trump for purposes of the fourth *Mazars* factor.

In light of the required narrowing of the Committee's subpoena as enumerated above, we hold that the Committee's legislative aims under its three investigative tracks, considered in combination, justify production of only the following subset of information encompassed by its subpoena: accounting records, source documents, and engagement letters from 2014–2018 that reference, indicate, or discuss any undisclosed, false, or otherwise inaccurate information about President Trump's or a Trump entity's reported assets, liabilities, or income; associated communications from 2014–2018 related to potential concerns that information provided was incomplete, inaccurate, or otherwise unsatisfactory; all requested documents from November 2016–2018 belonging to Trump Old Post Office LLC; all documents from November 2016–2018 referencing, indicating, discussing, or otherwise relating to, the Old Post Office lease; and all documents from 2017–2018 related to financial relationships, transactions, or ties between President Trump or a Trump entity and any foreign state or foreign state agency, the United States, any federal agency, any state or any state agency, or an individual government official.

As substantially narrowed in that fashion, we conclude that the Mazars subpoena is "no broader than reasonably necessary to support Congress's legislative objective[s]" across the Committee's three investigative tracks. *Mazars*, 140 S. Ct. at 2036. Again, the Committee need not show that it has a "demonstrated, specific need" for that subset of information, nor that the subset of information is "demonstrably critical" to its legislative purposes. *Id.* at 2032 (citations omitted). Rather, "reasonably necessary" is the relevant standard, *id.* at 2036, and we believe that standard is met when the subpoena is narrowed as set out in the preceding paragraph.

President Trump advances one last, overarching objection to our effort to render the subpoena consistent with the *Mazars* factors. In his view, once a court concludes that a congressional subpoena for presidential information is overbroad in any respect, the court cannot itself narrow the subpoena. Rather, he submits, the court must simply invalidate the overbroad subpoena and send the matter back to Congress to permit it to fashion a new subpoena. We disagree.

The Supreme Court's opinion in this case does not definitively resolve that issue. But in specifying that a court must "insist on a subpoena no broader than reasonably necessary," *id.* at 2036, we believe the Supreme Court intended to allow for a court reviewing a subpoena to conduct any required narrowing itself rather than to return the matter to Congress to start the process anew.

* * *

As for whether to order the parties to engage in further settlement negotiations, we recognize that disputes over congressional requests for a President's records have traditionally "been hashed out in the hurly-burly, the give-and-take of the political process between the legislative and the executive." *Mazars*, 140 S. Ct. at 2029 (quotation marks and citation omitted). But while the accommodation process is the preferred method for settling disputes between the political branches over access to the President's documents, the Supreme Court made clear that, when negotiations fail to resolve the matter, courts may step in to decide the interbranch dispute. The *Mazars* test inherently contemplates a situation in which the accommodation process fails to produce an amicable resolution and the dispute enters the courts.

Here, we see no reason to order the parties to negotiate further before we assess the validity of the Committee's subpoena. President Trump filed this lawsuit in April 2019, and the parties have had ample opportunity to arrive at an agreement in the years since. In June 2021, the district court directed the parties to "assess the possibility of an accommodation," but those efforts proved unsuccessful. 560 F. Supp. 3d at 58. Each side blames the other for the failure of the negotiations. President Trump contends that the Committee unreasonably demanded the ability to take physical possession of his papers. The Committee counters that it made "certain offers of confidentiality," but that President Trump insisted on unworkable restrictions on dissemination within Congress. House Reply Br. 24.

The accommodation process has proven unsuccessful. It now falls to this court to resolve the dispute in accordance with the framework laid down by the Supreme Court and based on the current record. This opinion endeavors to do so.

For the foregoing reasons, we affirm in part and reverse in part the judgment of the district court and remand for further proceedings consistent with this opinion.

So ordered.

Trump v. Mazars USA, LLC, 39 F.4th 774 (D.C. Cir. 2022). In applying the Supreme Court's four-part *Mazars* test, did the D.C. Circuit strike the right balance between the information-gathering needs of Congress and the burden on former President Trump? Was the D.C. Circuit correct in concluding that the district court had erred in applying a "*Mazars* lite" test because President Trump was no longer in office? How much difference should it make in terms of a separation of powers analysis if a congressional committee is seeking information from a former President, rather than a sitting President? Should it matter whether the incumbent President supports or opposes the position of the former President with respect to compliance with a congressional subpoena?

The Pecora Wall Street Investigation

Congressional investigations are frequently criticized as unnecessarily theatrical and overly partisan spectacles, but theatrics and partisanship are not necessarily antithetical to legislative accomplishments. The so-called "Pecora Hearings" that took place after the great stock market crash of 1929 illustrate how carefully orchestrated congressional hearings can generate both partisan political theater and significant legislative accomplishments. As Ferdinand Pecora said in his 1939 account of the hearings, "Never before in the history of the United States had so much wealth and power been required to render a public accounting." FERDINAND PECORA, WALL STREET UNDER OATH (Simon & Shuster 1939), p. 4. Corporate law scholar Joel Seligman described this masterful interweaving of politics and policy to produce the hearings that came to be known by Pecora's name in his 1982 book *The Transformation of Wall Street*, a comprehensive history of the Securities and Exchange Commission:

The Transformation of Wall Street

Joel Seligman (Houghton Mifflin Company 1982)

[*Excerpts from* Chapter One: After the Crash (footnotes omitted)]

The Securities and Exchange Commission was created at the conclusion of the Senate Banking and Currency Committee's 1932–1934 investigation of stock exchange practices, usually called the Pecora Hearings, in recognition of the decisive role played by the committee's counsel, Ferdinand Pecora. Between September 1, 1929, and July 1, 1932, the value of all stocks listed on the New York Stock Exchange shrank from a total of nearly $90 billion to just under $16 billion—a loss of 83 percent. In a comparable period, bonds listed on the New York Stock Exchange declined from a value of $49 billion to $31 billion. "The annals of finance," the Senate Banking Committee would write, "present no counterpart to this enormous decline in security prices." Nor did these figures, staggering as they were, fully gauge the extent of the 1929–1932 stock market crash. During the post-World War I decade, approximately $50 billion of new securities were sold in the United States. Approximately half or $25 billion would prove near or totally valueless. Leading "blue chip" securities, including General Electric, Sears, Roebuck, and U.S. Steel common stock, would lose over 90 percent of their value between selected dates in 1929 and 1932.

Formally, the purpose of Pecora's stock exchange hearings was to determine why these staggering decreases in security values had occurred and to propose legislation to prevent another stock market crash. The Pecora hearings also had an obvious political purpose. During the preceding twelve years, a majority of the country's voters had supported the laissez-faire economic policies suggested by Calvin Coolidge's often-quoted remark "This is a business country … and it wants a business government."

The revelations of the Pecora hearings were intended to diminish that faith in the nations' financial institutions. No other explanation can account for the attention lavished by Pecora on such matters as the salary levels and income tax returns of the financiers who appeared before him. Such data were virtually irrelevant to an investigation of the causes of the stock market crash. But in the political context in which the Senate Banking Committee functioned, such data seemed essential. In spite of the severity of the stock market crash, effective securities legislation might not have been enacted had Pecora's revelations not galvanized broad public support for direct federal regulation of the stock markets. President Roosevelt, personally, would attribute to the Pecora hearings a decisive role in making possible the legislation of the First Hundred Days of his administration. In retrospect, it is plain that the combination of the stock market crash and the Pecora hearings' revelations were instrumental in transforming national political sentiment from a laissez-faire ideology symbolized by the views of President Coolidge to a regulatory-reform ideology associated with Roosevelt's New Deal.

* * *

Ultimately the Senate Banking Committee's stock exchange hearings would transform American capitalism. They would be directly responsible for the Securities and Banking Acts of 1933, the Securities Exchange Act of 1934, and the creation of the Securities and Exchange Commission. But the hearings began like a Keystone Kops comedy.

Peter Norbeck was the dominant figure in the stock exchange inquiry for the first nine months. The South Dakotan characterized himself as a "Theodore Roosevelt Republican." John T. Flynn, both a political radical and a leading financial journalist of the day, more colorfully styled the senator "one of those Prairie Republicans—half Democrat, half other ingredients—but less than one-half of one percent Republican." Party labels were not particularly relevant. The former well-driller was an unabashed sectionalist and champion of farm-relief legislation. Norbeck's most visible achievement as senator would be helping to secure funds for the carving of the monument on Mount Rushmore.

By his own admission, Peter Norbeck was not qualified to be chairman of the Banking Committee. He knew little about finance. He had been named to the committee in 1921 in an attempt to give it greater geographic balance. At least once he tried to resign. However, in 1926, when unexpected election results made him the ranking Republican member, Norbeck feared he would suffer too great a loss of prestige if he did not accept the chairmanship of the influential committee. Besides, he observed, "as an authority on banking and currency he was the ablest well-driller in Congress."

Soon after his elevation to the chairmanship, Norbeck all but officially delegated full control of banking legislation to Carter Glass. When the depression heightened the importance of the Banking Committee's work, Norbeck acknowledged being flabbergasted by the pleas, suggestions, and criticisms he received. "I really begin to think," he wrote an acquaintance, "I am fortunate in the fact that part of the stuff goes over my head. I do not understand it all. If I did, maybe I wouldn't sleep."

Whatever Norbeck's technical limitations as chairman, he brought to the Senate Banking Committee as clear an anti-Wall Street bias as a prairie Progressive could muster. Flynn would go so far as to write, "It was Norbeck, big, honest, calm, filled with common sense, who made this an investigation of Wall Street, who kept doggedly at the probe ... and who, more than any other man, gave to the investigation its tone, its character, and direction."

* * *

Nine days after Roosevelt's election, Norbeck announced plans to resume the stock exchange hearings....

Norbeck then made his final contribution to securities law reform. After consultation with Senator Fetcher, the senior Democrat on the Banking Committee, Norbeck hired Ferdinand Pecora to be the committee's counsel. Born in Nicosia, Sicily, in 1882, Pecora had immigrated to New York City at the age of four. There his family lived in a cold water flat. As a schoolboy, Pecora worked a milk route in the morning and a paper route in the afternoon. Nevertheless, he graduated as valedictorian of his public school class. The future "hellhound of Wall Street" briefly applied himself to the pursuit of the Episcopal ministry, before a factory injury incapacitated his shoemaker father, requiring him to leave college and help support his family. His career in the law began when, at the age of fifteen, Pecora became a junior clerk in a one-man law office diagonally across the street from J.P. Morgan and Company. Five years later Pecora started part-time study at New York Law School. After graduating in 1906, Pecora served as a managing clerk in several firms before passing the bar in 1911.

He entered public life via local politics. In 1912, Pecora joined Theodore Roosevelt's National Progressive Party. An astute district leader, Pecora became vice president of the Bull Moose Party in New York State. Impressed with Woodrow Wilson's policies, Pecora switched his allegiance to the Democrats in 1916. The following year, the mayor of New York City rewarded Pecora's campaign efforts with a position in the office of New York City's district attorney.

There, Pecora thrived. District Attorney Joab H. Banton, who named Pecora his chief assistant in 1922, later credited Pecora with successful prosecution of over 150 fraudulent securities salesmen, and with the conviction of corrupt politicians in the city's Health Department and the Office of Comptroller of the State of New York. In a 1933 telegram to Senator Norbeck, Banton praised Pecora as "the best-qualified lawyer" in the country to lead the Banking Committee's investigation. Bainbridge Colby, Secretary of State under Wilson, after declining the counsel position himself, recommended Pecora to Senator Fletcher as "the most brilliant cross-examiner in New York."

Pecora was undeniably among the most theatrical. A compact, swarthy man with curling black and gray hair, he punctuated his courtroom appearances with the vigorous jabbing of a stubby finger. During the stock exchange hearings, Pecora's manner alternately could be genial, courtly, mocking, or belligerent. It was always relentless. (So relentless, in fact, that a startled J.P. Morgan, Jr., later would protest that Pecora pursued him as if he were "a horse thief.") He was given to intellectual excesses as well. A wholesale subscriber to the Brandeis bigness-is-badness thesis, he often treated Wall Street witnesses as if they had something to hide.

* * *

By mid-March [1933, Franklin] Roosevelt had established himself as political patron of the Pecora hearings. Wary of the unpredictable Carter Glass—who declined his offer to become Secretary of the Treasury—Roosevelt persuaded Duncan Fletcher to remain on the Banking Committee as its chairman, rather than use his seniority rights to claim the chairmanship of the Commerce Committee. The seventy-five-year-old Floridian was so soft-spoken, his voice was barely audible during the Banking Committee hearings. Often during the hearings, he appeared to doze in his chair. But Fletcher, a party loyalist, had actively campaigned for Franklin Roosevelt. A proverbially hard worker, Fletcher had, since 1908, favored regulation of the "gambling sharks and rascals in Wall Street." Soon after his inaugural, Roosevelt privately began meeting with Pecora as well. At Roosevelt's suggestion, Pecora and Fletcher agreed to make J.P. Morgan and Company the next target of the investigation.

Unlike Mitchell and the National City Bank, the House of Morgan opposed Pecora's requests for evidence. John W. Davis, the 1924 Democratic Party nominee for President, who served as attorney to Morgan, assumed that Pecora meant to conduct a "witch hunt." This sentiment no doubt was reinforced when Pecora demanded a meeting with Morgan in the unfurnished "shabby-looking office" his staff rented in uptown Manhattan, because Pecora professed to be "too busy" to meet Morgan in the banker's famous "house on the corner," as Morgan had requested. After examining the stock exchange practices enabling resolution, Davis counseled Morgan and his associates against permitting Pecora to examine the company's financial records. "I stated distinctly," Davis wrote, that the inquiry "was not directed to the investigation of investment bankers as such but to their dealings in securities." Following a March 22 meeting with Pecora, Morgan representatives refused to answer seven of twenty-three questions formally submitted by the Senate counsel. At Senator Fletcher's direction, Pecora returned to Washington, D.C., and drafted a new enabling resolution, which authorized the Banking Committee "to make a thorough and complete investigation of the operation by any person, firm, copartnership, company, association, corporation, or other entity of the business of banking, financing, and extending credit." Without a word of debate, Congress adopted the resolution on April 4.

The public investigation of the House of Morgan began on May 23. Days before, a special bank of telegraph lines was installed in the Senate Office Building so that reporters could wire intermittent reports. Because the noise of spectators inside and outside the Senate Banking Committee room repeatedly disrupted the hearings, the investigation was moved to the cavernous Senate Caucus Room. Kleig lights were installed in the Caucus Room's chandeliers to aid photographers. For twelve hearing days, newspapers gave the testimony front-page coverage, many printing it verbatim. "So completely," reported *The New Republic*, "has the Senate probe into the great House of Morgan blanketed all other issues on the Washington stage that it is impossible at this time to arouse interest in any other topic." News sources generally tinted their coverage in purple. *Time* magazine characterized the House of Morgan as "the greatest and most legendary private business of modern times." *Business Week* termed "Morgan & Co. ... unique in the magnitude of its operations and in the world prestige it enjoys." The *Richmond Times-Dispatch*, like many daily newspapers, seemed unable to contain its awe: "J. Pierpont Morgan, the twentieth-century embodiment of Croesus, Lorenzo the Magnificent, Rothschild; the lordly Mr. Morgan, financier and patron of arts; the unreachable Mr. Morgan, with his impregnable castle at Broad and Wall Streets and his private army of armed guards; the austere Mr. Morgan, to whose presence only the mighty are admitted, in a committee-room and upon his bare brow the gaze of the 'peepul.' Truly an extraordinary event!"

Although J.P. Morgan, Jr., dominated the attention of news reporters, the real target of Pecora's probe was the firm built by his father. J.P. Morgan and Company was the nation's leading private bank. Compared to commercial banks like the Chase or National City, Morgan and Company was a miniscule operation. As late of 1933, "the house on the corner" included only twenty partners. Drexel and Company, an allied company in Philadelphia, added but four partners to that number. Yet the firm's reputation for financial acumen persisted for two decades after the elder Morgan's death. These twenty-four partners held 126 directorships and trusteeships in eighty-nine firms with well over $20 billion in total resources. Fifty-two corporations, including American Telephone and Telegraph, Standard Oil of New Jersey, General Motors, Du Pont, and U.S. Steel, each maintained an average daily deposit of over $1 million for at least one of the years 1927 to 1932. Eighty-three other firms maintained an average daily balance of at least $100,000 each, vesting Morgan and Company with over half a billion dollars of monies to invest at the end of 1927. Most significantly, between January 1919 and May 1933, Morgan and Company had helped offer $6 billion in new securities.

This enormous sum was sold without the high-pressure sales efforts that characterized more aggressive firms, such as Mitchell's National City Company. Morgan and

Company did not employ salesmen. To maintain its status as a private bank totally exempt from state or federal regulation, it did not advertise even to the extent of placing a sign on the outer door of its Wall Street office. The firm's success, Morgan argued in an uncompromising opening statement written for him by John W. Davis, was the result of "the respect and esteem of the community." The private banker was "a national asset and not a national danger," because he was subject to a code of professional ethics so exacting that "we have never been satisfied with simply keeping within the law." Echoing his father's celebrated argument to the 1912 Pujo Committee that commercial credit was based on "character," not on "money or property," the younger Morgan insisted: "As to the theory that [a private banker] may become too powerful, it must be remembered that any power which he has comes, not from the possession of large means, but from the confidence of the people in his character and credit, and that that power, having no force to back it, would disappear at once if people thought that the character had changed or the credit had diminished."

It was Morgan and Company's reputation as a "national asset" that Pecora challenged in the stock exchange hearings. Five years later Pecora would write, "In truth, the investigation of the Morgan firm elicited no such glaring abuses" as he uncovered in his investigation of "other great banking institutions and personalities." But the fact that the name J.P. Morgan was, as *The New York Times* put it, "a magic one in American finance" caused the Morgan revelations to be the most influential of the stock exchange hearings.

As with Mitchell, Pecora began the Morgan hearings with a probe of income taxes. The revelation that the partners in the House of Morgan paid only $48,000 in income taxes in 1930 and none at all in 1931 and 1932 was treated by the press as the most sensational disclosure of the Morgan hearings. Even newspapers sympathetic to Morgan, like *The New York Times*, printed front-page headlines proclaiming, MORGAN PAID NO INCOME TAX FOR THE YEARS 1931 AND 1932 or TAX "EVASION" BY MORGAN IN LEGAL STOCK DEALINGS IS NOW HUNTED BY PECORA. But there was a crucial difference between the income tax disclosures about Morgan and the disclosures about Mitchell. J.P. Morgan, Jr., had violated no laws. Between 1917 and 1929, Morgan partners had paid over $57 million in income taxes, largely on their stock market profits. When the market plummeted, the Morgan partners reported no taxable income in 1931 and 1932, since their stock market losses exceeded all other taxable income. In fact, the net worth of Morgan and Company and Drexel and Company fell 55 percent between 1929 and 1931, declining from $119 million to $53 million. Pecora's scornful probe of the Morgan tax returns established that the firm, by delaying the admission of new partner S. Parker Gilbert until January 2, 1931, had been able to claim a capital loss of $21 million for 1931, which, under the existing tax laws, could be carried over until 1933. Had Gilbert been admitted in 1930, the tax loss could have been extended only until 1932. A subsequent examination by Internal Revenue agents found no illegality in this practice. As the *New York Evening Post* reported: "It is not criminality. Mr. Pecora only makes it seem so." At best, Pecora was able to show that Thomas S. Lamont, the son of Morgan and Company's managing partner, and himself a junior partner in the firm, illegally evaded paying income taxes by a paper "sale" of securities to his wife on December 30, 1930, and her "resale" of the securities to him three months later. But the younger Lamont evaded the Internal Revenue Code for no one but himself. Pecora's calculated blurring of the distinction between illegal tax evasion and permissible tax avoidance was devious, justifying on this one issue John Brook's assertion that the "righteous tribune of the people was one-quarter demagogic inquisitor."

* * *

Public reaction to the Morgan hearings was almost as condemnatory as that to the Charles E. Mitchell and National City Company revelations. Although the failure of the Morgan partners to pay income taxes and their use of the preferred lists won the greatest attention from journalists, the most serious editorial judgment was that the House of Morgan had forfeited its right to remain unregulated. "Why It Hurts" *The New York Times* titled an editorial as sorrowful as if it were describing the fall of the House of Thebes: "Here was a firm of bankers, perhaps the most famous and powerful in the whole world, which was certainly under no necessity of practicing the small arts of petty traders. Yet it failed under a test of its pride and prestige. By a mistake which had with the years swollen into a grievous fault, it sacrificed something intangible, imponderable, that had to do with the very highest repute." Walter Lippmann termed "the system of favoritism to insiders ... a system which can be explained but cannot be defended." He called on Washington to "reduce the sheer power of so much privately directed money." Though guilty of "no crude crime against the law," the House of Morgan, according to the *New York World-Telegram*, was guilty of "the far deeper, more dangerous offense of what Lord Bryce well calls 'The Submarine warfare which wealth can wage.' The country, the tone of its business, finance, and government, the whole capitalistic structure will be better, safer, and more stable when this long-standing notion of wealth's high prerogatives and immunities has gone finally into the discard." "No banking is private," *Business Week* insisted flatly. William Allen White summed up the hearings in his *Emporia Gazette*: "If the turmoil in the courts and in the Congressional committees stops, changes, or modifies the great thimble-rigging game of Wall Street, the depression of the last four years will have been worth all it cost."

The public response to the Morgan hearings was directly responsible for the passage of the Banking Act of 1933, which, among other things, required private banks to limit themselves either to receiving deposits or to providing investment services. Roosevelt had offered the bill only lukewarm support. Treasury Secretary Woodin favored delaying its adoption. But on the third day of the Morgan hearings, the Senate unexpectedly enacted the bill by a voice vote. The House soon followed suit.

The hearings also galvanized support for a new $100,000 appropriation for Pecora's investigation. But the most enthusiastic appreciation of Pecora's work came from the Executive Branch. On May 27, President Roosevelt signed into law the Securities Act of 1933, the most important consequence to that date of the stock exchange hearings. With a sideward glance toward Capitol Hill, Roosevelt stated:

The new law will also safeguard against the abuses of high-pressure salesmanship in security flotations. It will require full disclosure of all the private interests on the part of those who seek to sell securities to the public. The Act is thus intended to correct some of the evils which have been so glaringly revealed in the private exploitation of the public's money.

As the Seligman excerpt above suggests, the new laws enacted after the Pecora hearings were enormously important. They have also proved remarkably durable. The Securities Act of 1933, which regulates initial offerings of securities to the public, was soon followed by the Securities Exchange Act of 1934, which regulates stock exchanges and post-initial offering trading. The 1934 act also created the Securities and Exchange Commission. Although the 1933 and 1934 acts have been amended many times since their initial passage, they have not been repealed and they remain the statutory framework for regulation of the nation's capital markets. The Securities and Exchange Commission was viewed by many as "the crown jewel of the New Deal," and although it has suffered some notable setbacks (such as its failure to uncover the Bernard Madoff investor fraud scandal) it remains today, almost ninety years after its creation, among the most respected and powerful federal regulatory agencies. The scope of these legislative accomplishments, coupled with their remarkable longevity, demonstrates why the Pecora Hearings continue to be regarded as perhaps the most influential and productive congressional investigation in our nation's history.

Notes and Questions

1. **When History Judges, Results Matter.** The Pecora investigation is most lauded for the landmark legislative accomplishments it precipitated. Two decades earlier a predecessor investigation of Wall Street financing practices had failed to generate similar legislative reforms, and for that reason is not viewed with the same degree of historical reverence as is the Pecora Investigation. In 1912 a subcommittee of the House of Representatives Committee on Banking and Currency, called the "Pujo Committee" because it was chaired by Congressman Arsene P. Pujo of Louisiana, investigated the "money trust" and the influence of Wall Street bankers over the nation's economy. The Pujo Committee's efforts were hampered by President William Howard Taft's refusal to order the Comptroller of the Currency to assist the Committee by providing information sought by the Committee about the banks under the Comptroller's jurisdiction, and by the Committee's decision to limit its investigatory activities in the summer and fall of the year so as to avoid the appearance of acting to influence the 1912 presidential election. (The issues relating to the conduct of a congressional investigation, particularly an investigation of the incumbent administration, in an election year are discussed in more detail in Chapter 8, discussing the "9/11 Commission" investigation of 2003–2004.)

The Pujo Committee and its very capable chief counsel, Samuel Untermyer, succeeded in generating a great deal of public interest in its investigation, particularly when J.P. Morgan, Sr., was subpoenaed to testify before the committee, and the committee issued a report calling for both further investigation and comprehensive legislative reforms. The Committee's legislative recommendations were not acted upon, however, and the serious structural flaws in the country's banking and securities markets continued to metastasize over the next two decades, culminating in the stock market crash of 1929 and the Great Depression. Thus, while the Pujo Committee investigation of 1912 may have informed the public about Wall Street abuses, and doubtlessly provided good political theater, it produced neither the legislative accomplishments of the Pecora investigation nor the broad consensus support for strong congressional investigative powers that resulted from the Teapot Dome investigation.

   2. Timing Is Everything—in Congressional Investigations as in Life. As historian Donald A. Ritchie has observed, Pecora's timing was more advantageous than that of the previous congressional investigation of the Wall Street financial markets, the 1912 Pujo Committee hearings:

> Economic conditions, political support, and public interest all gave Pecora advantages denied to his predecessor, Samuel Untermyer, counsel for Pujo. Where the Pujo hearings had commenced in a relatively prosperous period, Pecora began his hearings at the nadir of the Depression. Where President William Howard Taft had withheld cooperation from Untermyer, President Franklin D. Roosevelt personally encouraged Pecora, endorsed the hearings, and incorporated their recommendations into his legislative program. The press, hostile to the earlier inquiry, lavished extensive coverage on Pecora, filling columns with his photographs and accounts of his activities. Pecora also benefited from Untermyer's mistakes. Recalling his unsuccessful attempts to obtain sufficient evidence, Pecora acquired far stronger subpoena powers than his predecessor. He marched his staff directly into the banks and brokerage houses rather than depend upon his witnesses to produce material voluntarily.

Donald A. Ritchie, *The Pecora Wall Street Expose, in* CONGRESS INVESTIGATES: A DOCUMENTED HISTORY 1792–1974, Vol. 4, at 2556.

   In fact, it is difficult to overstate the importance of the timing of the Pecora hearings. An excerpt from Ferdinand Pecora's 1939 book, "Wall Street Under Oath," illustrates the desperate environment in which his investigation was conducted:

> The examination before the Senate Committee of the officers of the National City Bank took place under most dramatic circumstances. It began on February 21, 1933, eleven days prior to the first inauguration of President Roosevelt. It lasted until March 2, 1933—just nine days, but in those nine days a whole era of American financial life passed away. It was the nadir of the depression. The leading officials of the National City testified against a background of collapsing banks, with "holidays" and moratoria spreading from state to state,

and an ever-mounting public hysteria and panic. On March 7, 1933, three days after Roosevelt's inauguration, every bank in the land, including National City, closed its doors.

FERDINAND PECORA, WALL STREET UNDER OATH (Simon & Schuster 1939), p. 70. To what extent should the success of the Pecora hearings be attributed to the desperate times in which they were held and the frantic search for legislative solutions to the country's dire economic woes, rather than the skill with which the hearings were conducted or the importance of the information they elicited?

3. **The Importance of Adequate Investigative Authority.** As recounted in the excerpted portion above from Joel Seligman's book *The Transformation of Wall Street*, Ferdinand Pecora initially met with resistance when he demanded information from J.P. Morgan and Company. The Morgan bank, at the advice of its counsel John W. Davis (a former congressman, ambassador to the United Kingdom, U.S. Solicitor General, and 1924 Democratic presidential candidate, whose eponymous law firm, now called Davis Polk, continues to this day to represent the interests of Wall Street financial institutions), took the position that Pecora lacked investigatory authority to obtain information about the internal affairs of J.P. Morgan and Company. Pecora promptly returned to Washington and drafted a new enabling resolution for the investigation, which committee chairman Senator Duncan Fletcher then brought to the floor of the Senate. The text of the new resolution and the statements of Senator Fletcher in seeking its approval follow:

Senate Resolution 56 and Floor Debate
April 3, 1933

Mr. Fletcher. Mr. President, from the Committee on Banking and Currency, I report back favorably, with an amendment, Senate Resolution 56, to enlarge the authority of that committee, and I ask unanimous consent for its immediate consideration.

The Vice President. The resolution will be read.

The Chief Clerk read Senate Resolution 56, submitted by Mr. Fletcher March 31, 1933, as follows:

> *Resolved*, That the Committee on Banking and Currency, or any duly authorized subcommittee thereof, in addition to the authority granted under Senate Resolution 84, Seventy-second Congress, agreed to March 4, 1932, and continued in force by Senate Resolution 239, Seventy-second Congress, agreed to June 21, 1932, and further continued by Senate Resolution 371, Seventy-second Congress, agreed to February 28, 1933, shall have authority and hereby is directed—
>
> 1. To make a thorough and complete investigation of the operation by any person, firm, copartnership, company, association, corporation, or

other entity, of the business of banking, financing, and extending credit; and of the business of issuing, offering, or selling securities;

2. To make a thorough and complete investigation of the business conduct and practices of security exchanges and of the members thereof;

3. To make a thorough and complete investigation of the practices with respect to the buying and selling and the borrowing and lending of securities which are traded in upon the various security exchanges, or on the over-the-counter markets, or on any other market, and of the values of such securities; and

4. To make a thorough and complete investigation of the effect of all such business operations and practices upon interstate and foreign commerce, upon the industrial and commercial credit structure of the United States, upon the operation of the national banking system and the Federal Reserve System, and upon the market for securities of the United States Government, and the desirability of the exercise of the taxing power of the United States with respect to any such business and any such securities, and the desirability of limiting or prohibiting the use of the mails, the telegraph, the telephone, and any other facilities of interstate commerce or communication with respect to any such operations and practices deemed fraudulent or contrary to the public interest.

For the purpose of this resolution the committee, or any duly authorized subcommittee thereof, is authorized to hold such hearings, to sit and act at such times and places, either in the District of Columbia or elsewhere, during the first session of the Seventy-third Congress or any recess thereof, and until the beginning of the second session thereof; to employ such experts and clerical, stenographic, and other assistants; to require by subpena or otherwise the attendance of such witnesses and the production and impounding of such books, papers, and documents; to administer such oaths and to take such testimony and to make such expenditures as it deems advisable. The cost of stenographic services to report such hearings shall not be in excess of 25 cents per hundred words.

The Vice President. The amendment of the committee will be stated.

The Chief Clerk. After the word "telephone" in line 20 it is proposed to insert the word "radio."

The Vice President. The Senator from Florida requests unanimous consent for the present consideration of the resolution.

* * * *

Mr. Borah. May I ask what change the amendment makes in the original resolution in the way of an additional authority? What is the purpose of the amendment?

Mr. Fletcher. It gives the committee somewhat larger jurisdiction. It extends that jurisdiction so as to enable the committee to make some inquiries it is desirous of making. The resolution is broadened so that there can be no objection to our making the investigation which we have been directed to make.

Mr. Borah. I know it broadens it, but what is undertaken to be covered by broadening it?

Mr. Couzens. Mr. President, may I answer the Senator's question?

Mr. Fletcher. I yield to the Senator from Michigan.

Mr. Couzens. May I point out that Mr. Pecora, the counsel for the Committee on Banking and Currency, asked the Morgan house to answer 23 questions? The Morgan house agreed to answer 17 of them; they distinctly refused to answer 1; and as to the other questions, they said they would take them under consideration. One of the questions, as I recall, that the counsel asked Morgan & Co. was how much they divided among the partners, and, as I understood, Mr. John W. Davis advised the Morgan house that they need not answer that question. This resolution extends the power of the Banking and Currency Committee so that they may require an answer to that question. That is just one of the elements which we thought necessitated the reporting of this resolution.

Mr. Borah. What I should like to know is, by what language or terms is it undertaken to compel them to answer that question? It presents a rather interesting point.

Mr. Fletcher. In large part this resolution is simply a repetition of the resolution heretofore adopted.

Mr. Borah. I understand that.

Mr. Fletcher. It enlarges the previous resolution so as to go into private banking or investment security concerns which raise some question about our authority to inquire into their affairs.

Mr. Borah. The resolution, then, includes private banking, and so forth?

Mr. Fletcher. I will say to the Senator that there are private bankers, for instance, in the city of New York—and there may be others elsewhere; but in New York, we will say—who are exempt from any supervision or control or suggestion from the bank commissioner of the State; they operate without any sort of supervision or regulation on the part of any State or National authority.

Mr. Borah. Have the committee been advised that they have the legal authority or right to make this additional inquiry?

Mr. Fletcher. Yes; we think beyond any doubt we have that authority. I will say, Mr. President, that this resolution was submitted last Friday; it has been printed, so that the substance of it is not entirely new. It was considered by the Banking and Currency Committee on Saturday and was reported out unanimously with only one amendment, and that was adding the word "radio" after the word "telephone." The resolution is here with the unanimous report of the committee. We feel that we ought to have this authority in order to proceed with the investigation.

* * *

The previous resolution, in effect at the time Pecora and Fletcher sought the amendment discussed above, read as follows:

Senate Resolution 84

March 4, 1932

Resolved, That the Committee on Banking and Currency, or any duly authorized subcommittee thereof, is authorized and directed (1) to make a thorough and complete investigation of the practices with respect to the buying and selling and the borrowing and lending of listed securities upon the various stock exchanges, the values of such securities, and the effect of such practices upon interstate and foreign commerce, upon the operation of the national banking system and the Federal reserve system, and upon the market for securities of the United States Government, and the desirability of the exercise of the taxing power of the United States with respect to any such securities; and (2) to report to the Senate as soon as practicable the results of such investigation and, if in its judgment such practices should be regulated, to submit with such report its recommendations for the necessary remedial legislation.

For the purposes of this resolution the committee, or any duly authorized subcommittee thereof, is authorized to hold such hearings, to sit and act at such times and places during the first session of the Seventy-second Congress, to employ such experts, and clerical, stenographic, and other assistants, to require by subpoena or otherwise the attendance of such witnesses and the production of such books, papers, and documents, to administer such oaths, and to take such testimony and to make such expenditures, as it deems advisable. The cost of stenographic services to report such hearings shall not be in excess of 25 cents per hundred words. The expenses of the committee, which shall not exceed $50,000, shall be paid from the contingent fund of the Senate upon vouchers approved by the chairman of the committee.

* * *

What language in the amended resolution expands the investigative jurisdiction set out in the earlier resolution, and in what manner? What is the answer to Senator Borah's question above, "I know it broadens it, but what is undertaken to be covered by broadening it?" What specific information about J.P. Morgan & Company do you think Pecora was seeking authority to obtain with the new enabling resolution? Why do you suppose he wanted that information, and what use do you think he intended to make of it?

4. Who Should Conduct the Actual Questioning of Witnesses? The Pujo Committee adopted the practice of having the committee's counsel, Samuel Untermyer, conduct the questioning of witnesses, rather than following the more customary congressional committee practice of having individual committee members conduct questioning, either alone or with the assistance of counsel. In this regard the Pecora investigation followed the Pujo Committee's example to good result, permitting Ferdinand Pecora to conduct the aggressive questioning of Wall Street financiers that established Pecora's place in history and created the record that supported the strong legislative reforms which followed the investigation. Not surprisingly, despite the obvious benefits of having an experienced counsel conduct a lengthy and uninterrupted line of questioning, members of Congress may be reluctant to cede their time in the spotlight to even the most able and experienced committee counsel. Moreover, some members of Congress have significant pre-congressional legal experience and consider themselves more than able to conduct an effective examination of even a recalcitrant witness. What are the advantages and disadvantages of direct member questioning of witnesses versus questioning by committee counsel? Can hybrid approaches that combine questioning by members and committee counsel offer the advantages of both approaches?

5. Congressional Investigations and Legal Reputations. In addition to their enormous power to obtain information and expose wrongdoing or questionable practices, congressional investigations have an unrivaled power to establish a lawyer's national reputation. In fact, until the relatively recent rise of blanket cable television news coverage and the Internet, nationally publicized congressional hearings were one of the very few legal proceedings that could focus the attention of the entire country on a lawyer and establish a national reputation almost overnight. Ferdinand Pecora and the hearings that are known by his name are an early example of this phenomenon, but there are many other examples, from both sides of the committee witness table. As discussed in Chapter 3, young Watergate committee minority counsel Fred Thompson's July 16, 1973 question to White House administrator Alexander P. Butterfield about the existence of "any listening devices in the Oval Office of the President" not only revealed to the nation the existence of the Nixon Watergate tapes, it also laid the cornerstone for a legal career that ultimately made Thompson a successful attorney, television and movie star, United States Senator, and 2008 presidential candidate. As discussed in Chapter 5, Oliver North's counsel in the Iran-Contra hearings, Brendan Sullivan, Jr., established his national reputation and simultaneously expanded the national lexicon when he famously declared "I am not a potted plant!" during those widely viewed televised congressional hearings.

6. A Final Note on Partisanship and the Appropriate Use of Congressional Investigative Power. As was the case at the outset of the Teapot Dome and Pecora hearings, every highly publicized congressional investigation will inevitably feature charges of political motivation and partisan efforts to misuse the congressional investigative power. Congress is a political institution, and its members are political animals, so no congressional investigation will be totally devoid of any political influence or overtones, and consequently there will always be at least some credible basis for cries of "partisanship" and improper "political" motives. In almost all cases, however, it will be the investigative results, as judged from the historian's perspective, rather than the political climate at the time, which will determine whether a particular inquiry is seen as a partisan "witch hunt" or a model of constitutional oversight. The remaining chapters of this book will explore further the important constitutional and public policy issues presented by the congressional investigative power.

Chapter Two

Mid-Century Developments

Overreaching and New Limits
on Congressional Investigative Powers

> *Let us not assassinate this lad further, Senator. You have done enough. Have you*
> *no sense of decency, sir, at long last? Have you left no sense of decency?*
>
> Special Counsel to the Army Joseph N. Welch, in response to
> Senator Joseph R. McCarthy, Army-McCarthy Hearings, June 9, 1954

Introduction: After Pecora

Congressional investigative activity continued apace after the Pecora hearings, although usually with less drama than those hearings had provided. One possible con-
tender for the kind of intense national attention that the Pecora hearings had generated
was the Senate Special Committee Investigating the Munitions Industry, known as the
Nye Committee because it was chaired by Republican Senator Gerald P. Nye of North
Dakota.[1] From 1934 to 1936, Nye's committee held a series of widely publicized hearings on war profiteering.[2] For a time it appeared that those hearings might succeed in

---

1. During his first term in the Senate, in 1927 and 1928, Nye had served as chair of the Senate
Committee on Public Lands and Surveys as it concluded the Teapot Dome investigation. A Nye biog-
rapher has observed that "Nye won nationwide publicity for his role in the [Teapot Dome] committee,
and the inquiry further emphasized for him the corrupting influence of great wealth upon the government and political parties." WAYNE S. COLE, SENATOR GERALD P. NYE AND AMERICAN FOREIGN
RELATIONS (Univ. Minn. Press 1962), pp. 48–49 (footnote reference omitted). Nye's experience with
Teapot Dome and other Senate inquiries also made him a strong proponent of congressional investigations and legislative oversight activities, as he explained in May 1933:

> Honest investigations, prosecuted by legislators determined to reach and develop the facts, and
> by legislators who in their work can and will abandon partisanship, are of the greatest value to
> the government and its people. They afford necessary knowledge basic to helpful legislation.
> They educate people to practices unfriendly to their best interests. They throw fear into men
> and interests who would by any means at their command move governments to selfish purpos-
> es. They command respect for government and for law. They tend to make government cleaner
> and more responsive to public needs and interests. We should have not less, but more legislative
> investigations.

Congressional Record, 73 Cong., 1st session, p. 4183 (1933) (quoted in COLE, *supra*, at 68–69).

2. An interesting historical footnote to the Nye Committee investigation of the munitions industry
is that the committee's staff counsel was Alger Hiss, who would later become the central character in
America's most celebrated and controversial spy case, the Alger Hiss/Whittaker Chambers affair. The

marshalling support for legislation to nationalize the munitions industries, a popular cause at that time. The hearings died with a political sputter rather than a legislative bang, however, when Chairman Nye angered his Democratic colleagues by questioning the veracity of deceased president Woodrow Wilson with respect to secret treaties among the World War I Allies. In retaliation for what Senator Carter Glass called "the unspeakable accusation against a dead President—dirt-daubing the sepulcher of Woodrow Wilson," the angry Democrats cut off further funding for Nye's investigation. Despite a voluminous hearing record and several lengthy reports, none of the Nye Committee's legislative recommendations were enacted. As a result, the Nye Committee hearings are now known more for contributing to U.S. isolationist sentiment during the 1930s than for any significant investigative findings or legislative accomplishments.

In terms of both practical importance and national political impact, there is little doubt as to what was the most significant congressional investigation of the period through the end of World War II. In early 1941, Senator Harry Truman of Missouri introduced a resolution in the Senate to create a special Senate investigative committee to investigate the national defense program. As Truman explained in a Senate floor speech on February 10, 1941, he was concerned about the concentration of defense facilities in certain geographic areas, favoritism in the awarding of defense contracts, and unwarranted preferences for large industrial corporations to the detriment of equally or better qualified smaller businesses. On March 1, 1941, Truman introduced a resolution to create "a special committee of seven Senators, to be appointed by the President of the Senate ... to make a full and complete study and investigation of the operation of the program for the procurement and construction of supplies, materials, munitions, vehicles, aircraft, vessels, plants, camps, and other articles and facilities in connection with the national defense...."[3] The resolution was adopted and Truman was appointed to chair the committee.

Although Truman's initial impetus for advocating the investigation may have been parochial political concerns about whether his Missouri constituents were receiving a fair share of the huge national defense pie, his conduct of the investigation quickly transcended politics. With the Japanese attack on Pearl Harbor on December 7, 1941, and the U.S. declaration of war against Japan the following day, the activities of Truman's committee assumed new importance in a much more complex political environment. Over the next three years, up until Truman resigned from the committee in August 1944 to become Roosevelt's vice presidential nominee in the November 1944 presidential election, Truman accomplished a political masterstroke. He con-

---

Hiss investigation, among other things, was instrumental in the political ascendancy of Richard M. Nixon, who as a California congressman first achieved national prominence through his relentless pursuit of the Hiss case. The Hiss case is discussed below in connection with the activities of the House Un-American Activities Committee. For a brief summary of the Hiss case with a focus on the role of the House Un-American Activities Committee and then-Representative Richard M. Nixon, see WALTER GOODMAN, THE COMMITTEE 244–71 (1968). *See also* RICHARD M. NIXON, SIX CRISES 1–71 (1962) (discussing the Hiss case).

3. Senate Resolution 71, March 1, 1941, Cong. Record, 77th Congress, 1st Session, 1615.

ducted a meaningful investigation of fraud and waste in the national defense effort without undermining support for Roosevelt's war policies or appearing unpatriotic or unsupportive of the national defense effort. The hearings also transformed Truman from a relatively obscure Missouri Senator to a national figure who commanded public respect and admiration. This investigative success led both to Truman's political ascendancy and the committee's great success as it carried on its work, without Truman, until 1948.[4] The scope of the Truman's Committee's accomplishments and the political impact of those accomplishments are described in the Senate's official history:

The Truman Committee[*]

No senator ever gained greater political benefits from chairing a special investigating committee than did Missouri's Harry S. Truman.

In 1940, as World War II tightened its grip on Europe, Congress prepared for eventual U.S. involvement by appropriating $10 billion in defense contracts. Early in 1941, stories of widespread contractor mismanagement reached Senator Truman. In typical fashion, he decided to go take a look. During his 10,000-mile tour of military bases, he discovered that contractors were being paid a fixed profit no matter how inefficient their operations proved to be. He also found that a handful of corporations headquartered in the East were receiving a disproportionately greater share of the contracts.

Convinced that waste and corruption were strangling the nation's efforts to mobilize itself for the war in Europe, Truman conceived the idea for a special Senate Committee to investigate the National Defense Program. Senior military officials opposed the idea, recalling the Civil War-era problems that the congressional Joint Committee on the Conduct of the War created for President Lincoln. Robert E. Lee had once joked that he considered the joint committee's harassment of Union commanders to be worth at least two Confederate divisions. Truman had no intention of allowing that earlier committee to serve as his model.

Congressional leaders advised President Franklin Roosevelt that it would be better for such an inquiry to be in Truman's sympathetic hands than to let it fall to those who might use it as a way of attacking his administration. They also assured the president that the "Truman Committee" would not be able to

---

4. Ironically, as discussed below, the Truman Committee was the predecessor to the Senate Permanent Subcommittee on Investigations, which was the vehicle used by Senator Joe McCarthy, after he assumed its chairmanship in 1953, to conduct the series of investigations into communist infiltration of government that added "McCarthyism" to the national lexicon and ultimately did much to bring both McCarthy and the institution of congressional investigation into national disrepute.

* United States Senate, Historical Minute Essays 1941–1963, March 1, 1941—The Truman Committee (available at http://www.senate.gov/artandhistory/history/minute/The_Truman_Committee. htm).

cause much trouble with a budget of only $15,000 to investigate billions in defense spending.

By unanimous consent on March 1, 1941, the Senate created what proved to be one of the most productive investigating committees in its entire history.

During the three years of Truman's chairmanship, the committee held hundreds of hearings, traveled thousands of miles to conduct field inspections, and saved millions of dollars in cost overruns. Earning nearly universal respect for his thoroughness and determination, Truman erased his earlier public image as an errand-runner for Kansas City politicos. Along the way, he developed working experience with business, labor, agriculture, and executive branch agencies that would serve him well in later years. In 1944, when Democratic party leaders sought a replacement for controversial Vice President Henry Wallace, they settled on Truman, thereby setting his course directly to the White House.

———————

Senator Charles Schumer of New York has argued that the Truman Committee should serve as a model for congressional oversight of the wars in Iraq and Afghanistan:

First, although Congress has frequently served in a critical oversight role in the conduct of military affairs, it has largely failed to oversee the war effort in Iraq and Afghanistan.

The Truman Committee, however, stands as perhaps the best and most compelling example of the worthy role Congress can play in overseeing a war effort—even when the first and second branches of government are ruled by the same party, as was the case during World War II. Established in March 1941, the Senate Special Committee to Investigate the National Defense Program (commonly known as the Truman Committee) was instituted to oversee war mobilization and defense production. Then-Senator Harry Truman's initiative created the panel shortly after his reelection to a second term and focused on whether or not defense contracts were being "fairly allocated within the country."

The Truman Committee toiled for seven years, from 1941 to 1948, and the resolution creating it authorized nearly unlimited authority to review the war effort—covering "almost all aspects of the war program except strategy and tactics." Indeed, the Committee had broad authority to (1) examine the continuing problems of war mobilization; (2) investigate shortages of critical materials and create specific programs to remedy them; (3) investigate programs related to the supply of equipment and facilities; and (4) investigate "war frauds" including fraudulent activities of war contractors and government officials.

The Committee's accomplishments included "trouble-shooting" the war effort by securing effective coordination. Its mediation of disputes between agencies played a large role in creating a functional mobilization program. The Committee also served as a major source of information about the war program. Wartime officials divulged little information about the conduct of the war to the public—partly out of security concerns and partly out of a desire to use the war as a manipulative tool, as secrecy was used to protect officials from criticism and to cover up mistakes and blunders. The Committee exerted considerable pressure on President Roosevelt to divulge "maximum information" about the conduct of the war and forced the government to justify withholding information. Meanwhile, the Committee generally avoided scapegoating or examining the motives of executive branch actors and usually provided them with advance copies of critical reports to avoid media sensationalism. The Truman Committee was astonishing in both its output and its impact. During its tenure, the Committee issued more than 50 reports, conducted 432 public hearings, and held 300 executive sessions. Thus, the Truman Committee serves as an exemplar for congressional investigations—even though Democrats controlled the Presidency and both houses of Congress during its time.

The important historical lesson is this: the aggressive work of the Truman Committee did not imperil the Presidency, upset the separation of powers, or undermine the war effort. Rather, it provided constructive criticism, benefited the treasury, and built public confidence in the military apparatus. And, it bears repeating, a Democratic Senator led this Committee to do work critical of a President belonging to his own party. Indeed, after three years of vigorously investigating the executive branch, Senator Truman was invited to join the Executive as Vice President.*

The creation of the Truman Committee by Senate Resolution on March 1, 1941 was to have a profound effect on American politics and, ultimately, world history. Truman's Senate committee work had made him a popular national figure and ultimately catapulted him to the presidency of the United States, as this 1945 account from *Harper's* magazine recounts:

Wesley McCune & John R. Beal, *The Job That Made Truman President*

Harper's Magazine, June 1945

With all due allowance for the accidents of mortality and politics, it is clear that Harry S. Truman was lifted into the White House by his performance as an investigator. In 1941 he was just another obscure junior Senator with no visible political future. Three years later he had made himself known, and respected, as the chairman of a special

---

* Charles E. Schumer, *Under Attack: Congressional Power in the Twenty-first Century*, HARV. L. + POL'Y REV. 14–16 (2007) (footnotes omitted).

committee investigating war production and, in consequence, the almost inevitable choice of his party as a compromise candidate for the Vice Presidency.

Truman's handling of that investigation throws a good deal of light on his character, methods, and capabilities. It also provides a noteworthy lesson in the handling of Congress' investigating power, one of the sharpest (and most hazardous) tools in the whole arsenal of government.

Plenty of other Senators and Representatives were running investigations at about the same time, in fields as important as Truman's. Most of them had greater political experience, and at least as much money and staff. Yet none was able to build himself into a national political figure. On the contrary, some—notably among the members of the Dies Committee—cut their political throats with spectacular thoroughness. Obviously Truman had learned, somehow, to wield his investigating tool with uncommon adroitness.

His training in the highly specialized business of Congressional inquiry began in 1936 under a master of the craft, Senator Burton K. Wheeler of Montana. Because Wheeler's isolationist views have dimmed his reputation during the war years, many people have forgotten that he earned fame as one of the most able, honest, and thorough of senator investigators. He and Truman sat together on the Interstate Commerce Committee and he chose the younger Senator to serve as his lieutenant in a special study of railway holding companies.

For two years this inquiry plodded along through some of the dullest hearings ever recorded at the Capitol. During the early months, Truman seldom opened his mouth. He watched the Montana maestro question an endless procession of witnesses; and he studied railway finance and corporate organization with a dogged intentness which his colleagues considered rather eccentric.

The public's indifference to the railroad inquiry was simply deafening. As the hearings dragged on, the other members (including Wheeler) lost interest, and Truman frequently was the only Senator who showed up for public sessions. Before no audience except his own counsel, the witness and his lawyers, and one or two weary newspapermen, he conducted the questioning with meticulous fairness and a growing knowledge of the nation's transport system. He made no reputation; indeed, his fellow Senators sometimes hinted that he was wasting time. But the investigation did result in a few important though obscure reforms. And a handful of industrialists and financiers began to speak of Truman as a strange sort of politician—a New Dealer who showed no desire to persecute business, a man who dug for his facts, used them surely, and tolerated no wool over his eyes.

This tedious schooling paid off handsomely when Truman decided early in 1941 to organize an investigation of his own. It was to be his first venture into the big-time political arena and its possibilities were not immediately apparent. There was no rivalry for the chairmanship, nor any stampede for seats on the committee. Consequently, Truman had an unusually free hand in indicating to the Senate leaders the men he wanted. * * *

The distinguishing mark of the original committee members—five Democrats and four Republicans—was a sort of unspectacular competence. All were junior senators from their respective states, with the exception of Tom Connally of Texas. They obviously were picked with an eye to their special knowledge of various phases of the war production program, and to the desirability of a balanced representation from every section of the country. * * *

* * * Truman outlined his plans for the committee, and emphasized the mistakes in the history of past investigations which he wanted to avoid. He did not conceive his job to be that of running the defense program; a Committee on the Conduct of the War had tried that during the Civil War, and had caused President Lincoln and the Union much grief. He did not want to sit by until scandals developed, and then try to assess the blame after it was too late to do any good; that had been tried after World War I, in 116 post mortem investigations (one lasting as late as 1935) which dug into everything in sight for every conceivable partisan purpose.

Both these pitfalls might be avoided, he believed, if the new committee tried an entirely new technique. It would undertake a current, continuing checkup on each major war program as it developed. The aim would be to keep an alert watch for bottlenecks, graft, waste, bureaucratic deadlocks, and other weaknesses, and to remedy them promptly before they could grow to ominous dimensions. What he wanted above all, he told Fulton, was facts. "I don't want to whitewash and I don't want to smear," he explained.

* * *

The results of Truman's unorthodox formula for running a Congressional inquiry surprised everyone—including the committee members. The performance differed in four important respects from that of most such investigations.

First of all, it got results. The accomplishments of the typical Congressional committee are at best minor, and at worst a sheer waste of time and money. All too often such inquiries begin with a fanfare of publicity, and then dribble away into confusion, bickering, and impotence. The Truman Committee, on the other hand, started modestly—and then proceeded to produce. * * *

A second distinguishing mark of the Truman group was its good administration. All investigation of this sort presents a more serious administrative problem than is generally recognized; while the number of people involved is relatively small, the committee members are likely to be prima donnas who are notoriously hard to handle.

Truman handled his colleagues with unobtrusive skill. Unlike many investigations, his did not turn into a one-man show; all, or nearly all, of the Senators contributed an uncommon amount of hard work. Truman carefully apportioned the fields to be covered among the members, so they did not get into each other's hair. He also made a point of spreading the credit and publicity, while he himself kept in the background as far as possible; as a result, internal jealousies never flared into open friction.

It is particularly significant that in four years of operation no committee member ever dissented from any report. Truman achieved this surprising unanimity by tireless search for all the facts, and then by consultation—no matter how tedious—until a set of conclusions was hammered out on which everyone could agree. Once a member objected when the committee prepared to spank an official from his own state for bungling one of the major war material programs. But after reviewing the case, the member decided against a minority report—the facts just couldn't be disputed. Senator Brewster summed it up in these words: "Reasonable men don't differ much when they have the facts." * * *

In the third place, the Truman committee demonstrated a sense of fairness and responsibility which inspired widespread confidence.

All too frequently Congressional investigators have set out to smear somebody, by fair means or foul and without giving their victims a chance for rebuttal. In contrast, Truman's group went to unheard-of lengths to make sure its facts were right, and that everyone concerned had a chance to check up on them. Its shipbuilding report, for example, was eighteen months in preparation. Several months before its release, the conclusions were circulated in draft to the WPB, Maritime Commission, and the Navy. All private shipbuilders mentioned in the document were consulted by telegram, and the maritime unions also were checked. Even the widow of a seaman was given opportunity to check the printer's proofs of her late husband's testimony. When the newspapers finally got the 75-page report, it was established as gospel. * * *

Finally, the committee displayed a brand of courage rare among politicians. It did not hesitate to criticize labor, when plainly at fault. Similarly, it pulled no punches in its reports on the misbehavior of several of the most powerful of industrial corporations. Truman went after some of the biggest brass hats, including General Somervell himself, at a time when no other civilian dared raise a voice against military encroachment into control of the civilian economy. Many a government agency—not excepting the White House—smarted under his blunt comments, at a time when Truman must have known he was being discussed as a possible vice presidential candidate.

Such apparently foolhardy behavior turned out, of course, to be good politics. It nearly always does. It is curious that most politicians still believe implicitly in the myth that conspicuous valor in the face of entrenched pressure groups means political suicide—in spite of contrary evidence piled up by scores of public men from Lincoln to George Norris. In the performance of his investigating committee, Truman proved once more that a politician can make honesty and courage pay off. Perhaps it is not too much to hope that in the White House he will remember his own lesson.

Notes and Questions

1. **Investigation for the Sake of Investigation?** The Truman Committee did not make legislative recommendations. The main purpose of the Truman hearings was to expose waste and fraud in the national defense program. The Committee published a number of reports that detailed its findings on a wide range of topics, such as military camp construction, rubber shortages, and gasoline rationing. The committee's findings were intended both to correct existing problems and to deter future waste and fraud.

Truman's efforts have been credited with saving huge amounts of money and the lives of many American soldiers. Is vigorous investigative oversight to expose waste and fraud in the executive branch as appropriate in peacetime as during war, or is there a special need for such aggressive oversight during wartime?

2. Respecting Separation of Powers. The Truman Committee was well aware of the special difficulties presented by efforts to exercise effective congressional oversight of the executive branch in times of war. During the Civil War a special Joint Committee on the Conduct of the War held hearings and conducted an investigation that has been criticized for encroaching upon and interfering with Lincoln's constitutional prerogatives as commander in chief. Truman was aware of that precedent and was anxious to avoid repeating the mistakes of the Civil War committee, so he focused his committee's efforts on identifying waste and fraud, rather than questioning military tactics and strategy. Truman described his concerns on this point in typically blunt fashion in 1954:

> One thing that added to my success as a committee chairman was that I made it my business to read the record of the Committee of the Conduct of the War Between the States. That way I found out what not to do. That committee tried to run the war for Lincoln and he wouldn't let them. If they had, they would have lost the war. Lee always figured the committee was worth three divisions to him.*

How do Truman's concerns apply to more recent conflicts, such as the Vietnam and Iraq wars? To what extent do such concerns explain—or justify—the reluctance of some members of Congress to "second-guess" the George W. Bush administration's policies in conducting the Iraq war?

3. Unintended Consequences. The important accomplishments and high public esteem of the Truman Committee led to the conversion of the committee to a permanent subcommittee of the Senate, the Permanent Subcommittee on Investigations of the Committee on Government Operations, in 1948. Ironically, it was this subcommittee that Senator Joe McCarthy chaired in the early 1950's and used to conduct the hearings and investigations that defined the McCarthy era. In 2003, when the executive sessions of the McCarthy subcommittee meetings were made public, subcommittee chairman Senator Carl Levin and ranking member Senator Susan M. Collins summarized the subcommittee's history and the impact of its McCarthy era activities:

> In 1948, the Senate established the Permanent Subcommittee on Investigations to continue the work of a special committee, first chaired by Missouri Senator Harry Truman, to investigate the national defense program during World War II. Over the next half century, the Subcommittee under our predecessor Chairmen, Senators John McClellan, Henry Jackson, Sam Nunn, William Roth, and John Glenn, conducted a broad array of hard-hitting investi-

---

* N.Y. Times Magazine, May 2, 1954, p. 66 (quoted in Telford Taylor, Grand Inquest: The Story of Congressional Investigations 109 & n.37 (1955).

gations into allegations of corruption and malfeasance, leading repeatedly to the exposure of wrongdoing and to the reform of government programs.

The phase of the Subcommittee's history from 1953 to 1954, when it was chaired by Joseph McCarthy, however, is remembered differently. Senator McCarthy's zeal to uncover subversion and espionage led to disturbing excesses. His browbeating tactics destroyed careers of people who were not involved in the infiltration of our government. His freewheeling style caused both the Senate and the Subcommittee to revise the rules governing future investigations, and prompted the courts to act to protect the Constitutional rights of witnesses at Congressional hearings. Senator McCarthy's excesses culminated in the televised Army-McCarthy hearings of 1954, following which the Senate voted overwhelmingly for his censure.

* * *

These hearings are a part of our national past that we can neither afford to forget nor permit to reoccur.

Carl Levin & Susan M. Collins, Preface to the Executive Sessions of the Senate Permanent Subcommittee on Investigations of the Committee on Government Operations, Vol. 1, Eighty-Third Congress, First Session 1953 (made public January 2003).

Excess and Abuse of Power: The Dies Committee and HUAC

Despite the historical importance of the Nye and Truman hearings, neither had a significant impact on the legal framework in which congressional investigations are conducted. The principal targets of Nye's investigation were the large industrial firms that produced munitions and explosives, such as the DuPont chemical company, and the Wall Street banks that provided credit to foreign governments, such as J.P. Morgan and Company. Although Nye could have scored political points by demonizing and abusing those witnesses, his committee generally treated its witnesses fairly.[5] Truman's hearings greatly increased public support and respect for the congressional investigative power—and certainly did so for Truman personally—but his hearings were conducted in a cautious, restrained manner and did not result in judicial proceedings

---

5. Historian John Edward Wiltz has noted that, despite a reputation for demagoguery and aggressive investigative tactics, the Nye Committee hearings were conducted fairly and respected the rights of witnesses:

> As for the treatment of witnesses, the Nye Committee's behavior was generally exemplary.... The committee allowed witnesses to make statements and exhibit documents even faintly relevant to the inquiry, and gave them ample opportunity to defend or explain their actions. Indeed it tended to treat representative of such corporate giants as DuPont and Morgan with considerable deference.

John Edward Wiltz, *The Nye Munitions Committee 1934*, in CONGRESS INVESTIGATES: A DOCUMENTED HISTORY 2763 (1975).

or legal controversies.[6] The great abuses of the congressional investigative power during the McCarthy era, and the eventual legal and political backlashes against those abuses, occurred later and arose out of America's concerns over the threat of communism during the Cold War. Their origins, however, can be found during the pre-World War II period in the formation and early activities of the Dies Committee and its evolution into the House Un-American Activities Committee, known as HUAC. John C. Grabow provides a succinct history of the HUAC saga in his 1988 treatise *Congressional Investigations Law and Practice*:

John C. Grabow,
Congressional Investigations Law and Practice
(1988)

HUAC's Creation

"McCarthyism": the term has become so associated with the notion of congressional abuse that it has entered our lexicon. The American Heritage Dictionary defines it as: "1. The political practice of publicizing accusations of disloyalty or subversion with insufficient regard to evidence. 2. The use of methods of investigation and accusation regarded as unfair, in order to suppress opposition." With the passage of time, the period of intense congressional scrutiny into the threat of Communist subversion during the late 1940s through the mid-1950s is often mistakenly attributed solely to the activities of Joseph R. McCarthy, the Senator from Wisconsin. In fact, much of this congressional activity occurred in the House of Representatives during a lengthy series of highly publicized investigations by the House Committee on Un-American Activities (HUAC).

HUAC spanned a period of thirty-seven years of investigations. Its roots were modest enough. HUAC was created as a special committee in 1938 to investigate:

> (1) the extent, character, and objects of un-American propaganda activities in the United States, (2) the diffusion within the United States of subversive and un-American propaganda that is instigated from foreign countries or of a domestic origin and attacks the principle of the form of government as guaranteed by our Constitution, and (3) all other questions in relation thereto that would aid Congress in any necessary remedial legislation.

The sponsor of the resolution creating the special committee, Martin Dies, won support from his colleagues in part with his statement that the committee's inquiry would last just seven months. Interestingly, though the dangers of communism were mentioned during the House debate on the enabling resolution, the greatest concern voiced was the threat of fascism, particularly Nazism. Dies was appointed Chairman

---

6. Telford Taylor described the work of the Truman Committee as having been conducted "with the sober and responsible purpose of focusing criticism in such a way as to assist the executive branch in surmounting the staggering obstacles and solving the grave issues of the war years." TELFORD TAYLOR, GRAND INQUEST: THE STORY OF CONGRESSIONAL INVESTIGATIONS 70 (1955).

of the committee, which from the period 1938 to the close of 1944 popularly became known as the Dies committee.

HUAC's first hearing was held on August 12, 1938. In his opening statement that day, Chairman Dies said that

> This Committee is determined to conduct its investigation upon a dignified plane and to adopt and maintain throughout the course of the hearings a judicial attitude. The Committee has no preconceived views of what the truth is respecting the subject matter of this inquiry.... We shall be fair and impartial at all times and treat every witness with fairness and courtesy.... This Committee will not permit any "character assassination" or any "smearing" of innocent people.... It is the Chair's opinion that the usefulness or value of any investigation is measured by the fairness and impartiality of the committee conducting the investigation. Neither the public nor the Congress will have any confidence in the findings of a committee which adopts a partisan or preconceived attitude.... It is easy to "smear" someone's name or reputation by unsupported charges or an unjustified attack, but it is difficult to repair the damage that has been done.... [W]hen any individual or organization is involved in any charge or attack made in the course of the hearings, that individual or organization will be accorded an opportunity to refute such charge or attack.

Equally remarkable, given what the committee was to become, the Chairman concluded his comments by cautioning the newsmen assembled in the hearing room against calling people "un-American" just because of "an honest difference of opinion with respect to some economic, political or social question."

The Dies Committee was extremely active that first year, conducting inquiries on such topics as the pro-Nazi German-American Bund and other Nazi activities, anti-Semitism, and Communist infiltration of the C.I.O., Brooklyn College, and the Farmer-Labor Party of Minnesota. However, the activity of HUAC steadily declined in the succeeding years through 1944 as it became essentially a one-man show under the flamboyant Dies.

HUAC's Resurrection

But for the efforts of Representative John Rankin, a combative white supremacist from Mississippi, HUAC would have undoubtedly died a quiet death in 1944 upon the retirement of Dies. Although there was little organized support for resurrecting what had become by that time a virtually dormant committee, Rankin on the first day of the new Congress surprised his fellow members with a motion to add HUAC to the list of standing committees of the House. Given the politically sensitive nature at that time of any kind of vote against investigations of un-American activities, a coalition of Republicans and Southern Democrats supported Rankin's resolution and, on January 4, 1945, voted to make HUAC a standing committee of the House.

Though Rankin, through his parliamentary maneuvering, had been able to obtain the necessary votes to continue the existence of HUAC, there was little active support for the committee among the Democratic leadership or general membership of the

House, and only scattered hearings were held in 1945 and 1946. HUAC came into its own only when the Republicans obtained control of the House in the 1946 congressional elections and J. Parnell Thomas of New Jersey became its new Chairman. Among the Republicans added to the committee that year was Representative Richard M. Nixon of California. Under Thomas, the committee no longer divided its time investigating the threat of subversive activity on the right and left. As postwar relations between the Soviet Union and the United States deteriorated, the unwavering focus of HUAC was on Communism. The often abusive ways of HUAC in the long string of hearings it held on this subject can be seen in two of the committee's most highly publicized inquiries—the Hollywood and Hiss-Chambers hearings.

The Hollywood Ten

In early 1947 HUAC turned its attention to communism in Hollywood, seeking, in the words of Max Lerner, to "track down the footprints of Karl Marx in movie land." In May of that year, a HUAC subcommittee of three members conducted field hearings in Hollywood, taking testimony of a dozen witnesses in closed session. Upon their return to Washington, the subcommittee members reported that "[s]cores of screen writers who are Communists have infiltrated into the various studios and it has been through this medium that most of the Communist propaganda has been injected into the movies," and that Communists "have employed subtle techniques in pictures in glorifying the Communist system and degrading our own system of Government and Institutions." Perhaps most incredible was the related charge that "some of the most flagrant communist propaganda films were produced as a result of White House pressure" from the administration of President Roosevelt.

Public hearings began in October 1947 under a carefully orchestrated plan that would be repeatedly utilized by the committee in future investigations as well. The committee began with a number of "friendly" witnesses, such as Robert Taylor, Gary Cooper, Jack L. Warner, Louis B. Mayer, Walt Disney, and Ronald Reagan. After these friendly witnesses finished their testimony about the dangers of Communist infiltration into the film industry, the committee turned to a series of "unfriendly" witnesses—suspected Communists or fellow travelers who were grilled about their alleged participation in subversive activity, invariably culminating with the now infamous question, "Are you now or have you ever been a member of the Communist Party of the United States?"

One of the unfriendly witnesses, the German playwright Bertolt Brecht, denied he was a Communist. The remaining witnesses, the so-called "Hollywood Ten," all refused to answer the question. None pled the Fifth Amendment right against self-incrimination; instead, they claimed that their First Amendment rights were violated by the inquiry. The tenor of the hearings can be seen in the following excerpt from the testimony of one of the Hollywood Ten, screenwriter John Howard Lawson:

> **Mr. [Robert E.] Stripling [chief investigator for the committee]:** Mr. Lawson, are you now, or have you ever been a member of the Communist Party of the United States?

Mr. Lawson: In framing my answer to that question I must emphasize the points that I have raised before. The question of communism is in no way related to this inquiry, which is an attempt to get control of the screen and to invade the basic rights of American citizens in all fields.

The question here relates not only to the question of my membership in any political organization, but this committee is attempting to establish the right—[The chairman pounding gavel.]

Mr. Lawson [continuing]: Which has been historically denied to any committee of this sort, to invade the rights and privileges and immunity of American citizens, whether they be Protestants, Methodist, Jewish or Catholic, whether they be Republicans or Democrats or anything else.

The Chairman [pounding gavel]: Mr. Lawson, just quiet down again. Mr. Lawson, the most pertinent question that we can ask is whether or not you have ever been a member of the Communist Party. Now, do you care to answer that question?

Mr. Lawson: You are using the old technique, which was used in Hitler Germany in order to create a scare here—

The Chairman [pounding gavel]: Oh—

Mr. Lawson: In order to create an entirely false atmosphere in which this hearing is conducted—[The Chairman pounding gavel.]

Mr. Lawson: In order that you can then smear the motion-picture industry, and you can proceed to the press, to any form of communication in this country.

The Chairman: You have learned—

Mr. Lawson: The Bill of Rights was established precisely to prevent the operation of any committee which could invade the basic rights of Americans. Now if you want to know—

Mr. Stripling: Mr. Chairman, the witness is not answering the question.

Mr. Lawson: If you want to know—[The chairman pounding gavel.]

Mr. Lawson: About the perjury that has been committed here and the perjury that is planned....

The Chairman [pounding gavel]: We are going to get the answer to that question if we have to stay here for a week.

Are you a member of the Communist Party, or have you ever been a member of the Communist Party?

Mr. Lawson: It is unfortunate and tragic that I have to teach this committee the basic principles of American—

The Chairman [pounding gavel]: That is not the question. That is not the question. The question is; Have you ever been a member of the Communist Party?

Mr. Lawson: I am framing my answer in the only way in which any American citizen can frame his answer to a question which absolutely invades his rights.

The Chairman: Then you refuse to answer that question; is that correct?

Mr. Lawson: I have told you that I will offer my beliefs, affiliations, and everything else to the American public, and they will know where I stand.

The Chairman [pounding gavel]: Excuse the witness—

Mr. Lawson: I have written Americanism for many years, and I shall continue to fight for the Bill of Rights, which you are trying to destroy.

The Chairman: Officers, take this man away from the stand—

In a technique utilized with all of the Hollywood Ten, the committee would then call one of its investigators as a witness, who would read into the record a detailed dossier of the witness' alleged subversive activities and affiliations. The committee cited all of the Hollywood Ten for contempt of Congress. All waived their right to a trial by jury and were found guilty. Each received the maximum penalty of one year in jail and $1,000 fine and were imprisoned.

As was typical of most of its investigations, given the dramatic charges that HUAC set out to prove about Communist propaganda being contained in Hollywood movies in a conspiracy with Roosevelt's blessing, the ultimate results of the hearings were meager at best. Most tellingly, the committee did not even submit a formal report of its findings to the House.

The Hiss-Chambers Hearings

Soon HUAC turned away from Hollywood (though the lure of Tinseltown proved irresistible and the committee would return again to the subject, with similar fanfare, in 1950) to what, with the passage of time, proved to be its most highly celebrated investigation—the 1948 Communist Espionage Hearings, popularly known as the Hiss-Chambers hearings. As was typical, the committee began these hearings with a somewhat less than open mind. For example, on the first day of public hearings, Representative Rankin stated that it was time that President Truman and New York Governor Dewey "got behind this committee and helped to clear this proposition up and drive these rats from the Federal, the State, and the municipal payrolls."

The public hearings began with the testimony of Elizabeth Bentley, who referred in lurid detail to her work during the war as a "courier" for the Communist Party. Bentley, adorned by the press with such names as the "beautiful blond spy queen" and the "nutmeg Mata Hari," provided the committee with numerous names of individuals who she alleged had been members of Communist "cells," designed to place their members in government jobs where they would have access to classified information.

Seeking to corroborate Bentley's story, the committee next turned to another former courier and member of the Communist Party, Whittaker Chambers, at the time an editor of *Time* magazine. Chambers' story proved to be even more sensational than that of Bentley. (Looking back at Chambers' initial testimony before HUAC, one cannot help but be struck with the similarity, in its rather portentous and self-dramatizing tone—"it is better to die on the losing side ... than to live under Communism"—to the more recent testimony of Oliver North.) The focus of the hearings thereafter focused on Chambers' charges.

The committee called before it many of the individuals named by Chambers (most of whom invoked the Fifth Amendment), but its primary focus was on Chambers's charge that Alger Hiss had been a member of the Communist Party and an active participant in the Washington cell of the Party. The committee's interest in Hiss was no doubt explainable at least in part by his prior ties to the Roosevelt administration, which made him a convenient symbol to many committee members of the evils of the New Deal. During his career in the State Department, Hiss had participated in the Dumbarten Oaks and Yalta Conferences; he was at the time of the hearings president of the Carnegie Endowment for International Peace. The committee's chief investigator, Stripling, would later write of "Alger Hiss, who sat with Roosevelt at Yalta when Poland and the rest of Eastern Europe were abandoned by the West."

On the same day that Chambers testified before HUAC, Hiss sent a cable denying that he knew Chambers and requesting the opportunity to appear before the committee to rebut Chambers' charges. On August 5, 1948, Hiss appeared and unequivocally denied that he had ever been a member or supporter of the Communist Party or that he had ever met Chambers. The committee then heard from Hiss and Chambers separately in closed session. Nixon examined Chambers about intimate family matters and other personal details about Alger Hiss; Chambers found it easy to answer many of these questions. Hiss told the committee that although he had never known a Whittaker Chambers, he knew a person named George Crosley who resembled the pictures of Chambers that Hiss had seen in the newspapers.

On August 17, 1948, Nixon arranged for Chambers and Hiss to meet face to face in executive session. The session began with Hiss saying, "I am perfectly prepared to identify this man as George Crosley." It ended with Hiss screaming at Chambers to make his accusations outside the presence of the committee where the statements would not be privileged from a libel suit. Hiss declared, "I challenge you to do it, and I hope you do it damned quickly."

On August 25, 1948, in a dramatic public confrontation, Hiss and Chambers testified together at a public hearing. Chambers identified Hiss; Hiss identified Chambers as the man he had known as George Crosley. Hiss again categorically denied Chambers' charges against him. Two days later, Chambers met Hiss's challenge to repeat his charges outside the protection of the committee and stated on *Meet the Press* (then a radio program) that "Alger Hiss was a Communist and may still be one." Several weeks later, Hiss brought an action for slander against Chambers in Baltimore federal district court.

Shortly thereafter, the Chambers-Hiss story took an even more dramatic turn when, in a deposition in the Hiss slander action, Chambers accused Hiss of espionage and produced a stack of papers which he alleged were copies of State Department documents given to Chambers by Hiss in 1938 to transfer to Soviet agents. After receiving hints from Chambers and his attorneys about these and related materials, the committee served a subpoena upon Chambers at his Maryland farm on December 3, at which time Chambers provided committee investigators with the infamous "Pumpkin Papers"—microfilms of even more government documents allegedly purloined by Hiss for transmission to the Soviets, which Chambers had kept for safekeeping in a hollowed-out pumpkin on his farm.

With this new development, Nixon, aboard a steamship to Panama, was taken off the ship by a Coast Guard plane and returned immediately to Washington. On December 7, the committee reopened its espionage hearings and heard from a number of witnesses, though not Chambers and Hiss themselves because both had been subpoenaed by a federal grand jury in New York. After several days of acrimonious negotiations with federal law enforcement officials, HUAC agreed to provide the grand jury with the "pumpkin" microfilms and to defer any public testimony by Hiss or Chambers. On December 15, 1948, a grand jury indicted Hiss on two counts of perjury. He was charged with lying under oath when he said he never gave Chambers documents from the State Department and that he never saw Chambers after January 1, 1937. On December 20, HUAC's Acting Chairman Karl E. Mundt (Thomas had recently been indicted for taking kickbacks from his office staff) announced that to prevent any adverse impact on the Hiss prosecution, the committee would hold no further public hearings on the matter. The committee, however, continued to question Chambers in executive session. In 1950, Hiss was convicted on both perjury counts in his second trial and was sentenced to five years in prison.

HUAC, in Retrospect

History, with considerable justification, has not looked kindly upon HUAC. HUAC's underlying fault throughout its tenure, well evidenced by the Hollywood and Chambers-Hiss hearings, was its preoccupation with the sensational exposure of individual wrongdoing. The committee often seemed to view itself as a combination "little FBI" and grand jury. Representative Rankin was fond of calling the committee "the grand jury of America." Many members of HUAC viewed their role as that of "the greatest open court in this country," sitting in judgment of the guilt or innocence of the hundreds of witnesses that appeared before it. In doing so, HUAC's methods created the climate for the tactics, even more damnable at times, of Joseph McCarthy in the Senate commencing in 1950.

This stress on individual wrongdoing caused the committee to ignore any serious attempt to examine the broader policy implications of the conduct at issue, the adequacy of existing statutes, or the need for any kind of curative legislation. Furthermore, given its prosecutorial bent, HUAC made no effort to provide the kinds of procedural protections that would be provided to an accused in a judicial setting (and that are now provided to some degree to congressional witnesses by the Senate and House rules). The committee had a few written procedures and no consistent policy in such areas as the decision to hear a witness in open or closed session, whether testimony would be held before the full committee or one of its ad hoc subcommittees, whether to provide impugned individuals a right to respond to charges from other witnesses, the right of witnesses to make opening statements, and the like.

A continuing controversy during HUAC hearings concerned the extent of a witness' right to the assistance of counsel. Though, as in all of these procedural areas, there was no consistent practice, the committee generally was hostile to any active role by a lawyer for an "unfriendly" witness appearing before it. During one executive session in 1946, the committee refused to let witnesses be accompanied by counsel, its Chairman explaining that

> During these hearings the committee policy has uniformly been that we do not permit lawyers in the committee room during executive sessions. If during the course of your examination any matter arises involving legal questions about which you desire to consult your counsel you can go out and consult with him.

A more frequent HUAC practice was to permit counsel to be present, but to cast aspersions upon witnesses who availed themselves of that opportunity. For example, HUAC made obvious its displeasure when Alger Hiss, in his fourth appearance before the committee, appeared for the first time accompanied by counsel.

An especially egregious incident concerning the role of counsel occurred during the Chambers-Hiss hearings. Chambers had accused Hiss of giving his old 1929 Ford roadster to a Communist Party member. Committee investigators had determined that the car was registered to a William Rosen, who, along with his wife, was subpoenaed to testify. Rosen refused to answer most of the committee's questions on Fifth Amendment grounds. After Rosen's counsel, Maurice Braverman, continued to instruct Rosen to assert his Fifth Amendment privilege and interrupted the questioning a number of times, the committee demanded that Braverman be sworn in so that he could be questioned. He refused, claiming that it was improper for the committee to ask him to disclose confidential attorney-client information. Braverman also refused to appear unless he could have his own counsel present. This provoked the often-quoted statement by Chairman Thomas that "[t]he rights you have are the rights given to you by this committee. We will determine what rights you have and what rights you have not got before the committee." Braverman refused again and the committee finally backed down that day. However, the committee did subpoena him, and the next day he appeared accompanied by his counsel. Braverman refused to answer any questions concerning his involvement with the Rosens or the Communist Party on the grounds that the committee's inquiry encroached upon the attorney-client relationship and his rights guaranteed by the First and Fifth Amendments.

As time passed, HUAC's popularity decreased. After the censure of Joseph McCarthy by the Senate in December 1954, interest in the committee plummeted. With the election of John F. Kennedy in 1960, the committee's activities were down to a few sporadic hearings. However, HUAC was not officially disbanded until 1975. (It had since been renamed the Internal Security Committee.) Given its long history of sensationalism, perhaps most surprising is that HUAC finally died with just a whimper.

Notes and Questions

1. Standing Committees Versus Special Committees. Arguably the most significant event in the life of the HUAC committee was its elevation to standing committee status in January 1945, as recounted by Grabow in the materials above. Standing committee status gave the investigation greater prominence and guaranteed continued funding for its activities. The audacious and creative manner in which standing committee status was attained is a fascinating example of parliamentary maneuvering and political manipulation. Congressman John E. Rankin of Mississippi pulled off this "coup" on the opening day of the seventy-ninth Congress:

> Then Rankin arose and offered an amendment to the rules—to make the Committee on Un-American Activities a standing committee of the House, with great latitude as to what it might investigate and how it chose to go about its investigating.

> The move took the House leadership by surprise, not only because it was in itself unorthodox, but because an understanding had been arrived at that any effort at reincarnating the Dies Committee would be given over to the mercies of [the Rules Committee]. By offering his amendment now, before the Rules Committee itself had been reestablished, the forewarned gentleman from Mississippi was attempting an end run. Rankin's main arguments, besides the rhetorical one that the Dies Committee had "performed a duty second to none," was that if the House did not act with dispatch, the files so assiduously collected by [the Dies Committee] might be removed by unnamed persons and thrown into the Potomac River. Rankin took care to remind his colleagues that the American Legion, whose political potential loomed very large indeed as the war neared its end, had lately asked Congress to continue the Committee and make it permanent.

> The leaders of the House had no inclination on this opening day to affront patriots by an insult to the memory of Martin Dies [who had just retired from Congress]. On the other hand, they had no enthusiasm for adopting his offspring as their own unto eternity. So they entrusted their cause to Representative McCormack, who explained in his passion-quelling way that he was certainly in favor of continuance of the Special Committee, but wanted the matter taken up in proper order, via the Rules Committee. He urged a vote against "the procedure that in 150 years of Constitutional history, no Congress ... has ever followed to establish a permanent committee of this kind." In a division on the question, Rankin's amendment was defeated by 134 to 146. Whereupon the Mississippian, with the experience of nearly a quarter century in the House, knew he had won. He asked for a roll call, and now the vote was 207 for the Committee and 186 against. Forty members, including the young man from Texas, Lyndon B. Johnson, voted a neutral "present." "I caught 'em flat-footed and flat-headed," Rankin rejoiced. A few minutes later, at 3:38 p.m., the House adjourned, having to its own astonishment and at

some cost to its traditions, created a permanent Committee on Un-American Activities.

WALTER GOODMAN, THE COMMITTEE 168–69 (1968).

2. Effects on the Lives of Ordinary Citizens. One aspect of HUAC's activities merits special mention and attention. Congressional investigations most often focus on political and governmental figures or on business entities and their leaders; they focus less frequently on the individual activities and personal lives of ordinary citizens. Perhaps the most pernicious aspect of the HUAC investigations was the depth and scope of the committee's efforts to root out and expose communists in all walks of life. The Supreme Court recognized the intrusive nature of these congressional investigations in a 1957 opinion:

> In the decade following World War II, there appeared a new kind of congressional inquiry unknown in prior periods of American history. Principally this was the result of the various investigations into the threat of subversion of the United States Government, but other subjects of congressional interest also contributed to the changed scene. This new phase of legislative inquiry involved a broad-scale intrusion into the lives and affairs of private citizens. It brought before the courts novel questions of the appropriate limits of congressional inquiry. Prior cases, like *Kilbourn*, *McGrain* and *Sinclair*, had defined the scope of investigative power in terms of the inherent limitations of the sources of that power. In the more recent cases, the emphasis shifted to problems of accommodating the interest of the Government with the rights and privileges of individuals. The central theme was the application of the Bill of Rights as a restraint upon the assertion of governmental power in this form.

Watkins v. United States, 354 U.S. 178, 195 (1957).

Although the Supreme Court's recognition of this new phenomenon in congressional investigative activities and the risk it posed to individual liberties was undoubtedly accurate, was it timely? Why did the Court wait until 1957, after years of well-publicized excesses by investigatory committees and terrible consequences for citizens who were investigated—ruined reputations, losses of jobs and livelihoods, and even suicides—before speaking out? In the years leading up to 1957, numerous cases involving committee investigations and individual rights worked through the federal trial and appellate courts, but the Supreme Court (with some narrow exceptions discussed below) declined to take any cases that presented those issues. Consider this timing issue in connection with the materials below on McCarthyism, particularly as to McCarthy's popularity in the early 1950s and his 1954 censure by the Senate and subsequent loss of political power and popular appeal.

3. Yet More Evidence of the Power, for Better or Worse, of Congressional Investigations to Launch National Political Careers. As noted above, the Truman Committee's success led to Harry Truman's selection as Roosevelt's running mate in the 1944 presidential election. The HUAC investigations, and particularly the Alger Hiss case, did the same for Richard Nixon, leading to his 1950 election to the Senate and his 1952 selection as Eisenhower's vice-presidential candidate. In a February 13, 1996, interview, Eisenhower's campaign adviser and Attorney General from 1953 to 1957, Herbert Brownell, Jr., described the role of the Hiss case in Nixon's political ascendancy:

> When it came to the selection of a Vice President in that '52 campaign, Eisenhower more or less left the choice up to Republican leaders and there is no doubt that while he finally approved the selection that they recommended, there is no doubt that a major factor in the selection of Nixon was his anti-Communist activities, especially his successful exposure of Alger Hiss. He really had brought to the attention of the American people in a way that nobody else had up to that time, some of the dangers that existed as to subversion in this country.
>
> Interviewer: So how important would you say was the Hiss case to Nixon's career?
>
> I think the Hiss case made Nixon. I don't think he would ever been selected as Vice President to the Presidential candidate without that, because he really would have been just another Senator.

National Security Archive, George Washington University, available at http://www. gwu.edu/~nsarchiv/coldwar/interviews/.

4. Lessons From the Hiss Case: A Cautionary Admonition for Witnesses in Congressional Investigations. It would be a mistake to view the Hiss case as a relic of history or a product of a different time with no relevance to the modern congressional investigative process. In 1996, on the occasion of Hiss's death, one of the authors commented on the lessons that can be learned from Hiss's case. Those observations are as relevant today as they were when written in 1996:

Stanley M. Brand, *Alger Hiss: How Not to Be a Congressional Witness*

The Hill, November 27, 1996

The death of Alger Hiss last week closed one of the most controversial, contested and written about criminal cases of the century, framed against the Cold War and the American confrontation with the post-war Soviet menace.

I reflect on the Hiss case not to take sides in the debate, but to examine it as a watershed in the long tradition of congressional investigation of the executive branch bureaucracy followed by Watergate, the Environmental Protection Agency Superfund, Iran-Contra and Whitewater scandals.

What struck me about reading the accounts and testimonial and investigative recapitulations of the Hiss case that were occasioned upon his death are the parallels faced by modern witnesses confronting congressional investigations. Not every witness faces his or her congressional accusers under the klieg lights, but the risks attendant to becoming the "subject" of congressional inquiry have become sufficient to render consideration of the "rules of the game" necessary.

Almost incredibly in the Hiss case, Whittaker Chambers' initial testimony about his alleged relationship with Hiss was greeted by indifference in the press. It was not until Hiss telegraphed the House Un-American Activities Committee and demanded to be heard under oath on the charges leveled by Chambers that the sleeping press was awakened by the drama of a confrontation between the two witnesses.

Lesson Number One: Never volunteer or seek to be brought before a congressional investigative committee, even if provoked by rivals or enemies to do so.

The congressional investigative forum simply is not a hospitable forum for personal vindication. Instead, it is driven by political and social forces the turn of which cannot be anticipated by a single witness. People caught up in a congressional investigative juggernaut need to look to God and their families for solace—none is available before a congressional investigative committee.

Also of great irony was Hiss's threat to sue Chambers if he dared repeat his defamatory charges of Communist Party membership outside the hearing room with its cloak of congressional immunity. So when Chambers stated on "Meet the Press" that "Alger Hiss was a Communist and may be now," Hiss sued for slander—a further mistake in his undoing. In response to questions during discovery in the case about the basis for his charges and whether he had any documents bearing Hiss's signature, Chambers produced secret documents purportedly provided to him by Hiss which he had hidden away in his nephew's elevator shaft, for just such an eventuality. These documents were also provided to the committee, in addition to the famous Pumpkin papers found on Chambers' farm which formed the basis for grand jury subpoenas to Hiss.

Lesson Number Two: Do not open oneself to collateral attack by seeking vindication in a lawsuit.

This turn of events also led to one of Hiss's other self-inflicted wounds after the testimony before Congress—investigation by a grand jury for perjury. Hiss was not the first, nor the last, to be trapped in the handoff from Congress to the Department of Justice. More recently, Michael Deaver was pilloried between the Scylla of Congress and the Charybdis of the grand jury. Exhausted from a seven-hour appearance before a congressional subcommittee testifying about acid rain and subsequent grand jury appearances, he was indicted and convicted for perjury. (Oliver North avoided such a trap by asserting his Fifth Amendment rights and obtaining immunity.)

Lesson Number Three: Do not lightly disavow constitutional protections designed by the framers to guard against overreaching by the government.

And in the final irony of the Hiss case, despite the evidence that he had spied for the Soviet Union, espionage charges could not be brought because they were barred by the statute of limitations. The only charges that could be brought were two counts of perjury: one count for denying that he had passed confidential State Department documents to Whittaker Chambers; and one count for denying that he knew Whittaker Chambers.

In a ritual repeated many times since, from Watergate to Rita Lavelle and James Watt, congressional witnesses have escaped substantive violations of law only to face perjury and obstruction charges that stem largely from their own false sense of invincibility.

Forty-six years ago Alger Hiss was convicted largely for failing to appreciate and understand that walking into a hostile congressional hearing is a life-threatening experience, proving an axiom perhaps truer in Washington than elsewhere. Those who do not heed the lessons of history are doomed to repeat them.

The other great congressional investigation cases that are mentioned in the article excerpted above—Watergate, the Environmental Protection Agency Superfund, Iran-Contra, and Whitewater—all are subjects of case studies in succeeding chapters of this book. The strategic considerations and tactical lessons that are discussed above also are explored in greater detail in succeeding chapters. The Hiss case, however, provides a good introduction to these points, while reinforcing the value of learning from history in this fascinating intersection of government, law, and politics.

The Nadir: McCarthyism Holds Sway

The modern era of the law of congressional investigations begins with the Teapot Dome investigation and resulting Supreme Court decisions that are included in Chapter 1 of this book. The modern era of the practice—as opposed to the law—of congressional investigations, however, probably did not begin until almost half a century later, in 1954, when the "Army-McCarthy" hearings were presented to a national television audience.[7] Richard H. Rovere, in his book *Senator Joe McCarthy*, described the unprecedented political impact of the Army-McCarthy hearings:

> Nothing remotely like the Army-McCarthy hearings had ever been seen in American history. As a spectacle of a political character enacted before an audience, there has never anywhere been anything to match it. [*Ed. Note: This*

----

7. Although their impact on public opinion may have been unprecedented, the Army-McCarthy hearings were not the first congressional proceedings to be broadcast on national television. As Telford Taylor noted in 1955:

Memories are short, and in this year of the graceless Army-McCarthy hearings it is an effort to recall that these were by no means the first Congressional investigative sessions to by viewed through the medium of television by millions of citizens. Nor were they the most widely viewed; in 1951 and 1952 several hearings of the Senate [organized] crime investigation—in which Senator Kefauver, the late Senator Tobey, counsel Rudolph Halley, and an extraordinary assortment of underworld characters such as Mr. Frank Costello played stellar roles—enjoyed the largest television audience that this type of program has ever reached. Even before that, the Un-American Activities Committee hearings in 1948 on the Hiss-Chambers accusations were televised and watched by millions.

TELFORD TAYLOR, GRAND INQUEST 240 (1955).

was written in 1959, before the Watergate hearings transfixed the nation and eclipsed the Army-McCarthy hearings as an example of the power of television to amplify public interest in political events.] The audience alone was almost beyond belief—upward of 20,000,000 at a time, or not much less than the population of the entire country just before the Civil War. The hearings ran for thirty-five days, or 187 hours on television, and several times 20,000,000 saw long stretches of it. Unlike the onlookers at most political spectacles, this audience had not been shanghaied. The compulsion to look—or, in the jargon of the medium, "to view"—came from the drama itself. Television, by the easy admission it gives to easy entertainment, has enormous power to distract, but no deliberate or commercial distraction, conceived and executed by professionals at great cost, has ever gripped the attention as this interminable, plotless, improvised, amateur production did in 1954.

RICHARD H. ROVERE, SENATOR JOE MCCARTHY 207 (1959).

While the Army-McCarthy hearings and their contribution to McCarthy's ultimate downfall provide a fascinating study on the fragile and fickle nature of political popularity in America, the significance of those hearings cannot be fully appreciated without a clear picture of the enormous political power McCarthy wielded in the early 1950s. In 2003, fifty years after the heyday of McCarthy's power and influence, Senate historian Donald A. Ritchie provided a summary of McCarthy's career in connection with the Senate's release of the record of the "executive sessions" of McCarthy's investigative subcommittee:

Donald A. Ritchie, *Introduction to 2003 Printing of the 1953–54 Executive Sessions of the Senate Permanent Subcommittee on Investigations of the Committee on Government Operations*

(2003)

The executive sessions of the Permanent Subcommittee on Investigations for the Eighty-third Congress, from 1953 to 1954, make sobering reading. Senator Joseph R. McCarthy assumed the chairmanship of the Government Operations Committee in January 1953 and exercised prerogative, under then existing rules, to chair the subcommittee as well. For the three previous years, Senator McCarthy had dominated the national news with his charges of subversion and espionage at the highest levels of the federal government, and the chairmanship provided him with a vehicle for attempting to prove and perhaps expand those allegations.

Elected as a Wisconsin Republican in 1946, Senator McCarthy had burst into national headlines in February 1950, when he delivered a Lincoln Day address in Wheeling, West Virginia, that blamed failures in American foreign policy on Communist infiltration of the United States government. He held in his hand, the senator asserted, a list of known Communists still working in the Department of State. When a special subcommittee of the Foreign Relations Committee investigated these charges and rejected them as "a fraud and a hoax," the issue might have died, but the outbreak of the Korean War, along with the conviction of Alger Hiss and arrest of Julius Rosenberg in 1950, lent new credibility to McCarthy's charges. He continued to make accusations that such prominent officials as General George C. Marshall had been part of an immense Communist conspiracy. In 1952, Dwight D. Eisenhower's election as president carried Republican majorities in both houses of Congress, and seniority elevated McCarthy to chairman of the Permanent Subcommittee on Investigations.

Jurisdictional lines of the Senate assigned loyalty issues to the Internal Security Subcommittee of the Judiciary Committee, but Senator McCarthy interpreted his subcommittee's mandate broadly enough to cover any government-related activity, including subversion and espionage. Under his chairmanship, the subcommittee shifted from searching out waste and corruption in the executive branch to focusing almost exclusively on Communist infiltration.

* * *

The Permanent Subcommittee on Investigations

Following the Legislative Reorganization Act of 1946, the Special Committee to Investigate the National Defense Program (popularly known as the Truman committee, for its chairman, Harry S. Truman) merged with the Committee on Expenditures in the Executive Departments to become the Permanent Subcommittee on Investigations. In 1953 the Committee on Executive Expenditures was renamed the Committee on Government Operations, and Senator Joseph R. McCarthy (1908–1957), who had joined the committee in 1947, became chairman of both the committee and its permanent subcommittee. Republicans won a narrow majority during the Eighty-third Congress, and held only a one-seat advantage over Democrats in the committee ratios. The influx of new senators since World War II also meant that except for the subcommittee's chairman and ranking member, all other members were serving in their first terms. Senator McCarthy had just been elected to his second term in 1952, while the ranking Democrat, Arkansas Senator John L. McClellan (1896–1977), had first been elected in 1942, and had chaired the Government Operations Committee during the Eighty-first and Eighty-second Congresses. The other members of the subcommittee included Republicans Karl Mundt (1900–1974), Everett McKinley Dirksen (1896–1969), and Charles E. Potter (1916–1979), and Democrats Henry M. Jackson (1912–1983) and Stuart Symington (1901–1988).

With senators serving multiple committee assignments, only on rare occasions would the entire membership of any committee or subcommittee attend a hearing. Normally, Senate committees operated with a few senators present, with members coming and going through a hearing depending on their conflicting commitments. Unique circumstances developed in 1953 to allow Senator McCarthy to be the sole senator present at many of the subcommittee's hearings, particularly those held away from Washington. In July 1953, a dispute over the chairman's ability to hire staff without consultation caused the three Democrats on the subcommittee to resign. They did not return until January 1954. McCarthy and his staff also called hearings on short notice, and often outside of Washington, which prevented the other Republican senators from attending. Senators Everett Dirksen and Charles Potter occasionally sent staff members to represent them (and at times to interrogate witnesses). By operating so often as a "one-man committee," Senator McCarthy gave witnesses the impression, as Harvard law school dean Erwin Griswold observed, that they were facing a "judge, jury, prosecutor, castigator, and press agent, all in one."

The Legislative Reorganization Act of 1946 had created a nonpartisan professional staff for each Senate committee. Originally, staff worked for the committee as a whole and were not divided by majority and minority. Chairman McCarthy inherited a small staff from his predecessor, Clyde Hoey, a Democrat from North Carolina, but a significant boost in appropriations enabled him to add many of his own appointees. For chief counsel, McCarthy considered candidates that included Robert Morris, counsel of the Internal Security Subcommittee, Robert F. Kennedy, and John J. Sirica, but he offered the job to Roy M. Cohn (1927–1986). The son of a New York State appellate division judge, Cohn had been too young to take the bar exam when he graduated from Columbia University Law School. A year later he became assistant United States attorney on the day he was admitted to the bar. In the U.S. attorney's office he took part in the prosecution of William Remington, a former Commerce Department employee convicted of perjury relating to his Communist party membership. Cohn also participated in the prosecution of Julius and Ethel Rosenberg, and in the trial of the top Communist party leaders in the United States. He earned a reputation as a relentless questioner with a sharp mind and retentive memory. In 1952, Cohn briefly served as special assistant to Truman's attorney general, James McGranery, and prepared an indictment for perjury against Owen Lattimore, the Johns Hopkins University professor whom Senator McCarthy had accused of being a top Soviet agent. Cohn's appointment also helped counteract the charges of prejudice leveled against the anti-Communist investigations. (Indeed, when he was informed that the B'nai B'rith was providing lawyers to assist the predominantly Jewish engineers suspended from Fort Monmouth, on the assumption of anti-Semitism, Cohn responded: "Well, that is an outrageous assumption. I am a member and an officer of B'nai B'rith.") In December 1952, McCarthy invited Cohn to become subcommittee counsel. "You know, I'm going to be the chairman of the investigating committee in the Senate. They're all trying to push me off the Communist issue...," Cohn recalled the senator telling him. "The sensible thing for me to do, they say, is start investigating the agriculture program or find out how many books they've got bound upside down at the Library of Congress. They want me to play it safe. I fought this Red issue. I won the primary on it. I won the election on it, and don't see anyone else around who intends to take it on. You can be sure that as chairman of this committee this is going to be my work. And I want you to help me."

At twenty-six, Roy Cohn lacked any previous legislative experience and tended to run hearings more like a prosecutor before a grand jury, collecting evidence to make his case in open session rather than to offer witnesses a full and fair hearing. Republican Senator Karl Mundt, a veteran investigator who had previously served on the

House Un-American Activities Committee, urged Cohn to call administration officials who could explain the policies and rationale of the government agencies under investigation, and to keep the hearings balanced, but Cohn felt disinclined to conduct an open forum. Arrogant and brash, he alienated others on the staff, until even Senator McCarthy admitted that putting "a young man in charge of other young men doesn't work out too well." Cohn's youth further distanced him from most of the witnesses he interrogated. Having reached maturity during the Cold War rather than the Depression, he could not fathom a legitimate reason for anyone having attended a meeting, signed a petition, or contributed to an organization with any Communist affiliation. In his memoirs, Cohn later recounted how a retired university professor once told him "that had I been born twelve or fifteen years earlier my world-view and therefore my character would have been very different."

An indifferent administrator, Senator McCarthy gave his counsel free rein to conduct investigations. In fact, he appointed Cohn without having first removed the subcommittee's previous chief counsel, Francis "Frip" Flanagan. To remedy this discrepancy, McCarthy changed Flanagan's title to general counsel, although he never delineated any differences in authority. When a reporter asked what these titles meant, McCarthy confessed that he did not know. The subcommittee's chief clerk, Ruth Young Watt, found that whenever a decision needed to be made, Cohn would say, "Ask Frip," and Flanagan would reply, "Ask Roy." "In other words," she explained, "I'd just end up doing what I thought was right."

The subcommittee held most of its hearings in room 357 of the Senate Office Building (now named the Russell Senate Office Building). Whenever it anticipated larger crowds for public hearings, it would shift to room 318, the spacious Caucus Room (now room 325), which better accommodated radio and television coverage. In 1953 the subcommittee also held extensive hearings in New York City, working out of the federal courthouse at Foley Square and the Waldorf-Astoria Hotel, while other executive sessions took place at Fort Monmouth, New Jersey, and in Boston. Roy Cohn had recruited his close friend, G. David Schine (1927–1996), as the subcommittee's unpaid "chief consultant." The two men declined to work out of the subcommittee's crowded office—Cohn did not even have a desk there. ("I don't have an office as such," Cohn later testified. "We have room 101 with 1 desk and 1 chair. That is used jointly by Mr. Carr and myself. The person who gets there first occupies the chair.") Instead, Cohn and Schine rented more spacious quarters for themselves in a nearby private office building. When the subcommittee met in New York, Schine made his family's limousine and suite at the Waldorf-Astoria available for its use. As the subcommittee's only unpaid staff member, he was not reimbursed for travel and other expenses, including his much-publicized April 1953 tour with Cohn of U.S. information libraries in Europe. In executive sessions, Schine occasionally questioned witnesses and even presided in Senator McCarthy's absence, with the chief counsel addressing him as "Mr. Chairman." Others on the staff, including James Juliana and Daniel G. Buckley, similarly conducted hearing-like interrogatories of witnesses. Schine continued his associations with the subcommittee even after his induction into the army that November—an event that triggered the chairman's epic confrontation with the army the following year.

The hectic pace and controversial nature of the subcommittee hearings during the Eighty-third Congress placed great burdens on the staff and contributed to frequent departures. Of the twelve staff members that McCarthy inherited, only four remained by the end of the year—an investigator, and three clerks. Of the twenty-one new staff added during 1953, six did not last the year. Research director Howard Rushmore (1914–1958) resigned after four months, and assistant counsel Robert Kennedy (1925–1968), after literally coming to blows with Roy Cohn, resigned in August, telling the chairman that the subcommittee was "headed for disaster." (The following year, Kennedy returned as minority counsel.) When Francis Flanagan left in June 1953, Senator McCarthy named J.B. Matthews (1894–1966) as executive director, hoping that the seasoned investigator would impose some order on the staff. Matthews boasted of having joined more Communist-front organizations than any other American, although he had never joined the Communist party. When he fell out of favor with radical groups in the mid-1930s, he converted into an outspoken anti-Communist and served as chief investigator for the House Un-American Activities Committee from 1939 to 1945. An ordained Methodist minister, he was referred to as "Doctor Matthews," although he held no doctoral degree. Just as McCarthy announced his appointment to head the subcommittee staff in June 1953, Matthews's article on "Reds in Our Churches" appeared in the *American Mercury* magazine. His portrayal of Communist sympathy among the nation's Protestant clergy caused a public uproar, and Republican Senator Charles Potter joined the three Democrats on the subcommittee in calling for Matthews's dismissal. Although Matthews resigned voluntarily, it was Senator McCarthy's insistence on maintaining the sole power to hire and fire staff that caused the three Democratic senators to resign from the subcommittee, while retaining their membership in the full Government Operations Committee. Senator McCarthy then appointed Francis P. Carr, Jr. (1925–1994) as executive director, with Roy Cohn continuing as chief counsel to direct the investigation.

The Rights of Witnesses

In their hunt for subversion and espionage, Senator McCarthy and chief counsel Cohn conducted hearings on the State Department, the Voice of America, the U.S. overseas libraries, the Government Printing Office, and the Army Signal Corps. Believing any method justifiable in combating an international conspiracy, they grilled witnesses intensely. Senator McCarthy showed little patience for due process and defined witnesses' constitutional rights narrowly. His hectoring style inspired the term "McCarthyism," which came to mean "any investigation that flouts the rights of individuals," usually involving character assassination, smears, mud-slinging, sensationalism, and guilt by association. "McCarthyism"—coined by the *Washington Post* cartoonist Herblock, in 1950—grew so universally accepted that even Senator McCarthy employed it, redefining it as "the fight for America." Subsequently, the term has been applied collectively to all congressional investigations of suspected Communists, including those by the House Un-American Activities Committee and Senate Internal Security Subcommittee, which bore no direct relation to the permanent subcommittee.

In these closed executive sessions, Senator McCarthy's treatment of witnesses ranged from abrasive to solicitous. The term "executive sessions" derives from the Senate's division of its business between legislative (bills and resolutions) and executive (treaties and nominations). Until 1929 the Senate debated all executive business in closed session, clearing the public and press galleries, and locking the doors. "Executive" thereby became synonymous with "closed." Committees held closed sessions to conduct preliminary inquiries, to mark up bills before reporting them to the floor, and to handle routine committee housekeeping. By hearing witnesses privately, the permanent subcommittee could avoid incidents of misidentification and could determine how forthcoming witnesses were likely to be in public. In the case of McCarthy, however, "executive session" took a different meaning. John G. Adams, who attended many of these hearings as the army's counsel from 1953 to 1954, observed that the chairman used the term "executive session" rather loosely. "It didn't really mean a closed session, since McCarthy allowed in various friends, hangers-on, and favored newspaper reporters," wrote Adams, "nor did it mean secret, because afterwards McCarthy would tell the reporters waiting outside whatever he pleased. Basically, 'executive' meant that Joe could do anything he wanted." Adams recalled that the subcommittee's Fort Monmouth hearings were held in a "windowless storage room in the bowels of the courthouse, unventilated and oppressively hot," into which crowded the senator, his staff, witnesses, and observers who at various times included trusted newspaper reporters, the governor of Wisconsin, the chairman's wife, mother-in-law and friends. "The 'secret' hearings were, after all, quite a show," Adams commented, adding that the transcripts were rarely released to the public. This ostensibly protected the privacy of those interrogated, but also gave the chairman an opportunity to give to the press his version of what had transpired behind closed doors, with little chance of rebuttal.

Roy Cohn insisted that the subcommittee gave "suspects" rights that they would not get in a court of law. Unlike a witness before a grand jury, or testifying on the stand, those facing the subcommittee could have their attorneys sit beside them for consultation. The executive sessions further protected the witnesses, Cohn pointed out, by excluding the press and the public. But Gen. Telford Taylor, an American prosecutor at Nuremberg, charged McCarthy with conducting "a new and indefensible kind of hearing, which is neither a public hearing nor an executive session." In Taylor's view, the closed sessions were a device that enabled the chairman to tell newspapers whatever he saw fit about what happened, without giving witnesses a chance to defend themselves or reporters a chance to check the accuracy of the accusations. Characteristically, Senator McCarthy responded to this criticism with an executive session inquiry into Gen. Taylor's loyalty. The chairman used other hearings to settle personal scores with men such as Edward Barrett, State Department press spokesman under Dean Acheson, and Edward Morgan, staff director of the Tydings subcommittee that had investigated his Wheeling speech.

Inclusion as a witness in these volumes in no way suggests a measure of guilt. Some of the witnesses who came before the permanent subcommittee in 1953 had been Communists; others had not. Some witnesses cooperated by providing names and other information; others did not. Some testified on subjects entirely unrelated to communism, subversion or espionage. The names of many of these witnesses appeared in contemporary newspaper accounts, even when they did not testify in public. About a third of the witnesses called in executive session did not appear at any public hearing, and Senator McCarthy often defined such witnesses as having been "cleared." Some were called as witnesses out of mistaken identity. Others defended themselves so resolutely or had so little evidence against them that the chairman and counsel chose not to pursue them. For those witnesses who did appear in public, the closed hearings served as dress rehearsals. The subcommittee also heard many witnesses in public session who had not previously appeared at a closed hearing, usually committee staff or government officials for whom a preliminary hearing was not deemed necessary. Given the rapid pace of the hearings, the subcommittee staff had little time for preparation. "No real research was ever done," Robert Kennedy complained. "Most of the investigations were instituted on the basis of some preconceived notion by the chief counsel or his staff members and not on the basis of any information that had been developed."

After July 1953, when the Democratic senators resigned from the subcommittee, other Republican senators also stopped attending the subcommittee's closed hearings, in part because so many of the hearings were held away from the District of Columbia and called on short notice. Witnesses also received subpoenas on such short notice that they found it hard to prepare themselves or consult with counsel. Theoretically the committee, rather than the chairman, issued subpoenas, Army Counsel John G. Adams noted. "But McCarthy ignored the Senate rule that required a vote of the other members every time he wanted to haul someone in. He signed scores of blank subpoenas which his staff members carried in their inside pockets, and issued as regularly as traffic tickets." Witnesses repeatedly complained that subpoenas to appear were served on them just before the hearings, either the night before or the morning of, making it hard for them to obtain legal representation. Even if they obtained a lawyer, the senator would not permit attorneys to raise objections or to talk for the witness. Normally, a quorum of at least one-third of the committee or subcommittee members was needed to take sworn testimony, although a single senator could hold hearings if authorized by the committee. The rules did not bar "one-man hearings," because senators often came and went during a committee hearing and committee business could come to a halt if a minimum number of senators were required to hold a hearing.

When the chairman acted as a one-man committee, the tone of the hearings more closely resembled an inquisition. Witnesses who swore that they never joined the Communist party or engaged in espionage or sabotage were held accountable for long-forgotten petitions they had signed a decade earlier or for having joined organizations that the attorney general later cited as Communist fronts. Seeking any sign of political unorthodoxy, the chairman and the subcommittee staff scrutinized the witnesses' lives and grilled them about the political beliefs of colleagues, neighbors and family members. In the case of Stanley Berinsky, he was suspended from the Army Signal Corps at Fort Monmouth after security officers discovered that his mother had once been a member of the Communist party:

The Chairman. Let's get this straight. I know it is unusual to appear before a committee. So many witnesses get nervous. You just got through telling us you did not know she was a Communist; now you tell us she resigned from the Communist party? As of when?

Mr. Berinsky. I didn't know this until the security suspension came up at Fort Monmouth.

The Chairman. When was that?

Mr. Berinsky. That was in 1952.

The Chairman. Then did your mother come over and tell you she had resigned?

Mr. Berinsky. I told her what happened. At that time she told me she had been out for several years.

The Chairman.... Well, did you ever ask her if she was a Communist?

Mr. Berinsky. No sir....

The Chairman. When you went to see her, weren't you curious? If somebody told me my mother was a Communist, I'd get on the phone and say, "Mother is this true"?... Did she tell you why she resigned?

Mr. Berinsky. It seems to me she probably did it because I held a government job and she didn't want to jeopardize my position.

The Chairman. In other words, it wasn't because she felt differently about the Communist party, but because she didn't want to jeopardize your position?

Mr. Berinsky. Probably.

The Chairman. Was she still a Communist at heart in 1952?

Mr. Berinsky. Well, I don't know how you define that.

The Chairman. Do you think she was a Communist, using your own definition of communism?

Mr. Berinsky. I guess my own definition is one who is a member of the party. No.

The Chairman. Let's say one who was a member and dropped out and is still loyal to the party. Taking that as a definition, would you say she is still a Communist?

Mr. Berinsky. Do you mean in an active sense?

The Chairman. Loyal in her mind.

Mr. Berinsky. That is hard to say.

The Chairman. Is she still living?

Mr. Berinsky. Yes.

Perhaps the most recurring phrase in these executive session hearings was not the familiar "Are you now or have you ever been a member of the Communist party?" That was the mantra of the public hearings. Instead, in the closed hearings it was "In other words," which prefaced the chairman's relentless rephrasing of witnesses' testimony into something with more sinister implications than they intended. Given Senator McCarthy's tendency toward hyperbole, witnesses objected to his use of inappropriate or inflammatory words to characterize their testimony. He took their objections as a sign they were covering up something:

The Chairman. Did you live with him when the apartment was raided by army security?

Mr. Okun. Senator, the apartment was not raided. He had been called and asked whether he would let them search it....

The Chairman. You seem to shy off at the word "raided." When the army security men go over and make a complete search of the apartment and find forty-three classified documents, to me that means "raided." You seem, both today and the other day to be going out of your way trying to cover up for this man Coleman.

Mr. Okun. No, sir. I do not want to cover up anything.

A few of those who appeared before the subcommittee later commented that the chairman was less intimidating in private than his public behavior had led them to expect. "Many of us have formed an impression of McCarthy from the now familiar Herblock caricatures. He is by no means grotesque," recalled Martin Merson, who clashed with the senator over the Voice of America. "McCarthy, the relaxed dinner guest, is a charming man with the friendliest of smiles." McCarthy's sometimes benign treatment of witnesses in executive session may have been a tactic intended to lull them into false complacency before his more relentless questioning in front of the television cameras, which certainly seemed to bring out the worst in him. Ruth Young Watt (1910–1996), the subcommittee's chief clerk from 1948 until her retirement in 1979, regarded the chairman as "a very kind man, very thoughtful of people working with him," but a person who would "get off on a tirade sometimes" in public hearings.

Senator McCarthy regularly informed witnesses of their right to decline to answer if they felt an answer might incriminate them, but he interpreted their refusal to answer a question as an admission of guilt. He also encouraged government agencies and private corporations to fire anyone who took the Fifth Amendment before a congressional committee. When witnesses also attempted to cite their First Amendment rights, the chairman warned that they would be cited for contempt of Congress. Although the chairman pointed out that membership in the Communist party was not a crime, many witnesses declined to admit their past connections to the party to avoid having to name others with whom they were associated. Some witnesses wanted to argue that the subcommittee had no right to question their political beliefs, but their attorneys advised them that it would be more prudent to decline to answer. During 1953, some seventy witnesses before the subcommittee invoked the Fifth Amendment and declined to answer questions concerning Communist activities. Five refused to answer on the basis of the First Amendment, two claimed marital privileges, and Harvard Professor Wendell Furry invoked no constitutional grounds for his failure to answer questions.

Some witnesses invoked the Fifth Amendment to avoid implicating those they knew to be Communists. Others invoked the Fifth Amendment as a blanket response to any questions about the Communist party, after being warned by their attorneys that if they answered questions about themselves they could be compelled to name their associates. In the case of *Rogers v. U.S.* (1951) the Supreme Court had ruled that a witness could not refuse to answer questions simply out of a "desire to protect others from punishment, much less to protect another from interrogation by a grand jury." The Justice Department applied the same reasoning to witnesses who refused to identify others to a congressional committee. Since the questions were relevant to the operation of the government, the department assured Senator McCarthy that it was his right as a congressional investigator to order witnesses to answer questions about whether they know any Communists who might be working in the government or in defense plants.

Senator McCarthy explained to witnesses that they could take the Fifth Amendment only if they were concerned that telling the truth would incriminate them, a reasoning that redefined the right against self-incrimination as incriminating in itself. Calling them "Fifth-Amendment Communists," he insisted that "an innocent man does not need the Fifth Amendment." At a public hearing, the chairman pressed one witness: "Are you declining, among other reasons, for the reason that you are relying upon that section of the Fifth Amendment which provides that no person may be a witness against himself if he feels that his testimony might tend to incriminate him? If you are relying upon that, you can tell me. If not, of course, you are ordered to answer. A Communist and espionage agent has the right to refuse on that ground, but not on any of the other grounds you cited."

Federal court rulings had given congressional investigators considerable leeway to operate. In the aftermath of the Teapot Dome investigation, the Supreme Court ruled in *McGrain v. Daugherty* (1927) that a committee could subpoena anyone to testify, including private citizens who were neither government officials nor employees. In *Sinclair v. U.S.* (1929), the Supreme Court recognized the right of Congress to investigate anything remotely related to its legislative and oversight functions. The court also upheld the Smith Act of 1940, which made it illegal to advocate overthrowing the U.S. government by force or violence. In 1948 the Justice Department prosecuted twelve Communist leaders for having conspired to organize "as a society, group and assembly of persons who teach and advocate the overthrow and destruction of the Government of the United States by force and violence." Upholding their convictions, in *Dennis v. U.S.* (1951), the Supreme Court denied that their prosecution had violated the First

Amendment, on the grounds that the government's power to prevent an armed rebellion subordinated free speech. During the next six years 126 individuals were indicted solely for being members of the Communist party. The Mundt-Nixon Act of 1950 further barred Communist party members from employment in defense installations, denied them passports, and required them to register with the Subversive Activities Control Board. In *Rogers v. U.S.* (1951) the Supreme Court declared that a witness who had testified that she was treasurer of a local Communist party and had possession of its records could not claim the Fifth Amendment when asked to whom she gave those records. Her initial admission had waived her right to invoke her privilege and she was guilty of contempt for failing to answer.

Not until after Senator McCarthy's investigations had ceased did the Supreme Court change direction on the rights of congressional witnesses, in three sweeping decisions handed down on June 17, 1957. In *Yates v. U.S.* the court overturned the convictions of fourteen Communist party members under the Smith Act, finding that organizing a Communist party was not synonymous with advocating the overthrow of the government by force and violence. As a result, the Justice Department stopped seeking further indictments under the Smith Act. In *Watkins v. U.S.*, the court specified that an investigating committee must demonstrate a legislative purpose to justify probing into private affairs, and ruled that public education was an insufficient reason to force witnesses to answer questions under the penalty of being held in contempt. These rulings confirmed that the Bill of Rights applied to anyone subpoenaed by a congressional committee.

If witnesses refused to cooperate, the chairman threatened them with indictment and incarceration. At the end of his first year as chairman, he advised one witness: "During the course of these hearings, I think up to this time we have some—this is just a rough guess—twenty cases we submitted to the grand jury, either for perjury or for contempt before this committee. Do not just assume that your name was pulled out of a hat. Before you were brought here, we make a fairly thorough and complete investigation. So I would like to strongly advise you to either tell the truth or, if you think the truth will incriminate you, then you are entitled to refuse to answer. I cannot urge that upon you too strongly. I have given that advice to other people here before the committee. They thought they were smarter than our investigators. They will end up in jail. This is not a threat; this is just friendly advice I am giving you. Do you understand that?" In the end, however, no witness who appeared before the subcommittee during his chairmanship was imprisoned for perjury, contempt, espionage, or subversion. Several witnesses were tried for contempt, and some were convicted, but each case was overturned on appeal.

Area of Investigation

Following the tradition of the Permanent Subcommittee on Investigations, the first executive session hearings in 1953 dealt with influence peddling, an outgrowth of an investigation begun in the previous Congress. Senator McCarthy absented himself from most of the influence-peddling hearings and left Senator Karl Mundt or Senator John McClellan, the ranking Republican and Democrat on the Government Operations Committee, to preside in his place. But the chairman made subversion and espionage his sole mission. On the day that the subcommittee launched a new set of hearings on influence peddling, it began hearings on the State Department's filing system, whose byzantine complexity Senator McCarthy attributed to either Communist infiltration or gross incompetence.

With the State Department investigation, Senator McCarthy returned to familiar territory. His Wheeling speech in 1950 had accused the department of harboring known Communists. The senator demanded that the State Department open its "loyalty files," and then complained that it provided only "skinny-ribbed bones of the files," "skeleton files," "purged files," and "phony files." The chairman's interest was naturally piqued in 1953 when State Department security officer John E. Matson reported irregularities in the department's filing system, and charged that personnel files had been "looted" of derogatory information in order to protect disloyal individuals. Although State Department testimony suggested that its system had been designed to protect the rights of employees in matters of career evaluation and promotion, Senator McCarthy contended that there had been a conspiracy to manipulate the files.

A brief investigation of homosexuals as security risks also grew out of previous inquiries. In 1950, Senator McCarthy denounced "those Communists and queers who have sold 400 million Asiatic people into atheistic slavery and have American people in a hypnotic trance, headed blindly toward the same precipice." He often laced his speeches with references to "powder puff diplomacy," and accused his opponents of "softness" toward communism. "Why is it that wherever it is in the world that our State Department touches the red-hot aggression of Soviet communism there is heard a sharp cry of pain—a whimper of confusion and fear?... Why must we be forced to cringe in the face of communism?" By contrast, he portrayed himself in masculine terms: in rooting out communism he "had to do a bare-knuckle job or suffer the same defeat that a vast number of well-meaning men have suffered over past years. It has been a bare-knuckle job. As long as I remain in the Senate it will continue as a bare-knuckle job." The subcommittee had earlier responded to Senator McCarthy's complaint that the State Department had reinstated homosexuals suspended for moral turpitude with an investigation in 1950 that produced a report on the *Employment of Homosexuals and Other Sex Perverts in Government*. The report had concluded that homosexuals' vulnerability to blackmail made them security risks and therefore "not suitable for Government positions."

The closed hearings shifted to two subsidiaries of the State Department, the Voice of America and the U.S. information libraries, which had come under the department's jurisdiction following World War II. Dubious about mixing foreign policy and propaganda, Secretary of State John Foster Dulles viewed the Voice of America as an unwanted appendage and was not unsympathetic to some housecleaning. It was not long, however, before the Eisenhower administration began to worry that McCarthy's effort to clean out the "left-wing debris" was disrupting its own efforts to reorganize the government. Senator McCarthy also looked into allegations of Communist literature on the shelves of the U.S. Information Agency libraries abroad. Rather than call the officials who administered the libraries, the subcommittees subpoenaed the authors of the books in question, along with scholars and artists who traveled abroad on Fulbright scholarships. These witnesses became innocent bystanders in the cross-fire between the subcommittee and the administration as the senator expanded his inquiry from examinations of files and books to issues of espionage and sabotage, warning audiences: "This is the era of the Armageddon—that final all-out battle between light and darkness foretold in the Bible." Zealousness in the search for subversives made the senator unwilling to accept bureaucratic explanations on such matters as personnel files and loyalty board procedures in the State Department, the Government Printing Office, and the U.S. Army.

Many of McCarthy's investigations began with a flurry of publicity and then faded away. Richard Rovere, who covered the subcommittee's hearings for the *New Yorker*, observed that investigation of the Voice of America was never completed. "It just stopped—its largest possibilities for tumult had been exhausted, and it trailed off into nothingness." Before completing one investigation, the subcommittee would have launched another. The hectic pace of hearings and the large number of witnesses it called strained the subcommittee's staff resources. Counsels coped by essentially asking the same questions of all witnesses. "For the most part you wouldn't have time to do all your homework on that, we didn't have a big staff," commented chief clerk Ruth Watt. As a result, the subcommittee occasionally subpoenaed the wrong individuals, and used the closed hearings to winnow out cases of mistaken identity. Some of those who were subpoenaed failed to appear. As Roy Cohn complained of the authors whose books had appeared in overseas libraries, "we subpoena maybe fifty and five show up."

When Senator McCarthy was preoccupied or uninterested in the subject matter, other senators would occasionally chair the hearings. Senator Charles Potter, for example, chaired a series of hearings on Korean War atrocities whose style, demeanor, and treatment of witnesses contrasted sharply with those that Senator McCarthy conducted; they are included in these volumes as a point of reference. Other hearings that stood apart in tone and substance concerned the illegal trade with the People's Republic of China, an investigation staffed by assistant counsel Robert F. Kennedy.

The subcommittee's investigations exposed examples of lax security in government agencies and defense contractors, but they failed to substantiate the chairman's accusations of subversion and espionage. Critics accused Senator McCarthy of gross exaggerations, of conducting "show trials" rather than fact-finding inquiries, of being careless and indifferent about evidence, of treating witnesses cavalierly and of employing irresponsible tactics. Indeed, the chairman showed no qualms about using raw investigative files as evidence. His willingness to break the established rules encouraged some security officers and federal investigators to leak investigative files to the subcommittee that they were constrained by agency policy from revealing. Rather than lead to the high-level officials he had expected to find, the leaked security files shifted his attention to lower-level civil servants. Since these civil servants lacked the freedom to fight back in the political arena, they became "easier targets to bully." Even Roy Cohn conceded that McCarthy invited much of the criticism "with his penchant for the dramatic," and "by making statements that could be construed as promising too much."

Having predicted to the press that his inquiry into conditions at Fort Monmouth would uncover espionage, Senator McCarthy willingly accepted circumstantial evidence as grounds for the dismissal of an employee from government-related service. The subcommittee's dragnet included a number of perplexed witnesses who had signed a nominating petition years earlier, belonged to a union whose leadership included alleged Communists, bought an insurance policy through an organization later designated a Communist front organization, belonged to a Great Books club that read Karl Marx among other authors, had once dated a Communist, had relatives who were Communists, or simply had the same name as a Communist. Those witnesses against whom strong evidence of Communist activities existed tended to be involved in labor organizing—hardly news since the Congress of Industrial Organizations (CIO) had already expelled such unions as the Federation of Architects, Engineers, Chemists and Technicians and the United Electrical Workers, whom McCarthy investigated. Those witnesses who named names of Communists with whom they had associated invariably described union activities, and none corroborated any claims of subversion and espionage.

Critics questioned Senator McCarthy's sincerity as a Communist hunter, citing his penchant for privately embracing those whom he publicly attacked; others considered him a classic conspiracy theorist. Once he became convinced of the existence of a conspiracy, nothing could dissuade him. He exhibited impatience with those who saw things differently, interpreted mistakes as deliberate actions, and suspected his opponents of being part of the larger conspiracy. He would not entertain alternative explanations and stood contemptuous of doubters. A lack of evidence rarely deterred him or undermined his convictions. If witnesses disagreed on the facts, someone had to be lying. The Fort Monmouth investigation, for instance, had been spurred by reports of information from the Army Signal Corps laboratories turning up in Eastern Europe. Since Julius Rosenberg had worked at Fort Monmouth, McCarthy and Cohn were convinced that other Communist sympathizers were still supplying secrets to the enemy. But the Soviet Union had been an ally during the Second World War, and during that time had openly designated representatives at the laboratories, making espionage there superfluous. Nevertheless, McCarthy's pursuit of a spy ring caused officials at Fort Monmouth to suspend forty-two civilian employees. After the investigations, all but two were reinstated in their former jobs.

Not until January 1954, did the remaining subcommittee members adopt rules changes that Democrats had demanded, and Senators McClellan, Jackson and Symington resumed their membership on the subcommittee. These rules changes removed the chairman's exclusive authority over staffing, and gave the minority members the right to hire their own counsel. Whenever the minority was unanimously opposed to holding a public hearing, the issue would go to the full committee to determine by majority vote. Also in 1954, the Republican Party Committee proposed rules changes that would require a quorum to be present to hold hearings, and would prohibit holding hearings outside of the District of Columbia or taking confidential testimony unless authorized by a majority of committee members. In 1955, the Permanent Subcommittee adopted rules similar to those the Policy Committee recommended.

Following the Army-McCarthy hearings of 1954, the Senate censured Senator McCarthy in December 1954 for conduct unbecoming of a senator. Court rulings in subsequent years had a significant impact on later congressional investigations by strengthening the rights of witnesses. Later in the 1950s, members and staff of the Permanent Subcommittee on Investigations joined with the Senator Labor and Public Welfare Committee to form a special committee to investigate labor racketeering, with Robert F. Kennedy as chief counsel. Conducted in a more bipartisan manner and respectful of the rights of witnesses, their successes helped to reverse the negative image of congressional investigations fostered by Senator McCarthy's freewheeling investigatory style.

* * *

Conclusion

McCarthy enjoyed remarkable political power and public support at the beginning of the Eisenhower administration. McCarthy's attacks on Democrats during the Truman administration were one thing, but when he continued his antics after a Republican administration took office it created difficult political problems for President Eisenhower. Haynes Johnson's 2005 book *The Age of Anxiety: McCarthyism to Terrorism* described Ike's travails in trying to deal with McCarthy:

> As McCarthy's contemptuous assaults on *his* State Department, *his* nominees, *his* policies, *his* right to lead America grew ever bolder, the president became increasingly furious beneath his grandfatherly public demeanor.

> Ike's White House advisers were divided on how to deal with the Wisconsin demagogue. Some wanted the president to take him on publicly, others counseled a strategy of caution. The wisest course, they argued, was to avoid a political slugging match with McCarthy. Stay above the fray, act presidential, let others in the new Republican administration and congressional majority work quietly behind the scenes to pacify McCarthy and lure him back onto the team. Besides, while Republicans now controlled Congress, they had only a one-vote margin in the Senate; all the more reason not to antagonize McCarthy. Eisenhower chose that path—but at a great price that always comes with appeasement.

HAYNES JOHNSON, THE AGE OF ANXIETY: MCCARTHYISM TO TERRORISM 264–65 (2005). For two years McCarthy and his chief counsel Roy Cohn conducted investigations and held public hearings on the Eisenhower administration's State Department, the Government Printing Office, the CIA, the Atomic Energy Commission, and defense manufacturing facilities. The end finally came when McCarthy and Cohn turned their attention to the Army, but not because of their investigative activities—the Achilles heel of McCarthyism was exposed through Cohn's efforts to obtain favorable treatment for his friend and committee staff colleague David Schine, who had been drafted into the Army.

The renowned author Tom Wolfe, in his characteristically elegant prose style, described the unintended consequences of Cohn's actions on behalf of Schine in "Dangerous Obsessions," a 1988 *New York Times* book review of two Cohn biographies:

> ... Cohn was more than Senator Joseph McCarthy, Republican of Wisconsin, could handle, in any case. McCarthy was not destroyed because he made wild charges concerning Communist influence in America. As polls showed repeatedly, so long as he stuck to that broad theme, he had tremendous bipartisan support. It was the sons of two established Democratic Party families who vied for the position of chief counsel to McCarthy's Senate Subcommittee on Internal Security. One was Roy Cohn. The other was Bobby Kennedy. Cohn won out because, among other considerations, he had, at age 26, vastly more experience as a prosecutor. Kennedy signed on as an assistant counsel, and Cohn treated him like a gofer, making him go out for sweet rolls and coffee refills, earning his eternal hatred. What did McCarthy in was his attack on the United States Army. It was Dwight Eisenhower's Army, and by now, 1953, Eisenhower was President of the United States. And who got McCarthy into his last, ruinous tarball battle with the Army? The little prince [Roy Cohn]....
>
> The thrust of the Army-McCarthy hearings was that McCarthy's attack on the Army had been nothing but an insidious attempt to get favored treatment for Cohn's friend Mr. Schine.
>
> So what? Cohn remained confident that he could win against any odds. But, as he would later admit to Mr. Zion, he was no match for the Army's counsel, the veteran Boston trial lawyer Joseph Welch. The hearings became a television drama that stopped America cold. The entire nation seemed to take time out to watch. The hearings had two famous punch lines, and Welch delivered them both.
>
> The most famous came when McCarthy violated a secret ... deal between Welch and Cohn. As Cohn and Mr. von Hoffman both tell it, Cohn had approached Welch and agreed not to reveal that one of Welch's young law associates, Frederick Fisher, had been a member of the National Lawyers Guild, reputed to be a Communist front, if Welch would not go into Cohn's inglorious armed-service record. Welch agreed, but McCarthy, infuriated by Welch's sarcastic, goading manner, blurted out the damning information about young Fisher, while Cohn mouthed the words, "No! No, Joe!" A wrangle ensued, climaxed by Welch's line: "Let us not assassinate this lad further, Senator. You have done enough. Have you no sense of decency, sir, at long last? Have you no sense of decency?"

Everyone in the hearing room except McCarthy's own team, even the reporters and photographers, rose up and cheered, and the McCarthy Era, as it was
known, was over.

Tom Wolfe, *Dangerous Obsessions*, NEW YORK TIMES, April 3, 1988 (book review of
The Autobiography of Roy Cohn by Sydney Zion and *Citizen Cohn* by Nicholas von
Hoffman).

Notes and Questions

1. **The Role of Committee Staff.** Heavy reliance on the work of key staff members,
usually attorneys acting as committee counsel, certainly is not unusual in congressional investigations. Chapter 1 of this book describes the key role that Ferdinand Pecora
played in the 1933–34 hearings that are known by his name. Even in this context,
however, Roy Cohn's role in the McCarthy investigations was unusual. Cohn was only
twenty-five years old when he went to work for McCarthy, but McCarthy nonetheless
allowed Cohn free rein to run the investigations. After beating out Robert F. Kennedy
for the position of McCarthy's chief counsel, Cohn clashed with Kennedy, who resigned from the staff with a notably prescient prediction that the subcommittee was
"headed for disaster." Despite Kennedy's reservations about Cohn's role, the extent of
Cohn's influence and resulting notoriety is well illustrated by a somewhat tongue-in-
cheek passage from Kennedy's 1960 book about his work in the 1950s as a Senate staff
counsel investigating organized crime's infiltration of labor unions:

> ... I was going into New York from La Guardia Airport when the cab driver
> turned around and said, "I know who you are. Now, let me see—" He thought
> for five minutes or so and just as he was about to let me out he said, "I know
> who you are—you're Roy Cohn!" I felt I had arrived in more ways than one.

ROBERT F. KENNEDY, THE ENEMY WITHIN: THE McCLELLAN COMMITTEE'S CRUSADE
AGAINST JIMMY HOFFA AND CORRUPT LABOR UNIONS 189 (1960).

2. **Eisenhower, McCarthy, and Executive Privilege.** As discussed above, President
Eisenhower was reluctant to oppose McCarthy's activities publicly, in part because he
feared that presidential opposition would only serve to give McCarthy more of the
publicity that McCarthy was so desperately seeking. When McCarthy turned his investigative attentions to the Army, however, it was more than Eisenhower could take, and
the Eisenhower administration then fought back with the weapon of the Cohn/Schine
special treatment allegations that were the subject of the Army-McCarthy hearings.
The battle that followed led not only to the televised hearings that precipitated McCarthy's eventual downfall, but also to the birth of the term "executive privilege" (although
the practice had been employed by presidents since Washington) and what historian
Arthur M. Schlesinger Jr. called "the most absolute assertion of presidential right to
withhold information from Congress ever uttered to that day in American history."
ARTHUR M. SCHLESINGER JR., THE IMPERIAL PRESIDENCY 155 (2004; orig. ed. 1973).
Eisenhower refused to permit administration officials to testify about the consultations
that led up to the Army's report on the Cohn/Schine affair, and in doing so couched

the president's power to withhold in extremely broad terms. A few years later, in 1958, Attorney General William P. Rogers used the term "executive privilege" to describe the then-rapidly growing practice of withholding executive branch information from Congress. As Schlesinger observed:

> Executive privilege had the advantage of sounding like a very old term. It passed rapidly into political discourse and very soon (though, so far as I have been able to discover, no President or Attorney General used it before the Eisenhower administration) acquired the patina of ancient and hallowed doctrine. What had been for a century and a half sporadic executive practice employed in very unusual circumstances was now in a brief decade hypostasized into sacred constitutional principle.

SCHLESINGER, THE IMPERIAL PRESIDENCY 159 (1973).

The subject of executive privilege will be discussed in more detail in Chapters 4 and 7. With respect to the breadth of the Eisenhower administration's executive privilege claims, and the role of Senator McCarthy in precipitating those claims, a candid acknowledgment of the extraordinary nature of those claims was provided by then-Assistant Attorney General and head of the Justice Department's Office of Legal Counsel Antonin Scalia, testifying in 1975 on behalf of the Ford administration during the "Pike Committee" investigation of U.S. intelligence agencies and activities:

> For example, some of the broadest assertions of executive privilege in history were made with respect to the McCarthy hearings, when the President just forbade any employee of the Department of Defense to appear. In ordinary circumstances, I would say that is not an appropriate manner of exercising executive privilege. In that circumstance, I think it was all right. But I don't know how a court could write an opinion to that effect and say, "Well, we think it is all right because we think this is a witch hunt and we don't like Joseph McCarthy."

U.S. Intelligence Agencies and Activities: Committee Proceedings, Nov. 14, 1975, House of Representatives Select Committee on Intelligence.

3. McCarthy's Censure by the Senate. Senator McCarthy was censured[8] by the Senate on December 2, 1954, by a vote of 67 to 22. The proceedings leading up to the final censure vote were long and acrimonious, and many of the charges that other Senators

---

8. The resolution that was approved by the Senate actually does not use the word "censure" and instead states that McCarthy's conduct "is hereby condemned." Sen. Res. 301, Dec. 2, 1954, Cong. Rec., 83rd Congress, 2nd Session, 16392. Notwithstanding this language, the proceedings leading up to the vote focused on whether McCarthy should be censured, and the resolution as originally introduced, before amendments, was to "censure" McCarthy. The Senate's final action was regarded as, and has since been referred to, as censuring McCarthy. One author has written that the issue of whether the final action should be regarded as a censure was resolved shortly after the vote, when "Senator Fulbright pulled out a dictionary and noted that *condemn* seemed to mean the same thing as *censure*, and that the word obviously covered the case." ARTHUR HERMAN, JOSEPH MCCARTHY: REEXAMINING THE LIFE AND LEGACY OF AMERICA'S MOST HATED SENATOR 293 (Free Press 2000).

brought against McCarthy were dropped before the vote on the final resolution. The final resolution contained only two charges against McCarthy, both of which related to his conduct in response to Senate investigations of his conduct; charges based upon his treatment of witnesses in committee hearings and his conduct on the Senate floor were dropped when it appeared that they might not command sufficient support. The irony of this outcome was noted by Telford Taylor in 1955, shortly after the censure vote:

> It is especially noteworthy, as Senator Monroney pointed out on the closing day of debate, that Senator McCarthy was not censured for his misuse of the Senate's investigatorial prerogatives, for his attack against the Executive branch, or for his treatment of anyone other than his fellow-Senators. He was censured only for his sulphurous reaction to the Senate's undertaking to investigate and judge him—i.e. for *obstructing* rather than *abusing* the Senate's power. In short, the Senate condemned Senator McCarthy as an individual, but it remains to be seen whether it checked McCarthyism.

TELFORD TAYLOR, GRAND INQUEST: THE STORY OF CONGRESSIONAL INVESTIGATIONS 135 (1955).

Although Taylor could not have known it in 1955, the Senate's censure vote and the resulting loss of status had a devastating effect on McCarthy. He was unable to adapt to the loss of public influence and political power, and his health declined as his abuse of alcohol increased. He died on May 2, 1957, before the end of his second Senate term, of liver failure that has been attributed to his alcohol abuse.

4. Recent Reexaminations of McCarthyism—Revisionist History or Correcting the Record? Even today, over fifty years after his death, McCarthy remains a polarizing and divisive figure. Historical scholarship and biographical accounts of his political career have been overwhelmingly negative, but in recent years some accounts have purported to "reexamine" his legacy and have argued that there was more merit to his efforts to combat Communism than has previously been recognized. These arguments rely heavily on recently obtained Cold War-era Soviet records, which show that at least some of the people McCarthy accused actually were involved in espionage activities on behalf of the Soviets. Other recent works continue to condemn McCarthy, arguing that there is no reason to revisit history's overwhelmingly negative assessment of his career. For a particularly thorough and detailed effort to paint a more sympathetic portrait of McCarthy, see ARTHUR HERMAN, JOSEPH MCCARTHY: REEXAMINING THE LIFE AND LEGACY OF AMERICA'S MOST HATED SENATOR (Free Press 2000). For a less sympathetic recent assessment of McCarthy's legacy, see HAYNES JOHNSON, THE AGE OF ANXIETY: MCCARTHYISM TO TERRORISM (Harcourt 2005).

Those who seek to defend McCarthy's motives, if not his excesses, are aided by the fact that surprising revelations about Cold War-era espionage continue to this day. For example, in November 2007, a *New York Times* article reported that "On Nov. 2, the Kremlin startled Western scholars by announcing that President Vladimir V. Putin had posthumously given the highest Russian award to a Soviet agent who penetrated the Manhattan Project to build the atomic bomb." William J. Broad, *A Spy's Path: Iowa to A-Bomb to Kremlin Honor*, NEW YORK TIMES, Nov. 12, 2007. The article goes on to describe how George Koval, an American-born Soviet agent trained by Stalin's bureau of military intelligence, succeeded in penetrating the Manhattan Project and may have passed on secrets of bomb manufacturing that helped the Soviets develop their own atomic bomb in an unexpectedly short time. Revelations of this nature keep the debate over "McCarthyism" alive by demonstrating that the dangers of Communist espionage cannot be dismissed as political grandstanding by McCarthy, Nixon, and other anti-Communists of that era. Information of this nature is also helpful when assessing the merits of the judicial responses to the HUAC and McCarthy era congressional investigations, which are discussed in the next section.

Aftermath:
The Supreme Court Sets Some Limits

The excesses of the HUAC and McCarthy congressional proceedings certainly did not go unnoticed by the federal courts, and by the late 1950s the Supreme Court was finally ready to impose some limitations on the investigative powers of congressional committees. The first indication that the Court was looking at congressional investigations in a new light came earlier, however, in a 1953 case involving a lobbying investigation by a special committee of the House of Representatives. In *United States v. Rumely*, 345 U.S. 41, 44 (1953), a case involving a criminal contempt citation against a publisher of political tracts that were distributed to members of Congress, Justice Frankfurter's majority opinion took judicial notice "that there is wide concern, both in and out of Congress, over some aspects of the exercise of the congressional power of investigation." The publisher had refused to reveal to the investigating committee the names of the purchasers of his publications, asserting that "under the Bill of Rights, that is beyond the power of your committee to investigate." The majority opinion avoided the ultimate constitutional issue by construing narrowly the phrase "lobbying activities" in the committee's enabling resolution so as to avoid any infringement on publishing activities protected by the First Amendment. (Justices Douglas and Black, in a concurring opinion by Justice Douglas, went further and concluded that the inquiry authorized by the resolution abridged First Amendment rights.)

The *Rumely* decision was an important harbinger of what was soon to come from the Supreme Court on the subject of the congressional investigative power. Particularly significant was the fact that the majority opinion was written by Justice Felix Frankfurter. During the Teapot Dome investigation Frankfurter had written an influential article, "Hands Off the Investigations," *The New Republic*, May 21, 1924, that championed a broad congressional investigative power:

> In conclusion, there is no substantial basis for criticism of the [Teapot Dome] investigations conducted by Senator Walsh and Senator Wheeler. Whatever inconveniences may have resulted are inseparable incidents of an essential exertion of governmental power, and to talk about these incidents is to deflect attention from wrong-doing and its sources.

The procedure of congressional investigation should remain as it is. No limitations should be imposed by congressional legislation or standing rules. The power of investigation should be left untrammeled, and the methods and forms of each investigation should be left for determination of Congress and its committees, as each situation arises. The safeguards against abuse and folly are to be looked for in the forces of responsibility which are operating from within Congress, and are generated from without.

Frankfurter's willingness, twenty-nine years after his Teapot Dome article, to recognize limitations on the congressional investigative power, even though the limitations were constitutionally based rather than the legislative limitations he had rejected in his article, was a signal that the Court was looking at congressional investigations in a new light. Subsequent Supreme Court cases confirmed that the era of carte blanch congressional investigative power was over, an unintended victim of the investigatory excesses of the HUAC/McCarthy investigations.

The next signal that the Supreme Court was concerned about the anti-communist congressional investigations came in 1955. That year the Court decided three cases on the same day that all involved contempt charges and assertions of the Fifth Amendment privilege against self-incrimination by witnesses in HUAC hearings. In the first case, *Quinn v. United States*, 349 U.S. 155, 164 (1955), the Court held that "no ritualistic formula is necessary to invoke the privilege.... Quinn's references to the Fifth Amendment were clearly sufficient to put the committee on notice of an apparent claim of privilege."[9] Chief Justice Warren then made quite clear that the Court was well aware

---

9. The other two 1955 cases, *Emspack v. United States*, 349 U.S. 190 (1955), and *Bart v. United States*, 349 U.S. 219 (1955), also construed broadly the application of the Fifth Amendment privilege in congressional investigations and demonstrated that the Court wished to safeguard the rights of witnesses appearing before congressional committees. In *Emspack*, Chief Justice Warren observed that "if it is true that in these times a stigma may somehow result from a witness' reliance on the Self-Incrimination Clause, a committee should be all the more ready to recognize a veiled claim of the privilege. Otherwise, the great right which the Clause was intended to secure might be effectively frustrated by private pressures." 349 U.S. at 195. The *Emspack* opinion also made clear that, in addition to possible stigma for asserting the Fifth Amendment privilege, the witnesses faced real risk of criminal prosecution if they answered the Committee's questions:

What was the setting—as revealed by the record—in which these questions were asked? Each of the named individuals had previously been charged with having Communist affiliations. On October 14, 1949, less than two months prior to petitioner's appearance before the committee, eleven principal leaders of the Communist Party in this country had been convicted under the Smith Act for conspiring to teach and advocate the violent overthrow of the United States. Petitioner was identified at their trial as a Communist and an associate of the defendants. It was reported that Smith Act indictments against other Communist leaders were being prepared. On November 23, 1949, two weeks prior to petitioner's appearance, newspapers carried the story that the Department of Justice "within thirty days" would take "an important step" toward the criminal prosecution of petitioner in connection with his non-Communist affidavit filed with the National Labor Relations Board. Under these circumstances, it seems clear that answers to the 58 questions concerning petitioner's associations "might be dangerous because injurious disclosure could result." To reveal knowledge about the named individuals—all of them having been previously charged with Communist affiliations—could well have furnished "a link in the

of—and strongly disapproved of—the use of "Fifth Amendment communist" charges by Senator McCarthy and similar disparagement of the Fifth Amendment privilege by others in the Congress:

> Particularly this is so if it is true, as the Government contends, that petitioner [in avoiding an unequivocal assertion of his Fifth Amendment privilege] feared the stigma that might result from a forthright claim of his constitutional right to refuse to testify. *It is precisely at such times—when the privilege is under attack by those who wrongly conceive of it as merely a shield for the guilty—that governmental bodies must be scrupulous in protecting its exercise.*

Id. (emphasis supplied).

The Supreme Court's decisions in *Rumely* and the HUAC Fifth Amendment cases made clear that witnesses before congressional committees did not forfeit their constitutional rights, and that the Court would be vigilant in protecting those rights, but those decisions did not fundamentally alter the Court's interpretation of the scope of the congressional investigative power. In 1957 the Court sought to do just that, announcing a new approach to judicial oversight of congressional investigations:

Watkins v. United States
354 U.S. 178 (1957)

Mr. Chief Justice Warren delivered the opinion of the Court....

We start with several basic premises on which there is general agreement. The power of the Congress to conduct investigations is inherent in the legislative process. That power is broad. It encompasses inquiries concerning the administration of existing laws as well as proposed or possibly needed statutes. It includes surveys of defects in our social, economic or political system for the purpose of enabling the Congress to remedy them. It comprehends probes into departments of the Federal Government to expose corruption, inefficiency or waste. But, broad as is this power of inquiry, it is not unlimited. There is no general authority to expose the private affairs of individuals without justification in terms of the functions of the Congress. This was freely conceded by the Solicitor General in his argument of this case. Nor is the Congress a law enforcement or trial agency. These are functions of the executive and judicial departments of government. No inquiry is an end in itself; it must be related to, and in furtherance of, a legitimate task of the Congress. Investigations conducted solely for the personal aggrandizement of the investigators or to "punish" those investigated are indefensible.

---

chain" of evidence needed to prosecute petitioner for a federal crime, ranging from conspiracy to violate the Smith Act to the filing of a false non-Communist affidavit under the Taft-Hartley Act.

Id. at 200 (footnotes and citations omitted). In *Bart*, the witness refused to answer four questions on grounds of pertinency and one question on grounds of the Fifth Amendment privilege; the Court held that the committee's "consistent failure to advise the witness of the committee's position as to his objections" prevented his subsequent prosecution for contempt. 349 U.S. at 223.

It is unquestionably the duty of all citizens to cooperate with the Congress in its efforts to obtain the facts needed for intelligent legislative action. It is their unremitting obligation to respond to subpoenas, to respect the dignity of the Congress and its committees and to testify fully with respect to matters within the province of proper investigation. This, of course, assumes that the constitutional rights of witnesses will be respected by the Congress as they are in a court of justice. The Bill of Rights is applicable to investigations as to all forms of governmental action. Witnesses cannot be compelled to give evidence against themselves. They cannot be subjected to unreasonable search and seizure. Nor can the First Amendment freedoms of speech, press, religion, or political belief and association be abridged....

Abuses of the investigative process may imperceptibly lead to abridgment of protected freedoms. The mere summoning of a witness and compelling him to testify, against his will, about his beliefs, expressions or associations is a measure of governmental interference. And when those forced revelations concern matters that are unorthodox, unpopular, or even hateful to the general public, the reaction in the life of the witness may be disastrous. This effect is even more harsh when it is past beliefs, expressions or associations that are disclosed and judged by current standards rather than those contemporary with the matters exposed. Nor does the witness alone suffer the consequences. Those who are identified by witnesses and thereby placed in the same glare of publicity are equally subject to public stigma, scorn and obloquy. Beyond that, there is the more subtle and immeasurable effect upon those who tend to adhere to the most orthodox and uncontroversial views and associations in order to avoid a similar fate at some future time. That this impact is partly the result of non-governmental activity by private persons cannot relieve the investigators of their responsibility for initiating the reaction.

The Court recognized the restraints of the Bill of Rights upon congressional investigations in *United States v. Rumely....* The magnitude and complexity of the problem of applying the First Amendment to that case led the Court to construe narrowly the resolution describing the committee's authority. It was concluded that, when First Amendment rights are threatened, the delegation of power to the committee must be clearly revealed in its charter.

Accommodation of the congressional need for particular information with the individual and personal interest in privacy is an arduous and delicate task for any court. We do not underestimate the difficulties that would attend such an undertaking. It is manifest that despite the adverse effects which follow upon compelled disclosure of private matters, not all such inquiries are barred. *Kilbourn v. Thompson* teaches that such an investigation into individual affairs is invalid if unrelated to any legislative purpose. That is beyond the powers conferred upon the Congress in the Constitution. *United States v. Rumely* makes it plain that the mere semblance of legislative purpose would not justify an inquiry in the face of the Bill of Rights. The critical element is the existence of, and the weight to be ascribed to, the interest of the Congress in demanding disclosures from an unwilling witness. We cannot simply assume, however, that every congressional investigation is justified by a public need that overbalances any private rights affected. To do so would be to abdicate the responsibility placed by the Constitution upon the judiciary to insure that the Congress does not unjustifiably encroach upon an individual's right to privacy nor abridge his liberty of speech, press, religion or assembly.

Petitioner has earnestly suggested that the difficult questions of protecting these rights from infringement by legislative inquiries can be surmounted in this case because there was no public purpose served in his interrogation. His conclusion is based upon the thesis that the Subcommittee was engaged in a program of exposure for the sake of exposure. The sole purpose of the inquiry, he contends, was to bring down upon himself and others the violence of public reaction because of their past beliefs, expressions and associations. In support of this argument, petitioner has marshalled an impressive array of evidence that some Congressmen have believed that such was their duty, or part of it.

We have no doubt that there is no congressional power to expose for the sake of exposure. The public is, of course, entitled to be informed concerning the workings of its government.[10] That cannot be inflated into a general power to expose where the predominant result can only be an invasion of the private rights of individuals. But a solution to our problem is not to be found in testing the motives of committee members for this purpose. Such is not our function. Their motives alone would not vitiate an investigation which had been instituted by a House of Congress if that assembly's legislative purpose is being served.

Petitioner's contentions do point to a situation of particular significance from the standpoint of the constitutional limitations upon congressional investigations. The theory of a committee inquiry is that the committee members are serving as the representatives of the parent assembly in collecting information for a legislative purpose. Their function is to act as the eyes and ears of the Congress in obtaining facts upon which the full legislature can act. To carry out this mission, committees and subcommittees, sometimes one Congressman, are endowed with the full power of the Congress to compel testimony. In this case, only two men exercised that authority in demanding information over petitioner's protest.

An essential premise in this situation is that the House or Senate shall have instructed the committee members on what they are to do with the power delegated to them. It is the responsibility of the Congress, in the first instance, to insure that compulsory process is used only in furtherance of a legislative purpose. That requires that

---

10. [Court's Note 33] We are not concerned with the power of the Congress to inquire into and publicize corruption, maladministration or inefficiency in agencies of the Government. That was the only kind of activity described by Woodrow Wilson in *Congressional Government* when he wrote: "The informing function of Congress should be preferred even to its legislative function." *Id.*, at 303. From the earliest times in its history, the Congress has assiduously performed an "informing function" of this nature. *See Landis, Constitutional Limitations on the Congressional Power of Investigation*, 40 Harv. L. Rev. 153, 168–194.

the instructions to an investigating committee spell out that group's jurisdiction and purpose with sufficient particularity. Those instructions are embodied in the authorizing resolution. That document is the committee's charter. Broadly drafted and loosely worded, however, such resolutions can leave tremendous latitude to the discretion of the investigators. The more vague the committee's charter is, the greater becomes the possibility that the committee's specific actions are not in conformity with the will of the parent House of Congress.

The authorizing resolution of the Un-American Activities Committee was adopted in 1938 when a select committee, under the chairmanship of Representative Dies, was created. Several years later, the Committee was made a standing organ of the House with the same mandate. It defines the Committee's authority as follows:

> The Committee on Un-American Activities, as a whole or by subcommittee, is authorized to make from time to time investigations of (1) the extent, character, and objects of un-American propaganda activities in the United States, (2) the diffusion within the United States of subversive and un-American propaganda that is instigated from foreign countries or of a domestic origin and attacks the principle of the form of government as guaranteed by our Constitution, and (3) all other questions in relation thereto that would aid Congress in any necessary remedial legislation.

It would be difficult to imagine a less explicit authorizing resolution. Who can define the meaning of "un-American"? What is that single, solitary "principle of the form of government as guaranteed by our Constitution"? There is no need to dwell upon the language, however. At one time, perhaps, the resolution might have been read narrowly to confine the Committee to the subject of propaganda. The events that have transpired in the fifteen years before the interrogation of petitioner make such a construction impossible at this date.

The members of the Committee have clearly demonstrated that they did not feel themselves restricted in any way to propaganda in the narrow sense of the word. Unquestionably the Committee conceived of its task in the grand view of its name. Un-American activities were its target, no matter how or where manifested. Notwithstanding the broad purview of the Committee's experience, the House of Representatives repeatedly approved its continuation. Five times it extended the life of the special committee. Then it made the group a standing committee of the House. A year later, the Committee's charter was embodied in the Legislative Reorganization Act. On five occasions, at the beginning of sessions of Congress, it has made the authorizing resolution part of the rules of the House. On innumerable occasions, it has passed appropriation bills to allow the Committee to continue its efforts.

Combining the language of the resolution with the construction it has been given, it is evident that the preliminary control of the Committee exercised by the House of Representatives is slight or non-existent. No one could reasonably deduce from the charter the kind of investigation that the Committee was directed to make....

The Government contends that the public interest at the core of the investigations of the Un-American Activities Committee is the need by the Congress to be informed of efforts to overthrow the Government by force and violence so that adequate legislative safeguards can be erected. From this core, however, the Committee can radiate outward infinitely to any topic thought to be related in some way to armed insurrection. The outer reaches of this domain are known only by the content of "un-American activities." Remoteness of subject can be aggravated by a probe for a depth of detail even farther removed from any basis of legislative action. A third dimension is added when the investigators turn their attention to the past to collect minutiae on remote topics, on the hypothesis that the past may reflect upon the present.

The consequences that flow from this situation are manifold. In the first place, a reviewing court is unable to make the kind of judgment made by the Court in United States v. Rumely, supra. The Committee is allowed, in essence, to define its own authority, to choose the direction and focus of its activities. In deciding what to do with the power that has been conferred upon them, members of the Committee may act pursuant to motives that seem to them to be the highest. Their decisions, nevertheless, can lead to ruthless exposure of private lives in order to gather data that is neither desired by the Congress nor useful to it. Yet it is impossible in this circumstance, with constitutional freedoms in jeopardy, to declare that the Committee has ranged beyond the area committed to it by its parent assembly because the boundaries are so nebulous.

More important and more fundamental than that, however, it insulates the House that has authorized the investigation from the witnesses who are subjected to the sanctions of compulsory process. There is a wide gulf between the responsibility for the use of investigative power and the actual exercise of that power. This is an especially vital consideration in assuring respect for constitutional liberties. Protected freedoms should not be placed in danger in the absence of a clear determination by the House or the Senate that a particular inquiry is justified by a specific legislative need.

It is, of course, not the function of this Court to prescribe rigid rules for the Congress to follow in drafting resolutions establishing investigating committees. That is a matter peculiarly within the realm of the legislature, and its decisions will be accepted by the courts up to the point where their own duty to enforce the constitutionally protected rights of individuals is affected. An excessively broad charter, like that of the House Un-American Activities Committee, places the courts in an untenable position if they are to strike a balance between the public need for a particular interrogation and the right of citizens to carry on their affairs free from unnecessary governmental interference. It is impossible in such a situation to ascertain whether any legislative purpose justifies the disclosures sought and, if so, the importance of that information to the Congress in furtherance of its legislative function. The reason no court can make this critical judgment is that the House of Representatives itself has never made it. Only the legislative assembly initiating an investigation can assay the relative necessity of specific disclosures.

Absence of the qualitative consideration of petitioner's questioning by the House of Representatives aggravates a serious problem, revealed in this case, in the relationship of congressional investigating committees and the witnesses who appear before them. Plainly these committees are restricted to the missions delegated to them, i.e., to acquire certain data to be used by the House or the Senate in coping with a problem that falls within its legislative sphere. No witness can be compelled to make disclosures on matters outside that area. This is a jurisdictional concept of pertinency drawn from the nature of a congressional committee's source of authority. It is not wholly different from nor unrelated to the element of pertinency embodied in the criminal statute under which petitioner was prosecuted. When the definition of jurisdictional pertinency is as uncertain and wavering as in the case of the Un-American Activities Committee, it becomes extremely difficult for the Committee to limit its inquiries to statutory pertinency....

The problem attains proportion when viewed from the standpoint of the witness who appears before a congressional committee. He must decide at the time the questions are propounded whether or not to answer. As the Court said in *Sinclair v. United States* ..., the witness acts at his peril. He is "* * * bound rightly to construe the statute." ... An erroneous determination on his part, even if made in the utmost good faith, does not exculpate him if the court should later rule that the questions were pertinent to the question under inquiry.

It is obvious that a person compelled to make this choice is entitled to have knowledge of the subject to which the interrogation is deemed pertinent. That knowledge must be available with the same degree of explicitness and clarity that the Due Process Clause requires in the expression of any element of a criminal offense. The "vice of vagueness" must be avoided here as in all other crimes. There are several sources that can outline the "question under inquiry" in such a way that the rules against vagueness are satisfied. The authorizing resolution, the remarks of the chairman or members of the committee, or even the nature of the proceedings themselves, might sometimes make the topic clear. This case demonstrates, however, that these sources often leave the matter in grave doubt.

The first possibility is that the authorizing resolution itself will so clearly declare the "question under inquiry" that a witness can understand the pertinency of questions asked him. The Government does not contend that the authorizing resolution of the Un-American Activities Committee could serve such a purpose. Its confusing breadth is amply illustrated by the innumerable and diverse questions into which the Committee has inquired under this charter since 1938. If the "question under inquiry" were stated with such sweeping and uncertain scope, we doubt that it would withstand an attack on the ground of vagueness....

There was an opening statement by the Committee Chairman at the outset of the hearing, but this gives us no guidance. In this statement, the Chairman did no more than paraphrase the authorizing resolution and give a very general sketch of the past efforts of the Committee....

No aid is given as to the "question under inquiry" in the action of the full Committee that authorized the creation of the Subcommittee before which petitioner appeared. The Committee adopted a formal resolution giving the Chairman the power to appoint subcommittees "* * * for the purpose of performing any and all acts which the Committee as a whole is authorized to do." In effect, this was a device to enable the investigations to proceed with a quorum of one or two members and sheds no light on the relevancy of the questions asked of petitioner....

The final source of evidence as to the "question under inquiry" is the Chairman's response when petitioner objected to the questions on the grounds of lack of pertinency. The Chairman then announced that the Subcommittee was investigating "subversion and subversive propaganda." This is a subject at least as broad and indefinite as the authorizing resolution of the Committee, if not more so....

The statement of the Committee Chairman in this case, in response to petitioner's protest, was woefully inadequate to convey sufficient information as to the pertinency of the questions to the subject under inquiry. Petitioner was thus not accorded a fair opportunity to determine whether he was within his rights in refusing to answer, and his conviction is necessarily invalid under the Due Process Clause of the Fifth Amendment.

We are mindful of the complexities of modern government and the ample scope that must be left to the Congress as the sole constitutional depository of legislative power. Equally mindful are we of the indispensable function, in the exercise of that power, of congressional investigations. The conclusions we have reached in this case will not prevent the Congress, through its committees, from obtaining any information it needs for the proper fulfillment of its role in our scheme of government. The legislature is free to determine the kinds of data that should be collected. It is only those investigations that are conducted by use of compulsory process that give rise to a need to protect the rights of individuals against illegal encroachment. That protection can be readily achieved through procedures which prevent the separation of power from responsibility and which provide the constitutional requisites of fairness for witnesses. A measure of added care on the part of the House and the Senate in authorizing the use of compulsory process and by their committees in exercising that power would suffice. That is a small price to pay if it serves to uphold the principles of limited, constitutional government without constricting the power of the Congress to inform itself.

The judgment of the Court of Appeals is reversed, and the case is remanded to the District Court with instructions to dismiss the indictment.

Notes and Questions

1. **Scope of the *Watkins* holding.** How broad is the application of the *Watkins* admonitions against ambiguity in the scope of a committee's investigative power? Do they apply to all witnesses in all kinds of congressional inquiries? Consider the observations of former Watergate Committee counsel James Hamilton:

> The Watkins case itself gives some clues as to the meaning of its interdiction against "exposure for the sake of exposure." This language, the Court indicated, applies only to exposure of *private* affairs; it has no applicability to the situation where *governmental* corruption, inefficiency, and waste are aired for public consumption. To the contrary, the informing function is perhaps most efficacious when it turns the legislative spotlight on derelictions in government.

JAMES HAMILTON, THE POWER TO PROBE 129 (1976). Are all aspects of the *Watkins* decision applicable only to congressional inquiries into the affairs of private citizens, or only the "exposure for the sake of exposure" aspects of the decision?

2. Subsequent Application of *Watkins*. Even when the activities of private citizens were at issue, the Supreme Court's subsequent application of the *Watkins* principles was somewhat more limited than the broad language of the opinion might suggest would be the case. Two years after its *Watkins* decision, the Court considered the case of Vassar College instructor Lloyd Barenblatt, who had been convicted of contempt of Congress for refusing to answer questions at a HUAC hearing about membership in the Communist Party and his activities while a graduate student at the University of Michigan. *Barenblatt v. United States*, 360 U.S. 109 (1959). Relying upon the "long and illuminating history" of HUAC's investigative activities,[11] a divided 5–4 Court concluded that the committee's "legislative authority to conduct the inquiry [into Communist influence in the field of education] presently under consideration is unassailable." *Id.* at 122. The Court also rejected any pertinency challenge by Barenblatt, because in the

---

11. The Court's reliance upon the committee's 1947 description of its "wide-range program in this field" of "investigation of Communist activities" is a telling indicator of the Court's reluctance, even in 1959, to disavow extremely wide-ranging congressional inquiries into the political beliefs and affiliations of private citizens. *Cf.* 360 U.S. at 118–19.

The scope of the program was as follows:

"1. To expose and ferret out the Communists and Communist sympathizers in the Federal Government.
2. To spotlight the spectacle of having outright Communists controlling and dominating some of the most vital unions in American labor.
3. To institute a countereducational program against the subversive propaganda which has been hurled at the American people.
4. Investigation of those groups and movements which are trying to dissipate our atomic bomb knowledge of the benefit of a foreign power.
5. Investigation of Communist influences in Hollywood.
6. Investigation of Communist influences in education.
7. Organization of the research staff so as to furnish reference service to Members of Congress and to keep them currently informed on all subjects relating to subversive and un-American activities in the United States.
8. Continued accumulation of files and records to be placed at the disposal of the investigative units of the Government and armed services." Report of the Committee on Un-American Activities to the United States House of Representatives, 80th Cong., 2d Sess., Dec. 31, 1948, 2–3 (Committee Print)."

360 U.S. at 119 n.11.

five-member majority's view, the focus of the hearing on Communist infiltration in the field of education had been made clear at the outset of the hearing, with none of the ambiguity that had been found in *Watkins*. *Id.* at 124–125. Finally, and perhaps most indicative of the Court's reluctance to apply *Watkins* too broadly, the Court rejected Barenblatt's First Amendment constitutional challenges under a balancing test that weighed his private interests against the public interest in preventing a communist overthrow of the United States government:

> That Congress has wide power to legislate in the field of Communist activity in this Country, and to conduct appropriate investigations in aid thereof, is hardly debatable. The existence of such power has never been questioned by this Court, and it is sufficient to say, without particularization, that Congress has enacted or considered in this field a wide range of legislative measures, not a few of which have stemmed from recommendations of the very Committee whose actions have been drawn in question here. In the last analysis this power rests on the right of self-preservation, 'the ultimate value of any society,' [citing *Dennis v. United States*, 341 U.S. 494 (1951)]. Justification for its exercise in turn rests on the long and widely accepted view that the tenets of the Communist Party include the ultimate overthrow of the Government of the United States by force and violence, a view which has been given formal expression by the Congress.

Id. at 127–28. Not surprisingly, when the balancing test was framed in this manner, Barenblatt's personal interests were found to be outweighed by the interest of the government in obtaining information about the Communist threat. A dissenting opinion by Justice Black, joined by Justice Douglas and Chief Justice Warren, bitterly denounced the use of a balancing test "in the realm of speech and association" to deny the First Amendment rights of witnesses. *Id.* at 140–53.

In two subsequent cases, also decided by 5–4 margins, the Supreme Court upheld convictions of witnesses who had refused to answer questions in HUAC hearings. In *Wilkinson v. United States*, 365 U.S. 399 (1961), the Court relied on *Barenblatt* to uphold the contempt conviction of Frank Wilkinson, a witness who had refused to answer the question "Are you now a member of the Communist Party?" at a HUAC subcommittee hearing in Atlanta. *See id.* at 407. After Wilkinson refused to answer, the committee's staff director, obviously mindful of the Court's *Watkins* decision, provided him with a lengthy explanation of "the reasons, the pertinency, and the relevancy" of the question, *id.* at 404 n.5, as well as evidence from prior hearings that the petitioner was a Communist, *id.* at 406. The Court found that the staff director's statement, coupled with the committee's resolution authorizing the Atlanta hearings, were sufficient to satisfy the requirements of *Watkins*. *Id.* at 410–13. The Court then relied on *Barenblatt* to summarily reject Wilkinson's First Amendment challenge to his conviction: "As the *Barenblatt* opinion makes clear, it is the nature of the Communist activity involved, whether the momentary conduct is legitimate or illegitimate politically, that establishes the Government's overbalancing interest." *Id.* at 414. *Braden v. United States*, 365 U.S. 399 (1961), a companion case to *Wilkinson* that was decided the same day, relied on the reasoning of *Wilkinson* and *Barenblatt* to conclude that a witness could be convicted of contempt for refusing to answer questions about his Communist Party affiliation at the time he signed a letter urging citizens to petition Congress in connection with legislative proposals relating to efforts to end segregation in the South. Despite the strong First Amendment interests implicated by such activities, the five-member majority concluded that the national interest in combating communism overcame any constitutional objections the witness might offer. The four dissenting Justices—Black, Brennan, Douglas, and Chief Justice Warren—would have distinguished *Barenblatt* (and the Court's much earlier, Teapot Dome decision in *Sinclair*, which had rejected as a defense to contempt charges a good-faith belief that the witness had a legal basis for refusing to answer committee questions) based on the strong First Amendment interests implicated by Braden's actions and the absence of any evidence in the record connecting Braden's anti-segregation activities to communism. *See id.* at 446–56 (dissenting opinion of Justice Douglas).

The holdings in the cases discussed above have caused some commentators to question whether the Court's subsequent application of *Watkins* supports the case's reputation as a judicial bulwark against congressional overreaching. Library of Congress constitutional law expert Louis Fisher has described the cases that followed *Watkins* as a retreat from aggressive judicial oversight of congressional investigative activities:

> The tone of the [*Watkins*] decision, containing reprimands aimed at Congress—together with other decisions handed down during that period—produced a groundswell of opposition from legislators. Various bills were introduced to curb the Court. In the face of this political pressure the Supreme Court, two years later [with the *Barenblatt* case, followed by the *Wilkinson* and *Braden* cases], retreated from its position.

Louis Fisher, Constitutional Conflicts Between Congress and the President 170–71 (4th ed. 1997). Other cases, however, support the more widely held view that *Watkins* signaled a more vigorous oversight role by the Court. For example, in *Deutch v. United States*, 367 U.S. 456 (1961), the Court held that a committee inquiring into communist activities "in the Albany area" could not ask questions relating to a contemnor's student years at Cornell University because "[i]t can hardly be seriously contended that Cornell University is in the Albany area," 367 U.S. at 470, and because the investigation related to communist infiltration into labor unions rather than to infiltration at Cornell or in educational institutions generally, *id.* at 467. *Deutch* provides a good example of the Court's unwillingness, after *Watkins*, to defer to congressional assertions of investigative jurisdiction.

3. Too Little Too Late, or Wise Accommodation of Valid National Interests? As the discussion in the immediately preceding note suggests, the *Watkins* decision undoubtedly forced Congress to give more consideration to the propriety of its investigative activities, but it did not prevent HUAC from continuing its wide-ranging investigations of "subversive" and "anti-American" activities. Although it is easy today to criticize the Supreme Court for not more vigorously applying the teachings of *Watkins* in subsequent cases or not doing more to protect the individual rights of witnesses, it is important to recall the atmosphere in which the Court was acting. The Cold War and the threat of Communist efforts to overthrow our government were very real concerns for Americans in the 1950s. In this regard, it may be a useful exercise in understanding the political and sociological context of the cases for you to substitute "al Qaeda" for "Communist" in the reports of the committee investigatory activity and the court cases reviewing those investigations. Does doing so alter to any extent your opinion of the committees' actions and the courts' responses?

4. Internal Rule Changes to Prevent Recurrence of McCarthy-Era Abuses. In addition to the limitations imposed by the court decisions that are discussed above, both chambers of Congress responded to the excesses of the McCarthy era by adopting changes to their rules that were intended to afford certain basic procedural protections to witnesses, and for the most part those changes remain in effect today. For example, in 1955 the House adopted "Hearing Procedures" under House Rule XI, clause 2(k) (1) that gave witnesses appearing at hearings important procedural rights. During the 117th Congress (2021–2022), those rules provided as follows:

Hearing procedures

(k)(1) The chair at a hearing shall announce in an opening statement the subject of the hearing.

(2) A copy of the committee rules and of this clause shall be made available to each witness on request.

(3) Witnesses at hearings may be accompanied by their own counsel for the purpose of advising them concerning their constitutional rights.

(4) The chair may punish breaches of order and decorum, and of professional ethics on the part of counsel, by censure and exclusion from the hearings; and the committee may cite the offender to the House for contempt.

(5) Whenever it is asserted by a member of the committee that the evidence or testimony at a hearing may tend to defame, degrade, or incriminate any person, or it is asserted by a witness that the evidence or testimony that the witness would give at a hearing may tend to defame, degrade, or incriminate the witness—(A) notwithstanding paragraph (g)(2), such testimony or evidence shall be presented in executive session if, in the presence of the number of members required under the rules of the committee for the purpose of taking testimony, the committee determines by vote of a majority of those present that such evidence or testimony may tend to defame, degrade, or incriminate any person; and (B) the committee shall proceed to receive such testimony in open session only if the committee, a majority being present, determines that such evidence or testimony will not tend to defame, degrade, or incriminate any person. In either case the committee shall afford such person an opportunity voluntarily to appear as a witness, and receive and dispose of requests from such person to subpoena additional witnesses.

(6) Except as provided in subparagraph (5), the chair shall receive and the committee shall dispose of requests to subpoena additional witnesses.

(7) Evidence or testimony taken in executive session, and proceedings conducted in executive session, may be released or used in public sessions only when authorized by the committee, a majority being present.

(8) In the discretion of the committee, witnesses may submit brief and pertinent sworn statements in writing for inclusion in the record. The committee is the sole judge of the pertinence of testimony and evidence adduced at its hearing.

(9) A witness may obtain a transcript copy of the testimony of such witness given at a public session or, if given at an executive session, when authorized by the committee.

Another important procedural protection, intended to prevent McCarthy's practice of holding hearings at which he was the only present committee member, is House Rule XI, clause 2(h)(2), which for the 117th Congress of 2021–2022 provided: "Each committee may fix the number of its members to constitute a quorum for taking testimony and receiving evidence, which may not be less than two."

It should be noted that these rule changes were not entirely self-initiated by Congress. To the contrary, some of these "reforms" to the internal rules of congressional procedure were adopted in direct response to Supreme Court decisions striking down prosecutions of congressional witnesses. For example, *Christoffel v. United States*, 338 U.S. 84 (1949), held that a committee at which a quorum was not present during utterance of a perjurious statement was not a "competent tribunal" under the federal perjury statute. For a more complete legislative history of the McCarthy-era congressional rule changes, see 101 Cong. Rec. 3569–3585 (1955) and Rules of Procedure for Senate Investigating Committees, Report of the Senate Committee on Rules and Administration, 84th Cong., 1st Sess. (1955).

These rule changes also expanded significantly the role that well-informed and well-prepared counsel can play in representing a witness at a congressional hearing. For example, during the House of Representatives investigation of U.S. investments by Ferdinand and Imelda Marcos, one of the authors represented an attorney who was called as a witness to testify about a Marcos purchase of New York City real estate. A rule in effect at that time, but since repealed, allowed a witness under subpoena to object to having his or her testimony broadcast on radio or television. The author used the rule to have the television cameras and radio microphones removed from the hearing room:

Mr. Solarz [Representative Stephen J. Solarz of New York]: At this point the committee will call its next witness Mr. Barry Knox.

I understand before Mr. Knox actually takes the witness stand—I would appreciate it if somebody on the staff could substitute Mr. Knox's name for Mr. Bullock's name in front of the witness table—that his attorneys would like to make a statement to the committee. For purposes of the record, if Mr. Knox's attorneys could identify themselves, that would be appreciated.

Mr. Brand: Stanley Brand.

Mr. Lowell: Abbe Lowell.

Mr. Solarz: Which of you two gentlemen would like to make a statement?

Mr. Brand: Mr. Chairman, pursuant to rule 11, clause 3(f)(2) of the House rules, rule 11 clause 3 and rule 21 of the committee rules, I hereby invoke on behalf of Mr. Knox the right afforded to him to require that all television and photographic lenses be covered and all microphones be covered or turned off during his testimony at this hearing.

Mr. Solarz: In view of the fact, Mr. Brand, you are a former counsel to the House in which capacity you served with great distinction, I have no reason to doubt the accuracy of your citation, but I hope you won't hold it against me if I ask your successor, who I think is present, or his assistant, to inform the committee as to whether, in fact, this request is indeed covered by the rules of the House.

Mr. Brand: As long as he gives the same answer I have no objection.

Mr. Tiefer: The answer given by the House rules, is that under the House rules, and I quote:

> No witness served with a subpoena by the committee shall be required against his or her will to be photographed at any hearing or to give evidence or testimony while the broadcasting of that hearing by radio or television is being conducted.
>
> [At] [t]he request of any such witness who does not wish to be subjected to radio, television, or still photograph coverage, all lenses shall be covered and all microphones used for coverage turned off.

Mr. Solarz: In view of the fact we have consistently throughout these hearings bent over backward to accommodate concerns of several of the witnesses who have come forward and in view of the fact that this request is consistent with the rules of the House and, indeed, seems to be in order, as chairman of the subcommittee, I will then ask television cameras to leave the room so that the witness, pursuant to his privilege under House rules, can testify without television cameras being present or if they can remain, I gather, I am told they can remain if you cover the lenses.

Also, all microphones of radio and other broadcast equipment used for coverage will have to be turned off. As soon as the Chair sees the cameras covered, I will ask the witness to take the witness stand.

The witness is within his rights to make this request and we have no alternative but to accede to it.

Mr. Brand, are you satisfied the request has been complied with?

Mr. Brand: Thank you Mr. Chairman.

Investigation of Philippine Investments in the United States, Hearings before the Subcommittee on Asian and Pacific Affairs of the Committee on Foreign Affairs, House of Representatives, Ninety-Ninth Congress, First and Second Sessions, 375–76 (1987). As noted above, the rule in question was revoked in 1997, and witnesses no longer have the right to object to television and radio broadcast of their testimony.

Criminal Contempt of Congress in the Modern Era

Watkins and the other McCarthy-era Supreme Court cases discussed above involved criminal prosecution of witnesses in congressional investigations for contempt of Congress. The federal statute that provides for prosecution of witnesses for contempt of Congress is 2 U.S.C. §192:

> Every person who having been summoned as a witness by the authority of either House of Congress to give testimony or to produce papers upon any matter under inquiry before either House, or any joint committee established by a joint or concurrent resolution of the two Houses of Congress, or any committee of either House of Congress, willfully makes default, or who, having appeared, refuses to answer any question pertinent to the question under inquiry, shall be deemed guilty of a misdemeanor, punishable by a fine of not more than [$100,000][12] nor less than $100 and imprisonment in a common jail for not less than one month nor more than twelve months.

An accompanying statute, 2 U.S.C. §194, provides the procedure for charging a witness with contempt of Congress:

> Whenever a witness summoned as mentioned in Section 192 of this title fails to appear to testify or fails to produce any books, papers, records, or documents, as required, or whenever any witness so summoned refuses to answer any question pertinent to the subject under inquiry before either House, or any joint committee established by a joint or concurrent resolution of the two Houses of Congress, or any committee or subcommittee of either House of Congress, and the fact of such failure or failures is reported to either House while Congress is in session or when Congress is not in session, a statement of fact constituting such failure is reported to and filed with the President of the Senate or the Speaker of the House, it shall be the duty of the said President of the Senate or Speaker of the House, as the case may be, to certify, and he shall so certify, the statement of facts aforesaid under the seal of the Senate or House, as the case may be, to the appropriate United States attorney, whose duty it shall be to bring the matter before the grand jury for its action.

---

12. Contempt of Congress is a Class A misdemeanor under current law, with a maximum fine of $100,000. *See* 18 U.S.C. §§3559, 3571 (2012).

These statutes create a complex procedure for prosecution of contempt of Congress, requiring actions by both the legislative and executive branches of the federal government. The Congressional Research Service has summarized this procedure and its purpose as follows:

> Under the procedure outlined in Section 194, "the following steps precede judicial proceedings under [the statute]: (1) approval by committee; (2) calling up and reading the committee report on the floor; (3) either (if Congress is in session) House approval of a resolution authorizing the Speaker to certify the report to the U.S. Attorney for prosecution, or (if Congress is not in session) an independent determination by the Speaker to certify the report; [and] (4) certification by the Speaker to the appropriate U.S. Attorney for prosecution."

> The criminal contempt statute and corresponding procedure are punitive in nature. It is used when the House or Senate wants to punish a recalcitrant witness and, by doing so, to deter others from similar contumacious conduct. The criminal sanction is not coercive because the witness generally will not be able to purge himself by testifying or supplying subpoenaed documents after he has been voted in contempt by the committee and the House or Senate. Consequently, once a witness has been voted in contempt, he lacks an incentive for cooperating with the committee. However, although the courts have rejected arguments that defendants had purged themselves, in a few instances the House has certified to the U.S. Attorney that further proceedings concerning contempts were not necessary where compliance with subpoenas occurred after contempt citations had been voted but before referral of the cases to grand juries.

> Under the statute, after a contempt has been certified by the President of the Senate or the Speaker, it is the "duty" of the United States Attorney "to bring the matter before the grand jury for its action." It remains unclear whether the "duty" of the U.S. Attorney to present the contempt to the grand jury is mandatory or discretionary.

Todd Garvey, *Congress's Contempt Power and the Enforcement of Congressional Subpoenas: Law, History, Practice, and Procedure*, Cong. Res. Service (May 12, 2017).

Since the McCarthy era, prosecutions for criminal contempt of Congress have been relatively rare. This likely is due, at least in part, to the requirements imposed by the Supreme Court in *Watkins* and other McCarthy-era cases. Another reason is that, as suggested by the language of the Congressional Research Service report quoted above, the Department of Justice often declines to present a congressional contempt citation to a federal grand jury for criminal prosecution. Since 1984, the Department of Justice has taken the position that, notwithstanding the "whose duty it shall be" language of 2 U.S.C. §194, Congress cannot compel the Department of Justice to initiate a prosecution for contempt of Congress:

> First, as a matter of statutory interpretation reinforced by compelling separation of powers considerations, we believe that Congress may not direct the

Executive to prosecute a particular individual without leaving any discretion to the Executive to determine whether a violation of the law has occurred. Second, as a matter of statutory interpretation and the constitutional separation of powers, we believe that the contempt of Congress statute was not intended to apply and could not constitutionally be applied to an Executive Branch official who asserts the President's claim of executive privilege in this context.

Prosecution for Contempt of Congress of an Executive Branch Official Who Has Asserted a Claim of Executive Privilege, 8 Op. O.L.C. 101, 102 (1984). The Department of Justice's interpretation of the criminal contempt statute, and the separation of powers issues that interpretation raises, are discussed in detail in Chapter 4. For purposes of this Chapter, however, it is sufficient to note that after the excesses of the McCarthy era, criminal prosecutions for contempt of Congress have been rare and largely confined to extreme cases of defiance of congressional subpoenas by recalcitrant witnesses. As you review the summary of those cases below, consider, in light of the HUAC and McCarthy committees' abuses of witnesses that are discussed in the first parts of the Chapter, whether criminal contempt is an appropriate and, in certain cases, even necessary remedy for contempt of Congress.

The rarity of criminal prosecutions for contempt of Congress is perhaps best illustrated by the fact that until Trump advisor Stephen Bannon was convicted of contempt of Congress in 2022, the last defendant to be tried and convicted of the crime of contempt of Congress was Watergate conspirator G. Gordon Liddy, who was convicted after a non-jury trial in May 1974. (The Watergate scandal is covered in Chapter 3. The Bannon conviction is discussed further below and in Chapter 1.) Liddy was charged with contempt after he defied a congressional subcommittee by refusing to answer questions or even raise his hand to be sworn in as a witness. Anthony Ripley, *Liddy Guilty of Contempt of Congress*, N.Y. TIMES (May 11, 1974). Liddy's conduct also provides an example of an extreme act of defiance of Congress by a completely uncooperative witness. As discussed below, Bannon took a similar approach in 2021, and was convicted after a jury trial in 2022.

While Liddy was the last person to be convicted of contempt of Congress after a trial up to the Bannon conviction in 2022, Reagan administration Environmental Protection Agency official Rita M. Lavelle was acquitted of contempt of Congress after a jury trial at which she testified in her own defense that she was too ill to travel from her home in California to testify before a House subcommittee investigating allegations of mismanagement at EPA. *See* Al Kamen, *EPA Ex-Official Cleared*, WASH. POST (July 23, 1983). Lavelle's acquittal is an example of the difficulties prosecutors may face in obtaining a conviction for contempt of Congress, and, as such, it may have contributed to the lack of criminal contempt prosecutions since her acquittal. (The Reagan administration EPA scandal is discussed in Chapter 4.)

Because criminal contempt of Congress is a misdemeanor offense, it can provide an attractive way to resolve a criminal investigation through a plea bargain that does not include more serious felony criminal charges. For example, during the Iran-Contra investigation, Independent Counsel Lawrence E. Walsh entered into a plea bargain with Reagan administration State Department official Elliott Abrams in which Abrams pleaded guilty to two misdemeanor counts of withholding information from Congress in violation of 2 U.S.C. §192. *United States v. Abrams*, Government's Statement of the Factual Basis for the Plea, U.S. District Court for the District of Columbia (Oct. 7, 1991). (The Reagan administration Iran-Contra scandal is covered in Chapter 5.) A similar plea bargain for contempt of Congress was used to resolve a criminal investigation of George W. Bush administration official Scott J. Bloch, who pleaded guilty to withholding information from congressional staff members who were investigating Bloch's role in deletions of emails on government computers. *Former Head of U.S. Office of Special Counsel Pleads Guilty to Criminal Contempt of Congress*, U.S. Attorney's Office, District of Columbia (April 27, 2010).

After lying dormant for almost three decades after the Lavelle acquittal, except as a plea-bargain vehicle in the *Abrams* and *Bloch* cases, the criminal contempt of Congress statute returned to the national spotlight when the Biden Justice Department acted on a criminal contempt of Congress referral by the House of Representatives[13] and obtained a federal grand jury indictment of former Trump White House official and Trump confidante Stephen K. Bannon for failing to comply with a subpoena issued to him by the House of Representatives Select Committee to Investigate the January 6 Attack on the United States Capitol:

---

13. In addition to the Bannon referral, the House of Representatives referred three other former Trump administration officials to the Department of Justice for prosecution for contempt of Congress after they had failed to comply with the January 6 Committee's subpoenas: Trump White House trade advisor Peter Navarro; Trump White House chief of staff Mark Meadows; and Trump White House deputy chief of staff for communications Dan Scavino. Bannon and Navarro were subsequently indicted, but the Department of Justice declined to prosecute Meadows and Scavino. Although the Department of Justice did not disclose its reasons for declining to prosecute Meadows and Scavino, they had cooperated to some degree, or at least negotiated, with the committee, while Bannon and Navarro defied the committee's subpoenas and refused to cooperate, citing executive privilege. With regard to their executive privilege claims, Bannon had not served in the White House since 2017, and Navarro's White House position did not involve the same degree of regular communication with President Trump as did Meadows's and Scavino's positions. Scavino was represented by one of the authors of this book.

Stephen K. Bannon Indicted for Contempt of Congress; Two Charges Filed for Failing to Honor House Subpoena from Select Committee Investigating Jan. 6 Capitol Breach

Department of Justice Press Release 21-1122 (Nov. 12, 2021)

Stephen K. Bannon was indicted today by a federal grand jury on two counts of contempt of Congress stemming from his failure to comply with a subpoena issued by the House Select Committee investigating the Jan. 6 breach of the U.S. Capitol.

Bannon, 67, is charged with one contempt count involving his refusal to appear for a deposition and another involving his refusal to produce documents, despite a subpoena from the House Select Committee to Investigate the January 6 Attack on the U.S. Capitol. An arraignment date has not yet been set in the U.S. District Court for the District of Columbia.

"Since my first day in office, I have promised Justice Department employees that together we would show the American people by word and deed that the department adheres to the rule of law, follows the facts and the law and pursues equal justice under the law," said Attorney General Merrick B. Garland. "Today's charges reflect the department's steadfast commitment to these principles."

"As detailed in the indictment, on Sept. 23, 2021, the Select Committee issued a subpoena to Mr. Bannon," said U.S. Attorney Matthew M. Graves for the District of Columbia. "The subpoena required him to appear and produce documents to the Select Committee, and to appear for a deposition before the Select Committee. According to the indictment, Mr. Bannon refused to appear to give testimony as required by subpoena and refused to produce documents in compliance with a subpoena."

In its subpoena, the Select Committee said it had reason to believe that Bannon had information relevant to understanding events related to Jan. 6. Bannon, formerly a Chief Strategist and Counselor to the President, has been a private citizen since departing the White House in 2017.

Each count of contempt of Congress carries a minimum of 30 days and a maximum of one year in jail, as well as a fine of $100 to $100,000. A federal district court judge will determine any sentence after considering the U.S. Sentencing Guidelines and other statutory factors.

An indictment is merely an allegation and all defendants are presumed innocent until proven guilty beyond a reasonable doubt in a court of law.

The case is being investigated by the FBI's Washington Field Office. The case is being prosecuted by the Public Corruption and Civil Rights Section of the U.S. Attorney's Office for the District of Columbia.

Bannon was indicted for two counts of violating 2 U.S.C. §192, one count for failing to provide testimony and one count for failing to provide documents. Not included in the Department of Justice press release above is Bannon's reason for refusing to comply with the congressional subpoena: Bannon had claimed that former President Donald Trump's assertion of executive privilege shielded him from compliance with the House Select Committee subpoena, even though Bannon was not serving in government at the time of the events under investigation and had not served in government since 2017. On July 22, 2022, Bannon was convicted of two misdemeanor counts of contempt of Congress, one for refusing to testify and one for refusing to produce documents to the January 6 Committee. (The January 6 Committee is discussed in Chapter 8.)

Notes and Questions

1. Criminal Prosecution or Political Persecution? In addition to claiming that former President Trump's invocation of executive privilege should shield him from compliance with the Select Committee subpoena, Bannon claimed that his prosecution was illegitimate and politically motivated. *See* David Yaffe-Bellany & Greg Farrell, *Bannon Vows Contempt Charges Will Become "Hell" for Democrats*, BLOOMBERG.COM (Nov. 15, 2021). How does the Bannon prosecution compare to other contempt of Congress prosecutions described in this Chapter? Do you think the Biden Justice Department's decision to charge Bannon was politically motivated, or was it a necessary and appropriate response to Bannon's refusal to comply with the Select Committee subpoena? Like the Gordon Liddy prosecution described above, Bannon refused to appear or cooperate in any manner with the congressional committee but, unlike Liddy, Bannon claimed to have a legal basis for his refusal to comply with the subpoena—Trump's assertion of executive privilege. Does the claim of executive privilege distinguish Bannon's case from Liddy's case? See Chapter 4 for further discussion of executive privilege and congressional efforts to subpoena executive branch officials.

2. Congressional Subpoenas: Separation of Powers and Power Politics. As the discussion above suggests, and as discussed further in Chapter 4, the Department of Justice position on prosecuting contempt of Congress charges referred by Congress, means that as a practical matter, contempt of Congress charges will only be brought when the executive branch chooses to bring criminal charges. Congress has no ready means of forcing the Department of Justice to present a contempt of Congress referral to a federal grand jury for potential indictment. As a consequence, bipartisan cooperation between the executive and legislative branches will be required when a presidential administration of one political party pursues contempt charges by a house of Congress controlled by the other political party. The Liddy and Lavelle prosecutions discussed above are the rare modern examples of such bipartisan cooperation. In the case of the Bannon prosecution, the change of administration from the Trump administration to the Biden administration made possible criminal charges that likely would never have been brought if President Trump had been re-elected. Does this undermine the legitimacy of the Bannon prosecution? Do you believe the Biden Justice

Department should have declined to prosecute Bannon? Or is the Bannon case the rare example where criminal contempt of Congress charges are necessary and appropriate, notwithstanding the political overtones surrounding the case?

3. Is a Neutral Arbiter Needed in Contempt of Congress Cases? One possible response to the political and separation of powers issues that arise when Congress seeks to compel the Department of Justice to prosecute a contempt of Congress charge is to have the decision made by a neutral and independent prosecutor. The Congressional Research Service has described how such a system could be implemented:

> Another proposed alternative for subpoena enforcement has been to establish statutorily a procedure for the appointment of an independent official responsible for prosecuting criminal contempt of Congress citations against executive branch officials. Such a law would seek to create an independent prosecutor authorized to make litigation and enforcement decisions, including the decision to initiate and pursue a criminal contempt prosecution pursuant to 2 U.S.C. §192 and §194 under reduced influence from the President and the DOJ. The independent prosecutor would retain prosecutorial discretion in enforcement decisions, but would arguably not be subject to the same "subtle and direct" political pressure and controls that a traditional U.S. Attorney may face. This office would likely be loosely modeled on the expired Office of Independent Counsel (Independent Counsel) established in the Independent Counsel Act of 1978 (Independent Counsel Act or ICA) and upheld by the Supreme Court in *Morrison v. Olson* [487 U.S. 654 (1988)].
>
> * * *
>
> Perhaps the chief criticism of the independent counsel statute, and arguably the reason the statute was permitted to expire, was the breadth of the Independent Counsel's jurisdiction. The ICA authorized the appointment of an independent counsel to investigate and prosecute a wide array of crimes, while also providing the option for the expansion of an appointed counsel's initial jurisdiction with the approval of the three-judge panel. Strictly limiting a new Independent Counsel's jurisdiction to only the investigation and prosecution of the specific criminal contempt of Congress citation approved by either the House or the Senate, with no option for jurisdictional expansion, might sufficiently restrict the authority of the Independent Counsel to alleviate some of those concerns.

Todd Garvey, *Congressional Subpoenas: Enforcing Executive Branch Compliance*, Congressional Research Service (Mar. 27, 2019) (footnotes omitted). One of the authors of this book proposed a similar approach in 1986, after the dispute over congressional access to Reagan administration EPA information. *See* Stanley M. Brand & Sean Connelly, *Constitutional Confrontations: Preserving a Prompt and Orderly Means by Which Congress May Enforce Investigative Demands Against Executive Branch Officials*, 36 CATHOLIC UNIV. L. REV. 71 (1986) (proposing "legislation that would provide for appointment of a special prosecutor in cases where a high-ranking executive official has thwarted the legislative will by refusing to produce materials demanded by Congress").

What do you think of the idea of having an "independent counsel" within the Department of Justice decide whether or not to bring criminal charges for contempt of Congress? Would that procedure address the separation of powers problem that the Department of Justice believes arises if Congress can direct an executive branch prosecutor to bring criminal charges? Should a President be able to "fire" an independent counsel who made a charging decision that displeases the President? Would insulating an independent counsel from dismissal by the President impinge too much on presidential authority? (See Chapter 3 for discussion of the Watergate investigation and the "Saturday Night Massacre" that culminated in the dismissal of Watergate special prosecutor Archibald Cox. See Chapter 4 for further discussion of the Independent Counsel Act and the *Morrison v. Olson* Supreme Court decision.) Finally, if an Independent Counsel had determined to prosecute Stephen Bannon, would the prosecution have greater legitimacy, or would it still be susceptible to challenge as politically motivated?

Chapter Three

Misconduct and Cover-Ups at the Highest Levels of Government

Congressional Investigation of the Watergate Scandal

It occurs to me that at this point, the central question, and in no way in deroga-tion of the importance of the great volume of material and the implications that flow from it, but the central question at this point is simply put. What did the President know and when did he know it?

Statement of Senator Howard H. Baker, Jr.,
Ranking Minority Member, Senate Select Committee on
Presidential Campaign Activities, during questioning of
former White House Counsel John W. Dean, III, June 28, 1973

The central thesis of this book is that effective legislative branch investigation and oversight is essential to our system of government. The materials in the preceding two chapters illustrate the importance of legislative oversight in exposing criminality and wrongdoing in the executive branch (the Teapot Dome investigation), providing a factual foundation and public support for vitally important remedial legislation (the Pecora hearings), and preventing waste and abuse in government operations and pro-curement (the Truman Committee). The McCarthy and HUAC materials in Chapter 2 illustrate that the legislative investigative power is a powerful and dangerous two-edged sword, which can be abused if employed for the wrong purposes or controlled by the wrong people. All of these themes coalesced in the greatest congressional investigation in our nation's history—Watergate.

The Watergate hearings exposed very serious criminal misconduct by a large num-ber of individuals in the executive branch, revealed striking abuses of the mechanisms of our government, and precipitated an extraordinarily wide range of remedial leg-islation. At its core, however, the Watergate scandal was most fundamentally about grave misconduct at the very highest levels of government—the president of the Unit-ed States and his closest advisers. Exposing and remedying misconduct at this level presents perhaps the greatest challenge to our legal and political systems. While the focus of this book is on congressional investigations, it is important to recognize that congressional investigations do not take place in a vacuum. They are almost always accompanied and influenced by two other vital components of our free democratic society—the criminal justice system and the press.

Watergate was a scandal so wide-ranging, so complex, and so vigorously covered up by the Nixon White House that it took the combined efforts of all three of the primary guardians of our democratic freedoms—the press, the criminal justice system, and the congressional investigative process—to expose and remedy its wrongs. The materials that follow focus on the congressional investigative process, but the contributions of the criminal justice system and the press are also recognized and should be studied carefully. Only by recognizing the importance of the contributions made by all three of these institutions can the student of Watergate appreciate how very close the cover-up came to succeeding.

Introduction: A Watergate Primer

The first key Watergate events took place in the criminal justice system and in the press reporting on those events.[1] The Watergate burglars, who were acting for President Nixon's Committee to Re-Elect the President (CRP), were caught in the Watergate of-fice building headquarters of the Democratic National Committee (DNC) in the early morning hours of June 17, 1972. This was actually the second Watergate break-in. A prior break-in had occurred on May 28, 1972, when electronic listening devices had been installed in the DNC headquarters offices. One purpose of the June 17 break-in was to repair a malfunctioning "bug" that had been placed on a telephone in the office of the chairman of the DNC during the previous break-in on May 28.

The Washington press, especially *Washington Post* reporters Carl Bernstein and Bob Woodward, aggressively pursued the Watergate break-in story. As Senator Sam Ervin later noted in his book on Watergate, *The Whole Truth: The Watergate Conspiracy*:

> Within a few weeks the *Washington Post* and other media of communications published astounding articles relating to the burglary. They disclosed that E. Howard Hunt was a consultant on the White House payroll with an office in the Executive Office Building, and that he and G. Gordon Liddy, the legal advisor to the Stans committee [the finance committee for Nixon's re-election campaign], had masterminded the burglary. They likewise revealed that at the direction of Jeb Stuart Magruder, deputy chairman of the Mitchell Committee [the political committee for Nixon's re-election campaign], Hugh W. Sloan, Jr., treasurer of the Stans Committee, had taken from safes in the quarters of the Stans committee substantial Nixon campaign funds in cash and delivered them to Liddy; and that the $4,500 in new $100 bills discovered by the Wash-

---

1. For a detailed chronology of Watergate events, including key press reports, see Watergate Special Prosecution Force Report, October 1975, Appendix K. For a summary of the events surrounding the Watergate break-in, see *id.* at pp. 4–5.

ington police on the persons and in the hotel rooms of the four Cubans on the day of their arrest represented a portion of the Nixon campaign funds which Sloan had delivered to Liddy.[2]

Federal prosecutors and FBI agents, working with a federal grand jury in Washington, investigated the Watergate break-in. The five Watergate burglars and their two handlers, G. Gordon Liddy and E. Howard Hunt, were charged with burglary, conspiracy, and wiretapping in connection with the June 17, 1972 break-in, and in January 1973 all seven defendants either pleaded guilty or were convicted at trial. To that point, payments of cash and vague assurances of future executive clemency had prevented the Watergate defendants from implicating anyone higher up in the Nixon campaign or at the White House. Hunt, Liddy, and the burglars maintained their silence at trial, and the prosecutors asserted at trial that there was no evidence of involvement by higher officials in the break-in. This allowed the Nixon White House to maintain through the 1972 presidential election that Hunt and Liddy had acted alone and that, in the words of Nixon press secretary Ronald Ziegler, the Watergate break-in was nothing more than "a third-rate burglary."

To understand the Watergate scandal fully, it is essential to recognize not only the falsity of the Nixon White House's original Watergate denials but also the reasons for the "cover up at any cost" mentality that drove the White House response. One reason for the cover-up was that the Watergate bugging was not an isolated incident. Far from being a rogue operation, Liddy and Hunt's actions grew out of a proposed secret political intelligence-gathering plan, called "Gemstone," that Liddy presented to then-Attorney General John Mitchell in Mitchell's office at the Department of Justice shortly before Mitchell left the Justice Department to chair Nixon's re-election campaign committee.[3] The original Gemstone plan—which included plans to use kidnapping, prostitutes, and extensive wiretapping and "bugging" of political opponents' communications—was rejected by Mitchell, deputy campaign chief Magruder, and then-White House counsel John Dean when Liddy first proposed the plan.[4]

---

2. Sam J. Ervin, Jr., The Whole Truth: The Watergate Conspiracy, at p. 9 (Random House 1980).

3. Liddy became general counsel to the Committee to Re-Elect the President, headed by Mitchell, after serving in the White House "Plumbers" unit, which is discussed below. The circumstances of Liddy's appointment and his role as "our man in charge of dirty tricks" at CRP are described in John Dean's book *Blind Ambition*, which recounts Dean's White House years. *See* John W. Dean III, Blind Ambition 76–77 (Simon & Schuster 1976). Liddy's Gemstone Plan itself was a successor to an earlier, much more ambitious "political intelligence" proposal called the "Huston Plan" because it had been developed by White House aide Tom Huston. That plan, which had sought to use wiretaps, mail intercepts, and burglaries to spy on left-wing groups in the U.S., had been approved by Nixon, but stalled when FBI Director J. Edgar Hoover refused to go along. *See id.* at 36–38. *See also* Sam J. Ervin, Jr., The Whole Truth: The Watergate Conspiracy, at 121–22 and 136 (Random House 1980). Documentation relating to the "Huston Plan" is reprinted in Hearings before the Select Committee on Presidential Campaign Activities, Book 3, at pp. 1319–1345.

4. *See* Hearings Before the Select Committee on Presidential Campaign Activities, Book 3, at 929–31 (testimony of John W. Dean, III, June 25, 1973). Dean provides a detailed description of Lid-

A scaled-back version of Gemstone was later implemented by Liddy, reporting to Magruder, and the Watergate break-in followed.[5] But Watergate was not Liddy's first break-in for the purpose of obtaining "political intelligence" for the Nixon White House. Liddy, Hunt, and some members of their team of Watergate burglars had previously burglarized the Beverly Hills office of Dr. Lewis Fielding, a psychiatrist who had treated Pentagon Papers whistleblower Daniel Ellsberg, in hopes of finding information in Ellsberg's psychiatric records that the White House could use to discredit him. Hunt and Liddy had been acting for White House aides Egil "Bud" Krogh and David Young. Krogh was a long-time protégé of Nixon's top domestic adviser, John Ehrlichman, and he and Young headed a special White House investigative unit, called the "Plumbers," that worked under Ehrlichman and White House special counsel Charles Colson.

Nixon had been outraged by Ellsberg's leaking of the Pentagon Papers to the press, and he authorized Ehrlichman to establish the "Plumbers" investigative unit in the White House to prevent further "leaks" and collect intelligence that could be used to discredit leakers. The burglary of the office of Ellsberg's psychiatrist was a Plumbers group operation overseen by Hunt and Liddy. Documents made public by the Senate Watergate Committee established that Ehrlichman approved the operation, so long as it was conducted in a manner that could not be traced back to the White House.[6]

The Plumbers group burglary of the office of Ellsberg's psychiatrist was not the only thing the Nixon White House had to hide at the time of the Watergate break-in. White House Chief of Staff H.R. Haldeman's assistant Gordon Strachan and Nixon appointments secretary Dwight Chapin had hired an old college friend of Chapin, California attorney Donald H. Segretti, to orchestrate a program of campaign "dirty tricks"

---

dy's original Gemstone proposal in *Blind Ambition. See* JOHN W. DEAN III, BLIND AMBITION 79–85 (Simon & Schuster 1976).

5. The Watergate Special Prosecution Force Report notes that "the original $1 million plan [referring to Liddy's initial "Gemstone" proposal] *from which the Watergate burglary evolved* included a proposal for mugging squads to rough up demonstrators." Watergate Special Prosecution Report, p. 69 (October 1975) (emphasis added).

6. For a summary of the "Plumbers" unit and the Fielding break-in, see Watergate Special Prosecution Report, pp. 60–62 (October 1975). The report states that Liddy and Hunt planned the Fielding burglary, that some of their Cuban-American associates carried it out, and that White House aides Egil Krogh and David Young had obtained the approval of John Ehrlichman for the burglary. Krogh later pleaded guilty to having conspired to violate Dr. Fielding's civil rights. *Id.* at 60–61. John Dean also described the "so-called 'plumbers' unit" in his June 25, 1973, testimony before the Senate Watergate Committee. *See* Hearings before the Select Committee on Presidential Campaign Activities of the United States Senate, Ninety-Third Congress, First Session, Book 3, at p. 921. The memorandum from Krogh and Young proposing that "a covert operation be undertaken to examine all the medical files still held by Ellsberg's psychoanalyst covering the two-year period in which he was undergoing analysis," with a notation by Ehrlichman approving the proposal "if done under your assurance that it is not traceable," is reprinted in Hearings Before the Select Committee on Presidential Campaign Activities, Book 6, at pp. 2644–45. For a summary of the evidence concerning the Plumbers unit's operation and activities, see SAM J. ERVIN, JR., THE WHOLE TRUTH: THE WATERGATE CONSPIRACY, at 105–07 (Random House 1980).

against the Democratic candidates in the 1972 presidential election.[7] In addition, E. Howard Hunt, while a member of the White House Plumbers operation, had worked for Colson on political dirty tricks projects, including falsifying State Department documents to make it appear that President John F. Kennedy had been involved in the 1963 assassination of the president of South Vietnam.[8]

The burglary of the office of Ellsberg's psychiatrist, the Segretti dirty tricks campaign, and the other misdeeds of Hunt, Liddy, and the White House Plumbers group were famously called "the White House horrors" by John Mitchell. It was the perceived absolute necessity of preventing disclosure of the "White House horrors" that made covering up the true facts about the Watergate break-in essential. As John Dean later explained, "Mitchell felt the hush money [paid to the Watergate break-in participants] would serve to protect not only himself but the President from the 'White House horrors' that Liddy and Hunt had carried out while working in the White House."[9]

And for several months the cover-up plan seemed to be working. Perjury in the original Watergate grand jury investigation, secret payments of hundreds of thousands of dollars for attorneys' fees and expenses, and carefully delivered suggestions of future executive clemency kept Hunt, Liddy, and the Watergate burglars quiet through the 1972 election and into the spring of 1973. The pressure on the convicted men was enormous, however, and after Hunt's wife died in a December 8, 1972 plane crash his demands increased. In addition, Watergate burglar James W. McCord, Jr., who like Hunt had previously been a CIA operative, became concerned that the Nixon White House might try to blame the Watergate break-in on the CIA. McCord was very protective of his former agency, and in a December 28, 1972 letter he warned the White House that if "the Watergate operation is laid at CIA's feet, where it does not belong, every tree in the forest will fall."[10]

Eventually, a tree did fall. In March 1973, prior to sentencing, McCord wrote a letter to the presiding judge, John J. Sirica, stating that the burglars had been under "political

---

7. For a summary of the "Dirty Tricks" operation, see Watergate Special Prosecution Report, pp. 55–57 (October 1975). Segretti later pleaded guilty to misdemeanor charges arising out of his conduct and provided testimony to the Watergate grand jury. Dwight Chapin was convicted of perjury for providing false testimony to the Watergate grand jury about his involvement in Segretti's activities. *Id.*

8. Senator Sam Ervin described Hunt's "gruesome task of falsifying State Department documents to defame the memory of former president John F. Kennedy" as part of a "first conspiracy" that predated the subsequent Watergate break-in cover-up conspiracy and also included the burglary of Ellsberg's psychiatrist's office, the Segretti dirty tricks campaign, and other illegal and improper campaign activities that were intended to secure Nixon's reelection. *See* SAM J. ERVIN, JR., THE WHOLE TRUTH: THE WATERGATE CONSPIRACY at 4–7 (Random House 1980).

9. JOHN W. DEAN III, BLIND AMBITION 123 (Simon & Schuster 1976).

10. *See* McCord letter to John Caulfield, reprinted in Hearings Before the Select Committee on Presidential Campaign Activities, Book 3, at p. 1235. In a December 31, 1972, letter to White House Special Counsel Charles Colson, Hunt warned Colson that, "My wife's death, the imminent trial, my present mental depression, and my inability to get any relief from my present situation, all contribute to a sense of abandonment by friends upon whom I had in good faith relied." Hunt went on to further warn that, "There is a limit to the endurance of any man trapped in a hostile situation and mine was reached on December 8th [the date his wife died in a plane crash]." *See id.* at 1234.

pressure" to plead guilty and remain silent and that perjury had occurred during the trial. The McCord letter, which Judge Sirica read in open court on March 23, 1973, was the first major step in the unraveling of the Watergate cover-up. The credit for that important event must go to the criminal justice system, and in particular to Judge Sirica for his efforts during the trial to make the burglars reveal more about their actions and who directed them.[11]

Although the McCord letter to Judge Sirica was the first major breach of the stonewall that the Nixon White House had attempted to construct around the Watergate break-in, congressional interest in Watergate was already intense when McCord's letter was made public in March 1973. In January, public disclosures during the trial of the Watergate burglars and press reports suggesting that the burglars were paid with CRP money and had been offered executive clemency in return for their silence during the break-in trial led to calls for a full-scale congressional investigation of the Watergate affair. On February 7, 1973, the Senate unanimously adopted Senate Resolution 60, which established a select committee on presidential campaign activities and authorized the committee to investigate the Watergate break-in and a wide range of other matters relating to the 1972 presidential campaign.

The Senate committee's investigation led to the second major event in the exposure of the Watergate cover-up—the dramatic congressional testimony of former Nixon White House Counsel John W. Dean III. The story of how the committee obtained Dean's testimony and how Dean's publicly televised testimony affected the American public's perception of Watergate and the Nixon presidency is an especially fascinating example of the unique power of congressional investigations to expose governmental wrongdoing.

---

11. Sam Dash, the chief counsel to the Senate Watergate Committee, described these events in his 1976 book *Chief Counsel: Inside the Ervin Committee—The Untold Story of Watergate*:

> During the trial, U.S. District Judge John J. Sirica pushed for answers. "Who hired you to go in there? Where did this money come from? Who was the money man? Who did the paying off?" He repeatedly told the chief prosecutor, Assistant U.S. Attorney Earl Silbert, that he was not satisfied with the investigation and that other witnesses should be questioned and called to testify. Although the suspicion of cover-up had not yet permeated public opinion, Judge Sirica's questions and remarks made many people throughout the country wonder.

> The morning [of February 2, 1973], Sirica said in an open court hearing on bail for McCord and Liddy:

> > Everybody knows there is going to be a congressional investigation in this case. I would hope frankly—not only as a judge, but as a citizen of a great country and one of millions of Americans who are looking for certain answers—I would hope that the Senate committee is granted power by Congress by a broad enough resolution to get to the bottom of what happened in this case.

SAMUEL DASH, CHIEF COUNSEL: INSIDE THE ERVIN COMMITTEE—THE UNTOLD STORY OF WATERGATE, at 5 (Random House 1976).

Star Witness:
John Dean's Nationally Televised
Indictment of the Nixon Administration

John Dean had been an assistant to Attorney General John Mitchell at the beginning of President Nixon's first term, and his work there led to his appointment in July 1970 as Counsel to the President, the top lawyer in the Nixon White House. Dean replaced John Ehrlichman in that position, and a year later, beginning immediately after the Watergate break-in, he played a key role in managing the cover-up that eventually led to Nixon's downfall. Dean's role as "the linchpin" in the Watergate cover-up, and the events leading up to Dean's nationally televised congressional testimony, were described by Watergate prosecutors Richard Ben-Veniste and George Frampton in their 1977 book *Stonewall: The Real Story of the Watergate Prosecution*:

> After a brief stint as a minority counsel for the House Judiciary Committee, Dean served for two years, from 1967 to 1969, on the staff of the National Commission on Reform of the Criminal Law. Ironically, it was in this capacity that he became one of the architects of the new federal immunity statute enacted by Congress in 1970, part of an omnibus anticrime measure strongly advocated by Nixon and Mitchell. The statute was instrumental in piercing the Watergate cover-up and opened the way for Dean to implicate Richard Nixon in Watergate before a national television audience.

> After his Reform Commission service, where he caught the eye of John Mitchell, Dean was brought by Mitchell to Justice as an "associate Deputy Attorney General"—an impressive-sounding title traditionally reserved for one or two bright young men on the Attorney General's staff. It was from there that he was called to the White House as counsel to the President, a position vacated when its previous occupant, John Ehrlichman, was promoted to coordinate the Administration's domestic programs. Dean's promotion was a result of his being "noticed" by the White House and later tapped by H.R. Haldeman after a personal interview at San Clemente. Mitchell was set against Dean's departure from Justice. "John," the Attorney General confided, "they'll eat you alive up there." But the lure of the big time proved too great.

* * *

The one substantive responsibility Dean inherited from John Ehrlichman was coordinating and disseminating domestic-intelligence reports that came to the White House from other law enforcement agencies. Dean soon learned of the voracious White House appetite for domestic intelligence. The President was titillated by it; Haldeman and Colson demanded more and more. The first year and a half of the Nixon Administration had seen continued Vietnam War protests, a series of criminal-conspiracy trials of political dissidents, the Cambodia invasion setting off a new wave of student protests throughout the nation, and finally the tragedy at Kent State. In the siege mentality that prevailed at the White House the President was perceived, in apocalyptic terms, to be involved in a many-faceted struggle against a single, undifferentiated "enemy." The struggle constituted no less than a total crisis of Presidential authority and credibility. The White House staff was especially eager for any intelligence that could be used as ammunition against this "enemy" (whether it be newsmen, students, politicians, or left-wing rabble rousers).

* * *

In mid-1971, when the White House began to plan in earnest for Richard Nixon's reelection campaign—another and even more critical battle in the President's struggle with his amorphous foe—Dean was asked to shoulder a greater intelligence load. But this task was soon turned over in large part to CRP. It had been decided that CRP should have its own "counsel" to handle the joint responsibilities of campaign funding law and "campaign intelligence." Dean himself helped locate the man for the job: G. Gordon Liddy.

When Liddy presented his proposal for a million-dollar CRP intelligence program to John Mitchell in January and February of 1972, Dean was invited to attend the meetings in his capacity as White House intelligence coordinator. He did not like what he saw. What with chase planes, kidnapping and hired prostitutes, the plan was something the White House should have nothing to do with. Dean reported as much to Haldeman. Haldeman agreed. It was all a little too flaky, a little too dangerous for the White House.

With the apprehension of Liddy's wiretap crew at the DNC offices in Watergate on June 17, however, Dean finally got the chance he had been waiting for to prove his mettle to the President's inner circle. Now the White House was presented a *fait accompli*. Like it or not, Liddy's program had gone forward and been bungled. With the election less than five months away, protection of the President's reelection became paramount. The political damage could be narrowly limited if the connection between the burglars and the CRP hierarchy could be concealed. The existence of the Liddy program that had been discussed at CRP and the White House would have to be kept secret.

No command decision was made to put a vast cover-up into motion. It was just instinct, political instinct, sharpened in the crucible of three years of White House paranoia, three years of White House struggle with the forces that were out to demolish "Presidential authority." The cover-up was another skirmish in this war. The Hunt-Liddy connection with the Plumbers and Hunt's previous work for Colson upped the ante. The Administration's abuses of power, what John Mitchell called "the White House horrors," had created a reservoir of secrets in the White House that had to be protected. Some could harm the President's reelection prospects even more than the truth about Watergate; thus the high priority of containing the investigation into the bugging. As John Dean told us in describing how and why the cover-up first began,

"There wasn't any articulated plan or motive. It was just assumed that this had to be done. It just happened."

* * *

So John Dean's big chance was at hand. Success was critical to the reputation of John Mitchell, Dean's sponsor and one of the President's closest friends. It was of utmost importance to the President's reelection. This would be Dean's major test in the eyes of Halderman and Ehrlichman: a test of loyalty, ability, discretion.

The word went out: Dean was "handling" Watergate for the White House. And handle it he did. It was no exaggeration to say, as Dean told the President in a taped conversation in March of 1973, that he was "all over the thing like a blanket."

When federal indictments of seven men, no one higher than Liddy, were finally returned on September 15 and Dean met personally with Haldeman and the President to receive the President's praise for his work, Dean felt that he had met the challenge. Nixon told Dean that, like the young hero in the Dutch legend, he had successfully "kept his fingers in the dike."

When the cover-up collapsed, the White House would claim that Dean had masterminded it. The charge was too severe. Dean's role could more accurately be likened to that of White House platoon sergeant: directing the daily battle order, keeping in touch with the flank unit at CRP, and keeping his commissioned officers informed. Like any good noncom Dean did not have to consult the White House brass at every step; he knew what was required. But the major decisions and strategic planning were theirs. In the final analysis they gave the orders; Dean carried them out.

By February of 1973 the storm clouds were on the horizon. Some of the seven men recently convicted in the Watergate trial were sure to be immunized by the federal prosecutors, the newly formed Ervin Committee, or both and forced to tell what they knew about higher-ups. They, in turn, were complaining vociferously that the financial commitments made to them had not been kept.

* * *

In February and March Dean began to meet with the President alone. They talked about the Gray hearings, the law of executive privilege, and Watergate. The President gave Dean the impression that he did not truly appreciate the dangers that lay in store for his Administration if the existence of the cover-up were revealed. A message Dean received from Howard Hunt in mid-March demanding an additional $120,000 shook even the cool young lawyer. If the money wasn't forthcoming, Hunt threatened, he would tell about the "seamy" things he had done for the White House, and that meant more than just Watergate.

Realizing that a critical moment was at hand, Dean decided to brief the President extensively on the details of the cover-up and the new Hunt threat. On the morning of March 21, Dean warned his President that Watergate was a "cancer on the Presidency" growing and compounding itself with every passing day. The young lawyer advised Nixon to seize the initiative and "cut his losses"—even if it meant sacrificing some White House aides, including Dean—before the President was too deeply involved personally to extricate himself. Dean warned the President that it was only a matter of time before the cover-up came unstuck.

Dean's "cancer on the Presidency" speech and the meetings that followed it on March 21 and 22 made little impact on Richard Nixon. The President did not comprehend the gravity of the situation. The cover-up would continue. The President himself was actively involved. The only decision to emerge was that Dean should write a "report" about Watergate purporting to set forth all the facts. What the President, Haldeman and Ehrlichman had in mind was a report that, in essence, implicated Magruder and others at CRP in the bugging, probably condemned Mitchell, played down and falsified the existence of any cover-up, and exonerated the White House entirely. If the true story later came out, the President could claim he relied on Dean's report.

Dean could not carry out his new assignment. If he wrote anything close to the truth, he would damn them all, the President included. If he wrote what was expected of him, the document would heavily incriminate Dean while protecting his superiors at the White House whose orders he had carried out.

On March 23 Dean's prediction about the cover-up was fulfilled when James McCord wrote a startling letter to Judge Sirica claiming that higher-ups were involved in Watergate and that perjury had been committed at the Watergate burglars' trial. McCord's information, Dean knew, was only hearsay, but it reached Magruder and Mitchell, and probably Dean. Mitchell, Dean knew, would not crack. But Magruder, who had testified at the trial and had indeed committed perjury, was something else. An "anonymous-source" news story reported on March 26 that Magruder and Dean had been implicated in the Watergate bugging. Dean sensed in telephone conversations with Magruder that Magruder was panicking—it wouldn't be long before he would break.

At the same time Dean was beginning to receive some disturbing signals from Haldeman and Ehrlichman, suggesting that the President and his two closest aides had decided to take Dean's advice and "cut their losses" by cutting loose John Dean. Dean would be made the sole White House scapegoat for deceiving the President and the President's aides. Haldeman and Ehrlichman would slip the noose.

Dean was at the crossroads of his life. The young lawyer considered the alternatives open to him and evaluated them in terms of probable long-range outcome. He decided he would be better off in the long run if he went to the prosecutors and told them what he knew about the bugging and a good part of what he knew of the cover-up—at least, the involvement of Haldeman, Ehrlichman, Colson, himself and the CRP officials. He was a dead duck anyway. If he were the first major figure to cooperate, he could expect to receive consideration for coming forward. He would insure that the full story came out, that he alone did not get blamed as the head honcho in the cover-up. Speed was now of the essence, for if Magruder and others beat him to the courthouse, Dean might lose the advantages that could accrue to an early, "voluntary cooperator."

RICHARD BEN-VENISTE & GEORGE FRAMPTON, STONEWALL: THE REAL STORY OF THE WATERGATE PROSECUTION 95–101 (Simon & Schuster 1977).

As this account makes clear, by the spring of 1973 John Dean had become the key figure in the Watergate investigation. Both the Watergate Special Prosecutor's Office and the Senate Watergate Committee desperately wanted John Dean's testimony, but Dean was refusing to testify without a grant of immunity. As noted in the Ben-Veniste & Frampton excerpt above, the then-new federal immunity statute allowed either federal prosecutors or Congress to grant Dean "use immunity" and compel him to testify about Watergate. Dean sought immunity and had engaged in lengthy negotiations with the prosecutors, both before and after Archibald Cox was appointed Watergate Special Prosecutor, but the prosecutors were reluctant to grant Dean immunity unless he agreed to plead guilty to at least one federal felony crime for his role in Watergate.[12]

Dean and his counsel then sought an immunity grant from the Senate Watergate Committee. Watergate Committee Chief Counsel Sam Dash, in his 1976 book *Chief Counsel: Inside the Ervin Committee—The Untold Story of Watergate*, described the importance of Dean's testimony to the Committee and the process by which it was obtained, including a series of three "secret meetings" with Dean and his counsel to determine whether Dean should be granted testimonial "use immunity" by the Senate Committee:

> As I sat in Dean's living room listening to the story that would be his sworn testimony, the unimaginable became startlingly real to me. Dean's evidence could destroy President Nixon. He was a witness to the President's actual statements and conduct in the Oval Office which directly implicated the President in the crime of obstructing justice in the Watergate investigation.

* * *

---

12. Dean ultimately reached an agreement with Cox's special prosecutors to plead guilty to one charge of conspiring to obstruct justice in the Watergate cover-up. He entered his guilty plea in federal court before Judge Sirica on Friday, October 19, 1973, the day before the infamous "Saturday night massacre" in which Nixon fired Cox. Richard Ben-Veniste and George Frampton, in *Stonewall: The Real Story of the Watergate Prosecution*, recount that Dean went through with the plea after being informed shortly before the court proceedings were to begin on Friday morning, October 19, that the prosecutors "didn't think Archie was going to be around after the weekend." *See* RICHARD BEN-VENISTE & GEORGE FRAMPTON, STONEWALL: THE REAL STORY OF THE WATERGATE PROSECUTION 130–31 (Simon & Schuster 1977).

I had prepared a long list of questions, based on my review of the prior two meetings with Dean, that required Dean to go over, point by point, most of the facts he had given me. I used this procedure for the double purpose of challenging information that had appeared vague or inconsistent when I reread my notes, and of checking Dean's retelling of the facts for discrepancies with his earlier version. Once again, Dean met this challenge by providing a sharper focus on the information he had previously given me and by producing new factual information, often with supporting documents, as a result of recollection refreshed by my questions.

I found that cross-examination failed to throw Dean off guard, but instead, provided an opportunity for him to strengthen his testimony. From my courtroom experiences as a prosecutor and a defense lawyer, I knew this to be characteristic of a truthful witness. I became more convinced of Dean's credibility and, consequently, his extraordinary importance as a public witness before the committee.

By the end of this third meeting Dean had given me most of the facts relating to the Watergate matter that he could recall. I suggested that he begin to prepare a complete written statement for the committee. When he had finished his first draft, I wanted to read it and cross-examine him on it.

* * *

The committee's rush toward public hearings seemed in marked contrast to the unhurried pace of the Watergate prosecution team at the federal courthouse. They had been fully staffed and had begun working on the investigation long before we did, and still they had not obtained new indictments. It was obvious that they would not be presenting their evidence publicly, at a trial, for at least another year. It was because of this delay in the criminal prosecutions that I knew we could not postpone our hearings. Senator Ervin was worried that the loss of confidence in government by the people had reached so critical a stage that a national calamity was imminent unless there was some highly visible and responsible action by a branch of government. At this time he believed that only a public airing of the facts of Watergate by our Senate Committee could meet the need for responsible government action.

It was especially fitting, Ervin thought, for a Senate select committee to serve this function, since, by so acting, it would be implementing the Constitution's concepts of separation of powers and checks and balances. "Where there is wrongdoing in the executive branch, Sam," he told me, citing Supreme Court authority, "it is the constitutional duty of the Congress to inform the public and provide remedial legislation." He was also fond of quoting President Wilson's statement that in a situation of corruption in the executive branch, "the public-informing function of Congress is even more important than its legislative function."

SAMUEL DASH, CHIEF COUNSEL: INSIDE THE ERVIN COMMITTEE—THE UNTOLD STORY OF WATERGATE 122–25 (Random House 1976).

Acting upon Dash's recommendation, the Senate Watergate Committee voted to confer immunity on Dean for his testimony before the committee. Dean presented his testimony to the committee in front of a national television audience for three full days in June 1973. The Senate Watergate Committee got what it bargained for when Dean provided his immunized testimony. Dean kicked off his testimony on June 25, 1973 by spending the entire day reading into the record a 250-page opening statement that presented a searing indictment of President Nixon's role in the Watergate cover-up. Some highlights of that testimony are excerpted below.

John Dean's Senate Testimony

Monday, June 25, 1973
U.S. Senate Select Committee on Presidential Campaign Activities
Washington, D.C.

The Select Committee met, pursuant to recess at 10:10 a.m., in room 318, Russell Senate Office Building, Senator Sam J. Ervin, Jr. (chairman), presiding.

Present: Senators Ervin, Talmadge, Inouye, Montoya, Baker, Gurney, and Weicker.

* * *

Senator ERVIN. The committee will come to order.

Counsel will call the first witness.

Mr. DASH. Mr. John W. Dean, III.

Senator ERVIN. Stand up and raise your right hand. Do you swear that the evidence that you shall give to the Senate Select Committee on Presidential Campaign Activities shall be the truth, the whole truth, and nothing but the truth so help you God.

Mr. DEAN. I do, so help me God.

* * *

Senator ERVIN. I would like for members of the committee, the witness and counsels for the witness to pay strict attention to what I shall say.

Mr. Dean appears before the committee and has appeared previously before the staff of the committee on obedience to subpoena from the committee.

Mr. Dean at all times has claimed that he is privileged against testifying by the self-incrimination clause of the fifth amendment on the ground that any testimony he might give to the committee concerning the matters the committee is authorized to investigate might incriminate him and, therefore, he appears involuntarily. The committee has unanimously in times past, requested His Honor, Judge Sirica, Chief Judge of the U.S. District Court of the District of Columbia, to enter an order of immunity for the witness under the provisions of sections 6002 and 6005 of title 18 of the United States. The committee pursuant to those statutes, gave 10 days notice to the Attorney

General of its application to Judge Sirica and at the instance of the Attorney General, Judge Sirica delayed entering an order until more than 20 days thereafter had expired. He then entered an order of immunity under the statutes, and Mr. Dean has now been informed of that fact and has previously been informed of that fact and he is now testifying under this order of immunity granted at the instance of the committee. He appears here involuntarily as a witness pursuant to this order, and he has heretofore been ordered by the committee to answer the questions and he has all the testimony he has previously given to the committee staff and all the testimony which he may give to this committee is given by him on the basis of the order of immunity. Is that correct?

Mr. SHAFFER. That is correct, Mr. Chairman.

* * *

Mr. DASH. Mr. Dean, you have a statement you wish to present to the committee.

Mr. DEAN. That is correct Mr. Dash. But before I commence reading the fairly lengthy statement I would just like to make a couple of comments. First of all, Mr. Chairman, and Mr. Vice Chairman and members of the committee, I sincerely wish I could say that it is my pleasure to be here today but I think you can understand why it is not.

Mr. DASH. Mr. Dean, could you please take the microphone and put it closer so we can all hear?

Mr. DEAN. Certainly. It is a very difficult thing for me to testify about other people. It is far more easy for me to explain my own involvement in this matter, the fact that I was involved in obstructing justice, the fact that I assisted another in perjured testimony, the fact that I made personal use of funds that were in my custody, it is far easier to talk about these things myself than to talk about what others did. Some of the people I will be referring to are friends, some are men I admire greatly and respect, and particularly with reference to the President of the United States, I would like to say this. It is my honest belief that while the President was involved that he did not realize or appreciate at any time the implications of his involvement, and I think that when the facts come out I hope the President is forgiven.

Pursuant to the request of the committee I will commence with a general description of the atmosphere in the White House prior to June 1972.

THE ATMOSPHERE AT THE WHITE HOUSE, PRE-JUNE 1972

To one who was in the White House and became somewhat familiar with its inner workings, the Watergate matter was an inevitable outgrowth of a climate of excessive concern over leaks, an insatiable appetite for political intelligence, all coupled with a do-it-yourself White House staff, regardless of the law. However, the fact that many of the elements of this climate culminated with the creation of a covert intelligence operation as a part of the President's reelection committee was not by conscious designs, but rather an accident of fate.

These, of course, are my conclusions but I believe they are well founded in fact. This committee, however, is not interested in my conclusions, rather it is interested in the facts as I know them. Rather than my characterizing the climate and attitudes, I shall—as requested—present the facts which themselves evidence the precursors of the Watergate incident.

* * *

Turning now to the so-called "plumbers" unit that was created to deal with leaks. I first heard of the plumbers unit in late July 1971. I do not recall ever being advised in advance that such a unit was being created in the White House, but I stumbled into it unknowingly when Mr. Egil Krogh happened to mention it to me. I was not involved in its establishment; I only know that Mr. Krogh and Mr. David Young were running it under Ehrlichman's direction. Shortly after Mr. Krogh told me about his unit, he told me that they were operating out of a supersecret location in the basement of the Executive Office Building. He invited me down to see the unit, which I did, and he showed me the sensor security system and scrambler phone.

I never discussed with Mr. Krogh or Mr. Young what they were doing or how they were doing it. It was through Jack Caulfield that I learned that Mr. Gordon Liddy was working with Mr. Krogh. I did not know Liddy personally, although I may have met him.

* * *

I did not realize that Mr. Howard Hunt worked—most of his time while he was at the White House—in the plumbers unit, until after June 17, 1972. I had seen Mr. Hunt on many occasions in Colson's office, and finally asked Mr. Colson who he was. He told me that he was doing some consultant work for him and introduced me. That was the only time I ever talked with Mr. Hunt.

* * *

LIDDY'S PLAN—MEETINGS IN MITCHELL'S OFFICE
* * *

After that, the next time I recall meeting Mr. Liddy was at a meeting in Mitchell's office on January 27, 1972. Magruder called my office to set up a meeting and only after I called Magruder to ask why he wanted me to attend the meeting did I learn that Liddy was going to present his intelligence plan. I met Magruder and Liddy at Mitchell's office. Liddy had a series of charts or diagrams which he placed on an easel and the presentation by Liddy began.

I did not fully understand everything Mr. Liddy was recommending at the time because some of the concepts were mind-boggling and the charts were in code names, but I shall attempt to reconstruct the high points that I remember as best I can. Liddy was in effect making a sales pitch. He said that the operations he had developed would be totally removed from the campaign and carried out by professionals. Plans called for mugging squads, kidnapping teams, prostitutes to compromise the opposition, and electronic surveillance.

* * *

Each major aspect of his proposal was on a chart with one chart showing the inter-relationship with the others. Each operation was given a code name. I have no recollection of these code names. With regard to surveillance, and I do not recall that this was necessarily limited to electronic surveillance, he suggested several potential targets. I cannot recall for certain if it was during this meeting or at the second meeting in early February that he suggested the potential targets. The targets that I recall he suggested were Mr. Larry O'Brien [then chair of the Democratic National Committee], the Democratic headquarters, and the Fontainebleau Hotel during the Democratic Convention. Mr. Liddy concluded his presentation by saying that the plan would cost approximately $1 million.

I do not recall Magruder's reaction during the presentation plan because he was seated beside me but I do recall Mitchell's reaction to the "Mission Impossible" plan. He was amazed. At one point I gave him a look of bewilderment and he winked. Knowing Mitchell, I did not think he would throw Liddy out of his office or tell him he was out of his mind, rather he did what I expected. He took a few long puffs on his pipe and told Liddy that the plan he had developed was not quite what he had in mind and the cost was out of the question. He suggested Liddy go back and revise his plan, keeping in mind that he was most interested in the demonstration problem.

* * *

The next time I became aware of any discussions of such plans occurred, I believe, on February 4, 1972. Magruder had scheduled another meeting in Mr. Mitchell's office on a revised intelligence plan. I arrived at the meeting very late and when I came in, Mr. Liddy was presenting a scaled down version of his earlier plan. I listened for a few minutes and decided I had to interject myself into the discussions. Mr. Mitchell, I felt, was being put on the spot. The only polite way I thought I could end the discussions was to inject that these discussions could not go on in the Office of the Attorney General of the United States and that the meeting should terminate immediately.

* * *

FIRST KNOWLEDGE OF WATERGATE INCIDENT
* * *

I next contacted Liddy and asked him to meet with me. He said he would come to my office. As he came into the office I was on the way out. I suggested we take a walk. It was shortly before noon and we walked down 17th Street toward the Corcoran Gallery.

I will try to reconstruct the conversation to the best of my memory. While I cannot recall every detail, I do indeed recall the major items we discussed.

Mr. Liddy told me that the men who had been arrested in the DNC were his men and he expressed concern about them. I asked him why he had his men in the DNC and he told me that Magruder had pushed him into doing it. He told me that he had not wanted to do it, but Magruder had complained about the fact that they were not getting good information from a bug they had placed in the DNC sometime earlier. He then explained something about the steel structure of the Watergate Office Building that was inhibiting transmission of the bug and that they had gone into the building to correct this problem. He said that he had reported to Magruder that during the earlier entry of the DNC offices they had seen documents—which I believe he told me were either Government documents or classified documents—and Magruder had told him to make copies of those documents.

Liddy was very apologetic for the fact that they had been caught and that Mr. Mc-Cord was involved. He told me that he had used Mr. McCord only because Magruder had cut his budget so badly. I asked him why one of the men had a check from Mr. Howard Hunt and he told me that these men were friends of Hunt and Hunt had put him in touch with them. I do not recall Liddy discussing any further involvement of Hunt, other than Hunt putting him in touch with the Cubans. I asked him if anyone from the White House was involved and he told me no.

As the conversation ended he again expressed his apology and his concern about the men in jail. I told him I couldn't help, and he said he understood. He also told me that he was a soldier and would never talk. He said if anyone wished to shoot him on the street, he was ready. As we parted I said I would be unable to discuss this with him further. He said he understood, and I returned to my office.

* * *

I met with Ehrlichman in the mid-afternoon and reported in full my conversation with Liddy. I also told Ehrlichman about the earlier meetings I had attended in Mitchell's office in late January and February and my subsequent conversation with Haldeman. He told me he wanted to meet later with Colson and told me to attend. Ehrlichman also requested that I keep him advised and find out from the Justice Department on [sic] what was going on.

* * *

Later that afternoon I attended a second meeting in Ehrlichman's office with Colson. I recall Ehrlichman asking where Hunt was. I said I had no idea and Colson made a similar statement. At that point, before the meeting had started, Ehrlichman instructed me to call Liddy and have him tell Hunt to get out of the country. I did this, without even thinking. Shortly after I made the call, however, I realized that no one in the White House should give such an instruction and raised the matter. A brief discussion ensued between Ehrlichman and myself. As I recall, Ehrlichman said that he was not a fugitive from justice, so why not. I said that I did not think it was very wise. At this point Colson chimed in that he also thought it unwise and Ehrlichman agreed. I immediately called Liddy again to retract the request but he informed me that he had already passed the message and it might be too late to retract.

* * *

MEETING WITH THE PRESIDENT—SEPTEMBER 15, 1972

On September 15 the Justice Department announced the handing down of the seven indictments by the Federal grand jury investigating the Watergate. Late that afternoon I received a call requesting me to come to the President's Oval Office. When I arrived at the Oval Office I found Haldeman and the President. The President asked me to sit down. Both men appeared to be in very good spirits and my reception was very warm and cordial. The President then told me that Bob—referring to Haldeman—had kept him posted on my handling of the Watergate case. The President told me I had done a good job and he appreciated how difficult a task it had been and the President was pleased that the case had stopped with Liddy. I responded that I could not take credit because others had done much more difficult things than I had done. As the President discussed the present status of the situation I told him that all that I had been able to do was to contain the case and assist in keeping it out of the White House. I also told him that there was a long way to go before this matter would end and that I certainly could make no assurances that the day would not come when this matter would start to unravel.

Early in our conversation the President said to me that former FBI Director Hoover had told him shortly after he had assumed office in 1969 that his campaign had been bugged in 1968. The President said that at some point we should get the facts out on this and use this to counter the problems that we were encountering.

The President asked me when the criminal case would come to trial and would it start before the election. I told the President that I did not know. I said that the Justice Department had held off as long as possible the return of the indictments, but much would depend on which judge got the case. The President said that he certainly hoped that the case would not come to trial before the election.

The President then asked me about the civil cases that had been filed by the Democratic National Committee, and the Common Cause case, and about the counter suits that we had filed. I told him that the lawyers at the reelection committee were handling these cases and that they did not see the Common Cause suit as any real problem before the election because they thought they could keep it tied up in discovery proceedings. I then told the President that the lawyers at the reelection committee were very hopeful of slowing down the civil suit filed by the Democratic National Committee because they had been making ex parte contacts with the judge handling the case and the judge was very understanding and trying to accommodate their problems. The President was pleased to hear this and responded to the effect that, "Well, that's helpful." I also recall explaining to the President about the suits that the reelection committee lawyers had filed against the Democrats as part of their counteroffensive.

* * *

The conversation then moved to the press conference of the Watergate incident and how the press was really trying to make this into a major campaign issue. At one point in this conversation I recall the President telling me to keep a good list of the press people giving us trouble, because we will make life difficult for them after the election. The conversation then turned to the use of the Internal Revenue Service to attack our enemies. I recall telling the President that we had not made much use of this because the White House did not have the clout to have it done, that the Internal Revenue Service was a rather Democratically oriented bureaucracy and it would be very dangerous to try any such activities. The President seemed somewhat annoyed and said that the Democratic administrations had used this tool well and after the election we would get people in these agencies who would be responsive to the White House requirements.

The conversation then turned to the President's postelection plans to replace people who were not on our team in all the agencies. It was at this point that Haldeman, I remember, started taking notes, and he also told the President that he had been developing information on which people should stay and which should go after the election. I recall that several days after my meeting with the President, I was talking to Dan Kingsley, who was in charge of developing the list for Haldeman as to people who should be removed after the election. I told Kingsley that this matter had come up during my conversation with the President, and he said he had wondered what had put new life into his project as he had received several calls from Higby about the status of his project within the last few days. The meeting ended with a conversation with the President about a book I was reading.

I left the meeting with the impression that the President was well aware of what had been going on regarding the success of keeping the White House out of the Watergate scandal and I also had expressed to him my concern that I was not confident that the coverup could be maintained indefinitely.

* * *

MEETING OF MARCH 13

This was a rather lengthy meeting, the bulk of which was taken up by a discussion about the Gray hearings and the fact that the Senate Judiciary Committee had voted to invite me to appear in connection with Gray's nomination. It was at this time we discussed the potential of litigating the matter of executive privilege and thereby preventing anybody from going before any Senate committee until that matter was resolved. The President liked the idea very much, particularly when I mentioned to him that it might be possible that he could also claim attorney/-client privilege on me so that the strongest potential case on executive privilege would probably rest on the counsel to the President. I told him that obviously this area would have to be researched. He told me that he did not want Haldeman and Ehrlichman to go before the Ervin hearings and that if we were litigating the matter on Dean, that no one would have to appear. Toward the end of the conversation, we got into a discussion of Watergate matters specifically. I told the President about the fact that there were money demands being made by the seven convicted defendants, and that the sentencing of these individuals was not far off. It was during this conversation that Haldeman came into the office. After this brief interruption by Haldeman's coming in, but while he was still there, I told the President about the fact that there was no money to pay these individuals to meet their demands. He asked me how much it would cost. I told him that I could only make an estimate that it might be as high as $1 million or more. He told me that that was no problem, and he also looked over at Haldeman and repeated the same statement. He then asked me who was demanding this money, and I told him it was principally coming from Hunt through his attorney. The President then referred to the fact that Hunt had been promised Executive clemency. He said that he had discussed this matter with Ehrlichman and, contrary to instructions that Ehrlichman had given Colson not to talk to the President about it, that Colson had also discussed it with him later. He expressed some annoyance at the fact that Colson had also discussed this matter with him.

The conversation then turned back to a question from the President regarding the money that was being paid to the defendants. He asked me how this was done. I told him I didn't know much about it other than the fact that the money was laundered so it could not be traced and then there were secret deliveries. I told him I was learning about things I had never known before, but the next time I would certainly be more knowledgeable. This comment got a laugh out of Haldeman. The meeting ended on this note, and there was no further discussion of the matter and it was left hanging just as I have described it.

PHONE CONVERSATION OF MARCH 20

When the President called and we had a rather rambling discussion, I told him at the conclusion of the conversation that evening that I wanted to talk with him as soon as possible about the Watergate matter because I did not think that he fully realized all the facts and the implication of those facts for people at the White House as well as himself. He said that I should meet with him the next morning about 10 o'clock.

Before going in to tell the President some of these things, I decided I should call Haldeman because I knew that his name would come up in the matter. I called Haldeman and told him what I was going to do, and Haldeman agreed that I should proceed to do so and inform the President of the situation.

MEETING OF MARCH 21

As I have indicated, my purpose in requesting this meeting particularly with the President was that I felt it necessary that I give him a full report of all the facts that I knew and explain to him what I believed to be the implication of those facts. It was my particular concern with the fact that the President did not seem to understand the implications of what was going on. For example, when I had earlier told him that I thought I was involved in an obstruction of justice situation he had argued with me to the contrary after I had explained it to him. Also, when the matter of money demands had come up previously he had very nonchalantly told me that that was no problem and I did not know if he realized that he himself could be getting involved in an obstruction of justice by having promised clemency to Hunt. What I had hoped to do in this conversation was to have the President tell me that we had to end the matter—now. Accordingly, I gave considerable thought to how I would present this situation to the President and try to make as dramatic a presentation as I could to tell him how serious I thought the situation was that the coverup continue.

I began by telling the President that there was a cancer growing on the Presidency and that if the cancer was not removed that the President himself would be killed by it. I also told him that it was important that this cancer be removed immediately because it was growing more deadly every day. I then gave him what I told him would be a broad overview of the situation and I would come back and fill in the details and answer any questions he might have about the matter.

I proceeded to tell him how the matter had commenced in late January and early February but that I did not know how the plans had finally been approved. I told him I had informed Haldeman what was occurring, and Haldeman told me I should have nothing to do with it. I told him I did not know if Mitchell had approved the plans but I had been told that Mitchell had been a recipient of the wiretap information and that Haldeman had also received some information through Strachan.

I then proceeded to tell him some of the highlights that had occurred during the coverup. I told him that Kalmbach had been used to raise funds to pay these seven individuals for their silence at the instructions of Ehrlichman. Haldeman, and Mitchell and I had been the conveyor of this instruction to Kalmbach. I told him that after the decision had been made that Magruder was to remain at the reelection committee, I had assisted Magruder in preparing his false story for presentation to the grand jury. I told him that cash that had been at the White House had been funneled back to the reelection committee for the purpose of paying the seven individuals to remain silent.

I then proceeded to tell him that perjury had been committed, and for this coverup to continue it would require more perjury and more money. I told him that the demands of the convicted individuals were continually increasing and that with sentencing imminent, the demands had become specific.

I told him that on Monday the 19th, I had received a message from one of the reelection committee lawyers who had spoken directly with Hunt and that Hunt had sent a message to me demanding money. I then explained to him the message that Hunt had told Paul O'Brien the preceding Friday to be passed on to me. I told the President I'd asked O'Brien why to Dean, and O'Brien had asked Hunt the same question. But Hunt had merely said you just pass this message on to Dean. The message was that Hunt wanted $72,000 for living expenses and $50,000 for attorney's fees and if he did not get the money and get it quickly that he would have a lot of seamy things to say about what he had done for John Ehrlichman while he was at the White House. If he did not receive the money, he would have to reconsider his options.

I informed the President that I had passed this message on to both Haldeman and Ehrlichman. Ehrlichman asked me if I had discussed the matter with Mitchell. I had told Ehrlichman that I had not done so and Ehrlichman asked me to do so. I told the President I had called Mitchell pursuant to Ehrlichman's request but I had no idea of what was happening with regard to the request.

I then told the President that this was just typical of the type of blackmail that the White House would continue to be subjected to and that I didn't know how to deal with it. I also told the President that I thought that I would as a result of my name coming out during the Gray hearings be called before the grand jury and that if I was called to testify before the grand jury or the Senate committee I would have to tell the facts the way I know them. I said I did not know if executive privilege would be applicable to any appearance I might have before the grand jury. I concluded by saying that it is going to take continued perjury and continued support of these individuals to perpetuate the coverup and that I did not believe it was possible to continue it; rather I thought it was time for surgery on the cancer itself and that all those involved must stand up and account for themselves and that the President himself get out in front of this matter.

I told the President that I did not believe that all of the seven defendants would maintain their silence forever, in fact, I thought that one or more would very likely break rank.

After I finished, I realized that I had not really made the President understand because after he asked a few questions, he suggested that it would be an excellent idea if I gave some sort of briefing to the Cabinet and that he was very impressed with my knowledge of the circumstances, but he did not seem particularly concerned with their implications.

It was after my presentation to the President and during our subsequent conversation the President called Haldeman into the office and the President suggested that we have a meeting with Mitchell, Haldeman, and Ehrlichman to discuss how to deal with this situation. What emerged from the discussion after Haldeman came into the office was that John Mitchell should account for himself for the pre-June 17 activities and the President did not seem concerned about the activities which had occurred after June 17.

After I departed the President's office I subsequently went to a meeting with Haldeman and Ehrlichman to discuss the matter further. The sum and substance of that discussion was that the way to handle this now was for Mitchell to step forward and if Mitchell were to step forward we might not be confronted with the activities of those in the White House involved in the coverup.

Accordingly, Haldeman, as I recall, called Mitchell and asked him to come down the next day for a meeting with the President on the Watergate matter.

In the late afternoon of March 21, Haldeman and Ehrlichman and I had a second meeting with the President. Before entering this meeting I had a brief discussion in the President's outer office of the Executive Office Building suite with Haldeman in which I told him that we had two options:

One is that this thing goes all the way and deals with both the preactivities and the postactivities, or the second alternative; if the coverup was to proceed we would have to draw the wagons in a circle around the White House and that the White House protect itself. I told Haldeman that it had been the White House protect itself. I told Haldeman that it had been the White House's assistance to the reelection committee that had gotten us into much of this problem and now the only hope would be to protect ourselves from further involvement.

The meeting with the President that afternoon with Haldeman, Ehrlichman, and myself was a tremendous disappointment to me because it was quite clear that the coverup as far as the White House was concerned was going to continue. I recall that while Haldeman, Ehrlichman, and I were sitting at a small table in front of the President in his Executive Office Building office that I for the first time said in front of the President that I thought that Haldeman, Ehrlichman, and Dean were all indictable for obstruction of justice and that was the reason I disagreed with all that was being discussed at that point in time.

I could tell that both Haldeman, and particularly Ehrlichman, were very unhappy with my comments. I had let them very clearly know that I was not going to participate in the matter any further and that I thought it was time that everybody start thinking about telling the truth.

I again repeated to them I did not think it was possible to perpetuate the coverup and the important thing now was to get the President out in front.

* * *

MEETING WITH THE PRESIDENT—APRIL 15

The President was very cordial when we met. I was somewhat shaken when I went in to meet him because I knew I had taken it upon myself to end the coverup and what I had started was going to cause serious problems for the President. I shall attempt to recall the highlights of the conversation that transpired on the meeting which occurred about 9 o'clock on April 15.

I told the President that I had gone to the prosecutors. And, I did not believe that this was an act of disloyalty but, rather in the end it would be an act of loyalty. I told him I felt this matter had to end. I informed the President that I told the prosecutors of my own involvement and the involvement of others. At one point in the conversation I recall the President asking me about Haldeman's knowledge of the Liddy plans. He asked me if I had told him earlier about the fact that I had met with Haldeman after the second meeting in Mitchell's office and told Haldeman what was going on. I told the President that I had reported this fact to him earlier. The President then made some reference to Henry Peterson asking about why Haldeman had not turned it off at that point and told me to testify that I had told Haldeman about the meeting in Mitchell's office. The President almost from the outset began asking me a number of leading questions, which was somewhat unlike his normal conversational relationships I had had with him, which made me think that the conversation was being taped and that a record was being made to protect himself. Although I became aware of this because of the nature of the conversation, I decided that I did not know it for a fact and that I had to believe that the President would not tape such a conversation.

Some question came up, by the President, as to whether I had immunity. As I can recall, I told him my lawyers had discussed this with the prosecutors but certainly I had no deal with the Government. He told me that he did not want to do anything to hurt my negotiations with the Government. I also recall that the conversation turned to the matter of Liddy not talking. He said something about Liddy was waiting for a signal and I told him that possibly what he was waiting for was a signal from the President.

I discussed with him the fact that maybe if Liddy's lawyer met with him that Liddy would begin to open up because I said that I thought that that would be very helpful if Liddy did talk. It was during this part of the conversation that the President picked up the telephone and called Henry Petersen and pretended with Petersen that I was not in the room but that the matter of Liddy's coming forward and talking had arisen during our conversation. The President relayed to Petersen that if Liddy's lawyer wanted to see him get a signal that the President was willing to do this.

The President also asked me about Petersen and I told him if anyone could give him good advice Henry Petersen could. The President also asked me if I remembered what day it was in March that I had reported to him on some of the details of the Watergate matter. He said that he thought it was the 21st but was not certain. I said that I could not recall for certain without checking.

At another point in the conversation the matter of the degree of discussions that I had had with the prosecutors came up and I informed the President that I had had no discussions with the prosecutors relating to conversations I had had with him or in anything in the area of national security. The President told me that I could not talk about national security areas and that I should not talk about the conversations I had had with him because they were privileged conversations.

Toward the end of the conversation the President recalled the fact that at one point we had discussed the difficulty in raising money and that he had said that $1 million was nothing to raise to pay to maintain the silence of defendants. He said that he had, of course, only been joking when he made that comment. As the conversation went on, and it is impossible for me to recall anything other than the high points of it, I became more convinced that the President was seeking to elicit testimony from me and put his perspective on the record and get me to agree to it.

The most interesting thing that happened during the conversation was, very near the end, he got up out of his chair, went behind his chair to the corner of the Executive Office Building and in a nearly inaudible tone said to me he was probably foolish to have discussed Hunt's clemency with Colson. I do not recall that I responded. The conversation ended shortly thereafter.

As I was on my way out of the office after exchanging parting pleasantries, I told the President that I hoped that my going to the prosecutors and telling the truth would not result in the impeachment of the President. He jokingly said, "I certainly hope so also," and he said that it would be handled properly.

MEETING WITH THE PRESIDENT—APRIL 16

I received word on Monday morning, April 16, that the President had requested I come to the oval office. I arrived at his office about 9:45, and rather than going to the reception entrance normally used by other members of the staff and myself, I went into Mr. Steve Bull's office. Mr. Bull is the one who had informed me that the President wanted to see me, so I went to his office.

Mr. Bull told me I would have to wait a few minutes because the President was in another meeting. A few minutes later Haldeman and Ehrlichman emerged laughing from the President's office and when they saw me in Mr. Bull's office their faces dropped. I said hello, they put on a serious—they said hello, put [on] a serious look and departed. I went into the President's office.

The President told me that he had been thinking about this entire matter and thought it might be a good idea if he had in his drawer a letter from me requesting that he accept my resignation or in the alternative an indefinite leave of absence. He said that he had prepared two letters for my signature and he would not do anything with them at this time but thought it would be good if he had them. The President said he had prepared the letters himself and that no one would know I had signed them. I read the letters and was amazed at what I was being asked to sign. I have submitted to the committee copies of the letter, but since they are very brief, I will read them.

> Dear Mr. President, in view of my increasing involvement in the Watergate matter, my impending appearance before the grand jury and the probability of its actions, I request an immediate and indefinite leave of absence from my position on your staff.

The second letter, which was even more incriminating, read:

> Dear Mr. President, as a result of my involvement in the Watergate matter, which we discussed last night and today, I tender you my resignation, effective at once.

After reading the letters, I looked the President squarely in the eye and told him that I could not sign the letters. He was annoyed with me, and somewhat at a loss for words. He said that maybe I would like to draft my own letter. I told him that the letters that he had asked me to sign were virtual confessions of anything regarding the Watergate. I also asked him if Ehrlichman and Haldeman had signed letters of resignation. I recall that he was somewhat surprised at my asking this and he said no, they had not but they had given him a verbal assurance to the same effect.

He then elaborated that Haldeman and Ehrlichman had said that if they were called before the grand jury they would seek an indefinite leave of absence. They had given him their verbal assurances. I then told the President that he had my verbal assurance to the same effect. It was a tense conversation, but I was not going to sign the letters under any circumstances.

As I sat there talking with the President, I had very much on my mind the laughter in Ehrlichman's and Haldeman's voices when they walked out of the office before they realized that I was waiting outside to see the President. To break the impasse the President said that he would like me to draft my own letter and report back to him later. He said that he was working on a statement regarding the Watergate and the recent developments that had come to his attention as a result of his meetings with Kleindienst and Petersen and would appreciate my thoughts. He said that he would also like a suggested draft letter for Haldeman and Ehrlichman or maybe a form letter that everyone could sign. I told him I would draft a letter and would report back to him.

The President called me to come to his EOB office about 4 that afternoon. He asked me if I had a draft letter [and] I said that I had as well as I had prepared some thoughts for his statement. He asked to see the letter, a copy of which I have submitted to the committee—but again shall read it because it is very brief:

> *Dear Mr. President: You have informed me that Bob Haldeman and John Ehrli-*
> *chman have verbally tendered their requests to be given an immediate and indef-*
> *inite leave of absence from your staff. By this letter I also wish to confirm my*
> *request that I be given such a leave of absence from your staff.*

Mr. DEAN. After the President read the letter, he handed it back to me and said it wasn't what he wanted. [Laughter.]

Senator ERVIN. The audience will please refrain from laughter.

Mr. DEAN. I then told him that I would not resign unless Haldeman and Ehrlichman resigned. I told him that I was not willing to be the White House scapegoat for the Watergate. He said that he understood my position and he wasn't asking me to be a scapegoat. I then gave him my recommendations of the draft statement. Before he read the draft statement he said that he had checked his records and it had been on March 21 that I had met with him and given him the report on the problems of the Watergate and its coverup. I have submitted to the committee a copy of the draft statement I prepared for the President.

* * *

Mr. DEAN. The gist of the statement was twofold: First the President had learned of new facts in the case over the weekend and as a result of this information coming to his staff had directed Henry Petersen to take charge and leave no stone unturned; secondly, that he had accepted requests from Haldeman, Ehrlichman and Dean to be placed on leave of absence. The President said virtually nothing about the statement and after reading it told me to talk with Len Garment, who he said was also preparing a draft statement. After departing from the President's office, I called Mr. Garment and told him that the President had requested I give him my input on the draft he was developing. Mr. Garment said he would come by my office, which he did. I gave him a copy of the draft statement, and he told me that he and I were thinking along similar lines, that is, that Haldeman, Ehrlichman, and Dean had to resign. I told him I was ready and willing but only if Haldeman and Ehrlichman resigned as well.

CALL FROM THE PRESIDENT—APRIL 17

The next time I heard anything about the draft statement was on April 17, when the President called and informed me that he had decided not to request any resignations until after the grand jury took action and that he would issue a statement very shortly. That statement of April 17 is a matter of public record. I would only like to point out one or two items about the statement. The President said that on March 21, as a result of serious charges which came to his attention, some of which were publicly report-ed, he began an intense new inquiry into this whole matter. I would merely refer the committee's attention back to my earlier testimony as to what the President did after my report to him on March 21 as to the White House's deep involvement in the cover-up. In short, the President commenced no investigation at all. Rather, the President, Haldeman, and Ehrlichman commenced to protect themselves against the unraveling of the coverup.

Secondly, I would also like to raise the paragraph that had been put in the statement that no one in a position of major importance in the administration should be given immunity from prosecution. While this statement went virtually unnoticed in the public, it was very evident to me what the President was saying: Dean will not be a witness against anyone so the Government might as well stop dealing with him.

THE DEAN SCAPEGOAT STATEMENT AND
REQUESTED RESIGNATION

On Monday night, April 16, I had learned that the President had informed the Government that he allegedly had taped a conversation in which I had told him I was seeking immunity from the Government in exchange for testimony on Haldeman and Ehrlichman. I have no recollection of ever telling the President that I was so negotiating with the Government and the President told me very specifically that he did not want to do anything to interfere with any negotiations I was having with the Government.

When I learned this from my attorney I suggested that he request that the Government call for the tape and listen to the tape because I told him it must be a reference to the meeting I had with the President on April 15, and if that conversation were taped the Government would have a pretty good idea of the dimensions of the case they were dealing with. I was referring to the fact the President had mentioned the million dollar conversation and the fact that he had talked to Colson about clemency for Hunt. I do not in fact know if such a tape exists but if it does exist and has not been tampered with and is a complete transcript of the entire conversation that took place in the President's office, I think that this committee should have that tape because I believe that it would corroborate many of the things that this committee has asked me to testify about.

When the President issued his statement on April 17 in which he was quite obviously trying to affect any discussions I was having with the Government regarding my testimony by inserting the phrase therein regarding "no immunity" and combined with the fact that he had requested that I sign a virtual confession on Monday of that week, I decided that indeed I was being set up and that it was time that I let the word out that I would not be a scapegoat. Accordingly, on April 19, I issued a statement to that effect.

After my statement of April 19, I had virtually no contact with the members of the White House staff. I did have occasion to speak with Mr. Garment, however. I recall asking him who had placed the "no immunity" paragraph in the President's statement. Garment said it had not been there in the earlier drafts, but was in the draft that emerged from Ehrlichman's consideration when Ehrlichman went over the final statement with the President.

On April 22, Easter Sunday, the President called me to wish me a Happy Easter. It was what they refer to at the White House as a "stroking" call.

On April 30, while out of the city, I had a call from my secretary in which she informed me that the wire services were carrying a story that my resignation had been requested and accepted and that Haldeman and Ehrlichman were also resigning.

Mr. Chairman, this concludes my rather lengthy statement. I apologize again for its length, but I have sought to comply with the committee's request to provide the committee with a broad overview of my knowledge of this matter.

SENATOR ERVIN: Without objection on the part of any member of the committee, the chairman at this time will admit into evidence all of the exhibits identified by the witness in the course of his testimony except exhibits Nos. 34-5, 34-6, 34-7, and 34-8 whose admissibility will be considered later by the committee.

The committee will stand in recess until 10 o'clock tomorrow morning.

Notes and Questions

1. Dean's Dilemma. John Dean was a relatively young lawyer in the Nixon White House when the Watergate scandal fell in his lap. As he recounts in his 1976 book *Blind Ambition*, he began by acting as a lawyer seeking to protect his clients in the White House but soon became a participant in a criminal conspiracy to cover-up the crimes of his associates. In carrying out the cover-up conspiracy he soon found himself committing serious crimes. Although distinguishable by its occurrence in the White House, Dean's situation is in many respects no different from that of any lawyer representing an organization who learns of prior misconduct by other members of the organization and must attempt to defend the organization. How does a lawyer, particularly a young lawyer with law school debts and limited economic means, resist the pressure to "go along" with improper conduct? Who is the "client" of a lawyer who represents an organization or an individual in his or her official capacity, as Dean represented Richard Nixon in his capacity as President of the United States? For the views of one of the authors on this subject, see Lance Cole, *The Government-Client Privilege After Office of the President v. Office of the Independent Counsel*, 22 J. LEGAL PROF. 15 (1997–98). *See also* Roger C. Cramton, George M. Cohen & Susan P. Koniak, *Legal and Ethical Duties of Lawyers After Sarbanes-Oxley*, 49 VILL. L. REV. 725 (2004); MARC I. STEINBERG, ATTORNEY LIABILITY AFTER SARBANES-OXLEY (Law Journal Press 2006).

2. Dean's Immunity. The wisdom of the federal prosecutors' decision to refuse to grant Dean immunity in exchange for his testimony is one of the most interesting legal questions of the entire Watergate saga. Both the original Watergate prosecution team from the U.S. Attorney's Office in Washington and the special prosecutor's office, under both Archibald Cox and his successor, Leon Jaworski, refused to grant Dean immunity in exchange for his testimony unless he agreed to plead guilty to at least one felony charge for his part in the Watergate cover-up. The refusals of Cox and Jaworski, who were independent of the Nixon White House and Justice Department, to grant Dean immunity support the decision of the original prosecution team to insist upon a guilty plea as a condition of an immunity grant. That decision is not without some taint of improper political influence, however. Assistant Attorney General Henry Peterson, the career official who headed the Justice Department's Criminal Division and supervised the initial Watergate investigation and prosecution, had been secretly providing Dean and President Nixon with information about the progress of the Watergate investigation.[13]

On April 17, 1973, when Dean was known by the White House to be in negotiations with the prosecutors, Nixon made a public statement on Watergate that included the disclosure that "I have expressed to the appropriate authorities my view that no individual holding, in the past or present, a position of major importance in the administration should be given immunity from prosecution." Dean's immunized testimony clearly would have threatened Nixon's top aides Haldeman and Ehrlichman, as well as Nixon himself. Whether acting upon the basis of independent prosecutorial judgment or in response to White House pressure, the Watergate prosecutors refused to grant Dean immunity unless he agreed to enter a felony guilty plea. For an explanation of the Watergate Special Prosecution Force's policies on granting immunity to witnesses, see *Watergate Special Prosecution Force Report* at 32–32 (October, 1975) (distinguishing prosecution of organized crime cases and noting that even a "low level" employee in the White House "has a great deal of power" and therefore "should take some responsibility for their actions").

Although the federal prosecutors declined to grant Dean's request for immunity, the Senate Watergate Committee later did so. Fred Thompson, who was the committee's chief minority (Republican) counsel, has explained how the Committee came to do what the federal prosecutors refused to do:

> The decision whether to grant immunity to Dean was not an easy one for the prosecutors, who were under extreme pressure. If they offered immunity to Dean, they could be accused of allowing the real culprit to go free. If they prosecuted Dean and he refused to cooperate, they might be accused of a cover-up themselves, and of passing up what might be their only opportunity to reach the big fish.

---

13. Peterson took several official actions that had the effect of lessening the likelihood that the Watergate cover-up would be exposed. He excused several Nixon White House and re-election committee officials from appearing in person before the Watergate grand jury, he provided Dean with FBI reports on the progress of the Watergate investigation, and he limited the original investigation to the break-in at the Watergate hotel, thereby preventing investigation of the burglary of the office of Daniel Ellsberg's psychiatrist and the Segretti "dirty tricks" operation. With respect to the latter action, Senator Sam Ervin observed that:

> Hindsight is easier than foresight. Nevertheless, it is reasonable to infer that, by their failure to follow up [on] Segretti's testimony to the grand jury, Peterson and [original Watergate prosecutor] Silbert muffed an opportunity to discover as early as August 1972 that two White House aides, Chapin and Strachan, and Nixon's personal attorney and fund dispenser Kalmbach [who paid Segretti and later provided payments to Hunt, Liddy, and the Watergate burglars], were seriously implicated in an important phase of the first [pre-cover-up] conspiracy.

SAM J. ERVIN, JR., THE WHOLE TRUTH: THE WATERGATE CONSPIRACY, at 12 (Random House 1980).

When it became apparent that the prosecution had serious reservations about a deal, Dean began round two of his campaign. If the prosecution would not grant immunity, perhaps the Watergate committee would. On Saturday, May 12, just five days before our hearing began, Charles Schaffer, Dean's lawyer, called Dash and said Dash could talk to Dean in Schaffer's office. At that session, Dean told Dash essentially what he had said to the prosecutors, but now he was beginning to imply other, more enticing, things. Having struck out when he used Haldeman and Ehrlichman as bait, Dean now began to dangle a larger prize—the president. News stories indicating that Dean would implicate Nixon began to trickle out.

When the committee met on Tuesday, May 15, Dash made his pitch. He said Dean had given "significant information" that was sufficient to justify immunity, but there was one problem: Dash could not report what Dean had told him because he had agreed not to. Dean, Dash said, was particularly fearful that once his story became known to the committee's Republican minority members the White House would be alerted in time to prepare a defense to Dean's charges. So the committee was being asked, in effect, to grant immunity to Dean without knowing his testimony, without being able to consider its value. If the prosecution had been asked to buy a pig in a poke, the committee was not being given a chance even to see the poke.

* * *

Dean was gambling that the committee could not resist his offer, and on his terms—and he was correct. Most committee and staff members were all but salivating at the prospect of Dean's testimony. Baker, having satisfied himself that there was no alternative, moved for a grant of immunity. [And the committee voted unanimously to grant Dean "use" immunity for his congressional testimony.]

FRED THOMPSON, AT THAT POINT IN TIME: THE INSIDE STORY OF THE SENATE WATERGATE COMMITTEE 61–62 (Quadrangle/N.Y. Times Book Co. 1975). Why did the Watergate Committee reach a different decision than the federal prosecutors on the question of whether Dean should receive immunity? What are the differences between the objectives of prosecutors in a criminal investigation and a congressional committee conducting a legislative investigation? Do those differences justify both the prosecutors' refusal to grant Dean immunity and the Watergate Committee's decision to grant him immunity? How might the outcome of the various Watergate investigations have been affected if the prosecutors had granted Dean immunity and as a result he had been less cooperative and forthcoming in his dealings with the Senate Committee? [*Ed. Note: Congressional immunity grants and their impact upon subsequent criminal prosecutions are discussed in Chapter 5.*]

3. Dean's Credibility. Dean's nationally televised congressional testimony accusing President Nixon of complicity in the Watergate cover-up placed Dean in direct conflict with the President of the United States and his former senior advisors, all of whom rallied around the President in an effort to discredit Dean and "stonewall"[14] the investigation. Many doubted that the conflicts between Dean's account and that of Nixon's other aides could ever be definitively resolved. The discovery a few weeks later that Nixon had taped his White House conversations dramatically escalated the stakes in the confrontation between Dean and Nixon's defenders.

One victim of the White House effort to discredit Dean was Nixon chief of staff H.R. Haldeman. As the above excerpts from Dean's testimony indicate, Dean testified that during a March 13, 1973 meeting with President Nixon and Haldeman, Nixon asked how much it would cost to continue paying the Watergate burglars. When Dean estimated that the cost could be as high as $1 million or more, Nixon responded that was no problem, and then repeated the response to Haldeman. On July 30, 1973, Haldeman testified under oath before the Senate Watergate Committee that he believed that the discussion actually occurred during a March 21, 1973 meeting, and that in April of that year he had listened to a tape recording of the March 21 meeting. Haldeman testified that on the tape recording of the meeting, "The President said 'there is no problem in raising $1 million, we can do that, but it would be wrong.'" The tape, however, contradicted Haldeman and confirmed Dean's account. Haldeman was later convicted of a felony perjury charge based upon his Senate testimony.[15]

As to Dean's credibility and the accuracy of his testimony, the Watergate Special Prosecution Force Report concluded that the tapes "substantially corroborated and added significantly to Dean's allegations." *See Watergate Special Prosecution Force Report* at 121 (October, 1975). In assessing Nixon's possible criminal liability and the credibility of Dean's allegations, the Report singled out the tape of the March 21, 1973 morning meeting among Nixon, Haldeman, and Dean:

President: How much money do you need?

Dean: I would say these people are going to cost, ah, a million dollars over the next, ah, few years.

President: We could get that.

---

14. Watergate prosecutors Richard Ben-Veniste and George Frampton chose "Stonewall" as the title of their 1977 book recounting "the real story of the Watergate prosecution." RICHARD BEN-VENISTE & GEORGE FRAMPTON, STONEWALL: THE REAL STORY OF THE WATERGATE PROSECUTION (Simon & Schuster 1977). Their book begins with this quote:

"I don't give a shit what happens. I want you all to stonewall it, let them plead the Fifth Amendment, cover-up or anything else, if it'll save it—save the plan. That's the whole point."

Richard Nixon, March 22, 1973, in a conversation with John Mitchell.

15. Haldeman's Senate testimony may also have tied Nixon's hands in terms of any ability to tamper with or erase the tape of that critical meeting. As Watergate prosecutors Richard Ben-Veniste and George Frampton have pointed out:

Obviously the President's eagerness to use the tape in his dispute with John Dean over the March 21 conversation had tied his hands. Once H.R. Haldeman reviewed the tape and testified about it in detail before the Ervin Committee, telling the committee that he had found no gaps on it, the President was locked into turning it over unharmed.

BEN-VENISTE & FRAMPTON, STONEWALL, at 206.

Dean: Um huh.

President: You, on, the money, you need the money. I mean, ah, you can get the money, but its ...

Dean: Well I think that we're

President: My point is, you can, you can get a million dollars, and you can get it in cash. Ah, I know where it can be got.

Dean: Um huh.

President: I mean, ah, it's not easy, but it could be done. But, ah, the question is, who the hell would handle it.

Dean: That is right. Ah.

President: Any ideas on that?

Dean: Well I would think that would be something Mitchell ought to be charged with.

President: I would think so too.

* * *

President: That's right, that's why, that's why your immediate thing, you've got no choice with Hunt with a hundred and twenty or whatever it is. Right?

Dean: That's right.

President: Would you agree that that's the buy time thing and you better damn well get that done.

Dean: I think that he ought to be given some signal anyway to, to ...

President: ... Well for Christ's sake get it, in a way that, ah—who, who's gonna talk to him? Colson? He's the one who is supposed to know him.

Id. at 120–121.

4. **Dean's Impact.** The press and the public had waited with great anticipation to see what Dean would say about the President. Dean's Senate testimony surpassed even the Army-McCarthy hearings some twenty years earlier in the degree to which it commanded the attention of a nationwide television audience, and it probably continues to stand as the high-water mark of the power of a congressional investigation to capture and influence public opinion. Although not readily apparent at the time, Dean's Senate testimony marked the beginning of the end of the Nixon presidency. Within a few weeks of Dean's testimony, Archibald Cox was appointed as Watergate Special Prosecutor, and shortly thereafter, the Senate investigation revealed to the nation the existence of Nixon's White House taping system. Those events ultimately led to the July 1974 Supreme Court ruling that Nixon must turn the tapes over to the Watergate Special Prosecutor, followed by Nixon's resignation on August 9, 1974. The discovery of the White House taping system is the subject of the next section. The battle for the tapes is the subject of the final section of this Chapter. The Nixon impeachment is discussed in Chapter 7.

The Revelation of the
White House Taping System

A good case can be made that the revelation of the Nixon tapes was the most important single piece of information revealed in all of the various Watergate investigations—and perhaps the greatest single evidentiary discovery in American legal history—because it was the contents of the tapes that ultimately forced Nixon to resign the presidency. As the details of Watergate recede into history, it may come as a surprise to many readers to learn how the existence of the taping system was revealed. The revelation did not come though the much-heralded investigative reporting of Woodward and Bernstein in the *Washington Post*. It also did not come through the aggressive federal grand jury investigation that was conducted by the Watergate special prosecutor's office, both before and after the "Saturday Night Massacre" when Nixon fired Archibald Cox. Rather, the nation learned of the White House taping system through the congressional investigative process.

Watergate buffs and diligent students of American history know that Fred Thompson, who then was chief minority counsel to the Watergate Committee, asked Nixon aide Alexander P. Butterfield the question that revealed the existence of a White House taping system to a national television audience. The full story of the revelation of the Nixon taping system through the Watergate Committee's investigation is less well-known. It is a story that is worth recounting in some detail, however, because it demonstrates how even the most seemingly mundane congressional investigative proceedings can reveal information of enormous public importance.

An excellent explanation of the importance of the tapes to the Watergate investigation was provided by Watergate prosecutors Richard Ben-Veniste and George Frampton in their book *Stonewall: The Real Story of the Watergate Prosecution*:

> On July 16 Alexander P. Butterfield, a former White House aide uninvolved in Watergate, startled a national television audience by revealing that Richard Nixon had been tape-recording his conversations since 1971. While the controversy still raged over whether Nixon had advance knowledge of the Watergate bugging, we were now told that the President had bugged his own White House. In the midst of the bitter debate about the truthfulness of Dean's allegations, here was the *deus ex machina* that could resolve the dispute. The most imaginative novelist would never have dared invent it.
>
> Butterfield, the author of this bombshell, had for several years managed the President's daily schedule in the Oval Office. In succeeding months we came to know the former Air Force colonel as an enigmatic figure with a military bearing, a plainly visible pride in his integrity and an eager-to-please manner that sometimes cloaked his intelligence. Butterfield's most distinguishing characteristic was a well-developed view of life in terms of personal duty. It was this code of duty, he said on television, that made him decide to reveal the

full story of the President's tapes when called in for a routine interview by Ervin Committee investigators.

RICHARD BEN-VENISTE & GEORGE FRAMPTON, STONEWALL: THE REAL STORY OF THE WATERGATE PROSECUTION 111 (Simon & Schuster 1977). For a detailed examination of the role of Alexander Butterfield in Watergate, see BOB WOODWARD, THE LAST OF THE PRESIDENT'S MEN (Simon & Schuster 2016).

In the committee's afternoon session of Monday, July 16, 1973, Thompson asked Butterfield the following questions:

> Thompson: Mr. Butterfield, are you aware of the installation of any listening devices in the Oval Office of the President?
>
> Butterfield: I was aware of listening devices; yes, sir.
>
> Thompson: When were those devices placed in the Oval Office?
>
> Butterfield: Approximately the summer of 1970. I cannot begin to recall the precise date. My guess, Mr. Thompson, is that the installation was made between—and this is a very rough guess—April or May of 1970 and perhaps the end of the summer or early fall 1970.
>
> Thompson: Are you aware of any devices that were installed in the Executive Office Building of the President?
>
> Mr. Butterfield: Yes, sir, at that time.

Thompson's questioning of Butterfield on that specific subject on that particular day was not a chance occurrence. Nor was it a chance occurrence that the questions were asked by the minority (Republican) counsel and not by majority (Democratic) counsel. To the contrary, the questions at the public hearing were the negotiated public outcome of a behind-the-scenes committee staff investigative process. The story of how the tapes came to be revealed through the congressional investigative process is the ultimate example of how investigative interviews that are expected to be routine and uneventful can yield bombshell revelations. Reprinted below are excerpts from accounts of the event provided in 1988 and 1989 by the Senate investigator whose questions led to the discovery of the Nixon tapes and the witness who revealed the existence of the White House taping system.

A. The Man Who Asked the Question: The Account of Senate Investigator Donald Sanders

Donald G. Sanders, *Watergate Reminiscences** *

Sixteen years have passed since the burglary of the Democratic National Committee headquarters in the Watergate Office Complex in Washington, D.C. The arrests of the burglars occurred in the very early hours of a Saturday morning, June 17, 1972. The Sunday edition of the *Columbia* (Missouri) *Tribune* had no report of the event. In the Monday *Tribune* there was a brief report at the bottom of page 1. Over the next week there was only one small follow-up story—on page 12. This initial treatment of the event by the press was not unusual. There was no immediate sense that this was the predicate for something very serious.

To view Watergate in perspective it is essential to remember that it occurred when presidential power was great—the weakening from Vietnam was still incipient. John F. Kennedy and Lyndon B. Johnson had been very powerful, dynamic executives. Richard M. Nixon's first term in office vastly consolidated power in the White House. I had already worked on the congressional staff for four years, and I specifically recall learning, in contrast to what I had been taught in high school civics, that the legislative branch was not nearly an equal to the executive branch. In such basic matters as congressional efforts to obtain executive branch witnesses for routine hearings or to gain access to even unclassified files, the executive branch response was cavalier. While Congress was already approving hundreds of millions of dollars for executive branch computers, for example, Congress itself was still in the Model A Ford category.

What I am leading to is the proposition that one did not then lightly contemplate serious battle with the White House nor lightly contemplate accusations of serious misconduct within the White House. And if one did, in contrast to the situation today, there was little expectation that access could be gained to White House documents, or that White House staff would not invoke executive privilege if called to testify. There was a very different aura about the infallibility and inaccessibility of the White House. The balloon had yet to be punctured.

I say this to underline how I felt, and to give you a sense of the pervasive disbelief that filled the room, soon after the Watergate Committee was organized, when Sen. Lowell Weicker (the Connecticut Republican on the committee) stated in a closed-door meeting that he felt culpability for the break-in could extend all the way to Bob Haldeman. Mind you, he wasn't even accusing the president—but to think that he was virtually accusing the president's right-hand man. Most of us were incredulous.

After reading of the arrest of the burglars in the Democratic National Committee office, I had a persistent feeling that it was more than a rogue operation. I thought

---

* THE JOURNAL OF AMERICAN HISTORY, Vol. 75, No. 4, at 1228–33 (Mar. 1989).

surely it would prove to be conscious design of the Committee for the Re-election of the President to gather political intelligence. I had absolutely no thought that it might extend into the White House. It did not seem remarkable to me that one campaign committee should try to collect data on another, but I was shocked that it involved breaking and entering. As the months passed, it seemed strange that the news accounts revealed no firm tie to the leaders of the reelection committee.

It was of paramount importance to the White House to keep the lid on until the November election. The White House strategy was to present the appearance that there was no one of higher rank than Gordon Liddy involved. In reality Liddy had cleared his illegal activities, and his $200,000 budget, with the executive director of the reelection committee, Jeb Magruder, and the Attorney General of the United States, John Mitchell—still in office, but serving as the de facto head of the reelection committee. Moreover, before the break-in, Liddy's overall plan for covert intelligence had been reported to Haldeman by John Dean.

And so, when the grand jury indictment of the burglars was made known in September 1972, with just fifty-two days to go to the election, the Department of Justice made the phenomenal pronouncement that there was no evidence of higher-up culpability.

When I learned in January 1973 that the Senate was forming an investigative committee, I made application for a staff position. I had been in Washington nine years, five at the headquarters of the Federal Bureau of Investigation (FBI) and four working as chief counsel for Congressman Dick Ichord (a Missouri Democrat). Of course, I would have liked to become chief counsel for Sam Ervin or Howard Baker. That was not to be. But despite my previous service with a House Democrat, my employment record attracted Baker and his new Chief Counsel, Fred Thompson. My job was to be deputy minority counsel.

I was impressed by Howard Baker's earnest instructions at one of my earliest meetings with him that we were to turn over every possible stone and, in his precise words, "let the chips fall where they may." My admiration and respect for Baker continued to grow. In public his behavior is gentlemanly and statesmanlike; he is exactly the same in private. While he deeply hoped the Republican National Committee, a distinct entity from the reelection committee, was not involved in the illegal conduct (it was eventually proved that it was not), he nevertheless urged us on to get all the facts. Baker served a vital role as negotiator and mediator between the Republican and Democratic parties.

Staff work began around the first of March 1973. We started with only slightly more than had been in the press. While hiring went on, Fred Thompson and I spent nights reading news reports—piecing together a mosaic of what was already known and who the key players were. We compiled a list of leads to be investigated. Some work had been started by a Senate subcommittee headed by Edward M. Kennedy and the House Banking and Currency Committee under Wright Patman. They withdrew when we began. Our objective was to try to trace a line of authority upward from Liddy.

In 1987, as the Iran-Contra affair was revealed, there was news coverage about Lt. Col. Oliver North's secretary, Fawn Hall. It shouldn't come as any surprise where we chose to start. Sure, with Gordon Liddy's secretary. When the big fellows refuse to talk with you, there's usually a coterie of others around them without whom they couldn't function. I must say, however, that attitudes about the inviolability of a personal secretary's knowledge have changed some since then. There were never any legal constraints on what a secretary could disclose, except for classified information or possibly something specified by contract, but there may have once been an unwritten code of honor about secrets she knew. Liddy's secretary had a melodious name: Sally Harmony. I conducted the interview with Sally Harmony, but I felt secret twinges of conscience in asking her to reveal her boss's business. It seemed somewhat akin to invading the attorney-client relationship.

Several sessions were required with Harmony. She lied at first to protect Liddy. She was not quite as eager as Fawn Hall. Eventually, she revealed that Liddy gave her wiretapped recordings of telephone conversations to transcribe, and that he sent political intelligence information to Jeb Magruder. She told us that Liddy was under supervision of Magruder and John Mitchell, although on paper Liddy was shown as counsel to the finance director. Liddy went to the trouble of ordering a special printing of stationery with brightly colored borders, emblazoned with his code word "Gemstone," which Harmony used to prepare reports of wiretapped conversations. The purpose of the stationery was to alert those to whom it was sent to be discreet in handling it. Harmony took the bill for this stationery directly to Magruder. He approved it but told Harmony to destroy the invoice. Bit by bit, the Watergate conspiracy was being pieced together.

As an aside, in speaking of Sally Harmony, I'm reminded of a rather unkind joke that circulated among staff and press concerning the way in which one committee senator questioned witnesses in the public hearings. As was customary, this senator had his staff assistant prepare questions for the senator to use in the hearings. Unfortunately, the senator had a habit of paying more attention to his questions than to the witness's answers. The story goes thus: "Now, Mrs. Harmony, tell me, did Gordon Liddy meet with John Mitchell on April 2, 1972?" Answer: "No, sir." Next question: "Well, then, tell me, Mrs. Harmony what did they discuss?"

One other early witness is of interest. She was the secretary to Liddy before Harmony—in January and February 1972, in the crucial period when Liddy was presenting to the attorney general, in the very office of the attorney general, his elaborate plans for political kidnapping, mugging, bugging, burglary, and prostitution. The secretary told me she recalled Liddy carrying into his office a thick pack of poster boards of large dimension, perhaps three feet by four feet. These were the graphic aids he used in his presentation to the attorney general.

The big break in the case however was the letter of Jim McCord to Judge John Sirica. McCord, you will recall, had been the hands-on supervisor of the burglary crew. As a Central Intelligence Agency (CIA) veteran, he did not like the indications that the CIA was being blamed for the burglary. Neither did he relish an impending stiff sentence from Judge Sirica, nor the information he had been hearing that some other defendants were receiving financial assistance.

McCord had no firsthand knowledge of the involvement of Liddy's superiors, but he had hearsay helpful to investigators. He accused Magruder of perjury before the grand jury, and he alleged that Magruder, Mitchell, and Dean had participated in the planning for covert intelligence. McCord's letter generated an epidemic of nervousness in Washington, and several individuals started talking.

The most notable witness was John Dean, who had frequent contact with the president. He testified for several days. In one of his scenarios, he said that in a conversation with the president in one of the president's offices, the president drew him to a corner of the room and in a quiet voice told Dean that he, Nixon, had been foolish in discussing clemency for one of the burglars with Chuck Colson. Dean seemed to suspect that there was some White House recording capability, but the discovery of it did not occur until two weeks later—on Friday the thirteenth, July 13, 1973.

Senator Ervin's staff scheduled an interview with Alexander Butterfield at 2:00 p.m. on July 13. It was to be held in a small, secure, windowless room in the basement of the Dirksen Senate Office Building. The room was big enough for only a desk, a table, and several chairs. Butterfield was then head of the Federal Aviation Administration, but he had been an assistant to Haldeman, and as such he had occupied a very small office immediately adjoining the Oval Office. It was his job to control, absolutely, the president's schedule, that is, to make it work. If someone was due to see the President at 1:12 p.m., Butterfield was responsible for ushering the person in at 1:12 p.m. He was the pivot point for papers and persons going into and out of the Oval Office.

Butterfield had been scheduled for an interview for two reasons: (1) he was one of a number of persons who had frequent contact with the president and key staff such as Haldeman, and (2) he could specifically provide insights to the White House methods for preserving on paper what transpired in the Oval Office.

I participated in the interview of Butterfield as Senator Baker's representative. Ervin's staff sent one attorney, an investigator, and a secretary. The investigator was Scott Armstrong, who later coauthored with Bob Woodward the best seller exposé of the United States Supreme Court entitled *The Brethren*. Bob Woodward was a very close friend of Armstrong. He was the *Washington Post* reporter who wrote *All the President's Men* with Carl Bernstein.

Scott Armstrong and the other attorney questioned Butterfield for about three hours concerning Nixon's office routine. Armstrong had a document from the White House containing some summaries of Dean's conversations with Nixon. It would be logical to question how they were constructed. Of course, they could have been put together immediately after a meeting by personal recollections and by reference to notes. But there was another dimension to the quality of those summaries, it seemed to me. I couldn't put my finger on it, but they had a measure of precision that went beyond those possibilities.

I had a fixed agreement with Ervin's staff; I would not interrupt or interfere with their conduct of an interview, and they were not to interfere with mine. Once they were finished, I would have whatever time I wanted for questioning. So, for three hours I simply listened and took notes, knowing that eventually it would be my turn.

As the minutes passed, I felt a growing certainty that the summaries had to have been made from a verbatim recording. I wondered whether Butterfield would be truthful if asked about a hidden recording system. I thought surely if such a system existed, the president would never have said anything incriminating on record. I wondered, if it existed, how it could therefore be of any value—remarks on it would be self-serving. Or, to consider it from a positive viewpoint, remarks on it would prove the president's innocence—in other words, contradict what John Dean was alleging. But if there were exculpatory recordings, why hadn't the president revealed the system and used it to his advantage? I was mystified that Ervin's staff hadn't asked Butterfield about tape recordings. I seriously considered the consequences of Butterfield revealing, in answer to *my* question, that there were recordings. If they were incriminating, did I want on my shoulders the fate of the presidency? It all seemed quite enormous. But Baker had said to let the chips fall where they might. It occurred to me that Butterfield would soon walk out of the room and this opportunity might not repeat itself. No matter how limited the circle of persons who would know of a recording system, I was sure Butterfield had to be included.

There was one other factor in my reasoning. I had served five years in FBI headquarters, on the fourth floor of the Department of Justice building, just below J. Edgar Hoover's fifth-floor suite. For years I heard comments about a built-in recorder in Hoover's office for use on occasions when he needed to preserve what was said. It was inconceivable to me that the office of the president (via the Secret Service) hadn't availed itself of a *technological* process that the FBI had.

And so my time came. It was no "cool-handed Luke" at work. My heart was pounding and my breath was shortened as I began questioning. I had resolved to go through with it only minutes before. I decided, for some unknown reason, not to bluntly ask if there was a tape recording system. After a few preliminaries, I asked Butterfield if he knew of any reason why the president would take John Dean to a corner of a room and speak to him in a quiet voice, as Dean had testified. His reply was stunning; he said, "I was hoping you fellows wouldn't ask me that. I've wondered what I would say. I'm concerned about the effect my answer will have on national security and international affairs. But I suppose I have to assume that this is a formal, official interview in the same vein as if I were being questioned by the committee under oath." I said, "That's right." He continued, "Well, yes, there's a recording system in the White House." We were all thunderstruck. Butterfield said the president wanted this kept absolutely secret, but he felt he had no other choice.

The system had been installed, he said, on Nixon's instructions, probably for historical use. There were microphones in the Oval Office, the Cabinet Room, the president's office in the Executive Office Building, the Lincoln Sitting Room on the second floor of the White House, in Aspen Lodge at Camp David, and in the telephones in all those rooms except the Cabinet Room.

When Butterfield finished it was 6:30. Knowing Armstrong's reputation for leaks, I asked Ervin's staff for renewed promises of secrecy. I then tracked down Fred Thompson at the pub across the street. Naturally, he was having a beer with a newsman. If I had appeared excited, the reporter would have been alerted, so I ordered a beer and engaged in small talk for awhile. Eventually, I asked Fred to step outside. On the street corner I told him the story, and he ran to telephone Senator Baker. I went home, late again for dinner. Senator Baker called me at home on Sunday for a firsthand account because Butterfield wanted to meet with him.

On Monday, after first resisting a committee subpoena, Butterfield testified before the committee in public, and you saw him on television. I couldn't believe we had kept the story from the *Washington Post*. We hadn't. I heard later through the grapevine that the *Post* had the story, but not enough corroboration to print it.

The battle for access to the tapes, and their erasures and disappearances, is another story, as is the impeachment proceeding. But the process was now irreversible.

B. The Man Who Answered the Question: The Account of Former Nixon Aide Alexander Butterfield

Conversations between Alexander P. Butterfield and David Thelen about the Discovery of the Watergate Tapes*

Introduction

The following document originated from a three-hour taped conversation between Alexander P. Butterfield and me at the O'Hare Hilton in Chicago, on June 22, 1988. After thinking over what he had said in Chicago, Butterfield called me on July 15 to elaborate on his answer. We then taped a one-hour telephone call on August 8, during which he was at a motel in Cedar Rapids, Iowa, and I was at the *Journal* office in Bloomington. I then edited and spliced the two transcripts into a single document, which I forwarded to him for his comments and elaborations. On October 12 he returned a heavily edited revision. I then suggested revisions to his revisions in which I left untouched most of his proposed changes but asked him to restore some of his omissions and inserted a few exchanges from our earlier conversations that I had not incorporated into the original transcript. Those changes he accepted with only minor alterations.

* * *

---

* THE JOURNAL OF AMERICAN HISTORY, Vol. 75, No. 4, at 1245–62 (Mar. 1989).

DT: Well, there must have been a point—especially as John Dean started to appear—when you thought: I know a way that we can confirm or refute Dean's claims. The record is there on the tapes.

AB: Yes, yes, OK, yes. Several people who know this story and who look back on the events of July '73 have said, "Gee, didn't you think that?" I did, but only fleetingly. I don't recall ever pondering over the matter. Please keep in mind that everyone was working like a son of a bitch. People don't just sit around and discuss newspaper stories—not anyone I know. We all worked from early morning to 9:00 and 10:00 and 11:00 p.m. day in and day out. I was a loyal Nixon man and a strong supporter. That's another reason I wouldn't be inclined to doubt or wonder about the president's veracity. In March of '73 I became administrator of the Federal Aviation Administration and was especially busy getting settled in there when in June, I think, John Dean began his long testimony.

I'll tell you all I thought of as I listened to Dean. "Everything John is saying makes perfect sense. I know the 'White House System' as well as anyone, and everything he's saying fits." But again, strange as it may seem, I did not follow the thought any further. I didn't let myself take the time to look deeper into the matter. Subconsciously, I may have had some suspicions about Richard Nixon, even then, quite early on, but only subconsciously. Otherwise, I was totally loyal.

DT: Would there have come a time when you would have thought that these tapes—or maybe the memos for the president's file you were talking about earlier—would refute or confirm somebody's story?

AB: I knew about [Nixon's] suspicion of everyone. I had learned by working there in the inner sanctum for so long that this was part of Nixon—part of his strangeness. He had deep resentments of people—resentments that seemed to have deepened over the years. If some senator or congressman weren't toeing the mark or were ultraliberal in his views or vocally anti-Nixon or had crossed Nixon in the past (he remembered those things like an elephant), he would say, "I don't want that son of a bitch to get any favors. Do you hear me? Not a goddamned one."

I knew, for instance, that they felt Ted Kennedy might have a girlfriend or two. The president wanted to, and did eventually, order the Secret Service to report on Teddy's activities. Naturally that's not the Secret Service's job; they (the agents) don't like to be put in those kinds of positions. But that's only an example of what went on—little sort of sneaky things like that were a far cry from my former "clean Gene" military world. But I must say, I took it in stride. I didn't, you know, think it was anything terribly shocking. I wasn't *that* naïve.

DT: But you knew one thing that very few people knew. You knew there was a tape being made of all these conversations to prove that either Nixon was right or Dean was right.

AB: Yes, and I thought about that. I thought that if those tapes were exposed—if that deep dark secret ever came to light—it would blow the whole issue, the whole national dilemma out of the water. When I was asked to come up to Capitol Hill [on Friday, July 13, 1973] and talk to some staff investigators of the Senate Watergate Committee, I knew very well that disclosure of the tapes information would be like a bombshell nationally and internationally. And because the taping system at the White House was known by only nine people, I made a conscious decision before going into that session not to reveal the taping system's existence unless, I want to repeat that, unless I were asked a very direct question pertaining to such a system. And of course I have to tell you I felt that was highly unlikely. I never dreamed they would ask a question having anything to do with the subject of taping or recording conversations. But if I were asked a direct question about the taping system, I would of course, answer appropriately. I knew in my mind that I would do that.

DT: Did you have any questions you thought they were much more likely to ask you about?

AB: No, I didn't prepare at all. I went up there on Friday afternoon directly from work. I didn't have to prepare. I knew what I knew, and I didn't know what I didn't know. They said they were going to ask me about how the White House works, how the staff functions. I guess I knew that about as well as anyone.

DT: Some people in that White House probably would have denied it or tried to evade it if asked. Why did you decide you would acknowledge it if you were asked?

AB: I never thought that I *couldn't* tell. You know what I mean? It seems so dumb now. People have pointed out to me that I could have taken the Fifth Amendment or something. I don't know about that kind of thing. I really don't. I mean I am not that kind of guy. This was a major investigation, and, if you want to get technical about it, Richard Nixon had said time and time again in public forums: "I want all of my people to come forward and be straightforward and open and honest. I want all the facts to come out." Well, I sort of knew that that was baloney, yet he was saying it, loudly and clearly.

The decision wasn't all that conscious. I simply knew I wouldn't lie. I would never lie. This may sound a little corny now, but this was an official investigation. I would never have thought of lying, whether under oath or not. But incidentally, I see now that I have been in the business world for a good many years that a hell of a lot of people do lie. Sometimes it seems that everyone lies, or would if money were involved. I didn't learn this until I was fifty-five years old. My whole upbringing was different. My father wouldn't have lied if his life had depended on it. I can't tell you how straight my parents were. In fact, I clearly recall my dad repaying back the government a portion of his travel allowance when he spent less than was allotted, or authorized, for a particular trip. He was a career naval aviator, a Naval Academy graduate.

The Interview

[*This is the account Butterfield wrote six weeks after our interview in Chicago.*]

AB: The session with the investigators began around 2:00 p.m. on Friday, July 13, 1973. And almost immediately I was shown a paper which appeared to me to be a transcript from the tapes. Well, I couldn't have been more surprised, though I don't think I expressed or demonstrated my surprise to my principal interrogator [Scott Armstrong]. It was a typed, seemingly verbatim, conversation the president was having with someone (I don't recall the other initials; it seems to me it was John Dean now that I think about it) and the question put to me was, "Where would something like this come from?" I suppose you could argue about how direct that was as a question, but no one had mentioned tapes, no one had mentioned recording devices, or even indicated that such was on his mind so I responded as though I were puzzled. I allowed as how the president had quite a fantastic retentive ability, but that particular paper I was holding in my hand seemed almost too detailed for one to have dictated its contents from memory. Then I mentioned that the president had kept a small mobile recording device in his desk drawer and occasionally dictated, on those small "tape belts," brief personal letters to friends, relatives, and others—letters which Rose Woods, his secretary, typed up for his signature. But I added that the transcript I was being shown was obviously not one of those "brief personal letters." So I sat there and scratched my head as though I were puzzled. And I was in a way. I couldn't believe that this was a transcript from the hidden recording system; yet what else could it be? Then, almost immediately, and to my great relief, the subject was dropped. It was as though the transcript had not been very important. The interview moved on to other matters, how the office of the president and the president's staff really worked, what the president's relationship was to members of his staff, what the relationships were one staff member to another, that type of thing. Well, some four hours later, it had to be close to 6:00 p.m., Don Sanders, the staff member representing the minority counsel, spoke. He'd been relatively quiet up to that point. He said, "Mr. Butterfield, getting back to that paper you were shown at the outset of this session, you mentioned the fact that the president had a small mobile dictating machine in his desk drawer. Was there ever any other kind of voice recording system in the president's office?" Those are close to his exact words, and I think you'll have to admit, as I did at the time to myself, that that indeed constituted a direct question. And there was just no way that I could be evasive or give a vague answer. It was either yes or no. I recall precisely my response. I said, "I hoped you all wouldn't ask that question. Yes, there was another recording system in the Oval Office." "Where was it?" he said. "Well, it was rather extensive system," I said. "In the Oval Office it was in two locations. There were microphones imbedded in the top of the president's desk and on fixtures over the mantel above the fireplace at the far end of the room, that is, at the opposite end of the room from the president's desk. There were also microphones in the Cabinet Room, and in the president's Executive Office Building (EOB) office, and on several of the president's most frequently used telephones."

Some people have asked since why I responded as I did, but that's an easy question for me to answer now. I thought it was easy to answer then, too. Because it was the truth; because he, Sanders, was a member of an official investigative body; because any other course of action would have been deceptive; because Richard Nixon (whether he meant it or not) had long since counseled his White House aides publicly to be cooperative and forthright with investigators; and, as if to emphasize his sincerity on that score, he had only some two months earlier released all of his aides from the executive privilege rule. Finally, I answered truthfully because I am a truthful person. I used to play that down to some considerable extent, but I see no reason to invent other reasons for having been open and honest and direct once the sixty-four-dollar question was put to me.

And the reason I prefaced my response to Don Sander's question with the statement, "I hoped you wouldn't ask that question," was because of the adverse impact I knew the news would have around the world … within diplomatic and other circles. For instance, British prime minister Harold Wilson, Golda Meir, and a host of other world leaders would know that their conversations with our president, in his office, had been surreptitiously recorded. The nation would clearly suffer embarrassment, as would the president's image. It concerned me greatly. But I didn't feel I had the luxury of choice in this matter.

DT: Did you feel relieved when they didn't get into the tapes after Armstrong finished? Or did you feel disappointed when they didn't get the tapes?

AB: Now you've brought up an interesting question. You've touched on an issue I've never before mentioned. I was just thinking coming in here today that I would have to admit to some suspicion going back to my White House days. I didn't think a lot in mid-1973 about John Dean being right and the president being wrong; but I thought to myself—often, as a matter of fact—that the tapes ought to be brought to light so that we could clear up this long and debilitating national mess. I certainly didn't see it as a means to put the screws to a president I enjoyed serving and very much respected. I just kept thinking, "Why doesn't the president refer to the tapes? Why don't we get on with the simple process of clearing this matter up?"

So, as I say, you asked an interesting question there. I had already said to myself that I was going to answer the big question if it were put to me directly. And I had already diverted the one not-so-direct question, and now the same subject, the same question, was coming at me again. But this time, this fellow,

Don Sanders, was asking about as directly as one could ask. Was there or was there not any kind of a taping system ever? Immediately after Sanders asked his question about a taping system, I said, "I am sorry you asked that question." Well, it's just possible that subconsciously I wasn't sorry. It's just possible that my impatience for the facts of the matter to be known, and for the debating to end, had its influence. I don't know; it's a psychological thing. Perhaps deep down I was delighted he asked that question. But then the initiative was his, not mine. And I'm as sure as I know I'm sitting here that if he hadn't asked, I would never have volunteered.

AB: [*Butterfield elaborated on this answer six weeks later:*] I remember occasional but only occasional, feelings of impatience at the time John Dean was testifying publicly in the summer of 1973. I found myself at times wanting something to happen, wanting the impasse, the debate, the stalemate, to end. What I'm saying, I think, is that I sense now in 1988 that I may have had a subconscious desire then, in 1973, to see an end to the debacle. There was a debilitating factor or aspect to the affair and knowing much or all of it could be brought to a close by the simple revelation of the hidden taping system, I was impatient. Do I think the subconscious impatience guided me? I'm not sure; I don't think so. I think I was guided by those things I mentioned early in our conversation. I was, however, strangely relieved. In speaking of this whole matter of impatience and the feeling of relief once the tapes information was out, I dare say that most people experienced a sense of relief. It was as though we had broken through a logjam and were now going to get on with it. I don't know if even the relief was a conscious thing in my case. It was just that I had this sense, subconsciously, that it sure would be great if everything would come out in the open. All one would have to do is expose the secret recording system. Then lo and behold, I'm in the dock and being asked the leading question. Does that mean that I somehow guided the event? I don't think so.

DT: After you revealed the tapes you must have thought something different than before Sanders asked the question. Did you think: Holy cow, the whole complexion of this issue is going to change, the Watergate Committee's actions are going to change, the press and so on, when it gets out?

AB: I knew very well that the complexion of the whole investigation was going to change, that the emphasis would shift immediately from who said what to whom to getting transcripts of the tapes, or the tapes themselves. I knew also how momentous the news would be. But perhaps naïvely, I thought the news, for a while at least, might be contained; and with that in mind, the first thing I did was gather Armstrong, Sanders, and the others right after the interview and express my hope that they would handle what they had heard from me wisely ... because of the embarrassment such news would surely bring to the president and the country. I actually said to them (it really was naïve, wasn't it?) that it would never do for this to get out to world leaders and others. I recall feeling upset—maybe depressed is the word—that I had been forced by circumstances, to preempt the president. I didn't know what in the hell was going to happen. But then I felt that I needed to talk to someone on the committee so I went to see Howard Baker a day and a half later, on Sunday [July 15].

DT: Why did you choose Howard Baker?

AB: Because he was the Republican leader of the committee, and I felt I knew him sufficiently well to tell everything that was on my mind. Moreover, I wanted to go to someone senior on the Republican side.

DT: Did you assume that he would know right away what you had said and would be discussing it with the White House?

AB: I didn't know that. I was a little naïve about that, too. When I went to see him that Sunday afternoon, I told him the whole story as though he knew nothing. But of course he knew it all and had known it within hours of the event on the previous Friday.

DT: He acted like he hadn't heard it?

AB: Yes, and now that I think about it, had he let me know right away, he could have saved me a lot of time. After I went through the entire story, I said to Howard, "I wish this thing weren't out. It's so big. How are you committee members going to contain it?" "Well," he said, "it's going to have to come out eventually." Then I said, "I sure as hell don't want to testify before the [full Ervin] Committee [about the tapes]. Perhaps you could get Haldeman to do that. I'm so peripheral to this Watergate business. Haldeman knows about the system and he's already a central figure." "Oh," he said, "I don't think you'll have to testify before the committee."

DT: Baker said that?

AB: Yes, he did. In fact, he said he'd lend a hand to quell the idea if it gained momentum. I felt pleased, as though I had a partner, someone in my corner. Then on Monday, July 16, I'm getting my hair cut prior to my scheduled departure for the Soviet Union the next day. I was at the barbershop at the Ritz-Carlton Hotel, watching the committee hearings on the barbershop TV. The phone rang, and it was for me. Committee staffer Jim Hamilton said: "Mr. Butterfield, we'd like you to come up to the committee. We are going to put you on this afternoon." Well, I was surprised to say the least. I'd felt comfortable after having talked to Howard Baker. Why hadn't I heard from Howard? What the hell was this all about? I felt myself getting angry. So, I said to Hamilton, "No way am I coming up there. I've talked to Howard Baker about this, and he said I probably would not have to testify publicly. So don't look for me. I won't be there. Besides you're interrupting my haircut." I then hung up. Then, within a half-minute I saw this guy on the tube walk onto the dais where the committee members were sitting, walk back behind the row of senators, stop at

Senator Ervin's chair, lean over and whisper in Ervin's ear. I actually saw him whisper into the old man's ear, and Ervin—you know how he had those eyebrows?—I could see those eyebrows go whoop, whoop, whoop, up and down; and it was a strange feeling, for I knew precisely what he was hearing—this guy Butterfield said no way is he coming up here. Well, no doubt the senator wasn't used to having people talk to him like that, even indirectly, so sure enough, a minute or two later the barbershop phone rang again. It was Hamilton. He said very calmly, "Mr. Butterfield, I have talked to Senator Ervin about what you said." I said: "I know, I saw you on television." Hamilton replied, "Senator Ervin told me to tell you that if you aren't up here in his office by 12:30 today, he'll have federal marshals pick you up on the street." Well, having seen this fellow on TV was funny, and it made me lighten up a bit. I apologized for my tough talk earlier and told him I'd be there … which I was. We moved to a small room. There was Senator Ervin, Senator Baker, Sam Dash, and Mr. Thompson, plus, as I recall one or two of the underlings. Howard was sort of apologetic. I sat on the table and spoke first. I said, "I am a very peripheral person here, but this is so big. I meant it when I said I didn't want to testify publicly. I think that if the taping system has to be made public, one of you all should simply announce it; or you should ask someone like Haldeman, who is already one of your witnesses, to give you the details."

DT: Why were you worried about it coming from you rather than Haldeman?

AB: I don't know. I don't know. Maybe because in my view it would give the appearance of me sort of running in the back door. I just felt that it wasn't up to me. At any rate, they said no, we have talked it over and we understand your point, Mr. Butterfield, but no way is it going to be contained. It is going to come out, and the best way for it to come out is for you to reveal it just as you did last Friday. You are the one who told us; therefore, you are the one who should tell the nation. So I said: OK, all right, let's go. I went in the washroom, washed my face, combed my hair, looked at myself in the mirror, and remember pausing for a second or two. Then I said to myself, son of a bitch, here goes. I didn't know precisely what I was going to say. But I knew I was going to answer questions, and I knew I wasn't going to have trouble answering them. Yet I wanted to say more. I wanted to get a message to the president somehow. I wanted him—especially him—to know and appreciate how all of this had come about.

DT: How did this revelation, do you think now, in retrospect fifteen years later change your life?

AB: It made it tough, I suppose, for a while. As it happened, I hadn't come to the White House to go on to a cushy job and make big money. That was not my motivation. Having come from a military background, myself, for some twenty-one years, money was clearly not my orientation. It was hard for me to leave the military in a way because I had had my cap set to go to the top. And, admittedly, I had been on a fairly fast track. But, yes I did think the White

House experience would in some ways be an enhancement to my new civilian career. And, yes, as a result of Watergate, it was not. So, while I've had a few tough years, I can't complain too loudly. Just look at all the colleagues of mine who went to prison. They have to have had a hell of a lot tougher time than I did. My case, where Watergate was concerned, was so different. I was neither a good guy nor a bad guy. I was an enigma. Business executives didn't rush in to pick up those who were involved with Watergate and dust them off and give them nice cushy jobs out in the private sector. So, generally speaking, those first ten years for me were not happy. In fact, it was a fairly miserable period. I think the inner sanctum, the Nixon lovers, are down on me to this day, as I am sure he is, because I screwed things up. But I doubt they understand the context in which all of this occurred.

DT: Do you ever talk about these events with people from the Nixon White House?

AB: I see Ehrlichman every now and then. I have dinner with him occasionally in Santa Fe.

DT: Do you ever talk about this stuff with him?

AB: Yes, I have a little bit with him, and with John Dean, too.

DT: Well, what do you say as you think back?

AB: We haven't gotten into too much. But I'd like to. I'd like to get them both alone. I would love to go off on a camping trip with Ehrlichman and Dean and hash everything out, but of course those two wouldn't go on the same camping trip. My guess is that they dislike each other still.

DT: Thinking of your cold-shoulder treatment by the Nixon White House....

AB: And I'd have to tell you by the Ford White House as well.

DT: Do you think the reputation, this decision, affected your chances of getting jobs?

AB: Without question. As I said, CEOs of companies don't want anything to do with you if they think you may be the subject of new and surprising revelations. One has to recapture his self-esteem. I don't think I actually lost my self-esteem, but I had to keep thinking: I am a good guy, and I have had bosses in the past under different conditions who thought I did a superb job for them. But while thinking this and telling myself how great I was, I was noticing on the job market that the CEOs I knew personally were shying away from me.

But I'm not going to sit here now in 1988 and be a bleeding heart. Things are just fine now. In fact, now I look back and feel very good indeed about the course of actions I chose—and about myself—and I rather enjoy looking the jerks, the people I know put selfish personal interests before probity, squarely in the eye. I feel that I have so much more than they do.

DT: Do you ever wonder why Nixon didn't burn the tapes after you revealed their existence?

AB: He didn't burn the tapes, when the chance was there, for one very simple reason. He didn't dream that he'd ever have to. He felt certain that there would be no need. He didn't know the snowball coming downhill was as big as it was, or that it was getting bigger by the day ... nor did he know how fast it was moving. The president's perception of the mounting trouble was not accurate because the White House never listens. There's so much power there, at the White House; there really is. You can pick up the phone and call almost anywhere and people will get in line to talk to you. You can do so much. You can have such tremendous influence, and on such a scale. It's almost awesome. So I don't think Mr. Nixon ever dreamed that the Watergate issue would come unraveled or get to the point where it might be wise not to have tapes around.

Significance

AB: I guess I told you that in this Trivial Pursuit game I'm "the man who revealed the existence of the tapes." That will be with me always. And of course I don't like that description or identification because it connotes or implies a foreknowledge of wrongdoing. It leads people to believe that I may well have been out to dump the president, that I went to the investigators, not that they came to me. Well maybe in 1974, but definitely not in 1973. But getting back to the Trivial Pursuit game, to me it's a shame the identifying statement can't read, "He was one of the few people who answered questions honestly."

DT: Well, if you could write the Trivial Pursuit question for you, what would you say? "The man who just told the truth"?

AB: Yes, something like that. This is not worth belaboring, but suffice it to say that I'd like truth or honesty or integrity to be the emphasis. After all, that's the way it really was. Why should it now be twisted? I didn't go forward saying to myself, "Here's a chance to be famous because, like George Washington, I chopped down the cherry tree." It seems funny, strange, actually, that what I did is exactly what all of us are supposed to do—what we teach our children to do—and yet that side of it, the simple motivation to be forthright never came out. What came out was that things seem sinister, dirty, suspicious.

DT: Now, knowing all that happened, would you have tried to avoid the summons?

AB: No. I'm glad I didn't try to avoid the summons.

DT: You're glad?

AB: Yes. I felt good about it then because I knew in my heart it was right. It was perfectly OK to tell what I knew to be the case. And human nature being what it is, I'm not sorry that I have some little place in history here, even though I realize that it's not the kind of place in history that might be admired by Nixon's progeny. It's not as though I went to my death for my country or burned at the stake like Joan of Arc or shot down thirty-nine enemy airplanes or something like that. My role was quite simple.

Butterfield added this comment when he returned the edited transcript in October 1988:

Let me summarize here the essence of the three principal points that I want to make:

1. In 1973 I did not go to the Watergate Committee; it came to me. I did not want to testify publicly and, in fact, refused until subpoenaed. I did not ask the questions; I only answered them.

2. While I do not feel that my memory of the events of 1973–74 has faded *or* that my perspectives have changed. I do realize now that during the fairly long period of John Dean's testimony before the Ervin Committee, I was, at times, impatient for the truth … which I knew the tapes would reveal. There was obviously a debate going on nationwide. Was the president involved, as Dean was telling us … or was the president free of complicity? I knew, of course, that the tapes would provide the answer and in some strange, deep-down, almost subconscious way was relieved myself by having the direct question asked of me by Mr. Sanders … even though I heard myself say first in response, "I'm sorry you gentlemen asked that question." In fact, I was sorry—very sorry—for the several reasons I've already mentioned, yet simultaneously there was this sense of relief that at last the taping system would be known, and with it the honest answers to a myriad of questions concerning the commission of illegal acts.

3. While I was very much a Nixon man and fan and an ardent and loyal appointee up to and through my July 1973 testimony, I was quite less than that a year later when I went before Peter Rodino's House Judiciary Committee as its first of eight witnesses. I then had a purpose and a cause. I knew, or at least felt I knew, that if the committee voted one or more articles of impeachment, Richard Nixon, understanding the House would follow, would be wise enough to close shop and step down. I was sure that what I had to say would greatly influence the committee membership and that no combination of wily tactics by Mr. St. Clair, the renowned Boston attorney representing the president, could throw me off course or render ineffective my factual contradictions of Nixon's oft-repeated lines about his negligence in monitoring and supervising his zealous aides, and about his preoccupations with the affairs of state.

Notes and Questions

1. Unintended Consequences. Although John Dean indicated during his Senate testimony that, on occasion, he suspected Nixon was taping their meetings, it was not Dean's testimony that was most directly responsible for the subsequent discovery of Nixon's secret taping system. As described by Donald Sanders in the account above, information provided to the committee by Nixon's White House counsel precipitated the questions that revealed the existence of the taping system. In an attempt to discredit John Dean during his Senate testimony, Nixon's White House counsel Fred Buzhardt gave Senate Watergate minority chief counsel Fred Thompson an extremely detailed account of key meetings between Nixon and John Dean. Thompson took detailed notes of the almost verbatim accounts that Buzhardt provided, then prepared a memorandum based upon those notes. *See* FRED THOMPSON, AT THAT POINT IN TIME: THE INSIDE STORY OF THE SENATE WATERGATE COMMITTEE, at 83 (Quadrangle/N.Y. Times Book Co. 1975). Sanders, a former FBI agent and experienced investigator, concluded that the Buzhardt account of the Nixon-Dean meetings was so detailed that it must have been prepared from a recording of the meeting. He then asked Butterfield the questions that led to the discovery of the taping system. Do you think Buzhardt made a tactical error in providing Thompson such a detailed account of the meetings? Did he expect that Thompson would use the information he provided only for his own preparation to cross-examine Dean and not share it with others? What if Buzhardt had told Thompson that the information came from tape recordings of the meetings and then had asked Thompson not to share that information with the committee's Democrats—would it have been improper for Thompson to have agreed to that request? Senate Watergate Committee majority chief counsel Sam Dash later recounted the Nixon White House attorneys' discomfort with the committee's characterization of Thompson's memo as "Buzhardt's reconstruction of the Dean-Nixon meetings." *See* SAMUEL DASH, CHIEF COUNSEL: INSIDE THE ERVIN COMMITTEE—THE UNTOLD STORY OF WATERGATE, at 159–60 (Random House 1976). In hindsight, it is easy to see why they were unhappy with the attention the document was receiving.

2. **The Importance of Persistent Questioning of Witnesses.** Butterfield's account indicates that he recalls Scott Armstrong did not follow up with additional questions when Butterfield feigned puzzlement over the source of the near-verbatim account of the Nixon-Dean meetings. Some four hours later, according to Butterfield's account, Sanders followed up on Armstrong's earlier question and forced Butterfield to reveal the existence of the taping system. Had Armstrong been more persistent in his initial questioning and asked Butterfield more pointed follow-up questions, then he, and not Donald Sanders, would be immortalized in historical accounts as the investigator who uncovered the Nixon tapes. For Armstrong's account of the interview, in which he portrays Butterfield's revelation of the taping system as at least in part a response to questions Armstrong had asked earlier in the interview about the Buzhardt memorandum, see Scott Armstrong, *Friday the Thirteenth*, J. AM. HIST., Vol. 75, No. 4, at 1245–62 (Mar. 1989).

3. **Investigative Etiquette.** The controversy over the discovery of the White House taping system also affected the conduct of the nationally televised Committee hearing at which Alexander Butterfield revealed the existence of the taping system. Ordinarily the initial questioning of Butterfield would have been conducted by majority counsel, followed by questioning by minority counsel. Majority chief counsel Sam Dash has recounted that ranking Republican Senator Howard Baker requested a different procedure for Butterfield's testimony:

Then a strange thing happened. Baker took me aside as we were leaving [Senate room] G-334 and said, "Since it was a minority staff member, Don Sanders, who asked the question which produced Butterfield's revelation of the taping system, I would appreciate it very much, Sam, if you would let Fred Thompson open up the questioning of Butterfield. This is going to be quite a blow to the administration, and I don't want the minority on the committee to look like it got caught with its pants down, when in fact it played a key role in discovering the tapes."

See SAMUEL DASH, CHIEF COUNSEL: INSIDE THE ERVIN COMMITTEE—THE UNTOLD STORY OF WATERGATE, at 182 (Random House 1976). Dash was "taken aback" by Baker's request because he had not previously been told that it was Sanders, and not Armstrong, who had asked Butterfield the critical question. After Armstrong reluctantly confirmed to Dash that indeed the key question had been asked by Sanders, Dash agreed to allow Thompson to question Butterfield first. Dash later wrote that he "personally resented it and felt cheated" because the discovery of the tapes "had indeed been the greatest find of our committee investigation," but he felt that he "had no choice but to let Fred Thompson develop the Butterfield material." *Id.* at 183. Why did Dash believe he had no choice but to allow Thompson to question Butterfield? What was the political and public opinion impact of having the disclosure of the White House taping system come as a result of nationally televised questioning by the minority counsel who worked for the Republican members of the committee? Did it give the proceedings a greater appearance of nonpartisanship and bipartisan cooperation than the underlying events warranted? By yielding to Thompson did Dash surrender the battle for primary credit for the discovery of the Nixon tapes but help win the war for public acceptance and support for the committee's work?

4. Recognizing Investigative "Clues" in Witness Testimony. In his prepared testimony describing his meeting with President Nixon on April 15, in which Dean first personally informed Nixon that he was meeting with the Watergate prosecutors, Dean included the following disclosure:

> The most interesting thing that happened during the conversation was, very near the end, he got up out of his chair, went behind his chair to the corner of the Executive Office Building Office and in a nearly inaudible tone said to me he was probably foolish to have discussed Hunt's clemency with Colson. I do not recall that I responded. The conversation ended shortly thereafter.

Put yourself in the position of a congressional investigator listening to Dean's testimony with no prior reason to believe that a taping system was in place in Nixon's offices. Would you have recognized that the event Dean described merited investigative attention? How strongly would you have followed up on the "clue" that Dean's testimony provided? Would you have connected Dean's testimony to the subsequent receipt of the extremely detailed "Buzhardt reconstruction" of Dean's meetings with Nixon and concluded that Nixon's meetings were taped?

The Battle for the Tapes

Butterfield's July 16, 1973, testimony revealing Nixon's taping system prompted both the Senate Committee and Watergate special prosecutor Archibald Cox to demand tapes of key meetings and conversations. Senate Watergate Committee counsel James Hamilton has described the historic nature of the subpoenas that were issued in an effort to obtain the tapes and the response of the Nixon White House to those subpoenas:

> The two subpoenas served on the President on July 23 were history's first congressional subpoenas to the chief executive. The first subpoena called for the tape recordings of five specific conversations between John Dean and the President. The second sought various materials relating to the involvement of twenty-five named individuals—including John Dean, H.R. Haldeman, John Ehrlichman, John Mitchell, Charles Colson, Jeb Magruder, and Howard Hunt—in any criminal activities connected with the 1972 presidential election. On the same day Special Prosecutor Cox delivered a grand jury subpoena to the President asking for nine specific tape recordings (including four requested by the Committee) and certain related documents.
>
> The President's response to the committee was prompt. Again relying on the need for confidentiality of presidential communications and papers, he declined to honor the two subpoenas. Moreover, he said, the tapes were under his personal control and not obtainable from any subordinate. He had thrown down the gauntlet.

JAMES HAMILTON, THE POWER TO PROBE, at 26 (Random House 1976). The battles that ensued when Nixon threw down the gauntlet and refused to comply with the subpoenas were fought in the federal courts. The outcomes of those battles are reflected in the two judicial opinions that are excerpted below. Even with an expedited review procedure, the Supreme Court's decision in the Watergate tapes case was not announced until July 24, 1974—almost exactly one year after the first tapes subpoenas were issued. Sixteen days later, on August 9, 1974, Richard Nixon resigned the presidency.

Senate Select Committee on Presidential Campaign Activities v. Nixon

498 F.2d 725 (D.C. Cir. 1974)
[Footnotes omitted.]

BAZELON, Chief Judge:

In this suit, the United States Senate Select Committee on Presidential Campaign Activities seeks a declaration that President Richard M. Nixon has a legal duty to comply with its subpoena *duces tecum*, directing him to produce "original electronic tapes" of five conversations between the President and his former Counsel, John W. Dean, III. By memorandum and order of February 8, 1974, the District Court for the District of Columbia denied the Committee's motion for summary judgment and dismissed the suit without prejudice. The Committee appeals. For the reasons stated herein, we affirm.

I.

The Select Committee was created on February 7, 1973, by a resolution of the Senate empowering the Committee to investigate "illegal, improper or unethical activities" occurring in connection with the presidential campaign and election of 1972, and "to determine ... the necessity or desirability of new congressional legislation to safeguard the electoral process by which the President of the United States is chosen." In testimony before the Committee on July 16, 1973, Alexander Butterfield, a former Deputy Assistant to the President, stated that certain presidential conversations, presumably including those about which Mr. Dean and others had previously testified, had been recorded on electronic tapes. The Committee thereupon attempted informally to obtain certain tapes and other materials from the President. When these efforts proved unsuccessful, the Committee issued the subpoena that is the subject of this appeal.

This subpoena directed the President to make available to the Committee taped recordings of five conversations that had occurred on specified dates "between President Nixon and John Wesley Dean, III, discussing alleged criminal acts occurring in connection with the Presidential election of 1972." The subpoena was duly served on the President, together with a second subpoena *duces tecum*, requiring production of all records that concerned, directly or indirectly, the "activities, participation, responsibilities or involvement" of twenty-five named persons "in any alleged criminal acts related to the Presidential election of 1972." Both subpoenas were returnable on July 26. By letter dated July 25, 1973, addressed to Senator Ervin as chairman of the Select Committee, the President declined to comply with either subpoena, asserting in justification the doctrine of executive privilege. The President stated that, although he had directed "that executive privilege not be invoked with regard to testimony by present and former members of [his] staff concerning possible criminal conduct," executive privilege was being asserted with respect to "documents and recordings that cannot be made public consistent with the confidentiality essential to the functioning of the Office of the President."

The Committee, in its own name and in the name of the United States, then brought this action to enforce the subpoenas. It alleged in its complaint that "the subpoenaed electronic tapes and other materials are vitally and immediately needed if the Select Committee's mandate and responsibilities ... are to be fulfilled." On August 29, the Committee filed a motion for summary judgment, seeking a declaration that the subpoenas were lawful and that the President's refusal to honor them, on the ground of executive privilege or otherwise, was illegal. On October 17, the District Court dismissed the Committee's action for want of statutory subject matter jurisdiction. The Committee appealed to this Court.

While the appeal was pending, the Senate on November 2 passed a resolution stating that the Select Committee is authorized to subpoena and sue the President and that the Committee, in subpoenaing and suing the President, was acting with valid legislative purposes and seeking information vital to the fulfillment of its legitimate legislative functions. The Select Committee asked this Court to hold its appeal in abeyance pending action on a bill, then before Congress, which conferred jurisdiction on the District Court for the District of Columbia in any civil action that the Committee theretofore or thereafter brought "to enforce or secure a declaration concerning the validity of any subpoena." This bill was enacted by Congress and the President having failed to exercise his veto, took effect on December 19, 1973. On December 28, in light of this new jurisdictional statute, we remanded the case to the District Court for further consideration.

Following the remand, on January 25, 1974, the District Court issued an order quashing the Committee's subpoena concerning twenty-five individuals. The Court found the subpoena "too vague and conclusory to permit a meaningful response" and, referring to our intervening opinion in *Nixon v. Sirica*, held the subpoena "wholly inappropriate given the stringent requirements applicable where a claim of executive privilege has been raised." No appeal was taken from this order and the matter is not before us.

At the same time, the District Court issued two orders concerning the subpoena of the five identified tapes. In the first, the Court requested the Watergate Special Prosecutor to submit a "statement concerning the effect, if any, that compliance with [the subpoena] would, in his opinion, be likely to have upon pending criminal cases or imminent indictments under his supervision." In the second order, finding the President's claim of executive privilege "too general and not sufficiently contemporaneous to enable the Court to determine the effect of that claim under the doctrine of *Nixon v. Sirica*," the Court requested the President to submit "a particularized statement addressed to specific portions of the subpoenaed tape recordings indicating whether he still wishes to invoke executive privilege as to these tapes and, with regard to those portions as to which the privilege is still asserted, if any, the factual ground or grounds for his determination that disclosure to the Select Committee would not be in the public interest." The President responded to this order by letter dated February 6, 1974. Rather than setting forth the particularized claims and reasons for which the District Court had called, the President reasserted executive privilege generally as to all of the subpoenaed material, citing as the bases for his claim the need for confidentiality of conversations that take place in the performance of his constitutional duties, and the possibly prejudicial effects on Watergate criminal prosecutions should the contents of the subpoenaed conversations become public. The latter concern was raised with reference to the President's constitutional duty to see that the laws are faithfully executed.

On February 8, the District Court entered the order at issue here. In the memorandum accompanying the order, the Court dealt first with the President's assertion that the matter before it constituted a non-justiciable political question. Finding the reasoning of this Court in *Nixon v. Sirica*, which concerned a grand jury subpoena, "equally applicable to the subpoena of a congressional committee," the District Court held that, under that case and the relevant Supreme Court precedents, the issues presented to it were justiciable. The Court then turned, in the terms of *Nixon v. Sirica*, to a weighing of "the public interests protected by the President's claim of privilege against the public interests that would be served by disclosure to the Committee in this particular instance." The Court found, first, that the Select Committee had failed to demonstrate either "a pressing need for the subpoenaed tapes or that further public hearings before the Committee concerning the content of those tapes will at this time serve the public interest." At the same time, however, the Court rejected the President's claim of privilege insofar as it was premised on the public interest in confidentiality, because, in its view, "the President's unwillingness to submit the tapes for the Court's *in camera ex parte* inspection or in any other fashion to particularize his claim of executive privilege precludes judicial recognition of that privilege on confidentiality grounds." The Court then, in the discharge of its duty as a court of equity, undertook independently to weigh the public interest in safeguarding pending criminal prosecutions from possibly prejudicial pretrial publicity, against the Committee's asserted need for the subpoenaed tapes. In the particular circumstances of this case, including the fact that the tapes had already been made available to the June, 1972, grand jury of this district, the Court found it necessary to assign priority to the public interest in "the integrity of the criminal process, rather than the Committee's need." It therefore dismissed the Committee's suit without prejudice.

II.

* * *

As in the present case, our attention in *Nixon v. Sirica* was directed solely to one species of executive privilege—that premised on "the great public interest in maintaining the confidentiality of conversations that take place in the President's performance of his official duties." We recognized this great public interest, analogizing the privilege, on the basis of its purpose, "to that between a congressman and his aides under the Speech and Debate Clause; to that among judges, and between judges and their law clerks; and ... to that contained in the fifth exemption to the Freedom of Information Act." We recognized, moreover, that protection of the presidential decision-making process requires a promise that, as a general matter, its confidentiality would not be invaded, even to the limited extent of a judicial weighing in every case of a claimed necessity for confidentiality against countervailing public interests of the moment.

* * *

We concluded that presidential conversations are "presumptively privileged," even from the limited intrusion represented by *in camera* examination of the conversations by a court. The presumption can be overcome only by an appropriate showing of public need by the party seeking access to the conversations. In *Nixon v. Sirica*, such a showing was made by the Special Prosecutor:

> We think that this presumption of privilege premised on the public interest in
> confidentiality must fail in the face of the uniquely powerful showing made by

the Special Prosecutor in this case. The function of the grand jury, mandated by the Fifth Amendment for the institution of federal criminal prosecutions for capital or other serious crimes, is not only to indict persons when there is probable cause to believe they have committed crime, but also to protect persons from prosecution when probable cause does not exist. As we have noted, the Special Prosecutor has made a strong showing that the subpoenaed tapes contain evidence peculiarly necessary to the carrying out of this vital function—evidence for which no effective substitute is available. The grand jury here is not engaged in a general fishing expedition, nor does it seek in any way to investigate the wisdom of the President's discharge of his discretionary duties. On the contrary, the grand jury seeks evidence that may well be conclusive to its decisions in on-going investigations that are entirely within the proper scope of its authority.

We concluded that this strong showing of need was sufficient to overcome the general presumption of privilege premised on the public interest in the confidentiality of the presidential decision-making process. We held that it was within the power of the District Court "[to] order disclosure of all portions of the tapes relevant to matters within the proper scope of the grand jury's investigations, unless the Court judges that the public interest served by nondisclosure of particular statements or information outweighs the need for that information demonstrated by the grand jury." It became, therefore, incumbent upon the President to make particularized showings in justification of his claims of privilege, and upon the District Court to follow procedures, including *in camera* inspection, requiring careful deliberation before even the demonstrated need of the grand jury might be satisfied.

III.

The staged decisional structure established in *Nixon v. Sirica* was designed to ensure that the President and those upon whom he directly relies in the performance of his duties could continue to work under a general assurance that their deliberations would remain confidential. So long as the presumption that the public interest favors confidentiality can be defeated only by a strong showing of need by another institution of government—a showing that the responsibilities of that institution cannot responsibly be fulfilled without access to records of the President's deliberations—we believed in *Nixon v. Sirica*, and continue to believe, that the effective functioning of the presidential office will not be impaired. Contrary, therefore, to the apparent understanding of the District Court, we think that *Nixon v. Sirica* requires a showing of the order made by the grand jury before a generalized claim of confidentiality can be said to fail, and before the President's obligation to respond to the subpoena is carried forward into an obligation to submit subpoenaed materials to the Court, together with particularized claims that the Court will weigh against whatever public interests disclosure might serve. The presumption against any judicially compelled intrusion into presidential confidentiality, and the showing requisite to its defeat, hold with at least equal force here.

Particularly in light of events that have occurred since this litigation was begun and, indeed, since the District Court issued its decision, we find that the Select Committee has failed to make the requisite showing. In its papers below and in its initial briefs to this Court, the Committee stated that it seeks the materials in question in order to resolve particular conflicts in the voluminous testimony it has heard, conflicts relating to "the extent of malfeasance in the executive branch," and, most importantly, the possible involvement of the President himself. The Committee has argued that the testimony before it makes out "a prima facie case that the President and his closest associates have been involved in criminal conduct," that "the materials sought bear on that involvement," and that these facts alone must defeat any presumption of privilege that might otherwise prevail.

It is true, of course, that the Executive cannot, any more than the other branches of government, invoke a general confidentiality privilege to shield its officials and employees from investigations by the proper governmental institutions into possible criminal wrongdoing. The Congress learned this as to its own privileges in *Gravel v. United States*, as did the judicial branch, in a sense, in *Clark v. United States*, and the executive branch itself in *Nixon v. Sirica*. But under *Nixon v. Sirica*, the showing required to overcome the presumption favoring confidentiality turned, not on the nature of the presidential conduct that the subpoenaed material might reveal, but, instead, on the nature and appropriateness of the function in the performance of which the material was sought, and the degree to which the material was necessary to its fulfillment. Here also our task requires and our decision implies no judgment whatever concerning possible presidential involvement in culpable activity. On the contrary, we think the sufficiency of the Committee's showing must depend solely on whether the subpoenaed evidence is demonstrably critical to the responsible fulfillment of the Committee's functions.

In its initial briefs here, the Committee argued that it has shown exactly this. It contended that resolution, on the basis of the subpoenaed tapes, of the conflicts in the testimony before it "would aid in a determination whether legislative involvement in political campaigns is necessary" and "could help engender the public support needed for basic reforms in our electoral system." Moreover, Congress has, according to the Committee, power to oversee the operations of the executive branch, to investigate instances of possible corruption and malfeasance in office, and to expose the results of its investigations to public view. The Committee says that with respect to Watergate-related matters, this power has been delegated to it by the Senate, and that to exercise its power responsibly, it must have access to the subpoenaed tapes.

We turn first to the latter contention. In the circumstances of this case, we need neither deny that the Congress may have, quite apart from its legislative responsibilities, a general oversight power, nor explore what the lawful reach of that power might be under the Committee's constituent resolution. Since passage of that resolution, the House Committee on the Judiciary has begun an inquiry into presidential impeachment. The investigative authority of the Judiciary Committee with respect to presidential conduct has an express constitutional source. Moreover, so far as these subpoenaed tapes are concerned, the investigative objectives of the two committees substantially overlap: both are apparently seeking to determine, among other things, the extent, if any, of presidential involvement in the Watergate "break-in" and alleged "cover-up." And, in fact, the Judiciary Committee now has in its possession copies of each of the tapes subpoenaed by the Select Committee. Thus, the Select Committee's immediate oversight need for the subpoenaed tapes is, from a congressional perspective, merely cumulative. Against the claim of privilege, the only oversight interest that the Select Committee can currently assert is that of having these particular conversations scrutinized simultaneously by two committees. We have been shown no evidence indicating that Congress itself attaches any particular value to this interest. In these circumstances, we think the need for the tapes premised solely on an asserted power to investigate and inform cannot justify enforcement of the Committee's subpoena.

The sufficiency of the Committee's showing of need has come to depend, therefore, entirely on whether the subpoenaed materials are critical to the performance of its legislative functions. There is a clear difference between Congress's legislative tasks and the responsibility of a grand jury, or any institution engaged in like functions. While fact-finding by a legislative committee is undeniably a part of its task, legislative judgments normally depend more on the predicted consequences of proposed legislative actions and their political acceptability, than on precise reconstruction of past events; Congress frequently legislates on the basis of conflicting information provided in its hearings. In contrast, the responsibility of the grand jury turns entirely on its ability to determine whether there is probable cause to believe that certain named individuals did or did not commit specific crimes. If, for example, as in *Nixon v. Sirica*, one of those crimes is perjury concerning the content of certain conversations, the grand jury's need for the most precise evidence, the exact text of oral statements recorded in their original form, is undeniable. We see no comparable need in the legislative process, at least not in the circumstances of this case. Indeed, whatever force there might once have been in the Committee's argument that the subpoenaed materials are necessary to its legislative judgments has been substantially undermined by subsequent events.

* * *

IV.

In approaching our judicial function, we have no doubt that the Committee has performed and will continue to perform its duties fully in the service of the nation. We must, however, consider the nature of its need when we are called upon, in the first such case in our history, to exercise the equity power of a court at the request of a congressional committee, in the form of a judgment that the President must disclose to the Committee records of conversations between himself and his principal aides. We conclude that the need demonstrated by the Select Committee in the peculiar circumstances of this case, including the subsequent and on-going investigation of the House Judiciary Committee, is too attenuated and too tangential to its functions to permit a judicial judgment that the President is required to comply with the Committee's subpoena. We therefore affirm the order dismissing the Committee's action without prejudice, although on grounds that differ from those announced by the District Court.

Affirmed.

United States v. Nixon

418 U.S. 683 (1974)
[Footnotes omitted except as indicated.]

Mr. Chief Justice BURGER delivered the opinion of the Court.

This litigation presents for review the denial of a motion, filed in the District Court on behalf of the President of the United States, in the case of *United States v. Mitchell et al.* (D.C. Crim. No. 74-110), to quash a third-party subpoena *duces tecum* issued by the United States District Court for the District of Columbia, pursuant to Fed. Rule Crim. Proc. 17(c). The subpoena directed the President to produce certain tape recordings and documents relating to his conversations with aides and advisers. The court rejected the President's claims of absolute executive privilege, of lack of jurisdiction, and of failure to satisfy the requirements of Rule 17(c).

* * *

On March 1, 1974, a grand jury of the United States District Court for the District of Columbia returned an indictment charging seven named individuals with various offenses, including conspiracy to defraud the United States and to obstruct justice. Although he was not designated as such in the indictment, the grand jury named the President, among others, as an unindicted coconspirator. On April 18, 1974, upon motion of the Special Prosecutor, a subpoena *duces tecum* was issued pursuant to Rule 17(c) to the President by the United States District Court and made returnable on May 2, 1974. This subpoena required the production, in advance of the September 9 trial date, of certain tapes, memoranda, papers, transcripts or other writings relating to certain precisely identified meetings between the President and others. The Special Prosecutor was able to fix the time, place, and persons present at these discussions because the White House daily logs and appointment records had been delivered to him. On April 30, the President publicly released edited transcripts of 43 conversations; portions of 20 conversations subject to subpoena in the present case were included. On May 1, 1974, the President's counsel filed a "special appearance" and a motion to quash the subpoena under Rule 17(c). This motion was accompanied by a formal claim of privilege. At a subsequent hearing, further motions to expunge the grand jury's action naming the President as an unindicted coconspirator and for protective orders against the disclosure of that information were filed or raised orally by counsel for the President.

On May 20, 1974, the District Court denied the motion to quash and the motions to expunge and for protective orders. 377 F. Supp. 1326. It further ordered "the President or any subordinate officer, official, or employee with custody or control of the documents or objects subpoenaed," *id.*, at 1331, to deliver to the District Court, on or before

May 31, 1974, the originals of all subpoenaed items, as well as an index and analysis of those items, together with tape copies of those portions of the subpoenaed recordings for which transcripts had been released to the public by the President on April 30. The District Court rejected jurisdictional challenges based on a contention that the dispute was nonjusticiable because it was between the Special Prosecutor and the Chief Executive and hence "intra-executive" in character; it also rejected the contention that the Judiciary was without authority to review an assertion of executive privilege by the President. The court's rejection of the first challenge was based on the authority and powers vested in the Special Prosecutor by the regulation promulgated by the Attorney General; the court concluded that a justiciable controversy was presented. The second challenge was held to be foreclosed by the decision in *Nixon v. Sirica*, 487 F.2d 700 (D.C. Cir. 1973).

The District Court held that the judiciary, not the President, was the final arbiter of a claim of executive privilege. The court concluded that under the circumstances of this case the presumptive privilege was overcome by the Special Prosecutor's *prima facie* "demonstration of need sufficiently compelling to warrant judicial examination in chambers ..." 377 F. Supp., at 1330. The court held, finally, that the Special Prosecutor had satisfied the requirements of Rule 17(c). The District Court stayed its order pending appellate review on condition that review was sought before 4 p.m., May 24. The court further provided that matters filed under seal remain under seal when transmitted as part of the record.

* * *

Against this background, the Special Prosecutor, in order to carry his burden, must clear three hurdles: (1) relevancy; (2) admissibility; (3) specificity. Our own review of the record necessarily affords a less comprehensive view of the total situation than was available to the trial judge and we are unwilling to conclude that the District Court erred in the evaluation of the Special Prosecutor's showing under Rule 17(c). Our conclusion is based on the record before us, much of which is under seal. Of course, the contents of the subpoenaed tapes could not at that stage be described fully by the Special Prosecutor, but there was a sufficient likelihood that each of the tapes contains conversations relevant to the offenses charged in the indictment. *United States v. Gross*, 24 F.R.D. 138 (S.D.N.Y. 1959). With respect to many of the tapes, the Special Prosecutor offered the sworn testimony or statements of one or more of the participants in the conversations as to what was said at the time. As for the remainder of the tapes, the identity of the participants and the time and place of the conversations, taken in their total context, permit a rational inference that at least part of the conversations relate to the offenses charged in the indictment.

We also conclude there was a sufficient preliminary showing that each of the subpoenaed tapes contains evidence admissible with respect to the offenses charged in the indictment. The most cogent objection to the admissibility of the taped conversations here at issue is that they are a collection of out-of-court statements by declarants who will not be subject to cross-examination and that the statements are therefore inadmissible hearsay. Here, however, most of the tapes apparently contain conversations to which one or more of the defendants named in the indictment were party. The hearsay rule does not automatically bar all out-of-court statements by a defendant in a criminal case. Declarations by one defendant may also be admissible against other defendants upon a sufficient showing, by independent evidence, of a conspiracy among one or more other defendants and the declarant and if the declarations at issue were in furtherance of that conspiracy. The same is true of declarations of coconspirators who are not defendants in the case on trial.... Accordingly, we cannot conclude that the District Court erred in authorizing the issuance of the subpoena *duces tecum.*

* * *

IV

THE CLAIM OF PRIVILEGE

A

Having determined that the requirements of Rule 17(c) were satisfied, we turn to the claim that the subpoena should be quashed because it demands "confidential conversations between a President and his close advisors that it would be inconsistent with the public interest to produce." App. 48a. The first contention is a broad claim that the separation of powers doctrine precludes judicial review of a President's claim of privilege. The second contention is that if he does not prevail on the claim of absolute privilege, the court should hold as a matter of constitutional law that the privilege prevails over the subpoena *duces tecum.*

In the performance of assigned constitutional duties each branch of the Government must initially interpret the Constitution, and the interpretation of its powers by any branch is due great respect from the others. The President's counsel, as we have noted, reads the Constitution as providing an absolute privilege of confidentiality for all Presidential communications. Many decisions of this Court, however, have unequivocally reaffirmed the holding of *Marbury v. Madison*, 1 Cranch 137 (1803), that "[i]t is emphatically the province and duty of the judicial department to say what the law is." *Id.* at 177.

No holding of the Court has defined the scope of judicial power specifically relating to the enforcement of a subpoena for confidential Presidential communications for use in a criminal prosecution, but other exercises of power by the Executive Branch and the Legislative Branch have been found invalid as in conflict with the Constitution.... Since this Court has consistently exercised the power to construe and delineate claims arising under express powers, it must follow that the Court has authority to interpret claims with respect to powers alleged to derive from enumerated powers.

Our system of government "requires that federal courts on occasion interpret the Constitution in a manner at variance with the construction given the document by another branch." *Powell v. McCormack....* And in *Baker v. Carr*, 369 U.S. at 211, the Court stated:

> [D]eciding whether a matter has in any measure been committed by the Constitution to another branch of government, or whether the action of that

branch exceeds whatever authority has been committed, is itself a delicate exercise in constitutional interpretation, and is a responsibility of this Court as ultimate interpreter of the Constitution.

Notwithstanding the deference each branch must accord the others, the "judicial Power of the United States" vested in the federal courts by Art. III, §1, of the Constitution can no more be shared with the Executive Branch than the Chief Executive, for example, can share with the Judiciary the veto power, or the Congress share with the Judiciary the power to override a Presidential veto. Any other conclusion would be contrary to the basic concept of separation of powers and the checks and balances that flow from the scheme of a tripartite government. The Federalist, No. 47, p. 313 (S. Mittell ed. 1938). We therefore reaffirm that it is the province and duty of this Court "to say what the law is" with respect to the claim of privilege presented in this case. *Marbury v. Madison, supra*, 1 Cranch at 177.

B

In support of his claim of absolute privilege, the President's counsel urges two grounds, one of which is common to all governments and one of which is peculiar to our system of separation of powers. The first ground is the valid need for protection of communications between high Government officials and those who advise and assist them in the performance of their manifold duties; the importance of this confidentiality is too plain to require further discussion. Human experience teaches that those who expect public dissemination of their remarks may well temper candor with a concern for appearances and for their own interests to the detriment of the decisionmaking process. Whatever the nature of the privilege of confidentiality of Presidential communications in the exercise of Art. II powers, the privilege can be said to derive from the supremacy of each branch within its own assigned area of constitutional duties. Certain powers and privileges flow from the nature of enumerated powers; the protection of the confidentiality of Presidential communications has similar constitutional underpinnings.

The second ground asserted by the President's counsel in support of the claim of absolute privilege rests on the doctrine of separation of powers....

However, neither the doctrine of separation of powers, nor the need for confidentiality of high-level communications, without more, can sustain an absolute, unqualified Presidential privilege of immunity from judicial process under all circumstances. The President's need for complete candor and objectivity from advisers calls for great deference from the courts. However, when the privilege depends solely on the broad, undifferentiated claim of public interest in the confidentiality of such conversations, a confrontation with other values arises. Absent a claim of need to protect military, diplomatic, or sensitive national security secrets, we find it difficult to accept the argument that even the very important interest in confidentiality of Presidential communications is significantly diminished by production of such material for *in camera* inspection with all the protection that a district court will be obliged to provide.

The impediment that an absolute, unqualified privilege would place in the way of the primary constitutional duty of the Judicial Branch to do justice in criminal prosecutions would plainly conflict with the function of the courts under Art. III. In designing the structure of our Government and dividing and allocating the sovereign power among three co-equal branches, the Framers of the Constitution sought to provide a comprehensive system, but the separate powers were not intended to operate with absolute independence.

* * *

To read the Art. II powers of the President as providing an absolute privilege as against a subpoena essential to enforcement of criminal statutes on no more than a generalized claim of the public interest in confidentiality of nonmilitary and nondiplomatic discussions would upset the constitutional balance of "a workable government" and gravely impair the role of the courts under Art. III.

C

Since we conclude that the legitimate needs of the judicial process may outweigh Presidential privilege, it is necessary to resolve those competing interests in a manner that preserves the essential functions of each branch....

The expectation of a President to the confidentiality of his conversations and correspondence, like the claim of confidentiality of judicial deliberations, for example, has all the values to which we accord deference for the privacy of all citizens and, added to those values, is the necessity for protection of the public interest in candid, objective, and even blunt or harsh opinions in Presidential decisionmaking. A President and those who assist him must be free to explore alternatives in the process of shaping policies and making decisions and to do so in a way many would be unwilling to express except privately. These are the considerations justifying a presumptive privilege for Presidential communications. The privilege is fundamental to the operation of Government and inextricably rooted in the separation of powers under the Constitution....

But this presumptive privilege must be considered in light of our historic commitment to the rule of law.... The very integrity of the judicial system and public confidence in the system depend on full disclosure of all the facts, within the framework of the rules of evidence. To ensure that justice is done, it is imperative to the function of courts that compulsory process be available for the production of evidence needed either by the prosecution or by the defense.

* * *

In this case the President challenges a subpoena served on him as a third party requiring the production of materials for use in a criminal prosecution; he does so on the claim that he has a privilege against disclosure of confidential communications. He does not place his claim of privilege on the ground they are military or diplomatic secrets....

* * *

No case of the Court, however, has extended this high degree of deference to a President's generalized interest in confidentiality. Nowhere in the Constitution, as we have noted earlier, is there any explicit reference to a privilege of confidentiality, yet to the extent this interest relates to the effective discharge of a President's powers, it is constitutionally based.

* * *

In this case we must weigh the importance of the general privilege of confidentiality of Presidential communications in performance of the President's responsibilities against the inroads of such a privilege on the fair administration of criminal justice.[16] The interest in preserving confidentiality is weighty indeed and entitled to great respect. However, we cannot conclude that advisers will be moved to temper the candor of their remarks by the infrequent occasions of disclosure because of the possibility that such conversations will be called for in the context of a criminal prosecution.

On the other hand, the allowance of the privilege to withhold evidence that is demonstrably relevant in a criminal trial would cut deeply into the guarantee of due process of law and gravely impair the basic function of the courts. A President's acknowledged need for confidentiality in the communications of his office is general in nature, whereas the constitutional need for production of relevant evidence in a criminal proceeding is specific and central to the fair adjudication of a particular criminal case in the administration of justice. Without access to specific facts a criminal prosecution may be totally frustrated. The President's broad interest in confidentiality of communications will not be vitiated by disclosure of a limited number of conversations preliminarily shown to have some bearing on the pending criminal cases.

We conclude that when the ground for asserting privilege as to subpoenaed materials sought for use in a criminal trial is based only on the generalized interest in confidentiality, it cannot prevail over the fundamental demands of due process of law in the fair administration of criminal justice. The generalized assertion of privilege must yield to the demonstrated, specific need for evidence in a pending criminal trial.

* * *

Affirmed.

Notes and Questions

1. Judicial Bias? Analytical Bases for the Nixon Tapes Judicial Decisions. How do the courts in the tapes opinions that are excerpted above analyze the relative needs for the tapes of the Senate committee and the Watergate Special Prosecutor? Do you perceive any "institutional bias" by the courts in favor of the fair trial and due process needs of the criminal justice system over the legislative and public informing needs of

---

16. [Note 19 of opinion:] We are not here concerned with the balance between the President's generalized interest in confidentiality and the need for relevant evidence in civil litigation, nor with that between the confidentiality interest and congressional demands for information, nor with the President's interest in preserving state secrets. We address only the conflict between the President's assertion of a generalized privilege of confidentiality and the constitutional need for relevant evidence in criminal trials.

the legislative branch? Consider in this regard the reaction of Senator Sam Ervin to the refusal of the federal courts to uphold the Senate committee's subpoenas:

> I submit that under our Constitution the power of a constitutionally created Senate committee to receive evidence relevant to an investigation it is conducting for legislative purposes is not dependent upon its satisfying the federal judiciary that its use of the evidence will serve the public interest or that it needs the evidence to perform its assigned task. These are matters for the determination of senators and not for judges.

SAM J. ERVIN, JR., THE WHOLE TRUTH: THE WATERGATE CONSPIRACY, at p. 9 (Random House 1980). To what extent does the legislative judgment as to the public interest merit judicial deference? *Cf. Chevron U.S.A., Inc. v. National Resources Defense Council*, 467 U.S. 837 (1984) (setting forth a deferential judicial approach to administrative agencies' interpretations of the laws they administer).

   2. Subpoena Enforcement Mechanisms: The Senate Suit. At the time the Ervin Committee issued its subpoena for the Nixon tapes and Nixon rebuffed the subpoena, there were two established legal procedures for enforcing subpoenas against recalcitrant witnesses—"self help" enforcement exercising a legislative body's "inherent" contempt power, in which the full House or Senate directs its sergeant at arms to arrest and imprison the recalcitrant party, and a criminal enforcement proceeding brought pursuant to a criminal contempt statute that Congress had first adopted in 1857, in which the full House or Senate refers a criminal contempt to the Department of Justice for prosecution. As Senate Watergate Committee counsel James Hamilton explained in his 1976 book *The Power to Probe*, neither of those approaches was viable when the recalcitrant subpoena recipient was the President of the United States:

> The committee could have instigated criminal contempt proceedings against the President. Several difficulties, however, hampered this course. The full Senate probably would not have supported such an attempt against the President. Substantial legal authority suggests that a President cannot be criminally tried before he is impeached; Special Prosecutor Jaworski subsequently adopted this position and instructed the grand jury investigating the Watergate cover-up not to indict Mr. Nixon while he was President. Also, a criminal contempt proceeding would have been a prolonged affair and would not have assured the committee prompt access to the materials it wanted. Perhaps most important, a criminal proceeding in the summer of 1973, when public outrage against President Nixon was not yet full-blown, appeared an unseemly course to take. A majority of the public probably would have opposed this tactic.
>
> The Senate has authority to dispatch its sergeant at arms to arrest and detain an individual who defies its process, but this alternative was obviously impractical. The sergeant at arms could not have reached the President, the public would have been incensed, and the full Senate, which must approve this procedure, would in all probability not have authorized its use.

The only feasible alternative, therefore, was to sue, although this choice also had its hazards. The committee was aware of the pitfalls, but, on Senator Howard Baker's motion, it voted without dissent to institute suit.

JAMES HAMILTON, THE POWER TO PROBE, at 27 (Random House 1976) (footnotes omitted). For a further explanation of the criminal contempt and self-help enforcement mechanisms available to the Ervin Committee, see *id.* at 85–97. Hamilton also recounted his personal experience of how the mere threat of the self-help enforcement remedy convinced a reluctant Alexander Butterfield to appear before the Ervin Committee:

> Ervin's rough persuasion also brought Alexander Butterfield to the witness table. Butterfield had told the committee's staff in executive session on Friday, July 16, 1973 [*sic*; the actual date was Friday, July 13, 1973], that President Nixon was taping his own conversations. On Monday, I was instructed to inform Butterfield that we wished his *public* testimony that very afternoon. Butterfield, preparing for a trip to Russia on FAA business, was, with some justification, infuriated by the short notice. In fact, he said, the pique evident in his voice, he would not appear.
>
> I reported Butterfield's retort to Senator Ervin, who was seated at the committee table listening to the testimony of Special Counsel to the President Richard Moore. Now, Ervin is not a man to be thwarted. As I conveyed Butterfield's response, the senator—his eyebrows cavorting and his jaws churning in anticipation of his next remark—grew visibly agitated. "Tell Mr. Butterfield," he said emphatically, "that if he is not here this afternoon I will send the sergeant at arms to fetch him." I faithfully relayed this declaration to Mr. Butterfield, whom I located in a barber's chair. Upon hearing Ervin's ultimatum, his defiance subsided. He would come, he said, as soon as he finished his haircut. Shortly after 1:30 p.m. he arrived—diffident, contrite, and nicely coiffed—to meet with Senators Ervin and Baker and staff. Later that afternoon he gave his electrifying testimony to the world.

Id. at 97.

Subsequent to Watergate, and in response to the jurisdictional difficulties identified by the federal courts in the Ervin Committee's Nixon tapes suit, Congress in 1978, as part of the Ethics in Government Act, adopted a new civil enforcement mechanism for Senate subpoenas, which authorizes the Senate Legal Counsel (a new staff office created in the aftermath of Watergate) to bring a civil suit in the U.S. District Court in the District of Columbia to enforce a Senate subpoena. *See* 2 U.S.C. §§288d and 28 U.S.C. 1365. That procedure applies only to Senate subpoenas, however, and not to House of Representatives subpoenas. Accordingly, the House of Representatives must rely on either self-help enforcement by the House sergeant at arms, which has not been used in recent decades, or the statutory criminal enforcement process, or file a civil suit in federal court seeking enforcement of its subpoena (as the House Judiciary Committee did in an effort to enforce its subpoenas to George W. Bush administration officials Joshua Bolten and Harriet Miers, discussed in Chapter 4 below).

The criminal enforcement process is not self-executing, however, because the U.S. Attorney to whom a criminal contempt citation is referred, who of course is an executive branch official, may decline to prosecute. (The issue of prosecutorial discretion to decline to prosecute a criminal contempt referral from Congress is discussed in Chapter 4.) The Department of Justice, through its Office of Legal Counsel, has adopted a policy of not prosecuting congressional contempt citations brought against executive branch officials who refuse to testify before Congress on the basis of instructions by the President to assert executive privilege. *See* Prosecution for the Contempt of Congress of an Executive Branch Official Who Has Asserted a Claim of Executive Privilege, 8 U.S. Op. Off. Legal Counsel 101 (1984); Response to Congressional Requests for Information Regarding Decisions Made Under the Independent Counsel Act, 10 U.S. Op. Off. Legal Counsel 68 (1986). For additional information on congressional subpoena enforcement procedures, see Morton Rosenberg & Todd B. Tatelman, *Congress's Contempt Power: A Sketch*, Congressional Research Service Report for Congress, Aug. 1, 2007; Louis Fisher, *Congressional Investigations: Subpoenas and Contempt Power*, Congressional Research Service Report for Congress, April 2, 2003. Criminal contempt prosecutions arising out of the House of Representatives investigation of the January 6, 2021, attack on the U.S. Capitol are discussed in Chapters 1 and 2.

3. Unintended Consequences: The Saturday Night Massacre. In the first round of judicial responses to the lawsuits brought to enforce the Nixon tapes subpoenas issued by the Ervin Committee and Watergate Special Prosecutor Cox, Judge Sirica ruled in favor of Cox's grand jury subpoena, but ruled against the Ervin Committee on jurisdictional grounds (see the discussion in Note 2 above on the statute that was subsequently enacted to give the Office of Senate Legal Counsel jurisdiction to bring civil enforcement proceedings for Senate subpoenas). President Nixon appealed Judge Sirica's decision to enforce the Cox subpoena, and on October 12, 1973, the U.S. Court of Appeals upheld Sirica, *Nixon v. Sirica*, 487 F.2d 700 (D.C. Cir. 1973). The ultimate outcome of the dispute over the Watergate Special Prosecutor's access to the Nixon tapes is the Supreme Court's unanimous 1974 decision in *United States v. Nixon*, excerpted above, but an event of epic historical magnitude occurred between the Court of Appeals decision on the first Cox subpoena and the subsequent Supreme Court decision upholding the special prosecutor's trial subpoena for additional tapes. Rather than submit to the Court of Appeals order to produce the subpoenaed tapes to the Watergate grand jury, President Nixon chose to order Attorney General Elliot Richardson to dismiss Cox. Richardson resigned rather than fire Cox, followed by the simultaneous resignation and dismissal of Deputy Attorney General William Ruckelshaus, who also refused to fire Cox. Solicitor General Robert Bork, who was next in line in seniority at the Justice Department, carried out Nixon's order and fired Cox. Those events—now known as the "Saturday Night Massacre"—resulted in a public backlash against Nixon the likes of which no President before or since has ever known.[17] Here, in notably detached and clinical prose, is the account of the Saturday Night Massacre and its aftermath provided in the Watergate Special Prosecution Force Report:

Dean's guilty plea and agreement to cooperate with the prosecutors came October 19, the last day for the President to seek Supreme Court review of the decision ordering him to produce the tapes. Instead of asking the Supreme Court to hear the case, he announced a proposed compromise: Senator John Stennis would listen to the tapes and review a statement of their contents; if verified by Stennis the statement would then be given to the Special Prosecutor and the grand jury. Under an integral part of the proposal, Cox would agree not to litigate further with respect to the nine tapes or to seek additional tapes in the future.

In a news conference the following day, Cox stated his reasons for not accepting the proposal. Edited summaries, he noted, probably would not be admissible as evidence in court. His agreement not to seek additional tapes would prevent WSPF from conducting its investigations thoroughly. And the order to accept the compromise terms, he said, was inconsistent with the pledge of independence he had received from Attorney General Richardson at the time of his appointment.

That evening, October 20, the White House announced the events that came to be known as the "Saturday Night Massacre": President Nixon ordered Attorney General Richardson to dismiss Cox for his refusal to accept the White House proposal; Richardson resigned rather than carry out the order, and Deputy Attorney General William Ruckelshaus was fired for his refusal to obey; finally, Solicitor General Robert Bork, next in seniority at the Justice Department, dismissed Cox as Special Prosecutor. Also on White House orders, agents of the FBI occupied the offices of WSPF, the Attorney General, and the Deputy Attorney General in order to prevent the removal of any documents. WSPF staff members, gathered in their offices, were informed that they would work henceforth as part of the Justice Department's Criminal Division.

* * *

The "Saturday Night Massacre" did not halt the work of WSPF, and the prosecutors resumed their grand jury sessions as scheduled the following Tuesday. Bork placed Assistant Attorney General Henry Petersen, head of the Criminal Division, in charge of the investigations WSPF had been conducting. Both men assured the staff that its work would continue with the cooperation of the Justice Department and without interference from the White House. Upon WSPF's request, Judge Sirica issued a protective order to limit access to,

---

17. For a summary of the public and Congressional reaction to Cox's firing, see the Watergate Special Prosecution Force Report at 184–85 (October 1975).

and prevent removal of, WSPF files. Despite their anger over Cox's dismissal and their doubts about the future of their office, the staff members, in a series of meetings, decided to continue their work for the time being.

Nevertheless, the dismissal of Cox and the President's refusal to produce the subpoenaed tapes provoked what one White House official called a "firestorm" of public criticism and serious talk of impeachment on Capitol Hill. In an abrupt reversal, the President announced on October 23 that he would comply with the grand jury subpoena and on October 26 that Bork would appoint a new Special Prosecutor who would have "total cooperation from the executive branch." While the President said he would be unwilling to produce additional White House tapes or other evidence that he considered privileged, he placed no restrictions on the new Special Prosecutor's authority to seek such evidence through the courts.

On November 1, the President announced that he would nominate Senator William B. Saxbe as the new Attorney General. Later that day, Acting Attorney General Bork announced his appointment of Leon Jaworski as Special Prosecutor. Jaworski, who was sworn into office November 5, was assured the same jurisdiction and guarantees of independence as Cox, with the additional provision that he could be dismissed, or his jurisdiction limited, only with consent of a bipartisan group of eight Congressional leaders. Three days after taking office, Jaworski told a House subcommittee that the continuity of WSPF operations had been restored and that the office's staff would remain intact.

Watergate Special Prosecution Force Report at 9–11 (October 1975).

More than any other event, the Saturday Night Massacre undermined public confidence in Nixon and paved the way for the impeachment proceedings in the House of Representatives that led to his resignation. What role did the contemporaneous Senate Watergate hearings play in shaping the public reaction to the Saturday Night Massacre? Senate Watergate Committee chief counsel Sam Dash has written that Nixon might well have succeeded in his containment strategy if not for the Committee's hearings:

> The irony is that Nixon would have succeeded had there been no Senate Watergate hearings that summer. To the uninformed public, the firing of the Special Prosecutor would have been just another political donnybrook in Washington. But, as the hearings progressed, the facts of the Watergate conspiracy and cover-up outraged the public; they came to understand how corrupt Nixon's firing of Cox really was. Millions of Americans wrote, called or telegraphed their outrage to the White House and Congress. This public outcry, then referred to as the "firestorm," was so fierce that Nixon was forced to appoint another special prosecutor, Leon Jaworski, to pick up where Cox left off.

Sam Dash, *Independent Counsel: No More, No Less a Federal Prosecutor*, 86 GEO. L. J. 2077, 2078 (1998). Do you agree with Dash's assessment of the importance of the Senate hearings in influencing public reaction to the Saturday Night Massacre? In light of the contents of the tapes, was it inevitable that some kind of "showdown" would occur between Nixon and those who were investigating Watergate? Did Nixon choose wisely in deciding to draw the line at Cox's subpoena? What alternatives did he have? Would the eventual outcome have been the same if he had produced the tapes and then, after indictments were brought, pardoned his subordinates who were criminally charged? Would the public outcry have been even greater if, rather than firing Cox, he had chosen to destroy the tapes on the grounds that it was not in the national interest to have them made public? With regard to this question, consider the public reaction to the discovery of the "18½ minute gap" in the tape of a June 20, 1972, conversation between Nixon and Haldeman, discussed in Note 5 below. Which course of action might have best preserved Nixon's ability to prevail if he was later impeached? Impeachment is discussed further in Chapter 7.

4. Presidential Machinations: The So-Called "Stennis Compromise." As the excerpt above from the Watergate Special Prosecution Force Report indicates, President Nixon attempted to avoid disclosure of the contents of his presidential tapes by offering the "Stennis compromise" in which Senator John C. Stennis, Democrat of Mississippi, would listen to the tapes and confirm the accuracy of Nixon-prepared summaries of the tapes. Nixon proposed that the summaries, verified by Stennis, would then be provided to the Ervin Committee and Special Prosecutor Cox. Nixon's choice of Stennis for this task was controversial and more than a little suspect. Although he was a Democrat, Stennis had been a strong supporter of Nixon to that point in the Watergate controversy. In addition, at the time he was proposed as an auditor of the accuracy of the tapes summaries, he was seventy-two years old, had poor hearing, and was recovering from gunshot injuries to the head that he had suffered as the victim of a robbery attempt. For additional details on the Stennis proposal and the response of the Watergate Special Prosecution Force to that proposal, see RICHARD BEN-VENISTE & GEORGE FRAMPTON, STONEWALL: THE REAL STORY OF THE WATERGATE PROSECUTION, at 129–30 (Simon & Schuster 1977).

Nixon's machinations did not end with whatever deficiencies Stennis might have brought to the role of a neutral and competent arbiter of the tapes' content, however. He also attempted to ratchet up the pressure on Cox by summoning Senators Baker and Ervin to the White House on Friday, October 19, 1973, and offered some version of the Stennis compromise to them (later accounts suggest that Nixon may have offered materially different versions to Stennis, to Cox through Attorney General Richardson, and to Senators Baker and Ervin at the October 19 meeting). In any event, after the meeting Nixon issued a statement that Baker and Ervin had agreed to his proposal, which had the effect of significantly increasing the pressure on Cox to accept the proposal. The next day Cox held his famous press conference at the National Press Club in Washington at which, after assuring the assembled press that he was not "out to get" President Nixon, Cox explained why he could not accept Nixon's proposal. The events now known as the "Saturday Night Massacre" followed.

What was Nixon seeking to do in putting forth the Stennis Compromise? Based upon what you now know of the contents of the tapes, do you think Nixon ever would actually have provided them to Senator Stennis? How does the analysis differ between the Watergate Special Prosecutor and the Senate Watergate Committee in terms of their ability to accept anything other than the actual tapes of the disputed conversations? Senator Ervin recalled that he and Senator Baker were offered transcripts of the relevant portions of the tapes, verified by Senator Stennis, and not summaries, and that he and Senator Baker, in their meeting with Nixon, did not accept the proposal and agreed only to present the proposal to their committee. *See* Sam J. Ervin, Jr., The Whole Truth: The Watergate Conspiracy, at 228–41 (Random House 1980). What is the significance of the distinction between transcripts and summaries of the taped conversations? Would either have been adequate for the Senate committee? Could the Watergate grand jury have accepted either transcripts or summaries in lieu of the actual tapes? What difficulties would have been presented at subsequent Watergate criminal trials if the grand jury had based indictments on either verified transcripts or summaries rather than the actual tapes?

5. Mysterious Deletions: The 18½ Minute Gap and the Sinister Force. The legal and political drama surrounding the Nixon tapes did not end when the subpoenaed tapes were eventually produced to the Watergate grand jury. In a turn of events that caused further erosion of public confidence in President Nixon, on November 21, 1973, White House Counsel Fred Buzhardt met with Judge Sirica and the Watergate special prosecutors to disclose a new problem with the tapes:

> At that meeting, Buzhardt announced that the subpoenaed tape of a conversation between President Nixon and H.R. Haldeman on June 20, 1972–3 days after the Watergate break-in—had been obliterated inexplicably by a buzzing sound lasting 18½ minutes. Haldeman's notes of that meeting indicated that the obliterated portion of the tape covered only that part of the conversation which was related to the break-in.
>
> The discovery of this tape gap led Judge Sirica to reopen the hearings [previously convened to determine why two other subpoenaed conversations had not been tape recorded], which continued for 7 days in late November and early December. The President's secretary, Rose Mary Woods, testified at the public hearing that she might have accidentally erased 4 or 5 minutes of the conversation. She explained that this possible erasure occurred when she inadvertently left her foot on the pedal controlling the tape recorder while answering the telephone and conducting a conversation. In addition to Ms. Woods' testimony, other White House aides, attorneys, and Secret Service personnel answered questions about the storage of the tape, the methods used to transcribe it, who had access to it, and the discovery of the gap. Testimony and access logs kept by custodians of the tapes revealed that, after being recorded, this tape had been routinely placed in a storage vault and not disturbed until September 28, 1973, two months after it had been subpoenaed by the grand jury. Any mishandling of the tape appeared to have occurred between that date and the discovery of the gap by White House counsel on November 14, 1973.

In a further effort to ascertain the cause of the 18½ minute gap, the court appointed a panel of six experts in acoustics and sound engineering approved by the White House and the WSPF. The panel was asked to determine the method by which the gap had been created, the kind of machine that had been used to create it, and the existence of any possibility of recovering the conversation. The experts began various tests on the tape early in December in the presence of representatives of the White House and WSPF. Their report, delivered to the court January 15, 1974, concluded that the gap had been produced by at least five separate hand operations of the stop and record buttons of a Uher 5000 machine, the same model used by Woods in transcribing the tape. The panel also concluded that recovery of the obliterated conversation would be impossible.

Since the experts' report made it clear that the gap had been caused by intentional erasures, and evidence produced at the hearings showed that the erasures had occurred after the tape had been subpoenaed, Judge Sirica referred the matter to the grand jury for further investigation of the possibility of obstruction of justice. A grand jury, assisted by WSPF and the FBI, began hearing witnesses January 28, 1974. It concluded from the testimony of over 50 people that a very small number of persons could have been responsible for the erasures, but it was unable to obtain evidence sufficient to prosecute any individual.

Watergate Special Prosecution Force Report, at 52 (October 1975).

This scrupulously factual and neutral account of the saga of the 18½ minute gap fails to capture the full flavor of the political and public opinion impact of the events. First, the White House offered the explanation that at least part of the erasure had occurred when Nixon's personal secretary Rose Mary Woods answered a telephone call while in the midst of transcribing the tape. Woods testified that when she answered the telephone she must have inadvertently both pushed the "record" button, rather than the "stop" button, and continued to press the foot pedal that kept the tape moving while speaking on the telephone. The efforts of Woods to recreate this unlikely chain of events, both in Judge Sirica's courtroom and a photographed session at her office in the White House, were met with widespread skepticism by the press and the public. The photographs of "the Rose Mary stretch" that appeared on the newspaper front pages further contributed to public skepticism of this White House explanation. For additional details on the discovery of the 18½ minute gap and the court inquiry into it, see RICHARD BEN-VENISTE & GEORGE FRAMPTON, STONEWALL: THE REAL STORY OF THE WATERGATE PROSECUTION, at 174–86 (Simon & Schuster 1977).

The Rose Mary Woods testimony was not the only public relations disaster for the Nixon White House that resulted from the judicial hearings that Judge Sirica conducted to investigate the 18½ minute tape gap. Another headline-generating event took place during the testimony of Nixon's new chief of staff (following Haldeman's ouster), Alexander Haig. Haig tried to rebut any suggestion that someone other than Rose Mary Woods was responsible for the 18½ minute erasure, dismissing a "devil theory" that some "sinister force" was responsible for the lengthy gap. *See* Ben-Veniste & Frampton, *supra* at 181–82. Subsequent analysis of the erased tapes by a panel of experts appointed by Judge Sirica and approved by both the Nixon White House and the Watergate Special Prosecutor indicated that the erasures were caused by the hand-operated tape recorder controls, not the foot pedal that Rose Mary Woods used when transcribing tapes, and that the 18½ minute gap was "caused by *at least five* distinct segments of erasure." *Id.* Haig's "sinister force" comment did not have the effect that he presumably intended, as it managed to both undermine the White House effort to explain the mysterious gap while also focusing unfavorable attention on what role President Nixon may have played in the erasure.

Only President Nixon and a very few of his aides had access to the tape. Neither the Watergate special prosecutors nor the subsequent House of Representatives impeachment proceedings were able to obtain sufficient evidence to accuse Nixon or any other individual of deliberately erasing the tape.

6. Aftermath: House Impeachment Hearings and Nixon's Resignation. The cumulative effect of Dean's Senate testimony, the Saturday Night Massacre, and the 18½ minute tape gap was a substantial erosion of political support for President Nixon. That erosion manifested itself in the impeachment proceedings against President Nixon that led to his resignation on August 9, 1974. The Nixon impeachment proceedings are discussed in Chapter 7.

7. Historical Perspective: The "Third-Rate Burglary" Label. The Watergate scandal encompassed a complex sequence of events that presented a host of difficult legal and constitutional issues. For that reason, it is difficult to summarize "Watergate" with the description of a single event, such as the actual Watergate break-in, or action, such as Nixon's "Saturday Night Massacre" dismissal of Archibald Cox. As noted in the text above, the Nixon White House steadfastly sought to maintain that, in the words of Nixon press secretary Ronald Ziegler, the Watergate break-in was nothing more than "a third-rate burglary." The "third-rate burglary" label continued to stick, however, even after the full range of Watergate activities and the degree of President Nixon's involvement in those activities had been exposed. The Watergate prosecutor who headed up the cover-up investigation recently sought to dispel the notion that Watergate was nothing more than a third-rate burglary:

> The break-in and burglary of the Democratic National Committee's head-quarters at the Watergate office building on June 17, 1972, was not the isolated and loopy "third-rate burglary" portrayed by the Nixon administration's spin control managers. It was a significant violation of law authorized by Nixon insiders at the highest level—if not the president himself—to *continue* illegal electronic eavesdropping and photographing of confidential records. For the same team had previously broken into the same DNC office; the June 17 break-in was supposed to replace a malfunctioning bug from the earlier intrusion.
>
> Indeed, it is a tribute to the skill of the Nixon spinmeisters that their "third-rate burglary" tag—coined to deflect attention from the higher-ups in-

volved—endures. The Watergate break-in was just one link in a chain of abuses that Nixon Attorney General John Mitchell aptly dubbed the "White House horrors." These included the break-in at a psychiatrist's office looking for information that could be used to smear Daniel Ellsberg, who had exposed the secret government history of the Vietnam War known as the Pentagon Papers; the misuse of the Internal Revenue Service and other federal agencies to punish those on the president's "enemies list;" the illegal wiretapping of journalists and members of Nixon's own administration; the deliberate falsification of government documents to enhance Nixon's political agenda; the proposed fire-bombing of the Brookings Institution as a diversion for the theft of documents; the surreptitious surveillance of political opponents; and the hiring of thugs to brutalize political protesters.

The subsequent cover-up was not an irrational reaction to an insignificant, stupid break-in. Rather, it was a reflexive attempt to counter the threat that the administration's widespread abuses of governmental authority would be exposed once investigators began asking questions. Nixon's imperial view of the presidency had encouraged a competition among his lieutenants. They catered to his dark side, disregarding legal boundaries to strike at and punish his adversaries and critics. As the cover-up unraveled, facts emerged about the extent of Nixon's willingness to misuse his power to prevent the truth from coming out. Nixon directed the deputy director of the CIA to tell the FBI, falsely, that the country's national security would be jeopardized by a full investigation of the money trail left by the Watergate burglars. Several of Nixon's top advisers committed perjury, including John Mitchell, who had been the nation's chief legal officer, as well as Nixon's chief of staff, H.R. Haldeman. There was more. Offers of presidential clemency were dangled before certain members of the burglary team, and all were paid significant sums of hush money from a secret slush fund—financed by campaign contributions controlled by the president and Haldeman and delivered by the president's personal attorney.

RICHARD BEN-VENISTE, THE EMPEROR'S NEW CLOTHES: EXPOSING TRUTH FROM WATERGATE TO 9/11 23–24 (St. Martin's Press 2009).

The Legacy of Watergate— From Reagan to Clinton to Trump

Watergate was arguably the most important and influential political and constitutional crisis of the latter twentieth century. It resulted in the only resignation by a President in American political history, and it provided the template for intense partisan political warfare that took place during subsequent presidential administrations, particularly the Reagan, Clinton, and Trump administrations. After Watergate, criminal investigations of sitting Presidents became almost commonplace, with Department of Justice special/independent counsels heading criminal probes that lasted years and dominated national news coverage. The Iran-Contra investigation of the Reagan administration, discussed in Chapter 5, led to criminal prosecutions of officials in the Reagan White House and highly publicized congressional hearings. The Whitewater investigation during the Clinton administration, discussed in Chapter 6, ultimately led to the impeachment of President Clinton, discussed in Chapter 7, albeit for matters that had little or no relationship to the original Whitewater investigation.

As significant as these investigations may have been, and it is difficult to overstate their political and historical importance, they did not result in another Supreme Court decision addressing a President's exposure to criminal investigation while in office.[18] The Nixon tapes case, discussed above, remained the leading Supreme Court authority for the remainder of the twentieth century and well into the twenty-first, until the administration of President Donald Trump, when the Supreme Court was called upon to decide whether a sitting President can be subject to a criminal investigation conducted by state prosecutors:

Trump v. Vance
591 U.S. ___, 140 S. Ct. 2412 (2020)
[Footnotes omitted except as indicated.]

CHIEF JUSTICE ROBERTS delivered the opinion of the Court.

In our judicial system, "the public has a right to every man's evidence." Since the earliest days of the Republic, "every man" has included the President of the United States. Beginning with Jefferson and carrying on through Clinton, Presidents have uniformly testified or produced documents in criminal proceedings when called upon by federal courts. This case involves—so far as we and the parties can tell—the first state criminal subpoena directed to a President. The President contends that the subpoena is unenforceable. We granted certiorari to decide whether Article II and the Supremacy Clause categorically preclude, or require a heightened standard for, the issuance of a state criminal subpoena to a sitting President.

I

In the summer of 2018, the New York County District Attorney's Office opened an investigation into what it opaquely describes as "business transactions involving multiple individuals whose conduct may have violated state law." Brief for Respondent Vance 2. A year later, the office—acting on behalf of a grand jury—served a subpoena *duces tecum* (essentially a request to produce evidence) on Mazars USA, LLP, the personal accounting firm of President Donald J. Trump. The subpoena directed Mazars to

---

18. During the Clinton administration, the Supreme Court ruled that a sitting President can be subject to a private civil lawsuit in federal court for alleged misconduct before becoming president, *see Clinton v. Jones*, 520 U.S. 681 (1997), but that case did not address criminal investigation or prosecution of a sitting President. See Chapters 4 and 9 for additional discussion and analysis of the separation of powers and other constitutional and legal issues arising out of criminal and congressional investigations of a sitting President.

produce financial records relating to the President and business organizations affiliated with him, including "[t]ax returns and related schedules," from "2011 to the present."

The President, acting in his personal capacity, sued the district attorney and Mazars in Federal District Court to enjoin enforcement of the subpoena. He argued that, under Article II and the Supremacy Clause, a sitting President enjoys absolute immunity from state criminal process. He asked the court to issue a "declaratory judgment that the subpoena is invalid and unenforceable while the President is in office" and to permanently enjoin the district attorney "from taking any action to enforce the subpoena." Amended Complaint in No. 1:19-cv-8694 (SDNY, Sept. 25, 2019), p. 19. Mazars, concluding that the dispute was between the President and the district attorney, took no position on the legal issues raised by the President.

[*Ed. Note: The Court described the procedural history of the case.*]

II

In the summer of 1807, all eyes were on Richmond, Virginia. Aaron Burr, the former Vice President, was on trial for treason. Fallen from political grace after his fatal duel with Alexander Hamilton, and with a murder charge pending in New Jersey, Burr followed the path of many down-and-out Americans of his day—he headed West in search of new opportunity. But Burr was a man with outsized ambitions. Together with General James Wilkinson, the Governor of the Louisiana Territory, he hatched a plan to establish a new territory in Mexico, then controlled by Spain. Both men anticipated that war between the United States and Spain was imminent, and when it broke out they intended to invade Spanish territory at the head of a private army.

But while Burr was rallying allies to his cause, tensions with Spain eased and rumors began to swirl that Burr was conspiring to detach States by the Allegheny Mountains from the Union. Wary of being exposed as the principal coconspirator, Wilkinson took steps to ensure that any blame would fall on Burr. He sent a series of letters to President Jefferson accusing Burr of plotting to attack New Orleans and revolutionize the Louisiana Territory.

Jefferson, who despised his former running mate Burr for trying to steal the 1800 presidential election from him, was predisposed to credit Wilkinson's version of events. The President sent a special message to Congress identifying Burr as the "prime mover" in a plot "against the peace and safety of the Union." 16 Annals of Cong. 39–40 (1807). According to Jefferson, Burr contemplated either the "severance of the Union" or an attack on Spanish territory. *Id.*, at 41. Jefferson acknowledged that his sources contained a "mixture of rumors, conjectures, and suspicions" but, citing Wilkinson's letters, he assured Congress that Burr's guilt was "beyond question." *Id.*, at 39–40.

The trial that followed was "the greatest spectacle in the short history of the republic," complete with a Founder-studded cast. N. Isenberg, Fallen Founder: The Life of Aaron Burr 351 (2007). People flocked to Richmond to watch, massing in tents and covered wagons along the banks of the James River, nearly doubling the town's population of 5,000. Burr's defense team included Edmund Randolph and Luther Martin, both former delegates at the Constitutional Convention and renowned advocates. Chief Justice John Marshall, who had recently squared off with the Jefferson administration in *Marbury v. Madison*, 1 Cranch 137 (1803), presided as Circuit Justice for Virginia. Meanwhile Jefferson, intent on conviction, orchestrated the prosecution from afar, dedicating Cabinet meetings to the case, peppering the prosecutors with directions, and spending nearly $100,000 from the Treasury on the five-month proceedings.

In the lead-up to trial, Burr, taking aim at his accusers, moved for a subpoena *duces tecum* directed at Jefferson. The draft subpoena required the President to produce an October 21, 1806 letter from Wilkinson and accompanying documents, which Jefferson had referenced in his message to Congress. The prosecution opposed the request, arguing that a President could not be subjected to such a subpoena and that the letter might contain state secrets. Following four days of argument, Marshall announced his ruling to a packed chamber.

The President, Marshall declared, does not "stand exempt from the general provisions of the constitution" or, in particular, the Sixth Amendment's guarantee that those accused have compulsory process for obtaining witnesses for their defense. *United States v. Burr*, 25 F. Cas. 30, 33–34 (No. 14,692d) (CC Va. 1807). At common law the "single reservation" to the duty to testify in response to a subpoena was "the case of the king," whose "dignity" was seen as "incompatible" with appearing "under the process of the court." *Id.*, at 34. But, as Marshall explained, a king is born to power and can "do no wrong." *Ibid.* The President, by contrast, is "of the people" and subject to the law. *Ibid.* According to Marshall, the sole argument for exempting the President from testimonial obligations was that his "duties as chief magistrate demand his whole time for national objects." *Ibid.* But, in Marshall's assessment, those demands were "not unremitting." *Ibid.* And should the President's duties preclude his attendance at a particular time and place, a court could work that out upon return of the subpoena. *Ibid.*

Marshall also rejected the prosecution's argument that the President was immune from a subpoena *duces tecum* because executive papers might contain state secrets. "A subpoena *duces tecum*," he said, "may issue to any person to whom an ordinary subpoena may issue." *Ibid.* As he explained, no "fair construction" of the Constitution supported the conclusion that the right "to compel the attendance of witnesses[] does not extend" to requiring those witnesses to "bring[] with them such papers as may be material in the defence." *Id.*, at 35. And, as a matter of basic fairness, permitting such information to be withheld would "tarnish the reputation of the court." *Id.*, at 37. As for "the propriety of introducing any papers," that would "depend on the character of the paper, not on the character of the person who holds it." *Id.*, at 34. Marshall acknowledged that the papers sought by Burr could contain information "the disclosure of which would endanger the public safety," but stated that, again, such concerns would have "due consideration" upon the return of the subpoena. *Id.*, at 37.

* * *

In the two centuries since the Burr trial, successive Presidents have accepted Marshall's ruling that the Chief Executive is subject to subpoena. In 1818, President Monroe received a subpoena to testify in a court-martial against one of his appointees. *See* Rotunda, *Presidents and Ex-Presidents as Witnesses: A Brief Historical Footnote*, 1975 U. Ill. L. Forum 1, 5. His Attorney General, William Wirt—who had served as a prosecutor during Burr's trial—advised Monroe that, per Marshall's ruling, a subpoena to testify may "be properly awarded to the President." *Id.*, at 5–6. Monroe offered to sit for a deposition and ultimately submitted answers to written interrogatories.

Following Monroe's lead, his successors have uniformly agreed to testify when called in criminal proceedings, provided they could do so at a time and place of their choosing. In 1875, President Grant submitted to a three-hour deposition in the criminal prosecution of a political appointee embroiled in a network of tax-evading whiskey distillers. See 1 R. Rotunda & J. Nowak, Constitutional Law §7.1(b)(ii), p. 996 (5th ed. 2012) (Rotunda & Nowak). A century later, President Ford's attempted assassin subpoenaed him to testify in her defense. *See United States v. Fromme*, 405 F. Supp. 578 (ED Cal. 1975). Ford obliged—from a safe distance—in the first videotaped deposition of a President. President Carter testified via the same means in the trial of two local officials who, while Carter was Governor of Georgia, had offered to contribute to his campaign in exchange for advance warning of any state gambling raids. See *Carter's Testimony, on Videotape, Is Given to Georgia Gambling Trial*, N.Y. Times, Apr. 20, 1978, p. A20 (Carter recounted that he "rejected the proposition instantly."). Two years later, Carter gave videotaped testimony to a federal grand jury investigating whether a fugitive financier had entreated the White House to quash his extradition proceedings. *See* Rotunda & Nowak §7.1(b)(vi), at 997. President Clinton testified three times, twice via deposition pursuant to subpoenas in federal criminal trials of associates implicated during the Whitewater investigation, and once by video for a grand jury investigating possible perjury. *See id.*, §7.1(c)(viii), at 1007–1008.

The bookend to Marshall's ruling came in 1974 when the question he never had to decide—whether to compel the disclosure of official communications over the objection of the President—came to a head. That spring, the Special Prosecutor appointed to investigate the break-in of the Democratic National Committee Headquarters at the Watergate complex filed an indictment charging seven defendants associated with President Nixon and naming Nixon as an unindicted co-conspirator. As the case moved toward trial, the Special Prosecutor secured a subpoena *duces tecum* directing Nixon to produce, among other things, tape recordings of Oval Office meetings. Nixon moved to quash the subpoena, claiming that the Constitution provides an absolute privilege of confidentiality to all presidential communications. This Court rejected that argument in *United States v. Nixon*, 418 U.S. 683 (1974), a decision we later described as "unequivocally and emphatically endors[ing] Marshall's" holding that Presidents are subject to subpoena. *Clinton v. Jones*, 520 U.S. 681, 704 (1997).

* * *

The Court thus concluded that the President's "generalized assertion of privilege must yield to the demonstrated, specific need for evidence in a pending criminal trial." *Id.*, at 713. Two weeks later, President Nixon dutifully released the tapes.

III

The history surveyed above all involved federal criminal proceedings. Here we are confronted for the first time with a subpoena issued to the President by a local grand jury operating under the supervision of a state court.

In the President's view, that distinction makes all the difference. He argues that the Supremacy Clause gives a sitting President absolute immunity from state criminal subpoenas because compliance with those subpoenas would categorically impair a President's performance of his Article II functions. The Solicitor General, arguing on behalf of the United States, agrees with much of the President's reasoning but does not commit to his bottom line. Instead, the Solicitor General urges us to resolve this case by holding that a state grand jury subpoena for a sitting President's personal records must, at the very least, "satisfy a heightened standard of need," which the Solicitor General contends was not met here.

A

We begin with the question of absolute immunity. No one doubts that Article II guarantees the independence of the Executive Branch. As the head of that branch, the President "occupies a unique position in the constitutional scheme." *Nixon v. Fitzgerald*, 457 U.S. 731, 749 (1982). His duties, which range from faithfully executing the laws to commanding the Armed Forces, are of unrivaled gravity and breadth. Quite appropriately, those duties come with protections that safeguard the President's ability to perform his vital functions. *See, e.g., ibid.* (concluding that the President enjoys "absolute immunity from damages liability predicated on his official acts"); *Nixon*, 418 U.S., at 708 (recognizing that presidential communications are presumptively privileged).

In addition, the Constitution guarantees "the entire independence of the General Government from any control by the respective States." *Farmers and Mechanics Sav. Bank of Minneapolis v. Minnesota*, 232 U.S. 516, 521 (1914). As we have often repeated, "States have no power ... to retard, impede, burden, or in any manner control the operations of the constitutional laws enacted by Congress." *McCulloch v. Maryland*, 4 Wheat. 316, 436 (1819). It follows that States also lack the power to impede the President's execution of those laws.

Marshall's ruling in *Burr*, entrenched by 200 years of practice and our decision in *Nixon*, confirms that federal criminal subpoenas do not "rise to the level of constitutionally forbidden impairment of the Executive's ability to perform its constitutionally mandated functions." *Clinton*, 520 U.S., at 702–703. But the President, joined in part by the Solicitor General, argues that state criminal subpoenas pose a unique threat of impairment and thus demand greater protection. To be clear, the President does not contend here that this subpoena, in particular, is impermissibly burdensome. Instead he makes a categorical argument about the burdens generally associated with state criminal subpoenas, focusing on three: diversion, stigma, and harassment. We address each in turn.

* * *

The President, however, believes the district attorney is investigating him and his businesses. In such a situation, he contends, the "toll that criminal process ... exacts from the President is even heavier" than the distraction at issue in *Fitzgerald* and *Clinton*, because "criminal litigation" poses unique burdens on the President's time and will generate a "considerable if not overwhelming degree of mental preoccupation."

But the President is not seeking immunity from the diversion occasioned by the prospect of future criminal liability. Instead he concedes—consistent with the position of the Department of Justice—that state grand juries are free to investigate a sitting President with an eye toward charging him after the completion of his term. *See* Reply Brief 19 (citing Memorandum from Randolph D. Moss, Assistant Atty. Gen., Office of Legal Counsel, to the Atty. Gen.: A Sitting President's Amenability to Indictment and Criminal Prosecution, 24 Op. OLC 222, 257, n. 36 (Oct. 16, 2000)). The President's objection therefore must be limited to the additional distraction caused by the subpoena itself. But that argument runs up against the 200 years of precedent establishing that Presidents, and their official communications, are subject to judicial process, *see Burr*, 25 F. Cas., at 34, even when the President is under investigation, *see Nixon*, 418 U.S., at 706.

The President next claims that the stigma of being subpoenaed will undermine his leadership at home and abroad. Notably, the Solicitor General does not endorse this argument, perhaps because we have twice denied absolute immunity claims by Presidents in cases involving allegations of serious misconduct. *See Clinton*, 520 U.S., at 685; *Nixon*, 418 U.S., at 687. But even if a tarnished reputation were a cognizable impairment, there is nothing inherently stigmatizing about a President performing "the citizen's normal duty of ... furnishing information relevant" to a criminal investigation. *Branzburg v. Hayes*, 408 U.S. 665, 691 (1972). Nor can we accept that the risk of association with persons or activities under criminal investigation can absolve a President of such an important public duty. Prior Presidents have weathered these associations in federal cases, and there is no reason to think any attendant notoriety is necessarily greater in state court proceedings.

* * *

Finally, the President and the Solicitor General warn that subjecting Presidents to state criminal subpoenas will make them "easily identifiable target[s]" for harassment. *Fitzgerald*, 457 U.S., at 753. But we rejected a nearly identical argument in *Clinton*, where then-President Clinton argued that permitting civil liability for unofficial acts would "generate a large volume of politically motivated harassing and frivolous litigation." *Clinton*, 520 U.S., at 708. The President and the Solicitor General nevertheless argue that state criminal subpoenas pose a heightened risk and could undermine the President's ability to "deal fearlessly and impartially" with the States. *Fitzgerald*, 457 U.S., at 752 (internal quotation marks omitted). They caution that, while federal prosecutors are accountable to and removable by the President, the 2,300 district attorneys in this country are responsive to local constituencies, local interests, and local prejudices, and might "use criminal process to register their dissatisfaction with" the President.

Brief for Petitioner 16. What is more, we are told, the state courts supervising local grand juries may not exhibit the same respect that federal courts show to the President as a coordinate branch of Government.

We recognize, as does the district attorney, that harassing subpoenas could, under certain circumstances, threaten the independence or effectiveness of the Executive. Even so, in *Clinton* we found that the risk of harassment was not "serious" because federal courts have the tools to deter and, where necessary, dismiss vexatious civil suits. 520 U.S., at 708. And, while we cannot ignore the possibility that state prosecutors may have political motivations, here again the law already seeks to protect against the predicted abuse.

* * * We generally "assume[] that state courts and prosecutors will observe constitutional limitations." *Dombrowski v. Pfister*, 380 U.S. 479, 484 (1965). Failing that, federal law allows a President to challenge any allegedly unconstitutional influence in a federal forum, as the President has done here. *See* 42 U.S.C. §1983; *Ex parte Young*, 209 U.S. 123, 155–156 (1908) (holding that federal courts may enjoin state officials to conform their conduct to federal law).

Given these safeguards and the Court's precedents, we cannot conclude that absolute immunity is necessary or appropriate under Article II or the Supremacy Clause. Our dissenting colleagues agree. Justice Thomas reaches the same conclusion based on the original understanding of the Constitution reflected in Marshall's decision in *Burr*. And Justice Alito, also persuaded by *Burr*, "agree[s]" that "not all" state criminal subpoenas for a President's records "should be barred." On that point the Court is unanimous.

We next consider whether a state grand jury subpoena seeking a President's private papers must satisfy a heightened need standard. The Solicitor General would require a threshold showing that the evidence sought is "critical" for "specific charging decisions" and that the subpoena is a "last resort," meaning the evidence is "not available from any other source" and is needed "now, rather than at the end of the President's term." Brief for United States as Amicus Curiae 29, 32 (internal quotation marks and alteration omitted). Justice Alito, largely embracing those criteria, agrees that a state criminal subpoena to a President "should not be allowed unless a heightened standard is met." *Post* (asking whether the information is "critical" and "necessary ... now").

We disagree, for three reasons. First, such a heightened standard would extend protection designed for official documents to the President's private papers. As the Solicitor General and Justice Alito acknowledge, their proposed test is derived from executive privilege cases that trace back to *Burr*. Brief for United States as Amicus Curiae 26–28; *post*, at 17. There, Marshall explained that if Jefferson invoked presidential privilege over executive communications, the court would not "proceed against the president as against an ordinary individual" but would instead require an affidavit from the defense that "would clearly show the paper to be essential to the justice of the case." *Burr*, 25 F. Cas., at 192. The Solicitor General and Justice Alito would have us apply a similar standard to a President's personal papers. But this argument does not account for the relevant passage from *Burr*: "If there be a paper in the possession of the executive, *which is not of an official nature*, he must stand, as respects that paper, in nearly the same situation with any other individual." *Id.*, at 191 (emphasis added). And it is only "nearly"—and not "entirely"—because the President retains the right to assert privilege over documents that, while ostensibly private, "partake of the character of an official paper." *Id.*, at 191–192.

Second, neither the Solicitor General nor Justice Alito has established that heightened protection against state subpoenas is necessary for the Executive to fulfill his Article II functions. Beyond the risk of harassment, which we addressed above, the only justification they offer for the heightened standard is protecting Presidents from "unwarranted burdens." In effect, they argue that even if federal subpoenas to a President are warranted whenever evidence is material, state subpoenas are warranted "only when [the] evidence is essential." But that double standard has no basis in law. For if the state subpoena is not issued to manipulate, the documents themselves are not protected, and the Executive is not impaired, then nothing in Article II or the Supremacy Clause supports holding state subpoenas to a higher standard than their federal counterparts.

Finally, in the absence of a need to protect the Executive, the public interest in fair and effective law enforcement cuts in favor of comprehensive access to evidence. Requiring a state grand jury to meet a heightened standard of need would hobble the grand jury's ability to acquire "all information that might possibly bear on its investigation." [*United States v.*] *R. Enterprises, Inc.*, 498 U.S., at 297. And, even assuming the evidence withheld under that standard were preserved until the conclusion of a President's term, in the interim the State would be deprived of investigative leads that the evidence might yield, allowing memories to fade and documents to disappear. This could frustrate the identification, investigation, and indictment of third parties (for whom applicable statutes of limitations might lapse). More troubling, it could prejudice the innocent by depriving the grand jury of exculpatory evidence.

* * *

Two hundred years ago, a great jurist of our Court established that no citizen, not even the President, is categorically above the common duty to produce evidence when called upon in a criminal proceeding. We reaffirm that principle today and hold that the President is neither absolutely immune from state criminal subpoenas seeking his private papers nor entitled to a heightened standard of need. The "guard[] furnished to this high officer" lies where it always has—in "the conduct of a court" applying established legal and constitutional principles to individual subpoenas in a manner that preserves both the independence of the Executive and the integrity of the criminal justice system. *Burr*, 25 F. Cas., at 34.

The arguments presented here and in the Court of Appeals were limited to absolute immunity and heightened need. The Court of Appeals, however, has directed that the case be returned to the District Court, where the President may raise further arguments as appropriate. 941 F.3d, at 646, n. 19.[19]

We affirm the judgment of the Court of Appeals and remand the case for further proceedings consistent with this opinion.

[*Ed. Note: Concurring and dissenting opinions omitted.*]

Notes and Questions

1. *Trump v. Vance* **and the Aaron Burr Case: Helpful History Lesson or Historical Cherry-Picking?** Chief Justice Roberts begins his *Trump v. Vance* majority opinion with a lengthy description of the Aaron Burr criminal trial in 1807, when Chief Justice John Marshall, sitting as a federal circuit judge rather than as Chief Justice of the Supreme Court, upheld a trial subpoena to President Thomas Jefferson. Reading the account of the Burr trial in Chief Justice Roberts's opinion would lead one to conclude that it provides legal and historical support for the majority's conclusion that a President should be subject to a state grand jury subpoena. The extent to which the Burr trial supports that conclusion, however, may be less clear than portrayed by Chief Justice Roberts:

> The Court's extended discussion of *Burr* made an appeal to originalism to support the result it reached. But, in doing so, the Court adopted an overly simplistic story of *Burr* and canonized it into the Court's separation of powers doctrine. * * *

> The Court invoked the Burr trial in a nod to originalism. The Court's holding was dictated by *Nixon* and *Clinton and its own separation of powers concerns. Yet Chief Justice Roberts took great pains to discuss the implications of Burr at length.* As the Court acknowledged, Chief Justice Marshall was sitting as Circuit Justice in the Burr trial—*Burr* was not a Supreme Court decision and has limited precedential value in the Court. Accordingly, the Court's use of *Burr* in *Clinton* and *Nixon* was ancillary to its central holdings. In *Vance,* however, the Court held up *Burr* as the foundation for the historical practice of Presidents complying with subpoenas. As it was not cited as precedent, nor used merely as background, the Court's extended discussion of the Burr trial is best understood as an attempt to shore up its holding by reference to original intent. * * *

> * * * One commentator has noted that Chief Justice Roberts "recounted a sanitized version of this seminal dispute,"[20] as evidenced by three key omis-

---

19. [Note 6 of opinion] The daylight between our opinion and Justice Thomas's "dissent" is not as great as that label might suggest. We agree that Presidents are neither absolutely immune from state criminal subpoenas nor insulated by a heightened need standard. We agree that Presidents may challenge specific subpoenas as impeding their Article II functions. And, although we affirm while Justice Thomas would vacate, we agree that this case will be remanded to the District Court.

20. [Note 92 of article] Josh Blackman, *Symposium: It Must Be Nice to Have John Marshall on Your Side,* SCOTUSBLOG (July 10, 2020, 2:40 PM), https://www.scotusblog.com/2020/07/symposium-it-must-be-nice-to-have-john-marshall-on-your-side [https://perma.cc/2C8Y-MSME].

sions. First, the Court did not make it clear that Jefferson agreed to produce the requested documents *before* he was aware of the subpoena. Therefore, Jefferson was not complying with the subpoena, and one cannot infer that he recognized it as a legitimate use of judicial power. Second, Jefferson wrote in his letter to the prosecutor that he agreed "*voluntarily* to furnish on all occasions ... whatever the purposes of justice may require," but the Court omitted the word "voluntarily" from its opinion, changing the tone of the phrase significantly and presenting Jefferson as much more amicable to the exercise of judicial power than he really was. Finally, though the Court acknowledged Jefferson's assertion that "[h]is 'personal attendance' ... was out of the question," it did not mention that the subpoena *required* Jefferson's presence and that, according to at least some interpreters, Jefferson "actively flouted the subpoena." In short, the originalist meaning of *Burr* is more complicated and nuanced than the Court's opinion in *Vance* may have suggested, partly because Jefferson and Marshall, two Founders, disagreed sharply on separation of powers issues. In retelling the story of Aaron Burr's trial, Chief Justice Roberts adhered to a more simplified understanding, presenting a story that supported the Court's result but was importantly incomplete. * * *

Vance was always going to mention *Burr*. It is a foundational case and was quoted in both *Nixon* and *Clinton*. However, *Burr* is not a binding precedent, and while history is and should be relevant to constitutional interpretation, the Court's recounting of Aaron Burr's treason trial simplified the dispute between Jefferson and Marshall and created the false impression of a singular original understanding of the President's amenability to subpoena. This incomplete version of history is now codified as Supreme Court precedent, and may well reverberate through American jurisprudence for generations to come.

Note, *Trump v. Vance*, 134 HARV. L. REV. 430 (Nov. 10, 2020) (footnotes omitted, except as indicated). Did Chief Justice Roberts rely too heavily on the *Burr* decision? Would removing the support of the *Burr* decision undercut the remaining analysis in *Trump v. Vance*? How hard should the Supreme Court strive for historical accuracy when deciding matters of great constitutional significance?

2. Does *Trump v. Vance* Understate the Risk That a State Criminal Investigation Could Impair a President's Ability to Perform the Duties of Office? Justice Kavanaugh, joined by Justice Gorsuch, concurred in the judgment in *Trump v. Vance* that a President does not have absolute immunity from state criminal process, but would have applied the heightened need standard of *United States v. Nixon* (the Watergate tapes case). Justice Kavanaugh was concerned about "a conflict between a State's interest in criminal investigation and the President's Article II interest in performing his or her duties without undue interference." In this regard, is it noteworthy that Justice Kavanaugh had worked for Independent Counsel Kenneth Starr during the Whitewater/Monica Lewinsky investigation of President Bill Clinton and therefore might have a greater appreciation than the other Supreme Court Justices for how much a criminal investigation can interfere with a President's ability to perform official duties? On this point, bear in mind that the private civil litigation the Supreme Court allowed to go forward in the 1997 *Clinton v. Jones* decision ultimately—but unforeseeably—led to the impeachment of President Clinton. Has the Supreme Court consistently under-emphasized the practical and political consequences of requiring sitting presidents to comply with civil (*Clinton v. Jones*) and criminal (*United States v. Nixon* and *Trump v. Vance*) judicial process?

3. Is Federalism a More Important Concern Than *Trump v. Vance* Recognizes? Justice Alito dissented in *Trump v. Vance*, arguing that under the Constitution, a President cannot be subject to state prosecution while in office, and therefore a state grand jury subpoena should not be enforced against a President "unless a heightened standard is met." Justice Alito was particularly concerned about the federalism issues presented by the New York grand jury subpoena—"whether the Constitution imposes restrictions on a State's deployment of its criminal law enforcement powers against a sitting President"—and the potential for interference with the President's ability to perform his constitutional duties—"[w]ithout a President who is able at all times to carry out the responsibilities of the office, our constitutional system could not operate, and the country would be at risk." In light of these federalism concerns, "we should not treat this subpoena like an ordinary grand jury subpoena and should not relegate a President to the meager defenses that are available when an ordinary grand jury subpoena is challenged." Justice Alito also took issue with the majority's reliance on the *Burr* case, which was a federal criminal case and therefore "entirely lacked the federalism concerns" present in *Vance*. Justice Alito warned that the majority's decision "threatens to impair the functioning of the presidency" by leaving the President insufficiently protected from harassment by politically motivated state law enforcement officials. How significant are the federalism concerns identified by Justice Alito? How likely is it, in the hyper-partisan political environment that has arisen after President Trump's refusal to concede defeat in the 2020 presidential election, that state prosecutors might seek to use their criminal law enforcement powers to harass a sitting President whose legitimacy they may dispute?

4. Who Won and Who Lost in *Trump v. Vance*? On first reading, it might appear that *Trump v. Vance* represents a clear loss for President Trump and for future Presidents who may find themselves caught up in state criminal investigations. It is difficult to gauge the damage this may do to future Presidents, but for President Trump, the case was not the loss it might have first appeared to be:

> Assessing President Trump's status requires us to know his goals. If his goal was to maximize the power of the president and to ensure that a sitting president was immune to subpoenas from grand juries and the Congress, he lost big time. His most grandiose claims for presidential power and executive authority were rejected by the Court, and the vote wasn't close. But if his primary concern was, as I believe it was, to ensure that his financial records, including especially his tax returns, remain hidden until after the November election, then he won big time. * * *

Although the Court ruled against him on his broad immunity claims, it left the door open for objections to specific subpoenaed documents based on grounds open to any litigant, like the claim that the subpoenas are intentionally harassing, unduly burdensome or issued in bad faith, as well as on grounds specific to the executive, such as the claim that the subpoenas are designed to interfere with the president's official duties or will impede him in carrying out those duties. Regardless of how these issues are resolved on remand, there seems no chance that the issues left open will be resolved before November.

* * * Trump also won some smaller doctrinal victories in *Vance*. In particular, the Court recognized that separation of powers issues exist even when it is the president's personal papers that are sought, and it regards as irrelevant the fact that subpoenas for a president's papers are directed to third parties rather than to the president.

Richard Lempert, *Winners and Losers in the Supreme Court Decisions on Trump's Finances*, Brookings Institution FixGov Blog (July 10, 2020). What is your view of the impact of the Supreme Court's decision in *Vance* and the accompanying *Mazars* decision, discussed in Chapter 1? As a practical matter, do these decisions result in the worst of all possible worlds—did they damage the institutional power of the presidency in the long run without resulting in any short-run public benefit? Or does the Court's strong endorsement in *Vance* of the principle that a President is not above the law represent a clear and enduring victory for our constitutional system of government?

Chapter Four

Separation of Powers and Disputes between the Political Branches of Government

Modern Era Cases from the Reagan, George W. Bush, Obama, and Trump Administrations

When you agree to let 17 members of a [congressional] subcommittee and staff see a document, that's as close to a waiver [of executive privilege] as you're going to get.

Stanley M. Brand, then-General Counsel to the Clerk of the House of Representatives, quoted in *The Washington Post*, p. A1, February 20, 1983

Introduction

One of the most difficult recurring problems in the law of congressional investigations and oversight is legislative branch access to confidential executive branch information, particularly with respect to congressional oversight of executive branch departments and agencies. While conflict between the legislative and executive branches in this area is as old as the Republic—extending back at least to 1792, when the House of Representatives successfully sought to obtain executive branch information about General St. Clair's troop losses in battle with Native American tribes—a generally accepted rule or procedure to resolve such disputes has yet to evolve. To the contrary, recent history suggests that the rift between the political branches on this vitally important separation of powers issue has grown larger. Moreover, the judicial branch has consistently displayed a particularly strong reluctance to intervene in legislative-executive disputes over access to information, so a judicial test of broad, general application has not been forthcoming. (In this regard, it is important to note that the most celebrated dispute over executive branch information in our national history, the Watergate special prosecutor's fight to gain access to the Nixon White House tapes, discussed in Chapter 3 above, was between two executive branch actors, President Nixon and the Watergate special prosecutor, in the context of a criminal investigation, so the Supreme Court's decision in that case is not necessarily applicable to disputes involving congressional demands for executive branch information.)

Conflicts between Congress and the executive over confidential executive branch information arise with some frequency and are typically resolved through political negotiation and compromise. The usual outcome is that Congress eventually receives access to some information, but Congress usually receives the information later and in a less complete form than it originally sought. Congress's most powerful tool to compel executive branch officials to turn over disputed information is its contempt power. When negotiations break down, a congressional committee can vote to hold an executive branch official in contempt of Congress for refusing to respond to the committee's information request. In modern times this procedure has been used with varying degrees of success against even top cabinet officials who have been instructed by the president to assert executive privilege in response to a congressional demand for information. Two notable examples that occurred more than twenty years apart and involved cabinet officials in administrations of both major political parties illustrate how this procedure has typically been employed.[1]

In 1975 the House Committee on Intelligence voted to hold Secretary of State Henry Kissinger in contempt for refusing to provide the committee with information regarding covert action recommendations by the State Department. More than two decades later, in 1997, the House Government Reform and Oversight Committee voted to hold Attorney General Janet Reno in contempt for refusing to produce to the committee Justice Department and FBI memoranda concerning possible appointment of an independent counsel to investigate campaign fundraising. In the Kissinger case the basis for refusing to provide information was a formal assertion of executive privilege by President Ford, who contended that providing the documents to Congress would jeopardize the executive branch's internal decision-making process. In the Reno case the Justice Department took the position that producing the documents would interfere with an ongoing criminal investigation and impinge upon independent prosecutorial decision-making. In both instances, however, the committees ultimately received some limited access to the documents at issue and the contempt proceedings against the cabinet officials were not taken up by the full House.[2] (A comparable scenario played out in the Senate in 1996, when the Senate Special Whitewater Committee sought notes of former White House associate counsel William Kennedy—a committee contempt vote and the threat of action by the full Senate resulted in production of the notes before the full Senate voted on the contempt resolution. That dispute is examined in Chapter 6.)

---

1. Additional information about these two disputes, as well as a comprehensive recounting of the history of Congress's use of its contempt power to compel information from recalcitrant executive branch officials, is provided in a 2003 Congressional Research Service Report for Congress on the topic. *See* Louis Fisher, *Congressional Investigations: Subpoenas and Contempt Power* (April 2, 2003).

2. One commentator has noted that the Reno campaign finance investigation matter is particularly significant because it "marked the first time that Congress was able to obtain significant prosecutorial recommendations in the midst of an active criminal investigation." *See* Todd D. Peterson, *Congressional Oversight of Open Criminal Investigations*, 77 NOTRE DAME L. REV. 1373, 1405 (2002).

The rationales for withholding documents from Congress that were asserted in the Kissinger and Reno examples—interference with confidential executive branch "deliberative process" decision-making and interference with ongoing prosecutorial activities—are frequently advanced as grounds for executive branch refusals to comply with legislative branch information requests.[3] In that regard, the Kissinger and Reno cases are representative of the kinds of disputes that most often arise in this area. Those two cases also illustrate a number of important common characteristics of legislative-executive disputes over information sought in connection with congressional oversight of executive branch agencies. First, such disputes are less likely to be resolved through compromise and accommodation when different political parties control the executive branch and the house of Congress that is seeking executive branch information, as was the case in both the Kissinger and Reno disputes. Second, a contempt vote by a congressional committee, with its accompanying national publicity and attendant threat of a contempt proceeding by a full house of Congress, often provides sufficient political pressure to break a negotiations logjam and yield a compromise. Finally, these disputes are usually resolved without either side resorting to court proceedings and seeking to involve the judicial branch in the matter.

Although most disputes over congressional access to executive branch information conform to these general observations, and most are ultimately resolved through political compromise and accommodation, that result does not always follow. When the positions of the two political branches harden and neither side is willing to compromise, the confrontation can escalate, and at that point both the process to be followed and the applicable law become much less clear and predictable. Until recently, such escalations and confrontations—with both a contempt finding against a senior executive branch official by a full house of Congress and an accompanying judicial proceeding—were rare.

During the Reagan administration, a conflict arose over a House of Representatives committee demand for information from the EPA about administration of the "Superfund" hazardous waste clean-up program. A similar dispute between the political branches arose when the House Judiciary Committee sought information from the George W. Bush White House about the 2006 removal of several United States At-

---

3. These bases for attempting to withhold information from Congress should be distinguished from assertions of executive privilege for confidential presidential communications. *See In re Sealed Case (Espy),* 121 F.3d 729 (D.C. Cir. 1997) (distinguishing the "presidential communications privilege" from the "deliberative process privilege"). In general, a claim of confidentiality for executive branch prosecutorial deliberations or general executive branch "deliberative process" decision-making that does not involve presidential communications are treated by the courts as weaker than claims of executive privilege for presidential communications with top advisors or for "a claim of need to protect military, diplomatic, or sensitive national security secrets." *See generally United States v. Nixon,* 418 U.S. 683, 706 (1974). *Cf. Prosecution for Contempt of Congress of an Executive Branch Official Who Has Asserted a Claim of Executive Privilege,* 8 Op. Off. Legal Counsel 101 (May 30, 1984) (collecting cases and arguing that the Supreme Court has suggested that "in some areas the President's executive privilege may be absolute and in some circumstances it is a qualified privilege that may be overcome by a compelling interest of another branch").

torneys. During the Obama administration, the House Oversight Committee sought information from the Department of Justice about "Operation Fast and Furious" and cross-border "gun-running" to Mexican drug cartels. More recently, during the Trump administration, House committees sought to obtain testimony from White House Counsel Donald McGahn in their investigations into possible Russian interference in the 2016 presidential election.

These four conflicts all resulted in federal court opinions on the power of Congress to investigate executive branch activities, although none of the cases reached the Supreme Court, and therefore, the law in this area remains unsettled. Despite this lack of definitive Supreme Court guidance, these four conflicts provide instructive examples of the difficult separation of powers issues that such cases can present. For those reasons, these four conflicts are the principal subjects of this Chapter and are reviewed in greater detail below.

The House of Representatives EPA "Superfund" Investigation and the Anne Gorsuch Burford Contempt Proceedings

The factual background of the Reagan administration EPA dispute and the policy issues it presented were summarized by one of the authors of this book in a law review article that was published shortly after the matter was resolved:

Stanley M. Brand & Sean Connelly,
Constitutional Confrontations: Preserving a Prompt and Orderly Means by Which Congress May Enforce Investigative Demands Against Executive Branch Officials
36 CATHOLIC UNIVERSITY LAW REVIEW 71 (1986)
(footnotes omitted)

Congress possesses the inherent constitutional authority to inquire into all matters that potentially may be the subject of legislation. This investigatory authority, however, would be quite meaningless absent "some means of compulsion ... to obtain what is needed." Accordingly, Congress has the power, also inherent in the Constitution, to issue investigatory subpoenas and punish witnesses who fail to comply therewith. In addition, Congress has enacted legislation whereby a recalcitrant witness is certified as being in contempt of Congress, and the case is forwarded to a United States Attorney for criminal prosecution.

One of the most important areas of congressional inquiry relates to oversight of the Executive Branch. Although there is arguably no constitutional impediment to the use of compulsion against an Executive Branch official who has refused to comply with a congressional subpoena, there are nevertheless several practical constraints in such a case, especially where the recalcitrant witness is a high-ranking official claiming executive privilege....

Congressional demands for information from the executive branch are nothing new. Indeed, disputes between Congress and the President regarding the latter's obligation to produce requested information date back to the administration of George Washington. Until recently, however, no high-ranking official had ever been voted in contempt by the full House or Senate. The legislative history of the congressional contempt statute nevertheless makes clear that it was intended "to punish equally the Cabinet officer and the culprit who may have insulted the dignity of the House...." Furthermore, the Justice Department has recognized that instances might arise where an executive branch official would be cited for contempt of Congress, in which case the official would be forced to retain private counsel.

In 1982, however, a dispute broke out between a House subcommittee and the executive branch regarding the latter's duty to provide information pertinent to congressional oversight of the Environmental Protection Agency (EPA). The confrontation eventually resulted in the citation of EPA Administrator Anne Gorsuch Burford by the full House for contempt of Congress. The Burford case is deserving of close scrutiny, both for its historical import and for its dramatic exposure of the inadequacies in the present system of congressional compulsion against the executive branch.

The historic dispute in the Burford case had its genesis on March 10, 1982 when the House Subcommittee on Investigations and Oversight of the Committee on Public Works and Transportation (Levitas subcommittee) opened a series of hearings regarding EPA enforcement of federal environmental statutes, including the so-called Superfund Act. These hearings, according to a subsequent committee report, "raised a number of concerns about the adequacy of the Superfund law, and the extent to which the EPA's efforts to carry it out are both satisfactory and in keeping with the intent of the law." In a letter to EPA Administrator Gorsuch (Burford) dated September 15, 1982, Chairman Levitas requested that certain Superfund information be made available to his subcommittee. Although indicating a willingness to make some materials available to the subcommittee, EPA refused to make available any materials contained in files relating to open investigations. After extensive negotiations proved unsatisfactory to the subcommittee, it caused a subpoena to be served upon EPA Administrator Burford on November 22, 1982. The subpoena required Burford to appear before the subcommittee on December 2, 1982 for the purpose of giving testimony and producing documents relating to EPA Superfund enforcement.

Prelude to a Showdown:
The Reagan Administration Asserts
Executive Privilege

With the benefit of hindsight, it appears that the Reagan administration Justice Department may have seized upon the EPA dispute as a "test case" in which it could assert a more robust view of the scope of executive privilege than had prevailed in the period immediately following the Watergate scandal.[4] When reviewing the materials below, consider the political environment that existed at the time: Reagan, a popular Republican president (the EPA dispute occurred before President Reagan's political standing was weakened by the Iran-Contra scandal, which is the subject of Chapter 5), was fighting numerous political and policy battles with an assertive House of Representatives controlled by the Democrats (the Democratic majority in the House of Representatives, led by its politically adept Speaker Thomas P. "Tip" O'Neill, opposed many of President Reagan's economic and social policy initiatives[5]). Reproduced below are the Reagan Executive Orders, Justice Department legal memoranda, and House of Representatives legal memoranda that gave rise to the criminal contempt of Congress proceeding against EPA Administrator Anne Gorsuch Burford.

The White House

Washington, D.C., November 4, 1982

Memorandum for the Heads of Executive
Departments and Agencies

**Subject: Procedures Governing Responses to Congressional
Requests for Information**

The policy of this Administration is to comply with Congressional requests for information to the fullest extent consistent with the constitutional and statutory obligations of the Executive Branch. While this Administration, like its predecessors, has an obligation to protect the confidentiality of some communications, executive privilege will be asserted only in the most compelling circumstances, and only after careful

---

4. *See generally Report Relating to the Contempt Citation of Anne M. (Gorsuch) Burford*, H.R. No. 98-323 at 7–10 (July 27, 1983) (recounting the circumstances in which the Reagan administration Department of Justice reversed an initial position of the EPA's Deputy Administrator granting access to the disputed Superfund enforcement files and thereafter took the position "that a congressional inquiry into these types of matters would wrest from the Executive its ability to 'take care that the laws be faithfully executed,' as set forth in Section 3, Article II of the U.S. Constitution"). *See also* ANNE M. BURFORD WITH JOHN GREENYA, ARE YOU TOUGH ENOUGH? 154 (McGraw Hill 1986) ("The whole idea of raising the test case with Congress by refusing to release 'enforcement sensitive' documents had come from Justice Department lawyers in the first place...."); 258–60 (quoting former Congressman Elliot Levitas observing that the Justice Department was seeking an opportunity to assert broad executive privilege claims "about documents that no President of the United States will ever see in his life").

5. *See* JOHN A. FARRELL, TIP O'NEILL AND THE DEMOCRATIC CENTURY 563–606 (Little, Brown & Co. 2001).

review demonstrates that assertion of the privilege is necessary. Historically, good faith negotiations between Congress and the Executive Branch have minimized the need for invoking executive privilege, and this tradition of accommodation should continue as the primary means of resolving conflicts between the Branches. To ensure that every reasonable accommodation is made to the needs of Congress, executive privilege shall not be invoked without specific Presidential authorization.

The Supreme Court has held that the Executive Branch may occasionally find it necessary and proper to preserve the confidentiality of national security secrets, deliberative communications that form a part of the decision-making process, or other information important to the discharge of the Executive Branch's constitutional responsibilities. Legitimate and appropriate claims of privilege should not thoughtlessly be waived. However, to ensure that this Administration acts responsibly and consistently in the exercise of its duties, with due regard for the responsibilities and prerogatives of Congress, the following procedures shall be followed whenever Congressional requests for information raise concerns regarding the confidentiality of the information sought:

1. Congressional requests for information shall be complied with as promptly and as fully as possible, unless it is determined that compliance raises a substantial question of executive privilege. A "substantial question of executive privilege" exists if disclosure of the information requested might significantly impair the national security (including the conduct of foreign relations), the deliberative processes of the Executive Branch or other aspects of the performance of the Executive Branch's constitutional duties.

2. If the head of an executive department or agency ("Department Head") believes, after consultation with department counsel, that compliance with a Congressional request for information raises a substantial question of executive privilege, he shall promptly notify and consult with the Attorney General through the Assistant Attorney General for the Office of Legal Counsel, and shall also promptly notify and consult with the Counsel to the President. If the information requested of a department or agency derives in whole or in part from information received from another department or agency, the latter entity shall also be consulted as to whether disclosure of the information raises a substantial question of executive privilege.

3. Every effort shall be made to comply with the Congressional request in a manner consistent with the legitimate needs of the Executive Branch. The Department Head, the Attorney General and the Counsel to the President may, in the exercise of their discretion in the circumstances, determine that executive privilege shall not be invoked and release the requested information.

4. If the Department Head, the Attorney General or the Counsel to the President believes, after consultation, that the circumstances justify invocation of executive privilege, the issue shall be presented to the President by the Counsel to the President, who will advise the Department head and the Attorney General of the President's decision.

5. Pending a final Presidential decision on the matter, the Department Head shall request the Congressional body to hold its request for the information in abeyance. The Department Head shall expressly indicate that the purpose of this request is to

protect the privilege pending a Presidential decision, and that the request itself does not constitute a claim of privilege.

6. If the President decides to invoke executive Privilege, the Department Head shall advise the Requesting Congressional body that the claim of executive privilege is being made with the specific approval of the President.

Any questions concerning these procedures or related matters should be addressed to the Attorney General, through the Assistant Attorney General for the Office of Legal Counsel, and to the Counsel to the President.

/s/ Ronald Reagan

The White House

Washington, D.C., November 30, 1982

Memorandum for the Administrator, Environmental Protection Agency

Subject: Congressional Subpoenas for Executive Branch Documents

I have been advised that the Subcommittee on Oversight and Investigations of the Energy and Commerce Committee of the House of Representatives has issued a subpoena requiring you, as Administrator of the Environmental Protection Agency ("EPA"), to produce documents from open law enforcement files assembled as part of the enforcement of the Comprehensive Environmental Response, Compensation, and Liability Act of 1980 ("CERCLA") against three specific sites which have been utilized in the past for the dumping of hazardous wastes located in Michigan, California and Oklahoma. I further understand that you have also received a subpoena from the Subcommittee on Investigations and Oversight of the Public Works and Transportation Committee of the House of Representatives apparently intended to secure similar files regarding an additional approximately 160 hazardous waste sites.

It is my understanding that in response to requests by the Energy and Commerce Subcommittee during its investigation of the EPA's enforcement program under CERCLA, the EPA has either produced or made available for copying by the Subcommittee approximately 40,000 documents. I am informed that in response to the Public Works and Transportation Subcommittee, the EPA estimates that it has produced, will produce, or will make available for inspection and copying by the Subcommittee approximately 787,000 documents at a cost of approximately $223,000 and an expenditure of more than 15,000 personnel hours. I further understand that a controversy has arisen between the EPA and each of these Subcommittees over the EPA's unwillingness to permit copying of a number of documents generated by attorneys and other enforcement personnel within the EPA in the development of potential civil or criminal enforcement actions against private parties. These documents, from open law enforcement files, are internal deliberative materials containing enforcement strategy and statements of the Government's position on various legal issues which may be raised in enforcement actions relative to the various hazardous waste sites by the EPA or the Department of Justice under CERCLA.

The Attorney General, at my direction, has sent the attached letter to Chairman Dingell of the Energy and Commerce Subcommittee setting forth the historic position of the Executive Branch, with which I concur, that sensitive documents found in open law enforcement files should not be made available to Congress or the public except in extraordinary circumstances. Because dissemination of such documents outside the Executive Branch would impair my solemn responsibility to enforce the law, I instruct you and your agency not to furnish copies of this category of documents to the Subcommittees in response to their subpoenas. I request that you insure that the Chairman of each Subcommittee is advised of my decision.

I also request that you remain willing to meet with each Subcommittee to provide such information as you can, consistent with these instructions and without creating a precedent that would violate the Constitutional doctrine of separation of powers.

/s/ RONALD REAGAN

Office of the Attorney General

Washington, D.C., November 30, 1982

Hon. ELLIOTT H. LEVITAS, *Chairman,*
Subcommittee on Investigations and Oversight,
Committee on Public Works and Transportation,
House of Representatives, Washington, D.C.

DEAR MR. CHAIRMAN:

I have had occasion to reiterate, in the attached letter to Chairman Dingell of the Subcommittee on Oversight and Investigations of the House Committee on Energy and Commerce, the historic position of the Executive Branch that it is not in the public interest for sensitive documents found in open law enforcement files to be given to Congress or its committees except in extraordinary circumstances. I am aware that your Subcommittee has issued to Administrator Gorsuch of the Environmental Protection Agency ("EPA") a subpoena apparently seeking copies of some 787,000 documents found in open law enforcement files related to approximately 160 hazardous waste sites located throughout the United States. At least 23 and probably more documents covered in your Subcommittee's subpoena are of that class covered by my letter to Chairman Dingell, since they reflect prosecutorial strategy and other internal deliberations regarding prosecution of the particular cases involved.

Because the principles articulated in the attached letter to Chairman Dingell are fully applicable to some of the documents arguably within the scope of your Subcommittee's subpoena, I believe it appropriate to provide you with a copy of that letter at this time. Because neither I nor my staff have previously communicated directly with you on this particular matter, I would also like to express my hope that, after you have had the benefit of my views on this issue, set in their historical perspective, you will no longer seek to compel production of this class of documents from the Administrator. Should you wish to discuss this matter further prior to the Subcommittee's scheduled

December 2 hearing, I would ask that you contact Assistant Attorney General McConnell of my Office of Legislative Affairs at your convenience.

I would also add that I am confident that the legislative needs of your Subcommittee can be met without the production by the Administrator of sensitive documents in open law enforcement files. That is certainly the lesson that history teaches, and I believe you will agree that it is incumbent on both of our Branches to avoid constitutional confrontations so long as the needs and prerogatives of each Branch can be harmonized.

Sincerely,

WILLIAM FRENCH SMITH,
Attorney General

Office of the Attorney General
Washington, D.C., November 30, 1982

Hon. JOHN D. DINGELL, *Chairman,*
Subcommittee on Oversight and Investigations,
Committee on Energy and Commerce,
House of Representatives Washington, D.C.

DEAR MR. CHAIRMAN:

This letter responds to your letter to me of November 8, 1982, in which you, on behalf of the Subcommittee on Oversight and Investigations of the Committee on Energy and Commerce of the House of Representatives, continue to seek to compel the production to your Subcommittee of copies of sensitive open law enforcement investigative files (referred to herein for convenience simply as "law enforcement files") of the Environmental Protection Agency ("EPA"). Demands for other EPA files, including similar law enforcement files, have also been made by the Subcommittee on Oversight and Investigations of the Public Works and Transportation Committee of the House of Representatives.

Since the issues raised by these demands and others like them are important ones to two separate and independent Branches of our Nation's Government, I shall reiterate at some length in this letter the longstanding position of the Executive Branch with respect to such matters. I do so with the knowledge and concurrence of the President.

As the President announced in a memorandum to the Heads of all Executive Departments and Agencies on November 4, 1982, "[t]he policy of this Administration is to comply with Congressional requests for information to the fullest extent consistent with the constitutional and statutory obligations of the Executive Branch.... [E]xecutive privilege will be asserted only in the most compelling circumstances, and only after careful review demonstrates that assertion of the privilege is necessary." Nevertheless, it has been the policy of the Executive Branch throughout this Nation's history generally to decline to provide committees of Congress with access to or copies of law enforcement files except in the most extraordinary circumstances. Attorney General Robert Jackson, subsequently a Justice of the Supreme Court, restated this position to Congress over forty years ago:

"It is the position of [the] Department [of Justice], restated now with the approval of and at the direction of the President, that all investigative reports are confidential documents of the executive department of the Government, to aid in the duty laid upon the President by the Constitution to 'take care that the laws be faith-fully executed,' and that congressional or public access to them would be not in the public interest.

"Disclosure of the reports could not do otherwise than seriously prejudice law enforcement. Counsel for a defendant or prospective defendant, could have no greater help than to know how much or how little information the Government has, and what witnesses or sources of information it can rely upon. This is exactly what these reports are intended to contain."

This policy does not extend to all material contained in investigative files. Depending upon the nature of the specific files and the type of investigation involved, much of the information contained in such files may and is routinely shared with Congress in response to a proper request. Indeed, in response to your Subcommittee's request, considerable quantities of documents and factual data have been provided to you. The EPA estimates that approximately 40,000 documents have been made available for your Subcommittee and its staff to examine relative to the three hazardous waste sites in which you have expressed an interest. The only documents which have been withheld are those which are sensitive memoranda or notes by EPA attorneys and investigators reflecting enforcement strategy, legal analysis, lists of potential witnesses, settlement considerations and similar materials the disclosure of which might adversely affect a pending enforcement action, overall enforcement policy, or the rights of individuals.

I continue to believe, as have my predecessors, that unrestricted dissemination of law enforcement files would prejudice the cause of effective law enforcement and, because the reasons for the policy of confidentiality are as sound and fundamental to the administration of justice today as they were forty years ago, I see no reason to depart from the consistent position of previous presidents and attorneys general. As articulated by former Deputy Assistant Attorney General Thomas E. Kauper over a decade ago: "the Executive cannot effectively investigate if Congress is, in a sense, a partner in the investigation. If a congressional committee is fully apprised of all details of an investigation as the investigation proceeds, there is a substantial danger that congressional pressures will influence the course of the investigation."

Other objections to the disclosure of law enforcement files included the potential damage to proper law enforcement which would be caused by the revelation of sensitive techniques, methods or strategy, concern over the safety of confidential informants and the chilling effect on sources of information if the contents of files are widely disseminated, sensitivity to the rights of innocent individuals who may be identified in law enforcement files but who may not be guilty of any violation of law, and well-founded

fears that the perception of the integrity, impartiality and fairness of the law enforcement process as a whole will be damaged if sensitive material is distributed beyond
those persons necessarily involved in the investigation and prosecution process. Our
policy is premised in part on the fact that the Constitution vests in the President and
his subordinates the responsibility to "take Care that the Laws be faithfully executed".
The courts have repeatedly held that "the Executive Branch has exclusive authority and
absolute discretion to decide whether to prosecute a case...." *United States v. Nixon*,
418 U.S. 683, 693 (1974).

The policy which I reiterate here was first expressed by President Washington and
has been reaffirmed by or on behalf of most of our Presidents, including Presidents
Jefferson, Jackson, Lincoln, Theodore Roosevelt, Franklin Roosevelt, and Eisenhower.
I am aware of no President who has departed from this policy regarding the general
confidentiality of law enforcement files.

I also agree with Attorney General Jackson's view that promises of confidentiality
by a congressional committee or subcommittee do not remove the basis for the policy
of nondisclosure of law enforcement files. As Attorney General Jackson observed in
writing to Congressman Carl Vinson, then Chairman of the House Committee on
Naval Affairs, in 1941:

> "I am not unmindful of your conditional suggestion that your counsel will
> keep this information 'inviolate until such time as the committee determines
> its disposition.' I have no doubt that this pledge would be kept and that you
> would weigh every consideration before making any matter public. Unfortu-
> nately, however, a policy cannot be made anew because of personal confidence
> of the Attorney General in the integrity and good faith of a particular commit-
> tee chairman. We cannot be put in the position of discriminating between
> committees or of attempting to judge between them, and their individual
> members, each of whom has access to information once placed in the hands
> of the committee."

Deputy Assistant Attorney General Kauper articulated additional considerations in
explaining why congressional assurances of confidentiality could not overcome concern over the integrity of law enforcement files:

> "[S]uch assurances have not led to a relaxation of the general principle that
> open investigative files will not be supplied to Congress, for several reasons.
> First, to the extent the principle rests on the prevention of direct congressional
> influence upon investigations in progress, dissemination to the Congress, not
> by it, is the critical factor. Second, there is the always present concern, often
> factually justified, with 'leaks.' Third, members of Congress may comment or
> publicly draw conclusions from such documents, without in fact disclosing
> their contents."

It has never been the position of the Executive Branch that providing copies of law
enforcement files to congressional committees necessarily will result in the documents'
being made public. We are confident that your Subcommittee and other congressional

committees would guard such documents carefully. Nor do I mean to imply that any particular committee would necessarily "leak" documents improperly although, as you know, that phenomenon has occasionally occurred. Concern over potential public distribution of the documents is only a part of the basis for the Executive's position. At bottom, the President has a responsibility vested in him by the Constitution to protect the confidentiality of certain documents which he cannot delegate to the Legislative Branch.

With regard to the assurance of confidential treatment contained in your November 8, 1982 letter, I am sensitive to Rule XI, cl. 2, §7606c of the Rules of the House of Representatives which provides that "[a]ll committee hearings, records, data, charts, and files ... shall be the property of the House and *all Members of the House shall have access thereto.* ..." In order to avoid the requirements of this rule regarding access to documents by all Members of the House, your November 8 letter offers to receive these documents in "executive session" pursuant to Rule XI, cl. 2, §712. It is apparently on the basis of §712 that your November 8 letter states that providing these materials to your Subcommittee is not equivalent to making the documents "public." But, as is evident from your accurate rendition of §712, the only protection given such materials by that section and your understanding of it is that they shall not be made public, in your own words, "without the consent of the Subcommittee."

Notwithstanding the sincerity of your view that §712 provides adequate protection to the Executive Branch, I am unable to accept and therefore must reject the concept that an assurance that documents would not be made public "without the consent of the Subcommittee" is sufficient to provide the Executive the protection to which he is constitutionally entitled. While a congressional committee may disagree with the President's judgment as regards the need to protect the confidentiality of any particular documents, neither a congressional committee nor the House (or Senate, as the case may be) has the right under the Constitution to receive such disputed documents from the Executive and sit in final judgment as to whether it is in the public interest for such documents to be made public.[6] To the extent that a congressional committee believes that a presidential determination not to disseminate documents may be improper, the House of Congress involved or some appropriate unit thereof may seek

---

6. [Note 1] Your November 8 letter points out that in my opinion of October 13, 1981 to the President a passage from the Court's opinion in *United States v. Nixon*, 418 U.S. 682 (1974), was quoted in which the word "public" as it appears in the Court's opinion was inadvertently omitted. That is correct, but the significance you have attributed to it is not. The omission of the world "public" was a technical error made in the transcription of the final typewritten version of the opinion. This error will be corrected by inclusion of the word "public" in the official printed version of that opinion. However, the omission of that word was not material to the fundamental points contained in the opinion. The reasoning contained therein remains the same. As the discussion in the text of this letter makes clear, I am unable to accept your argument that the provision of documents to Congress is not, for purposes of the President's Executive Privilege, functionally and legally equivalent to making the documents public, because the power to make the documents public shifts from the Executive to a unit of Congress. Thus, for these purposes the result under *United States v. Nixon* would be identical even if the Court had itself not used the word "public" in the relevant passage.

judicial review (*See Senate Select Committee v. Nixon*, 498 F.2d 725 (D.C. Cir. 1974)), but it is not entitled to be put in a position unilaterally to make such a determination. The President's privilege is effectively and legally rendered a nullity once the decision as to whether "public" release would be in the public interest passes from his hands to a subcommittee of Congress. It is not up to a congressional subcommittee but to the courts ultimately " ' to say what the law is' with respect to the claim of privilege presented in [any particular] case." *United States v. Nixon*, 418 U.S. at 705, *quoting Marbury v. Madison*, 1 Cranch 137, 177 (1803).

I am unaware of a single judicial authority establishing the proposition which you have expounded that the power properly lies only with Congress to determine whether law enforcement files might be distributed publicly, and I am compelled to reject it categorically. The crucial point is not that your Subcommittee, or any other subcommittee, might wisely decide not to make public sensitive information contained in law enforcement files. Rather, it is that the President has the constitutional responsibility to take care that the laws are faithfully executed; if the President believes that certain types of information in law enforcement files are sufficiently sensitive that they should be kept confidential, it is the President's constitutionally required obligation to make that determination.[7]

These principles will not be employed to shield documents which contain evidence of criminal or unethical conduct by agency officials from proper review. However, no claims have been advanced that this is the case with the files at issue here. As you know, your staff has examined many of the documents which lie at the heart of this dispute to confirm that they have been properly characterized. These arrangements were made in the hope that that process would aid in resolving this dispute. Furthermore, I understand that you have not accepted Assistant Attorney General McConnell's offer to have the documents at issue made available to the Members of your Subcommittee at the offices of your Subcommittee for an inspection under conditions which would not have required the production of copies and which, in this one instance, would not have irreparably injured our concerns over the integrity of the law enforcement process. Your apparent rejection of that offer would appear to leave no room for further compromise of our differences on this matter.

In closing, I emphasize that we have carefully reexamined the consistent position of the Executive Branch on this subject and we must reaffirm our commitment to it. We believe that this policy is necessary to the President's responsible fulfillment of his constitutional obligations and is not in any way an intrusion on the constitutional duties of Congress. I hope you will appreciate the historical perspective from which these views are now communicated to you and that this assertion of a fundamental right by

---

7. [Note 2] It was these principles that were embodied in Assistant Attorney General McConnell's letters of October 18 and 25, 1982 to you. Under these principles, your criticism of Mr. McConnell's statements made in those letters must be rejected. Mr. McConnell's statements represent an institutional viewpoint that does not, and cannot, depend upon the personalities involved. I regret that you chose to take his observations personally.

the Executive will not, as it should not, impair the ongoing and constructive relationship that our two respective Branches must enjoy in order for each of us to fulfill our different but equally important responsibilities under our Constitution.

Sincerely,

WILLIAM FRENCH SMITH,
Attorney General

Office of the Clerk,
U.S. House of Representatives
Washington, D.C., December 8, 1982

Re: Attorney General's Letter Concerning Subpoena For Documents to Administrator of Environmental Protection Agency

To: Honorable Elliott H. Levitas, Chairman, Subcommittee on Investigations and Oversight, House Committee on Public Works and Transportation

From: Stanley M. Brand, General Counsel to the Clerk

This memorandum responds to the assertions made in the Attorney General's letter of November 30, 1982 concerning a subpoena for documents directed to the Administrator of the Environmental Protection Agency ("EPA") related to hazardous waste sites throughout the United States. The letter of the Attorney General is a copy of the same letter directed to the Honorable John D. Dingell, Chairman of the Subcommittee on Oversight and Investigations of the House Committee on Energy and Commerce in response to a subpoena that Subcommittee issued to the EPA concerning some of the same documents.

The Attorney General's opinion that EPA need not provide the information required for your Subcommittee inquiry rests on two premises: (1) that the information is beyond the reach of congressional subpoena power because it is "sensitive" material in "law enforcement files" and (2) that a Subcommittee's offer to receive the information in executive session is not a basis for providing it. Neither point is well taken. I have addressed the second premise because it forms a basis of the letter, although it appears more relevant to the issue of confidentiality raised in Chairman Dingell's letter of November 8, 1982 in connection with that subcommittee's subpoena. The Attorney General's discussion of executive session proceedings and the rules governing conduct of such proceedings is nevertheless disturbing because it is based on a complete misunderstanding of the constitutional basis for Congress' authority to receive "secret" information.

Regarding the Attorney General's first premise that Congress cannot subpoena material in law enforcement files, the Attorney General's opinion cites no caselaw to support this proposition; indeed, he could not because none exists to support him. Nothing is better established than that Congress's investigative power "encompasses inquiries concerning the administration of existing laws as well as proposed or possibly needed statutes.... [I]t comprehends probes into departments of the Federal Government to expose corruption, inefficiency or waste." *Watkins v. United States*, 354 U.S. 178, 187 (1957).

Of particular importance here is the history of legislative oversight of the Justice Department and its enforcement of the law. Indeed, past congressional investigations have focused on the Department's efforts in particular cases, rather than general or abstract policies.[8] In *McGrain v. Daugherty*, 273 U.S. 135 (1926) a Senate committee investigated charges that the Department of Justice had failed to prosecute public corruption, antitrust and other matters. The Supreme Court expressly recognized congressional authority to examine and inquire into specific enforcement decisions by the Department of Justice whether to prosecute as an incident of the legislative function:

> The subject to be investigated was the administration of the Department of Justice—whether its functions were being properly discharged or were being neglected or misdirected, and particularly *whether the Attorney General and his assistants were performing or neglecting their duties in respect of the institution and prosecution of proceedings*... the subject... would be materially aided by the information [sought]... the functions of the Department of Justice, the powers and duties of the Attorney general and the duties of his assistants, are all subject to regulation by congressional legislation, and... the department is maintained and its activities are carried on under such appropriations as in the judgment of Congress are needed from year to year. (273 U.S. at 177–78.) (Emphasis added.)

This principle applies with equal, if not greater, force to the Environmental Protection Agency. Congress has every right to see how the laws it passes are being administered and enforced, and whether those charged with responsibility "in respect of the institution and prosecution of proceedings," *id.*, are adequately and properly performing their responsibility.

The Attorney General does not discuss the congressional reach of investigatory power established by *McGrain*, and he does not distinguish it from the situation here. Instead, he argues that special principles, hitherto raised by the Justice Department primarily to defend nondisclosure of *criminal investigations* of the Justice Department itself, should be extended to contexts such as EPA's preparations for civil suits and

---

8. [1] In fact, some of these investigations have focused on issues such as interference with grand juries and special treatment in cases of White House influence. *See, e.g., Charges of Illegal Practices of the Department of Justice: Hearings Before a Subcommittee of the Committee of the Judiciary of the United States Senate*, 66th Cong., 3d Sess. (1921); *Investigation of Hon. Harry M. Daugherty, formerly Attorney General of the United States, Hearings Before the Select Committee on Investigations of the Attorney General of the United States Senate*, 60th Cong., 1st Sess. Vols. 1–3, 1924; *Consent Decree Program of the Department of Justice, Hearings Before the Antitrust Subcommittee, Subcommittee No. 51 of the House Committee on the Judiciary*, 85th Cong., 1st & 2d Sess., pts. I and II (1957–58); *Mercury Pollution and Enforcement of the Refuse Act of 1899, Hearings Before a Subcommittee of the Committee on Government Operations of the House of Representatives*, 92nd Cong., 2d Sess., pts. 1–3 (1971–72).

settlements. Without denigrating the importance of this EPA work, which is, of course, the Subcommittee's reason for its inquiry, those preparations for civil suits or settlements do not raise the concerns involved in release of Justice Department criminal investigation files, such as the danger that prejudicial pretrial publicity will deny criminal defendants a fair trial or that the safety of FBI informants will be jeopardized. The Attorney General's opinion placed its principal reliance on the 1941 opinion of Attorney General Jackson concerning nondisclosure of the FBI's investigative files. Yet the Attorney General cites no precedent for extending the policy regarding FBI criminal investigation files, with their special concerns, throughout the government whenever any matter may relate to civil suits—an enormous extension of secrecy.

Even where the concerns regarding pretrial publicity and due process for defendants have been raised, the courts have not blocked the exercise of the congressional investigative power. For instance, when a witness under indictment in state court on charges relating to the same matters about which the Senate committee sought to interrogate the witness, his challenge to the committee subpoena based on a contention that legislative questioning would aid in the state prosecution resulting in a denial of due process was rejected. *Hutcheson v. United States*, 369 U.S. 599 (1962). As the court explained:

> The suggestion made in dissent that the questions which petitioner refused to answer were 'outside the power of a committee to ask' under the Due Process Clause because they touched on matters then pending in judicial proceedings cannot be accepted for several reasons: First, the reasoning underlying this proposition is that these inquiries constituted a legislative encroachment on the judicial function. But such reasoning can hardly be limited to inquiries that may be germane to existing judicial proceedings; it would surely apply as well to inquiries calling for answers that might be used to the prejudice of the witness in any future judicial proceeding. If such were the reach of 'due process' it would turn a witness' privilege against self-incrimination into a self-operating restraint on congressional inquiry, and would in effect *pro tanto* obliterate the need for that constitutional protection. (369 U.S. at 613 n. 16.)

Finally, on this point, litigants have asserted that the conduct of concurrent congressional investigations have [*sic*] prejudiced their right to obtain a fair trial owing to the attendant publicity generally by public congressional hearings. These claims have also been rarely accepted by the courts. We know of only one case reversing a conviction on the basis of prejudicial publicity generated by a congressional investigation, *Delany v. United States*, 199 F.2d 107 (1st Cir. 1952) (reversal of conviction for failure of trial court to grant continuance until pretrial publicity generated by House committee investigation into subject matter subsided), and even in such rare instances, the holdings run to the *consequences* of concurrent congressional proceedings on the criminal prosecution, not to the *authority* of the Congress to conduct a hearing and summon witnesses. In *United States v. Romano*, 583 F.2d 1, 4 (1st Cir. 1978), the Senate committee determined not to heed warnings from the Department of Justice that insistence on defendant's testimony would threaten or absolutely bar successful future prosecution, and the conviction was upheld nonetheless. *See also Beck v. Washington*, 369 U.S. 541, 544 (1962) (upholding conviction of defendant called as a witness before congressional committee five days after indictment).

These cases demonstrate that even in instances where the Congress determines to make public information it has received relative to law enforcement matters, it does not necessarily mean that the concerns raised by the Attorney General are implicated. Even less so, then, unless and until the committee decides in its wisdom to make any portion of the documents public.

Even where FBI intelligence gathering has been at issue, Congress has not foregone its power of inquiry in appropriate circumstances.[9] Yet here, those weightier concerns are not even present. In their absence, the Attorney General would block congressional inquiry on the basis of two much weaker arguments.

First, concern is expressed that congressional inquiry is somehow inconsistent with the absolute prosecutorial discretion vested in the Executive branch, a point not in dispute. The Attorney General has once again confused congressional oversight with interference in prosecutorial decision-making. *See* Letter from William French Smith to President Reagan, Oct. 13, 1981 *reprinted in Congressional Proceedings Against Interior Secretary James G. Watt for Withholding Subpoenaed Documents and For Failure to Answer Questions Relating to Reciprocity Under the Mineral Lands Leasing Act, Report of the Committee on Energy and Commerce*, H.R. Rep. 89d, 97th Cong., 2d Sess. 42, 54 (1982). By reviewing these records, the committee seeks not to influence individual enforcement decisions, but rather to review the integrity and effectiveness of EPA's enforcement program and to evaluate the adequacy of existing law.

Second, concern is expressed that congressional oversight calls for information which reflects the government's strategy or the methods or weaknesses of its investigations. Yet if this type of concern were recognized as blocking congressional inquiry,

---

9. [1] Two recent congressional inquiries have focused on the conduct of investigation by the FBI: the Billy Carter inquiry in 1980 and the various inquiries into ABSCAM in 1982. As more extensive examples, in the mid-1970's House and Senate committees probed allegations concerning domestic intelligence gathering by the FBI and by units of the Justice Department such as the Interdivision Information Unit (IDIU). *See Intelligence Activities and the Rights of Americans, Book II, Final Report of the Senate Select Committee to Study Governmental Operations with Respect to Intelligence Activities*, S. Rep. No. 94-755 at 78 (IDIU) and 86 (Cointelpro) (1976); *FBI Oversight, Hearings Before the Subcommittee on Civil and Constitutional Rights of the Committee on the Judiciary of the House of Representatives*, 94th Cong., 1st & 2d Sess., pts. 1 & 2 (1975–76). These investigating committees and the General Accounting Office examined hundreds of individual cases of domestic intelligence gathering in order to determine the necessity for legislation in the area. The Senate Intelligence Committee declared as its "most important lesson to be derived from our experience," S. Rep. No. 94-755 at IX n. 7, a conclusion characteristic of many of the other investigations of the Justice Department: "effective oversight is impossible without regular access to the underlying working documents.... Top level briefings do not adequately describe the realities. For that the documents are a necessary supplement and at times the only source."

it would end a major portion of all such inquiry. Congressional inquiry into foreign affairs and military matters calls for information on strategy and weaknesses in national security matters; congressional inquiry into waste, fraud, and inefficiency, *Watkins v. United States, supra*, in domestic operations calls for information on strategy and weaknesses in combating these. Congress does not forego [*sic*] inquiry simply because it may produce information on the government's strategies and weaknesses; the only way to correct either bad law or bad administration is to examine these matters.

Nor does the fact that these matters may be the subject of civil suit mean that congressional inquiry should be blocked. There is unbroken precedent that Congress may investigate subjects relevant to its legislative function which are concurrently the subject matter of pending suit or likely to come before the courts. No court has ever held, and the Attorney General cites none, that exercise of Congress' investigative power concurrently with the prosecution of cases before the courts interferes in the administration of justice. In fact, the courts have held directly contrary. *See McGrain v. Daugherty, supra* at 180; *Sinclair v. United States*, 279 U.S. 263, 295 (1929) (authority of Senate "to require pertinent disclosures in aid of its own constitutional power is not abridged because the information sought to be elicited may also be of use in such suits").

In any event, claims by litigants that concurrent congressional investigations violate constitutional precepts of fairness of due process, also an apparent concern of the Attorney General, have largely been rejected. *United States v. Mitchell*, 397 F. Supp. 166, 179–180 (D.D.C. 1974), *aff'd sub. nom. United States v. Haldeman*, 559 F.2d 31 D.D.C. 1976), *cert. denied*, 431 U.S. 933 (1977); *United States v. Mitchell*, 372 F. Supp. 1239, 1259–60 (S.D.N.Y. 1973).

The Attorney General's second premise is that the Subcommittee's offer to receive information in executive session is not a legal basis for providing that information. The Attorney General argues that "promises of confidentiality by a congressional committee or subcommittee do not remove the basis for the policy of nondisclosure of law enforcement files," because the Subcommittee could decide, by formal vote, to use material in public session, and therefore providing the Subcommittee with that material would mean the executive had "lost control" over the material. While the Attorney General quotes previous Department of Justice statements to this effect, he does not cite any judicial or statutory precedent, nor any aspect of the historic role of the receipt of information in executive session, to support his view. Indeed, the Attorney General's opinion professes complete ignorance of judicial opinions regarding the significance in this context of executive session.[10]

---

10. [1] "I am unaware of a single judicial authority establishing the propositions which you have expounded that the power properly lies only with Congress to determine whether law enforcement files might be distributed publicly, and I am compelled to reject it categorically." Opinion of the Attorney General at 7.

However, there is extensive judicial, statutory, and historic precedent for disclosure of the most sensitive material to congressional committees in executive session, notwithstanding the asserted "lost control." The Framers anticipated that Congress would need to receive sensitive information requiring secret treatment, and provided expressly for it in the Journal Clause, Art. I, §5, Cl. 3, which requires the Senate and House to keep and publish Journals, "except such parts as may in their judgment require secrecy."

Contemporary judicial opinions recognize the significance of that constitutional authority, noting that "Congress has undoubted authority to keep its records secret, authority rooted in the Constitution, longstanding practice, and current congressional rules." *Goland v. Central Intelligence Agency*, 607 F.2d 339, 346 (D.C. Cir. 1978), *cert. denied*, 445 U.S. 927 (1980). The very reason the Framers conferred this authority on Congress to keep its record secret was so that it could receive sensitive information, such as information about "negotiations about treaties," from the executive.[11] *See generally*, Kaye, *Congressional Papers, Judicial Subpoenas, and the Constitution*, 24 U.C.L.A. L. Rev. 253, 533 (1977) (secrecy clause protects Congress's proceedings concerning negotiation of treaties and planning of military operations in wartime).

In light of this, the availability of executive sessions as a means of receiving information without disclosure, and congressional commitments about confidentiality, have been given strong weight by the courts. Private parties have frequently objected, as the Attorney General has done in this instance, to receipt by congressional committees of information from law enforcement agencies; their objections relied on the ground urged by the Attorney General, that a committee might subsequently use executive session material in public. The courts have uniformly given this objection short shrift, holding that disclosure to congressional committees is not tantamount to public disclosure. *Exxon Corp. v. FTC*, 589 F.2d 582, 589 (D.C. Cir. 1978), *cert. denied*, 441 U.S. 943 (1979). The courts "presume that the committees of Congress will exercise their powers responsibly and with due regard for the rights of affected parties." *FTC v. Owens-Corning Fiberglass Corp.*, 626 F.2d 966, 970 (D.C. Cir. 1980).

Similarly, a leading Supreme Court case notes the importance of executive session as a basis for receiving testimony when there is parallel litigation. In *Hutcheson v. United States, supra*, the Court ruled that Congress could obtain testimony even from a defendant facing a pending state criminal case. As Justice Brennan noted in his seminal

---

11. [2] *See* R. Berger, *Executive Privilege: A Constitutional Myth* 204–05 (1975). A clear early example of the link between the Executive providing material, and Congress receiving it in executive session, occurred in 1800. The Senate, in response to a request from President Adams that his instructions to envoys negotiating with the French be treated in strictest confidence, adopted a resolution—which, with limited changes, is currently Senate Rule XXXIX—specifically requiring that treaties and confidential communications be kept secret until the Senate by resolution removes that injunction of secrecy. *See Inquiry into the Matter of Billy Carter and Libya: Hearings Before the Subcom. to Investigate the Activities of Individuals Representing the Interests of Foreign Governments of the Senate Comm. on the Judiciary*, 96th Cong. 2d Sess. 1690 (1980) (Congressional Research Service memorandum describing history of executive session treatment of material).

concurring opinion, "Surely it cannot be said that a fair criminal trial and a full power of [congressional] inquiry are interests that defy accommodation ... [by means such as] postponement of inquiry until after an immediately pending trial, *or the taking of testimony in executive session*—or that the State grant a continuance in the trial" 369 U.S. at 624–25.

Three examples directly contradict the Attorney General's view that the availability of executive session is not a basis for providing sensitive information. First, both the House and Senate receive extensive secret intelligence material through their intelligence committees, precisely because both the House and Senate have rules that such material shall be kept secret by the committees. *See* H.R. Rule 48(7), Rules of the House of Representatives §944, H.R. Doc. No 398, 96th Cong., 2d Sess. 659, 665, (1981); Senate Resolution 400, 94th Cong., 2d Sess., §8 (1976). Second, authorized House and Senate committees receive confidential tax information, precisely because they receive it in executive session. *See* 265 U.S.C. §6103(f)(3), §6103(f)(4)(B).

Third, the Justice Department itself has disclosed confidential information to House and Senate committees, such as wiretap information from a pension fraud and bribery investigation, based on the receipt of such information in executive session and commitments concerning nondisclosure. A defendant challenged this arrangement in court as insufficiently protecting him against public release of this information, but the court upheld the arrangement as sufficiently protective and the objection was overruled. *United States v. Allen M. Dorfman, et al.*, No. 81 CR 269 (bench opinion, July 1, 1981), *reprinted in Court Proceedings and Actions of Vital Interest to the Congress No. 14; Current to Sept. 1, 1981*, at 407–411 (House Judiciary Committee Print 1982).

In sum, the spectre raised by the Attorney General that Congress compromises the prosecution of cases by concurrently investigating the subject matter, even in advance of any decision to make public the information it obtains, is unfounded. It is also inconsistent with the prior position of the Department of Justice. For example, in 1979, the representatives of the Department testified in connection with an investigation into fraudulent oil pricing and Congress requested access to open civil litigation files in a specific case. The Department stated it has "[n]o objection, except that we would ask that because of the pending litigation that they not be made public at this juncture, *unless the committee has some compelling need.*" *White Collar Crime in the Oil Industry: Joint Hearings Before the Subcomm. on Energy and Power of the House Comm. on Interstate and Foreign Commerce and the Subcomm. on Crime of the House Comm. on Judiciary*, 96th Cong., 1st Sess. 157 (1979) (testimony of John C. Keeney, Deputy Assistant Attorney General, Criminal Division, Department of Justice) (emphasis added).

Thus, there is ample precedent for congressional inquiries into the conduct by the Executive of investigations and litigation. There is ample precedent for receipt in executive session as a basis for providing sensitive material. There is no reason for extending the secrecy principles hitherto reserved for FBI criminal investigative files to the entire government.

Showdown in U.S. District Court

As the correspondence above suggests, each side of the EPA dispute had taken legal positions that were not conducive to reaching an accommodation or compromise to resolve the matter. Battle was joined when the full House of Representatives voted to hold EPA Administrator Burford in contempt, and the Speaker of the House referred the matter to the Justice Department for criminal prosecution. In a remarkable and unprecedented turn of events, the Reagan Justice Department not only refused to prosecute Burford, whom they viewed as having acted lawfully and at the express direction of the president, but also took the extraordinary step of filing a civil lawsuit against the House of Representatives in federal court in Washington, D.C. The result was one of the most oddly captioned lawsuits in American legal history, *United States v. House of Representatives of the United States.*

Before reviewing the court's opinion in that case, which is reproduced in full below, consider the following summary of the positions of the parties and the ultimate outcome of the matter, taken from Brand & Connelly, *supra*, 36 CATH. UNIV. L. REV. at 79–81 (footnotes omitted):

> When Burford appeared before the subcommittee on December 2, she refused to produce certain documents covered by the subpoena, citing a memorandum from President Reagan. [*Ed. Note: Reproduced in full above.*] The Levitas subcommittee then voted to hold Burford in contempt. After still further negotiations proved unsuccessful, the full committee voted, on December 10, 1982, to certify Burford in contempt and to forward the matter to the full House for its consideration. On December 16, 1982, the House passed, by a vote of 259 to 105, a resolution citing Burford for contempt of Congress. The Speaker of the House, acting pursuant to 2 U.S.C. §194, then certified the contempt, whereupon a copy of the certification was delivered to the United States Attorney for the District of Columbia.
>
> Immediately after the House vote and prior to the delivery of the contempt citation, however, the Justice Department filed a complaint in the name of the United States seeking declaratory and injunctive relief against numerous House of Representatives defendants. The requested relief included an injunction that would have prevented "any further action to enforce the outstanding subpoena" against Burford. The United States Attorney, whose name was listed on the Justice Department complaint, declined to present the Burford matter to a grand jury, claiming that "it would not be appropriate for me to consider bringing this matter before a grand jury until the civil action has been resolved."
>
> The House defendants almost immediately moved to dismiss the suit. The memorandum in support of the House motion identified numerous jurisdictional and constitutional defects in the Justice Department complaint. The barriers to suit identified by the House defendants included the Speech or Debate Clause and Article III of the Constitution.

On February 3, 1983, the court granted the House defendants' motion to dismiss. [*Ed. Note: The full opinion of the court is reproduced below.*] Choosing to avoid most of the House's specific arguments, the court instead relied upon the more generalized notion in the House memorandum that the Justice Department lawsuit was an inappropriate vehicle for resolving the merits of the constitutional confrontation. The court stated that "constitutional claims and other objections to congressional investigatory procedures may be raised as defenses in a criminal prosecution." Further, it added that resolution of the executive privilege claim would become necessary only if Burford became a defendant in either a criminal contempt proceeding or some other legal action initiated by Congress. The court, therefore, held that the civil action should be dismissed. In so holding, it distinguished *United States v. American Telephone & Telegraph Co. (AT&T)*, 552 F.2d 384 (D.C. Cir. 1976), in which the District of Columbia Circuit upheld jurisdiction over a lawsuit brought by the executive branch seeking to prevent a private party from complying with a congressional subpoena. According to the court, the *AT&T* case was distinguishable because, absent a need for prior judicial intervention in a civil context, the executive branch would never have been able to raise its claim of executive privilege.

The Justice Department never took an appeal from this dismissal. EPA Administrator Burford resigned from her position on March 9, 1983, and the disputed documents were turned over to a House committee that same day upon a promise by the committee to preserve confidentiality.

United States v.
House of Representatives of the United States
556 F. Supp. 150 (D.D.C. 1983)

John Lewis Smith, Jr., District Judge.

The United States of America and Anne M. Gorsuch, in her official capacity as Administrator of the Environmental Protection Agency (EPA), bring this action under the Declaratory Judgment Act, 28 U.S.C. §2201. Plaintiffs ask the Court to declare that Administrator Gorsuch acted lawfully in refusing to release certain documents to a congressional subcommittee. Defendants in the action are: The House of Representatives of the United States; The Committee on Public Works and Transportation; The Honorable James J. Howard, Chairman of the Committee on Public Works and Transportation; The Subcommittee on Investigations and Oversight of the Committee on Public Works and Transportation; The Honorable Elliott J. Levitas, Chairman of the Subcommittee on Investigations and Oversight of the Committee on Public Works and Transportation; The Honorable Thomas P. O'Neill, Speaker of the House of Representatives; Edmund L. Henshaw, Jr., Clerk of the House of Representatives; Jack Russ, Sergeant at Arms of the House of Representatives; and James T. Molloy, Doorkeeper of the House of Representatives. The individual defendants are sued only in their official capacities. The case is now before the Court on defendants' motion to dismiss.

The essential facts are undisputed. On November 22, 1982, a subpoena was served upon Anne Gorsuch by the Subcommittee on Investigations and Oversight (the Subcommittee) of the Committee on Public Works and Transportation (the Committee). The subpoena required Administrator Gorsuch to appear before the Subcommittee on December 2, 1982, and to produce at that time the following documents:

> all books, records, correspondence, memorandums, papers, notes and documents drawn or received by the Administrator and/or her representatives since December 11, 1980, including duplicates and excepting shipping papers and other commercial or business documents, contractor and/or other technical documents, for those sites listed as national priorities pursuant to Section 105(8)(B) of P.L. 96-510, the "Comprehensive Environmental Response, Compensation and Liability Act of 1980."

On November 30, 1982, President Reagan sent a Memorandum to Administrator Gorsuch instructing her to withhold from the Subcommittee any documents from open law enforcement files assembled as part of the Executive Branch's efforts to enforce the Comprehensive Environmental Response, Compensation and Liability Act of 1980. On December 2, 1982, the return date of the subpoena, Administrator Gorsuch appeared before the Subcommittee. She advised the Subcommittee that the EPA had begun to gather for production all documents responsive to the subpoena, but "... sensitive documents found in open law enforcement files will not be made available to the Subcommittee." 149 Cong. Rec. H10037. The Committee passed a Resolution reporting the matter to the full House of Representatives on December 10, 1982. The full House cited Administrator Gorsuch for contempt of Congress on December 16, 1982. The initial complaint in this case was filed on the same day, one day before the contempt resolution was certified to the United States Attorney for the District of Columbia for presentment to the grand jury. To date, the United States Attorney has not presented the contempt citation to the grand jury for its consideration.

Section 192 of Title 2 of the United States Code provides that a subpoenaed witness who refuses "to produce papers upon any matter under inquiry before either House ... or any committee of either House of Congress", shall be guilty of a misdemeanor "punishable by a fine of not more than $1,000 nor less than $100 and imprisonment in a common jail for not less than one month nor more than twelve months." Once an individual has been found in contempt by either House of Congress, a contempt order is presented to the President of the Senate or the Speaker of the House of Representatives for certification. 2 U.S.C. §194. The President or Speaker in turn delivers the contempt citation to the appropriate United States Attorney. *The United States Attorney is then required to bring the matter before the grand jury. Id.* [*Ed. Note: Emphasis added; see Note 1 below.*]

The Executive Branch, through the Justice Department, has chosen an alternate route, however, in bringing this civil action against the House of Representatives and individual members of the Legislative Branch. Plaintiffs ask the Court to resolve the controversy by deciding whether Administrator Gorsuch acted lawfully in withholding certain documents under a claim of executive privilege.

Defendants raise several challenges to the propriety of plaintiffs' cause of action. Included among defendants' grounds for dismissal are lack of subject matter jurisdiction, lack of standing, and the absence of a "case or controversy" as required by Article III, §2 of the United States Constitution. In addition, defendants claim that they are immune from suit under the Speech and Debate Clause, Article I, §6, cl. 1. Plaintiffs have addressed and opposed each of these threshold challenges.

The Legislative and Executive Branches of the United States Government are embroiled in a dispute concerning the scope of the congressional investigatory power. If these two co-equal branches maintain their present adversarial positions, the Judicial Branch will be required to resolve the dispute by determining the validity of the Administrator's claim of executive privilege. Plaintiffs request the Court to provide immediate answers, in this civil action, to the constitutional questions which fuel this controversy. Defendants, however, have indicated a preference for established criminal procedures in their motion to dismiss this case. Assuming there are no jurisdictional bars to this suit, therefore, the Court must initially determine whether to resolve the constitutional controversy in the context of a civil action, or defer to established statutory procedures for deciding challenges to congressional contempt citations.

The statutory provisions concerning penalties for contempt of Congress, 2 U.S.C. §192 and §194, constitute "an orderly and often approved means of vindicating constitutional claims arising from a legislative investigation." *Sanders v. McClellan*, 463 F.2d 894, 899 (D.C.Cir.1972). Under these provisions, constitutional claims and other objections to congressional investigatory procedures may be raised as defenses in a criminal prosecution. *See Barenblatt v. United States*, 360 U.S. 109 (1959); *Ansara v. Eastland*, 442 F.2d 751 (D.C.Cir.1971); *United States v. Tobin*, 306 F.2d 270, 276 (D.C. Cir.1962). Courts have been extremely reluctant to interfere with the statutory scheme by considering cases brought by recalcitrant witnesses seeking declaratory or injunctive relief. *See, e.g., Eastland v. United States Servicemen's Fund*, 421 U.S. 491 (1975); *Ansara v. Eastland*, 442 F.2d at 754. Although the Court of Appeals for this Circuit has entertained one civil action seeking to block compulsory legislative process, that action was brought by the Executive Branch to prevent a private party from complying with a congressional subpoena. *See United States v. American Telephone and Telegraph Company*, 551 F.2d 384 (D.C.Cir.1976). Significantly, therefore, in that case the Executive Branch was not able to raise its claim of executive privilege as a defense to criminal contempt proceedings.

Courts have a duty to avoid unnecessarily deciding constitutional issues. *United States v. Rumely*, 345 U.S. 41 (1952). When constitutional disputes arise concerning the respective powers of the Legislative and Executive Branches, judicial intervention should be delayed until all possibilities for settlement have been exhausted. *See United States v. American Telephone and Telegraph*, 551 F.2d at 393–395. Judicial restraint is essential to maintain the delicate balance of powers among the branches established by the Constitution. *See id.* Since the controversy which has led to *United States v. House of Representatives* clearly raises difficult constitutional questions in the context of an intragovernmental dispute, the Court should not address these issues until circumstances indicate that judicial intervention is necessary.

The gravamen of plaintiffs' complaint is that executive privilege is a valid defense to congressional demands for sensitive law enforcement information from the EPA. Plaintiffs have, thus, raised this executive privilege defense as the basis for affirmative relief. Judicial resolution of this constitutional claim, however, will never become necessary unless Administrator Gorsuch becomes a defendant in either a criminal contempt proceeding or other legal action taken by Congress. *See, e.g., Ansara v. Eastland,* 441 F.2d at 753–754. The difficulties apparent in prosecuting Administrator Gorsuch for contempt of Congress should encourage the two branches to settle their differences without further judicial involvement. Compromise and cooperation, rather than confrontation, should be the aim of the parties. The Court, therefore, finds that to entertain this declaratory judgment action would be an improper exercise of the discretion granted by the Declaratory Judgment Act, 28 U.S.C. §2201. *See Hanes Corp. v. Millard,* 531 F.2d 585, 591 (D.C.Cir.1976). In light of this determination, the Court will not address the additional grounds for dismissal raised by defendants.

Accordingly, defendants' motion to dismiss is granted.

Aftermath:
Granting Access and "Purging" Contempt

The court's refusal to grant the relief sought by the Justice Department and its admonition that the parties should pursue "[c]ompromise and cooperation, rather than confrontation" had the desired effect and quickly led to a settlement of the dispute. The Reagan administration granted the House subcommittee access to the disputed documents, subject to some conditions. *See Report Relating to the Contempt Citation of Anne M. (Gorsuch) Burford,* H.R. No. 98-323 (July 27, 1983) (detailing the terms of the negotiated resolution of the dispute). The subcommittee chairman, in return, agreed to introduce a resolution "purging" the contempt resolution. The report that accompanied that resolution appeared to declare victory in the dispute over the EPA documents, by noting that the subcommittee "now has that information, in the form of total access to the EPA Superfund program files: copies of the Superfund program records and other documents it was seeking through its subpoena, including those considered 'enforcement sensitive' by the EPA and the Department of Justice; and can now discharge its investigative duties and assist the Congress, through the oversight process, in carrying out its legislative responsibilities." *See id.* at 3. The report also made clear that the House continued to maintain its position that "the statutory means of compulsion provided by law for compliance with subpoenas is applicable to executive branch officials." *See id.* at 2. The Reagan Justice Department, in turn, thereafter memorialized its contrary legal position in a formal opinion of the Office of Legal Counsel (discussed further in Note 1 below). *See Prosecution for Contempt of Congress of an Executive Branch Official Who Has Asserted a Claim of Executive Privilege*, 8 Op. Off. Legal Counsel 101 (May 30, 1984). These diametrically opposed views of the law of executive privilege have since remained the positions of the legislative and executive branches, even as control of both branches has shifted between the two major political parties. It is not surprising that disputes have continued to arise in the area, but it is perhaps surprising that it took over two decades before a dispute again spilled over into the judicial branch. The next section of this Chapter will examine that dispute.

Notes and Questions

1. **Contempt of Congress, Separation of Powers, and Prosecutorial Discretion.** In addition to its refusal to grant the Department of Justice's request for a declaratory judgment that EPA Administrator Burford had acted lawfully in refusing on grounds of executive privilege to produce subpoenaed information to Congress, the court in the opinion above states that a U.S. Attorney, on receipt of a criminal contempt referral from Congress, is "required to bring the matter before a grand jury" for prosecution. The interpretation of the criminal contempt of Congress statute as a mandatory directive appears to be consistent with the statutory language, which provides that Congress can certify a contempt resolution to a U.S. Attorney "*whose duty it shall be* to bring the matter before a grand jury for its action." *See* 2 U.S.C. §194 (emphasis added). The Department of Justice, however, rejected that interpretation of the contempt statute. In a 1984 opinion by the Justice Department's Office of Legal Counsel on the EPA dispute, Assistant Attorney General for the Office of Legal Counsel Theodore B. Olson took the position that "[a]s a matter of statutory construction and separation of powers analysis, a United States Attorney is not required to refer a congressional contempt citation to a grand jury or otherwise to prosecute an Executive Branch official who carries out the President's instruction to invoke the President's claim of executive privilege before Congress." *Prosecution for Contempt of Congress of an Executive Branch Official Who Has Asserted a Claim of Executive Privilege*, 8 Op. Off. Legal Counsel 101 (May 30, 1984).

The 1984 OLC opinion is based upon two core conclusions concerning the proper interpretation and application of the criminal contempt of Congress statute. First, the OLC opinion concludes that a mandatory directive from Congress requiring the executive branch to prosecute a particular individual who has been held in contempt of Congress violates separation of powers principles: "First, as a matter of statutory interpretation reinforced by compelling separation of powers considerations, we believe Congress may not direct the Executive to prosecute a particular individual without leaving any discretion to the Executive to determine whether a violation of law has occurred." The separation of powers concerns relied upon in the OLC opinion are predicated on a broad conception of executive privilege and a corollary belief that an assertion of executive privilege is presumptively valid, making a criminal prosecution for assertion of executive privilege a constitutionally impermissible burden on the President's ability to assert executive privilege: "If one House of Congress could make it a crime simply to assert the President's presumptively valid claim, even if a court subsequently were to agree that the privilege claims were valid, the exercise of the privilege would be so burdened as to be nullified."

The second core conclusion of the 1984 OLC opinion is that, properly interpreted, the criminal contempt of Congress statute has no application to senior executive branch officials. The opinion asserts that the legislative history to the criminal contempt statute contains no indication "that Congress intended the statute to provide a remedy for refusals to produce documents pursuant to a Presidential claim of executive privilege." The opinion buttresses this assertion by noting that "until the citation of the EPA Administrator in 1982, 125 years after the contempt statute was enacted, neither house of Congress had ever voted to utilize the contempt statute against a presidential assertion of executive privilege." In rejecting the application of the contempt statute to executive branch officials as contrary to separation of powers principles, the 1984 OLC opinion contains notably colorful language: "By wielding the cudgel of criminal contempt, however, Congress seeks to invoke the power of the third branch, not to resolve a dispute between the Executive and Legislative Branches and to obtain documents it claims it needs, but to punish the Executive, indeed to punish the official who carried out the President's constitutionally authorized commands, for asserting a constitutional privilege." Although the 1984 opinion begins with "the caveat that our conclusions are limited to the unique circumstances that gave rise to these questions in late 1982 and early 1983," its conclusion on the separation of powers issue appears to extend beyond the Anne Gorsuch Burford EPA case: "The balancing required by the separation of powers demonstrates that the contempt of Congress statute cannot be constitutionally applied to an executive official in the context under consideration." The "context under consideration" presumably includes any senior executive branch official who asserts executive privilege at the direction of the President.

Do you agree with the 1984 OLC opinion's conclusions on the separation of powers issues? Is it constitutionally impermissible for Congress to require criminal prosecution of persons who are held in contempt of Congress? If so, how does a statute that requires prosecution of those persons differ from statutes requiring prosecution of persons who commit other offenses that Congress has defined as criminal? Under the OLC opinion's interpretation could a U.S. Attorney decline to prosecute a private citizen for contempt of Congress, for example if the U.S. Attorney believed that Congress had overstepped its constitutional authority in seeking information from that individual? What if the private individual is a former senior government official who has been subpoenaed by Congress to provide information about his or her activities while serving in government? (For further examination of the latter issue, see the discussion of the *McGahn* case later in this Chapter.)

In congressional testimony in 1983 one of the authors of this book took strong issue with the legal position taken by OLC regarding the proper interpretation of the criminal contempt of Congress statute:

Testimony of Stanley M. Brand,
General Counsel to the Clerk of the
House of Representatives

Examining and Reviewing the Procedures That Were Taken by the Office of the U.S. Attorney for the District of Columbia In Their Implementation of a Contempt Citation That Was Voted by the Full House of Representatives Against Then Administrator of the Environmental Protection Agency, Anne Gorsuch Burford, Hearing of the Committee on Public Works and Transportation, U.S. House of Representatives, 98th Con., 1st Sess. (June 16, 1983).

Mr. BRAND. Thank you, Mr. Chairman. I think, as everyone recalls, I was—

The CHAIRMAN. For the record, please tell your position.

Mr. BRAND. General Counsel to the Clerk of the House of Representatives.

As I think you will recall, I was responsible for rendering legal advice to the committee with respect to the issuance of its subpoena and the subsequent lawsuit, proceedings, and negotiations which ensued.

The statutory scheme enacted by Congress as a means of compulsion for subpoenas has been used hundreds of times since 1857, as Chairman Levitas pointed out. It was not until the late hours of December 16, 1982, however, that a serious challenge to its viability was raised by the Department. Rather than proceed under the statute as it had done hundreds of times in the past through the U.S. Attorney, it filed an unprecedented suit alleging that the law was unconstitutional, could never be invoked against any executive officials, and seeking the declaratory and injunctive relief against the House of Representatives.

As everyone knows by now, the suit was dismissed by motion of the House of Representatives and shortly thereafter, pursuant to negotiations, full access to the documents was obtained.

However, because of the Department's position in the suit and in the public statements it made during the pendency of the suit, questions have been raised about the viability of the law which Congress passed in 1857.

I am convinced that the statute is a good statute and is alive and well. Nothing in the Department's brief or in its civil suits or submissions to the House Judiciary Committee on this issue convinced me that it is not. Reduced to simple dimensions, I think the Department's position was, like the boy who came to the game with a ball, he didn't like the rules, and goes home with the ball during the game. That is not a perfect metaphor, but I think it illustrates the point.

The ball in this case is the prosecutorial discretion they say they have to—vested in the U.S. Attorney—to refuse to go forward. The other players are the Congress and the courts. They invoke prosecutorial discretion and go home.

Congress sits by on the sidelines, frustrated, in a way totally frustrated in their ability to obtain a judicial resolution.

But, let's look at the law in the cases and see why that position is not supportable.

The concept on which they rely and, quickly reviewing Mr. [Stanley] Harris' prepared statement of prosecutorial discretion is well known.[12] It permits a prosecutor to determine generally which cases to bring, how to bring them, and whether particular facts warrant prosecution given the policies and reasons advanced by the law.

This much no one disputes. Where we depart is its relevance to the statute at issue. In our view, the Department and the U.S. Attorney did not exercise any prosecutorial discretion as we know it; rather, they boldly stated that they would never under any circumstances and for any reason bring a prosecution. This is not discretion.

This is recalcitrance, which shades perilously close to obstruction. But the statute provides not in any way that impinges on prosecutorial discretion that the matter shall merely be presented to the grand jury and it does not otherwise circumscribe the discretion that all prosecutors have in bringing cases.

As we know from the cases and the sources of—other sources of authority, the U.S. Attorney is merely an adviser to the grand jury. As stated in one original case:

> What is the place of the U.S. Attorney in the functioning of the grand jury? You must naturally accord him the respect due an officer of the government, but you do not forget he is, from the viewpoint of the grand jury, only a lawyer, an agent of the Federal Department of Justice, and by law he is only the legal adviser to the grand jury.

As Judge Smith stated in describing the statute's provisions in the lawsuit, after certification the U.S. Attorney is "then required to bring the matter before the grand jury."

And under the statutory scheme, it is to the judiciary that Congress has delegated responsibility to protect it from contumacious witnesses. I notice in the U.S. Attorney's prepared statement that he indicates the legislative history reflects Congress felt obliged to transfer contempt adjudications to the executive branch.

I must respectfully disagree.

I have with me the legislative history of the 1857 statute, and Congressman Marshall states the intent:

> If it is the sense of the House that sufficient authority for the purposes does not now reside in the House of Congress, then let the bill invoke the aid of the judiciary.

The Supreme Court has picked up on that legislative history and has continually sounded the note that it is conscious intent to enlist the aid of the judiciary in prosecuting contumacious conduct. This is a quote from the *United States v. Russell*, a 1962 U.S. Supreme Court case:

---

12. *[Ed. Note: Stanley Harris was the U.S. Attorney for the District of Columbia from 1982 to 1983, and was appointed to the D.C. District in 1983 to succeed Judge Smith, the author of* United States v. House of Representatives.*]*

When Congress provided that no one could be prosecuted under 2 U.S.C. §192 except upon an indictment, Congress made the basic decision that only a grand jury could determine whether a person could be held to answer in a criminal trial for refusing to give testimony pertinent to a question under congressional committee inquiry.

In that Congress enlists the aid of the judiciary to enforce its subpoenas and the grand jury is clearly more an arm of the courts to the extent that it is a part of any branch; the Department's refusal is a refusal to permit the Congress to invoke judicial process which commences when the House votes to certify the matter to the U.S. Attorney.

Finally, there are no prior examples of the Department construing the statute in this manner. Indeed, we have the opposite.

* * *

In conclusion, I submit that the prosecutorial discretion waived [*sic*] about in this case was a high-sounding euphemism for recalcitrance, a smoke screen to distract us from the Department's decision in this matter to place the mere assertion of a claim of privilege above the responsibility to enforce a valid law hundreds of times.

I again had an opportunity to peruse the U.S. Attorney's statement and I would make only one other point. The U.S. Attorney discusses that the words of the statute are that he shall present the matter to the grand jury and that "shall" has been interpreted in other statutory frameworks to be an admonition, not a mandatory requirement.

It has also been interpreted to be a mandatory requirement in cases, including the famous impoundment cases with which this committee was no doubt familiar.

In the Nixon administration, the Department took the position on a number of—in a number of instances that when Congress said that the Executive shall appropriate money, it didn't mean "shall," it meant "may."

The courts resoundingly rejected that proposition, said when Congress mandated that the money be spent, that that language imposed a duty upon the executive branch.

I would also point out that in Mr. Harris' statement he says he is not free to discuss the merits of the Burford contempt matter but that illustratively the grand jury would be entitled to know that she was following the instructions of the President of the United States in conducting herself as she did.

I am not sure that they would. Reading the cases, that is not an element of the offense. Clearly the statute requires willful—an element of the statute is willfulness. The willfulness that is required though is not necessarily a state of mind which borders on evil intent to refuse to comply. It is that the willfulness is not to present yourself and testify or produce documents as the case may be. That might be an issue for the jury, and her instructions from the President might be an issue for the jury to consider in determining whether the elements of the offense have been established.

I am unaware of any instance in which that kind of defense has been presented to the grand jury in making out a case under the statute.

The one example we have, I think, is the *Tobin* case, which is an early case in this circuit involving the New York Port Authority director. He raised executive privilege in a court proceeding that was a matter that the court dealt with at trial, and so I would like to put that on the record as well.

That concludes my statement.

For a law review article providing further refutation of the Justice Department's "prosecutorial discretion" argument, see Brand & Connelly, 36 CATH. UNIV. L. REV. at 87–88 (footnotes omitted, except as noted):

> It was further argued by the Executive Branch during the Burford controversy that Congress could not constitutionally interfere with the Executive's prosecutorial discretion in determining what cases to bring before a grand jury. There are serious questions, however, as to whether the Executive Branch truly exercised prosecutorial discretion in the Burford matter.[13] In a more general vein, constitutional claims of prosecutorial discretion are, in any event, unpersuasive in this context. As recently stated by a leading commentator, Article II of the Constitution "is a duty, not a license; it imposes an obligation on the President to enforce duly enacted laws." Even assuming that Congress could not constitutionally interfere with the Executive's prosecutorial discretion based upon the individualized facts of a given case (an assumption that itself is far from clear), there should be little doubt as to the constitutionality of a statutory scheme constraining the Executive's discretion over broad categories of cases. It is constitutionally permissible, therefore, for Congress to decree that every person cited by a House of Congress for contempt be brought before a grand jury.

The position taken in the 1984 OLC opinion was subsequently reiterated in a 1986 Office of Legal Counsel Opinion, *Response to Congressional Requests for Information Regarding Decisions Made Under the Independent Counsel Act*, 10 Op. Off. Legal Counsel 68 (April 28, 1986). The 1986 opinion reaffirmed OLC's earlier view that executive privilege can be asserted to refuse to produce law enforcement files to Congress:

---

13. [Note 112] "Prosecutorial discretion" concerns, *inter alia*, a determination to decline prosecution where no substantial federal interest would be served, the putative defendant is subject to prosecution in another jurisdiction, or there exists an adequate noncriminal alternative. UNITED STATES DEPARTMENT OF JUSTICE, PRINCIPLES OF FEDERAL PROSECUTION 5–14 (July 1980). Among the factors that a prosecutor may consider are the likelihood of conviction, the choice of a strong case to test uncertain law, the degree of criminality, the weight of evidence, precedent, policy, the climate of public opinion, and the gravity of the offense. *See Smith v. United States*, 375 F.2d 242, 247 (5th Cir.), *cert. denied*, 389 U.S. 841 (1967). The elements of the congressional contempt statute are not difficult or complicated to prove, and none of the factors identified by the courts as relevant to the exercise of discretion were present. On the contrary, the only articulated reasons for the bold and unequivocal refusal of the Justice Department to proceed was that prosecution would impose a 'heavy burden' upon the assertion of executive privilege. This is hardly the exercise of discretion; it is simply a variation upon the theory that any executive official following orders is excused from the obligation to respond to valid congressional demands.

Moreover, the policy of the Executive Branch throughout our Nation's history has generally been to decline to provide committees of Congress with access to, or copies of, open law enforcement files except in extraordinary circumstances. This policy with respect to Executive Branch investigations was first expressed by President Washington and has been reaffirmed by or on behalf of most or our Presidents, including Presidents Jefferson, Jackson, Lincoln, Theodore Roosevelt, Franklin Roosevelt, and Eisenhower. No President, to our knowledge, has departed from this position affirming the confidentiality and privileged nature of open law enforcement files.

The 1986 opinion also restated the conclusion of the prior 1984 OLC opinion that "Congress could not, as a matter of statutory or constitutional law, invoke the criminal contempt of Congress procedure set out in 2 U.S.C. §§192 and 194 against the head of an Executive Branch agency, if he acted on the instructions of the President to assert executive privilege in response to a congressional subpoena."

Experts at the Congressional Research Service have disputed the OLC's assertion that the legislative history of the criminal contempt statute indicates that it was not intended to be used against senior executive branch officials:

> The assertion that the legislative history of the 1857 statute establishing the criminal contempt process demonstrates that it was not intended to be used against executive branch official [*sic*] is not supported by the historical record. The floor debates leading to enactment of the statute make clear that the legislation was intended as an alternative to, not a substitute for, inherent contempt authority. This understanding has been reflected in numerous Supreme Court opinions upholding the use of the criminal contempt statute. A close review of the floor debates indicates that Representative H. Marshall expressly pointed out that the broad language of the bill "proposes to punish equally the Cabinet officer and the culprit who may have insulted the dignity of this House by an attempt to corrupt a Representative of the people."

Morton Rosenberg & Todd B. Tatelman, *Congress's Contempt Power: Law, History, Practice, and Procedure*, CRS Report for Congress (updated April 15, 2008).

Despite the controversy and uncertainty surrounding the legal positions taken in the 1984 and 1986 OLC opinions, subsequent presidential administrations from both parties have not taken action to rescind them, and they continue to represent the official position of the Department of Justice. For two decades after those opinions were published Congress and the executive branch continued to skirmish frequently over access to information, but a conflict of the scope and intensity of the Burford EPA dispute did not arise again until the George W. Bush administration and the dispute over U.S. Attorney dismissals that is the subject of the next section of this Chapter.

2. Collateral Damage. The congressional investigation into EPA's administration of the Superfund and the accompanying executive privilege dispute ultimately led to the resignation of EPA Administrator Anne Gorsuch Burford and a number of her subordinates. Burford concluded her 1986 autobiography with a notably frank (some might say bitter) summary of those events:

> Ronald Reagan is touted as being the greatest team player, the greatest loyalist of his own administration. If that is the case, we are all in deep trouble. As Stanley Brand so aptly pointed out, when congressional criticism began to touch the presidency, Mr. Reagan solved *his* problem by jettisoning me and my people, people whose only "crime" was loyal service, following orders. I was not the first to receive his special brand of benevolent neglect, a form of conveniently looking the other way, while his staff continues to do some very dirty work. The current management vacuum at EPA is a direct result of Presidential neglect. Those slots would not be vacant if there were a real concern for the environment.
>
> When President Reagan asked me to head the Environmental Protection Agency, I understood that he wanted me to carry out his policies of New Federalism and regulatory reform, and to get better environmental results with fewer people and less money. I took the job because I wanted to bring a politically conservative approach to solving management problems of environmental protection. And I took the job because I thought Ronald Reagan shared that philosophy.
>
> Having to face the fact that he does not is probably the hardest thing I have had to do, and I am still uncomfortable with it. Ronald Reagan has always been a personal and political hero of mine, and concluding that he doesn't care about the environment hurts.

Anne M. Burford with John Greenya, Are You Tough Enough? 281–82 (McGraw-Hill 1986) (emphasis in original).

Another senior EPA official, Assistant Administrator Rita M. Lavelle, suffered even worse consequences. Lavelle was convicted of perjury and obstruction of justice in connection with testimony she provided to Congress about her activities at EPA. *See United States v. Lavelle*, 751 F.2d 1266 (D.C. Cir. 1985) (affirming conviction on perjury and obstruction of justice charges); *see also* P.J. Meitl, *The Perjury Paradox: The Amazing Under-Enforcement of the Laws Regarding Lying to Congress*, 25 Quinnipiac Univ. L. Rev. 547, 553–54 (2007) (describing Rita Lavelle's conviction after "the jury listened to Lavelle testify in her own defense for five hours, and found her denials of wrongdoing unconvincing"). The EPA matter is an example of how the spotlight of a congressional investigation can expose problems in administration and compliance with the law at federal agencies, and can even lead to criminal charges if agency officials knowingly and intentionally provide false information or attempt to mislead Congress. The public's perception of the scope of the problems at EPA was serious enough that President Reagan recruited the EPA's first administrator, William D. Ruckelshaus, to return to the agency and help restore its credibility and effectiveness. Ruckelshaus, of course, was a particularly good candidate for a "Mr. Clean" role at EPA because of his national reputation for independence and probity that resulted from his forced resignation as Deputy Attorney General for refusing to follow President Nixon's order to fire Watergate special prosecutor Archibald Cox. (See Chapter 3 for more information about Watergate and the "Saturday Night Massacre" resignations of Ruckelshaus and Attorney General Elliot Richardson.)

3. Investigating the Investigation—Illegal Obstruction? The contentious and protracted conflict between Congress and the Reagan administration over the EPA matter did not end with EPA Administrator Burford's resignation. The aggressive posture taken by the Department of Justice in the matter had ruffled more than a few feathers in Congress, and it precipitated an "investigation of the EPA investigation" in which the House Judiciary Committee conducted an extensive investigation of the role of the conduct of the Department of Justice. Justice Antonin Scalia described those events in his dissenting opinion in the Supreme Court case that followed:

> The present case began when the Legislative and Executive Branches became "embroiled in a dispute concerning the scope of the congressional investigatory power," *United States v. House of Representatives of United States*, 556 F. Supp. 150, 152 (D.D.C. 1983), which—as is often the case with such interbranch conflicts—became quite acrimonious. In the course of oversight hearings into the administration of the Superfund by the Environmental Protection Agency (EPA), two Subcommittees of the House of Representatives requested and then subpoenaed numerous internal EPA documents. The President responded by personally directing the EPA Administrator not to turn over certain of the documents, *see* Memorandum of November 30, 1982, from President Reagan for the Administrator, Environmental Protection Agency, reprinted in H.R.Rep. No. 99-435, pp. 1166–1167 (1985), and by having the Attorney General notify the congressional Subcommittees of this assertion of executive privilege, *see* Letters of November 30, 1982, from Attorney General William French Smith to Hon. John D. Dingell and Hon. Elliott H. Levitas, reprinted, *id.* at 1168–1177. In his decision to assert executive privilege, the President was counseled by appellee Olson, who was then Assistant Attorney General of the Department of Justice for the Office of Legal Counsel, a post that has traditionally had responsibility for providing legal advice to the President (subject to approval of the Attorney General). The House's response was to pass a resolution citing the EPA Administrator, who had possession of the documents, for contempt. Contempt of Congress is a criminal offense. *See* 2 U.S.C. § 192. The United States Attorney, however, a member of the Executive Branch, initially took no steps to prosecute the contempt citation. Instead, the Executive Branch sought the immediate assistance of the Third Branch by filing a civil action asking the District Court to declare that the EPA Administrator had acted lawfully in withholding the documents under a claim of executive privilege. *See ibid.* The District Court declined (in my view correctly) to get involved in the controversy, and urged the other two Branches to try "[c]ompromise and cooperation, rather than confrontation." 556 F. Supp. at 153. After further haggling, the two Branches eventually reached an agree-

ment giving the House Subcommittees limited access to the contested documents.

Congress did not, however, leave things there. Certain Members of the House remained angered by the confrontation, particularly by the role played by the Department of Justice. Specifically, the Committee remained disturbed by the possibility that the Department had persuaded the President to assert executive privilege despite reservations by the EPA; that the Department had "deliberately and unnecessarily precipitated a constitutional confrontation with Congress"; that the Department had not properly reviewed and selected the documents as to which executive privilege was asserted; that the Department had directed the United States Attorney not to present the contempt certification involving the EPA Administrator to a grand jury for prosecution; that the Department had made the decision to sue the House of Representatives; and that the Department had not adequately advised and represented the President, the EPA and the EPA Administrator. H.R. Rep. No. 99-435, p. 3 (1985) (describing unresolved "questions" that were the basis of the Judiciary Committee's investigation). Accordingly, staff counsel of the House Judiciary Committee were commissioned (apparently without the knowledge of many of the Committee's members) to investigate the Justice Department's role in the controversy. That investigation lasted 2 1/2 years, and produced a 3,000-page report issued by the Committee over the vigorous dissent of all but one of its minority-party members. That report, which among other charges questioned the truthfulness of certain statements made by Assistant Attorney General Olson during testimony in front of the Committee during the early stages of its investigation, was sent to the Attorney General, along with a formal request that he appoint an independent counsel to investigate Mr. Olson and others.

Morrison v. Olson, 487 U.S. 654, 699–701 (1988) (Scalia, J., dissenting).

As this summary by Justice Scalia suggests, the majority report issued by the Judiciary Committee found fault with the actions of senior Justice Department officials in responding to the committee's requests for information about the department's actions in connection with the EPA inquiry. The most serious charges leveled by the Judiciary Committee were that the Deputy Attorney General and the Assistant Attorney General for the Land and Natural Resources Division "had wrongfully withheld certain documents from the Committee, thus obstructing the Committee's investigation" and that Theodore Olson, the head of the Office of Legal Counsel "had given false and misleading testimony." *See id.* at 666 (majority opinion by Chief Justice Rehnquist). The Judiciary Committee requested that the Attorney General appoint an independent counsel, under the independent counsel statute that was then in effect, to investigate the three senior Justice Department officials. After a preliminary investigation, as provided for in the statute, the Attorney General concluded that a referral to an independent counsel was warranted only as to Olson. The independent counsel investigation of Olson concluded without any criminal charges being brought against Olson, although the independent counsel's final report concluded that Olson's congressional testimony was "not always forthcoming" and in at least one instance was "disingenuous and misleading." *See Report of the Independent Counsel Concerning Theodore B. Olson and Robert M. Perry* (Redacted Version) 25 and 197–98, D.C. Cir., Div. for Purpose of Appointing Independent Counsels, Div. No. 86-1 (Dec. 27, 1988). Olson, of course, survived the incident with his professional reputation intact and later served as lead counsel for George W. Bush in the *Bush v. Gore* Supreme Court case and as Solicitor General of the United States in the George W. Bush administration.

4. Unintended Consequences. The most significant legal development that ultimately resulted from the EPA dispute—the Supreme Court decision in *Morrison v. Olson* upholding the independent counsel statute—would have been difficult to predict at the outset of Congress's inquiry and is an example of how congressional investigations can have unexpected and unintended consequences. As discussed in the previous Note, at the end of a two-year inquiry into the handling of the EPA matter by the Justice Department, the House Judiciary Committee formally requested that Attorney General Edwin Meese follow the procedures of the independent counsel statute for appointment of an independent counsel to investigate possible criminal conduct by three senior Justice Department officials. Meese ultimately determined that seeking an independent counsel investigation was appropriate in the case of only one of the three officials, Assistant Attorney General for the Office of Legal Counsel Theodore B. Olson (after concluding, controversially and contrary to the recommendations of his own staff review of the matter, that the other two officials "lacked the requisite 'criminal intent' to obstruct the committee's investigation," *see Morrison v. Olson*, 487 U.S. 654, 666 n.11 (1988)). When the Independent Counsel, Alexia Morrison, served Olson and the two other senior Justice Department officials with grand jury subpoenas, they refused to comply with the subpoenas and asserted that the independent counsel statute was unconstitutional. In the resulting litigation, a federal district court in Washington held that the act was constitutional, but the appeals court reversed, holding that the act was unconstitutional. *See In re Sealed Case*, 838 F.2d 476 (D.C. Cir. 1988). The case then went to the Supreme Court under the caption *Morrison v. Olson*.

Morrison v. Olson presented extraordinarily important constitutional and legal issues. At stake in the case was not only the principal post-Watergate congressional reform to protect against executive branch misconduct but also the broader Reagan administration "unitary executive" theory that all executive branch functions should be subject to unfettered presidential control. It also bears noting that the political environment at the time that *Morrison v. Olson* reached the Supreme Court could not have been more highly charged. Independent Counsel Lawrence Walsh's investigation of the Iran-Contra affair (which is the subject of Chapter 5 below) was in full swing at the time, so the potential import of the case was enormous in both legal and political terms.

A complete analysis of the Supreme Court's decision in *Morrison v. Olson* is beyond the scope of this Note, but in an unexpectedly unified 7–1 decision the court upheld the constitutionality of the independent counsel statute, finding that both the statute's judicial appointment process and its limits on Attorney General removal of independent counsels were constitutionally permissible. With respect to the core separation of powers issue, Chief Justice Rehnquist's majority opinion concluded that "[n]otwithstanding the fact that the counsel is to some degree 'independent' and free from Executive supervision to a greater extent than other federal prosecutors, in our view, these [removal and other] features of the Act give the Executive Branch sufficient control over the independent counsel to ensure that the President is able to perform his constitutionally assigned duties." 487 U.S. at 696. With respect to this crucial issue, the Court's conclusion was a major setback not only for Mr. Olson personally but also for the Reagan administration's broader effort to consolidate executive branch power under presidential control. The opinion also cleared the way for the continued investigation of the Reagan administration by Independent Counsel Walsh (see Chapter 5, discussing the Iran-Contra affair) and the subsequent investigation of President Clinton by Independent Counsel Kenneth Starr (see Chapter 6, discussing the Whitewater investigation).

The lone dissenter in *Morrison v. Olson* was Justice Antonin Scalia. Scalia took strong issue with the majority, arguing that the independent counsel statute violated core constitutional separation of powers principles. Justice Scalia also emphasized what he saw as serious practical flaws in the operation of the independent counsel statute. Many would conclude that his concerns appear strikingly prescient in light of the events that transpired a few years later when Independent Counsel Starr investigated President Clinton:

> The independent counsel thus selected proceeds to assemble a staff. As I observed earlier, in the nature of things, this has to be done by finding lawyers who are willing to lay aside their current careers for an indeterminate amount of time, to take on a job that has no prospect of permanence and little prospect for promotion. One thing is certain, however: it involves investigating and perhaps prosecuting a particular individual. Can one imagine a less equitable manner of fulfilling the Executive responsibility to investigate and prosecute? What would be the reaction if, in an area not covered by this statute, the Justice Department posted a public notice inviting applicants to assist in an investigation and possible prosecution of a certain prominent person? Does this not invite what Justice Jackson described as "picking the man and then searching the law books, or putting investigators to work, to pin some offense on him"? To be sure, the investigation must relate to the area of criminal offense specified by the life-tenured judges. But that has often been (and nothing prevents it from being) very broad—and should the independent counsel or his or her staff come up with something beyond that scope, nothing prevents him or her from asking the judges to expand his or her authority or, if that does not work, referring it to the Attorney General, whereupon the whole process would recommence and, if there was "reasonable basis to believe" that further investigation was warranted, that new offense would be referred to the Special Divi-

sion, which would in all likelihood assign it to the same independent counsel. It seems to me not conducive to fairness. But even if it were entirely evident that unfairness was in fact the result—the judges hostile to the administration, the independent counsel an old foe of the President, the staff refugees from the recently defeated administration—*there would be no one accountable to the public to whom the blame could be assigned.*

487 U.S. at 730–31 (Scalia, J., dissenting) (emphasis in original).

Reacting in part to public discomfort with the length and cost of the investigations of independent counsels Walsh and Starr, Congress allowed the independent counsel statute to expire without renewal in 1999 (the statute had previously expired in 1992, but was reauthorized in 1994; that reauthorization led to the replacement of Whitewater special counsel Robert Fiske, who had been appointed by Attorney General Janet Reno, with Independent Counsel Kenneth Starr, who was appointed by the judicial panel provided for in the statute). Who had the better arguments in the *Morrison v. Olson* case? Should Congress have reauthorized the independent counsel statute when it expired in 1999? Are special counsels appointed by the Attorney General, such as Archibald Cox for the Watergate investigation and Patrick Fitzgerald for the more recent Valerie Plame Wilson CIA leak case, an adequate substitute for a statutory independent counsel? For historical analysis and a comparison of the roles of Justice Department special counsels and statutory independent counsels, see Harold H. Bruff, *Independent Counsel and the Constitution*, 24 WILLAMETTE L. REV. 539 (1988). *See also In re Olson*, 818 F.2d 34 (D.C. Cir. 1987) (summarizing Justice Department special counsel investigations in the Teapot Dome, Truman administration, Watergate, Iran-Contra, and Olson matters). Assuming that the *Morrison v. Olson* precedent addresses potential constitutional objections, should Congress pass a statute providing for independent counsels to prosecute criminal contempt of Congress charges such as the one in the Anne Gorsuch Burford case? For one of the author's views on that question, see Stanley M. Brand & Sean Connelly, *Constitutional Confrontations: Preserving a Prompt and Orderly Means by Which Congress May Enforce Investigative Demands Against Executive Branch Officials*, 36 CATH. UNIV. L. REV. 71 (1986). For an in-depth account of the *Morrison v. Olson* case, see Kevin M. Stack, *The Story of* Morrison v. Olson: *The Independent Counsel and Independent Agencies in Watergate's Wake, in* PRESIDENTIAL POWER STORIES (Curtis Bradley & Christopher Schroeder eds., 2008). Finally, for an interesting historical comparison, consider one of the most celebrated contempt of Congress prosecutions in recent history, the prosecution of G. Gordon Liddy for refusing to be sworn in and provide testimony to a congressional committee in an investigation relating to the Watergate scandal:

> In a few instances, members of Congress and Congressional committees referred matters to the [Watergate] Special Prosecutor's office for investigation. Any such allegation that merited full investigation was fully pursued. Others either did not fall within [the Special Prosecutor's] jurisdiction or proved to lack potential after initial inquiry. In one instance, a referral by a committee

resulted directly in a conviction. On September 10, 1973, after G. Gordon Liddy refused to be sworn in to testify before the House Armed Services Committee's Subcommittee on Intelligence, the House of Representatives voted to cite Liddy for contempt of Congress. The case was referred by the U.S. Attorney for the District of Columbia to [the Watergate Special Prosecutor]. Liddy was subsequently indicted on March 4, 1974, for refusing to testify or produce papers before a Congressional committee, and he was found guilty on May 10, 1974.

Watergate Special Prosecution Force Report 206–07 (Oct. 1975). Does the Watergate Special Prosecutor's prosecution and conviction of Liddy for failing to cooperate with a congressional investigation support the argument that contempt of Congress prosecutions of individuals in or closely associated with the executive branch should be referred to a special counsel rather than a politically appointed U.S. Attorney? (Congressional investigation of the Watergate scandal is discussed in Chapter 3, and the impeachment proceedings against President Nixon that resulted from Watergate are discussed in Chapter 7.)

5. **An Impressive Legislative Legacy.** The EPA/Superfund controversy was not an inconsequential "inside the beltway" spat between the legislative and executive branches. The Democratic Congress of the 1980s subsequently racked up an impressive string of significant legislative actions in the area of environmental protection, including the Hazardous and Solid Waste Amendments of 1984, the Safe Drinking Water Act Amendments of 1986, the Superfund Amendments and Reauthorization Act of 1986, and the Water Quality Act of 1987. It is particularly noteworthy that these important environmental legislative initiatives were passed into law at the same time that the Reagan administration was pursuing an aggressive environmental deregulation agenda.

6. **The Futility of Collateral Attacks on Congressional Subpoenas.** The lack of success of the attempt by the Department of Justice to obtain a declaratory judgment upholding the Reagan administration's executive privilege claims illustrates the difficulty subpoena recipients face in bringing collateral attacks on congressional subpoenas in the federal courts. In the EPA case the collateral attack was brought by the Department of Justice in the name of the United States (at least in the view of the Department, although Congress did not accept that characterization) and on the basis of an official, written assertion of executive privilege by the President of the United States. The lawsuit was nonetheless dismissed almost immediately. Other litigants face even more daunting obstacles in attempting to pursue collateral attacks on congressional subpoenas. One of the authors of this book summarized the relevant legal authorities in a 1983 memorandum to Congressman John Dingell and the Subcommittee on Oversight and Investigations of the House Committee on Energy and Commerce:

Office of the Clerk, U.S. House of Representatives

Washington, D.C., March 21, 1983

[MEMORANDUM]

Re: Civil Suits Commenced By Witnesses To Block
    Congressional Subpoenas

Hon. JOHN D. DINGELL, *Chairman,*
Subcommittee on Oversight and Investigations,
Committee on Energy and Commerce.

You have inquired concerning the effect, if any, of a civil suit filed on behalf of a witness subpoenaed to appear before the Subcommittee seeking to enjoin implementation of the subpoenas or declare it illegal or unconstitutional.[14]

It is settled beyond peradventure of doubt that the courts will not interfere in the legislative process by way of enjoining implementation of a subpoena or declaring that it is an illegal or unconstitutional exercise of legislative authority. *Eastland v. United States Servicemen's Fund*, 421 U.S. 491 (1975).

> ... The issuance of a subpoena pursuant to an authorized investigation is similarly an indispensable ingredient of lawmaking; without it our recognition that the act "of authorizing" is protected would be meaningless. To hold that Members of Congress are protected for authorizing an investigation, but not for issuing a subpoena in exercise of that authorization, would be a contradiction denigrating the power granted to Congress in Art. I and would indirectly impair the deliberation of Congress.

421 U.S. at 505.

Even before the Supreme Court's pronouncement in *Eastland*, the law of this circuit clearly established that a witness could not obtain injunctive or declaratory relief against a congressional subpoena, and attempts to do so have been universally rejected on several grounds.[15] *Pauling v. Eastland*, 288 F.2d 126 (1960) (action for declaration that Senate subpoena was unconstitutional); *Cole v. McClellan*, 439 F.2d 534 (D.C. Cir. 1970) (same); *Sanders v. McClellan*, 463 F.2d 894 (D.C. Cir. 1972) (same): *Ansara v. Eastland*, 442 F.2d 751 (D.C. Cir. 1971) (same); *See also, Hearst v. Black*, 87 F.2d 68 (1936) (action to enjoin Senate from copying and using telegraphic messages allegedly obtained from illegal search and seizure); *Methodist Federation for Social Action v. East-*

---

14. [1] I understand that the lawyer representing Rita M. Lavelle has filed such a suit, although as of today service of the complaint has not been achieved.

15. [2] This memorandum will address *only* the threshold issue whether a witness can obtain injunctive or declaratory relief against a congressional subpoena and nothing herein should be construed to concede or recognize the validity of any claims the witness has respecting alleged infirmities in the subpoena. To the extent the witness has such claims, the exclusive avenue for judicial review is through the criminal contempt statute. 2 U.S.C. §§192–194.

land, 141 F. Supp. 729 (D.D.C. 1956) (three-judge court) (action to declare unconstitutional resolution authorizing printing and distribution of a report charging plaintiffs were a communist front organization); *Doe v. McMillan*, 412 U.S. 306 (1973) (action seeking to declare unconstitutional and illegal authorization by committee to print and distribute report).

If there remained a scintilla of doubt concerning the fatal defects in suits against the implementation of congressional subpoenas, those doubts should have been laid to rest last month when Judge John Lewis Smith decided the case of *United States v. House of Representatives* Civil Action No. 82-3583 (D.D.C. issued Feb. 1, 1983), an action for injunctive and declaratory relief filed against the House and certain of its members by the Department of Justice following the citation of Anne (Gorsuch) Burford for contempt of Congress.

In granting the House of Representatives' motion to dismiss the suit, Judge Smith recognized that a witness is confined to challenging a congressional subpoena through the "orderly and often approved means" of the criminal contempt statute.

> The statutory provisions concerning penalties for contempt of Congress, 2 U.S.C. § 192 and § 194, constitute "an orderly and often approved means of vindicating constitutional claims arising from a legislative investigation." *Sanders v. McClellan*, 463 F.2d 894, 899 (D.C. Cir. 1972). Under these provisions, constitutional claims and other objections to congressional investigatory procedures may be raised as defenses in a criminal prosecution.

United States v. House of Representatives, Civil Action No. 82-3583, *supra*, Slip Op. at 5.

Accordingly, the suit is wholly without basis or validity and the committee may proceed without reference to any such suit.

Stanley M. Brand
General Counsel to the Clerk

Proceedings Against Rita M. Lavelle, Report of the Committee on Energy and Commerce, Appendix V at 20–21 (May 16, 1983).

As the memorandum above indicates, there is no avenue for collateral attack on a congressional subpoena. That is, one cannot preemptively enjoin or declare illegal a congressional subpoena or proceeding before a criminal referral or other enforcement proceeding ripens. Former President Donald Trump learned this lesson when he failed in his effort to prevent the National Archives from providing documents from his presidency to the House Select Committee to Investigate the January 6th Attack on the United States Capitol. *See Trump v. Thompson*, 595 U.S. ___, 142 S. Ct. 680 (2021). (The investigation of the House January 6 Committee is discussed in Chapter 8.) A subject of a subpoena can, however, seek damages for unconstitutional actions taken outside the legitimate legislative sphere. *See McSurely v. McClellan*, 553 F.2d 1277, 1286 (D.C. Cir. 1976) (*per curiam*) (*en banc*); *see also Hutchinson v. Proxmire*, 443 U.S. 111 (1976).

The Bush Administration U.S. Attorneys Removal Investigation and the Miers/Bolten Contempt Proceedings

If the extraordinary events of the EPA case described above were a one-time occurrence, then they might be dismissed as an anomaly in the history of relations between the executive and legislative branches of government, and the fact that there was not any definitive resolution of the issues involved would be of lesser importance. That is not the case, however. History to a large degree repeated itself some two decades later when the House Judiciary Committee investigated the George W. Bush administration's dismissal of several sitting U.S. Attorneys. Once again, despite a contempt vote by the full House of Representatives and an adversarial judicial proceeding pitting the two political branches against one another, the matter was concluded without any definitive resolution of the constitutional and legal issues in dispute.

A. Background on U.S. Attorneys

The chief federal prosecutor in federal judicial districts is known as the "United States Attorney." The relevant federal statute sets forth the legal procedures for appointment and removal of U.S. Attorneys:

> (a) The President shall appoint, by and with the advice and consent of the Senate, a United States attorney for each judicial district.

> (b) Each United States attorney shall be appointed for a term of four years. On the expiration of his term, a United States attorney shall continue to perform the duties of his office until his successor is appointed and qualifies.

> (c) Each United States attorney is subject to removal by the President.

28 U.S.C. §541. Another federal statute defines the duties of U.S. Attorneys:

> (1) prosecute for all offenses against the United States;

> (2) prosecute or defend, for the Government, all civil actions, suits or proceedings in which the United States is concerned;

> (3) appear in behalf of the defendants in all civil actions, suits or proceedings pending in his district against collectors, or other officers of the revenue or customs for any act done by them or for the recovery of any money exacted by or paid to these officers, and by them paid into the Treasury;

> (4) institute and prosecute proceedings for the collection of fines, penalties, and forfeitures incurred for violation of any revenue law, unless satisfied on investigation that justice does not require the proceedings; and

> (5) make such reports as the Attorney General may direct.

28 U.S.C. §546. U.S. Attorneys generally are not removed by the President except when they have engaged in misconduct, except that "U.S. Attorneys have typically been removed from office by a new President so that the new President could appoint his own U.S. Attorneys." Kevin M. Scott, *CRS Report for Congress: U.S. Attorneys Who Have Served Less than Full Four-year Terms, 1981–2006* (Feb. 22, 2007). A U.S. Attorney's Office is staffed with "Assistant United States Attorneys" or "AUSAs" who assist the U.S. Attorney in fulfilling these statutory responsibilities and function as the line attorneys who appear for the United States in federal court. AUSAs are appointed, and subject to removal, by the Attorney General of the United States. 28 U.S.C. §543.

As the chief federal prosecutors in judicial districts around the country, U.S. Attorneys must follow Department of Justice rules and procedures, but they also exercise considerable independent judgment and have a great deal of power and discretion in deciding matters such as what criminal cases will be pursued by the United States, what charges will be brought in those cases, and what kinds of plea bargains will be accepted. Supreme Court Justice Antonin Scalia has observed that "[o]nly someone who has worked in the field of law enforcement can fully appreciate the vast power and the immense discretion that are placed in the hands of a prosecutor with respect to the object of his investigation," and he amplified this point by quoting an influential speech on the role of federal prosecutors by Attorney General and later Supreme Court Justice Robert Jackson:

> There is a most important reason why the prosecutor should have, as nearly as possible, a detached and impartial view of all groups in his community. Law enforcement is not automatic. It isn't blind. One of the greatest difficulties of the position of prosecutor is that he must pick his cases, because no prosecutor can even investigate all of the cases in which he receives complaints. If the Department of Justice were to make even a pretense of reaching every probable violation of federal law, ten times its present staff will be inadequate. We know that no local police force can strictly enforce the traffic laws, or it would arrest half the driving population on any given morning. What every prosecutor is practically required to do is to select the cases for prosecution and to select those in which the offense is the most flagrant, the public harm the greatest, and the proof the most certain.

> If the prosecutor is obliged to choose his case, it follows that he can choose his defendants. Therein is the most dangerous power of the prosecutor: that he will pick people that he thinks he should get, rather than cases that need to be prosecuted. With the law books filled with a great assortment of crimes, a prosecutor stands a fair chance of finding at least a technical violation of some act on the part of almost anyone. In such a case, it is not a question of discovering the commission of a crime and then looking for the man who has committed it, it is a question of picking the man and then searching the law books, or putting investigators to work, to pin some offense on him. It is in this realm—in which the prosecutor picks some person whom he dislikes or desires to embarrass, or selects some group of unpopular persons and then looks

for an offense, that the greatest danger of abuse of prosecuting power lies. It is
here that law enforcement becomes personal, and the real crime becomes that
of being unpopular with the predominant or governing group, being attached
to the wrong political views, or being personally obnoxious to or in the way of
the prosecutor himself.

Morrison v. Olson, 487 U.S. 654, 727–28 (1988) (Scalia, J., dissenting) (quoting Robert
Jackson, The Federal Prosecutor, Address Delivered at the Second Annual Conference
of United States Attorneys, April 1, 1940).[16]

The observation and supporting quotation offered by Justice Scalia illustrate the
complexity of the role that U.S. Attorneys play in our system of justice. Although
U.S. Attorneys are political appointees who are confirmed by the Senate and subject
to removal by the President without cause, they are universally viewed as ethically
obliged to exercise their power and authority in a neutral, nonpartisan manner, and
any attempt to influence or interfere with their official actions based upon partisan
political motives clearly would be improper—even if it did not rise to the level of a
criminal obstruction of justice. These were the considerations that caught the attention of congressional members and staff when questions arose in 2007 about whether
improper political considerations had played a role in the removal in 2006 of several
U.S. Attorneys.

B. The House Judiciary Committee Investigates the U.S. Attorneys Matter

The events that have since become known as "The U.S. Attorneys Scandal" were
summarized in a succinct and objective manner by two law professors who are experts
on prosecutorial conduct and ethics:

> In December of 2006, DOJ forced eight U.S. Attorneys [*Ed. Note: The num-
> ber of forced removals was later determined to be nine, see "An Investigation Into
> the Removal of Nine U.S. Attorneys in 2006," Report of the Office of the Inspector
> General and Office of Professional Responsibility, Department of Justice (Sep-
> tember 2008).*] to resign and appointed replacements who, under a recent an-

---

16. Justice Scalia went on to explain how he believes our constitutional system of government
adequately controls the "awesome" power and discretion delegated to federal prosecutors:

Under our system of government, the primary check against prosecutorial abuse is a political
one. The prosecutors who exercise this awesome discretion are selected, and can be removed,
by a President whom the people have trusted enough to elect. Moreover, when crimes are not
investigated and prosecuted fairly, nonselectively, with a reasonable sense of proportion, the
President pays the cost in political damage to his administration. If federal prosecutors "pick
people that [they] thin[k] [they] should get, rather than cases that need to be prosecuted," if
they amass many more resources against a particular prominent individual, or against a particular class of political protesters, or against members of a particular political party, than the
gravity of the alleged offenses or the record of successful prosecutions seems to warrant, the
unfairness will come home to roost in the Oval Office.

Morrison v. Olson, 487 U.S. 654, 728–29 (1988) (Scalia, J., dissenting).

ti-terrorism law, could avoid Senate confirmation. Eventually the media took notice, questioning the motivation for the discharges. The Department initially characterized the firings as routine personnel matters, but both houses of Congress, led by a Democratic majority, were skeptical and commenced investigation. To date, the propriety of the discharges has not been determined to Congress's satisfaction. Congress has not had complete access to potential evidence for various reasons. Witnesses have refused to testify publicly and under oath, asserting the Fifth Amendment or executive privilege, or have testified that they do not recall significant conversations. Relevant documents have been withheld, again based on executive privilege. Other documentary evidence has been deleted and not yet recovered. The evidence has been emerging slowly and tortuously.

The explanations originally emanating from DOJ were that the U.S. Attorneys had been asked to resign because of deficiencies in their administrative or leadership abilities or because of inadequate commitment to official Department policy. Some discharged U.S. Attorneys allegedly failed to vigorously pursue voter fraud cases, which had been established as a departmental priority. Another allegedly did not adequately prosecute immigration cases.

Testimony from the fired U.S. Attorneys and other DOJ personnel cast doubt on these explanations, which some observers have dismissed as implausible.

Commentators have offered other possible explanations for the discharges. Some surmise that the underlying motivation was to replace prosecutors who had failed to ally themselves sufficiently with partisan Republican ends, either by investigating or charging Republican officials (or those with ties to them) for corruption or by not prosecuting Democratic officials for alleged corruption and other Democrats for alleged violations of voter registration laws.

Other observers have speculated that the Bush administration sought to advance the careers of lawyers loyal to the administration by appointing them in the place of the discharged U.S. Attorneys.

Bruce A. Green & Fred C. Zacharias, *"The U.S. Attorneys Scandal" and the Allocation of Prosecutorial Power*, 69 Ohio St. L.J. 187 (2008).

In early 2007 the House Judiciary Committee began investigating the U.S. Attorney dismissals. (The following summary of events is taken from the opinion in *Committee on the Judiciary, United States House of Representatives v. Miers*, 558 F. Supp. 2d 53 (D.D.C. 2008), portions of which are reproduced below.) The Judiciary Committee initially heard hearing testimony from six of the dismissed U.S. Attorneys and then took testimony from a number of senior Justice Department officials, including Attorney General Alberto Gonzales. A former Justice Department liaison to the White House, Monica Goodling, was compelled to provide testimony after being granted immunity to overcome her assertion of her Fifth Amendment privilege against self-incrimination (congressional immunity grants are discussed further in Chapter 5). A former White House Political Director, Sara M. Taylor, appeared before the committee and provided testimony, but invoked executive privilege in response to some questions.

The Judiciary Committee's initial investigation of the matter revealed that no one at the Department of Justice—including former Deputy Attorney General James B. Comey, who had been the senior official responsible for supervision of U.S. Attorneys—could identify who was responsible for the dismissals. The Committee then sought to determine what role senior presidential advisor Karl Rove and former White House Counsel Harriet Miers had played in the dismissals. Negotiations for voluntary interviews and production of relevant White House documents broke down when White House Counsel Fred Fielding took the position that the interviews of White House officials had to be conducted without oaths or transcripts and could not be followed by subsequent issuance of subpoenas, and that no internal White House documents would be produced to the Committee. The Judiciary Committee refused to accept those conditions, and both House Judiciary Committee Chairman John Conyers and Senate Judiciary Committee Chairman Patrick Leahy wrote letters to Fielding seeking to reach an accommodation to resolve the dispute. Those efforts were unsuccessful, and on June 13, 2007 the House Judiciary Committee issued subpoenas seeking testimony from Miers and production of White House documents by White House Chief of Staff Joshua Bolten. Fielding then wrote Conyers and Leahy advising them that President Bush was asserting executive privilege, and also wrote a letter to the private attorney representing Miers directing that she should not provide testimony to the Committee.

After additional correspondence and subcommittee actions, the full House Judiciary Committee adopted a resolution on July 25, 2007, recommending that the House of Representatives find Bolten and Miers in contempt for failing to comply with the subpoenas. On November 5, 2007, the Committee filed its report recommending contempt proceedings, and Conyers again wrote to Fielding reiterating the Committee's desire to resolve the matter in a cooperative manner and suggesting a proposal for resolving the dispute. Fielding rejected that proposal and responded that the White House and the Committee were "at a most regrettable impasse." On February 14, 2008, the full House of Representatives voted 223–32 to hold Bolten and Miers in contempt of Congress. (Many of the Republican members of the House walked out of the Chamber in protest, so the 223–32 vote total does not reflect the full membership of the House.) The contempt vote was the first time since the Anne Gorsuch Burford EPA contempt proceeding, and only the second time in U.S. history, that a full house of Congress had voted to hold a senior executive branch official in contempt for refusing to provide information in response to a congressional subpoena.[17]

---

17. In 1983 the House of Representatives voted 413–0 to hold EPA Assistant Administrator Rita Lavelle in contempt for defying a House Energy and Commerce Committee subpoena to testify, but Lavelle's contempt sanction was based upon her refusal to testify about her personal conduct at EPA, and not an institutional executive privilege issue, as evidenced by the unanimous bipartisan vote to

The resolutions that accompanied the contempt vote authorized Speaker of the House Nancy Pelosi to certify the contempt vote to the U.S. Attorney for the District of Columbia for criminal prosecution of Bolten and Miers. Pelosi did so, but Attorney General Michael Mukasey (who had replaced Gonzales), relying on the 1984 Office of Legal Counsel opinion addressing the EPA dispute, ordered the U.S. Attorney not to present the contempt charges to a grand jury. Attorney General Mukasey's position on the matter is explained in the letter below to Speaker Pelosi:

Office of the Attorney General

Washington, D.C., February 29, 2008

The Honorable Nancy Pelosi,
Speaker, House of Representatives,
Washington, D.C. 20515

Dear Madam Speaker:

As you know, the President, asserting executive privilege, directed that Joshua Bolten, Chief of Staff to the President, and Harriet Miers, the former Counsel to the President, not release certain documents or provide related testimony subpoenaed by the Committee on the Judiciary of the House of Representatives. The President also directed Ms. Miers to invoke her constitutional immunity from compelled congressional testimony and to decline to appear before the Committee. These directives were based on legal opinions from the Department of Justice advising that the assertions of privilege and immunity were legally proper.

Notwithstanding the President's directives, on July 25, 2007, the House Committee on the Judiciary adopted a resolution recommending that the House of Representatives cite Mr. Bolten and Ms. Miers for contempt. On November 5, 2007, the Committee referred its report on the resolution to the full House. On February 14, 2008, the House adopted a contempt resolution, which you referred on February 28, 2008, to the United States Attorney for the District of Columbia for prosecution under the criminal contempt of Congress statute, 2 U.S.C. §§192, 194 (2000).

As explained in our July 24, 2007 letter to Judiciary Committee Chairman Conyers, a copy of which is enclosed, the Department of Justice's longstanding position taken during Administrations of both parties is "that the contempt of Congress statute was not intended to apply and could not constitutionally be applied to an Executive Branch official who asserts the President's claim of

---

hold her in contempt. She was subsequently acquitted on the contempt charge but found guilty on perjury and obstruction of justice charges for testimony she had provided in her Senate confirmation hearing about her recusal from participating in EPA Superfund program matters that involved her former employer. *See United States v. Lavelle*, 751 F.2d 1266 (D.C. Cir. 1985) (affirming conviction on perjury and obstruction of justice charges).

executive privilege." *Prosecution for Contempt of Congress of an Executive Branch Official Who Has Asserted a Claim of Executive Privilege*, 8 Op. O.L.C. 101, 102 (1984). Further, as we also explained in the letter to Chairman Conyers, the same principles that preclude prosecuting an Executive Branch official for abiding by a presidential claim of executive privilege also preclude prosecuting a senior presidential adviser for lawfully invoking her constitutional immunity from compelled congressional testimony. Here, the President directed Ms. Miers to invoke her constitutional immunity, and the President's directive was based upon a legal opinion from the Department of Justice advising that such an invocation of immunity would be legally proper.

Accordingly, the Department has determined that the non-compliance by Mr. Bolten and Ms. Miers with the Judiciary Committee subpoenas did not constitute a crime, and therefore the Department will not bring the congressional contempt citations before a grand jury or take any other action to prosecute Mr. Bolten or Ms. Miers.

Please do not hesitate to contact me if you would like to discuss this matter further.

Sincerely,

/s/

Michael B. Mukasey
Attorney General

Enclosure

cc: The Honorable John Boehner
The Honorable John Conyers, Jr.
The Honorable Lamar Smith

U.S. Department of Justice, Office of Legislative Affairs

Office of the Assistant Attorney General,
Washington, D.C. 20530,
July 24, 2007

The Honorable John Conyers, Jr.
Chairman, Committee on the Judiciary
U.S. House of Representatives
Washington, D.C. 20515

Dear Mr. Chairman:

We understand that the Judiciary Committee is voting tomorrow on resolutions calling for the House of Representatives to refer contempt of Congress citations against Josh Bolton, the Chief of Staff to the President, and Harriet Miers, the former Counsel to the President, to the United States Attorney for the District of Columbia for prosecution pursuant to the criminal contempt of Congress statute, 2 U.S.C. §§192, 194 (2000).

As you know, the President has asserted executive privilege and directed that certain documents and related testimony not be provided in response to subpoenas issued by the Judiciary Committee in connection with its inquiry into the decision of the Department of Justice to request the resignations of several United States Attorneys in 2006. The President also directed Ms. Miers to invoke her immunity from compelled congressional testimony and decline to appear in response to a subpoena from the Judiciary Committee. These directives were based on legal opinions from the Department advising that the assertion of privilege and immunity were legally proper. *See* Letter for the President from Paul D. Clement, Solicitor General and Acting Attorney General (June 27, 2007) (addressing assertion of executive privilege); Memorandum for the Counsel to the President from Steven G. Bradbury, Principal Deputy Assistant Attorney General, Office of Legal Counsel, *Re: Immunity of Former Counsel to the President from Compelled Congressional Testimony* (July 10, 2007).

As it considers the contempt resolutions, we think it is important that the Committee appreciate fully the longstanding Department of Justice position, articulated during Administrations of both parties, that "the criminal contempt of Congress statute does not apply to the President or presidential subordinates who assert executive privilege." *Application of 28 U.S.C. §458 to Presidential Appointment of Federal Judges*, 19 Op. O.L.C. 350, 356 (1995). As expressed by Office of Legal Counsel Assistant Attorney General Theodore B. Olson more than twenty years ago, when an Executive Branch official complies in good faith with the President's assertion of executive privilege, "a United States Attorney is not required to refer a contempt citation ... to a grand jury or otherwise to prosecute [the] Executive Branch official who is carrying out the President's instruction...." *Prosecution for Contempt of Congress of an Executive Branch Official Who Has Asserted a Claim of Executive Privilege*, 8 Op. O.L.C. 101, 102 (1984) (*"Prosecution for Contempt of Congress"*). Two legal conclusions support the longstanding Department position:

> First, as a matter of statutory interpretation reinforced by compelling separation of powers considerations, we believe that Congress may not direct the Executive to prosecute a particular individual without leaving any discretion to the Executive to determine whether a violation of the law has occurred. Second, as a matter of statutory interpretation and the constitutional separation of powers, we believe that the contempt of Congress statute was not intended to apply and could not constitutionally be applied to an Executive Branch official who asserts the President's claim of executive privilege in this context.

Id.

The position Mr. Olson articulated was based on prior Department positions and has been consistently followed ever since, including in an explicit statement in a published OLC opinion by Assistant Attorney General Walter Dellinger during the Clinton Administration, recognizing that "the criminal contempt of Congress statute does not apply" in this context, because "application of the contempt statute against an assertion of executive privilege would seriously disrupt the balance between the President and Congress." *Application of 28 U.S.C. §458 to Presidential Appointment of Federal Judges*, 19 Op. O.L.C. at 356.

It is the Department's view that the same position necessarily also applies to Ms. Miers's lawful invocation of her immunity from compelled congressional testimony. The principles that protect an Executive Branch official from prosecution for declining to comply with a congressional subpoena based on a directive from the President asserting executive privilege similarly shield a current or former immediate adviser to the President from prosecution for invoking his or her immunity from compelled congressional testimony—especially when, as here, the President instructs the official to do so.

Please do not hesitate to contact us if you would like further information concerning the Department's position on the pending contempt of Congress resolutions. We would be pleased to provide a fuller explanation of our views on this important matter.

Sincerely,

/s/

Brian A. Benczkowski
Principal Deputy Assistant
Attorney General

cc: The Honorable Lamar Smith

No doubt anticipating the position taken by the Attorney General on criminal prosecution, the House Judiciary Committee had included in the contempt proceedings against Bolten and Miers a resolution authorizing Judiciary Committee Chairman John Conyers to file a civil lawsuit in federal court to enforce the committee's subpoenas. When the suit was brought it was assigned to United States District Judge John D. Bates, who before being appointed to the federal bench by President George W. Bush in 2001 had served as a career federal prosecutor and a top deputy to Independent Counsel Kenneth Starr. If the litigants or observers of the case questioned whether Judge Bates's long service in the executive branch might influence his legal analysis in favor of the Bush administration's legal arguments, however, they quickly learned otherwise. On July 31, 2008, Judge Bates issued the opinion that is reproduced in part below.

Committee on Judiciary, U.S. House of Representatives v. Miers

558 F. Supp. 2d 53 (D.D.C. 2008)

This dispute pits the political branches of the federal government against one another in a case all agree presents issues of extraordinary constitutional significance. The heart of the controversy is whether senior presidential aides are absolutely immune from compelled congressional process. But as is often true of lawsuits that raise important separation of powers concerns, there are many obstacles to the invocation of the jurisdiction of the federal courts that must first be addressed.

The Committee on the Judiciary ("Committee"), acting on behalf of the entire House of Representatives, asks the Court to declare that former White House Counsel Harriet Miers must comply with a subpoena and appear before the Committee to testify regarding an investigation into the forced resignation of nine United States Attorneys in late 2006, and that current White House Chief of Staff Joshua Bolten must produce a privilege log in response to a congressional subpoena. Ms. Miers and Mr. Bolten (collectively "the Executive")[18] have moved to dismiss this action in its entirety on the grounds that the Committee lacks standing and a proper cause of action, that disputes of this kind are non-justiciable, and that the Court should exercise its discretion to decline jurisdiction. On the merits, the Executive argues that sound principles of separation of powers and presidential autonomy dictate that the President's closest advisors must be absolutely immune from compelled testimony before Congress, and that the Committee has no authority to demand a privilege log from the White House.

Notwithstanding that the opposing litigants in this case are co-equal branches of the federal government, at bottom this lawsuit involves a basic judicial task—subpoena en-

---

18. [Court's Note 1] The Court will refer to the defendants in this action, and to the executive branch and the current administration generally, as "the Executive."

forcement—with which federal courts are very familiar. The executive privilege claims that form the foundation of the Executive's resistance to the Committee's subpoenas are not foreign to federal courts either. After all, from *Marbury v. Madison* [citation omitted] (1803) ("[i]t is emphatically the province and duty of the judicial department to say what the law is"), through *United States v. Nixon* [citation omitted] (1974) (the judiciary is the ultimate arbiter of claims of executive privilege), to *Boumediene v. Bush* [citation omitted] (2008) (rejecting regime in which the political branches may "switch the Constitution on or off at will" and, rather than the judiciary, "say 'what the law is'"), the Supreme Court has confirmed the fundamental role of the federal courts to resolve the most sensitive issues of separation of powers. In the thirty-four years since *United States v. Nixon* was decided, the courts have routinely considered questions of executive privilege or immunity, and those issues are now "of a type that are traditionally justiciable" in federal courts, and certainly not unprecedented, as the Executive contends.

Indeed, the aspect of this lawsuit that is unprecedented is the notion that Ms. Miers is absolutely immune from compelled congressional process. The Supreme Court has reserved absolute immunity for very narrow circumstances, involving the President's personal exposure to suits for money damages based on his official conduct or concerning matters of national security or foreign affairs. The Executive's current claim of absolute immunity from compelled congressional process for senior presidential aides is without any support in the case law. The fallacy of that claim was presaged in *United States v. Nixon* itself [citation omitted]:

> neither the doctrine of separation of powers, nor the need for confidentiality of high-level communications, without more, can sustain an absolute, unqualified Presidential privilege of immunity from judicial [or congressional] process under all circumstances.

It is important to note that the decision today is very limited. To be sure, most of this lengthy opinion addresses, and ultimately rejects, the Executive's several reasons why the Court should not entertain the Committee's lawsuit, but on the merits of the Committee's present claims the Court only resolves, and again rejects, the claim by the Executive to absolute immunity from compelled congressional process for senior presidential aides. The specific claims of executive privilege that Ms. Miers and Mr. Bolten may assert are not addressed—and the Court expresses no view on such claims. Nor should this decision discourage the process of negotiation and accommodation that most often leads to resolution of disputes between the political branches. Although standing ready to fulfill the essential judicial role to "say what the law is" on specific assertions of executive privilege that may be presented, the Court strongly encourages the political branches to resume their discourse and negotiations in an effort to resolve their differences constructively, while recognizing each branch's essential role. To that end, the Court is reminded of Justice Jackson's observations in his concurring opinion in *Youngstown Sheet & Tube Co. v. Sawyer* [citation omitted] (1952):

> While the Constitution diffuses power the better to secure liberty, it also contemplates that practice will integrate the dispersed powers into a workable

government. It enjoins upon its branches separateness but interdependence, autonomy but reciprocity. Presidential powers are not fixed but fluctuate, depending upon their disjunction or conjunction with those of Congress.

* * *

[*Ed. Note: The opinion then reviews the background of the case (summarized above) and rejects all of the executive branch arguments that the court should dismiss the case, concluding that the court has jurisdiction over the dispute, the dispute is ripe for adjudication, the Judiciary Committee has standing to enforce its duly issued subpoena through a civil lawsuit, and that judicial resolution of a subpoena enforcement dispute is appropriate.*]

The Executive cannot identify a single judicial opinion that recognizes absolute immunity for senior presidential advisors in this or any other context. That simple yet critical fact bears repeating: the asserted absolute immunity claim here is entirely unsupported by existing case law. In fact, there is Supreme Court authority that is all but conclusive on this question and that powerfully suggests that such advisors do not enjoy absolute immunity. The Court therefore rejects the Executive's claim of absolute immunity for senior presidential aides.

* * *

Unfortunately for the Executive, this line of argument has been virtually foreclosed by the Supreme Court. In *Harlow v. Fitzgerald*, [citation omitted] (1982), the plaintiff sued "senior White House aides" for civil damages arising out of the defendants' official actions. [citation omitted] The defendants argued that they were "entitled to a blanket protection of absolute immunity as an incident of their offices as Presidential aides." [citation omitted] The Supreme Court rejected that position. Notwithstanding the absolute immunity extended to legislators, judges, prosecutors, and the President himself, the Court emphasized that "[f]or executive officials in general, however, our cases make plain that qualified immunity represents the norm." [citation omitted] Although there can be no doubt regarding "the importance to the President of loyal and efficient subordinates in executing his duties of office, ... these factors, alone, [are] insufficient to justify absolute immunity." [citation omitted].

* * *

The Executive's concern that "[a]bsent immunity ... there would be no effective brake on Congress's discretion to compel the testimony of the President's advisers at the highest level of government" is also unfounded. To begin with, the process of negotiation and accommodation will ensure that most disputes over information and testimony are settled informally. Moreover, political considerations—including situations where Congress or one House of Congress is controlled by the same political party that holds the Presidency—will surely factor into Congress's decision whether to deploy its compulsory process over the President's objection. In any event, the historical record produced by the Committee reveals that senior advisors to the President have often testified before Congress subject to various subpoenas dating back to 1973. Thus, it would hardly be unprecedented for Ms. Miers to appear before Congress to testify and assert executive privilege where appropriate. Still, it is noteworthy that in an environment where there is *no* judicial support whatsoever for the Executive's claim of absolute immunity, the historical record also does not reflect the wholesale compulsion by Congress of testimony from senior presidential advisors that the Executive fears.

Significantly, although the Supreme Court has established that the President is absolutely immune from civil suits arising out of his official actions, even the President may not be absolutely immune from compulsory process more generally. In *United States v. Nixon*, the Supreme Court held that the President is entitled only to a presumptive privilege that can be overcome by the requisite demonstration of need. [citation omitted] There, the Supreme Court indicated that "an absolute, unqualified privilege would place [an impediment] in the way of the primary constitutional duty of the Judicial Branch to do justice in criminal prosecutions ... [and] would plainly conflict with the function of the courts under Art. III." [citation omitted] Seizing on that passage, the Executive insists that this case is distinguishable because it does not involve a core function of another constituent branch but rather a peripheral exercise of Congress's power. That is mistaken. As discussed above, Congress's power of inquiry is as broad as its power to legislate and lies at the very heart of Congress's constitutional role. Indeed, the former is necessary to the proper exercise of the latter: according to the Supreme Court, the ability to compel testimony is *"necessary to the effective functioning of courts and legislatures."* [*United States v.*] *Bryan* [citation omitted]. Thus, Congress's use of (and need for vindication of) its subpoena power in this case is no less legitimate or important than was the grand jury's in *United States v. Nixon*. Both involve core functions of a co-equal branch of the federal government, and for the reasons identified in *Nixon*, the President may only be entitled to a presumptive, rather than an absolute, privilege here.[19] And it is certainly the case that if the President is entitled only to a presumptive privilege, his close advisors cannot hold the superior card of absolute immunity.

* * *

Tellingly, the only authority that the Executive can muster in support of its absolute immunity assertion are two OLC opinions authored by Attorney General Janet Reno and Principal Deputy Assistant Attorney General Steven Bradbury, respectively. *See Assertion of Executive Privilege with Respect to Clemency Decision* [citation omitted] (O.L.C. 1999); *Immunity of Former Counsel to the President from Compelled Congressional Testimony* [citation omitted] (O.L.C. 2007). Those opinions conclude that immediate advisors to the President are immune from compelled congressional testimony.

---

19. [Court's Note 35] The Executive also contends that *United States v. Nixon* has no force outside of the criminal context. For the reasons set forth above, the Court disagrees—indeed, the D.C. Circuit has rejected that view. *See In re Sealed Case* ("It fell to the remaining *Nixon* cases to address the scope of the presidential communications privilege in other contexts.... [Those] cases established the contours of the presidential communications privilege. The President can invoke the privilege when asked to produce documents or other materials that reflect presidential decisionmaking and deliberations and that the President believes should remain confidential. If the President does so, the documents become presumptively privileged. However, the privilege is qualified, not absolute, and can be overcome by an adequate showing of need.").

The question, then, is how much credence to give to those opinions. Like the Olson and Cooper OLC opinions, the Reno and Bradbury opinions represent only persuasive authority. Hence, the Court concludes that the opinions are entitled to only as much weight as the force of their reasoning will support. [*Ed. Note: The memoranda by Assistant Attorneys General Theodore Olson and Charles Cooper are discussed in Note 2 following this case.*]

With that established, the Court is not at all persuaded by the Reno and Bradbury opinions. Unlike the Olson and Cooper OLC opinions, which are exhaustive efforts of sophisticated legal reasoning, bolstered by extensive citation to judicial authority, the Reno and Bradbury OLC opinions are for the most part conclusory and recursive. Neither cites to a single judicial opinion recognizing the asserted absolute immunity. Indeed, the three-page Bradbury OLC opinion was hastily issued on the same day that the President instructed Ms. Miers to invoke absolute immunity, and it relies almost exclusively upon the conclusory Reno OLC opinion and a statement from a memorandum written by then-Assistant Attorney General William Rehnquist in 1971. *See* [citation omitted]. Mr. Rehnquist wrote:

> The President and his immediate advisers—that is, those who customarily meet with the President on a regular or frequent basis—should be deemed absolutely immune from testimonial compulsion by a congressional committee. They not only may not be examined with respect to their official duties, but they may not even be compelled to appear before a congressional committee.

Mr. Rehnquist also wrote that the rationale supporting the proposed immunity for senior advisors is grounded in the fact that those individuals "are presumptively available to the President 24 hours a day, and the necessity of either accommodating a congressional committee or persuading a court to arrange a more convenient time, could impair that availability." *Id.*

Significantly, Mr. Rehnquist referred to his conclusions as "tentative and sketchy," *see id.*, and then later apparently recanted those views. *See U.S. Government Information Policies and Practices—The Pentagon Papers: Hearings Before the Subcomm. on Foreign Operations and Gov't Info. of the H. Comm. on Gov't Operations*, 92nd Cong. 385 (1971) (testimony of William H. Rehnquist, Assistant Att'y Gen.) ("[M]embers[s] of the executive branch ... have to report, give [their] name and address and so forth, and then invoke the privilege."). In *Clinton v. Jones*, then-Chief Justice Rehnquist joined in holding that even the demands of the President's schedule could not relieve him of the duty to give a civil deposition. [citation omitted] ("The burden on the President's time and energy that is a mere byproduct of such review surely cannot be considered as onerous as the direct burden imposed by judicial review and the occasional invalidation of his official actions. We therefore hold that the doctrine of separation of powers does not require federal courts to stay all private actions against the President until he leaves office."). Whatever force the Rehnquist memorandum[20] had when written, then,

---

20. [Court's Note 36] The Rehnquist memorandum actually provides no support for absolute immunity for Ms. Miers because at the time she received her subpoena she was no longer an executive

it retains little vitality in light of *Clinton v. Jones*. If the President[21] must find time to comply with compulsory process in a civil lawsuit, so too must his senior advisors for a congressional subpoena.

At oral argument, counsel for the Executive stated that, as a fall back position, even if Ms. Miers is not entitled to absolute immunity, a qualified immunity analysis should apply. That was, after all, the ultimate disposition in *Harlow*: senior presidential advisors are entitled to qualified immunity against damages actions. The qualified immunity inquiry, however, does not fit comfortably in the present context. Nevertheless, qualified immunity might conceivably be appropriate in some situations involving national security or foreign affairs. Similarly, it might apply where Congress is not utilizing its investigation authority for a legitimate purpose but rather aims simply to harass or embarrass a subpoenaed witness.

In any event, the Court need not decide whether qualified immunity can be applied as a general matter in a setting involving declaratory relief and congressional subpoenas because, even assuming that it can, Ms. Miers is not entitled to such immunity. It bears repeating that this inquiry does not involve the sensitive topics of national security or foreign affairs. Congress, moreover, is acting pursuant to a legitimate use of its investigative authority. Notwithstanding its best efforts, the Committee has been unable to discover the underlying causes of the forced terminations of the U.S. Attorneys. The Committee has legitimate reasons to believe that Ms. Miers's testimony can remedy that deficiency. There is no evidence that the Committee is merely seeking to harass Ms. Miers by calling her to testify. Importantly, moreover, Ms. Miers remains able to assert privilege in response to any specific question or subject matter. For its part, the Executive has not offered any independent reasons that Ms. Miers should be relieved from compelled congressional testimony beyond its blanket assertion of absolute immunity. The Executive's showing, then, does not support either absolute or qualified immunity in this case.

The Court once again emphasizes the narrow scope of today's decision. The Court holds only that Ms. Miers (and other senior presidential advisors) do not have absolute immunity from compelled congressional process in the context of this particular subpoena dispute. There may be some instances where absolute (or qualified) immunity is

---

branch official, thereby relieving her of the need to be available to the President twenty-four hours a day.

21. [Court's Note 37] There is some ambiguity over the scope of the President's involvement in the decision to terminate the U.S. Attorneys in this case. The Committee contends that the White House has asserted that the "President was not involved in any way ... and that he did not receive advice from his aides about the U.S. Attorneys and he did not make a decision to fire any of them." *See* Pl.'s Opp'n & Reply at 12. That assertion is based on a statement made by Acting White House Press Secretary Dana Perino on March 27, 2007. The Executive, however, now maintains that the Committee "substantially overstates the record on this point." *See* Tr. at 57. As the Executive sees it, the record simply indicates that "the President was not involved in decisions about who would be asked to resign from the department," but "does not reflect that the President had no future involvement" in any capacity. *Id.* Given the Court's limited decision here, it is unnecessary to address this factual dispute at this time. The Court notes, however, that the degree and nature of the President's involvement may be relevant to the proper executive privilege characterization under *In re Sealed Case* [citation omitted].

appropriate for such advisors, but this is not one of them. For instance, where national security or foreign affairs form the basis for the Executive's assertion of privilege, it may be that absolute immunity is appropriate. Similarly, this decision applies only to *advisors*, not to the President. The Court has no occasion to address whether the President can be subject to compelled congressional process—the Supreme Court held in *Harlow* that the immunity inquiries for the President and senior advisors are analytically distinct. Similarly, there is no need to address here whether the Vice President could be subject to compelled congressional process. Most importantly, Ms. Miers may assert executive privilege in response to any specific questions posed by the Committee. The Court does not at this time pass judgment on any specific assertion of executive privilege.

There are powerful reasons supporting the rejection of absolute immunity as asserted by the Executive here. If the Court held otherwise, the presumptive presidential privilege could be transformed into an absolute privilege and Congress's legitimate interest in inquiry could be easily thwarted. Indeed, even in the Speech or Debate context—which has an explicit textual basis and confers absolute immunity—Members of Congress must still establish that their actions were legislative in nature before invoking the protection of the Clause. *See, e.g., Rayburn*, [citation omitted]; *Jewish War Veterans of the U.S. v. Gates* [citation omitted] (D.D.C. 2007). Members cannot simply assert, without more, that the Speech or Debate Clause shields their activities and thereby preclude all further inquiry. Yet that is precisely the treatment that the Executive requests here.

Similarly, if the Executive's absolute immunity argument were to prevail, Congress could be left with no recourse to obtain information that is plainly *not* subject to any colorable claim of executive privilege. For instance, surely at least some of the questions that the Committee intends to ask Ms. Miers would not elicit a response subject to an assertion of privilege; so, too, for responsive documents, many of which may even have been produced already. The Executive's proposed absolute immunity would thus deprive Congress of even non-privileged information. That is an unacceptable result.

Clear precedent and persuasive policy reasons confirm that the Executive cannot be the judge of its own privilege and hence Ms. Miers is not entitled to absolute immunity from compelled congressional process. Ms. Miers is not excused from compliance with the Committee's subpoena by virtue of a claim of executive privilege that may ultimately be made. Instead, she must appear before the Committee to provide testimony, and invoke executive privilege where appropriate.[22] And as the Supreme Court has direct-

---

22. [Court's Note 38] Relying on *Cheney v. United States District Court for the District of Columbia*, [citation omitted] (2004), the Executive insists that invocation of executive privilege on a question-by-question basis is insufficient protection for its institutional interests. The Executive, however, misreads *Cheney*. There, the issue was whether "the assertion of executive privilege is a necessary precondition to [entertaining] the Government's separation-of-powers objections" to civil subpoenas that were unacceptably overbroad. Because the assertion of executive privilege sets "coequal branches of the Government ... on a collision course," [citation omitted], the Court explained that a district court may entertain separation of powers objections to overly broad document requests prior to the formal invocation of executive privilege. Here, however, the Executive attempts to utilize absolute

ed, the judiciary remains the ultimate arbiter of an executive privilege claim, since it is the duty of the courts to declare what the law is. *See United States v. Nixon* [citation omitted]; *see also Marbury v. Madison* [citation omitted].

* * *

CONCLUSION

For the foregoing reasons, the Court will deny the Executive's motion to dismiss and grant the Committee's motion for partial summary judgment. A separate Order accompanies this Memorandum Opinion.

———

In another parallel to the Reagan administration EPA dispute more than twenty-five years earlier, after the federal district court rejected the Bush administration's broad executive privilege claim, the parties ultimately reached a compromise that allowed the House of Representatives to obtain almost everything that it had sought in its subpoenas. The terms of that compromise are set out in the agreement that is reproduced below, which was made available to the public on the House Judiciary Committee website. *See* http://judiciary.house.gov/hearings/pdf/Agreement090304.pdf.

Agreement Concerning Accommodation

Committee on the Judiciary, US House of Representatives v. Harriet Miers et al.
Civil Action No. 08-0409 (JDB)

This document describes the terms of an accommodation agreement between the Bush Administration and the House Judiciary Committee to resolve the U.S. Attorneys matter finally. The parties agree in good faith to resolve any outstanding questions with a view toward ending the entire matter between the parties. The Obama Administration and the House Judiciary Committee will execute a separate agreement concerning the final disposition of the ongoing litigation.

Interviews

- The House Judiciary Committee (the "Committee") will interview Karl Rove and Harriet Miers, but there will be no additional interviewees / witnesses (subject to the one exception below). The interviews will be conducted as soon as possible,

---

immunity, the basis of which is rooted in notions of executive privilege. The "collision course" that the Supreme Court feared in *Cheney*, then, has already been set in motion by the Executive. In any event, the Court indicated only that "the Executive Branch [does not] bear the onus of critiquing ... unacceptable discovery requests line by line." [citation omitted]. Indeed, the D.C. Circuit had already determined that the "discovery requests [were] anything but appropriate." In *Cheney*, the Supreme Court focused on the heavy burden imposed by the wide breadth of the request for information. There is no similar burden created by Ms. Miers invoking executive privilege in response to specific, targeted questions. Here, the Executive does not claim that the Committee's questions will be overly broad; instead, it asserts that Ms. Miers need not provide any response whatsoever. That contention finds no support in *Cheney*.

consistent with needed preparation time and the availability of the witnesses and their counsel. After the conclusion of the interviews, the Committee reserves its right to seek public testimony from Mr. Rove and Ms. Miers.

- ○ The Committee has no current intention to seek interviews of any additional former Bush White House personnel. However, if information comes to light necessitating an interview from former Bush White House official William Kelley, the interview will be conducted pursuant to the terms of this agreement.

- Transcripts of interviews will be created and promptly provided to all involved parties.

- The scope of the interviews will be limited to: (1) facts relating to the evaluation of, decision to dismiss, or decision to replace the former U.S. Attorneys in question; the alleged decisions to retain certain U.S. Attorneys; and any allegations of selective prosecution related thereto; and (2) testimony or representations made by Department of Justice officials to Congress on the U.S. Attorneys matter. For the period beginning on March 9, 2007 (the date of the Committee's first written demand for information from the White House), interviews will not include the content of conversations involving: (i) Mr. Rove and members of the White House Counsel's office; or (ii) Ms. Miers and members of the White House Counsel's office. In the case of Mr. Rove, the interview also will include facts relating to the prosecution of Alabama governor Don Siegelman.

- As to official privileges, counsel will direct witnesses not to respond to questions only when questions relate to communications to or from the President or when questions are outside the scope of questioning set forth above.

- The following counsel may attend the interviews: counsel for the interviewee, Committee majority, Committee minority, the President, and the former President.

- Interviewees will be allowed a reasonable period of time to review relevant documents in advance of the interview.

- Reasonable logistical details (*e.g.*, venue, time limitation, etc.) will be set in advance.

Documents

- With the exception of 4 pages of particularly sensitive privileged material (which will be described for Committee staff by a representative of the former President), Committee staff (majority and minority) will be allowed to review the documents for the period December 2004 through March 8, 2007. Documents subpoenaed by the Committee from Harriet Miers will be treated in the same manner.

- The foregoing documents will be provided to Committee staff (majority and minority) at a reasonable time in advance of the interviews.

- As to documents post-dating March 8, 2007, the following will be made available for Committee review only and a copy will not be produced to the Committee:

- The final draft of the Scudder Memorandum;

- Any factual chronology prepared by the Department of Justice Office of Legal Counsel in the possession of the White House; and

- Any documents showing White House inputs or edits to Congressional testimony of Department of Justice officials on the subject of the U.S. Attorneys matter.

Copies of the aforementioned documents will be made available for the Committee's use during interviews conducted pursuant to this agreement. The Committee will return and will not retain any such copies at the conclusion of the respective interviews.

- In addition, the former Administration will conduct a timely review to identify: (1) any documents sent to/from White House personnel to/from third parties other than Department of Justice personnel; and (2) any documents referenced in the aforementioned Scudder Memorandum or OLC chronologies shown to the Committee. The former Administration will consider making some or all of the above material available to the Committee (in the same manner as the other post-March 8, 2007 documents described above). This process will be completed and the issue resolved prior to the interviews described in this agreement.

- Documents and their contents will remain confidential through the time of completion of the last interview. At that time, copies of documents provided to the Committee and/or contents of documents reviewed by the Committee may be made public. The transcripts discussed above may be made public after the completion of the last interview and after counsel has had a reasonable opportunity to review them for accuracy. No document or part of any document and no description or partial description of any document shall be disclosed to any other person until after the completion of the last interview.

Litigation

- The existing litigation will be stayed or the briefing schedule extended in such a way as to serve as the equivalent of a stay until at least the completion of the interviews.

- The Committee retains its rights to challenge any assertion of privilege over questions and documents for the period December 2004 through March 8, 2007.

- The Committee will not argue that this accommodation operates as a bar or waiver of the current or former Administration's existing rights, including but not limited to the right to argue jurisdictional objections, claims of immunity, or claims of executive privilege.

Notes and Questions

1. Terms of Settlement. Review carefully the terms of the settlement agreement set out above. What are the noteworthy aspects of the agreement? Does the agreement require Rove and Miers to provide testimony under oath? Why would the House Judiciary Committee have agreed not to seek testimony from other Bush administration officials (with one exception) before they had obtained the testimony of Rove and Miers? Is the "scope of the interviews" as limited by the agreement adequate to ensure that the Judiciary Committee can satisfy its oversight responsibilities (for additional information relevant to this question, see Note 2 below)? With respect to the agreement on production of documents, what might be the explanation for the Judiciary Committee not being permitted to review the "4 pages of particularly sensitive privileged material" that instead is to be "described for committee staff by a representative of the former President"? If those four pages reflect direct communications with President Bush, would describing them to committee staff constitute a waiver of executive privilege, and if so does the final section of the agreement protect against such a waiver claim? Why are three categories of "documents post-dating March 8, 2007" subject to special treatment under the agreement? The "Scudder memorandum" is a reference to a "timeline" chronology of events relating to the U.S. Attorney dismissals prepared by Associate White House Counsel Michael Scudder in 2007 in connection with a White House internal review of the matter. A September 2008 joint report by the Department of Justice Office of the Inspector General and Office of Professional Responsibility noted that the White House had provided the DOJ IG investigators with only a "heavily redacted" version of the Scudder memorandum and that they believed "the refusal to provide us with an unredacted copy of this document hampered our investigation." *See An Investigation Into the Removal of Nine U.S. Attorneys in 2006*, Office of the Inspector General and Office of Professional Responsibility, Department of Justice 94 (September 2008). In a September 18, 2008, letter appended to the September 2008 DOJ OIG/OPR report, Deputy Counsel to the President Emmet T. Flood took this position with respect to the Scudder Memorandum:

> In our view, to make available to OIG/OPR a draft chronology of this sort, prepared under the circumstances described above, would threaten a very significant chilling effect for counsel and White House officials, and complete disclosure would have an adverse impact on the effective provision of legal advice within the White House. That impact, as we perceived it, was not outweighed by OIG/OPR's stated need for the information, at least not to the extent we understood that need as articulated in our discussions with your offices. Accordingly, we did not make the draft chronology available *in its entirety*.

> At the same time, the White House recognized that OIG and OPR—which are components of an executive branch agency—had a genuine, and potentially significant, interest in reviewing those factual portions of the draft chronology for which OIG/OPR had a substantial need and no other available source. With these competing interests in mind, the White House attempted to strike

a balance respectful of both concerns. In view of the draft chronology's origins and purpose, we viewed the situation as in some sense analogous to civil discovery efforts to obtain an opponent's attorney work-product material. *See Hickman v. Taylor,* 329 U.S. 495 (1947); Fed. R. Civ. P. 26(b)(3). Accordingly, after several meetings with OIG/OPR to discuss the question of our respective offices' interests in this matter, the White House provided for OIG/OPR review a redacted copy of the draft chronology. The unredacted portions made available to OIG/OPR contained factual information for which the White House understood OIG/OPR to have expressed a substantial need and for which OIG/OPR had no alternative available source that could provide the same or equivalent information. As to portions not made available, the decision not to provide them resulted from our not receiving from OIG/OPR a focused showing of substantial need for the non-disclosed portions and an understanding that the undisclosed material (or its equivalent) was unavailable from another source.

In this partial disclosure, as noted above, we sought to balance the needs of your investigation with the White House's confidentiality interests. That impact, as we perceived it, was not outweighed by OIG/OPR's need for the undisclosed information, at least to the extent we understood that need as articulated in our discussions with your office.

Id. at Appendix A. The DOJ OIG/OPR report contains the following conclusion:

In sum, we believe that the process used to remove the nine U.S. Attorneys in 2006 was fundamentally flawed. While Presidential appointees can be removed for any reason or for no reason, as long as it is not an illegal or improper reason, Department officials publicly justified the removals as the result of an evaluation that sought to replace underperforming U.S. Attorneys. In fact, we determined that the process implemented largely by Kyle Sampson, Chief of Staff to the Attorney General, was unsystematic and arbitrary, with little oversight by the Attorney General, the Deputy Attorney General, or any other senior Department official. In choosing which U.S. Attorneys to remove, Sampson did not adequately consult with the Department officials most knowledgeable about their performance, or even examine formal evaluations of each U.S. Attorney's Office, despite his representations to the contrary.

We also determined that the U.S. Attorneys were not given an opportunity to address concerns about their performance or provided the reasons for their removal, which led to widespread speculation about the true reasons for their removal, including that they were removed for improper partisan political reasons. And to make matters worse, after the removals became public the statements and congressional testimony provided by the Attorney General, the Deputy Attorney General, Sampson, and other Department officials about the reasons for the removals were inconsistent, misleading, and inaccurate in many respects. We believe the primary responsibility for these serious failures rest [*sic*] with senior Department leaders—Attorney General Alberto Gonzales and Deputy Attorney General Paul McNulty—who abdicated their responsibility to adequately oversee the process and to ensure that the reasons for removal of each U.S. Attorney were supportable and not improper. These removals were not a minor personnel matter—they were an unprecedented removal of a group of high-level Department officials that was certain to raise concerns if not handled properly. Yet, neither the Attorney General nor the Deputy Attorney General provided adequate oversight or supervision of this process. We also concluded that Sampson bears significant responsibility for the flawed and arbitrary removal process. Moreover, they and other Department officials are responsible for failing to provide accurate and truthful statements about the removals and their role in the process.

We believe our investigation was able to uncover most of the facts relating to the reasons for the removal of most of the U.S. Attorneys. However, as described in this report, there are gaps in our investigation because of the refusal of certain key witnesses to be interviewed by us, including former White House officials Karl Rove, Harriet Miers, and William Kelley, former Department of Justice White House Liaison Monica Goodling, Senator Pete Domenici, and his Chief of Staff. In addition, the White House would not provide us internal documents related to the removals of the U.S. Attorneys.

The most serious allegation that we were not able to fully investigate related to the removal of David Iglesias, the U.S. Attorney for New Mexico, and the allegation that he was removed to influence voter fraud and public corruption prosecutions. We recommend that a counsel specially appointed by the Attorney General assess the facts we have uncovered, work with us to conduct further investigation, and ultimately determine whether the evidence demonstrates that any criminal offense was committed with regard to the removal of Iglesias or any other U.S. Attorney, or the testimony of any witness related to the U.S. Attorney removals.

The Department's removal of the U.S. Attorneys and the controversy it created severely damaged the credibility of the Department and raised doubts about the integrity of Department prosecutive decisions. We believe that this investigation, and final resolution of the issues raised in this report, can help restore confidence in the Department by fully describing the serious failures in the process used to remove the U.S. Attorneys and by providing lessons for the Department in how to avoid such failures in the future.

Id. at 356–58.

2. Presidential Control of Federal Prosecutors. How much control and influence should a President, or for that matter the Attorney General and the central administration of the Department of Justice, often referred to as "Main Justice" by federal prosecutors in the field, have over U.S. Attorneys? Should U.S. Attorneys be completely independent and insulated from direct supervision by the President or the Attorney general? Or should U.S. Attorneys be treated much like regional officials in other cabinet departments and subject to strict supervision and control by political appointees at Main Justice in Washington? If U.S. Attorneys should be treated differently, what is the reason and what should be the limits on supervision and influence over their action by political appointees? For an exploration of these and related questions, see Bruce A. Green & Fred C. Zacharias, *"The U.S. Attorneys Scandal" and the Allocation of Prosecutorial Power*, 69 OHIO ST. L.J. 187 (2008). Professors Green and Zacharias offer an interesting perspective on the issue of whether U.S. Attorneys should be more insulated from political interference by high-ranking political officials:

> A call to give lower-level prosecutors greater independence from higher ranked officials would be strikingly at odds with one of the primary themes of contemporary commentary on prosecutorial ethics. Prosecutorial misconduct traditionally is considered to be the product of too much independence, particularly on the part of rogue prosecutors on the front lines. A more contemporary insight is that even well-intentioned prosecutors are subject to biases that must be kept in check. Proposed solutions include the implementation of internal policies constraining individual prosecutors' discretion, increased oversight and decision making by supervisory personnel, and dis-aggregation of decision-making authority.

Id. at 189–90. Do these considerations influence your thinking about the need for centralized oversight of federal prosecutors in the field?

Professor Sara Sun Beale has observed that "[t]he current structure of the Department of Justice is anomalous" and "I am not aware of any agency other than the Justice Department in which the head of each small domestic field office is a presidential appointee subject to Senate confirmation." Sara Sun Beale, *Rethinking the Role and Identity of United States Attorneys*, 6 OHIO ST. J. CRIM. L. 369, 371–72 (2009). Professor Beale considers whether the current system of political appointments of U.S. Attorneys should be replaced with one in which U.S. Attorneys are career civil servants:

> I conclude that, on balance, converting the U.S. Attorneys to a career civil service role is neither politically feasible nor desirable. No one doubts that the Attorney General and the heads of the divisions within the Department (which I will refer to collectively as the leadership of "Main Justice") are and will always be political appointees. The appointment of these officials is the mechanism by which each new presidential administration establishes and carries out its policies and priorities. As long as the U.S. Attorneys remain subject to the oversight and direction of the political leadership at Main Justice, it will not be possible to preclude entirely the possibility that political considerations might improperly influence decisions in individual prosecutions. Nor would it be desirable to eliminate the requirement of Senate confirmation for U.S. Attorneys.
>
> The current appointment process for U.S. Attorneys has several advantages. It creates a desirable counterweight to Main Justice in two distinct ways. First,

it provides a political counterweight, because the U.S. Attorneys have their own political influence and constituencies. Second, because the U.S. Attorneys are political figures drawn from their districts and confirmed with the support of their home-state senators, they also serve as a counterweight to excessive centralization and uniformity within the federal system. There is real value in a structure that delegates federal prosecutorial power to local districts, reinforcing federalism and allowing federal law to be adapted to different conditions. The current system also has several other major advantages. A presidential appointment gives the U.S. Attorney desirable prestige that helps him or her carry out the federal law enforcement mission and it increases the accountability of the U.S. Attorneys. Bringing in an outsider may also increase the fairness and accuracy of federal prosecuting by reducing institutional tunnel vision.

Id. at 372–73. Do you agree with Professor Beale's conclusions? If not, how would you change the current system, if at all?

3. The Reagan Administration OLC Opinions, Turned Against the Bush Administration? A portion of Judge Bates's opinion in the *Miers* case that is not reproduced above analyzed the application of the 1984 and 1986 Office of Legal Counsel opinions on executive privilege assertions by senior executive branch officials (discussed in the preceding section of this Chapter). Note the way Judge Bates relied upon the views expressed in those opinions to reject the Bush administration's argument that he should decline to enforce the Judiciary Committee's subpoenas because judicial intervention in the dispute would be inappropriate:

> Two significant OLC opinions issued during the Reagan administration warrant examination at this point. In 1984, an opinion by Acting Assistant Attorney General Theodore Olson confirmed the viability of a federal civil suit brought by a House of Congress to enforce subpoenas issued to executive officials. *See Prosecution for Contempt of Congress of an Executive Branch Official Who Has Asserted a Claim of Executive Privilege*, 8 U.S. Op. Off. Legal Counsel 101, 137 (1984) (hereinafter "Olson OLC Opinion"). As OLC opined, Congress has three options available to enforce a subpoena against a recalcitrant respondent: (1) referral to the U.S. Attorney for prosecution of a criminal contempt of Congress charge; (2) detention and prosecution pursuant to Congress's inherent contempt authority; or (3) a civil action to enforce the subpoena in a federal district court. When the respondent is a member of the executive branch who refuses to comply on the basis of executive privilege, however, OLC stated that the "contempt of Congress statute does not require and *could not constitutionally* require a prosecution of that official, or even, we believe, a referral to a grand jury of the facts relating to the alleged contempt." *Id.* at 142 (emphasis added). That conclusion is rooted in concerns over both the Executive's traditional prosecutorial discretion, *see id.* at 140, as well as the "concomitant chilling effect" that might impair presidential advice if the possibility of criminal prosecution loomed over the President's close advisors, *see id.* at 142. Significantly, OLC also determined that "the same reasoning that suggests

that the statute could not constitutionally be applied against a Presidential assertion of privilege applies to Congress' inherent contempt powers as well." *Id.* at n.42. Thus, neither criminal prosecution nor inherent contempt could be employed against a recalcitrant executive branch official, as OLC saw it.

Instead, "Congress [can] obtain a judicial resolution of the underlying privilege claim and vindicate its asserted right to obtain any documents by a civil action for enforcement of a congressional subpoena." *Id.* at 137. As OLC put it, a civil action would be superior because:

> Congress has a legitimate and powerful interest in obtaining any unprivileged documents necessary to assist it in its lawmaking function ... [and][a] civil suit to enforce the subpoena would be aimed at the congressional objective of obtaining the documents, not at inflicting punishment on an individual who failed to produce them. Thus, even if criminal sanctions were not available against an executive official who asserted the President's claim of privilege, Congress would be able to vindicate its legitimate desire to obtain documents if it could establish that its need for the records outweighed the Executive's interest in preserving confidentiality.

Id. In fact, after examining *Senate Select Comm. III* [*Ed. Note: a case in which the Senate Watergate Committee sought access to the Nixon White House tapes (see Chapter 3)*], the OLC concluded that "there is little doubt that, at the very least, Congress may authorize civil enforcement of its subpoenas and grant jurisdiction to the courts to entertain such cases." *Id.* at 137 n.36. There is no suggestion whatsoever in the Olson OLC Opinion that such a civil suit would encounter any Article III obstacles because Congress (or a committee) would lack standing or because the dispute would not be considered traditionally amenable to judicial resolution. To the contrary, OLC rather emphatically concluded that a civil action would be the *least* controversial way for Congress to vindicate its investigative authority.

A 1986 OLC opinion authored by Assistant Attorney General Charles Cooper reached the same conclusion. *See Response to Congressional Requests for Information Regarding Decisions Made Under the Independent Counsel Act*, 10 U.S. Op. Off. Legal Counsel 68 (1986) (hereinafter "Cooper OLC Opinion"). In that opinion, OLC restated its position that Congress may institute "a civil suit seeking declaratory enforcement of [a] subpoena." *Id.* at 83. Likewise, OLC indicated that although inherent contempt is theoretically available to Congress and could ultimately be challenged by the executive branch through a writ of habeas corpus brought by the detained official, "it seems most unlikely that Congress could dispatch the Sergeant-at-Arms to arrest and imprison an Executive Branch official who claimed executive privilege." *Id.* at 86.

Ultimately, OLC concluded that "although the civil enforcement route has not been tried by the House, it would appear to be a viable option." *Id.* at 88;

see also id. at 88 n. 33 ("Any notion that the courts may not or should not review [subpoena enforcement disputes between the political branches] is dispelled by *United States v. Nixon* ... in which the Court clearly asserted its role as ultimate arbiter of executive privilege questions."). In fact, the Cooper OLC Opinion stated that the "rationale used by the Department [in *AT&T I*] would appear to *apply equally to suits filed by a House of Congress* seeking enforcement of its subpoena against executive privilege claims." *Id.* at 88 (emphasis added). There can be no doubt, then, that at least one prior administration regarded a civil suit by Congress to enforce a subpoena as presenting a justiciable controversy—and, indeed, to be the preferred method for resolving such inter-branch disputes. *See id.* at 88 n.33 ("[O]nly judicial intervention can prevent a stalemate between the other two branches that could result in a particular paralysis of government operations.").

558 F. Supp. 2d 75–77. At a later point in the *Miers* opinion, Judge Bates again relied on the 1984 and 1986 OLC opinions to refute arguments of the Bush administration against enforcing the Judiciary Committee subpoena:

> Still, the Executive takes the Committee to task for failing to utilize its inherent contempt authority. But there are serious problems presented by the prospect of inherent contempt, not the least of which is that the Executive is attempting to have it both ways on this point. To begin with, prosecution pursuant to inherent contempt is a method of "inflicting punishment on an individual who failed" to comply with a subpoena. *See* Olson OLC Opinion at 137. As OLC has recognized, a civil action, by contrast, is directed towards "obtaining any unprivileged documents necessary to assist [Congress's] lawmaking function." *Id.* Put another way, the two remedies serve different purposes, although it is true that threatening prosecution under inherent contempt may lead to the production of documents. But unlike a civil action for subpoena enforcement, that is not the primary goal of inherent contempt. Second, imprisoning current (and even former) senior presidential advisors and prosecuting them before the House would only exacerbate the acrimony between the two branches and would present a grave risk of precipitating a constitutional crisis. Indeed, one can easily imagine a stand-off between the Sergeant-at-Arms and executive branch law enforcement officials concerning taking Mr. Bolten into custody and detaining him. *See* Cooper OLC Opinion at 86 ("[I]t seems most unlikely that Congress could dispatch the Sergeant-at-Arms to arrest and imprison an Executive Branch official who claimed executive privilege."). Such unseemly, provocative clashes should be avoided, and there is no need to run the risk of such mischief when a civil action can resolve the same issues in an orderly fashion. Third, even if the Committee did exercise inherent contempt, the disputed issue would in all likelihood end up before this Court, just by a different vehicle—a writ of habeas corpus brought by Ms. Miers and Mr. Bolten. In either event there would be judicial resolution of the underlying issue.

Indeed this administration, along with previous executive administrations, has observed that inherent contempt is *not* available for use against senior executive branch officials who claim executive privilege. In this very case, the Executive has questioned "whether [inherent contempt] would even countenance the arrest of the President or his closest aides for refusing to testify or provide privileged documents ... at the President's direction." The Executive has described that possibility as a "dubious proposition." Previous administrations have gone even further. The Olson OLC Opinion explained that "the same reasoning that suggests that the [criminal contempt] statute could not constitutionally be applied against a Presidential assertion of privilege applies to Congress' inherent contempt powers as well." *See* Olson OLC Opinion at 140 n. 42. The Cooper OLC Opinion concurred: the inherent contempt alternative "may well be foreclosed by advice previously rendered by this Office." *See* Cooper OLC Opinion at 83. Thus, there are strong reasons to doubt the viability of Congress's inherent contempt authority vis-a-vis senior executive officials. To be sure, the executive branch's opinion is not dispositive on this question, and the Court need not decide the issue. At the very least, however, the Executive cannot simultaneously question the sufficiency and availability of an alternative remedy but nevertheless insist that the Committee must attempt to "exhaust" it before a civil cause of action is available.

558 F. Supp. 2d at 91–92. Finally, Judge Bates returned to the 1986 OLC opinion as an authority supporting his rejection of the Bush administration's argument that he should exercise judicial discretion and dismiss the Judiciary Committee's lawsuit rather than intervening in a dispute between the two political branches of government:

As the Cooper OLC Opinion put it, "only judicial intervention can prevent a stalemate between the other two branches that could result in a particular paralysis of government operations." *See* Cooper OLC Opinion at 88 n.33. Although the identity of the litigants in this case necessitates that the Court proceed with caution, that is not a convincing reason to decline to decide a case that presents important legal questions. Rather than running roughshod over separation of powers principles, the Court believes that entertaining this case will reinforce them. Two parties cannot negotiate in good faith when one side asserts legal privileges but insists that they cannot be tested in court in the traditional manner. That is true whether the negotiating partners are private firms or the political branches of the federal government. Accordingly, the Court will deny the Executive's motion to dismiss.

558 F. Supp. 2d at 99.

4. Textual Ambiguity: Is the Core Problem Here a Lack of Textual Constitutional Guidance? There is no explicit textual provision in the Constitution for either the power of Congress to investigate or the right of a President to withhold information from Congress based on "executive privilege." As discussed in Chapter 1 above, in the Teapot Dome-era case of *McGrain v. Daugherty*, 273 U.S. 135 (1927), the Supreme Court recognized that the power to investigate is inherent in the power to legislate that is granted to Congress in Article I of the Constitution. During the McCarthy era, discussed in Chapter 2 above, the Court recognized the broad scope of the congressional investigative power in *Watkins v. United States*, 354 U.S. 178, 187 (1957): "The power of the Congress to conduct investigations is inherent in the legislative process. That power is broad. It encompasses inquiries concerning the administration of existing laws as well as proposed or possibly needed statutes.... [And it] comprehends probes into departments of the Federal Government to expose corruption, inefficiency, or waste." Two decades later the Court reexamined the power of Congress to investigate and confirmed that "[t]he scope of its power of inquiry ... is as penetrating and far-reaching as the potential power to enact and appropriate under the Constitution." *Eastland v. United States Servicemen's Fund*, 421 U.S. 491, 504 n.15 (1975) (quoting *Barenblatt v. United States*, 360 U.S. 109, 111 (1950)). Despite the breadth and strength of these pronouncements, however, the fact remains that the congressional power to investigate is not based upon an explicit textual reference in the Constitution, and for that reason it is more vulnerable to changing judicial interpretations than powers and privileges that are explicitly delineated in the Constitution's text.

The same is true of the "executive privilege" doctrine. As the Justice Department OLC, consistently one of the strongest governmental proponents of executive privilege, has recognized:

> The Constitution nowhere states that the President, or the Executive Branch generally, enjoys a privilege against disclosing information requested by the courts, the public, or the legislative branch. The existence of such a privilege, however, is a necessary corollary of the executive function vested in the President by Article II of the Constitution, has been asserted by numerous Presidents from the earliest days of our Nation, and has been explicitly recognized by the Supreme Court.

Response to Congressional Requests for Information Regarding Decisions Made Under the Independent Counsel Act, 10 Op. Off. Legal Counsel 68 (April 28, 1986) (citing *United States v. Nixon*, 418 U.S. 683, 705–06 (1974)).

To what extent does the difficulty of resolving the disputes between Congress and the executive branch that are the subject of this Chapter stem from the fact that both sides are asserting legal doctrines that are not grounded in specific textual provisions of the Constitution? Does this lack of an explicit textual mooring in the Constitution explain to some degree the hesitance of the courts to intervene in these cases? For a comprehensive examination of the law and politics of executive privilege claims, see Louis Fisher, The Politics of Executive Privilege (Carolina Academic Press 2004). For an in-depth analysis of the issue of congressional access to law enforcement information, see Todd D. Peterson, *Congressional Oversight of Open Criminal Investigations*, 77 Notre Dame L. Rev. 1373 (2002). Finally, consider the analysis of the "constitutional text" issue provided by Judge Bates in a portion of the *Miers* opinion that is not reproduced above:

Against that backdrop [of Supreme Court precedent on implied rights of action in the federal courts], the Committee's argument is straightforward. Article I, the Committee asserts, provides Congress with an implied right to investigate in furtherance of its legislative function. That right has been recognized by the Supreme Court, which has also held that it carries with it a necessary corollary that Congress may rely upon compulsory process to enforce its investigative authority. Indeed, according to the Committee the Supreme Court has already "establishe[d] a framework for implying remedies pursuant to Congress's powers under Article I." *See* Pl.'s Opp'n & Reply at 39. In *Marshall v. Gordon*, [citation omitted] (1917), the Court explained that Congress's implied inherent contempt authority "rests solely upon the right of self-preservation to enable the public powers given to be exerted." [citation omitted] This implied power derives "from the right to prevent acts which, in and of themselves, inherently obstruct or prevent the discharge of legislative duty." *Id.* [citation omitted]. For the same reasons that the Supreme Court implied a power of inherent contempt in *Marshall*, the Committee argues, this Court should imply a cause of action to vindicate the right of Congress to carry out its legislative duty. [Footnote: Indeed, as the Committee would have it, the Supreme Court's implied remedy in *Marshall*—inherent contempt—is more drastic than the civil cause of action that the Committee pursues here, and hence this Court should take comfort in the fact that the Supreme Court has already crafted a more severe remedy.]

In response, the Executive insists that the Supreme Court "has made clear that implied causes of action under the Constitution arise only where there is a constitutionally-explicit *right* to be vindicated." *See* Defs.' Reply at 26 (emphasis in original). Article I, the Executive says, creates no such explicit right. True enough, but the Executive overlooks the fact that the Supreme Court has already construed Article I in *McGrain*, *Eastland*, and other cases to find an implied right of investigation, and indeed an implied right to compel compliance with that investigative power, accruing to Congress. *See, e.g., Eastland*, [citation omitted] ("The power to investigate and to do so through compulsory process plainly falls within [the] definition [of Congress's legislative function]."). This Court is equally bound by constitutional constructions issued by the Supreme Court as it is by the text of Article I itself.

558 F. Supp. 2d at 89–90.

5. Resolving Executive Privilege Disputes—Is a Legislative Solution Possible? As the materials above suggest, the current system for resolving disputes over congressional subpoenas for executive branch information is unworkable. Enforcement through the criminal contempt process is likely to be unavailable if the executive branch refuses to bring criminal contempt charges, as occurred in the EPA and Miers/Bolten cases. Inherent contempt proceedings remain a theoretical possibility, but most likely are not a politically realistic alternative. The decision of Judge Bates in the *Miers* case certainly enhances the viability of civil enforcement remedy, but that approach is neither assured nor satisfactory. Although the *Miers* decision is carefully reasoned and supported with thorough legal analysis, it is the decision of a lower federal court, and another court in a different case could reach a different conclusion on the core jurisdictional issues. More important, even if one views the *Miers* case as a victory by the House Judiciary Committee, success came too late and after too much effort to provide a practical solution in future disputes. In fact, some would say that the *Miers* case shows how a recalcitrant executive branch can use the legal process to "run out the clock" on a congressional subpoena and delay surrender of information long enough to effectively frustrate the oversight responsibilities of Congress.

Is there anything Congress can do to strengthen its hand in these disputes? After the EPA dispute, one of the authors of this book argued for a new law that would provide for court appointment of an independent counsel to prosecute criminal contempt of Congress charges against high-ranking executive branch officials. *See* Stanley M. Brand & Sean Connelly, *Constitutional Confrontations: Preserving a Prompt and Orderly Means by Which Congress May Enforce Investigative Demands Against Executive Branch Officials*, 36 CATH. UNIV. L. REV. 71 (1986). Legislation of that nature was never enacted, however, and since that time the independent counsel statute has been allowed to lapse and the use of independent counsels has fallen out of favor with Congress and the public (see Note 4 following the section above on the EPA dispute for more discussion of the independent counsel statute). As a result, barring some dramatic change in public perception and political popularity of independent counsels, that approach is unlikely to be taken up by Congress.

Another possible solution is to enact legislation to confirm the jurisdiction of the federal courts to hear civil enforcement actions for congressional subpoenas and provide for expedited judicial review in such cases. That approach was suggested by Emily Berman of the Brennan Center for Justice at New York University Law School. *See* Emily Berman, *Executive Privilege: A Legislative Remedy*, Brennan Center for Justice, New York University Law School (2009). Berman proposed that Congress adopt a new "Executive Privilege Codification Act" that contains the following provisions:

Section 105 Standing and Authorization to Sue

A House of Congress that elects by a majority vote of the whole House to bring a specific civil action under this statute, or a committee or subcommittee of a House of Congress authorized by a majority vote of the whole House to bring a specific civil action under this statute, has standing and may bring that civil action in the federal District Court for the District of Columbia to compel compliance with a subpoena duly issued to any witness, including an officer or employee of the United States, if that witness has failed to comply with the terms of the subpoena on the basis of a claim of executive privilege. When a House of Congress, or an authorized committee or subcommittee, brings such a suit in the federal courts, the courts shall exercise their jurisdiction over the action.

Section 106 Jurisdiction

In addition to the subject matter jurisdiction available under 28 U.S.C. §1331, the District Court for the District of Columbia shall have original, exclusive jurisdiction over any civil action, brought by either House of Congress, or any duly authorized committee or subcommittee thereof, with respect to any claim of executive privilege asserted before either House or any committee of either House.

Sec. 107 Mootness

The expiration of a Congress shall not be deemed to render any civil action brought pursuant to this statute moot on prudential grounds. The subsequent Congress shall possess all the rights and powers under this statute that its predecessor possessed.

Sec. 108 Three-Judge Panel

Any civil action brought pursuant to this statute shall be heard and adjudicated by three judges appointed in accordance with 28 U.S.C. §2284. Any party may appeal the decision of the panel directly to the Supreme Court in accordance with 28 U.S.C. §1253.

Sec. 109 Expedited Schedule

The federal courts shall place any action filed pursuant to this statute on an expedited schedule and make its timely resolution a priority.

Sec. 110 Mutual Accommodation & Exhaustion

Members of Congress and the Executive shall seek all means of mutually accommodating one another's needs with respect to congressional information requests. No House of Congress, or any committee or subcommittee thereof, shall bring a civil action as authorized herein until it has attempted to secure the subpoenaed information through negotiations with the Executive.

Id. at 56–57. Changing the law in this manner would allow civil subpoena enforcement actions to be heard by a special federal three-judge district court panel, already available under existing law, and decided on an expedited schedule, with direct appeal to the Supreme Court, also already available under existing law, so as to resolve such disputes as expeditiously as is possible under our legal system. In addition to providing for prompt resolution, this approach would place responsibility for making the final decision on executive privilege disputes with the Supreme Court. This process would also have several important practical advantages that are particularly well-suited to resolving subpoena disputes involving high-level executive branch officials. The availability of an expedited judicial enforcement and appeals process makes it less likely that a recalcitrant executive branch official with dubious executive privilege claims (as the court determined was the case with the claim asserted in the Miers/Bolten dispute that executive officials have an "absolute privilege" from appearing before Congress) could try to "run out the clock" on a congressional investigation. This is a significant step forward from the current unworkable system, which leaves Congress with no realistic means available to it to enforce its subpoenas within a reasonable period of time.

What do you think of the Berman proposal? Should Congress enact the recommended statutory provisions? If Congress enacted them, would they withstand judicial review? Do they avoid the separation of powers concerns that are expressed in the 1984 and 1986 OLC opinions discussed above? Can you suggest any better solution for appropriately balancing the legitimate interests of the executive and legislative branches in executive privilege disputes?

6. The Power of Congressional Staff—A Cautionary Tale for Executive Branch Officials. A legal newspaper's 2009 article profiling Bruce Cohen, then Senate Judiciary Committee staff director and long-time aide to Senator Patrick Leahy of Vermont, provides some behind-the-scenes insights into how failing to satisfy questions and concerns of congressional staff can have unpleasant consequences for executive branch officials:

> Winning over Cohen can be critical for those with interests before the Judiciary Committee. D. Kyle Sampson found out the hard way in 2007, when he was chief of staff to [then-Attorney General Alberto] Gonzales. Leahy and Sen. Dianne Feinstein (D-Calif.) had sent a letter to Gonzales asking about initial media reports of the U.S. Attorneys firings. Sampson then went to Capitol Hill to try to reassure the Senators' staffs that the Justice Department was justified in removing the prosecutors. In a meeting in Cohen's office in the Dirksen Senate Office Building, Cohen and Jennifer Duck, Feinstein's chief counsel, pressed Sampson for details. They weren't satisfied with what they heard, according to a report by the Justice Department's internal watchdogs, and Democrats began organizing the first hearing on the matter—a move that led to the eventual ouster of Gonzales, Sampson, and other top DOJ officials.

David Ingram, *The Gatekeeper: Bruce Cohen Holds the Keys to Leahy's Committee*, LEGAL TIMES (April 13, 2009). (Further information about this meeting can be found at pages 58–60 of the September 2008 DOJ OIG/OPR Report that is discussed in Note 1 above.) Adding this account to what you have learned from this Chapter about relations between the executive branch and Congress, what advice would you give executive branch officials about dealings with members of Congress and their staffs? To what extent does your advice differ if you are advising an official of the executive branch that is controlled by one political party when the other political party controls one or both houses of Congress? In this regard, it is noteworthy that in *Gravel v. United States*, 408 U.S. 606, 617 (1972), the Supreme Court held that, for purposes of applying legislative immunity to the performance by legislative aides of acts that would be protected if performed by a legislator, legislative staff were "alter egos" of the elected legislators and therefore also entitled to immunity.

An inaccurate or inadequate response to a congressional inquiry, even one from a member of the minority party of one of the houses of Congress, can have damaging political consequences. A particularly instructive example arose during the Obama administration, as discussed in the following section.

The Obama Administration "Operation Fast & Furious" Investigation and the Holder Contempt Proceedings

In 2011 Senator Charles E. Grassley of Iowa was the ranking member of the Senate Judiciary Committee, which has oversight authority over the Department of Justice. In that capacity, Senator Grassley wrote to the acting director of the U.S. Bureau of Alcohol, Tobacco, Firearms and Explosives ("ATF") , a bureau within the Department of Justice, with questions about whether ATF had allowed "straw purchasers" of firearms along the Mexican border to supply weapons to Mexican drug cartels. Senator Grassley is known for welcoming "whistleblower" reports of misconduct in government, and he advised ATF that members of the Judiciary Committee had received reports that weapons purchased by straw buyers had been allowed to "walk" across the border and that two of the weapons were subsequently used in the shooting death of a federal officer.

The Department of Justice responded to Grassley's inquiry with a strongly worded letter on February 4, 2011, denying that ATF had allowed guns to "walk" across the border after having been purchased by straw buyers. That denial subsequently proved to be inaccurate, and Grassley, who was in the minority in the Senate, referred the matter to the House of Representatives Committee on Oversight & Government Reform. The House Oversight Committee focused on the February 4, 2011 letter, which was formally withdrawn by the Department of Justice in December 2011. The committee continued to seek information about the February 4 letter and its retraction. The Obama Justice Department produced materials related to the drafting of the letter, but resisted producing documents created after February 4. The Committee subpoenaed those documents, and in June 2012, President Obama, at Attorney General Eric Holder's request, asserted executive privilege over the documents. The House of Representatives then voted to hold Attorney General Holder in contempt of Congress. This was the first time in American history that a sitting cabinet member had been held in contempt of Congress, and it set the stage for another judicial battle over congressional access to executive branch information. (For a more detailed account of the Fast & Furious dispute, which criticizes the Obama Justice Department's handling of the matter and President Obama's assertion of executive privilege, see Louis Fisher, *Obama's Executive Privilege and Holder's Contempt: "Operation Fast & Furious"*, PRESIDENTIAL STUDIES QUARTERLY, Vol. 43, No. 1 (March 2013).)

Committee on Oversight &
Government Reform v. Holder

979 F. Supp. 2d 1 (D.D.C. 2013)

AMY BERMAN JACKSON, District Judge.

The Committee on Oversight and Government Reform of the United States House of Representatives has filed this action to enforce a subpoena it issued to the Attorney General of the United States, Eric H. Holder, Jr. The Attorney General refused to produce a portion of the records called for by the subpoena on the grounds that they are covered by the executive privilege, and the Committee seeks a declaration that the invocation of the privilege is invalid in this instance and that the documents must be produced. The matter is before the Court on defendant's motion to dismiss the complaint under Federal Rules of Civil Procedure 12(b)(1) and 12(b)(6): the Attorney General takes the position that a dispute between the legislative and executive branches must be resolved through negotiation and accommodation, and that the judiciary may not, or at least, should not, get involved.

The motion to dismiss will be denied. The fact that this case arises out of a dispute between two branches of government does not make it nonjusticiable; Supreme Court precedent establishes that the third branch has an equally fundamental role to play, and that judges not only may, but sometimes must, exercise their responsibility to interpret the Constitution and determine whether another branch has exceeded its power. In the Court's view, endorsing the proposition that the executive may assert an unreviewable right to withhold materials from the legislature would offend the Constitution more than undertaking to resolve the specific dispute that has been presented here. After all, the Constitution contemplates not only a separation, but a balance, of powers. * * *

The Court is mindful that "federal courts may exercise power only in the last resort ... and only when adjudication is consistent with a system of separated powers and [the dispute is one] traditionally thought to be capable of resolution through the judicial process." *Allen v. Wright*, 468 U.S. 737, 752 (1984) (internal citations and quotation marks omitted). But here, the narrow legal question posed by the complaint is precisely the sort of crisp legal issue that courts are well-equipped to address and routinely called upon to resolve.

The defendant warns that an assumption of jurisdiction in this case would mark an unprecedented expansion of the role of an Article III court. But there has been binding precedent to the contrary in this Circuit for more than thirty-five years. In *United States v. AT&T*, 551 F.2d 384, 390 (D.C. Cir. 1976), the Court of Appeals declared: "the mere fact that there is a conflict between the legislative and executive branches over a congressional subpoena does not preclude judicial resolution of the conflict." And five years ago, another court in this District carefully considered and rejected the same arguments being advanced by the Attorney General here. In a case involving a different Congress and a different President, *Committee on the Judiciary v. Miers*, 558 F. Supp. 2d 53 (D.D.C. 2008), the court concluded in a persuasive opinion that it had jurisdiction to resolve a similar clash between the branches.

For the reasons set forth in *Miers*, as well as those detailed below, the Court finds that neither the Constitution nor prudential considerations require judges to stand on the sidelines. There is federal subject matter jurisdiction over this complaint, and it alleges a cause of action that plaintiff has standing to bring. The Court cautions that this opinion should not be taken as any indication of its views on the merits of the dispute, which have yet to be briefed, argued, or considered in any way. The defendant's pleadings stress the importance of the privilege and the role it plays encouraging candor in executive branch deliberations and decision making. But at this stage of the proceedings, the sole question before the Court is whether it can and should exercise jurisdiction to hear the case—not whether the documents are covered by the privilege. This opinion does not grapple with the scope of the President's privilege: it simply rejects the notion that it is an unreviewable privilege when asserted in response to a legislative demand. * * * [*Ed. Note: The court's detailed review of the background of the dispute and the procedural history of the case is omitted.*]

The defendant does not attempt to suggest that the *Miers* case is distinguishable in any way from the instant action; he simply urges the Court to come to a different conclusion. But the Court is persuaded by the reasoning of the *Miers* opinion and by its own review of the authorities discussed in detail in that opinion. The Court rejects the notion that merely hearing this dispute between the branches would undermine the foundation of our government, or that it would lead to the abandonment of all negotiation and accommodation in the future, leaving the courts deluged with subpoena enforcement actions. Indeed, one cannot help but observe that in the five years that have elapsed since the *Miers* decision, the dire consequences prophesied by the Department have not come to pass. In the end, the civics lesson set out in the Department's brief is flawed and selective, and it ignores the fact that almost 40 years ago the Supreme Court unequivocally rejected the notion that the separation of powers doctrine would bar judicial review of a Presidential claim of privilege.

In *United States v. Nixon*, 418 U.S. 683 [(1974)], the Court acknowledged that each branch of government is empowered to interpret the Constitution in the first instance when defining and performing its own constitutional duties, and that one branch's interpretation of its own powers is due deference from the others. *Id.* at 703. But the Court reviewed the history of its own jurisprudence, beginning with *Marbury v. Madison*, and it pointed out that it had repeatedly been called upon to decide whether the executive branch or the legislature had exercised its power in conflict with the Constitution. *Id.* at 703–04. The Court quoted *Powell v. McCormack*: "Our system of government 'requires that federal courts on occasion interpret the Constitution in a manner at variance with the construction given the document by another branch.'" *Id.* at 704, quoting 395 U.S. 486. And it repeated what it had set forth in *Baker v. Carr*: "[D]eciding whether a matter has in any measure been committed by the Constitution to another branch of government, or whether the action of that branch exceeds whatever authority has been committed, is itself a delicate exercise in constitutional interpretation, and is a responsibility of this Court as ultimate interpreter of the Constitution." *Id.*, quoting 369 U.S. 186, 211 (1962).

Ultimately, the Supreme Court held that it was "the province and duty" of the Court "to say what the law is" with respect to the claim of executive privilege that was presented in that case. *Id.* at 705, quoting *Marbury v. Madison*, 5 U.S. (1 Cranch) 137, 177 (1803). "Any other conclusion would be contrary to the basic concept of separation of powers and the checks and balances that flow from the scheme of a tripartite government." *Id.* at 704. Those principles apply with equal force here. To give the Attorney General the final word would elevate and fortify the executive branch at the expense of the other institutions that are supposed to be its equal, and do more damage to the balance envisioned by the Framers than a judicial ruling on the narrow privilege question posed by the complaint. * * *

There is simply no binding precedent that requires the Court to dismiss this case on the grounds that it presents a political dispute. That conclusion is reinforced by the fact that the executive branch has itself invoked the jurisdiction of the courts when it sought to enjoin compliance with a Congressional subpoena, see *AT&T I*, 551 F.2d at 384, or to obtain a declaration concerning the validity of a claim of executive privilege asserted in response to a House request. See *United States v. House of Representatives*, 556 F. Supp. 150, 150–51 (D.D.C. 1983). As the court commented in *Miers*, "[t]he Court does not understand why separation of powers principles are more offended when the Article I branch sues the Article II branch than when the Article II branch sues the Article I branch." *Miers*, 558 F. Supp. 2d at 96. The Attorney General has advanced several other grounds for declining jurisdiction, most of which are variations on the same theme. The defendant moves to dismiss the case on the grounds that there is no statutory provision conferring federal subject matter jurisdiction in this case, that the plaintiff lacks standing, and that the complaint seeking a declaratory judgment does not allege a cause of action. Finally, the Attorney General argues that even if this court has jurisdiction to hear the case, it should decline to exercise it in its discretion. None of these arguments carries the day, and they will be addressed in turn below. * * *

The Court finds, as did the court in *Miers*, that this case presents a federal question and that therefore, the court has jurisdiction under 28 U.S.C. §1331. 558 F. Supp. 2d at 64. That was not a controversial finding in *Miers*, since both sides conceded that section 1331 provided subject matter jurisdiction over the dispute. *Id.* But the court went on to observe that since the case involved a failure to comply with a duly issued congressional subpoena, and the subpoena power derives implicitly from Article I of the Constitution, the case arose under the Constitution for purposes of section 1331. The Court agrees. This determination comports with Circuit precedent set forth in *AT&T I*, where the Court of Appeals recognized the existence of subject matter jurisdiction under section 1331 in a similar subpoena enforcement dispute due to the "fundamental constitutional rights ... involved." 551 F.2d at 388–89.

Notwithstanding its previous concession, the Department of Justice now insists that subject matter jurisdiction is lacking. Defendant argues that the fact that there is a specific statute that vests jurisdiction in the District Court for the District of Columbia for actions brought by the Senate to enforce its subpoenas means that in the absence of a parallel statute, this court does not have jurisdiction over an action brought on behalf of the House. But this does not follow either explicitly or implicitly from 28 U.S.C. §1365.

* * *

The first problem with the defendant's argument is that section 1365 specifically states that it does not have anything to do with cases involving a legislative effort to enforce a subpoena against an official of the executive branch withholding records on the grounds of a governmental privilege. 28 U.S.C. §1365(a). So the statute would not confer jurisdiction in an action similar to this one brought by the Senate either, and the Court would be required look to section 1331 only in any event.

Second, the chronology of events surrounding the enactment of section 1365 reveals that the jurisdictional gap it was meant to cure was not a lack of jurisdiction over actions like this one. In 1973, when the Senate Committee investigating the Watergate scandal brought an action to enforce a subpoena issued to President Nixon, the court held that it lacked jurisdiction because it was impossible to assign a monetary value to the plaintiff's claim, and therefore, it could not be shown that the case satisfied the amount-in-controversy requirement that was included in section 1331 at that time. *Senate Select Comm. on Presidential Campaign Activities v. Nixon*, 366 F. Supp. 51, 60–61 (D.D.C.1973). Congress promptly remedied the situation, passing legislation that vested jurisdiction for Senate Select Committee suits in the U.S. District Court for the District of Columbia. *See Senate Select Comm.*, 498 F.2d at 727, citing Pub. L. No. 93-190 (Dec. 18, 1973), 87 Stat. 736 (Dec. 18, 1973). Then, in 1976, as the D.C. Circuit observed in *AT&T I*, Congress turned its attention to section 1331, and it amended the provision to eliminate the amount-in-controversy requirement for "any ... action brought against the United States, any agency thereof, or any officer or employee thereof in his official capacity." *See* 551 F.2d at 389 n.7; Pub. L. No. 94-574, 90 Stat. 2721 (Oct. 21, 1976). Thus, at the time that section 1365 was enacted as part of the Ethics in Government Act in 1978, it was not necessary to remedy any lack of jurisdiction for actions brought against a federal officer acting in his official capacity. *See* S.Rep. No. 95-170 at 91–92 (1977) ("This exception in the statute is not intended to be a Congressional finding that the Federal courts do not now have the authority to hear a civil action to enforce a subp[o]ena against an officer or employee of the Federal government.").

* * * Thus, the cases cited by the defense are inapplicable, and section 1364 [*Ed. note: error in original; should read "section 1365"*], which addresses the enforcement of Senate subpoenas against private parties, is not germane here.

* * * [*Ed. Note: The court holds that the committee has standing to bring suit and the suit alleges a cause of action for which declaratory relief can be sought.*]

Finally, the Attorney General takes the position that even if the Court is authorized to hear the lawsuit, it should exercise the discretion embodied in the Declaratory Judgment Act and its equitable discretion to decline to do so in favor of a negotiated resolution. His chief argument is the same one that the Court has already rejected: that this case is an inappropriate attempt by legislators to bring a political dispute into a judicial forum, threatening the separation of powers. But he also insists that that the suit was brought before the possibilities for compromise had been exhausted. The amici echo that sentiment, taking the position that the process of negotiation and accommodation was still underway at the time the Committee made a precipitous decision to file suit. Both the defendant and the House amici take particular umbrage at what they characterize as a rush to the contempt vote, but the contempt citation is not a matter that is before the Court. For its part, the Committee takes the position that the Attorney General's position was fixed and that further negotiation would have been pointless.

Based on everything that has been presented to the Court to date, and the amount of time that has elapsed since this dispute arose, the Court does not believe that a discretionary dismissal is warranted. Moreover, it finds that the equitable considerations tend to favor the assumption of jurisdiction in this instance. While the defense presents its motion as a request that the court remain neutral while the other two bodies work out their difficulties, dismissing the case without hearing it would in effect place the court's finger on the scale, designating the executive as the victor based solely on his untested assertion that the privilege applies. * * *

In the end, it is the defendant's own brief that makes the best case for why the Court should not predicate its ruling on equitable grounds. The Attorney General argues: "[t]he prudential bases for refusing jurisdiction are especially strong here, where substantial accommodation was continuing and has continued, and where Congress's legitimate informational interests have been largely satisfied." He goes on: "the Committee had little need to resort to the judicial process in order to conduct meaningful oversight." Making a decision that turns upon on the "legitimacy" of the inquiry, the "need" for the documents, or how "meaningful" the oversight would be would require the Court to wade thigh high into the very waters the defendant spent the first forty pages of his brief telling it to avoid. Getting into the question of who bears responsibility for the impasse here—who negotiated properly or fairly, whether the appropriate amount of time was spent, whether any accommodation offered was "substantial" or merely superficial, and the relative merits of the grounds for the withholding and the stated need for the material—would put the Court squarely in the position of second guessing political decisions and take it well outside of its comfortable role of resolving legal questions that are amenable to judicial determination. And the Court would be wading into the muck without boots: in this case, it is the equitable issues, and not the legal questions posed by the complaint, that lack clear standards to apply and implicate political considerations that the court should be reluctant to assess.

Therefore, following the approach adopted by the court in *Miers*, this Court will not undertake to assign blame for the impasse—it is supposed to be accepting the complaint on its face at this point in the proceedings in any event. It is sufficient that it finds the conclusion that there is an impasse to be inescapable, and that under those circumstances, it does not appear that there would be any point to sending this matter back. * * *

CONCLUSION

Since for all of the reasons set forth above, neither legal nor prudential considerations support the dismissal of this action, the defendant's motion to dismiss the action will be denied. A separate order will issue.

Notes and Questions

1. A Subsequent Ruling on the Merits Rejects the Obama Executive Privilege Claim. Almost three years after the court's initial decision that it had jurisdiction over the dispute, it finally reached a judgment on the merits, rejecting the Obama administration's executive privilege claims:

> There is no need for the Court to invade the province of the legislature and undertake its own assessment of the legitimacy of the Committee's investigation, because the Department of Justice has conceded the point: it has repeatedly acknowledged the legitimacy of the investigation. [Citations omitted.]
>
> Furthermore, there is no need to balance the need against the impact that the revelation of any record could have on candor in future executive decision making, since any harm that might flow from the public revelation of the deliberations at issue here has already been self-inflicted: the emails and memoranda that are responsive to the subpoena were described in detail in a report by the Department of Justice Inspector General that has already been released to the public. *See* A Review of ATF's Operation Fast and Furious and Related Matters (Redacted), Office of the Inspector General Oversight and Review Division, U.S. Dep't of Justice (Sept. 2012) ("IG Report"), https://oig.justice.gov/reports/2012/s1209.pdf.
>
> Therefore, the Court finds, under the unique and limited circumstances of this case, that the qualified privilege must yield, given the executive's acknowledgment of the legitimacy of the investigation, and the fact that the Department itself has already publicly revealed the sum and substance of the very material it is now seeking to withhold. Since any harm that would flow from the disclosures sought here would be merely incremental, the records must be produced. The Court emphasizes that this ruling is not predicated upon a finding of wrongdoing.

Committee on Oversight & Government Reform v. Lynch, 156 F. Supp. 3d 101 (D.D.C. 2016). This holding on executive privilege paved the way for an eventual settlement of the dispute, albeit long after the parties had ceased to be invested in the dispute.

2. Congressional Institutional Hypocrisy?—Deliberative Process Executive Privilege vs. the Speech or Debate Clause. One commentator has pointed out an inconsistency between Congress's efforts to obtain executive branch deliberative process information and the protection Congress enjoys against such incursion by the executive branch into congressional decision-making under the Speech or Debate Clause of the Constitution:

Ironically, congressional deliberations are not available to the other branches or the public without the express consent of Congress as a result of the Speech or Debate Clause. As with the Executive, Congress desires to protect against the chilling of open and honest deliberations that would accompany exposing representatives' statements to the public. Information protected under the Speech or Debate Clause is that of legitimate "legislative acts," and a reviewing court must interpret that protection broadly to protect the free expression of ideas among legislators who would otherwise fear political backlash in raising concerns. This broad interpretation ensures the independent operation of Congress. Accordingly, Congress clearly appreciates the values undergirding a deliberative process privilege and other similar confidentiality interests, but it does not think such assertions have merit when made by the Executive in the context of congressional oversight requests.

Andrew McCanse Wright, *Constitutional Conflict and Congressional Oversight*, 98 Marquette L. Rev. 881, 957 (2014) (footnotes omitted). What do you think about Wright's comparison of executive privilege and Speech or Debate Clause protections? Does it make sense that under the Constitution the Congress enjoys near-absolute protection from inquiry into its deliberative process, while the executive branch receives only qualified executive privilege protection for its deliberative process, and that privilege can be overcome in appropriate cases, as in the Fast and Furious decision quoted in Note 1 above? Is it important that Congress is a collegial body that operates largely under public scrutiny, with open committee hearings, floor debate and votes, while the executive branch powers are vested in a single person who largely acts in private? For an argument that executive privilege should be understood as a presidential immunity, which is absolute in shielding a president from congressional oversight demands except in impeachment proceedings, see Jonathan David Shaub, *The Executive's Privilege*, 70 Duke L.J. 1 (2020).

3. Aftermath—Another Negotiated Settlement, Again After Significant Passage of Time. While the U.S. Attorneys' dismissal investigation that was the subject of the *Miers* decision was resolved in a little over two years, the litigation over the Fast & Furious investigation was not resolved until 2019, seven years after the House voted to hold Attorney General Holder in contempt. Perhaps even more noteworthy than the passage of time is the odd result that, in agreeing to settle the matter, both sides requested that the court vacate its previous orders in the case. Why would both sides seek to have those orders vacated? Consider this summary of the outcomes during the long-running litigation:

Overall, throughout the litigation, Congress has prevailed in its efforts to obtain rulings designed to pry more records from the department related to Operation Fast and Furious. However, both Congress and the executive branch lost on long-held—and cherished—legal arguments they had deployed in the tussle over information access. * * *

The Justice Department lost its arguments that the court didn't have authority to decide the case. It had moved to dismiss the lawsuit on the grounds that "the court did not have—or should decline to exercise—jurisdiction over a case the Justice Department characterized as a political dispute between the executive and legislative branches of government." Judge Jackson rejected that argument in a 2013 order (apparently not among the vacatur requests), citing *United States v. Nixon*, and determined that the court "had not only the authority, but the responsibility, to resolve the conflict."

The Oversight Committee lost its argument that [the executive branch's] deliberative process privileges don't apply to [subpoenas from] Congress. Congress has long maintained that the deliberative process privilege—designed to shield confidential internal executive branch deliberations from disclosure—was unavailable, as a matter of law, in response to a congressional subpoena. Congress had long argued that it was a common law, rather than constitutional, privilege, and therefore had no basis to defeat a congressional request for information. Judge Jackson disagreed. In the new ruling rejecting the settlement conditions, the court described the holding of its 2014 order: "It determined that there is a constitutional dimension to the deliberative process aspect of the executive privilege, and that the privilege could be properly invoked in response to a legislative demand." * * * [T]his was a significant doctrinal loss for Congress.

The Justice Department lost its argument that it could assert privilege over document categories. The department argued that materials created about how to respond to the congressional investigation, after some faulty information had been provided to Sen. Charles Grassley (R-Iowa) in early 2011, were beyond congressional need and that such "meta-investigations" invaded separation of powers. In the 2014 order, the Justice Department lost that battle. Instead, the court endorsed a congressional need for those documents but required privilege determinations on a document-by-document basis. The court also required the department to create a document-level privilege log, which it had been long resisting.

The Oversight Committee lost its argument that deliberative process privilege did not cover meta-investigations. Thereafter, the committee argued, as a categorical matter, that deliberative process privileges do not apply to intra-agency communications about how to respond to Congress or the media. The court again rejected this second version of a categorical argument, but held that the privilege, while applicable, "is a qualified one that can be overcome by a sufficient showing of need for the material."

The Justice Department lost its argument that disclosure to the inspector general did not waive privilege. Rather than engage in that balancing of congressional need against executive confidentiality, the court held in its 2016 order that the Justice Department had "already disclosed" the documents by providing them to the department's inspector general. From the Justice Department perspective, that was a disclosure within the executive branch that requires a different constitutional analysis than a disclosure to Congress and should not amount to a waiver of privilege. That ruling creates an incentive for executive branch agencies to withhold materials they deem privileged from the relevant inspectors general if doing so would establish a waiver of privilege vis-à-vis Congress.

Andrew M. Wright, *(Not So) Fast and Furious Settlement in Congressional Subpoena Case*, JUST SECURITY (Oct. 26, 2018). As this summary demonstrates, both sides had reasons to join together in seeking to have the prior orders vacated, but the court refused to do so. The matter was finally resolved when the parties entered into an agreement that neither side would invoke the rulings against the other in future cases, and with that understanding, the court approved the final settlement in January 2019. *See* Testimony of Morton M. Rosenberg Before the Special Committee on the Climate Crises on the Investigatory Authority of House Committees (Oct. 29, 2019) (summarizing the outcome of the Fast and Furious investigation and litigation).

4. Bipartisan Judicial Consensus—But Only Temporarily? In the *Miers* and *Holder* cases, two federal judges appointed by two Presidents of different political parties reached largely the same conclusions respecting the role of the federal courts in disputes over congressional efforts to obtain executive branch information from the administrations of two Presidents from different political parties (and in each case, in holding that judicial involvement was appropriate, the court had sided with the "opposition party" that had not appointed that judge to the bench). After those cases were resolved, it appeared that perhaps the law in this area was beginning to stabilize, particularly as to whether federal courts should always defer to the "accommodation" process of negotiation between the political branches. This changed with the Trump administration, when a dispute over access to testimony and documents from the White House Counsel introduced new uncertainty and unpredictability into the legal equation. That case is the subject of the next section of this Chapter.

The Trump Administration Russia Election Interference Investigation and the McGahn Subpoena Litigation

On May 7, 2017, shortly after the inauguration of President Donald J. Trump, Deputy Attorney General Rod J. Rosenstein appointed former FBI Director Robert S. Mueller III to serve as a Department of Justice Special Counsel to investigate allegations of Russian interference in the 2016 presidential election. Rosenstein made the appointment as Acting Attorney General, after then-Attorney General Jeff Sessions recused himself from the matter because of prior contacts with the Russian ambassador to the United States while working on the Trump campaign. Special Counsel Mueller completed his investigation in March 2019 and filed his report with the Department of Justice. The report reviewed evidence of Russian interference in the 2016 election and related matters, including whether President Trump had obstructed justice in the Russia investigation. The report stated that it "does not exonerate" President Trump, but explained that the Office of Special Counsel "accepted" the longstanding Department of Justice position that a President cannot be indicted while in office. *See* Special Counsel Robert S. Mueller, III, Report on the Investigation Into Russian Interference in the 2016 Presidential Election (March 2019).

On March 4, 2019, the Judiciary Committee of the House of Representatives, under control of the Democrats after the mid-term elections of 2018, opened an investigation into allegations of misconduct by President Trump, including possible obstruction of justice. The Judiciary Committee focused on whether the possible obstruction of justice described in the Special Counsel's report warranted the Committee initiating impeachment proceedings against President Trump. One of the key witnesses cited in the obstruction of justice sections in the Special Counsel's report was White House Counsel Donald F. McGahn. The Judiciary Committee initially requested that McGahn voluntarily provide documents to the Committee. Then, after not receiving documents in response to that request, the Committee subpoenaed McGahn in April 2019, seeking testimony and documents concerning possible obstruction of justice by President Trump. President Trump instructed McGahn not to appear before the Committee, and the White House Counsel, relying on an opinion from the Department of Justice Office of Legal Counsel, *see Testimonial Immunity Before Cong. of the Former Counsel to the President*, 43 Op. O.L.C., Slip. Op. at 17 (May 20, 2019), advised the Committee that as a former senior advisor to the President, McGahn was subject to "testimonial immunity" and could not be compelled to provide information about his official duties to the Committee. After extensive negotiations, in which the Committee invoked the prior *Miers* decision that a former White House Counsel must appear for testimony, the Committee and the Trump White House reached agreement as to production of a privilege log for subpoenaed documents, but were unable to reach agreement as to McGahn's testimony before the Committee. On August 7, 2019, the Committee filed a civil lawsuit seeking to have the court compel McGahn to testify.

A. Initial Federal District Court Decision in the McGahn Case

Judge (now Justice) Ketanji Brown Jackson, the federal district judge who initially heard the *McGahn* case, agreed with the holdings of the two federal district judges who had decided the *Miers* and *Holder* cases on the important question of whether the federal courts have subject matter jurisdiction over disputes between the executive and legislative branches concerning congressional oversight of the executive branch:

> In 2008, in the context of a dispute over whether the Committee on the Judiciary of the House of Representatives ("the Judiciary Committee") had the power to compel former White House Counsel Harriet Miers and then-White House Chief of Staff Joshua Bolten to testify and produce documents in connection with a congressional investigation, the Department of Justice ("DOJ") made three legal contentions of "extraordinary constitutional significance." *Comm. on Judiciary, U.S. House of Representatives v. Miers*, 558 F. Supp. 2d 53, 55 (D.D.C. 2008) (Bates, J.). First, DOJ argued that a duly authorized commit-

tee of Congress acting on behalf of the House of Representatives cannot invoke judicial process to compel the appearance of senior-level aides of the President for the purpose of receiving sworn testimony. *See id.* at 66–67, 78. Second, DOJ maintained that a President can demand that his aides (both current and former) ignore a subpoena that Congress issues, on the basis of alleged absolute testimonial immunity. *See id.* at 100. And, third, DOJ asserted that the federal courts cannot exercise subject-matter jurisdiction over any such subpoena-related stalemate between the Legislature and the Executive branch, on separation of powers grounds. *See id.* at 72–73, 93–94. The district court that considered these propositions rejected each one in a lengthy opinion that thoroughly explained why the federal courts have subject-matter jurisdiction over such disputes, *see id.* at 64–65; why the Judiciary Committee had standing to sue and a cause of action to proceed in federal court, *see id.* at 65–94; and why the claim that a President's senior-level aides have absolute testimonial immunity is meritless, *see id.* at 99–107. Most importantly, the *Miers* opinion also persuasively demonstrated that DOJ's conception of the limited power of both Congress and the federal courts relative to the expansive authority of the President—which, purportedly, includes the power to shield himself and his aides from being questioned about any aspect of their present or former White House work—is not grounded in the Constitution or in any other federal law. *See id.* at 99, 106–07; *cf. Comm. on Oversight & Gov't Reform v. Holder*, 979 F. Supp. 2d 1, 10–11 (D.D.C. 2013).

The more things change, the more they stay the same. On May 20, 2019, President Donald J. Trump directed former White House Counsel Donald F. McGahn II to decline to appear before the Judiciary Committee in response to a subpoena that the Committee had issued to McGahn in connection with its investigation of Russia's interference into the 2016 presidential election and the Special Counsel's findings of fact concerning potential obstruction of justice by the President. Months of negotiations ensued, which produced no testimony from McGahn, and on August 7, 2019, the Judiciary Committee filed the instant lawsuit. Invoking Article I of the U.S. Constitution, the Judiciary Committee implores this Court to "[d]eclare that McGahn's refusal to appear before the Committee in response to the subpoena issued to him was without legal justification" (Compl., ECF No. 1, at 53), and it also seeks an "injunction ordering McGahn to appear and testify forthwith before the Committee."

* * * In short, this Court agrees with Judge Bates's conclusion that federal courts have subject-matter jurisdiction to resolve legal disputes that arise between the Legislature and the Executive branch concerning the scope of each branch's subpoena-related rights and duties, under section 1331 of Title 28 of the United States Code and the Constitution. *See Miers*, 558 F. Supp. 2d at 64–65. Jurisdiction exists because the Judiciary Committee's claim presents a legal question, and it is "emphatically" the role of the Judiciary to say what the law is. *Marbury v. Madison*, 5 U.S. (1 Cranch) 137, 177 (1803). It also plainly

advances constitutional separation-of-powers principles, rather than subverts them, when a federal court decides the question of whether a legislative subpoena that a duly authorized committee of the House of Representatives has issued to a senior-level aide of the President is valid and enforceable, or, alternatively, is subject to the President's invocation of absolute testimonial immunity. Furthermore, *Miers* was correct to conclude that, given the indisputable Article I power of the House of Representatives to conduct investigations of potential abuses of power and subpoena witnesses to testify at hearings concerning such investigations, the Judiciary Committee has both standing and a cause of action to file an enforcement lawsuit in federal court if the Executive branch blocks a current or former presidential aides' performance of his duty to respond to a legislative subpoena. *See id.* at 65–75, 78–94.

DOJ's arguments to the contrary are rooted in "the Executive's interest in 'autonomy[,]'" and, therefore, "rest[] upon a discredited notion of executive power and privilege." *Id.* at 103. Indeed, when DOJ insists that Presidents can lawfully prevent their senior-level aides from responding to compelled congressional process and that neither the federal courts nor Congress has the power to do anything about it, DOJ promotes a conception of separation-of-powers principles that gets these constitutional commands exactly backwards. In reality, it is a core tenet of this Nation's founding that the powers of a monarch must be split between the branches of the government to prevent tyranny. *See* The Federalist No. 51 (James Madison); *see also Buckley v. Valeo*, 424 U.S. 1, 120 (1976). Thus, when presented with a case or controversy, it is the Judiciary's duty under the Constitution to interpret the law and to declare government overreaches unlawful. Similarly, the House of Representatives has the constitutionally vested responsibility to conduct investigations of suspected abuses of power within the government, and to act to curb those improprieties, if required. Accordingly, DOJ's conceptual claim to unreviewable absolute testimonial immunity on separation-of-powers grounds—essentially, that the Constitution's scheme countenances unassailable Executive branch authority—is baseless, and as such, cannot be sustained.

* * * Instead, this Court concurs with the thrust of *Miers's* conclusion that, whatever the scope of the President's executive privilege with respect to the information that Congress seeks to compel, and whatever the merits of DOJ's assertion that senior-level aides are the President's "alter egos" for the purpose of invoking an immunity, DOJ has failed to bridge the yawning gap between a presidential aide's right to withhold privileged information in the context of his or her compelled congressional testimony (which no one disputes), and the President's purported power to direct such aides to refuse to show up and be questioned *at all* (which appears only in a string of OLC opinions that do not themselves constitute legal precedents and are manifestly inconsistent with the constitutional jurisprudence of the Supreme Court and the D.C. Circuit in many respects).

Thus—to be crystal clear—what is at issue in this case is solely whether senior-level presidential aides, such as McGahn, are legally required to respond to a subpoena that a committee of Congress has issued, by appearing before the committee for testimony despite any presidential directive prohibiting such a response. The Court distinguishes this issue from the very different question of whether the specific information that high-level presidential aides may be asked to provide in the context of such questioning can be withheld from the committee on the basis of a valid privilege. In other words, "the Court only resolves, and again rejects, the claim by the Executive to absolute immunity from compelled congressional process for senior presidential aides." *Miers*, 558 F. Supp. 2d at 56; *see also id.* (noting that "[t]he specific claims of executive privilege that [a subpoenaed presidential aide] may assert are not addressed—and the Court expresses no view on such claims"). And in reaching this conclusion, "[t]he Court holds only that [McGahn] (and other senior presidential advisors) do not have absolute immunity from compelled congressional process in the context of this particular subpoena dispute." *Id.* at 105–06. Accordingly, just as with Harriet Miers before him, Donald McGahn "must appear before the Committee to provide testimony, and invoke executive privilege where appropriate." *Id.* at 106.

Committee on the Judiciary v. McGahn, 415 F. Supp. 3d 148, 152–55 (D.D.C. 2019) (footnotes omitted).

The *McGahn* district court opinion included a particularly strong rejection of the argument, asserted by the Trump administration Justice Department, that a senior White House advisor enjoys "absolute immunity" from being compelled to testify before Congress:

C. The President Does Not Have the Power To Prevent His Aides
  From Responding To Legislative Subpoenas On The Basis Of Absolute
  Testimonial Immunity

The merits legal issues that the instant dispute between the House Judiciary Committee and the Executive branch raises are straightforward. The Committee claims that it has issued a lawful subpoena to former White House Counsel Donald F. McGahn II; that McGahn has refused to appear before the Committee to provide testimony as required; and that "[t]here is no lawful basis for McGahn's refusal to appear before the Judiciary Committee." For its part, DOJ asserts that, consistent with its understanding of the longstanding view of the Department's Office of Legal Counsel, there *is* a lawful basis for McGahn's defiance of the Committee's valid subpoena: the President has ordered him not to. DOJ asserts that current and former senior-level presidential aides have "absolute testimonial immunity" from compelled congressional process, as a matter of law; therefore, if the President invokes "executive privilege" over a current or former aides' testimony—as he has done with respect to McGahn—that aide need not accede to the lawful demands of Congress. Thus, it is important to note at the outset, what is *not* at issue in the instant case. No one contests the lawfulness of the Judiciary's subpoena, and no one maintains that, if McGahn has the legal duty to testify before the Committee, that a senior-level aide in his position has no right to invoke executive privilege to withhold certain information in the course of his testimony, as appropriate.

For the reasons that follow, this Court finds that the President does not have (and, thus, cannot lawfully assert) the power to prevent his current and former senior-level aides from responding to congressional subpoenas. As Judge Bates explained in *Miers*, as a matter of law, such aides do not have absolute testimonial immunity. Therefore, as it relates to them, a valid legislative subpoena issued by a duly authorized committee of Congress gives rise to a legally enforceable duty to perform. The President cannot override this duty, notwithstanding OLC's ostensible recognition of such power. Accordingly, if a duly authorized committee of Congress issues a valid legislative subpoena to a current or former senior-level presidential aide, the law requires the aide to appear as directed, and assert executive privilege as appropriate. *See Miers*, 558 F. Supp. 2d at 106.

[*Ed. Note: The court then explains that* Miers, *"the only recorded case in our Nation's history that directly addresses the legal argument that a senior-level presidential aide is immune to a legislative subpoena seeking testimony when the President directs him to ignore that congressional mandate," rejected the absolute immunity argument as "entirely unsupported by case law." The court adopts the* Miers *absolute immunity analysis in full. The court also notes that the Holder "Fast and Furious" case involved only a dispute over documents, not a subpoena for testimony, and therefore did not present the same issue of absolute immunity from providing testimony as the subpoenas for testimony in* Miers *and Mc-Gahn.*]

2. OLC's Long-Held View That Senior-Level Presidential Aides Have
   Absolute Testimonial Immunity Is Neither Precedential Nor Persuasive

That all said, it is certainly true that OLC has long been of the view that senior-level presidential aides have absolute testimonial immunity; indeed, as *Miers* indicates, the first recorded statement of the agency that specifically commits this view to writing was authored in 1971. See Mem. from William H. Rehnquist, Assistant Attorney General, Office of Legal Counsel, to John D. Ehrlichman, Assistant to the President for Domestic Affairs, *Power of Congressional Committee to Compel Appearance or Testimony of "White House Staff"* (Feb. 5, 1971) ("1971 Memorandum"). In that year, then-Assistant Attorney General William Rehnquist produced a memorandum on the point that maintained (without direct citation) that "[t]he President and his immediate advisers—that is, those who customarily meet with the President on a regular or frequent basis—should be deemed absolutely immune from testimonial compulsion by a congressional committee." *Id.* at 7. This OLC memorandum further indicated that such persons "not only may not be examined with respect to their official duties, but they may not even be compelled to appear before a congressional committee." *Id.* But, of course, as definitive as this statement of law sounds, OLC serves as legal counsel to the Executive branch, and "the Executive cannot be the judge of its own privilege[.]" *Miers*, 558 F. Supp. 2d at 106. Consequently, its statement of the law is "entitled to only as much weight as the force of [its] reasoning will support." *Id.* at 104.

In this Court's view, the persuasiveness of OLC opinion that senior-level presidential aides enjoy immunity from compelled congressional process turns on two familiar factors: the authority that is provided in support of this proposition, and the reasons that are provided for why the author reached this conclusion. With respect to the first consideration, it cannot be overstated that the 1971 Memorandum does not cite to a single case that stands for the asserted proposition, and the ten-plus subsequent statements by OLC that DOJ points to in support of this immunity simply reference back to the 1971 Memorandum without providing any court authority. It goes without saying that longevity alone does not transform an unsupported notion into law.

As for the logic behind the view, the original memorandum appears to reason by by analogy. It begins by recognizing the breadth of Congress' power of inquiry, which admittedly "carries with it the power to compel the testimony of a witness." 1971 Mem. at 1. And then as if providing the solution to a problem that it had not yet identified, the memo states that "if White House staff personnel are to be exempt from appearing or testifying before a congressional committee, it is because they have some special immunity or privilege not accorded others." *Id.* at 1. The remainder of the 8-page document devotes itself to developing potential reasons for such a privilege. It suggests, for example, "a certain analogy to judicial proceedings[,]" in which a "distinction" is made "between a claim of absolute immunity from even being sworn in as a witness, and a right to claim privilege in answering certain questions in the course of one's testimony as a witness." *Id.* at 4.

Ultimately, the 1971 Memorandum pushes for the former, on the basis of a handful of historical examples in which former assistants to various Presidents blatantly refused to appear before Congress in response to a legislative subpoena. *See id.* at 5–6. At least one of these folks was apparently polite enough to write a letter to the committee that "grounded his refusal on the confidential nature of his relationship with the President." *Id.* at 5. But others merely sent congressional subpoenas back with the simple statement that "[i]n each instance the President directed me, in view of my duties as his Assistant, not to appear before your subcommittee." *Id.* at 5; *see also id.* at 6.

Tellingly, the 1971 Memorandum does not purport to suggest that the law already countenanced such behavior. Rather, the posture of the Memorandum appears to be a policy piece that provides its client with arguments for why it should be thus. Moreover, as *Miers* notes, Rehnquist admitted that "his conclusions [were] 'tentative and sketchy,'" *Miers*, 558 F. Supp. 2d at 104 (quoting 1971 Mem. at 7), and in his later role as a Supreme Court Justice, he "apparently recanted those views[,]" *id.* In one especially candid moment in the text of the Memorandum, Rehnquist admits that the historical precedents for refusing a congressional subpoena "are obviously quite inconclusive" but that "[i]n a strictly tactical sense, the Executive Branch has a headstart in any controversy with the Legislative Branch, since the Legislative Branch wants something the Executive Branch has, and therefore the initiative lies with the former." 1971 Mem. at 7. He continued: "[a]ll the Executive has to do is maintain the *status quo* and he prevails." *Id.* It is not surprising that, per this initial internal effort to establish the ways in which certain White House staff could prevail in any conflict with Congress over their legally enforceable duty to appear for testimony when subpoenaed, OLC subsequently developed an entire series of statements, each of which references the 1971 Memorandum, but none of which specifically acknowledges that the initial basis for this conclusion was seemingly formed out of nothing.

This inauspicious start does not bode well for this Court's determination of whether OLC's persistent opinion that senior-level aides to the President are absolutely immune from having to respond to compelled congressional process should be credited. Additionally, subsequent developments in caselaw have cast doubt on the 1971 Memorandum's suggestion that the matter of the President's own absolute immunity was settled because "[e]veryone associated with the Executive Branch from [the prosecution of Aaron Burr] until now, so far as I know, has taken the position that the President himself is absolutely immune from subpoena by anyone[.]" 1971 Mem. at 3; *see also Clinton v. Jones*, 520 U.S. 681 (1997); *United States v. Nixon*, 418 U.S. 683 (1974). Moreover, in this first formal floating of the principle of absolute testimonial immunity for certain aides of the President, the author was also crystal clear that the "absolute immun[ity] from testimonial compulsion by a congressional committee" that he was proposing was primarily due to the fact that such "immediate advisors" are "presumptively available to the President 24 hours a day, and the necessity of either accommodating a congressional committee or persuading a court to arrange a more convenient time, could impair that availability." 1971 Mem. at 7. Of course, that analysis does not support the extension of absolute immunity to former senior-level aides that DOJ has pressed in recent times.

In fairness, over time, the initial take on absolute testimonial immunity evolved. It appears that OLC's subsequent statements in support of this proposition were beefed up with various other reasons for why one could plausibly assert that certain aides of the President should be absolutely immune from having to testify before Congress, which reasons largely invoke constitutional separation of powers concerns, including potential harassment of the aides (and thus, the President), the risk of disclosure of information covered by executive privilege, and the appearance that the Executive branch is subordinate to the Legislature. *See, e.g., Testimonial Immunity Before Congress of the Assistant to the President and Senior Counselor to the President*, 43 Op. O.L.C. ___, at *2 ("Absent immunity, congressional committees could wield their compulsory power to attempt to supervise the President's actions, or to harass those advisers in an effort to influence their conduct, retaliate for actions the committee disliked, or embarrass and weaken the President for partisan gain." (quotation marks and citation omitted)); *McGahn OLC Mem.*, 43 Op. O.L.C. ___, at *5 ("The President is a separate branch of government. He may not compel congressmen to appear before him. As a matter of separation of powers, Congress may not compel him to appear before it." (quotation marks and citation omitted)); *Immunity of the Assistant to the President*, 38 Op. OLC at *4 ("The pressure of compelled live testimony about White House activities in a public congressional hearing would … create an inherent and substantial risk of inadvertent or coerced disclosure of confidential information relating to presidential decisionmaking—thereby ultimately threatening the President's ability to receive candid and carefully considered advice from his immediate advisers."). Many of these reasons appear in the brief that DOJ has submitted to support absolute immunity in the context of this case. But, unfortunately for DOJ, its mere recantation of these aspirational assertions does not make the proposition any more persuasive, and in fact, given the history of how OLC's opinion has developed, it appears that an endorsement of the principles that OLC espouses would amount to adopting the absolute testimonial immunity for senior-level presidential aides by *ipse dixit*. Furthermore, because there are few, if any, well-formulated justifications for categorically excusing current and former senior-level presidential aides from responding to compelled congressional process, it would be difficult to do so consistent with existing case law, traditional norms of practice under our constitutional system of government, and common sense.

3. There Is No Principled Basis For Concluding That Senior-Level Presidential Aides Should Have Absolute Testimonial Immunity

DOJ maintains that its contention that senior-level presidential aides should enjoy absolute testimonial immunity plainly follows from two related premises: (1) that the President himself has absolute testimonial immunity from compelled congressional process, and (2) that, as a derivative matter, so too must his "immediate advisors … with whom the President customarily meets on a regular or frequent basis." In *Miers*, Judge Bates ably explains that both of these assumptions stand on shaky footing after *United States v. Nixon, Clinton v. Jones*, and *Harlow v. Fitzgerald*. *See Miers*, 558 F. Supp. 2d at 100–05. This Court agrees with *Miers*'s analysis, and it also observes that none of the differences that DOJ has highlighted between the instant case, on the one hand, and *Clin-*

ton and *Nixon*, on the other, actually matters. The following brief observations further demonstrate that the proposition that senior-level presidential aides are entitled to absolute testimonial immunity has no principled justification, which further undermines DOJ's assertion that such immunity must exist.

First of all, the concept of absolute immunity from compelled congressional process cannot be gleaned from cases that endorse absolute testimonial immunity for legislators, or those that accept absolute immunity *from civil damages* for a variety of public officials. For example, DOJ's reliance on *Gravel v. United States*, 408 U.S. 606 (1972), is obviously misplaced, because legislative aides derive their absolute immunity from the Constitution's provision of absolute testimonial immunity to congresspersons through the Speech and Debate Clause. *See id.* at 615–17. As *Miers* explained, the Supreme Court in *Harlow* specifically addressed the argument that such immunity applies to senior-level executive aides, then concluded that, in contrast to legislative aides, senior-level executive aides are only entitled to *qualified* immunity. *Harlow*, 457 U.S. at 809.

Nor can DOJ reasonably rely on the well-established body of case law that applies to the very different circumstance of immunity from civil damages. There are *reasons* why courts have determined that judges, and legislators, and presidents cannot be held liable for civil damages for discretionary decisions that they make in the course of their duties. *See, e.g., Forrester v. White*, 484 U.S. 219, 225 (1988) (finding that absolute immunity from civil damages for judicial acts protects "the finality of judgments[,] discourage[s] inappropriate collateral attacks, [and] protect[s] judicial independence by insulating judges from vexatious actions prosecuted by disgruntled litigants" (citation omitted)); *Nixon v. Fitzgerald*, 457 U.S. 731, 751 (1982) (holding that the President is absolutely immune from civil damages due to "the singular importance of the President's duties," and that "diversion of his energies by concern with private lawsuits would raise unique risks to the effective functioning of government"); *Tenney v. Brandhove*, 341 U.S. 367, 375 (1951) (explaining that legislators "must be free to speak and act without fear of criminal and civil liability" as the reason for the absolute immunity endowed by the Speech and Debate Clause and similar provisions in "[f]orty-one of forty-eight State[]" constitutions); *see also Imbler v. Pachtman*, 424 U.S. 409, 424 (1976) (explaining the purpose of absolute immunity from civil damages for prosecutorial acts is to allow a prosecutor "to exercise his best judgment both in deciding which suits to bring and in conducting them in court"). And at least one of these justifications does not seem at all applicable to the reasons why one might have immunity from compelled congressional process. One cannot simply assume that the same rationale that compels the conclusion that those who hold certain civil functions are absolutely immune *from civil damages* necessitates absolute immunity *from compelled congressional process*, even for those same individuals.

DOJ's conception of absolute testimonial immunity for senior-level aides also turns out to be overbroad in application, which results in its imposing unwarranted societal costs. To understand why this is so, it is helpful to reflect on a hypothetical that the Court posed during the motions hearing. The Court posed to DOJ counsel a scenario in which an authorized House committee is interested in determining whether to appropriate special funding to improve the décor and the infrastructure-related working environment inside the White House. The committee wishes to evaluate the need for such additional funding, and it wants to talk to everyone who works there, and to compel this witness testimony, if needed. The Court asked DOJ counsel whether, if subpoenas issue, could the White House Counsel invoke absolute testimonial immunity to excuse the participation of senior-level presidential aides?

After engaging briefly with the Court in a humorous exchange about the Executive branch's interest in addressing certain issues that currently exist with the White House, DOJ counsel responded that "the President would probably allow his most sensitive aides to go testify" but "if the person has testimonial immunity and the President has asserted it ... then, yes, [the committee] wouldn't be able to compel the person." Upon reflection, looking at it logically, one has to wonder why that is the case? Those aides' status as senior-level assistants to the President seems irrelevant—*i.e.*, when it comes to being asked about the decor in the White House, either *no* White House worker should have to be bothered with Congress's questions, or *everyone* who is called should have to appear. Therefore, the distinction between aides with heightened knowledge, access to the President, and special responsibilities (*i.e.*, senior-level presidential aides) makes no difference where the topic of Congress's investigation does not even conceivably implicate such distinction. Why, then, should senior-level presidential aides always get to play a special trump card with respect to such congressional requests? Judge Bates reflected on a similar concern in *Miers*, and DOJ has yet to explain why "Congress should be left with no recourse to obtain information that is plainly not subject to any colorable claim of executive privilege." *Miers*, 558 F. Supp. 2d at 106.

On the other hand, if Congress seeks to explore with certain senior-level White House aides topics of a potentially sensitive nature, it is widely accepted that the President can exert executive privilege with respect to his aides' answers, as appropriate, to protect any privileged information. *Miers*, 225 F. Supp. 2d at 106. Given this, the question becomes why, then, would such senior-level aides *need* absolute immunity? In other words, even without a total exemption from compelled congressional process, senior-level White House aides can withhold the kinds of confidential and privileged information that distinguishes them from everybody else; they can do so by asserting an appropriate privilege if needed, when legislators ask questions that probe too deeply. Thus, it appears that absolute testimonial immunity serves only the indefensible purpose of blocking testimony about *non*-protected subjects that are relevant to a congressional investigation and that such an aide would otherwise have a legal duty to disclose.

Notably, this would appear to be the case even with respect to aides who, like White House Counsels, are "at the hub of all presidential activity." To be sure, White House Counsels and other similar aides have unfettered access to the President on a regular basis, and their roles with the Executive branch involve daily contact with copious amounts of information that is confidential in nature, including information that has been classified for our national security. But DOJ has not persuasively explained why such access warrants absolute testimonial immunity, where such an individual would be counseled in any sworn communications with Congress, and would have ample opportunity to invoke executive privilege or any other lawful basis for withholding information, as needed to protect the legitimate interests of the Executive branch. And, of course, if such an aide cannot lawfully invoke any privilege to protect information in response to the committee's questions, then there is no rational basis for maintaining that he should be immune from responding to Congress's valid subpoena in the first place.

It is also the case that the other rationale that such senior-level presidential aides might hope to rely on—"I'm too busy"—is unavailable in the wake of the Supreme Court's conclusion that even the President himself must find the time. *See Miers*, 558 F. Supp. 2d at 104. In any event, no such excuse could possibly apply to *former* senior-level aides, who have long departed from the White House, because such individuals no longer have proximity to power. What, then, justifies *their* right to be excused from the duty to respond to a call from Congress, especially when other private citizens have no choice? At a minimum, this perplexing question raises the following conceptual conundrum: if the purpose of providing certain senior-level presidential aides with absolute testimonial immunity is that the practicalities of their special roles demand it, then what justifies allowing that entitlement to follow them when they return to private life? As a matter of pure logic, it would seem that if one's access to the Oval Office is the reason that a categorical exemption from compelled congressional process is warranted, then that trump card should, at most, be a raincheck, and not the lifetime pass that DOJ proposes.

DOJ's apparent response to the concern that absolute testimonial immunity for current and former senior-level aides serves no purpose is its suggestion in its briefs that such broad immunity serves three more systematic goals. First, it asserts that absolute testimonial immunity facilitates frank communications in the White House, and without it, the potential "public spectacle" of having to appear before a congressional committee "would surely exert influence over [senior-level aides'] conduct in office, and could adversely affect the quality and candor of the counsel" that they offer to the President. DOJ provides no evidence to support this representation. And it appears to contradict the lived experience of the many government officials who have testified before Congress, seemingly without consequence, over the years. *See Miers*, 558 F. Supp. 3d at 102 (observing that "the historical record produced by the Committee reveals that senior advisors to the President have often testified before Congress subject to various subpoenas dating back to 1973").

DOJ's assertions about the chilling effect of compelled congressional process also imply that congressional questioning is needlessly intrusive and unwarranted, and that characterization drastically discounts the reasons why executive branch officials, including members of the President's staff, are called to testify. As the Supreme Court has suggested on numerous occasions, Congress brings in witnesses not as punishment, but to provide the Legislature with the information that it needs to perform its critical legislative and oversight functions. *Watkins*, 354 U.S. at 187; *McGrain*, 273 U.S. at 175. Thus, the idea that having to testify truthfully about the inner workings of government is a threat that would actually be sufficient to prevent key public servants from competently performing as assistants to the President seems anomalous. Moreover, if the institutions of our government are all, in fact, pushing in the same direction as they should be—*i.e.*, toward developing and implementing policies that are in the best interests of the People of the United States—then the possibility that one of the public servants who work within the government might be called upon to cooperate with Congress, and thereby perform his public duty of giving authorized legislators the means of performing their own constitutional functions, provides no reasonable grounds for fear. And if it does, as DOJ here suggests, then that is all the more reason why such testimony is critical. In short, DOJ's implicit suggestion that compelled congressional process is a "zero-sum" game in which the President's interest in confidentiality invariably outweighs the Legislature's interest in gathering truthful information, such that current and former senior-level presidential aides should be always and forever immune from answering probing questions, is manifestly inconsistent with a governmental scheme that can only function properly if its institutions work together. *See* The Federalist No. 51 (James Madison).

DOJ's second systematic concern is similarly discordant. DOJ insists that, without absolute testimonial immunity for senior-level presidential aides, the Executive branch would grind to a halt from the weight of the subpoenas that would be thrust upon it. This representation is plainly speculative. Furthermore, such speculation seems unreasonable, given two known facts. First of all, as DOJ itself admits, Congress has long demanded information from high-level members of the Executive branch, apparently without incident. *See Mazars*, 940 F.3d at 721 (noting that Presidents have "been the subjects of Congress's legislative investigations" as far back as 1832, and that "fewer of these have required judicial intervention"). As the Supreme Court commented in *Clinton v. Jones*, the President's "predictive judgment finds little support in either history or the relatively narrow compass of the issues raised in this particular case." *Clinton*, 520 U.S. at 702 (citations omitted)); *see also id.* ("As we have already noted, in the more than 200-year history of the Republic, only three sitting Presidents have been subjected to suits for their private actions. If the past is any indicator, it seems unlikely that a deluge of such litigation will ever engulf the Presidency.").

In addition, as relevant here, we have a test case by which we can prove, or disprove, DOJ's theory. The second significant fact is that it has been more than a decade since Judge Bates released the *Miers* decision, which plainly announced that senior-level presidential aides lack absolute immunity from compelled congressional process. Ironically, *Miers* itself observed that "[i]t is noteworthy that in an environment where there is no judicial support whatso-ever for the Executive's claim of absolute immunity, the historical record also does not reflect the wholesale compulsion by Congress of testimony from se-nior presidential advisors that the Executive fears." *Miers*, 558 F. Supp. 2d at 102. And the absence of such history seems even more noteworthy at present. Surely if Congress was inclined to utilize its subpoena power to harass the Executive branch unjustifiably, then *Miers*'s own holding would have given it sufficient impetus to do so. Yet, even DOJ must acknowledge that no such parade of horribles has happened.

DOJ's third argument for the necessity of absolute testimonial immunity for systematic reasons places it back in the familiar refuge of its constitutional separation-of-powers contentions. In this regard, DOJ maintains, that "the public spectacle of haling [current and] former advisors to a sitting President before a committee of Congress ... promote[s] the perception of Executive subservience to the Legislature," which, in its view of what the Constitution permits, is improper, because "[a] committee of Congress could not, consis-tent with the separation of powers, hale the President before it to compel him to testify under oath, any more than the President may compel congressmen to appear before him." Here, once again, DOJ calls on separation-of-powers principles to do work that the Framers never intended. Indeed, *the entire point of segregating the powers of a monarch into the three different branches of government was to give each branch certain authority that the others did not possess. Thus, while the branches might well be conceived of as co-equals (in the sense that one cannot unlawfully subvert the prerogatives of another), that does not mean that all three branches must be deemed to have the *same* pow-ers. To the contrary, the President cannot hale members of Congress into the White House for questioning *precisely because* the power of inquiry resides with the Legislature, and also because the Constitution itself expressly pre-vents the Executive branch from becoming inquisitors by inflicting its own subpoena power on members of Congress for political reasons.[23]

---

23. [Court's Note 33] The Speech and Debate Clause mandates that members of the House and Senate and their aides "may not be made to answer—either in terms of questions or in terms of de-fending himself from prosecution—for the events that occurred" as part of the legislative process. *See Gravel*, 408 U.S. at 614–16. The Constitution, therefore, makes legislators and their aides immune to

Therefore, DOJ's argument that the House of Representatives, which unquestionably possesses the constitutionally authorized power of inquiry and also the power of impeachment, should *not* be able to issue subpoenas to executive branch officials because the President cannot do the same to them, simultaneously appreciates traditional separation-of-powers principles *and* subverts them, and as such, truly makes no sense. *See Miers*, 558 F. Supp. 2d at 103 (explaining that the Executive branch's separation-of-powers interest in "[p]residential autonomy, such as it is, cannot mean that the Executive's actions are totally insulated from scrutiny by Congress. That would eviscerate Congress's historical oversight function").

4. Concluding That Presidential Aides Enjoy Absolute Testimonial Immunity At The President's Discretion Conflicts With Core Constitutional Norms

Finally, the Court turns to DOJ's contention that, quite apart from the accepted ability of a President to invoke executive privilege to protect confidential information during the course of aides' testimony before Congress, as a matter of law, it is the President who controls whether such aide provides any testimony whatsoever. During the motions hearing, DOJ's counsel repeatedly emphasized that the power to invoke absolute testimonial immunity with respect to current and former senior-level aides *belongs to the President*. And when asked whether this power of the Executive is limited to such aides' communications with Congress in particular, or also extends to preventing his aides from speaking to anyone else (*e.g.*, the media) even after their departure from the White House, counsel indicated that while the Executive branch has "not taken a position on that," it was "definitely not disclaiming that." This single exchange—which brings to mind an Executive with the power to oversee and direct certain subordinates' communications for the remainder of their natural lives—highlights the startling and untenable implications of DOJ's absolute testimonial immunity argument, and also amply demonstrates its incompatibility with our constitutional scheme.

Stated simply, the primary takeaway from the past 250 years of recorded American history is that Presidents are not kings. *See* The Federalist No. 51 (James Madison); The Federalist No. 69 (Alexander Hamilton); 1 Alexis de Tocqueville, Democracy in America 115–18 (Harvey C. Mansfield & Delba Winthrop eds. & trans., Univ. of Chicago Press 2000) (1835). This means that they do not have subjects, bound by loyalty or blood, whose destiny they are

---

the force of subpoena with respect to protected legislative activity. The Supreme Court has explained that the Speech and Debate Clause derives from a similar provision of the English Bill of Rights of 1689, which served to address successive monarchs' use of "criminal and civil law to suppress and intimidate critical legislators." *See United States v. Johnson*, 383 U.S. 169, 179 (1966). Thus, the purpose of the Speech and Debate Clause is to protect legislators from intimidating and/or hostile executive and judicial inquiry, a common abuse of power in seventeenth century England. *See id.* at 181–82. And, notably, the Constitution includes nothing akin to the Speech and Debate Clause for the Executive branch.

entitled to control. Rather, in this land of liberty, it is indisputable that current and former employees of the White House work for the People of the United States, and that they take an oath to protect and defend the Constitution of the United States. Moreover, as citizens of the United States, current and former senior-level presidential aides have constitutional rights, including the right to free speech, and they retain these rights even after they have transitioned back into private life.

To be sure, there may well be circumstances in which certain aides of the President possess confidential, classified, or privileged information that cannot be divulged in the national interest and that such aides may be bound by statute or executive order to protect. But, in this Court's view, the withholding of such information from the public square in the national interest and at the behest of the President is a duty that the aide herself possesses. Furthermore, as previously mentioned, in the context of compelled congressional testimony, such withholding is properly and lawfully executed on a question-by-question basis through the invocation of a privilege, where appropriate.[24] As such, with the exception of the recognized restrictions on the ability of current and former public officials to disclose certain protected information, such officials (including senior-level presidential aides) still enjoy the full measure of freedom that the Constitution affords. Thus, DOJ's present assertion that the absolute testimonial immunity that senior-level presidential aides possess is, ultimately, owned by the President, and can be invoked by the President to overcome the aides' own will to testify, is a proposition that cannot be squared with core constitutional values, and for this reason alone, it cannot be sustained.

*　*　*

To make the point as plain as possible, it is clear to this Court for the reasons explained above that, with respect to senior-level presidential aides, absolute immunity from compelled congressional process simply does not exist. Indeed, absolute testimonial immunity for senior-level White House aides appears to be a fiction that has been fastidiously maintained over time through the force of sheer repetition in OLC opinions, and through accommodations that have permitted its proponents to avoid having the proposition tested in the crucible of litigation. And because the contention that a President's top advisors cannot be subjected to compulsory congressional process simply has no basis in the law, it does not matter whether such immunity would theoretically be available to only a handful of presidential aides due to the sensitivity

---

24. [Court's Note 34] With respect to such withholding, the President can certainly identify sensitive information that he deems subject to executive privilege, *United States v. Nixon*, 418 U.S. at 713, and his doing so gives rise to a legal duty on the part of the aide to invoke the privilege on the President's behalf when, in the course of his testimony, he is asked a question that would require disclosure of that information. But the invocation of the privilege by a testifying aide is an order of magnitude different than DOJ's current claim that the President essentially owns the *entirety* of a senior-level aide's testimony such that the White House can order the individual not to appear before Congress *at all*.

of their positions, or to the entire Executive branch. Nor does it make any difference whether the aides in question are privy to national security matters, or work solely on domestic issues. And, of course, if *present* frequent occupants of the West Wing or Situation Room must find time to appear for testimony as a matter of law when Congress issues a subpoena, then any such immunity most certainly stops short of covering individuals who only purport to be cloaked with this authority because, at some point in the past, they *once* were in the President's employ. This was the state of law when Judge Bates first considered the issue of whether former White House Counsel Harriet Miers had absolute testimonial immunity in 2008, and it remains the state of law today, and it goes without saying that the law applies to former White House Counsel Don McGahn, just as it does to other current and former senior-level White House officials.

Thus, for the myriad reasons laid out above as well as those that are articulated plainly in the prior precedents of the Supreme Court, the D.C. Circuit, and the U.S. District Court for the District of Columbia, this Court holds that individuals who have been subpoenaed for testimony by an authorized committee of Congress must appear for testimony in response to that subpoena—*i.e.*, they cannot ignore or defy congressional compulsory process, by order of the President or otherwise. Notably, however, in the context of that appearance, such individuals are free to assert any legally applicable privilege in response to the questions asked of them, where appropriate.

V. CONCLUSION

The United States of America has a government of laws and not of men. The Constitution and federal law set the boundaries of what is acceptable conduct, and for this reason, as explained above, when there is a dispute between the Legislature and the Executive branch over what the law requires about the circumstances under which government officials must act, the Judiciary has the authority, and the responsibility, to decide the issue. Moreover, as relevant here, when the issue in dispute is whether a government official has the duty to respond to a subpoena that a duly authorized committee of the House of Representatives has issued pursuant to its Article I authority, the official's defiance unquestionably inflicts a cognizable injury on Congress, and thereby, substantially harms the national interest as well. These injuries give rise to a right of a congressional committee to seek to vindicate its constitutionally conferred investigative power in the context of a civil action filed in court.

Notably, whether or not the law requires the recalcitrant official to release the testimonial information that the congressional committee requests is a separate question, and one that will depend in large part on whether the requested information is itself subject to withholding consistent with the law on the basis of a recognized privilege. But as far as the duty to appear is concerned, this Court holds that Executive branch officials are not absolutely immune from compulsory congressional process—no matter how many times the Executive branch has asserted as much over the years—even if the President expressly directs such officials' non-compliance.

This result is unavoidable as a matter of basic constitutional law, as the *Miers* court recognized more than a decade ago. Today, this Court adds that this conclusion is inescapable precisely because compulsory appearance by dint of a subpoena is a legal construct, not a political one, and per the Constitution, no one is above the law. That is to say, however busy or essential a presidential aide might be, and whatever their proximity to sensitive domestic and national-security projects, the President does not have the power to excuse him or her from taking an action that the law requires. Fifty years of say so within the Executive branch does not change that fundamental truth. Nor is the power of the Executive unfairly or improperly diminished when the Judiciary mandates adherence to the law and thus refuses to recognize a veto-like discretionary power of the President to cancel his subordinates' legal obligations. To the contrary, when a duly authorized committee of Congress issues a valid subpoena to a current or former Executive branch official, and thereafter, a federal court determines that the subpoenaed official does, as a matter of law, have a duty to respond notwithstanding any contrary order of the President, the venerated constitutional principles that animate the structure of our government and undergird our most vital democratic institutions are preserved. * * *

Committee on the Judiciary v. McGahn, 415 F. Supp. 3d 148, 199–200, 204–15 (D.D.C. 2019) (footnotes omitted except as indicated).

B. A Panel of the D.C. Circuit Introduces New Uncertainty into the Law

As of 2019, after three lengthy and largely consistent judicial decisions by federal district court judges appointed by both Democratic and Republican Presidents, it appeared that the law regarding the power of Congress to compel testimony from the Executive Branch was moving toward more settled predictability. Then the *McGahn* district court decision was appealed, and a divided three-judge panel of the D.C. Circuit initially ruled that the Judiciary Committee lacked Article III standing because of separation of powers principles and historical practice. *Committee on the Judiciary v. McGahn*, 951 F.3d 510 (D.C. Cir. 2019). The Committee then sought *en banc* review of that decision, and in August 2020, the D.C. Circuit issued an *en banc* decision reversing the divided three-judge panel on the standing issue, vacating the panel's separation of powers decision and confirming that the Committee has standing to sue in federal court to enforce its subpoenas:

> McGahn begins his separation of powers objections by maintaining that if the Committee has standing, then Congress will have been provided "'a blueprint for extensive expansion of the legislative power' by allowing Congress to

'arrogate power to itself,'" empowering Congress to unilaterally resolve informational disputes without engaging in the historical practice of negotiating informational disputes with the Executive Branch. Courts must take care not to disrupt the "longstanding practice" of accommodation between the political branches. *Mazars*, 140 S. Ct. at 2031. But there is no congressional "arrogation" of power here and no threat that the court's decision will disrupt the historical practice of accommodation. To the contrary, permitting Congress to bring this lawsuit preserves the power of subpoena that the House of Representatives is already understood to possess. Rather, it is McGahn's challenge to the Committee's standing that seeks to alter the *status quo ante* and aggrandize the power of the Executive Branch at the expense of Congress.

For more than forty years this circuit has held that a House of Congress has standing to pursue a subpoena enforcement lawsuit in federal court. See *Comm. on Oversight & Gov't Reform v. Holder*, 979 F. Supp. 2d 1, 20–22 (D.D.C. 2013); *Comm. on the Judiciary, U.S. House of Representatives v. Miers*, 558 F. Supp. 2d 53, 68–78 (D.D.C. 2008); *United States v. AT&T*, 551 F.2d 384, 391 (D.C. Cir. 1976); *Senate Select Comm.*, 498 F.2d at 728. McGahn does not suggest that any court, prior to the vacated panel majority in the present case, has ever ruled to the contrary. Congress and the Executive Branch have long operated under the assumption that Congress may, if necessary, seek enforcement of a subpoena in federal court.

Accepting McGahn's position that the Committee lacks standing would significantly curtail the possibility of accommodation. That outcome would upset settled expectations and dramatically alter bargaining positions in the accommodation process over informational disputes in the future. Without the possibility of enforcement of a subpoena issued by a House of Congress, the Executive Branch faces little incentive to reach a negotiated agreement in an informational dispute. Indeed, the threat of a subpoena enforcement lawsuit may be an essential tool in keeping the Executive Branch at the negotiating table. For example, President Clinton and a Senate subcommittee "[e]ventually . . . reached an agreement" over an informational dispute only after "a Senate threat to seek judicial enforcement of the subpoena." *Mazars*, 140 S. Ct. at 2030. Without that possibility, Presidents could direct widescale non-compliance with lawful inquiries by a House of Congress, secure in the knowledge that little can be done to enforce its subpoena — as President Trump did here. Traditional congressional oversight of the Executive Branch would be replaced by a system of voluntary Presidential disclosures, potentially limiting Congress to learning only what the President wants it to learn. And the power of impeachment, the "essential check . . . upon the encroachments of the executive," Federalist No. 66 (A. Hamilton), would be diminished because a President would be unlikely to voluntarily turn over information that could lead to impeachment.

* * *

Accordingly, we hold that the Committee has Article III standing to seek enforcement in federal court of its duly issued subpoena in the performance of constitutional responsibilities. Therefore, we affirm the judgment of the district court in part. Consideration of McGahn's other contentions—including threshold pre-merits objections that there is no subject matter jurisdiction and no applicable cause of action, and potential consideration of the merits if reached—remain to be decided and are remanded to the panel to address in the first instance.

Committee on the Judiciary v. McGahn, 968 F.3d 755, 771, 778 (D.C. Cir. 2020) (*en banc*).

As noted at the conclusion of its holding set out above, the D.C. Circuit held that that Judiciary Committee had standing, but it did not address the separate issue of whether the federal courts have subject matter jurisdiction to decide such a case. That issue was remanded to the same panel that had initially held that the Judiciary Committee lacked standing to sue. Less than a month later, the same divided three-judge panel issued another opinion in the case—one that introduced further uncertainty into the law on judicial enforcement of congressional subpoenas:

> The *en banc* court held that the Committee has Article III standing, but the Committee "also need[s] a cause of action to prosecute" its case in federal court. *Make the Road N.Y. v. Wolf*, 962 F.3d 612, 631 (D.C. Cir. 2020). Here, the Committee argues that it has an implied cause of action under Article I, that it can invoke the traditional power of courts of equity to enjoin unlawful executive action, and that the Declaratory Judgment Act provides a separate basis for this suit. We disagree.

> * * *

> In this case, Congress has *declined* to authorize lawsuits like the Committee's twice over. First, Congress has granted an express cause of action to the Senate—but not to the House. See 2 U.S.C. §288d; 28 U.S.C. §1365(b). Second, the Senate statute expressly *excludes* suits that involve executive-branch assertions of "governmental privilege." 28 U.S.C. §1365(a). The expression of one thing implies the exclusion of the other, and authorizing the Committee to bring its lawsuit would conflict with two separate statutory limitations on civil suits to enforce congressional subpoenas. When determining whether to "recognize any causes of action not expressly created by Congress," "our watchword is caution," *Hernandez* [*v. Mesa*], 140 S. Ct. at 742, and we should not ignore Congress's carefully drafted limitations on its authority to sue to enforce a subpoena.

> The Committee next suggests that—even if Article I alone doesn't provide a cause of action—the court may exercise its "traditional equitable powers" to grant relief. *Ziglar* [*v. Abbasi*], 137 S. Ct. at 1856. But even those equitable powers remain "subject to express and implied statutory limitations," *Armstrong v. Exceptional Child Ctr., Inc.*, 575 U.S. 320, 327 (2015), and are further limited to

relief that was "traditionally accorded by courts of equity," *Grupo Mexicano de Desarrollo S.A. v. All. Bond Fund, Inc.*, 527 U.S. 308, 319 (1999). Again, "implied statutory limitations" foreclose suits by the House and suits that implicate a governmental privilege; this one checks both boxes, so Congress itself has precluded us from granting the requested relief to the Committee.

In any event, there is also nothing "traditional" about the Committee's claim. The Committee cannot point to a single example in which a chamber of Congress brought suit for injunctive relief against the Executive Branch prior to the 1970s. True enough, the en banc court rejected McGahn's argument that "federal courts have not historically entertained congressional subpoena enforcement lawsuits," but the full court also recognized the "relative recency" of lawsuits to enforce subpoenas. *McGahn*, 2020 WL 4556761, at *14. When determining the scope of our equitable authority, however, "relatively recent" history isn't enough. In *Grupo Mexicano*, the Supreme Court explained that we "must ask whether the relief" that the Committee requests "was traditionally accorded *by courts of equity*." 527 U.S. at 319 (emphasis added). The relief requested here—an injunction issued against a former Executive Branch official in an interbranch information dispute—cannot possibly have been traditionally available in courts of equity, because the "separate systems of law and equity" in our federal system ceased to exist in 1938. *SCA Hygiene Prods. Aktiebolag v. First Quality Baby Prods., LLC*, 137 S. Ct. 954, 960 (2017). The Committee's smattering of examples from the 1970s comes (at least) thirty years too late.

* * *

The dissent's contrary arguments fail. First, the dissent suggests that the court may infer a cause of action from the Committee's Article I power to issue subpoenas. The dissent quotes *McGrain v. Daugherty*, which held that the "power of inquiry—with process to enforce it—is an essential and appropriate auxiliary to the legislative function." 273 U.S. 135, 174 (1927); see also *Quinn v. United States*, 349 U.S. 155, 160–61 (1955) (similar). But the Supreme Court has also explained that "[a]uthority to exert the powers of the [House] to compel production of evidence *differs widely* from authority to invoke judicial power to that purpose." *Reed v. Cty. Comm'rs of Del. Cty.*, 277 U.S. 376, 389 (1928) (emphasis added). And neither of the cases that the dissent cites says that Article I gives the Committee power to file a civil suit to enforce its subpoenas. *McGrain* arose out of a habeas corpus suit filed after the Senate exercised its *inherent* contempt power to arrest the Attorney General's brother. See *McGrain*, 273 U.S. at 153–54. And although *Quinn* stated that Congress has "the authority to compel testimony" through "its own processes" or a "judicial trial," that case arose out of a criminal conviction for contempt of Congress—a violation of a criminal statute. 349 U.S. at 160–61. These cases do not demonstrate that Article I creates a cause of action for the Committee. To the contrary, they show that Congress has long relied on its own devices—either its inherent contempt power, *see, e.g., Anderson v. Dunn*, 19 U.S. (6 Wheat.) 204 (1821), or the criminal contempt statute enacted in 1857, see *McGrain*, 273 U.S. at 167.

Our circuit has already recognized these limits on Congress's power to enforce subpoenas. As we explained, "Prior to 1978 Congress had *only two* means of enforcing compliance with its subpoenas: [1] a statutory criminal contempt mechanism and [2] the inherent congressional contempt power." *In re U.S. Senate Permanent Subcomm. on Investigations*, 655 F.2d 1232, 1238 (D.C. Cir. 1981) (emphasis added) (footnote omitted). Although Congress "[r]espond[ed] to this deficiency" by enacting a "mechanism for civil enforcement of *Senate* subpoenas" in 1978, that statute "does not ... include civil enforcement of subpoenas by the House of Representatives." *Id.* at 1238 & n.28 (emphasis added). Our precedent thus plainly presupposes that the Constitution alone does not provide a cause of action.

* * *

Because the Committee lacks a cause of action to enforce its subpoena, this lawsuit must be dismissed. We note that this decision does not preclude Congress (or one of its chambers) from ever enforcing a subpoena in federal court; it simply precludes it from doing so without first enacting a statute authorizing such a suit. The Constitution's Necessary and Proper Clause vests Congress with power to "make all Laws which shall be necessary and proper for carrying into Execution" its constitutional powers, and that Clause gives Congress—and certainly not the federal courts—the broad discretion to structure the national government through the legislative process.

If Congress (rather than a single committee in a single chamber thereof) determines that its current mechanisms leave it unable to adequately enforce its subpoenas, it remains free to enact a statute that makes the House's requests for information judicially enforceable. Indeed, Congress has passed similar statutes before, authorizing criminal enforcement in 1857 and civil enforcement for the Senate in 1978. See *Senate Permanent Subcomm.*, 655 F.3d at 1238 & n.26. Because no "legislation pursues its purposes at all costs," *CTS Corp. v. Waldburger*, 573 U.S. 1, 12 (2014) (internal quotation marks omitted), any such statute might, for example, carve out certain categories of subpoenas, or create unique procedural protections for defendants. That's exactly what Congress has done in the past. The 1857 statute, for instance, stated that "no person examined and testifying" before Congress "shall be held to answer criminally ... for any fact or act [about] which he shall be required to testify." *In re Chapman*, 166 U.S. 661, 665 n.1 (1897). And the Senate's civil enforcement statute exempts from suit any defendant asserting a "governmental privilege." 28 U.S.C. § 1365(a).

Balancing the various policy considerations in crafting an enforcement statute is a legislative judgment. For that reason, the Constitution leaves to Congress—and not to the federal courts—the authority to craft rights and remedies in our constitutional democracy. Perhaps "new conditions" "might call for a wrenching departure from past practice" and for a new statute allowing the House to leverage the power of federal courts to compel testimony or the production of documents. *Grupo Mexicano*, 527 U.S. at 322. But if any institution is well-positioned to "perceive" those new conditions, to assess Congress's needs, to balance those needs against the countervailing policy considerations, and then "to design the appropriate remedy," that institution is Congress. *Id.*

The judgment of the district court is reversed, and the case is remanded for further proceedings consistent with this opinion.

Committee on the Judiciary v. McGahn, 973 F.3d 121, 123–26 (D.C. Cir. 2020).

This decision by the divided three-judge panel, at the end of August 2020, effectively meant that the case would not be resolved before the 2020 presidential election. The case remained pending when the Biden administration took office in January 2021. In May 2021, the Biden Justice Department and the Judiciary Committee reached agreement on an "accommodation" to resolve the case that would permit the Committee to conduct a "transcribed interview" of McGahn. *See* Joint Motion to Postpone Oral Argument, *Judiciary Committee v. McGahn*, No. 19-5331 (D.C. Cir. May 12, 2021). Consistent with this agreement, on July 13, 2021, the D.C. Circuit entered an *en banc* order that vacated the divided three-judge panel decision on subject matter jurisdiction and dismissed the case. *See* Order, *Judiciary Committee v. McGahn*, No. 19-5331 (D.C. Cir. July 13, 2021). This ended the *McGahn* case after two years of litigation without any definitive resolution of the absolute testimonial immunity issue.

Notes and Questions

1. New Uncertainty in an Already Complex Area of Law. The D.C. Circuit's July 13, 2021, order vacated the decision of the divided three-judge panel that the federal courts lack subject-matter jurisdiction to enforce subpoenas issued by the House of Representatives,, but it did not resolve the issue. "While there were some issues specific to a subpoena directed at an executive branch official, some of its reasoning could have led to similar challenges by private sector parties subpoenaed by Congress. By vacating the judgment, the full D.C. Circuit vindicated House subpoena power for now. However, because the *en banc* panel did not reject the logic or reasoning of the prior opinion, Congress may face a similar challenge to its enforcement remedies in future litigation." Andrew M. Wright, et al., *The End of the McGahn Litigation Saga: House Subpoena Power is Vindicated, For Now*, NAT. L. REV. No. 321 (Aug. 2, 2021). How much validity does the three-judge panel's subject-matter jurisdiction analysis retain after having been vacated by an *en banc* order of the D.C. Circuit? How likely are future litigants to seek to rely on the subject-matter jurisdiction argument to challenge congressional subpoenas? Does the subject matter jurisdiction challenge give new ammunition to private parties battling congressional subpoenas? Does it matter that the August 7, 2021, D.C. Circuit opinion upholding the Judiciary Committee's standing to sue relied in part on the fact that the Judiciary Committee was exercising its constitutional power of impeachment?

2. Absolute Testimonial Immunity—Still a Viable Theory? It is important to note that none of the D.C. Circuit opinions in the *McGahn* litigation addressed the merits of the absolute testimonial immunity for present and former senior presidential advisors that was asserted by McGahn and the Trump Justice Department:

> A few points are critical to understanding the agreement the parties made [in the *McGahn* case]. The first is that at no point has the appeals court weighed in on the merits of McGahn's claim of immunity. The district court has rejected it, but both D.C. Circuit opinions dealt with antecedent questions: whether the committee has standing to sue and whether a cause of action exists under which to do so. The district court opinion, of course, is not binding precedent, so by settling this case now, the executive branch preserves its ability to argue for testimonial immunity for senior presidential advisers in the future.

Quinta Jurecic & Bejamin Wittes, *Trump's White House Counsel Will Testify Before Congress: What Now?*, LAWFARE, May 17, 2021. Do you think the absolute immunity theory has merit? What are the separation of powers implications if the theory were to become law? For a scholarly argument in favor of such immunity, see Jonathan David Shaub, *The Executive's Privilege*, 70 DUKE L.J. 1 (2020).

3. Running Out the Clock—The New Normal? A striking similarity of the *Miers*, *Holder*, and *McGahn* cases is that in all three cases, the executive branch was able to use litigation to "run out the clock" on a congressional demand for information and all three cases were resolved only after a new administration, of a different political party, took office. Does this make it likely that future presidential administrations will again seek to use litigation, including the arguably unresolved "absolute testimonial immunity" theory, to run out the clock and avoid compliance with congressional subpoenas? Does it suggest that new legislation is necessary to establish federal court jurisdiction and ensure faster judicial resolution of such disputes? For an argument that Congress should pass legislation to clarify its investigative powers, see Bob Bauer & Jack Goldsmith, *Congress Should Seize this Chance to Get its Power Back*, POLITICO (Oct. 5, 2021) (arguing for enactment of the Protecting Our Democracy Act "to restore some congressional authority in this area by strengthening Congress's hand in enforcing its subpoenas").

Chapter Five

The Fifth Amendment Privilege against Self-Incrimination and Congressional Grants of Immunity

The Iran-Contra Investigation

I believe during the past week we have participated in creating and developing very likely a new American hero.

> Statement of Senator Daniel K. Inouye at the conclusion of
> Col. Oliver L. North's testimony before the Joint House-Senate
> Committees Investigating the Iran-Contra Affair, July 14, 1987

As the materials in the preceding Chapters demonstrate, effective congressional investigation and oversight is heavily dependent upon obtaining the testimony of knowledgeable witnesses. Although Congress has very broad investigative subpoena power, that power can be thwarted in certain instances. For example, in investigations of federal government activities and misconduct, assertions of executive privilege can hamper the congressional investigative process. The case studies that were examined in Chapter 4 illustrate how this may occur.

Executive privilege is not the only legal doctrine that can be invoked to impede congressional efforts to obtain witness testimony. Two other legal doctrines are often asserted as grounds for witnesses to refuse to provide congressional testimony. If the personal conduct of a witness is in any way at issue, the witness may choose to assert the Fifth Amendment privilege against self-incrimination and refuse to testify. If testimony is sought about legal advice provided to a witness, or provided by a witness if the witness is an attorney, then the attorney-client privilege may be asserted as grounds to withhold testimony. This Chapter examines the application of the Fifth Amendment privilege against self-incrimination to congressional proceedings. The attorney-client privilege is examined in Chapter 6.

Background on the Fifth Amendment and Immunity Grants

Fifth Amendment law is surprisingly complex, given the fundamental nature of the right against self-incrimination and the plain language by which the Constitution guarantees that right:

> No person ... shall be compelled in any criminal case to be a witness against himself....

U.S. Constitution, Amendment V. For example, persons who are not well-versed in constitutional criminal procedure are surprised to learn that voluntarily created personal writings, such as private notes and diaries, are not necessarily protected by the Fifth Amendment and generally must be produced in response to a government subpoena.[1] Similarly, most people do not expect that the government can compel them to disclose incriminating information about their closest friends and family members, as for example took place when the mother of White House intern Monica Lewinsky was compelled to testify about her daughter in Independent Counsel Kenneth Starr's grand jury investigation.[2] The Lewinsky example illustrates two critically important points of Fifth Amendment law. First, the right against self-incrimination is personal in nature, and therefore it cannot be invoked to protect even very close friends or family members. Second, even when one's testimony may be personally incriminatory, the right against self-incrimination can be overcome by an immunity grant. Immunity grants, and in particular their use in congressional investigations, are the primary focus of this Chapter.

Congressional immunity grants create special legal and policy problems that are not present when executive branch prosecutors determine that a witness should be granted immunity. Two knowledgeable commentators have described the special problems presented by congressional immunity grants as follows:

> The history of the Watergate and Iran-Contra investigations by Congress shows that grants of testimonial or "use" immunity are very often indispensable tools of major congressional investigations. Yet, such grants of immunity intensify the conflict between key purposes of Congressional investigations

---

1. In some instances the "act of production" of personal writings may be incriminating, and in those instances the Fifth Amendment privilege can be asserted as grounds for refusing to produce the documents. Even in those cases, however, it is the "act of production" and not the documents themselves or their contents, that is protected by the Fifth Amendment. *See generally*, Lance Cole, *The Fifth Amendment and Compelled Production of Personal Documents After* United States v. Hubbell—*New Protection for Private Papers?*, 29 Am. J. Crim. L. 123 (2002).

2. *See* Findings of Independent Counsel Kenneth W. Starr on President Clinton and the Lewinsky Affair ("Starr Report"), Part I. B. 3, "Ms. Lewinsky's Confidants" (1998). Starr also compelled testimony from Ms. Lewinsky's psychologist, her counselor, her aunt, a former boyfriend, and several of her closest friends. *See id.* Although some or all of this testimony may have been incriminatory as to Ms. Lewinsky, the Fifth Amendment privilege against self-incrimination did not apply to testimony by Ms. Lewinsky's confidants about what she had done or what she had told them she had done.

and those of the criminal justice system by erecting a potentially formidable barrier to subsequent criminal prosecutions. If they are not properly timed or employed once made, grants of testimonial immunity may block otherwise successful criminal prosecutions by making it more difficult or impossible for prosecutors to meet their "heavy burden" of demonstrating that their cases are not tainted by the immunized testimony given before the Congress.

Improperly made grants of immunity may also result in failed congressional investigations. If an immunity is granted prematurely, a thorough investigation may not be able to be conducted. Immunity also may be granted improvidently, by giving it to a witness who should not be immunized, thus assisting an individual who should be prosecuted to escape prosecution. Finally, even when an immunity is granted, it may not be able to be enforced so that an investigation can proceed.

Given this tension between the need for congressional investigations to employ use immunity and the possibility that using it may defeat the ends of the criminal justice system, one of the first orders of business for a major congressional investigation which precedes or parallels related criminal investigations or prosecutions will be to navigate the shoals of use immunity.

George W. Van Cleve & Charles Tiefer, *Navigating the Shoals of "Use" Immunity and Secret International Enterprises in Major Congressional Investigations: Lessons of the Iran-Contra Affair*, 55 Mo. L. Rev. 43 (1990). The issues identified by Van Cleve and Tiefer, beginning with the procedure for congressional immunity grants and the concept of "use" immunity, must be examined further to appreciate fully the implications of the congressional grants of immunity in the Iran-Contra investigation.

Procedure for Congressional Immunity Grants

The law governing grants of immunity to witnesses to compel their testimony despite their assertion of a Fifth Amendment privilege against self-incrimination has changed markedly over time. The current federal immunity statute, 18 U.S.C. §6002, provides as follows:

Whenever a witness refuses, on the basis of his privilege against self-incrimination, to testify or provide other information in a proceeding before or ancillary to—

(1) a court or grand jury of the United States,

(2) an agency of the United States, or

(3) either House of Congress, a joint committee of the two Houses, or a committee or a subcommittee of either House,

and the person presiding over the proceeding communicates to the witness an order issued under this title, the witness may not refuse to comply with the order on the basis of his privilege against self-incrimination; but no testimony or other information compelled under the order (or any information directly or indirectly derived from such testimony or other information) may be used against the witness in any criminal case, except a prosecution for perjury, giving a false statement, or otherwise failing to comply with the order.

The procedure by which a congressional immunity grant can be obtained is set out in a companion statute, 18 U.S.C. §6005:

(a) In the case of any individual who has been or may be called to testify or provide other information at any proceeding before or ancillary to either House of Congress, or any committee, or any subcommittee of either House, or any joint committee of the two Houses, a United States district court shall issue, in accordance with subsection (b) of this section, upon the request of a duly authorized representative of the House of Congress or the committee concerned, an order requiring such individual to give testimony or provide other information which he refuses to give or provide on the basis of his privilege against self-incrimination, such order to become effective as provided in section 6002 of this title.

(b) Before issuing an order under subsection (a) of this section, a United States district court shall find that—

(1) in the case of a proceeding before or ancillary to either House of Congress, the request for such an order has been approved by an affirmative vote of a majority of the Members present of that House;

(2) in the case of a proceeding before or ancillary to a committee or a subcommittee of either House of Congress or a joint committee of both Houses, the request for such an order has been approved by an affirmative vote of two-thirds of the members of the full committee; and

(3) ten days or more prior to the day on which the request for such order was made, the Attorney General was served with notice of an intention to request the order.

(c) Upon application of the Attorney General, the United States district court shall defer the issuance of any order under subsection (a) of this section for such period, not longer than twenty days from the date of the request for such order, as the Attorney General may specify.

Several aspects of the procedure outlined in the statute should be noted. First, although the immunity order is entered by a federal court, the court has no discretion to refuse to grant a properly submitted congressional request for such an order. In other words, so long as a house or committee of Congress has complied with the terms of the statute, the court must—as directed by the "shall issue" language in subsection (a)—grant the request and enter the immunity order. The court does not have discretion to review the merits of the decision to employ an immunity grant as an investigative tool or even to decline to grant immunity to a particular witness. The judicial branch therefore cannot second-guess the legislative branch's policy decision to grant immunity. Similarly, although the Attorney General must receive at least ten days' advance notice that an immunity order request will be filed with the court, the Attorney General cannot prevent the Congress from submitting a request for an immunity order. This remains true even if the executive branch can otherwise make a compelling case that granting immunity to a particular witness will prevent subsequent prosecution of that person or undermine the process of investigating and prosecuting other culpable persons. As Iran-Contra Independent Counsel Lawrence E. Walsh summarized the law in his final report, "The law was clear that Congress controlled the political decision of whether immunity grants were justified by the importance of the hearings even though they could destroy a criminal prosecution." Final Report of the Independent Counsel for Iran/Contra Matters, Vol. I, Investigations and Prosecutions, at 32 (1993).

Even after a congressional immunity order request is submitted to the court, the Attorney General, representing the prosecutorial interests of the executive branch, cannot "veto" or otherwise block a congressional immunity request. The most the Attorney General can do is require the court to defer entering the immunity order for an additional twenty days after the date the request is submitted to the court. This procedure ensures that prosecutors will have at least thirty days to document and segregate all of their evidence against the immunized witness, if they wish to retain the option to pursue a prosecution after the immunized testimony is provided. (This procedure is discussed further in the section on The Oliver North Phenomenon, below.) Moreover, as is the case with the request for the immunity order itself, the court has no discretion to deny an Attorney General's request for the twenty-day extension (again, note the "shall defer" language in the statute). The net practical effect of the statutory procedure is to make the role of the court, while essential to the process of immunizing a witness, more ministerial than judicial.

Other noteworthy aspects of the statutory procedure pertain more to practical political considerations than legal process. Although the decision to obtain an immunity order can be made solely by the legislative branch, the procedures set out in the statute ensure that at least some degree of bipartisan cooperation is likely to be necessary in the House of Congress that seeks the order. When congressional committees seek to immunize a witness, the statute requires approval of two-thirds of the committee members (which may be more difficult to obtain than two-thirds of the committee members present and voting, because members who wish to oppose the immunity grant without going on record by voting against it can simply fail to attend the committee meeting and their absence will have the same effect as a vote against immunity). The statute requires only a majority of those present and voting in the full chamber of either House of Congress to approve an immunity request, but in the case of Senate witnesses a filibuster by the minority party can block the immunity grant. To invoke cloture in the Senate and overcome a filibuster at least sixty votes will be required in favor of the immunity grant, so as a practical matter bipartisan support likely will be required when the full Senate votes on an immunity request. The effect of these statutory provisions and procedural requirements is to make it unlikely that a witness in a congressional proceeding can be granted immunity without some measure of bipartisan support for the immunity grant.

"Use" Immunity Compared to "Transactional" Immunity

Beyond these procedural requirements for obtaining an immunity order, it is important to understand the nature of the immunity protection provided by an order issued pursuant to the current federal immunity statute. The Fifth Amendment protects against compulsory self-incrimination, so immunity from prosecution can eliminate any Fifth Amendment concern by obviating the risk that a witness's statements would incriminate him or her. Nevertheless, the scope of immunity that must be provided to satisfy the Fifth Amendment has varied over time with shifting decisions of the Supreme Court. One of the authors of this book has summarized those changes as follows:

> For much of our history, the assumption was that a valid assertion of the Fifth Amendment privilege against self-incrimination could be overcome only by a grant of full transactional immunity, which would prohibit subsequent prosecution of the witness asserting the privilege. In 1892, the Supreme Court reviewed a challenge to an 1868 immunity statute that provided an immunized witness protection only from the "use" of immunized testimony. In *Counselman v. Hitchcock* [142 U.S. 547 (1892)] the Court rejected this "use" immunity as failing to provide protection adequate to override a defendant's Fifth Amendment privilege against self-incrimination. Broad language in *Counselman*[3] suggested that transactional immunity was the only means by which the government could constitutionally overcome a witness's assertion of the Fifth Amendment privilege. In any event, as the ... [Supreme] Court subsequently observed, a grant of use immunity "was plainly deficient in its failure to prohibit the use against the immunized witness of evidence derived from his compelled testimony."[4]

> In 1893 Congress passed a "transactional" immunity statute in response to the *Counselman* decision. By providing that "no person shall be prosecuted or subjected to any penalty or forfeiture for or on account of any transaction, matter or thing, concerning which he may testify, or produce evidence, documentary or otherwise," the new statute gave an immunized witness full transactional immunity from prosecution. This statute remained in place until 1970, when Congress enacted 18 U.S.C. §§6002 and 6003, which provide only

---

3. [353] "In view of the [Fifth Amendment] constitutional provision, a statutory enactment, to be valid, must afford absolute immunity against future prosecution for the offence to which the question relates." 142 U.S. at 585–586.

4. [355] *United States v. Hubbell*, 530 U.S. 27, 39 n.21 (2000).

use and derivative use immunity and therefore "do[] not 'afford [the] absolute immunity against future prosecution' referred to in *Counselman*."[5]

In 1972, the Supreme Court decided *Kastigar v. United States* and approved the use and derivative use immunity provided by the new federal statute as "coextensive with the privilege against self-incrimination." The Court's reasoning turned on its conception of the extent of the protection afforded by the Fifth Amendment:

> While a grant of immunity must afford protection commensurate with that afforded by the privilege, it need not be broader. Transactional immunity, which affords full immunity from prosecution for the offense to which the compelled testimony relates, affords the witness considerably broader protection than does the Fifth Amendment privilege. The privilege has never been construed to mean that one who invokes it cannot subsequently be prosecuted.... Immunity from the use of compelled testimony, as well as evidence derived directly and indirectly therefrom, affords this protection. It prohibits the prosecutorial authorities from using the compelled testimony in *any* respect, and it therefore insures that the testimony cannot lead to the infliction of criminal penalties on the witness.

By permitting subsequent prosecution of an immunized witness, *Kastigar* appeared to have altered the balance of power between witnesses who asserted their privilege against self-incrimination with respect to their testimony and prosecutors who were seeking that testimony but did not wish to forgo all opportunity to prosecute the witness who possessed the information.

The extent of the change brought about by *Kastigar*'s approval of the use and derivative use immunity statute ultimately was tempered by the difficulty of proving that the prosecution had made no improper use of the immunized testimony. [*Ed. Note: This was the legal issue that faced the federal trial courts when they were called upon to review the legal challenges to the prosecutions of key Iran-Contra figures, such as Oliver North and John Poindexter, who had provided immunized congressional testimony about matters related to the conduct that was the basis of the criminal charges against them.*]

Lance Cole, *The Fifth Amendment and Compelled Production of Personal Documents After* United States v. Hubbell—*New Protection for Private Papers?*, 29 Am. J. Crim. L. 123, 178–79 (2002) (footnotes omitted, except as indicated).

The materials below provide background information on the Iran-Contra Affair and explore the legal issues that were presented when the Iran-Contra Independent Counsel, Lawrence E. Walsh, prosecuted Reagan Administration National Security Council officials John M. Poindexter and Oliver L. North after Congress had granted

---

5. [358] *See Kastigar v. United States*, 406 U.S. 441, 452 (1972).

them immunity and compelled them to provide public testimony about their roles in the events that gave rise to their subsequent prosecutions.

Iran-Contra and the Immunized Testimony of North and Poindexter

A. Background

Lawrence E. Walsh, *Final Report of the Independent Counsel for Iran/Contra Matters*

Independent Counsel
August 4, 1993

The Basic Facts of Iran/contra

The Iran/contra affair concerned two secret Reagan Administration policies whose operations were coordinated by National Security Council staff. The Iran operation involved efforts in 1985 and 1986 to obtain the release of Americans held hostage in the Middle East through the sale of U.S. weapons to Iran, despite an embargo on such sales. The contra operations from 1984 through most of 1986 involved the secret governmental support of contra military and paramilitary activities in Nicaragua, despite congressional prohibition of this support.

The Iran and contra operations were merged when funds generated from the sale of weapons to Iran were diverted to support the contra effort in Nicaragua. Although this "diversion" may be the most dramatic aspect of Iran/contra, it is important to emphasize that both the Iran and contra operations, separately, violated United States policy and law. The ignorance of the "diversion" asserted by President Reagan and his cabinet officers on the National Security Council in no way absolves them of responsibility for the underlying Iran and contra operations.

The secrecy concerning the Iran and contra activities was finally pierced by events that took place thousands of miles apart in the fall of 1986. The first occurred on October 5, 1986, when Nicaraguan government soldiers shot down an American cargo plane that was carrying military supplies to contra forces; the one surviving crew member, American Eugene Hasenfus, was taken into captivity and stated that he was employed by the CIA. A month after the Hasenfus shootdown, President Reagan's secret sale of U.S. arms to Iran was reported by a Lebanese publication on November 3. The joining of these two operations was made public on November 25, 1986, when Attorney General Meese announced that Justice Department officials had discovered that some of the proceeds from the Iran arms sales had been diverted to the contras.

When these operations ended, the exposure of the Iran/contra affair generated a new round of illegality. Beginning with the testimony of Elliott Abrams and others in October 1986 and continuing through the public testimony of Caspar W. Weinberger on the last day of the congressional hearings in the summer of 1987, senior Reagan Administration officials engaged in a concerted effort to deceive Congress and the public about their knowledge of and support for the operations.

Independent Counsel has concluded that the President's most senior advisers and the Cabinet members on the National Security Council participated in the strategy to make National Security staff members [National Security Advisor Robert "Bud"] McFarlane, Poindexter, and North the scapegoats whose sacrifice would protect the Reagan Administration in its final two years. In an important sense, this strategy succeeded. Independent Counsel discovered much of the best evidence of the cover-up in the final year of active investigation, too late for most prosecutions.

* * *

The Operational Conspiracy

The operational conspiracy was the basis for Count One of the 23-count indictment returned by the Grand Jury March 16, 1988, against Poindexter, North, [Gen. Richard] Secord, and [Albert] Hakim. It charged the four with conspiracy to defraud the United States by deceitfully:

(1) supporting military operations in Nicaragua in defiance of congressional controls;

(2) using the Iran arms sales to raise funds to be spent at the direction of North, rather than the U.S. Government; and

(3) endangering the Administration's hostage-release effort by overcharging Iran for the arms to generate unauthorized profits to fund the contras and for other purposes.

The charge was upheld as a matter of law by U.S. District Judge Gerhard A. Gesell even though the Justice Department, in a move that Judge Gesell called "unprecedented," filed an amicus brief supporting North's contention that the charge should be dismissed. Although Count One was ultimately dismissed because the Reagan Administration refused to declassify information necessary to North's defense, Judge Gesell's decision established that high Government officials who engaged in conspiracy to subvert civil laws and the Constitution have engaged in criminal acts. Trial on Count One would have disclosed the Government-wide activities that supported North's Iran and contra operations.

Within the NSC, McFarlane pleaded guilty in March 1988 to four counts of withholding information from Congress in connection with his denials that North was providing the contras with military advice and assistance. McFarlane, in his plea agreement, promised to cooperate with Independent Counsel by providing truthful testimony in subsequent trials.

Judge Gesell ordered severance of the trials of the four charged in the conspiracy indictment because of the immunized testimony given by Poindexter, North and Hakim to Congress. North was tried and convicted by a jury in May 1989 of altering and destroying documents, accepting an illegal gratuity, and aiding and abetting in the obstruction of Congress. His conviction was reversed on appeal in July 1990 and charges against North were subsequently dismissed in September 1991 on the ground that trial witnesses were tainted by North's nationally televised, immunized testimony before Congress. Poindexter in April 1990 was convicted by a jury on five felony counts of conspiracy, false statement, destruction and removal of records and obstruction of Congress. The Court of Appeals reversed his conviction in November 1991 on the immunized testimony issue.

The Flow of Funds

The off-the-books conduct of the two highly secret operations circumvented normal Administration accountability and congressional oversight associated with covert ventures and presented fertile ground for financial wrongdoing. There were several funding sources for the contras' weapons purchases from the covert-action Enterprise formed by North, Secord and Hakim:

(1) donations from foreign countries;

(2) contributions from wealthy Americans sympathetic to President Reagan's contra support policies; and

(3) the diversion of proceeds from the sale of arms to Iran.

Ultimately, all of these funds fell under the control of North, and through him, Secord and Hakim.

North used political fundraisers Carl R. Channell and Richard R. Miller to raise millions of dollars from wealthy Americans, illegally using a tax-exempt organization to do so. These funds, along with the private contributions, were run through a network of corporations and Swiss bank accounts put at North's disposal by Secord and Hakim, through which transactions were concealed and laundered. In late 1985 through 1986 the Enterprise became centrally involved in the arms sales to Iran. As a result of both the Iran and contra operations, more than $47 million flowed through Enterprise accounts.

Professional fundraisers Channell and Miller pleaded guilty in the spring of 1987 to conspiracy to defraud the Government by illegal use of a tax-exempt foundation to raise contributions for the purchase of lethal supplies for the contras. They named North as an unindicted co-conspirator.

Secord pleaded guilty in November 1989 to a felony, admitting that he falsely denied to Congress that North had personally benefited from the Enterprise. Hakim pleaded guilty to the misdemeanor count of supplementing the salary of North. Lake Resources Inc., the company controlled by Hakim to launder the Enterprise's money flow, pleaded guilty to the corporate felony of theft of Government property in diverting the proceeds from the arms sales to the contras and for other unauthorized purposes. Thomas G. Clines was convicted in September 1990 of four tax-related felonies for failing to report all of his income from the Enterprise.

* * *

From the outset both Congress and the Independent Counsel understood that the key witnesses in an investigation of the Iran-Contra Affair were John Poindexter and Oliver North. In fact, as North frequently noted in his immunized congressional testimony, he was the only individual named in the court order authorizing an independent counsel investigation of Iran-Contra. The congressional committees investigating Iran-Contra desperately wanted to obtain the testimony of North and Poindexter, and the Independent Counsel desperately wanted to avoid any congressional testimony that would compromise a later effort to prosecute the key Iran-Contra figures. North and his counsel of course wanted to avoid a criminal prosecution of North. As a consequence, the committees were forced to negotiate with both the Independent Counsel and with North's personal counsel in order to obtain his testimony. The Independent Counsel summarized the outcome of his negotiation with the committees as follows:

> Under a Memorandum of Understanding dated March 24, 1987, the Committees agreed not to vote on immunizing North before June 4, not to question him privately before June 15, and not to call him for public testimony before June 23. In exchange, Independent Counsel agreed not to seek an automatic 20-day deferral of North's immunity grant, as he was entitled to under the federal use immunity statute. For Poindexter, the Committees agreed not to vote on immunity before April 20, not to question him privately before May 2 or three days before the start of public hearings, and not to call him to testify publicly before June 15. To insure against leaks of Poindexter's private testimony, the Committees agreed that only three attorneys and a court reporter would be present and that the notes of the private session would not be transcribed or removed from a Committee vault before June 15. The attorneys who questioned Poindexter privately would not disclose his answers to Committee members or others before June 15 except under "certain extraordinary circumstances"—that is, if he provided evidence of an impeachable offense. Independent Counsel agreed in return not to seek a 20-day deferral of Poindexter's immunity grant.

Final Report of the Independent Counsel for Iran/Contra Matters, Vol. I, Investigations and Prosecutions, at 33 n.21 (1993).

Careful readers of the Final Report excerpt above will note that, in addition to the extraordinary provision for evidence of an impeachable offense, the summary is remarkable for what it does not contain—any mention of procedures governing private testimony sessions with Oliver North. The reason for this is that North and his counsel took a "hard line" with the committees and refused to make North available for either private or public testimony:

> Given Lt. Col. Oliver L. North's Fifth Amendment objections when subpoenaed, the only way to obtain his testimony was to compel it through a grant of use immunity. The Committees' decision to grant him use immunity was not an easy one. Because North was a principal target of the criminal investigation, the Independent Counsel strenuously urged the Committees to forego [sic] any grant of immunity to North. At the same time, it was clear that the Committees' failure to obtain North's testimony would leave the record incomplete.
>
> After weighing the need for North's testimony against the arguments of the Independent Counsel, the Committees decided to strike a balance.... [See the summary above of the agreement between the Committees and the Independent Counsel.]
>
> On June 15, 1987, the U.S. District Court for the District of Columbia issued an immunity order compelling North to testify. Thereupon, the Committees again subpoenaed North to testify and produce documents. North, through counsel, vigorously objected and argued that, despite the immunity orders, he would be severely prejudiced in his defense of any subsequent criminal charges were he required to testify unconditionally in private and public sessions. North's counsel maintained that compelling North's testimony at such a late stage deprived North of the full benefits of use immunity and thus unfairly stripped him of a criminal defendant's most important right—to remain silent.
>
> North's counsel demanded, *inter alia*, that the Committees agree to limit North's testimony to a maximum of 3 days and not to recall him under any circumstances. He demanded also that the Committees agree not to require North to produce documents until immediately prior to his appearance for testimony. If such demands were not met, North's counsel informed the Committees that he would advise his client to disobey the subpoenas and defend against criminal contempt charges.
>
> The Committees were thus confronted with another difficult decision. Criminal contempt proceedings could take years to complete and, even if successful, would not necessarily result in obtaining North's testimony. The penalty for criminal contempt is imprisonment, not compulsion of the recalcitrant witness' testimony. Although civil contempt proceedings do coerce testimony from the witness, serious statutory questions arose as to whether the Committees could successfully mount civil contempt charges against North, given his status as a Government employee.* Although the Committees

---

* Title 28 U.S.C. §1324. [*Ed. Note: See the discussion of contempt remedies in Chapter 4.*]

firmly believed that North's legal arguments were without merit, it was not clear that the jury in a criminal contempt case would agree. Furthermore, certain of North's arguments were persuasive to the Committees as a matter of fundamental fairness to an individual facing likely criminal prosecution.

Accordingly, the Committees again struck a balance. The Committees decided to restrict North's private testimony, in advance of his public appearance, to a single session limited to the subject of the involvement and knowledge, if any, of the President regarding "the diversion." Also, the Committees reaffirmed their intention to try to complete North's testimony in 4 days and not to recall him for further testimony unless extraordinary developments created a compelling need therefore. It should be noted that the Committees had not recalled any witness prior to North's appearance, nor did they afterward. Robert McFarlane testified for a second time, following North's appearance, only at his own request. (The Committees declined to commit to limit North's testimony to 4 days. His public testimony actually continued for 6 days, and he was not recalled thereafter.) The Committee rejected all of North's other demands.

The Committees' decisions regarding North's testimony were made to accommodate the legitimate concerns expressed by his counsel without sacrificing the Committee's power or the integrity of the proceedings. As a result, North appeared in response to the committees' subpoenas, produced his notebooks and other relevant documents, and submitted to extensive questioning.

Report of the Congressional Committees Investigating the Iran-Contra Affairs, Appendix at 687–88 (November 1987).

With these tripartite agreements in place among the Committees, the Independent Counsel, and North and his counsel, the stage was set for the most dramatic congressional testimony since Watergate.

B. The Oliver North Phenomenon

The legal issues presented by the Iran-Contra Affair and the prosecutions of Oliver North and John Poindexter cannot be fully understood without an appreciation of the dramatic and unprecedented public impact of Oliver North's congressional testimony. In the summer of 1987, North delivered an Oscar-worthy testimonial performance and surpassed John Dean's summer 1973 Watergate testimony to become history's most celebrated congressional investigation witness. Historian David Thelen described the Iran-Contra hearings and the impact of North's congressional testimony in these dramatic terms:

From the opening gavel on May 5 to the closing one on August 3, millions of Americans drew large parts of the hearings into their lives that summer. When General Secord testified on the first afternoon, 37 percent of Americans told pollsters that they watched the hearings, and the three commercial networks reported that 11.7 million television sets were switched to the hearings. By the second day the Cable News Network (CNN) reported a 70 percent increase in its audiences over those for the programs the hearings replaced. Within weeks CNN announced that the hearings attracted audiences that were three times larger than those for its regular programs. By the climax of the hearings, when the three commercial networks returned to televise Oliver North's July testimony, the audience reached 55 million viewers, roughly five times that for the most popular daytime television program, "General Hospital." More than seven of every ten Americans watched and told pollsters that they were "somewhat" or "very" interested in the hearings.

* * *

By the time North left the stand on July 14, viewers had transformed the hearings into a popular debate on the meaning of patriotism and heroism. Viewers reached for phones, for paper, for cards, to encourage, to chastise, to advise legislators. The volume of calls, letters, and telegrams from citizens to legislators exploded in July. One Democratic senator received 4,000 calls over a three-day period at his Washington and constituency offices, and his Capitol Hill receptionist described the volume as "the worst in my seven years here." Receptionists for Jim Courter answered over 200 calls on a single day of North's appearance, and those for Jack Brooks counted 392 calls on a single day. On one day, July 10, staff answering Senate Select Committee telephones logged 1,409 calls before they staggered home for the night. Over the course of the hearings the number of incoming letters and telegrams ranged from the 3,000 delivered to reticent Congressman William Broomfield (R-Mich.) to the 16,000 to outspoken Jack Brooks. Among senators, 8,200 pieces of mail were delivered to William Cohen, 10,000 to David Boren (D-Okla.), and 11,000 to Paul Sarbanes. By July 27, about a week before adjournment of the hearings, George Mitchell had received 7,207 letters and telegrams and 2,623 phone calls related to the hearings. By the time of its adjournment in early August the Senate Select Committee had received—in addition to letters to individual legislators—49,500 letters, 28,000 telegrams, and enough telephone calls to bring the combined total to well over 100,000 communications. The House Select Committee received at least the same volume.

The half-million letters, telegrams, and phone calls that Americans sent to the committeemen over three months in the summer of 1987 together represented perhaps the largest spontaneous popular response to a congressional activity in American legislative history. Among them, Jack Brooks, Lee Hamilton, and Louis Stokes had represented the Texas Gulf Coast, the hilly countryside of southeastern Indiana, and the heart of Cleveland for three-quarters of a century. They had risen to positions of great prestige and visibility within the House of Representatives. And they all agreed with Stokes that the letters and phone calls they received on the Iran-Contra hearings constituted "the greatest public outpouring" they had seen in their careers. The same popular response overwhelmed Republican legislators; an aide to Jim Courter called the magnitude "unprecedented."

DAVID THELEN, BECOMING CITIZENS IN THE AGE OF TELEVISION 18–19 (Univ. of Chicago Press 1996).

North's testimony was a masterwork of public-opinion management through the use of television. He appeared in full Marine Corps military uniform, even though his duties at the National Security Council were bureaucratic, not military, and he had not worn his Marine Corps uniform at work. During his six days of televised public testimony, North proceeded to turn the tables on his congressional interrogators and inspire massive public support for his actions and the causes he espoused, all while he and his aggressive counsel, Brendan V. Sullivan, Jr., protested that his rights were being abridged by forcing him to testify. Ironically, as discussed in more detail below, this same compelled testimony ultimately saved North from criminal convictions arising out of his conduct in the Iran-Contra Affair.

The testimony excerpts that are set out below are intended to provide some of the flavor and tone of North's historic performance. The initial questioning of North was by House of Representatives Chief Counsel John W. Nields, Jr., after which Senate Chief Counsel Arthur L. Liman questioned North, and then individual members of the House and Senate committees were provided a limited time to question North. Liman has described how from the very outset North's testimony did not go as the congressional committees and their counsels had planned:

> Oliver North.
>
> I share responsibility for making him into a national hero. In retrospect, I think it was almost inevitable. North, boyishly handsome and photogenic, sat in his Marine uniform with his medals at a simple table, alone with his lawyer. Arrayed against him, on an elevated two-tier platform, sat eleven Senators and fifteen members of the House committee, plus all their aides and staff. Steven Spielberg later told me that North was televised at the hero's angle, looking up as though from a pit at the committees, who resembled two rows of judges at the Spanish Inquisition. Spielberg called that the villain's angle. Unfortunately, the committees had built the platform without any advice from a movie director.

* * *

> With North, as with all other witnesses, Nields and I divided the questioning. Nields's questions, like a direct examination at trial, were designed to bring out North's basic story, including his lying to Congress, his shredding of documents, his creating the Enterprise, the diversion, and his accepting the role of fall guy. I, in turn, would examine North about allegations that he had misappropriated money from the Enterprise for personal use.

* * *

I had rarely, if ever, seen a cooperating witness in a criminal case who admitted more than North did. But there was one salient difference. Even when making these admissions, North acted like a hostile witness. He was combative even when agreeing with Nields's questions, and he made all his illegal acts—the lying to Congress, the diversion, the formation of the Enterprise, the cover-up—seem logical and patriotic.

Somehow, it got to John Nields, some realization perhaps that whatever crimes he'd committed, North was nevertheless emerging a national hero. Normally a mild and gentle examiner, Nields became unexpectedly and unnecessarily acrimonious. Before the eyes of the nation, an old conflict was reprised, the Vietnam veterans against the protesters—North, with his crew cut, pressed uniform, and upright military bearing, Nields with his long hair—and with it an old national perception, born out of the frustration of those years, that, even if the war had been wrong, somehow the protesters had been wrong too.

The longer the examination went on, the angrier Nields grew. And then, suddenly, he started questioning North about possible misappropriations of money—the very matters we'd agreed I would cover.

I don't know at what moment Nields decided to do this, but the tactic backfired. North managed to deflect Nields's angry allegations. In a bravura performance, North, the can-do Marine, became the victim of Nields—an unlikely switch but one that took place right before the cameras—and the result was the overshadowing of all that Nields had accomplished in bringing out North's story by a series of essentially petty matters. In response to Nields's probing, North testified that he'd built the security fence to protect his family against a terrorist threat, and that Calero's traveler's checks had merely reimbursed him for money laid out of his own pocket for the Contras.

Essentially a spectator to Nields's examination, I also got my first glimpse of how the networks were covering it. At least one of the network anchormen kept describing the hearing like a sporting event—and clearly he had North ahead on points. It didn't seem to make a particle of difference to him—supposedly a seasoned observer of the political scene—that North was describing a deliberate and systematic operation to subvert the Constitution. The anchorman couldn't have cared less.

But not even the television coverage prepared me—or any of us—for the extraordinary public response. A veritable tidal wave of telegrams poured in to the committee members in support of North. We had no idea, at the time, that Western Union was offering a discount rate for a stock telegram supporting North, while telegrams supporting the committees were transmitted at regular rates, but at the same time North's supporters were flooding the telephone lines of the members of the committee with calls. When I questioned North myself, I received thousands of threatening letters, including a number of ugly anti-Semitic ones, and for several days, Inouye and I had to be given special police protection.

ARTHUR L. LIMAN, LAWYER: A LIFE OF LAW AND CONTROVERSY 336–339 (Public Affairs 1998). As you read the excerpts of North's testimony reproduced below, bear in mind the identity, role, and political party affiliation of the different interrogators and note how North adeptly and skillfully tailored his responses to each questioner.

C. Oliver North's Congressional Testimony

Joint Hearings on the Iran-Contra Investigation, Testimony of Oliver L. North

Tuesday, July 7, 1987

SENATE SELECT COMMITTEE ON SECRET MILITARY
ASSISTANCE TO IRAN AND THE NICARAGUAN OPPOSITION
AND
HOUSE SELECT COMMITTEE TO INVESTIGATE
COVERT ARMS TRANSACTIONS WITH IRAN

Washington, D.C.

The Select Committees met, pursuant to call, at 9:00 a.m., in room 325, Russell Senate Office Building, Hon. Daniel K. Inouye (chairman of the Senate Select Committee) and Hon. Lee H. Hamilton (chairman of the House Select Committee) presiding.

CHAIRMAN INOUYE. The hearing will please come to order.

* * * *

Colonel North, please rise.

[Witness sworn.]

TESTIMONY OF LT. COL. OLIVER L. NORTH: QUESTIONING BY COUNSELS

CHAIRMAN INOUYE. Please be seated.

Last evening, at 9:30, the committee received a letter from the counsel to Lt. Col. Oliver L. North, and I wish to read this letter. It is addressed to the chair and to Mr. Liman.

"Dear Chairman Inouye: Lt. Col. North would like to give an opening statement in the event he testifies tomorrow morning. We request that Rule 5.3 be waived, and that as an immunized witness, he be permitted to make the statement. In view of the extraordinary vilification and the many comments by committee members regarding Lt. Col. North's conduct and his credibility, fairness warrants a waiver of the rule.

"We have not been able to review the massive quantities of documents which you provided to us under severe restrictions over the course of the last six days. Moreover, we were advised this afternoon that 7 hours of tape recordings were located today as a result of our persistent requests. We simply do not have the time to review that information and large quantities of other material prior to the scheduled start of testimony on July 7th, 1987, at 9:00 a.m.

"As you know, there are many documents and slides which we have requested but which have not been forthcoming. These factors have severely hampered Lt. Col. North's preparation for interrogation by numerous counsel and 26 members of the committee.

"We appreciate your cooperation.

"Respectfully yours, Brendan V. Sullivan, Jr."

I think the record should show that the July 7th hearing date was at the request of Colonel North and his counsel. I am certain the record will also show that we had suggested a later date at or about the middle of this month. But bowing to the wishes of the witness and his counsel, we did reluctantly agree to the July 7th opening. Therefore, I would hope that counsel will keep in mind that if he is having troubles, it is not because of our doing.

Secondly, as to the opening statement, I wish to read the pertinent parts of the rule. I am certain that counsel and witness have studied the hearing rules very carefully and I am certain they know what they stand for.

Five point three says the following: "Any witness desiring to make an introductory statement shall file 20 copies of the statement with the chairman or chief clerk 48 hours in advance of the appearance." The opening statement was filed with this committee 45 minutes ago.

"Unless the chairman determines that there is good cause for a witness's failure to do so, a witness may be required to summarize a prepared statement if it exceeds 10 minutes. Unless the committee determines otherwise, a witness who appears before the committee under a grant of immunity shall not be permitted to make a statement or testify except to respond directly to questions posed by committee members or committee staff."

We have been here sitting for several weeks and we will continue to do so to receive testimony and consider one thing above others: the rule of law. Here, once again, the witness is asking us to bend the law and to suggest that he may be above the law.

We will abide with his wishes; however, we will insist upon following the rule of law, and if the colonel wishes to make the opening statement, he may do so Thursday morning, which is 48 hours from this date.

Mr. Nields, please proceed.

MR. SULLIVAN. Mr. Chairman?

CHAIRMAN INOUYE. Yes, sir.

MR. SULLIVAN. Thank you, sir, for reading my letter that was delivered to you yesterday.

In fairness, I think that the committee should be aware of some very important facts. In order to prepare for Colonel North's testimony, we wrote a letter to this committee, to you and to counsel, on March 19, 1987, many months ago. At that time, Mr. Chairman, we specifically requested that the committee make records available to us in order for Colonel North to testify fully and accurately before this committee about his five years of service to the country. That letter specifically requested that we be provided with all of his documents.

Let me read the short letter, please, addressed to you, sir, and to Mr. Hamilton, in care of your counsel, and to Mr. Culvahouse at the White House.

"Gentlemen: In the event Lt. Col. North is called to testify about the subject matter under investigation by the Congress, it will be necessary for him to have prior access to the voluminous documentation and other materials which we believe are in your custody and control. A witness cannot be expected to accurately recall all of the facts related to years of intensive work as a government official without having access to those materials. We request that you provide us with all of the relevant materials well in advance to facilitate complete and accurate testimony."

That letter was delivered to the committee and we heard nothing for months.

The next significant event, Mr. Chairman, is that on June 30, 1987, just 7 days ago, we were provided with Colonel North's records under the most unusual circumstances. They were delivered to us in five boxes. They were shuffled by date and subject matter so that one could not even begin to understand what those records said, much less read them all. And I say to you that this is the first time in my career I have ever had to appear with a client in circumstances in which I have not been able to read all the records.

On June 30, when those records were delivered, we were so stunned by the volume of them and the lateness of their arrival that we actually tried to humor ourselves a little bit by piling the documents end on end and taking a photograph of them so we could demonstrate how serious our problem was. The documents piled together exceed the height of Colonel North and cannot possibly be read, studied in a week.

Sir, I assure you, and I think you know, that we have worked very hard with you and with counsel to facilitate the important work of this committee, while giving proper deference to the rights of one citizen. I don't come up here to the Congress. My life is spent a few blocks away in the courthouse where we as defense lawyers focus on individual rights.

We are not asking that the law be bended. We are not suggesting that Colonel North is above the law. We are simply requesting that you understand the needs of this particular citizen. This is the most extraordinary proceeding I think, Mr. Chairman, in our 200 years.

As a defense lawyer, I have never been in a position where a client is forced to testify about all matters which are the subject of a pending indictment. We believe he has an absolute right not to testify under the fifth amendment.

The committee has worked hand in glove with the independent counsel in order to facilitate two things: One, so you can get your factual account; and, secondly, to defeat—to defeat—the benefits of the immunity statute.

CHAIRMAN INOUYE. May I request that the counsel cut his statement a bit shorter?

MR. SULLIVAN. Yes, sir.

CHAIRMAN INOUYE. Under our rules, it is your responsibility to advise our witness, your client, not to advise the committee.

MR. SULLIVAN. Yes, sir. I appreciate that, and I will conclude.

Let me just say that the thing that bothers counsel the most, and no doubt you all understand that my duty is to focus on the rights of Colonel North. The thing that bothers me the most is to have listened over the last many weeks when snippets of evidence have been introduced in the hearings, when false conclusions have been drawn, when members of this committee have said on national television that Colonel North is guilty, when members of this committee ridicule his assertion of his constitutional rights, when members of the committee suggest that when he appears, Mr. Chairman, he will not tell the truth. That is what some members have said.

And in the most astounding circumstance, even one member asks a witness whether—whether he would be believed if he took the stand—

CHAIRMAN INOUYE. May I advise counsel the witness will have ample opportunity to speak his mind, sir.

MR. SULLIVAN. Yes, sir. I understand. I just ask for reconsideration, Mr. Chairman. It is very important for the rights of this individual, that he—

CHAIRMAN INOUYE. We will make certain, sir, that every right that the witness has under the Constitution of the United States will be reserved for him.

May I also comment on what you have just said, sir? In your March letter, you indicated that in the event your client should decide to become a witness, those are important words. We had no idea and the Nation had no idea whether Colonel North was going to testify before this committee; and, in fact, a week ago, it was your proposal that we exchange documents simultaneously, 5 days before this date, and we acceded to your wishes, sir. I am certain you recall that.

And, secondly, if I may remind you again, sir, this date, July 7, was at your recommendation. We strongly suggested to you that it would be in the best interests of your client and also in the best interests of the proceedings to begin the interrogation at a later date.

We also strongly suggested that it would be in the best interests of your client, and the best interests of these proceedings, if we had the opportunity to meet with your client for interrogation, deposition, and interviews before this public hearing.

But it was your suggestion that we should limit these executive meetings and we should begin on this date.

Therefore, Mr. Nields, please proceed.

MR. SULLIVAN. Mr. Chairman, just one more thought, if I may, sir? The reference in the letter—

CHAIRMAN INOUYE. Mr. Nields?

MR. SULLIVAN. Mr. Chairman, could I make one more objection to the proceeding, just for the record, please?

CHAIRMAN INOUYE. Please state it.

MR. SULLIVAN. It is my request that the committee withdraw the subpoenas to Colonel North in view of the fact that we believe that the immunity statute as applied in this circumstance is unconstitutional in view of the many statements made by various members of the committee already indicating that Colonel North is guilty of some crime.

We believe that his rights are adversely affected and we request that you put congressional prerogatives secondary to the rights of this particular citizen.

Thank you, sir.

CHAIRMAN INOUYE. Your objection has been noted and overruled. Mr. Nields.

MR. SULLIVAN. Could I ask one more question, please, sir, and I will be brief. I apologize. Just one more.

Since the committee refuses to permit Colonel North to give an opening statement—

CHAIRMAN INOUYE. We have not refused. He may do so Thursday morning.

MR. SULLIVAN. I understand. Would it be—

CHAIRMAN INOUYE. Pursuant to our rules, he may do so Thursday morning.

MR. SULLIVAN. Would you consider, sir, permitting him to give his opening statement during the lunch break today, utilizing this room after the committee adjourns?

CHAIRMAN INOUYE. You may not, sir.

Mr. Nields?

MR. NIELDS. Colonel North, were you involved in the use of the proceeds of sales of weapons to Iran for the purpose of assisting the Contras in Nicaragua?

MR. NORTH. Counsel, on advice of counsel, I respectfully decline to answer the question, based on my constitutional fifth amendment rights.

CHAIRMAN INOUYE. Colonel North, you are appearing here today pursuant to subpoenas issued on behalf of the Senate and House Select Committees. I hereby communicate to you orders issued by the U.S. District Court for the District of Columbia at the request of the committees, providing that you may not refuse to provide any evidence to these committees on the basis of your privilege against self-incrimination, and providing further that no evidence or other information obtained under the oath or any information directly or indirectly derived from such evidence may be used against you in any criminal proceeding.

I therefore, pursuant to such orders, direct you to answer the questions put to you.

CHAIRMAN HAMILTON. Colonel North, I communicate a similar order obtained by the House Select Committee which is also at the witness table, and I, too, direct you to answer the questions put to you.

MR. SULLIVAN. We understand that Colonel North is here pursuant to compulsion of subpoenas issued by both the House and the Senate; is that correct, sir?

CHAIRMAN INOUYE. You are correct, sir.

Mr. Nields, proceed.

MR. NIELDS. Colonel North, you were involved in two operations of this government of great significance to the people of this country; is that correct?

MR. NORTH. At least two, yes, sir.

MR. NIELDS. One of them involved the support of the Contras during the time the Boland Amendment was in effect and another one involved the sale of arms to Iran; is that correct?

MR. NORTH. Yes. And it also involved support for the Democratic outcome in Nicaragua, both before and after the Boland Amendment was in effect.

MR. NIELDS. And these operations were carried out in secret?

MR. NORTH. We hope so.

MR. NIELDS. They were covert operations?

MR. NORTH. Yes, they were.

MR. NIELDS. And covert operations are designed to be secrets from our enemies?

MR. NORTH. That is correct.

MR. NIELDS. But these operations were designed to be secrets from the American people?

MR. NORTH. Mr. Nields, I am at a loss as to how we can announce it to the American people and not have the Soviets know about it. I am not trying to be flippant, but I just don't see how you can possibly do it.

MR. NIELDS. Well in fact, Colonel North, you believe that the Soviets were aware of our sale of arms to Iran, weren't you?

MR. NORTH. We came to a point in time when we were concerned about that.

MR. NIELDS. But it was designed to be kept a secret from the American people?

MR. NORTH. I think what is important, Mr. Nields, is that we somehow arrive at some kind of understanding right here and now as to what a covert operation is. I mean, if we could find a way to insulate with a bubble over these hearings that are being broadcast in Moscow, and talk about covert operations to the American people without it getting into the hands of our adversaries, I am sure we would do that. We haven't found a way to do it.

MR. NIELDS. But you put it somewhat differently to the Iranians with whom you were negotiating on the 8th and 9th of October in Frankfurt, Germany, didn't you? You said to them that Secretary of Defense Weinberger in our last session with the President said, "I don't think we should send one more screw"—talking about the HAWK parts—"until we have our Americans back from Beirut because when the

American people find out that this has happened, they'll impeach you," referring to the President.

MR. SULLIVAN. Objection. Apparently counsel is reading from a transcript of a tape recording, Mr. Chairman, which Colonel North may have caused to be made. And we have not been provided with a copy of that material. I think it is inappropriate for questions to be asked of the colonel when counsel has a copy of the tape but we do not have it.

Thank you, sir.

MR. NIELDS. Colonel North does have a copy of it. It was sent—

CHAIRMAN INOUYE. Objection is overruled.

MR. NIELDS. It was sent to him over the weekend, and it is in a notebook in front of counsel.

MR. SULLIVAN. Fine. Thank you, Mr. Nields.

MR. NIELDS. Titled "Second Channel."

MR. SULLIVAN. As I walked in the door, 5 minutes after I was handed all these notebooks, which I am now looking at for the first time. Do you want to direct my attention to where it is, sir? Which book and what's in it.

MR. NIELDS. In a notebook titled "Second Channel Transcripts" at tab 5.

I believe it is the top notebook that you put your papers on top of.

MR. SULLIVAN. Tab 5, sir?

MR. NIELDS. Tab 5.

MR. SULLIVAN. What page, sir?

MR. NIELDS. It's right at tab 5, on that page.

MR. SULLIVAN. Would you give us a moment to read it, sir?

MR. NIELDS. Yes.

MR. SULLIVAN. Could you help us out, Mr. Nields? Do I begin reading right on tab 5 or the page behind it?

MR. NIELDS. Right on tab 5 and my question is simple. Did you tell the Iranians with whom you were negotiating on October 8 and 9 that the Secretary of Defense had told the President at his most recent meeting. "When the American people find out that this has happened, they will impeach you?"

That is the entire question. Did you say that to the Iranians?

MR. SULLIVAN. Does it say that on this page, sir?

MR. NIELDS. Yes. At the very top.

MR. NORTH. Mr. Nields, this is apparently one of the transcripts of tape recordings that I caused to be made of my discussions with the Iranians. I would like to note that for every conversation, whenever it was possible, I asked for the assistance of our intelligence services to trans—to tape record and transcribe every single session so that when I returned there would be no doubt as to what I said.

I am the one who created these tapes, plus the 7 hours of tape recordings that your committee found yesterday, because I knew where they were, and I kept trying to alert you to them, and I am the one who created those tapes so there would never be any doubt in the minds of my superiors as to what I had said or why I had said it. That is a bald-faced lie told to the Iranians. And I will tell you right now, I'd have offered the Iranians a free trip to Disneyland if we could have gotten Americans home for it.

MR. NIELDS. The question was, did you say it?

MR. NORTH. I absolutely said it. I said a lot of other things to the Iranians. To get our hostages home.

MR. NIELDS. And when the Hasenfus plane went down in Nicaragua, the U.S. Government told the American people that the U.S. Government had no connection whatsoever with that airplane.

Is that also true?

MR. NORTH. When the Hasenfus airplane went down, I was in the air headed for Europe, so I do not know what the initial statements were and I couldn't comment on them.

MR. SULLIVAN. Who in the Government and when, sir? Are you asking him generally did someone in the Government make a statement?

MR. NIELDS. We have had testimony—that Elliott Abrams—

CHAIRMAN INOUYE. Address the chair if you have any questions to ask.

MR. SULLIVAN. Yes, sir. I think that we would perhaps make more progress if he asked what the colonel did, what he said, what he heard with respect to his actions.

A statement indicating that what someone in the American Government had said seems to me to be a little far afield, sir. That is my only comment.

CHAIRMAN INOUYE. Mr. Nields, proceed.

MR. NIELDS. That was not true, was it, Colonel North?

MR. NORTH. Which was not true, Mr. Nields?

MR. NIELDS. It is not true the U.S. Government had no connection with Mr. Hasenfus' airplane that went down in Nicaragua?

MR. NORTH. No, it was not true. I had an indirect connection with that flight, and many others I would point out.

MR. NIELDS. In certain Communist countries, the Government's activities are kept secret from the people, but that is not the way we do things in America, is it?

MR. NORTH. Counsel, I would like to go back to what I said just a few moments ago.

I think it is very important for the American people to understand that this is a dangerous world, that we live at risk, and that this Nation is at risk in a dangerous world.

And that they ought not be led to believe as a consequence of these hearings that this Nation cannot or should not conduct covert operations.

By their very nature, covert operations or special activities, are a lie. There is great deceit—deception practiced in the conduct of covert operations.

They are at essence a lie.

We make every effort to deceive the enemy as to our intent, our conduct, and to deny the association of the United States with those activities.

The intelligence committees hold hearings on all kinds of these activities conducted by our intelligence services. The American people ought not to be led to believe by the way you are asking that question that we intentionally deceived the American people or had that intent to begin with.

The effort to conduct these covert operations was made in such a way that our adversaries would not have knowledge of them, or that we could deny American association with them, or the association of this Government with those activities.

And that is not wrong.

MR. NIELDS. The American people were told by this Government that our Government had nothing to do with the Hasenfus airplane, and that was false, and it is a principal purpose of these hearings to replace secrecy and deception with disclosure and truth, and that is one of the reasons we have called you here, sir.

And one question the American people would like to know the answer to is what did the President know about the diversion of the proceeds of Iranian arms sales to the Contras.

Can you tell us what you know about that, sir?

MR. NORTH. You just took a long leap from Mr. Hasenfus' airplane.

As I told this committee several days ago, and if you will indulge me, counsel, in a brief summary of what I said, I never personally discussed the use of the residuals or profits from the sale of United States weapons to Iran for the purpose of supporting the Nicaraguan Resistance with the President.

I never raised it with him and he never raised it with me during my entire tenure at the National Security Council staff. Throughout the conduct of my entire tenure at the National Security Council, I assumed that the President was aware of what I was doing and had, through my superiors, approved it.

I sought approval of my superiors for every one of my actions, and it is well documented.

I assumed when I had approval to proceed from either Judge Clark, Bud McFarlane, or Admiral Poindexter, that they had, indeed, solicited and obtained the approval of the President.

To my recollection, Admiral Poindexter never told me that he met with the President on the issue of using residuals from the Iranian sales to support the Nicaraguan

Resistance. Or that he discussed the residuals or profits for use by the Contras with the President, or that he got the President's specific approval, nor did he tell me that the President had approved such a transaction.

But again, I wish to reiterate that throughout, I believed that the President had indeed authorized such activity. No other person with whom I was in contact during my tenure at the White House told me that he or she ever discussed the issue of the residuals or profits with the President.

In late November, two other things occurred which relate to this issue.

On or about Friday, November 21, I asked Admiral Poindexter directly, "Does the President know?" He told me he did not.

And on November 25, the day I was reassigned back to the U.S. Marine Corps for service, the President of the United States called me. In the course of that call, the President said to me, words to the effect that, "I just didn't know."

Those are the facts as I know them, Mr. Nields. I was glad that when you introduced this, you said that you wanted to hear the truth. I came here to tell you the truth, the good, the bad, and the ugly.

I am here to tell it all—pleasant and unpleasant, and I am here to accept responsibility for that which I did.

I will not accept responsibility for that which I did not do.

CHAIRMAN INOUYE. Before proceeding, may I make an inquiry of the witness.

Was that response from a written text?

MR. NORTH. Those are from notes that I made in preparation for this session, sir.

CHAIRMAN INOUYE. It is not a verbatim written text?

MR. NORTH. No, sir, it is not.

CHAIRMAN INOUYE. Mr. Nields.

MR. NIELDS. Colonel North, you left something out, didn't you?

MR. SULLIVAN. What is it, counsel?

MR. NIELDS. You have testified that you assumed that the President had authorized the diversion. Lieutenant colonels in the Marine Corps do not divert millions of dollars from arms sales to Iran for the benefit of the Contras based on assumptions, do they?

You had a basis for your assumption.

MR. NORTH. I had the approval of my superiors as I did for all other things that I did, Mr. Nields.

* * *

MR. NIELDS. I would like to return to the HAWK transaction.

Sometime in mid-November of 1986, were you asked to prepare summaries of the U.S. Government's involvement in arms sales to Iran?

MR. NORTH. My recollection, Mr. Nields, is that I was asked shortly after the revelations in *Al Shiraa* and then subsequent pickup by [*sic*] that by the American media, to prepare a chronology of the facts. And my recollection is that the very first of those was prepared during a rather frantic period of time during the first week or so of November and that my first effort at that was probably about the 7th of November.

And it was simply an effort to factually recount what had happened.

I think there are two things, if I may just explain something to you, to explain some of the bewilderment you may be seeing not only in me, but in perhaps other witnesses who worked at the NSC.

We all sincerely believed that when we sent a PROF message [*Ed. Note: The "PROF" system was the early form of email used by North and Poindexter at the National Security Council; see discussion at Note 1.B, below*] to another party and punched the button "delete," that it was gone forever.

Wow, were we wrong.

And you have before you now recollections of facts or collections of facts as they were communicated back and forth to one another, for example, in November of 1985 or December of 1985, that we did not have at our disposal in November of 1986.

MR. NIELDS. You are saying that when you pushed the delete button on a PROF message, you thought it was gone from the system forever?

MR. NORTH. That is correct.

MR. NIELDS. Are you also saying that if it was gone from the system, that you could pretend it never happened?

MR. NORTH. That is not what I said, counsel.

What I was trying to explain to you is perhaps one of the reasons why some people seem to be confused about events a year earlier. OK?

When they didn't have much of what transpired in terms of authorities and descriptions and facts in 1985, they didn't have in their files anymore. Those weren't retrieved until after the Tower Commission found a way to pull them all back up.

MR. NIELDS. When you pushed the delete button on the PROF system, it didn't erase your memory, did it, sir?

MR. NORTH. No.

MR. NIELDS. And you recall, do you not, being intimately involved in the shipment of 18 HAWKs to Iran in November of 1985?

MR. NORTH. I was indeed intimately involved in the shipment of HAWKs to Iran in 1985.

MR. NIELDS. And that wasn't erased from your memory when you erased, pushed the delete button on the PROF message?

MR. NORTH. Not at all.

* * *

[MORNING SESSION, July 8, 1987]

MR. NIELDS: And you already knew then that [Iranian arms dealer Manucher] Ghorbanifar was willing to pay $10,000 per TOW [a kind of anti-tank missile]?

MR. NORTH: No. What I knew then was Ghorbanifar was willing to get $10,000 per TOW. I, to this day, don't know—first of all, in the September transactions, we were never able to determine that I can recall whether or not Mr. Ghorbanifar ever paid a penny for the TOW's that were shipped from Israel. And what we did know is that Mr. Ghorbanifar was willing to receive at least $10,000. I was subsequently told that Mr. Ghorbanifar had actually gotten thirteen or thirteen-and-a-half thousand, $13,500, maybe $14,000 apiece from the Iranians. When we opened the second channel and did a transaction with the second channel, Mr. [Amiram] Nir [an Israeli diplomat] was extraordinarily upset that we weren't charging the same "high price."

Now, in fairness to Mr. Nir, Mr. Nir very clearly wanted to support other activities as he put it, through these transactions. There were a number of proposals made. Some of those are referenced in the files that I gave you. I believe that those are very, very sensitive documents. And, as I said yesterday, I would have believed that executive privilege should have prevented those documents [from being] turned over, and certainly not disclosed to the world—because those operations can affect the lives of Americans. But those were proposals that Mr. Nir had, and that some of the residuals would be used to fund those operations. And I sought approval from my superiors for those operations. I discussed those operations directly with [CIA] Director [William] Casey, and there were various code names as you saw—TA-1, TH-1, et cetera—in my documents referred to, as Mr. Nir defined them.

Incidentally, just one last point, if you'll indulge me. I realize that people snicker when they refer to the code sheet. The reason we were using the code sheet was not some joke or some childish code from Captain Midnight. We were talking on open telephone lines. And I will tell you right now that, were it not for that code and the fact that we were able to talk over open telephone lines, we might not have been able to capture the terrorists who sea-jacked the Achille Lauro and killed Leon Klinghoffer.

MR. NIELDS: I think the only question has to do with price.

MR. NORTH: I know it has to do with price.

MR. NIELDS: I think the only question has to do with price.

MR. SULLIVAN: Mr. Nields, Mr. Chairman, if the witness believes that something is related to the subject matter of the question he should be permitted to answer.

CHAIRMAN INOUYE: The question related to price and I hope that the witness will respond to the question.

MR. NORTH: Mr. Chairman, I tried to respond to the question of price.

CHAIRMAN INOUYE: We have been—

MR. NORTH: The way the question was asked, Mr. Chairman, was, who authorized $17 million etc. to go to that account? And I'm saying that what I was authorized to do was to allow that account to be used to further these transactions and the purposes to which the residuals generated by those transactions would be used, and I sought approval for that and I was granted approval for that.

CHAIRMAN INOUYE: And we permitted you over 10 minutes to make that explanation. The question now is price, please respond to that.

[Ed. Note: North's counsel charges that North is the victim of a "stall job."]

MR. SULLIVAN: Mr. Chairman, I object to that. Colonel North is attempting to do the very best he can. And I want to state to the Chairman, and I should put it on the record right now, that I believe that we're being subjected to a stall job. We met with you, Mr. Chairman—

CHAIRMAN INOUYE: Who is responsible for the stall, sir?

MR. SULLIVAN: Counsel. Let me, let me clarify one thing, sir, please. When you and I, and Senator Rudman, and Mr. Hamilton sat across the table and tried to arrive at a solution in which we balanced the interests of Colonel North and weighed his constitutional rights against the Committee's need to obtain the facts, we left that meeting and those negotiations relying upon the intention—not promise—the intention of the Committee to resolve its questioning of Colonel North within four days. A letter was sent to me by Counsel after that meeting saying that you intended to conclude these—the question by July 10th.

Over the last day and several hours, I must say that the rambling questions and the inability to finish the subject matter and proceed to another has caused me concern. When Colonel North wants to give an answer which seems to tell the story, he's cut off, and Mr. Nields keeps saying to him, "Well, we'll get back to that, we'll get back to that." I'd suggest that if you give Colonel the opportunity to tell the story, he can tell the story.

I was disheartened last night, Mr. Chairman, when I saw on the national news, two Senators make reference to the fact that these hearings were likely to go into next week. I don't know why they should go into next week. The intention of the Committee was that there be four days; that there be 30 questioners. I don't know what's happened, and I don't want to prejudge the Committee, as some members of the Committee have prejudged Colonel North, but I suspect, sir, that what's happening here is we're meandering through questions in a disjointed fashion so that when it comes Friday, you can say, Mr. Chairman, that it's necessary to continue on Monday, or perhaps Tuesday.

You know, as a trial lawyer I know a stall when I see one. There's never been a lawyer that tried a case that didn't know that stalling and putting a weekend in between a witness' testimony so you can dissect his examination and ask further questions on Monday is not a good tactic. So I would request, Mr. Chairman, that if Colonel North is given the opportunity to answer the questions fully, as he believes—as he's trying to do, I would suggest that we'd make a great deal of progress and that the Committee would be able to fulfill its promise to us—its stated intentions that we finish this matter on Friday, and we're doing our best to do that.

And I might add, that we're willing, if the Committee is willing, to sit a longer day. For example yesterday, with a two hour lunch, and concluding at 5:00, those kinds of shortened schedules are likely to lead us into next week. So we earnestly request and respectfully request—and I hope the Committee hasn't changed its intention despite the statement of a couple of Senators last night—our goal here is to finish this by the close of business Friday, and I know Colonel North is trying his hardest to do that, and I'm trying to do so as well. Thank you, sir.

SENATOR GEORGE MITCHELL: (D-Me): Mr. Chairman?

CHAIRMAN INOUYE: May the record show that it took four and a half minutes to explain the stall.

(Laughter)

Senator Mitchell.

MR. SULLIVAN: Mr. Chairman, I thought that if I did lay out, clearly and respectfully to you, what my concern was that perhaps it would facilitate speeding up instead of trying to drag this proceeding into next week, and submit Col. North to the incessant questioning of 30 people. Thank you, sir.

SEN. MITCHELL: Mr. Chairman, may I be recognized?

CHAIRMAN INOUYE: Yes, sir.

SEN. MITCHELL: Mr. Chairman, I was present at the meeting to which Mr. Sullivan referred, and I believe the record should show that at that meeting I stated to Mr. Sullivan that in my judgment his two requests, one that there be no prior private testimony, and second, that the testimony in public be limited to 30 hours, were inconsistent and incompatible, and that the inevitable effect of not having prior private testimony would be to make the public testimony much longer than would otherwise be the case. And, that in my view, if he insisted in pursuing his demand for no prior private testimony, as he did, and as this Committee acceded to his demand, that inevitably Counsel would have to in public go over many areas that they would not have to do in private.

And, as you will recall, Mr. Chairman, and members of the Committee, it was at my insistence, anticipating that precisely this type of statement would be made at some point in the proceedings, but I insisted that the letter of intention include an explicit statement to the effect that this was not any binding commitment, and depending on the scope and nature of the testimony, and other facts and circumstances as they may arise, that the testimony might go beyond that.

Therefore, Mr. Chairman, I think the record should show that in my judgment, I believe the committee members should know this objection is wholly unfounded, without any merit, and I believe the Counsel should be permitted to question as he has, because he's not had the opportunity to question in private, and therefore he must cover these areas as thoroughly as he can.

MR. SULLIVAN: May I respond, Mr. Chairman?

CHAIRMAN INOUYE: I thank the senator from Maine, and may the record also show that as far as the Chair is concerned, Mr. Nields has been carrying on in a very orderly and professional manner.

MR. SULLIVAN: Mr.—may I respond briefly, Mr. Chairman, please?

CHAIRMAN INOUYE: Briefly, sir.

MR. SULLIVAN: Yes. This—Mr. Mitchell accurately describes the views that he presented at the meeting, and apparently those views were overruled, because I received a letter from Counsel, in paragraph 5, which says as follows: Quote, "The committees intend to complete Lt. Col. North's testimony by the close of the hearing on July 10th, 1987, and do not intend to recall Lt. Col. North for further testimony."

I'm leaving out some of the remaining words.

CHAIRMAN INOUYE: Read the whole paragraph in.

(Laughter)

MR. SULLIVAN: I'll be glad to. (Laughter) I'll be glad to. (Laughter continues.) I'd like to make this a part of the record. I left out the words because it's unrelated to this particular issue. I'll read it again. Quote: "The committees intend to complete Lt. Col. North's testimony by the close of the hearing on July 10th, 1987, and do not intend to recall Lt. Col. North for further testimony, unless (emphasizing) extraordinary developments create a compelling need therefore, and that any such recall"—not initial testimony, Mr. Mitchell—"recall would be limited to the matters that necessitated the recall."

My point is that in order to accommodate Lt. Col. North—

SEN. MITCHELL: Would you read the whole paragraph?

CHAIRMAN INOUYE: Read the whole paragraph.

MR. SULLIVAN: Yes, sir. Would you like to see it?

Mr. _____: Mr. Chairman—

MR. SULLIVAN: Let me make clear—this is—we were told—this is not a binding agreement. I don't want to mislead you. (Laughter) This is the intention, the stated, a stated intention of Mr. Hamilton and Chairman Inouye. We are relying on the stated intention to go forward. I find it a little disheartening, last night, to see two senators say that they're going to go into next week. Now what happened yesterday, that all of a sudden the intention is not able to be complied with? It's just an intention. We're asking that the intention that we relied upon be kept.

CHAIRMAN INOUYE: I believe you've had enough time. May I just, for the record, so that the record will be clear, read the rest of this paragraph?

"Although it is not now the intention of the Committee, the scope and nature of Lt. Col. North's testimony could result in his testimony continuing beyond four days, and in his later recall. Matters on which the Committees are not waiving their power, and we understand that you are not waiving any rights."

MR. SULLIVAN: Mr. Chairman, I ask that the whole letter be put into the record as an exhibit.

CHAIRMAN INOUYE: It is so ordered. And your objection is overruled.

* * *

[*Ed. Note: North testifies about funds that were used to pay for a security system at his home.*]

MR. NIELDS: Col. North, did you have any interest—personal interest I'm talking about, now—in any of the monies that flowed from the arms sales to Iran, or that were kept in Swiss accounts under Gen. Secord's control?

MR. NORTH: Not one penny.

MR. NIELDS: There has been testimony, as I'm sure you're aware, that a death benefit account was set up by Mr. Hakim with the name Button, for the benefit of your family in the event of your death. Were you aware of any such account?

MR. NORTH: No. Totally unaware of it. First I heard of it was through these hearings. I have never heard of it before and it was a shock. An absolute shock.

MR. NIELDS: There is a—a testamentary document which has been introduced in evidence, relating to a particular $2 million sub-account set up also by Mr. Hakim, which provides that in his death Gen. Secord can control the use of the funds and in the event of his death, you can control the use of the funds and it also contains a provision that if everybody dies, it will be distributed to their estates. Were you aware of such a document?

MR. NORTH: No. I never heard of it until these hearings started. I still don't believe it. I was shocked and I have absolutely no idea where that came from, whatsoever. Never heard of it before.

MR. NIELDS: And you never heard of the idea, either. I take it?

MR. NORTH: No. Ever. I—I do want to make one point clear. I did at one point express concern, after I would guess in February, March, April, somewhere, after I'd met Mr. Hakim, became aware what his role was in the financial network that had been established, I did at some point express concern to Gen. Secord, "Suppose both you guys go down on the same airplane, flitting back and forth to Europe or wherever you're going, what happens then?" And I was told, "Don't worry about it, arrangements will be made so that these operations can continue." But nobody ever told me that a single penny was set aside for my purposes, for my benefit, whatsoever. Ever. And I never heard of buttons or bellybuttons until these hearings began.

MR. NIELDS: I'd like to separate out, then, the two issues raised by this will or this testamentary document. You're indicating that the portion of it that provides for the monies being distributed to the estates of the individuals is a foreign notion to you.

MR. SULLIVAN: Excuse me, Mr. Chairman. Could we please have a copy of the document—

MR. NIELDS: It's Exhibit 169—

MR. SULLIVAN:—which the counsel's referring to?

MR. NIELDS: One-sixty-nine.

MR. SULLIVAN: Object to the term "will." Mr. Chairman, I believe the term has been used 50 times in these hearings, prior to today. This is not a will, and any lawyer in the room knows it's not a will. (Pause while Lt. Col. North studies the document.)

MR. NORTH: It's the first time I've ever seen this document, ever.

MR. NIELDS: Understood. You've said that. I just want to separate out the issues. There's a part of the document that provides for distribution to individuals' estates in event of death. It's on the second page. And I take it your testimony is that that concept—not only have you not seen the document, but that concept is foreign to you. You never heard of anything like it?

MR. NORTH: I never heard of it before. I don't know how much more clearly I can put it, Counsel. I never, ever heard that proposal before, that suggestion.

MR. NIELDS: There's a second part of the document that relates, simply, to control over the use of the funds; and that's on the first page of it, second paragraph. And I take it that, although you never saw the document, the concept that you would control disposition of the funds—I don't mean in your personal capacity, but in your governmental capacity, in the event of the death of Hakim and Secord—that's not foreign to you, is it?

MR. NORTH: Well I—I never professed to have control over a—over a single penny of this. I elicited the cooperation of General Secord. To my knowledge, he cooperated in every case with the things that we asked him to do. But I never, once, saw those words; nor do I want to leave you with the impression that this was what I had in mind when I said to them, "What happens if both you guys drop dead?" I was more than willing to have anybody else they wanted, so that we could continue the activities. But I didn't necessarily wish to become the person who had to fly back and forth to Switzerland. I've never ever been in a Swiss bank.

MR. NIELDS: There's been testimony that several thousand dollars was spent on a fence, security system that was put in at your residence, and that the monies to pay for it came from Gen. Secord. And my question to you is, were you aware—I take it there was a security system put in at your residence?

MR. NORTH: There is a security system in at my residence. It has since this April been sufficiently supplemented that it is now extraordinary.

MR. NIELDS: And I take it—were you aware that that security system was paid for by Gen. Secord?

MR. NORTH: I'm going to waffle an answer. I'm going to say yes-and-no. And if you'll indulge me, I will give you another one of my very straightforward, but rather lengthy, answers. The issue of the security system was first broached immediately after a threat on my life by Abu Nidal. Abu Nidal is, as I'm sure you and the intelligence committees know, the principal, foremost assassin in the world today. He is a brutal murderer.

When I was first alerted to that threat by the Federal Bureau of Investigation in late April, I was simply told that there was a threat that had been promulgated by Abu Bahar who is the press spokesman for the Fateh Revolutionary Council, which is the name of the Abu Nidal group. He targeted me for assassination. We then made an effort over the course of several days to have the story killed and not run in the US—not me, but the story, killed and not run on the US media. Nonetheless it ran, and I believe the date was the 28th of April. The initial assessment was that this was a response to the attack on Libya, which we had run a preemptive kind of terrorist raid on Libya on the 14th of April, [in] which I had a small role to play. CBS chose to run the film anyway. The FBI was then contacted again and told—asked—what protection can be offered. The FBI correctly said, "We don't offer protection." I then sought other types of protection.

I went to my superiors and said, "What can be done?" Contrary to what was said some days ago, this lieutenant-colonel was not offered at that time any protection by the government of the United States, Sen. Rudman. I asked for and I was told that the only thing that I could do is to immediately PCS—Permanent Change of Station. You and I, as Marines, know well what that means—jerked out of home and sent to Camp Lejune. In that I was preparing at the time to go to Teheran, and we didn't want to tell the whole world that, that was deemed not to be an appropriate thing to do. The next thing that we looked to try to do is to find a secure telephone to put in my home to justify the installation of a US security system. That, too, was impossible or not feasible or couldn't be done. The next thing I did was to ask for a list of who installs these things for the US government, maybe I can get a better price by calling them. I believe it was someone in the Secret Service gave me a list of three or four of these companies that do that kind of installation. I called two or three of them. It is now late April, early May, it's within days of this threat, and I called and I asked, can you come out and do a survey and give me an estimate. And in each case, I think it was two or three of them—and I was at that point relatively busy—I was told it would be several weeks before we can come out and do an estimate and a survey, and it will be several more weeks or months before we can complete the installation because, after all, summertime is our busy time.

At some point along in there, either General Secord raised with me or I raised with him this threat. And I told him I couldn't get US government protection, I couldn't find a contractor to come out and do it myself, and he said, "Don't worry about that. I've got a good friend"—or an "associate," I don't remember the words—"who's an expert. This guy has a company that does these things." And he shortly thereafter, I believe it was around the 5th of May, introduced me to Mr. Glenn Robinette. He was introduced to me as a man who, one, had been a former CIA—or perhaps, I understood at the time, FBI, I don't remember—technical expert, a man who owned a security company, and a man who could immediately go out and do a survey and an estimate. He did.

Over the course of the next few days, he went out to my home, I called my wife—or told my wife, whatever—that he'd be out. He went through the situation and he came up with an estimate of $8500 "max"—as I recall it was $8000 to $8500—and he could furthermore immediately install the system.

[Ed. Note: North issues a challenge to the terrorist Abu Nidal and testifies about threats to his family and his life.]

Now, I want you to know that I'd be more than willing—and if anybody else is watching overseas, and I'm sure they are—I'll be glad to meet Abu Nidal on equal terms anywhere in the world. Okay? There's an even deal for him. But I am not willing to have my wife and my four children meet Abu Nidal or his organization on his terms. And I want you to know what was going through my mind. I was about to leave for Teheran. I had already been told by Director Casey that I should be prepared to take my own life. I had already been told that the government of the United States, on an earlier proposal for a trip, might even disavow the fact that I had gone on the trip, on an earlier proposal, and we can come back to that at some time if you like. And so having been asked—having asked for some type of US government protection for my wife and children, and having been denied that—and perhaps for fully legitimate reasons. And if there is a law that prevents the protection of American government employees and their families from people like Abu Nidal, then gentlemen, please fix it, because this kid won't be around much longer, as I'm sure you know. But there will be others, if they take activist steps to address the problem of terrorism, who will be threatened. And I would like to just, if I may, just read to you a little bit about Mr. Abu Nidal, just so you know my mental state at the time. "Abu Nidal, the radical Palestinian guerilla leader linked to last Friday's attacks in Rome and Vienna,"—and that was the so-called "Christmas massacre"—"in which 19 people died and 200 were wounded, is the world's most wanted terrorist." That's the Christian Science Monitor. When you look at his whole career, Abu Nidal makes the infamous terrorist Carlos look like a Boy Scout.

Abu Nidal himself, quoted in Der Spiegel, "Between America and us, there exists a war to the death. In the coming months and years, Americans will be thinking about us." "For sheer viciousness, Abu Nidal has few rivals in the underworld of terrorism." Newsweek.

Our own State Department, and we have copies of these that we can make available for insertion into the record, but the State Department's summary on Abu Nidal, not exactly an overstatement, notes that his followers, who number an estimated 500, have killed as many as 181 persons, and wounded more than 200 in two years. Abu Nidal does not deny these things.

We also have an exhibit that we can provide for you that shows what Abu Nidal did in the Christmas massacres. One of the people killed in the Christmas massacre, and I do not wish to overdramatize this, but the Abu Nidal terrorist in Rome who blasted the 11-year old American Natasha Simpson to her knees, deliberately zeroed in and fired an extra burst at her head, just in case. Gentlemen, I have an 11-year old daughter, not perhaps a whole lot different than Natasha Simpson, and so, when Mr. Robinette told me, on or about the 10th of May, that he could immediately install a security system, I said, "Please try to keep it to the $8,000 to $8,500. I am, after all, a Marine Lieutenant Colonel, and I live on my salary." And, he installed that system.

Now, let me go to your next question because I know it's coming and deserves an answer. I never got a bill, and it is, after all—

MR. NIELDS: Wait. Before you go to the next—

MR. NORTH: It is, after all, the answer to your question. It is the answer to your question.

MR. NIELDS: I am—

MR. NORTH: You asked me where it came from, and I'm trying to tell you.

MR. NIELDS: I am going to ask you that question, but—

MR. NORTH: You've already asked me the question. You asked me whether or not the money came from General Secord.

MR. NIELDS: Correct.

MR. NORTH: And, I'm getting there.

MR. NIELDS: All right. Okay.

MR. NORTH: Okay? When that system was installed, it was practically—it was totally complete. It allowed, for example, that when my wife would trigger an alarm, an alarm would ring in the central station, and the Fairfax police would immediately be notified, and that arrangement was worked out with—this wasn't surreptitious. Fairfax police came out—you pays your taxes in Fairfax County, but you gets your money's worth—and by golly they came out, and they photographed the house, and they did the normal precautionary things to respond to the kind of terrorist alert that they had been briefed on by the FBI. And that's the best that they could do, and it was at that point, with the security system installed, it was adequate; that instantly, they would respond to one of those emergency alarms. And Mr. Robinette provided it.

Now, I then went on the trip to Teheran. I came back. I never got a bill. I didn't ask for a bill, and I never received one. I never asked, "Where's the bill?" until well after it was too late. And I'll cover that.

When I didn't get a bill, I basically understood what had happened. And I don't know exactly how it worked out, but I—I believe that an accommodation was worked between Mr. Robinette and Gen. Secord to make a gift out of that security system, that I did not pay for.

When I came to the end of my tenure at the NSC, it was, to say the least, a busy time. There were other things to be done besides shredding documents when I left. There was a lot of work to be done. And one of the things that I did was to sit and contemplate the previous five and a half years of my work. And I am proud of that work. I believe that we accomplished a lot.

But there was one thing that just didn't look right. And that was that for the first time in my life, I had accepted something that I hadn't paid for. And even though I honestly believe that the government of the United States should have paid for it, should have put it in, I then picked up the phone and asked for a bill. I got a bill. In fact, I got two of them. I didn't ask that they be back-dated; but after all, Mr. Robinette is an old hand in the CIA. (Laughter.)

All right. The bills came with the old original dates, and I think there was another bill with a later date on it. And then, as I told you yesterday, I was going to tell you the truth—the good, the bad, and the ugly. This is the truth. I did probably the grossest misjudgment that I have made in my life. I then tried to paper over that whole thing, by sending two phony documents back to Mr. Robinette. It was not an exercise in good judgment.

I don't believe I have any particular monopoly on bad judgment. I think it was a gross error in judgment for this Committee to put my home address upon the screen for the whole world to see, when I've got 20 security agents guarding my wife, my children, and me right now.

I'd also like to point out that it's not quite as bad as it originally seemed. This year, and these things kind of come in Aprils, I guess, but this April, the FBI called again. This April the FBI called and told me that there was another threat on my life. The big difference was, this year I was back with a band of brothers that has a long reputation for taking care of its own. And the United States Marine Corps and the Naval Intelligence—Naval Investigative Service of Naval Intelligence, got together and immediately put security on me and my home, where my wife and children are protected.

I can't tell you how grateful I am for that. The security system that was installed by Mr. Robinette with Gen. Secord's money, or the Enterprise's money or Mr. Hakim's money, or I don't know whose money, was put in and supplemented, enormously, by the folks, some of which are sitting in this room right now. Some of whom are at my home, right now. Some of whom drive me around in an armored motorcade that makes it look like a European potentate. But the fact is, I am grateful for that assistance, beyond measure. Because when you think about what could happen, when somebody like that is out to kill you and doesn't care if he takes out your children with you, you run out of options in a big hurry. I ran out of options, I think the government of the United States should have stepped up to it, and didn't. Whether it's because of laws or regulations, I don't know.

I admit to making a serious, serious, judgment error in what I then did to paper it over and I'm willing to sit here and admit to that. But I'm also suggesting to you gentlemen, that if it was Gen. Secord who paid the bill, whatever it was, I thought it was $8 thousand, didn't learn until the hearing started, it was more. I also suggest to you that if it was Gen. Secord, first of all, "Thank you, Gen. Secord." And second of all, you guys ought to write him a check because the government should have done it to begin with. Thank you, sir.

MR. NIELDS: Thank you, Col. North. I need to ask you one other question on this subject.

MR. NORTH: I'll make my second answer shorter.

MR. NIELDS: The documents which I believe you had reference to that you wrote and back-dated, are Exhibits 172 and Exhibit 173.

MR. NORTH: Yes.

MR. NIELDS: Before I get to the document. Who was it that you made the request for security to, and who turned you down?

MR. NORTH: Well I—I went to—well first of all I asked the FBI what they could do about it. And the FBI told me and I have since checked and I was since told this, again this April, when they called about a threat this spring, that the FBI is not in the business of providing protection. And they indeed, are not. I'm not—I'm not necessarily, by the way, saying that I think they should have, because it is clearly not within their jurisdiction, I suppose. But, I then asked if there was anything that could be done at the White House.

MR. NIELDS: And who was it, who was it that you asked at the White House?

MR. NORTH: I asked Admiral Poindexter, and I was referred to Mr. McDaniel. I was then—it was then suggested that there's only two things that can be done. You can either get a secure phone—find a secure telephone and put it in your home and use that to justify the installation of a security system. Well, for whatever reasons, no secure telephone could be found. And I'm not—that may well be the case. I don't know. I was also told that the other alternative was immediate PCS to Camp Lejune or another military installation, which did not seem entirely practical, given that I was getting ready to go to Teheran. Thus, there were no answers.

MR. NIELDS: That was Adm. Poindexter or Mr. McDaniel who told you that you could be transferred to Camp Lejune?

MR. NORTH: I don't recall which one it was. I know that that issue came up and was dismissed.

MR. NIELDS: Okay. Turning now to Exhibits 172 and 173, I take it what you're saying is that they were both typed on the same day.

MR. NORTH: No. Actually, I think they were typed on two different days, or maybe even three different days. But they're both phony documents. I mean, I've admitted to that. I'm here to tell you the truth, even when it hurts, okay? They're phony.

MR. NIELDS: The second one, Exhibit 173, there are three letters from the typewriter that don't type correctly. How was that arranged?

MR. NORTH: It wasn't arranged. That's the way the wheel on the thing was when I typed it. And the wheel was defective. It was simply that way.

MR. NIELDS: Were the two letters typed on the same typewriter?

MR. NORTH: No.

MR. NIELDS: Were they typed in the same place?

MR. NORTH: No. Actually, one letter I think was typed on one typewriter that was similar to the other one, and I couldn't find a decent ball or the wheel thing that worked right, and that was the only one that was there. And I dummied up even the explanation on the bottom of it.

MR. NIELDS: When you say you dummied up the explanation—

MR. NORTH: That's the way it was.

MR. NIELDS: So you didn't drop the ball?

MR. NORTH: No. I mean, after all, thinking that you were—this was not typed at the White House. It was typed after I left. Incidentally, no one else knew about this besides me. I mean, this was my own little stupidity all on my own.

MR. NIELDS: And what was the purpose of writing an explanation at the bottom of Exhibit 173?

MR. NORTH: Well, the only letter that you sent with a ball that doesn't work—it was a demonstrator model in a store that I typed it on. And you've got to provide some kind of an explanation as to why supposedly a White House typewriter doesn't write. So I explained it on the bottom by saying I dropped the ball—"the ball" being the explanation for the defective type.

MR. NIELDS: Why did you dummy up the explanation?

MR. NORTH: Well, theoretically, I mean if—

MR. SULLIVAN: I object. Now, Mr. Chairman, Col. North has frankly admitted what he did here. I must believe that the United States Congress has better things to do than focus on two phony letters after the witness has admitted that they're phony. Could we please move on to another subject?

CHAIRMAN INOUYE: We will proceed in the fashion we wish to.

MR. NORTH: The fact is, this letter was typed on a machine, but dated as though I were still at the White House. Right? 1 October '86, I was still at the White House. And the machine didn't work well, didn't write right. Somebody had screwed up the—the wheel on this demonstrator. And thus, I had to explain why a White House typewriter, where they usually work pretty well, didn't work well. And so I put that note at the bottom. It was simply an explanation for why the typewriter didn't work as I had hoped it to. It's not more sinister than it appears.

[Ed. Note: North testifies about his use of traveler's checks.]

MR. NIELDS: There's been testimony about use of traveler's checks. I'd like to give you an opportunity to answer or explain that testimony. I take it you have it in mind.

MR. NORTH: I do have it in mind, Counsel. I appreciate the opportunity. Again, you'll have to indulge me a bit. When I began the covert operation in 1986—excuse me, in 1984 in support of the resistance, we had enormous problems trying to solve near-time, real-time—what I call operational problems. The end result of that was that

I talked to Director Casey about the difficulties. He—he had suggested establishing an operational account, and I did so. There were two sources of monies for that operational account. One was traveler's checks from Adolfo Calero, and the other one was cash, eventually from Gen. Secord.

My recollection is that the very first traveler's checks came either very late '84, or certainly early 1985, and that the sum total of traveler's checks was probably in excess of $100,000, or thereabouts. I also had cash, which I estimate today to be somewhere around $150,000 to $175,000. At various points in time, there would be considerable sums in it; and at various points in time, there would be none in it.

My recollection is that I got the traveler's checks in packages of less than $10,000. I understand that others have remembered elsewise, but that's how I remember it. Those funds were used to support the operations that we were conducting. They were used to support the covert operation in Nicaragua, and then eventually were used to support other activities as well. The fact that I had those funds available was known to Mr. McFarlane, to Admiral Poindexter, to Director Casey, and eventually, to Admiral Art Moreau over at the Pentagon.

It was also—came to be known to others, that—some of whom you've had testify here—the funds were used, initially, only to support the Nicaragua program. But eventually, it was broadened to include other activities as well. Let me give you some examples.

In the Nicaragua program, operational support was provided to a whole host of Nicaraguan resistance leaders, either directly by me from the fund, or through couriers that I used to carry it out. Other resistance activities inside Nicaragua were supported, of a less military nature in some cases. Europeans who helped us with both the public affairs aspect, and the acquisition of other arms, through a separate channel outside that you've already heard about from Gen. Secord, or Gen. Singlaub, were paid for out of this account. Money was mailed from this account to addresses in Caracas, San Jose, Tegucigalpa, and San Salvador, among other places, to support activities inside Managua. The Indian movement, the Atlantic coast Indian movement, was supported from this account, and meetings with the Atlantic Coast Indians, both the Misurasata and the Miskito movement itself, were supported from this account. And eventually, the fund was used to support other activities, such as a DEA hostage recovery activity and the assistance of another European, who we have agreed not to talk about.

What's important that you realize is that meticulous records were kept on all of this. I kept a detailed account of every single penny that came into that account and left that account. All of the transactions were recorded on a ledger that Director Casey gave me for that purpose. Every time I got a travelers—group of travelers checks in, I would record them. And I would record them when they went out, even going so far as to record the travelers checks' numbers themselves.

The ledger for this operational account was given to me by Director Casey. And when he told me to do so, I destroyed it, because it had within it the details of every single person who had been supported by this fund, the addresses, their names, and placed them at extraordinary risk.

Every transaction that you showed on that chart that you had up on the wall or the screen, or wherever it was, hard to tell when you see it on a videotape, but when you had it up there, you showed a group of travelers checks with my name on it. Every single one of those travelers checks which bore my name were used by me to defray an actual operational expense as it happened. I'd cash a check, for example, at Miami Airport and hand the money to a resistance person who I met with there. Or I flew myself off to someplace; because we were trying to avoid the use of appropriated funds, we used this account to live within Boland and to hide the fact that NSC travel was being conducted.

Unlike the CIA, an NSC travel voucher system doesn't have a covert cover. We had one dickens of a time trying to protect my travel. And as you undoubtedly know, gentlemen, I made an enormous amount of travel. The schedule was brutal. Much of it was paid for out of that operational account.

There were times when that account was down to zero, no money in it. I didn't have any travelers checks, and I'd handed out all the cash, not to myself, but to others. Under those circumstances I would use my own money, Lieutenant Colonel Oliver North's paycheck money, his own money that he had earned, and I would use it for an operational expense. I would therefore make a notation in the ledger: spent $250 on going to Atlanta to meet with somebody. And the next time I got cash or traveler's checks, I would use those checks to reimburse myself.

Every single penny on the checks that you saw that came to me was used to pay an operational expense on the scene or to reimburse myself. I never took a penny that didn't belong to me. Every single one of those checks—and I would also point out to you, Counsel, that you don't have them all, because by my own recognition and memory, there were checks used in 1986, and the ones that you depicted earlier were only 1985. And I used those travelers checks right up until shortly before I was fired, but only for the purposes that you saw.

And I realize that it—that this hearing is a difficult thing. Believe me, gentlemen, it isn't as difficult for you as it is for a guy that's got to come up here and tell the truth, and that's what I'm trying to do. And I want to make it very clear that when you put up things like "Parklane Hosiery" and you all snicker at it, and you know that I've got a beautiful secretary, and the good Lord gave her the gift of beauty, and the people snicker that Ollie North might have been doing a little hanky-panky with his secretary, Ollie North has been loyal to his wife since the day he married her. And the fact is I went to my best friend and I asked her, "Did I ever go to Parklane Hosiery?" And you know what she told me? "Of course you did, you old buffoon, you went there to buy leotards for our two little girls." And the reason I wrote the check to Parklane Hosiery, just like the checks at Giant, is because I was owed my money for what I had spent in pursuing that covert operation.

You gentlemen may not agree that we should have been pursuing covert operations at the NSC, but we were. We had an operational account and we used the money for legitimate purposes within that covert operation. Does that answer your question, sir?

MR. NIELDS: Yes.

MR. NORTH: Thank you.

MR. NIELDS: I have a couple of more on that subject. When was the ledger destroyed?

MR. NORTH: My recollection is that the ledger—and I—I'm—anticipating your question, I have tried as best I can to reconstruct not only that, but when a lot of the more intensified destruction began. My sense is that it was probably destroyed along about the 4th or the 5th of November, and I say "probably" because the initial discussions I had with [CIA] Director Casey about this operation coming unraveled began right after the Hasenfus shootdown, which was early October. I think it was the 4th or the 5th of October, and then the discussions that he had shortly thereafter with Mr. Furmark, who told him that, "Oh, by the way, a lot of people happen to know that Ollie North has been using money from the Iranian arms transactions to support the contras," or words to that effect.

I then went on in a very intensive period of travel, and I must tell you that we intensified our efforts considerably. Knowing that this operation was coming apart, we made an extraordinary effort to get the second channel going, to open it up, and to get as many Americans out as we possibly could before it all came down.

I believe that it was right after I returned from one of my early November trips. I had a meeting with Director Casey. Director Casey said, "Look. This revelation that's either occurring or about to occur is the end." At that point in time, he told me, "You ought to go out and get a lawyer."

Now, from one of the guys who's one of the best lawyers in the world by my book—he used to remind me a lot not to say bad things about lawyers,—I've been reminded about that since—Director Casey told me to get a lawyer because there was probably going to be a civil suit against me by associates of Mr. Furmark to recover their money. And, so in that whole process, somewhere between what I would judge to be the 13th of October and the 4th of November, he told me specifically, "Get rid of things. Get rid of that book because that book has in it the names of everybody, the addresses of everybody. Just get rid of it, and clean things up." And, I did so.

MR. NIELDS: Where did the money come from?

MR. NORTH: The two sources that I remember very vividly were Mr. Calero, by traveler's checks, sometimes given by him to me directly or couriered to me, and then also cash from General Secord.

MR. NIELDS: Did you ever—you've indicated that on occasion you've advanced your own money and reimbursed yourself out of this fund. Were there occasions when it was the other way around?

MR. NORTH: I don't understand.

MR. NIELDS: You borrowed from the fund—

MR. NORTH: Never.

MR. NIELDS: —for personal purposes—

MR. NORTH: Never.

MR. NIELDS: —and then reimbursed?

MR. NORTH: Never.

MR. NIELDS: Did you ever permit Fawn Hall to do that?

MR. NORTH: I did, I, as I recall, it was a very late, probably a Friday or Saturday night, and I had told her that she could take the weekend off, and she didn't have any money. And, she needed—she was driving to the beach or somewhere. And I, as I recall, gave her two or three checks, made the appropriate notation in the ledger, and told her that I had to have the money back as soon as she could cash a check, and she did. And I put the money back in the account. To my recollection, I never advanced anybody anything out of the account. I never advanced myself out of that.

MR. NIELDS: There has been testimony about efforts to route money to you through your wife out of the Swiss bank accounts. I'd like to give you an opportunity to respond to those that—testimony on that subject, if you wish.

MR. NORTH: I'd be glad to. Again, if you'll allow me to go back in time a little bit, in February of 1986, we had the first direct meetings with the Iranians in five-plus years—between US government officials and the Iranians, other than the discussions that were going on in Europe over settlement of accounts. In those meetings, in the latter days of February, it was decided that there would be two trips to Teheran—that I would go on an advance trip with Gen. Secord, the purpose of which would be to establish an agenda for a higher-level trip to take place in April. My advance trip was to have taken place in March.

Because the US government had been unable to provide a translator for that session, Mr. Hakim came to that session and acted as translator. And that was, to my recollection, the very first time I had heard of Mr. Hakim. I think it is the first time I had actually met with Mr. Hakim, and I have no recall to the contrary. Mr. Hakim thought that this idea of an advance trip was lunacy. I mean, he put it in the strongest possible terms that this was not a good thing to do. The CIA officer who was with me at that meeting agreed with him. When the discussion transpired, it was actually pointed out that you could never be heard from on this trip again. The risks were known to Mr. Hakim very clearly because he is, after all, an Iranian. He fled the revolution that we now seek to get along with. The CIA officer thought that the trip was very high risk.

When I later talked to Director Casey—and this was within days of this whole event, Director Casey raised another issue, and that was, first of all, the trip—because it is so black, this advance trip is so hidden that we're going to use non-US government assets throughout, European or Middle Eastern airlines, no US air registration, air flights, you might never be heard from again. The government might disavow the entire thing. And, furthermore, I, Bill Casey, am not going to let you go unless you are prepared to deal with the issue of torture. We knew by then that Bill Buckley, a man who I knew, was probably dead, and that he had been tortured. We knew that he had given as much as a 400-page confession under torture that we were making every effort to recover. And Director Casey told me that he would not concur in my going on the advance trip unless I took with me the means by which I could take my own life. I did not tell my wife and children that, and they may be hearing it for the first time right now.

In the course of that discussion, Mr. Hakim said to me, "If you don't come back, I will do something for your family." He did not say "we," that I recall, he said "I." Now by that point in time, I had come to know that Mr. Hakim was a wealthy man in his own right. I was grateful for the assistance that he had been providing in translating over several very difficult days of discussions with the Iranians. And several days thereafter, when he suggested that my wife meet with his lawyer in Philadelphia, I agreed that my wife should do so. The purpose, as I understood it, of that meeting was that my wife would be in touch with the person who would, if I didn't return, do something for my family.

My wife went to the meeting in Philadelphia several days thereafter. And you have notations in the notebooks that I surrendered to you about what happened. She went to the very brief meeting. There was no money mentioned, no account mentioned, no amount mentioned, no will mentioned, no arrangement. The meeting focused on how many children I had, their ages, and a general description of my family. A brief meeting in the offices, as I remember, of Touche Ross, a respectable firm in Philadelphia, with a lawyer. I then went, and, thank God, returned safely, from Iran. After that trip, there was one more call to my wife from the lawyer. On or about the first of June, almost immediately after my return from Teheran, the lawyers called again and asked for the name of an adult executor for our family, in the event, I suppose that neither my wife nor I were around. I told my wife, "Do not call him back. It is unnecessary." She never did. She never heard from him again, and she has never made contact with him again. No money was ever transferred to my possession, control, account, or that of my wife, or that of my children. I never ever heard about "belly buttons" until these hearings began. Does that answer your question, Counsel?

MR. NIELDS: Yes, and I take it that in answering the question, you've been telling us what happened at certain meetings that I take it were attended only by your wife, and I take it you are testifying to what you've been told by her?

MR. NORTH: On advice of counsel, I have not revealed any of our confidential marital communications. I have given you a surmise, based on what I know the facts to be.

MR. SULLIVAN: In other words, Counsel, don't call his wife up here.

MR. NIELDS: No. That wasn't the question, at all. The question was simply what the source of the information was, and I take it, it's your wife?

MR. NORTH: Counsel, I gave you a long story, and the sources are multiple for that story, but accurate.

MR. NIELDS: Well, other than your wife, what are the sources?

MR. NORTH: Some of the information may be privileged or a work product of my attorney.

MR. SULLIVAN: In other words, we've done a little of our own investigation—Excuse me, Mr. Chairman—a little of our own investigation regarding these allegations, and have amassed some evidence and have concluded that they're absolutely baseless. From that information, Col. North has been able to draw certain conclusions, and if you have any proof to the contrary, why don't you present it?

MR. NIELDS: So, what he is testifying to is based on what he's been told by his wife and his attorneys?

MR. SULLIVAN: Not necessarily so. There are other factors as well.

MR. NIELDS: Okay, what else?

MR. NORTH: I, I'm just telling you all that I know about the event. No money ever was received. [Counsel conferring with witness.]

MR. NORTH: I obviously had a conversation with Mr. Hakim that initiated this entire business back in February or early March.

MR. NIELDS: Can you give the Committee any information that would shed light on why Mr. Zucker was meeting with a lawyer in Switzerland in October of 1986, seeking to find a way of routing a substantial sum of money to you through your wife?

MR. NORTH: No. I can give you absolutely no insight to that.

MR. SULLIVAN: Objection to your question, "routing a substantial sum of money." There's no predicate to that.

MR. NORTH: I cannot, Counsel, and I think it's important for you to know that the very first time I heard these things was as a consequence of these hearings, and I was shocked. I never ever got a penny from those accounts. The only thing that it can be said that I ever received as a consequence of what I did in the course of these activities, or as a result of perhaps one of those accounts, is the security system which is at my home, and I still, to this day, don't know exactly who paid for it.

MR. NIELDS: Mr. Chairman, I have no further questions for the morning.

CHAIRMAN INOUYE: The joint panel will stand in recess until 2:00 p.m.

* * *

[AFTERNOON SESSION, July 8, 1987]

* * *

MR. NIELDS: Was the President of the United States aware of your—the fact that you were running a resupply operation in Nicaragua?

MR. NORTH: Again, I have absolutely no idea of what the President's knowledge [was] specifically about what I was doing. I made every effort to keep my superiors fully apprised as to what I was doing, and the effect that it was having in the region.

And you have tons of documents taken from me, some of which I personally surrendered to you and you alone, and others that were taken from my files, that make that abundantly clear.

I don't know, to this day, what the President knew I, personally, was doing. I hope to God that people were keeping him apprised as to the effect of it. Because if we hadn't done it, there wouldn't have been a Nicaraguan resistance around when the Congress got around to putting up $100 million for it—sir.

MR. NIELDS: Did you obtain from Mr. Dutton a book of photographs?

MR. NORTH: From who? Oh yes, I did.

MR. NIELDS: And did you tell him that you were—wanted that book of—and this was, I take it, a book of photographs of various aspects of the resupply operation?

MR. NORTH: That's correct—

MR. NIELDS: Planes—

MR. NORTH: And other things, too. I don't recall specifically what was in the book, then, but that is correct.

MR. NIELDS: And did you tell them that you wanted that book so that you would have something to show the President about the good work that they were doing?

MR. NORTH: I'm not sure that I put it that way. I—you know, I—I want to get away from this "Ollie North wanted to get the credit" stuff, because I didn't. I think what I wanted to do was to—if I said something to that effect: "I think the President ought to see this." And I think I made an effort to send it up to the President through the National Security Advisor. And I don't know whether it ever got to the President or not.

But if the book is still around, somebody ought to send it to him. Because the President ought to be aware of what a handful of people did to keep the Nicaraguan resistance alive at a time when nobody in this Congress seemed to care. And it's important that the President know that good men gave inordinate amounts of time, and some gave their lives to support that activity. And some of them have been brutally treated by what has come about in these two parallel investigations—brutally treated.

MR. NIELDS: How did you go about making efforts—(pause)—how did you go about making efforts—

MR. NORTH: I would like to correct something I just said, Mr. Chairman. And I apologize to those who did care, because there were many members of this—this body who cared a lot. And eventually a majority cared again, and chose to appropriate $100 million to support that resistance. And I apologize to those of you who have backed them all the way. And I pray to God you will not stop because what I have done or what I have failed to do, I desperately believe that if nothing else comes of these hearings, that you will have sufficient reason to vote, again, to appropriate monies to that cause. And I ask your apologies for overstating what I just did.

* * *

MR. NIELDS: And there came a time, did there not, when you had an—an interview with members of the House Intelligence Committee—

MR. NORTH: I did.

MR. NIELDS: —and staff?

MR. NORTH: I don't remember if there was any staff or not. I defer to Chairman Hamilton; he convened his group in the White House Situation Room, and I met with him there.

MR. NIELDS: There's a memorandum which was done by staff, which is Exhibit 126. Do you have that in front of you?

MR. NORTH: I do.

MR. NIELDS: And it's dated August 6, 1986. Is that at or about the time when you had this interview?

MR. NORTH: I—again, I defer to the Committee and Chairman Hamilton. I had such a meeting. If that's when it was, I don't remember the date.

MR. NIELDS: And this was you personally talking to them?

MR. NORTH: It was on instructions of the National Security Advisor. I was instructed to meet with Chairman Hamilton and, I believe, many of the members of the Committee.

MR. NIELDS: And they were interested in finding out the answers to the questions raised by the resolution of inquiry—

MR. NORTH: Exactly.

MR. NIELDS: —your fund-raising activities—

MR. NORTH: Precisely.

MR. NIELDS: —military support for the contras—

MR. NORTH: That's right.

MR. NIELDS: —questions about Mr. Owen, General Singlaub, and John Hull?

(Long pause)

MR. NORTH: Yes.

MR. NIELDS: The beginning of this memorandum that appears to be a description of what you said during that meeting, it says "from Boland Amendment on North explains strictures to contras." Is that true? Did you explain the strictures to the contras?

MR. NORTH: I explained to them that there was no US Government money until more was appropriated, yes.

MR. NIELDS: And it says "never violated stricture. Gave advice on Human Rights Civil Action Program."

MR. NORTH: I did do that.

MR. NIELDS: But I take it you did considerably more, which you did not tell the committee about.

MR. NORTH: I have admitted that here before you today, knowing full well what I told the committee then. I think—and I'm—I think we can abbreviate this in hopes that we can move on so that I can finish this week. I will tell you right now, counsel, and all the members here gathered that I misled the Congress. I mis—

MR. NIELDS: At that meeting?

MR. NORTH: At that meeting.

MR. NIELDS: Face-to-face?

MR. NORTH: Face-to-face.

MR. NIELDS: You made false statements to them about your activities in support of the contras?

MR. NORTH: I did. Furthermore, I did so with a purpose, and I did so with the purpose of hopefully avoiding the very kind of thing we have before us now and avoiding a shutoff of help to the Nicaraguan resistance and avoiding an elimination of the resistance facilities in three Central American countries—

MR. NIELDS: We—

MR. NORTH: —where—wherein we had promised those heads of state. On my specific orders, I had—on specific orders to me, I had gone down there and assured them of our absolute and total discretion.

MR. NIELDS: We do—do live in a democracy, don't we?

MR. NORTH: We do, sir. Thank God.

MR. NIELDS: In which it is the people, not one Marine Lieutenant Colonel, that get to decide the important policy decisions for the nation.

(Long silence)

MR. NORTH: Yes. And, I—

MR. NIELDS: And, part of the democratic process—

MR. NORTH: And, I would point out that part of that answer is that this Marine Lieutenant Colonel was not making all of those decisions on his own. As I indicated in my testimony yesterday, MR. NIELDS, I sought approval for everything that I did.

MR. NIELDS: But, you denied Congress the facts—

MR. NORTH: I did.

MR. NIELDS: You denied the elected representatives of our people the facts upon which they needed—

MR. NORTH: I did.

MR. NIELDS: —to make a very important decision for this nation.

MR. NORTH: I did because of what I have just described to you as our concerns, and I did it because we have had incredible leaks, from discussions with closed committees of the Congress. I, I, I was a part of, as people now know, the coordination for the mining of the harbors in Nicaragua. When that one leaked, there were American lives at stake, and it leaked from a member of one of the committees, who eventually admitted it. When there was a leak on the sensitive intelligence methods that we used to help capture the Achille Lauro terrorists, it almost wiped out that whole channel of communications.

I mean, those kinds of things are devastating. They are devastating to the national security of the United States, and I desperately hope that one of the things that can derive from all of this ordeal is that we can find a better way by which we can communicate those things properly with the Congress. I'm not admitting that what happened in this is proper. I'm not admitting, or claiming rather, that what I did and my role in it in communicating was proper.

MR. NIELDS: Were you instructed to do it?

MR. NORTH: I was not specifically instructed, no.

MR. NIELDS: Were you generally instructed?

MR. NORTH: Yes.

MR. NIELDS: By whom?

MR. NORTH: My superiors. I prepared draft answers that they signed and sent. And, I would also point out—

MR. NIELDS: What superior?

MR. NORTH: Well who—look who sign—I didn't sign those letters to the—to this body.

MR. NIELDS: I'm talking about the last—I'm talking about the oral meeting in August of 1986.

MR. NORTH: I went down to that oral meeting with the same kind of understanding that I prepared those memos in 1985 and other communications.

MR. NIELDS: Well, you had a different boss, and in fairness, you ought to tell us whether he instructed you to do it, understood you to do it, knew about it afterwards, or none of those?

MR. NORTH: He did not specifically go down and say, "Ollie, lie to the committee." I told him what I had said afterwards, and he sent me a note saying, "Well done."

Now I would also like to point out one other thing. I deeply believe that the President of the United States is also an elected official of this land. And by the Constitution, as I understand it, he is the person charged with making and carrying out the foreign policy of this country. I believed, from the moment I was engaged in this activity in 1984, that this was in furtherance of the foreign policy established by the President. I still believe that.

MR. NIELDS: Even—

MR. NORTH: I'm not saying that what I did here was right. And I have just placed myself, as you know, counsel, in great jeopardy.

MR. NIELDS: Even the President is elected by the people.

MR. NORTH: I just said that.

MR. NIELDS: And the people have the right to vote him out of office, if they don't like his policies.

MR. NORTH: That's true.

MR. NIELDS: And they can't exercise that function, if the policies of the President are hidden from them.

MR. NORTH: Wait a second. Yesterday, we talked about the need for this nation, which is a country at risk in a dangerous world, having the need to conduct covert operations and secret diplomacy, carry out secret programs. I mean, we talked at some length about that. And that can certainly be the subject of great debate. And this great institution can pass laws that say no such activities can ever be conducted again. But that would be wrong, and you and I know that.

The fact is, this country does need to be able to conduct those kinds of activities. And the President ought not to be in a position, in my humble opinion, of having to go out and explain to the American people, on a biweekly basis or any other kind, that I, the President, am carrying out the following secret operations. It just can't be done. No nation in the world will ever help us again—and we desperately need that kind of help—if we are to survive, given our adversaries.

And what I'm saying to you, Mr. Nields, is the American people, I think, trust that the President will, indeed, be conducting these kinds of activities. They trust that he will do so with a good purpose and good intent.

I will also admit to you that I believe there has to be a way of consulting with the Congress. There must be. I would also point out to you, Mr. Nields, that, in June of 1986, not the Tower Commission—I gave a speech before the American Bar Association, on very short notice. I stood on the podium with Sen. Moynihan, and I advocated the formation of a small, discreet, joint intelligence committee, with a very professional, small staff, in which the Administration would feel comfortable confiding and planning and conducting and funding these kinds of activities. I still believe that that could be a good and thoughtful thing to do. There has to be that kind of proposal that allows the Administration to talk straightforwardly with the Congress.

* * *

[Thursday, July 9, 1987, Morning Session]

CHAIRMAN INOUYE: The hearing will please come to order. This morning, the panel will resume the questioning of Lt. Col. North. May the record indicate that on 8:15 a.m., on July 7, 1987, the Select Committees of the House and Senate received a statement, the opening statement of Colonel North. This statement, pursuant to the rules, has been examined and determined there are no inadvertent disclosures of classified material, further, that we are satisfied that the statement does not exceed the bounds set forth by the court in the grant of immunity, and although the statement obviously exceeds ten minutes, we will not insist upon a summary of it. And if the Colonel wishes to present his opening statement at this time; he may do so in total.

MR. NORTH: Thank you, Mr. Chairman.

CHAIRMAN INOUYE: Please proceed.

MR. NORTH: As you all know by now, my name is Oliver North, Lieutenant Colonel, United States Marine Corps. My best friend is my wife Betsy, to whom I have been married for 19 years, and with whom I have had four wonderful children, aged 18, 16, 11 and 6.

I came to the National Security Council six years ago to work in the administration of a great president. As a staff member, I came to understand his goals and his desires. I admired his policies, his strength, and his ability to bring our country together. I observed the President to be a leader who cared deeply about people, and who believed that the interests of our country were advanced by recognizing that ours is a nation at risk in a dangerous world, and acting accordingly. He tried, and in my opinion succeeded, in advancing the cause of world peace by strengthening our country, by acting to restore and sustain democracy throughout the world, and by having the courage to take decisive action when needed.

I also believe that we must guard against a rather perverse side of American life, and that is the tendency to launch vicious attacks and criticism against our elected officials. President Reagan has made enormous contributions, and he deserves our respect and admiration.

The National Security Council is, in essence, the President's staff. It helps to formulate and coordinate national security policy. Some, perhaps on this Committee, believe that the NSC was devoid of experienced leadership. I believe that is wrong. While at the NSC, I worked most closely with three people: Mr. Robert C. McFarlane, Admiral John Poindexter, and CIA Director William Casey. Bud McFarlane is a man who devoted nearly thirty years of his life to public service in a number of responsible positions. At the NSC, he worked long hours, made great contributions, and I admire him for those efforts. Admiral Poindexter is a distinguished naval officer who served in a number of important positions of responsibility. He, too, was a tireless worker with a similar record of public service, and I, too, admire him greatly. William Casey was a renowned lawyer, a war veteran of heroic proportions, and a former chairman of the SEC. I understood that he was also a close personal friend and adviser to President Reagan.

There is nearly a century of combined public service by these three men. As a member of the NSC staff, I knew that I held a position of responsibility. But I knew full well what my position was. I did not engage in fantasy that I was the President or Vice President or Cabinet member, or even Director of the National Security Council. I was simply a staff member with a demonstrated ability to get the job done. Over time, I was made responsible for managing a number of complex and sensitive covert operations that we have discussed here to date. I reported directly to Mr. McFarlane and to Admiral Poindexter. I coordinated directly with others, including Director Casey. My authority to act always flowed, I believe, from my superiors. My military training inculcated in me a strong belief in the chain of command. And so far as I can recall, I always acted on major matters with specific approval, after informing my superiors of the facts, as I knew them, the risks, and the potential benefits. I readily admit that I was action-oriented, that I took pride in the fact that I was counted upon as a man who got the job done. And I don't mean this by way of criticism, but there were occasions when my superiors, confronted with accomplishing goals or difficult tasks, would simply say, "Fix it, Ollie," or, "Take care of it."

Since graduating from the Naval Academy in 1968, I have strived to be the best Marine officer that one can be. In combat, my goal was always to understand the objective, follow orders, accomplish the mission, and to keep alive the men who served under me. One of the good things that has come from the last seven months of worldwide notoriety has been the renewed contact that I've had with some of the finest people in the world—those with whom I served in Vietnam. Among the 50,000 or so messages of support that have arrived since I left the NSC are many from those who recount the horrors we lived through, and who now relate stories of their families and careers. After Vietnam, I worked with my fellow officers to train good Marines to be ready in case we were called upon elsewhere in the world, but at the same time to hope that we never were. I honestly believed that any soldier who has ever been to a war truly hopes he will never see one again.

My Marine Corps career was untracked in 1981, when I was detailed to the National Security Council. I was uneasy at the beginning, but I came to believe that it was important work, and as years passed and responsibilities grew, I got further from that which I loved, the Marine Corps and Marines.

During 1984, '85, and '86, there were periods of time when we worked two days in every one. My guess is that the average workday lasted at least 14 hours. To respond to various crises, the need for such was frequent, and we would often go without a night's sleep, hoping to recoup the next night or thereafter. If I had to estimate the number of meetings and discussions and phone calls over that five years, it would surely be in the tens of thousands. My only real regret is that I virtually abandoned my family for work during these years, and that work consisted of my first few years on the staff, as the project officer for a highly classified and compartmented National Security project, which is not a part of this inquiry.

I worked hard on the political military strategy for restoring and sustaining democracy in Central America, and in particular, El Salvador. We sought to achieve the democratic outcome in Nicaragua that this administration still supports, which involved keeping the contras together in both body and soul. We made efforts to open a new relationship with Iran, and recover our hostages. We worked on the development of a concerted policy regarding terrorists and terrorism and a capability for dealing in a concerted manner with that threat.

We worked on various crises, such as TWA 847, the capture of Achille Lauro, the rescue of American students in Grenada and the restoration of democracy on that small island, and the US raid in Libya in response to their terrorist attacks. And, as some may be willing to admit, there were efforts made to work with the Congress on legislative programs.

There were many problems. I believed that we worked as hard as we could to solve them, and sometimes we succeeded, and sometimes we failed, but at least we tried, and I want to tell you that I, for one, will never regret having tried.

I believe that this is a strange process that you are putting me and others through. Apparently, the President has chosen not to assert his prerogatives, and you have been permitted to make the rules. You called before you the officials of the Executive Branch. You put them under oath for what must be collectively thousands of hours of testimony. You dissect that testimony to find inconsistencies and declare some to be truthful and others to be liars. You make the rulings as to what is proper and what is not proper. You put the testimony which you think is helpful to your goals up before the people and leave others out. It's sort of like a baseball game in which you are both the player and the umpire. It's a game in which you call the balls and strikes and where you determine who is out and who is safe. And in the end you determine the score and declare yourselves the winner.

From where I sit, it is not the fairest process. One thing is, I think, for certain—that you will not investigate yourselves in this matter. There is not much chance that you will conclude at the end of these hearings that the Boland Amendments and the frequent policy changes therefore were unwise or that your restrictions should not have been imposed on the Executive Branch. You are not likely to conclude that the Administration acted properly by trying to sustain the freedom fighters in Nicaragua when they were abandoned, and you are not likely to conclude by commending the President of the United States who tried valiantly to recover our citizens and achieve an opening that is strategically vital—Iran. I would not be frank with you if I did not admit that the last several months have been difficult for me and my family. It has been difficult to be on the front pages of every newspaper in the land day after day, to be photographed thousands of times by bands of photographers who chase us around since November just because my name arose at the hearings. It is difficult to be caught in the middle of a constitutional struggle between the Executive and legislative branches over who will formulate and direct the foreign policy of this nation. It is difficult to be vilified by people in and out of this body, some who have proclaimed that I am guilty of criminal conduct even before they heard me. Others have said that I would not tell the truth when I came here to testify, and one member asked a person testifying before this body whether he would believe me under oath. I asked when I got here—if you don't believe me, why call me at all? It has been difficult to see questions raised about my character and morality, my honesty, because only partial evidence was provided. And, as I indicated yesterday, I think it was insensitive of this Committee to place before the cameras my home address at a time when my family and I are under 24-hour armed guard by over a dozen government agents of the Naval Investigative Service because of fear that terrorists will seek revenge for my official acts and carry out their announced intentions to kill me.

It is also difficult to comprehend that my work at the NSC—all of which was approved and carried out in the best interests of our country—has led to two massive parallel investigations staffed by over 200 people. It is mind-boggling to me that one of those investigations is criminal and that some here have attempted to criminalize policy differences between co-equal branches of government and the Executive's conduct of foreign affairs.

I believe it is inevitable that the Congress will in the end blame the Executive Branch, but I suggest to you that it is the Congress which must accept at least some of the blame in the Nicaraguan freedom fighters' matter. Plain and simple, the Congress is to blame because of the fickle, vacillating, unpredictable, on-again off-again policy toward the Nicaraguan Democratic Resistance—the so-called Contras. I do not believe that the support of the Nicaraguan freedom fighters can be treated as the passage of a budget. I suppose that if the budget doesn't get passed on time again this year, it will be inevitably another extension of another month or two.

But, the contras, the Nicaraguan freedom fighters are people—living, breathing, young men and women who have had to suffer a desperate struggle for liberty with sporadic and confusing support from the United States of America.

Armies need food and consistent help. They need a flow of money, of arms, clothing and medical supplies. The Congress of the United States allowed the executive to encourage them, to do battle, and then abandoned them. The Congress of the United States left soldiers in the field unsupported and vulnerable to their communist enemies. When the executive branch did everything possible within the law to prevent them from being wiped out by Moscow's surrogates in Havana and Managua, you then had this investigation to blame the problem on the executive branch. It does not make sense to me.

In my opinion, these hearings have caused serious damage to our national interests. Our adversaries laugh at us, and our friends recoil in horror. I suppose it would be one thing if the intelligence committees wanted to hear all of this in private and thereafter pass laws which in the view of Congress make for better policies or better functioning government. But, to hold them publicly for the whole world to see strikes me as very harmful. Not only does it embarrass our friends and allies with whom we have worked, many of whom have helped us in various programs, but it must also make them very wary of helping us again.

I believe that these hearings, perhaps unintentionally so, have revealed matters of great secrecy in the operation of our government. And sources and methods of intelligence activities have clearly been revealed to the detriment of our security.

As a result of rumor and speculation and innuendo, I have been accused of almost every crime imaginable. Wild rumors have abounded. Some media reports have suggested that I was guilty of espionage for the way I handled US intelligence. Some have said that I was guilty of treason, and suggested in front of my 11-year-old daughter, that I should be given the death penalty. Some said I stole 10 million dollars. Some said I was second only in power to the President of the United States, and others that I condoned drug-trafficking to generate funds for the contras, or that I personally ordered assassinations, or that I was conducting my own foreign policy. It has even been suggested that I was the personal confidant of the President of the United States. These and many other stories are patently untrue.

I don't mind telling you that I'm angry at what some have attempted to do to me and my family. I believe that these committee hearings will show that you have struck some blows. But, I am going to walk from here with my head high and my shoulders straight because I am proud of what we accomplished. I am proud of the efforts that we made, and I am proud of the fight that we fought. I am proud of serving the administration of a great president. I am not ashamed of anything in my professional or personal conduct. As we go through this process I ask that you continue to please keep an open mind. Please be open minded, and able to admit that, perhaps, your preliminary conclusions about me were wrong. And please, also, do not mistake my attitude for lack of respect. I am in awe of this great institution just as I am in awe of the presidency. Both are equal branches of government with separate areas of responsibility under the constitution that I have taken an oath to support and defend, and I have done so, as many of you have. And although I do not agree with what you are doing, or the way that it is being done, I do understand your interest in obtaining the facts and I have taken an oath to tell the truth and helping you to do so. In closing, Mr. Chairman, and I thank you for this opportunity, I would just simply like to thank the tens of thousands of Americans who have communicated their support, encouragement and prayers for me and my family in this difficult time. Thank you, sir.

CHAIRMAN INOUYE: Thank you very much, Colonel North. I wish the record to show that the panel did not amend, delete or strike out any word, or words—or phrases from this opening statement. Furthermore, we did not put on testimony words which we thought were helpful to our goals and leave the rest out. I am certain you will agree with me, Colonel, that every word you wanted to present to the people of the United States was presented. Isn't that correct, sir?

MR. NORTH: Yes, Mr. Chairman it was, and I was not referring to my testimony but that which preceded me, sir—about me.

CHAIRMAN INOUYE: And secondly, you have suggested that these hearings have disclosed matters of great secrecy in the operation of our government and sources and methods of intelligence activities have clearly been revealed to the detriment of our national security. May I, once again, advise you that according to the director of the National Security Agency, General Odom, not a single bit of classified material has been leaked by activities of this joint panel. Questioning will be resumed by Mr. Van Cleve. Mr. Van Cleve?

* * *

MR. VAN CLEVE: Colonel North, I have the, what I regard as the personal and painful task of asking you the following questions: You've admitted before this committee that you lied to representatives of the Iranians in order to try and release the hostages. Is that correct?

MR. NORTH: I lied every time I met with the Iranians.

MR. VAN CLEVE: And, you've admitted that you lied to General Secord with respect to conversations that you supposedly had with the President? Is that correct?

MR. NORTH: In order to encourage him to stay with the project, yes.

MR. VAN CLEVE: And, you've admitted that you lied to the Congress. Is that correct?

MR. NORTH: I have.

MR. VAN CLEVE: And, you admitted that you lied in creating false chronologies of these events. Is that correct?

MR. NORTH: That is true.

MR. VAN CLEVE: And you've admitted that you created false documents that were intended to mislead investigators with respect to a gift that was made to you. Is that correct?

(Long pause)

MR. NORTH: No.

MR. VAN CLEVE: I think I understand the reason for your hesitation. You certainly have admitted that the documents themselves were completely false. Is that correct?

MR. NORTH: That is correct.

MR. VAN CLEVE: And, they were intended to create a record of an event that never occurred. Is that correct?

MR. NORTH: That is correct.

MR. VAN CLEVE: Can you assure this committee that you are not here now lying to protect your Commander in Chief?

MR. NORTH: I am not lying to protect anybody, counsel. I came here to tell the truth. I told you that I was going to tell it to you, the good, the bad, and the ugly. Some of it has been ugly for me. I don't know how many other witnesses have gone through the ordeal that I have before arriving here and seeing their names smeared all over the newspapers, and by some members of this committee, but I committed when I raised my right hand and took an oath as a midshipman that I would tell the truth, and I took an oath when I arrived here before this committee to tell the truth, and I have done so, painful though it may be for me and for others. I have told you the truth, counsel, as best I am able.

MR. VAN CLEVE: I have no further questions for this witness, Mr. Chairman.

CHAIRMAN INOUYE: Thank you very much. When we resume our hearings at 2:00, Mr. Arthur Liman will continue the questioning. We'll stand in recess until 2:00 p.m.

AFTERNOON SESSION, July 9, 1987

CHAIRMAN INOUYE: The hearings will please come to order. Before proceeding, may I advise the guests that the chair will not tolerate any demonstrations. Mr. Liman.

* * *

MR. LIMAN: Now, did I understand you to say a moment ago that if Admiral Poindexter had not told you on Friday that he had not told the President you, quote "may well have told the Attorney General that the President did know"?

MR. NORTH: No, I would—

MR. SULLIVAN: That's a very confusing question, Mr. Chairman—

MR. LIMAN: Well—

MR. SULLIVAN: Could you restate it, sir?

MR. LIMAN: Did you just testify a few moments ago that had Admiral Poindexter not told you on Friday that the President was unaware of the diversion, you might well have told the Attorney General on that Sunday that the President knew? Is that what you said?

MR. NORTH: Well, let me cast this the right way because I don't want to leave any false impressions. In the conversations that I had with the Admiral on Friday, all of which related to, as I recall them, my departure, the safety of the hostages and the second channel, the cleanup of the files—if that's an acceptable way of putting it—I asked the Admiral pointedly that day, "Did the President, or does the President, know about the fact that we used these monies to support the resistance?" And he told me, then, "No." I think that's the last conversation I ever had with the Admiral about that aspect of it.

Thus I, having assumed all along that those things which required presidential approval indeed had them, think I conveyed to the Attorney General on Sunday just exactly those sentiments. My recollection of it is that when he asked me, "Did the President approve these?" I told him, "I guess he didn't," or "He didn't," or what—something like that. Because that's what the Admiral had told me on Friday.

MR. LIMAN: And what you meant to say before, at least what I think you were trying to say, is that you had assumed, for some nine months, that the President of the United States knew and approved of the diversion. Correct?

MR. NORTH: I had assumed, from the day I took my post at the National Security Council, that those things which required the approval of the President—and I sent forward memoranda soliciting that approval, and I got the authority to proceed on various initiatives—had indeed received the approval of the President. I've testified to that.

MR. LIMAN: And it wasn't until Admiral Poindexter answered your question, that that assumption was shaken.

MR. NORTH: It wasn't shaken. He simply denied that the President knew.

MR. LIMAN: Did you ask him: "Admiral Poindexter, why did you not discuss this with the President?"

MR. NORTH: No.

MR. LIMAN: Why not?

MR. NORTH: First of all, I'm not in the habit of questioning my superiors. If he deemed it not to be necessary to ask the President, I saluted smartly and charged up the hill. That's what lieutenant colonels are supposed to do. I have no problem with that. I don't believe that what we did, even under those circumstances, is wrong or illegal.

MR. LIMAN: And have—

MR. NORTH: I've told you, I thought it was a good idea to begin with.

MR. LIMAN: And—

MR. NORTH: I still think it was a good idea, counsel.

MR. LIMAN: And have you wondered why, if it was a good idea, that the President of the United States dismissed you because of it?

MR. NORTH: Let me—let me just make one thing very clear, counsel. This Lieutenant Colonel is not going to challenge a decision of the Commander in Chief, for whom I still work. And I am proud to work for that Commander in Chief. And if the Commander in Chief tells this Lieutenant Colonel to go stand in the corner and sit on his head, I will do so. And if the Commander in Chief decides to dismiss me from the NSC staff, this Lieutenant Colonel will proudly salute, and say, "Thank you for the opportunity to have served," and go. And I am not going to criticize his decision, no matter how he relieves me, sir.

MR. LIMAN: Has anyone given you an explanation, Col. North, on behalf of the President, of why he did not think it was "a good idea," and dismissed you?

MR. NORTH: The President of the United States saw fit to call me later the same day, and in the course of that call, which was also intensely personal, he told me words to the effect, "I just didn't know." I have no reason to disbelieve what the Commander in Chief told me, sir.

MR. LIMAN: Did you say to him, "I received my approval from Admiral Poindexter and Director Casey."?

MR. NORTH: I did not say those words to the Commander in Chief. I simply expressed my thanks for having been able to serve him for five and half years, and my regrets that my service had brought forth a political firestorm and difficulties, when all I sought to do was to help. And that what I may have done was to hurt him.

* * *

MR. LIMAN: Did you tell Admiral Poindexter that you were going to be shredding documents other than the diversion documents which you had said you had already gotten rid of?

MR. NORTH: I don't—again, I don't recall specifically saying that. But I do recall assuring them on a number of occasions that I had taken care of my files, that I had shredded things, that basically the files were cleaned up. That was the basic input.

MR. LIMAN: I want to move to another topic, Colonel.

MR. NORTH: Can I—before we leave that if we may, Counsel. Again, I well recognize that there are certainly people who think it might have been something else, but the efforts to destroy those documents over the course of that period of time beginning in October, I never once believed to be anything criminal at all. I did not believe that anything I had done to that point was criminal. And I didn't think that it was anything other than preserving the integrity of activities and operations, the lives of people who were out there at stake, the various things that I had done that no longer were relevant—some of them were history and never would be done again—they simply didn't need to be exposed in any way. And one cannot be certain in the expansive answer to your comment, that whoever came in would be chosen by a national security adviser. I'm not certain that one ought to rest with the assurance that the person that comes in to replace you shares your same values or necessarily shares the same perspective that you have on a number of things. And I'm not saying that I have an exclusive view of what is right or wrong. I believe that things I did were right, and I believe that the lives of the people with whom I worked needed to be protected. I knew that the successor that was coming in wasn't going to do that. The CIA was not back actively engaged in the support of the Nicaraguan resistance. And the names and addresses and the places and the people with whom I worked during the period of time in which the CIA was not engaged, need not be exposed to anybody. And I want you to know that that was a lot of what was going through my mind.

MR. LIMAN: Colonel, since you chose to give that answer, I'm not going to leave the subject for a moment. First, let me make a statement, that it will probably provide no comfort to you for you to understand that we're not prosecutors here, and we're not here to assess criminal responsibility. I understand that there is an independent counsel somewhere working in other offices, but you should understand that our assessment is of a different nature.

MR. NORTH: Counsel, I understand that you're saying that, but I have heard members of this Committee who have said that I did wrong, that I wouldn't even need counsel, or that I wouldn't have abided by my rights under the Constitution but for the fact that I had done wrong, and I didn't believe it then, and I don't believe it now.

MR. LIMAN: Are you saying, sir, that you do not believe that it was wrong to misrepresent facts to the Congress of the United States?

MR. NORTH: I have admitted that, but I didn't think it was criminal.

MR. LIMAN: I'm not talking about what was criminal, you just chose the word "wrong." Are you saying, sir, that it wasn't wrong to misrepresent facts to the Attorney General of the United States?

MR. NORTH: (Confers with counsel.) I have testified as to what I believed to be right and wrong before—

MR. LIMAN: Now—

MR. NORTH: —and you have had that, and it's on the record.

MR. LIMAN: Now, Colonel, you have talked about the fact that you didn't know who your successor would be, and that was one of the reasons for engaging in all of this activity in the days before you left office, correct?

MR. NORTH: That is correct.

MR. LIMAN: The one thing you knew, was that people taking tours of the White House couldn't go into your office and look at the files there, right?

MR. NORTH: Not without the combination to my door.

MR. LIMAN: And the other thing you knew—(Pauses while North confers with his attorney.) And the other thing that you knew was that the President of the United States, the Commander in Chief whom you respect and revere, and I suspect love, had asked the Attorney General to do a fact finding mission, that's correct, isn't it?

MR. NORTH: Actually I don't know that Admiral Poindexter, when he told me about the fact finding inquiry on the 21st, that he specified that it was the President who had asked that that be done, but I did come to know that, that is correct.

MR. LIMAN: Would it have made a difference to you in your actions if you felt that the Attorney General was proceeding on the specific instructions of the President as opposed to the Admiral?

MR. NORTH: Would what have made a difference—that my actions be any different?

MR. LIMAN: Yes, sir.

MR. SULLIVAN: Objection, it's a hypothetical question—

MR. LIMAN: Would you—

MR. SULLIVAN: It's just pure speculation.

MR. LIMAN: You say that you were not sure whether the Attorney General was conducting this inquiry at the request of the President, or at the request of the Admiral. That's what I heard you say.

MR. NORTH: No. What I said was, I don't know that the Admiral told me, on the 21st, that the President—at least, I don't recall knowing at the time—that the Admiral told me that this was being done at the request of the President. He may well have told me that.

[Ed. Note: North's counsel tells the committee "I'm not a potted plant."]

MR. LIMAN: Would you have shredded less documents on the 22nd if you had been told that the Attorney General was acting at the specific request of the President, your Commander in Chief?

MR. SULLIVAN: Objection.

CHAIRMAN INOUYE: What is the basis of your objection, sir?

MR. SULLIVAN: It is pure speculation—dreamland. It has two "ifs" in it. And Mr. Liman knows better than most that—

CHAIRMAN INOUYE: May I remind—

MR. SULLIVAN: —those kinds of questions, Mr. Chairman, are wholly inappropriate, not just because of rules of evidence, not because you couldn't say it in a court, but because it's just dreamland. It's speculation. He says, "If you'd done this, and if you'd done that, and if you'd done that—what about this?" Come on, let's have, Mr. Chairman—

CHAIRMAN INOUYE: I'm certain counsel—

MR. SULLIVAN: —plain fairness, plain fairness. That's all we're asking.

CHAIRMAN INOUYE: May I speak, sir? May I speak?

MR. SULLIVAN: Yes, sir.

CHAIRMAN INOUYE: I'm certain counsel realizes that this is not a court of law.

MR. SULLIVAN: I—believe me, I know that.

CHAIRMAN INOUYE: And I'm certain you realize that the rules of evidence do not apply in this inquiry.

MR. SULLIVAN: That I know as well. I'm just asking for fairness—fairness. I know the rules don't apply. I know the Congress doesn't recognize attorney-client privilege, a husband and wife privilege, priest-penitent privilege. I know those things are all out the window—

CHAIRMAN INOUYE: We have attempted to be as fair as we can.

MR. SULLIVAN: —and we rely on just fairness, Mr. Chairman. Fairness.

CHAIRMAN INOUYE: Let the witness object, if he wishes to.

MR. SULLIVAN: I'm not a potted plant. I'm here as the lawyer. That's my job. (Laughter.)

CHAIRMAN INOUYE: Mr. Liman, please proceed with that question.

MR. NORTH: Let me answer it with a hypothetical answer.

MR. LIMAN: Colonel, you testified, when I put a question to you, that you did not recall whether the—the Admiral had told you that the President had requested the Attorney General to act. Do you recall that?

MR. NORTH: I do.

MR. LIMAN: You are the person who volunteered that fact, in response to one of my questions. Do you recall that?

MR. NORTH: I do.

MR. LIMAN: And my question to you was, would that have made a difference? You're the person who surfaced it.

MR. NORTH: Don't get angry, Counsel. I'm going to answer your question. If the Admiral had told me that the President had asked the Attorney General to conduct a fact-finding inquiry into all of the aspects of what I had done, and that I should tell the Attorney General everything, then I would have done so. Does that answer your question, sir?

And, the Admiral did not tell me that.

MR. LIMAN: And, if the Admiral had told you that, you wouldn't have done the quantity of shredding that you did. Is that correct?

MR. NORTH: We can play hypothetical games all night. If the Admiral had told me not to shred, I wouldn't have shredded.

MR. SULLIVAN: If the—

MR. LIMAN: Did you tell the Admiral that you were going to shred?

MR. NORTH: Pardon.

MR. LIMAN: Did you tell the Admiral that you were going to shred?

MR. NORTH: I told the Admiral that I was cleaning up my files. I told him that well before this began. I assured him on the 21st that I'd already done most of it.

MR. SULLIVAN: Mr. Chairman, may I object please. There has to be a reasonable limit to questions posed about shredding. I mean, how many hours, how many days, how many times? The Colonel has admitted shredding. I would say, conservatively, 125 times. I, please, respectfully ask, could we move on?

MR. NORTH: I honestly think, and I'm not trying to be light about it, we spent more time talking about it than I spent doing it. I honestly mean that. I shredded. I was never told not to shred. I shredded because I thought it was the right thing to do. When I didn't have a shredder, I put it in the burnbag and they were burned, and when the time came that I saw the entire situation change, and I was faced with the possibility of being the victim of a criminal prosecution, I then took action to protect myself. I took my notebooks home, and I took papers home, and I kept them until I turned them over to you.

MR. LIMAN: Now, let's—

MR. NORTH: And, to the White House.

* * *

MR. LIMAN: Now, is it correct, sir, that you were put in a position in which everybody who's eager and content to have Ollie North do whatever was necessary to energize the contras—to keep them together as a fighting force, to instill democratic values in them, to open up a southern front, to promote unity, to provide them with intelligence, to provide them with advice on munitions, to help provide them with that air base in a Central American country. They were all content and eager for you to do this as long as you didn't create a record pinning it on them?

MR. NORTH: You'd have to ask them.

MR. LIMAN: Well, do you remember, Oliver North, that you had a conversation once with the Chief of the Central American Task Force at the CIA right after Boland was passed? And that—and I'm going to show it to you, if you don't remember—and that you got criticized for being indiscreet in mentioning what you were doing, and you were told, "be more discreet next time," not that you shouldn't do it.

MR. NORTH: I recall the event, I don't recall the time.

MR. LIMAN: It's an Exhibit here, it's—we don't have to go over it.

MR. NORTH: I recall it.

MR. LIMAN: But that really was the spirit, wasn't it, of it all: don't infect other people with knowledge—

MR. NORTH: "Unnecessary knowledge" is the term.

MR. LIMAN: You do it, you provide the deniable link, you take the rap, if it gets exposed. That was what this was all about, right?

MR. NORTH: I have testified to that.

MR. LIMAN: And it's also fair to say that the people who chose you for this knew and appreciated your qualities?

MR. NORTH: You're asking me to put myself in the minds of other people, Counsel.

MR. LIMAN: Well—

MR. NORTH: I don't believe that any of those people foresaw the outcome of what has happened—

MR. LIMAN: Well—

MR. NORTH: I certainly didn't. I do honestly believe that they expected that Ollie would go quietly. And Ollie intended to do so right up until the day that somebody decided to start a criminal prosecution.

MR. LIMAN: Colonel, you characterized yourself, you described yourself—(pause) You described yourself as an action-oriented person, correct?

MR. NORTH: That's correct.

MR. LIMAN: You were the person, I think in your own statement, people would say, "Ollie, fix it." Right?

MR. NORTH: That's correct.

MR. LIMAN: And it would get fixed, right?

MR. NORTH: Usually.

MR. LIMAN: And you could cut through red tape, right?

MR. NORTH: Didn't say that in the statement. Well, but we did.

MR. LIMAN: That's—we understand each other, I've read enough of what you've written—

MR. NORTH: Mr. Liman, let me just say one thing, I think it's important for everybody to understand. I don't believe that people for whom I still have an enormous amount of respect, like Mr. McFarlane, or Admiral Poindexter, would have ever placed me in jeopardy of a criminal prosecution. I don't believe that those men—whether or not the President knew, and I don't think the President would have done that—I don't think anybody intended that Ollie North have to endure having his name be the only one to appear on the appointment order for an independent counsel. I think we all saw—I certainly did—that what we were doing was within the limits of the law—

MR. LIMAN: But—

MR. NORTH: —that there were great liabilities and that they were principally political, that the liabilities included the protection of the lives of other people, some of whom were at great risk, and some of whom have died. But—

MR. LIMAN: Oliver North, I hear you saying that if you weren't on the order for the appointment of an independent counsel, if there was an agreement that there was no criminal liability here, people would expect you to come before Congress and say, "I did it! It's not their fault"—

MR. NORTH: I did do—

MR. LIMAN: —"I was that loose cannon."

MR. NORTH: I did do it. I am not, as I said in my statement, at all ashamed of any of the things that I did. I was given a mission and I tried to carry it out.

MR. LIMAN: But part of that mission was to shield the others who were giving you the orders.

MR. NORTH: That is the part of any subordinate. Every centurion had a group of shields out in front of him, a hundred of 'em.

MR. LIMAN: Well, would you agree with this proposition, Colonel, that—and I think you would, because I think those medals represent—

MR. NORTH: No, those medals represent the heroism of the young Marines that I led. That's what they represent. And I—

MR. LIMAN: You still have those values, don't you?

MR. NORTH: I never called myself a hero. Those words were used by other people who describe me. I am grateful for those words, but I have never called myself such.

MR. LIMAN: Colonel—Colonel, five and a half years in the White House hasn't destroyed those values?

MR. NORTH: Not at all.

MR. LIMAN: Nor has this investigation destroyed those values.

MR. NORTH: Not in the least.

MR. LIMAN: And I want to talk about those values, because I think this is important for the American people. And you would agree with the proposition, wouldn't you, that in our desire to promote democracy abroad, including Nicaragua and elsewhere, we must never sacrifice our democratic values here?

MR. NORTH: I couldn't agree more.

MR. LIMAN: And that part of those democratic values are that sometimes Congress is going to disagree with the Executive branch?

MR. NORTH: True enough.

MR. LIMAN: And sometimes you, as a military officer, are going to disagree with what the President or the Congress decide as a matter of policy—correct?

MR. NORTH: Certainly.

MR. LIMAN: And you believe very firmly in civilian control?

MR. NORTH: Absolutely.

MR. LIMAN: And you do not share the view that was expressed and retracted by your secretary that sometimes you must rise above the written law?

MR. NORTH: I do not believe in rising above the law at all, and I do not [think] that I have ever stated that.

MR. LIMAN: And you—

MR. NORTH: I haven't—I have not.

MR. LIMAN: And when you, Colonel North, had to—in order to protect this operation and your superiors—engage in deception of Congress, in deception of other members of the Executive branch, it is particularly painful for you in view of the honor code that you subscribed to at Annapolis, isn't that so?

MR. NORTH: That is correct.

* * *

SEN. HATCH: And I have to say to you, I think these hearings are very important in spite of that, but I think that's something we have to be concerned about and I agree with you. In that regard, would you agree that if we must ever have these kinds of hearings at all they should not be turned into forums where persons, especially those under investigation by the Independent Counsel are prematurely judged and accused of criminal conduct.

MR. NORTH: It would have been nice, sir.

SEN. HATCH: I saw a lot of premature judging in—in the—the process—in this process, and I kind of resented it then, and I still resent it today. Along these lines a scholar once wrote, "How individuals who have been pilloried by Congressional investigating committees can be guaranteed a fair trial before an unprejudiced jury is hard to see unless the jury be illiterate." Would you agree with that?

MR. NORTH: At the very least, sir.

SEN. HATCH: And would you also agree with another statement by the same author when he states, "If the investigative power of Congress is unlimited, the separation of powers and systems of checks and balances must break down." Is that correct?

MR. NORTH: That was the position I've taken throughout, sir.

SEN. HATCH: Well, these statements were written, by the way, by one Arthur Lawrence Liman in the thesis entitled "Limited Government and Unlimited Investigation." This was in partial fulfillment—I—I know that he's going to appreciate my comments and—before I get through.

(Laughter)

MR. NORTH: I thought I had written them, sir.

SEN. HATCH: Well, let me tell you, they were true then and they're true today. It was in partial fulfillment of the requirements for the Bachelor's Degree at the Harvard University, April 2, 1954, shortly after the McCarthy Hearings. And I happ—and I'm personally happy to say that regardless of what others have done her, Arthur Liman has, for the most part, conducted himself in accordance with what he wrote 33 years ago.

* * *

TESTIMONY OF LT. COL. OLIVER L. NORTH: CLOSING STATEMENTS BY COMMITTEE MEMBERS

* * *

SEN. SARBANES: Well, Colonel, let me—I just want to close here because my time is almost up. First of all, let me say to you that we appreciate your appearance before the Committee. I want you to know I don't think there's any member of the Committee who has not been touched by your very heartfelt statement about the pressures that were, that you were feeling that were applied and imposed upon your family. And I think your concern for their security and your very moving statement in that regard is a matter that touched all of us, and it's regrettable that that problem could not have been addressed in some other way, and that it led to it being dealt with as it was and the difficulties that flowed from that, and the statement you made about the whole letters exchange being a mistake, but we understand the motivation that was behind that.

I want to make this observation. You know, we put up in the Capitol and in other places quotes from our respected leaders to draw lessons and morals from. There's one in the Capitol of the United States quoting Justice Brandeis, and it says, "The greatest dangers to liberty lurk in insidious encroachments, by men of zeal, well meaning, but without understanding." And I think the understanding that Justice Brandeis was talking about, is that in a democracy, reasonable people can differ on the substance of policy. In fact, that's the essence of democracy. And the thing we fault in the totalitarian regimes, to which we are opposed, is the fact that they don't permit those differences and establish a system for resolving them peacefully.

It's part of our system that you have a respect and tolerance for the views of others, no matter how deeply your own policy views may be held, and that a civility ought to exist between us. Others may equally hold strong policy views. In fact, they may even agree with your goals, but disagree with the methods or tactics by which you hope to achieve them. Many of the goals about which you have spoken before this Committee, I think are goals that are subscribed to by members of the Committee, and by the American people. Some members agreed with the tactics you wanted to use, others disagreed with it.

In countries where they don't have a process for resolving those sharp differences, they resort to violence. Here we have a constitutional system that established procedures for resolving those differences and we make our policy through an interaction between the Congress and the President. If one loses in that process, the constitutional system guarantees you the right to come back and to seek to make your policy views prevail. We protect people's right to do that. We recognize they may feel deeply, and they may not prevail as the process works. The other side may prevail. But we guarantee their right to come back. But if we have a system where policymakers are seeking to implement their views regardless of the decisions that have been made constitutionally, then we're undermining the integrity of the political process.

That's the concern about these private networks, that go outside of the established way of reaching a decision. Decisions that are very controversial, in which there are very sharp differences. But once we start going down the path of people saying, we're not going to respect that decision that has been made through the constituted channels, we're going to go outside of it, shrouded in secrecy, then, I think, we're facing very deep difficulties. And that's why I simply close by making the point that the depth of one's conviction, and the well-meaning aspect to it, is not enough, in and of itself, that view has to prevail. Now, you've been very persuasive. You've been persuasive in the past as you've dealt with—with the Congress and with others. But the essence of our constitutional system, the thing that makes it respected throughout the world, that commands the allegiance and the support of the American people, is that it gives us a process by which we can resolve these sharply held differences amongst ourselves. And we have to maintain that process. The substantive goal does not justify compromising the means we have put into place. Thank you, Mr. Chairman.

* * *

REP. STOKES: Colonel, at the beginning of your testimony, you told us that you came to tell the truth—the good, the bad, and the ugly. And I want to commend you for keeping your word. I think it has been good; I think it has been bad; and I think it has been ugly. I suppose that what has been most disturbing to me about your testimony is the ugly part. In fact, it has been more than ugly. It has been chilling, and, in fact, frightening. I'm not talking just about your part in this, but the entire scenario—about government officials who plotted and conspired, who set up a straw man, a fall guy. Officials who lied, misrepresented, and deceived. Officials who planned to superimpose upon our government a layer outside of our government, shrouded in secrecy and only accountable to the conspirators.

I could go on and on, but we both know the testimony, and it is ugly. In my opinion it is a prescription for anarchy in a democratic society.

In the course of your testimony, I thought often about the honor code at the US Naval Academy. For 19, now almost 20 years, I have appointed young men to that Academy. I've always taken great pride in those appointees, knowing that they would be imbued with the highest standard of honor, duty and responsibility toward their government. The Academy catalog speaks of the honor concept of being more than an administrative device, that it fosters the development of lasting and moral principles, it becomes part and parcel of the professionalism expected of graduates as commissioned officers.

But more than that, I think of the young students all over America sitting in civics and government courses. You've said many times that you worry about the damage these hearings are creating for the United States around the world. I worry, Colonel, about the damage to the children of America, the future leaders of America. I worry about how we tell them that the ugly things you've told us about in our government is not the way American government is conducted. That is not our democracy's finest hour.

And then lastly, Colonel, I was touched yesterday by the eloquence of Senator Mitchell who spoke so poignantly about the rule of law and what our Constitution means to immigrants. He spoke eloquently of how all Americans are equal under our law. Senator Mitchell's words meant a great deal to another class of Americans, blacks and minorities, because, unlike immigrants, they have not always enjoyed full privileges of justice and equality under the Constitution which we now celebrate in its 200th year. If any class of Americans understand and appreciate the rule of law, the judicial process and constitutional law, it is those who've had to use that process to come from a status of nonpersons in American law to a status of equality under the law. We had to abide by the slow and arduous process of abiding by law until we could change the law through the judicial process.

In fact, Colonel, as I sit here this morning looking at you in your uniform, I cannot help but remember that I wore the uniform of this country in World War II in a segregated army. I wore it as proudly as you do, even though our government required black and white soldiers in the same army to live, sleep, eat, and travel separate and apart, while fighting and dying for our country. But because of the rule of law, today's servicemen in America suffer no such indignity.

Similar to Senator Mitchell's humble beginnings, my mother, a widow, raised two boys. She had an eighth-grade education. She was a domestic worker who scrubbed floors. One son became the first black mayor of a major American city. The other sits today as Chairman of a House Intelligence Committee. Only in America, Colonel North. Only in America. And while I admire your love for America, I hope too that you will never forget that others too love America just as much as you do and that others too will die for America, just as quick as you will.

Thank you, Mr. Chairman.

* * *

SEN. SARBANES: Mr. Chairman, because of the assertions which will appear on the printed record questioning the fairness of this Committee, I think it's important to place on the printed record a demonstration of Committee fairness, which I think has been very visible and obvious to all of us as we have sat through this hearing and to those who have watched it, and that is that Colonel North's counsel has had unlimited scope throughout these proceedings to defer his responses to questions while they engaged in consultation and counsel. And that has happened frequently and often, and I simply underscore it to place it on the printed record because, although it is very visible, unless a statement is made about it, it will not appear in the printed record reflecting, I think, a very significant measure of fairness extended to the colonel and his testimony before this committee.

* * *

CHAIRMAN INOUYE: Thank you very much. Colonel North, Mr. Sullivan, I think we're now at the end of a long 6 days. The questions I have cannot be answered because some of those who could have answered these questions are not here with us. And furthermore, I'm certain you'll agree that we've had enough questions.

* * *

I believe during the past week we have participated in creating and developing very likely a new American hero. Like you, as one who has felt the burning sting of bullet and shrapnel, and heard the unforgettable and frightening sounds of incoming shells, I salute you, sir, as a fellow combat man. And the rows of ribbons that you have on your chest will forever remind us of your courageous service and your willingness—your patriotic willingness to risk your life and your limb. I'm certain the life and the burdens of a hero will be difficult and heavy. And so, with all sincerity, I wish you well as you begin your journey into a new life. However, as an interested observer and as one who has participated in the making of this new American hero, I've found certain aspects of you testimony to be most troubling. Chairman Hamilton has most eloquently discussed them—because, as a result of your very gallant presence and your articulate statements, your life, I'm certain, will be emulated by many, many young Americans. I'm certain we will all of us receive an abundance of requests from young citizens throughout the land for entrance into the privileged ranks of cadets of the military services. These young citizens having been imbued with the passion of patriotism will do so. And to these young men and women, I wish to address a few words.

In 1964, when Col. North was a cadet, he took an oath of office, like all hundreds throughout the service academies. And he also said that he will abide with the regulations which set forth the cadet honor concept. The first honor concept—first, because it's so important, over and above all others, is a very simple one: a member of the brigade does not lie, cheat, or steal. And in this regulation of 1964, the word "lie" was defined as follows, quote: "A deliberate oral or written untruth, it may be an oral statement which is known to be false or a simple response to a question in which the answer is known to be false." End of quote. The words, "mislead" or "deceive," were defined as follows: "A deliberate misrepresentation of a true situation by being untruthful or withholding or omitting or subtlly wording information in such a way, as to leave an erroneous or false impression of the known true situation."

And when the Colonel put on his uniform and the bars of a second lieutenant, he was well aware that he was subject to the Uniform Code of Military Justice. It's a special code of laws that apply to our men and women in uniform. It's a code that has been applicable to the conduct and activities of Colonel North throughout his military career, and even at this moment. And that code makes it abundantly clear, that orders of a superior officer must be obeyed by subordinate members—but it is lawful orders.

The Uniform Code makes it abundantly clear that it must be the lawful orders of a superior officer. In fact, it says, members of the military have an obligation to disobey unlawful orders. This principle was considered so important, that we—we, the government of the United States, proposed that it be internationally applied, in the Nuremberg trials. And so, in the Nuremberg trials, we said that the fact that the defendant—

MR. SULLIVAN: —Mr. Chairman. May I please register an objection.—

CHAIRMAN INOUYE: —May I continue my statement.—

MR. SULLIVAN: —I find this offensive! I find you engaging in a personal attack on Colonel North, and you're far removed from the issues of this case. To make reference to the Nuremberg trials, I find personally and professionally distasteful, and I can no longer sit here and listen to this.

CHAIRMAN INOUYE: You will have to sit there, if you want to listen.

MR. SULLIVAN: Mr. Chairman, please don't conclude these hearings on this unfair note. I have strong objections to many things in the hearings, and you up there speak about listening to the American people. Why don't you listen to the American people and what they've said as a result—(Chairman Inouye bangs the gavel)—of the last week. There are 20,000 telegrams in our room outside the corridor here that came in this morning. The American people—

CHAIRMAN INOUYE: I'm sure that there are.

MR. SULLIVAN: The American people have spoken and please stop this personal attack against Colonel North.

CHAIRMAN INOUYE: I have sat here, listened to the Colonel without interrupting. I hope you will accord me the courtesy of saying my piece.

MR. SULLIVAN: Sir, you may give speeches on the issues, it seems to me. You may ask questions, but you may not attack him personally. This has gone too far, in my opinion, with all due respect.

CHAIRMAN INOUYE: I'm not attacking him personally.

MR. SULLIVAN: That's the way I hear it, sir.

CHAIRMAN INOUYE: Colonel North, I'm certain it must have been painful for you, as you stated, to testify that you lied to senior officials of our government, that you lied and misled our Congress. And believe me, it was painful for all of us to sit here and listen to that testimony. It was painful. It was equally painful to learn from your testimony that you lied and misled because of what you believed to be a just cause—supporters of Nicaragua freedom fighters, the contras.

You have eloquently articulated your opposition to Marxism and communism and I believe that all of us—I'm certain that all of us on this panel are equally opposed to Marxism and communism. But should we, in the defense of democracy, adopt and embrace one of the most important tenets of communism and Marxism—the ends justify the means?

This is not one of the commandments of democracy. Our government is not a government of men. It is still a government of laws. And finally, to those thousands upon thousands of citizens who have called, sent telegrams, written letters, I wish to thank all of you most sincerely and commend you for your demonstrated interest in the well-being of our government, of our freedoms and our democracy. Your support or opposition of what is happening in this room is important—important because it dramatically demonstrates the strength of this democracy.

We Americans are confident in our strength to openly and without fear put into action one of the important teachings of our greatest Founding Fathers, Thomas Jefferson, who spoke of the right to dissent, the right to criticize the leaders of this government and he said, "The spirit of resistance to government is so valuable on certain occasions that I wish it to be always kept alive. It will often be exercised when wrong, but better so, than not be exercised at all."

Unlike communism, in a democracy such as ours, we are not afraid to wash our dirty linen in public. We're not afraid to let the world know that we do have failures and we do have shortcomings. I think all of us should recall the open invitation that we send to the press of the world to view the spaceflights, to record our successes and record our failures. We permit all to film and record our spaceflights. We don't, after the fact, let the world know only of our successes. And I think we should recall that we did not prohibit any member of the world press to film and record one of the bloodiest chapters of our domestic history, the demonstration and riots in the civil rights period. This was not easy to let the world know that we had police dogs and police officers with whips and clubs denying fellow citizens their rights. But I've always felt that, as long as we daily reaffirm our belief in and support of our Constitution and the great principles of freedom that were long ago enunciated by our Founding Fathers, we'll continue to prevail and flourish.

I'd like to make one make more closing remark. Throughout the past 10 days, many of my colleagues on this panel, in opening their questions to the colonel, prefaced their remarks by saying, "Colonel, I'm certain you know that I voted for aid to the contras." Ladies and gentlemen and Colonel North, I voted against aid to the contras. I did so not as a communist. I did so not as an agent of the KGB. I did so upon information that I gathered as a member of the bipartisan commission on Central America, based upon information that I gathered as chairman of the Foreign Operations Committee, based upon information that I gathered as a senior member of the Defense subcommittee, and based upon information that I gathered as chairman and member of the Senate Intelligence Committee.

I voted against aid to the contras. It wasn't easy to vote against your Commander-in-Chief. It's not easy to stand before my colleagues and find yourself in disagreement, but that is the nature of democracy. I did so because I was firmly convinced that to follow the path or the course that was laid down by the Reagan proposal was—would certainly and inevitably lead to a point where young men and women of the United States would have to be sent into the conflict. And, Colonel; I am certain, having experience warfare, that is not what we want our young people to go through again. You have lost many friends, and their names now are engraved on the black marble. I have lost many friends who are buried throughout this land.

I know that the path of democ—diplomacy is frustrating—at times angering. But I would think that we should give it a chance, if it means that, with some patience, we could save even one life. So that is why I wish my colleagues to know that I voted against aid to the Nicaraguan freedom fighters.

This has been a long day. I know that all of us are desirous of a rest. Col. North, with all sincerity, I thank you for your assistance these past six days. You have been most cordial, and your presence should make your fellow officers very proud of the way you have presented yourself. And to your lady, I wish her the best. She has sat there throughout these days with patience and grace. You have a fine lady.

The panel will stand in recess for ten minutes.

Notes and Questions

1. Lessons from the North testimony. The portions of North's testimony that are excerpted above were selected for two purposes. The primary purpose, noted above, is to illustrate how effectively North used his congressional testimony to build public support for himself and the causes he espoused. The second purpose, which is the focus of this Note, is to identify some practical lessons that are illustrated by exchanges that occurred during North's testimony:

A. *A congressional investigation is not a judicial proceeding, and rules of evidence do not apply.* When House Chief Counsel John Nields questioned North about his initial meeting with Attorney General Ed Meese about the Iran-Contra matter, with Nields using notes of the meeting prepared by someone other than North, North's counsel objected that, "It is appropriate to ask what he said at the meeting, but not with respect to someone else's notes as if it gives authority to what is transcribed in the notes." Committee chair Senator Daniel Inouye's ruling on the objection was swift and sure: "For the purposes of a congressional inquiry, the question is proper. Objection is overruled. Please proceed."

B. *When counseling a witness, always assume that email and other electronic communications are never really erased; when conducting an investigation, always obtain the email and other electronic communications.* The use of email and electronic communication today is commonplace and ubiquitous. At the time of the Iran-Contra hearings, email was a far more esoteric mode of communication. The "PROF notes" email messages among North and his colleagues proved a rich source of evidence for investigators. As North acknowledged under questioning by John Nields, "We all sincerely believed that when we sent a PROF message to another party and punched the button 'delete,' that it was gone forever. Wow, were we wrong."

The Iran-Contra email "PROF notes" actually were discovered during the Tower Commission (a special three-member commission appointed by President Reagan to investigate the Iran-Contra matter) investigation that preceded the Iran-Contra congressional investigation:

> On 11 February [1987], Kenneth Krieg, a Pentagon analyst assigned to work on the commission's staff, informed Tower that he had discovered a wealth of computer files on NSC activity during the period of the arms shipments to Iran and the contra resupply effort. The files were part of an internal communications network known as Professional Office System (PROFS) software. An early form of e-mail, the PROFS network was used as a means of sending private communications between top NSC officials. The individuals using the system assumed that messages saved to memory were well protected from outside scrutiny and could be deleted on command.
>
> They were wrong. White House technicians routinely copied saved materials onto the main White House computer to safeguard important files. The FBI was aware of this and had already tried, unsuccessfully, to access the saved messages. Krieg was highly skilled at manipulating the system, however, and was able to deliver where the bureau had failed.
>
> The recovered PROFS notes, assembled into a stack almost 4 feet high, painted a damning picture of NSC involvement in the events of Iran-Contra. Oliver North had made particularly heavy use of the computer system. The resulting paper trail erased any lingering doubts regarding his central role in shaping the Iran initiative. To a lesser degree the notes also incriminated McFarlane and Poindexter. This was the proof the commission so desperately needed. It corroborated much of McFarlane's testimony and made North and Poindexter's refusal to testify [before the Tower Commission] less consequential. Tower later compared the impact of the discovery to "switching on a bright overhead light" in a darkened room. As testimony to the importance of the breakthrough, both the congressional investigators and the independent counsel made heavy use of the PROFS evidence in their own reports.

Kenneth Kitts, *Presidential Commissions & National Security: The Politics of Damage Control* 115–16 (Lynne Rienner Publishers 2006). (Special investigative commissions are the subject of Chapter 8.)

C. *Playing "hardball" can be a two-edged sword.* North's counsel, Brendan Sullivan, objected vigorously to the "rambling questions and the inability to finish the subject matter and proceed to another" that Sullivan argued was a "stall job" to prolong unnecessarily North's testimony. Senator George Mitchell countered Sullivan's objection with the observation that because of North's refusal to appear for a full private deposition prior to his public testimony Sullivan's "objection [was] wholly unfounded, without any merit, and I believe the Counsel should be permitted to question as he has, because he's not had the opportunity to question in private, and therefore he must cover these areas as thoroughly as he can." Chairman Inouye then overruled the objection.

D. *Never underestimate the impact of dramatic excess, when skillfully and effectively deployed.* One area of vulnerability for North was his failure to pay for a home security system arranged by his private sector confederates Hakim and Secord. When asked about the security system during his congressional testimony, North invoked an assassination threat against him by notorious international terrorist Abu Nibal, and added this dramatic flourish: "Now, I want you to know that I'd be more than willing—and if anybody else is watching overseas, and I'm sure they are—I'll be glad to meet Abu Nibal on equal terms anywhere in the world. Okay? There's an even deal for him. But I am not willing to have my wife and my four children meet Abu Nidal or his organization on his terms. And I want you to know what was going through my mind." This comment, with the subsequent lengthy explanation of the dangers presented by the Abu Nibal organization, went quite far toward expunging any public condemnation of North for accepting the security system. North effectively used similar dramatic license to refute suggestions of sexual misconduct arising out of his use of Contra cashier's checks to purchase items at a ladies' hosiery shop:

> And I realize that it—that this hearing is a difficult thing. Believe me, gentlemen, it isn't as difficult for you as it is for a guy that's got to come up here and tell the truth, and that's what I'm trying to do. And I want to make it very clear that when you put up things like "Parklane Hosiery" and you all snicker at it, and you know that I've got a beautiful secretary, and the good Lord gave her the gift of beauty, and the people snicker that Ollie North might have been doing a little hanky-panky with his secretary, Ollie North has been loyal to his wife since the day he married her. And the fact is I went to my best friend and I asked her, "Did I ever go to Parklane Hosiery?" And you know what she told me? "Of course you did, you old buffoon, you went there to buy leotards for our two little girls." And the reason I wrote the check to Parklane Hosiery, just like the checks at Giant, is because I was owed my money for what I had spent in pursuing that covert operation.

As illustrated by these two examples, North's testimony set new standards for the use of dramatic presentations during televised congressional hearings to defuse potentially damaging investigative findings.

E. *Be prepared to guard and preserve privileges.* At one point in North's testimony the questioning focused on communications between North and his wife. North and his counsel were prepared to avoid any suggestion that he was waiving his confidential marital communications privilege:

> MR. NIELDS: Yes, and I take it that in answering the question, you've been telling us what happened at certain meetings that I take it were attended only by your wife, and I take it you are testifying to what you've been told by her?
>
> MR. NORTH: On advice of counsel, I have not revealed any of our confidential marital communications. I have given you a surmise, based on what I know the facts to be.
>
> MR. SULLIVAN: In other words, Counsel, don't call his wife up here.
>
> MR. NIELDS: No. That wasn't the question, at all. The question was simply what the source of the information was, and I take it, it's your wife?

MR. NORTH: Counsel, I gave you a long story, and the sources are multiple for that story, but accurate.

MR. NIELDS: Well, other than your wife, what are the sources?

MR. NORTH: Some of the information may be privileged or a work product of my attorney.

MR. SULLIVAN: In other words, we've done a little of our own investigation—Excuse me, Mr. Chairman—a little of our own investigation regarding these allegations, and have amassed some evidence and have concluded that they're absolutely baseless. From that information, Col. North has been able to draw certain conclusions, and if you have any proof to the contrary, why don't you present it?

MR. NIELDS: So, what he is testifying to is based on what he's been told by his wife and his attorneys?

MR. SULLIVAN: Not necessarily so. There are other factors as well.

MR. NIELDS: Okay, what else?

MR. NORTH: I, I'm just telling you all that I know about the event. No money ever was received. (Pause) I obviously had a conversation with Mr. Hakim that initiated this entire business back in February or early March.

As discussed in more detail in Chapter 6 below, evidentiary privileges that are not constitutionally based, such as the confidential marital communications privilege, will not necessarily be recognized in congressional investigative proceedings. Nevertheless, voluntarily providing congressional testimony that reveals information that otherwise would be protected by a privilege could be construed as a waiver of that privilege in a subsequent civil or criminal judicial proceeding, so the prudent course of action is to avoid any suggestion of waiver, as North and his counsel did in the exchange above.

F. *A good one-liner can make a reputation—and even define a career.* Despite the gravity of the constitutional and political issues that were the subject of the Iran-Contra hearings, perhaps the most-remembered and often-quoted line from the entire proceedings is Brendan Sullivan's retort to Chairman Inouye's admonition that he should allow the witness to answer the question: "I'm not a potted plant. I'm here as the lawyer. That's my job."

G. *What you say now can come back to haunt you later.* Senator Orrin Hatch deftly and gently scored some political points (and probably conveyed a subtle but effective warning) when he quoted Senate Majority Chief Counsel Arthur Liman's senior thesis as a Harvard undergraduate, written during the McCarthy era, describing the dangers of excessive zeal in congressional investigations. Mr. Liman probably could not have imagined when he wrote those words that they would be quoted back to him over thirty years later in a congressional investigation. The best politicians are always mindful of this phenomenon, and often temper their remarks out of concern that they might one day be in the position of the person or group they currently oppose.

H. *Finally, always recall that in the age of television, visual images matter.* As discussed in the excerpt quoted above from Arthur Liman's book *Lawyer: A Life of Counsel and Controversy*, North's military uniform and medals, and the angle from which he was photographed by the television cameras, had a dramatic impact on the public's perception of the proceedings. Liman tried to counter the impact of North's military uniform and medals at the outset of the subsequent testimony of Admiral John Poindexter on July 15, 1987:

> MR. LIMAN. Admiral, without unduly intruding on your privacy, I just want to go over some facts in your biography.
>
> You are 50 years of age.
>
> MR. POINDEXTER. That is correct.
>
> MR. LIMAN. What is your present position?
>
> MR. POINDEXTER. I am a Special Assistant to the chief of Naval Operations.
>
> MR. LIMAN. And you are a vice admiral in the Navy?
>
> MR. POINDEXTER. Technically, I am a rear admiral at this point.
>
> MR. LIMAN. And you were a graduate of the United States Naval Academy at Annapolis in 1958?
>
> MR. POINDEXTER. Yes.
>
> MR. LIMAN. And you had the distinction of graduating first in a class of some 900 midshipmen?
>
> MR. POINDEXTER. I did.
>
> MR. LIMAN. And you obtained a doctorate in nuclear physics at the California Institute of Technology?
>
> MR. POINDEXTER. I did.
>
> MR. LIMAN. And after that, you have served in various position of command and staff in the Navy until you joined the National Security Council staff; is that correct?
>
> MR. POINDEXTER. Yes.
>
> MR. LIMAN. It is also fair to say, is it not, admiral, that if you were wearing your uniform today, it would be bedecked with a number of medals and ribbons, including the Legion of Merit, the Meritorious Service Medal, the Naval Expeditionary Medal, the National Defense Service Medal?
>
> MR. POINDEXTER. Yes, Mr. Liman.
>
> If I may, I would like to say something about that at this point. I know some people wonder why I am not wearing my uniform, and I would like to make that point clear in the beginning.
>
> I am very proud of my uniform and I am very proud of the United States Navy, but this issue is not a Navy issue. When the President decided in Decem-

ber 1985 to appoint me as the National Security Adviser, he gave me a separate commission, a commission essentially as a political appointee filling the position that although not required to be civilian, often has been in the past.

Under this commission, I reported directly to the President on matters that were appropriate, which I will get into later.

In addition to that commission, I also retained my commission as a naval officer, as a vice admiral in the United States Navy.

All during my time as National Security Adviser, I tried to make a very clear distinction between the two hats that I wore, one National Security Adviser, the other a vice admiral in the United States Navy.

Because these hearings are basically on issues that I handled as National Security Adviser, I chose to appear here in civilian clothes, which I think is entirely appropriate given the nature of the matters under consideration.

Despite the merits of Poindexter's reasons for not wearing his Naval uniform during his testimony, there is no doubt that North garnered considerable public support by appearing in his Marine Corps uniform. The importance of visual appearances in the age of television is undeniable, and has been so at least since Richard Nixon's haggard appearance during his 1960 televised debate with John F. Kennedy, which some believe caused Nixon to lose the presidential election. In the age of YouTube, TikTok, and twenty-four-hour news and politics channels, anyone who ignores the visual element does so at great peril.

2. Comparing the roles of counsel and members in questioning witnesses. The excerpts of North's testimony provided above show the considerable difference between the nature and objectives of questioning by committee counsel and subsequent questioning by committee members. In proceedings where counsel is charged with eliciting the facts and exploring the underlying legal issues, the questioning by members is less about obtaining information than about scoring political points. For example, consider the moving remarks of Congressman Louis Stokes about the special meaning that the rule of law holds for African-Americans. Although North may have privately taken umbrage at some of Stokes's remarks, he was wise not to try to debate the issues with the congressman. The best-prepared witnesses, like North in this instance, know when to engage in political exchanges with members and when to "cut your losses" and simply not respond. Moreover, those with legislative experience know that in congressional proceedings the time of the proceeding is not dictated by whether or not every question has been asked, but rather by whether or not every questioner has had an opportunity to ask. Particularly where questioning by members is concerned, redundancy and repetition are to be expected, and objecting to the inefficiency of the process will not succeed in persuading the chair to cut off a member who is within his or her allotted time for questioning.

3. The importance of closing remarks. Portions of some committee members' closing remarks are reproduced above. Often those statements will be among the most important in a proceeding, particularly for the individual members. Members and their staff are likely to spend a disproportionate amount of their time focusing on closing remarks, and they often are tailored to important constituencies such as the voters "back home" or the members of a voting bloc the member wishes to reach. Despite their importance, the delivery of effective closing remarks is a dicey business, requiring a subtle balance between eloquence and demagoguery. Read the closing remarks excerpted above and draw your own conclusions as to which speakers struck or missed this balance.

The North and Poindexter Use Immunity Grants in the Courts

A. The Initial Decision in *United States v. North* (*North I*)

In May 1989, almost two years after his immunized congressional testimony, North was convicted of three criminal offenses arising out of the events that he had recounted in his congressional testimony. In the July 1990 decision excerpted below, the United States Court of Appeals for the District of Columbia addressed the impact of his prior immunized testimony on the government's ability to prosecute North. The complete decision covers 117 pages in the Federal Reporter; the portions below are taken from the section of the opinion that addresses the use of North's immunized congressional testimony.

United States v. North

910 F.2d 843 (D.C. Cir. 1990)

PER CURIAM:

Introduction

In November of 1986, a Lebanese newspaper reported that the United States had secretly sold weapons to Iran. Two months later, Congress established two committees charged with investigating the sales of arms to Iran, the diversion of proceeds therefrom to rebels (or "Contras") fighting in Nicaragua, and the attempted cover-up of these activities (controversial events popularly known as "the Iran/Contra Affair"). In July of 1987, Lieutenant Colonel Oliver L. North, a former member of the National Security Council ("NSC") staff, testified before the Iran/Contra congressional committees. North asserted his Fifth Amendment right not to testify before the committees, but the government compelled his testimony by a grant of use immunity pursuant to 18 U.S.C. §6002. North testified for six days. His testimony was carried live on national television and radio, replayed on news shows, and analyzed in the public media.

Contemporaneously with the congressional investigation, and pursuant to the Independent Counsel statute, 28 U.S.C. §§591–99 [*Ed. Note: This statute has since expired and was not renewed by Congress*], the Special Division of this Court … appointed Lawrence E. Walsh as Independent Counsel ("IC") and charged him with the investigation and prosecution of any criminal wrongdoing by government officials in the

Iran/Contra events. As a result of the efforts of the IC, North was indicted and tried on twelve counts arising from his role in the Iran/Contra Affair. After extensive pretrial proceedings and a twelve-week trial, North was convicted in May of 1989 on three counts: aiding and abetting an endeavor to obstruct Congress in violation of 18 U.S.C. §§1505 and 2 ("Count 6"); destroying, altering, or removing official NSC documents in violation of 18 U.S.C. §2071 ("Count 9"); and accepting an illegal gratuity, consisting of a security system for his home, in violation of 18 U.S.C. §201(c)(1)(B) ("Count 10"). North now appeals his convictions on these counts.

I. Use of Immunized Testimony

A. *Introduction*

> No person ... shall be compelled in any criminal case to be a witness against himself....

U.S. Const. amend. V

North argues that his Fifth Amendment right against self-incrimination was violated, asserting that the District Court failed to require the IC to establish independent sources for the testimony of witnesses before the grand jury and at trial and to demonstrate that witnesses did not in any way use North's compelled testimony. North further argues that his Fifth Amendment right was violated by the District Court's failure to determine whether or not the IC made "nonevidentiary" use of the immunized testimony.

* * *

The prohibition against compelled testimony is not absolute, however. Under the rule of *Kastigar v. United States*, 406 U.S. 441 (1972), a grant of use immunity under 18 U.S.C. §6002 enables the government to compel a witness's self-incriminating testimony. This is so because the statute prohibits the government both from using the immunized testimony itself and also from using any evidence derived directly or indirectly therefrom. Stated conversely, use immunity conferred under the statute is "coextensive with the scope of the privilege against self-incrimination, and therefore is sufficient to compel testimony over a claim of the privilege.... [Use immunity] prohibits the prosecutorial authorities from using the compelled testimony in *any* respect...." *Kastigar*, 406 U.S. at 453 (emphasis in original). *See also Braswell v. United States*, 487 U.S. 99, 117 (1988) ("Testimony obtained pursuant to a grant of statutory use immunity may be used neither directly nor derivatively.").

* * *

C. *Analysis*

North's primary *Kastigar* complaint is that the District Court failed to require the IC to demonstrate an independent source for each item of evidence or testimony presented to the grand jury and the petit jury, and that the District Court erred in focusing almost wholly on the IC's leads to witnesses, rather than on the content of the witnesses' testimony. North also claims that the IC made an improper nonevidentiary use of the immunized testimony (as by employing it for purposes of trial strategy), or at least that the District Court failed to make a sufficient inquiry into the question. North also protests that his immunized testimony was improperly used to refresh the recollection of witnesses before the grand jury and at trial, that this refreshment caused them to alter their testimony, and that the District Court failed to give this question the careful examination it deserved. In our discussion here, we first consider alleged nonevidentiary use of immunized testimony by the IC. We will then proceed to consider the use of immunized testimony to refresh witnesses' recollections. Finally, we will address the distinction between use of immunized testimony as a lead to procure witnesses and use insofar as it affects the substantive content of witnesses' testimony.

Assuming without deciding that a prosecutor cannot make nonevidentiary use of immunized testimony, we conclude that the IC here did not do so and that the District Court's inquiry and findings on this issue are not clearly erroneous. Thus, we do not decide the question of the permissibility or impermissibility of nonevidentiary use. However, contrary to the District Court, we conclude that the use of immunized testimony by witnesses to refresh their memories, or otherwise to focus their thoughts, organize their testimony, or alter their prior or contemporaneous statements, constitutes evidentiary use rather than nonevidentiary use. The District Court on remand is to hold the searching type of *Kastigar* hearing described in detail below, concerning North's allegations of refreshment. Finally, because the District Court apparently interpreted *Kastigar* as prohibiting the government only from using immunized testimony *as a lead* rather than *using it at all*, we hold that the District Court's truncated *Kastigar* inquiry was insufficient to protect North's Fifth Amendment right to avoid self-incrimination.

* * *

We cannot agree with the District Court that the use of immunized testimony to refresh the memories of witnesses is a nonevidentiary matter and that therefore refreshment should not be subject to a *Kastigar* hearing because "[n]o court has ever so required, nor did *Kastigar* suggest anything of the kind." [*Ed. Note: Citation to the District Court's preliminary decision on North's Kastigar claims,* United States v. *Poindexter, 698 F. Supp. 300 (D.D.C. 1988), which is hereinafter cited by the court as "Kastigar Memo."*] In our view, the use of immunized testimony by witnesses to refresh their memories, or otherwise to focus their thoughts, organize their testimony, or alter their prior or contemporaneous statements, constitutes *indirect evidentiary* not *nonevidentiary use.* This observation also applies to witnesses who studied, reviewed, or were exposed to the immunized testimony in order to prepare themselves or others as witnesses.

Strictly speaking, the term *direct evidentiary use* may describe only attempts by the prosecutors to offer the immunized testimony directly to the grand jury or trial jury, as by offering the testimony as an exhibit. But the testimony of other witnesses is also *evidence* that is to be considered by the grand jury or the trial jury. When the government puts on witnesses who refresh, supplement, or modify that evidence with compelled testimony, the government uses that testimony to indict and convict. The fact that the government violates the Fifth Amendment in a circuitous or haphazard fashion is cold comfort to the citizen who has been forced to incriminate himself by threat of imprisonment for contempt. The stern language of *Kastigar* does not become lenient because the compelled testimony is used to form and alter evidence in oblique ways exclusively, or at a slight distance from the chair of the immunized witness. Such a looming constitutional infirmity cannot be dismissed as merely nonevidentiary. This type of use by witnesses is not only evidentiary in any meaningful sense of the term; it is at the core of the criminal proceeding.

In summary, the use of immunized testimony—before the grand jury or at trial—to augment or refresh recollection is an evidentiary use and must be dealt with as such.

2. Refreshment

Both the trial and the grand jury proceedings involved "a considerable number" of witnesses who had "their memories refreshed by the immunized testimony," *Kastigar Memo,* 698 F. Supp. at 313, a use of compelled testimony that the District Court treated as nonevidentiary. *Id.* The District Court stated that "[t]here is no way a trier of fact can determine whether the memories of these witnesses would be substantially different if it had not been stimulated by a bit of the immunized testimony itself" and that "there is no way of determining, except possibly by a trial before the trial, whether or not any defendant was placed in a substantially worse position by the possible refreshment of a witness' memory through such exposure." *Id.* at 314. The District Court found that such taint occurs in the "natural course of events" because "[m]emory is a mysterious thing that can be stirred by a shaggy dog or a broken promise." *Id.* at 313.

This observation, while likely true, is not dispositive of the searching inquiry *Kastigar* requires. The fact that a sizable number of grand jury witnesses, trial witnesses, and their aides apparently immersed themselves in North's immunized testimony leads us to doubt whether what is in question here is simply "stimulation" of memory by "a bit" of compelled testimony. Whether the government's use of compelled testimony occurs in the natural course of events or results from an unprecedented aberration is irrelevant to a citizen's Fifth Amendment right. *Kastigar* does not prohibit simply "a whole lot of use," or "excessive use," or "primary use" of compelled testimony. It prohibits "*any* use," direct or indirect. From a prosecutor's standpoint, an unhappy byproduct of the Fifth Amendment is that *Kastigar* may very well require a trial within a trial (or a trial before, during, or after the trial) if such a proceeding is necessary for the court to determine whether or not the government has in any fashion used compelled testimony to indict or convict a defendant.

We readily understand how court and counsel might sigh prior to such an undertaking. Such a *Kastigar* proceeding could consume substantial amounts of time, personnel, and money, only to lead to the conclusion that a defendant—perhaps a guilty defendant—cannot be prosecuted. Yet the very purpose of the Fifth Amendment under these circumstances is to prevent the prosecutor from transmogrifying into the inquisitor, complete with that officer's most pernicious tool—the power of the state to force a person to incriminate himself. As between the clear constitutional command and the convenience of the government, our duty is to enforce the former and discount the latter.

* * *

It may be that it is possible in the present case to separate the wheat of the witnesses' unspoiled memory from the chaff of North's immunized testimony, but it may not. There at least should be a *Kastigar* hearing and specific findings on that question. If it proves impossible to make such a separation, then it may well be the case that the prosecution cannot proceed. Certainly this danger is a real one in a case such as this where the immunized testimony is so broadly disseminated that interested parties study it and even casual observers have some notion of its content. Nevertheless, the Fifth Amendment requires that the government establish priorities before making the immunization decision. The government must occasionally decide which it values more: immunization (perhaps to discharge institutional duties, such as congressional fact-finding and information-dissemination) or prosecution. If the government chooses immunization, then it must understand that the Fifth Amendment and *Kastigar* mean that it is taking a great chance that the witness cannot constitutionally be indicted or prosecuted.

* * *

We conclude that the District Court's reliance on warnings to witnesses (to avoid testifying as to anything they had learned from North's immunized testimony) was not sufficient to ensure that North's testimony was not used. As North argues, "witnesses could not possibly filter each answer through the court's hypothetical 'prior knowledge' test." The fact that the District Court reviewed transcripts of testimony before the grand jury *in camera* would have alerted the Court to the presence of North's immunized testimony only if it were clearly identified as such. Such a review could not have disclosed the unattributed inclusion of immunized testimony in other evidence and is defective. The only proper remedy is the searching *Kastigar* inquiry....

* * *

The convictions are vacated and the case is remanded to the District Court. On remand, if the prosecution is to continue, the District Court must hold a full *Kastigar* hearing that will inquire into the *content* as well as the *sources* of the grand jury and trial witnesses' testimony. That inquiry must proceed witness-by-witness; if necessary, it will proceed line-by-line and item-by-item. For each grand jury and trial witness, the prosecution must show by a preponderance of the evidence that no use whatsoever was made of any of the immunized testimony either by the witness or by the Office of Independent Counsel in questioning the witness. This burden may be met by establishing that the witness was never exposed to North's immunized testimony, or that the allegedly tainted testimony contains no evidence not "canned" by the prosecution before such exposure occurred. Unless the District Court can make express findings that the government has carried this heavy burden as to the content of all of the testimony of each witness, that testimony cannot survive the *Kastigar* test. We remind the prosecution that the *Kastigar* burden is "heavy" not because of the evidentiary standard, but because of the constitutional standard: the government has to meet its proof only by a preponderance of the evidence, but *any* failure to meet that standard must result in exclusion of the testimony.

If the District Court finds that the government has failed to carry its burden with respect to any item or part of the testimony of any grand jury or trial witness, it should then consider whether that failure is harmless beyond a reasonable doubt. If the District Court concludes that the government's failure to carry its burden with respect to that particular witness or item is harmless beyond a reasonable doubt, the District Court should memorialize its conclusions and rationales in writing. If the government has in fact introduced trial evidence that fails the *Kastigar* analysis, then the defendant is entitled to a new trial. If the same is true as to grand jury evidence, then the indictment must be dismissed.

* * *

Notes and Questions

1. As a practical matter, how should a trial judge apply the *North* court's holding that when a previously immunized witness is prosecuted it is necessary to conduct an inquiry into any use of the immunized testimony that "must proceed witness-by-witness; if necessary, it will proceed line-by-line and item-by-item"? What kind of judicial proceedings are needed to comply with this requirement? What is the burden of proof that the prosecution must meet? *See generally* Ronald F. Wright, *Congressional Use of Immunity Grants After Iran-Contra*, 80 MINN. L. REV. 407, 445–48 (1995) (discussing the various burdens of proof for exclusionary rule hearings).

2. Is the real problem in the *North* case not the grant of immunity, but rather the process by which Congress determined to grant North immunity? In Watergate John Dean provided a complete proffer, albeit under unusual circumstances that did not include participation by minority counsel (see Chapter 3), before the committee voted to grant Dean immunity. In Iran-Contra the congressional committees granted North immunity with only limited prior knowledge of what his testimony would be (see above). Senate Watergate committee chief counsel Sam Dash has written that the Iran-Contra committees made a mistake in granting North immunity without a full proffer:

> The Senate Watergate Committee faced the same problem when Watergate Special Prosecutor Cox urged the Committee not to give immunity to John Dean and Jeb Magruder, key targets of the Cox investigation. Like the Iran-Contra Committees, the Senate Watergate Committee turned down Cox. It was Chairman Sam Ervin's view that, in light of the Watergate crisis facing the nation, including the possible involvement of the President, the full story should be quickly communicated to the public on television, even though as a consequence some individuals might avoid conviction and prison. As the former Chief Counsel of the Senate Watergate Committee and a participant in the Committee's decision to go ahead with the grants of immunity, I still believe we made the right decision. However, I am much less sure of the justification to grant immunity to North, Poindexter and Hakim. In brief, I believe that the Iran-Contra Committees, particularly in North's case, so handicapped

themselves by the compromises they made to obtain North's immunized testimony, that they accomplished little more than exhibiting a notorious witness on television, without fulfilling their congressional responsibility to inform the public.

Samuel Dash, *Independent Counsel: No More, No Less A Federal Prosecutor*, 86 Geo. L.J. 2077, 2089 (1998). Is Dash correct, or is it unlikely that a proffer from North would have made a difference? In particular, consider whether the committees could have refused to grant North immunity even if they had concluded after a full proffer that he either was not entirely truthful in his testimony, would be a "notorious" witness, or both.

3. Does the *North* opinion in effect transform use immunity into transactional immunity, at least for any witness whose congressional testimony is publicly broadcast or reported in the news media? *See generally* R.S. Ghio, Note, *The Iran-Contra Prosecutions and the Failure of Use Imm*unity, 45 Stan. L. Rev. 229 (1992) (arguing that derivative use immunity is equivalent in practical effect to transactional immunity). Keep this question in mind as you study the section below on Application of the *North* Decision. Even if *North* does result in what is effectively transactional immunity for some witnesses, is this necessarily an undesirable result? If there is a problem, does it stem from the broad nature of the immunity under *North* or from the fact that the immunity decision is made by the legislative branch rather than by executive branch prosecutors? One commentator has suggested that the congressional grants of immunity are unconstitutional under separation of powers doctrine. *See* Hannah Metkis Volokh, Note, *Congressional Immunity Grants and Separation of Powers: Legislative Vetoes of Federal Prosecutors*, 85 Geo. L. J. 2017 (2007).

4. Is the decision to compel congressional testimony through immunity grants really a policy decision that should be made by the legislative branch? Some language in the *North* decision suggests that the panel deciding the case may have viewed it as such:

> Nevertheless, the Fifth Amendment requires that the government establish priorities before making the immunization decision. The government must occasionally decide which it values more: immunization (perhaps to discharge institutional duties, such as congressional fact-finding and information-dissemination) or prosecution. If the government chooses immunization, then it must understand that the Fifth Amendment and *Kastigar* mean that it is taking a great chance that the witness cannot constitutionally be indicted or prosecuted.

North I, 910 F.2d 843, 862 (D.C. Cir. 1990). Bear this issue in mind as you read the materials below.

5. Has the impact of the *North* decision been overstated? The Iran-Contra Independent Counsel observed that even in the Watergate investigation, no witness who was granted immunity and refused to plead guilty was ever convicted at trial. John Dean and Charles Colson chose to plead guilty despite their prior congressional immunity grants, and the only immunized witness who was charged in the Watergate cover-up indictment, Gordon Strachan, never went to trial because the Watergate Special Prosecutor was concerned that his prior immunity grant would undermine the prosecution. *See Final Report of the Independent Counsel for Iran/Contra Matters*, Vol. I, Investigations and Prosecutions, at 559 (1993). In light of that prior experience, is the outcome of the *North* case as remarkable as it might first appear to be?

B. Application of the *North* Decision

The Iran-Contra Independent Counsel petitioned the U.S. Court of Appeals for rehearing on the court's application of *Kastigar* to North's immunized testimony and subsequent conviction, but the court concluded that the Independent Counsel's arguments for a less stringent *Kastigar* test "lack[ed] merit." *See United States v. North*, 920 F.2d 940, D.C. Cir. 1990 ("*North II*"). Then-Chief Judge Judge Patricia Wald dissented vigorously from the majority's application of *Kastigar* to North's congressional testimony:

> Since, as the IC's petition forcefully points out, my colleagues' original opinion effectively transformed a limited use immunity into a sweeping transaction immunity, I would grant the IC's petition for rehearing on the *Kastigar* issue. By exalting form over substance, the original *per curiam* eviscerates both the use-immunity and independent-counsel statutes; its consequences for future cases of public import are ominous.

* * *

> By mandating additional—and practically unattainable—requirements not found in *Kastigar* itself, my colleagues have upset this tension. They have rendered impossible in virtually all cases the prosecution of persons whose immunized testimony is of such national significance as to be the subject of congressional hearings and media coverage. In their opinions, my colleagues have ruled that *Kastigar* requires at least *four* distinct showings, only the first two of which can be derived from *Kastigar* itself. First, the prosecutors must demonstrate that they avoided "significant exposure" to the immunized testimony. Majority Opinion ("Maj. op.") at 859. Second, the prosecution must demonstrate that its identification and questioning of witnesses was based solely on "independent leads"—without the use of immunized testimony. Maj. op. at 863. Third—a new requirement, appearing for the first time in the opinion denying rehearing—the prosecution must demonstrate that the immunized testimony did not "*motivate[ ]* " its witnesses to testify. Opinion on Petition for Rehearing at 942. And fourth, the prosecution must demonstrate that the testimony of witnesses "exposed" to immunized matter has been "'canned' by the prosecution before such exposure." Maj. op. at 872.

> The last and most stringent of these requirements—that witness testimony be pre-recorded—is certainly an unwarranted departure from current law. For this reason, it deserves quotation at some length.

> > [T]he District Court must hold a full *Kastigar* hearing that will inquire into the *content* as well as the *sources* of the grand jury and trial witness-

es' testimony. That inquiry must proceed witness-by-witness; if necessary, it will proceed line-by-line and item-by-item. For each grand jury and trial witness, the prosecution must show by a preponderance of the evidence that no use whatsoever was made of any of the immunized testimony either by the witness or by the Office of Independent Counsel in questioning the witness. *This burden may be met by establishing that the witness was never exposed to North's immunized testimony, or that the allegedly tainted testimony contains no evidence not "canned" by the prosecution before such exposure occurred.*

Maj. op. at 872–873 (latter emphasis supplied). Although my colleagues now maintain that they did not intend to rule that pre-recording was the *only* way the prosecution could demonstrate that the testimony of a witness exposed to immunized testimony was admissible, the words of the *per curiam* are clear: either can the witness or can his testimony. [Footnote omitted.]

* * *

The consequences of a pre-recording requirement are both predictable and troubling. Prospective targets of grand juries in national scandals would line up to testify before Congress, in exchange for what is effectively transaction immunity. A requirement of "nonuse" would be converted into a guarantee of nonprosecution. Moreover, as the IC notes, with regard to crimes involving government corruption, the IC and Congress have *parallel* responsibilities. A pre-recording requirement compels Congress to delay congressional hearings until all of the testimony of all potential witnesses has been pre-recorded; in doing so, this requirement unduly burdens Congress' exercise of its legitimate authority to hold important public hearings.

The Supreme Court has said that use immunity "grants neither pardon nor amnesty." *Kastigar*, 406 U.S. at 461. But the majority's excruciatingly heightened *Kastigar* requirements run counter to Congress' express assertion that "the [use-immunity] provision is not an 'immunity bath.'" H. Rep. No. 91-1188, 91st Cong., 2d Sess. at 12 (1970) (citing *United States v. Monia*, 317 U.S. 424, 63 S.Ct. 409 (1943)).

* * *

As the IC's petition highlights, the central conceptual weakness of the majority's analysis is its failure to recognize that a prosecutor's exposure to immunized testimony and a witness' independent exposure to such testimony raise related but distinct issues. By holding to the same standard witnesses who have "thoroughly soaked" themselves in immunized testimony and prosecutors who have assiduously avoided the slightest taint, the majority renders virtually impossible any prosecution of an immunized defendant who testifies publicly.

* * *

Whether or not the best resolution of these values lies in burden shifting, the important thing is that the use-immunity statute be construed so as to accommodate the real difference between prosecutorial exposure and use—the central danger posed by use immunity—and witness exposure, which is more diffuse and beyond the immediate control of the prosecution. Respecting this critical difference, this court should seek to provide a workable and attainable standard that guarantees the integrity of use immunity while allowing for a cautious and untainted prosecution.

The majority opinion countered Judge Wald's arguments as follows:

Finally, and perhaps at the heart of the dissent's concerns, is the argument that a straightforward application of *Kastigar* in cases where a witness testifies before Congress, after Congress grants immunity under section 6005, unduly restricts Congress' role in exposing wrongdoing in the nation—including wrongdoing in the executive branch. She even contends that witnesses who wished to frustrate prosecutors would "line up to testify before Congress [] in exchange for ... immunity." Dissent on Pet. for Reh'g at 953. We do not think Congress would be so naive as lightly to grant use immunity to such prospective defendants. Surely Congress does so only when its perception of the national interest justifies this extraordinary step. When Congress grants immunity before the prosecution has completed preparing its "case," the prosecutor, whoever that may be, can warn that the grant of immunity has its institutional costs; in this case, the IC indeed warned Congress that "any grant of use and derivative use immunity would create serious—and perhaps insurmountable—barriers to the prosecution of the immunized witness." Memorandum of the Independent Counsel Concerning Use Immunity 1 (Jan. 13, 1987) (submitted to the Joint Congressional Iran/Contra Committees). The decision as to whether the national interest justifies that institutional cost in the enforcement of the criminal laws is, of course, a political one to be made by Congress. Once made, however, that cost cannot be paid in the coin of a defendant's constitutional rights. That is simply not the way our system works. The political needs of the majority, or Congress, or the President never, never, never, should trump an individual's explicit constitutional protections. Indeed, the government may not even use immunized testimony to prevent a defendant's subsequent perjury. *See New Jersey v. Portash*, 440 U.S. 450, 459 (1979) ("Testimony given in response to a grant of legislative immunity is the essence of coerced testimony.... [In the case of immunized testimony,] we deal with the constitutional privilege against compulsory self-incrimination in its most pristine form. Balancing, therefore, is not simply unnecessary. It is impermissible.").

The Iran-Contra Independent Counsel provided a detailed analysis of his views on the implications of the *North* and *Poindexter* decisions in his Final Report:

Lawrence E. Walsh, *Final Report of the Independent Counsel for Iran/Contra Matters*

Independent Counsel, August 4, 1993

Part X

Political Oversight and the Rule of Law

* * *

Background

It was apparent from the outset of the Iran/contra investigation that congressional grants of use immunity to the principals in the affair would make prosecution of those persons problematic. The Office of Independent Counsel noted that concern in its first Interim Report, issued in April 1987, explaining that the award of immunity "will have a serious and possibly destructive impact upon a subsequent prosecution" and "might preclude future prosecution of those [immunized] individuals." The Office pointed out that, under *Kastigar v. United States*, 406 U.S. 441, 458 (1972), a grant of use immunity results in "a sweeping proscription of any use, direct or indirect, of the compelled testimony and any information derived therefrom." The Office accordingly took extensive steps to avoid this danger. It expedited the elements of its investigation most likely to be the subject of congressional inquiry. It memorialized the statements of potential trial witnesses—in the vernacular, "canning" them—that were made prior to the time that immunized testimony became publicly available. It implemented prophylactic procedures designed to shield prosecutors and investigators from exposure to immunized disclosures. And it urged Congress to be conservative in granting immunity.

When Congress nevertheless chose to compel testimony from North and Poindexter, these prophylactic procedures continued before the Grand Jury and at the *North* and *Poindexter* trials. Grand Jury witnesses were instructed by the Government to "make sure that your answers to our questions are based solely on your own personal knowledge and recollection of the events in question. Do not relate to us anything which you learned for the first time as a result of listening to or reading or hearing about immunized testimony." The district judge gave a similar instruction to all witnesses at the *North* trial.

The district judge presiding in the *Poindexter* case took even more extensive precautions. Prior to trial he reviewed statements made by potential trial witnesses before Poindexter's immunized testimony became publicly available, finding that all of the proposed testimony of most of these witnesses had been memorialized by that date. As for those witnesses whose trial testimony would not be limited to that "canned" prior to Poindexter's congressional appearance, the district judge found that the proposed trial testimony of most of them concerned subjects that Poindexter did not address in his immunized statements.

This left the Government still to prove that five of its potential witnesses were free of taint. The district judge ordered these witnesses to appear at a pretrial hearing. Of the three of these witnesses who subsequently testified at trial, two credibly affirmed at the hearing that their anticipated trial testimony would not be affected in any way by Poindexter's immunized statements.

The third witness, North, took a different tack. He stated at the hearing that he was unable, with respect to any relevant subject, to distinguish between what he had personally done, observed or experienced and what he had heard about the events by way of Poindexter's immunized testimony. As for Poindexter's destruction of the December 1985 presidential Finding, North acknowledged that he had seen Poindexter destroy a piece of paper, but insisted that he did not know that the document was the Finding until Poindexter stated that fact before Congress.

The district court, however, rejected North's testimony at the hearing as incredible. Basing its ruling on North's demeanor, on inconsistencies in North's testimony, and on other objective indicia that North had an untainted memory of events, the court found that North "appears to have been embarked at that time upon the calculated course of attempting to assist his former colleague and co-defendant ... by prevaricating on various issues, including most notably the issue whether he had to rely for his recollection of events on Poindexter's immunized testimony." North accordingly was permitted to testify.

The North and Poindexter Decisions

Both convictions were set aside by divided panels on appeal. In the *North* case, the appeals court concluded that receipt of testimony from witnesses whose memories had been refreshed by exposure to North's immunized disclosures constituted improper "evidentiary use" of North's statements. The majority accordingly directed the district court to determine on remand as to each witness whether it was possible to separate out "unspoiled memory" from that influenced by North's testimony and, if not, to exclude evidence presented by such witnesses.

The court of appeals also concluded that the trial judge's instructions to witnesses were inadequate to prevent them from testifying to matters that they had first learned from North's immunized disclosures, accepting North's argument that such witnesses could not filter their answers through the district court's "prior knowledge" test. The court therefore held that the trial judge was obligated, on remand, to hold a full hearing "that will inquire into the *content* as well as the *sources* of the Grand Jury and trial witnesses' testimony. That inquiry must proceed witness-by-witness; if necessary, it will proceed line-by-line and item-by-item." The court explained that the district judge was required to "make express findings that the government has carried [its] heavy burden as to the content of all of the testimony of each witness."

Then-Chief Judge Patricia M. Wald dissented, declining to find that the district judge's "prodigious and conscientious efforts to protect North's Fifth Amendment rights were in any way so ineffectual as to require reversal on the formalistic grounds the majority advances." She noted that virtually all of the Grand Jury evidence relating to the counts on which North was convicted had been presented *prior* to North's congressional appearance. And she found it "indeed striking that North's counsel cannot point to a single instance of alleged witness testimony tainted by exposure to North's immunized testimony." In all, she observed that the procedural regime imposed by the majority "makes a subsequent trial of any congressionally immunized witness virtually impossible."[6]

On remand, the prosecution of North was dismissed when Independent Counsel concluded that satisfaction of the court of appeals' requirements would be both very difficult and enormously burdensome.

A different panel of the appeals court reversed Poindexter's convictions. The majority concluded that all of his convictions had to be set aside because, in its view, the trial court's measures failed to ensure that Poindexter's immunized testimony was not used against him at trial. In reaching this conclusion, the court of appeals restated the standard set out in *North*: "that a prohibited 'use' [of immunized testimony] occurs if a witness' recollection is refreshed by exposure to the defendant's immunized testimony, or if his testimony is in any way 'shaped, altered, or affected,' by such exposure." Under this standard, the court explained, "'the Government must demonstrate affirmatively that the immunized testimony did not ... [have] an influence on [the trial witnesses'] thinking, even one for which they cannot at this time consciously account.'"

Although the *Poindexter* case was tried prior to the decision in *North*, the court of appeals declined to remand for new findings under the *North* standard. Focusing on North's testimony at the *Poindexter* trial, the court held that the district judge's finding that North lied when he denied having an independent recollection could not be used to support the proposition that North *did* have an untainted memory. The court of appeals also went on to reason that the district judge's finding of differences between North's account and Poindexter's immunized testimony was irrelevant, holding that a "substantially exposed witness" who had not "canned" his testimony may give evidence at trial only when he "persuasively claim[s] that he can segregate the effects of his exposure."

Chief Judge Abner J. Mikva dissented in part. Although he did not take issue with the *North* standard, he complained that in *North* "the Court changed the standards the special prosecutor had to meet; today we refuse to let him try to meet them." The majority's failure to accord any weight to the district judge's credibility findings, Chief

---

6. [1] The court reaffirmed its initial conclusions when it denied rehearing. It did, however, appear to modify its opinion in two respects. It retreated somewhat from the suggestion in its initial opinion that the Government could establish a lack of taint only by showing that a witness never had been exposed to the immunized testimony or that all of his evidence had been "canned" prior to exposure. At the same time, however, the court added another element to the showing required on remand: whether Government witnesses were motivated to testify by the immunized disclosures. Chief Judge Wald again dissented. She concluded that the procedures used by the district court—under which the Government effectively made a showing that no illegal use of the immunized testimony was made—were adequate; she suggested that the majority's contrary conclusion "represents an unneeded and unprecedented incursion into the trial court's discretion in managing a fair trial." She also faulted the majority for failing to realize that any use of the tainted evidence may have been too attenuated to raise constitutional concerns, noting that the question "is a deep and unsettled one in current constitutional law."

Judge Mikva added, tells future defendants that all they need to evade responsibility [to testify at trial] is a well-timed case of amnesia."[7]

The Implications of *North* and *Poindexter*

The decisions in *North* and *Poindexter* have significant implications for the interplay between congressional oversight and law enforcement. While it may affect any case in which immunity is granted, the holding in *North* will have its most profound impact on prosecutions involving public immunized testimony—in particular, testimony before Congress—that is widely disseminated. In such cases, the court of appeals' ruling on refreshed recollection will require a complex psychological inquiry into the thought processes and memory of every witness. At the same time, the large number of witnesses potentially exposed to immunized congressional testimony in cases involving newsworthy events means that the court of appeals' draconian procedural requirements will, as Judge Wald observed, "consume[] countless extra weeks or months of trial." In all, then, the *North* ruling may, again in Judge Wald's words, amount to "an absolute deterrent of any prosecution after a grant of immunity in a high-profile case."

The decision in *Poindexter* took the *North* ruling a step further. The court purported to state its procedural holding in modest terms: focusing on North's testimony at the Poindexter trial, the court said "only that where a substantially exposed witness does not persuasively claim that he can segregate the effects of his exposure, the prosecution does not meet its burden merely by pointing to other statements of the same witness that were not themselves shown to be untainted." But while it is difficult to quarrel with that statement in the abstract, the real effect of the court's holding is significantly broader. In fact, the court held that the Government could not carry its burden by pointing either to persuasive evidence that a witness was lying when he denied having an untainted recollection of the relevant events or to other forms of circumstantial indicia that the witness had not been affected by the immunized testimony. It bears emphasis that the court of appeals decided more than that the district judge applied the wrong standard in assessing such evidence; by refusing to remand the case, the court concluded as a matter of law that such evidence *never* may be used to carry the Government's burden. It thus is manifest that, unless the court retreats from its rule, testimony from a witness whose testimony has not been "canned" and who asserts

---

7. [2] There are grounds to doubt the correctness of the court of appeals' decisions in *North* and *Poindexter*. There is considerable authority for the proposition that a finding that a witness lied may be used to establish "'that the truth is the opposite of his story'" (*NLRB v. Walton Mfg. Co.*, 369 U.S. 404, 408 (1962) (per curiam), quoting *Dyer v. MacDougall*, 201 F.2d 265, 269 (2d Cir. 1952) (L. Hand, J.))—which means that the finding that North lied when he denied having an untainted memory could have been used to establish that he *did* have an untainted memory. And the Supreme Court repeatedly has applied attenuation concepts in deciding whether evidence must be excluded under the Fourth or Fifth Amendments—concepts that were rejected by the court of appeals in *North* and *Poindexter*. See, e.g., *Nix v. Williams*, 467 U.S. 431, 442 (1984); *United States v. Crews*, 445 U.S. 463, 471 (1980). The Supreme Court denied Independent Counsel's petitions for certiorari in both cases, however, and further analysis of the constitutional issues is beyond the scope of this report.

that he has been affected by exposure to immunized disclosures will not be admitted at trial, no matter how improbable or internally inconsistent his claim of exposure to immunized testimony.

These rules will have obvious practical consequences. They will make almost impossible the prosecution of any case involving public immunized statements that requires testimony by persons sympathetic to the accused, such as co-conspirators or other associates. And the dangers of abuse and manipulation are magnified by the court of appeals' view, expressed in *North*, that a witness inclined to assist the defense may become disqualified from testifying at trial by the simple expedient of soaking *himself* in the defendant's immunized statements.[8] As the outcome of the *North* and *Poindexter* prosecutions makes clear, these consequences have particular importance because the cases most sharply affected by the D.C. Court of Appeals holdings will, by definition, be prosecutions involving conduct that has far-flung implications for national policy—those where Congress has determined that the national interest requires an immediate public examination of the activity at issue.

Notes and Questions

1. Compare the conclusions in Walsh's 1993 Final Report to the concerns expressed in Judge Patricia Wald's 1990 dissenting opinion in *North II*.

2. The conventional wisdom among knowledgeable practitioners is that the *North* and *Poindexter* decisions in effect make it impossible to prosecute anyone who has provided immunized congressional testimony. Do you agree with that general conclusion? To what extent does the degree of publicity surrounding the immunized testimony influence the likelihood of a successful subsequent prosecution? Can persons who are likely to be witnesses in a subsequent criminal trial effectively "sabotage" the prosecution in the manner Judge Wald identified, by "soaking themselves" in the immunized testimony and later stating that they cannot separate their independent recollections from what they learned from the immunized testimony?

3. Some courts have declined to follow the North and Poindexter holdings. *See, e.g., United States v. Koon*, 34 F.3d 1416 (9th Cir. 1994). If you were a judge in a jurisdiction in which *North* and *Poindexter* were not controlling precedent, would you follow the holdings in those cases in deciding how to balance the Fifth Amendment rights of immunized witnesses against the ability to prosecute criminal wrongdoing effectively?

---

8. [3] As the court of appeals put it, persons sympathetic to the defense "could have held evening classes in 'the Parsing and Deconstruction of *Kastigar*' for the very purpose of 'derailing' the [Independent Counsel's] prosecution, and such a curriculum would have been simply irrelevant to the question of whether or not the prosecution's case made use of North's compelled testimony."

C. Historical Perspective and Final Observations on Iran-Contra

In 1995, five years after the *North* and *Poindexter* decisions, Professor Ronald F. Wright observed that:

> Anecdotal evidence suggests that the *North* and *Poindexter* decisions have discouraged congressional committees from using immunities in particular cases:
>
> 1) The House Energy and Commerce Committee decided, several days after the issuance of the *North* opinion in 1990, not to grant immunity to Michael Milken during an investigation of junk bonds dealing, at least until after his criminal sentencing.
>
> 2) The Senate Ethics Committee, during its investigation of several senators implicated in the Charles Keating affair, declined in 1991 to request an immunity order for Keating because of the importance of a later criminal prosecution.
>
> 3) Senator John Kerry established a policy of making no grants of immunity during the inquiry by the POW/MIA Committee into whether American servicemen were knowingly left in Vietnam.
>
> 4) The Committee on House Administration, during its 1992 investigation of the House Post Office, voted not to request immunity orders for three key witnesses because of a possible conflict with an ongoing criminal investigation. More recently, the House decided to postpone further an Ethics Committee investigation into the Post Office, again citing concern about interference with criminal investigations.
>
> 5) The Senate Permanent Subcommittee on Investigations decided against using immunities during its 1993 investigation of the misuse of student grants from the Department of Education.
>
> 6) Senator Arlen Specter, chair of a subcommittee of the Senate Judiciary Committee, declared before hearings on the shooting incident between FBI agents and Randy Weaver at Ruby Ridge, Idaho, that the subcommittee would seek no grants of immunity.

Ronald F. Wright, *Congressional Use of Immunity Grants After Iran-Contra*, 80 Minn. L. Rev. 407, 431–33 (1995) (footnotes omitted).

The trend documented by Professor Wright has continued, and since Iran-Contra no major figure in a congressional investigation who was or might have been subject to criminal prosecution has been granted immunity. During the Senate Whitewater investigation, the Republican majority sought to grant immunity to David Hale, who had publicly accused President Clinton of improprieties, but the Democrats on the committee voted against granting immunity and the majority was unable to obtain the two-thirds vote required by the immunity statute. *See* Final Report, Senate Special

Committee to Investigate Whitewater Development Corporation and Related Matters, 371–72 (June 17, 1996).

In one more-recent instance, a congressional committee has conferred immunity on an Executive Branch witness who was potentially the subject of a criminal prosecution, but that witness was a relatively minor player in the matter under investigation. In May 2007, in its investigation of whether U.S. Attorneys had been removed from office for political or other improper reasons, the House Judiciary Committee compelled Monica M. Goodling, a mid-level official in the George W. Bush Administration Justice Department, to testify under a grant of use immunity. Goodling testified that some of her personnel actions at the Justice Department "crossed the line" of what was permitted under federal law, but she was not subsequently prosecuted. Presumably, one factor influencing the decision not to bring charges against her was that any prosecution would have to meet the *North-Poindexter* tests for proving that her immunized testimony had not been used against her.

Does this history of reluctance on the part of Congress to grant immunity after the *North* and *Poindexter* decisions support the admonitions and concluding observations of the Iran-Contra Independent Counsel in the portion of his Final Report that is reproduced below?

Lawrence E. Walsh, *Final Report of the Independent Counsel for Iran/Contra Matters*

Independent Counsel, August 4, 1993

Part X

Political Oversight and the Rule of Law

The Iran/contra prosecutions illustrate in an especially stark fashion the tension between political oversight and enforcement of existing law. Congress's decision to compel immunized testimony from a number of Iran/contra figures pursuant to 18 U.S.C. §6002—most notably Lt. Col. Oliver L. North and Vice Adm. John M. Poindexter—was thought important both to address an immediate crisis of political confidence and to shed light on flaws in the functioning of the national security apparatus. Ultimately, however, that decision also was fatal to the prosecutions of North and Poindexter, and made a full and equitable accounting for criminal wrongdoing impossible. That outcome holds important lessons for the future.

* * *

The Competing Roles of Congress and the Independent Counsel

With this as background, the competing roles of Congress and the Executive (here represented by Independent Counsel) must be borne in mind. As Independent Counsel recognized from the outset of his investigation, it is Congress (in the case of the Iran/contra affair, its Select Committees) that is primarily responsible for the accurate public disclosure of the facts concerning transactions such as the Iran/contra matters. Ultimately, it is Congress that is empowered to legislate in a manner that not only will preclude future similar transactions in a narrow sense, but that also will facilitate the effective management of foreign policy and that will discourage disregard for existing legal strictures.

Although the Independent Counsel also has a reporting function, his first responsibility, in contrast, is the prosecution of criminal conduct. Accordingly, it is not primarily his duty to develop for the public a knowledge of what occurred.

When a conflict between the oversight and prosecutorial roles develops—as plainly occurred in the Iran/contra affair—the law is clear that it is Congress that must prevail. This is no more than a recognition of the high political importance of Congress's responsibility. It also is the appropriate place to strike the balance, as resolution of this conflict calls for the exercise of a seasoned political judgment that must take a broad view of the national interest.

In exercising this judgment, however, it is imperative that Congress be sensitive to the dangers posed by grants of immunity to the successful prosecution of criminal conduct—and that it bear in mind, as well, the importance of the even-handed application of criminal justice. In recent years Congress has granted use immunity with some frequency, in cases including many of the most notable examples of misconduct involving public officials or matters of public policy: in addition to the Iran/contra affairs, the list includes the Watergate, "Koreagate," and ABSCAM scandals; congressional ethics inquiries; impeachment proceedings against federal judges; inquiries into narcotics trafficking, assassinations, and organized crime; investigations of fraud, corruption, and mismanagement on Indian reservations; and most recently, allegations of misconduct at the Department of Housing and Urban Development and of improper favors for savings and loan officials. In all, Congress has conferred use immunity on more than 300 witnesses over the last two decades.

In the past, members of Congress may have been of the view that the experience of the Watergate case suggests that grants of use immunity do not significantly impede successful prosecution. Even at that time, that would not have been the proper lesson to draw from Watergate. Although two immunized witnesses in the Watergate matter—John Dean and Charles Colson—subsequently pleaded guilty, no immunized Watergate witness who refused to plead guilty was successfully tried and convicted. Gordon Strachan, the only immunized witness who was charged in the Watergate cover-up indictment, never went to trial because the Watergate Special Prosecutor concluded that there was a significant possibility that Strachan eventually might prevail on his claim of taint.[9] The same thing happened in the case of Felipe De Diego, who was granted immunity by state authorities in connection with the break-in at the office of Daniel Ellsberg's psychiatrist.[10] But in any event, the decisions in *North* and *Poindexter* should lay to rest any lingering sense that a congressional grant of use immunity is not a serious bar to future prosecution.

---

9. [4] See Strachan, *Self-Incrimination, Immunity and Watergate*, 56 Tex. L. Rev. 791, 814–820 (1978).

10. [5] See *United States v. De Diego*, 511 F.2d 818, 822–825 (D.C. Cir. 1975).

Congressional action that precludes prosecution—or, as in Iran/contra, that makes it impossible to sustain a successful prosecution—imposes costs on society that far transcend the failure to convict a few lawbreakers. There is significant inequity when (again as in Iran/contra) the more peripheral players are convicted while the central figures in the criminal enterprise escape punishment. And perhaps more fundamentally, the failure to punish governmental lawbreakers feeds the perception that public officials are not wholly accountable for their actions. It also may lead the public to believe that no real wrongdoing took place. That is a danger in the Iran/contra affair, where Oliver North hailed the ultimate dismissal of the prosecution against him as a personal vindication. While it was, of course, nothing of the sort—North was found guilty beyond a reasonable doubt of serious criminal offenses, and the court of appeals' decision setting aside his conviction cast no doubt on his factual guilt—the risk of public confusion on the point is substantial.

This background strongly suggests that Congress should compel public testimony from a Government official suspected of criminal misconduct only in the most extraordinary circumstances. Before doing so, it should determine whether there is substantial evidence that the prospective witness was involved in a criminal transaction, whether he or she ordinarily would be a logical subject for prosecutive consideration, and whether the prospective witness had a leading or substantial role in the criminal enterprise. If so, Congress also should determine whether a less culpable person could supply the evidence sought, and what the likelihood is that the witness to be immunized will supply honest, useful and necessary information. Only if no less culpable person is available—and if the need for obtaining the information is compelling—should the prospective witness be granted immunity.

Part XI
Concluding Observations

The underlying facts of Iran/contra are that, regardless of criminality, President Reagan, the secretary of state, the secretary of defense, and the director of central intelligence and their necessary assistants committed themselves, however reluctantly, to two programs contrary to congressional policy and contrary to national policy. They skirted the law, some of them broke the law, and almost all of them tried to cover up the President's willful activities.

What protection do the people of the United States have against such a concerted action by such powerful officers? The Constitution provides for congressional oversight and congressional control of appropriations, but if false information is given to Congress, these checks and balances are of lessened value. Further, in the give and take of the political community, congressional oversight is often overtaken and subordinated by the need to keep Government functioning, by the need to anticipate the future, and by the ever-present requirement of maintaining consensus among the elected officials who are the Government.

The disrespect for Congress by a popular and powerful President and his appointees was obscured when Congress accepted the tendered concept of a runaway conspiracy of subordinate officers and avoided the unpleasant confrontation with a powerful President and his Cabinet. In haste to display and conclude its investigation of this unwelcome issue, Congress destroyed the most effective lines of inquiry by giving immunity to Oliver L. North and John M. Poindexter so that they could exculpate and eliminate the need for the testimony of President Reagan and Vice President Bush.

Immunity is ordinarily given by a prosecutor to a witness who will incriminate someone more important than himself. Congress gave immunity to North and Poindexter, who incriminated only themselves and who largely exculpated those responsible for the initiation, supervision and support of their activities. This delayed and infinitely complicated the effort to prosecute North and Poindexter, and it largely destroyed the likelihood that their prompt conviction and appropriate sentence would induce meaningful cooperation.

These important political decisions were properly the responsibility of Congress. It was for the Committees to decide whether the welfare of the nation was served or endangered by a continuation of its investigation, a more deliberate effort to test the self-serving denials presented by Cabinet officers and to search for the full ramifications of the activities in question. Having made this decision, however, no one could gainsay the added difficulties thrust upon Independent Counsel. These difficulties could be dealt with only by the investment of large amounts of additional time and large amounts of expense.

The role of Independent Counsel is not well understood. Comparisons to United States attorneys, county district attorneys, or private law offices do not conceive the nature of Independent Counsel. Independent Counsel is not an individual put in charge of an ongoing agency as an acting U.S. attorney might be; he is a person taken from private practice and told to create a new agency, to carry out the mission assigned by the court. It is not as though he were told to step in and try a case on the calendar of an ongoing office with full support of the Government behind him, as it would be behind the United States attorney. He is told to create an office and to confront the Government without any expectation of real cooperation, and, indeed, with the expectation of hostility, however veiled. That hostility will manifest itself in the failure to declassify information, in the suppression of documents, and in all of the evasive techniques of highly skilled and large, complex organizations.

The investigation into Iran/contra nevertheless demonstrates that the rule of law upon which our democratic system of government depends can be applied to the highest officials even when they are operating in the secret areas of diplomacy and national security.

Despite extraordinary difficulties imposed by the destruction and withholding of records, the need to protect classified information, and the congressional grants of immunity to some of the principals involved, Independent Counsel was able to bring criminal charges against nine government officers and five private citizens involved in illegal activities growing out of the Iran/contra affair.

More importantly, the investigation and the prosecutions arising out of its investigation have provided a much more accurate picture of how two secret Administration policies—keeping the contras alive "body and soul" during the Boland cutoff period and seeking the release of Americans held hostage by selling arms to Iran—veered off into criminality.

Evidence obtained by Independent Counsel establishes that the Iran/contra affair was not an aberrational scheme carried out by a "cabal of zealots" on the National Security Counsel staff, as the congressional Select Committees concluded in their majority report.[11] Instead, it was the product of two foreign policy directives by President Reagan which skirted the law and which were executed by the NSC staff with the knowledge and support of high officials in the CIA, State and Defense departments, and to a lesser extent, officials in other agencies.

Independent Counsel found no evidence of dissent among his Cabinet officers from the President's determination to support the contras after federal law banned the use of appropriated funds for that purpose in the Boland Amendment in October 1984. Even the two Cabinet officers who opposed the sale of arms to Iran on the grounds that it was illegal and bad policy—Defense Secretary Caspar W. Weinberger and Secretary of State George P. Schultz—either cooperated with the decision once made, as in the case of Weinberger, or stood aloof from it while being kept informed of its progress, as was the case of Schultz.

In its report section titled "Who Was Responsible," the Select Committees named CIA Director William Casey, National Security Advisers Robert C. McFarlane and John M. Poindexter, along with NSC staff member Oliver L. North, and private sector operatives Richard V. Secord and Albert Hakim. With the exception of Casey who died before he could be questioned by the OIC, Independent Counsel charged and obtained criminal convictions of each of the men named by Congress. There is little doubt that, operationally, these men were central players.

But the investigation and prosecutions have shown that these six were not out-of-control mavericks who acted alone without the knowledge or assistance of others. The evidence establishes that the central NSC operatives kept their superiors—including Reagan, Bush, Shultz, Weinberger and other high officials—informed of their efforts generally, if not in detail, and their superiors either condoned or turned a blind eye to them. When it was required, the NSC principals and their private sector operatives received the assistance of high-ranking officers in the CIA, the Defense Department, and the Department of State.

Of the 14 persons charged criminally during the investigation, four were convicted of felony charges after trial by jury, seven pleaded guilty either to felonies or misdemeanors, and one had his case dismissed because the Administration refused to declassify information deemed necessary to the defendant by the trial judge. Two cases that were awaiting trial were aborted by pardons granted by President Bush. As this report

---

11. [1] Majority Report, p. 22.

explained earlier, many persons who committed crimes were not charged. Some minor crimes were never investigated and some that were investigated were not solved. But Independent Counsel believes that to the extent possible, the central Iran/contra crimes were vigorously prosecuted and the significant acts of obstruction were fully charged.

* * *

The Role of Independent Counsel

Given the enormous autonomous power of both the Legislative and Executive branches in the modern state, the rightly celebrated constitutional checks and balances are inadequate, alone, to preserve the rule of law upon which our democracy depends.

As Watergate demonstrated, the checks and balances reach their limits in the case of criminal wrongdoing by Executive branch officials. The combination of an aggressive press, simple crimes, the White House tapes, and principled defiance by Department of Justice-appointed counsel all combined to bring Watergate to its conclusion without an independent counsel statute. It was apparent then, however, as it should be now in light of Iran/Contra, that the competing roles of the attorney general, as a member of the Cabinet and presidential adviser on the one hand and chief law enforcement officer on the other, create an irreconcilable conflict of interest.

As Iran/contra demonstrated, congressional oversight alone cannot make up for deficiencies that result when an attorney general abandons that law-enforcement role in cases of Executive branch wrongdoing. Well before Attorney General Meese sought an independent counsel in December 1986, he had already become, in effect, the President's defense lawyer, to the exclusion of his responsibilities as the nation's top law enforcement officer. By that time, crucial documents had already been destroyed and false testimony given.

Congress, with all the investigatory powers it wields in the investigatory process, was not able to uncover many of these documents or disprove much of that false testimony. That inability is structural, and does not result from ill will, impatience, or character flaw on the part of any legislator. With good reason, Congress's interest in investigating Executive branch wrongdoing extends no further than remedying perceived imbalances in its relations with the Executive branch. Except in cases of impeachment, Congress's interest does not, and should not, extend to the law enforcement goals of deterrence, retribution and punishment.

In normal circumstances, these law-enforcement goals are the province of the Justice Department, under the direction of the attorney general. As the chief law enforcement officer of the United States, the attorney general represents the people of the United States — not the President, the Cabinet or any political party. When the attorney general cannot so represent the people, the rule of law requires that another, independent institution assume that responsibility. That is the historic role of the independent counsel.

Problems Posed by Congressional Immunity Grants

The magnitude of Iran/contra does not by itself explain why Independent Counsel took so long to complete the task assigned by the Special Division which appointed him. The word "independent" in Independent Counsel is not quite accurate as a description of his work. Time and again this Independent Counsel found himself at the mercy of political decisions of the Congress and the Executive branch. From the date of his appointment on December 19, 1986, Independent Counsel had to race to protect his investigations and prosecutions from the congressional grants of immunity to central Enterprise conspirators. At the same time, he had to wait almost one year for records from Swiss banks and financial organizations vital to his work. Once Congress granted immunity, Independent Counsel had to insulate himself and his staff from immunized disclosures, postponing the time he could get a wider view of the activities he was investigating.

Despite extraordinary efforts to shield the OIC from exposure to immunized testimony, the North and Poindexter convictions were overturned on appeal on the immunity issue. While the appellate panels did not find the prosecution was "tainted" by improper exposure to the immunized testimony of North or Poindexter, they ruled that the safeguards utilized by the trial courts did not ensure that witnesses' testimony was not affected by the immunized testimony.

Although Independent Counsel warned the Select Committees of the possibility that granting use immunity to principals in the Iran/contra matter might make it impossible to prosecute them successfully, he has never contended that Congress should refrain from granting use immunity to compel testimony in such important matters as Iran/contra. In matters of great national concern, Independent Counsel recognizes that intense public interest and the need for prompt and effective congressional oversight of intelligence activities may well force the Congress to act swiftly and grant immunity to principals.

But, in light of the experience of Independent Counsel in the Iran/contra cases, Congress should be aware of the fact that future immunity grants, at least in such highly publicized cases, will likely rule out criminal prosecution.

Congressional action that precludes, or makes it impossible to sustain, a prosecution has more serious consequences than simply one less conviction. There is a significant inequity when more peripheral players are convicted while central figures in a criminal enterprise escape punishment. And perhaps more fundamentally, the failure to punish governmental lawbreakers feeds the perception that public officials are not wholly accountable for their actions. In Iran/contra, it was President Reagan who first asked that North and Poindexter be given immunity so that they could exculpate him from responsibility for the diversion. A few months later, the Select Committees did that—granting immunity without any proffer to ensure honest testimony.

* * *

Final Thoughts

The Iran/contra investigation will not end the kind of abuse of power that it addressed any more than the Watergate investigation did. The criminality in both affairs did not arise primarily out of ordinary venality or greed, although some of those charged were driven by both. Instead, the crimes committed in Iran/contra were motivated by the desire of persons in high office to pursue controversial policies and goals even when the pursuit of those policies and goals was inhibited or restricted by executive orders, statutes or the constitutional system of checks and balances.

The tone in Iran/contra was set by President Reagan. He directed that the contras be supported, despite a ban on contra aid imposed on him by Congress. And he was willing to trade arms to Iran for the release of Americans held hostage in the Middle East, even if doing so was contrary to the nation's stated policy and possibly in violation of the law.

The lesson of Iran/contra is that if our system of government is to function properly, the branches of government must deal with one another honestly and cooperatively. When disputes arise between the Executive and Legislative branches, as they surely will, the laws that emerge from such disputes must be obeyed. When a President, even with good motive and intent, chooses to skirt the laws or to circumvent them, it is incumbent upon his subordinates to resist, not join in. Their oath and fealty are to the Constitution and the rule of law, not to the man temporarily occupying the Oval Office. Congress has the duty and the power under our system of checks and balances to ensure that the President and his Cabinet officers are faithful to their oaths.

Notes and Questions

1. **Principled Investigation or Politically Motivated Witch Hunt?** Independent Counsel Lawrence Walsh's lengthy investigation of the Iran-Contra Affair was and remains controversial. Was Walsh a principled public servant who sought to overcome deliberate obstruction in his efforts to enforce the law, or was he an unaccountable "runaway prosecutor" who used his investigation to criminalize legitimate policy differences? It may be too early for history to return a final verdict on Walsh, but there is little doubt that disapproval of his investigation had important repercussions. Although Walsh was a life-long Republican with an impressive history of public service, his investigation inspired great hostility from Republican critics. That hostility, particularly among congressional Republicans, coupled with widespread dissatisfaction among congressional Democrats with Independent Counsel Kenneth Starr, were the principal reasons that Congress ultimately declined to extend the Independent Counsel Act.

2. Independent Counsel Walsh argued, in the above excerpt of his final report, that the attorney general's "competing roles" of presidential adviser and chief law enforcement officer create "an irreconcilable conflict of interest" that makes an independent counsel statute necessary. Congress disagreed and in 1999 allowed the independent counsel statute to expire without renewal. In large measure, the failure of Congress to renew the statute stemmed from bipartisan disenchantment with Walsh's Iran/Contra investigation (particularly among Republicans, who condemned Walsh's investigation as too long, too costly, and too partisan) and Kenneth Starr's Whitewater/Lewinski investigation (particulary among Democrats, who condemned Starr's investigation as too long, too costly, and too partisan). Consider events subsequent to the 1999 expiration

of the independent counsel statute, particularly Department of Justice Special Counsel Patrick Fitzgerald's investigation of the Valerie Plame Wilson matter and Special Counsel Robert Mueller's investigation of Russian influence on the 2016 presidential election (see Chapters 4 and 7). Do these more recent experiences suggest that a new independent counsel statute is needed, or do they suggest that the system can adequately police executive branch wrongdoing without an independent counsel statute? Ironically, among the long list of renowned attorneys who have served as special counsels and independent counsels, the three whose reputations were most enhanced, or at least not damaged, by their service—Archibald Cox, Leon Jaworski, and Patrick Fitzgerald—were Justice Department special counsels and not statutory independent counsels.

3. Has Congress Deferred Too Much to the Interests of the Criminal Justice System? In his Final Report, the Iran-Contra Independent Counsel observed that, except in cases of impeachment, Congress should not take action to further "the law enforcement goals of deterrence, retribution and punishment." Since Iran-Contra the Congress has largely deferred to the Department of Justice or Independent Counsels in their pursuit of these goals. Has Congress done so at the expense of its own constitutional duties? Professor Ronald F. Wright has argued that in some cases Congress may have been too deferential to the criminal justice system:

> Preserving criminal prosecution may be the foremost concern in some incidents of alleged wrongdoing. But when full and immediate congressional investigation of matters of public import, such as Whitewater or the FBI's conduct at Ruby Ridge, are delayed or diminished out of deference to criminal investigation, then one must ask whether the public has been best served. The choice of the criminal forum over the legislative forum in such cases is troubling because of the cynicism about Congress that the choice displays. It suggests that little worthwhile can come of a congressional hearing, and that any prospect of a criminal conviction should be enough reason to forego the pointless spectacle of hearings. Whether or not this is a sound judgment, it corrodes public faith to hear members of Congress themselves declare this judgment.

> Further, it is certainly worth asking whether a criminal prosecution provides the appropriate sort of accountability for misconduct in public office. If congressional hearings, rather than a criminal proceeding, were to become the main event for public scrutiny of a political figure, then political crimes would receive political punishments. And the decisionmakers—both the members of Congress and the interested public—would be better equipped to decide the issues than the often ill-informed jurors who must decide criminal cases under current juror selection rules.

> It is now unfashionable to praise congressional hearings. Yet there is a long history in this country of defending the virtues of congressional investigations as a genuine forum for public debate. As defenders have pointed out over the

years, congressional hearings can achieve a wider range of objectives than a judgment and sentence in a criminal case. Hearings will sometimes result in genuine punishment for wrongdoers who have not, strictly speaking, violated a criminal law. Hearings can inform Congress about the need for new legislation. They can also lead to public scrutiny of poor governance, and quicker and more certain accountability of government officials—accountability in a broader sense than the criminal law can achieve.

The costs of slow and incomplete congressional investigations are diffuse, but they have serious consequences for the health of the republic. Obstacles to the use of immunity grants do not, standing alone, cause ineffective congressional hearings. But when Congress inquires into governmental conduct with possible criminal ramifications, immunities are the central source of conflict between congressional and criminal investigations. If Congress can improve its practices with immunities, it will do more than improve its inner workings. It will reaffirm its own legitimacy as a place for meaningful debate and accountability. It could foster, in a small way, the conditions for democratic debate and self-governance.

Ronald F. Wright, *Congressional Use of Immunity Grants After Iran-Contra*, 80 MINN. L. REV. 407, 465–68 (1995) (footnotes omitted). Recall the materials on Watergate in Chapter 3 and the importance of John Dean's congressional testimony in that investigation. Is it a serious problem for our system of government if the likely effect of the *North* and *Poindexter* decisions is to prevent a John Dean from obtaining immunity in a congressional investigation?

4. Was the Iran-Contra Affair a Harbinger of Executive Branch Excesses Yet to Come? In this regard, consider the comments of historian Theodore H. Draper, in the concluding paragraph of his review of Independent Counsel Walsh's Final Report:

Can something on the order of the Iran-contra affairs happen again in the United States? I am not sanguine that we have been inoculated against some sort of repetition. The presidency has become so inflated and Congress so flabby, the secrecy of government so pervasive, and the distance between the electorate and their representatives so great, that only a self-denying president may save us from another such disgrace. After all, the deal with Iran was made public as a result of its exposure by an obscure Lebanese magazine, not by the vigilance of the American press or Congress. The Iran-contra events may be more important as a warning of what can go wrong in the American system than as a bar to its going wrong again.

Theodore H. Draper, *Walsh's Last Stand*, NEW YORK REVIEW OF BOOKS, Mar. 3, 1994. Consider also the discussions in Chapter 4 of President Donald Trump's assertions of executive privilege and blanket refusal to cooperate with Congress, as well as the discussion in Chapter 8 of the congressional investigation of the January 6, 2021, attack on the U.S. Capitol. Has Mr. Draper's warning proved prescient?

Waiver of the Fifth Amendment Privilege in Congressional Testimony: The Lois Lerner Dispute

One final legal issue relating to the application of the Fifth Amendment to congressional testimony merits consideration: When will a witness's opening statement or responses to questions waive the witness's Fifth Amendment privilege against self-incrimination? That issue arose in 2013, when the House Committee on Oversight and Government Reform sought the testimony of Internal Revenue Service official Lois G. Lerner in connection with the committee's investigation of reports that the IRS had improperly scrutinized the applications for tax-exempt status submitted by conservative political groups:

> Previously, in 2012, the House Committee on Oversight and Government Reform (Committee) had received reports that the Internal Revenue Service (IRS) improperly targeted conservative political groups applying for tax-exempt status by scrutinizing their applications for additional information, such as the identity of applicant donors, and delaying their applications. In 2013, Lois G. Lerner, who was serving as the IRS's Director of Exempt Organizations at the time, publicly acknowledged that the agency had inappropriately targeted conservative groups.[12]
>
> In response, the Committee commenced an investigation of the IRS's targeting program, which included conducting interviews with IRS officials and obtaining testimony and documents related to the program. The Committee, in particular, considered Ms. Lerner's testimony critical because, as the Director of the Exempt Organizations division, "[s]he was at the epicenter of the targeting program." The Committee hoped that Ms. Lerner would answer "important outstanding questions" about why the IRS targeted conservative organizations. On May 14, 2013, the Committee sent a letter to Ms. Lerner asking her to testify at a May 22, 2013 hearing about the IRS's handling of applications for tax-exempt status. Ms. Lerner, through counsel, confirmed her attendance at the hearing, but indicated that she would invoke her Fifth Amendment privilege against self-incrimination instead of answering questions. Subsequently, on May 20, 2013, the Committee issued a subpoena to compel Ms. Lerner's

---

12. [*Ed. Note: Ms. Lerner had acknowledged the agency's actions at an American Bar Association event in May 2013.* "So our line people in Cincinnati who handled the applications did what we call centralization of these cases. They centralized work on these in one particular group.... However, in these cases, the way they did the centralization was not so fine. Instead of referring to the cases as advocacy cases, they actually used case names on this list. They used names like Tea Party or Patriots and they selected cases simply because the applications had those names in the title. That was wrong, that was absolutely incorrect, insensitive, and inappropriate—that's not how we go about selecting cases for further review. We don't select for review because they have a particular name." Rick Hasen, Transcript of Lois Lerner's Remarks at Tax Meeting Sparking IRS Controversy, ELECTION LAW BLOG *(May 11, 2013, 7:37 a.m.), http://electionlawblog.org/?p=50160.*]

testimony. Ms. Lerner, through counsel, again invoked her Fifth Amendment right not to answer any questions. In response, Committee Chairman Darrell Issa advised Ms. Lerner that the subpoena remained in effect, and that her attendance at the hearing was expected because she was "uniquely qualified" to testify about the IRS's actions.

On May 22, 2013, Ms. Lerner appeared before the Committee. In an opening statement, she denied any wrongdoing or unlawful activity as the Director of Exempt Organizations at IRS, but maintained that she would assert her Fifth Amendment privilege not to testify or answer any questions relating to the Committee's investigation. Following the hearing, on June 28, 2013, the Committee, by a 22–17 vote, approved a resolution finding that Ms. Lerner had waived her Fifth Amendment privilege by making a voluntary opening statement and denying her involvement in unlawful activity. Thus, on February 25, 2014, Chairman Issa advised Ms. Lerner's counsel by letter that she was expected to comply with the subpoena and present testimony before the Committee at a reconvened hearing on March 5, 2014. Ms. Lerner appeared before the Committee on March 5, 2014.

At the beginning of the hearing, Chairman Issa advised Ms. Lerner that, because the Committee had determined that she waived her Fifth Amendment privilege, it reserved the option of recommending a contempt resolution against her if she refused to answer any questions. Nevertheless, Ms. Lerner continued to invoke her Fifth Amendment privilege. Several weeks later, on April 10, 2014, the Committee, by a 21–12 vote, approved a contempt resolution against Ms. Lerner for her refusal to comply with the subpoena.

On May 7, 2014, the House voted 231–187 to adopt the Committee's resolution, and directed the Speaker, pursuant to 2 U.S.C. §§192 and 194, to certify the contempt citation to the U.S. Attorney for the District of Columbia for prosecution.

Todd Garvey, *Congress's Contempt Power and the Enforcement of Congressional Subpoenas: Law, History, Practice, and Procedure*, Congressional Research Service (May 12, 2017) (footnotes omitted).

The content and language of Lerner's opening statement was central to the dispute over whether she had waived her Fifth Amendment rights. In her opening statement she denied that she had violated any laws:

> Good morning, Mr. Chairman and members of the Committee. My name is Lois Lerner, and I'm the Director of Exempt Organizations at the Internal Revenue Service.
>
> I have been a government employee for over 34 years. I initially practiced law at the Department of Justice and later at the Federal Election Commission. In 2001, I became—I moved to the IRS to work in the Exempt Organizations office, and in 2006, I was promoted to be the Director of that office.

Exempt Organizations oversees about 1.6 million tax-exempt organizations and processes over 60,000 applications for tax exemption every year. As Director I'm responsible for about 900 employees nationwide, and administer a budget of almost $100 million. My professional career has been devoted to fulfilling responsibilities of the agencies for which I have worked, and I am very proud of the work that I have done in government.

On May 14th, the Treasury inspector general released a report finding that the Exempt Organizations field office in Cincinnati, Ohio, used inappropriate criteria to identify for further review applications for organizations that planned to engage in political activity which may mean that they did not qualify for tax exemption. On that same day, the Department of Justice launched an investigation into the matters described in the inspector general's report. In addition, members of this committee have accused me of providing false information when I responded to questions about the IRS processing of applications for tax exemption.

I have not done anything wrong. I have not broken any laws. I have not violated any IRS rules or regulations, and I have not provided false information to this or any other congressional committee.

And while I would very much like to answer the Committee's questions today, I've been advised by my counsel to assert my constitutional right not to testify or answer questions related to the subject matter of this hearing. After very careful consideration, I have decided to follow my counsel's advice and not testify or answer any of the questions today.

Because I'm asserting my right not to testify, I know that some people will assume that I've done something wrong. I have not. One of the basic functions of the Fifth Amendment is to protect innocent individuals, and that is the protection I'm invoking today. Thank you.

The IRS: Targeting Americans for Their Political Beliefs: Hearing before the H. Comm. on Oversight & Gov't Reform, 113th Cong. 22 (May 22, 2013) (H. Rpt. 113-33) (statement of Lois Lerner, Director, Exempt Orgs., IRS).

Whether or not this statement had waived Lerner's Fifth Amendment privilege against self-incrimination was hotly disputed. One of the authors of this book provided the following statement to the Committee prior to the Lerner contempt vote and subsequent criminal contempt referral to the Department of Justice:

Statement of Stanley M. Brand, Esq. Regarding Lois Lerner's Assertion of Constitutional Privilege

Dated: June 27, 2013

Counsel for the Committee on Oversight and Government Reform (Minority) has asked me to provide a brief statement concerning my view of whether Lois Lerner, an IRS official who appeared before the Committee on

May 22, 2013 in connection with its inquiry into the Internal Revenue Service's consideration of applications for tax exempt status by certain groups, waived her rights under the Fifth Amendment by giving a brief prefatory statement during her appearance. As I stated at the time of her appearance, I do not believe her comments would be construed as a waiver under current judicial interpretations of the Fifth Amendment. It is well settled that the Fifth Amendment privilege against being compelled to testify against oneself is available in congressional proceedings. *Quinn v. United States*, 349 U.S. 155 (1955); *Emspack v. United States*, 349 U.S. 190 (1955). What is also well settled is that the Courts will afford witnesses wide latitude in assessing the sufficiency of the words used to assert the privilege. As the Court in *Quinn* stated "no ritualistic formula is necessary to invoke the privilege.... Quinn's references to the Fifth Amendment were clearly sufficient to put the Committee on notice of an apparent claim of privilege." 349 U.S. at 164.

Ms. Lerner's brief introductory statement to the Committee, not given in response to any specific question, was simply a profession of her innocence, offered prior to the commencement of Member questioning regarding the substance of the Committee's inquiry. It contained no factual representations relating to the subject matter of the hearing and generally denied wrongdoing.

Indeed, in the *Quinn* case itself, a lengthy colloquy between the witness asserting the privilege and the Committee propounding the questions occurred during the witnesses' appearance. When sworn and questioned, Quinn stated "I would like to make a statement along the lines that [an earlier witness] made yesterday in regard to a question of that nature, I feel that the political beliefs, opinions and associations of the American people can be held secret if they so desire." *Id.*, at 158, n.8. The witness went on in response to further questions from the committee".... I may add I feel I have no other choice in this matter, because the defense of the Constitution, I hold sacred, I don't feel I am hiding behind the Constitution, but in this case I am standing before it, defending it, as small as I am." *ld.* Despite this extended expression by the witness, the Court upheld his claim of privilege.

As with all constitutional privileges that protect individuals against governmentally compelled testimony, the Courts have insisted on a knowing and unequivocal waiver before divesting a witness of such privileges. *See, e.g. United States v. Helstoski*, 442 U.S. 477, 493 (1979) (the constitutional privilege for congressional speech or debate requires "an explicit and unequivocal waiver").

Based on the foregoing, I do not believe that Ms. Lerner's brief introductory profession of innocence, in which she offered no substantive testimony or evidence constitutes a waiver of her Fifth Amendment rights.

The Department of Justice ultimately declined to prosecute Lerner. In a letter to Speaker of the House John A. Boehner dated March 31, 2015, U.S. Attorney for the District of Columbia Ronald C. Machen, Jr. explained that his office would not present the contempt citation to a grand jury for prosecution. Machen summarized his office's analysis and conclusions as follows:

> Under 2 U.S.C. §192, a person is guilty of contempt of Congress if he or she, "having been summoned as a witness by the authority of either House of Congress to give testimony or to produce papers upon any matter under inquiry before ... any committee of either House of Congress, willfully ... refuses to answer any question pertinent to the question under inquiry." Where the House of Representatives has voted to find a witness in contempt, 2 U.S.C. §194 directs the Speaker of the House to "certify" the matter "to the appropriate United States attorney, whose duty it shall be to bring the matter before the grand jury for its action."
>
> Upon receipt of your referral, a team of experienced career prosecutors in this United States Attorney's Office was assigned to assess the matter. As discussed in more detail below, after extensive analysis of the facts of this matter and the applicable law, it was the team's conclusion that the Committee followed proper procedures in notifying Ms. Lerner that it had rejected her claim of privilege and gave her an adequate opportunity to answer the Committee's questions. Thus, Ms. Lerner's refusal to answer would be "willful" under Section 192 unless otherwise excused. However, the team also concluded that Ms. Lerner did not waive her Fifth Amendment privilege by making an opening statement on May 22, 2013, because she made only general claims of innocence. Thus, the Fifth Amendment to the Constitution would provide Ms. Lerner with an absolute defense should she be prosecuted under Section 192 for her refusal to testify.
>
> Given this assessment, we have further concluded that it is not appropriate for a United States Attorney to present a matter to the grand jury for action where, as here, the Constitution prevents the witness from being prosecuted for contempt. We respectfully inform you that we will therefore not bring the Congressional contempt citation before a grand jury or take any other action to prosecute Ms. Lerner for her refusal to testify on March 5, 2014.

* * *

> We wish to assure you that the Department of Justice does not question the authority of Congress "to summon witnesses before either House or before their committees," or "to pass laws 'necessary and proper' to carry into effect its power to get testimony." *See Adams v. Maryland*, 347 U.S. 179, 183 (1954) (citing U.S. Const. art. I, §8). Thus, in appropriate circumstances, a United States Attorney's Office will refer to a grand jury under Section 192 witnesses who contumaciously withhold testimony or other information that Congress has legitimately sought to compel in the exercise of its legislative or oversight

responsibilities. Because, however, the authority of any branch of the United States government to compel witness testimony is limited by the protections of the Constitution, and Ms. Lerner did not waive those protections in this matter, the United States Attorney's Office will not bring the instant contempt citation before a grand jury.

Notes and Questions

1. Wise Strategy or Unnecessary Risk? Although Lerner ultimately prevailed and was not prosecuted for contempt of Congress, she remained at risk of prosecution for almost two years after she gave her opening statement denying wrongdoing. Did the benefits to her of giving a blanket denial of wrongdoing justify the subsequent risk of prosecution? Is your conclusion affected if you factor in the cost of legal fees for the protracted dispute over whether she had waived her privilege against self-incrimination? Would you advise a client in a congressional investigation to take the approach Lerner did?

2. Did Lerner Prevail as a Matter of Law or Politics? As discussed in Chapter 4, the Department of Justice has long maintained that it retains prosecutorial discretion to decide whether or not to present contempt of Congress cases to a grand jury, notwithstanding the "whose duty it shall be to bring the matter before the grand jury for its action" language of 2 U.S.C. §194. Was Lerner's position clearly correct as a matter of law, or was she fortunate that her referral for criminal prosecution was by a Republican majority in the House of Representatives and the decision to prosecute was made by a U.S. Attorney in a Democratic presidential administration? Consider the views of one commentator on this issue:

> This is not to say that Machen's conclusion on waiver is unreasonable. As I have said, this is a close legal question, and reasonable people can disagree on the outcome. The issue is whether the decision should be made by the U.S. Attorney or by a court.
>
> This brings us to Machen's third point. Notwithstanding the apparently clear language of the statute requiring that a congressional contempt be presented to a grand jury (see, for example, then-Speaker Pelosi's position in the *Miers* case), [*Ed. Note: The* Miers *case is discussed in Chapter 4.*] Machen contends that the decision is within his discretion. He further maintains that under DOJ policies that [*sic*] it is not proper to bring the matter before a grand jury unless he is convinced that Lerner's privilege claim is invalid. Machen's position here conflicts with both statutory text and congressional intent, IMHO, although I am not particularly surprised that he has taken this stance.
>
> Essentially the U.S. Attorney's office is reserving the right to make its own independent judgment about the legitimacy of a congressional contempt citation, even if that means resolving a close legal question in a way that protects a witness in an investigation that could embarrass the administration he

serves. It is another in a long line of examples demonstrating Congress's institutional weakness in controlling the executive.

Michael Stern, *The U.S. Attorney's Troubling Decision in the Lois Lerner Case*, POINT OF ORDER (April 1, 2015). See also Brian P. Ketcham, *Waiving the Fifth Amendment Before Congress—Not as Easy as Congress Might Hope*, THE CHAMPION (Aug. 2013).

3. Look again at Lerner's opening statement that is quoted in full above. Is it clear that she provided no testimony and only offered a general denial of wrongdoing? Is it significant that Lerner was not appearing before the committee voluntarily, but rather had been compelled to appear by issuance of a subpoena, even after her counsel had advised the committee that she would assert her Fifth Amendment privilege against self-incrimination and not provide testimony? Professor James Duane explained the difference between Lerner's position and that of a criminal or civil defendant who voluntarily decides to testify at trial:

> When a criminal or civil defendant chooses to voluntarily testify at his trial in his own defense, it has always been universally understood that he cannot—after testifying fully to his one-sided version of the facts in response to questions from his own lawyer on direct examination—then "take the Fifth" and refuse to answer any questions from the prosecutor on cross-examination. *Brown v. United States*, 356 U.S. 148, 154–55 (1957). This is a reflection of the special nature of the right of cross-examination at civil and criminal trials, and of the inherent unfairness in allowing a witness to potentially interfere with "the function of courts of justice to ascertain the truth." *Id.* at 156. These concerns apply with special force in a criminal trial, because the Double Jeopardy clause of the Fifth Amendment gives the prosecution only one shot at trying to prove its case against the accused.

> But this is not the same as the rule for witnesses like Lois Lerner, who attempted to invoke the Fifth Amendment in response to questions put to her at an investigative hearing where she was ordered to appear under subpoena. *See Brown*, 356 U.S. at 155 (distinguishing between "a witness who is compelled to testify" and the situation "when a witness voluntarily testifies," and noting that the Fifth Amendment is more readily waived in the latter situation). She did not appear voluntarily, did not give a complete presentation of her side of the case on direct examination, and her generic denial of wrongdoing—even without the equivalent of cross-examination—did not pose the slightest threat to the investigative work of this Committee.

> In *Brown*, the Supreme Court noted the special danger that would result at a trial if a witness who voluntarily testified at length were allowed to put her version of the facts before the judge or jury, thus potentially influencing the verdict and the outcome of the case, without allowing herself to be subject to meaningful cross examination. The Court reasoned that the value of cross-examination in that context would be vastly superior to the unacceptable alternative of "striking the witness' testimony" and asking the judge or jury to put

it out of their minds. *Brown*, 356 U.S. at 156 n.5. But that danger is simply not present in a situation like the one before this Committee, when a witness claims the Fifth Amendment after giving a generic denial of wrongdoing not at a trial but during an investigative proceeding such as a police interview, a grand jury proceeding, or a Congressional committee. In such settings the ultimate objective is gathering information—as much as possible—not necessarily reaching any final determinations of fact or liability, and so there is no grave threat of injustice if a witness in such a setting invokes the Fifth Amendment to prevent the government agency or investigator from getting an answer to every question it would prefer to have answered. This is especially true in a case like this one, where a Congressional committee has heard nothing from a witness other than a generic denial of wrongdoing; surely no member of this distinguished Committee (unlike the jurors at an ordinary trial) would have the slightest difficulty disregarding those unexplained and conclusory denials in light of her refusal to answer specific questions pertaining to those denials.

Thank Goodness Professor Dershowitz is Wrong About the Fifth Amendment, Written Statement of Professor James J. Duane, Submitted to the House Committee on Oversight and Government Reform, June 28, 2013. Professor Duane's analysis demonstrates why, even if you conclude that Lerner's strategy was wise in the politically charged context of a congressional hearing, the approach taken by Lerner should not be attempted by a defendant in a judicial proceeding.

Chapter Six

The Attorney-Client Privilege in Congressional Investigations

The Whitewater Notes Dispute and the January 6 Committee Investigation of the Attack on the U.S. Capitol

> *I express at the outset my concern about some of the legal arguments which have been raised that the attorney-client privilege does not apply to Congress, to congressional investigations.*
>
> Statement of Senator Arlen Specter during
> floor debate on civil enforcement of a subpoena for
> Whitewater attorney notes, December 20, 1995

> *Dr. Eastman and President Trump launched a campaign to overturn a democratic election, an action unprecedented in American history. Their campaign was not confined to the ivory tower—it was a coup in search of a legal theory. The plan spurred violent attacks on the seat of our nation's government, led to the deaths of several law enforcement officers, and deepened public distrust in our political process.... If Dr. Eastman and President Trump's plan had worked, it would have permanently ended the peaceful transfer of power, undermining American democracy and the Constitution. If the country does not commit to investigating and pursuing accountability for those responsible, the Court fears January 6 will repeat itself.*
>
> U.S. District Judge David O. Carter,
> in *Eastman v. Thompson* (C.D. Cal. 2022)

As suggested by the statement of Senator Arlen Specter quoted above, the law is not settled on the issue of whether or not the attorney-client privilege applies to congressional proceedings. The essence of the arguments on either side of the issue can be stated succinctly. One argument is that the attorney-client privilege is an evidentiary rule that was developed by the judicial branch of government for use in judicial proceedings, and as a co-equal branch of government the Congress is not bound to recognize the doctrine. The strongest opposing argument is that, notwithstanding the judicial branch origins of the privilege, the right to counsel that is guaranteed by the Sixth Amendment gives the attorney-client privilege a constitutional dimension that must be recognized by the Congress. The materials that follow examine both sides of this issue, beginning with background information on the attorney-client privilege and then focusing on attorney-client privilege disputes that arose during investigations by the Senate Whitewater Committee in 1995 and the House Select Committee to Investigate the January 6 Attack on the United States Capitol in 2022.

The Attorney-Client Privilege and the Work Product Doctrine

The attorney-client privilege occupies a special place in the American legal system and, like the Fifth Amendment privilege against self-incrimination, is one of the few legal doctrines that is almost universally known to the general public. Like the privilege against self-incrimination, however, the specifics of attorney-client privilege law are more complex than most non-lawyers would ever imagine. One of the authors of this book has summarized the history and basic elements of attorney-client privilege law as follows:

Lance Cole, *Revoking Our Privileges: Federal Law Enforcement's Multi-Front Assault on the Attorney-Client Privilege (And Why It Is Misguided)*

48 Villanova L. Rev. 469, 474–98 (2003)
(footnotes omitted except as indicated)

The Importance of the Attorney-Client Privilege in the American Legal System.

A. Relevant Historical Background.

Almost every article, case, and treatise on the attorney-client privilege begins with the observation that the attorney-client privilege is the oldest evidentiary privilege recognized in Anglo-American common law....

1. Origins and Historical Development of the Privilege.

The attorney-client privilege is recognized in the federal judicial system and in all state judicial systems. The roots of the privilege extend back to Roman law and the notion that the loyalty a lawyer owes to a client disqualifies the lawyer from serving as a witness in the client's case. In English common law the rule of confidentiality for attorney testimony came to be grounded in the client's right to have his secrets protected, rather than the lawyer's right not to be compelled to testify. Although the existence of the privilege was established in English common law by the beginning of the nineteenth century, its scope and boundaries were not well settled.

The early American cases recognizing the privilege did little to resolve the ambiguities surrounding it, although they did establish the availability of the privilege when legal advice was "related directly to pending or anticipated litigation." In the United States, two principal influences served to define the privilege and establish the policy grounds upon which it came to rest during the twentieth century. One of those influences, not surprisingly, was the United States Supreme Court. The other, and perhaps the more important, influence was the treatise on evidence published by then-Professor and later Dean John Henry Wigmore of the Northwestern Law School shortly after the turn of the century.[1]

Wigmore's original treatise on evidence made two especially significant contributions to the development of attorney-client privilege law in the United States. First, ... Wigmore sought to articulate a policy basis for the privilege that both justified its continued existence and answered the arguments of its critics. That policy basis is discussed below. Second, and perhaps most important to the orderly development of privilege law, Wigmore sought to define the privilege in terms of its essential elements and "to group them in natural sequence." This undertaking, which Wigmore described as "a matter of some difficulty," led to the now-classic definition of the privilege:

(1) Where legal advice of any kind is sought (2) from a professional legal adviser in his capacity as such, (3) the communications relevant to that purpose, (4) made in confidence (5) by the client, (6) are at his instance permanently protected (7) from disclosure by himself or by the legal adviser, (8) except the client waives the protection.

Wigmore organized the discussion and analysis of the privilege in his treatise according to these numbered elements. The influence and acceptance of Wigmore's treatise as the leading authority in the field resulted in a widely accepted definition of the privilege and contributed to an orderly development of the law in this area.[2]

---

1. [15] John Henry Wigmore, A TREATISE ON THE SYSTEM OF EVIDENCE IN TRIALS AT COMMON LAW, Vol. IV (1st ed. 1905) (hereinafter, "Wigmore, First Edition").

2. [22] A widely cited judicial test for application of the privilege is that of Judge Wyzanski in *United States v. United Shoe Machinery Corp.*, 89 F. Supp. 357, 358 (1950):

The privilege applies only if (1) the asserted holder of the privilege is or sought to become a client; (2) the person to whom the communication was made (a) is a member of the bar of a court, or his subordinate and (b) in connection with this communication is acting as a lawyer; (3) the communication relates to a fact of which the attorney was informed (a) by his client (b) without the presence of strangers (c) for the purpose of securing primarily either (i) an opinion on law (ii) legal services or (iii) assistance in some legal proceeding, and not (d) for the purpose of committing a crime or tort; and (4) the privilege has been (a) claimed and (b) not waived by the client.

Judge Wyzanski did not cite Wigmore (or any other authority) in support of his test for application of privilege, but both the organization (numbered elements) and content (generally tracking Wigmore's definition) suggest Wigmore's influence. (Judge Wyzanski appears to have been reading Wigmore at

... In the first edition of his treatise, Wigmore identified four elements that must be present before any privilege should be recognized:

(1) The communications must originate in a *confidence* that they will not be disclosed; (2) This element of *confidentiality must be essential* to the full and satisfactory maintenance of the relation between the parties; (3) The *relation* must be one which in the opinion of the community ought to be sedulously *fostered*; and (4) The *injury* that would inure to the relation by the disclosure of the communications must be *greater than the benefit* thereby gained for the correct disposal of litigation.

He concluded that all four elements were present in the case of the attorney-client privilege. He also stated categorically that the "modern theory" of the policy underlying the privilege was to promote freedom of consultation of legal advisers by clients.

In embracing the modern theory of the privilege, Wigmore defended the privilege against its most influential nineteenth century critic, Jeremy Bentham. Bentham's argument against the privilege, in short, was that deterring a guilty client from seeking legal advice was not cause for concern, while an innocent client had nothing to fear if the privilege were not available, and thus would not be deterred. Wigmore exposed both the naivete and the flawed premises underlying Bentham's argument. First, Wigmore observed that (even in the relatively simpler times in which he wrote), "[t]here is in civil cases often *no hard-and-fast line between guilt and innocence*," and in many cases neither party will be completely in the right or completely in the wrong in a moral sense. Wigmore made the case that in actual practice, unlike in Bentham's abstract argument, the reality of the legal system is much more complex, and the costs of depriving one party of confidential legal advice is higher, than Bentham's argument would suggest.[3]

---

the time. Although he did not cite Wigmore in that case, he repeatedly cited Wigmore, referring to him as one of "the masters of the law of evidence," in a companion case involving the same parties and decided the same day addressing an issue arising under the hearsay rule. *See United Shoe*, 89 F. Supp. at 351–52. *Cf.* David J. Fried, "*Too High a Price for Truth: The Exception to the Attorney-Client Privilege for Contemplated Crimes and Frauds,*" 64 N.C. L. Rev. 443, n.1 (1986) ("Judge Wyzanski's statement of the Rule of privilege is an expansion of Professor Wigmore's version [Wigmore quotation omitted]."). For a [more] contemporary definition of the privilege see the Restatement (Third) of Law Governing Lawyers. §68 (2000) ("[T]he attorney-client privilege may be invoked ... with respect to: (1) a communication (2) made between privileged persons (3) in confidence (4) for the purpose of obtaining or providing legal assistance for the client.").

3. [30] Wigmore observed that "the abstinence from seeking legal advice in a good cause is by hypothesis an evil which is fatal to the administration of justice; and even Bentham does not go so far as to question this hypothesis." Wigmore, First Edition at §2291, at p. 3202. The United States Supreme Court expressed a similar view in *Upjohn Co. v. United States*, 449 U.S. 383, 393 n.2 (1981) ("an individual trying to comply with the law or faced with a legal problem also has strong incentive to disclose information to his lawyer, yet the common law has recognized the value of the privilege in further facilitating communications"). The Court's privilege analysis in *Upjohn* is discussed further [below].

A second flaw in Bentham's argument, exposed by Wigmore, was the assumption that no social good would be served by fostering access to legal counsel by those with weak or wrongfully advanced causes. Wigmore made the point that in many cases principled legal counsel would persuade clients not to pursue such causes or would pursue an appropriate settlement of cases that had limited merit. Wigmore's careful refutation of Bentham's attack on the privilege provided a compelling and influential catalogue of the utilitarian benefits of a broadly available privilege. Thanks to the broad acceptance of the arguments made by Wigmore, throughout the twentieth century there has been a widespread acceptance that those benefits outweigh the costs, in terms of withheld testimony, imposed by a widely available attorney-client privilege.

The second major influence on the development of the attorney-client privilege in the United States was the Supreme Court. The Court's views on the subject were in accord with the arguments Wigmore advanced in his treatise. It appears that by the late nineteenth century the Supreme Court had enthusiastically embraced the "modern" rationale for the attorney-client privilege. In an 1876 case involving a dispute over a life insurance policy, *Connecticut Mutual Life Ins. Co. v. Schaefer*,[4] the Court described the interests served by the privilege in particularly strong terms: "If a person cannot consult his legal adviser without being liable to have the interview made public the next day by an examination enforced by the courts, the law would be little short of despotic. It would be a prohibition upon professional advice and assistance." The Court made this statement in support of its conclusion that the attorney-client privilege had been properly invoked to block testimony by an attorney about conversations with a client whom he had represented in a divorce. The defendant insurance company had sought to examine the attorney about statements the client had made to him about her deceased ex-husband that, if admitted into evidence, might have proved that false statements were made in the insurance application. The Court upheld the assertion of privilege and applauded the protection of confidential communications to one's attorney as dictated by the "wise and liberal policy" quoted above. This case indicates that by the late nineteenth century the Supreme Court had enthusiastically embraced the attorney-client privilege.

Subsequent cases support this conclusion and demonstrate that the regard in which the Court holds the privilege has not wavered, despite considerable criticism of the privilege by academics and commentators. In 1888 the Supreme Court described the policy grounds for the privilege as "founded upon the necessity, in the interest and administration of justice, of the aid of persons having knowledge of the law and skilled in its practice, which assistance can only be safely and readily availed of when free from consequences or the ap-

---

4. [34] 94 U.S. 457 (1876).

prehension of disclosure."[5] Several important points are implicit in this description. First, the Court recognized that laypersons cannot function in our legal system without the expert advice that can be obtained only from those with special training in law. In other words, one can no longer be "self-taught" in law—it is simply too complex a field to master without expert assistance. Second, our justice system will not function properly if laypersons do not seek out and obtain such expert advice. Our legal system is neither particularly user-friendly nor self-executing, and the legal advice provided by trained attorneys is what keeps the system functioning. Finally, and perhaps most important, laypersons will not seek out this advice if the system creates impediments to their doing so or if they believe that doing so will have adverse consequences for them....

  2. The Attorney Work-Product Doctrine Described and Distinguished.

Another important historical development involving the Supreme Court that merits discussion before reviewing the Court's more recent attorney-client privilege cases is the Court's approval of the attorney work-product doctrine in 1947 in *Hickman v. Taylor*.[6] The concept of protecting attorney work-product, such as an attorney's notes of witness interviews, from discovery by opponents in litigation was a new development in the law of evidence. Prior to the liberalization of pre-trial discovery rules, work-product protection was not needed because adversaries generally did not seek information from one another. In *Hickman* the Court held that attorney work-product has a qualified immunity from discovery in litigation. The protection is qualified because the Court was careful to note that if written statements and documents in an attorney's files contain facts that are "essential to the preparation of [an adversary's] case, discovery may properly be had." A detailed analysis of the protections provided by the work-product doctrine is not necessary for purposes of this [Chapter] ..., and a brief overview of the work-product doctrine, focusing on the important distinctions between the work-product doctrine and the attorney-client privilege, will suffice. What is more important for purposes of this [Chapter] ... is a comparison of the policy grounds underlying the privilege and the work-product doctrine....

Since *Hickman* was decided the work-product doctrine has been codified in the Federal Rules of Civil Procedure[7] and the Federal Rules of Criminal Procedure.[8] As it has evolved, the work-product doctrine recognizes a distinction between so-called "opinion work-product"—an attorney's mental impressions and legal theories—and the underlying factual information contained in an attorney's work-product. The work-product doctrine does not

---

5. [40] Hunt v. Blackburn, 128 U.S. 464, 470 (1888).
6. [45] 329 U.S. 495 (1947).
7. [50] Fed. R. Civ. P. 26(b)(3).
8. [51] Fed. R. Crim. P. 16(b)(2).

limit or deter independent efforts by adversaries to collect factual information, even if the same information has previously been collected by an adversary and incorporated into her work-product. As a leading commentator has explained the difference, "[m]ental impressions are fully protected; facts, on the other hand, seem to be fully discoverable."[9]

Another distinguishing aspect of the work-product doctrine is the extent of the protection provided. The attorney-client privilege applies only to confidential communications between an attorney and a client for the purpose of giving or receiving legal advice, while the work-product doctrine protects a broader range of materials prepared by or at the direction of an attorney in preparation for or in anticipation of litigation. For example, an attorney's notes of an interview or discussion with a third-party witness would not be protected by the attorney-client privilege, but would be protected by the work-product doctrine. Similarly, an attorney's notes of her legal analysis or litigation strategy, assuming they did not reflect communications with her client, would not be protected by the privilege but would be subject to the highest level of protection as "opinion work-product."

The differences between the protections provided by the two legal doctrines are significant, particularly in the real world of litigation practice, and analytically it is important always to distinguish between the two separate and distinct legal doctrines. Commentators have tended to focus on the differing policy grounds that are promoted by the two doctrines. The attorney-client privilege is often described as promoting the interests of the client in access to legal advice, while the work-product doctrine is often described as serving the interests of the attorney in preparing for litigation. Most commentators do recognize, albeit implicitly in many instances, that both policy grounds ultimately promote the same core value of efficient administration of justice and effective functioning of our legal system. What is often not adequately considered, however, is another core value that both doctrines serve—protecting the interest of the client in effective legal representation.

This latter value, which was explicitly embraced by the Supreme Court in *Hickman v. Taylor*,[10] is one that merits attention when analyzing the … [issue of whether the attorney-client privilege and the work product doctrine should be available in congressional investigations]. A fundamental policy objective underlying the work-product doctrine is protection of the attorney-client relationship—the same policy objective that underlies the "modern theory" of the attorney-client privilege. The Supreme Court's enthusiastic embrace of the work-product doctrine in *Hickman* and thereafter demonstrates its respect

---

9. [53] Stephen A. Saltzburg, *Privileges and Professionals: Lawyers and Psychiatrists*, 66 VA. L. REV. 597, 613–14 (1980).

10. [64] *See* 329 U.S. 495, 511 ("And the interests of the clients and the cause of justice would be poorly served [without the protections of the work-product doctrine].").

and concern for the attorney-client relationship, and its desire to protect that relationship from unnecessary outside interference....

B. The Supreme Court's Recent Decisions Affirming the Importance of the Attorney-Client Privilege and the Work-Product Doctrine.

1. Privilege Issues Decided by the Supreme Court Since 1980.

In view of the historical importance attached to the attorney-client privilege in our adversarial system of justice, it is perhaps surprising that the United States Supreme Court has addressed attorney-client privilege issues on relatively few occasions. What is remarkable about the Supreme Court's privilege jurisprudence is not its quantity, but rather the consistency with which the Court has upheld both the application of the privilege and the policy grounds, discussed above, that underlie it. In recent decades the Supreme Court has decided four significant attorney-client privilege cases.... As the discussion below indicates, the cases make clear that the Court is strongly "pro-attorney-client privilege" and therefore is unlikely to look with favor on actions ... that unnecessarily undercut or curtail the availability of the privilege.

a. *Upjohn Co. v. United States* and the Corporate Attorney-Client Privilege.

In 1981 the Supreme Court decided the *Upjohn* [*v. United States*] case and unanimously rejected the "control group" test for availability of the privilege in the corporate context.[11] [*Ed. Note: The "control group" test would have applied the privilege to communications between a corporation's lawyer and the people who control the corporation, but not communications between the corporation's lawyer and lower-level employees.*] In *Upjohn* then-Associate Justice William H. Rehnquist emphasized the public policy basis for the privilege. He recognized that by encouraging full and frank communication between attorneys and clients the privilege promotes broader public interests in compliance with the law and the administration of justice. He described the privilege as "recognizing that sound legal advice or advocacy serves public ends and that such advice or advocacy depends upon the lawyer's being fully informed by the client." His opinion for the Court concluded that the control group test was inconsistent with these public policy objectives because it would limit the persons within a corporation who received confidential legal advice from the corporation's attorneys while at the same time limiting the amount of information that corporate attorneys received from employees and agents of the corporation. The opinion acknowledged that complications arise when the attorney-client privilege is applied to an artificial entity such as a corporation, particularly where middle-level and lower-level employees are involved, but concluded that limiting application of the privilege to the high-level "control group" of a corporation was untenable because to do so would frustrate "the

---

11. [88] Upjohn Co. v. United States, 449 U.S. 383 (1981).

very purpose of the privilege" and could "limit the valuable efforts of corporate counsel to ensure their client's compliance with the law."

Significantly, the core rationale of the *Upjohn* decision is the belief that confidentiality is essential if the societal interest in fostering compliance with the law is to be served. Without an assurance of confidentiality, clients are unlikely to confide in their attorneys, and if they do not obtain fully informed legal advice they are less likely to comply with the law. Any doubt that the Court wished to emphasize this point is dispelled by the frequently quoted statement in *Upjohn* that "[a]n uncertain privilege, or one which purports to be certain but results in widely varying applications by the courts, is little better than no privilege at all." This rationale has remained constant in the Court's other privilege cases that have been decided since *Upjohn*, notwithstanding the passage of [four] decades and the changes in the make-up of the Court that have occurred in that time.

b. *Commodity Futures Trading Commission v. Weintraub* and Bankruptcy Trustees.

In 1984 the Court revisited the application of the privilege to a corporate entity, this time in the context of a corporate bankruptcy. In *Commodity Futures Trading Comm'n v. Weintraub*[12] the Court held that control over a bankrupt corporation's attorney-client privilege passes to the bankruptcy trustee. Justice Marshall, writing for a unanimous Court, concluded that in the case of a corporate bankruptcy the trustee in bankruptcy, by virtue of the management powers the trustee assumes, is analogous to the board of directors of a solvent corporation. Because the officers and directors of a solvent corporation exercise the power to waive the corporation's attorney client privilege, the trustee should assume that power when the bankruptcy court has appointed a trustee and stripped managerial power from the bankrupt company's officers and directors.

Like Justice Rehnquist in *Upjohn*, Justice Marshall in *Weintraub* recognized that the administration of the attorney-client privilege raises "special problems" in the corporate context, because a corporation is an inanimate entity and cannot speak directly to its lawyers. He described *Upjohn* and *Weintraub* as presenting "related" questions arising out of the application of the privilege to corporations. The key point from *Weintraub* for purposes of this [Chapter] is that Justice Marshall based his analysis on the same core rationale that Justice Rehnquist relied on in *Upjohn*—that by promoting full and frank communications between attorneys and their clients the privilege "encourages observance of the law and aids in the administration of justice." This concern with not unduly interfering with attorney-client communications is evident in the portion of the *Weintraub* opinion that dismisses the argument that vesting

---

12. [97] 471 U.S. 343 (1984).

power to waive the privilege in the trustee of a bankrupt corporation "will have an undesirable chilling effect on attorney-client communications." Rather than rejecting the underlying premise that chilling attorney-client communications should be avoided, Justice Marshall dismissed the argument because the chilling effect with a bankruptcy trustee is no greater than in the case of solvent corporation that undergoes a change of management. In both cases the corporation's prior management loses its control over assertion and waiver of the corporation's attorney-client privilege. In essence the *Weintraub* Court began its analysis with explicit approval of the public policy objectives identified in *Upjohn* that are served by the attorney-client privilege and concluded its analysis with an implicit recognition of the importance of those same public policy objectives.

  c. *United States v. Zolin* and the Crime-Fraud Exception.

Five years later, the Supreme Court's next venture into the attorney-client privilege arena resulted in an even stronger affirmation of the rationale underlying the privilege and the public policy objectives the privilege promotes. In *United States v. Zolin*[13] the Court grappled with the "crime-fraud exception" to the attorney-client privilege, which arguably is one of the most vexing areas of privilege law. In yet another unanimous decision the Court concluded that a court may use *in camera* review to determine whether the crime-fraud exception applies to attorney-client communications—but only if the party challenging the privilege presents evidence sufficient to support a reasonable belief that *in camera* review may establish that the exception is applicable. The *Zolin* Court also rejected the "independent evidence rule" that the purportedly privileged communications themselves cannot be considered by the court *in camera*, concluding that such a rule would create "too great an impediment to the adversary process."

On first examination, *Zolin* might appear to signal diminished support for the privilege by the Supreme Court, but a close reading of the opinion proves that is not the case. In *Zolin*, as it had done in *Upjohn* and *Weintraub*, the Court began its attorney-client privilege analysis by explaining that the privilege is intended to encourage full and frank communications between attorneys and their clients, which promotes the broader public policy interests in observance of law and administration of justice. The *Zolin* Court expressed its support of this core principle, which it articulated as "the centrality of open client and attorney communication to the proper functioning of our adversary system of justice." Rather than departing from this concept of the role and importance of the attorney-client privilege in our legal system, the *Zolin* opinion recognized an important limitation on it—that the privilege does not ap-

---

13. [110] 491 U.S. 554 (1989).

ply if the communications further ongoing or future wrongdoing. In those circumstances, the policy reasons for recognizing the privilege are not present, and therefore the privilege should not be available.

The conclusion in *Zolin* that the privilege should not be available to shield communications in furtherance of a future crime or fraud is neither remarkable nor inconsistent with the policy interests the privilege is intended to serve, and does not detract from the Court's strong support for the privilege when properly invoked to shield the confidentiality of legitimate legal advice. The *Zolin* Court made this point clear in its analysis of whether *in camera* judicial review should be conducted whenever a party asserts that the crime-fraud exception is applicable to attorney-client communications. The primary reason that the Court rejected a blanket rule that *in camera* judicial review should always be conducted when a party challenged the privilege on crime-fraud grounds was concern that such a rule "would place legitimate disclosure between attorneys and clients at undue risk." The Court was unwilling to endorse a rule that would deter full and frank communications between clients and their lawyers. The Court went so far as to condemn any approach to the crime-fraud problem that would "permit opponents of the privilege to engage in groundless fishing expeditions." This refusal to permit such fishing expeditions, even when it is alleged that the privilege has been misused to further an ongoing or future crime or fraud, is consistent with the Court's prior support for the privilege and the policy interests it serves, as previously demonstrated in *Upjohn* and *Weintraub*.

The test that the Court adopted in *Zolin* for when an *in camera* review should be conducted also reflects the Court's concern that the availability of the privilege not be unduly curtailed. A requirement that evidence sufficient to support a "reasonable belief" that *in camera* review may yield evidence establishing that the crime-fraud exception is applicable to the privilege communications at issue means that a court must be presented concrete evidence of future criminal or fraudulent conduct—mere unsubstantiated allegations will be insufficient to breach the privilege. Moreover, the use of the term "reasonable belief" demonstrates that the Court intended that an objective standard should apply to the initial determination of whether a legitimate crime-fraud exception challenge to the privilege is being advanced. An objective standard limits the discretion of individual judges and screens out weak and spurious challenges to the privilege. Thus both the rejection of a blanket rule permitting *in camera* review rule and the objective standard that the Court established for availability of such review indicate that the Court's primary concern in *Zolin* was to avoid any unwarranted invasion of the privilege. This solicitude for the continued vitality of the privilege and hesitance to formulate a rule that might deter legitimate attorney-client communications demonstrate that the *Zolin* Court remained committed to the core principle that the privilege is a vital element of our legal system.

d. *Swidler & Berlin v. United States* and the Deceased Client.

The Court's most recent attorney-client privilege case provides even stronger confirmation that the Court remains strongly opposed to any unnecessary encroachment on the protections provided by the attorney-client privilege. In *Swidler & Berlin v. United States*[14] the office of Independent Counsel Kenneth W. Starr sought to obtain the handwritten notes taken by Swidler & Berlin attorney James Hamilton during an initial interview with a client, then-Deputy White House Counsel Vincent W. Foster, Jr., shortly before Foster committed suicide. Two unusual aspects of this case made for a dramatic confrontation between the public interests served by the privilege and the evidentiary costs it imposes by excluding potentially relevant evidence. First, the case involved that most sacred form of attorney work product recording client communications: an attorney's handwritten notes of an initial interview with a client. Second, the information was sought in connection with a criminal investigation of the President of the United States. The combination of these two factors created a test case with a unique juxtaposition of competing public policy interests—those served by the privilege and those presented by allegations of wrongdoing by the country's chief law enforcement officer. Perhaps surprisingly to those who question the importance of the privilege in our modern legal system, the Supreme Court lined up squarely behind the attorney-client privilege.

Read as a whole, the *Swidler & Berlin* opinion reflects an overwhelming reluctance on the part of the Court to accept a change to existing privilege law that would be contrary to the interest of clients and therefore might undermine clients' reliance on the privilege and willingness to provide their attorneys with full and frank disclosure of relevant information. In rejecting the Independent Counsel's argument for extending "posthumous curtailment of the privilege" beyond cases involving disputes among a deceased client's heirs, the Court emphasized that the rationale for overcoming the privilege in those cases is that doing so furthers the client's intent. The Court's concern with protecting the interest of the client in maintaining the confidentiality of communications with counsel was most evident in its response to the argument advanced by the Independent Counsel that after the client's death "the interest in determining whether a crime had been committed should trump client confidentiality." Here the Court focused on the concerns a client might have, beyond concern with criminal prosecution, which could cause him to withhold information from counsel if confidentiality was not assured. The Court identified concerns about reputation, civil liability, and possible harm to friends or family as reasons a client might withhold information. The Court was unwilling to accept the risk that clients' willingness to confide in counsel would be impaired, even if the exception to the privilege applied only in criminal cases.

---

14. [123] 524 U.S. 399 (1998).

The *Swidler & Berlin* Court also expressed concern about injecting additional uncertainty into the privilege's application. This concern is consistent with the Court's core objective, consistently applied since its decision in the *Upjohn* case, that the application of the privilege should encourage clients to communicate with their lawyers. In advancing this objective, the Court embraced a broad concept of the privilege, extending beyond client concerns about prosecution in criminal cases, to client confidences about personal and family matters that must be revealed to obtain legal advice. Even these kinds of client confidences, perhaps only tangentially related to the legal advice provided in the course of such communications, was deemed worthy of protection by the Court. Taken as a whole, the *Swidler & Berlin* case represents perhaps the strongest affirmation yet of the value of the attorney-client privilege by the Supreme Court.

2. Conclusion.

For purposes of this [discussion of the application of the privilege to congressional investigations], it is important to note that all of these cases involved efforts by law enforcement officials to overcome assertions of privilege by parties subject to government regulatory proceedings or criminal prosecutions. In all instances the Court sustained the availability of the privilege and rejected efforts by the government to limit its protections. Moreover, as discussed above, in all four of the cases the Court consistently upheld the policy grounds that historically have been recognized as supporting the privilege. In short, these cases demonstrate consistent support of the privilege by the Supreme Court over the past two decades.

The Supreme Court's holding in the Foster attorney-notes case, *Swidler & Berlin v. United States*, provides an appropriate point of departure for examination of a principal topic of this Chapter, the 1995 efforts of the Senate Whitewater Committee to obtain notes prepared by Associate Counsel to the President William H. Kennedy, III, during a November 1993 meeting of White House attorneys and private attorneys representing President and Mrs. Clinton in the various Whitewater investigations. That dispute required a floor vote of the United States Senate before the matter was resolved and the notes were produced to the committee. Before turning to the materials on that dispute, consider the following Notes and Questions.

Notes and Questions

1. An Open Question. This Chapter began by describing the as-yet-unresolved issue of whether the attorney-client privilege must be recognized in congressional proceedings. Now that you have reviewed the history and additional background information on the privilege that is provided in the section immediately above, and in particular the views expressed by the Supreme Court in *Upjohn v. United States*, consider the more nuanced presentation of the issue by one of the leading practitioners in the area, James Hamilton, and his co-authors in a recent law review article:

> The availability of the attorney-client privilege in the context of congressional investigations has been a subject of considerable debate. Very few judicial decisions have addressed this issue, and those that have done so fail to resolve the matter conclusively. However, in recent decades a number of congressional committees have taken the position that the attorney-client and other common law privileges do not apply as of right in their proceedings but instead fall within the committee's discretion. The Subcommittee on Oversight and Investigations of the House Energy and Commerce Committee expressed this view in 1977 and 1983. In 1985, a subcommittee of the House Committee on Foreign Affairs, adopting the same position, cited an attorney for contempt because he refused to answer questions about the American business activities of his client, former Philippine President Ferdinand Marcos. That same year, another House subcommittee rejected a claim that the work product privilege precluded it from questioning a former Amtrak employee about an internal investigation conducted on behalf of the company's attorneys.

> Several arguments have been advanced in support of this discretionary view. First, it has been contended that a non-constitutional privilege cannot override Congress's inherent investigative authority, which, as we have seen, derives from the Constitution. According to this argument, subjecting Congress to the requirements of the privilege would "permit the judiciary to determine congressional procedures" and thus would undermine Congress's constitutional authority to establish its own rules. Another argument contends that the policy justifications for the privilege relate solely to the adversary system and are inapplicable to investigations, which are non-adversarial and do not involve the adjudication of witnesses' interests. In addition, it is argued that the precedents of the British Parliament and those of Congress support the conclusion that the privilege is discretionary.

> None of these arguments survives close scrutiny. First, the fact that Congress's power to investigate is constitutionally-based does not necessarily render the privilege inapplicable to congressional inquiries. Grand jury investigations likewise have a constitutional foundation, and yet common law privileges clearly apply in that context. Moreover, it has been shown that the courts and Congress historically have understood the attorney-client privilege to be a substantive common law right, not merely a procedural rule governing the administration of judicial proceedings.

> The argument that the policies advanced by the attorney-client privilege do not apply in the investigative setting also is unpersuasive. As the Supreme Court has recognized in *Upjohn Co. v. United States*:

>> [The privilege's] purpose is to encourage full and frank communication between attorneys and their clients and thereby promote broader public

interests in the observance of law and administration of justice. The privilege recognizes that sound legal advice or advocacy serves public ends and that such advice or advocacy depends on the lawyer being fully informed by the client.

These policy interests are not confined to the adversarial setting. Clearly, the prospect of an attorney being called before Congress to reveal client secrets is at odds with the encouragement of full and frank communications between attorneys and clients. Indeed, the *Upjohn* Court recognized that "if the purpose of the attorney-client privilege is to be served, the attorney and client must be able to predict with some degree of certainty whether particular discussions will be protected." Such certainty cannot be achieved if the decision to honor the privilege is a matter of committee discretion.

The grand jury analogy provides an additional response to the argument that the attorney-client privilege is inapplicable outside the adversarial context. A grand jury proceeding is not adversarial in nature, but, as noted, the privilege is recognized in that setting. It is unclear why the protections of the privilege should apply in that type of investigative proceeding but not in a congressional hearing, which involves similar features.

As to the contention that history supports the discretionary view, it should be noted that the precedents in this area are not determinative. While Congress has declined to observe the privilege in some instances, many committees historically have recognized common law privileges when properly raised. Moreover, the legislative history of the congressional contempt statute reveals significant concern on the part of many legislators about the protection of the attorney-client and other common law privileges.

In view of the foregoing, it appears likely that a court would recognize the attorney-client privilege if confronted with such a claim in a contempt prosecution. Nevertheless, the absence of clear judicial authority in this area renders the outcome uncertain. Therefore, a witness relying on the privilege as grounds for noncompliance with a committee order acts at his or her peril.

James Hamilton, Robert F. Muse & Kevin Amer, *Congressional Investigations: Politics and Process*, 44 Am. Crim. L. Rev. 1115, 1147–50 (2007) (footnotes omitted).

Careful readers will recall that James Hamilton was the Assistant Chief Counsel to the Senate Select Committee on Presidential Campaign Activities, known as the Ervin Committee, that investigated Watergate and is a subject of Chapter 3 of this book. As a lawyer in private practice some twenty years after Watergate, Hamilton was retained by then-Deputy White House Counsel Vince Foster in July 1993 to advise Foster with respect to anticipated congressional hearings on White House Travel Office employee dismissals. Nine days after retaining Hamilton, Foster committed suicide. Whitewater Independent Counsel Kenneth Starr subpoenaed Hamilton's handwritten notes of his initial meeting with Foster. Hamilton asserted attorney-client privilege and refused to turn over the notes. The battle over the notes eventually went all the way to the Supreme

Court, where Hamilton and his law firm, Swidler & Berlin, prevailed. *See Swidler & Berlin v. United States,* 524 U.S. 399 (1998). Hamilton's successful defense of the attorney-client privilege in the Foster notes case gives special credibility to his views on the issue of whether the privilege should be available as a matter of right in congressional proceedings. Bear in mind the observations of Hamilton and his co-authors as you consider the issues presented by the Whitewater Notes dispute that is the subject of the next section of this Chapter. For additional arguments supporting recognition of the attorney-client privilege in congressional proceedings, see Bradley J. Bondi, *No Secrets Allowed: Congress's Treatment and Mistreatment of the Attorney-Client Privilege and the Work-Product Protection in Congressional Investigations and Contempt Proceedings,* 25 J. OF L. & POL. 145 (2009), and Jonathan P. Rich, *The Attorney-Client Privilege in Congressional Investigations,* 88 COLUM. L. REV. 145 (1988).

2. Why it Matters—the Specter of Waiver. A logical question for you to ask yourself at this point is "What's all the fuss about—why does it matter if Congress refuses to recognize the attorney-client privilege?" In some cases, of course, the divulging of specific confidential information shared with an attorney may, in and of itself, be the reason for concern about congressional questioning about communications with the attorney. More often, however, the cause for concern stems from the potential legal consequences of revealing confidential attorney-client communications—a broad "subject-matter waiver" of the protection of the attorney-client privilege. President and Mrs. Clinton's private attorneys at the Washington law firm William & Connolly, in their legal memorandum opposing surrender of the Kennedy notes to the Senate Whitewater Committee, described the waiver problem as follows:

> ... As every lawyer well knows, counsel must be scrupulous not to allow even the smallest intrusion into the attorney-client relationship. Once there is any such intrusion, no matter if only a single disclosed document, adversaries can be counted upon to demand more. They would argue that there has been a waiver of the privilege with respect to all communications on the same subject matter and with the same counsel. There can be no doubt that the various investigators would do just that, and a court would have to decide, ultimately, the scope of the waiver, if any. Thus, any disclosure of communications, like the subpoenaed notes, that are a part of the personal legal relationship, no matter how narrow, necessarily places the Clintons' basic right and ability to talk to their lawyers in confidence at unacceptable risk. A lawyer and a client who believe a communication was privileged must protect it if they are to protect their relationship.

Report of the Special Committee to Investigate Whitewater Development Corporation and Related Matters to Accompany S. Res. 199, Refusal of William H. Kennedy, III, to Produce Notes Subpoenaed by the Special Committee to Investigate Whitewater Development Corporation and Related Matters, Dec. 19, 1995, Exhibit C, Dec. 12, 1995 Submission of Williams & Connolly to the Special Senate Committee Regarding Whitewater and Related Matters, at 93.

3. A Separation of Powers Issue (Yet Again). As you review the materials on the Whitewater Notes dispute in the section that follows, focus your attention on the separation of powers issue presented by the dispute—whether or not the judicial branch origins and purposes of the attorney-client privilege give Congress a basis for declining to recognize the privilege. In that regard, consider the fact that the attorney-client privilege is routinely asserted against (and respected by) executive branch law enforcement agencies and authorities. Why might a different result arguably be appropriate for the legislative branch? Is a distinction supported by the fact that the executive branch commonly—but not always, particularly in areas of criminal and regulatory agency law enforcement—enforces the law through judicial branch proceedings? One commentator has argued that recognition of the attorney-client privilege by executive branch administrative agencies in internal agency proceedings is especially relevant to the issue of whether federal courts should require recognition of the privilege by Congress:

> Lower federal courts have also ruled that the attorney-client privilege must be respected in administrative investigations, while several have indicated that the privilege must exist in any governmental proceeding. In the words of one court, "[t]he attorney-client privilege is deeply imbedded and is part of the warp and woof of the common law. In order to abrogate it in whole or in part as to any proceeding whatsoever, affirmative legislation would be required that is free from ambiguity" [quoting *Civil Aeronautics Bd. v. Air Transport Ass'n of Am.*, 201 F. Supp. 318 (D.D.C. 1961)]. Since administrative agencies act as quasi-legislative bodies based on authority delegated by Congress, these holdings provide further support for the applicability of the privilege in congressional proceedings.

Jonathan P. Rich, *The Attorney-Client Privilege in Congressional Investigations*, 88 COLUM. L. REV. 145, 168 (1988) (footnotes omitted). With respect to the argument that the attorney-client privilege has a constitutional dimension by virtue of the Sixth Amendment right to counsel, the same court that is quoted by Rich in the law review article excerpt above went on to say, in the sentence immediately following the quote, "The very existence of the right of counsel necessitates the attorney-client privilege in order that a client and his attorney may communicate between themselves freely and confidentially." *Civil Aeronautics Bd. v. Air Transport Ass'n of Am.*, 201 F. Supp. 318 (D.D.C. 1961).

The William Kennedy
Whitewater Notes Dispute

All of the legal and policy issues that are described above came to a head in 1995 in perhaps the most politically charged circumstance one might imagine—an assertion of attorney-client privilege by a sitting President, who was facing a re-election challenge, in response to a subpoena issued by a special congressional investigative committee that was controlled by the opposition political party. The Senate committee report that is excerpted below contains the views of the committee's Republican majority, voting unanimously to enforce the subpoena, and the Democratic minority, voting unanimously to oppose enforcing the subpoena.

Refusal of William H. Kennedy, III, to Produce Notes Subpoenaed by the Special Committee to Investigate Whitewater Development Corporation and Related Matters

REPORT OF THE SPECIAL COMMITTEE TO INVESTIGATE WHITEWATER DEVELOPMENT CORPORATION AND RELATED MATTERS

ADMINISTERED BY THE COMMITTEE ON BANKING, HOUSING, AND URBAN AFFAIRS UNITED STATE SENATE

TO ACCOMPANY

S. Res. 199

TOGETHER WITH MINORITY AND ADDITIONAL VIEWS

December 19, 1995

The Special Committee to Investigate Whitewater Development Corporation and Related Matters reports an original resolution to direct the Senate Legal Counsel to bring a civil action to enforce the Committee's subpoena to William H. Kennedy, III, and recommends that the resolution be agreed to.

PURPOSE

On December 8, 1995, the Committee issued a subpoena *duces tecum* to William H. Kennedy, III, former Associate Counsel to the President and now of counsel to the Rose Law firm of Little Rock, Arkansas, to produce notes that he took at a meeting held on November 5, 1993, at the law firm of Williams & Connolly. The purpose of this meeting, which was attended by both personal counsel for the President and Mrs. Clinton and by White House officials, was to discuss Whitewater Development Corporation ("Whitewater") and related matters. The meeting occurred at a critical time with regard to the "Washington phase" of the Whitewater matter, and Mr. Kennedy's notes of this meeting may relate to at least six matters of inquiry specified in Senate Resolution 120, including allegations that the White House improperly handled confidential government information about Whitewater. Nevertheless, Mr. Kennedy, at the instruction of counsel for both the President and Mrs. Clinton and the White House, has refused to comply with the Committee's subpoena for his notes.

This report recommends that the Senate adopt a resolution authorizing the Senate Legal Counsel to bring a civil action to compel Mr. Kennedy to comply with the Committee's subpoena. In accordance with section 705(c) of the Ethics in Government Act of 1978, 2 U.S.C. §288d(c) (1994), this report discusses the following:

(A) the procedure followed by the Committee in issuing its subpoena;

(B) the extent to which Mr. Kennedy has complied with the subpoena;

(C) the objections or privileges to the subpoena raised by counsel for the President and Mrs. Clinton, the White House, and Mr. Kennedy; and

(D) the comparative effectiveness of (i) bringing a civil action, (ii) certifying a criminal action for contempt of Congress, and (iii) initiating a contempt proceeding before that Senate.

To place the Committee's request for civil enforcement of its subpoena in proper context, this report first provides the background of the November 5, 1993 meeting and its relevance to the Committee's investigation.

BACKGROUND

A. The Committee's Investigation and Subpoena Authority

Acting pursuant to Senate Resolution 120, the Special Committee to Investigate Whitewater Development Corporation and Related Matters ("the Committee") is currently investigating and holding public hearings into a number of matters, including:

(1) whether the White House improperly handled confidential Resolution Trust Corporation ("RTC") information about Madison Guaranty Savings & Loan Association ("Madison") and Whitewater;

(2) whether the Department of Justice improperly handled RTC criminal referrals relating to Madison and Whitewater;

(3) the operations of Madison;

(4) the activities, investments and tax liability of Whitewater, its officers, directors, and shareholders;

(5) the handling by the RTC and other federal regulators of civil or administrative actions against any parties regarding Madison; and

(6) the sources of funding and lending practices of Capital Management Services, and its supervision by the Small Business Administration ("SBA"), including any alleged diversion of funds to Whitewater.

Section 5(b)(1) of Senate Resolution 120 authorizes the Committee to issue subpoenas for the production of documents. Under section 5(b)(10) of the Resolution, the Committee is authorized to report to the Senate recommendations for civil enforcement with respect to the willful failure or refusal of any person to produce any document or other material in compliance with any subpoena.

B. The November 5, 1993 Whitewater Defense Meeting

On November 5, 1993, a meeting was held at the law offices of Williams & Connolly, which had recently been retained by the President and Mrs. Clinton to act as their personal counsel for Whitewater-related matters. Seven persons attended the meeting; three lawyers in private practice and four White House officials:

David Kendall, a partner at the Washington, D.C. law firm of Williams & Connolly and the most recently retained private counsel to the President and Mrs. Clinton on the Whitewater matter.

Stephen Engstrom, a partner at the Little Rock law firm of Wilson, Engstrom, Corum, Dudley & Coulter, who also had been retained by the President and Mrs. Clinton to provide personal legal advice on the Whitewater matter.

James Lyons, a lawyer in private practice in Colorado, who had provided legal advice to then-Governor and Mrs. Clinton on the Whitewater matter during the 1992 presidential campaign.[15]

Then-Counsel to the President Bernard Nussbaum.

Then-Associate Counsel to the President William Kennedy, who while a partner at the Rose Law Firm, provided some legal services to the Clintons in 1990–92 in connection with their investment in Whitewater.

Then-Associate Counsel to the President Neil Eggleston.

Then-Director of White House Personnel Bruce Lindsey. The White House claims that Mr. Lindsey, a lawyer, provided legal services to the President with regard to the Whitewater matter while serving as White House Personnel Director. (Williams & Connolly, 12/12/95 Mem. p. 15). As set forth more fully below, however, Mr. Lindsey has testified that he never provided advice to the President regarding Whitewater matters. (Lindsey, 7/21/94 Dep. pp. 39–40).

Kendall organized this meeting, which lasted for more than two hours, during which time Mr. Kennedy took extensive notes.

* * *

White House spokesman Mark Fabiani has stated that the purpose of the meeting was to "pass the torch between the White House lawyers who had been handling Whitewater to the newly hired attorney, David Kendall." (New York Post, 11/29/95 p. 16).

The President and Mrs. Clinton's personal counsel, Mr. Kendall, has offered a more detailed explanation of the purpose of the meeting. According to Mr. Kendall, the meeting was held

> to provide new private counsel with a briefing about "Whitewater" issues from counsel for the Clintons who had been involved with those matters, to brief the White House Counsel's office and new personal counsel on the knowledge of James M. Lyons, personal attorney for the Clintons who had conducted an investigation of Whitewater Development Corporation in the 1992 Presidential Campaign, to analyze the pending issues, and, finally, to discuss a division of labor between personal and White House counsel for handling future Whitewater issues (Williams & Connolly, 12/12/95 Mem. p. 13).

---

15. [1] The President and Mrs. Clinton have agreed not to assert the attorney-client privilege with regard to any communications that occurred during the 1992 presidential campaign, including communications they may have had with Lyons.

C. The Relevance of Mr. Kennedy's Notes to the Committee's Investigation

Mr. Kennedy's notes may be relevant to at least six areas of inquiry outlined above that the Committee is now investigating pursuant to Senate Resolution 120.

* * *

DISCUSSION

A. The Procedure Followed by the Committee in Issuing the Subpoena to Mr. Kennedy

* * *

On December 5, 1995, Mr. Kennedy appeared before the Committee. He was questioned about the November 5 meeting, but, at the direction of counsel for both the President and Mrs. Clinton and the White House, refused to answer any questions about the substance of the meeting.

* * *

On December 8, 1995, the Committee issued a subpoena *duces tecum* to Mr. Kennedy directing him to "[p]roduce any and all documents, including but not limited to, notes, transcripts, memoranda, or recordings, reflecting, referring or relating to a November 5, 1993 meeting attended by William Kennedy at the offices of Williams & Connolly." The Committee advised Mr. Kennedy that, if he had objections to subpoenas, he was invited to submit a legal memorandum to the Committee by December 12, 1995.[16]

B. The Extent to Which Mr. Kennedy Has Complied with the Committee's Subpoena

Mr. Kennedy has refused to comply with the Committee's subpoena. On December 12, 1995, the Committee received separate submissions from counsel for Mr. Kennedy, the President and Mrs. Clinton, and the White House raising objections to the Committee's subpoena. Mr. Kennedy's counsel advised the Committee that Mr. Kennedy had been instructed by the President and Mrs. Clinton's personal counsel and by the White House Counsel not to produce to the Committee the subpoenaed notes of the November 5 meeting.

On December 14, 1995, the Chairman of the Committee, pursuant to Senate Resolution 120, convened a meeting of the Committee to rule on the objections raised by Mr. Kennedy's counsel, the President and Mrs. Clinton's personal counsel and the White House counsel. After careful consideration of the arguments, and after receiving the advice of the Committee's counsel, the Chairman overruled the objections to the

---

16. [2] Counsel for Mr. Kennedy subsequently informed the Committee by letter that he was "somewhat uncertain about the status of the subpoena" because it had been delivered to him rather than Mr. Kennedy. The Committee believes that the December 8, 1995, subpoena was validly served on counsel for Mr. Kennedy, who had represented Mr. Kennedy in connection with the Committee's present investigation and had regularly communicated with the Committee on Mr. Kennedy's behalf. In any event, on December 15, 1995, the Committee voted to issue another subpoena, which was personally served on Mr. Kennedy in Little Rock that same day.

subpoena. The Committee then voted to order and direct Mr. Kennedy to produce the subpoenaed documents by 9:00 a.m. on December 15, 1995. After Mr. Kennedy failed to comply with this order, the Committee voted on December 15, 1995, to report to the Senate the resolution that accompanies this report.

* * *

C. Objections to the Subpoena

Counsel to the President and Mrs. Clinton and the White House have interposed three objections to the Committee's subpoena for Mr. Kennedy's notes: (i) the attorney-client privilege; (ii) the common interest doctrine, which has been raised in conjunction with the attorney-client privilege; and (iii) the work product doctrine.

* * *

2. The attorney-client privilege does not shield the Kennedy notes from disclosure to this Committee

The primary objection to the Committee's subpoena interposed by the President and Mrs. Clinton is the attorney-client privilege. In conjunction with that objection, the Clintons have also raised the so-called "common interest" or "joint defense" doctrine. The Committee is firmly of the view that the attorney-client privilege cannot shield Mr. Kennedy's notes from disclosure to the Committee.

It is within the sound discretion of Congress to decide whether to accept a claim of attorney-client privilege. See Morton Rosenberg, "Investigative Oversight: An Introduction to the Law, Practice, and Procedure of Congressional Inquiry." CRS Report No. 95-464A, at 43 (April 7, 1995). Unlike some other testimonial privileges, such as the privilege against compulsory self-incrimination, see U.S. Const. Amend. V, the attorney-client privilege itself is not rooted in the Constitution. See *Maness v. Meyers*, 419 U.S. 449, 466 n.15 (1975); *Cluchette v. Rushen*, 770 F.2d 1469, 1471 (9th Cir. 1985), cert. denied, 475 U.S. 1088 (1986). Rather, the attorney-client privilege is a product of the common law and is observed in federal courts by virtue of the Federal Rules of Evidence. See Fed. R. Evid. 501.

In deciding questions of privilege, committees of Congress have consistently recognized their plenary authority to rule on any claim of non-constitutional privilege. See Proceedings Against Ralph Bernstein and Joseph Bernstein, H. Rep. No. 99-462, 99th Cong., 2d Sess. 13, 14 (1986); Hearings, International Uranium Cartel, Before the Subcommittee on Oversight and Investigations, House Committee on Interstate and Foreign Commerce, 85th Cong., 1st Sess. 60, 123 (1977). The Constitution affirmatively grants each house of Congress the authority to establish its own rules of procedure. See U.S. Const., Art. I, §5, cl. 2. The conclusion that recognition of privileges is a matter of congressional discretion is consistent, moreover, with both traditional English parliamentary procedure, and the Congress' [sic] historical practice. See *Rosenberg, supra*, at 44–49.

Although this Committee has honored valid claims of attorney-client privilege in the course of its investigation, it need not recognize such claims of privilege in the same manner as would a court of law. A congressional committee must make its own determination regarding the propriety of recognizing the privilege in the course of a congressional investigation taking into account the Senate's constitutionally-based responsibility to oversee the activities of the Executive Branch.[17] In this instance, it is the Committee's considered judgment that the President and Mrs. Clinton's claim of privilege is not well taken.

* * *

There can be no privilege protecting Mr. Kennedy's notes from disclosure to this Committee unless the notes reflect the substance of a confidential communication of the President or Mrs. Clinton. Cf. *American Standard, Inc. v. Pfizer Inc.*, 828 F.2d 734, 745 (Fed. Cir. 1988) (attorney's written legal opinion held not privileged because "it did not reveal, directly or indirectly, the substance of any confidential communication"). Given that President Clinton did not attend the November 5 meeting and did not communicate with anyone during the course of the meeting, it is unlikely that the Kennedy notes reflect much, if anything, in the way of President Clinton's confidential communications. Moreover, to the extent that the notes reveal information about Whitewater obtained from persons other than the President and Mrs. Clinton, they cannot be privileged.

In sum, based upon the facts before the Committee about the November 5 meeting, the President and Mrs. Clinton have not satisfied the Committee that the Kennedy notes are protected from disclosure to the Committee by the attorney-client privilege.

> *b. The presence of government lawyers at the November 5 meeting bars any claim of attorney-client privilege for Mr. Kennedy's notes*

Because the November 5 meeting was attended by four government attorneys—Messrs. Nussbaum, Kennedy and Eggleston of the White House Counsel's office, and by Mr. Lindsey, then the White House Personnel Director—the attorney-client privilege does not protect communications with those attorneys.

* * *

> *ii. No "official" attorney-client privilege may be asserted against a congressional subpoena*

Even assuming there was an official interest of the presidency at stake in underlying Whitewater matters discussed at the November 5 meeting, no "official" attorney-client privilege can shield communications by government lawyers from disclosure to a congressional committee.

The acceptance of an absolute attorney-client privilege to shield all communications within the Executive Branch at which any one of its numerous attorneys is present

---

17. [3] Even in a judicial setting, "[t]he party asserting the attorney-client privilege has the burden of establishing the relationship and the privileged nature of the communication." *Ralls v. United States*, 52 F.3d 223, 225 (9th Cir. 1995). Moreover, "[b]ecause the attorney-client privilege obstructs the truth-finding process, it is construed narrowly." *Westinghouse Elec. Corp.*, 951 F.2d 1413, 1423 (3d. Cir. 1991).

would give the Executive Branch the power substantially to impair the Congress's ability to perform its constitutional responsibility to "probe[] into departments of the Federal Government to expose corruption, inefficiency or waste." *Watkins v. United States*, 354 U.S. 178, 184 (1957).

The submissions to the Committee by counsel for the White House and the President and Mrs. Clinton fail to provide any support for the existence of an official governmental attorney-client privilege against the Congress. In prior instances in which committees of the Senate or the House have chosen to respect properly supported claims of attorney-client privilege, as far as the Committee has been able to determine, the privilege was asserted in each case on behalf of a private individual or organization, not by another branch of the government.

* * *

iii. No "common interest" exists between the President and Mrs. Clinton's private interests and the interests of the United States

The Committee rejects the argument of counsel for the President and Mrs. Clinton and the White House that the communications made during the November 5 meeting are privileged, notwithstanding the presence of two sets of lawyers representing different clients, on grounds that the lawyers representing the President's official interests, and those representing his private interests, shared a common interest. (Williams & Connolly, 12/12/95 Memo. pp. 26–31; White House, 12/12/95 Mem. pp. 15–17). Although the Committee does not rule out the possibility that the common interest or joint defense theory might apply to government attorneys, cf. *United States v. AT&T*, 642 F.2d 1285 (D.C. Cir. 1980) (recognizing that government lawyers and private lawyers may share a common interest with respect to work product), the Clintons' private interests were simply not in common with the government's official interests in these matters.

The Clintons' private interest was to avoid any liability to the public arising out of the failure of Madison Guaranty, the Rose Law Firm's representation of Madison in certain questionable transactions, the Clintons' investment in Whitewater, or any tax deficiency. The Clintons' interest was thus directly antagonistic to the government's interest in attempting to determine whether such liability exists and if so to pursue appropriate remedies for that liability.

In sum, the presence of four government lawyers at the November 5 meeting, whose allegiance and duty runs to the United States and not to the personal legal interests of the President and Mrs. Clinton, bars application of the attorney-client privilege.

* * *

3. The work product doctrine does not shield the Kennedy notes from disclosure to the committee

In addition to asserting the attorney-client privilege, the President and Mrs. Clinton contend that the so-called "work product" doctrine protects the Kennedy notes from disclosure to the Committee. The work product doctrine shields from disclosure in some instances work prepared by an attorney in anticipation of litigation. See *Hickman v. Taylor, supra.* "The party seeking to assert the attorney-client privilege or the work product doctrine as a bar to discovery has the burden of establishing that either or both is applicable." *Barclays American Corp. v. Kane*, 746 F.2d 653, 656 (10th Cir. 1984).

The notes in question are the work product of Mr. Kennedy. There is no evidence, however, that Mr. Kennedy was acting in anticipation of litigation during the November 5 meeting. Quite to the contrary, Mr. Kennedy has testified that he was not representing anyone at the meeting. (Kennedy, 11/28/95 Hrg. pp. 44, 46).

Moreover, "the work product doctrine is clearly a qualified privilege which may be defeated by a showing of good cause." *Central Nat'l Ins. Co. v. Medical Protection Co.*, 107 F.R.D. 393, 395 (E.D. Mo. 1985) (citing *Hickman*); accord *Armstrong v. Trico Marine, Inc.*, No. 89-4309, U.S. Dist. Lexis 2434, *3 (E.D. La. Feb. 26, 1992). Indeed, when first recognizing the work product doctrine, the Supreme Court specifically stated that "we do not mean to say that all materials obtained or prepared ... with an eye toward litigation are necessarily free from discovery in all cases." *Hickman*, 329 U.S. at 511.

The Committee has determined that it must have access to Mr. Kennedy's notes of the November 5 meeting if it is to discharge responsibly its constitutional oversight function. In the Committee's view, this constitutes sufficient cause to override any claim based upon the work product doctrine.

D. Comparative Effectiveness of a Civil Action or a Certification to the United States Attorney for Criminal Prosecution

The Committee has considered the comparative effectiveness of a civil action to enforce the Committee's subpoena compared to an immediate referral to the United States Attorney for a criminal prosecution.[18]

In a civil action under 28 U.S.C. §1365 (1994), the Committee would apply, upon authorization of the Senate, to the United States District Court for the District of Columbia for an order requiring the witness to produce the subpoenaed documents. If the district court determines that the witness has no valid reason to refuse to produce the subpoenaed documents, the court would direct the witness to produce them. Disobedience of that order would subject the witness to sanctions to induce compliance. The witness could free himself of the sanctions by producing the subpoenaed documents. Sanctions could not continue beyond the Senate's need for the subpoenaed documents.

The civil enforcement statute excludes from its coverage actions against "an officer or employee of the Federal Government acting within his official capacity." 28 U.S.C. §1365(a) (1994). The legislative history of this provision explains that this limitation "should be construed narrowly. Therefore, a subpoena against Federal government officers or employees *not acting within the scope of their official duties* is not excluded

---

18. [4] The Senate has not used in decades its power to try a recalcitrant witness before the bar of the Senate, as the available judicial remedies have proven adequate.

from the coverage of this jurisdictional statute." Public Officials Integrity Act of 1977, S. Rep. No. 170, 95th Cong., 1st Sess. 92 (1977) (emphasis added).

The Committee has concluded that section 1365(a) does not bar an action against Mr. Kennedy, who is now a private citizen. Section 1365(a) was enacted so that disputes between the Legislative and Executive Branches implicating separation of powers concerns would be resolved extra-judicially. President Clinton, however, has not invoked executive privilege with respect to the Kennedy notes but only the attorney-client privilege. In any event, Mr. Kennedy was not acting within his official capacity during the November 5 meeting. Mr. Kennedy testified that "I was not at that meeting representing anyone." (Kennedy, 12/5/95 Hrg. p. 44; see also *id.* at 46).

The fact that Mr. Kennedy kept his notes of the November 5 meeting after he left government service further supports the Committee's view that he was not acting within the scope of his official activities.

In a criminal referral under 2 U.S.C. §§192, 194 (1994), the Senate would direct the President pro tempore to certify to the United States Attorney for the District of Columbia the facts concerning the witness' refusal to produce the subpoenaed documents. The United States Attorney would then present the matter to a grand jury, which could indict the witness for contempt of Congress. If convicted, the witness could receive a sentence of up to a year in prison and a $100,000 fine.

The Committee recommends that the Senate bring a civil action to compel Mr. Kennedy to comply with the Committee's subpoena. The Committee's objective is to obtain Mr. Kennedy's notes of the November 5 meeting and any other documents he may possess responsive to the Committee's subpoena. Civil enforcement will likely satisfy that objective since failure to comply with the subpoena would result in the imposition of a coercive sanction. At the same time, the Committee understands that, in refusing to comply with the Committee's subpoena, Mr. Kennedy has been acting upon the instruction of counsel for the President and Mrs. Clinton and the White House. The Committee is not inclined at this time to seek criminal punishment of Mr. Kennedy for the decisions of others.

Accordingly, the Committee recommends that the Senate authorize a civil enforcement proceeding to compel Mr. Kennedy to comply with the Committee's subpoena.

Committee's Rollcall Vote

In compliance with paragraph 7 (b) and (c) of Rule XXVI of the Standing Rules of the Senate, the record of the rollcall vote of the Special Committee to Investigate Whitewater Development Corporation and Related Matters to report the original resolution favorably was as follows:

YEAS	NAYS
Mr. D'Amato	Mr. Sarbanes
Mr. Shelby	Mr. Dodd
Mr. Bond	Mr. Kerry
Mr. Mack	Mr. Bryan

Mr. Faircloth	Mrs. Boxer
Mr. Bennett	Mrs. Mosely-Braun
Mr. Grams	Mrs. Murray
Mr. Domenici	Mr. Simon
Mr. Hatch	
Mr. Murkowski	

MINORITY VIEWS

Special Committee to Investigate Whitewater Development Corporation and Related Matters

I. INTRODUCTION

The President's lawyers have made a well-founded assertion, supported by respected legal authorities, that the November 5, 1993 meeting at Williams & Connolly was protected by the attorney-client privilege. If the President's lawyers are correct in their assertion, then the production of William Kennedy's notes of the meeting to the Special Committee would result in a general waiver of the Clintons' attorney-client privilege that might go far beyond the discussions at the November 5, 1993 meeting.

* * *

Several legal scholars who have examined the November 5, 1993 meeting have concluded that a valid claim of privilege has been asserted. For example, University of Pennsylvania law professor Geoffrey C. Hazard, Jr., a specialist in legal ethics and the attorney-client privilege, provided a legal opinion that communications between White House lawyers and the President's private lawyers are protected by the attorney-client privilege.[19] Professor Hazard reasoned that the President "has two sets of lawyers, engaged in conferring with each other. On that basis there is no question that the privilege is effective. Many legal consultations for a client involve the presence of more than one lawyer." Professor Hazard added that the President has "two legal capacities, that is, the capacity ex officio—in his office as President—and the capacity as an individual." Thus, there are "two clients," and the matters discussed at the meeting "were of concern to the President in each capacity as client." Since the lawyers for the two different clients conferred about matters of mutual concern to each client, "the attorney-client privilege is not lost by either client."

Other legal experts agree with Professor Hazard's analysis. New York University law school professor Stephen Gillers stated the following:

> The oddity here is that Clinton is in both sets of clients, in one way with his presidential hat on and in one way as a private individual. The lawyers who represent the President have information that the lawyer who represents the Clintons legitimately needs, and that's the common interest. It's true that government lawyers cannot handle the private matters of government officials.

---

19. [5] December 14, 1995 letter from Geoffrey C. Hazard, Jr. to John M. Quinn. A copy of this letter is attached as Exhibit A to this report.

However, perhaps uniquely for the President, private and public are not distinct categories so while the principle is clear the application is going to be nearly impossible.[20]

University of Colorado law professor Christopher Mueller stated that "[b]oth as chief executive and as a citizen the President has a right to counsel" and "the fact that he's the President of the United States doesn't mean that he lacks the privilege."[21]

* * *

2. THE COMMON INTEREST DOCTRINE

The common interest doctrine enables counsel for clients with common interests "to exchange privileged communications and attorney work product in order to adequately prepare a defense without waiving either privilege."[22] The November 5, 1993 meeting entailed all of the elements necessary for a valid assertion of the common interest privilege. All of the attorneys represented the Clintons in either their private or their official capacities. All shared the common interest of representing the Clintons—both personally and officially—with respect to Whitewater-related matters. Finally, the attorneys met in private at the law offices of the Clintons' personal counsel and considered their conversation to be confidential.[23] The presence of White House attorneys at the meeting does not vitiate the privilege since private and government attorneys may share a common interest.[24]

Leading legal experts in the field have supported the assertion of privilege here. Professor Hazard has reviewed the events of November 5, 1993 and concluded that: "Inasmuch as the White House lawyers and the privately engaged lawyers were addressing a matter of common interest to the President in both legal capacities, the attorney-client privilege is not waived or lost as against third parties."[25] Professor Gillers, in concluding that the meeting was privileged, noted that "[t]he lawyers who represent the President have information that the lawyer who represents the Clintons needs, and that's the common interest."[26]

---

20. [6] *Id.*

21. [7] R. Marcus & S. Schmidt, "Legal Experts Uncertain on Prospects of Clinton Privilege Claim," Washington Post, Dec. 14, 1995 at A13.

22. [8] *Haines v. Liggett Group, Inc.*, 975 F.2d 81, 94 (3d Cir. 1992); *see also Waller v. Financial Corp. of America*, 828 F.2d 579, 583 n.7 (9th Cir. 1987) ("communications by a client to his own lawyer remain privileged when the lawyer subsequently shares them with co-defendants for purposes of a common defense").

23. [10] The privilege encompasses notes and memoranda of statements made at meetings among counsel and their clients with a common interest, as well as the statements themselves. *In re Grand Jury Subpoena Dated Nov. 16, 1974*, 406 F. Supp. 381, 384–94 (S.D.N.Y. 1975).

24. [11] *United States v. American Telephone and Telegraph, Co.*, 642 F.2d 1285, 1300–01 (D.C. Cir. 1980) (applying the common interest privilege to materials shared between MCI and the government).

25. [12] December 14, 1995 Hazard letter (Exhibit A) at p. 2.

26. [13] R. Marcus & S. Schmidt, "Legal Experts Uncertain on Prospects of Clinton Privilege Claim," Washington Post, Dec. 14, 1995 at A13.

3. THE WORK PRODUCT DOCTRINE

The work product doctrine is "broader than the attorney-client privilege; it protects materials prepared by the attorney, whether or not disclosed to the client, and it protects material prepared by agents for the attorney."[27] The work product doctrine protects "the work of the attorney done in preparation for litigation."[28] Litigation need only be contemplated at the time the work is performed,[29] and the term litigation is defined broadly to encompass administrative and federal investigations.[30] Furthermore, work product which reveals counsel's "opinions, judgments, and thought processes" receives a "higher level of protection, and a party seeking discovery must show extraordinary justification" to obtain such materials.[31]

Under these standards, the President's lawyers appear to have made a legitimate assertion of the attorney work product privilege. Kennedy's notes presumably contain the mental impressions and opinions of the seven lawyers who met in confidence to discuss the legal aspects of Whitewater-related maters that had been raised in news articles published in late October and early November 1993. Equally important, the Committee has not demonstrated the requisite extraordinary need for the notes, particularly in view of the fact that Kendall and the White House have offered the Committee the opportunity to discover why the meeting was called, what was known prior to the meeting, who was present at the meeting, and what was done after the meeting was held.

* * *

1. CONGRESS HISTORICALLY HAS RESPECTED THE ATTORNEY-CLIENT PRIVILEGE

Congress has long respected the attorney-client privilege. Indeed, the Congress first acknowledged the confidentiality of attorney-client discussions in 1857.[32] A century later, in the aftermath of the McCarthy hearings, the Senate considered a rule that would have expressly recognized the testimonial privileges that traditionally are protected in litigation. The Senate ultimately decided that the rule was unnecessary:

> With few exceptions, it has been committee practice to observe the testimonial privileges of witnesses with respect to communications between clergyman

---

27. [14] *In re Grand Jury Proceedings*, 601 F.2d 162, 171 (5th Cir. 1979) (citations omitted).

28. [15] *In re Grand Jury Proceedings*, 33 F.3d 342, 348 (4th Cir. 1994).

29. [16] *See Holland v. Island Creek Corp.*, 885 F. Supp. 4, 7 (D.D.C. 1995).

30. [17] *In re Sealed Case*, 676 F.2d 793 (D.C. Cir. 1982) (applying work-product doctrine to documents created by counsel rendering legal advice in connection with SEC and IRS investigations).

31. [18] *In re Sealed Case*, 676 F.2d 793, 809–10 (D.C. Cir. 1982); *accord Upjohn Co. v. United States*, 440 U.S. at 401 (opinion work product "cannot be disclosed simply on a showing of substantial need and inability to obtain the equivalent without undue hardship").

32. [19] Jonathan P. Rich, Note, *The Attorney-Client Privilege in Congressional Investigations*, 88 COLUM. L. REV. 145, 152–55 (1988) ("Attorney-Client Privilege in Congressional Investigations").

and parishioner, doctor and patient, *lawyer and client*, and husband and wife. Controversy does not appear to have arisen in this connection.[33]

As recently as 1990, Senate Majority Leader George Mitchell stated that: "[a]s a matter of actual experience ... Senate committees have customarily honored the [attorney-client] privilege where it has been validly asserted."[34]

Even in politically charged investigations, the Senate has respected the attorney-client privilege. During the Iran-Contra investigation, for example, Gen. Richard Secord and Lt. Col. Oliver North successfully asserted the attorney-client privilege in refusing to answer questions posed to them by the Senate Counsel.[35] Similarly, during proceedings against Judge Alcee Hastings, the impeachment trial committee considered Judge Hastings' claim of attorney-client privilege in ruling that testimony would not be received into evidence.[36]

The Senate's most recent experience with the attorney-client privilege arose during its disciplinary proceedings against Senator Bob Packwood. Prior to the controversy over Senator Packwood's diaries, the Select Committee on Ethics considered Senator Packwood's assertion that certain documents (other than the diaries) were covered by the attorney-client or work-product privileges. To resolve that claim, the Ethics Committee appointed a former jurist (Kenneth W. Starr) as a hearing examiner to make recommendations to the Committee and accepted his recommendation that the privilege be sustained.[37]

With respect to the diaries, the Committee agreed "to protect Senator Packwood's privacy concerns by allowing him to mask information dealing with attorney-client and physician-patient privileged matters, and information dealing with personal, private family matters."[38] The Committee's hearing examiner (Judge Starr) reviewed Senator Packwood's assertions of attorney-client privilege. The Committee abided by all of the examiner's determinations and did not call upon the court to adjudicate any of the attorney-client privilege claims.

---

33. [20] Rules of Procedure for Senate Investigating Committees, 83d Cong., 2d Sess. 27 (Comm. Print 1955), *quoted in* T. Millet, *The Applicability of Evidentiary Privileges for Confidential Communications Before Congress*, JOHN MARSHALL L. REV. 309, 316 (1988) (emphasis added).

34. [21] 136 Cong. Rec. S7613 (daily ed. June 7, 1990) (Sen. Mitchell).

35. [22] Iran-Contra Investigation: Joint Hearings Before the House Select Committee to Investigate Covert Arms Transactions with Iran and the Senate Select Committee on Secret Military Assistance to Iran and the Nicaraguan Opposition, 100th Cong., 1st Sess. 199 (1987) (Secord); N.Y. Times, July 10, 1987, at A8, col. 4 (North).

36. [23] Report of the Senate Impeachment Trial Committee on the Articles Against Judge Alcee L. Hastings: Hearings Before the Senate Impeachment Trial Comm., pt. 2A, 101st Cong., 1st Sess. 64 (1989).

37. [24] Select Committee on Ethics: Documents Related to the Investigation of Senator Robert Packwood, S. Rpt. No. 30, vol. 9, 104th Cong., 1st Sess. 37 (1995).

38. [25] S. Rep. No. 164, 103d Cong., 1st Sess. 2 (1993). *See also Senate Select Committee on Ethics v. Packwood*, 845 F. Supp. 17, 19 (D.D.C. 1994).

2. The Clintons' Assertion of the Attorney-Client Privilege Deserves the Same Respect that the Committee Has Afforded to Witnesses in this Investigation

As noted above, the Special Committee has honored the attorney-client privilege on several occasions throughout its proceedings.

* * *

In determining whether to recognize attorney-client privilege claims, the Congress traditionally has weighed "the legislative need for disclosure against any possible resulting injury."[39] As discussed below, the balance in this instance favors respecting the attorney-client privilege and rejecting the Resolution put forth by the Special Committee.

3. The Senate Should Avoid a Needless Constitutional Confrontation by Pursuing a Negotiated Resolution to This Dispute

Congressional attempts to inquire into privileged executive branch communications are rare, and with good reason. By definition, such efforts provoke constitutional confrontations.

Moreover, Congress' efforts to invade privileged executive branch communications have met with little success. The courts have resisted adjudicating congressional attempts to inquire into privileged communications. For example, the United States District Court for the District of Columbia (the same court that would hear the current dispute) refused to determine whether Reagan Administration E.P.A. Administrator Anne Gorsuch properly withheld documents subpoenaed by a committee of the House of Representatives. Instead, the court "encourage[d] the two branches to settle their differences without further judicial involvement."[40]

Only once in the history of the nation have the courts required the disclosure of confidential Presidential communications; and even then, the courts ordered disclosure to a grand jury while denying disclosure to the Congress.[41] In the words of then-Assistant Attorney General Antonin Scalia, it would be "erroneous" to interpret that singular event "as an indication that the Supreme Court is either willing or able to adjudicate the issue of privilege when it arises in the context of a Legislative-Executive dispute."[42]

The United States Court of Appeals for the District of Columbia Circuit has long held that presidential communications are "presumptively privileged."[43] Accordingly,

---

39. [26] Hearings, "International Uranium Cartel," Subcomm. on Oversight and Investigations, House Comm. on Interstate and Foreign Commerce, 95th Cong., 1st Sess., Vol. 1, 123 (1977).

40. [27] *United States v. House of Representatives*, 556 F. Supp. 150, 152 (D.D.C. 1983).

41. [28] *United States v. Nixon*, 418 U.S. 683, 712, n. 19 (1974) (noting that the compelling need arising out of the criminal process merited a breach of executive privilege and observing that the same need was not present in a congressional inquiry).

42. [29] Statement of Antonin Scalia, Hearings on S. 2170 before the Subcomm. on Intergovernmental Relations, Senate Comm. on Govt. Operations, 94th Cong., 1st Sess. 116 (Oct. 23, 1975).

43. [30] *Nixon v. Sirica*, 487 F.2d 700, 705 (D.C. Cir. 1973).

a congressional committee seeking to inquire into presidential communications bears a heavy burden to demonstrate that it has a proper basis to do so. That burden can be met "only by a strong showing of need by another institution of government—a showing that the responsibilities of that institution cannot responsibly be fulfilled without access to records of the President's deliberations...."[44] Moreover, the Committee must prove that "the subpoenaed evidence is demonstrably critical to the responsible fulfillment of the Committee's functions."[45]

Where, as here, the competing constitutional interests of the legislative and executive branches are implicated, the courts have balanced alternative interests and proposals to determine "which would better reconcile the competing constitutional interests."[46] In this regard, the United States Court of Appeals for the District of Columbia Circuit has stated that "each branch should take cognizance of an implicit constitutional mandate to seek optimal accommodation through a realistic evaluation of the needs of the conflicting branches in the particular fact situation.[47] As former Attorney General William French Smith noted:

> The accommodation required is not simply an exchange of concessions or a test of political strength. It is an obligation of each branch to make a principled effort to acknowledge, and if possible to meet, the legitimate needs of the other branch.[48]

Thus, even if the Special Committee had demonstrated a compelling need for the privileged information, the Senate still should balance that need for the information against the competing interests identified by Williams & Connolly and the White House. Such a balance weighs heavily against the course pursued by the Special Committee.

Although the Kennedy notes may be relevant to the Committee's inquiry, the Committee's need for the notes is not sufficiently compelling to justify a federal court action to enforce the subpoena. As noted previously, the White House has offered to make Kennedy's notes available to the Committee if certain conditions are met. The Committee has not explained why accommodating those conditions would interfere with the Committee's investigation. Therefore, the Committee has not demonstrated the requisite compelling need to invade privileged presidential communications.

VII. CONCLUSION

For more than a century, the Senate has recognized and respected the attorney-client relationship. Senate action that needlessly forces a waiver of the privilege would deprive

---

44. [31] *Senate Select Comm. on Pres. Campaign Activities v. Nixon*, 498 F.2d 725 (D.C. Cir. 1974).
45. [32] *Id.* at 731.
46. [33] *United States v. American Telephone and Telegraph Co. (ATT I)*, 551 F.2d 384, 394 (D.C. Cir. 1976).
47. [34] *United States v. American Telephone and Telegraph Co. (ATT II)*, 567 F.2d 121, 127 (D.C. Cir. 1977).
48. [35] Opinion of the Attorney General for the President, "Assertion of Executive Privilege in Response to a Congressional Subpoena," 5 Op. O.L.C. 27, 31 (1981) (Smith Opinion).

the President and Mrs. Clinton of the right to communicate in confidence with their counsel—a basic right afforded to all Americans. Because the information the Committee seeks is available to it without forcing a constitutional conflict, the Senate should not move forward to seek enforcement of the Committee's subpoena to William Kennedy.

PAUL S. SARBANES
CHRISTOPHER J. DODD
JOHN F. KERRY
RICHARD H. BRYAN
BARBARA BOXER
CAROL MOSELEY-BRAUN
PATTY MURRAY
PAUL SIMON

Notes and Questions

1. **The Procedural Context of the Kennedy Notes Report.** The report above was prepared by the Senate Whitewater Committee to accompany a proposed Senate resolution that would direct the Senate Legal Counsel to initiate a civil lawsuit requesting a federal court to order Mr. Kennedy to produce his notes of the November 5 meeting to the Committee. As discussed in Chapters 3 and 4 above, a law passed by Congress in 1978 as part of the Ethics in Government Act gives the Senate Legal Counsel authority to bring a lawsuit in federal court to enforce a Senate subpoena "when directed to do so by the adoption of a resolution by the Senate." *See* 2 U.S.C. §288b. Another statutory provision requires a majority vote of the committee issuing the subpoena and an accompanying report supporting the resolution that "contains a statement of—

(A) the procedure followed in issuing such subpena;

(B) the extent to which the party subpenaed has complied with such subpena;

(C) any objections or privileges raised by the subpenaed party; and

(D) the comparative effectiveness of bringing a civil action under this section, certification of a criminal action for contempt of Congress, and initiating a contempt proceeding before the Senate."

See 2 U.S.C. §288d. The Whitewater Committee report is drafted to satisfy these statutory requirements.

Another statute, enacted at the same time, explicitly gives the federal court in Washington, D.C. "original jurisdiction, without regard to the amount in controversy," to hear civil suits brought by the Senate to enforce Senate subpoenas, to issue orders to parties who have refused to comply with Senate subpoenas, and to impose contempt sanctions upon any parties who fail to comply with the court's order to enforce a Senate subpoena. *See* 28 U.S.C. §1365.

These statutes apply only to efforts to enforce Senate subpoenas. Congress did not enact a civil enforcement mechanism for House of Representatives subpoenas, and as of the time of this writing, it has not done so. The reasons that a House of Representatives civil enforcement mechanism was not included in the 1978 legislation are set out in the House report on the legislation:

> The Senate bill establishes an office of congressional legal counsel to defend the constitutional powers of Congress in proceedings before the courts and confers jurisdiction on the courts to enforce congressional subpenas. The managers on the part of the House recede and concur in an amendment of the Senate bill which establishes an office of Senate Legal Counsel and confers jurisdiction on the courts to enforce Senate subpenas.

> The appropriate committees in the House have not considered the Senate's proposal to establish a joint, House-Senate Office of Congressional Legal Counsel. The Senate has twice voted to establish a joint office. Because the House is not prepared to agree to a joint office at this time, the Senate desires to establish its own Office of Senate Legal Counsel to defend its interests in court. The managers agree that the Senate Legal Counsel should, whenever, appropriate, cooperate and consult with the House in litigation matters of interest to both Houses.

> The appropriate committees in the House also have not considered the Senate's proposal to confer jurisdiction on the courts to enforce subpenas of House and Senate Committees. The Senate has twice voted to confer such jurisdiction on the courts and desires at this time to confer jurisdiction on the courts to enforce Senate subpoenas.

P.L. 95-521, Ethics In Government Act of 1978, House Conference Report No. 95-1756, Oct. 11, 1978.

Commentators have puzzled over this imbalance of subpoena enforcement powers between the House and Senate. "The Senate provision provides advantages in resolving disputes and avoiding drawn out contempt proceedings. It is surprising that the House has not yet enacted a similar enforcement proceeding." James Hamilton, Robert F. Muse, & Kevin Amer, *Congressional Investigations: Politics and Process*, 44 AM. CRIM. L. REV. 1115, 1136 n.112 (2007). Notwithstanding the advantages of the Senate's civil enforcement mechanism, it has not been frequently used in the years since its enactment. A 2007 report for Congress prepared by the Congressional Research Service noted that "[s]ince the statute's enactment in 1979, the Senate has authorized the Office of Senate Legal Counsel to seek civil enforcement of a document subpoena at least 6 times, the last in 1995." Morton Rosenberg & Todd B. Tatelman, *Congress's Contempt Power: A Sketch (CRS Report for Congress)*, Aug. 1, 2007, at CRS-14. In addition to the Kennedy Whitewater notes dispute that is the focus of this Chapter, a noteworthy use of the Senate civil enforcement mechanism was the successful civil suit to enforce a 1993 subpoena for the personal diaries of Senator Bob Packwood. *See Senate Select Comm. on Ethics v. Packwood*, 845 F. Supp. 17 (D.D.C. 1994). The Packwood matter and the approach of the Senate Ethics Committee to attorney-client privilege matters are discussed in the Minority Views portion of the Whitewater Committee report that is excerpted above.

2. Differing Approaches of the Republican Majority and the Democratic Minority. As the Majority Report and Minority Views excerpts above demonstrate, the Republican majority and the Democratic minority members of the Senate Whitewater Committee took notably different approaches in their responses to the Kennedy notes attorney-client privilege issue. The Majority Report took a categorical position that a congressional committee need not accept an assertion of attorney-client privilege, if it chooses not to do so, and that in any event the Kennedy notes were not covered by the attorney-client privilege, the joint defense/common interest privilege, or the attorney work product doctrine. The Minority Views portion of the report took a less resolute position, arguing that the President's lawyers had "made a well-founded assertion" that the notes were privileged and that the better approach would be to seek a negotiated resolution rather than risk a court confrontation that could create a precedent that might be unfavorable to the Senate. Are these differing approaches to the legal issue unavoidable results of the procedural stage of the dispute—presenting arguments to the full Senate on whether or not to enforce the subpoena—or are they the product of larger political forces? In particular, does it appear that the majority was prepared to challenge the Clintons on every legal and policy front, while the minority was hesitant to provide unqualified support to the Clintons? Is the minority's failure to declare unequivocally that the notes are privileged and that Congress should recognize the privilege an indication of some reservations about whether the privilege should be available in the particular circumstances before the committee?

3. The Governmental Attorney-Client Privilege. In some instances the Majority Report seems to stretch to dismiss the application of the privilege to the Kennedy notes, such as the argument that because "President Clinton did not attend the November 5 meeting and did not communicate with anyone during the course of the meeting, it is unlikely that the Kennedy notes reflect much, if anything, in the way of President Clinton's confidential communications." Majority Report at p. 12. On another point, however, subsequent judicial decisions have adopted the position taken by the Majority Report. The Majority Report argued that "[t]he presence of government lawyers at the November 5 meeting bars any claim of attorney client privilege for Mr. Kennedy's notes" because "Government attorneys may not represent the President on private legal matters." Report of the Special Committee to Investigate Whitewater Development Corporation and Related Matters to Accompany S. Res. 199, Refusal of William H. Kennedy, III, to Produce Notes Subpoenaed by the Special Committee to Investigate Whitewater Development Corporation and Related Matters, Dec. 19, 1995, 13–14. Two federal appeals courts subsequently reached a similar conclusion in their review of efforts by Independent Counsel Kenneth Starr to obtain attorney notes in Starr's Whitewater investigation:

> In two cases Starr's office convinced federal appeals courts to reject assertions of attorney-client privilege by government attorneys.[49] These cases involved

---

49. [212] *See In re Grand Jury Subpoena Duces Tecum*, 112 F.3d 910, 921 (8th Cir. 1997); *In re Lindsey*, 158 F.3d 1263, 1276 (D.C. Cir. 1998) (per curiam).

assertions of privilege by White House attorneys for communications with President Clinton and First Lady Hillary Rodham Clinton. In simplest terms, Starr's office convinced the courts in both cases that federal government attorneys should not be permitted to assert a governmental attorney-client privilege as a basis for withholding information from a federal grand jury conducting a criminal investigation.[50] The legal issues involved in the cases are complex, however, and the reviewing courts were deeply divided as to the appropriate resolution of those issues.[51]...

Starr's office's first attack on the governmental attorney-client privilege arose out of a Whitewater investigation grand jury subpoena for handwritten notes taken by attorneys in the White House Counsel's office at two meetings with Hillary Clinton.[52] Starr's office took the position that applying the attorney-client privilege to those meetings "would be tantamount to establishing a

---

50. [213] *See Subpoena Duces Tecum*, 112 F.3d at 925–26 ("To sum up, we hold that neither the attorney-client privilege nor the attorney work product doctrine is available to the White House in the circumstances of this case."); 158 F.3d at 1278 ("In sum, it would be contrary to tradition, common understanding, and our governmental system for the attorney-client privilege to attach to White House Counsel in the same manner as private counsel.").

51. [214] Although Starr's office prevailed in both cases at the court of appeals level and the Supreme Court denied certiorari in both cases, leaving the court of appeals opinions as the final authorities, the reviewing courts were more deeply divided than this outcome might suggest at first glance. In both cases the federal district judge that initially heard the case concluded that a governmental attorney-client privilege could be asserted by the White House (although the lower court in the *Lindsey* case ruled that Starr's office had made a sufficient showing of need and unavailability to overcome the privilege, *see* 158 F.3d at 1267), and in both cases the appellate panels that ruled in favor of Starr's office did so by 2–1 votes over vigorous dissents. By simply doing the math, one is left with the result that the eight federal judges at the district court and appeals court levels who reviewed the cases were evenly divided, four to four, on the key question of whether White House attorneys could assert a governmental attorney-client privilege in response to a grand jury subpoena. That fact alone demonstrates that the cases involved an extremely difficult legal judgment on the core privilege issue. The Supreme Court's denial of certiorari is not inconsistent with this conclusion, as two Justices objected strongly to the denial of certiorari in the *Lindsey* case. *See Office of President v. Office of Indep. Counsel*, 525 U.S. 996 (1998). As Justice Breyer aptly observed: "The divided decision of the Court of Appeals makes clear that the legal question presented by this petition has no clear legal answer and is open to serious legal debate." *Id.* at 996....

52. [217] *See Subpoena Duces Tecum*, 112 F.3d at 913–14. The court described the attorney notes at issue as follows:

The first set of documents comprises notes taken by Associate Counsel to the President Miriam Nemetz on July 11, 1995, at a meeting attended by Mrs. Clinton, Special Counsel to the President Jane Sherburne, and Mrs. Clinton's personal attorney, David Kendall. The subject of this meeting was Mrs. Clinton's activities following the death of Deputy Counsel to the President Vincent W. Foster, Jr. The documents in the second collection are notes taken by Mrs. Sherburne on January 26, 1996, during meetings attended by Mrs. Clinton, Mr. Kendall, Nicole Seligman (a partner of Mr. Kendall's), and, at times, John Quinn, Counsel to the President. These meetings, which took place during breaks in and immediately after Mrs. Clinton's testimony before a federal grand jury in Washington, D.C., concerned primarily the discovery of certain billing records from the Rose Law Firm in the residence area of the White House.

Id. at 914.

new privilege," while the White House took the position that under established privilege law the communications that took place at the meetings should be protected. The federal district court concluded that both the attorney-client privilege and the work-product doctrine applied to the notes, and Starr's office appealed to the Eighth Circuit Court of Appeals.

Finding little case law on point, the appeals court relied on "general principles," to analyze the privilege issue, and concluded that the governmental attorney-client privilege should not be available to thwart a federal grand jury subpoena because of the "important differences between the government and non-governmental organizations such as business corporations." The key differences identified by the court were that a business corporation can be subjected to criminal liability based upon the actions of its agents, while a governmental agency like the Office of the President cannot, and that "a general duty of public service" requires government employees, including White House attorneys, to favor disclosure over concealment. These considerations were sufficient to cause the court to agree with Starr's office that the White House should not be able to rely upon the attorney-client privilege to withhold the notes from a grand jury conducting a criminal investigation.[53]

Employing essentially the same reasoning, the court also concluded that the attorney work-product doctrine did not apply to the attorneys' notes. Because the White House attorneys were not working in anticipation of litigation involving the White House, and because the White House as a governmental entity was not the subject or target of the grand jury investigation, the court concluded that the work-product doctrine was not applicable. In the court's view, the "essential element" necessary for attorney work-product protection, preparation for an adversarial proceeding involving one's client, was not present because the White House lawyers did not represent Mrs. Clinton in her personal capacity, and it was in that capacity that she was being investigated by Starr's office.

Finally, the court rejected the application of the common interest doctrine based upon the presence of Mrs. Clinton's private counsel at the meetings at which the notes were taken. In what is perhaps the most remarkable assertion in the entire opinion, the court categorically declared: "The OIC's investigation can have no legal, factual, or even strategic effect on the White House as an institution."[54] The court went on to reject demands upon the time of White

---

53. [224] *See id.* at 921 ("An official who fears he or she may have violated the criminal law and wishes to speak with an attorney in confidence should speak with a private attorney, not a government attorney.").

54. [227] *Id.* at 923. The OIC's subsequent criminal referral to the House of Representatives in the Lewinsky matter, and the resulting impeachment trial of President Clinton by the Senate, certainly seems to call into question the validity of the court's categorical statement, but presumably the court's response would be that those events affected only President Clinton personally and not "the White House as an institution." That response seems dubious at best, however. *Cf. In re Lindsey*, 158 F.3d

House staff, vacancies in positions if staff members were indicted, and other "political concerns" as legitimate "common interests" between the White House and Mrs. Clinton in her personal capacity.[55] Accordingly, the court rejected the application of the common interest doctrine to the White House attorneys' notes.

The Eighth Circuit's rejection of any governmental attorney-client privilege, work-product doctrine, or common interest doctrine protection for the White House attorneys' notes has been widely criticized by commentators. It also was the subject of a strongly worded dissenting opinion by one of the three judges on the appellate panel that heard the case. Whether or not one agrees with the court's decision, however, it is indisputable that the case introduced new uncertainty into the application of the attorney-client privilege to a huge category of attorney-client communications—those that involve government lawyers. That uncertainty was compounded by a subsequent case in which Starr's office sought to overcome the assertions of a governmental attorney-client privilege.

Starr's office's second attempt to overcome assertions of governmental attorney-client privilege involved another White House attorney, Deputy White House Counsel Bruce Lindsey, and a different investigation, the Monica Lewinsky investigation.[56] In seeking to compel Lindsey's testimony about discussions with President Clinton concerning Lewinsky, Starr's office took the position that permitting Lindsey to assert a governmental attorney-client privilege before the grand jury would be inconsistent with the proper role of a government lawyer, and that President Clinton should be required to rely only upon his private attorneys for fully confidential counsel. The district court concluded that the President does possess a governmental attorney-client privilege for official consultations with White House attorneys, but ruled that the privilege was qualified in the grand jury subpoena context and could be overcome by a showing of sufficient need and unavailability of the subpoenaed information from other sources. The district court concluded that Starr's office had made a sufficient showing to overcome the qualified governmental

---

1263, 1282, n.16 (D.C. Cir. 1998) (per curiam) ("Impeachment may remove the person, but no one could reasonably controvert that it affects the Office of the President as well. Even if there will always be a President and an Office of the President, it is unrealistic to posit that the Presidency will not be diminished by an impeachment.... The possibility of impeachment implicates institutional concerns of the White House, and White House Counsel, representing the Office of the President, would presumably play an important role in defending the institution of the Presidency.") (citations omitted). As with so many other aspects of the Clinton presidency and the Starr investigation, history will be the final judge of whether the OIC's actions had any effect on the White House as an institution. *Cf.* BOB WOODWARD, SHADOW: FIVE PRESIDENTS AND THE LEGACY OF WATERGATE (Simon & Schuster 1999).

55. [228] *See id.* ("But even if we assume that it is proper for the White House to press political concerns upon us, we do not believe that any of these incidental effects on the White House are sufficient to place that governmental institution in the same canoe as Mrs. Clinton, whose personal liberty is potentially at stake.").

56. [232] *See Lindsey,* 158 F.3d at 1276.

attorney-client privilege, and the parties appealed to the D.C. Circuit Court of Appeals.

The D.C. Circuit undertook its own analysis of the governmental attorney-client privilege issue, and did not base its conclusions on the Eighth Circuit's prior opinion on that issue.[57] After a detailed review of authorities, the D.C. Circuit concluded that a federal government attorney should not be permitted to assert the governmental attorney-client privilege in response to a federal grand jury subpoena:

> In sum, it would be contrary to tradition, common understanding, and our governmental system for the attorney-client privilege to attach to White House Counsel in the same manner as private counsel. When government attorneys learn, through communications with their clients, of information related to criminal misconduct, they may not rely on the government attorney-client privilege to shield such information from disclosure to a grand jury.

President Clinton also argued that Lindsey's interactions with the President's private counsel should be protected by the common interest doctrine. In analyzing the common interest doctrine issue, the D.C. Circuit, unlike the Eighth Circuit in the case involving Mrs. Clinton, seemed to accept the proposition that "the President in his private persona" may some share common interests with the Office of the President as an institution, such as concerns relating to impeachment.[58] In the court's view, however, the "overarching duties of Lindsey in his role as a government attorney prevent him from withholding information about possible criminal misconduct from the grand jury."[59] As a result, the D.C. Circuit, like the Eighth Circuit, refused to permit use of the common interest doctrine by government attorneys to frustrate a grand jury subpoena in a criminal investigation.

Also like the Eighth Circuit's government attorney-client privilege decision, the D.C. Circuit opinion provoked a vigorous dissent and has been widely criticized by commentators....

Lance Cole, *Revoking Our Privileges: Federal Law Enforcement's Multi-Front Assault on the Attorney-Client Privilege (And Why It Is Misguided)*, 48 VILL. L. REV. 469 (2003) (footnotes omitted except as indicated). In the aftermath of the cases described above, the federal courts of appeals have divided on the issue of how the attorney-client privilege should apply to government attorneys. *See* Nancy Leong, Note, *Attorney-Client*

---

57. [235] *See id.* at 1267–78. The D.C. Circuit did cite the Eighth Circuit opinion on the governmental attorney-client privilege issue, albeit well into the D.C. Circuit's independent analysis of the issue. *See id.* at 1274 (citing the Eight Circuit opinion's conclusion that "to allow any part of the federal government to use its in-house attorneys as a shield against the production of information relevant to a criminal investigation would represent a gross misuse of public assets").

58. [239] *See Lindsey*, 158 F.3d at 1282 & n.16.

59. [240] *Id.* at 1283.

Privilege in the Public Sector: A Survey of Government Attorneys, 20 Geo. J. Legal Ethics 163 (2007) (collecting cases).

To what extent do the judicial decisions described above validate the legal positions taken by the Republican majority of the Senate Whitewater Committee in the Kennedy notes dispute? What are the larger implications of these holdings for government lawyers who find themselves advising public officials in matters where the officials' personal conduct is at issue? Is it realistic for the judiciary to require a "bright-line division" between government counsel and personal counsel in all cases where there are allegations of personal misconduct by governmental officials? For the views of one of the authors of this book on these issues, see Lance Cole, *The Government-Client Privilege after Office of the President v. Office of the Independent Counsel*, 22 J. Legal Prof. 15 (1997–98).

4. The Special Problem of Former Government Officials. The application of the attorney-client privilege to government officials in congressional investigations is a murky legal area, and uncertainty is compounded when the issue is the application of the privilege to former government officials whose testimony is sought on matters occurring while they were in government service. In the Senate the issue is even further complicated by the provision in the civil enforcement jurisdictional statute forbidding use of the civil enforcement procedure for a subpoena issued to "an officer or employee of the Federal Government acting within his official capacity." *See* 28 U.S.C. §1365(a). At the time that the Senate Whitewater Committee sought William Kennedy's notes, he was no longer in government service, so the committee's majority took the position that the civil enforcement statute could be used against him:

> The Committee has concluded that section 1365(a) does not bar an action against Mr. Kennedy, who is now a private citizen. Section 1365(a) was enacted so that disputes between the Legislative and Executive Branches implicating separation of powers concerns would be resolved extra-judicially. President Clinton, however, has not invoked executive privilege with respect to the Kennedy notes, but only the attorney-client privilege. In any event, Mr. Kennedy was not acting within his official capacity during the November 5 meeting. Mr. Kennedy testified that "I was not at that meeting representing anyone." (Kennedy, 12/5/95 Hrg. p. 44; see also *id.* at 46).

> The fact that Mr. Kennedy kept his notes of the November 5 meeting after he left government service further supports the Committee's view that he was not acting within the scope of his official activities.

Report of the Special Committee to Investigate Whitewater Development Corporation and Related Matters to Accompany S. Res. 199, Refusal of William H. Kennedy, III, to Produce Notes Subpoenaed by the Special Committee to Investigate Whitewater Development Corporation and Related Matters, Dec. 19, 1995, 19.

What is the significance of the fact that Mr. Kennedy was no longer in government service at the time of the dispute over his notes of the Whitewater defense meeting? Does the Whitewater Committee Majority Report that is excerpted above acknowledge, at least implicitly, that if it could be established conclusively that Mr. Kennedy was acting in his official capacity as a government attorney at the time he made his notes, then use of the Senate civil enforcement mechanism would be unlawful? Would the fact that he had subsequently left government service and was a private citizen at the time of the dispute affect the analysis of that issue? Does it seem contradictory that two federal appeals courts have held that government attorneys cannot assert an attorney-client privilege against an Executive Branch criminal proceeding (see Note 3 above), but the statute providing for civil enforcement of Senate subpoenas specifically exempts federal government employees who are acting within the scope of their official duties? What is the explanation for the different treatment of government officials in these two contexts?

A similar issue arose, in the context of a presidential claim of executive privilege, in 2008 when the House Judiciary Committee sought testimony from former White House Counsel Harriet Miers on the Bush administration's dismissals in 2006 of nine United States Attorneys. The Judiciary Committee was investigating whether the dismissals were prompted by improper political considerations. Miers was White House Counsel at the time of the dismissals, but she was no longer in government in June 2007 when she was subpoenaed by the Judiciary Committee. President Bush, through White House Counsel Fred F. Fielding, asserted executive privilege and directed Miers not to provide testimony in response to the subpoena, and she declined to appear before the committee in response to the subpoena. In March 2008 the House Judiciary Committee filed a civil complaint in federal court in Washington, D.C, seeking to compel Miers to comply with the subpoena. The committee also sued White House Chief of Staff Joshua Bolten to enforce a subpoena for White House documents relating to the dismissals of the U.S. Attorneys. The outcome of the Judiciary Committee's suit is discussed in Chapter 4.

Aftermath: Production of the Kennedy Notes to the Whitewater Committee

On December 20, 1995, the United States Senate debated the resolution to enforce the subpoena for the Kennedy notes and then voted on the resolution. The resolution passed by a 51–45 margin that was divided strictly by party affiliation, just as the earlier committee vote had been divided along party lines. The day after the Senate vote to enforce the subpoena, the White House agreed to make the notes available to the Whitewater Committee, so a civil enforcement proceeding was not initiated. The Clinton White House was able to change its position on withholding the notes after the Senate vote because Independent Counsel Kenneth Starr and the House of Representatives Banking and Financial Services Committee, both conducting Whitewater investigations at the time, agreed not to treat production of the notes to the Senate as a waiver of the attorney-client privilege.

Although the legal issues surrounding the Kennedy notes are of considerable interest, the content of the notes did not disappoint in terms of providing drama and igniting controversy. Perhaps the most controversial and closely scrutinized portion of Kennedy's notes was an entry with a line containing the word "Vacuum" followed by space and then the words "Rose Law files" followed by more space and the words "WWDC docs—subpoena" at the end of the line. Directly beneath that line was an entry that said "*Documents—never know go out" with "Quietly (?)" on the line directly below.

Not surprisingly, these cryptic entries generated considerable interest, particularly on the part of the majority members of the Senate Whitewater Committee and their chief counsel, Michael Chertoff, and required a great deal of skeptically received testimony by Mr. Kennedy in his efforts to explain the meaning of his notes. Drama surrounding the meaning of the entries was heightened by the fact that in January 1996, shortly after the controversy over the Kennedy notes had been resolved, previously missing Rose Law Firm billing records, relating to the law firm's representation of Madison Guaranty Savings and Loan Association, were found in the White House residence. The billing records had been under subpoena by several federal investigative authorities, including the Senate Whitewater Committee, which raised questions as to how the records came to be lost and then later found in the White House residence.

The discovery of the Rose Law Firm billing records was very much on the minds of the Senate Whitewater Committee members and their counsel in January 1996 when Mr. Kennedy and other participants in the November 1993 Whitewater defense meeting appeared before the committee. Portions of the Whitewater Committee testimony about the Kennedy notes are excerpted below. Read the testimony and the notes and then draw your own conclusions about the meaning and significance of the disputed entries in the notes.

Investigation of Whitewater Development Corporation and Related Matters

Tuesday, January 16, 1996

U.S. SENATE, COMMITTEE ON BANKING, HOUSING, AND URBAN AFFAIRS, SPECIAL COMMITTEE TO INVESTIGATE WHITEWATER DEVELOPMENT CORPORATION AND RELATED MATTERS, *Washington, D.C.*

The Committee met at 10:05 a.m., in room 216 of the Hart Senate Office Building, Senator Alfonse M. D'Amato (Chairman of the Committee) presiding.

* * *

I'm going to ask our witnesses to stand for the purpose of taking the oath.

[Whereupon, William H. Kennedy, Attorney, Rose Law Firm, Bruce R. Lindsey, Deputy Counsel to the President and Assistant to the President, and Neil Eggleston, Partner, Howrey & Simon, former Associate Counsel to the President were called as witnesses and, having first been duly sworn, were examined and testified as follows:]

The Chairman. I'm going to ask if any of the witnesses, Mr. Kennedy, Mr. Lindsey, or Mr. Eggleston, have any statements that they would like to make prior to our starting?

Mr. Kennedy.

SWORN TESTIMONY OF WILLIAM H. KENNEDY, III
ATTORNEY, ROSE LAW FIRM

Mr. Kennedy. I do not, Mr. Chairman.

The Chairman. Mr. Lindsey.

SWORN TESTIMONY OF BRUCE R. LINDSEY
DEPUTY COUNSEL TO THE PRESIDENT AND ASSISTANT TO THE PRESIDENT

Mr. Lindsey. Mr. Chairman, just for the record, I am Bruce Lindsey, Deputy Counsel to the President and Assistant to the President. I have no opening statement.

The Chairman. Mr. Eggleston.

SWORN TESTIMONY OF W. NEIL EGGLESTON
PARTNER, HOWREY & SIMON
FORMER ASSOCIATE COUNSEL TO THE PRESIDENT

Mr. Eggleston. Mr. Chairman, again, my name is Neil Eggleston. I was Associate Counsel to the President from about September 1993 to about September 1994. I am now no longer affiliated with the White House. I have no statement, sir.

The Chairman. Mr. Chertoff.

Mr. Chertoff. Thank you, Mr. Chairman.

Mr. Kennedy, on November 5, 1993, you met with Mr. Kendall and other individuals at his offices in Williams & Connolly; is that correct?

Mr. Kennedy. It is, Mr. Chertoff.

Mr. Chertoff. Mr. Lindsey, you were at that meeting?

Mr. Lindsey. Yes, sir.

Mr. Chertoff. Mr. Kennedy, you were at the meeting?

Mr. Kennedy. I was.

Mr. Chertoff. Mr. Kennedy, you prepared notes of the meeting in your own handwriting?

Mr. Kennedy. That is correct, Mr. Chertoff.

Mr. Chertoff. You later typed up those notes yourself, right?

Mr. Kennedy. That's correct.

Mr. Chertoff. And you furnished the handwritten and the typed notes to the Committee, right?

Mr. Kennedy. That is correct.

Mr. Chertoff. You also furnished them to the White House; right?

Mr. Kennedy. That is correct also.

Mr. Chertoff. Mr. Eggleston, have you had an opportunity to look at the notes?

Mr. Eggleston. I have.

Mr. Chertoff. Have you looked at the package of material the White House prepared to go out in connection with the notes?

Mr. Eggleston. I have.

Mr. Chertoff. Mr. Lindsey, same true for you?

Mr. Lindsey. Yes, sir.

* * *

Mr. Ben-Veniste [Minority Chief Counsel]. Now much has been made of the line in the notes, and I am referring to S 12534. If you would have that page in front of you, please.

Mr. Eggleston. Is that the typewritten version?

Mr. Ben-Veniste. Yes, it is. You have that handy?

Mr. Eggleston. I do, sir.

Mr. Ben-Veniste. Where it says, "Vacuum," and then, "Rose Law files." Let me ask you very directly because this is an important question. Was there any discussion about removing, or destroying, or obliterating, or otherwise making unavailable any files that were believed to be in existence at the Rose Law Firm during that meeting?

Mr. Eggleston. Absolutely not.

Mr. Ben-Veniste. Your prior background was as a Federal prosecutor; is that correct?

Mr. Eggleston. That's correct.

Mr. Ben-Veniste. Would you have tolerated any such discussion had such discussion arisen?

Mr. Eggleston. I would not have.

Mr. Ben-Veniste. Did you have any reason to believe at the point in that meeting that there were any files in the Rose Law Firm that were in any way the subject of interest or controversy at that time?

Mr. Eggleston. I don't think I had it as to any particular files, no. But I want to emphasize, as clearly as I can, there was absolutely no discussion at that meeting of anybody destroying any files. I would not have tolerated it; Mr. Kendall wouldn't have tolerated it. I had known Mr. Nussbaum for a period of time before that. He would not have tolerated that. That conversation did not occur at this meeting.

Mr. Ben-Veniste. Mr. Kennedy, let me ask you to look at those notes, and look at your handwritten notes, which are at page S 12523.

Mr. Kennedy. Yes, sir.

Mr. Ben-Veniste. I feel confident I am not asking you this question for the first time. What did you mean, to the best of your recollection, when you wrote this note—"Vacuum," space, "Rose Law files"?

Mr. Kennedy. We were referring to at the meeting that there was an information vacuum, that when you tried to get your arms around Whitewater, in this case referring to the real estate investment, it is impossible to do. The records were a shambles. I had personal knowledge of that. You are dealing with an information vacuum.

The Rose Law files, as they related to Whitewater documents, would—if you had gotten your hands on them, they would not have meant anything to you because of the condition of the records.

Mr. Ben-Veniste. Let me ask you very directly the same question I asked Mr. Eggleston. Did you or anybody at that meeting suggest in any way, shape or form that files then existing at the Rose Law Firm should be destroyed or hidden or otherwise made unavailable?

Mr. Kennedy. Absolutely not. And I don't have a prosecutorial background but I wouldn't have tolerated it either.

* * *

The Chairman. Before I turn to Senator Bond, Mr. Kennedy, let me ask you to look at your notes with the relevant testimony, and have them put up on the [video screen]. Your handwritten note about Rose Law files, the "vacuum" page.

Mr. Chertoff. 12523.

The Chairman. Look at that line, starting with "vacuum," would you read that for me, it says, "vacuum," what else? Read it.

Mr. Kennedy. It says, "Vacuum," space, "Rose Law files, Whitewater docs," dash, "subpoena."

The Chairman. What did you mean by that?

Mr. Kennedy. By what, Mr. Chairman?

The Chairman. What did you mean by that whole thing?

Mr. Kennedy. What I just testified about, Mr. Chairman.

The Chairman. The Whitewater documents were subpoenaed?

Mr. Kennedy. They were not.

The Chairman. Were you concerned about the subpoena?

Mr. Kennedy. We did not anticipate a subpoena, Mr. Chairman. We did not anticipate a subpoena, Mr. Chairman.

The Chairman. If you did not anticipate a subpoena, why did you put that down?

Mr. Kennedy. We did not have an expectation that a subpoena would be issued.

The Chairman. Then the question is, why did you write "Whitewater documents subpoena"?

Mr. Kennedy. The discussion was that if a subpoena were issued, files that had once been at the Rose Law Firm would no longer be there, with regard to Whitewater.

The Chairman. I believe that, absolutely. Let's go over the next one. "Documents, never know go out," underlined. Is that what it says? Read it.

Mr. Kennedy. Yes, sir. Asterisk, "Documents," with an arrow, "never know go out."

The Chairman. What did you mean by that?

Mr. Kennedy. I was talking about how the Whitewater documents, and I am talking about the Whitewater corporate records as they relate to Whitewater as a corporation and with regard to the real estate—

The Chairman. Aren't you talking about the Rose Law firm policy concerning documents?

Mr. Kennedy. Rose Law firm policy?

The Chairman. Wasn't there a policy?

Mr. Kennedy. What policy, Mr. Chairman?

The Chairman. A policy that the documents would not go out? Did you hear the testimony of your former partner last week?

Mr. Kennedy. Not all of it, no sir.

The Chairman. You heard the testimony relating to Mr. Foster coming to him and asking him to remove certain documents and to give them to him, the file? Do you remember that?

Mr. Kennedy. Yes, sir.

The Chairman. This was unusual wasn't it?

Mr. Kennedy. Well.

The Chairman. Weren't you the managing partner then?

Mr. Kennedy. Yes, sir.

The Chairman. You were the managing partner?

Mr. Kennedy. Mr. Chairman—

The Chairman. Now wait a minute. I ask the questions.

Mr. Kennedy. Yes, sir, I understand that.

The Chairman. Did you have a policy relating to what files and documents could or couldn't be removed from the firm?

Mr. Kennedy. I don't believe we had a written policy on it at that time, no, sir.

The Chairman. Did you have a policy?

Mr. Kennedy. Yes, sir, generally understood, yes.

The Chairman. What was the policy?

Mr. Kennedy. Without the client's consent, documents shouldn't be removed from the firm.

The Chairman. So, doesn't this refer basically to that policy, "Documents," arrow, "never know go out"?

Mr. Kennedy. Absolutely not, Mr. Chairman.

The Chairman. What does it mean?

Mr. Kennedy. It relates to the fact that there is—as far as I know, still is—a mystery about how the Whitewater documents—again I wish to stress these are the corporate records and real estate records relating to Whitewater as an investment—got from the Rose Law Firm to the campaign in 1992.

The Chairman. You didn't know that your partner, Mr. Foster, had asked for them? You didn't know that?

Mr. Kennedy. Mr. Chairman, these are apples and oranges. Yes, sir.

The Chairman. You didn't know that some of these—what about the billing records?

Senator Sarbanes. Let him answer.

Mr. Kennedy. Mr. Chairman—

The Chairman. Did you ask for the files on Madison?

Mr. Kennedy. I did not.

The Chairman. Then how did you know there were no files?

Mr. Kennedy. Mr. Chairman, you are confusing apples and oranges. I wish to state again, if you will allow me to answer, that what we are talking about here are the Whitewater records relating to Whitewater as a corporation and the real estate records to Whitewater's actual real estate. These did not relate to Madison files as they were described in Mr. Massey's testimony.

The Chairman. Did you know that Mr. Foster was looking for the Madison files?

Mr. Kennedy. I was aware that Mr. Foster was looking for the Madison files during the 1992 campaign, yes, sir.

The Chairman. Did you know he took them to the campaign?

Mr. Kennedy. No, sir, I am not aware of that.

The Chairman. You were surprised when you heard for the first time last week that Mr. Foster took the files to the campaign?

Mr. Kennedy. Mr. Chairman, I did not hear all of Mr. Massey's testimony. I don't know if he testified about that, about that as a fact, or not.

The Chairman. Did you know about this prior to last week?

Mr. Kennedy. Know about what, Mr. Chairman?

The Chairman. That the Madison files were brought to the campaign committee and that Mr. Foster was the person who asked for them?

Mr. Kennedy. Mr. Chairman, I was aware at the time that Mr. Foster was looking, on behalf of the law firm, at the Madison representation, so that the law firm could make a response to the issues that had come up in the campaign.

The Chairman. Do you know that the campaign acquired possession of the files?

Mr. Kennedy. I do not know that for a fact, no, sir.

The Chairman. You still don't know that for a fact?

Mr. Kennedy. I still don't know that the campaign actually got the Madison records.

The Chairman. You weren't aware they were removed?

Mr. Kennedy. No, sir.

The Chairman. Let me ask you about the next line. You said, "Documents, never know go out," and then the next line is—

Mr. Kennedy. Say that again, Mr. Chairman?

The Chairman. The next line, would you read the next line? There is a word that's underlined twice.

Mr. Kennedy. Mr. Chairman—

The Chairman. I am waiting for this one.

Mr. Kennedy. I bet you are. There is a long answer to this one.

The Chairman. Creative answer. Go ahead.

Mr. Kennedy. Characterize it as you wish.

The Chairman. If it is what has been reported in the media through spokespeople, we will let the general public decide, as well as Members of the Committee.

Mr. Kennedy. I am totally comfortable with that.

The Chairman. What is the next word?

Senator Sarbanes. Let him respond.

Mr. Kennedy. When I typed the—what is in front of you is the typed version of these notes. It was done at the request of my counsel, long before any of—either one of us knew that these notes would ever become public. It was done at the request of my counsel. This won't surprise anybody in this room. My handwriting is difficult to read. But it was done on a quick and dirty basis, it was not done with the expectation that I would be answering questions about these notes.

And as anyone who has examined them against the handwritten notes, the actual notes themselves, I dropped some lines, I left some words out. I did not do a perfect job.

One of the things that I have found most aggravating about the press reports and the commentary on these notes is, after the word "quietly" in the typewritten version there is a question mark, put there by me because I wasn't sure at the time whether the word was "quietly" or "quality."

That question mark has never appeared in anybody's commentary or in any press reports—that's something I have to live with—but that question mark is there. And the word is not "quietly," it is "quality." I have taken a magnifying glass, applied it to the originals and that is the word.

Now that ties in with the discussion about the quality of the Whitewater records that I once had in my possession, received from Mrs. Clinton.

The Chairman. "Vacuum Rose Law files." What does that mean?

Mr. Kennedy. The words stand not as a complete sentence, Mr. Chairman, or not as even a complete phrase. The word "Vacuum" stands by itself. There is a space between it and "Rose files."

The Chairman. What does it mean?

Mr. Kennedy. If you're referring to the handwritten notes.

The Chairman. What does it mean?

Mr. Kennedy. As I previously testified, Mr. Chairman, it refers to the fact that surrounding the Whitewater, again the real estate investment, the Whitewater corporation, there was and is an information vacuum.

The Chairman. How much time did you spend discussing Whitewater during this meeting—no, I will withdraw that. We will get back to that later because we need more time to develop this. I have impinged on my colleague's time, and I will ask that he be given additional time and I will give additional time to this side.

* * *

Mr. Chertoff. I just have one last area I want to ask you about, very briefly. This is back where we started with, "Vacuum Rose Law files." The reference to "Documents never go out," and your typed version says, "quietly," I just want to be clear on this. You typed up a translation of your handwritten notes for your lawyer.

Mr. Kennedy. That's correct.

Mr. Chertoff. And I assume you tried to be as accurate as reasonably possible for your lawyer?

Mr. Kennedy. Mr. Chertoff, as I have testified, I did it on a very quick and dirty basis. I never dreamed I would be typing notes for posterity.

Mr. Chertoff. You still wanted to be as accurate as you reasonably could. There is no percentage, Mr. Kennedy, in trying to fool your own lawyer, is there?

Mr. Kennedy. Mr. Chertoff, certainly I wasn't trying to fool my own lawyer, but as the typed translation indicates, I did not do a perfect job. I am here testifying in front of you, it was quick, it was dirty, it was done in a hurry simply to help them read my handwriting.

Mr. Chertoff. The word you typed was "quietly."

Mr. Kennedy. That is correct, with a question mark in parentheses afterward.

Mr. Chertoff. When was it you picked up the magnifying glass and it became "Documents never go out quality"?

Mr. Kennedy. When this became an issue of some significance.

Notes and Questions

1. A Lawyer's Worst Nightmare? Lawyers often work under the erroneous assumption that their handwritten notes, reflecting their thoughts and mental impressions about legal matters they are handling, will be absolutely immune from discovery under the attorney-client privilege, the work product doctrine, or both. Without intending any comment upon the contents of Mr. Kennedy's notes, it is a fact of life that, because lawyers assume that their handwritten notes are and will remain confidential, they may be less careful about what they write in such notes than they are about the contents of their other writings. This lack of care may be reflected in notes that characterize facts at issue in litigation, assess the strength of a legal argument, or simply contain basic errors in spelling, grammar, and punctuation. Having to produce such notes in litigation and endure examination on their contents by opposing counsel is bad enough, but to have the process play out in nationally televised congressional hearings, as was the case for Mr. Kennedy, may well be a lawyer's worst nightmare.

2. An Important Lesson. It is easy to dismiss the Kennedy notes situation by saying lawyers in the White House or lawyers representing the President of the United States should expect special scrutiny of all that they do and should act accordingly, even when they take notes in meetings. To do so would be a mistake, however. A lawyer cannot predict whether what today seems to be a routine legal matter—a real estate closing, a business transaction, or a civil deposition—may later prove to be a matter of intense local or even national interest. For example, the lawyers at the Rose Law Firm who worked on routine legal matters for a small Arkansas savings and loan association, Madison Guaranty, could not have expected that their billing records would later be scrutinized in nationally televised congressional hearings. The careful lawyer is always mindful of this possibility, however, and is always precise and circumspect when taking notes of a meetings or witness interview, preparing a routine "file memorandum" to document an event or communication with a client, and even when preparing personal "timesheets" used to bill clients. The authors of this book advise their law students to adhere to a *"New York Times* Rule"—assume that anything you write as a lawyer may one day appear on the front page of the *New York Times* (or your local or state newspaper).

3. The Crime-Fraud Exception to the Attorney-Client Privilege. The risk of unwelcome exposure of a lawyer's work product is compounded by the potential application of an important legal doctrine. The crime-fraud exception to the attorney-client privilege and the work product doctrine removes the protection of those doctrines for any communication between a lawyer and a client that is used to further a crime or fraud. What many lawyers mistakenly assume is that because they are not involved in, or aware of, any criminal or fraudulent activity, then their communications with the client will remain privileged. That assumption is incorrect. The law is clear that the determinative factor is the actions and intentions of the client in receiving legal advice. In other words, the lawyer can be completely innocent, pure of heart and mind, and unaware of the client's misconduct, but the crime-fraud exception will apply if the client was acting wrongfully. One of the authors has described the role of the crime-fraud exception in our legal system as follows:

> The crime-fraud exception protects against the most egregious class of abuses of the privilege—instances in which a client misuses legal advice to commit a crime or perpetrate a fraud. The Supreme Court has stated that "the purpose of the crime-fraud exception to the attorney-client privilege [is] to assure that the 'seal of secrecy' ... between lawyer and client does not extend to communications 'made for the purpose of getting advice for the commission of a fraud' or a crime."[60] The rationale for the exception is well established and follows from the policy goals that underlie recognition of the attorney-client privilege in the first instance—the attorney-client privilege is intended to promote the administration of justice, and any use of the privilege that is inconsistent with that end should not be permitted. The crime-fraud exception prevents use of the privilege to protect communications that do not further legitimate purposes and therefore do not promote the administration of justice. It is important to recognize, however, that the exception applies even if the attorney is completely innocent and unaware of the client's wrongdoing; it is the intent and actions of the client that determine whether or not the exception applies. Of course the exception also applies if the attorney acts in furtherance of criminal or fraudulent activity.

Although the rationale for the crime-fraud exception is widely accepted, the application of the exception in actual cases poses difficulties. As one appellate court has explained, "[t]he crime/fraud exception to the attorney-client privilege cannot be successfully invoked merely upon a showing that the client communicated with counsel while the client was engaged in criminal activity."[61] The party seeking to overcome the privilege must present evidence of something more than ongoing criminal activity involving the client to establish that the crime-fraud exception applies to communications between a client and an attorney. Defining precisely what evidence must be presented to trigger application of the exception and what process should be followed in evaluating that evidence has proved difficult for the courts.

The Supreme Court weighed in on the issues presented by application of the crime-fraud exception in 1989 with its decision in *United States v. Zolin,*[62] discussed above [in this Chapter].... Unfortunately, the *Zolin* opinion does

---

60. [144] *United States v. Zolin*, 491 U.S. 554, 563 (1989) (quoting *Clark v. United States*, 289 U.S. 1, 15 (1933) and *O'Rourke v. Darbishire*, [1920] A.C. 581, 604 (P.C.)). The lower federal courts have formulated the exception in similar terms: "[t]he attorney-client privilege does not apply where the client consults an attorney to further a crime or fraud." *See In re Richard Roe, Inc.*, 168 F.3d 69, 71 (2d 1999); *United States v. Martin*, 278 F.3d 988, 1001 (9th Cir. 2002); *Alexander v. FBI*, 198 F.R.D. 306, (D.C. Cir. 2000); *In re* Impounded, 241 F.3d 308 (3d Cir. 2001).

61. [151] *Subpoenas Duces Tecum*, 798 F.2d at 34.

62. [155] 491 U.S. 554 (1989).

not provide further guidance as to what constitutes sufficient proof to establish applicability of the crime-fraud exception and does not suggest how that quantum of proof exceeds the showing necessary to obtain an *in camera* inspection. The lower federal courts have been left to grapple with those issues, and the law in this difficult area is still evolving.

The crime-fraud exception is a difficult area of the law, but it provides an important limitation on availability of the attorney-client privilege. Moreover, the procedure for asserting a claim that the exception applies is sufficiently clear, at least since the Supreme Court's *Zolin* decision, to permit government officials readily to obtain judicial review of improper assertions of privilege. The relatively low showing required by *Zolin* to obtain *in camera* [judicial] review [of a privileged communication], coupled with *Zolin's* rejection of an independent evidence rule, means that if law enforcement authorities have credible evidence that legal advice is being or has been misused, they can obtain judicial review to determine if the crime-fraud exception should be invoked. Although they may be frustrated if courts do not always conclude that the exception is applicable, that frustration is both predictable and desirable in our adversary system of justice. In light of the importance of the policies served by the attorney-client privilege, it is appropriate that decisions about its availability be made by neutral judicial officers, rather than by government officials who are responsible for law enforcement. Absent some evidence that the crime-fraud exception is not adequate to protect against abuses of the system, law enforcement officials should rely upon it to overcome wrongful assertions of privilege on a case-by-case basis, and should not seek to undercut the overall availability of the privilege in our legal system.

Lance Cole, *Revoking Our Privileges: Federal Law Enforcement's Multi-Front Assault on the Attorney-Client Privilege (And Why It Is Misguided)*, 48 VILL. L. REV. 469, 500–07 (2003) (footnotes omitted except as indicated).

Recent events suggest that the crime-fraud exception "works in the real world" of law enforcement and litigation. For example, in one of the most highly publicized criminal investigation in our national history, Independent Counsel Kenneth Starr's investigation of President Clinton and Monica Lewinsky, a federal court in Washington, D.C. applied the crime-fraud exception in a situation where the lawyer involved was innocent of any wrongdoing. In *In re Grand Jury Subpoena to Francis D. Carter*, 1998 U.S. Dist. LEXIS 19497, at 4–5 (D.D.C. April 28, 1998), the court held that Monica Lewinsky's communications with the attorney who assisted her with preparation of an affidavit stating that she did not engage in sexual relations with President Clinton was subject to the crime-fraud exception. The court explicitly noted that "[t]he attorney does not need to know about his client's potential wrongdoing for the exception to apply." Mr. Carter was compelled to testify before the Starr Grand Jury about his representation of Ms. Lewinsky and produce his files pertaining to that representation.

The important lesson to take from this case and the many other, less celebrated, cases like it is clear. A prudent attorney never assumes that his notes and other work product will be immune from discovery.

The January 6 Committee and the Crime-Fraud Exception

As politically charged and contentious as the Senate Whitewater Committee investigation was in 1995–96, it pales in comparison to the level of partisan conflict and national political discord that accompanied the investigation of the House Select Committee to Investigate the January 6 Attack on the United States Capitol (the January 6 Committee) in 2021–22. (The January 6 Committee is discussed further in Chapter 8.) In early 2022 the January 6 Committee sought information from one of former President Donald Trump's legal advisers, giving rise to an attorney-client privilege dispute:

Eastman v. Thompson

594 F. Supp. 3d 1156 (C.D. Cal. 2022)

[*Ed. Note: footnotes omitted, except as indicated.*]

Plaintiff Dr. John Eastman ("Dr. Eastman"), a former law school dean at Chapman University, is a "political conservative who supported former President [Donald] Trump" and a self-described "activist law professor." While he was a professor at Chapman, Dr. Eastman worked with President Trump and his campaign on legal and political strategy regarding the results of the November 3, 2020 election.

This case concerns the House of Representatives Select Committee to Investigate the January 6 Attack on the US Capitol's ("Select Committee") attempt to obtain emails sent or received by Dr. Eastman on his Chapman email account between November 3, 2020 and January 20, 2021. The parties disagree on whether the documents are privileged or if they should be disclosed.

The Court previously ordered the parties to begin with documents from January 4–7, 2021. Dr. Eastman reviewed each document and claimed privilege over some, and the Select Committee objected to a number of his claims. At this point, the parties disagree on whether 111 documents from those dates are privileged. The parties submitted briefing, and the Court held a hearing on the privilege claims on March 8, 2022. The Court then personally reviewed the 111 challenged documents, which were provided by Dr. Eastman.

I. BACKGROUND

A. Facts

1. Election fraud claims

Dr. Eastman claims that the 2020 presidential election was "one of the most controversial in American history." Despite the lack of evidence of election tampering, "a significant portion of the population came to believe the election was tainted by fraud, disregard of state election law, misconduct by election officials and other factors."

In the months after the election, President Trump and Dr. Eastman helped foster those public beliefs and encouraged state legislators to question the election results. Dr. Eastman testified before and met with "state legislators[] to advise them of their constitutional authority … to direct the 'manner' of choosing presidential electors." Relying on public interviews with attendees, the Select Committee states that on January 2, 2021, President Trump and Dr. Eastman hosted a briefing urging several hundred state legislators from states won by President Biden to "decertify" electors.

President Trump also made personal appeals to state officials. On January 2, he called Georgia Secretary of State Brad Raffensperger to discuss allegations of election fraud. During the call, President Trump repeatedly claimed it was impossible for him to have lost the popular vote in Georgia, and repeatedly mentioned his "current margin [of] only 11,779" votes. He explained to Secretary Raffensperger that he did not care about specific fraud numbers as long as he won, "[b]ecause what's the difference between winning the election by two votes and winning it by half a million votes[?]" When Secretary Raffensperger pushed back against these requests, the President warned of public anger and threatened criminal consequences. The President interspersed the conversation with specific fraud claims—dead people voting, absentee ballot forgeries, trucks ferrying illegal ballots, and machines stuffed with "unvoted" ballots. Mr. Raffensperger debunked the allegations "point by point" and explained that "the data you have is wrong;" however, President Trump still told him, "I just want to find 11,780 votes."

The next day, President Trump attempted to elevate Jeffrey Clark to Acting Attorney General, based on Mr. Clark's statements that he would write a letter to contested states saying that the election may have been stolen and urging them to decertify electors. The White House Counsel described Mr. Clark's proposed letter as a "murder-suicide pact" that would "damage everyone who touches it" and commented "we should have nothing to do with that letter." President Trump eventually did not promote Mr. Clark after multiple high-ranking members of the Department of Justice threatened mass resignations that would leave the Department a "graveyard."

In the months following the election, numerous credible sources—from the President's inner circle to agency leadership to statisticians—informed President Trump and Dr. Eastman that there was no evidence of election fraud. One week after the election, the Cybersecurity and Infrastructure Security Agency declared "[t]he November 3rd election [] the most secure in American history" and found "no evidence that any voting system deleted or lost votes, changed votes, or was in any way compromised." An internal Trump Campaign memo concluded in November that fraud claims related to Dominion voting machines were baseless. In early December, Attorney General Barr publicly stated there was no evidence of fraud, and on December 27, Deputy Attorney General Donoghue privately told President Trump that after "dozens of investigations, hundreds of interviews," the Department of Justice had concluded that "the major allegations [of election fraud] are not supported by the evidence developed."

Still, President Trump repeatedly urged that "the Department [of Justice] should publicly say that the election is corrupt or suspect or not reliable."

By early January, more than sixty court cases alleging fraud had been dismissed for lack of evidence or lack of standing.

2. Plan to disrupt electoral count

In response to alleged fraud, Dr. Eastman researched and planned a strategy for President Trump to win the election. Just after Christmas, Dr. Eastman wrote a now-public two-page memo proposing that Vice President Pence refuse to count certified electoral votes from states contested by the Trump campaign: Arizona, Georgia, Michigan, Nevada, New Mexico, Pennsylvania, and Wisconsin. The memo outlines the two ways in which Dr. Eastman's plan ensures "President Trump is re-elected." If Vice President Pence refused to count electoral votes from all seven contested states, President Trump would win 232 votes to 222. Alternatively, if Congress claimed that a candidate could not win without reaching 270 votes, Vice President Pence could send the election to the Republican-majority House of Representatives, which would then elect President Trump. The memo emphasizes that "[t]he main thing here is that Pence should do this without asking for permission—either from a vote of the joint session or from the Court."

On January 3, 2021, Dr. Eastman drafted a six-page memo expanding on his plan and analysis, which he later disclosed to the media. This memo "war gam[ed]" four potential scenarios for January 6, only some of which would lead to President Trump winning reelection. Claiming that "[t]he stakes could not be higher," Dr. Eastman concludes his memo stating that his plan is "BOLD, Certainly. But this Election was Stolen by a strategic Democrat plan to systematically flout existing election laws for partisan advantage; we're no longer playing by Queensbury Rules."

On January 4, President Trump and Dr. Eastman invited Vice President Pence, the Vice President's counsel Greg Jacob, and the Vice President's Chief of Staff Marc Short to the Oval Office to discuss Dr. Eastman's memo. Dr. Eastman presented only two courses of action for the Vice President on January 6: to reject electors or delay the count. During that meeting, Vice President Pence consistently held that he did not possess the authority to carry out Dr. Eastman's proposal.

The Vice President's counsel and chief of staff were then directed to meet separately with Dr. Eastman the next day to review materials in support of his plan. Dr. Eastman opened the meeting on January 5 bluntly: "I'm here asking you to reject the electors." Vice President's counsel Greg Jacob and Dr. Eastman spent the majority of the meeting in a Socratic debate on the merits of the memo's legal arguments. Over the course of their discussion, Dr. Eastman's focus pivoted from requesting Vice President Pence reject the electors to asking him to delay the count, which he presented as more "palatable." Ultimately, Dr. Eastman conceded that his argument was contrary to consistent historical practice, would likely be unanimously rejected by the Supreme Court, and violated the Electoral Count Act on four separate grounds. Despite receiving pushback,

President Trump and Dr. Eastman continued to urge Vice President Pence to carry out the plan. At 1:00 am on January 6, President Trump tweeted, "If Vice President @Mike_Pence comes through for us, we will win the Presidency ... Mike can send it back!" At 8:17 a.m., the President tweeted again, "States want to correct their votes ... All Mike Pence has to do is send them back to the States, AND WE WIN. Do it Mike, this is a time for extreme courage!"

Following his tweets, President Trump placed two calls to Vice President Pence directly. After not being able to connect with the Vice President around 9:00 am, they spoke at approximately 11:20 am. Vice President Pence's National Security Advisor, General Keith Kellogg, Jr., was present and described President Trump as berating the Vice President for "not [being] tough enough to make the call" to delay or reject electoral votes.

3. Attack on the Capitol

On January 6, 2021, tens of thousands of people gathered outside the White House to protest the lawful transition of power from President Trump to President Joseph Biden. Both Dr. Eastman and President Trump gave speeches to relay the plan not just to the thousands gathered at the Ellipse but also to those watching at home. President Trump's personal attorney, Rudy Giuliani, introduced Dr. Eastman before he spoke as the "professor" who would "explain ... what happened last night, how they cheated, and how it was exactly the same as what they did on November 3." Dr. Eastman declared to the crowd:

> And all we are demanding of Vice President Pence is this afternoon at 1:00 he let the legislators of the state look into this so we get to the bottom of it, and the American people know whether we have control of the direction of our government, or not. We no longer live in a self-governing republic if we can't get the answer to this question. This is bigger than President Trump. It is a very essence of our republican form of government, and it has to be done. And anybody that is not willing to stand up to do it, does not deserve to be in the office. It is that simple.

President Trump then took the podium. He began with praise for Dr. Eastman and his plan to have Vice President Pence disrupt the count:

> Thank you very much, John. ... John is one of the most brilliant lawyers in the country, and he looked at this and he said, "What an absolute disgrace that this can be happening to our Constitution." ... Because if Mike Pence does the right thing, we win the election. All he has to do, all this is, this is from the number one, or certainly one of the top, Constitutional lawyers in our country. He has the absolute right to do it.

Before the Joint Session of Congress began, Vice President Pence publicly rejected President Trump and Dr. Eastman's plan: "It is my considered judgment that my oath to support and defend the Constitution constrains me from claiming unilateral authority to determine which electoral votes should be counted and which should not."

At 1:00 pm, members of Congress began the Joint Session as required by the Twelfth Amendment and the Electoral Count Act.

Soon after, President Trump finished his speech by urging his supporters to walk with him to the Capitol:

> Now, it is up to Congress to confront this egregious assault on our democracy. And after this, we're going to walk down, and I'll be there with you, we're going to walk down, we're going to walk down.... [W]e're going to try and give our Republicans, the weak ones because the strong ones don't need any of our help. We're going to try and give them the kind of pride and boldness that they need to take back our country. So let's walk down Pennsylvania Avenue.

After President Trump's speech, several hundred protesters left the rally and stormed the Capitol building. As the D.C. Circuit described it:

> Shortly after the speech, a large crowd of President Trump's supporters—including some armed with weapons and wearing full tactical gear—marched to the Capitol and violently broke into the building to try and prevent Congress's certification of the election results. The mob quickly overwhelmed law enforcement and scaled walls, smashed through barricades, and shattered windows to gain access to the interior of the Capitol. Police officers were attacked with chemical agents, beaten with flag poles and frozen water bottles, and crushed between doors and throngs of rioters.[63]

President Trump returned to the White House after his speech. At 2:02 pm, Mark Meadows, the White House Chief of Staff, was informed about the violence unfolding at the Capitol. Mr. Meadows immediately went to relay that message to President Trump. Even as the rioters continued to break into the Capitol, President Trump tweeted at 2:24 pm: "Mike Pence didn't have the courage to do what should have been done to protect our Country and our Constitution, giving States a chance to certify a corrected set of facts, not the fraudulent or inaccurate ones which they were asked to previously certify. USA demands the truth!"

During the riot, Vice President Pence, Members of Congress, and workers across the Capitol were forced to flee for safety. Seeking shelter during the attack, Vice President Pence's counsel Greg Jacob emailed Dr. Eastman that the rioters "believed with all their hearts the theory they were sold about the powers that could legitimately be exercised at the Capitol on this day." Mr. Jacob continued, "[a]nd thanks to your bullshit, we are now under siege."

---

63. [49] *Trump v. Thompson*, 20 F.4th 10, 15–16 (D.C. Cir. 2021), cert. denied, No. 21-932, 2022 WL 516395 (U.S. Feb. 22, 2022) (citing STAFF REP. OF S. COMM. ON HOMELAND SECURITY & GOVERNMENTAL AFFS. & S. COMM. ON RULES & ADMIN., 117TH CONG., EXAMINING THE U.S. CAPITOL ATTACK: A REVIEW OF THE SECURITY, PLANNING, AND RESPONSE FAILURES ON JANUARY 6, at 23–29 (June 8, 2021) ("Capitol Attack Senate Report"), and Hearing on the Law Enforcement Experience on January 6th Before the H. Select Comm. to Investigate the January 6th Attack on the U.S. Capitol, 117th Cong., at 2 (July 27, 2021)).

President Trump later published a video expressing support for the rioters but urging them to leave the Capitol: "We love you, you're very special. You've seen what happens, you see the way others are treated that are so bad and so evil. I know how you feel." At 6:00 pm, President Trump reiterated: "These are the things and events that happen when a sacred landslide election victory is so unceremoniously & viciously stripped away from great patriots who have been badly & unfairly treated for so long. Go home with love & in peace. Remember this day forever!"

As the attack progressed, Dr. Eastman continued to urge Vice President Pence to reconsider his decision not to delay the count. In an email to Vice President Pence's counsel Greg Jacob at 2:25 pm on January 6, Dr. Eastman wrote: "The 'siege' is because YOU and your boss did not do what was necessary to allow this to be aired in a public way so the American people can see for themselves what happened." At 6:09 pm, Dr. Eastman "remain[ed] of the view" that "adjourn[ing] to allow the state legislatures to continue their work" was the "most prudent course." At 11:44 pm, Dr. Eastman sent one final email to persuade Jacob to change his mind: "I implore you to consider one more relatively minor violation and adjourn for 10 days...."

After the riot had subsided, the Joint Session of Congress reconvened. "It was not until 3:42 a.m. on January 7 that Congress officially certified Joseph Biden as the winner of the 2020 presidential election."

The rampage on January 6 "left multiple people dead, injured more than 140 people, and inflicted millions of dollars in damage to the Capitol." As the House of Representatives later wrote, January 6, 2021 was "one of the darkest days of our democracy."

4. Investigation into the attack

In response to the attack, the House of Representatives created the Select Committee to "investigate and report upon the facts, circumstances, and causes relating to the January 6, 2021, domestic terrorist attack upon the United States Capitol Complex ... and relating to the interference with the peaceful transfer of power."

On November 8, 2021, the Select Committee issued a subpoena to Dr. Eastman. In the accompanying cover letter, Chairman Thompson stated that Dr. Eastman was "instrumental in advising President Trump that Vice President Pence could determine which electors were recognized on January 6, a view that many of those who attacked the Capitol apparently also shared."

Dr. Eastman declined to produce any documents or communications to the Select Committee and asserted his Fifth Amendment privilege against production. During his deposition, Dr. Eastman asserted his Fifth Amendment privilege 146 times.

The Select Committee subsequently issued a subpoena to obtain Dr. Eastman's communications from his former employer, Chapman University, on January 18, 2022. The subpoena ordered Chapman to produce Dr. Eastman's documents stored on Chapman's servers "that are related in any way to the 2020 election or the January 6, 2021 Joint Session of Congress, ... during the time period November 3, 2020 to January 20, 2021." Chapman initially collected over 30,000 responsive documents. The Select

Committee then worked with Chapman to tailor search terms, resulting in just under 19,000 responsive documents.

* * *

II. LEGAL STANDARD

Federal common law governs the attorney-client privilege when courts adjudicate issues of federal law. "As with all evidentiary privileges, the burden of proving that the attorney-client privilege applies rests not with the party contesting the privilege, but with the party asserting it." The "party asserting the attorney-client privilege has the burden of establishing the relationship and the privileged nature of the communication." The party must assert the privilege "as to each record sought to allow the court to rule with specificity." It is "extremely disfavored" when a "subpoena [i]s met by blanket assertions of privilege." "Because it impedes full and free discovery of the truth, the attorney-client privilege is strictly construed." The same burden applies to the party asserting work product protection.

III. DISCUSSION

The Court will first consider Dr. Eastman's assertions of attorney-client privilege, then his assertions of work product protection. For each category, the Court will examine whether the privilege attached in the first place, whether it was waived, and whether an exception applies.

* * *

1. Existence of attorney-client relationship

The Select Committee argues that Dr. Eastman has not met his burden of proving that an attorney-client relationship existed between him and President Trump. An attorney-client relationship is formed when an attorney advises a client who has consulted him seeking legal assistance. Attorney-client relationships may be express or implied. Among other factors, courts consider "the intent and conduct of the parties" and "whether the client believed an attorney-client relationship existed."

In response to the Court's request for evidence of an attorney-client relationship, Dr. Eastman provided only an unsigned, undated retainer agreement between him, President Trump as candidate, and President Trump's campaign committee. However, strong evidence establishes that Dr. Eastman had an attorney-client relationship with President Trump and his campaign between January 4 and 6, 2021. * * * The evidence clearly supports an attorney-client relationship between President Trump, his campaign, and Dr. Eastman during January 4–7, 2021.

* * *

3. Crime-fraud exception

Based on the Court's previous analysis, there are eleven remaining protected documents. The Court now considers whether any of those documents should be disclosed based on the crime-fraud exception, as the Select Committee argues.

The crime-fraud exception applies when (1) a "client consults an attorney for advice that will serve [them] in the commission of a fraud or crime," and (2) the communications are "sufficiently related to" and were made "in furtherance of" the crime. It is irrelevant whether the attorney was aware of the illegal purpose or whether the scheme was ultimately successful. The exception extinguishes both the attorney-client privilege and the work product doctrine. The party seeking disclosure must prove the crime-fraud exception applies by a preponderance of the evidence, meaning "the relevant facts must be shown to be more likely true than not."

The Court first analyzes whether President Trump and Dr. Eastman likely committed any of the crimes alleged by the Select Committee, and then whether the eleven remaining documents relate to and further those crimes.

a. Potential crimes or fraud

The Select Committee alleges that the crime-fraud exception applies based on three offenses:

(1) President Trump attempted to obstruct "Congress's proceeding to count the electoral votes on January 6," in violation of 18 U.S.C. §1512(c)(2);

(2) "President Trump, Plaintiff [Dr. Eastman], and several others entered into an agreement to defraud the United States by interfering with the election certification process," in violation of 18 U.S.C. §371; and

(3) "President [Trump] and members of his Campaign engaged in common law fraud in connection with their efforts to overturn the 2020 election results."

The Court will now determine whether President Trump and Dr. Eastman likely committed these offenses.

i. Obstruction of an official proceeding

The Select Committee alleges that President Trump violated 18 U.S.C. §1512(c)(2), which criminalizes obstruction or attempted obstruction of an official proceeding. It requires three elements: (1) the person obstructed, influenced or impeded, or attempted to obstruct, influence or impede (2) an official proceeding of the United States, and (3) did so corruptly.

Attempts to obstruct

Section 1512(c)(2) requires that the obstructive conduct have a "nexus ... to a specific official proceeding" that was "either pending or was reasonably foreseeable to [the person] when he engaged in the conduct." President Trump attempted to obstruct an official proceeding by launching a pressure campaign to convince Vice President Pence to disrupt the Joint Session on January 6.

President Trump facilitated two meetings in the days before January 6 that were explicitly tied to persuading Vice President Pence to disrupt the Joint Session of Congress. On January 4, President Trump and Dr. Eastman hosted a meeting in the Oval Office with Vice President Pence, the Vice President's counsel Greg Jacob, and the Vice

President's Chief of Staff Marc Short. At that meeting, Dr. Eastman presented his plan to Vice President Pence, focusing on either rejecting electors or delaying the count. When Vice President Pence was unpersuaded, President Trump sent Dr. Eastman to review the plan in depth with the Vice President's counsel on January 5. Vice President Pence's counsel interpreted Dr. Eastman's presentation as being on behalf of the President.

On the morning of January 6, President Trump made several last-minute "revised appeal[s] to the Vice President" to pressure him into carrying out the plan. At 1:00 am, President Trump tweeted: "If Vice President @Mike_Pence comes through for us, we will win the Presidency ... Mike can send it back!" At 8:17 am, President Trump tweeted: "All Mike Pence has to do is send them back to the States, AND WE WIN. Do it Mike, this is a time for extreme courage!" Shortly after, President Trump rang Vice President Pence and once again urged him "to make the call" and enact the plan. Just before the Joint Session of Congress began, President Trump gave a speech to a large crowd on the Ellipse in which he warned, "[a]nd Mike Pence, I hope you're going to stand up for the good of our Constitution and for the good of our country. And if you're not, I'm going to be very disappointed in you. I will tell you right now." President Trump ended his speech by galvanizing the crowd to join him in enacting the plan: "[L]et's walk down Pennsylvania Avenue" to give Vice President Pence and Congress "the kind of pride and boldness that they need to take back our country."

Together, these actions more likely than not constitute attempts to obstruct an official proceeding.

Official proceeding

The Court next analyzes whether the Joint Session of Congress to count electoral votes on January 6, 2021, constituted an "official proceeding" under the obstruction statute. The United States Code defines "official proceeding" to include "a proceeding before the Congress." The Twelfth Amendment outlines the steps to elect the President, culminating in the President of the Senate opening state votes "in the presence of the Senate and House of Representatives." Dr. Eastman does not dispute that the Joint Session is an "official proceeding." While there is no binding authority interpreting "proceeding before the Congress," ten colleagues from the District of Columbia have concluded that the 2021 electoral count was an "official proceeding" within the meaning of section 1512(c)(2), and the Court joins those well-reasoned opinions.[64]

---

64. [221] *United States v. Sandlin*, ___ F. Supp. 3d ___, No. 21-CR-00088-DLF, 2021 WL 5865006 (D.D.C. Dec. 10, 2021); *United States v. Caldwell*, ___ F. Supp. 3d ___, No. 21-CR-00028-APM, 2021 WL 6062718 (D.D.C. Dec. 20, 2021); *United States v. Mostofsky*, ___ F. Supp. 3d ___, No. 21-CR-00138-JEB, 2021 WL 6049891 (D.D.C. Dec. 21, 2021); *United States v. Nordean*, ___ F. Supp. 3d ___, No. 21-CR-00175-TJK, 2021 WL 6134595 (D.D.C. Dec. 28, 2021); *United States v. Montgomery*, No. 21-CR-00046-RDM, 2021 WL 6134591 (D.D.C. Dec. 28, 2021); *McHugh*, ___ F. Supp. 3d ___, 2022 WL 296304; *United States v. Grider*, No. 21-CR-00022-CKK, 2022 WL 392307 (D.D.C. Feb. 9, 2022); *United States v. Miller*, No. 21-CR-00119-CJN, 2022 WL 823070 (D.D.C. Mar. 7, 2022); *United States v. Andries*, No. 21-CR-00093-RC, 2022 WL 768684 (D.D.C. Mar. 14, 2022); *United States v. Puma*, No. 21-CR-00454-PLF, 2022 WL 823079 (D.D.C. Mar. 19, 2022).

Corrupt intent

A person violates § 1512(c) when they obstruct an official proceeding with a corrupt mindset. The Ninth Circuit has not defined "corruptly" for purposes of this statute. However, the court has made clear that the threshold for acting "corruptly" is lower than "consciousness of wrongdoing," meaning a person does not need to know their actions are wrong to break the law. Because President Trump likely knew that the plan to disrupt the electoral count was wrongful, his mindset exceeds the threshold for acting "corruptly" under § 1512(c).

President Trump and Dr. Eastman justified the plan with allegations of election fraud—but President Trump likely knew the justification was baseless, and therefore that the entire plan was unlawful. Although Dr. Eastman argues that President Trump was advised several state elections were fraudulent, the Select Committee points to numerous executive branch officials who publicly stated[65] and privately stressed to President Trump[66] that there was no evidence of fraud. By early January, more than sixty courts dismissed cases alleging fraud due to lack of standing or lack of evidence, noting that they made "strained legal arguments without merit and speculative accusations"[67] and that "there is no evidence to support accusations of voter fraud."[68] President Trump's repeated pleas for Georgia Secretary of State Raffensperger clearly demonstrate that his justification was not to investigate fraud, but to win the election: "So what are we going to do here, folks? I only need 11,000 votes. Fellas, I need 11,000 votes. Give me a break." Taken together, this evidence demonstrates that President Trump likely knew the electoral count plan had no factual justification.

---

65. [225] On November 12, 2020, the Cybersecurity and Infrastructure Security Agency published a statement that "[t]he November 3rd election was the most secure in American history" and that "[t]here is no evidence that any voting system deleted or lost votes, changed votes, or was in any way compromised." Similarly, Attorney General Barr publicly disagreed with President Trump's claims of election improprieties.

66. [226] In a December 15, 2020 meeting, high-ranking advisors emphasized to President Trump that with respect to allegations of fraud, "people are telling you things that are not right." On December 27, 2020, Deputy Attorney General Donoghue told President Trump "in very clear terms" that the Department of Justice had done "dozens of investigations, hundreds of interviews" and concluded that "the major allegations [of election fraud] are not supported by the evidence developed."

67. [228] *Donald J. Trump for President, Inc. v. Boockvar*, 502 F. Supp. 3d 899, 906 (M.D. Pa.), aff'd sub nom. *Donald J. Trump for President, Inc. v. Sec'y of Pennsylvania*, 830 F. App'x 377 (3d Cir. 2020), and appeal dismissed, No. 20-3384, 2021 WL 807531 (3d Cir. Jan. 7, 2021) ("[T]his Court has been presented with strained legal arguments without merit and speculative accusations, unpled in the operative complaint and unsupported by evidence. In the United States of America, this cannot justify the disenfranchisement of a single voter, let alone all the voters of its sixth most populated state. Our people, laws, and institutions demand more.").

68. [229] *Stoddard v. City Election Comm'n*, No. 20-014604-CZ, slip op. at 4 (Mich. Cir. Ct. Nov. 6, 2020) ("A delay in counting and finalizing the votes from the City of Detroit without any evidentiary basis for doing so, engenders a lack of confidence in the City of Detroit to conduct full and fair elections. The City of Detroit should not be harmed when there is no evidence to support accusations of voter fraud."). *See also Ward v. Jackson*, No. CV-20-0343-AP/EL, 2020 WL 8617817, at *2 (Ariz. Dec. 8, 2020), cert. denied, 141 S. Ct. 1381 (2021) ("[Plaintiff] fails to present any evidence of 'misconduct[]' [or] 'illegal votes.'").

The plan not only lacked factual basis but also legal justification. Dr. Eastman's memo noted that the plan was "BOLD, Certainly." The memo declared Dr. Eastman's intent to step outside the bounds of normal legal practice: "we're no longer playing by Queensbury Rules." In addition, Vice President Pence "very consistent[ly]" made clear to President Trump that the plan was unlawful, refusing "many times" to unilaterally reject electors or return them to the states. In the meeting in the Oval Office two days before January 6, Vice President Pence stressed his "immediate instinct [] that there is no way that one person could be entrusted by the Framers to exercise that authority."

Dr. Eastman argues that the plan was legally justified as it "was grounded on a good faith interpretation of the Constitution." But "ignorance of the law is no excuse," and believing the Electoral Count Act was unconstitutional did not give President Trump license to violate it. Disagreeing with the law entitled President Trump to seek a remedy in court, not to disrupt a constitutionally-mandated process. And President Trump knew how to pursue election claims in court—after filing and losing more than sixty suits, this plan was a last-ditch attempt to secure the Presidency by any means.

The illegality of the plan was obvious. Our nation was founded on the peaceful transition of power, epitomized by George Washington laying down his sword to make way for democratic elections. Ignoring this history, President Trump vigorously campaigned for the Vice President to single-handedly determine the results of the 2020 election. As Vice President Pence stated, "no Vice President in American history has ever asserted such authority." Every American—and certainly the President of the United States—knows that in a democracy, leaders are elected, not installed. With a plan this "BOLD," President Trump knowingly tried to subvert this fundamental principle.

Based on the evidence, the Court finds it more likely than not that President Trump corruptly attempted to obstruct the Joint Session of Congress on January 6, 2021.

ii. Conspiracy to defraud the United States

The Select Committee also alleges that President Trump, Dr. Eastman, and others conspired to defraud the United States by disrupting the electoral count, in violation of 18 U.S.C. §371. That crime requires that (1) at least two people entered into an agreement to obstruct a lawful function of the government (2) by deceitful or dishonest means, and (3) that a member of the conspiracy engaged in at least one overt act in furtherance of the agreement.

Agreement to obstruct a lawful government function

As the Court discussed at length above, the evidence demonstrates that President Trump likely attempted to obstruct the Joint Session of Congress on January 6, 2021. While the Court earlier analyzed those actions as attempts to obstruct an "official proceeding," Congress convening to count electoral votes is also a "lawful function of government" within the meaning of 18 U.S.C. §371, which Dr. Eastman does not dispute.

An "agreement" between co-conspirators need not be express and can be inferred from the conspirators' conduct. There is strong circumstantial evidence to show that there was likely an agreement between President Trump and Dr. Eastman to enact the plan articulated in Dr. Eastman's memo. In the days leading up to January 6, Dr. Eastman and President Trump had two meetings with high-ranking officials to advance the plan. On January 4, President Trump and Dr. Eastman hosted a meeting in the Oval Office to persuade Vice President Pence to carry out the plan. The next day, President Trump sent Dr. Eastman to continue discussions with the Vice President's staff, in which Vice President Pence's counsel perceived Dr. Eastman as the President's representative. Leading small meetings in the heart of the White House implies an agreement between the President and Dr. Eastman and a shared goal of advancing the electoral count plan. The strength of this agreement was evident from President Trump's praise for Dr. Eastman and his plan in his January 6 speech on the Ellipse: "John is one of the most brilliant lawyers in the country, and he looked at this and he said, 'What an absolute disgrace that this can be happening to our Constitution.'"

Based on these repeated meetings and statements, the evidence shows that an agreement to enact the electoral count plan likely existed between President Trump and Dr. Eastman.

Deceitful or dishonest means

Obstruction of a lawful government function violates §371 when it is carried out "by deceit, craft or trickery, or at least by means that are dishonest." While acting on a "good faith misunderstanding" of the law is not dishonest, "merely disagreeing with the law does not constitute a good faith misunderstanding... because all persons have a duty to obey the law whether or not they agree with it."

The Court discussed above how the evidence shows that President Trump likely knew that the electoral count plan was illegal. President Trump continuing to push that plan despite being aware of its illegality constituted obstruction by "dishonest" means under §371.

The evidence also demonstrates that Dr. Eastman likely knew that the plan was unlawful. Dr. Eastman heard from numerous mentors and like-minded colleagues that his plan had no basis in history or precedent. Fourth Circuit Judge Luttig, for whom Dr. Eastman clerked, publicly stated that the plan's analysis was "incorrect at every turn." Vice President Pence's legal counsel spent hours refuting each part of the plan to Dr. Eastman, including noting there had never been a departure from the Electoral Count Act and that not "a single one of [the] Framers would agree with [his] position."

Dr. Eastman himself repeatedly recognized that his plan had no legal support. In his discussion with the Vice President's counsel, Dr. Eastman "acknowledged" the "100 percent consistent historical practice since the time of the Founding" that the Vice President did not have the authority to act as the memo proposed. More importantly, Dr. Eastman admitted more than once that "his proposal violate[d] several provisions of statutory law," including explicitly characterizing the plan as "one more relatively minor violation" of the Electoral Count Act. In addition, on January 5, Dr. Eastman conceded that the Supreme Court would unanimously reject his plan for the Vice President to reject electoral votes. Later that day, Dr. Eastman admitted that his "more palatable" idea to have the Vice President delay, rather than reject counting electors, rested on "the same basic legal theory" that he knew would not survive judicial scrutiny.

Dr. Eastman's views on the Electoral Count Act are not, as he argues, a "good faith interpretation" of the law; they are a partisan distortion of the democratic process. His plan was driven not by preserving the Constitution, but by winning the 2020 election:

> [Dr. Eastman] acknowledged that he didn't think Kamala Harris should have that authority in 2024; he didn't think Al Gore should have had it in 2000; and he acknowledged that no small government conservative should think that that was the case.

Dr. Eastman also understood the gravity of his plan for democracy—he acknowledged "[y]ou would just have the same party win continuously if [the] Vice President had the authority to just declare the winner of every State."

The evidence shows that Dr. Eastman was aware that his plan violated the Electoral Count Act. Dr. Eastman likely acted deceitfully and dishonestly each time he pushed an outcome-driven plan that he knew was unsupported by the law.

Overt acts in furtherance of the conspiracy

President Trump and Dr. Eastman participated in numerous overt acts in furtherance of their shared plan. As detailed at length above, President Trump's acts to strong-arm Vice President Pence into following the plan included meeting with and calling the Vice President and berating him in a speech to thousands outside the Capitol. Dr. Eastman joined one of those meetings, spent hours attempting to convince the Vice President's counsel to support the plan, and gave his own speech at the Ellipse "demanding" the Vice President "stand up" and enact his plan.

iii. Common law fraud

As the Court discusses below, review of the eleven remaining documents reveals no further efforts to spread false claims of election fraud. Accordingly, the Court does not reach whether President Trump likely engaged in common law fraud.

b. Actions in furtherance of crime or fraud

The Court now determines whether any of the remaining eleven documents were in furtherance of the two crimes the Court found evidence of above, obstruction of an official proceeding and conspiracy to defraud the United States by attempting to persuade Vice President Pence to reject or delay electoral votes on January 6, 2021.

The crime-fraud exception applies when the "communications for which production is sought are 'sufficiently related to' and were made 'in furtherance of [the] intended, or present, continuing illegality.'" In a civil case, the burden of proof for the party seeking disclosure under the crime-fraud exception is preponderance of the evidence, meaning more likely than not.

"[T]he crime-fraud exception does not require a completed crime or fraud but only that the client have consulted the attorney in an effort to complete one." The exception applies even if the attorney does not participate in the criminal activity, and "and even

[if] the communication turns out not to help (and perhaps even to hinder) the client's completion of a crime." An attorney's wrongdoing alone may pierce the privilege, regardless of the client's awareness or innocence.[69]

Nine of the eleven documents were emails or attachments discussing active lawsuits in state and federal courts. They include drafting filings, conferring about oral arguments, or planning future litigation strategy. While these suits might have dealt with claims of election fraud, pursuing legal recourse itself did not advance any crimes, and the contents of the emails are cabined to those narrow litigation purposes. As such, these nine emails were not in furtherance of any of the offenses alleged by the Select Committee, so the crime-fraud exception does not apply.

The tenth document is an email sent at 4:03 pm MST on January 6, 2021, during the resumption of the Joint Session of Congress after the attack on the Capitol. The email responded to a request to participate in Dr. Eastman's work on behalf of President Trump. While the email discusses Vice President Pence's refusal to reject or delay the electoral count, the email was not "itself in furtherance" of the plan and thus does not fall within the crime-fraud exception.

The eleventh document is a chain forwarding to Dr. Eastman a draft memo written for President Trump's attorney Rudy Giuliani. The memo recommended that Vice President Pence reject electors from contested states on January 6. This may have been the first time members of President Trump's team transformed a legal interpretation of the Electoral Count Act into a day-by-day plan of action. The draft memo pushed a strategy that knowingly violated the Electoral Count Act, and Dr. Eastman's later memos closely track its analysis and proposal. The memo is both intimately related to and clearly advanced the plan to obstruct the Joint Session of Congress on January 6, 2021. Because the memo likely furthered the crimes of obstruction of an official proceeding and conspiracy to defraud the United States, it is subject to the crime-fraud exception and the Court ORDERS it to be disclosed.

* * *

IV. DISPOSITION

Dr. Eastman and President Trump launched a campaign to overturn a democratic election, an action unprecedented in American history. Their campaign was not confined to the ivory tower—it was a coup in search of a legal theory. The plan spurred violent attacks on the seat of our nation's government, led to the deaths of several law enforcement officers, and deepened public distrust in our political process. More than a year after the attack on our Capitol, the public is still searching for accountability. This case cannot provide it. The Court is tasked only with deciding a dispute over a

---

69. [269] See In re Sealed Case, 107 F.3d 46, 49 n.2 (D.C. Cir. 1997) ("[T]here may be rare cases . . . in which the attorney's fraudulent or criminal intent defeats a claim of privilege even if the client is innocent."); In re Impounded Case (Law Firm), 879 F.2d 1211, 1213 (3d Cir. 1989) ("We cannot agree" that "the crime-fraud exception does not apply to defeat the client's privilege where the pertinent alleged criminality is solely that of the law firm").

handful of emails. This is not a criminal prosecution; this is not even a civil liability suit. At most, this case is a warning about the dangers of "legal theories" gone wrong, the powerful abusing public platforms, and desperation to win at all costs. If Dr. Eastman and President Trump's plan had worked, it would have permanently ended the peaceful transition of power, undermining American democracy and the Constitution. If the country does not commit to investigating and pursuing accountability for those responsible, the Court fears January 6 will repeat itself. With this limited mandate, the Court finds the following ten documents privileged: 4553; 4793; 4794; 4828; 5097; 5101; 5113; 5412; 5424; 5719. The Court ORDERS Dr. Eastman to disclose the other one hundred and one documents to the House Select Committee.

Dated: March 28, 2022

David O. Carter
United States District Judge

Notes and Questions

1. An Historic Decision—Or Judicial Overreach? Judge Carter's decision was reported to be the first instance in American history in which a federal court concluded that evidence indicated a sitting President had committed a crime. Although the decision is the conclusion of only one federal judge, and the decision notes that the evidentiary standard applied is the "more likely than not" preponderance of the evidence standard of civil cases, rather than the more stringent "beyond a reasonable doubt" standard that applies in criminal cases, how significant do you believe this decision to be? Is your conclusion influenced by the fact that Judge Carter is a registered Democrat who was appointed to the federal bench by President Bill Clinton? Should it be?

2. Impeachable Offenses? Judge Carter's decision concludes that it is "more likely than not" that President Trump committed federal crimes. The Constitution provides in Article II, §4, that "The President ... shall be removed from Office on Impeachment for, and Conviction of, Treason, Bribery, or other high Crimes and Misdemeanors." The House of Representatives impeached President Trump in 2021 for incitement of insurrection, but he was acquitted by the Senate. Do you believe that Judge Carter's analysis supports impeachment and conviction of President Trump? This question and the 2021 impeachment proceedings against President Trump are explored further in Chapter 7.

3. Why Did the Committee Rely Upon the Crime-Fraud Exception? As discussed at the beginning of this Chapter, congressional committees have sometimes taken the position that the attorney-client privilege does not necessarily apply in congressional proceedings, because it is a common law judicial branch privilege and is not a constitutional privilege, so committees have discretion to override it and compel compliance. One obvious answer, as discussed in Chapter 4, is the difficulty of enforcement if a subpoena recipient is recalcitrant and refuses to comply. It also may be that the recent *Mazars* Supreme Court decision, discussed in Chapter 1, weakened the argument that

Congress can overcome assertions of attorney-client privilege. Consider the following analysis of two experienced practitioners:

Andy Wright: * * * The specific issue that we wanted to talk about today is the attorney-client privilege, which every lawyer graduating from college thinks is sacrosanct. People and clients rely on it to tell their deepest and darkest secrets to their lawyers without fear of it being exposed to the light of day.

But Congress has always taken the position that the attorney-client privilege is not legally binding for congressional investigations because they are not judicial proceedings—it's a common law privilege. What's really been fascinating over the last year since the Supreme Court decided the *Trump v. Mazars* case is that, there's been a shift towards strengthening attorney-client privilege claims asserted before Congress. It started with the chief justice's statement in *Mazars* that recipients of congressional subpoenas "have long been understood to retain common law and constitutional privileges."

While that statement is accurate with respect to constitutional privileges, I think the House definitely did not agree with the idea that the common law privileges apply in congressional investigations and what we're seeing now in the context of current investigations—most notably with respect to the Jan. 6 attack on the Capitol—is that a lot of parties are asserting the attorney-client privilege in investigations before Congress now. It seems that some courts are accepting those claims or at least assuming that they are valid and the House doesn't seem to be pressing its legal position that they don't apply.

David Rybicki: I would add that the issue in *Mazars* with respect to common law privileges is something that has been quite contentious over the years and federal courts have never definitely resolved the issue. Congress' position has always been that respecting the attorney-client privilege was a discretionary question for the chair of the congressional committee conducting the inquiry.

We'll see whether *Mazars* has changed all that, but when you look at the federal court litigation in California involving the potentially protected communications between professor John Eastman and members of the then-White House during the aftermath of the 2020 election you see that this issue is still very much a live issue and that the Eastman litigation could create significant new federal precedent with respect to where the privilege applies or doesn't apply. Preliminarily, it seems that the judge in the Eastman case is taking the view, without having ruled formally, that the privilege does in fact apply.

At one point the judge asked, "Where is the line between an attorney and a political adviser?" That question is relevant in the traditional analysis that asks whether or not communications between a lawyer and a client are privileged. And that analysis is far less interesting than the fact that we're conducing the analysis itself, which means that at least this judge is inclined to rule that the privilege applies in the context of the Jan. 6 inquiry.

* * *

NLJ: Looking ahead, what ought to be done to address the issue?

AW: I have great respect for congressional investigative power. I spent several years on the Hill and was a staff director in an investigative committee on the House side. I think it's a very broad and important power. But I think that Congress ought to formally recognize the validity and importance of attorney-client privilege. It's not that it could never be pierced but there ought to be a formal recognition of confidentiality interests as an important principle that should be respected in Congress. And then they could maybe formalize the rules when investigative interests outweigh those important confidentiality interests.

Both of us probably agree that it is something that ought to be recognized, whether it's Congress doing it itself versus judicially imposed recognition—but I think it's an important principle that most people agree should be part of our legal system.

DR: I agree that formal recognition, in addition to the de facto recognition that many congressional committees already apply to the attorney-client privilege, should be formalized in the rules of the most active investigative committees. That would be a big step. I don't think federal courts will be opining on these issues directly and I think that's where the issue arises in the Jan. 6 investigation—it would be best for Congress to move forward on this rather than for a court or a judge.

AW: It would help settle expectations on what to expect when you go into it rather than a committee-by-committee, staffer-by-staffer, chairman-by-chairman kind of rule, which is where things stand right now.

David Rybicki & Andrew Wright, *Q&A: Attorney-Client Privilege May Be on Shaky Grounds in Congressional Investigations*, Nat'l L.J. (March 30, 2022).

Do you agree with Rybicki and Wright that Congress should formally recognize the attorney-client privilege? If committees of this Congress did so, would the position be binding on committees in subsequent Congresses? Does this suggest Congress should pass a law recognizing that the attorney-client privilege applies to its proceedings? Would doing so be in Congress's interests?

4. Culpability of the Client vs. Culpability of the Attorney. As Judge Carter's opinion discusses, a key issue in crime-fraud exception cases is the wrongful intent of the client vs. the wrongful intent and knowledge of the attorney. The most important point to understand is that the crime-fraud exception can apply even if the attorney is completely unaware of the client's intention to misuse the legal advice that the attorney is providing. A completely innocent and nonculpable attorney can be compelled to testify about otherwise privileged communications if the client has the requisite wrongful intent. For example, as the footnotes in Judge Carter's opinion discuss, President Trump received briefings from senior Justice Department officials that debunked the claims that voter fraud had affected the outcome of the election. If President Trump failed to share this information with his private attorneys, and they believed that such voter fraud had occurred, the crime-fraud exception would still apply based on President Trump's knowledge and culpability, even if his private attorneys did not have the same knowledge and culpability. As the opinion establishes, however, that was not the case, and by January 6, both President Trump and his attorneys knew that evidence of significant voter fraud affecting the outcome of the election was lacking.

A less likely, but still theoretically possible, situation, which Judge Carter's opinion also recognizes, is that an attorney might be culpable and have the requisite wrongful intent, but the client does not have the same knowledge and culpability. In that case, the crime-fraud exception would still apply, based on the wrongful conduct of the attorney. For example, if, despite the briefings he received from senior Justice Department officials, President Trump had continued to believe that widespread voter fraud occurred and he should have won the election, but his attorneys knew otherwise, and despite that knowledge, continued to promote a false narrative, in legal proceedings and public statements, the crime-fraud exception would still apply. Again, however, it is important to note that the facts establish, as Judge Carter's opinion emphasizes, that both President Trump and his attorneys knew by January 6 that there was no widespread voter fraud and President Trump had lost the election.

The complexity of the points discussed above illustrate why the crime-fraud exception to the attorney-client privilege is both an extremely important and exceedingly difficult area of the law. Consider the analysis and illustrative example provided in the excerpted law review article below written by one of the authors of this book:

I. Overview of the Crime-Fraud Exception

The crime-fraud exception is essential to the proper functioning of the attorney-client privilege because it provides a means for the legal system to screen out instances in which clients seek to misuse the attorney-client relationship to commit a crime, perpetrate a fraud, or cover up ongoing crimes or frauds. The rationale for the crime-fraud exception is well established and follows from the policy goals that underlie recognition of the attorney-client privilege in the first instance; the attorney-client privilege is intended to promote the administration of justice, and any use of the privilege that is inconsistent with that end should not be permitted. The crime-fraud exception is intended to prevent use of the attorney-client privilege to protect communications that do not further legitimate purposes and therefore do not promote the administration of justice.

It is important to recognize that the crime-fraud exception applies even if the attorney is completely innocent and unaware of the client's wrongdoing; it is the intent and actions of the client—not the attorney—that determine whether or not the exception applies. It is equally important to recognize that the exception will apply when an innocent and unknowing attorney's advice and representation is used to conceal or hide ongoing criminal activity, such as a conspiracy to hide past misconduct or obstruct justice.

Although the rationale for the crime-fraud exception is widely accepted, the application of the exception in actual cases poses difficulties. As one appellate court has explained, "The crime/fraud exception to the attorney-client privilege cannot be successfully invoked merely upon a showing that the client communicated with counsel while the client was engaged in criminal activity." The party seeking to overcome the privilege must present evidence of something more than ongoing criminal activity involving the client to establish that the crime-fraud exception applies to communications between a client and an attorney. Defining precisely what evidence must be presented to trigger application of the exception and what process should be followed in evaluating that evidence has proved difficult for the courts.

The crime-fraud exception is a difficult area of the law, but it provides an important limitation on availability of the attorney-client privilege. If the exception is not properly applied by the courts, unscrupulous clients can misuse the attorney-client relationship to further or cover up their crimes and misconduct.... Because of the importance of the policies served by the attorney-client privilege, it is essential that prosecutors and civil litigants be able to ascertain where the boundary is between appropriate attorney-client consultations and misuse of the attorney-client privilege by clients who are acting in bad faith and seeking to abuse the justice system. This Article seeks to clarify this important area of law....

B. Monica Lewinsky

... In the late 1990s Whitewater Independent Counsel Kenneth W. Starr shifted his focus from the Whitewater land deal in Arkansas to President Clinton's relationship with White House intern Monica Lewinsky. Early in its investigation of the Lewinsky affair, Independent Counsel Starr's office invoked the crime-fraud exception to compel grand jury testimony and production of documents from Lewinsky's attorney....

For purposes of the analysis in this Article, Lewinsky's retention of Washington, D.C. attorney Francis D. Carter to represent her in connection with the Paula Jones civil sexual harassment lawsuit against President Clinton and to prepare an affidavit stating that Lewinsky did not have a sexual relationship with President Clinton is the important aspect of the Monica Lewinsky investigation. In early 1998, shortly after Starr's office began investigating the Lewinsky matter, it issued grand jury subpoenas to Carter calling for him to provide testimony and produce documents relating to his representation of Lewinsky. Carter moved to quash the subpoenas, arguing, among other things, that the subpoenas improperly sought to invade Lewinsky's attorney-client privilege and work-product doctrine protections. Starr's office countered with the argument that the crime-fraud exception applied and therefore Carter should be compelled to produce the subpoenaed documents and testify before the grand jury.

Chief Judge Norma Holloway Johnson analyzed the application of the crime-fraud exception to Lewinsky's engagement of Carter to prepare the affidavit. Based upon an in camera submission of evidence by Starr's office, Chief Judge Johnson concluded that the crime-fraud exception was applicable and overruled the assertions of attorney-client privilege. The evidence contained in the in camera submission was sufficient to convince the court that Lewinsky "committed perjury when she signed her affidavit, procured as a result of Mr. Carter's legal advice, and used her false affidavit as part of a broader scheme to obstruct justice."[70] Judge Johnson also concluded that the crime-fraud exception should overcome the assertion of work-product doctrine protection because Lewinsky consulted Carter for the purpose of committing perjury and obstruction of justice and used his work-product for that purpose. Based upon those conclusions, the court ordered Carter to testify and to produce the subpoenaed documents.[71]

… [T]he Lewinsky case supports the basic crime-fraud exception principle set forth above—that if a lawyer's services are being used to submit false information to the government as part of an effort to further or conceal a crime or fraud, then the attorney-client privilege should be vitiated and the attorney can and should be compelled to testify about communications with the client.…

Lance Cole, *Paul Manafort, Monica Lewinsky, and the Penn State Three Case: When Should the Crime-Fraud Exception Vitiate the Attorney-Client Privilege?*, 91 TEMP. L. REV. 555 (Spring 2019) (footnotes omitted, except as indicated).

Compare the circumstances of the Lewinsky case to Judge Carter's application of the crime-fraud exception in the Eastman case. Are the two cases consistent? Did Judge Carter properly apply the crime-fraud exception?

5. The January 6 Committee and the Governmental Attorney-Client Privilege. John Eastman was not the only witness subpoenaed by the January 6 Committee who asserted attorney-client privilege as a basis for refusing to provide information to the committee. Former senior Department of Justice official Jeffrey B. Clark was subpoenaed by the January 6 Committee on October 13, 2021, and he appeared for a commit-

---

70. [48] In a footnote to the quoted statement, Judge Johnson explained that she was not concluding that Lewinsky necessarily had committed those crimes: "The Court finds here that the OIC has met its burden under the crime-fraud exception. It expressly does not find, however, that Ms. Lewinsky in fact committed those crimes." In another portion of the opinion, Judge Johnson made clear that "there is no suggestion that Mr. Carter knew about any of the alleged wrongdoing."

71. [50] The court did accept Carter's arguments that forcing him to produce certain items that Lewinsky had given to him would violate Lewinsky's Fifth Amendment right against self-incrimination. That portion of Judge Johnson's opinion was reversed by the D.C. Circuit Court. *See Sealed Case III*, 162 F.3d 670, 675 (D.C. Cir. 1998) (citing *Fisher v. United States*, 425 U.S. 391 (1976)) (concluding that, because no attorney-client privilege existed, there would be no compulsion in violation of Lewinsky's Fifth Amendment privilege in forcing Carter to produce the subpoenaed items). The D.C. Circuit Court affirmed Judge Johnson's ruling that the crime-fraud exception applied, rejecting Lewinsky's materiality and intent arguments.

tee deposition on November 5, 2021. At the deposition, Mr. Clark refused to answer questions from committee staff and members. Among the grounds Mr. Clark and his counsel gave for refusing to answer was attorney-client privilege. That prompted committee counsel to ask the following question:

> At the time of these events, Mr. Clark was an employee of the Department of Justice, right, and his client was the people of the United States, not President Trump or anyone else. So help me understand how any attorney-client privilege could possibly be implicated when a Department of Justice official, a member of the executive branch, in the course of his professional responsibilities, is engaged in talking to his superiors or anyone else within the executive branch?

Clark Nov. 5, 2021 Deposition, p. 35. Mr. Clark's counsel responded that "I think we have, you know, reached an impasse and, consequently, we—.... We're done." Mr. Clark stated "I would say that we've not reached an impasse, and there have been repeated efforts to characterize the position as absolutist. It's not. We're inviting a dialogue in the letter [from Mr. Clark's counsel that was delivered to the committee shortly before the deposition began]. But for today, I think we're done." Clark Nov. 5, 2021 Deposition, pp. 35–36. Shortly thereafter, Mr. Clark and his counsel left the deposition, after committee members and staff asked that the deposition continue after a one-hour recess to allow the committee chair to review the letter from Mr. Clark's counsel and rule on the objections and assertions of privilege. Clark Nov. 5, 2021 Deposition, p. 39.

On December 2, 2021, the January 6 Committee voted unanimously in favor of a resolution to hold Mr. Clark in contempt of Congress. At the time of this writing, the full House of Representatives had not voted on the committee's resolution to hold Mr. Clark in contempt.

In cases arising out of the Whitewater Independent Counsel investigation, two federal appeals courts ruled that executive branch attorneys working in the White House could not assert attorney-client privilege as grounds for refusing to provide information in response to a federal grand jury subpoena. *See In re Grand Jury Subpoena Duce Tecum*, 112 F.3d 910 (8th Cir. 1997), *cert. denied*, 117 S. Ct. 2482 (1997); *In re Lindsey*, 158 F.3d 1263 (D.C. Cir. 1998). The *Lindsey* court summarized the reasons for its holding as follows:

> In these expedited appeals, the principal question is whether an attorney in the Office of the President, having been called before a federal grand jury, may refuse, on the basis of a government attorney-client privilege, to answer questions about possible criminal conduct by government officials and others. To state the question is to suggest the answer, for the Office of the President is a part of the federal government, consisting of government employees doing government business, and neither legal authority nor policy nor experience suggests that a federal government entity can maintain the ordinary common law attorney-client privilege to withhold information relating to a federal criminal offense.... The public interest in honest government and in exposing

wrongdoing by government officials, as well as the tradition and practice, acknowledged by the Office of the President and by former White House Counsel, of government lawyers reporting evidence of federal criminal offenses
whenever such evidence comes to them, lead to the conclusion that a government attorney may not invoke the attorney-client privilege in response to
grand jury questions seeking information relating to the possible commission
of a federal crime.

As one of the authors of this book has observed, "[G]overnment attorneys can no longer assume that the attorney-client privilege will protect discussions with government
officials if a prosecutor or grand jury later seeks to obtain information about those
discussions." Lance Cole, *The Government-Client Privilege After* Office of the President
v. Office of the Independent Counsel, 22 J. LEGAL PROF. 15, 27 (1997–98).

With this information about the governmental attorney-client privilege, consider
the question to Jeffrey Clark by the January 6 Committee counsel that is quoted above.
Does the D.C. Circuit decision in the *Lindsey* case apply to Mr. Clark's assertion of attorney-client privilege for communications with President Trump? How important is it
that the *Lindsey* case involved a federal grand jury subpoena issued in connection with
a criminal investigation conducted by the executive branch of government, while in
the Clark matter, a committee of the legislative branch had directed a subpoena to Mr.
Clark for information involving his activities as an attorney in the executive branch?
Does the reasoning of the *Lindsey* court apply to the Clark situation even though it is
a different branch of government seeking to overcome an assertion of governmental
attorney-client privilege? Does the fact that the two governmental attorney-client privilege cases cited above both involved criminal investigations, while the Clark situation
involved a congressional investigation, make the holdings of those cases inapplicable
to Mr. Clark's assertion of attorney-client privilege? As you consider these questions,
recall that congressional committees have no power to charge or prosecute crimes,
and that the power to prosecute federal crimes is solely within the executive branch of
government, through the Department of Justice.

Chapter Seven

Impeachment

What, it may be asked, is the true spirit of [impeachment] itself? Is it not de-signed as a method of NATIONAL INQUEST *into the conduct of public men?"*

Federalist No. 65 (Alexander Hamilton)

[A]n impeachable offense is whatever a majority of the House of Representatives considers [it] to be at a given moment in history; conviction results from what-ever offense or offenses two-thirds of the other body [the Senate] considers to be sufficiently serious to require removal of the accused from office."

Then-House Minority Leader Gerald R. Ford, arguing for the impeachment of Supreme Court Associate Justice William O. Douglas (April 15, 1970)

Whether ours shall continue to be a government of laws and not of men is now for Congress and ultimately the American people.

Statement of dismissed Watergate Special Prosecutor Archibald Cox, issued after the "Saturday Night Massacre" of October 20, 1973

Overview of the Impeachment Process

Impeachment is the most dramatic exercise of Congress's oversight power. The im-peachment power is explicitly set out in the Constitution but, like Congress's power to legislate, depends to some degree on an implied power to conduct investigations and to compel the testimony of witnesses and the production of documents. In 1974, during the impeachment investigation of President Nixon, the House Judiciary Committee provided a summary of the relevant constitutional provisions in a report prepared by the committee's staff:

The Constitution deals with the subject of impeachment and conviction at six places. The scope of the power is set out in Article II, Section 4:

The President, Vice President and all civil Officers of the United States, shall be removed from Office on Impeachment for, and Conviction of, Treason, Bribery, or other high Crimes and Misdemeanors.

Other provisions deal with procedures and consequences. Article I, Section 9 states:

The House of Representatives ... shall have the sole Power of Impeachment.

Similarly, Article I, Section 3, describes the Senate's role:

The Senate shall have the sole Power to try all Impeachments. When sitting for that Purpose, they shall be on Oath or Affirmation. When the President of the United States is tried, the Chief Justice shall preside: And no Person shall be convicted without the Concurrence of two thirds of the Members present.

The same section limits the consequences of judgment in cases of impeachment:

Judgment in Cases of Impeachment shall not extend further than to remove from Office, and disqualification to hold and enjoy any Office of honor, Trust or Profit under the United States; but the Party convicted shall nevertheless be liable and subject to Indictment, Trial, Judgment and Punishment, according to Law.

Of lesser significance, although mentioning the subject, are: Article II, Section 9:

The President ... shall have Power to grant Reprieves and Pardons for Offences against the United States, except in Cases of Impeachment.

Article III, Section 9:

The Trial of all Crimes, except in Cases of Impeachment, shall be by Jury....

Constitutional Grounds for Presidential Impeachment, Report by the Staff of the Committee on the Judiciary, House of Representatives 35 (Feb. 1974).

Several points concerning the constitutional provisions quoted above merit emphasis. First, the Constitution is clear that the impeachment power extends not just to the President and Vice President, but to all civil officers of the United States. While the four presidential impeachments (and President Nixon's near-impeachment) garner the most attention, the impeachment power has been used most frequently against federal judges because of the life tenure they enjoy after appointment. A few others have been impeached, including one cabinet officer, Secretary of War William W. Belknap, who was acquitted in the Senate in 1876, after he had resigned. In 1797, the House of Representatives impeached a Senator, William Blount, who had been expelled by the Senate prior to his impeachment. The Senate dismissed the case against Blount without holding a trial, amid doubts concerning whether members of Congress are among the "civil Officers" subject to impeachment.[1]

---

1. The 1974 House Judiciary Committee report summarized the proceedings against Blount in the Senate as follows:

Before Blount's impeachment, the Senate expelled him for "having been guilty of a high misdemeanor, entirely inconsistent with his public trust and duty as a Senator." At the [Senate]

This Chapter will focus on the impeachment proceedings that were initiated against President Richard Nixon, who resigned before an impeachment vote would have taken place in the House of Representatives, and Presidents Bill Clinton and Donald Trump, who were acquitted by the Senate after being impeached by the House of Representatives. In the nineteenth century, President Andrew Johnson was also impeached, and he too was acquitted by the Senate, although by a much narrower margin (35–19 in favor of conviction, one vote short of the required two-thirds majority) than Presidents Clinton and Trump.[2] Clinton was acquitted on his two articles of impeachment by votes of 45–55 and 50–50, and Trump was acquitted by votes of 48–52, 47–53, and 43–57.

A second noteworthy aspect of the impeachment provisions in the Constitution is the unique nature of the procedures they specify. Impeachment requires separate actions in the two houses of Congress, with a vote on articles of impeachment in the House of Representatives and then, if the House votes to impeach, a vote on the impeachment charges in the Senate. The provision for a two-thirds vote to convict in the

---

trial a plea was interposed on behalf of Blount to the effect that (1) a Senator was not a "civil officer," (2) having already been expelled, Blount was no longer impeachable, and (3) no crime or misdemeanor in the execution of office had been alleged. The Senate voted 14 to 11 that the plea was sufficient in law that the Senate ought not to hold jurisdiction. The impeachment was dismissed.

Constitutional Grounds for Presidential Impeachment, Report by the Staff of the Committee on the Judiciary, House of Representatives, Appendix B, "American Impeachment Cases," 42 (Feb. 1974) (footnote references omitted).

2. A widely read summary of the law of impeachment, written for laypersons by a law professor, summarized the Johnson impeachment proceedings as follows:

... The remaining case was that of President Andrew Johnson. He was impeached, substantially, for having removed the secretary of war, a holdover from Lincoln's administration, in alleged violation of a Tenure in Office Act passed by the Reconstruction Congress, and for attempting to bring disgrace and ridicule on Congress—itself a ridiculous charge. He was acquitted, but by a vote just one short of the two-thirds needed to convict; such an "acquittal" is not a satisfactory legal precedent on [the question of what constitutes an] "impeachable offense." ... [T] he acquittal was almost certainly not on the facts, but on the belief that no impeachable offense had been charged—but with the weakness as precedent just mentioned. Moreover, the Johnson impeachment is, to say the least, by no means universally regarded today as a paradigm of propriety or of unimpassioned law.

CHARLES L. BLACK, JR., IMPEACHMENT: A HANDBOOK 51–52 (Yale Univ. Press 1974). For the reasons provided by Professor Black, and because we now have more recent examples provided by the impeachment proceedings against Presidents Nixon, Clinton, and Trump, the impeachment of President Andrew Johnson is not a major focus of this Chapter. For an in-depth study of the Johnson impeachment, see DAVID O. STEWART, IMPEACHED: THE TRIAL OF PRESIDENT ANDREW JOHNSON AND THE FIGHT FOR LINCOLN'S LEGACY (Simon & Schuster 2009); see also WILLIAM H. REHNQUIST, GRAND INQUESTS: THE HISTORIC IMPEACHMENTS OF JUSTICE SAMUEL CHASE AND PRESIDENT ANDREW JOHNSON (1992). Stewart reports the extraordinary amount of "corruption and bribery that surrounded the Senate trial" of Andrew Johnson and observes that the Nixon and Clinton presidential impeachment "episodes pale when compared to the fervor that rocked the nation in 1868, when ... only the impeachment clauses of the Constitution stood between the nation and a second Civil War." STEWART, supra, at 4.

Senate suggests that the Framers intended removal from office to be an extraordinary remedy that would be imposed only when a high level of political consensus favored doing so. Although our present two-party political system was not in place at the time, the Framers of the Constitution nonetheless put in place a system that makes it difficult to obtain an impeachment conviction as a partisan political tactic.[3] A leading scholar of the federal impeachment process has noted that the two-thirds supermajority requirement for the Senate vote was an innovation of the American constitutional convention, with no parallel in prior English precedents, and demonstrated the creative and independent approach of the Framers in fashioning an impeachment process:

> Even though many of the delegates were familiar with the English experience with impeachment, their general agreement to deviate from English impeachment is noteworthy because it shows that from the convention's outset the delegates put a uniquely American stamp on the federal impeachment process. For example, the delegates vigorously debated the definitions for impeachable offenses, whereas the English Parliament had always refused to constrain its jurisdiction over impeachments by restrictively defining impeachable offenses. The delegates also agreed to limit impeachment to office-holders, but in England, anyone, except for a member of the royal family, could be impeached. Whereas the English House of Lords could convict upon a bare majority, the American delegates required a supermajority vote of the members of the Senate present. In addition, the House of Lords could order any punishment upon conviction, but the delegates limited the punishments in the federal constitution to those typically found—removal and disqualification—in state constitutions. Moreover, the English people had no means by which to discipline their king, while the Framers agreed to make the president impeachable for certain offenses. Thus, the constitutional convention debates about impeachment confirm that the federal impeachment process is, in many critical aspects, uniquely American.

MICHAEL J. GERHARDT, THE FEDERAL IMPEACHMENT PROCESS: A CONSTITUTIONAL AND HISTORICAL ANALYSIS 10–11 (Univ. Chicago Press, 2d ed. 2000) (footnote references omitted).

Another important consideration is the manner in which impeachment fits within the greater scheme of law enforcement and judicial review provided for in the Constitution. As to law enforcement, the Constitution is explicit that impeachment is not the sole available remedy for misconduct by federal officials. Article I, §3 clearly provides that the consequences of impeachment cannot exceed removal from office and disqualification from future service. It also is clear that further punishment for the same misconduct can be imposed through the legal system, so there is no basis for

---

3. Interestingly, however, the impeachment itself requires only a bare majority in the House, leading to the possibility that the House could impeach a President without any support from Representatives of the President's party. That possibility was realized in 2019 when Donald Trump was impeached (the first time) without any Republican votes in favor of impeachment.

any "double jeopardy" argument in impeachment cases. This point is illustrated by the fact that President Clinton—even after being acquitted by the Senate—had to reach a separate agreement with the Independent Counsel's office to resolve possible criminal charges arising out of the same conduct that led to his impeachment (discussed further below).

The Roles of the Senate and the Judiciary in Impeachment Trials

The Federalist No. 65
(Alexander Hamilton)

* * * A well-constituted court for the trial of impeachments is an object not more to be desired than difficult to be obtained in a government wholly elective. The subjects of its jurisdiction are those offenses which proceed from the misconduct of public men, or, in other words, from the abuse or violation of some public trust. They are of a nature which may with peculiar propriety be denominated POLITICAL, as they relate chiefly to injuries done immediately to the society itself. The prosecution of them, for this reason, will seldom fail to agitate the passions of the whole community, and to divide it into parties more or less friendly or inimical to the accused. In many cases it will connect itself with the pre-existing factions, and will enlist all their animosities, partialities, influence, and interest on one side or on the other; and in such cases there will always be the greatest danger that the decision will be regulated more by the comparative strength of parties, than by the real demonstrations of innocence or guilt.

The delicacy and magnitude of a trust which so deeply concerns the political reputation and existence of every man engaged in the administration of public affairs, speak for themselves. The difficulty of placing it rightly, in a government resting entirely on the basis of periodical elections, will as readily be perceived, when it is considered that the most conspicuous characters in it will, from that circumstance, be too often the leaders or the tools of the most cunning or the most numerous faction, and on this account, can hardly be expected to possess the requisite neutrality towards those whose conduct may be the subject of scrutiny. * * *

What, it may be asked, is the true spirit of the institution itself? Is it not designed as a method of NATIONAL INQUEST into the conduct of public men? If this be the design of it, who can so properly be the inquisitors for the nation as the representatives of the nation themselves? It is not disputed that the power of originating the inquiry, or, in other words, of preferring the impeachment, ought to be lodged in the hands of one branch of the legislative body; will not the reasons which indicate the propriety of this arrangement strongly plead for an admission of the other branch of that body to a share of the inquiry? The model from which the idea of this institution has been borrowed, pointed out that course to the Convention: In Great Britain it is the province of the house of commons to prefer the impeachment; and of the house of lords to decide upon it. Several of the State constitutions have followed the example. As well the latter as the former seem to have regarded the practice of impeachments, as a bridle in the hands of the legislative body upon the executive servants of the government. Is not this the true light in which it ought to be regarded?

Where else, than in the Senate could have been found a tribunal sufficiently dignified, or sufficiently independent? What other body would be likely to feel *confidence enough in its own situation*, to preserve, unawed and uninfluenced, the necessary impartiality between an *individual* accused, and the *representatives of the people, his accusers?*

Could the Supreme Court have been relied upon as answering this description? It is much to be doubted whether the members of that tribunal would, at all times, be endowed with so eminent a portion of fortitude, as would be called for in the execution of so difficult a task; & it is still more to be doubted, whether they would possess the degree of credit and authority, which might, on certain occasions, be indispensable, towards reconciling the people to a decision, that should happen to clash with an accusation brought by their immediate representatives. A deficiency in the first, would be fatal to the accused; in the last, dangerous to the public tranquillity. The hazard in both these respects could only be avoided, if at all, by rendering that tribunal more numerous than would consist with a reasonable attention to œconomy. The necessity of a numerous court for the trial of impeachments is equally dictated by the nature of the proceeding. This can never be tied down by such strict rules, either in the delineation of the offense by the prosecutors, or in the construction of it by the Judges, as in common cases serve to limit the discretion of courts in favor of personal security. There will be no jury to stand between the Judges, who are to pronounce the sentence of the law and the party who is to receive or suffer it. The awful discretion, which a court of impeachments must necessarily have, to doom to honor or to infamy the most confidential and the most distinguished characters of the community, forbids the commitment of the trust to a small number of persons.

These considerations seem alone sufficient to authorize a conclusion, that the Supreme Court would have been an improper substitute for the Senate, as a court of impeachments. There remains a further consideration, which will not a little strengthen this conclusion. It is this. The punishment, which may be the consequence of conviction upon impeachment, is not to terminate the chastisement of the offender. After having been sentenced to a perpetual ostracism from the esteem and confidence, and honors and emoluments of his country; he will still be liable to prosecution and punishment in the ordinary course of law. Would it be proper that the persons, who had disposed of his fame and his most valuable rights as a citizen in one trial, should in another trial, for the same offense, be also the disposers of his life and his fortune? Would there not be the greatest reason to apprehend, that error in the first sentence would be the parent of error in the second sentence? That the strong bias of one decision would be apt to overrule the influence of any new lights, which might be brought to vary the complexion of another decision? Those who know any thing of human nature, will not hesitate to answer these questions in the affirmative; and will be at no loss to perceive, that by making the same persons Judges in both cases, those who might happen to be the objects of prosecution would in a great measure be deprived of the double security, intended them by a double trial. The loss of life and estate would often be virtually included in a sentence, which, in its terms, imported nothing more than dismission from a present, and disqualification for a future, office. It may be said, that the intervention of a jury, in the second instance, would obviate the danger. But juries are frequently influenced by the opinions of Judges. They are sometimes induced to find special verdicts, which refer the main question to the decision of the court. Who would be willing to stake his life and his estate upon the verdict of a jury acting under the auspices of Judges who had predetermined his guilt?

Would it have been an improvement of the plan, to have united the Supreme Court with the Senate, in the formation of the court of impeachments? This Union would certainly have been attended with several advantages; but would they not have been overballanced by the signal disadvantage, already stated, arising from the agency of the same Judges in the double prosecution to which the offender would be liable? To a certain extent, the benefits of that Union will be obtained from making the Chief Justice of the Supreme Court the President of the court of impeachments, as is proposed to be done in the plan of the Convention; while the inconveniences of an intire incorporation of the former into the latter will be substantially avoided. This was perhaps the prudent mean. I forbear to remark upon the additional pretext for clamor, against the Judiciary, which so considerable an augmentation of its authority would have afforded.

Would it have been desirable to have composed the court for the trial of impeachments of persons wholly distinct from the other departments of the government? There are weighty arguments, as well against, as in favor of such a plan. To some minds, it will not appear a trivial objection, that it could tend to increase the complexity of the political machine; and to add a new spring to the government, the utility of which would at best be questionable. But an objection, which will not be thought by any unworthy of attention, is this—A court formed upon such a plan would either be attended with heavy expense, or might in practice be subject to a variety of casualties and inconveniences. It must either consist of permanent officers stationary at the seat of government, and of course entitled to fixed and regular stipends, or of certain officers of the State governments, to be called upon whenever an impeachment was actually depending. It will not be easy to imagine any third mode materially different, which could rationally be proposed. As the court, for reasons already given, ought to be numerous; the first scheme will be reprobated by every man, who can compare the extent of the public wants, with the means of supplying them; the second will be espoused with caution by those, who will seriously consider the difficulty of collecting men dispersed over the whole union; the injury to the innocent, from the procrastinated determination of the charges which might be brought against them; the advantage to the guilty, from the opportunities which delay would afford to intrigue and corruption; and in some cases the detriment to the State, from the prolonged inaction of men, whose firm and faithful execution of their duty might have exposed them to the persecution of an intemperate or designing majority in the House of Representatives. Though this latter supposition may seem harsh, and might not be likely often to be verified; yet it ought not to be forgotten, that the demon of faction will at certain seasons extend his sceptre over all numerous bodies of men.

But though one or the other of the substitutes which have been examined, or some other that might be devised, should be thought preferable to the plan, in this respect, reported by the Convention, it will not follow, that the Constitution ought for this reason to be rejected. If mankind were to resolve to agree in no institution of government, until every part of it had been adjusted to the most exact standard of perfection, society would soon become a general scene of anarchy, and the world a desert. Where is the standard of perfection to be found? Who will undertake to unite the discordant opinions of a whole community, in the same judgment of it; and to prevail upon one conceited projector to renounce his *infallible* criterion for the *fallible* criterion of his more *conceited neighbor*? To answer the purpose of the adversaries of the Constitution, they ought to prove, not merely, that particular provisions in it are not the best, which might have been imagined; but that the plan upon the whole is bad and pernicious.

PUBLIUS.

––––––––––

Federalist No. 65 points to some of the problems that would arise if impeachment trials were conducted by the part of government most accustomed to conducting trials: the Article III judiciary. Hamilton's argument on this point is two-pronged. First, he notes the peculiar character of impeachment trials as determining an official's fitness for office. For that reason, argues Hamilton, members of Congress—representatives of the people—are best suited to decide whether to impeach and whether to convict because they are best able to determine whether the official in question has violated the trust of the people that the members of Congress represent. Second, involving the judiciary in an impeachment might prejudice the courts in the event that a second trial were held concerning the same conduct that led to the impeachment. Recall that the consequence of impeachment and conviction "shall not extend further than to removal from Office, and disqualification to hold and enjoy" any future federal office. U.S. Const., art. I, §3. If the impeached official has committed a crime, he would be "liable and subject to Indictment, Trial, Judgment, and Punishment, according to Law." *Id.* Hamilton feared that if judges took part in impeachments, the impeached official could not receive a fair hearing before a judge who had already convicted him in an impeachment trial.

Do such concerns require that the judiciary be completely excluded from reviewing the legality of an impeachment or an impeachment trial? If an official were impeached and convicted because of racial prejudice, because of partisanship, or purely on the basis of a coin flip, could the official appeal to the courts for relief?[4] The Supreme Court

––––––––––

4. The Framers likely did not intend impeachment convictions in the Senate to be subject to judicial review. As Professor Gerhardt has explained:

addressed the issue of judicial review of impeachment proceedings for the first time in a 1993 decision involving the impeachment of federal district judge Walter Nixon:

(Walter L.) Nixon v. United States
506 U.S. 224 (1993)

Petitioner Walter L. Nixon, Jr., asks this Court to decide whether Senate Rule XI, which allows a committee of Senators to hear evidence against an individual who has been impeached and to report that evidence to the full Senate, violates the Impeachment Trial Clause, Art. I, §3, cl. 6. That Clause provides that the "Senate shall have the sole Power to try all Impeachments." But before we reach the merits of such a claim, we must decide whether it is "justiciable," that is, whether it is a claim that may be resolved by the courts. We conclude that it is not.

Nixon, a former Chief Judge of the United States District Court for the Southern District of Mississippi, was convicted by a jury of two counts of making false statements before a federal grand jury and sentenced to prison. The grand jury investigation stemmed from reports that Nixon had accepted a gratuity from a Mississippi businessman in exchange for asking a local district attorney to halt the prosecution of the businessman's son. Because Nixon refused to resign from his office as a United States District Judge, he continued to collect his judicial salary while serving out his prison sentence.

On May 10, 1989, the House of Representatives adopted three articles of impeachment for high crimes and misdemeanors. The first two articles charged Nixon with giving false testimony before the grand jury and the third article charged him with bringing disrepute on the Federal Judiciary.

---

it would have been unusual or novel for judges to have reviewed (as opposed to having participated as parts of the trial bodies in) impeachment actions, because judicial review of impeachment proceedings simply had not occurred prior to the Constitution's drafting and ratification either in the states or in England. To be sure, the Framers did not discuss judicial review much at all, but this was so because they were familiar with judicial review of written documents, including state constitutions and legislation, and, thus, expected there would be judicial review of statutory questions or constitutional challenges to legislation. Given that judicial review of impeachments would have been unprecedented for the Framers, however, it is reasonable to believe that if they had wanted this to have become part of the constitutional design they would have had to make explicit provision for it or at least to have acknowledged or discussed the possibility explicitly.

MICHAEL J. GERHARDT, THE FEDERAL IMPEACHMENT PROCESS: A CONSTITUTIONAL AND HISTORICAL ANALYSIS 127 (Univ. Chicago Press, 2d ed. 2000). Although it is not inconceivable that the Framers could have adopted a completely unprecedented procedure governing impeachment proceedings, as they in fact did with the Senate's supermajority requirement for conviction, Professor Gerhardt's point is well taken that such a radical departure could be expected to have been explicitly reflected in the text of the Constitution. Professor Gerhardt also notes that the Framers made a considered decision not to include impeachment in the list of "heads of jurisdiction" that ultimately came to define the Article III judicial power (art. III, §2). *See id.* at 127–28.

After the House presented the articles to the Senate, the Senate voted to invoke its own Impeachment Rule XI, under which the presiding officer appoints a committee of Senators to "receive evidence and take testimony." Senate Impeachment Rule XI, reprinted in Senate Manual, S. Doc. No. 101-1, 186 (1989).[5] The Senate committee held four days of hearings, during which 10 witnesses, including Nixon, testified. Pursuant to Rule XI, the committee presented the full Senate with a complete transcript of the proceeding and a Report stating the uncontested facts and summarizing the evidence on the contested facts. Nixon and the House impeachment managers submitted extensive final briefs to the full Senate and delivered arguments from the Senate floor during the three hours set aside for oral argument in front of that body. Nixon himself gave a personal appeal, and several Senators posed questions directly to both parties. The Senate voted by more than the constitutionally required two-thirds majority to convict Nixon on the first two articles. The presiding officer then entered judgment removing Nixon from his office as United States District Judge.

Nixon thereafter commenced the present suit, arguing that Senate Rule XI violates the constitutional grant of authority to the Senate to "try" all impeachments because it prohibits the whole Senate from taking part in the evidentiary hearings. See Art. I, §3, cl. 6. Nixon sought a declaratory judgment that his impeachment conviction was void and that his judicial salary and privileges should be reinstated. The District Court held that his claim was nonjusticiable, and the Court of Appeals for the District of Columbia Circuit agreed. We granted certiorari.

A controversy is nonjusticiable—*i.e.*, involves a political question—where there is "a textually demonstrable constitutional commitment of the issue to a coordinate political department; or a lack of judicially discoverable and manageable standards for resolving it...." *Baker v. Carr*, 369 U.S. 186 (1962). But the courts must, in the first instance, interpret the text in question and determine whether and to what extent the issue is textually committed. *See ibid.* As the discussion that follows makes clear, the

---

5. [1] Specifically, Rule XI provides:

"[I]n the trial of any impeachment the Presiding Officer of the Senate, if the Senate so orders, shall appoint a committee of Senators to receive evidence and take testimony at such times and places as the committee may determine, and for such purpose the committee so appointed and the chairman thereof, to be elected by the committee, shall (unless otherwise ordered by the Senate) exercise all the powers and functions conferred upon the Senate and the Presiding Officer of the Senate, respectively, under the rules of procedure and practice in the Senate when sitting on impeachment trials.

"Unless otherwise ordered by the Senate, the rules of procedure and practice in the Senate when sitting on impeachment trials shall govern the procedure and practice of the committee so appointed. The committee so appointed shall report to the Senate in writing a certified copy of the transcript of the proceedings and testimony had and given before such committee, and such report shall be received by the Senate and the evidence so received and the testimony so taken shall be considered to all intents and purposes, subject to the right of the Senate to determine competency, relevancy, and materiality, as having been received and taken before the Senate, but nothing herein shall prevent the Senate from sending for any witness and hearing his testimony in open Senate, or by order of the Senate having the entire trial in open Senate."

concept of a textual commitment to a coordinate political department is not completely separate from the concept of a lack of judicially discoverable and manageable standards for resolving it; the lack of judicially manageable standards may strengthen the conclusion that there is a textually demonstrable commitment to a coordinate branch. * * *

Petitioner argues that the word "try" [implies] that the proceedings must be in the nature of a judicial trial. From there petitioner goes on to argue that this limitation precludes the Senate from delegating to a select committee the task of hearing the testimony of witnesses, as was done pursuant to Senate Rule XI. "'[T]ry' means more than simply 'vote on' or 'review' or 'judge.' In 1787 and today, trying a case means hearing the evidence, not scanning a cold record." Brief for Petitioner 25. Petitioner concludes from this that courts may review whether or not the Senate "tried" him before convicting him.

There are several difficulties with this position which lead us ultimately to reject it. The word "try," both in 1787 and later, has considerably broader meanings than those to which petitioner would limit it. Older dictionaries define try as "[t]o examine" or "[t]o examine as a judge." See 2 S. Johnson, A Dictionary of the English Language (1785). In more modern usage the term has various meanings. For example, try can mean "to examine or investigate judicially," "to conduct the trial of," or "to put to the test by experiment, investigation, or trial." Webster's Third New International Dictionary 2457 (1971). Petitioner submits that "try," as contained in T. Sheridan, Dictionary of the English Language (1796), means "to examine as a judge; to bring before a judicial tribunal." Based on the variety of definitions, however, we cannot say that the Framers used the word "try" as an implied limitation on the method by which the Senate might proceed in trying impeachments. * * *

The conclusion that the use of the word "try" in the first sentence of the Impeachment Trial Clause lacks sufficient precision to afford any judicially manageable standard of review of the Senate's actions is fortified by the existence of the three very specific requirements that the Constitution does impose on the Senate when trying impeachments: The Members must be under oath, a two-thirds vote is required to convict, and the Chief Justice presides when the President is tried. These limitations are quite precise, and their nature suggests that the Framers did not intend to impose additional limitations on the form of the Senate proceedings by the use of the word "try" in the first sentence.

Petitioner devotes only two pages in his brief to negating the significance of the word "sole" in the first sentence of Clause 6. As noted above, that sentence provides that "[t]he Senate shall have the sole Power to try all Impeachments." We think that the word "sole" is of considerable significance. Indeed, the word "sole" appears only one other time in the Constitution—with respect to the House of Representatives' "*sole* Power of Impeachment." Art. I, §2, cl. 5 (emphasis added). The commonsense meaning of the word "sole" is that the Senate alone shall have authority to determine whether an individual should be acquitted or convicted. The dictionary definition bears this out. "Sole" is defined as "having no companion," "solitary," "being the only one," and "functioning ... independently and without assistance or interference." Webster's Third New International Dictionary 2168 (1971). If the courts may review the actions of the Senate in order to determine whether that body "tried" an impeached official, it is difficult to see how the Senate would be "functioning ... independently and without assistance or interference." * * *

Petitioner finally argues that even if significance be attributed to the word "sole" in the first sentence of the Clause, the authority granted is to the Senate, and this means that "the Senate—not the courts, not a lay jury, not a Senate Committee—shall try impeachments." Brief for Petitioner 42. It would be possible to read the first sentence of the Clause this way, but it is not a natural reading. Petitioner's interpretation would bring into judicial purview not merely the sort of claim made by petitioner, but other similar claims based on the conclusion that the word "Senate" has imposed by implication limitations on procedures which the Senate might adopt. Such limitations would be inconsistent with the construction of the Clause as a whole, which, as we have noted, sets out three express limitations in separate sentences.

The history and contemporary understanding of the impeachment provisions support our reading of the constitutional language. The parties do not offer evidence of a single word in the history of the Constitutional Convention or in contemporary commentary that even alludes to the possibility of judicial review in the context of the impeachment powers. This silence is quite meaningful in light of the several explicit references to the availability of judicial review as a check on the Legislature's power with respect to bills of attainder, *ex post facto* laws, and statutes.

The Framers labored over the question of where the impeachment power should lie. Significantly, in at least two considered scenarios the power was placed with the Federal Judiciary. See 1 Farrand 21–22 (Virginia Plan); *id.*, at 244 (New Jersey Plan). Indeed, James Madison and the Committee of Detail proposed that the Supreme Court should have the power to determine impeachments. See 2 *id.*, at 551 (Madison); *id.*, at 178–179, 186 (Committee of Detail). Despite these proposals, the Convention ultimately decided that the Senate would have "the sole Power to try all Impeachments." Art. I, §3, cl. 6. According to Alexander Hamilton, the Senate was the "most fit depositary of this important trust" because its Members are representatives of the people. *See The Federalist No. 65*, p. 440 (J. Cooke ed. 1961). The Supreme Court was not the proper body because the Framers "doubted whether the members of that tribunal would, at all times, be endowed with so eminent a portion of fortitude as would be called for in the execution of so difficult a task" or whether the Court "would possess the degree of credit and authority" to carry out its judgment if it conflicted with the accusation brought by the Legislature—the people's representative. *See id.*, at 441. In addition, the Framers believed the Court was too small in number: "The awful discretion, which a court of impeachments must necessarily have, to doom to honor or to infamy the most confidential and the most distinguished characters of the community, forbids the commitment of the trust to a small number of persons." *Id.*, at 441–442.

There are two additional reasons why the Judiciary, and the Supreme Court in particular, were not chosen to have any role in impeachments. First, the Framers recognized that most likely there would be two sets of proceedings for individuals who commit impeachable offenses—the impeachment trial and a separate criminal trial. In fact, the Constitution explicitly provides for two separate proceedings. See Art. I, §3, cl. 7. The Framers deliberately separated the two forums to avoid raising the specter of bias and to ensure independent judgments:

> "Would it be proper that the persons, who had disposed of his fame and his most valuable rights as a citizen in one trial, should in another trial, for the same offence, be also the disposers of his life and his fortune? Would there not be the greatest reason to apprehend, that error in the first sentence would be the parent of error in the second sentence? That the strong bias of one decision would be apt to overrule the influence of any new lights, which might be brought to vary the complexion of another decision?" *The Federalist No. 65*, p. 442 (J. Cooke ed. 1961).

Certainly judicial review of the Senate's "trial" would introduce the same risk of bias as would participation in the trial itself.

Second, judicial review would be inconsistent with the Framers' insistence that our system be one of checks and balances. In our constitutional system, impeachment was designed to be the *only* check on the Judicial Branch by the Legislature. On the topic of judicial accountability, Hamilton wrote:

> "The precautions for their responsibility are comprised in the article respecting impeachments. They are liable to be impeached for mal-conduct by the house of representatives, and tried by the senate, and if convicted, may be dismissed from office and disqualified for holding any other. *This is the only provision on the point, which is consistent with the necessary independence of the judicial character, and is the only one which we find in our own constitution in respect to our own judges.*" *Id.*, No. 79, at 532–533 (emphasis added).

Judicial involvement in impeachment proceedings, even if only for purposes of judicial review, is counterintuitive because it would eviscerate the "important constitutional check" placed on the Judiciary by the Framers. See *id.*, No. 81, at 545. Nixon's argument would place final reviewing authority with respect to impeachments in the hands of the same body that the impeachment process is meant to regulate.

Nevertheless, Nixon argues that judicial review is necessary in order to place a check on the Legislature. Nixon fears that if the Senate is given unreviewable authority to interpret the Impeachment Trial Clause, there is a grave risk that the Senate will usurp judicial power. The Framers anticipated this objection and created two constitutional safeguards to keep the Senate in check. The first safeguard is that the whole of the impeachment power is divided between the two legislative bodies, with the House given the right to accuse and the Senate given the right to judge. *Id.*, No. 66, at 446. This split of authority "avoids the inconvenience of making the same persons both accusers and judges; and guards against the danger of persecution from the prevalency of a factious spirit in either of those branches." The second safeguard is the two-thirds superma-jority vote requirement. Hamilton explained that "[a]s the concurrence of two-thirds of the senate will be requisite to a condemnation, the security to innocence, from this additional circumstance, will be as complete as itself can desire." *Ibid.*

In addition to the textual commitment argument, we are persuaded that the lack of finality and the difficulty of fashioning relief counsel against justiciability. *See Baker v. Carr*, 369 U.S. at 210. We agree with the Court of Appeals that opening the door of judicial review to the procedures used by the Senate in trying impeachments would "expose the political life of the country to months, or perhaps years, of chaos." 938 F.2d at 246. This lack of finality would manifest itself most dramatically if the President were impeached. The legitimacy of any successor, and hence his effectiveness, would be impaired severely, not merely while the judicial process was running its course, but during any retrial that a differently constituted Senate might conduct if its first judg-ment of conviction were invalidated. Equally uncertain is the question of what relief a court may give other than simply setting aside the judgment of conviction. Could it order the reinstatement of a convicted federal judge, or order Congress to create an additional judgeship if the seat had been filled in the interim?

Petitioner finally contends that a holding of nonjusticiability cannot be reconciled with our opinion in *Powell v. McCormack*, 395 U.S. 486 (1969). The relevant issue in *Powell* was whether courts could review the House of Representatives' conclusion that Powell was "unqualified" to sit as a Member because he had been accused of misappro-priating public funds and abusing the process of the New York courts. We stated that the question of justiciability turned on whether the Constitution committed authority to the House to judge its Members' qualifications, and if so, the extent of that com-mitment. Article I, §5 provides that "Each House shall be the Judge of the Elections, Returns and Qualifications of its own Members." In turn, Art. I, §2 specifies three requirements for membership in the House: The candidate must be at least 25 years of age, a citizen of the United States for no less than seven years, and an inhabitant of the State he is chosen to represent. We held that, in light of the three requirements specified in the Constitution, the word "qualifications"—of which the House was to be the Judge—was of a precise, limited nature. *Id.* at 522.

Our conclusion in *Powell* was based on the fixed meaning of "[q]ualifications" set forth in Art. I, §2. The claim by the House that its power to "be the Judge of the Elec-tions, Returns and Qualifications of its own Members" was a textual commitment of unreviewable authority was defeated by the existence of this separate provision spec-ifying the only qualifications which might be imposed for House membership. The decision as to whether a Member satisfied these qualifications *was* placed with the House, but the decision as to what these qualifications consisted of was not.

In the case before us, there is no separate provision of the Constitution that could be defeated by allowing the Senate final authority to determine the meaning of the word "try" in the Impeachment Trial Clause. We agree with Nixon that courts possess power to review either legislative or executive action that transgresses identifiable textual limits. * * * But we conclude, after exercising that delicate responsibility, that the word "try" in the Impeachment Trial Clause does not provide an identifiable textual limit on the authority which is committed to the Senate.

For the foregoing reasons, the judgment of the Court of Appeals is

Affirmed.

[*Ed. Note: The opinions of Justice Stevens, concurring; Justice White, joined by Justice Blackmun, concurring in the judgment; and Justice Souter, concurring in the judgment, are omitted.*]

Notes and Questions

1. Judicial Review of Impeachment Proceedings After the *Nixon* Case. Does the Supreme Court's "nonjusticiability" holding with respect to the procedures used by the Senate in Judge Nixon's impeachment trial mean that judicial review is never available in challenges to impeachment proceedings? One way to think about that question is to ask what the Court's rationale in *Nixon* was. Did the Court hold that the case presented a political question because "try" "lacks precision" and thus the Senate's procedure did not violate the Constitution? Or did the Court hold that the courts have no authority to determine whether the Senate's procedure violated the Constitution?

What if an impeached official argues that his impeachment fails to identify conduct amounting to "Treason, Bribery, or other high Crimes and Misdemeanors" under Article II, §4? Does the reasoning by which the Supreme Court distinguished *Powell v. McCormack* in Judge Nixon's case suggest that an impeachment challenge based upon the "Treason, Bribery, or other high Crimes and Misdemeanors" language might be subject to judicial review? Read carefully the last two paragraphs of the *Nixon* decision with this question in mind.

On the larger issue of whether some provision for judicial review of compliance with constitutional limitations on impeachment proceedings is desirable, consider the views expressed by one of the leading modern impeachment scholars (views that were expressed prior to the Supreme Court's decision in the *Walter Nixon* case):

> Constitutional limits, as *Powell v. McCormack* again reminds us, are subject to judicial enforcement; and I would urge that judicial review of impeachments is required to protect the other branches from Congress' arbitrary will. It is hardly likely that the Framers, so devoted to "checks and balances," who so painstakingly piled one check of Congress on another, would reject a crucial check at the nerve center of the separation of powers. They scarcely contemplated that their wise precautions must crumble when Congress dons its "judicial" hat, that then Congress would be free to shake the other branches to their very foundations. Before we swallow such consequences, the intention of the Framers to insulate congressional transgressions of the "limits" they imposed upon impeachment should be proved, not casually assumed. The Con-

stitution, said the Supreme Court, condemns "all arbitrary exercise of power;" "there is no place in our constitutional system for the exercise of arbitrary power." The "sole power to try" affords no more exemption from that doctrine than does the sole power to legislate, which, it needs no citation, does not extend to arbitrary acts.

Finally, if it be assumed that the "sole power to try" conferred insulation from review, it must yield to the subsequent Fifth Amendment provision that "no person" shall "be deprived of life, liberty, or property without due process of law." * * * "Due process" has been epitomized by the Court as the "protection of the individual against arbitrary action." One who enters government services does not cease to be a "person" within the Fifth Amendment; and an impeachment for offenses outside constitutional authorization would deny him the protection afforded by "due process." It would be passing strange to conclude that a citizen may invoke the judicial "bulwark" against a twenty-dollar fine but not against an unconstitutional impeachment, removal from and perpetual disqualification to hold federal office. Here protection of the individual coincides with preservation of the separation of powers; and the interests of the assaulted branch, as Judge George Wythe perceived, are one with the interest of the "whole community." Those interests counsel us to give full scope to the "strong American bias in favor of a judicial determination of constitutional and legal issues," and to deny insulation from review of impeachments in defiance of constitutional bounds.

RAOUL BERGER, IMPEACHMENT: THE CONSTITUTIONAL PROBLEMS 125–26 (Harvard Univ. Press/Bantam Books ed. 1974) (footnote references omitted).

2. **The Influence of Partisanship on Impeachment Proceedings.** As noted in the text above, although impeachment by a partisan majority in the House is possible, the history to date suggests that the Framers of the Constitution adequately protected against partisan removal from office with the two-thirds supermajority requirement for conviction in the Senate:

> ... [I]n the nineteenth century, Congress never succeeded in removing any official for purely partisan reasons. That lesson has carried over into the twentieth century. The impeachment threats against both Chief Justice Warren and William O. Douglas never came close to being realized....

In addition, even though partisanship was fervent in Congress throughout most of the 1980s, Judges Hastings and Nixon were each convicted by a Democratically controlled Senate. While Harry Claiborne—a Democrat—was convicted by a Republican-controlled Senate in 1986, his convictions were based on strongly bipartisan votes on three of the four articles of impeachment against him.

In the 1990s, partisanship has been on the rise, culminating in President Clinton's historic impeachment by the House and acquittal by the Senate. Partisanship was clearly evident in the voting patterns in every phase of President

Clinton's impeachment proceedings. For example, the House Judiciary committee approved four impeachment articles against President Clinton in votes that broke along party lines. Moreover, over ninety-five percent of the Republicans in the House voted to impeach the President for perjury and obstruction of justice, while over ninety-five percent of House Democrats voted not to impeach the President. In the Senate, one hundred percent of the votes that were cast to convict the President were cast by Republicans, while all of the Democrats voted to acquit him on the two impeachment articles approved by the House. In addition, the votes on the floors of both the House and the Senate to block a separate vote on censure overwhelmingly followed party divisions. While these voting patterns reflect party biases, they led to acquittal rather than conviction. Thus, they dramatically signal that removal is feasible only if those seeking conviction are able to build bipartisan support for their cause. If an impeached official's party controls enough seats in the Senate to block conviction and if all of those senators remain unified in opposing removal, removal is a practical impossibility.

MICHAEL J. GERHARDT, THE FEDERAL IMPEACHMENT PROCESS: A CONSTITUTIONAL AND HISTORICAL ANALYSIS 135–36 (Univ. Chicago Press, 2d ed. 2000) (footnote references omitted).

Despite this history, is there reason for concern about the role of partisanship in the impeachment process? In the modern era of intense partisanship, is it too easy for a partisan majority to vote an impeachment in the House, yet at the same time is it too difficult to obtain a bipartisan two-thirds majority vote for conviction in the Senate? Do the failed Clinton and Trump impeachments demonstrate that obtaining conviction in the Senate is virtually impossible so long as Senators refuse to cross party lines in an impeachment vote? Does this political reality explain why House Speaker Nancy Pelosi never supported efforts by some members of the House to impeach President George W. Bush? If so, what changed to cause Pelosi to support the impeachment of President Donald Trump?

3. A Different Standard for Judicial Impeachments? Gerald Ford is often criticized for his statement (appearing at the beginning of this Chapter) that an impeachable offense is whatever a majority of the House of Representatives considers it to be at a given moment in history. Commentators take issue with the suggestion that impeachment is a purely political exercise with no fixed standards. Taking this single quote out of the context in which it was originally offered, however, does not do justice to the argument that then-Congressman and House Minority Leader Ford was advancing. Rather than arguing for a standardless impeachment process, Ford was actually advancing a textualist constitutional argument that the standard for bringing impeachment proceedings against federal judges should differ from that applicable to other federal officials:

> [C]ontrary to a widespread misconception, Federal judges and the justices of the Supreme Court are *not* appointed for life. * * * To me the Constitution is perfectly clear about the tenure, or term of office, of all Federal Judges—it is

"during good behaviour." It is implicit in this that when behaviour ceases to be good, the right to hold judicial office ceases also. Thus, we come quickly to the central question: What constitutes "good behaviour" or, conversely, un-good or disqualifying behaviour?

The words employed by the Framers of the Constitution were, as the proceedings of the convention detail, chosen with exceedingly great care and precision. Note, for example, the word "behaviour." It relates to action, not merely to thoughts or opinions; further, it refers not to a single act but to a pattern or continuing sequence of action. We cannot and should not remove a Federal judge for the legal views he holds—this would be as contemptible as to exclude him from serving on the Supreme Court for his ideology or past decisions. Nor should we remove him for a minor or isolated mistake—this does not constitute behaviour in the common meaning.

What we should scrutinize in sitting judges is their continuing pattern of action, their behaviour. The Constitution does not demand that it be "exemplary" or "perfect." But it does have to be "good."

Naturally, there must be orderly procedure for determining whether or not a Federal judge's behaviour is good. The courts, arbiters in most such questions of judgment, cannot judge themselves. So the Founding Fathers vested this ultimate power where the ultimate sovereignty of our system is most directly reflected—in the Congress, in the elected representatives of the people and of the States. * * *

Article II, dealing with the Executive Branch, states in Section 4:

"The President, Vice President, and all civil Officers of the United States, shall be removed from office on impeachment for, and conviction of, Treason, Bribery or other high crimes and misdemeanors."

This has been the most controversial of the Constitutional references to the impeachment process. No consensus exists as to whether, in the case of Federal judges, impeachment must depend upon conviction of one of the two specified crimes of Treason or Bribery or be within the nebulous category of "other high crimes and misdemeanors." There are pages upon pages of learned argument whether the adjective "high" modifies "misdemeanors" as well as "crimes," and over what, indeed, constitutes a "high misdemeanor."

In my view, one of the specific or general offenses cited in Article II is required for removal of the indirectly-elected President and Vice President and all appointed civil officers of the executive branch of the Federal government, whatever their terms of office. But in the case of members of the Judicial Branch, Federal judges and justices, I believe an additional and much stricter requirement is imposed by Article II [sic], namely, "good behaviour."

Finally, and this is a most significant provision, Article One of the Constitution specifies:

"Judgment in Cases of Impeachment shall not extend further than to removal from Office, and disqualification to hold and enjoy any office of honor, Trust or Profit under the United States: but the Party convicted shall nevertheless be liable and subject to Indictment, Trial, Judgment and Punishment, according to Law."

In other words, Impeachment resembles a regular criminal indictment and trial but it is *not* the same thing. It relates solely to the accused's right to hold civil office; not to the many other rights which are his as a citizen and which protect him in a court of law. By pointedly voiding any immunity an accused might claim under the double jeopardy principle, the Framers of the Constitution clearly established that impeachment is a unique political device; designed explicitly to dislodge from public office those who are patently unfit for it, but cannot otherwise be promptly removed.

The distinction between impeachment and ordinary criminal prosecution is again evident when impeachment is made the *sole* exception to the guarantee of Article III, Section 3 that trial of all crimes shall be by jury—perhaps the most fundamental of all Constitutional protections.

We must continually remember that the writers of our Constitution did their work with the experience of the British Crown and Parliament freshly in mind. There is so much that resembles the British system in our Constitution that we sometimes overlook the even sharper differences—one of the sharpest is our divergent view on impeachment.

In Great Britain the House of Lords sits as the court of highest appeal in the land, and upon accusation by Commons the Lords can try, convict and punish *any* impeached subject—private person or official—with any lawful penalty for his crime—including death.

Our Constitution, on the contrary, provides only the relatively mild penalties of removal from Office, and disqualification for future office—the worst punishment the U.S. Senate can mete out is *both* removal and disqualification.

Moreover, to make sure impeachment would not be frivolously attempted or easily abused, and further to protect officeholders against political reprisal, the Constitution requires a two-thirds vote of the Senate to convict.

With this brief review of the law, of the Constitutional background for impeachment, I have endeavored to correct two common misconceptions: first, that Federal judges are appointed for life and, second, that they can be removed only by being convicted, with all ordinary protections and presumptions of innocence to which an accused is entitled, of violating the law.

This is not the case. Federal judges can be and have been impeached for improper personal habits such as chronic intoxication on the bench, and one of the charges brought against President Andrew Johnson was that he delivered "intemperate, inflammatory and scandalous harangues."

I have studied the principal impeachment actions that have been initiated over the years and frankly, there are too few cases to make very good law. About the only thing the authorities can agree upon in recent history, though it was hotly argued up to President Johnson's impeachment and the trial of Judge Swayne, is that an offense need *not* be indictable to be impeachable. In other words, something less than a criminal dereliction of duty may nevertheless be sufficient grounds for impeachment and removal from public office.

What, then, is an impeachable offense?

The only honest answer is that an impeachable offense is whatever a majority of the House of Representatives considers to be at a given moment in history; conviction results from whatever offense or offenses two-thirds of the other body considers to be sufficiently serious to require removal of the accused from office. Again, the historical context and political climate are important; there are few fixed principles among the handful of precedents.

I think it is fair to come to one conclusion, however, from our history of impeachments: a higher standard *is* expected of Federal judges than of any other "civil Officers" of the United States. The President and Vice President, and all persons holding office at the pleasure of the President, can be thrown out of office by the voters at least every four years. To remove them in midterm (it has been tried only twice and never done) would indeed require crimes of the magnitude of treason and bribery. Other elective officials, such as Members of the Congress, are so vulnerable to public displeasure that their removal by the complicated impeachment route has not even been tried since 1790. But nine Federal judges, including one Associate Justice of the Supreme Court, have been impeached by this House and tried by the Senate; four were acquitted; four convicted and removed from office; and one resigned during trial and the impeachment was dismissed.

House Floor Speech: Impeach Justice Douglas (April 15, 1970), Box D29, Gerald R. Ford Congressional Papers, Gerald R. Ford Library.

What do you think of Ford's argument? How important is the "during good Behaviour" language in Article III, §1? For contemporaneous scholarly analysis of the issues Ford raised, see John D. Feerick, *Impeaching Federal Judges: A Study of the Constitutional Provisions*, 39 FORDHAM L. REV. 1 (1970), and Frank Thompson & Daniel C. Pollitt, *Impeachment of Federal Judges: An Historical Overview*, 49 N.C. L. REV. 87 (1970). For more recent analyses of the legal issues involved in the impeachment of federal judges, see Warren S. Grimes, *Hundred-Ton-Gun Control: Preserving Impeachment as the Exclusive Removal Mechanism for Federal Judges*, 38 U.C.L.A. L. REV. 1209 (1991), and Peter M. Shane, *Who May Discipline or Remove Federal Judges?: A Constitutional Analysis*, 142 U. PA. L. REV. 209 (1993).

4. Should Cabinet Officers Ever Be Impeached? As the portion of Gerald Ford's statement that is reproduced in Note 3 above suggests, impeachment is generally not considered necessary for cabinet officers and other political appointees who serve at the pleasure of the President because the people can effectively remove those officials through the presidential election process. Congress has impeached a cabinet-level official on only one occasion. That effort, against Secretary of War William W. Belknap in 1876, was unsuccessful (although the failure to convict Belknap in the Senate may have been in part due to his resignation):

SECRETARY OF WAR WILLIAM W. BELKNAP (1876)

a. Proceedings in the House

In 1876 the Committee on Expenditures in the War Department unanimously recommended Impeachment of Secretary Belknap "for high crimes and misdemeanors while in office," and the House unanimously adopted the resolution.

b. Articles of Impeachment

Five articles of impeachment were drafted by the Judiciary Committee and adopted by the House, all relating to Belknap's allegedly corrupt appointment of a military post trader. The House agreed to the articles as a group, without voting separately on each.

Article I charged Belknap with "high crimes and misdemeanors in office" for unlawfully receiving sums of money, in consideration for the appointment, made by him as Secretary of War.

Article II charged Belknap with a "high misdemeanor in office" for "willfully, corruptly, and unlawfully" taking and receiving money in return for the continued maintenance of the post trader.

Article III charged that Belknap was "criminally disregarding his duty as Secretary of War, and barely prostituting his high office to his lust for private gain," when he "unlawfully and corruptly" continued his appointee in office, "to the great injury and damage of the officers and soldiers of the United States" stationed at the military post. The maintenance of the trader was also alleged to be "against public policy, and to the great disgrace and detriment of the public service."

Article IV alleged seventeen separate specifications relating to Belknap's appointment and continuance in office of the post trader.

Article V enumerated the instances in which Belknap or his wife had corruptly received "divert large sums of money."

c. Proceedings in the Senate

The Senate failed to convict Belknap on any of the articles, although majorities favored conviction, in votes ranging from 35–25 to 37–25.

d. Miscellaneous

In the Senate trial, it was argued that, because Belknap had resigned prior to his impeachment the case should be dropped. The Senate, by a vote of 37 to 29, decided that Belknap was amenable to trial by impeachment. Twenty-two of the Senator[s] voting not guilty on each article, nevertheless indicated that in their view the Senate had no jurisdiction.

Constitutional Grounds for Presidential Impeachment, Report by the Staff of the Committee on the Judiciary, House of Representatives, Appendix B, "American Impeachment Cases," 49–50 (Feb. 1974) (footnote references omitted).

Despite the fact that no cabinet-level official has ever been successfully removed from office through impeachment, and despite the passage of almost a century and a half since the impeachment proceedings against Secretary Belknap, impeachment nonetheless remains at least theoretically available as a means to remove a cabinet official in an appropriate case. When, if ever, should impeachment be used against a cabinet-level official? Consider in this regard a May 2007 op-ed by law professor Frank Bowman, calling for the impeachment of then-Attorney General Alberto Gonzales:

> If Alberto Gonzales will not resign, Congress should impeach him. Article II of the Constitution grants Congress the power to impeach "the president, the vice president and all civil officers of the United States." The phrase "civil officers" includes the members of the cabinet (one of whom, Secretary of War William Belknap, was impeached in 1876).
>
> Impeachment is in bad odor in these post-Clinton days. It needn't be. Though provoked by individual misconduct, the power to impeach is at bottom a tool granted Congress to defend the constitutional order. Mr. Gonzales's behavior in the United States attorney affair is of a piece with his role as facilitator of this administration's claims of unreviewable executive power.
>
> A cabinet officer, like a judge or a president, may be impeached only for commission of "high crimes and misdemeanors." But as the Nixon and Clinton impeachment debates reminded us, that constitutional phrase embraces not only indictable crimes but "conduct ... grossly incompatible with the office held and subversive of that office and of our constitutional system of government." * * *
>
> The right of Congress to demand explanations imposes on the president, and on inferior executive officers who speak for him, the obligation to be truthful. An attorney general called before Congress to discuss the workings of the Justice Department can claim the protection of "executive privilege" and, if challenged, can defend the (doubtful) legitimacy of such a claim in the courts. But having elected to testify, he has no right to lie, either by affirmatively misrepresenting facts or by falsely claiming not to remember events. Lying to Congress is a felony—actually three felonies: perjury, false statements and obstruction of justice.
>
> A false claim not to remember is just as much a lie as a conscious misrepresentation of a fact one remembers well. Instances of phony forgetfulness seem to abound throughout Mr. Gonzales's testimony, but his claim to have no memory of the November Justice department meeting at which he authorized

the attorney firings left even Republican stalwarts like Jeff Sessions of Alabama gaping in incredulity. The truth is almost surely that Mr. Gonzales's forgetfulness is feigned—a calculated ploy to block legitimate Congressional inquiry into questionable decisions made by the Department of Justice, White House officials and, quite possibly, the president himself.

Even if perjury were not a felony, lying to Congress has always been understood to be an impeachable offense. As James Iredell, later a Supreme Court justice, said in 1788 during the debate over the impeachment clause, "The president must certainly be punishable for giving false information to the Senate." The same is true of the president's appointees.

The president may yet yield and send Mr. Gonzales packing. If not, Democrats may decide that to impeach Alberto Gonzales would be politically unwise. But before dismissing the possibility of impeachment, Congress should recognize that the issue here goes deeper than the misbehavior of one man. The real question is whether Republicans and Democrats are prepared to defend the constitutional authority of Congress against the implicit claim of an administration that it can do what it pleases and, when called to account, send an attorney general of the United States to Capitol Hill to commit amnesia on its behalf.

Frank Bowman, *He's Impeachable, You Know*, N.Y. TIMES (May 3, 2007).

Attorney General Gonzales resigned in September 2007 as congressional criticism mounted over testimony he had provided concerning the forced resignations of a number of U.S. Attorneys in 2006. (The U.S. Attorneys matter is one of the topics of Chapter 4; the consequences of giving false or misleading testimony in congressional proceedings is one of the topics of Chapter 9.) What do you think of Professor Bowman's argument? When, if ever, should Congress seek to impeach a cabinet-level official? What about lower-level officials? Would you distinguish between senior political appointees and career government employees, or does your answer turn solely upon the nature of the conduct involved and not upon the status of the official in question? Consider in your analysis the following explanation of the relationship between impeachment and presidential removal of executive-branch officials:

> Impeachment, Madison explained, had a special purpose: it was designed to reach a bad officer sheltered by the President, who "could be removed even against the will of the President; so that the declaration in the Constitution was intended as a supplemental security for the good behavior of the public officers." This point was made again and again. Impeachment, said Elias Boudinot, enables the House "to pull down an improper officer, although he should be supported by all the power of the Executive." "Favoritism," said Abraham Baldwin, also a Framer, could not protect a man from the power of the House "in despite of the President" to "drag him from his place." The point bears emphasis because it reveals, first, that the Founders had learned from the English history of the need for power to remove evil favorites, presidential no less

than royal, and also that impeachment was in essence not an exclusive medium of removal but a breach in the separation of powers for the purpose of "supplemental security," "an exception to a principle."

RAOUL BERGER, IMPEACHMENT: THE CONSTITUTIONAL PROBLEMS 146–47 (Harvard Univ. Press/Bantam Books ed. 1974) (footnote references omitted).

Impeachment and Parallel Criminal Proceedings: President Richard M. Nixon

No president has been removed from office by an impeachment vote in the Senate, and three presidents—Andrew Johnson, Bill Clinton, and Donald Trump (twice)—have been acquitted in impeachment trials in the Senate. This summary is incomplete, however, because it omits the exception that proves the rule of presidential removal by impeachment—the resignation of President Richard Nixon in the face of impeachment proceedings arising out of the Watergate scandal. Watergate is the topic of Chapter 3, so this section will not reexamine the details of the Watergate scandal and will instead focus on selected issues relating to the impeachment proceedings against President Nixon.

The House Judiciary Committee approved three articles of impeachment against President Nixon, but Nixon resigned before the full House voted on those articles. Thus, Nixon was not impeached, but the impeachment articles that were approved by the Committee are important and instructive, particularly as a point of comparison with the later impeachments of Bill Clinton and Donald Trump.

Articles of Impeachment against President Richard M. Nixon

Adopted by the House Judiciary Committee, July 27, 1974

RESOLUTION

Impeaching Richard M. Nixon, President of the United States, of high crimes and misdemeanors.

Resolved, That Richard M. Nixon, President of the United States, is impeached for high crimes and misdemeanors, and that the following articles of impeachment be exhibited to the Senate:

Articles of impeachment exhibited by the House of Representatives of the United States of America in the name of itself and of all of the people of the United States of America, against Richard M. Nixon, President of the United States of America, in maintenance and support of its impeachment against him for high crimes and misdemeanors.

ARTICLE I

In his conduct of the office of President of the United States, Richard M. Nixon, in violation of his constitutional oath faithfully to execute the office of President of the

United States and, to the best of his ability, preserve, protect, and defend the Constitution of the United States, and in violation of his constitutional duty to take care that the laws be faithfully executed, has prevented, obstructed, and impeded the administration of justice, in that:

On June 17, 1972, and prior thereto, agents of the Committee for the Re-election of the President committed unlawful entry of the headquarters of the Democratic National Committee in Washington, District of Columbia, for the purpose of securing political intelligence. Subsequent thereto, Richard M. Nixon, using the powers of his high office, engaged personally and through his close subordinates and agents, in a course of conduct or plan designed to delay, impede, and obstruct the investigation of such illegal entry; to cover up, conceal and protect those responsible; and to conceal the existence and scope of other unlawful covert activities.

The means used to implement this course of conduct or plan included one or more of the following:

1. making false or misleading statements to lawfully authorized investigative officers and employees of the United States;

2. withholding relevant and material evidence or information from lawfully authorized investigative officers and employees of the United States;

3. approving, condoning, acquiescing in, and counselling witnesses with respect to the giving of false or misleading statements to lawfully authorized investigative officers and employees of the United States and false or misleading testimony in duly instituted judicial and congressional proceedings;

4. interfering or endeavoring to interfere with the conduct of investigations by the Department of Justice of the United States, the Federal Bureau of Investigation, the office of Watergate Special Prosecution Force, and Congressional Committees;

5. approving, condoning, and acquiescing in, the surreptitious payment of substantial sums of money for the purpose of obtaining the silence or influencing the testimony of witnesses, potential witnesses or individuals who participated in such unlawful entry and other illegal activities;

6. endeavoring to misuse the Central Intelligence Agency, an agency of the United States;

7. disseminating information received from officers of the Department of Justice of the United States to subjects of investigations conducted by lawfully authorized investigative officers and employees of the United States, for the purpose of aiding and assisting such subjects in their attempts to avoid criminal liability;

8. making or causing to be made false or misleading public statements for the purpose of deceiving the people of the United States into believing that a thorough and complete investigation had been conducted with respect to allegations of misconduct on the part of personnel of the executive branch of the United States

and personnel of the Committee for the Re-election of the President, and that there was no involvement of such personnel in such misconduct: or

9. endeavoring to cause prospective defendants, and individuals duly tried and convicted, to expect favored treatment and consideration in return for their silence or false testimony, or rewarding individuals for their silence or false testimony.

In all of this, Richard M. Nixon has acted in a manner contrary to his trust as President and subversive of constitutional government, to the great prejudice of the cause of law and justice and to the manifest injury of the people of the United States.

Wherefore Richard M. Nixon, by such conduct, warrants impeachment and trial, and removal from office.

ARTICLE II

Using the powers of the office of President of the United States, Richard M. Nixon, in violation of his constitutional oath faithfully to execute the office of President of the United States and, to the best of his ability, preserve, protect, and defend the Constitution of the United States, and in disregard of his constitutional duty to take care that the laws be faithfully executed, has repeatedly engaged in conduct violating the constitutional rights of citizens, impairing the due and proper administration of justice and the conduct of lawful inquiries, or contravening the laws governing agencies of the executive branch and the purposes of these agencies.

This conduct has included one or more of the following:

1. He has, acting personally and through his subordinates and agents, endeavored to obtain from the Internal Revenue Service, in violation of the constitutional rights of citizens, confidential information contained in income tax returns for purposes not authorized by law, and to cause, in violation of the constitutional rights of citizens, income tax audits or other income tax investigations to be initiated or conducted in a discriminatory manner.

2. He misused the Federal Bureau of Investigation, the Secret Service, and other executive personnel, in violation or disregard of the constitutional rights of citizens, by directing or authorizing such agencies or personnel to conduct or continue electronic surveillance or other investigations for purposes unrelated to national security, the enforcement of laws, or any other lawful function of his office; he did direct, authorize, or permit the use of information obtained thereby for purposes unrelated to national security, the enforcement of laws, or any other lawful function of his office; and he did direct the concealment of certain records made by the Federal Bureau of Investigation of electronic surveillance.

3. He has, acting personally and through his subordinates and agents, in violation or disregard of the constitutional rights of citizens, authorized and permitted to be maintained a secret investigative unit within the office of the President, financed in part with money derived from campaign contributions, which unlawfully utilized the resources of the Central Intelligence Agency, engaged in covert

and unlawful activities, and attempted to prejudice the constitutional right of an accused to a fair trial.

4. He has failed to take care that the laws were faithfully executed by failing to act when he knew or had reason to know that his close subordinates endeavored to impede and frustrate lawful inquiries by duly constituted executive, judicial and legislative entities concerning the unlawful entry into the headquarters of the Democratic National Committee, and the cover-up thereof, and concerning other unlawful activities including those relating to the confirmation of Richard Kleindienst as Attorney General of the United States, the electronic surveillance of private citizens, the break-in into the offices of Dr. Lewis Fielding, and the campaign financing practices of the Committee to Re-elect the President.

5. In disregard of the rule of law, he knowingly misused the executive power by interfering with agencies of the executive branch, including the Federal Bureau of Investigation, the Criminal Division, and the Office of Watergate Special Prosecution Force, of the Department of Justice, and the Central Intelligence Agency, in violation of his duty to take care that the laws be faithfully executed.

In all of this, Richard M. Nixon has acted in a manner contrary to his trust as President and subversive of constitutional government, to the great prejudice of the cause of law and justice and to the manifest injury of the people of the United States.

Wherefore Richard M. Nixon, by such conduct, warrants impeachment and trial, and removal from office.

ARTICLE III

In his conduct of the office of President of the United States, Richard M. Nixon, contrary to his oath faithfully to execute the office of President of the United States and, to the best of his ability, preserve, protect, and defend the Constitution of the United States, and in violation of his constitutional duty to take care that the laws be faithfully executed, has failed without lawful cause or excuse to produce papers and things as directed by duly authorized subpoenas issued by the Committee on the Judiciary of the House of Representatives on April 11, 1974, May 15, 1974, May 30, 1974, and June 24, 1974, and willfully disobeyed such subpoenas. The subpoenaed papers and things were deemed necessary by the Committee in order to resolve by direct evidence fundamental, factual questions relating to Presidential direction, knowledge or approval of actions demonstrated by other evidence to be substantial grounds for impeachment of the President. In refusing to produce these papers and things Richard M. Nixon, substituting his judgment as to what materials were necessary for the inquiry, interposed the powers of the Presidency against the the lawful subpoenas of the House of Representatives, thereby assuming to himself functions and judgments necessary to the exercise of the sole power of impeachment vested by the Constitution in the House of Representatives.

In all of this, Richard M. Nixon has acted in a manner contrary to his trust as President and subversive of constitutional government, to the great prejudice of the cause of law and justice, and to the manifest injury of the people of the United States.

Wherefore, Richard M. Nixon, by such conduct, warrants impeachment and trial, and removal from office.

————

Because Watergate was the subject of a criminal investigation conducted by a Department of Justice special prosecutor (initially Archibald Cox, fired by Nixon in the infamous "Saturday Night Massacre" discussed in Chapter 3, and then Cox's successor, Leon Jaworski), the Nixon impeachment proceedings focused national attention on the relationship between impeachment proceedings and simultaneous criminal-justice-system proceedings. Two aspects of this unprecedented circumstance of "parallel proceedings" warrant further consideration. One important unresolved issue is the relationship between impeachment and indictment of a sitting President, and more specifically whether a sitting President can be indicted without first having been impeached. (As discussed at the beginning of this Chapter, the Constitution in Article I, §3 makes clear that an impeached president "shall nevertheless be liable and subject to Indictment, Trial, Judgment and Punishment, according to Law." Therefore, an impeached president can be indicted, tried, and convicted based upon the same conduct that supported impeachment.) The second important issue presented by the Nixon impeachment proceedings was what should be the relationship between the special prosecutor's investigation and the impeachment proceedings in the House of Representatives, and, more specifically, what assistance and support, if any, the special prosecutor should provide to the impeachment proceedings in the House. Both issues were addressed in the Watergate Special Prosecution Force Report issued in October 1975:

Actions Related to President Nixon's Possible Criminal Liability

Watergate Special Prosecution Force Report 119–32 (Oct. 1975)

Determining Whether to Seek the President's Indictment

Counsel to the Special Prosecutor and his staff conducted extensive legal research to resolve whether the Constitution contemplated the impeachment process as the exclusive means for adjudicating the culpability of an incumbent President. As they found, that issue had been largely ignored or only obliquely alluded to at the time of the Constitutional Convention and in the ensuing 186 years.

The question of the President's indictability, which was viewed in the office as obviously momentous in terms of its consequences for the country, resulted in an intense debate among members of the Special Prosecutor's staff. After examining the Constitution, relevant case law, and the historical and contemporary arguments, there appeared to be no textual basis in the Constitution for concluding that an incumbent President—any more than any other Federal official subject to the impeachment process—is immune from the ordinary process of criminal law prior to impeachment and removal from office. Consequently, one approach was that, if a *prima facie* case of obstruction of justice existed on the basis of known evidence, an indictment of the President would be essential to vindicate the principles that there should be equal justice for all and that no one is above the law. This view held that a failure to indict the incumbent President, in the face of evidence of his criminal activity, would seriously impair the integrity of the criminal process. Such impairment would be all the more severe because the President was the very man in whom the Constitution reposes the final obligation to ensure that the law is obeyed and enforced, and because his actions appeared to have been designed to place himself and other individuals beyond the reach of the law.

The other approach was that the impeachment process should take precedence over a criminal indictment because the Constitution was ambivalent on this point and an indictment provoking a necessarily lengthy legal proceeding would either compel the President's resignation or substantially cripple his ability to function effectively in the domestic and foreign fields as the Nation's Chief Executive Officer. Those consequences, it was argued, should result from the impeachment mechanism explicitly provided by the Constitution, a mechanism in which the elected representatives of the public conduct preliminary inquiries and, in the event of the filing of a bill of impeachment of the President, a trial based upon all the facts. Any indictment could then be brought after those proceedings were completed. Under this view, a single, unelected prosecutor should be hesitant to invoke the criminal justice system, prior to the completion of pending impeachment hearings, especially when the constitutionality of such a course remained in doubt. There was also concern that an indictment of the President would suspend the impeachment proceedings until after his criminal trial.

The Special Prosecutor concluded that the Supreme Court, if presented with the question, would not uphold an indictment of the President for the crimes of which he would be accused. Accordingly, he thought it would not be responsible conduct to recommend that the grand jury return an indictment against the President, particularly when the impeachment proceedings were ongoing. Since the Special Prosecutor's charter mandated his investigating allegations against the President and authorized reports to the Congress, he then examined the legality of a grand jury presentment concerning President Nixon, and the possible transmission of evidence pertinent to the question of his involvement to the House of Representatives. After additional legal research and deliberation within the office, the Special Prosecutor determined that this course of action would be both constitutional and appropriate. It was his view that the House of Representatives, in the first instance, was the appropriate body under the Constitution to examine evidence relating to the president, and to determine whether he should be charged with conduct justifying impeachment and removal from office. Many alternatives for the form of such a report were considered; the possibilities included a presentment detailing all the evidence in narrative form, a conclusory summary of grand jury findings of fact and conclusions of law, or a transmission of relevant witness testimony without comment or conclusions. The Special Prosecutor advised the grand jury to submit a report with evidence relating to the President to Judge Sirica, and to recommend that the judge transmit such evidence to the House Judiciary Committee.

In order to avoid any claim of unilateral action on the part of the Special Prosecutor in the event that he should name the President as a co-conspirator during pre-trial proceedings in the Watergate case, Jaworski also sought the grand jury's judgment on his opinion that the President was a member of the charged conspiracy and that evidentiary considerations at a cover-up trial mandated naming the President as a participant in the conspiracy. Thus, when the grand jury voted to indict seven men in connection with the Watergate cover-up, it also voted to name Richard M. Nixon as one of the 18 unindicted co-conspirators in an alleged conspiracy to obstruct justice.

At the time the grand jury handed up the indictment on March 1, it also submitted a Report and Recommendation advising the Chief Judge that it "had heard evidence that it regards as having a material bearing on matters within the primary jurisdiction" of the House Judiciary Committee in its impeachment inquiry, but that it ought "to defer to the House of Representatives" in determining what action was warranted by the evidence. The grand jury recommended that the sealed materials accompanying the report be transmitted to the House Judiciary Committee. The materials included 12 recordings of Presidential conversations and testimony pertinent to President Nixon's involvement in the Watergate matter.

In a March 6 hearing before Judge Sirica on the disposition of the grand jury report, James St. Clair announced for the President that he would furnish to the Judiciary Committee all the materials that had previously been furnished to the Special Prosecutor's office. The Special Prosecutor's counsel argued that the materials the White House had agreed to supply to the Committee were not necessarily the same as those the grand jury asked the court to transmit to the Committee. John Doar and Albert Jenner, appearing on behalf of the Committee, requested that the Court deliver the grand jury report to enable the Committee to discharge its constitutional obligation with the aid of the best information available. In a March 8 letter from Committee Chairman Peter Rodino to Judge Sirica, Rodino stated that a unanimous resolution of the Committee reflected its view that in constitutional terms it would be unthinkable if the material was kept from the House of Representatives. Judge Sirica ruled on March 18 that the grand jury report and accompanying materials should be delivered to the Committee.

On March 20, two defendants named in the Watergate cover-up indictment, H.R. Haldeman and Gordon Strachan, filed a petition for a writ of mandamus with the Court of Appeals to block the delivery of the materials to the Committee. The next day, the Court denied the petition, stating that the President, as the focus of the grand jury report and the person who presumably would have the greatest interest in its disposition, interposed no objection to the District Court's action. As a result, the report was delivered to the House Judiciary Committee on March 26. In addition, the President delivered to the Committee the materials he had given to the Special Prosecutor. These included 12 recordings related to Watergate, seven related to ITT, dairy, and "Plumbers" matters, and numerous documents relevant to these areas.

Cooperation with the House Judiciary Committee

H. Res. 803, adopted by the House of Representatives on February 6, by a vote of 410 to 4, explicitly authorized the House Judiciary Committee to investigate whether grounds existed for the impeachment of Richard Nixon. The resolution also granted the Committee the power of subpoena for its investigation. Preliminary discussions on liaison between the staff of the House Judiciary Committee and the Special Prosecutor's office had been held more than two months earlier. In a meeting on November 20, 1973, between attorneys from the Special Prosecutor's office and the Judiciary Committee, Deputy Special Prosecutor Ruth had assured the Committee of WSPF's cooperation so long as such cooperation did not interfere with WSPF investigations and trials and investigative sources were protected. * * *

The Special Prosecutor's office also supplied information directly to the Committee throughout the impeachment inquiry. The basis for WSPF's action was set forth in a May 8 letter from Jaworski to Doar in which the Special Prosecutor stated his understanding that, although WSPF was being asked to provide the information voluntarily, the Committee was prepared to fulfill its responsibilities by issuing subpoenas. On the basis of this understanding, Jaworski determined that his office would furnish such relevant information requested by the Committee as it possessed, within the bounds of relevant laws and regulations. Jaworski also informed Doar that WSPF staff attorneys would contact Committee staff attorneys to coordinate the furnishing of requested information.

On May 9, Ruth notified WSPF task force leaders of the procedures to be followed in providing information to the Committee: there could be no disclosure of testimony presented before a grand jury; no disclosure of information received from the White House (Doar was arranging to receive from St. Clair what the White House had supplied to the Special Prosecutor); documentary evidence would be furnished only when the source of the information consented (the same procedure used with the Senate Select Committee); only information directly related to possible Presidential involvement would be furnished; confidentiality of witnesses would be preserved if necessary; and no notes of office interviews were to be supplied. Ruth further directed that WSPF staff members recommend the name of witnesses to be interviewed by the Committee and the topics to be covered in such interviews. * * *

As a result of the Committee's investigation, on June 18 and 19, 1974, Doar presented to the Committee a "Statement of Information" containing evidence on the events that led to the appointment of Elliot Richardson as Attorney General, the creation of the Watergate Special Prosecution Force, the appointment of Archibald Cox, the authority and jurisdiction of the Special Prosecutor's office, the investigations initiated by the Special Prosecutor and the response of President Nixon to those investigations, the issuance of subpoenas to the President, the litigation arising out of his refusal to comply with those subpoenas, the firing of Cox, the appointment of Leon Jaworski, and the court hearings on the 18½ minute erasure on the June 20, 1972, tape.

On July 29, by a vote of 28 to 10, the Committee adopted a second Article of Impeachment against President Nixon. Article II charged that the President had:

> ... repeatedly engaged in conduct violating the constitutional rights of citizens, impairing the due and proper administration of justice and the conduct

of lawful inquiries, or contravening the laws governing agencies of the executive branch and the purposes of these agencies.

As an example of such conduct, the Committee stated:

> In disregard of the rule of law, he knowingly misused the executive power by interfering with agencies of the executive branch, including the Federal Bureau of Investigation, the Criminal Division and the Office of Watergate Special Prosecution Force, of the Department of Justice, and the Central Intelligence Agency, in violation of his duty to take care that the laws be faithfully executed.

As supporting evidence for its conclusion that President Nixon had impeded the Special Prosecutor's investigation, the Committee noted the White House delay in making information available to the Special Prosecutor and, in some cases, withholding documents, the concealment of the White House taping system, the firing of Cox, and the refusal to cooperate with Jaworski.

The President's Resignation; Further Consideration of Indictment

On July 24, 1974, the Supreme Court announced its unanimous decision in *United States v. Nixon* and ordered the President to turn over additional tape recordings of Presidential conversations subpoenaed for use in the Watergate cover-up trial then scheduled to begin in September. Among the subpoenaed conversations were those of June 23, 1972, between H.R. Haldeman and the President. On Monday, August 5, St. Clair and Alexander Haig, the President's chief of staff, telephoned Jaworski to inform him that the June 23 tape recording revealed the President's early knowledge of the Watergate cover-up and a possible violation of law in his misuse of a Federal agency. On Thursday, August 8, Jaworski met with Haig, at the latter's request. Jaworski later told members of his staff that Haig had called the meeting to inform him of the President's decision to resign, but that during the meeting no promises or understandings of any kind had been either requested or offered. In a statement issued immediately after the President's resignation announcement, the Special Prosecutor said:

> There has been no agreement or understanding of any sort between the President or his representatives and the Special Prosecutor relating in any way to the President's resignation.

> The Special Prosecutor's Office was not asked for any such agreement or understanding and offered none. Although I was informed of the President's decision this afternoon, my office did not participate in any way in the President's decision to resign.

President Nixon's resignation became effective at noon on Friday, August 9. Shortly thereafter Jaworski was contacted by Herbert J. Miller, Jr., an attorney for the former President. During several meetings between Jaworski and Miller in August, Miller argued that the former President should not be indicted because the massive publicity resulting from both the impeachment proceedings and his resignation would make it impossible to select an impartial jury. On September 4, Miller submitted to the Special Prosecutor an extensive memorandum supporting this view. Research by the WSPF staff disputed Miller's position, however, and Jaworski concluded that any prosecution of the former President might require a nine-month to one-year delay in bringing a case to trial in order to allow existing and foreseeable pre-trial publicity to dissipate.

Another question raised in the wake of the resignation was whether the former President should be included as a defendant in the Watergate cover-up case. Jaworski invited members of WSPF's legal staff to submit their views on this question and other issues surrounding possible criminal action against the former President, and many did. Since it was evident to the Special Prosecutor and to staff members that inclusion of the former President would entail considerable if not indefinite delay of the trial, which was then scheduled to begin on October 1, Jaworski decided against such inclusion. He also decided to defer any criminal action against the former President until the cover-up jury was sequestered, to eliminate the possibility that the jurors might be subjected to additional pre-trial publicity.

The Pardon * * *

On September 8 President Ford granted a "full, free and absolute" pardon to former President Nixon for all offenses committed during Mr. Nixon's tenure as President (January 20, 1969, through August 9, 1974). President Ford's action generated extensive discussion and legal research by WSPF.

This focused upon two possible theories to challenge the pardon. First, was it invalid because it preceded any indictment or conviction? And second, despite the President's inherent constitutional powers to control all law enforcement decisions, whether by directing that an investigation not proceed, ordering an indictment dismissed, or granting a pardon, had the president voluntarily bound himself through the Special Prosecutor's charter not to exercise his constitutional pardon powers when the exercise of that power would interfere with the independent judgment of the Special Prosecutor to decide whom to prosecute?

* * * [A]fter the Watergate trial jury had been sequestered, [Special Prosecutor Jaworski] stated the basis of his decision not to challenge the validity of the pardon in a letter to Attorney General William Saxbe, dated October 12, which accompanied his letter of resignation as Special Prosecutor:

> Although not appropriate for comment until after the sequestering of the jury in *United States v. Mitchell, et al.*, in view of suggestions that an indictment be returned against former President Richard M. Nixon questioning the validity of the pardon granted him, I think it proper that I express to you my views on this subject to dispel any thought that there may be some relation between my resignation and that issue.
>
> As you realize, one of my responsibilities, not only as an officer of the court, but as a prosecutor, as well, is not to take a position in which I lack faith or which my judgment dictates is not supported by probable cause. The provision in the Constitution investing the President with the right to grant pardons, and the recognition by the Untied States Supreme Court that a pardon may be

granted prior to the filing of charges are so clear, in my opinion, as not to admit of doubt. Philip Lacovara, then Counsel to the Special Prosecutor, by written memorandum on file in this office, came to the same conclusion, pointing out that: "… the pardon power can be exercised at any time after a federal crime has been committed and it is not necessary that there be any criminal proceedings pending. In fact, the pardon power has been used frequently to relieve federal offenders of criminal liability and other penalties and disabilities attaching to their offenses even where no criminal proceedings against the individual are contemplated."

I have also concluded, after thorough study that there is nothing in the charter and guidelines appertaining to the office of the Special Prosecutor that impairs or curtails the president's free exercise of the constitutional right of pardon. * * *

Thus, in light of these conclusions, for me to procure an indictment of Richard M. Nixon for the sole purpose of generating a purported court test on the legality of the pardon, would constitute a spurious proceeding in which I had no faith; in fact, it would be tantamount to unprofessional conduct and violative of my responsibility as prosecutor and officer of the court.

Notes and Questions

1. The Indictment Question—Should a Sitting President Be Subject to Indictment Prior to Impeachment? How persuasive do you find the argument of some members of the Watergate Special Prosecutor's office, described above, that "an indictment of the President would be essential to vindicate the principles that there should be equal justice for all and that no one is above the law"? Although the text of the Constitution arguably is ambiguous, does the combination of detailed procedures for impeachment and explicit recognition that the impeached officer "shall nevertheless be liable and subject to Indictment, Trial, Judgment and Punishment, according to Law" suggest that the Framers intended that impeachment and removal from office would precede any criminal proceedings?

The constitutional text makes no distinction between the President and the other "civil Officers" subject to impeachment, in terms of whether impeachment must be pursued before the commencement of criminal proceedings. Should the President *alone* be immune from indictment while he is in office? Of what import, if any, is the fact that several federal judges have been impeached *after* they were convicted of criminal conduct? Vice President Spiro Agnew was indicted while in office, despite his protests that his accusers should have had to pursue impeachment. Professor Michael J. Gerhardt has argued that the historical practice of indicting some impeachable officials indicates that indictment is available against a sitting President as well: "Federal prosecutors in the Justice Department have prosecuted impeachable officers, such as federal judges, for years. If those prosecutions are not unconstitutional bypasses of the impeachment process, it is difficult to conceive how the prosecutions of other impeachable officials should be." MICHAEL J. GERHARDT, THE FEDERAL IMPEACHMENT PROCESS: A CONSTITUTIONAL AND HISTORICAL ANALYSIS 10–11 (Univ. Chicago Press, 2d ed. 2000). *See also Nixon v. Sirica*, 487 F.2d 700, 711 n.50 (D.C. Cir. 1973) (*en banc*) (*per curiam*) ("Because impeachment is available against all 'civil Officers of the United States,' not merely against the President, U.S. Const. art. II, §4, it is difficult to understand how any immunities peculiar to the President can emanate by implication from the fact of impeachability.").

Does the President's position at the head of the executive branch—the part of the government responsible for bringing prosecutions—itself suggest that any federal prosecution of a sitting President should be unavailable absent the President's own acquiescence? Robert Bork, while Solicitor General, offered such an interpretation in explaining why Vice President Agnew could be indicted while in office, but the President could not: "The Framers could not have contemplated prosecution of an incumbent President because they vested him complete power over the execution of the law, which includes, of course, the power to control prosecutions." *In re: Proceedings of the Grand Jury Impaneled December 5, 1972, Application of Spiro T. Agnew, Vice President of the United States*, Case Number Civil 73-965, Memorandum for the United States Concerning the Vice President's Claim of Constitutional Immunity, Oct. 5, 1973, at p.20. Bork's interpretation of Article II is consistent with the "unitary-executive" thesis, which notes that the Constitution vests (all of) the executive power in a single President of the United States. Although that view of Article II continues to claim adherents, it appears to have been rejected by the Supreme Court. *See Morrison v. Olson*, 487 U.S. 654, 685–96 (1988); *United States v. Nixon*, 418 U.S. 683, 692–97 (1974). *Compare Morrison*, 487 U.S. at 705 (Scalia, J., dissenting) ("[S]ince the [independent-counsel] statute vests some purely executive power in a person who is not the President of the United States, it is void.").

Relying in part on *Morrison*'s upholding of the independent-counsel statute, constitutional scholar Ronald Rotunda argued in a memo to Kenneth Starr, the Independent Counsel investigating President Clinton, that a sitting President could be indicted. According to Rotunda, Bork's argument depends on the President's "power to control prosecutions," and *Morrison* demonstrated that limits could be placed on that power. *See* Letter from Ronald D. Rotunda to Hon. Kenneth W. Starr re: Indictability of the President, May 13, 1998, at 32–33 (hereinafter Rotunda, Indictability of the President).[6] Rotunda also argued that the Supreme Court's decision in *Clinton v. Jones*, which refused to give the President an immunity from *civil* suits while in office, implied that there should not be an immunity from *criminal* process either:

> If public policy and the Constitution allow a private litigant to sue a sitting
> President for alleged acts that are not part of the President's official duties—and

---

6. Professor Rotunda also emphasized that President Clinton could hardly claim that the President had the exclusive power to control prosecutions, since he lobbied for and signed the independent-counsel law that, it was clear, would lead to an investigation of his own activities. *See* Rotunda, Indictability of the President, *supra*, at 32.

that is what *Clinton v. Jones* squarely held—then one would think that an indictment is constitutional because the public interest in criminal cases is greater than the public interest in civil cases.

Rotunda, Indictability of the President, *supra*, at 27–28 (emphasis deleted). Do you believe that Rotunda is correct to point to the greater public interest in prosecuting criminal offenses compared to the interest in pursuing justice for a single civil plaintiff, or do you think that criminal charges are likely to prove to be a greater distraction to the President, resulting in harm to the public interest from the President's inability to give complete attention to the duties of his office?

Further, Rotunda noted that the Constitution, in Article I, §6, clause 1, contains two explicit privileges applicable to members of Congress—the privilege from arrest during congressional sessions and the speech-or-debate privilege—but does not contain any explicit privilege for the President:

> The existence of these two privileges and the absence of any similarly clear language creating any source of Presidential privilege is significant. If the Framers of our Constitution had wanted to create some constitutional privilege to shield the President or any other member of the Executive Branch from criminal indictment (or to prevent certain officials from being indicted before they were impeached), they could have drafted such a privilege. They certainly knew how to draft immunity language, for they drafted a very limited immunity for the federal legislature.

Rotunda, Indictability of the President, *supra*, at 17–18. Finally, note that even if the President may constitutionally be indicted or tried, it does not necessarily follow that he may be imprisoned following a conviction. Imprisonment would likely effect a "constructive removal of the President from office," and might, therefore, have to wait until the President has left office as the result of the expiry of his term, a conviction after impeachment, or resignation. *Nixon v. Sirica*, 487 F.2d 700, 711 (D.C. Cir. 1973) (*en banc*) (*per curiam*). If imprisonment of a sitting President would be unconstitutional because it would impair the functioning of the Executive Branch, would indictment lead to an impairment that is any less significant? Additionally, is it appropriate for a grand jury in a single judicial district to impose on the rest of the country whatever difficulties might result from an indictment? Whatever other flaws the impeachment process may contain, at least (as Alexander Hamilton realized in *Federalist* No. 65) it vests the awesome power of being "the inquisitors for the nation" in the members of Congress—"the representatives of the nation themselves."

Does the cumulative weight of these issues suggest that Watergate Special Prosecutor Leon Jaworski reached the correct decision when he determined that the impeachment process should precede the criminal indictment process? For additional analysis of these questions, see *Must Impeachment Precede Indictment?*, the Epilogue to Raoul Berger, Impeachment: The Constitutional Problems 315–52 (Harvard Univ. Press/Bantam Books ed. 1974).

2. The "Unindicted-Coconspirator" Designation. The portion of the Watergate Special Prosecution Force Report that is reproduced above contains the somewhat cryptic statement that "evidentiary considerations at a cover-up trial mandated naming the President as a participant in the conspiracy." The decision to name a sitting President of the United States as an "unindicted coconspirator" in an ongoing criminal prosecution was undoubtedly one of the most extraordinary actions of the Watergate Special Prosecutor's office, arguably comparable in its audacity to Archibald Cox's earlier refusal to bow to presidential orders to drop his demand for the White House tapes, which culminated in the "Saturday Night Massacre" and Cox's dismissal. The fascinating internal politics and the complex legal issues involved in applying the unindicted-coconspirator label to President Nixon have been described by the Watergate task force prosecutor who conceived the tactic:

> As we approached the time for presenting our indictment of the Big Three—Mitchell, Haldeman, and Ehrlichman, the most powerful and influential men in Nixon's administration—the decision on what to do about the president loomed large. The evidence pointed unmistakably to Nixon's participation in the cover-up, but the law was uncertain as to whether a sitting president could be subjected to a criminal indictment while in office. The combination of the potential chaos such an action might bring and the availability of the constitutional remedy of impeachment in the wings solidified Jaworski's determination that indictment of the president was not an option. I agreed, at least while impeachment remained a viable alternative. But a number of issues related to Nixon's role had to be resolved. As time passed, it became clear that Jaworski was unwilling to have the grand jury characterize Nixon's role in any way. Ordinarily, prosecutors either identified unindicted coconspirators in the body of the indictment used to charge those named as defendants, or deferred naming unindicted coconspirators until a "bill of particulars" filed at some point before trial. While Jaworski agreed with us regarding the sufficiency of the evidence against the president, his conservative instincts led him to the unshakable conclusion that he would not get ahead of the curve in characterizing Nixon's role. This should be left to Congress, once it got up to speed on the evidence supporting impeachment. But the courts had denied Congress access to the tapes, the contents of which remained secret, since we had obtained them pursuant to a grand jury subpoena and because we had stringently observed the requirement of grand jury secrecy.

> Numerous meetings, accompanied by voluminous written memoranda discussing these issues, took place among various factions within the office. Finally, we were able to persuade Leon that transmittal of the tapes and other evidence we had obtained, assembled in the form of a nonaccusatory "road map," could be presented by the grand jury to Judge Sirica with the request that he allow the package to be transmitted to the House Judiciary Committee while it considered articles of impeachment.

The issue of grand jury action regarding Nixon was more difficult. Jaworski bristled whenever I sought to bring up the subject of Nixon as coconspirator. But under the rules of evidence, the tape recordings of Nixon and his coterie, which were essential to our proof against the Big Three, would be inadmissible hearsay unless Nixon's role as a coconspirator were accepted by the trial judge as an exception to the hearsay rule. Under settled rules of evidence, once the prosecution established the existence of a criminal conspiracy, the statements of any of its members in furtherance of the conspiracy are admissible in evidence against all other members of the conspiracy.[7] This argument appealed to Jaworski the trial lawyer, but Jaworski the establishmentarian was adamant: There would be no mention of Nixon as a coconspirator in the indictment.

After many sleepless nights, I came up with a solution that I thought we might be able to sell to Leon. At some point before trial, a judge would order us to provide a list of unindicted coconspirators in a bill of particulars. At that juncture, we would have to identify Nixon as a member of the conspiracy or risk having the tapes—all of which involved Nixon as an active participant—deemed inadmissible. Jaworski would then be subject to an attack from the White House that he had supplanted the grand jury to brazenly name Nixon when the grand jury itself had done no such thing. Instead, how about allowing the grand jury to vote *now* to authorize the special prosecutor to name a designated list of unindicted coconspirators *later*? There were at least a dozen men who had entered plea bargains or otherwise agreed to cooperate who would eventually be named as unindicted coconspirators. If the grand jury had the opportunity to vote on authorizing Jaworski to name Nixon later, this would accommodate Leon's desire to avoid getting ahead of the curve now and provide cover for him later when the time came to name the coconspirators. I had never heard of any such procedure being employed before, but the circumstances called for some level of creativity. It would also provide us peace of mind that Jaworski wouldn't get cold feet when the time came to speak up.

I put the proposal to Jaworski at a mid-February dinner party [Watergate task force prosecutor] Jill Wine hosted at her home, which we had planned several weeks before to welcome the Jaworskis to Washington. I omitted the part about cold feet. Leon listened impassively and said he would get back to us. We waited on tenterhooks for forty-eight hours before Leon gave his assent.

Leon addressed the grand jury personally to explain why Richard Nixon was not included as a named defendant in our proposed indictment. He then explained the procedure for the jury to vote on authorization for him to name

---

7. [*Ed. Note: Federal Rule of Evidence 801(d)(2)(E) defines a statement made by a "party's coconspirator during and in furtherance of the conspiracy" as non-hearsay.*]

specific unindicted coconspirators at the appropriate time prior to trial. As I read the names of the list of proposed unindicted coconspirators, arranged in alphabetical order, the stenographer's eyes opened wide when I got to Richard M. Nixon.

RICHARD BEN-VENISTE, THE EMPEROR'S NEW CLOTHES: EXPOSING THE TRUTH FROM WATERGATE TO 9/11, at 37–39 (St. Martin's Press 2009).

3. The Assistance Question—How Much Assistance Should a Federal Prosecutor Investigating a Sitting President Provide to the House of Representatives' Impeachment Proceedings? As the excerpt above from the Watergate Special Prosecution Force Report indicates, Watergate Special Prosecutor Leon Jaworski followed a cautious and restrained course in providing information about President Nixon to the House Judiciary Committee. The Watergate Special Prosecutor did not advocate for Nixon's impeachment, but instead provided the Judiciary Committee with a "roadmap" to the evidence against Nixon. Two of the Watergate prosecutors have described how this "roadmap" approach was used to provide the relevant information to the Judiciary Committee without extraneous advocacy or characterization of the evidence:

> The form * * * chosen for the report was a series of "statements of fact," most of which were one or a few sentences long. Each "statement of fact" was numbered. Each was followed by a list of evidence that supported the numbered statement: a tape, a few pages of recorded grand-jury testimony, a document. (Later, we were flattered by the fact that the House Judiciary Committee staff copied our format precisely for presenting all of its impeachment evidence to the committee members and the public.) We wanted to be sure that everything we had gathered that contributed to the case against President Nixon was sent over to the Judiciary Committee. More important, we wanted the road map to make "perfectly clear" how each piece of evidence fit together in the overall scheme.

RICHARD BEN-VENISTE & GEORGE FRAMPTON, STONEWALL: THE REAL STORY OF THE WATERGATE PROSECUTION 129–30 (Simon & Schuster 1977). Did the Watergate Special Prosecutor follow the right approach, or should he have aggressively advocated that the Judiciary Committee impeach Nixon? Compare the approach followed by the Watergate Special Prosecutor to the approach taken by Independent Counsel Kenneth Starr in the Clinton impeachment proceedings, discussed in the next section of this Chapter.

4. Disclosure of Grand Jury Material to a House Impeachment Inquiry. As the Watergate Special Prosecution Force Report notes, Watergate defendants H.R. Haldeman and Gordon Strachan unsuccessfully sued to prevent grand jury material from being disclosed to the House of Representatives. Federal Rule of Criminal Procedure 6(e) generally prohibits the disclosure of "a matter occurring before the grand jury," subject to exceptions listed in Rule 6(e)(3). Rule 6(e)(3)(E)(i) provides that the court may authorize disclosure "preliminarily to or in connection with a judicial proceeding." Accordingly, the issue became whether an impeachment trial qualified as a "judicial proceeding" such that disclosure to the House could be authorized.[8] Chief Judge Sirica did order the material to be transmitted to the House, and that decision was affirmed by the D.C. Circuit. *Haldeman v. Sirica*, 501 F.2d 714 (D.C. Cir. 1974).

The issue returned to the courts during the Trump Administration, when the House demanded grand jury material that had been redacted from the publicly released version of the Mueller Report, which examined Russian interference in the 2016 presidential election. The Department of Justice opposed disclosure, arguing that a congressional impeachment inquiry was not a "judicial proceeding." The district court disagreed, and ordered the material disclosed. *In re: Application of the Committee on the Judiciary, U.S. House of Representatives*, 414 F. Supp. 3d 129 (D.D.C. 2019). The court held that an impeachment *trial* was a "judicial proceeding," even if conducted by the Senate, and so the House's impeachment inquiry was "preliminar[y] to or in connection with a judicial proceeding," and thus authorized by Rule 6(e). The D.C. Circuit affirmed in the opinion reproduced below, 951 F.3d 589 (D.C. Cir. 2020). The Supreme Court later ordered both opinions vacated as moot, 142 S. Ct. 46 (2021).

In re: Committee on the Judiciary, U.S. House of Representatives

951 F.3d 589 (D.C. Cir. 2020), *vacated as moot*
142 S. Ct. 46 (2021)

ROGERS, Circuit Judge. * * *

The constitutional text confirms that a Senate impeachment trial is a judicial proceeding. Article I provides that "[t]he Senate shall have the sole Power to try all Impeachments" and further states that when the President "is tried, the Chief Justice shall preside." U.S. Const. art. I, §3, cl. 6. The Framers of the Constitution also understood impeachment to involve the exercise of judicial power. For instance, Alexander Hamilton referred to the Senate's "judicial character as a court for the trial of impeachments." The Federalist No. 65, at 396 (Clinton Rossiter ed., 1961). The district court here properly concluded that "the Federalist Papers, the text of the Constitution, and Supreme Court precedent all make clear" that "impeachment trials are judicial in nature and constitute judicial proceedings." *App. for Mueller Report Grand Jury Materials*, 414 F. Supp.3d at 153; see id. at 152–58.

---

8. The D.C. Circuit has held that Rule 6(e) prohibits disclosures except as permitted by the exceptions (or, presumably, by statute). *See McKeever v. Barr*, 920 F.3d 842 (D.C. Cir. 2019), *cert. denied* 140 S. Ct. 597 (2020). *See also Pitch v. United States*, 953 F.3d 1226, 1234–38 (11th Cir.) (*en banc*), *cert. denied*, 141 S. Ct. 624 (2020); *United States v. McDougal*, 559 F.3d 837, 840 (8th Cir. 2009); *In re: Grand Jury 89-4-72*, 932 F.2d 481, 488 (6th Cir. 1991). *Cf. In re: Petition for Order Directing Release of Records*, 27 F.4th 84, 91–95 (1st Cir. 2022) (holding that, assuming there is inherent authority to disclose grand jury material, such authority would apply only to further the fair administration of justice and not merely because the material is of historical interest). Other courts of appeals, however, have concluded that district courts possess inherent authority to disclose grand jury material. *See Carlson v. United States*, 837 F.3d 753, 766–67 (7th Cir. 2016); *In re: Craig*, 131 F.3d 99, 103 (2d Cir. 1997).

* * * The term "judicial proceeding" has long and repeatedly been interpreted broadly, and courts have authorized the disclosure of grand jury materials "in an array of judicial and quasi-judicial contexts" outside of Article III court proceedings—such as administrative proceedings before the United States Tax Court, *App. for Mueller Report Grand Jury Materials*, 414 F.Supp.3d at 150 (collecting cases). So understood, the term "judicial proceeding" encompasses a Senate impeachment trial over which the Chief Justice of the Supreme Court presides and the Senators constitute the jury. * * *

Additionally, the historical practice supports interpreting Rule 6(e) to encompass impeachment. Rule 6(e) was adopted in 1946 to "codif[y] the traditional rule of grand jury secrecy" that was applied at common law. As summarized by the district court, Congress has repeatedly obtained grand jury material to investigate allegations of election fraud or misconduct by Members of Congress. *App. for Mueller Report Grand Jury Materials*, 414 F.Supp.3d at 157–59. The Department dismisses this practice because no example involved impeachment proceedings. But these examples evince a common-law tradition, starting as early as 1811, of providing grand jury materials to Congress to assist with congressional investigations. And historical practice reflects at least one example of a court-ordered disclosure of grand jury materials to the Committee—prior to the Rule's enactment—for use in its impeachment investigation of two federal judges. Conduct of Albert W. Johnson and Albert L. Watson, U.S. District Judges, Middle District of Pennsylvania: Hearing before Subcomm. of the H. Comm. on the Judiciary, 79th Cong., at 63 (1945).

Since Rule 6(e) was enacted, federal courts have authorized the disclosure of grand jury materials to the House for use in impeachment investigations involving two presidents and three federal judges. *See generally In re 1972 Grand Jury Report*, 370 F. Supp. 1219 (D.D.C. 1974) (President Nixon); Order, *In re Madison Guar. Sav. & Loan Ass'n, Div. No. 94-1* (D.C. Cir. Spec. Div. July 7, 1998) (*per curiam*) (President Clinton); *In re Request for Access to Grand Jury Materials Grand Jury No. 81-1, Miami* ("*Hastings*"), 833 F.2d 1438 (11th Cir. 1987) (Judge Alcee Hastings); Order, *Nixon v. United States*, Civ. No. H88-0052(G) (S.D. Miss. 1988) (Judge Walter Nixon), referenced in H.R. Rep. No. 101-36, at 15H.R. Rep. No. 101-36, at 15 (1989); and Order, *In re Grand Jury Investigation of U.S. District Judge G. Thomas Porteous, Jr.*, No. 2:09-mc-04346-CVSG (E.D. La. Aug. 6, 2009). It is only the President's categorical resistance and the Department's objection that are unprecedented. In interpreting the Rule, this established practice deserves "significant weight." * * *

The Committee has established a particularized need for the redacted grand jury materials it seeks. The party requesting the grand jury information must show (1) the material "is needed to avoid a possible injustice in another judicial proceeding," (2) "the need for disclosure is greater than the need for continued secrecy," and (3) the "request is structured to cover only material so needed." * * * [The district court did not abuse its discretion in concluding that] any remaining secrecy interests in the redacted grand jury materials were readily outweighed by the Committee's compelling need for the materials in order to determine whether, or to what extent, links existed between the Russian government's efforts to interfere in the 2016 United States presidential election proceedings and individuals associated with President Trump's election campaign. * * *

Furthermore, the Committee's request was tailored to its need. The Committee requested three categories of grand jury materials: (1) all portions of the Mueller Report that were redacted pursuant to Rule 6(e); (2) any portions of grand jury transcripts or exhibits referenced in those redactions; and (3) any underlying grand jury testimony and exhibits that relate directly to certain individuals and events described in the Mueller Report. Additionally, the Committee proposed a staged disclosure, starting with the first two categories of materials. The district court reasonably granted this request given the Committee's compelling need to be able to make a final determination about the President's conduct described in the Mueller Report, and stated that the Committee could file further requests articulating its need for the grand jury materials in the third category. * * *

The Committee's request for the grand jury materials in the Mueller Report is directly linked to its need to evaluate the conclusions reached and not reached by the Special Counsel. In the Special Counsel Mueller's own estimation, his Report "contains ... that information necessary to account for the Special Counsel's prosecution and declination decisions and to describe the investigation's main factual results." The Committee states that it needs the unredacted material to review these findings and make its own independent determination about the President's conduct. The district court had no reason to question the Committee's representation because the Mueller Report itself made clear why the grand jury materials in Volume I were necessary for the Committee to review and evaluate in exercise of its constitutional duty. Courts must take care not to second-guess the manner in which the House plans to proceed with its impeachment investigation or interfere with the House's sole power of impeachment. *Cf. Walter Nixon*, 506 U.S. at 230–31.

Of course, courts must not simply rubber stamp congressional requests for grand jury materials. In cases where the connection between the grand jury materials and the Committee's impeachment investigation is not obvious, further inquiry by the district court may be needed. For instance, Committee counsel could be permitted to review the unredacted grand jury materials *in camera* to enable a more detailed explanation of the relevance of particular witnesses, portions of transcripts, or records. Or the district court, in the exercise of its discretion, might decide it should review the unredacted materials *in camera*, as occurred here at the Department's suggestion, with respect to Volume II of the Mueller Report.

But here, where the Special Counsel stopped short of making any "ultimate conclusions about the President's conduct," Mueller Report, Vol. II at 8, in part to avoid preempting the House's sole power of impeachment, *see id.* at 1, the Committee has established that it cannot "fairly and diligently" make a final determination about the conduct described in both volumes of the Mueller Report "without the grand jury material referenced" therein. *App. for Mueller Report Grand Jury Materials*, 414 F. Supp.

3d at 178. * * * Given the Committee's tailored request in the instant case, this court has no occasion to decide whether granting a request for "all" of the redacted grand jury materials would have been an abuse of discretion; that question remains for another day. Here, for reasons explained, the district court did not abuse its discretion by ordering the disclosure of all portions of the Mueller Report redacted pursuant to Rule 6(e) and any grand jury transcripts or exhibits referenced in those redactions without scrutinizing the Committee's need as to each redaction.

Accordingly, because a Senate impeachment trial qualifies as a "judicial proceeding" pursuant to Rule 6(e) and the Committee has established a particularized need for the requested portions of grand jury materials, the district court's Order is affirmed. * * *

The Constitutional Grounds for Presidential Impeachment: President Bill Clinton

Although President Clinton's conduct in the Monica Lewinsky affair is regarded by many as indefensible, there is far less agreement as to whether it falls within the definition of impeachable "high Crimes and Misdemeanors." On the one hand, perjury, suborning perjury, and obstruction of justice, in the abstract, do seem to be the kinds of serious offenses that could lead to impeachment; indeed, they formed part of the allegations against President Nixon. On the other hand, the tawdry context of President Clinton's misbehavior suggests to many that his misdeeds are not the kind of "high" crimes that justify removal from office. At the same time, many condemn the zeal and tactics used by Independent Counsel Kenneth Starr in investigating Clinton's affair with Lewinsky and in advocating for Clinton's impeachment. The Clinton impeachment is considered here as a vehicle for addressing—and perhaps debating—the meaning of the grounds for impeachment set out in the Constitution. That still-unresolved topic will be central to our examination of the first Trump impeachment, later in this Chapter.

A. The Starr Referral

Referral to the United States House of Representatives pursuant to Title 28, United States Code, § 595(c)

Submitted by the Office of the Independent Counsel,
September 9, 1998

[*Ed. Note: Footnote references omitted.*]

Introduction

As required by Section 595(c) of Title 28 of the United States Code, the Office of the Independent Counsel ("OIC" or "Office") hereby submits substantial and credible information that President William Jefferson Clinton committed acts that may constitute grounds for an impeachment.

The information reveals that President Clinton:

> lied under oath at a civil deposition while he was a defendant in a sexual harassment lawsuit;

> lied under oath to a grand jury;

> attempted to influence the testimony of a potential witness who had direct knowledge of facts that would reveal the falsity of his deposition testimony;

> attempted to obstruct justice by facilitating a witness's plan to refuse to comply with a subpoena;

> attempted to obstruct justice by encouraging a witness to file an affidavit that the President knew would be false, and then by making use of that false affidavit at his own deposition;

> lied to potential grand jury witnesses, knowing that they would repeat those lies before the grand jury; and

> engaged in a pattern of conduct that was inconsistent with his constitutional duty to faithfully execute the laws.

The evidence shows that these acts, and others, were part of a pattern that began as an effort to prevent the disclosure of information about the President's relationship with a former White House intern and employee, Monica S. Lewinsky, and continued as an effort to prevent the information from being disclosed in an ongoing criminal investigation.

Factual Background

In May 1994, Paula Corbin Jones filed a lawsuit against William Jefferson Clinton in the United States District Court for the Eastern District of Arkansas. Ms. Jones alleged that while he was the Governor of Arkansas, President Clinton sexually harassed her during an incident in a Little Rock hotel room. President Clinton denied the allegations. He also challenged the ability of a private litigant to pursue a lawsuit against a sitting President. In May 1997, the Supreme Court unanimously rejected the President's legal argument. The Court concluded that Ms. Jones, "[l]ike every other citizen who properly invokes [the District Court's] jurisdiction ... has a right to an orderly disposition of her claims," and that therefore Ms. Jones was entitled to pursue her claims while the President was in office. A few months later, the pretrial discovery process began.

One sharply disputed issue in the *Jones* litigation was the extent to which the President would be required to disclose information about sexual relationships he may have had with "other women." * * *

In late 1997, the issue was presented to United States District Judge Susan Webber Wright for resolution. Judge Wright's decision was unambiguous. For purposes of pretrial discovery, President Clinton was required to provide certain information about his alleged relationships with other women. In an order dated December 11, 1997, for example, Judge Wright said: "The Court finds, therefore, that the plaintiff is entitled to information regarding any individuals with whom the President had sexual relations or proposed or sought to have sexual relations and who were during the relevant time frame state or federal employees." Judge Wright left for another day the issue whether any information of this type would be admissible were the case to go to trial. But for purposes of answering the written questions served on the President, and for purposes of answering questions at a deposition, the District Court ruled that the President must respond.

In mid-December 1997, the President answered one of the written discovery questions posed by Ms. Jones on this issue. When asked to identify all women who were state or federal employees and with whom he had had "sexual relations" since 1986, the President answered under oath: "None." For purposes of this interrogatory, the term "sexual relations" was not defined.

On January 17, 1998, President Clinton was questioned under oath about his relationships with other women in the workplace, this time at a deposition. Judge Wright presided over the deposition. The President was asked numerous questions about his relationship with Monica Lewinsky, by then a 24-year-old former White House intern, White House employee, and Pentagon employee. Under oath and in the presence of Judge Wright, the President denied that he had engaged in a "sexual affair," a "sexual relationship," or "sexual relations" with Ms. Lewinsky. The President also stated that he had no specific memory of having been alone with Ms. Lewinsky, that he remembered few details of any gifts they might have exchanged, and indicated that no one except his attorneys had kept him informed of Ms. Lewinsky's status as a potential witness in the *Jones* case. * * *

On April 1, 1998, Judge Wright granted President Clinton's motion for summary judgment, concluding that even if the facts alleged by Paula Jones were true, her claims failed as a matter of law. Ms. Jones has filed an appeal, and as of the date of this Referral, the matter remains under consideration by the United States Court of Appeals for the Eighth Circuit.

After the dismissal of Ms. Jones's lawsuit, the criminal investigation continued. It was (and is) the view of this Office that any attempt to obstruct the proper functioning of the judicial system, regardless of the perceived merits of the underlying case, is a serious matter that warrants further inquiry. After careful consideration of all the evidence, the OIC has concluded that the evidence of wrongdoing is substantial and credible, and that the wrongdoing is of sufficient gravity that it warrants referral to Congress.

The Significance of the Evidence of Wrongdoing

It is not the role of this Office to determine whether the President's actions warrant impeachment by the House and removal by the Senate; those judgments are, of course, constitutionally entrusted to the legislative branch. This Office is authorized, rather, to conduct criminal investigations and to seek criminal prosecutions for matters within its jurisdiction. In carrying out its investigation, however, this Office also has a statutory duty to disclose to Congress information that "may constitute grounds for an impeachment," a task that inevitably requires judgment about the seriousness of the acts revealed by the evidence.

From the beginning, this phase of the OIC's investigation has been criticized as an improper inquiry into the President's personal behavior; indeed, the President himself suggested that specific inquiries into his conduct were part of an effort to "criminalize my private life." The regrettable fact that the investigation has often required witnesses to discuss sensitive personal matters has fueled this perception.

All Americans, including the President, are entitled to enjoy a private family life, free from public or governmental scrutiny. But the privacy concerns raised in this case are subject to limits, three of which we briefly set forth here.

First. The first limit was imposed when the President was sued in federal court for alleged sexual harassment. The evidence in such litigation is often personal. At times, that evidence is highly embarrassing for both plaintiff and defendant. As Judge Wright noted at the President's January 1998 deposition, "I have never had a sexual harassment case where there was not some embarrassment." Nevertheless, Congress and the Supreme Court have concluded that embarrassment-related concerns must give way to the greater interest in allowing aggrieved parties to pursue their claims. Courts have long recognized the difficulties of proving sexual harassment in the workplace, inasmuch as improper or unlawful behavior often takes place in private. To excuse a party who lied or concealed evidence on the ground that the evidence covered only "personal" or "private" behavior would frustrate the goals that Congress and the courts have sought to achieve in enacting and interpreting the Nation's sexual harassment laws. That is particularly true when the conduct that is being concealed—sexual relations in the workplace between a high official and a young subordinate employee—itself conflicts with those goals.

Second. The second limit was imposed when Judge Wright required disclosure of the precise information that is in part the subject of this Referral. A federal judge specifically ordered the President, on more than one occasion, to provide the requested information about relationships with other women, including Monica Lewinsky. The fact that Judge Wright later determined that the evidence would not be admissible at trial, and still later granted judgment in the President's favor, does not change the President's legal duty at the time he testified. Like every litigant, the President was entitled to object to the discovery questions, and to seek guidance from the court if he thought those questions were improper. But having failed to convince the court that his objections were well founded, the President was duty bound to testify truthfully and fully. Perjury and attempts to obstruct the gathering of evidence can never be an acceptable response to a court order, regardless of the eventual course or outcome of the litigation.

The Supreme Court has spoken forcefully about perjury and other forms of obstruction of justice:

> In this constitutional process of securing a witness' testimony, perjury simply
> has no place whatever. Perjured testimony is an obvious and flagrant affront to

the basic concepts of judicial proceedings. Effective restraints against this type of egregious offense are therefore imperative.

The insidious effects of perjury occur whether the case is civil or criminal. Only a few years ago, the Supreme Court considered a false statement made in a civil administrative proceeding: "False testimony in a formal proceeding is intolerable. We must neither reward nor condone such a 'flagrant affront' to the truth-seeking function of adversary proceedings.... Perjury should be severely sanctioned in appropriate cases." Stated more simply, "[p]erjury is an obstruction of justice."

Third. The third limit is unique to the President. "The Presidency is more than an executive responsibility. It is the inspiring symbol of all that is highest in American purpose and ideals." When he took the Oath of Office in 1993 and again in 1997, President Clinton swore that he would "faithfully execute the Office of President." As the head of the Executive Branch, the President has the constitutional duty to "take Care that the Laws be faithfully executed." The President gave his testimony in the *Jones* case under oath and in the presence of a federal judge, a member of a co-equal branch of government; he then testified before a federal grand jury, a body of citizens who had themselves taken an oath to seek the truth. In view of the enormous trust and responsibility attendant to his high Office, the President has a manifest duty to ensure that his conduct at all times complies with the law of the land.

In sum, perjury and acts that obstruct justice by any citizen—whether in a criminal case, a grand jury investigation, a congressional hearing, a civil trial, or civil discovery—are profoundly serious matters. When such acts are committed by the President of the United States, we believe those acts "may constitute grounds for an impeachment." * * *

There is substantial and credible information supporting the following eleven possible grounds for impeachment:

1. President Clinton lied under oath in his civil case when he denied a sexual affair, a sexual relationship, or sexual relations with Monica Lewinsky.

2. President Clinton lied under oath to the grand jury about his sexual relationship with Ms. Lewinsky.

3. In his civil deposition, to support his false statement about the sexual relationship, President Clinton also lied under oath about being alone with Ms. Lewinsky and about the many gifts exchanged between Ms. Lewinsky and him.

4. President Clinton lied under oath in his civil deposition about his discussions with Ms. Lewinsky concerning her involvement in the *Jones* case.

5. During the *Jones* case, the President obstructed justice and had an understanding with Ms. Lewinsky to jointly conceal the truth about their relationship by concealing gifts subpoenaed by Ms. Jones's attorneys.

6. During the *Jones* case, the President obstructed justice and had an understanding with Ms. Lewinsky to jointly conceal the truth of their relationship from the judicial process by a scheme that included the following means: (i) Both the President and

Ms. Lewinsky understood that they would lie under oath in the *Jones* case about their sexual relationship; (ii) the President suggested to Ms. Lewinsky that she prepare an affidavit that, for the President's purposes, would memorialize her testimony under oath and could be used to prevent questioning of both of them about their relationship; (iii) Ms. Lewinsky signed and filed the false affidavit; (iv) the President used Ms. Lewinsky's false affidavit at his deposition in an attempt to head off questions about Ms. Lewinsky; and (v) when that failed, the President lied under oath at his civil deposition about the relationship with Ms. Lewinsky.

7. President Clinton endeavored to obstruct justice by helping Ms. Lewinsky obtain a job in New York at a time when she would have been a witness harmful to him were she to tell the truth in the *Jones* case.

8. President Clinton lied under oath in his civil deposition about his discussions with Vernon Jordan concerning Ms. Lewinsky's involvement in the *Jones* case.

9. The President improperly tampered with a potential witness by attempting to corruptly influence the testimony of his personal secretary, Betty Currie, in the days after his civil deposition.

10. President Clinton endeavored to obstruct justice during the grand jury investigation by refusing to testify for seven months *and* lying to senior White House aides with knowledge that they would relay the President's false statements to the grand jury—and did thereby deceive, obstruct, and impede the grand jury.

11. President Clinton abused his constitutional authority by (i) lying to the public and the Congress in January 1998 about his relationship with Ms. Lewinsky; (ii) promising at that time to cooperate fully with the grand jury investigation; (iii) later refusing six invitations to testify voluntarily to the grand jury; (iv) invoking Executive Privilege; (v) lying to the grand jury in August 1998; and (vi) lying again to the public and Congress on August 17, 1998—all as part of an effort to hinder, impede, and deflect possible inquiry by the Congress of the United States.

The first two possible grounds for impeachment concern the President's lying under oath about the nature of his relationship with Ms. Lewinsky. The details associated with those grounds are, by their nature, explicit. The President's testimony unfortunately has rendered the details essential with respect to those two grounds, as will be explained in those grounds.

[*Ed. Note: The report then provides detailed information about the matters listed above, including information about President Clinton's sexual contacts with Monica Lewinsky.*]

B. The Clinton Articles of Impeachment

Articles of Impeachment against President William Jefferson Clinton

H. Res. 611, 105th Cong., 2d Sess. [Exhibited to Senate on January 7, 1999]

RESOLUTION

Impeaching William Jefferson Clinton, President of the United States, for high crimes and misdemeanors.

Resolved, That William Jefferson Clinton, President of the United States, is impeached for high crimes and misdemeanors, and that the following articles of impeachment be exhibited to the United States Senate:

Articles of impeachment exhibited by the House of Representatives of the United States of America in the name of itself and of the people of the United States of America, against William Jefferson Clinton, President of the United States of America, in maintenance and support of its impeachment against him for high crimes and misdemeanors.

ARTICLE I

In his conduct while President of the United States, William Jefferson Clinton, in violation of his constitutional oath faithfully to execute the office of President of the United States and, to the best of his ability, preserve, protect, and defend the Constitution of the United States, and in violation of his constitutional duty to take care that the laws be faithfully executed, has willfully corrupted and manipulated the judicial process of the United States for his personal gain and exoneration, impeding the administration of justice, in that:

On August 17, 1998, William Jefferson Clinton swore to tell the truth, the whole truth, and nothing but the truth before a Federal grand jury of the United States. Contrary to that oath, William Jefferson Clinton willfully provided perjurious, false and misleading testimony to the grand jury concerning one or more of the following: (1) the nature and details of his relationship with a subordinate Government employee; (2) prior perjurious, false and misleading testimony he gave in a Federal civil rights action brought against him; (3) prior false and misleading statements he allowed his attorney to make to a Federal judge in that civil rights action; and (4) his corrupt efforts to influence the testimony of witnesses and to impede the discovery of evidence in that civil rights action.

In doing this, William Jefferson Clinton has undermined the integrity of his office, has brought disrepute on the Presidency, has betrayed his trust as President, and has acted in a manner subversive of the rule of law and justice, to the manifest injury of the people of the United States.

Wherefore, William Jefferson Clinton, by such conduct, warrants impeachment and trial, and removal from office and disqualification to hold and enjoy any office of honor, trust, or profit under the United States.

ARTICLE II

In his conduct while President of the United States, William Jefferson Clinton, in violation of his constitutional oath faithfully to execute the office of President of the United States and, to the best of his ability, preserve, protect, and defend the Constitution of the United States, and in violation of his constitutional duty to take care that the laws be faithfully executed, has prevented, obstructed, and impeded the administration of justice, and has to that end engaged personally, and through his subordinates and agents, in a course of conduct or scheme designed to delay, impede, cover up, and conceal the existence of evidence and testimony related to a Federal civil rights action brought against him in a duly instituted judicial proceeding.

The means used to implement this course of conduct or scheme included one or more of the following acts:

(1) On or about December 17, 1997, William Jefferson Clinton corruptly encouraged a witness in a Federal civil rights action brought against him to execute a sworn affidavit in that proceeding that he knew to be perjurious, false and misleading.

(2) On or about December 17, 1997, William Jefferson Clinton corruptly encouraged a witness in a Federal civil rights action brought against him to give perjurious, false and misleading testimony if and when called to testify personally in that proceeding.

(3) On or about December 28, 1997, William Jefferson Clinton corruptly engaged in, encouraged, or supported a scheme to conceal evidence that had been subpoenaed in a Federal civil rights action brought against him.

(4) Beginning on or about December 7, 1997, and continuing through and including January 14, 1998, William Jefferson Clinton intensified and succeeded in an effort to secure job assistance to a witness in a Federal civil rights action brought against him in order to corruptly prevent the truthful testimony of that witness in that proceeding at a time when the truthful testimony of that witness would have been harmful to him.

(5) On January 17, 1998, at his deposition in a Federal civil rights action brought against him, William Jefferson Clinton corruptly allowed his attorney to make false and misleading statements to a Federal judge characterizing an affidavit, in order to prevent questioning deemed relevant by the judge. Such false and misleading statements were subsequently acknowledged by his attorney in a communication to that judge.

(6) On or about January 18 and January 20–21, 1998, William Jefferson Clinton related a false and misleading account of events relevant to a Federal civil rights action brought against him to a potential witness in that proceeding, in order to corruptly influence the testimony of that witness.

(7) On or about January 21, 23, and 26, 1998, William Jefferson Clinton made false and misleading statements to potential witnesses in a Federal grand

jury proceeding in order to corruptly influence the testimony of those witnesses. The false and misleading statements made by William Jefferson Clinton were repeated by the witnesses to the grand jury, causing the grand jury to receive false and misleading information.

In all of this, William Jefferson Clinton has undermined the integrity of his office, has brought disrepute on the Presidency, has betrayed his trust as President, and has acted in a manner subversive of the rule of law and justice, to the manifest injury of the people of the United States.

Wherefore, William Jefferson Clinton, by such conduct, warrants impeachment and trial, and removal from office and disqualification to hold and enjoy any office of honor, trust, or profit under the United States.

Passed the House of Representatives December 19, 1998.

NEWT GINGRICH,
Speaker of the House of Representatives

Address to the Senate by Former Senator Dale Bumpers of Arkansas at the Conclusion of President Clinton's Impeachment Trial in the Senate

145 Cong. Rec. 145, No. 10, pp. S844–S848, Jan. 21, 1999[9]

Mr. Counsel Bumpers. * * *

We are here today because the President suffered a terrible moral lapse of marital infidelity—not a breach of the public trust, not a crime against society, the two things Hamilton talked about in Federalist Paper No. 65—which I recommend it to you before you vote—but it was a breach of his marriage vows. It was a breach of his family trust. It is a sex scandal. H.L. Mencken once said, "When you hear somebody say, 'This is not about money,' it's about money."

[Laughter.]

And when you hear somebody say, "This is not about sex," it's about sex. * * *

The House managers have said shame and embarrassment is no excuse for lying. The question about lying—that is your decision. But I can tell you, put yourself in his position—and you have already had this big moral lapse—as to what you should do. We are, none of us, perfect. Sure, you say, he should have thought of all that beforehand. And indeed he should have, just as Adam and Eve should have, just as you and you and you and you and millions of other people who have been caught in similar circumstances should have thought of it before. As I say, none of us is perfect. * * *

---

9. *See also* Appendix: Address to the Senate, in DALE BUMPERS, THE BEST LAWYER IN A ONE-LAW-YER TOWN 277–93 (Random House 2003). Senator Bumpers had just retired from serving four terms in the Senate when the Clinton defense team asked him to present a closing argument in the Senate impeachment trial. *See id.* at 259–76.

Make no mistake about it: Removal from office is punishment. It is unbelievable punishment, even though the Framers didn't quite see it that way. Again, they said—and it bears repeating over and over again—they said they wanted to protect the people. But I can tell you this: The punishment of removing Bill Clinton from office would pale compared to the punishment he has already inflicted on himself. There is a feeling in this country that somehow or another Bill Clinton has gotten away with something. Mr. Leader, I can tell you, he hasn't gotten away with anything. And the people are saying, "Please don't protect us from this man. Seventy-six percent of us think he's doing a fine job; 65 to 70 percent of us don't want him removed from office." * * *

... I have tried 300, 400, maybe 500 divorce cases.... In all those divorce cases, I would guess about 80 percent of the contested cases perjury was committed. Do you know what it was about? Sex. Extramarital affairs. But there is a very big difference in perjury about a marital infidelity in a divorce case and perjury about whether I bought the murder weapon, or whether I concealed the murder weapon or not. And to charge somebody with the first and punish them as though it were the second stands our sense of justice on its head.

There is a total lack of proportionality, a total lack of balance in this thing. The charge and the punishment are totally out of sync. All of you have heard or read the testimony of the five prosecutors who testified before the House Judiciary Committee—five seasoned prosecutors. Each one of them, veterans, said that under the identical circumstances of this case, they would never charge anybody because they would know they couldn't get a conviction. In this case, the charges brought and the punishment sought are totally out of sync. There is no balance, there is no proportionality.

But even stranger—you think about it—is that if this case had originated in the courthouse rather than the Capitol, you would never have heard of it. How do you reconcile what the prosecutors said with what we're doing here? * * *

This is one of the most important points of this entire presentation. First of all, the term "treason and bribery"—nobody quarrels with that. We are not debating treason and bribery here in this Chamber. We are talking about other high crimes and misdemeanors. And where did "high crimes and misdemeanors" come from? It came from the English law. They found it in English law under a category which said distinctly "political" offenses against the state.

Let me repeat that. They said "high crimes and misdemeanors" was to be because they took it from English law where they found it in the category that said offenses distinctly "political" against the state.

So colleagues, please, for just one moment, forget the complexities of the facts and the tortured legalisms—we have heard them all brilliantly presented on both sides. And I'm not getting into that.

But ponder this: If high crimes and misdemeanors was taken from English law by George Madison [sic], which listed high crimes and misdemeanors as "political" offenses against the state, what are we doing here? If, as Hamilton said, it had to be a crime against society or a breach of the public trust, what are we doing here? Even perjury, concealing, or deceiving an unfaithful relationship does not even come close to being an impeachable offense. Nobody has suggested that Bill Clinton committed a political crime against the state.

So, colleagues, if you honor the Constitution, you must look at the history of the Constitution and how we got to the impeachment clause. And, if you do that, and you do that honestly, according to the oath you took, you cannot—you can censor [*sic*] Bill Clinton; you can hand him over to the prosecutor for him to be prosecuted, but you cannot convict him. And you cannot indulge yourselves the luxury or the right to ignore this history. * * *

Colleagues, this is easily the most important vote you will ever cast. If you have difficulty because of an intense dislike of the President—and that is understandable—rise above it. He is not the issue. He will be gone. You won't. So don't leave a precedent from which we may never recover and almost surely will regret.

If you vote to acquit, Mr. Leader, you know exactly what is going to happen. * * * You are going to get on with your legislative agenda. * * * But if you vote to convict, you can't be sure what is going to happen.

James G. Blaine was a Member of the House [*sic*] when Andrew Johnson was tried in 1868, and 20 years later he recanted. He said, "I made a bad mistake." And he said, "As I reflect back on it, all I can think about is that having convicted Andrew Johnson would have caused much more chaos and confusion in this country than Andrew Johnson could ever conceivably have created."

And so it is with William Jefferson Clinton. If you vote to convict, in my opinion you are going to be creating more havoc than he could ever possibly create. After all, he only has 2 years left. So don't, for God's sake, heighten the people's alienation, which is at an all time high, toward their government. The people have a right, and they are calling on you to rise above politics, rise above partisanship. They are calling on you to do your solemn duty, and I pray you will.

Thank you, Mr. Chief Justice.

––––––––––

President Clinton was acquitted by the Senate on February 12, 1999. On Article I, the vote was 45 guilty, 55 not guilty; on Article II, the vote was 50 guilty, 50 not guilty. *See* 145 Cong. Rec. S1458–S1459 (1999).

Post-Impeachment:
Final Resolution of the Independent Counsel
Investigation of President Clinton

As noted at the outset of this Chapter, the Constitution is clear that an impeachment conviction does not foreclose the possibility of criminal prosecution for the same conduct. *See* U.S. Const., art. I, §3. By the same token, an impeachment acquittal, as occurred in President Clinton's impeachment, does not preclude subsequent criminal prosecution for the same conduct. After the Senate acquittal of President Clinton in February 1999, it took almost two years to resolve the Independent Counsel's criminal investigation of President Clinton. The settlement of the criminal proceedings was announced on January 19, 2001, the day before President Clinton left office. The President agreed to accept a five-year suspension of his Arkansas law license, paid a $25,000 fine to cover counsel fees, and acknowledged that "certain of my responses to questions about Ms. Lewinsky were false." Independent Counsel Robert Ray, who had succeeded Kenneth Starr, agreed to decline prosecution of the President as to all matters within the Independent Counsel's jurisdiction.

Notes and Questions

1. **The Assistance Question Redux—Did Starr Go Too Far?** As the materials above indicate, Whitewater Independent Counsel Kenneth W. Starr followed a different approach in his impeachment referral against President Clinton in the Monica Lewinsky affair than that followed by Watergate Special Prosecutor Leon Jaworski. Rather than following Jaworski's relatively restrained "roadmap" approach to providing evidence of impeachable offenses to the House Judiciary Committee, Starr wrote a long and detailed referral that characterized the evidence against President Clinton and drew legal conclusions based upon that evidence. In response to criticism over his referral, Starr argued that his actions were required by the impeachment referral provisions of the independent counsel statute that was then in effect. *See* 28 U.S.C. §595(c) ("An independent counsel shall advise the House of Representatives of any substantial and credible information which such independent counsel receives, in carrying out the independent counsel's responsibilities under this Chapter, that may constitute grounds for an impeachment.").

One prominent member of Starr's staff took strong exception to Starr's actions in connection with the impeachment referral. Starr had earlier appointed Samuel Dash, a Georgetown University law professor and legal-ethics expert who had served as chief counsel to the Senate Watergate Committee, to serve as Starr's ethics adviser in the investigation of President Clinton. Dash, who had helped write the independent counsel law after his service on the Senate Watergate Committee, concluded that, in appearing before the House Judiciary Committee and aggressively advocating for President Clinton's impeachment, Starr violated his obligations under the independent counsel statute and unlawfully intruded on the power of impeachment, which the Constitution gives solely to the House of Representatives. Dash resigned in protest over Starr's actions, and made public the following letter of resignation on Friday, November 20, 1998:

Dear Ken,

I hereby submit my resignation as outside consultant and adviser to you and your Office of Independent Counsel, effective at noon today.

My decision to leave has nothing whatsoever to do with the many unfounded and misinformed attacks on your conduct as independent counsel. Through most of your tenure, I have been fully informed by you and your staff on all major decisions made by your office. I have advised you on these matters and have approved most of the decisions made. On some I agreed with you and your staff at the outset. As to others, where I disagreed, you showed your willingness to be open to my advice and you came to different decisions.

From my special vantage point, as an experienced professional outsider with no personal or professional stake in the outcome of your investigations, I found that you conducted yourself with integrity and professionalism as did your staff of experienced federal prosecutors.

I resign for a fundamental reason. Against my strong advice, you decided to depart from your usual professional decision-making by accepting the invitation of the House Judiciary Committee to appear before the committee and serve as an aggressive advocate for the proposition that the evidence in your referral demonstrates that the president committed impeachable offenses.

In doing this you have violated your obligations under the independent counsel statute and have unlawfully intruded on the power of impeachment which the Constitution gives solely to the House. As independent counsel you have only one narrow duty under the statute relating to the House's power of impeachment. That one duty, under Section 595(c) of the statute, is to objectively provide for the House substantial and credible information that may constitute grounds for impeachment.

The statute does not, and could not constitutionally give the independent counsel any role in impeachment other than this single informing function. The House is not dependent on the independent counsel for information related to its impeachment role. It can get its information from many sources, including through its own process, and does not need a referral of information from the independent counsel before it can decide to have an impeachment inquiry. The referral you made to the House was proper under the statute.

But your role and authority as a provider of information to the House stopped there. You have no right or authority under the law, as independent counsel, to advocate for a particular position on the evidence before the Judiciary Committee or to argue that the evidence in your referral is strong enough to justify the decision by the committee to recommend impeachment. Constitutionally, as you have recognized, the House has the sole power of impeachment. As an executive branch independent prosecutor you may not intrude on that sole power, even if invited by the committee.

Your referral to the House under the statute presented all the evidence you had about the Lewinsky matter which you believed was substantial and credible. As I have said, that was your only lawful responsibility under the statute governing your office. The House committee has excellent lawyers advising it and did not need you to summarize your referral and to argue for impeachment. Indeed the committee does not have a right to impose upon you as independent counsel to be its prosecuting counsel for impeachment.

By your willingness to serve in this improper role you have seriously harmed the public confidence in the independence and objectivity of your office. Frequently you have publicly stated that you have sought my advice in major decisions and had my approval. I cannot allow that inference to continue regarding your present abuse of your office and have no other choice but to resign.

Sincerely,

/s/

Samuel Dash

Dash's letter is an unusually strong condemnation and accusation of unprofessional conduct against Starr. Was the disagreement between Starr and Dash merely "an academic dispute about the role of the independent counsel," as then-House Judiciary Committee member Lindsey Graham described it at the time, *see* Susan Schmidt & Ruth Marcus, *Starr's Ethics Advisor Quits Over Testimony*, WASH. POST A1 (Nov. 21, 1998), or is there a more fundamental separation-of-powers question at issue? What would you have done if you had been in Starr's position? How would you justify taking a different approach than that followed by Leon Jaworski in the Watergate investigation? For contemporaneous reports of the views of several prominent practicing lawyers and academic experts, see Schmidt & Marcus, *supra*.

2. **The Clinton Impeachment and the Law of Perjury, Part I — The Materiality Issue.** In his "closing argument" to the Senate, reproduced in part above, Senator Bumpers sought to distinguish charges of perjury about sex and an extramarital affair from more "serious" perjury charges, such as perjury committed by a witness in a murder case. The law of perjury, of course, does not recognize such a distinction, although it does require that a false statement be "material" to the legal proceedings in which it was made. The first "possible ground[] for impeachment" against President Clinton in Independent Counsel Starr's referral to the House of Representatives, reproduced in part above, was that President Clinton "lied under oath at a civil deposition while he was a defendant in a sexual harassment lawsuit" (the Paula Jones case). President Clinton's attorneys and political defenders argued that even if he did make false statements about his relationship with Monica Lewinsky during his deposition in the Paula Jones civil litigation, those statements were not "material" to the case and therefore

would not meet the legal definition of perjury. One of the four articles of impeachment against President Clinton that were passed by the House Judiciary Committee charged that President Clinton had committed perjury in the *Jones* litigation, but that article was defeated in the full House of Representatives by a vote of 229 to 205.

After President Clinton's acquittal in the Senate impeachment trial, the federal judge who presided over the Paula Jones sexual harassment case found President Clinton in civil contempt of court for having "violated this Court's discovery Orders regarding disclosure of information deemed by this Court to be relevant to plaintiff's lawsuit." *See Jones v. Clinton*, 36 F. Supp. 2d 1118, 1131 (E.D. Ark. 1999). The judge concluded that President Clinton had made "intentionally false" statements during his deposition testimony:

> It is difficult to construe the President's sworn statements in this civil lawsuit concerning his relationship with Ms. Lewinsky as anything other than a willful refusal to obey this Court's discovery Orders. Given the President's admission that he was misleading with regard to the questions being posed to him and the clarity with which his falsehoods are revealed by the record, there is no need to engage in an extended analysis of the President's sworn statements in this lawsuit. Simply put, the President's deposition testimony regarding whether he had ever been alone with Ms. Lewinsky was intentionally false, and his statements regarding whether he had ever engaged in sexual relations with Ms. Lewinsky likewise were intentionally false, notwithstanding tortured definitions and interpretations of the term "sexual relations."

Id. at 1130 (footnotes omitted). Does this judicial finding that President Clinton made "intentionally false" statements during his deposition regarding information "relevant to the plaintiff's lawsuit" establish that President Clinton committed perjury in the *Jones* case, or does the materiality defense remain even after the court's findings? Consider in this regard the following explanation of the distinction between "materiality" and "relevance" offered by the D.C. Circuit in a McCarthy-era false-statements case: "'Material' when used in respect to evidence is often confused with 'relevant,' but the two terms have wholly different meanings. To be 'relevant' means to relate to the issue. To be 'material' means to have probative weight, *i.e.*, reasonably likely to influence the tribunal in making a determination required to be made. A statement may be relevant but not material." *Weinstock v. United States*, 231 F.2d 699, 701 (D.C. Cir. 1956). The same court later said that the test for materiality under the federal perjury statute is "whether the false statement has a natural tendency to influence, or was capable of influencing, the decision of the tribunal in making a determination required to be made." *United States v. Moore*, 613 F.2d 1029, 1038 (D.C. Cir. 1979), *quoting Weinstock*, 231 F.2d at 701–02. Applying these tests, would President Clinton's false statements during his deposition in the *Jones* litigation constitute perjury? Professor Richard Uviller has argued that they would not:

> Even an intentionally false statement does not amount to the federal crime of perjury unless it concerns a *material* matter. At this stage, remember, Pres-

ident Clinton is being deposed on an alleged incident in a hotel room between himself and Paula Jones while he was Governor of Arkansas. The question he falsely answered at the deposition concerned sexual interactions between himself and Monica Lewinsky years later in the White House. How is the matter elicited by these questions material to the issues in the Jones lawsuit? Those who have not studied the Federal Rules of Evidence might be tempted to say the Lewinsky business revealed a sexual predator with weak judgment or control, or went to prove a pattern of seductive conduct likely to be repeated. Maybe so, but those familiar with the Federal Rules—and, in particular, Rule 404(a)—know that character is inadmissible to show that this is just the sort of thing a person like that would do. Even if one—or more than one—prior, unrelated incident establishes a pattern, patterns to prove propensity to prove the conduct at issue are clearly (if counter-intuitively) excluded. In fact, Judge Wright correctly ruled that the answers to the Lewinsky questions would be inadmissible in the trial of the Jones case.

Can a false answer to a question impermissible under the Rules of Evidence be material? Judge Wright also ruled (erroneously, I thought) that the question was nevertheless allowed at the deposition because the Rules of Evidence do not apply at pre-trial discovery. True, but there are limits at discovery too. A question may not be asked at discovery if there is little chance that it will lead to admissible evidence. Since the whole Lewinsky affair was inadmissible at the Jones trial, it is hard to see how the question at issue might discover admissible evidence.

H. Richard Uviller, *Poorer But Wiser: The Bar Looks Back at Its Contribution to the Impeachment Spectacle*, 68 FORDHAM L. REV. 897, 904–05 (1999) (footnote references omitted). For additional analysis of this issue, see Alan Heinrich, *Clinton's Little White Lies: The Materiality Requirement for Perjury in Civil Discovery*, 32 LOY. L.A. L. REV. 1303 (1999). *See also* Daniel H. Pollitt, *Sex in the Oval Office and Cover-Up Under Oath: Impeachable Offense?*, 77 N.C. L. REV. 259 (1998).

3. The Law of Perjury, Part II—The "Literal Truth" Defense, or Does It in Fact Matter "What the Meaning of 'Is' Is"? The "materiality" argument is not the only technical defense that can be asserted to avoid a criminal conviction for perjury. In one of the best-known Supreme Court cases reviewing perjury charges, the following exchange between an attorney and a witness in a corporate bankruptcy proceeding was at issue:

> Q. Do you have any bank accounts in Swiss banks, Mr. Bronston?
>
> A. No, sir.
>
> Q. Have you ever?
>
> A. The company had an account there for about six months, in Zurich.
>
> Q. Have you any nominees who have bank accounts in Swiss banks?
>
> A. No, sir.

Q. Have you ever?

A. No, sir.

It is undisputed that for a period of nearly five years, between October 1959 and June 1964, petitioner had a personal bank account at the International Credit Bank in Geneva, Switzerland, into which he made deposits and upon which he drew checks totaling more than $180,000. It is likewise undisputed that petitioner's answers were literally truthful. (a) Petitioner did not at the time of questioning have a Swiss bank account. (b) Bronston Productions, Inc. did have the account in Zurich described by petitioner. (c) Neither at the time of questioning nor before did petitioner have nominees who had Swiss accounts. The Government's prosecution for perjury went forward on the theory that in order to mislead his questioner, petitioner answered the second question with literal truthfulness but unresponsively addressed his answer to the company's assets and not to his own—thereby implying that he had no personal Swiss bank account at the relevant time.

Bronston v. United States, 409 U.S. 352, 354–55 (1973). The Supreme Court unanimously reversed the defendant's perjury conviction and held that an answer to a question, even if intentionally evasive, is not perjury "simply because a wily witness succeeds in derailing the questioner—so long as the witness speaks the literal truth." *Id.* at 360. The Court placed a heavy burden on the lawyer asking the question in such situations:

It is the responsibility of the lawyer to probe; testimonial interrogation, and cross-examination in particular, is a probing, prying, pressing form of inquiry. If a witness evades, it is the lawyer's responsibility to recognize the evasion and to bring the witness back to the mark, to flush out the whole truth with the tools of adversary examination.

Id. at 358–59. Does *Bronston* provide any possible insights into what President Clinton meant when, during his August 17, 1998 grand jury testimony, he made the following statements about his deposition in the *Jones* litigation? "I wanted to be legal without being particularly helpful" and "[m]y goal in this deposition was to be truthful but ... I did not wish to do the work of the Jones lawyers" and "I was determined to walk through the mine field of this deposition without violating the law, and I believe I did." (The quotes here are taken from the January 19, 2001, letter of President Clinton's attorney David Kendall to Independent Counsel Robert W. Ray, and the emphases are in Mr. Kendall's letter.)

If President Clinton, a former law professor, recalled the *Bronston* case, might he have been attempting to use the rule of *Bronston* during his civil deposition testimony to give evasive but literally true testimony, and thus avoid committing perjury? Senator Arlen Specter, in his floor statement explaining his "not proved" vote on the Clinton impeachment (discussed further in Note 5 below), recognized the application of *Bronston* to President Clinton's testimony: "Utilizing the holding in *Bronston* to the utmost, the President couched his answers with great care relying on the questioner not to pursue the unanswered questions." *See* 145 Cong. Rec. S1537 (Feb. 12, 1999) (floor statement of Senator Specter). Would that strategy explain his famously tortured interpretation of the term "sexual relations" and his widely derided statement during his August 17, 1998, videotaped grand jury testimony that whether or not his counsel Robert Bennett's statement during the *Jones* deposition that there is no sex of any kind with Monica Lewinsky was a false statement "depends upon what the meaning of the word 'is' is" (because at the time Bennett made the statement the sexual relationship had stopped)?[10] If President Clinton was trying to use the rule of *Bronston* to avoid committing perjury, was it a wise legal strategy? Consider in this regard the following scathing indictment of the Clinton defense by federal judge, law professor, and prolific legal commentator Richard Posner, discussing a November 6, 1998, letter signed by several hundred law professors urging Congress not to impeach President Clinton and the failure of the American bar to take issue with the law professors' letter:

> The silence of the bar could be thought to condone the tactics employed by the President (himself a lawyer, remember) and his lawyers, tactics that conform to the lay intuition that what lawyers mainly do is drive a wedge between law and justice. The lawyers' defense of the President against the charge of perjury was grounded in quibbling, hairsplitting equivocation, brazen denial of the obvious, truncated quotation and quotation out of context, and mischaracterization of the law. The impression that many lay observers must have taken from this spectacle was that perjury is an unimportant technical offense, that a skillful liar is beyond its reach, and that a clever lawyer can beat any perjury charge (and perhaps any charge, period) by spinning a web of sophistries.

---

10. For an in-depth account of Clinton's civil deposition and grand jury testimony, see JOHN F. HARRIS, THE SURVIVOR: BILL CLINTON IN THE WHITE HOUSE (Random House 2005). Harris describes Clinton's preparation for his deposition in the Paula Jones sexual harassment case and the compromise that resulted in the definition used during the deposition of "sexual relations" as "contact with the genitalia, anus, groin, breast, inner thigh, or buttocks of any person with an intent to gratify the sexual desire of any person," which Harris notes "would in time be seen as his salvation." *Id.* at 302–03. Harris also described Clinton's videotaped grand jury testimony and the "meaning of 'is' is" exchange:

> Most of all, he masterfully obscured what prosecutors believed were the clear facts of the case in a cloud of verbiage. Some of it was prim and punctilious, as when he explained the legalistic definition of sexual relations in the Jones case meant that Lewinsky had had sexual relations with him, but not vice versa. "If the deponent is the person who has oral sex performed on him, then contact is not with anything on that list, but with the lips of another person."

> The Starr team was furious at what it regarded as the president's pettifogging. [Prosecutor Robert] Bittman recalled that in the Jones deposition, Robert Bennett had assured the judge and the plaintiff's lawyers that "there is no sex of any kind in any manner, shape, or form" between the president and Lewinsky. Wouldn't you agree, Bittman sneered, that "was an utterly false statement"?

> Clinton smiled and said, "It depends on what the meaning of 'is' is.... If 'is' means is and never has been, that is one thing. If it means, there is none, that was a completely true statement." A few minutes later, he added, "I was not trying to give you a cute answer on that."

> Of course, he had been doing that—and he paid for his cuteness. That throwaway line turned out to be one of Clinton's entrants in *Bartlett's Familiar Quotations*.

Id. at 340.

Richard A. Posner, An Affair of State: The Investigation, Impeachment, and Trial of President Clinton 242 (Harvard Univ. Press 1999). Do you agree with Judge Posner's critique of the Clinton defense, or do you believe that Clinton had a right—and his lawyers had an obligation—to assert any available legal defenses during the impeachment proceedings, including highly technical arguments like the "materiality" and "literal truth" arguments that are discussed above?

4. *Clinton v. Jones* in Hindsight. If the fault for President Clinton's deception and his subsequent legal troubles lies primarily with Clinton himself, and perhaps secondarily with his lawyers, should the Supreme Court also bear a measure of fault for its ruling that a sitting President could be subjected to private civil litigation while in office for acts occurring before he assumed office? *See Clinton v. Jones*, 520 U.S. 681 (1997) (holding unanimously that Paula Jones could proceed with her lawsuit against President Clinton). Shortly after the Clinton impeachment, Professor Akhil Reed Amar offered the following critique of *Clinton v. Jones* and the case that he views as its predecessor, *United States v. Nixon* (the Watergate tapes case):

> [L]ike *Nixon*, *Jones* reflected a remarkably self-satisfied view of federal judges. Trust us federal judges, said *Jones*, to sensitively manage lawsuits against the President. Against this institutional smugness, is it impolite to note that the entire national agenda of the last year has been derailed because of a legal error of Judge Wright's? Under a proper view of Fourth Amendment privacy and Federal Rules of Civil Procedure 26(c) and 45(c), Monica Lewinsky should never have been asked about her purely consensual sexual activity. Nor should Clinton have been forced to answer, given that his answer could implicate serious privacy interests of a non-party to this civil suit (Lewinksy) in the absence of a compelling need. But on this key issue Judge Wright was Judge Wrong when it counted (at the deposition), and had it not been for this error, the relevant "crimes" that hijacked the Clinton presidency would never have occurred. * * * In wrongly requiring disclosure of intimate and confidential relations, however, Judge Wright was in a way merely following the logic of *Nixon*, and its insistence on evidence over privacy.

Akhil Reed Amar, *Nixon's Shadow*, 83 Minn. L. Rev. 1405, 1416 (1999). Do you agree with Professor Amar's assessment? Did the Supreme Court err when it allowed the Paula Jones lawsuit to go forward during Clinton's presidency, rather than deferring it until after he left office? If so, what should be the rule governing when a sitting president can be sued for private conduct and when should such suits be deferred? For an essay arguing that "[t]he Supreme Court got it just right in ruling that President Clinton has no constitutional immunity, as Chief Executive, from responding to a lawsuit brought against him by Paula Jones," see Alan M. Dershowitz, *The Supreme Court is Right in the* Jones *Case*" (June 1997), *in* Sexual McCarthyism: Clinton, Starr, and the Emerging Constitutional Crisis 111–114 (Basic Books 1998).

5. **More on the Influence of Partisanship on Impeachment Proceedings—Partisanship and the Clinton Impeachment.** As explained above, impeachment is a unique

procedure—a political process, but with a constitutionally defined legal framework. What role, if any, should partisanship play in impeachment proceedings? In thinking about this question, consider the following historical analysis of American impeachment proceedings:

> Four of the six perfectly partisan votes [in the history of American impeachments] took place during the Clinton episode. The first was the House Judiciary Committee's vote for a formal investigation; the other three also involved that body in voting for Articles I, III, and IV of impeachment, while the vote on Article II saw only one Republican defect. Of the twelve votes taken on Clinton
>
> - Four were 100 percent vs. 100 percent;
> - Two were 90 percent vs. 100 percent;
> - Two were 80 percent vs. 100 percent;
> - Two were 90 percent vs. 90 percent;
> - One was 80 percent vs. 90 percent;
> - And, one was 60 percent vs. 90 percent.
>
> If one accepts this method of measuring partisanship, then the impeachment effort against Clinton clearly qualifies as perhaps the very definition of partisan politics.
>
> As for Clinton's acquittal, it can again be argued that the president survived because senators decided his behavior did not meet the legal requirements of high crimes and misdemeanors. In contrast to the [Andrew] Johnson acquittal, however, when Republicans had the votes for removal even if the Democrats voted as a block (which they did), there was no chance of removing Clinton if the Democrats were to vote as a block (which they did). The 45 Democrats clearly had different legal opinions than did at least 45 of the Republicans. Senator Arlen Specter's (R-PA) dramatic vote of "not proven" pointed up the possibility that the law was more important than politics.
>
> The *Washington Post* observed, however, that the Republicans failed "because four New England moderates and one from Pennsylvania joined with the 45 Senate Democrats to produce a 50–50 vote" that was partly attributable to the fact that "three of the moderates—Senators John Chafee (RI), James M. Jeffords (VT), and Olympia J. Snowe (ME)—were up for reelection ... in states where Clinton enjoy[ed] substantial popularity." The *Post* concluded: "In contrast to the battle in the House, where GOP moderates were pressured by the GOP leadership to support impeachment simply to 'keep the process going,' moderates in the Senate felt no such pressure. There was no chance for the necessary 67 votes to convict Clinton, and so the Senate moderates, in effect, were given a pass by their leadership." Republicans charged the Democrats with being partisan because of their block voting in the two Senate votes, apparently forgetting that they, too, had voted as a block five times during the process, including the first two votes that got the process started.

William B. Perkins, *The Political Nature of Presidential Impeachment in the United States*, *in* CHECKING EXECUTIVE POWER: PRESIDENTIAL IMPEACHMENT IN COMPARATIVE PERSPECTIVE 37–38 (Jody C. Baumgartner & Naoko Kada eds., Praeger Publishers 2003) (footnote references omitted). Should Senators be expected to put aside their partisan political affiliations during impeachment votes? Would it be desirable for them to do so? Is it naïve and unrealistic to believe they *could* ever do so? Does the famous "not proved" vote of then-Republican Senator Arlen Specter of Pennsylvania, referenced above, reflect nonpartisan legal analysis or was it just a politician's attempt to "have it both ways" on a difficult question? Senator Specter offered the following explanation of his vote on President Clinton's impeachment:

> My position in the matter is that the case has not been proved. I have gone back to Scottish law where there are three verdicts: guilty, not guilty, and not proved. I am not prepared to say on this record that President Clinton is not guilty. But I am certainly not prepared to say that he is guilty. There are precedents for a Senator voting present. I hope that I will be accorded the opportunity to vote not proved in this case.

145 Cong. Rec. S1535 (Feb. 12, 1999). (Senator Specter's vote was recorded as a "not guilty" vote, and as such his vote was one of the five by "moderate" Republicans who joined with the 45 Democrats to yield a 50–50 acquittal on Article II, which charged President Clinton with obstruction of justice in the Paula Jones litigation. *See* 145 Cong. Rec. S1459 (Feb. 12, 1999) (recording roll call vote).) Is Senator Specter's "not proved" vote an appropriate last word on the Clinton impeachment?

6. The Meaning of "High Crimes and Misdemeanors." The Constitution's Framers adopted the "high Crimes and Misdemeanors" standard from England, where it was the standard for impeachment by Parliament. Nevertheless, it is clear that, at least in some respects, the American Framers did not want to render executive branch officials responsible to Congress in the same way that governmental ministers—indeed, all British subjects—are responsible to Parliament. If executive-branch officials could be impeached and removed from office because of policy disagreements with Congress, or even because of Congress's view that the executive branch officials lack ability, impeachment would amount to something close to a vote of no confidence—and the executive's independence under the American separation of powers would be undermined. For that reason, when George Mason proposed adding "maladministration" to the list of impeachable offenses, James Madison objected. Madison argued that "[s]o vague a term" as "maladministration" would allow the Senate to remove a President at will. (The Framers also rejected "malpractice or neglect of duty" and "neglect of duty [and] malversation.") The Framers thereupon added "high Crimes and Misdemeanors."

The meaning of "high Crimes and Misdemeanors" is discussed further in the next section, which considers whether non-criminal conduct can satisfy the standard. For now, consider the adjective "high." That word, as well as Parliamentary practice, signaled that not every crime would amount to an impeachable offense. Even if a government official could be convicted of the crime of reckless driving, for example, that crime might not be a "high Crime" justifying his removal from office. Rather, "high Crimes" are offenses against the constitutional system or, as Hamilton wrote in *Federalist* No. 65, an "abuse or violation of some public trust." Justice Story's treatise on constitutional law distinguished impeachable "political offenses" from "crimes of a strictly legal character." Only "abuse of high offices of trust" — "personal mis-conduct, or gross neglect, or usurpation, or habitual disregard of the public interests, in the discharge of the duties of public office" — could satisfy the constitutional standard. Thus, while we might expect "high" to mean "serious," that does not appear to be the way in which the Framers used the term.

Did President Clinton's behavior amount to a high crime or misdemeanor? Is making a false statement, while intending to deceive a different branch of government, necessarily an offense against the constitutional system and therefore an impeachable offense? Are you persuaded by the argument of former-Senator Bumpers that the context of President Clinton's behavior rendered it something other than a crime against the state? Would it be any more of a "high" crime if President Clinton had lied in a tax case or a murder case? What if he lied under oath about his use of marijuana? (In 1992, Clinton infamously admitted having "experimented" with marijuana but claimed that "I didn't inhale." That statement, however, was not made under oath.)

First Impeachment of Donald Trump

In the last section, we saw that the impeachment of President Clinton raised concerns about partisanship in the impeachment process, as well as questions about the meaning of "high Crimes and Misdemeanors." Both of those issues returned to the forefront when President Trump was impeached (for the first time) in 2019. After the impeachment resolution, which is reprinted immediately below, we will consider legal issues raised by each of the two articles of impeachment, which respectively alleged abuse of power and obstruction of Congress.

A. The (First Two) Trump Articles of Impeachment

Resolution
Impeaching Donald John Trump,
President of the United States, for High Crimes and Misdemeanors

Resolved, That Donald J. Trump, President of the United States, is impeached for high crimes and misdemeanors and that the following articles of impeachment be exhibited to the United States Senate:

Articles of impeachment exhibited by the House of Representatives of the United States of America in the name of itself and of the people of the United States of America, against Donald J. Trump, President of the United States of America, in maintenance and support of its impeachment against him for high crimes and misdemeanors.

ARTICLE I: ABUSE OF POWER

The Constitution provides that the House of Representatives "shall have the sole Power of Impeachment and that the President shall be removed from Office on Impeachment for, and Conviction of, Treason, Bribery, or other high Crimes and Misdemeanors". In his conduct of the office of President of the United States—and in violation of his constitutional oath faithfully to execute the office of President of the United States and, to the best of his ability, preserve, protect, and defend the Constitution of the United States, and in violation of his constitutional duty to take care that the laws be faithfully executed—Donald J. Trump has abused the powers of the Presidency, in that:

Using the powers of his high office, President Trump solicited the interference of a foreign government, Ukraine, in the 2020 United States Presidential election. He did so through a scheme or course of conduct that included soliciting the Government of Ukraine to publicly announce investigations that would benefit his reelection, harm the election prospects of a political opponent, and influence the 2020 United States Presidential election to his advantage. President Trump also sought to pressure the Government of Ukraine to take these steps by conditioning official United States Government acts of significant value to Ukraine on its public announcement of the investigations. President Trump engaged in this scheme or course of conduct for corrupt purposes in pursuit of personal political benefit. In so doing, President Trump used the powers of the Presidency in a manner that compromised the national security of the United States and undermined the integrity of the United States democratic process. He thus ignored and injured the interests of the Nation.

President Trump engaged in this scheme or course of conduct through the following means:

(1) President Trump—acting both directly and through his agents within and outside the United States Government—corruptly solicited the Government of Ukraine to publicly announce investigations into—

(A) a political opponent, former Vice President Joseph R. Biden, Jr.; and

(B) a discredited theory promoted by Russia alleging that Ukraine—rather than Russia—interfered in the 2016 United States Presidential election.

(2) With the same corrupt motives, President Trump—acting both directly and through his agents within and outside the United States Government—conditioned two official acts on the public announcements that he had requested—

(A) the release of $391 million of United States taxpayer funds that Congress had appropriated on a bipartisan basis for the purpose of providing vital military and security assistance to Ukraine to oppose Russian aggression and which President Trump had ordered suspended; and

(B) a head of state meeting at the White House, which the President of Ukraine sought to demonstrate continued United States support for the Government of Ukraine in the face of Russian aggression.

(3) Faced with the public revelation of his actions, President Trump ultimately released the military and security assistance to the Government of Ukraine, but has persisted in openly and corruptly urging and soliciting Ukraine to undertake investigations for his personal political benefit.

These actions were consistent with President Trump's previous invitations of foreign interference in United States elections.

In all this, President Trump abused the powers of the Presidency by ignoring and injuring national security and other vital national interests to obtain an improper personal political benefit. He has also betrayed the Nation by abusing his high office to enlist a foreign power in corrupting democratic elections.

Wherefore President Trump, by such conduct, has demonstrated that he will remain a threat to national security and the Constitution if allowed to remain in office, and has acted in a manner grossly incompatible with self-governance and the rule of law. President Trump thus warrants impeachment and trial, removal from office, and disqualification to hold and enjoy any Office of honor, trust, or profit under the United States.

ARTICLE II: OBSTRUCTION OF CONGRESS

The Constitution provides that the House of Representatives "shall have the sole Power of Impeachment" and that the President "shall be removed from Office on Impeachment for, and Conviction of, Treason, Bribery, or other high Crimes and Misdemeanors". In his conduct of the office of President of the United States—and in violation of his constitutional oath faithfully to execute the office of President of the United States and, to the best of his ability, preserve, protect, and defend the Constitution of the United States, and in violation of his constitutional duty to take care that the laws be faithfully executed—

Donald J. Trump has directed the unprecedented, categorical, and indiscriminate defiance of subpoenas issued by the House of Representatives pursuant to its sole Power of Impeachment. President Trump has abused the powers of the Presidency in a manner offensive to, and subversive of, the Constitution, in that:

The House of Representatives has engaged in an impeachment inquiry focused on President Trump's corrupt solicitation of the Government of Ukraine to interfere in the 2020 United States Presidential election. As part of this impeachment inquiry, the Committees undertaking the investigation served subpoenas seeking documents and testimony deemed vital to the inquiry from various Executive Branch agencies and offices, and current and former officials.

In response, without lawful cause or excuse, President Trump directed Executive Branch agencies, offices, and officials not to comply with those subpoenas. President Trump thus interposed the powers of the Presidency against the lawful subpoenas of the House of Representatives, and assumed to himself functions and judgments necessary to the exercise of the "sole Power of Impeachment" vested by the Constitution in the House of Representatives. President Trump abused the powers of his high office through the following means:

(1) Directing the White House to defy a lawful subpoena by withholding the production of documents sought therein by the Committees.

(2) Directing other Executive Branch agencies and offices to defy lawful subpoenas and withhold the production of documents and records from the Committees—in response to which the Department of State, Office of Management and Budget, Department of Energy, and Department of Defense refused to produce a single document or record.

(3) Directing current and former Executive Branch officials not to cooperate with the Committees—in response to which nine Administration officials defied subpoenas for testimony, namely John Michael "Mick" Mulvaney, Robert B. Blair, John A. Eisenberg, Michael Ellis, Preston Wells Griffith, Russell T. Vought, Michael Duffey, Brian McCormack, and T. Ulrich Brechbuhl.

These actions were consistent with President Trump's previous efforts to undermine United States Government investigations into foreign interference in United States elections.

Through these actions, President Trump sought to arrogate to himself the right to determine the propriety, scope, and nature of an impeachment inquiry into his own conduct, as well as the unilateral prerogative to deny any and all information to the House of Representatives in the exercise of its "sole Power of Impeachment". In the history of the Republic, no President has ever ordered the complete defiance of an impeachment inquiry or sought to obstruct and impede so comprehensively the ability of the House of Representatives to investigate "high Crimes and Misdemeanors". This abuse of office served to cover up the President's own repeated misconduct and to seize and control the power of impeachment and thus to nullify a vital constitutional safeguard vested solely in the House of Representatives.

In all of this, President Trump has acted in a manner contrary to his trust as President and subversive of constitutional government, to the great prejudice of the cause of law and justice, and to the manifest injury of the people of the United States.

Wherefore, President Trump, by such conduct, has demonstrated that he will remain a threat to the Constitution if allowed to remain in office, and has acted in a manner grossly incompatible with self-governance and the rule of law. President Trump thus warrants impeachment and trial, removal from office, and disqualification to hold and enjoy any office of honor, trust, or profit under the United States.

B. First Trump Impeachment, Article I: Abuse of Power

President Trump's first impeachment charged him with soliciting Ukrainian assistance in his 2020 re-election campaign. The principal basis for the charge was the President's July 25, 2019, phone call with Ukrainian President Volodymyr Zelenskyy, the content of which is reprinted below. In the call, President Trump asked President Zelenskyy to investigate the behavior of former U.S. Vice President (and prospective 2020 presidential candidate) Joe Biden, as well as the business dealings of Biden's son Hunter.

In 2014, while Joe Biden was Vice President and involved with the Obama Administration's policy with respect to Ukraine, Hunter Biden joined the board of directors of a Ukrainian energy company named Burisma. Hunter was paid $50,000 per month, despite having no qualifications for such a post. Two years later, Joe Biden pressured Ukraine to fire its prosecutor general, Viktor Shokin, by threatening to withhold loan guarantees. Although Shokin later claimed that he was fired because he was investigating Burisma, Shokin was widely believed—by the European Union, the World Bank, the International Monetary Fund, and officials of both U.S. political parties—to be corrupt. Whether or not Shokin was investigating Burisma, there is no evidence that Biden had him fired to protect Hunter or his business interests. Nevertheless, the appearance of a conflict of interest struck many—including, apparently, President Trump—as suspicious.

President Trump also appeared to ask the Ukrainian president for assistance investigating "Crowdstrike"—the cybersecurity firm hired by the Democratic National Committee after the DNC's servers were hacked by Russia as part of an attempt to interfere in the 2016 U.S. presidential election. Although President Trump suggested that there might be a Ukrainian connection to Crowdstrike—perhaps as a way of undermining the conclusion that Russia was responsible for the DNC hacks—there is no evidence for such a connection.

Memorandum of Telephone Conversation

SUBJECT: Telephone Conversation with President Zelenskyy of Ukraine
Participants: President Zelenskyy of Ukraine
Notetakers: The White House Situation Room
Date, Time July 25, 2019, 9:03–9:33 am EDT and
Place: Residence

The President: Congratulations on a great victory. We all watched from the United States and you did a terrific job. The way you came from behind, somebody who wasn't given much of a chance, and you ended up winning easily. It's a fantastic achievement. Congratulations.

President Zelenskyy: You are absolutely right Mr. President. We did win big and we worked hard for this. We worked a lot but I would like to confess to you that I had an opportunity to learn from you. We used quite a few of your skills and knowledge and were able to use it as an example for our elections and yes it is true that these were unique elections. We were in a unique situation that we were able to achieve a unique success. I'm able to tell you the following; the first time you called me to congratulate me when I won my presidential election, and the second time you are now calling me when my party won the parliamentary election. I think I should run more often so you can call me more often and we can talk over the phone more often.

The President: (laughter) That's a very good idea. I think your country is very happy about that.

President Zelenskyy: Well yes, to tell you the truth, we are trying to work hard because we wanted to drain the swamp here in our country. We brought in many many new people. Not the old politicians, not the typical politicians, because we want to have a new format and a new type of government. You are a great teacher for us and in that.

The President: Well it is very nice of you to say that. I will say that we do a lot for Ukraine. We spend a lot of effort and a lot of time. Much more than the European countries are doing and they should be helping you more than they are. Germany does almost nothing for you. All they do is talk and I think it's something that you should really ask them about. When I was speaking to [German Chancellor] Angela Merkel she talks Ukraine, but she doesn't do anything. A lot of the European countries are the same way so I think it's something you want to look at but the United States has been very very good to Ukraine. I wouldn't say that it's reciprocal necessarily because things are happening that are not good but the United States has been very very good to Ukraine.

President Zelenskyy: Yes you are absolutely right. Not only 100%, but actually 1000% and I can tell you the following; I did talk to Angela Merkel and I did meet with her I also met and talked with [French President Emmanuel] Macron and I told them that they are not doing quite as much as they need to be doing on the issues with the sanctions. They are not enforcing the sanctions. They are not working as much as they should work for Ukraine. It turns out that even though logically, the European Union should be our biggest partner but technically the United States is a much bigger partner than the European Union and I'm very grateful to you for that because the United States is doing quite a lot for Ukraine. Much more than the European Union especially when we are talking about sanctions against the Russian Federation. I would also like to thank you for your great support in the area of defense. We are ready to continue to cooperate for the next steps specifically we are almost ready to buy more Javelins from the United States for defense purposes.

The President: I would like you to do us a favor though because our country has been through a lot and Ukraine knows a lot about it. I would like you to find out what happened with this whole situation with Ukraine, they say Crowdstrike.... I guess you have one of your wealthy people.... The server, they say Ukraine has it. There are a lot of things that went on, the whole situation. I think you're surrounding yourself with some of the same people. I would like to have the Attorney General call you or your people and I would like you to get to the bottom of it. As you saw yesterday, that whole nonsense ended with a very poor performance by a man named Robert Mueller, an incompetent performance, but they say a lot of it started with Ukraine. Whatever you can do, it's very important that you do it if that's possible.

President Zelenskyy: Yes it is very important for me and everything that you just mentioned earlier. For me as a President, it is very important and we are open for any future cooperation. We are ready to open a new page on cooperation in relations between the United States and Ukraine. For that purpose, I just recalled our ambassador from

United States and he will be replaced by a very competent and very experienced ambassador who will work hard on making sure that our two nations are getting closer. I would also like and hope to see him having your trust and your confidence and have personal relations with you so we can cooperate even more so. I will personally tell you that one of my assistants spoke with Mr. Giuliani just recently and we are hoping very much that Mr. Giuliani will be able to travel to Ukraine and we will meet once he comes to Ukraine. I just wanted to assure you once again that you have nobody but friends around us. I will make sure that I surround myself with the best and most experienced people. I also wanted to tell you that we are friends. We are great friends and you Mr. President have friends in our country so we can continue our strategic partnership. I also plan to surround myself with great people and in addition to that investigation, I guarantee as the President of Ukraine that all the investigations will be done openly and candidly. That I can assure you.

The President: Good because I heard you had a prosecutor who was very good and he was shut down and that's really unfair. A lot of people are talking about that, the way they shut your very good prosecutor down and you had some very bad people involved. Mr. Giuliani is a highly respected man. He was the mayor of New York City, a great mayor, and I would like him to call you. I will ask him to call you along with the Attorney General. Rudy very much knows what's happening and he is a very capable guy. If you could speak to him that would be great. The former ambassador from the United States, the woman, was bad news and the people she was dealing with in the Ukraine were bad news so I just want to let you know that. The other thing, There's a lot of talk about Biden's son, that Biden stopped the prosecution and a lot of people want to find out about that so whatever you can do with the Attorney General would be great. Biden went around bragging that he stopped the prosecution so if you can look into it.... It sounds horrible to me.

President Zelenskyy: I wanted to tell you about the prosecutor. First of all, I understand and I'm knowledgeable about the situation. Since we have won the absolute majority in our Parliament, the next prosecutor general will be 100% my person, my candidate, who will be approved, by the parliament and will start as a new prosecutor in September. He or she will look into the situation, specifically to the company that you mentioned in this issue. The issue of the investigation of the case is actually the issue of making sure to restore the honesty so we will take care of that and will work on the investigation of the case. On top of that, I would kindly ask you if you have any additional information that you can provide to us, it would be very helpful for the investigation to make sure that we administer justice in our country with regard to the Ambassador to the United States from Ukraine as far as I recall her name was Ivanovich. It was great that you were the first one who told me that she was a bad ambassador because I agree with you 100%. Her attitude towards me was far from the best as she admired the previous President and she was on his side. She would not accept me as a new President well enough.

The President: Well, she's going to go through some things. I will have Mr. Giuliani give you a call and I am also going to have Attorney General Barr call and we will get to the bottom of it. I'm sure you will figure it out. I heard the prosecutor was treated very badly and he was a very fair prosecutor so good luck with everything. Your economy is going to get better and better I predict. You have a lot of assets. It's a great country. I have many Ukrainian friends, they're incredible people.

President Zelenskyy: I would like to tell you that I also have quite a few Ukrainian friends that live in the United States. Actually last time I traveled to the United States, I stayed in New York near Central Park and I stayed at the Trump Tower. I will talk to them and I hope to see them again in the future. I also wanted to thank you for your invitation to visit the United States, specifically Washington DC. On the other hand, I also want to ensure you that we will be very serious about the case and will work on the investigation. As to the economy, there is much potential for our two countries and one of the issues that is very important for Ukraine is energy independence. I believe we can be very successful and cooperating on energy independence with United States. We are already working on cooperation. We are buying American oil but I am very hopeful for a future meeting. We will have more time and more opportunities to discuss these opportunities and get to know each other better. I would like to thank you very much for your support.

The President: Good. Well, thank you very much and I appreciate that. I will tell Rudy and Attorney General Barr to call. Thank you. Whenever you would like to come to the White House, feel free to call. Give us a date and we'll work that out. I look forward to seeing you.

President Zelenskyy: Thank you very much. I would be very happy to come and would be happy to meet with you personally and get to know you better. I am looking forward to our meeting and I also would like to invite you to visit Ukraine and come to the city of Kyiv which is a beautiful city. We have a beautiful country which would welcome you. On the other hand, I believe that on September 1 we will be in Poland and we can meet in Poland hopefully. After that, it might be a very good idea for you to travel to Ukraine. We can either take my plane and go to Ukraine or we can take your plane, which is probably much better than mine.

The President: Okay, we can work that out. I look forward to seeing you in Washington and maybe in Poland because I think we are going to be there at that time.

President Zelenskyy: Thank you very much Mr. President.

The President: Congratulations on a fantastic job you've done. The whole world was watching. I'm not sure it was so much of an upset but congratulations.

President Zelenskyy: Thank you Mr. President bye-bye.

Notes and Questions

1. **High *Crimes*?** The first article of impeachment charged President Trump with abuse of power. But while abuse of power may be the essence of what differentiates impeachable "high" crimes from ordinary crimes (see the discussion at the end of the previous section), there is no crime denominated "abuse of power." Does the Constitu-

tion permit the President to be impeached for a "high Crime" that is not a crime at all, in the ordinary sense of the word?

Given that there was no federal criminal code at the time the Constitution was drafted, it is quite unlikely that the Constitution requires impeachable offenses to be pre-existing crimes defined by federal statute. Nevertheless, President Trump's lawyers argued that a "high Crime" must at least be "crime-like." They argued that "high Crimes and Misdemeanors" should be interpreted in context—and they pointed out that the phrase comes third in the list of impeachable offenses, following treason and bribery. Thus, they argued, the President may be impeached for offenses that are neither treason nor bribery, but they must represent threats to the constitutional system *akin to* treason and bribery. *See* 166 Cong. Rec. S316 (Jan. 21, 2020) (President's brief) ("'[O] ther high Crimes and Misdemeanors' must be understood to have the same qualities—in terms of seriousness and their effect on the functioning of government—as the crimes of 'Treason' and 'Bribery.'").

The President's lawyers further argued that an unduly expansive interpretation of "high Crimes and Misdemeanors"—one that would permit the President to be impeached whenever Congress judged him to have abused his power—would in practice permit the President to be impeached for "maladministration," which the Framers rejected as being insufficient to protect presidential independence from Congress.

Do you think "abuse of power" is too vague or manipulable to be a "high Crime[or] Misdemeanor"? Or does it appropriately distinguish "high Crimes and Misdemeanors" from unimpeachable offenses by focusing on what *Federalist* No. 65 called an "abuse or violation of some public trust"? Is "abuse of power" really just another way of *defining* "high Crimes and Misdemeanors"? If so, is it appropriate for "abuse of power" to be an impeachment charge, or should the House have to do a better job of specifying what high crime or high misdemeanor it believes was committed?

2. Potential Limits on an "Abuse of Power" Charge. Nobody claims that Congress should be able to impeach an executive branch official over a policy disagreement. Nevertheless, one might worry that relatively minor inter-branch conflicts—concerning, for example, whether the President has made too much use of executive orders—could be described as "abuses of power" by political opponents and thereby made into impeachable offenses.[11] To avoid such a result, we might try to identify the kinds of abuses of power that are sufficiently serious (and that rise above mere partisan concerns) to

---

11. As an illustration of the potentially broad use of the impeachment power—or of the singularity of President Trump—consider the following: "[B]efore the Ukraine affair, [House Judiciary C]ommittee staff members had drafted ten Articles of Impeachment. These would have covered everything from collusion with Russia, obstruction of the Mueller investigation, giving hush money to deceive the public about an extramarital affair, dangling pardons to encourage people not to testify against him, violating the Emoluments Clause, and spending money in ways unauthorized by Congress. The Tenth Article was blank, entitled 'The Next High Crime.'" Victoria F. Nourse, The Impeachments of Donald Trump 117 n.70 (2021) (citing Norm Eisen, A Case for the American People: The United States v. Donald Trump (2020) and Peter Baker, *House Democrats Considered 10 Impeachment Articles Before Narrowing Their Case Against Trump*, N.Y. Times, July 22, 2020)).

be impeachable. Drawing on some work by other scholars, Professor Victoria Nourse has collected some possible abuse-of-power standards. *See* VICTORIA F. NOURSE, THE IMPEACHMENTS OF DONALD TRUMP 114–16 (2021). Consider whether any of these standards would be appropriate, and whether they would establish a clear enough line identifying impeachable high crimes and misdemeanors.

a. *Whether a reasonable person would consider the behavior "abusive and wrong, without reference to partisan politics or differences of opinion on policy." Id.* at 115 (quoting CHARLES L. BLACK, JR. & PHILIP BOBBITT, IMPEACHMENT: A HANDBOOK 30 (2018)). While this standard purports to rule out partisanship as a justification for impeachment, the "abusive and wrong" standard may be thought to be so elastic as practically to invite partisanship. Further, whether a given behavior violates that standard would seem to depend on the level of generality at which the behavior is described. For example, we might agree that "cheating in a presidential election" or "extorting a foreign country" would be "abusive and wrong," although we might not agree about whether those phrases are apt descriptions of President Trump's behavior with respect to Ukraine.

b. *Whether the behavior undermines the electoral system.* Perhaps abuses of power should not be impeachable unless they attack our democracy. As long as our electoral system is functioning, we might expect the voters to sort out potential abuses of power, but if those abuses themselves disrupt the functioning of the electoral process, then impeachment is necessary to re-impose necessary checks. House managers repeatedly pointed to President Trump's alleged efforts to "cheat" in the 2020 election, in arguing that impeachment was essential. On the other hand, there are problems with this standard. For one thing, all abuses of power, by definition, undermine the electoral process in some form, by exercising power that the people did not authorize that official to exercise. For another thing, some of the worst abuses of power—use of the military to assassinate congressional leaders, for example—might not relate directly to elections, yet we all might agree that they would be impeachable.

c. *Whether the situation is too urgent to wait until the next election.* As with the sub-versive-of-democracy standard discussed above, we might reserve impeachment for those misbehaviors that cannot be corrected by the normal electoral process. Even if the electoral system is functioning properly, the next election might be so far away that a rogue President might be able to cause too much damage in the interim. But where that is not the case, and the voters can decide for themselves whom to trust with power, perhaps that should be the preferred approach.

d. *Whether a different President should be impeached for the same conduct.* To check our partisanship, we might ask ourselves whether we would support impeachment if the same behavior were performed by a different President. If our instinct is to defend an accused President because we admire him, we should ask ourselves whether we would feel the same way if the President were someone we disliked; if our instinct is to support impeachment of the current President, we should ask ourselves whether we would feel the same way if the President were one we admired. Although the desire to eliminate consideration of partisanship may be admirable, this standard, like the others, is vulnerable to people's tendency to rationalize their partisanship.

e. *Whether impeachment is the only available constitutional remedy.* Finally, we might reserve impeachment as a last resort. If there is another method of checking a presidential abuse of power—by challenging the executive's action in court, for example—then impeachment should not be invoked. Because the judicial process takes time, however, litigation might not be thought to be an adequate remedy to address an ongoing abuse of power.

3. Conditioning Foreign Aid and a White House Meeting on Announcing an Investigation. The first article of impeachment charged that President Trump "conditioned two official acts" on Ukraine's announcement of an investigation into the Bidens. Those two acts were the release of $391 million for military and security assistance and a meeting at the White House. The aid was delayed but eventually released (long before Russia's 2021 invasion of Ukraine), despite the lack of any Ukrainian investigation into the Bidens. The Impoundment Control Act (ICA), 2 U.S.C. §684, permits the President to decline to spend congressionally appropriated funds in certain circumstances, but not simply because the President disagrees with the policy behind the appropriation—and obviously not because of the President's desire to improve his re-election chances. Presidents have also temporarily withheld appropriated funds for "programmatic" reasons that make it impractical to spend the funds. *See generally* PETER M. SHANE ET AL., SEPARATION OF POWERS LAW: CASES AND MATERIALS 197–202 (4th ed. 2018).

In a report issued in 2020, the Government Accountability Office concluded that the withholding of Ukraine's aid violated the ICA, because the withholding "f[ell] squarely within the scope of an impermissible policy deferral" and was not justified as programmatic. U.S. Government Accountability Office, Office of Management and Budget—Withholding of Ukraine Security Assistance, File No. B-331564, Jan. 16, 2020, at 6. Would temporarily withholding Ukraine's aid be an impeachable offense? Does the answer depend on whether the deferral violates the ICA? Does the answer depend on whether President Trump subjectively thought the Bidens' conduct deserved an investigation or, instead, whether President Trump was trying to gain an electoral advantage through an investigation of conduct that he knew was not illegal?

Would anything change if the President had encouraged DOJ or the IRS to look into suspicious behavior of a political opponent? The question is not merely hypothetical; the second article of impeachment against President Nixon, approved by the House Judiciary Committee but not by the full House, charged that Nixon had attempted to use the IRS to harass certain Democrats: The article alleged that Nixon "endeavored . . . to cause, in violation of the constitutional rights of citizens, income tax audits or other income tax investigations to be initiated or conducted in a discriminatory manner." Nixon's counsel, John Dean, had given a list of about 200 prominent Democrats to IRS head Johnnie Mac Walters, and had told Walters that the White House wanted them "investigated and some put in jail." Walters took the list to Treasury Secretary

George Shultz, who told Walters to lock the list in a safe. Because of Walters and Shultz's defiance of the White House, no politically motivated tax investigations occurred. Several other presidential administrations—including Presidents Coolidge, Franklin Roosevelt, Kennedy, Clinton, George W. Bush, and Obama have been accused of misusing the IRS for political purposes (although, unlike Nixon, those Presidents were not recorded on tape telling an advisor to "go[] after their tax returns").

What about the second "official act"—the White House meeting with Ukrainian officials—referenced in the Trump impeachment? Is it an impeachable offense to condition the President's *time* on support for the President's electoral prospects? Would you be surprised to learn that a President was more willing to meet with members of his party or donors to his campaign than with his political opponents? Is such a meeting distinguishable from the head-of-state meeting at the White House that President Trump was accused of withholding?

4. The Significance of Former Vice President Biden as the Subject of the Investigation. House managers stressed that President Trump's actions regarding Ukraine were directed at the behavior of former Vice President Biden, Trump's potential opponent in the 2020 presidential election. Had President Trump urged an investigation into another American, it would have been more difficult for the House to claim that Trump was trying to "cheat" in the election. How significant is the fact that Biden and his son were at the center of the potential investigation?

Does the answer depend on President Trump's motives? If he were genuinely concerned about potentially unethical behavior by the former Vice President and his family, would it have been improper for him to ask Ukraine to investigate the matter?

C. First Trump Impeachment, Article II: Obstruction of Congress

The second article of impeachment against President Trump charged that he obstructed the House's impeachment investigation by directing White House officials not to testify before Congress, and by directing executive-branch officials not to turn over documents subpoenaed by House committees. The President's lawyers responded that the President was under no duty to cooperate with a "sham" process that they viewed as unfair and the product of partisanship. Further, they argued that the President's close advisors were absolutely immune from testifying before Congress, and that Congress's subpoenas requested privileged material. (Cases involving the "absolute immunity" argument for presidential advisors are discussed in Chapter 4.) As you will see below, the House managers responded largely by arguing that the President should not be able to determine the rules for his own impeachment, and that if a President were able to keep damaging testimony and documents away from a House committee investigating potential grounds for impeachment, then the threat of impeachment would be toothless.

The Constitution does not require any particular procedures for the House of Representatives to follow in considering impeachment; it states only that each house of

Congress "may determine the Rules of its Proceedings." U.S. Const., art. I, §5. Nevertheless, an impeachment inquiry usually begins with the House voting to authorize the Judiciary Committee to conduct the inquiry. Such a vote may be controversial and politically costly for some members of Congress, and arguments over the Committee's procedures might delay passage. For these reasons, some members of the House might believe it expedient to avoid such a vote—and others might want to demand one.

The first Trump impeachment, breaking with past practice in presidential impeachments, began when Speaker Pelosi simply announced that the House would undertake an impeachment inquiry. Although the House later voted—with no Republicans voting in favor—to establish procedures for the Intelligence and Judiciary Committees' proceedings, there was never a formal House vote to initiate the inquiry.

President Trump objected to this deviation from past practice and argued that the process adopted by the House in his case was unfair. In the letter to House leaders reprinted below, the Counsel to the President announced that the President "cannot participate in [House Democrats'] partisan and unconstitutional inquiry." That failure to cooperate—specifically, the refusal to allow testimony by certain presidential aides and the refusal to respond to committee requests for seventy-one categories of documents from six agencies—became the basis of the second article of impeachment.

Letter from Counsel to the President Pat Cippolone to Speaker Pelosi and House Committee Chairmen

October 8, 2019

Dear Madam Speaker and Messrs. Chairmen:

I write on behalf of President Donald J. Trump in response to your numerous, legally unsupported demands made as part of what you have labeled—contrary to the Constitution of the United States and all past bipartisan precedent—as an "impeachment inquiry." As you know, you have designed and implemented your inquiry in a manner that violates fundamental fairness and constitutionally mandated due process.

For example, you have denied the President the right to cross-examine witnesses, to call witnesses, to receive transcripts of testimony, to have access to evidence, to have counsel present, and many other basic rights guaranteed to all Americans. You have conducted your proceedings in secret. You have violated civil liberties and the separation of powers by threatening Executive Branch officials, claiming that you will seek to punish those who exercise fundamental constitutional rights and prerogatives. All of this violates the Constitution, the rule of law, and *every past precedent*. Never before in our history has the House of Representatives—under the control of either political party—taken the American people down the dangerous path you seem determined to pursue. Put simply, you seek to overturn the results of the 2016 election and deprive the American people of the President they have freely chosen. Many Democrats now apparently view impeachment not only as a means to undo the democratic results of the last election, but as a strategy to influence the next election, which is barely more than a year away. As one member of Congress explained, he is "concerned that if we don't impeach the President, he will get reelected." Your highly partisan and unconstitutional effort threatens grave and lasting damage to our democratic institutions, to our system of free elections, and to the American people. * * *

* * * Your unprecedented actions have left the President with no choice. In order to fulfill his duties to the American people, the Constitution, the Executive Branch, and all future occupants of the Office of the Presidency, President Trump and his Administration cannot participate in your partisan and unconstitutional inquiry under these circumstances.

I. Your "Inquiry" Is Constitutionally Invalid and Violates Basic Due Process Rights and the Separation of Powers.

Your inquiry is constitutionally invalid and a violation of due process. In the history of our Nation, the House of Representatives has never attempted to launch an impeachment inquiry against the President without a majority of the House taking political accountability for that decision by voting to authorize such a dramatic constitutional step. Here, House leadership claims to have initiated the gravest inter-branch conflict contemplated under our Constitution by means of nothing more than a press conference at which the Speaker of the House simply announced an "official impeachment inquiry." Your contrived process is unprecedented in the history of the Nation,[12] and lacks the necessary authorization for a valid impeachment proceeding.

The Committees' inquiry also suffers from a separate, fatal defect. Despite Speaker Pelosi's commitment to "treat the President with fairness," the Committees have not established any procedures affording the President even the most basic protections demanded by due process under the Constitution and by fundamental fairness. Chairman Nadler of the House Judiciary Committee has expressly acknowledged, at least when the President was a member of his own party, that "[t]he power of impeachment ... demands a rigorous level of due process," and that in this context "due process mean[s] ... the right to be informed of the law, of the charges against you, the right to confront the witnesses against you, to call your own witnesses, and to have the assistance of counsel" [citing statements of Rep. Nadler during the Obama and Clinton Administrations]. All of these procedures have been abandoned here.

These due process rights are not a matter of discretion for the Committees to dispense with at will. To the contrary, they are constitutional requirements. The Supreme

---

12. [4] Since the Founding of the Republic, under unbroken practice, the House has never undertaken the solemn responsibility of an impeachment inquiry directed at the President without first adopting a resolution authorizing a committee to begin the inquiry. The inquiries into the impeachments of Presidents Andrew Johnson and Bill Clinton proceeded in multiple phases, each authorized by a separate House resolution. See, e.g., H.R. Res. 581, 105th Cong. (1998); H.R. Res. 525, 105th Cong. (1998); III Hinds' Precedents §§2400–02, 2408, 2412. And before the Judiciary Committee initiated an impeachment inquiry into President Richard Nixon, the Committee's chairman rightfully recognized that "a[n] [inquiry] resolution has always been passed by the House" and "is a necessary step." III Deschler's Precedents ch. 14, §15.2. The House then satisfied that requirement by adopting H.R. Res. 803, 93rd Cong. (1974).

Court has recognized that due process protections apply to all congressional investigations.[13] Indeed, it has been recognized that the Due Process Clause applies to impeachment proceedings.[14] And precedent for the rights to cross-examine witnesses, call witnesses, and present evidence dates back nearly 150 years. Yet the Committees have decided to deny the President these elementary rights and protections that form the basis of the American justice system and are protected by the Constitution. No citizen—including the President—should be treated this unfairly.

To comply with the Constitution's demands, appropriate procedures would include—at a minimum—the right to see all evidence, to present evidence, to call witnesses, to have counsel present at all hearings, to cross-examine all witnesses, to make objections relating to the examination of witnesses or the admissibility of testimony and evidence, and to respond to evidence and testimony. Likewise, the Committees must provide for the disclosure of all evidence favorable to the President and all evidence bearing on the credibility of witnesses called to testify in the inquiry. The Committees' current procedures provide none of these basic constitutional rights.

In addition, the House has not provided the Committees' Ranking Members with the authority to issue subpoenas. The right of the minority to issue subpoenas—subject to the same rules as the majority—has been the standard, bipartisan practice in all recent resolutions authorizing presidential impeachment inquiries. The House's failure to provide co-equal subpoena power in this case ensures that any inquiry will be nothing more than a one-sided effort by House Democrats to gather information favorable to their views and to selectively release it as only they determine. The House's utter disregard for the established procedural safeguards followed in past impeachment inquiries shows that the current proceedings are nothing more than an unconstitutional exercise in political theater.

As if denying the President basic procedural protections were not enough, the Committees have also resorted to threats and intimidation against potential Executive Branch witnesses. Threats by the Committees against Executive Branch witnesses who assert common and longstanding rights destroy the integrity of the process and brazenly violate fundamental due process. In letters to State Department employees, the Committees have ominously threatened—without any legal basis and before the Committees even issued a subpoena—that "[a]ny failure to appear" in response to a mere letter *request* for a deposition "shall constitute evidence of obstruction." Worse, the Committees have broadly threatened that if State Department officials attempt to insist upon the right for the Department to have an agency lawyer present at depositions to protect legitimate Executive Branch confidentiality interests—or apparently if they make any effort to protect those confidentiality interests *at all*—these officials will have their salaries withheld.

---

13. [8] *See, e.g., Watkins v. United States*, 354 U.S. 178, 188 (1957); *Quinn v. United States*, 349 U.S. 155, 161 (1955).

14. [9] *See Hastings v. United States*, 802 F. Supp. 490, 504 (D.D.C. 1992), *vacated on other grounds*, 988 F.2d 1280 (D.C. Cir. 1993).

The suggestion that it would somehow be problematic for anyone to raise long-established Executive Branch confidentiality interests and privileges in response to a request for a deposition is legally unfounded. Not surprisingly, the Office of Legal Counsel at the Department of Justice has made clear on multiple occasions that employees of the Executive Branch who have been instructed not to appear or not to provide particular testimony before Congress based on privileges or immunities of the Executive Branch cannot be punished for following such instructions.[15] Current and former State Department officials are duty bound to protect the confidentiality interests of the Executive Branch, and the Office of Legal Counsel has also recognized that it is unconstitutional to exclude agency counsel from participating in congressional depositions. In addition, any attempt to withhold an official's salary for the assertion of such interests would be unprecedented and unconstitutional.[16] The Committees' assertions on these points amount to nothing more than strong-arm tactics designed to rush proceedings without any regard for due process and the rights of individuals and of the Executive Branch. Threats aimed at intimidating individuals who assert these basic rights are attacks on civil liberties that should profoundly concern all Americans.

II. The Invalid "Impeachment Inquiry" Plainly Seeks To Reverse the Election of 2016 and To Influence the Election of 2020.

The effort to impeach President Trump—without regard to any evidence of his actions in office—is a naked political strategy that began the day he was inaugurated, and perhaps even before. In fact, your transparent rush to judgment, lack of democratically accountable authorization, and violation of basic rights in the current proceedings make clear the illegitimate, partisan purpose of this purported "impeachment inquiry." The Founders, however, did not create the extraordinary mechanism of impeachment so it could be used by a political party that feared for its prospects against the sitting President in the next election. The decision as to who will be elected President in 2020 should rest with the people of the United States, exactly where the Constitution places it.

Democrats themselves used to recognize the dire implications of impeachment for the Nation. For example, in the past, Chairman Nadler has explained:

> The effect of impeachment is to overturn the popular will of the voters. We must not overturn an election and remove a President from office except to defend our system of government or our constitutional liberties against a dire threat, and we must not do so without an overwhelming consensus of the American people. There must never be a narrowly voted impeachment or an impeachment supported by one of our major political parties and opposed by

---

15. [14] *See, e.g., Testimonial Immunity Before Congress of the Former Counsel to the President*, 43 Op. O.L.C. ___, *19 (May 20, 2019); *Prosecution for Contempt of Congress of an Executive Branch Official Who Has Asserted a Claim of Executive Privilege*, 8 Op. O.L.C. 101, 102, 140 (1984) ("The Executive, however, must be free from the threat of criminal prosecution if its right to assert executive privilege is to have any practical substance.").

16. [16] *See* President Donald J. Trump, Statement by the President on Signing the Consolidated Appropriations Act, 2019 (Feb. 15, 2019); *Authority of Agency Officials To Prohibit Employees From Providing Information to Congress*, 28 Op. O.L.C. 79, 80 (2004).

another. Such an impeachment will produce divisiveness and bitterness in our politics for years to come, and will call into question the very legitimacy of our political institutions.[17]

Unfortunately, the President's political opponents now seem eager to transform impeachment from an extraordinary remedy that should rarely be contemplated into a conventional political weapon to be deployed for partisan gain. These actions are a far cry from what our Founders envisioned when they vested Congress with the "important trust" of considering impeachment.[18] Precisely because it nullifies the outcome of the democratic process, impeachment of the President is fraught with the risk of deepening divisions in the country and creating long-lasting rifts in the body politic. Unfortunately, you are now playing out exactly the partisan rush to judgment that the Founders so strongly warned against. The American people deserve much better than this. * * *

Given that your inquiry lacks any legitimate constitutional foundation, any pretense of fairness, or even the most elementary due process protections, the Executive Branch cannot be expected to participate in it. Because participating in this inquiry under the current unconstitutional posture would inflict lasting institutional harm on the Executive Branch and lasting damage to the separation of powers, you have left the President no choice. Consistent with the duties of the President of the United States, and in particular his obligation to preserve the rights of future occupants of his office, President Trump cannot permit his Administration to participate in this partisan inquiry under these circumstances.

Your recent letter to the Acting White House Chief of Staff argues that "[e]ven if an impeachment inquiry were not underway," the Oversight Committee may seek this information as a matter of the established oversight process. Respectfully, the Committees cannot have it both ways. The letter comes from the Chairmen of three different Committees, it transmits a subpoena "[p]ursuant to the House of Representatives' impeachment inquiry," it recites that the documents will "be collected as part of the House's impeachment inquiry," and it asserts that the documents will be "shared among the Committees, as well as with the Committee on the Judiciary as appropriate." The letter is in no way directed at collecting information in aid of legislation, and you simply cannot expect to rely on oversight authority to gather information for an unauthorized impeachment inquiry that conflicts with all historical precedent and rides roughshod over due process and the separation of powers. If the Committees wish to return to the regular order of oversight requests, we stand ready to engage in that process as we have in the past, in a manner consistent with well-established bipartisan constitutional protections and a respect for the separation of powers enshrined in our Constitution.

For the foregoing reasons, the President cannot allow your constitutionally illegitimate proceedings to distract him and those in the Executive Branch from their work

---

17. [18] 144 Cong. Rec. HI 1786 (daily ed. Dec. 18, 1998) (statement of Rep. Jerrold Nadler).
18. [19] The Federalist No. 65 (Alexander Hamilton).

on behalf of the American people. The President has a country to lead. * * * We hope that, in light of the many deficiencies we have identified in your proceedings, you will abandon the current invalid efforts to pursue an impeachment inquiry and join the President in focusing on the many important goals that matter to the American people.

Sincerely,

Pat A. Cipollone
Counsel to the President

Notes and Questions

1. Reversing the Result of an Election? Throughout the first Trump impeachment, the President's defenders argued that impeachment would amount to overturning the result of the 2016 election, and that the voters should have been permitted to decide whether President Trump should continue in office. Such a characterization is an exaggeration. Conviction and removal would not have installed Hillary Clinton (who lost to Trump in 2016) as President, nor would it have installed any other Democrat. Rather, the result would have been that Vice President Pence would have become President. *See* U.S. Const. Amend. XXV. Should that fact have any bearing on how hesitant we should be about impeaching a President?

In another sense, of course, a successful impeachment *would* overturn the result of the last presidential election—the winner of that election would no longer be President. But that is obviously and nearly always the result of impeachment and conviction. If impeachment of a President is ever appropriate, it would oust the choice of the voters in the prior election. Was there anything special about the Trump impeachment in this regard?

2. Due Process. Mr. Cipollone's letter repeatedly characterized House procedures not only as unfair, but as unconstitutional violations of due process. (The Fifth Amendment requires the government to provide due process before depriving someone of life, liberty, or property; presumably the President's due process rights would be triggered because of his "liberty" interest in continuing in office, as well as in his eligibility for future office, plus his "property" interest in his salary.) Is the House bound to comply with due process in considering whether to impeach? If so, what procedures are constitutionally required? Does the Constitution require the minority party in the House to have subpoena power, for example? Is the Senate constitutionally obligated to provide due process during an impeachment trial? After the *Walter Nixon* case, which appears earlier in this Chapter, it seems clear that judicial review would not be available to test any allegation that either the House or the Senate violated due process, but the Constitution may impose an obligation to provide fair procedures even if that obligation is not judicially enforceable.

3. Congress's Power of Impeachment Versus Its Power to Legislate. In Chapter 1, we explored Congress's power to compel the President to provide testimony and documents so that Congress can fulfill its legislative function. As you may recall, *Trump* *v. Mazars USA, LLP* placed some limits on Congress's powers; Congress cannot use subpoenas to harass the President if it is possible for Congress to obtain the needed information without relying on the executive branch. *Mazars* did not, however, decide on the scope of Congress's power to compel testimony and documents in impeachment investigations.

Although the issue has never been resolved, it has been suggested ever since the Washington Administration that Congress's powers might be broader in an impeachment context than in the legislative context. In 1796, when the House of Representatives requested information relating to the negotiation of the Jay Treaty, President Washington refused the request. In a letter to the House, he explained that "the inspection of the papers asked for cannot be relative to any purpose under the cognizance of the House of Representatives, *except that of an impeachment*, which the resolution has not expressed." George Washington, Message to the House of Representatives Regarding Documents Relative to the Jay Treaty, March 30, 1796 (emphasis added). Should Congress have broader powers in an impeachment inquiry? If Congress's powers to compel testimony and documents are greater in impeachment investigations, should those greater powers apply only when the full House votes to open an impeachment inquiry, or would they apply as well if the Speaker announces the initiation of such an inquiry by holding a press conference?

4. Who Should Have to Compromise? As noted above, congressional committees requested that the executive branch provide more than seventy categories of documents, resulting in the President's blanket refusal to cooperate. Thus, it appears that the House did little to ensure that its requests were as narrow as possible, and the President did nothing to ensure that his invocations of privilege were as narrow as possible. Should either Congress or the President be required to defer to the other's understanding of the amount of disclosure that is reasonable? Is there any other alternative to placing one branch at the mercy of the other?

House managers argued that allowing the President to decide how much cooperation to provide would make the impeachment power ineffective because impeachment "depends on Congress's ability to discover, and then to thoroughly and effectively investigate, Presidential misconduct. Without the ability of Congress to do that, the impeachment power is a nullity." 166 Cong. Rec. S456 (Jan. 22, 2020) (statement of Rep. Schiff). They argued that deferring to the President would, for that same reason, amount to making the President the judge in his own case. They also argued that the House's "sole" power of impeachment implied that the House was to be the "sole" body responsible for determining the appropriate process in an impeachment inquiry, including the amount of cooperation required from the executive branch.

The President argued the converse: that giving the House the unreviewable power to demand testimony, documents, and information from the executive branch could cripple the latter while the House engaged in a proverbial fishing expedition—a danger that the President alleged was particularly acute when the impeachment inquiry itself was infected by partisanship.

While one might argue that the courts should be available to resolve such disputes between the branches, there are problems there too. In the first place, courts might lack jurisdiction, either because the case presents a political question or because of a lack of standing. Even if a court could hear such a case, however, the litigation process (complete with appeals) would likely take far too much time; an impeachment could hardly be delayed for several months while courts decide claims of privilege.

For a case in point, consider *Committee on the Judiciary, United States House of Representatives v. McGahn*, 415 F. Supp. 3d 148 (D.D.C. 2019). As discussed in Chapter 4, Don McGahn, President Trump's former White House Counsel, was subpoenaed by the House Judiciary Committee to give testimony relating to the Mueller investigation into Russian interference in the 2016 election. President Trump ordered McGahn not to appear, and the Committee brought an action for a declaratory judgment and an injunction forcing McGahn to testify. Judge Jackson (who was subsequently elevated to the D.C. Circuit and then to the Supreme Court by President Biden) ruled in the Committee's favor, but a panel of the D.C. Circuit held that the Committee lacked standing to bring the action. 951 F.3d 510 (D.C. Cir. 2020). The *en banc* D.C. Circuit reversed the panel's decision on standing and remanded the case to the three-judge panel. 968 F.3d 755 (D.C. Cir. 2020) (*en banc*). The panel again ruled against the Committee's ability to go to court, 973 F.3d 121 (D.C. Cir. 2020), and the D.C. Circuit again took the case *en banc*. 2020 U.S. App. LEXIS 32573 (D.C. Cir. 2020). Before the court could hear the case for a second time *en banc*, the House and DOJ settled the case. Thus it is not clear under the law of the D.C. Circuit that there is federal jurisdiction to hear such suits.

Jurisdiction or no, the drawn-out process of litigation should give us reason to doubt the judiciary's ability to resolve conflicts between the branches when Congress demands cooperation from the executive. But the merits of the *McGahn* controversy are important (regardless of the lack of precedential value of the case itself) for another reason: assessing the charge that President Trump obstructed Congress by refusing to allow his aides to testify. Everyone conceded that aides, if they were to testify, could properly refuse to answer questions that called for confidential information protected by executive privilege. The key question was whether those aides had to respond to the subpoena and invoke executive privilege on a question-by-question basis, or whether they could refuse to testify at all.

The Office of Legal Counsel had long maintained that close presidential advisors—"those who customarily meet with the President on a regular or frequent basis," Memorandum for John D. Ehrlichman, Assistant to the President for Domestic Affairs, from William H. Rehnquist, Assistant Attorney General, Office of Legal Counsel, *Re: Power of Congressional Committee to Compel Appearance or Testimony of "White House Staff"* (Feb. 5, 1971) at 7—were immune from being forced to testify before Congress. President Trump relied on that conclusion in defending against the claim that he had obstructed Congress by refusing to allow his advisors to testify.

The testimonial-immunity claim has been tested in court only twice (both times in the D.C. District)—and twice it has lost. The issue is hardly settled, however, as neither case produced an appellate opinion on the merits. A portion of the *McGahn* court's decision is reproduced below, but first consider the opinion of the Office of Legal Counsel, arguing that close aides of the President have absolute immunity from compelled congressional testimony.

Office of Legal Counsel, U.S. Department of Justice

Testimonial Immunity Before Congress of the Former Counsel to the President
(May 20, 2019), 2019 WL 6047057

Memorandum Opinion for the Counsel to the President

On April 22, 2019, the Committee on the Judiciary of the House of Representatives subpoenaed Donald F. McGahn II, the former Counsel to the President, to testify about matters described in the report of Special Counsel Robert S. Mueller, III. You have asked whether Mr. McGahn is legally required to appear.

We provide the same answer that the Department of Justice has repeatedly provided for nearly five decades: Congress may not constitutionally compel the President's senior advisers to testify about their official duties. This testimonial immunity is rooted in the constitutional separation of powers and derives from the President's independence from Congress. * * *

This testimonial immunity is distinct from, and broader than, executive privilege. Like executive privilege, the immunity protects confidentiality within the Executive Branch and the candid advice that the Supreme Court has acknowledged is essential to presidential decision-making. But the immunity extends beyond answers to particular questions, precluding Congress from compelling even the appearance of a senior presidential adviser—as a function of the independence and autonomy of the President himself. In this regard, the President's immediate advisers are constitutionally distinct from the heads of executive departments and agencies, whose offices are created by acts of Congress, whose appointments require the Senate's advice and consent, and whose responsibilities entail the administration of federal statutes. Those officers can and do testify before Congress. The President's immediate advisers, however, exercise no statutory authority and instead act solely to advise and assist the President. Their independence from Congress reflects that of the President.

The President stands at the head of a co-equal branch of government. Yet allowing Congress to subpoena the President to appear and testify would "promote a perception that the President is subordinate to Congress, contrary to the Constitution's separation of governmental powers into equal and coordinate branches." [*Immunity of the Assistant to the President and Director of the Office of Political Strategy and Outreach from Congressional Subpoena*, 38 Op. O.L.C. at *3 (July 15, 2014) ("*Immunity of the Assistant to the President*").] As Assistant Attorney General Theodore Olson explained in 1982: "The President is a separate branch of government. He may not compel congressmen to appear before him. As a matter of separation of powers, Congress may not compel him to appear before it." [Memorandum for Edward C. Schmults, Deputy Attorney General, from Theodore B. Olson, Assistant Attorney General, Office of Legal Counsel at 2 (July 29, 1982) ("Olson Memorandum").] The President's immediate advisers are an extension of the President and are likewise entitled to absolute immunity from compelled congressional testimony. * * * The demands of the office require the President to rely on senior advisers who serve "as the President's alter ego, assisting him on a daily basis in the formulation of executive policy and resolution of matters affecting the military, foreign affairs, and national security and other aspects of his discharge of his constitutional responsibilities."

There are dozens of congressional committee and subcommittees with the authority to conduct hearings and subpoena witnesses. Recognizing a congressional authority to compel the President's immediate advisers to appear and testify at the times and places of their choosing would interfere directly with the President's ability to faithfully discharge his responsibilities. It would allow congressional committees to "wield their compulsory power to attempt to supervise the President's actions, or to harass those advisers in an effort to influence their conduct, retaliate for actions the committee disliked, or embarrass and weaken the President for partisan gain." *Immunity of the Assistant to the President*, 38 Op. O.L.C. at *3. And in the case of the President's current advisers, preparing for such examinations would force them to divert time and attention from their duties to the President at the whim of congressional committees. This "would risk significant congressional encroachment on, and interference with, the President's prerogatives and his ability to discharge his duties with the advice and assistance of his closest advisers," ultimately subordinating senior presidential advisers to Congress rather than the President. *Id.*

The immunity of senior presidential advisers also protects the Executive Branch's strong interests in confidentiality as well as the President's ability to obtain sound and candid advice. * * * While a senior presidential adviser, like other executive officials, could rely on executive privilege to decline to answer specific questions at a hearing, the privilege is insufficient to ameliorate several threats that compelled testimony poses to the independence and candor of executive councils.

First, compelled congressional testimony "create[s] an inherent and substantial risk of inadvertent or coerced disclosure of confidential information," despite the availability of claims of executive privilege with respect to the specific questions asked during such testimony. *Immunity of the Assistant to the President*, 38 Op. O.L.C. at *4. As we explained in 2014, senior presidential advisers

> could be asked, under the express or implied threat of contempt of Congress, a wide range of unanticipated and hostile questions about highly sensitive deliberations and communications. In the heat of the moment, without the opportunity for careful reflection, the adviser might have difficulty confining his remarks to those that do not reveal such sensitive information. Or the adviser could be reluctant to repeatedly invoke executive privilege, even though validly applicable, for fear of the congressional and media condemnation she or the President might endure.

Id.

Second, even "[t]he prospect of compelled interrogation by a potentially hostile congressional committee about confidential communications with the President or among the President's immediate staff could chill presidential advisers from providing unpopular advice or from fully examining an issue with the President or others." *Immunity of the Assistant to the President*, 38 Op. O.L.C. at *4. This is true whether or not the President might ultimately assert executive privilege over the testimony in question, given the adviser's uncertainty over whether a particular matter will become the subject of future congressional inquiry and whether the President would choose to incur the political costs associated with invoking the privilege.

Finally, given the frequency with which the testimony of a senior presidential adviser—whose sole and daily responsibility is to advise and assist the President—would fall within the scope of executive privilege, compelling the adviser's appearance is not likely to promote any valid legislative interests. Coercing senior presidential advisers into situations where they must repeatedly decline to provide answers, citing executive privilege, would be inefficient and contrary to good-faith governance. The President's immediate advisers, if compelled to testify, are unlikely to answer many of the Members' questions, suggesting that the hearing itself will not serve any legitimate purpose for the Committee. * * *

The immunity of the President's immediate advisers from compelled congressional testimony on matters related to their official responsibilities has long been recognized and arises from the fundamental workings of the separation of powers. This immunity applies to the former White House Counsel. Accordingly, Mr. McGahn is not legally required to appear and testify about matters related to his official duties as Counsel to the President.

Steven A. Engel
Assistant Attorney General
Office of Legal Counsel

Committee on the Judiciary,
United States House of Representatives v. McGahn

415 F. Supp. 3d 148 (D.D.C. 2019), vacated for lack of jurisdiction,
973 F.3d 121 (D.C. Cir. 2020)

JACKSON, J. * * *

DOJ maintains that its contention that senior-level presidential aides should enjoy absolute testimonial immunity plainly follows from two related premises: (1) that the President himself has absolute testimonial immunity from compelled congressional process, and (2) that, as a derivative matter, so too must his "immediate advisors ... with whom the President customarily meets on a regular or frequent basis." In [*Committee on the Judiciary v.*] *Miers* [558 F. Supp. 2d 53 (D.D.C. 2008)], Judge Bates ably explains that both of these assumptions stand on shaky footing after *United States v. Nixon, Clinton v. Jones*, and *Harlow v. Fitzgerald. See Miers*, 558 F. Supp. 2d at 100–05.

This Court agrees with *Miers*'s analysis, and it also observes that none of the differences that DOJ has highlighted between the instant case, on the one hand, and *Clinton* and *Nixon*, on the other, actually matters. The following brief observations further demonstrate that the proposition that senior-level presidential aides are entitled to absolute testimonial immunity has no principled justification, which further undermines DOJ's assertion that such immunity must exist.

First of all, the concept of absolute immunity from compelled congressional process cannot be gleaned from cases that endorse absolute testimonial immunity for legislators, or those that accept absolute immunity *from civil damages* for a variety of public officials. For example, DOJ's reliance on *Gravel v. United States*, 408 U.S. 606 (1972), is obviously misplaced, because legislative aides derive their absolute immunity from the Constitution's provision of absolute testimonial immunity to congresspersons through the Speech and Debate Clause. *See id.* at 615–17. As *Miers* explained, the Supreme Court in *Harlow* specifically addressed the argument that such immunity applies to senior-level executive aides, and concluded that, in contrast to legislative aides, senior-level executive aides are only entitled to *qualified* immunity. *Harlow*, 457 U.S. at 809.

Nor can DOJ reasonably rely on the well-established body of case law that applies to the very different circumstance of immunity from civil damages. * * * One cannot simply assume that the same rationale that compels the conclusion that those who hold certain civil functions are absolutely immune *from civil damages* necessitates absolute immunity *from compelled congressional process*, even for those same individuals.

* * * [T]he distinction between aides with heightened knowledge, access to the President, and special responsibilities (i.e., senior-level presidential aides) makes no difference where the topic of Congress' investigation does not even conceivably implicate such distinction. Why, then, should senior-level presidential aides always get to play a special trump card with respect to such congressional requests? * * *

[I]f Congress seeks to explore with certain senior-level White House aides topics of a potentially sensitive nature, it is widely accepted that the President can exert executive privilege with respect to his aides' answers, as appropriate, to protect any privileged information. *Miers*, 558 F. Supp. 2d at 106. Given this, the question becomes why, then, would such senior-level aides *need* absolute immunity? In other words, even without a total exemption from compelled congressional process, senior-level White House aides can withhold the kinds of confidential and privileged information that distinguishes them from everybody else; they can do so by asserting an appropriate privilege if needed, when legislators ask questions that probe too deeply. Thus, it appears that absolute testimonial immunity serves only the indefensible purpose of blocking testimony about *non*-protected subjects that are relevant to a congressional investigation and that such an aide would otherwise have a legal duty to disclose.

Notably, this would appear to be the case even with respect to aides who, like White House Counsels, are "at the hub of all presidential activity." To be sure, White House Counsels and other similar aides have unfettered access to the President on a regular basis, and their roles within the Executive branch involve daily contact with copious amounts of information that is confidential in nature, including information that has been classified for our national security. But DOJ has not persuasively explained why such access warrants absolute testimonial immunity, where such an individual would be counseled in any sworn communications with Congress, and would have ample opportunity to invoke executive privilege or any other lawful basis for withholding information, as needed to protect the legitimate interests of the Executive branch. And, of course, if such an aide cannot lawfully invoke any privilege to protect information in response to the committee's questions, then there is no rational basis for maintaining that he should be immune from responding to Congress' valid subpoena in the first place.

It is also the case that the other rationale that such senior-level presidential aides might hope to rely on—"I'm too busy"—is unavailable in the wake of the Supreme Court's conclusion [in *Clinton v. Jones*] that even the President himself must find the time. In any event, no such excuse could possibly apply to *former* senior-level aides, who have long departed from the White House, because such individuals no longer have proximity to power. What, then, justifies *their* right to be excused from the duty to respond to a call from Congress, especially when other private citizens have no choice? At a minimum, this perplexing question raises the following conceptual conundrum: if the purpose of providing certain senior-level presidential aides with absolute testimonial immunity is that the practicalities of their special roles demand it, then what justifies allowing that entitlement to follow them when they return to private life? As a matter of pure logic, it would seem that if one's access to the Oval Office is the reason that a categorical exemption from compelled congressional process is warranted, then that trump card should, at most, be a raincheck, and not the lifetime pass that DOJ proposes.

DOJ's apparent response to the concern that absolute testimonial immunity for current and former senior-level aides serves no purpose is its suggestion in its briefs that such broad immunity serves three more systematic goals. First, it asserts that absolute testimonial immunity facilitates frank communications in the White House, and without it, the potential "public spectacle" of having to appear before a congressional committee "would surely exert influence over [senior-level aides'] conduct in office, and could adversely affect the quality and candor of the counsel" that they offer to the President. DOJ provides no evidence to support this representation. And it appears to contradict the lived experience of the many government officials who have testified before Congress, seemingly without consequence, over the years.

DOJ's assertions about the chilling effect of compelled congressional process also imply that congressional questioning is needlessly intrusive and unwarranted, and that characterization drastically discounts the reasons why executive branch officials, including members of the President's staff, are called to testify. As the Supreme Court has suggested on numerous occasions, Congress brings in witnesses not as punishment, but to provide the Legislature with the information that it needs to perform its critical legislative and oversight functions. *Watkins*, 354 U.S. at 187; *McGrain*, 273 U.S. at 175. Thus, the idea that having to testify truthfully about the inner workings of government is a threat that would actually be sufficient to prevent key public servants from competently performing as assistants to the President seems anomalous. Moreover, if the institutions of our government are all, in fact, pushing in the same direction as they should be—i.e., toward developing and implementing policies that are in the best interests of the People of the United States—then the possibility that one of the public servants who work within the government might be called upon to cooperate with Congress, and thereby perform his public duty of giving authorized legislators the means of performing their own constitutional functions, provides no reasonable grounds for fear. And if it does, as DOJ here suggests, then that is all the more reason why such testimony is critical. In short, DOJ's implicit suggestion that compelled congressional process is a "zero-sum" game in which the President's interest in confidentiality invariably outweighs the Legislature's interest in gathering truthful information, such that current and former senior-level presidential aides should be always and forever immune from answering probing questions, is manifestly inconsistent with a governmental scheme that can only function properly if its institutions work together.

DOJ's second systematic concern is similarly discordant. DOJ insists that, without absolute testimonial immunity for senior-level presidential aides, the Executive branch would grind to a halt from the weight of the subpoenas that would be thrust upon it. This representation is plainly speculative. Furthermore, such speculation seems unreasonable, given two known facts. First of all, as DOJ itself admits, Congress has long demanded information from high-level members of the Executive branch, apparently without incident. * * *

In addition, as relevant here, we have a test case by which we can prove, or disprove, DOJ's theory. The second significant fact is that it has been more than a decade since Judge Bates released the *Miers* decision, which plainly announced that senior-level presidential aides lack absolute immunity from compelled congressional process. * * * Surely if Congress was inclined to utilize its subpoena power to harass the Executive branch unjustifiably, then *Miers*'s own holding would have given it sufficient impetus to do so. Yet, even DOJ must acknowledge that no such parade of horribles has happened.

DOJ's third argument for the necessity of absolute testimonial immunity for systematic reasons places it back in the familiar refuge of its constitutional separation-of-powers contentions. In this regard, DOJ maintains, that "the public spectacle of haling [current and] former advisors to a sitting President before a committee of Congress ... promote[s] the perception of Executive subservience to the Legislature," which, in its view of what the Constitution permits, is improper, because "[a] committee of Congress could not, consistent with the separation of powers, hale the President before it to compel him to testify under oath, any more than the President may compel congressmen to appear before him." Here, once again, DOJ calls on separation-of-powers principles to do work that the Framers never intended. Indeed, *the entire point* of segregating the powers of a monarch into the three different branches of government was to give each branch certain authority that the others did not possess. Thus, while the branches might well be conceived of as co-equals (in the sense that one cannot unlawfully subvert the prerogatives of another), that does not mean that all three branches must be deemed to have the *same* powers. To the contrary, the President cannot hale members of Congress into the White House for questioning *precisely because* the power of inquiry resides with the Legislature, and also because the Constitution itself expressly prevents the Executive branch from becoming inquisitors by inflicting its own subpoena power on members of Congress for political reasons.[19]

Therefore, DOJ's argument that the House of Representatives, which unquestionably possesses the constitutionally authorized power of inquiry and also the power of impeachment, should *not* be able to issue subpoenas to Executive branch officials because the President cannot do the same to them, simultaneously appreciates traditional separation-of-powers principles *and* subverts them, and as such, truly makes no sense. * * *

To make the point as plain as possible, it is clear to this Court for the reasons explained above that, with respect to senior-level presidential aides, absolute immunity from compelled congressional process simply does not exist. Indeed, absolute testimonial immunity for senior-level White House aides appears to be a fiction that has been fastidiously maintained over time through the force of sheer repetition in OLC opinions, and through accommodations that have permitted its proponents to avoid having the proposition tested in the crucible of litigation. And because the contention that a President's top advisors cannot be subjected to compulsory congressional process simply has no basis in the law, it does not matter whether such immunity would theoretically be available to only a handful of presidential aides due to the sensitivity of their positions, or to the entire Executive branch. Nor does it make any difference whether the aides in question are privy to national security matters, or work solely on domestic issues. And, of course, if *present* frequent occupants of the West Wing or Situation Room must find time to appear for testimony as a matter of law when Congress issues a subpoena, then any such immunity most certainly stops short of covering individuals who only purport to be cloaked with this authority because, at some point in the past, they *once* were in the President's employ. * * *

[T]his Court holds that individuals who have been subpoenaed for testimony by an authorized committee of Congress must appear for testimony in response to that subpoena—i.e., they cannot ignore or defy congressional compulsory process, by order of the President or otherwise. * * *

Notably, whether or not the law requires the recalcitrant official to release the testimonial information that the congressional committee requests is a separate question, and one that will depend in large part on whether the requested information is itself subject to withholding consistent with the law on the basis of a recognized privilege.

---

19. [33] The Speech and Debate Clause mandates that members of the House and Senate and their aides "may not be made to answer—either in terms of questions or in terms of defending himself from prosecution—for the events that occurred" as part of the legislative process. *See Gravel*, 408 U.S. at 614–16. The Constitution, therefore, makes legislators and their aides immune to the force of subpoena with respect to protected legislative activity. * * * [T]he purpose of the Speech and Debate Clause is to protect legislators from intimidating and/or hostile executive and judicial inquiry, a common abuse of power in seventeenth century England. And, notably, the Constitution includes nothing akin to the Speech and Debate Clause for the Executive branch.

But as far as the duty to appear is concerned, this Court holds that Executive branch officials are not absolutely immune from compulsory congressional process—no matter how many times the Executive branch has asserted as much over the years—even if the President expressly directs such officials' non-compliance. * * *

Notes and Questions

1. **Immunity from Testifying.** Assuming that executive privilege would excuse executive branch officials from answering questions that would disclose confidential material, why would presidential advisors be privileged from appearing before Congress and answering questions *not* implicating executive privilege? Are you more convinced by the Office of Legal Counsel's arguments for such a broad testimonial immunity or by Judge Jackson's arguments for insisting that the privilege be asserted on a question-by-question basis?

2. **Turnabout Is Fair Play.** Judge Jackson was not impressed by OLC's argument that just as the President cannot compel members of Congress to meet with him, Congress should not be able to compel the President or his close advisors to testify before congressional committees. Was the analogy apt, or is there a crucial difference between the two branches' ability to compel testimony?

3. **Immunity of the President Himself?** If you agree with Judge Jackson that presidential aides simply have no immunity from appearing before Congress, would you reach the same conclusion with respect to the President himself? Could the House have subpoenaed President Trump himself and impeached him if he failed to appear? If you think the President himself is immune, then why not extend that immunity to aides who are the President's "alter egos"? Does OLC have a good argument that close presidential aides should derivatively receive the President's immunity, just like congressional aides are able to assert their bosses' Speech-or-Debate-Clause immunity?

4. **Immunity of Former Aides.** By the time McGahn was subpoenaed, he was no longer Counsel to the President. (The same was true with respect to Harriet Miers in 2007.) Review the arguments offered by OLC for protecting the testimonial privilege of presidential aides. Which of those arguments apply to *former* aides? Does the criminal conviction of former Trump aide Stephen Bannon for contempt of Congress in 2022, after he refused to cooperate with the congressional investigation of the January 6, 2021 attack on the U.S. Capitol (discussed in Chapter 1), affect your thinking on this issue?

5. **Is There a Duty of the Executive Branch to Cooperate with an Impeachment?** In some ways, Judge Jackson's opinion was an appeal to first principles. Although the executive branch had, for decades, asserted that presidential aides have a constitutional immunity against being forced to give congressional testimony, Judge Jackson concluded that the OLC opinions were a house of cards—that the immunity was based solely on "the force of sheer repetition in OLC opinions" and "simply does not exist." Judge Jackson was willing to accept, however, that Congress "unquestionably" had the power of inquiry, and that such a power included the power to force officials in the executive branch to cooperate with such an inquiry.

Why not view the Constitution as establishing a greater separation of powers be-tween the executive and legislative branches, *i.e.*, permitting Congress to impeach executive-branch officials, but not permitting Congress to demand executive-branch cooperation in impeachments? Was the President's "stonewalling" an obstruction of Congress or just an insistence that Congress do its own work? Reconsider *McGrain* and *Mazars*, which were discussed in Chapter 1. Are those cases correct that Congress can command assistance from the executive branch in fulfilling Congress's legislative function? Should the powers of Congress to demand executive-branch cooperation be any greater or lesser when Congress is considering impeachment?

6. A Partisan Impeachment; a Partisan Acquittal. The Senate acquitted President Trump on both articles of impeachment. On the first article, which charged abuse of power, Republican Mitt Romney became the first Senator in U.S. history to vote to con-vict a President of his own party, joining all 47 Democrats in voting to convict.[20] The outcome was never in much doubt, however, and the 48 guilty votes were well short of the 67 necessary for conviction. The vote on the second article was completely along party lines: 47 Democrats for conviction and 53 Republicans for acquittal.

What lessons should be drawn about the nearly complete partisanship throughout the entire impeachment? In the House, nearly all Democrats voted for both articles of impeachment, and no Republicans voted for either article. In the Senate, all Democrats voted to convict and nearly all Republicans voted to acquit. Surely such a partisan split is unfortunate—but should the blame be placed with Democrats who went forward with an impeachment despite the lack of bipartisan support, or with Republicans who did not join the Democrats in calling for President Trump's ouster?

Second Impeachment of Donald Trump: Incitement of Insurrection

On January 6, 2021—the day Congress was to count the electoral votes that gave Joe Biden the presidency—rioters stormed the Capitol. The rioters were supporters of President Trump and believed that Trump was the rightful victor of the 2020 election. They overpowered law enforcement, entered the Capitol by force, and occupied it for approximately four hours before departing.

President Trump had alleged that the 2020 election was tainted by fraud, and falsely claimed that he had won the election in a "landslide." His allegations of fraud had been

---

20. The Senate's Democratic Caucus at the time of the first Trump impeachment was comprised of 45 members of the Democratic Party and 2 Independents (Bernie Sanders of Vermont and Angus King of Maine). For ease of reference, all 47 are referred to here as Democrats. Similarly, in 2021, the Democrats became the "majority" party even though the Senate was technically comprised of 50 Republicans, 48 Democrats, and 2 Independents. Again, we will refer to the Democratic-leaning Independents as Democrats and treat the Senate during the second Trump impeachment as made up of 50 Democrats and 50 Republicans, rather than unduly complicating the discussion by saying "48 Democrats and 2 Independents who caucus with the Democrats."

brought to the courts in the weeks after the election, but the President was unable to demonstrate in any of those cases that fraud occurred. Nevertheless, he continued to urge his supporters to "stop the steal," and he reinforced that message on January 6, in a speech to thousands of his supporters at the White House.

Rioters breached the security barriers at the Capitol while the President was speaking, and the certification of the electoral vote was disrupted, as members of Congress fled. One rioter was fatally shot, scores of rioters and law-enforcement personnel were injured, a Capitol Police officer died of a stroke after the attack, and other law enforcement officers committed suicide after the attack. Several rioters stated their desire to attack or kill members of Congress and the Vice President, and although the rioters entered several areas of the Capitol, including the Speaker's office and the Senate chamber, fortunately no member of Congress was physically harmed, and neither was Vice President Pence. Eventually, after President Trump tweeted that the rioters should leave the Capitol, they did so. Congress completed the electoral-vote certification, confirming Biden's election, later that night. One week later, the House impeached President Trump for "incitement of insurrection." One week remained in President Trump's term of office, but the Senate did not hold a trial until after President Biden's inauguration on January 20, 2021.

President Trump's January 6, 2021, speech appears below, followed by the article of impeachment passed by the House. Most of the text of President Trump's speech is reproduced below, including his allegations of election fraud, because the context is vital if one is to assess the incitement-of-insurrection charge. By including the fraud allegations, however, we do not mean to suggest their validity. Readers interested in the merits of President Trump's claims of fraud may consult the court opinions in the cases challenging the election results, *e.g.*, *Donald J. Trump for President, Inc. v. Boockvar*, 502 F. Supp. 3d 899 (M.D. Pa.), *aff'd*, 830 Fed. Appx. 377 (3d Cir. 2020).

Speech by President Donald J. Trump

January 6, 2021, Washington, D.C.

Well, thank you very much. This is incredible.

Media will not show the magnitude of this crowd. Even I, when I turned on today, I looked, and I saw thousands of people here. But you don't see hundreds of thousands of people behind you because they don't want to show that.

We have hundreds of thousands of people here and I just want them to be recognized by the fake news media. Turn your cameras please and show what's really happening out here because these people are not going to take it any longer. They're not going to take it any longer. Go ahead. Turn your cameras, please. Would you show? They came from all over the world, actually, but they came from all over our country.

I just really want to see what they do. I just want to see how they covered. I've never seen anything like it. But it would be really great if we could be covered fairly by the media. The media is the biggest problem we have as far as I'm concerned, single biggest problem. The fake news and the big tech.

Big tech is now coming into their own. We beat them four years ago. We surprised them. We took them by surprise and this year they rigged an election. They rigged it like they've never rigged an election before. And by the way, last night they didn't do a bad job either if you notice.

I'm honest. And I just, again, I want to thank you. It's just a great honor to have this kind of crowd and to be before you and hundreds of thousands of American patriots who are committed to the honesty of our elections and the integrity of our glorious republic.

All of us here today do not want to see our election victory stolen by emboldened radical-left Democrats, which is what they're doing. And stolen by the fake news media. That's what they've done and what they're doing. We will never give up, we will never concede. It doesn't happen. You don't concede when there's theft involved.

Our country has had enough. We will not take it anymore and that's what this is all about. And to use a favorite term that all of you people really came up with: We will stop the steal. Today I will lay out just some of the evidence proving that we won this election and we won it by a landslide. This was not a close election.

You know, I say, sometimes jokingly, but there's no joke about it: I've been in two elections. I won them both and the second one, I won much bigger than the first. OK. Almost 75 million people voted for our campaign, the most of any incumbent president by far in the history of our country, 12 million more people than four years ago.

And I was told by the real pollsters—we do have real pollsters—they know that we were going to do well and we were going to win. What I was told, if I went from 63 million, which we had four years ago, to 66 million, there was no chance of losing. Well, we didn't go to 66, we went to 75 million, and they say we lost. We didn't lose.

And by the way, does anybody believe that Joe had 80 million votes? Does anybody believe that? He had 80 million computer votes. It's a disgrace. There's never been anything like that. You could take third-world countries. Just take a look. Take third-world countries. Their elections are more honest than what we've been going through in this country. It's a disgrace. It's a disgrace.

Even when you look at last night. They're all running around like chickens with their heads cut off with boxes. Nobody knows what the hell is going on. There's never been anything like this.

We will not let them silence your voices. We're not going to let it happen, I'm not going to let it happen.

(Audience chants: "Fight for Trump.")

Thank you.

And I'd love to have if those tens of thousands of people would be allowed. The military, the secret service. And we want to thank you and the police law enforcement. Great. You're doing a great job. But I'd love it if they could be allowed to come up here with us. Is that possible? Can you just let him come up, please?

And Rudy, you did a great job. He's got guts. You know what? He's got guts, unlike a lot of people in the Republican Party. He's got guts. He fights, he fights.

And I'll tell you. Thank you very much, John. Fantastic job. I watched. That's a tough act to follow, those two. John is one of the most brilliant lawyers in the country, and he looked at this and he said, "What an absolute disgrace that this can be happening to our Constitution."

And he looked at Mike Pence, and I hope Mike is going to do the right thing. I hope so. I hope so.

Because if Mike Pence does the right thing, we win the election. All he has to do, all this is, this is from the number one, or certainly one of the top, Constitutional lawyers in our country. He has the absolute right to do it. We're supposed to protect our country, support our country, support our Constitution, and protect our constitution.

States want to revote. The states got defrauded, They were given false information. They voted on it. Now they want to recertify. They want it back. All Vice President Pence has to do is send it back to the states to recertify and we become president and you are the happiest people.

And I actually, I just spoke to Mike. I said: "Mike, that doesn't take courage. What takes courage is to do nothing. That takes courage." And then we're stuck with a president who lost the election by a lot and we have to live with that for four more years. We're just not going to let that happen.

Many of you have traveled from all across the nation to be here, and I want to thank you for the extraordinary love. That's what it is. There's never been a movement like this, ever, ever. For the extraordinary love for this amazing country, and this amazing movement, thank you.

(Audience chants: "We love Trump.") * * *

We're gathered together in the heart of our nation's capital for one very, very basic and simple reason: To save our democracy.

You know most candidates on election evening and, of course, this thing goes on so long. They still don't have any idea what the votes are. We still have congressional seats under review. They have no idea. They've totally lost control. They've used the pandemic as a way of defrauding the people in a proper election.

But you know, you know, when you see this and when you see what's happening. Number one, they all say, "Sir, we'll never let it happen again." I said, "That's good. But what about eight weeks ago?" You know they try and get you to go.

They said, "Sir, in four years, you're guaranteed." I said: "I'm not interested right now. Do me a favor, go back eight weeks. I want to go back eight weeks. Let's go back eight weeks."

We want to go back and we want to get this right because we're going to have somebody in there that should not be in there and our country will be destroyed and we're not going to stand for that.

For years, Democrats have gotten away with election fraud and weak Republicans. And that's what they are. There's so many weak Republicans. And we have great ones. Jim Jordan and some of these guys, they're out there fighting. The House guys are fighting. But it's, it's incredible.

Many of the Republicans, I helped them get in, I helped them get elected. I helped Mitch get elected. I helped. I could name 24 of them, let's say, I won't bore you with it. And then all of a sudden you have something like this. It's like, "Oh gee, maybe I'll talk to the president sometime later." No, it's amazing.

They're weak Republicans, they're pathetic Republicans and that's what happens.

If this happened to the Democrats, there'd be hell all over the country going on. There'd be hell all over the country. But just remember this: You're stronger, you're smarter, you've got more going than anybody. And they try and demean everybody having to do with us. And you're the real people, you're the people that built this nation. You're not the people that tore down our nation.

The weak Republicans, and that's it. I really believe it. I think I'm going to use the term, the weak Republicans. You've got a lot of them. And you got a lot of great ones. But you got a lot of weak ones. They've turned a blind eye, even as Democrats enacted policies that chipped away our jobs, weakened our military, threw open our borders and put America last. * * *

And you have to get your people to fight. And if they don't fight, we have to primary the hell out of the ones that don't fight. You primary them. We're going to. We're going to let you know who they are. I can already tell you, frankly.

But this year, using the pretext of the China virus and the scam of mail-in ballots, Democrats attempted the most brazen and outrageous election theft and there's never been anything like this. So pure theft in American history. Everybody knows it.

That election, our election was over at 10 o'clock in the evening. We're leading Pennsylvania, Michigan, Georgia, by hundreds of thousands of votes.

And then late in the evening, or early in the morning, boom, these explosions of bull——.

And all of a sudden. All of a sudden it started to happen.

(Audience chants: "Bull——.")

Don't forget when Romney got beat. Romney, hey. Did you see his? I wonder if he enjoyed his flight in last night. But when Romney got beaten, you know, he stands up like you're more typical, "Well, I'd like to congratulate the victor." The victor? Who is the victor, Mitt? "I'd like to congratulate." They don't go and look at the facts. No, I don't know. He got, he got slaughtered. Probably, maybe it was OK, maybe it was. But that's what happened.

But we look at the facts and our election was so corrupt that in the history of this country we've never seen anything like it. You can go all the way back.

You know, America is blessed with elections. All over the world they talk about our elections. You know what the world says about us now? They said, we don't have free and fair elections.

And you know what else? We don't have a free and fair press. Our media is not free, it's not fair. It suppresses thought, it suppresses speech and it's become the enemy of the people. It's become the enemy of the people. It's the biggest problem we have in this country.

No third-world countries would even attempt to do what we caught them doing. And you'll hear about that in just a few minutes.

Republicans are, Republicans are constantly fighting like a boxer with his hands tied behind his back. It's like a boxer. And we want to be so nice. We want to be so respectful of everybody, including bad people. And we're going to have to fight much harder.

And Mike Pence is going to have to come through for us, and if he doesn't, that will be a, a sad day for our country because you're sworn to uphold our Constitution.

Now, it is up to Congress to confront this egregious assault on our democracy. And after this, we're going to walk down, and I'll be there with you, we're going to walk down, we're going to walk down.

Anyone you want, but I think right here, we're going to walk down to the Capitol, and we're going to cheer on our brave senators and congressmen and women, and we're probably not going to be cheering so much for some of them.

Because you'll never take back our country with weakness. You have to show strength and you have to be strong. We have come to demand that Congress do the right thing and only count the electors who have been lawfully slated, lawfully slated.

I know that everyone here will soon be marching over to the Capitol building to peacefully and patriotically make your voices heard. * * *

[W]e were going to sit home and watch a big victory and everybody had us down for a victory. It was going to be great and now we're out here fighting. I said to somebody, I was going to take a few days and relax after our big electoral victory. 10 o'clock it was over. But I was going to take a few days.

And I can say this. Since our election, I believe, which was such a catastrophe, when I watch. And even these guys knew what happened. They know what happened. They're saying: "Wow, Pennsylvania's insurmountable. Wow, Wisconsin." Look at the big leads we had, right. Even though the press said we would lose Wisconsin by 17 points. Even though the press said, Ohio's going to be close, we set a record; Florida's going to be close, we set a record; Texas is going to be close, Texas is going to be close, we set a record.

And we set a record with Hispanic, with the Black community, we set a record with everybody.

Today we see a very important event though. Because right over there, right there, we see the event going to take place. And I'm going to be watching. Because history is going to be made. We're going to see whether or not we have great and courageous leaders, or whether or not we have leaders that should be ashamed of themselves throughout history, throughout eternity they'll be ashamed.

And you know what? If they do the wrong thing, we should never, ever forget that they did. Never forget. We should never ever forget.

With only three of the seven states in question, we win the presidency of the United States. And by the way, it's much more important today than it was 24 hours ago, because I don't. I spoke to David Perdue, what a great person, and Kelly Loeffler, two great people, but it was a setup.[21]

And you know, I said, "We have no backline anymore." The only backline, the only line of demarcation, the only line that we have is the veto of the president of the United States. So this is now, what we're doing, a far more important election than it was two days ago. * * *

As you know, the media has constantly asserted the outrageous lie that there was no evidence of widespread fraud. Have you ever seen these people? While there is no evidence of fraud. Oh, really? Well, I'm going to read you pages. I hope you don't get bored listening to it. Promise? Don't get bored listening to it, all those hundreds of thousands of people back there. * * *

All they, all these people, don't get bored, don't get angry at me because you're going to get bored because it's so much.

The American people do not believe the corrupt, fake news anymore. They have ruined their reputation. But you know, it used to be that they'd argue with me. I'd fight. So I'd fight, they'd fight, I'd fight, they'd fight. Pop pop. You'd believe me, you'd believe them. Somebody comes out. You know, they had their point of view, I had my point of view, but you'd have an argument.

Now what they do is they go silent. It's called suppression and that's what happens in a communist country. That's what they do, they suppress. You don't fight with them anymore. Unless it's a bad story. They have a little bad story about me, they make it 10 times worse and it's a major headline. * * *

* * * We don't have a fair media anymore. It's suppression. And you have to be very careful with that and they've lost all credibility in this country.

We will not be intimidated into accepting the hoaxes and the lies that we've been forced to believe.

Over the past several weeks, we've amassed overwhelming evidence about a fake election. This is the presidential election. Last night was a little bit better because of the fact that we had a lot of eyes watching one specific state, but they cheated like hell anyway. * * *

---

21. [*Ed. Note: President Trump is here referring to Georgia's run-off elections the previous day for two seats in the U.S. Senate. Democrats won both seats, giving that party control of the Senate.*]

Today, for the sake of our democracy, for the sake of our Constitution, and for the sake of our children, we lay out the case for the entire world to hear. You want to hear it?

(Audience responds: "Yeah")

In every single swing state, local officials, state officials, almost all Democrats, made illegal and unconstitutional changes to election procedures without the mandated approvals by the state legislatures.

That these changes paved a way for fraud on a scale never seen before. I think we go a long way outside of our country when I say that.

So, just in a nutshell, you can't make a change or voting for a federal election unless the state legislature approves it. No judge can do it. Nobody can do it. Only a legislature.

So as an example, in Pennsylvania, or whatever, you have a Republican legislature, you have a Democrat mayor, and you have a lot of Democrats all over the place. They go to the legislature. The legislature laughs at them, says we're not going to do that. They say, thank you very much and they go and make the changes themselves, they do it anyway. And that's totally illegal. That's totally illegal. You can't do that.

In Pennsylvania, the Democrat secretary of state and the Democrat state Supreme Court justices illegally abolished the signature verification requirements just 11 days prior to the election.

So think of what they did. No longer is there signature verification. Oh, that's OK. We want voter ID by the way. But no longer is there a signature verification. Eleven days before the election they say we don't want it. You know why they don't want to? Because they want to cheat. That's the only reason.

Who would even think of that? We don't want to verify a signature?

There were over 205,000 more ballots counted in Pennsylvania. Think of this, you had 205,000 more ballots than you had voters. That means you had two. Where did they come from? You know where they came from? Somebody's imagination, whatever they needed.

So in Pennsylvania, you had 205,000 more votes than you had voters. And the number is actually much greater than that now. That was as of a week ago. And this is a mathematical impossibility unless you want to say it's a total fraud.

So Pennsylvania was defrauded. Over 8,000 ballots in Pennsylvania were cast by people whose names and dates of birth match individuals who died in 2020 and prior to the election. Think of that. Dead people, lots of dead people, thousands. And some dead people actually requested an application. That bothers me even more.

Not only are they voting, they want an application to vote. One of them was 29 years ago, died. It's incredible. Over 14,000 ballots were cast by out-of-state voters, so these are voters that don't live in this state.

And by the way, these numbers are what they call outcome-determinative, meaning these numbers far surpass. I lost by a very little bit. These numbers are massive, massive.

More than 10,000 votes in Pennsylvania were illegally counted, even though they were received after Election Day. In other words, they were received after Election Day. Let's count them anyway.

And what they did in many cases is, they did fraud. They took the date and they moved it back so that it no longer is after Election Day. And more than 60,000 ballots in Pennsylvania were reported received back. They got back before they were ever supposedly mailed out. In other words, you got the ballot back before you mailed it, which is also logically and logistically impossible, right?

Think of that one. You got the ballot back. Let's send the ballots. Oh, they've already been sent. But we got the ballot back before they were sent. I don't think that's too good, right?

Twenty-five thousand ballots in Pennsylvania were requested by nursing home residents, all in a single giant batch, not legal, indicating an enormous, illegal ballot harvesting operation. You're not allowed to do it, it's against the law.

The day before the election, the state of Pennsylvania reported the number of absentee ballots that had been sent out. Yet this number was suddenly and drastically increased by 400,000 people. It was increased, nobody knows where it came from, by 400,000 ballots, one day after the election.

It remains totally unexplained. They said, "Well, ah, we can't figure that." Now, that's many, many times what it would take to overthrow the state. Just that one element. Four hundred thousand ballots appeared from nowhere right after the election.

By the way, Pennsylvania has now seen all of this. They didn't know because it was so quick. They had a vote. They voted. But now they see all this stuff, it's all come to light. Doesn't happen that fast. And they want to recertify their votes. They want to recertify. But the only way that can happen is if Mike Pence agrees to send it back. Mike Pence has to agree to send it back.

(Audience chants: "Send it back.")

And many people in Congress want it sent back.

And think of what you're doing. Let's say you don't do it. Somebody says, "Well, we have to obey the Constitution." And you are, because you're protecting our country and you're protecting the Constitution. So you are.

But think of what happens. Let's say they're stiffs and they're stupid people, and they say, well, we really have no choice. Even though Pennsylvania and other states want to redo their votes. They want to see the numbers. They already have the numbers. Go very quickly. And they want to redo their legislature because many of these votes were taken, as I said, because it wasn't approved by their legislature. You know, that, in itself, is legal. And then you have the scam, and that's all of the things that we're talking about.

But think of this. If you don't do that, that means you will have a president of the United States for four years, with his wonderful son. You will have a president who lost all of these states. Or you will have a president, to put it another way, who was voted on by a bunch of stupid people who lost all of these states.

You will have an illegitimate president. That's what you'll have. And we can't let that happen. * * *

In Wisconsin, corrupt Democrat-run cities deployed more than 500 illegal, unmanned, unsecured drop boxes, which collected a minimum of 91,000 unlawful votes. It was razor-thin, the loss. This one thing alone is much more than we would need. But there are many things.

They have these lockboxes. And, you know, they'd pick them up and they disappear for two days. People would say where's that box? They disappeared. Nobody even knew where the hell it was.

In addition, over 170,000 absentee votes were counted in Wisconsin without a valid absentee ballot application. So they had a vote, but they had no application, and that's illegal in Wisconsin. Meaning those votes were blatantly done in opposition to state law and they came 100% from Democrat areas such as Milwaukee and Madison, 100%.

In Madison, 17,000 votes were deposited in so-called human drop boxes. You know what that is, right? Where operatives stuff thousands of unsecured ballots into duffle bags on park benches across the city, in complete defiance of cease-and-desist letters from state legislature.

Your state legislatures said don't do it. They're the only ones that can approve it. They gave tens of thousands of votes. They came in in duffle bags. Where the hell did they come from?

According to eyewitness testimony, Postal Service workers in Wisconsin were also instructed to illegally backdate approximately 100,000 ballots. The margin of difference in Wisconsin was less than 20,000 votes. Each one of these things alone wins us the state. Great state. We love the state. We won the state.

In Georgia, your secretary of state who, I can't believe this guy's a Republican. He loves recording telephone conversations. You know, that was? I thought it was a great conversation personally. So did a lot of other. People love that conversation because it says what's going on.[22]

These people are crooked. They're 100%, in my opinion, one of the most corrupt, between your governor and your secretary of state. And now you have it again last night. Just take a look at what happened. What a mess.

And the Democrat Party operatives entered into an illegal and unconstitution—unconstitutional settlement agreement that drastically weakened signature verification and other election security procedures.

Stacey Abrams. She took them to lunch. And I beat her two years ago with a bad candidate, Brian Kemp. But they took, the Democrats took the Republicans to lunch

---

22. [*Ed. Note: President Trump is referring to a phone call he made to Georgia Secretary of State Brad Raffensperger on January 2, 2021, urging him to "find" enough votes to give Trump a victory in the state.*]

because the secretary of state had no clue what the hell was happening. Unless he did have a clue. That's interesting. Maybe he was with the other side.

But we've been trying to get verifications of signatures in Fulton County, they won't let us do it. The only reason they won't is because we'll find things in the hundreds of thousands. Why wouldn't they let us verify signatures in Fulton County, which is known for being very corrupt. They won't do it. They go to some other county where you would live.

I said, "That's not the problem." The problem is Fulton County, home of Stacey Abrams. She did a good job, I congratulate her. But it was done in such a way that we can't let this stuff happen. We won't have a country if it happens.

As a result, Georgia's absentee ballot rejection rate was more than 10 times lower than previous levels because the criteria was so off.

Forty-eight counties in Georgia, with thousands and thousands of votes, rejected zero ballots. There wasn't one ballot. In other words, in a year in which more mail-in ballots were sent than ever before, and more people were voting by mail for the first time, the rejection rate was drastically lower than it had ever been before.

The only way this can be explained is if tens of thousands of illegitimate votes were added to the tally. That's the only way you could explain it.

By the way, you're talking about tens of thousands. If Georgia had merely rejected the same number of unlawful ballots as in other years, they should have been approximately 45,000 ballots rejected. Far more than what we needed to win, just over 11,000. They should find those votes. They should absolutely find that. Just over 11,000 votes, that's all we need. They defrauded us out of a win in Georgia, and we're not going to forget it.

There's only one reason the Democrats could possibly want to eliminate signature matching, opposed voter ID, and stop citizenship confirmation. "Are you a citizenship [sic]?" You're not allowed to ask that question, because they want to steal the election.

The radical left knows exactly what they're doing. They're ruthless and it's time that somebody did something about it. And Mike Pence, I hope you're going to stand up for the good of our Constitution and for the good of our country. And if you're not, I'm going to be very disappointed in you. I will tell you right now. I'm not hearing good stories.

In Fulton County, Republican poll watchers were ejected, in some cases, physically from the room under the false pretense of a pipe burst. Water main burst, everybody leave. Which we now know was a total lie.

Then election officials pull boxes, Democrats, and suitcases of ballots out from under a table. You all saw it on television, totally fraudulent. And illegally scanned them for nearly two hours, totally unsupervised. Tens of thousands of votes. This act coincided with a mysterious vote dump of up to 100,000 votes for Joe Biden, almost none for Trump. Oh, that sounds fair. That was at 1:34 a.m.

The Georgia secretary of state and pathetic governor of Georgia, have reached, although he says I'm a great president. You know, I sort of maybe have to change. He said the other day, "Yes, I do. I disagree with president, but he's been a great president." Good, thanks. Thank you very much.

Because of him and others, you have Brian Kemp. Vote him the hell out of office, please. Well, his rates are so low. You know, his approval rating now, I think it just reached a record low.

They've rejected five separate appeals for an independent and comprehensive audit of signatures in Fulton County. Even without an audit, the number of fraudulent ballots that we've identified across the state is staggering.

Over 10,300 ballots in Georgia were cast by individuals whose names and dates of birth match Georgia residents who died in 2020 and prior to the election.

More than 2,500 ballots were cast by individuals whose names and dates of birth match incarcerated felons in Georgia prison. People who are not allowed to vote.

More than 4,500 illegal ballots were cast by individuals who do not appear on the state's own voter rolls.

Over 18,000 illegal ballots were cast by individuals who registered to vote using an address listed as vacant, according to the Postal Service.

At least 88,000 ballots in Georgia were cast by people whose registrations were illegally backdated.

Sixty-six thousand votes, each one of these is far more than we need. Sixty-six thousand votes in Georgia were cast by individuals under the legal voting age.

And at least 15,000 ballots were cast by individuals who moved out of the state prior to November 3 election. They say they moved right back. They moved right back. Oh, they moved out, they moved right back. OK. They missed Georgia that much. I do. I love Georgia, but it's a corrupt system.

Despite all of this, the margin in Georgia is only 11,779 votes.

Each and every one of these issues is enough to give us a victory in Georgia, a big beautiful victory. Make no mistake, this election was stolen from you, from me and from the country.

And not a single swing state has conducted a comprehensive audit to remove the illegal ballots. This should absolutely occur in every single contested state before the election is certified.

In the state of Arizona, over 36,000 ballots were illegally cast by non-citizens. Two thousand ballots were returned with no address. More than 22,000 ballots were returned before they were ever supposedly mailed out. They returned, but we haven't mailed them yet.

Eleven thousand six hundred more ballots and votes were counted, more than there were actual voters. You see that? So you have more votes again than you have voters.

One hundred and fifty thousand people registered in Maricopa County after the registration deadline. One hundred and three thousand ballots in the county were sent for electronic adjudication with no Republican observers.

In Clark County, Nevada, the accuracy settings on signature verification machines were purposely lowered before they were used to count over 130,000 ballots.

If you signed your name as Santa Claus, it would go through.

There were also more than 42,000 double votes in Nevada. Over 150,000 people were hurt so badly by what took place. And 1,500 ballots were cast by individuals whose names and dates of birth match Nevada residents who died in 2020 prior to November 3 election. More than 8,000 votes were cast by individuals who had no address and probably didn't live there.

The margin in Nevada is down at a very low number, any of these things would have taken care of the situation. We would have won Nevada, also. Every one of these we're going over, we win.

In Michigan, quickly, the secretary of state, a real great one, flooded the state with unsolicited mail-in ballot applications sent to every person on the rolls in direct violation of state law.

More than 17,000 Michigan ballots were cast by individuals whose names and dates of birth match people who were deceased.

In Wayne County, that's a great one. That's Detroit. One hundred and seventy-four thousand ballots were counted without being tied to an actual registered voter. Nobody knows where they came from.

Also, in Wayne County, poll watchers observed canvassers rescanning batches of ballots over and over again, up to three or four or five times.

In Detroit, turnout was 139% of registered voters. Think of that. So you had 139% of the people in Detroit voting. This is in Michigan. Detroit, Michigan.

A career employee of the Detroit, City of Detroit, testified under penalty of perjury that she witnessed city workers coaching voters to vote straight Democrat while accompanying them to watch who they voted for. When a Republican came in, they wouldn't talk to him.

The same worker was instructed not to ask for any voter ID and not to attempt to validate any signatures if they were Democrats. She also told to illegally, and was told, backdate ballots received after the deadline and reports that thousands and thousands of ballots were improperly backdated. That's Michigan.

Four witnesses have testified under penalty of perjury that after officials in Detroit announced the last votes had been counted, tens of thousands of additional ballots arrived without required envelopes. Every single one was for a Democrat. I got no votes.

At 6:31 a.m. in the early morning hours after voting had ended, Michigan suddenly reported 147,000 votes. An astounding 94% went to Joe Biden, who campaigned brilliantly from his basement. Only a couple of percentage points went to Trump.

Such gigantic and one-sided vote dumps were only observed in a few swing states and they were observed in the states where it was necessary.

You know what's interesting? President Obama beat Biden in every state other than the swing states where Biden killed them, but the swing states were the ones that mattered.

They're always just enough to push Joe Biden barely into the lead. We were ahead by a lot and within a number of hours we were losing by a little.

In addition, there is the highly troubling matter of Dominion Voting Systems. In one Michigan county alone, 6,000 votes were switched from Trump to Biden and the same systems are used in the majority of states in our country.

Senator William Ligon, a great gentleman, chairman of Georgia's senate judiciary subcommittee. Senator Ligon, highly respected, on elections has written a letter describing his concerns with Dominion in Georgia.

He wrote, and I quote, The Dominion Voting Machines employed in Fulton County had an astronomical and astounding 93.67% error rate. It's only wrong 93% of the time in the scanning of ballots requiring a review panel to adjudicate or determine the voter's interest in over 106,000 ballots out of a total of 113,000.

Think of it. You go in and you vote and then they tell people who you supposed to be voting for. They make up whatever they want. Nobody's ever even heard.

They adjudicate your vote. They say, Well, we don't think Trump wants to vote for Trump. We think he wants to vote for Biden. Put it down for Biden.

The national average for such an error rate is far less than 1% and yet you're at 93%. The source of this astronomical error rate must be identified to determine if these machines were set up or destroyed to allow for a third party to disregard the actual ballot cast by the registered voter.

The letter continues. There is clear evidence that tens of thousands of votes were switched from President Trump to former Vice President Biden in several counties in Georgia.

For example, in Bibb County, President Trump was reported to have 29,391 votes at 9:11 p.m. Eastern time, while simultaneously Vice President Joe Biden was reported to have 17,213. Minutes later, just minutes, at the next update, these vote numbers switched with President Trump going way down to 17,000 and Biden going way up to 29,391. And that was very quick, a 12,000 vote switch all in Mr. Biden's favor.

So, I mean, I could go on and on about this fraud that took place in every state, and all of these legislatures want this back. I don't want to do it to you because I love you and it's freezing out here. But I could just go on forever. I can tell you this.

(Audience chants: "We love you.")

So when you hear, when you hear, while there is no evidence to prove any wrongdoing, this is the most fraudulent thing anybody has, this is a criminal enterprise. This is a criminal enterprise. And the press will say, and I'm sure they won't put any of that on there, because that's no good. And you ever see, while there is no evidence to back President Trump's assertion.

I could go on for another hour reading this stuff to you and telling you about it. There's never been anything like it.

Think about it. Detroit had more votes than it had voters. Pennsylvania had 205,000 more votes than it had more. But you don't have to go any. Between that, I think that's almost better than dead people if you think, right? More votes than they had voters. And many other states also.

It's a disgrace that the United States of America, tens of millions of people, are allowed to go vote without so much as even showing identification.

In no state is there any question or effort made to verify the identity, citizenship, residency or eligibility of the votes cast.

The Republicans have to get tougher. You're not going to have a Republican Party if you don't get tougher. They want to play so straight. They want to play so, sir, yes, the United States. The Constitution doesn't allow me to send them back to the States. Well, I say, yes it does, because the Constitution says you have to protect our country and you have to protect our Constitution, and you can't vote on fraud. And fraud breaks up everything, doesn't it? When you catch somebody in a fraud, you're allowed to go by very different rules.

So I hope Mike has the courage to do what he has to do. And I hope he doesn't listen to the RINOs and the stupid people that he's listening to.

It is also widely understood that the voter rolls are crammed full of non-citizens, felons and people who have moved out of state and individuals who are otherwise ineligible to vote. Yet Democrats oppose every effort to clean up their voter rolls. They don't want to clean them up. They're loaded.

And how many people here know other people, that when there are hundreds of thousands and then millions of ballots got sent out, got three, four, five, six, and I heard one, who got seven ballots. And then they say you didn't quite make it, sir.

We won in a landslide. This was a landslide. They said it's not American to challenge the election. This the most corrupt election in the history, maybe of the world.

You know, you could go third-world countries, but I don't think they had hundreds of thousands of votes and they don't have voters for them. I mean no matter where you go, nobody would think this.

In fact, it's so egregious, it's so bad that a lot of people don't even believe it. It's so crazy that people don't even believe it. It can't be true. So they don't believe it.

This is not just a matter of domestic politics, this is a matter of national security.

So today, in addition to challenging the certification of the election, I'm calling on Congress and the state legislatures to quickly pass sweeping election reforms, and you better do it before we have no country left.

Today is not the end, it's just the beginning. * * *

We must stop the steal and then we must ensure that such outrageous election fraud never happens again, can never be allowed to happen again. * * *

With your help, we will finally pass powerful requirements for voter ID. You need an ID to cash a check. You need an ID to go to a bank, to buy alcohol, to drive a car. Every person should need to show an ID in order to cast your most important thing, a vote.

We will also require proof of American citizenship in order to vote in American elections. We just had a good victory in court on that one, actually.

We will ban ballot harvesting and prohibit the use of unsecured drop boxes to commit rampant fraud. These drop boxes are fraudulent. Therefore, they get disapp—they disappear, and then all of a sudden they show up. It's fraudulent.

We will stop the practice of universal unsolicited mail-in balloting.

We will clean up the voter rolls that ensure that every single person who casts a vote is a citizen of our country, a resident of the state in which they vote and their vote is cast in a lawful and honest manner.

We will restore the vital civic tradition of in-person voting on Election Day so that voters can be fully informed when they make their choice.

We will finally hold big tech accountable. * * * All of these tech monopolies are going to abuse their power and interfere in our elections, and it has to be stopped. And the Republicans have to get a lot tougher, and so should the Democrats. They should be regulated, investigated, and brought to justice under the fullest extent of the law. They're totally breaking the law.

Together, we will drain the Washington swamp and we will clean up the corruption in our nation's capital. We have done a big job on it, but you think it's easy. It's a dirty business. It's a dirty business. You have a lot of bad people out there. * * *

As this enormous crowd shows, we have truth and justice on our side. We have a deep and enduring love for America in our hearts. We love our country.

We have overwhelming pride in this great country and we have it deep in our souls. Together, we are determined to defend and preserve government of the people, by the people and for the people.

Our brightest days are before us. Our greatest achievements, still away.

I think one of our great achievements will be election security. Because nobody until I came along had any idea how corrupt our elections were.

And again, most people would stand there at 9 o'clock in the evening and say I want to thank you very much, and they go off to some other life. But I said something's wrong here, something is really wrong, can have happened.

And we fight. We fight like hell. And if you don't fight like hell, you're not going to have a country anymore.

Our exciting adventures and boldest endeavors have not yet begun. My fellow Americans, for our movement, for our children, and for our beloved country.

And I say this despite all that's happened. The best is yet to come.

So we're going to, we're going to walk down Pennsylvania Avenue. I love Pennsylvania Avenue. And we're going to the Capitol, and we're going to try and give.

The Democrats are hopeless, they never vote for anything. Not even one vote. But we're going to try and give our Republicans, the weak ones because the strong ones don't need any of our help. We're going to try and give them the kind of pride and boldness that they need to take back our country.

So let's walk down Pennsylvania Avenue.

I want to thank you all. God bless you and God Bless America.

Thank you all for being here. This is incredible. Thank you very much. Thank you.

Resolution

Impeaching Donald John Trump,
President of the United States, for high crimes and misdemeanors

Resolved, That Donald John Trump, President of the United States, is impeached for high crimes and misdemeanors and that the following article of impeachment be exhibited to the United States Senate:

Article of impeachment exhibited by the House of Representatives of the United States of America in the name of itself and of the people of the United States of America, against Donald John Trump, President of the United States of America, in maintenance and support of its impeachment against him for high crimes and misdemeanors.

ARTICLE I: INCITEMENT OF INSURRECTION

The Constitution provides that the House of Representatives "shall have the sole Power of Impeachment" and that the President "shall be removed from Office on Impeachment for, and Conviction of, Treason, Bribery, or other high Crimes and Misdemeanors". Further, section 3 of the 14th Amendment to the Constitution prohibits any person who has "engaged in insurrection or rebellion against" the United States from "hold[ing] any office … under the United States". In his conduct while President of the United States—and in violation of his constitutional oath faithfully to execute the office of President of the United States and, to the best of his ability, preserve, protect, and defend the Constitution of the United States, and in violation of his constitutional duty to take care that the laws be faithfully executed—Donald John Trump engaged in high Crimes and Misdemeanors by inciting violence against the Government of the United States, in that:

On January 6, 2021, pursuant to the 12th Amendment to the Constitution of the United States, the Vice President of the United States, the House of Representatives, and the Senate met at the United States Capitol for a Joint Session of Congress to count the votes of the Electoral College. In the months preceding the Joint Session, President Trump repeatedly issued false statements asserting that the Presidential election results were the product of widespread fraud and should not be accepted by the American people or certified by State or Federal officials. Shortly before the Joint Session commenced, President Trump, addressed a crowd at the Ellipse in Washington, DC. There, he reiterated false claims that "we won this election, and we won it by a landslide". He also willfully made statements that, in context, encouraged—and foreseeably resulted in—lawless action at the Capitol, such as: "if you don't fight like hell you're not going to have a country anymore". Thus incited by President Trump, members of the crowd he had addressed, in an attempt to, among other objectives, interfere with the Joint Session's solemn constitutional duty to certify the results of the 2020 Presidential election, unlawfully breached and vandalized the Capitol, injured and killed law enforcement personnel, menaced Members of Congress, the Vice President, and Congressional personnel, and engaged in other violent, deadly, destructive, and seditious acts.

President Trump's conduct on January 6, 2021, followed his prior efforts to subvert and obstruct the certification of the results of the 2020 Presidential election. Those prior efforts included a phone call on January 2, 2021, during which President Trump urged the secretary of state of Georgia, Brad Raffensperger, to "find" enough votes to overturn the Georgia Presidential election results and threatened Secretary Raffensperger if he failed to do so.

In all this, President Trump gravely endangered the security of the United States and its institutions of Government. He threatened the integrity of the democratic system, interfered with the peaceful transition of power, and imperiled a coequal branch of Government. He thereby betrayed his trust as President, to the manifest injury of the people of the United States.

Wherefore, Donald John Trump, by such conduct, has demonstrated that he will remain a threat to national security, democracy, and the Constitution if allowed to remain in office, and has acted in a manner grossly incompatible with self-governance and the rule of law. Donald John Trump thus warrants impeachment and trial, removal from office, and disqualification to hold and enjoy any office of honor, trust, or profit under the United States.

A. The Senate's Jurisdiction

By the time President Trump's Senate trial began on February 9, 2021, he was no longer in office. That fact raised two questions: First, did the Senate have "jurisdiction" to try a former President? Second, if the Senate were to hold a trial, who would preside? The second question is the easier of the two. The Constitution (Article I, §3) provides that "When the President of the United States is tried, the Chief Justice shall preside." But at the time of the trial, the President of the United States was Joe Biden, not Donald Trump. Because only one person can be President at any one time, and because the Constitution says that the Chief Justice shall preside when "the" (not "a") President is tried, the text of the document suggests that the Chief Justice should not preside at the trial of a former President.

In addition, there are functional reasons to reach the same conclusion. A key reason for the Chief Justice's participation in a trial of the current President would be absent in a trial of a former President. According to the Constitution, "[t]he Vice President of the United States shall be President of the Senate" (art. I, §3), and thus would ordinarily be the presiding officer in an impeachment trial. When the current President is tried, the Vice President would have a conflict of interest because a conviction would cause the Vice President to become President. *See* U.S. Const. amend. XXV. In a trial of a *former* President, however, there is no such conflict of interest. Regardless of the result of President Trump's second impeachment trial, Vice President Harris was going to remain Vice President.

Accordingly, Vice President Harris could have presided at the second Trump impeachment, but she chose not to do so. Instead, the presiding officer at the second Trump impeachment was Senator Patrick Leahy, the president *pro tempore*—that is, the Senate's presiding officer in the absence of the Vice President—by virtue of being the Senator of the majority (Democratic) party with the greatest number of years of continuous service.

The jurisdictional question produced much more controversy. Obviously, a conviction in the Senate could not remove former-President Trump from office, but a conviction would not have been strictly academic or symbolic. According to the Constitution (Article II, §4), a convicted official "shall be removed from Office," but the Senate may also disqualify a convicted official from *future* service: "Judgment in Cases of Impeachment shall not extend further than to removal from Office, and disqualification to hold and enjoy any Office of honor, Trust or Profit under the United States" (Article I, §3).

The President's lawyers argued that the Constitution's use of "and" implied that the Senate could disqualify the official from future service only if it also removed him from office. And because the Senate could not order former-President Trump removed from an office that he had already vacated, it was without jurisdiction to hold the trial at all: "Conviction and removal are inextricably intertwined. If removal no longer is possible, neither is an impeachment conviction.... There is no authority granted to Congress to impeach and convict persons who are not 'civil officers of the United States.' It's as simple as that." 167 Cong. Rec. S608 (Feb. 9, 2021) (statement of Mr. Schoen).

The House managers countered by pointing to the Constitution's literal language. The Constitution did not say that disqualification was available only in conjunction with removal; all it said was that the Senate was powerless to impose a punishment greater than removal plus future disqualification. Just as the Senate could remove a convicted official without also ordering disqualification, the Senate could disqualify a former officeholder even if removal were no longer an available remedy.

Further, the President's lawyers argued that if Article I, §3 requires the Chief Justice to preside only when "the [*current*] President" is tried, then Article II, §4, which specifies the officers who are subject to impeachment, should be similarly construed to apply only to current officeholders. That is, Article I, §3 provides that impeachment trials of "the President" shall have the Chief Justice as the presiding officer. And Article II, §4 provides that "[t]he President" shall be removed from office upon impeachment and conviction. If Donald Trump was no longer "the President" for purposes of Article I, §3, so that the presiding officer did not need to be the Chief Justice, then Donald Trump was no longer "[t]he President" for purposes of Article II, §4, and he was not subject to impeachment at all. *See* 167 Cong. Rec. S606 (Feb. 9, 2021) (statement of Mr. Schoen). Were Senate Democrats trying to have it both ways by holding that former-President Trump was subject to an impeachment trial with Senator Leahy presiding?

In addition to that textual argument, the House managers offered an argument based in policy. The President's argument, they contended, would create a "January exception," according to which no amount of wrongdoing in the final month of a presidential administration could result in impeachment and conviction because the official would be out of office by the time a judgment could be reached. (Presumably the same result would obtain at any point during a presidential administration if the official resigned before the end of the Senate trial.) Although the House managers characterized the January exception as allowing a President who committed high crimes and misdemeanors to escape without any consequence, it should be remembered that the official would be subject to criminal indictment and trial even if impeachment were no longer available. The official would, however, escape the lifetime ban on officeholding that might result from conviction.

Until 2021, no former President had ever been subject to an impeachment trial, but Secretary of War William Belknap had been impeached in 1876, shortly after resigning his cabinet position. His Senate trial was held the following month, after a motion to dismiss failed, 29–37. That vote did not fully resolve the constitutional question of the Senate's power to try a former official, however; despite widespread agreement that Belknap was guilty of bribery, 25 Senators voted to acquit, and 22 justified their vote on the ground that they believed that the Senate lacked jurisdiction. Those 25 votes were sufficient to secure an acquittal.

There was also British precedent for conducting a trial of a former official. Warren Hastings, the former Governor-General of Bengal, was impeached in 1787 and tried between 1788 and 1795, even though he had left India in 1785. He was ultimately acquitted, but the Framers of the U.S. Constitution, writing in 1787, would certainly have been aware of the incident. Thus, had they wanted American impeachments to be limited to current officeholders, the Framers might have been expected to say so explicitly. On the other hand, it is always dangerous to rely on British precedents to answer separation-of-powers questions under the American Constitution, because it is clear that the Framers intended to depart—at least to some degree—from the British precedents. For example, the American impeachment power is unquestionably more limited than its British counterpart in forbidding Congress from imposing a punishment beyond removal from office and future disqualification. Perhaps that limitation implied that British precedent was of dubious value in deciding whether the U.S. Senate could try former officeholders.

In the Trump impeachment trial, the Senate ultimately determined that it had jurisdiction. Senator Rand Paul moved to dismiss the impeachment because President Trump was no longer in office, but the motion was defeated 45–55. Five Republicans joined the unanimous Democratic caucus to defeat the motion. But, as in 1876 in the Belknap impeachment trial, some Republican Senators pointed to what they believed to be the Senate's questionable jurisdiction in explaining their later votes to acquit.

B. Incitement and Freedom of Speech

On the merits, the President's defenders argued that he did not "incite" an "insurrection." They pointed out that the Capitol had been breached even before President Trump finished his speech, and therefore the speech could not have been the "incitement." The House managers replied that throughout his administration, the President encouraged (or at least condoned) violence, and his lies about a stolen election had given his supporters a target. The combination, they argued, made violence the likely, if not inevitable, result. Thus, when President Trump told his supporters to "fight like hell. And if you don't fight like hell, you're not going to have a country anymore," they might have been expected to take that statement more literally than would supporters of a different politician.

The President's lawyers further argued that his speech on January 6 was protected by the First Amendment. Supreme Court precedent holds that incitement is not constitutionally protected, but there is an extremely high threshold for the kind of speech that qualifies as incitement. According to the leading case, *Brandenburg v. Ohio*, 395 U.S. 444 (1969) (*per curiam*), "the constitutional guarantees of free speech and free press do not permit a State to forbid or proscribe advocacy of the use of force or of law violation except where such advocacy is directed to inciting or producing imminent lawless action and is likely to incite or produce such action." *Id.* at 447. Thus, even if President Trump's speech on January 6 were "likely" to produce imminent violence—and assessing likelihood after the fact is bound to be difficult—the speech would be protected unless it were "directed to" producing such violence. The President's lawyers argued that the *Brandenburg* standard required the House to demonstrate that President Trump *intended* to instigate violence, and that they could not make such a showing.

The House managers stressed President Trump's language—particularly his call to his supporters to "fight"—in arguing that violence was exactly what he had in mind. They also argued that if President Trump had not intended the violence, he would have acted more quickly to stop it once he became aware of it. President Trump's lawyers responded that "fight" was a commonplace metaphor, particularly in political rhetoric, and that the use of that word could not reasonably be taken to suggest that President Trump had meant to encourage physical violence. The President's lawyers even played a lengthy video compilation of Democratic politicians exhorting their supporters to "fight." Further, President Trump's lawyers pointed to the portion of the speech in which the President urged his supporters to protest "peacefully and patriotically" in arguing that it was peaceful protest, not violence, that he was trying to inspire. Supporters of conviction, however, argued that context is crucial, and that President Trump's use of violent imagery on that occasion—addressing a huge crowd of angry people, a short distance from where the electoral votes were counted, after telling them for months that the election had been stolen—was an incitement of violence even where use of "fight" in other contexts would not rise to that level. As one of the House managers argued,

> This was not just one reference or a message to supporters by a politician to fight for a cause. He had assembled thousands of violent people, people he knew were capable of violence, people he had seen be violent. They were standing now in front of him. And then he pointed at us, lit the fuse, and sent an angry mob to fight the perceived enemy—his own Vice President and the Members of Congress as we certified an election.

167 Cong. Rec. S632 (daily ed., Feb. 10, 2021) (statement of Manager Dean).

More fundamentally, it is not clear that the *Brandenburg* standard applies in impeachments. That is, even accepting that President Trump had a First Amendment right to give his speech (in the sense that he could not be criminally punished or civilly sued for making the speech), could Congress nevertheless convict him of "high Crimes and Misdemeanors" for exercising those rights irresponsibly?

Letter by Constitutional Law Scholars on President Trump's First Amendment Defense

Feb. 5, 2021

Next week the Senate will conduct an impeachment trial to determine whether former President Trump should be disqualified from holding future office for inciting insurrection and subverting America's constitutional democratic process in multiple respects. At that trial, President Trump's lawyers plan to defend his actions on January 6 by arguing that the First Amendment shields him from conviction. We, the undersigned constitutional law scholars, write to explain why this is wrong.

The First Amendment is no bar to the Senate convicting former President Trump and disqualifying him from holding future office. Although we differ from one another in our politics, disagree on many questions of constitutional law, and take different approaches to understanding the Constitution's text, history, and context, we all agree that any First Amendment defense raised by President Trump's attorneys would be legally frivolous. In other words, we all agree that the First Amendment does not prevent the Senate from convicting President Trump and disqualifying him from holding future office.

I. The First Amendment does not apply in impeachment proceedings, so it cannot provide a defense for President Trump.

Many of us believe that the First Amendment simply does not apply here. The First Amendment limits the government's ability to make it unlawful to engage in speech, practice a religion, peaceably assemble, or petition the government. Thus, when lawyers say that a defendant established a First Amendment defense in a court case, what they mean is that the defendant demonstrated that the government could not make their conduct *unlawful*.

But Congress's power to impeach is not limited to *unlawful* acts. Instead, federal officers can be impeached for *lawful* conduct, and violations of an officer's oath of office can constitute impeachable "high Crimes or misdemeanors" under the Constitution even if no law has been violated. For example, federal judges can be—and have been—impeached for presiding over trials while intoxicated. That is not a federal crime, but it is a violation of the judicial oath to faithfully and impartially execute a federal judge's duties. Likewise, a President or a Secretary of Defense could be impeached for not defending the United States against a foreign attack. Again, that is not necessarily a violation of any criminal law, but it is certainly a violation of an oath to defend the United States Constitution. And for the same reason, a President could be impeached for publicly renouncing their oath "to preserve, protect, and defend the Constitution of the United States." Imagine a President who publicly announces, "I no longer promise to preserve the Constitution." Such a declaration would not be illegal—indeed, the First Amendment would almost certainly bar Congress from making it illegal—but the President could still be impeached for betraying the oath of office.

As a result, asking whether President Trump was engaged in lawful First Amendment activity misses the point entirely. Regardless of whether President Trump's conduct on and around January 6 was lawful, he may be constitutionally convicted in an impeachment trial if the Senate determines that his behavior was a sufficiently egregious violation of his oath of office to constitute a "high Crime[] or misdemeanor[]" under the Constitution. If so, he can be convicted and disqualified from future office regardless of whether he would have a First Amendment defense in a subsequent criminal prosecution.

II. Even if the First Amendment applies in impeachment proceedings, it does not prohibit conviction and disqualification for violating the President's Oath of Office.

Many of us believe that, regardless of whether the First Amendment does or does not apply to impeachment, President Trump can be convicted and disqualified because he is accused of violating his oath through an "extraordinary, unprecedented repudiation of the President's duties to protect the government" through his "further acts and omissions after he incited the crowd to attack the Capitol"—namely, by allegedly watching the mob storm Congress on television and "not immediately taking action to protect Congress and the Capitol." While reasonable people can disagree as to the scope of free speech rights in specific contexts (such as the scope of the government's power to limit its own employees' public expression), no reasonable scholar or jurist could conclude that President Trump had a First Amendment right to incite a violent attack on the seat of the legislative branch, or then to sit back and watch on television as Congress was terrorized and the Capitol sacked.

On the contrary, the Constitution imposes an affirmative duty on the President to "take care that the laws be faithfully executed," and willful violations of that duty are an impeachable offense. Accordingly, if the Senate concludes that President Trump willfully failed to intervene to protect Congress from a mob—indeed, one he incited—in violation of the presidential duty to take care to faithfully execute the law, the First Amendment offers him no protection at all from impeachment. The First Amendment protects the freedoms of speech, press, religion, assembly, and petition; it does not grant the President the freedom to engage in a willful dereliction of duty.

III. The President's speech and conduct around January 6 constitute unprotected incitement.

Even if the principles of First Amendment law are applicable in the impeachment context (and many of us believe they are not), many of us believe there is an extraordinarily strong argument that the Supreme Court's standards, articulated in *Brandenburg v. Ohio*, for when the government may *criminally* punish an individual's deliberate incitement of others to engage in imminent lawless acts are satisfied in this case. President Trump's speech, and the overall course of his conduct, advanced the factually baseless position that the election had been "stolen" and, further, that *immediate* action was necessary to prevent Vice President Pence and Congress from counting and confirming the votes of Electors that had been submitted (and certified) by the States. The evidence shows that President Trump deliberately assembled the crowd of supporters; that he steeled his supporters for action and knew that they were ready to take immediate action; that he directed them to take such immediate action; that President Trump said he would be with them in such action and supported such action; that he intended such action to accomplish the unlawful disruption of the constitutional processes of Congress in counting the votes of Electors and certifying the results; and that many persons in the mob that attacked Congress and the Capitol understood themselves to be doing exactly what President Trump had directed and intended for them to do.

In this context and under the circumstances, many of us believe there is a powerful case that even under the Supreme Court's narrow standards for when speech inciting violence is not constitutionally protected, President Trump's words and conduct were unprotected. His words and conduct were, in the words of the *Brandenburg* case, "directed to inciting or producing imminent lawless action and ... likely to ... produce such action."

* * *

As scholars of constitutional law, we know there are many difficult questions of First Amendment law. But the permissibility of President Trump's impeachment trial is not one of them. The First Amendment is no defense to the article of impeachment leveled against the former President, because the First Amendment does not apply in impeachment proceedings; because the president does not have a First Amendment right to incite a mob and then sit back and do nothing as the hostile mob invades the Capitol and terrorizes Congress; or because, in context, President Trump engaged in unlawful incitement. Accordingly, while we express no view here on the ultimate question of whether the Senate should convict President Trump and disqualify him from future office, we urge the Senate not to base its decision on the erroneous understanding of the First Amendment urged by President Trump's lawyers.

Notes and Questions

1. Frivolous? Are the scholars correct that a First Amendment defense would be "legally frivolous"? If so, is that because the First Amendment does not apply in impeachment proceedings, or because President Trump's speech falls within an exception to the First Amendment's protection? Is it paradoxical to argue that Congress's impeachment power—itself created by the Constitution—can be exercised without regard for the remainder of the Constitution? Does the scholars' letter essentially argue that then-Congressman Ford was correct that "[a]n impeachable offense is whatever a majority of the House of Representatives considers [it] to be at a given moment in history"?

2. Which Portions of the Constitution Apply to Impeachments? If you think the First Amendment does not apply to impeachment proceedings, is the same true with regard to the rest of the Constitution? Recall that President Trump's lawyers argued that the procedures used in his first impeachment violated due process. Does Congress have any obligation to provide due process in impeachment proceedings?

Imagine that Congress believes gun violence, climate change, or illegal immigration to be a critical threat to the nation. Could Congress impeach the President for vetoing bills designed to deal with those problems? Should the President be able to defend himself by pointing out that the Constitution grants him the veto power, or should Congress be able to impeach and convict the President for using his veto power in a manner that Congress believes is harmful to the country? Could Congress impeach the President for invoking executive privilege—even as to materials protected by *United States v. Nixon*? What if the President exercised the pardon power in a way that favored his supporters—for example, by pardoning all of the people involved in the January 6 riot, or pardoning the former spouse of a large campaign contributor (as President Clinton did when he pardoned Marc Rich on the last day of his presidency)?

3. Presidential Power and the Johnson Impeachment. The country's first presidential impeachment, in 1868, charged that President Andrew Johnson had violated the Tenure of Office Act by dismissing Secretary of War Edwin Stanton. The Act purported to require the Senate's advice and consent before the dismissal of any official for whose appointment the Senate's advice and consent was required. The Constitution explicitly requires senatorial advice and consent for certain appointments, but it is silent as to what role, if any, Congress should play in removals of executive-branch officials. Johnson was impeached by the House and came within one vote of conviction in the Senate. Years later, the Supreme Court held that the Constitution gave the President the unilateral power to remove purely executive officials, if restrictions on the President's removal power would undermine his ability to carry out his constitutionally assigned functions.[23] Thus, President Johnson's removal of Secretary of War Stanton was consti-

---

23. *See Morrison v. Olson*, 487 U.S. 654, 696 (1988); *Myers v. United States*, 272 U.S. 52 (1925). *Compare Humphrey's Executor v. United States*, 295 U.S. 602 (1935) (upholding restrictions on a Pres-

tutional, and the Tenure of Office Act was unconstitutional (at least in the view of the Supreme Court). Does it follow that President Johnson should have been acquitted?

C. Failing to Defend the Capitol

President Trump's second impeachment contained only one article—the charge of inciting an insurrection. President Trump's defense was that (assuming the Senate had jurisdiction to try him) he did not intend to instigate violence; he did not in fact incite the violence at the Capitol; he had a constitutional right to give the speech that he gave; and he should not be held responsible for the actions of others, even if the rioters were his supporters. Whatever you think of the incitement charge or President Trump's defense, the President certainly may be held responsible for his own actions in *response* to the violence at the Capitol. The President takes an oath to "preserve, protect, and defend the Constitution"; did he violate that oath by failing to protect the Congress and the counting of the electoral votes? Should he have been charged with that offense instead of, or in addition to, incitement?

Consider this sequence of events, as related first by House Manager Cicilline and then by House Manager Castro:

> Mr. Manager CICILLINE of Rhode Island. * * * [O]n January 6, Donald Trump did not once condemn this attack. He did not once condemn the attackers. In fact, on January 6, the only person he condemned was his own Vice President, Mike Pence, who was hiding in this building with his family in fear for his life.
>
> In the first crucial hours of this violent attack, he did nothing to stop it, nothing to help us.
>
> By all accounts, from the people that were around him, he was delighted. And here is the last thing Donald Trump said that day * * *. At 6 p.m. on January 6, after all the destruction that you just saw, Capitol Police and the National Guard fighting to secure this building, here is what Donald Trump tweeted:
>
> > These are the things and events that happen when a sacred landslide election victory is so unceremoniously & viciously stripped away from great patriots who have been badly & unfairly treated for so long. Go home with love & in peace. Remember this day forever!
>
> He got what he incited, and according to Donald Trump, we got what we deserve. Donald Trump's incitement of this insurrection, including his dereliction of his duty as Commander in Chief to defend the Capitol and the people in it, his complete refusal to condemn the attack while it was going on, and his continuing to incite the violence during the attack require impeachment. * * *

---

ident's removal authority concerning a member of an independent regulatory commission whose duties were not purely executive).

[W]ithin minutes of Donald Trump's speech ending, there were significant reports of escalating violence that began to surface. Buildings around the Capitol were starting to be evacuated, and by 1:15, an explosive device had been found at the DNC, and a pipe bomb had been found at the RNC about 15 minutes earlier. The House Sergeant at Arms had called for immediate assistance. At 1:34 p.m., the mayor of Washington, DC, called for additional National Guard troops. * * *

For 40 minutes, while buildings were being cleared, pipe bombs were being found, and his supporters were literally breaching the perimeter of the Capitol and overwhelming law enforcement. You saw the violence that was occurring. We heard nothing from the President of the United States. We didn't hear anything from Donald Trump until 1:49 p.m., when, while all of this is unfolding, President Trump sent out a tweet.

This was the first thing he did when he learned the U.S. Capitol, with all the Members of Congress and his own Vice President, was under violent attack. What was that tweet? Nearly an hour after the rioters breached the Capitol perimeter at 1:49, Donald Trump released a propaganda reel of his "Save America" speech that he had given an hour before.

I want to be clear. The events I just described—the rioters breaching the Capitol, attacking law enforcement, the violence that is being broadcast all over the television for the whole world to see, including the President of the United States—I want to show you: This is what is happening right before Donald Trump sends that video out again and as he does it.

(Text of video presentation of 1-6-2021.)

President TRUMP. Our country has had enough. We will not take it anymore and that's what this is all about. And to use a favorite term that all of you people really came up with: We will stop the steal. Because you'll never take back our country with weakness. You have to show strength, and you have to be strong.

Even if President Trump claims he didn't know the extent of the violence that would follow his speech, it was now happening in plain view, broadcast on television. His supporters were attacking law enforcement. The mayor and the police chief were calling for help. Members of Congress and the Vice President were inside scared for their lives.

He doesn't send help, and he doesn't try to stop it. He doesn't even acknowledge the attack. Instead, our Commander in Chief tweeted the video of the speech that he had given before, that included language like "our country has had enough. We will not take it anymore and that's what this is all about.... You have to be strong."

Those around Donald Trump—this was later reported—were disgusted. His close aides, his advisers, those working for him, former officials, and even his family were begging him to do something. Kellyanne Conway, the President's close adviser, called to "add her name" to the chorus of aides urging Donald Trump to take action. Ivanka Trump, the President's own daughter, went to the Oval Office "as soon as" the rioting escalated, and as was confirmed by Senator Graham, "trying to get [Trump] to speak out, to tell everyone to leave."

Minority Leader Kevin McCarthy called Jared Kushner, "pleading with him to persuade Trump to issue a statement" or to do something. And Kushner, too, went down to the White House after that call.

And it wasn't just the people at the White House. Members of Congress from both parties, who were trapped here, were calling the White House to ask for help. Some Members even appealed directly to Donald Trump. These Members who had "been loyal Trump supporters and were even willing to vote against the electoral college results, were now scared for their lives."

Minority Leader Kevin McCarthy repeatedly even got into a screaming match as the attack was under way, demanding that Mr. Trump do something, issue a statement denouncing the mob.

I imagine many of you sitting here today picked up your phone and tried to reach somebody at the White House to ask for help. This wasn't partisan politics. These were Americans from all sides trying to force our Commander in Chief to protect and defend our country. He was required to do that.

Now, the extent of how many people tried to reach the President to get him to act is not known. But what is clear, what we know without any doubt, is that from the very beginning, the people around Donald Trump lobbied him to take command. What is also clear is what Donald Trump, our Commander in Chief, did in those initial hours to protect us. Nothing. Not a thing. He knew it was happening. The attack was on TV. We all know that President Trump had the power to stop these attacks. He was our Commander in Chief. He had the power to assess the security situation, send backup, and send help.

He also had incited these violent attacks. They were listening to him. He could have commanded them to leave, but he didn't.

The first critical hour and a half of this bloody attack, Donald Trump tweeted his rally speech and did nothing else. And we know why. We know his state of mind that prompted his utter, complete refusal to defend us. It was reported by those around him.

The President, as reported by sources at the time, was delighted. As he watched the violence unfold on television, President Trump was reportedly "borderline enthusiastic because it meant the certification was being derailed."

Senator Ben Sasse relayed a conversation with senior White House officials that President Trump was "walking around the White House confused about why other people on his team weren't as excited as he was."

Mr. Trump's reaction to this attack, reportedly, genuinely freaked people out. I understand why. We just suffered a very serious attack, an attack on our country. And we saw them—the people around him—do it. But when Donald Trump saw it, he was delighted.

Now, what President Trump did next confirms why he was so delighted, why he wanted this, because it shows that his singular focus that day—the day we were attacked—was not protecting us, was not protecting you, was not protecting the Capitol, but it was stopping the certification of the election results.

The evidence is clear. Shortly after 2 p.m., as the siege was fully under way, then-President Trump made a call. This is the first call that we are aware he made to anyone inside the Capitol during the attack. He didn't call the Vice President to ask how he could help defend the Capitol. He didn't call the next two in line to succession of the Presidency to check on their safety or well-being.

Instead, he * * * spent 5 to 10 minutes talking to Senator Tuberville, urging him to delay the election results * * *.

(Video presentation.)

You saw Senator Lankford stop speaking and leave the floor quickly in that clip because the insurgents had broken through the barricades and entered the building. And as these armed insurrectionists banged on the doors, Members of Congress were told to put on their gas masks, to put bags over their heads for safety, and prepare to evacuate. And Donald Trump was calling to ask the Senator to delay the certification process. Let that sink in.

Donald Trump didn't get to finish that call. It was cut off because the Senators had to move to another location, for your security. And thank God they did because as the call was occurring, the rioters got closer to the Senate Chamber, and as we all know now, but for the heroism of Capitol Police Officer Eugene Goodman and other law enforcement officers who took them in a different direction to the police line, they very likely would have gotten here.

Think about that. Armed insurrectionists with guns, weapons, zip ties, brass knuckles, they were coming for us. They were inside the United States Capitol, trying to stop the certification process. The police were outnumbered. And but for the grace of God, they would have gotten us, all of us.

And our Commander in Chief makes a call about an hour after the siege began, not to preserve, protect, and defend you and our country and the Capitol but to join forces with the mob and pressure a Senator to stop certification. We just can't get numb to this kind of behavior. * * *

[W]hile we were under armed attack and being evacuated, while our law enforcement officers were fighting for their lives, our Commander in Chief was calling not to determine how to best secure the building and the people in it but to continue to pressure Senators to stop the certification process and a peaceful transfer of power, just as he incited the mob to do earlier in the day. This was a breathtaking dereliction of his duty and a violation of his oath as our Commander in Chief. * * *

It can't be that the Commander in Chief can incite a lawless, bloody insurrection and then utterly fail in his duty as Commander in Chief to defend us from the attack, to defend our law enforcement officers from that attack, and just get away with it. Donald Trump abdicated his duty to us all. We have to make this right, and you can make it right.

Mr. Manager CASTRO of Texas. My fellow manager David Cicilline showed you what President Trump did and did not do in those first critical hours of the attack.

He sent a tweet at 1:49 p.m., where he reposted a video of the speech that incited the attack, and he called a Senator to ask him to delay the certification as the Senator was being evacuated for his own safety.

We left off around 2:15 p.m. At this point, insurgents were inside the Senate and the House, and the Senate had been evacuated for everyone's safety. As you saw, Vice President Mike Pence and his family even had to be evacuated for their safety.

Now, you will recall Donald Trump had made Vice President Pence a target. He attacked the Vice President at the rallies, in speeches, and on Twitter. And during President Trump's speech that morning of the attack, he ramped it up again. After privately pressuring Mike Pence in front of thousands in the crowd, he called Mike Pence out 11 times, including saying:

(Text of video presentation of 1-6-2021.)

Mike Pence, I hope you're going to stand up for the good of our Constitution and for the good of your country. And if you're not, I'm [going] to be … disappointed in you. I will tell you right now.

And this was the crowd's response to Donald Trump's days of relentless attacks on his own Vice President:

(Text of video presentation.)

(People chanting: "Hang Mike Pence.")

By 2:15 p.m., the crowd was chanting in unison "Hang Mike Pence" outside the very building he had been evacuated from with his family.

Now, even if President Trump didn't know that his inflammatory remarks about his Vice President would result in chants of "Hang Mike Pence," by 2:15 p.m., he surely knew. The attack was all over television. They were doing this out in the open. This was a Vice President whose life, whose family's life, was being threatened by people whom the President had summoned to the Capitol. And what did President Trump do in response? Did he stop? Did he tell his base: No, don't attack my Vice President? Even when President Trump knew what his words were causing, he didn't do any of those things to stop the crowd. In fact, he did the opposite. He fueled the fire.

At 2:24 p.m., he tweeted:

Mike Pence didn't have the courage to do what should have been done to protect our country and our Constitution.... USA demands the truth.

Over an hour and a half into the attack, and this is what he tweeted. And he still, even at this point, did not acknowledge the attack on the Capitol, let alone condemn it. Instead, he further incites the mob against his own Vice President, whose life was being threatened.

Well, some of you may say: Well, who was paying attention anyway? Well, that mob was paying attention.

(Text of video presentation.)

Unidentified Speaker. Mike Pence didn't have the courage to do what should have been done to protect our country and our Constitution, giving States a chance to certify or correct a set of facts, not (inaudible) defraud ones or inaccurate ones, which they were asked to previously certify. U.S. demands the truth.

Unidentified Speaker. Mike Pence, anarchist. Mike Pence, anarchist.

Unidentified Speaker. (Inaudible.) Can I speak to Pelosi? Yeah, we're coming, b****. Oh, Mike Pence, we're coming for you, too, f*****g traitor.

Unidentified Speaker. Donald J. Trump better (inaudible).

Unidentified Speaker. Full house.

Unidentified Speaker. (Inaudible) Mike Pence let us down. Mike Pence let us down, people. If you want to get something done, you are going to have to do it yourself.

The insurgents amplified President Trump's tweet attacking the Vice President with a bullhorn. They were paying attention, and they also followed instructions. In fact, the insurgents were at one point, as you saw, 60 feet away from the Vice President and the Vice President's family. Some of these insurgents were heard saying "that they hoped to find Vice President Mike Pence and execute him by hanging him from a Capitol Hill tree as a traitor," and then they erected a gallows with a noose.

This is what Donald Trump incited. Please take a close look at that picture. It hearkens back to our Nation's worst history of lynching.

A President's words have the power to move people to action, and these were the results.

And why did the President incite such rage against the Vice President? He was fulfilling his constitutional duty, as we all were that day. Vice Presidents in this country have been carrying out this constitutional duty—overseeing the certification of election results—without incident, without contest, without a word, for the entirety of our Nation. It is part of our peaceful transition of power in the United States.

The Vice President said he reviewed the Constitution and he could not block certification, as President Trump wanted him and was pressuring him to do. He told the President in a letter that morning, a few hours before President Trump's tweet:

> [I will] approach this moment with [a] sense of duty and an open mind, setting politics and personal interests aside, and do [my] part to faithfully discharge our duties under the Constitution. I also pray that we will do so with humility and faith.

And the President's response to that statement was to attack Mike Pence while he was with his family under the threat of a violent mob. The Vice President was following his faith, his duty, and his oath to our Nation.

The Vice President and I don't agree on too much in politics, but he is a man who upholds his oath, his faith, his duty, and most of all upholds the Constitution. And Mike Pence is not a traitor to this country. He is a patriot. And he and his family, who was with him that day, didn't deserve this, didn't deserve a President unleashing a mob on them, especially because he was just doing his job.

As this was unfolding and the crowd grew more violent, the President, of course, was not alone at the White House, and the people closest to him—his family and advisers—who saw this unfolding in realtime, begged him, implored him to stop the attack.

An aide to Mark Meadows, the President's Chief of Staff, urged his boss to go see the President, saying: "They are going to kill people."

"They are going to kill people." That is what those around President Trump feared, and still nothing. It wasn't until 2:38 p.m., nearly 2 hours after the start of the siege, that Donald Trump even acknowledged the attack. And when he finally did acknowledge the attack, here is what he said * * *:

> Please support our Capitol Police and Law Enforcement. They are truly on the side of our Country. Stay peaceful!

Much has been made of the fact that in this tweet he says, "Stay peaceful." Senators, "Stay peaceful"? Think about that for a second. These folks were not peaceful. They were breaking windows, pushing through law enforcement officers, waving the flag as they invaded this Capitol Building. This was a violent, armed attack.

"Stay peaceful"? How about: Stop the attack. Stop the violence.

"Stay peaceful"? How about you say: Immediately leave. Stop.

And he said: "Please support our Law Enforcement." How about he actually support our law enforcement by telling these insurgents to leave the Capitol immediately, which he never did. He didn't because, the truth is, he didn't want it to stop. He wanted them to stay and to stop the certification. And his failure had grave and deadly consequences.

By 2:45 p.m., the warnings were tragically proven correct. Ashli Babbitt was shot by an officer as she tried to break through a glass door to reach the Speaker's Lobby.

At this point, the pleas to Donald Trump, publicly and privately, grew even more desperate. At 2:54 p.m., Alyssa Farah, a former strategic communications director, begged the President:

Condemn this now. You are the only one they will listen to. For our country!

Mick Mulvaney, the President's former Chief of Staff, his right-hand man at one point, tweeted at 3:01:

The President's tweet is not enough. He can stop this now and needs to do exactly that. Tell these folks to go home.

He can stop this now. Tell these folks to go home.

At 3:06 p.m., Representative McCarthy appeared on FOX News. Here is what he said.

(Text of video presentation of 1-6-2021.)

Mr. McCARTHY. I could not be sadder or more disappointed with the way our country looks at this very moment. People are getting hurt. Anyone involved in this, if you're hearing me, hear me very loud and clear: This is not the American way.

He is saying on FOX News, which the President watches: This is not the American way. Stop the attack.

Representative Gallagher, at 3:11 p.m., while secured in his own office, posted a video to Twitter.

(Text of video presentation of 1-6-2021.)

Mr. GALLAGHER. Mr. President, you have got to stop this. You are the only person who can call this off. Call it off.

And then, when the President didn't answer his pleas on Twitter, Representative Gallagher went on live television.

(Text of video presentation of 1-6-2021.)

Mr. GALLAGHER. I mean, this is insane. I mean—I—I have not seen anything like this since I deployed to Iraq in 2007 and 2008. I mean, this is America, and this is what is happening right now. We need—the President needs to call it off. Like, call it off. Call it off.

Representative Gallagher, you see there, said he had not seen anything like this since he was deployed in Iraq.

The message around the President was clear, from everyone: You need to call this off. Stop it.

But does he? No. His next tweet was not until about 3:13 p.m. Once again, it is important to consider what was happening between Donald Trump's 2:38 p.m. tweet and his next tweet at 3:13 p.m. [The tweet said, "I am asking for everyone at the U.S. Capitol to remain peaceful. No violence! Remember, WE are the Party of Law & Order—respect the Law and our great men and women in Blue. Thank you!"] * * *

You will notice one of the things he says to his mob, to these insurrectionists, rather than to stop or to leave, was to say thank you. Thank you. Thank you for what? Thank you for shattering the windows and destroying property? Thank you for injuring more than 140 police officers? Thank you for putting in danger all of our lives and the lives of our families?

How about, instead of "thank you," Donald Trump, on that day, acted like our Commander in Chief and stopped this, as only he could, and told those people to leave. * * *

Senators, ask yourselves this: How easy would it have been for the President to give a simple command, a simple instruction, just telling them: Stop. Leave.

This was a dereliction of duty, plain and simple, and it would have been for any President who had done that. And that brings me to my next point. You heard from my colleagues that when planning this attack, the insurgents predicted that Donald Trump would command the National Guard to help them.

There is a lot that we don't know yet about what happened that day, but here is what we do know: Donald Trump did not send help to these officers who were badly outnumbered, overwhelmed, and being beaten down. Two hours into the insurrection, by 3 p.m., President Trump had not deployed the National Guard or any other law enforcement to help, despite multiple pleas to do so.

President Donald Trump was at the time our Commander in Chief of the United States of America. He took a solemn oath to preserve, protect, and defend this country, and he failed to uphold that oath. In fact, there is no indication that President Trump ever made a call to have the Guard deployed or had anything to do with the Guard being deployed when it ultimately was.

Shortly after 3:04 p.m., the Acting Defense Secretary announced that the Guard had been activated and listed the people he spoke with prior to this activation, including Vice President Mike Pence, Speaker Pelosi, Leader McConnell, Senator Schumer, and Representative Hoyer. But that list did not include the President. This omission of his name was reportedly not accidental. According to reports, "Trump initially rebuffed requests to mobilize the

National Guard and required interference by other officials," including his own White House Counsel. And later, "as a mob of Trump supporters breached police barricades and seized the Capitol," Trump reportedly was "disengaged in discussions with Pentagon leaders about deploying the National Guard to aid the overwhelmed U.S. Capitol Police." President Trump was reportedly "completely, totally out of it. He made no attempt to reach [the National Guard.]" And it was Vice President Pence, still under threat for his life, who reportedly spoke to the Guard.

President Trump's conduct confirms this too. At no point on January 6 did Donald Trump even reference the National Guard. The only thing that we heard connecting the President to the Guard was from his Press Secretary, who tweeted about the Guard being deployed at the President's direction over half an hour later, at 3:36 p.m.

We have seen what Donald Trump does when he tries to take credit for something, and yet, even when the National Guard was finally deployed, he didn't even acknowledge it. In fact, he didn't say a word about the National Guard the entire day. Think about that: the bloodiest attack we have seen on our Capitol since 1812 and our President couldn't be bothered to even mention that help was on its way.

These insurgents had been attacking our government for over 4 hours by that point. And we may have been the target, but it was the brave men and women who protect our Capitol who were out there combating thousands of armed insurgents in a fight for their lives, and that is who Donald Trump left entirely unprotected.

* * * I think it is important to understand what the Capitol Police were facing, how severely they were outnumbered while our Commander in Chief, whose job it was to protect and defend them, was just watching, doing nothing for hours, refusing to send help. If he wanted to protect these officers, if he cared about their safety, as he tweeted about, he would have told his supporters to leave. He would have sent help right away.

One brave officer was killed. Others took their lives after the attack. More than 140 police officers were injured, including cracked ribs, smashed spinal discs. One officer will lose an eye. Another was stabbed with a metal fence stake. They were completely and violently overwhelmed by a mob and needed help, and our Commander in Chief, President Trump, refused to send it.

Senators, you have seen all the evidence so far, and this is clear: On January 6, President Trump left everyone in this Capitol for dead. For the next hour after President Trump's 3 p.m. tweet, he still did nothing. Not until 4:17 p.m., over 3½ hours after the violence started, did our President send a message finally asking the insurgents to go home.

On the right, you will see what happened that day in the hours leading up to his prerecorded video. On the left, you will see his message. Let's watch.

(Text of video presentation.)

President TRUMP. I know your pain, I know you're hurt, we had an election that was stolen from us. It was a landslide election and everyone knows it, especially the other side. But you have to go home now. We have to have peace. We have to have law and order. We have to respect our great people in law and order. We don't want anybody hurt. It's a very tough period of time. There's never been a time like this, where such a thing happened, where they could take it away from all of us. From me, from you, from our country. This was a fraudulent election, but we can't play into the hands of these people. We have to have peace. So go home. We love you, you're very special. We've seen what happens, you see the way others are treated that are so bad and so evil. I know how you feel. But go home and go home in peace.

This is the first time our Commander in Chief spoke publicly at all since the attack began, over 3½ hours after it started, and these are the entirety of the words the President spoke out loud to the American people or to the attackers that entire day.

Nowhere in that video, not once did he say: I condemn this insurrection. I condemn what you did today.

Nowhere did he say: I am sending help immediately. Stop this.

Here is what he said instead:

I know your pain, I know you're hurt. We had an election that was stolen.

Even after all the things we witnessed, even after all of that carnage, he goes out and tells the same big lie, the same big lie that enraged and incited the attack. He repeated this while the attack was ongoing and while we were still under threat.

And here is what else he said:

Go home in peace.

We love you, you're very special.

Senators, you were here. You saw this with your own eyes. You faced that danger. And when President Trump had an opportunity to confront them as the leader of us all, as our Commander in Chief, what did he tell them?

We love you, you're very special.

This was not a condemnation; this was a message of consolation, of support, of praise. And if there is any doubt that his supporters, these insurgents, took this as a message of support and praise, watch for yourselves.

(Text of video presentation.)

Mr. Angeli [the rioter dressed in horns]. Donald Trump asked everybody to go home. He just said—he just put out a tweet. It is a minute long. He asked everybody to go home.

Unidentified Speaker. Why do you think so?

Mr. Angeli. Because we won the f*****g day. We f*****g won.

Unidentified Speaker. How did we win?

Mr. Angeli. Well, we won by sending a message to the Senators and the Congressmen, we won by sending a message to Pence, OK, that if they don't do as—as it is their oath to do, if they don't uphold the Constitution, then we will remove them from office, one way or another.

I suspect you recognize that man. You will hear him say that "we won the day." Who won the day? We know that at least five people lost their lives that day. The House and the Senate were in life-threatening danger, and so was the Vice President, and think of everyone else here as well. Who won on January 6? That is not a win for America, but it is a win for Donald Trump unless we hold him accountable.

Now, a little over an hour after that video, the brave members of law enforcement secured the Capitol, and we as a Congress got ready to continue certifying the results of our free and fair election.

A half hour after that, President Trump issued another tweet. In case there was any doubt as to whether he was happy with the people who did this, as to whether he had incited this, he commemorated what happened on January 6.

At 6:01 p.m. on January 6, he tweeted:

These are the things and events that happen when a sacred landslide election victory is so unceremoniously & viciously stripped away from great patriots who have been badly & unfairly treated for so long.

Ending with:

Remember this day forever!

My colleague Manager Cicilline started with this tweet because this tweet shows exactly how Donald Trump felt about what happened on January 6. "These are the things . . . that happen." He is saying this was foreseeable. He is saying: I told you this was going to happen if you certified the election for anyone else, and you got what you deserved for trying to take my power away.

[G]reat patriots. . . . Go home with love & in peace. Remember this day forever!

He is saying to them: You did good. He is not regretful. He is not grieving. He is not sad. He is not angry about the attack. He is celebrating it. He is commemorating it.

This is the entirety of what President Trump said to the public once the attack began—five tweets and a prerecorded video. On the day of the most-bloody insurrection we faced in generations, our Commander in Chief, who is known for sending 108 tweets in a normal day, sent 5 tweets and a prerecorded video. That is the entirety of President Trump's public statements from when the attack began until he went to bed on January 6. That is all he did despite all the people we know who begged him to preserve, protect, and defend. That was our Commander in Chief's response.

He began the day with "Our country has had enough, we will not take it anymore, and that's what this is all about," and he ended the attack with letting us know that we got what he forewarned that morning.

We will, of course, each of us, remember that day forever, but not in the way that President Trump intended, not because of the actions of these violent, unpatriotic insurrectionists. I will remember that day forever because despite President Trump's vicious attempts throughout the day to encourage the siege and block the certification, he failed. At 8:06 p.m., the Senate gaveled into session, and the counting of the electoral votes continued. About an hour later, the House followed suit. And close to 4 a.m., after spending a significant part of the day evacuated or on the floor or hiding, this great body fulfilled the will of the people and certified the electoral college vote.

And I am proud to be part of Congress. I am proud that we ensured that the will of the American people finally prevailed on that day. And I am proud that I and everyone in this room abided by our oath of office even if the President didn't abide by his.

President Trump, too, took an oath as President. He swore on a Bible to preserve, protect, and defend. And who among us can honestly say they believe that he upheld that oath? Who among us will let his utter dereliction of duty stand?

Cong. Rec. S639–S643.

Notes and Questions

1. **"I Guess These People Are More Upset About the Election Than You Are."** In addition to the presentation above, the House managers sought to introduce a statement by Republican Representative Jaime Herrera Beutler concerning a statement that President Trump made to House Minority Leader Kevin McCarthy during the riot. After a disagreement about whether there would be depositions of Rep. Beutler and others who might corroborate the story, the parties stipulated that if Rep. Beutler were to testify, she would say the following:

When McCarthy finally reached the president on January 6 and asked him to publicly and forcefully call off the riot, the president initially repeated the falsehood that it was antifa that had breached the Capitol. McCarthy refuted that and told the president that these were Trump supporters. That's when, according to McCarthy, the president said, "Well, Kevin, I guess these people are more upset about the election than you are."

2. **Is Ineptitude Impeachable?** Suppose President Trump did not *desire* the violence at the Capitol, but he nonetheless did too little, in Congress's judgment, to stop it. Could

he be impeached for such a failure? What if the President exercised his commander-in-chief responsibilities in a particularly inept manner, *e.g.*, the ill-fated invasion of Cuba at the Bay of Pigs? If impeachment is available in such situations, what difference is there between "high Crimes and Misdemeanors" and "maladministration"?

3. How Would You Vote? Suppose you were a member of the Senate. If you believed that President Trump's speeches and other conduct did not rise to the level of inciting an insurrection, but you did believe he was culpable in failing to respond adequately to the ongoing violence, how should you have voted in the trial? Would you have voted to acquit, on the rationale that the charged crime was not proven (and the proven crime was not charged), or would you have voted to convict, on the rationale that the charged crime was closely enough related to the "high Crime[or] Misdemeanor[]" that President Trump did commit? The January 6, 2021, attack on the U.S. Capitol is discussed further in Chapter 8.

Chapter Eight

Special Independent Investigative Commissions

The Roberts Commission, the Warren Commission, and the 9/11 Commission

Blue-ribbon commissions are the ghosts of US politics. Like apparitions, they materialize from time to time and wade into the middle of public debate—for example, the Kennedy assassination, Social Security reform, 11 September 2001 ('9/11')—then disappear in the blink of an eye. Left behind are the dusty accounts of tragedy and scandal, the well-intended recommendations, and the warnings that so often go unheeded.

KENNETH KITTS, PRESIDENTIAL COMMISSIONS &
NATIONAL SECURITY: THE POLITICS OF DAMAGE CONTROL 1 (2006)

In Chapter 1 we observed that congressional investigations fulfill a vital role in our society. They are a primary means by which our elected representatives in government address our social problems and respond to our national crises and scandals. But, as the materials in the first seven chapters of this book demonstrate, congressional investigations by their very nature have a substantial and unavoidable political component. As one historian observed:

> In theory, congressional investigations proceed in an atmosphere of calm, reason, detachment, and impartiality toward their "informing function." In practice they proceed in the buffeting winds of fears and fancies, the ethnic, religious, and political pressures that mark a society at a particular time. Too often they reflect opinion rather than present information necessary for the legislative process. Too often they are clearly vulnerable to partisan exploitation.[1]

In most instances these inherent shortcomings in the congressional investigative process are not fatal flaws; some politics and partisanship are both expected and ac-

---

1. H. Lew Wallace, *The McCarthy Era 1954*, in CONGRESS INVESTIGATES: A DOCUMENTED HISTORY 1792–1974, Vol. V, at 3746.

cepted as the price that must be paid to obtain a legislative solution to a problem or response to a crisis.[2] There are notable exceptions to this general rule, however. Some events are too calamitous, and some problems are too important and intractable, for the public to tolerate partisan political gamesmanship. And, from a political perspective, some situations are too politically hazardous for a President to leave the response entirely to the congressional investigative process. In these situations, the most frequently employed solution is to create a special "blue-ribbon" commission to investigate and report on the matter. Those commissions and the investigations they conduct are the subject of this Chapter. The primary focus will be on the special commission investigations that followed the three most traumatic national events of the last century: the Japanese attack on Pearl Harbor and the Roberts Commission investigation; the assassination of President Kennedy and the Warren Commission investigation; and the terrorist attacks on September 11, 2001 and the 9/11 Commission investigation.

Overview of American Investigative Commissions

These three investigations are probably the most highly publicized and controversial special investigative commissions in our national history to date, but they are only a small sample of the wide range of national governmental commissions. Before focusing on these three landmark examples, it is useful to survey briefly the larger body of special commissions. Government special commissions come in different forms and derive their investigative mandates and powers from different sources. They have been used in this country since President George Washington sent a special commission of three members to investigate the Whiskey Rebellion in western Pennsylvania,[3] and Washington's use of a special commission was probably inspired by the longstanding

---

2. The chair and vice chair of the 9/11 Commission commented upon the impediments to effective and timely congressional responses to national issues:

> We learned that the United States Congress needs help. Too often, Congress cannot deal with the toughest questions facing the nation. Because of the divisiveness in the country, the dizzying twenty-four-hour news cycle, the constant need to raise funds and travel back and forth to a home district, the complexity of some bills, and the pressure on members to be partisan team players, it is harder for Congress to take the time to work through issues and build consensus. So many tough issues now get foisted off on commissions.

THOMAS H. KEAN & LEE H. HAMILTON, WITH BENJAMIN RHODES, WITHOUT PRECEDENT: THE INSIDE STORY OF THE 9/11 COMMISSION 318 (Alfred A. Knopf 2006) (hereinafter KEAN & HAMILTON).

3. *But see* THOMAS R. WOLANIN, PRESIDENTIAL ADVISORY COMMISSIONS: TRUMAN TO NIXON 5 (Univ. Wisconsin Press 1975) ("It is often claimed that commissions were first used by President Washington and have been one of the techniques available to chief executives ever since. This view is in error. Washington's commission was a small group of men sent in 1794 to try to persuade the rebellious farmers of Pennsylvania to yield to the federal government during the Whiskey Rebellion. They were unsuccessful, and the militia were ultimately sent to end the rebellion. This commission was a group of conciliators and negotiators who, upon failing in their task, advised the President that sterner measures were needed. They were an operational group dealing directly with a crisis, and therefore more analogous to Clark Clifford's mission to Detroit during the urban riot of 1965 at the

practice in England of employing royal commissions to address national problems.[4] Since Washington's presidency the use of special commissions has waxed and waned, with limited use in the nineteenth century and steadily increased use beginning with the administration of President Theodore Roosevelt and continuing throughout the twentieth century. They are now a fixture of our national government, and some categorization is necessary to organize the many variations that exist.

One useful means of categorizing national government commissions is to distinguish "policy" commissions from "investigative" commissions. Although the division is inexact, and some commissions straddle both sides of the division,[5] it does provide a useful means of separating those commissions that are created to seek solutions to a particularly vexing public policy problem from those that are created to conduct a factual investigation of a specific event and provide a report to government and the public at large. One commentator summarized the distinctions between these categories as follows:

> There are two principal types of citizens' commissions. The first is a *prepolicy, advisory* commission appointed to assist the executive or legislative branches of government in performing their respective responsibilities. Such commissions primarily inquire into and analyze social conditions or circumstances and render advice and recommendations for government intervention. For example, the President's Committee on Civil Rights, appointed by President Truman in 1946, was prompted by several incidents indicating that the civil rights of Black Americans were being violated throughout the country. A more recent example of such a commission is the President's Commission on Organized Crime, appointed by President Reagan in 1983. This pre-policy, advisory function is performed by Royal Commissions in England and Canada.
>
> The second type of citizens' commission is what may be characterized as a *specific event* inquiry commission. Such commissions, described elsewhere as

---

behest of President Johnson than to presidential advisory commissions as they have operated in the twentieth century." (citations omitted)).

4. For a comparison of British royal commissions to U.S. blue-ribbon commissions, see Kenneth Kitts, Presidential Commissions & National Security: The Politics of Damage Control 2–4 (Lynne Rienner Publishers 2006). An early study of presidential commissions noted that the "partisan and political bias" that accompanies legislative commissions in the United States, coupled with the "separation of powers" that distinguished the United States government from the British parliamentary structure, has prevented legislative commissions from achieving the stature and prestige accorded to British royal commissions. See Carl Marcy, Presidential Commissions 4–5 (King's Crown Press 1945).

5. For example, the report of the National Commission on Terrorist Attacks Upon the United States (the 9/11 Commission), which is a principal focus of this Chapter, provided a comprehensive factual narrative of the September 11, 2001 terrorist attacks and the events that preceded those attacks (see The 9/11 Commission Report, chapters 1–11), and also set out a detailed and comprehensive set of policy recommendations that were aimed at preventing future terrorist attacks (see The 9/11 Commission Report, chapters 12–13).

"'post mortems,'" are appointed in the aftermath of some public scandal, tragedy, or government misconduct. Examples of this type of commission are the Roberts Commission appointed in 1941 by President Roosevelt to inquire into the circumstances surrounding the Japanese attack on Pearl Harbor, and the Space Shuttle Challenger Accident Commission appointed in February 1986 by President Reagan to inquire into the space shuttle disaster that killed seven astronauts. In England, Canada, and Israel, this type of commission is called a tribunal of inquiry.[6]

When this nomenclature is employed, the focus on this Chapter is the investigative/specific event inquiry commission, and not on the prepolicy/advisory type of commission.

Another way to describe this fundamental difference among national commissions is to distinguish between "administrative" commissions that seek to improve the administration of government and so-called "boards of inquiry" that focus upon a particular event or perceived failure of government:

> The essential distinction is that the commissions described as engaged in administrative studies are bodies seeking to improve administration as such. They may be created as a result of charges that government is expensive, its methods antiquated, or that red tape is rampant. Boards of inquiry on the other hand are bodies looking for wrongdoing. They are trying to pin guilt on someone or some organization. They are usually created as a result of an obvious failure of government or a disaster for which the public demands a complete explanation.[7]

Again, our focus is on "boards of inquiry," and not "administrative" commissions.

A different way to categorize national commissions is to distinguish "presidential" commissions from those created by an act of Congress. For example, the Roberts Commission and the Warren Commission were created by presidential executive orders, while the 9/11 Commission was created by a statute passed by Congress. Even this distinction is less exacting than it might first appear, however. To create a "congressional" commission, the President must sign legislation that Congress has passed (if one puts aside the unlikely prospect of Congress overriding a presidential veto of legislation creating a Commission), and no commission requiring access to government information is likely to succeed without presidential support. By the same token, presidential commissions that seek to do more than make policy recommendations are likely to need compulsory process, which only Congress can confer upon a commission. As is discussed in greater detail below, both the Roberts Commission and the Warren

---

6. Carl E. Singly, *The MOVE Commission: The Use of Public Inquiry Commissions to Investigate Government Misconduct and Other Matters of Vital Importance*, 59 TEMPLE L.Q. 303, 304–05 (1986).

7. CARL MARCY, PRESIDENTIAL COMMISSIONS 89 (King's Crown Press 1945). Marcy argued that "administrative studies are most thorough and successful if undertaken under the auspices of the Executive" and that "investigations which seek to uncover wrongdoing are most appropriately undertaken under the auspices of Congress." *Id.*

Commission sought and obtained subpoena power from Congress through joint resolutions enacted after the commissions had been formed.

These abstract categorizations come to life when applied to actual commissions
in our nation's history. The Roberts Commission that President Roosevelt created to
investigate the Pearl Harbor attacks falls clearly into the investigative commission/
board of inquiry category, and it was without question a presidential commission even
though, as noted above, after it was formed it obtained subpoena power through a congressional joint resolution.[8] Other Roosevelt-era commissions, such as the President's
Committee on Economic Security, which laid the groundwork for the Social Security
Act of 1935, and the President's Committee on Civil Service Improvements, chaired by
Supreme Court Justice Stanley Reed, are classic examples of, respectively, "policy" and
"administrative" commissions.

The same distinctions can be drawn between the work of the Warren Commission, a
classic presidential "board of inquiry" created to perform a predominately fact-finding
function, and other landmark Johnson administration commissions. The President's
Commission on Law Enforcement and the Administration of Justice, chaired by Attorney General Nicolas Katzenbach and known as the Katzenbach Commission, is
a presidential commission that falls more neatly into the policy and administrative
categories than the fact-finding and board of inquiry categories. President Johnson's
National Advisory Commission on Civil Disorders, known as the Kerner Commission,
was created to investigate urban unrest in the U.S. in the mid-1960s and is more difficult to categorize. This categorization difficulty is apparent from President Johnson's
remarks at the signing of the Executive Order creating the Kerner Commission:

> No society can tolerate massive violence, any more than a body can tolerate
> massive disease. And we in America shall not tolerate it.
>
> But just saying that does not solve the problem. We need to know the an-
> swers, I think, to three basic questions about these riots:
>
> — What happened?
>
> — Why did it happen?
>
> — What can be done to prevent it from happening again and again?[9]

The three questions identified by President Johnson obviously gave the commission
a broad mandate that encompassed both fact-finding and policy recommendations.
More recent examples of this categorization difficulty are the 9/11 Commission, which
was responsible for both investigating the 9/11 attacks and making policy recommendations to prevent future terrorist attacks, and the Silberman-Robb WMD Commis-

---

8. *See* Report of the Commission Appointed by the President of the United States to Investigate
and Report the Facts Relating to the Attack Made by Japanese Armed Forces Upon Pearl Harbor in the
Territory of Hawaii on December 7, 1941 (the Roberts Commission Report) 1 (Jan. 23, 1942) (Senate
Doc. No. 159, 77th Cong., 2d Sess.).

9. President Lyndon B. Johnson, Remarks Upon Signing Order Establishing the National Advisory
Commission on Civil Disorders, July 29, 1967.

sion, which was responsible for assessing the intelligence capabilities of the United States regarding weapons of mass destruction and making policy recommendations to improve the U.S. Intelligence Community.

The difficulties in categorizing independent commissions notwithstanding, the use of blue-ribbon commissions has steadily increased in recent decades. One commentator has sought to explain the unlikely continued proliferation of blue-ribbon commissions and advisory committees in the following terms:

> In the federal government, the independent advisory commission enjoys no lawmaking power; no one is obligated to pay any attention to its conclusions; and it is held to minimal, if any, standards of legal or political accountability. Yet its proliferation throughout the twentieth century suggests that it fills a gap in the legislative and executive's array of authorities by enabling deliberative, expert, and independent consideration of a controversial issue, whether that issue arises from a traumatic event like the 9/11 attacks, or more quotidian policy issues that stymie legislative and regulatory action, or symbolic issues that the President, Congress, or an executive branch agency wishes to acknowledge.[10]

An in-depth analysis of the reasons for the proliferation of independent commissions is beyond the scope of this Chapter and is not necessary for our main purpose, which is to compare the investigative processes of these commissions to congressional investigations. The three examples we will examine provide particularly fertile grounds for comparison of congressional investigations and independent commission investigations. The Roberts Commission and the Warren Commission were perceived as less than fully successful inquiries, and as a result suffered the ignominy of having their investigations reopened and reexamined by congressional panels. The 9/11 Commission, in contrast, was created in large measure because a prior congressional investigation had not satisfied the public demand for a complete accounting of the 9/11 attacks. All three investigations are fascinating and extraordinarily complex topics of study, as evidenced by the fact that each one has been the subject of numerous book-length studies and critiques. For that reason, the discussion that follows in this Chapter should not be viewed as a comprehensive analysis of these three landmark investigative commissions, but rather as a selective examination of key topics relating to independent commission investigative procedures and practices as they compare to those of congressional investigations.

The Pearl Harbor attack was the worst military defeat in our nation's history and the only successful attack on the U.S. homeland in the twentieth century. The John F. Kennedy assassination was the only presidential assassination in the last hundred years and, in the words of Senator Arlen Specter, "the single most investigated event in world

---

10. Mark Fenster, *Designing Transparency: The 9/11 Commission and Institutional Form*, 65 WASH. & LEE L. REV. 1239, 1246 (2008) (citations omitted).

history, with the possible exception of the crucifixion of Christ."[11] It is not surprising that both of these events precipitated an immediate governmental response in the form of a special blue-ribbon national investigative commission. What may be surprising is the manner in which those two investigations were conducted and the amount of controversy they fostered.

The Roberts Commission and Pearl Harbor

Within days of the December 7, 1941 Japanese surprise attack on Pearl Harbor, President Roosevelt decided to create a special commission to investigate the matter. The President's decision and the membership of the commission were announced on December 17. On December 18, the commission's mandate was formalized with the issuance of an Executive Order signed by President Roosevelt:

Executive Order 8983 Establishing a Commission to Investigate the Pearl Harbor Attack.

December 18, 1941

Pursuant to the authority in me vested by the Constitution of the United States, I hereby appoint as a commission to ascertain and report the facts relating to the attack made by Japanese armed forces upon the Territory of Hawaii on December 7, 1941, the following:

Associate Justice Owen J. Roberts, United States Supreme Court, Chairman;

Admiral William H. Standley, United States Navy, Retired;

Rear Admiral Joseph M. Reeves, United States Navy, Retired;

Major General Frank R. McCoy, United States Army, Retired;

Brigadier General Joseph T. McNarney, United States Army.

The purposes of the required inquiry and report are to provide bases for sound decisions whether any derelictions of duty or errors of judgment on the part of United States Army or Navy personnel contributed to such successes as were achieved by the enemy on the occasion mentioned, and if so, what these derelictions or errors were, and who were responsible therefor.

The Commission will convene at the call of its Chairman at Washington, D. C., will thereafter proceed with its professional and clerical assistants to Honolulu, Territory of Hawaii, and any other places it may deem necessary to

---

11. Arlen Specter with Charles Robbins, Passion for Truth 3 (William Morrow 2000) (hereinafter Specter). As is discussed in greater detail below, Senator Specter served on the staff of the Warren Commission and is credited with developing the "single-bullet theory" (which he prefers to call "the single-bullet conclusion" because he believes its accuracy has been established) to explain the assassination. *See id.* at 1–4.

visit for the completion of its inquiry. It will then return to Washington, D.C., and submit its report directly to the President of the United States.

The Commission is empowered to prescribe its own procedure, to employ such professional and clerical assistants as it may deem necessary, to fix the compensation and allowances of such assistants, to incur all necessary expenses for services and supplies, and to direct such travel of members and employees at public expense as it may deem necessary in the accomplishment of its mission. Each of the members of the Commission and each of its professional assistants, including civilian advisers and any Army, Navy, and Marine Corps officers so employed, detailed, or assigned shall receive payment of his actual and necessary expenses for transportation, and in addition and in lieu of all other allowances for expenses while absent from the place of his residence or station in connection with the business of the Commission, a per diem allowance of twenty-five dollars. All of the expenses of the Commission shall be paid by Army disbursing officers from allocations to be made to the War Department for that purpose from the Emergency Fund for the President.

All executive officers and agencies of the United States are directed to furnish the Commission such facilities, services, and cooperation as it may request of them from time to time.

White House   (signed) Franklin D. Roosevelt

It is noteworthy that the Roberts Commission was chaired by Supreme Court Justice Owen Roberts. Two decades earlier Roberts had served as a Department of Justice special prosecutor for the Teapot Dome scandal, which is examined in Chapter 1. Subsequently, as a member of the Supreme Court, Roberts had been the subject of national attention when he shifted his judicial stance on constitutional challenges to President Roosevelt's New Deal programs in the famous "switch in time that saved nine," that upheld the New Deal and averted a potential constitutional crisis over Roosevelt's "court-packing" plan.[12] While Roberts's prior Teapot Dome investigative experience and position as a Supreme Court Justice made him a natural choice to head a Pearl Harbor investigative commission, the other members of the commission all were from the military and therefore subject to question in terms of their ability to investigate aggressively and evaluate objectively the actions of the armed services. Moreover, the executive order charged the commission with investigating "whether any derelictions of duty or errors of judgment on the part of United States Army or Navy personnel contributed to such successes as were achieved by the enemy," an investigative mandate that arguably omitted evaluation of whether high-level civilian government officials

---

12. The Roberts shift from anti-New Deal to pro-New Deal voting in Supreme Court decisions is described in Barry Friedman, *The History of Countermajoritarian Difficulty, Part Four: Law's Politics*, 148 U. Pa. L. Rev. 971, 974 (2000).

were at fault.[13] Add to these vulnerabilities the fact that the commission was an organ of the executive branch charged with investigating a failure of core executive branch military preparedness responsibilities, and the potential for second-guessing and loss of credibility is evident.

Immediately after its formation, the Roberts Commission promptly proceeded to compound the structural problems noted above by embarking on a series of actions that further exposed it to criticism and undermined the credibility of its investigative efforts.[14] The commission's initial interviews of high-ranking military officials in Washington were neither conducted under oath nor transcribed, a procedure that was criticized during subsequent congressional inquiries. The commission then traveled to Hawaii to conduct further fact-finding on site, where witnesses were questioned under oath and on-the-record. The commission then returned to Washington and by the end of January presented its report, which cast blame heavily on the field military officers in Hawaii. The three key conclusions of the commission were that:

> 16. The failure of the commanding general, Hawaiian Department, and the commander in chief, Pacific Fleet, to confer and cooperate with respect to the meaning of the warnings received and the measures necessary to comply with the orders given them under date of November 27, 1941, resulted largely from a sense of security due to the opinion prevalent in diplomatic, military, and naval circles, and in the public press, that any immediate attack by Japan would be in the Far East. The existence of such a view, however prevalent, did not relieve the commanders of the responsibility for the security of the Pacific Fleet and our most important outpost.

> 17. In the light of the warnings and directions to take appropriate action, transmitted to both commanders between November 27 and December 7, and the obligation under the system of coordination then in effect for joint cooperative action on their part, it was a dereliction of duty on the part of each of them not to consult and confer with the other respecting the meaning and intent of the warnings, and the appropriate measures of defense required by the imminence of hostilities. The attitude of each, that he was not required to inform himself of, and his lack of interest in, the measures undertaken by the other to carry out the responsibility assigned to such other under the provisions of the plans then in effect, demonstrated on the part of each a lack of appreciation of the responsibilities vested in them and inherent in their positions as commander in chief, Pacific Fleet, and commanding general, Hawaiian Department.

---

13. *See* KENNETH KITTS, PRESIDENTIAL COMMISSIONS & NATIONAL SECURITY: THE POLITICS OF DAMAGE CONTROL 26–27 (Lynne Rienner Publishers 2006) (discussing Admiral Standley's concerns about the breadth of the commission's investigative mandate).

14. The events summarized here are described in more detail in KITTS, *supra*, at 23–38.

18. The Japanese attack was a complete surprise to the commanders and they failed to make suitable dispositions to meet such an attack. Each failed properly to evaluate the seriousness of the situation. These errors of judgment were the effective causes for the success of the attack.

Report of the Commission Appointed by the President of the United States to Investigate and Report the Facts Relating to the Attack Made by Japanese Armed Forces Upon Pearl Harbor in the Territory of Hawaii on December 7, 1941 (the Roberts Commission Report), p. 20–21 (Jan. 23, 1942) (Senate Doc. No. 159, 77th Cong., 2d Sess.).

These three conclusions, and the commission's investigation generally, did not fare well under subsequent official and historical scrutiny. The Roberts Commission has been criticized for adopting an unduly restrictive investigative mandate, placing too much blame on the field commanders in Hawaii, failing to investigate adequately secret signals intelligence that might have prompted greater readiness had it been shared with the Pearl Harbor commanders, permitting too much involvement in its work by senior civilian military officials who more properly should have been treated as within its investigative purview, and relying on investigative procedures that may have been inadequate for an investigation of such monumental importance. For all of these reasons, the Roberts Commission cannot be judged a complete success. The most compelling evidence of failure is the extent to which subsequent investigations were viewed as necessary to resolve questions regarded as either left open or addressed inadequately by the Roberts Commission. The Senate Committee on Governmental Affairs report that accompanied proposed legislation to create a commission to investigate the September 11 terrorist attacks summarized the Roberts Commission investigation and the successor investigations as follows:

Pearl Harbor investigations

In the aftermath of the December 7, 1941, attack on United States military installations at Pearl Harbor in the Hawaiian Islands, four major panels were established to conduct investigations of that event. The first of these entities was created on December 18, 1941, by E.O. 8983, "to ascertain and report the acts relating to the attack." The President's chartering order named Supreme Court Associate Justice Owen J. Roberts as chair and two retired Navy admirals and two retired Army generals as members of the panel. After interviewing 127 witnesses in Washington and Hawaii, the commission concluded its work on January 23, 1942, when it presented its report of findings—placing responsibility for the disaster with the senior Army and Navy commanders in Hawaii—to the President.

The Roberts Commission was followed by three additional inquiries. On June 13, 1944, the President signed S.J. Res. 133, directing the Secretary of War and the Secretary of the Navy "to proceed forthwith with an investigation into the facts surrounding the [Pearl Harbor] catastrophe." The Army Pearl Harbor Board was in continuous session from July 24, 1944, to October 20, 1944, conducting a fact-finding investigation; the board heard a total of 151 witnesses. It assessed responsibility over a wider spectrum than did the Roberts report, and placed its findings in the context of United States relations with Japan before December 7, 1941. The Navy Court of Inquiry on the Pearl Harbor attack convened on July 24, 1944 and concluded its inquiry on October 19, 1944. An additional investigation ordered by the Navy was conducted during May 2, 1945, to July 12, 1945. The Navy's inquiry concentrated on the guilt or innocence of the interested parties and did not analyze as comprehensively the background of the attack or assess the responsibilities of Washington officials.

With S. Con. Res. 27 of September 11, 1945, Congress mandated the Joint Committee on the Investigation of the Pearl Harbor Attack to "make a full and complete investigation of the facts relating to the events and circumstances leading up to and following the attack made by Japanese armed forces upon Pearl Harbor." Chaired by Senator Alben W. Barkley (D-KY), the panel was composed of five Senators and five Representatives, three Democrats and two Republicans in each case. It held hearings between November 11, 1945, and May 31, 1946, and reviewed the work of the Roberts Commission and Army and Navy panels investigating the Pearl Harbor attack. The bipartisan majority report of the committee, supported by eight members of the panel, blamed the American performance at Pearl Harbor on the national defense system.

Senate Report 107–150, To Establish the National Commission on Terrorist Attacks Upon the United States, and for Other Purposes (May 14, 2002).

For purposes of this book and our central thesis that congressional investigations play a vital role in our system of government, it is noteworthy that two of the three principal investigations that followed the Roberts Commission were the result of congressional action, acquiesced in by President Roosevelt, demonstrating the lack of congressional satisfaction with the Roberts Commission's "presidential commission" investigation.

A similar fate befell the other preeminent presidential commission in our nation's history, the Warren Commission, but while the Roberts Commission is generally perceived as conducting a flawed and inadequate investigation, history's verdict on the Warren Commission is less clear.

Notes and Questions

1. **Timing and Deadlines.** A remarkable aspect of the Roberts Commission investigation was the extraordinary speed with which it completed its investigation and reported its conclusions to President Roosevelt, just over one month after it was formed. How should the need for a fast public report on an event of overwhelming national interest be balanced against the competing need for adequate time to conduct a thorough and complete investigation? Both the Warren Commission's investigation of the Kennedy assassination and the 9/11 Commission's investigation of the September 11 terrorist attacks, discussed below, were greatly influenced by completion deadlines. As you review the materials below on those investigations, imagine that you are a member

of Congress and ask yourself how much time you would consider to be necessary for an independent commission to conduct an investigation of that magnitude.

2. Investigative Procedures. As noted above, the Roberts Commission has been criticized for its early investigative activities, when key officials were interviewed informally without administering oaths or making a transcription of the interviews. The issue of what investigative procedures an independent investigative commission should follow is a recurring question that commissions have faced. Under current law it is likely that any false or misleading statements by a witness could be criminally prosecuted under the federal false statements statute, 18 U.S.C. §1001, but many witnesses may not be aware of the broad application of that statute and may not appreciate (particularly if they are not advised by competent counsel) that this law is applicable even when an oath is not administered.[15] Moreover, it may be viewed as coercive or intimidating for commission investigators to emphasize the statute's application to a witness interview or testimony at a commission hearing. A uniform practice of swearing witnesses, on the other hand, arguably impresses upon all witnesses the importance of providing complete and truthful testimony.

Similar issues surround the preparation of verbatim transcripts of all witness interviews. Using court reporters or professional stenographers for every witness statement is expensive and can be inefficient, particularly for routine background interviews. Having stenographers present also may be impractical when testimony involves classified information or national security issues. On the other hand, it is impossible to predict when a presumably routine witness may provide "bombshell" testimony (for an example of how that may occur, see the discussion in Chapter 3 on Alexander Butterfield's testimony in the Watergate congressional investigation that revealed the presence of the Nixon White House taping system). Also, as a practical matter, a verbatim transcript may be the only definitive means of resolving after-the-fact disputes about exactly what a witness said in his or her testimony. Technological advances in audio and video recording may provide solutions for some of these obstacles, however, as is discussed in subsequent sections of this Chapter.

As you review the materials in this Chapter on special commission investigations, consider how those investigations differ from congressional inquiries and how those differences may affect the investigative procedures that are employed. Are there any universal rules that should apply, or must each commission make its own determination as to what investigative procedures should govern its investigation? See the Notes following the discussion below of the 9/11 Commission investigation for further examination of the issues surrounding independent commissions' investigative procedures.

---

15. Major league baseball player Miguel Tejada pled guilty to making false statements in a congressional investigation of steroid use in major league baseball. *See* Michael S. Schmidt, *Tejada Pleads Guilty to Lying to Congress*, N.Y. Times (Feb. 11, 2009). The statements that were the basis for the false statements charge against Tejada were made to congressional staff investigators during a 2005 interview in a Baltimore hotel room, not sworn testimony during a congressional hearing. *See Tejada Charged with Lying to Congress About Drugs*, Denver Post (Feb. 10, 2009).

3. Comparison to Congressional Investigations. As you review the materials below on the Warren Commission, you should compare the investigation conducted by the Warren Commission to that of the Roberts Commission and to the various congressional investigations that are described in the preceding chapters of this book. What are the advantages and disadvantages of presidential commission investigations compared with congressional investigations? Does Congress inevitably err when it cedes investigative authority to a presidential commission? In three of the case studies included in this book—the Pearl Harbor investigations, the Kennedy assassination investigations, and the Iran-Contra investigations—initial investigations by presidential commission have proved inadequate and have been supplemented by subsequent full-blown congressional investigations. Are the congressional investigations a superior means of finding and making public the essential facts about events of great public importance? If so, why?

The Warren Commission and the John F. Kennedy Assassination

Perhaps no governmental investigation in our nation's history has been subject to more reexamination, second-guessing, and public skepticism than the Warren Commission's investigation of the assassination of President John F. Kennedy. The work of the Warren Commission and its conclusion that Lee Harvey Oswald acted alone in assassinating President Kennedy has been under attack for more than fifty years. Legions of assassination experts, conspiracy theorists, and critics of both the way the investigation was conducted and the conclusions it reached have significantly eroded public confidence in the Warren Commission's work. Kennedy assassination terminology such as "the single bullet theory" and "the grassy knoll" have become part of our national lexicon. In 2007 writer and former Charles Manson prosecutor Vincent Bugliosi published *Reclaiming History*, a 1,500-page tome on the Kennedy assassination that aimed to refute and discredit the numerous Kennedy assassination conspiracy theories. In the Introduction to *Reclaiming History*, Bugliosi summarized forty years of conspiracy theories and Warren Commission critiques as follows:

> The hard-core conspiracy theorists believe not only that there was a massive conspiracy to kill the president, but that the Warren Commission learned about this conspiracy, and, as pawns of the U.S. government, entered into a new conspiracy to cover it up. "The Warren Commission engaged in a cover-up of the truth and issued a report that misrepresented or distorted almost every relevant fact about the crime," Howard Roffman writes in his book, *Presumed Guilty*. Gerald D. McKnight, a professor of history, no less, writes that the Warren Commission members were "men intent on deceiving the nation." Just in the area of the president's autopsy, he says, "the Commission sanctioned perjury, connived at the destruction of the best evidence, boycotted key witnesses, and deliberately and knowingly suppressed material medical records and legal documents." There were "two conspiracies," conspiracy theorist Jim Marrs confidently asserts. "One was the conspiracy to kill the president. The

second conspiracy was the conspiracy to cover up the first conspiracy," the second conspiracy being committed by "officials high within the U.S. government to hide the truth from the American public."

One of the first purveyors of this silliness was New Orleans district attorney Jim Garrison. During his investigation of Clay Shaw for the president's murder, he said that "the United States government—meaning the present administration, Lyndon Johnson's administration—is obstructing the investigation.... It has concealed the true facts, to be blunt about it, to protect the individuals involved in the assassination of John Kennedy." The promotional literature for conspiracy theorist Carl Oglesby's 1992 book, *Who Killed JFK?*, likewise reflects this commonly held belief of the conspiracy community, which it accepts as a mosaic truth: "In this clear, readable book, prominent assassination researcher Carl Oglesby proves that JFK must have been killed by a conspiracy, not a lone gunman. Even scarier, he knows that the U.S. government has been, *and still is* covering up that conspiracy." If we're to believe Oglesby, our current federal government (as well as all previous ones since 1963) is engaged in a conspiracy to cover up the truth in the assassination.

Apparently, then, such distinguished Americans as Chief Justice Earl Warren, Senators John Sherman Cooper and Richard B. Russell, Representatives Gerald Ford and Hale Boggs, former CIA director Allen Dulles and former president of the World Bank John J. McCoy (the members of the Warren Commission), as well as the Commission's general counsel, J. Lee Rankin, a former solicitor general of the United States, and fourteen prominent members of the American Bar (assistant counsels to the Commission), people of impeccable honor and reputation, got together in some smoky backroom and *all* of them agreed, for some ungodly reason, to do the most dishonorable deed imaginable—give organized crime, the CIA, the military-industrial complex, or whoever was behind the assassination, a free pass in the murder of the president of the United States. And in the process, not only risk destroying everything they had worked for—their reputation and legacy to their families—but expose themselves to prosecution for the crime of accessory after the fact to murder. Ask yourself this: would Earl Warren, for instance, risk being remembered as the chief justice of the United States Supreme Court who was an accessory after the fact to the murder of this nation's president, one who disgraced himself, his country, and the highest court in the land? The mere asking of the question demonstrates the absurdity of the thought. As political columnist Charles Krauthammer put it, it is preposterous to believe that "Earl Warren, a liberal so principled that he would not countenance the conviction of one Ernesto Miranda [of *Miranda v. Arizona* fame] on the grounds that police had neglected to read him his rights, was an accessory to a fascist coup d'etat." Indeed, why would any of the members of the Warren Commission and their staff stake their good reputation on a report they prepared which they knew to be fraudulent?

And if the conspiracy to kill Kennedy was as obvious as conspiracy theorists want us to believe, how then could the Warren Commission members have had any confidence that the conspiracy's existence would not have surfaced in the future? Moreover, if we adopt the cover-up theory, did all seven Commission members, on their own, decide to suppress the truth? Or was there a ringleader or architect of the cover-up, like Warren? If the latter, how was he able to get the other six members (and, necessarily, a significant number of the Commission's assistant counsels and staff) to go along with his nefarious scheme? Indeed, not knowing what their response might be, wouldn't he have been deathly afraid to even approach them with such a monumentally base and criminal proposal? The whole notion is too ridiculous to even contemplate. Adding a touch of humor to it all, as Commission member Gerald Ford said, "The thought that Earl Warren and I would conspire on anything is preposterous."

* * *

The point should be made that even if a sense of honor and duty were not the primary motivating factors in the Warren Commission's work, simple self-interest would naturally have induced its members not to try to cover up the existence of a conspiracy if, in fact, they found one. As Commission assistant counsel David Slawson, whose area of responsibility, along with William T. Coleman, Jr., was to determine if there was a conspiracy, told me, "We were all motivated to find something unexpected, such as other gunmen or a hidden conspiracy. *It would have made us heroes.* But these hopes gradually disappeared as the evidence that it was just Oswald rolled in." (Kenneth Klein, assistant deputy chief counsel for the later HSCA [House of Representatives Select Committee on Assassinations], said essentially the same thing in his article, "Facts Knit the Single Bullet Theory": "Since the validity of the Warren Commission's finding that Lee Harvey Oswald was the lone assassin rested firmly on the validity of the single-bullet theory, the staff members of the Select Committee would have been thrilled to have disproved it. To have done so would surely have led to fame and fortune. Only one thing prevented us from doing so, the evidence.—Goodbye fame. Goodbye fortune.")

* * *

In his memoirs, Chief Justice Earl Warren, after pointing out that his commission uncovered "no facts upon which to hypothesize a conspiracy," and that separate investigations by the FBI, Central Intelligence Agency, Secret Service, and Departments of State and Defense could not find "any evidence of conspiracy," wrote, "To say now that these [agencies], as well as the Commission, suppressed, neglected to unearth, or overlooked evidence of a conspiracy would be an indictment of the entire government of the United States. It would mean the whole structure was absolutely corrupt from top to bottom, not one person of high or low rank willing to come forward to expose the villainy, in spite of the fact that the entire country bitterly mourned the death of its young President."

* * *

Yet the conspiracy theorists are convinced that even before the Warren Commission, the whole purpose of President Lyndon Johnson establishing it was to whitewash what really happened, either because he was complicit himself or because he was fearful that if it came out that Russia or Cuba was behind the assassination, it might precipitate a nuclear war. But this ignores the fact that the Warren Commission (five of whose members were Republican, unlikely candidates to cover up anything, much less a murder, for a Democratic president) wasn't even LBJ's idea. As far as is known, Yale Law School's Walt Rostow first suggested it to LBJ's press secretary, Bill Moyers, in a telephone conversation on the morning of November 24, 1963, the day after the assassination. ("My suggestion is that a presidential commission be appointed of very distinguished citizens in the very near future. Bipartisan and above politics," Rostow told Moyers.) Almost concurrently, the *Washington Post*, lobbied by LBJ's own Justice Department (particularly Deputy Attorney General Nicholas Katzenbach), let it be known to the White House that it favored the idea also.

LBJ, in fact, was originally strongly opposed to the idea, saying it was "very bad" and the inquiry into the assassination should be a "state matter" handled by the attorney general of the state of Texas with only the assistance of the FBI.

* * *

Conspiracy theorists can find little comfort in the finding of the HSCA that President Kennedy "was probably assassinated as a result of a conspiracy." Nowhere did the HSCA conclude that any of the groups frequently mentioned by the theorists, such as the CIA, FBI, Secret Service, organized crime, Cuban government, anti-Castro Cuban exiles, and so on, were involved in any conspiracy to kill the president. To the contrary, the select committee specifically concluded just the opposite, that they were "not involved." For example, the HSCA said, "Based on the Committee's entire investigation, it concluded that the Secret Service, FBI, and CIA were not involved in the assassination." The sole basis for the HSCA's conclusion that there was a conspiracy was its contested and far less-than-unanimous belief that in addition to the three shots it determined that Oswald fired from the Book Depository Building (two of which, it concluded, struck the president), there was a "high probability" that a fourth shot, which it said did not hit the president, was fired from the grassy knoll. If such were actually the case, a conclusion of conspiracy would be compelled—unless one drew the unrealistic inference that two people, acting totally independent of each other, just happened to try and kill the president at the same place and moment in time.

The basis for this fourth-shot conclusion was an acoustical analysis of a police Dictabelt recording from Dallas police headquarters containing sounds, the HSCA believed, from a police motorcycle in Dealey Plaza whose radio transmitting switch was stuck in the "on" position. HSCA acoustic experts thought the sounds heard on the tape were probably those of four gunshots. However, as is discussed in considerable depth in an endnote, this fourth-shot conclusion has been completely discredited and proved to be in error by subsequent analyses of the Dictabelt. In 1982, twelve of the most prominent experts in ballistic acoustics in the country were commissioned by the National Research Council to reexamine the Dictabelt. The panel found "conclusively" from other concurrent and identifiable background noise on the Dictabelt that the sound which the HSCA experts believed to be a fourth shot actually occurred "about one minute after the assassination," when the presidential limousine was long gone down Stemmons Freeway on its way to Parkland Memorial Hospital.

* * *

When one removes the Dictabelt "fourth shot" from the USCA findings, all that is really left is the HSCA's conclusion that Oswald killed Kennedy, and the fact that the committee found no evidence of any person or group being conspired with Oswald, the identical findings of the Warren Commission.

As the Bugliosi excerpt above suggests, the Warren Commission has been the subject of numerous books and studies, scholarly and otherwise. An in-depth examination of Kennedy assassination literature is beyond the scope of this Chapter, but it is noteworthy that the many of the most influential works focus on the investigative activities of the Warren Commission. These works share a common thesis that, rather than seeking the truth about the Kennedy assassination, the Warren Commission instead sought to establish "political truth"[16] or "official truth"[17] by confirming that Oswald acted alone, and in so doing ignored evidence that tended to disprove that thesis—or may even have manipulated the evidence to support that thesis.

Keep these critiques in mind as you review the materials on the Warren Commission that are set out below (which, it should be noted, provide at best only a cursory introduction to the topic). Also keep in mind that despite the extraordinary efforts to disprove the Warren Commission's conclusion over the past six-plus decades, includ-

---

16. *See* EDWARD J. EPSTEIN, INQUEST: THE WARREN COMMISSION AND THE ESTABLISHMENT OF POLITICAL TRUTH, Part One, "Political Truth" (Viking Press 1966). "Quite clearly, a serious discussion of this problem [evidence of a second assassin] would in itself have undermined the dominant purpose of the Commission, namely the settling of doubts and suspicions. Indeed, if the Commission had made it clear that very substantial evidence indicated the presence of a second assassin, it would have opened a Pandora's box of doubts and suspicions. In establishing its version of the truth, the Warren Commission acted to reassure the nation and protect the national interest." *Id.* at 125.

17. *See* GERALD D. MCKNIGHT, BREACH OF TRUST: HOW THE WARREN COMMISSION FAILED THE NATION AND WHY, Chapter One, "Assembling the 'Official Truth' in Dallas," (University Press of Kansas 2005). "That same weekend Johnson, Hoover, and Deputy Attorney General Nicholas deB. Katzenbach settled upon the 'official truth' of the assassination, the politically accepted version fabricated for public consumption." *Id.* at 19.

ing efforts to use new technological and forensic tools[18] to shed additional light on the events of November 22, 1963, the core conclusions of the Warren Commission have never been convincingly rebutted.

The mandate of the Warren Commission was set out in Executive Order 11130, which created the Commission:

Executive Order 11130 Appointing a Commission to Report Upon the Assassination of President John F. Kennedy.

Released November 30, 1963. [Dated November 29, 1963]

PURSUANT to the authority vested in me as President of the United States, I hereby appoint a Commission to ascertain, evaluate, and report upon the facts relating to the assassination of the late President John F. Kennedy and the subsequent violent death of the man charged with the assassination. The Commission shall consist of—

The Chief Justice of the United States, Chairman;
Senator Richard B. Russell;
Senator John Sherman Cooper;
Congressman Hale Boggs;
Congressman Gerald R. Ford;
The Honorable Allen W. Dulles;
The Honorable John J. McCloy.

The purposes of the Commission are to examine the evidence developed by the Federal Bureau of Investigation and any additional evidence that may hereafter come to light or be uncovered by Federal or State authorities; to make such further investigation as the Commission finds desirable; to evaluate all the facts and circumstances surrounding such assassination, including the subsequent violent death of the man charged with the assassination, and to report to me its findings and conclusions.

The Commission is empowered to prescribe its own procedures and to employ such assistants as it deems necessary.

Necessary expenses of the Commission may be paid from the "Emergency Fund for the President."

---

18. For example, in 1978 the House Special Committee on Assassinations convened a panel of photographic science experts and used computer enhancement analysis conducted by the Los Alamos Scientific Laboratory, the Rochester Institute of Technology, the University of Southern California, and Aerospace Corp. to evaluate motion picture and photographic images that Warren Commission critics had asserted showed additional gunmen near the assassination site. *See generally* Appendix to Hearings before the Select Committee on Assassinations, United States House of Representatives, Vol. VI, Photographic Evidence (March 1979). The panel of experts concluded that "There is no definitive visible evidence of any gunmen in the streets, sidewalks, or areas adjacent to Dealey Plaza. Nor was any evidence discerned of a flash of light or puff of smoke." *Id.* at 109.

All Executive departments and agencies are directed to furnish the Commission with such facilities, services, and cooperation as it may request from time to time.

LYNDON B. JOHNSON

———

The Warren Commission was granted subpoena power and the power to confer immunity on witnesses by a special joint resolution of Congress:

Public Law 88-202
88th Congress, S.J. Res. 137
December 13, 1963
Joint Resolution

Authorizing the Commission established to report upon the assassination of President John F. Kennedy to compel the attendance and testimony of witnesses and the production of evidence.

Resolved by the Senate and House of Representatives of the United States of America in Congress assembled, That

(a) for the purposes of this joint resolution, the term "Commission" means the Commission appointed by the President by Executive Order 11130, dated November 29, 1963.

(b) The Commission, or any member of the Commission when so authorized by the Commission, shall have power to issue subpoenas requiring the attendance and testimony of witnesses and the production of any evidence that relates to any matter under investigation by the Commission. The Commission, or any member of the Commission or any agent or agency designated by the Commission for such purpose, may administer oaths and affirmations, examine witnesses, and receive evidence. Such attendance of witnesses and the production of such evidence may be required from any place within the United States at any designated place of hearing.

(c) In case of contumacy or refusal to obey a subpoena issued to any person under subsection (b), any court of the United States within the jurisdiction of which the inquiry is carried on or within the jurisdiction of which said person guilty of contumacy or refusal to obey is found or resides or transacts business, upon application by the Commission shall have jurisdiction to issue to such person an order requiring such person to appear before the Commission, its member, agent, or agency, there to produce evidence if so ordered, or there to give testimony touching the matter under investigation or in question; and any failure to obey such order of the court may be punished by said court as a contempt thereof.

(d) Process and papers of the commission, its members, agent, or agency, may be served either upon the witness in person or by registered mail or by telegraph or by leaving a copy thereof at the residence or principal office or place of business of the person required to be served. The verified return by the individual so serving the same, setting forth the manner of such service, shall be proof of the same, and the return post office receipt or telegraph receipt therefore when registered and mailed or telegraphed as aforesaid shall be proof of service of the same. Witnesses summoned before the commission, its members, agent, or agency, shall be paid the same fees and mileage that are paid witnesses in the courts of the United States, and witnesses whose depositions are taken and the persons taking the same shall severally be entitled to the same fees as are paid for like services in the courts of the United States.

(e) No person shall be excused from attending and testifying or from producing books, records, correspondence, documents, or other evidence in obedience to a subpoena, on the ground that the testimony or evidence required of him may tend to incriminate him or subject him to a penalty or forfeiture; but no individual shall be prosecuted or subjected to any penalty or forfeiture (except demotion or removal from office) for or on account of any transaction, matter or thing concerning which he is compelled, after having claimed his privilege against self-incrimination, to testify or produce evidence, except that such individual so testifying shall not be exempt from prosecution and punishment for perjury committed in so testifying.

(f) All process of any court to which application may be made under this Act may be served in the judicial district wherein the person required to be served resides or may be found.

Approved December 13, 1963.

Although the Warren Commission was created by a presidential executive order, it required congressional action to grant the Commission subpoena power (see subsection b above) and the power to confer immunity on witnesses (see subsection e above). Thus the investigative mandate of the Warren Commission and the investigative powers it could use to implement that mandate were established by cooperative actions of the executive and legislative branches of government. The judicial branch also played a role, albeit indirectly and involuntarily, by contributing the services of Chief Justice Earl Warren to head the Commission. The story of Warren's participation is a fascinating historical anecdote that also raises important legal and policy issues regarding the make-up of investigative commissions and the proper role of the judiciary.

While the benefits of having a Supreme Court Justice lead a special national investigative commission, in terms of bestowing credibility and negating suggestions of partisan influence, are substantial, it is not clear that service on such a commission by a sitting federal judge is advisable, or even appropriate. Warren, for example, did not wish to serve in that capacity, but despite his strong misgivings about undertaking the assignment he was unable to resist the legendary persuasive powers of President Lyndon Johnson. Arlen Specter, who played a key role in the Warren Commission's investigation as the staff member who developed the "single bullet theory," has provided an insider's account of the Chief Justice's decision to head up the commission's investigation:

> Chief Justice Warren delivered our charge at an early staff meeting. All the lawyers gathered around the conference table in the commission hearing room to receive an indoctrination message from the chief justice. Earl Warren had tremendous presence, but even more so on this occasion, when he spoke of duty. His stature derived largely from his position as chief justice and the moral tone he had set for America, but he also radiated great strength as a man.

> At the outset of his indoctrination talk, the chief justice explained his reasons for serving on the commission. He addressed the question that had troubled many, about the propriety of a Supreme Court justice's undertaking such an assignment. Justice Robert Jackson had drawn heavy criticism for serving as a prosecutor in the Nuremberg War Crimes Trials following World War II. Likewise, Justice Owen J. Roberts had drawn objections for his work on the commission that had investigated the Pearl Harbor attack. The Kennedy assassination probe was an especially sensitive subject, since the Supreme Court might one day have to review the prosecution then pending against Jack Ruby, or other matters arising from the assassination.

> The chief justice told us he had taken on the commission job very reluctantly. "Archibald Cox, the solicitor general, came to see me and said, 'Mr. Chief Justice, I've been instructed to ask you to be chairman of the commission to investigate the assassination of President Kennedy.'" And Warren said, "I told Archibald Cox no. The Deputy Attorney General Nicholas Katzenbach came to talk to me. And I similarly told him no."

> Attorney General Robert Kennedy did not come to talk to the chief justice. The next call came from the White House, less than two hours later. "And then President Johnson asked me to come to the Oval Office, and asked me to do it," Warren said, "and I said no." The chief justice again declined, on the ground that he should not be involved in any such task, given his responsibility to the Supreme Court. The president persisted. He told Chief Justice Warren that only he could lend the credibility the country and the world so desperately needed as the people tried to understand why their heroic young president had been slain. Conspiracy theories involving communists, the U.S.S.R., Cuba, the military-industrial complex, and even the new president were already swirling. The Kennedy assassination could lead America into a nuclear war that could kill 40 million people, the president warned. President Johnson stressed that it was crucial to have men of prestige and ability to reassure the people that the whole truth was being aired. "Then the president said to me, 'Chief Justice Warren, would you refuse to put on the uniform of your country in time of national emergency, if requested by the commander in chief?'"

"Of course not," the chief justice said. Well, the president said, that was the situation they now faced. "I could hardly refuse that," Warren told us. "So I accepted."

ARLEN SPECTER WITH CHARLES ROBBINS, PASSION FOR TRUTH 53–54 (William Morrow 2000). The question of whether or not a sitting Supreme Court Justice should serve on a national investigative commission is closely related to the larger question of what level of activity and commitment of available professional time should be expected of commission members. (See Note 1 below for additional discussion of this issue.)

A second noteworthy structural characteristic of the Warren Commission concerns the backgrounds of its members and staff. For better or worse, the Warren Commission was a commission of lawyers. In addition to the seven commissioners, all of whom were lawyers, the Warren Commission had a staff comprised of a General Counsel, former Solicitor General of the United States J. Lee Rankin, and fourteen Assistant Counsels, who conducted the Commission's investigation with support from twelve additional staff members and the Federal Bureau of Investigation. The Warren Commission divided its investigative mandate into six major areas and staffed each area with a senior assistant counsel and a junior assistant counsel. The counsels then worked with the FBI and other federal agencies to conduct the Commission's investigation. The Warren Commission's reliance on the FBI for investigative support, rather than employing a staff of professional investigators, has been a source of criticism and controversy almost from the outset of the Commission's work. As an early and influential Warren Commission critic noted in 1966:

> The Commission conducted an independent investigation without independent investigators. The Commission found it unnecessary "to employ investigators other than the members of the Commission's legal staff," because it felt that it could rely on the facilities and investigative reports of the FBI and other federal agencies. Although the Commission in fact relied mainly on the FBI, the investigation in theory was independent, because the legal staff "critically reassessed" the reports and work of the FBI and conducted further investigations where necessary. J. Lee Rankin said, "Our lawyers were the only independent investigators that we needed."

EDWARD J. EPSTEIN, INQUEST: THE WARREN COMMISSION AND THE ESTABLISHMENT OF TRUTH 72 (Viking Press 1966) (footnotes omitted). Epstein, like other Warren Commission critics, found fault with the Commission's reliance on the FBI for investigative support and concluded that the Commission's investigation "was by no means exhaustive or even thorough." *Id.* at 125. The issue of investigative support for independent commission investigative activities is discussed further in the Notes below.

Other critics of the Warren Commission have ascribed even more nefarious motives to the role of the FBI in the Warren Commission's investigation. Gerald D. McKnight argued that FBI Director J. Edgar Hoover decided immediately after the assassination that Oswald must have acted alone, and then manipulated the entire FBI investigative effort to support that conclusion:

Limiting the investigation from the outset to the alleged lone assassin would have consequences: All the evidence allowed to come forward in the case—ballistics, fingerprints and palm prints, fiber analysis, and other technical data—would be slanted and misrepresented to establish that Oswald, and only Oswald, fired the shots that killed Kennedy and wounded Connally.

GERALD D. MCKNIGHT, BREACH OF TRUST: HOW THE WARREN COMMISSION FAILED THE NATION AND WHY 15 (University Press of Kansas 2005) (footnote omitted).

Although separated by almost thirty years, the Epstein and McKnight books that are quoted above share a common focus and a common conclusion that is particularly relevant to this Chapter's focus on special national investigative commissions. Both Epstein and McKnight focused their books on the investigative activities of the Warren Commission. And both contended that the fundamental purpose of the Warren Commission was not to find and report the true facts of the Kennedy assassination, but rather to establish the "official truth" (McKnight)[19] or the "political truth" (Epstein)[20] that Oswald was the assassin and acted alone in killing Kennedy. Both charged the Warren Commission with slanting the evidence to support the lone assassin conclusion and ignoring evidence that they contended supports the conclusion that Oswald did not act alone. The failure of the Warren Commission to dispel these kinds of doubts about the legitimacy of its investigation makes it a particularly important topic for further study in this Chapter's examination of special national investigative commissions.

Even a cursory analysis of the voluminous literature on the Kennedy assassination is beyond the scope of this Chapter, but it is instructive to focus on the core findings of the Commission's report that have precipitated the criticism and skepticism reflected in the Epstein and McKnight books quoted above. The following is from the Narrative of Events section in Chapter One, Summary and Conclusions, of the Warren Commission Report:

> The President's car which had been going north made a sharp turn toward the southwest onto Elm Street. At a speed of about 11 miles per hour, it started down the gradual descent toward a railroad overpass under which the motorcade would proceed before reaching the Stemmons Freeway. The front of the

---

19. *See* GERALD D. MCKNIGHT, BREACH OF TRUST: HOW THE WARREN COMMISSION FAILED THE NATION AND WHY, Chapter One, "Assembling the 'Official Truth' in Dallas" (University Press of Kansas 2005). "That same weekend Johnson, Hoover, and Deputy Attorney General Nicholas deB. Katzenbach settled upon the 'official truth' of the assassination, the politically accepted version fabricated for public consumption." *Id.* at 19.

20. *See* EDWARD J. EPSTEIN, INQUEST: THE WARREN COMMISSION AND THE ESTABLISHMENT OF POLITICAL TRUTH, Part One, "Political Truth" (Viking Press 1966). "Quite clearly, a serious discussion of this problem [evidence of a second assassin] would in itself have undermined the dominant purpose of the Commission, namely the settling of doubts and suspicions. Indeed, if the Commission had made it clear that very substantial evidence indicated the presence of a second assassin, it would have opened a Pandora's box of doubts and suspicions. In establishing its version of the truth, the Warren Commission acted to reassure the nation and protect the national interest." *Id.* at 125.

Texas School Book Depository was now on the President's right, and he waved to the crowd assembled there as he passed the building. Dealey Plaza—an open, landscaped area marking the western end of downtown Dallas stretched out to the President's left. A Secret Service agent riding in the motorcade radioed the Trade Mart that the President would arrive in 5 minutes.

Seconds later shots resounded in rapid succession. The President's hands moved to his neck. He appeared to stiffen momentarily and lurch slightly forward in his seat. A bullet had entered the base of the back of his neck slightly to the right of the spine. It traveled downward and exited from the front of the neck, causing a nick in the left lower portion of the knot in the President's necktie. Before the shooting started, Governor Connally had been facing toward the crowd on the right. He started to turn toward the left and suddenly felt a blow on his back. The Governor had been hit by a bullet which entered at the extreme right side of his back at a point below his right armpit. The bullet traveled through his chest in a downward and forward direction, exited below his right nipple, passed through his right wrist which had been in his lap, and then caused a wound to his left thigh. The force of the bullet's impact appeared to spin the Governor to his right, and Mrs. Connally pulled him down into her lap. Another bullet then struck President Kennedy in the rear portion of his head, causing a massive and fatal wound. The President fell to the left into Mrs. Kennedy's lap.

It is not an exaggeration to say that no finding or conclusion of any government study or investigation has been as controversial or subject to as much criticism as the Warren Commission's conclusion that a single bullet passed through President Kennedy's body and then caused all of Governor Connally's injuries. In a book chapter entitled "Birth of the 'Single-Bullet' Fabrication," historian Gerald D. McKnight notes that, "If there is a Rosetta stone for the Kennedy assassination that exposed the deception of the government's investigation into the crime, it is what in time came to be referred to as the 'single bullet' theory." McKnight then asserts that the single bullet theory "was an ad hoc invention or fabrication to meet the Commission's requirements for a lone-assassin, no-conspiracy explanation of the Kennedy assassination."[21]

No one is more entitled to respond to this harsh assessment of the single bullet theory than the theory's originator, Senator Arlen Specter. In 1964 Specter was an assistant counsel to the Warren Commission and was the staff member who developed the single bullet theory or, as Specter prefers to call it, the "single bullet conclusion":

> I had developed the Single-Bullet Theory more than thirty years earlier as a staff lawyer on the President's Commission on the Assassination of President John F. Kennedy, more commonly known as the Warren Commission. I now call it the Single-Bullet Conclusion. It began as a theory, but when a theory is established by the facts, it deserves to be called a conclusion. The conclusion

---

21. McKnight, *supra*, at 181.

is that the same bullet sliced through President John F. Kennedy's neck and then tore through Texas Governor John Connally's chest and wrist, finally lodging in the governor's thigh, as the presidential motorcade wound through downtown Dallas on November 22, 1963. The Warren Commission adopted the Single-Bullet Conclusion as its official explanation.[22]

Specter's spirited defense of the single bullet theory has a substantial personal dimension, because when he says "I had developed the Single Bullet Theory" he is not exaggerating or self-aggrandizing—he was the staff attorney who formulated the single bullet theory. This aspect of the Warren Commission investigation, that a single staff member was responsible for what proved to be the most important investigative conclusion within the commission's mandate, reflects the importance of establishing an adequate staff support structure at the outset of a commission's work. The issue of providing adequate staffing for independent investigative commissions is discussed in the Notes at the conclusion of this Chapter.

Like the Roberts Commission investigation of Pearl Harbor, the Warren Commission investigation of the Kennedy assassination is not regarded, at least if public perception and widespread acceptance of its conclusions are the applicable metrics, as a completely successful independent commission investigation. Although the single-bullet theory has never been disproved, and no credible evidence has ever been revealed to undermine the core conclusion of the Warren Commission that Oswald acted alone, enormous public doubt and skepticism about the Commission's conclusions remain. The negative historical assessments of both the Roberts Commission and the Warren Commission were well-known to the members of the 9/11 Commission when it undertook its investigation, which is the subject of the next section of this Chapter.

Notes and Questions

1. **Judicial Leadership.** Both the Roberts Commission and the Warren Commission were chaired by sitting members of the United States Supreme Court, and in the case of the Warren Commission by the Chief Justice of the United States. The leadership of these commissions by members of the highest court in the land undoubtedly was intended to increase public confidence in the commissions' work, and likely did so. The question remains, however, whether service on such a commission by a sitting federal judge is advisable, or even appropriate. Warren, for example, did not wish to serve in that capacity and only agreed to do so after being "persuaded" by President Johnson to serve, and there is little doubt that Warren's responsibilities as Chief Justice detracted from his ability to devote his full time and attention to the Warren Commission. Should judges take on these assignments? For an analysis of the legal and ethical issues, see Robert B. McKay, *The Judiciary and Nonjudicial Activities*, 35 L. CONTEMP. PROBS. 9 (1970); Solomon Slonim, *Extrajudicial Activities and the Principle of the Separation*

---

22. *See* SPECTER, *supra*, at 1–2.

of Powers, 49 CONN. B. J. 391 (1975). For a summary of extrajudicial assignments undertaken by Supreme Court Justices and federal lower court judges, see Andrew D. Herman, *The WTO Dispute Settlement Review Commission: An Unwise Extension of Extrajudicial Roles*, 47 HASTINGS L.J. 1635, 1643–1647 (1996). Herman's article also provides additional perspective on Chief Justice Warren's service as chairman of the Warren Commission:

> Justice Jackson's year-and-a-half absence from the Court when he was the principal prosecutor at Nuremberg was an embarrassment to the Court. Chief Justice Warren's solution in connection with the investigation of the Kennedy assassination was scarcely better when he sought to perform two crucial tasks concurrently. That Warren succeeded as well as he did is a testimonial to his capacity, not to the merit of the idea. [Citing McKay, *supra*, at 25.]

In explaining why he originally declined to serve, Chief Justice Warren stated:

> I told [Deputy Attorney General] Katzenbach and [Solicitor General] Cox that I had more than once expressed myself to that effect for several reasons. First, it is not in the spirit of constitutional separation of powers to have a member of the Supreme Court serve on a presidential commission; second, it would distract a Justice from the work of the Court, which had a heavy docket; and, third, it was impossible to foresee what litigation such a commission might spawn, with resulting disqualification of the Justice from sitting in such cases. I then told them that, historically, the acceptance of diplomatic posts by Chief Justices Jay and Ellsworth had not contributed to the welfare of the Court, that the service of five Justices on the Hayes-Tilden Commission had demeaned it, that the appointment of Justice Roberts as chairman to investigate the Pearl Harbor disaster had served no good purpose, and that the action of Justice Robert Jackson in leaving the Court for a year to become chief prosecutor at Nuremberg after World War II had resulted in divisiveness and internal bitterness on the Court.

Earl Warren, *The Memoirs of Earl Warren* 356 (1977).

Herman, *supra* at note 69.

2. Investigative Support. As noted above, one of the most controversial aspects of the Warren Commission's investigation was its reliance on the FBI as its investigative arm, rather than assembling its own staff of independent investigators. Warren Commission critics have asserted that the FBI was more concerned with protecting its own reputation and that of its director, J. Edgar Hoover, than it was committed to supporting the commission's investigation. For a critical account of the Bureau's alleged failings, see "FBI Blunders and Cover-Ups," Chapter 10 of Gerald McKnight's *Breach of Trust: How the Warren Commission Failed the Nation and Why* 247–81 (2005). Perhaps the most serious question surrounding the FBI's conduct concerns the Bureau's failure to provide the Secret Service with Lee Harvey Oswald's name prior to President Kennedy's visit to Dallas, when Oswald was already under FBI surveillance, and whether the FBI subsequently "covered up" information about Oswald's prior contacts with the FBI Dallas office that might have reflected poorly on the Bureau.

In fairness to the work of the Warren Commission, however, it should be noted that the FBI did not escape unscathed in the commission's report. After laying out the details of the FBI's role in the complex chain of events that preceded the Kennedy assassination, the report concluded:

> As reflected in this testimony, the officials of the FBI believed that there was no data in its files which gave warning that Oswald was a source of danger to President Kennedy. While he had expressed hostility at times toward the State Department, the Marine Corps, and the FBI as agents of the Government, so far as the FBI knew he had not shown any potential for violence. Prior to November 22, 1963, no law enforcement agency had any information to connect Oswald with the attempted shooting of General Walker. It was against this background and consistent with the criteria followed by the FBI prior to November 22 that agents of the FBI in Dallas did not consider Oswald's presence in the Texas School Book Depository Building overlooking the motorcade route as a source of danger to the President and did not inform the Secret Service of his employment in the Depository Building.

> The Commission believes, however, that the FBI took an unduly restrictive view of its responsibilities in preventive intelligence work, prior to the assassination. The Commission appreciates the large volume of cases handled by the FBI (636,371 investigative matters during fiscal year 1963). There were no Secret Service criteria which specifically required the referral of Oswald's case to the Secret Service; nor was there any requirement to report the names of defectors. However, there was much material in the hands of the FBI about Oswald: the knowledge of his defection, his arrogance and hostility to the United States, his pro-Castro tendencies, his lies when interrogated by the FBI, his trip to Mexico where he was in contact with Soviet authorities, his presence in the School Book Depository job and its location along the route of the motorcade. All this does seem to amount to enough to have induced an alert agency, such as the FBI, possessed of this information to list Oswald as a potential threat to the safety of the President. This conclusion may be tinged with hindsight, but is stated primarily to direct the thought of those responsible for the future safety of our President to the need for a more imaginative and less narrow interpretation of their responsibilities.

> It is the conclusion of the Commission that, even in the absence of Secret Service criteria which specifically required the referral of such a case as Oswald's to the Secret Service, a more alert and carefully considered treatment of the Oswald case by the Bureau might have brought about such a referral.

The President's Commission on the Assassination of President Kennedy: Report 443 (U.S. Government Printing Office 1964).

Notwithstanding this willingness of the Warren Commission to criticize the agency that it relied upon for investigative support, it is fair to ask whether the Commission received full cooperation from the FBI in areas where the Bureau's conduct was at issue. As is discussed in more detail in the section below, the 9/11 Commission took a different approach, assembling its own investigative staff rather than relying on the FBI or other government investigative agencies. What are the costs and benefits of each approach? To what extent does the public perception—and perhaps the practical reality—of unbiased investigative neutrality that accompanies an independent investigative staff outweigh the considerable cost, in terms of resources and time, necessary to assemble a staff and bring them up to speed to cover investigative ground that other government agencies may have already plowed? Should an independent investigative commission always have its own investigative staff, or are there situations when it may make more sense to rely on other agencies of government for investigative support? Is it ever acceptable to allow an agency whose conduct is within the investigative mandate of an independent commission, as was the case with the FBI in both the Kennedy assassination investigation and the 9/11 investigation, to take the lead investigative role supporting the commission's work?

3. Transparency and Public Access. The Warren Commission had a mixed record in terms of transparency and public access. Almost all of the meetings of the Warren Commission were closed "executive" sessions (the exception being the testimony of attorney Mark Lane, who requested an open session), which have since been made public but were not open to the public and press at the time they took place. On the other hand, the Warren Commission published extensive appendices to its report containing the transcripts of the testimony of the 552 witnesses who appeared before the Commission and its staff (*Warren Commission Report*, Appendix V, "List of Witnesses" at 483). Ironically, the practical effect of the process followed by the Warren Commission seems to have been the "worst of both worlds" in terms of fostering public acceptance of their findings. Conspiracy theorists used the closed sessions of Warren Commission to suggest nefarious cover-ups and improper activity, while at the same time poring over the voluminous information in the appendices to find any conceivable inconsistency or flaw in the Commission's investigative process. The net result was that the Warren Commission unwittingly was its own worst enemy in terms of building public support for its findings and conclusions.

The chair and vice chair of the 9/11 Commission have acknowledged that when they set out to investigate the 9/11 terrorist attacks they hoped to avoid the doubts and conspiracy theories that have plagued the Warren Commission since its report was released:

> History also gave us a powerful incentive to be open about what level of access—to people and government documents—we were being given. This was a lesson we could take from the Warren Commission, which had looked at the John F. Kennedy assassination. For decades, the Warren Commission's findings have been poked and prodded by conspiracy theorists, in large measure because the commission is not perceived as having had full access to the

most secretive materials in the government. Lee Harvey Oswald may have acted alone, but over the years people could point in different directions and say to the commission, "You didn't look at this document about U.S. policy toward Cuba; you didn't talk to so-and-so; you didn't turn over this stone." To avoid such accusations, we had to be able to stand up in front of the American people and say, "We have asked for everything that has to do with the 9/11 story, and have seen everything we asked for."

THOMAS H. KEAN & LEE H. HAMILTON, WITHOUT PRECEDENT: THE INSIDE STORY OF THE 9/11 COMMISSION 25 (Alfred A. Knopf 2006). Unlike the Warren Commission, the 9/11 Commission held its hearings and took testimony from witnesses in open public sessions whenever possible. Although this increased public awareness of the Commission's work, it also left the Commission open to charges that it (or particular members of the Commission) were "grandstanding" and playing too much to the press. How should a high-profile investigative commission balance these competing risks? If too much of a commission's work is done in private, will it create public doubts and leave the commission's work too vulnerable to cover-up charges? If a commission holds extensive public sessions, will it backfire and lead to a loss of public respect and acceptance of the commission's work? Keep these questions in mind as you consider the materials below on the 9/11 Commission.

The 9/11 Commission

As noted in the introduction to this Chapter, there is no doubt that the terrorist attacks of September 11, 2001, were the most traumatic incident in our recent national history. It is not surprising that the 9/11 attacks were the subject of a blue-ribbon commission investigation. What is more surprising about the 9/11 Commission investigation is the timing and the order of events. Typically a special investigative commission is put in place quickly, to respond to public concerns and demonstrate a serious government commitment to a perceived national crisis. And in most instances, as with the Roberts Commission and the Warren Commission, national investigative commissions are created at the direction of the President (albeit reluctantly in the case of President Johnson and the Warren Commission), rather than Congress, which is often hesitant to cede primary investigative authority to a commission.

The 9/11 Commission turned these typical expectations upside-down. The George W. Bush administration had vigorously resisted calls for an independent commission investigation after the 9/11 attacks, and the initial investigation of the 9/11 attack was conducted as a congressional investigation—a special joint investigation by the House and Senate intelligence committees. This congressional "Joint Inquiry" was not a complete and comprehensive investigation of the 9/11 attacks, however. The focus of the Joint Inquiry was on whether intelligence failures had allowed the attacks to succeed and whether Congress needed to change federal laws in response. In addition, because the Joint Inquiry was a congressional investigation conducted in the Legislative Branch of government, the Bush administration relied upon constitutional separation of powers arguments to limit the Joint Inquiry's access to executive branch information. The Bush White House also refused to permit key administration officials to testify in the Joint Inquiry investigation. For these and other reasons, the ten-month congressional Joint Inquiry investigation failed to satisfy the families of 9/11 victims and the many others who were calling for a full and complete investigation of the attacks, particularly after the Bush administration blocked the release of some twenty-seven pages of the Joint Inquiry's final report "that related to the Saudi government and the assistance that government gave to some and possibly all of the September 11 terrorists."[23]

The result of this lack of satisfaction with the Joint Inquiry investigation was a remarkable example of how continued pressure from concerned citizens can ultimately force governmental action even in the face of resistance at the highest levels. The former chair and vice-chair of the 9/11 Commission have described how this occurred:

> All of these factors pointed toward the need for an independent, bipartisan commission with complete access to government documents and officials. Senator Lieberman introduced legislation on this in the spring of 2002, while the Joint Inquiry was still at work, and there was extended debate through the summer about the need for an independent commission. The chief obstacle was the White House, which argued that the congressional inquiry was continuing, and that an independent investigation would distract the government from waging the ongoing war on terrorism. At several points, it appeared that the proposal to create a 9/11 Commission was dead.
>
> This is when the 9/11 families made their voices heard....
>
> Over the summer of 2002, 9/11 families met with members of Congress and White House officials. Senators Lieberman and McCain, and Congressmen Roemer, Shays, and Chris Smith (R-N.J.) worked hard on Capitol Hill. Meanwhile the American people showed a powerful interest in the information about the 9/11 attacks coming out in the Joint Inquiry and in press reports. In September, the White House ended its opposition and announced that it would back the creation of a commission—with Press Secretary Ari Fleischer directly crediting the 9/11 families by saying, "the administration has

---

23. SENATOR BOB GRAHAM WITH JEFF NUSSBAUM, INTELLIGENCE MATTERS: THE CIA, THE FBI, SAUDI ARABIA, AND THE FAILURE OF AMERICA'S WAR ON TERROR 215 (Random House 2004). The lack of satisfaction with the Joint Inquiry investigation stemmed at least in part from the fact that, despite the many restrictions placed upon it, the Joint Inquiry discovered and made public a number of important facts and policy issues regarding the 9/11 attacks. *See generally id.* at 159–77 (describing "Discoveries in San Diego" by Joint Inquiry investigators, including the fact that two of the 9/11 hijackers had been living in San Diego with an FBI informant prior to the attacks, and recounting the impact of the Joint Inquiry public staff statement revealing areas in which the Bush administration had refused to allow the Joint Inquiry to make public certain of its investigative findings).

met with some of the families of the 9/11 groups, who have talked about the need for a commission to look into a host of issues, and they have made compelling arguments."...

The day before Thanksgiving—November 27, 2002—before an audience that included many of the 9/11 families, President Bush signed the bill creating the 9/11 Commission.[24]

As this summary demonstrates, the 9/11 Commission definitely was a child of the legislative branch, not a presidential commission offspring of the executive branch like the Roberts Commission and the Warren Commission. In important respects, however, the 9/11 Commission was more akin to an orphan, left without parental support from either of the political branches of government. As a preliminary matter, the 9/11 Commission was not funded adequately:

The bill was not what [then-Senate Democratic Leader Tom] Daschle, Mc-Cain, and the families had wanted. It provided the commission with an insultingly small budget—$3 million over eighteen months, compared with more than $40 million for the federal commission that investigated the *Challenger* [space shuttle] disaster. "The budget was a joke," Daschle said.[25]

Beyond the issue of funding, the legislation gave the 9/11 Commission an extraordinarily broad investigative mandate and an exceedingly tight timetable within which to fulfill that mandate. The legislation creating the 9/11 Commission contained this investigative mandate:

Sec. 602. Purposes.

The purposes of the Commission are to—

(1) examine and report upon the facts and causes relating to the terrorist attacks of September 11, 2001, occurring at the World Trade Center in New York, New York, in Somerset County, Pennsylvania, and at the Pentagon in Virginia;

(2) ascertain, evaluate, and report on the evidence developed by all relevant governmental agencies regarding the facts and circumstances surrounding the attacks;

(3) build upon the investigations of other entities, and avoid unnecessary duplication, by reviewing the findings, conclusions, and recommendations of—

---

24. THOMAS H. KEAN & LEE H. HAMILTON, WITHOUT PRECEDENT: THE INSIDE STORY OF THE 9/11 COMMISSION 19–21 (Alfred A. Knopf 2006). *See also* Public Law 107-306, Nov. 27, 2002, Title VI—National Commission on Terrorist Attacks Upon the United States.

25. PHILIP SHENON, THE COMMISSION: THE UNCENSORED HISTORY OF THE 9/11 INVESTIGATION 31 (Hachette Book Group USA 2008).

(A) the Joint Inquiry of the Select Committee on Intelligence of the Senate and the Permanent Select Committee on Intelligence of the House of Representatives regarding the terrorist attacks of September 11, 2001, (hereinafter in this title referred to as the "Joint Inquiry"); and

(B) other executive branch, congressional, or independent commission investigations into the terrorist attacks of September 11, 2001, other terrorist attacks, and terrorism generally;

(4) make a full and complete accounting of the circumstances surrounding the attacks, and the extent of the United States' preparedness for, and immediate response to, the attacks; and

(5) investigate and report to the President and Congress on its findings, conclusions, and recommendations for corrective measures that can be taken to prevent acts of terrorism.

Despite this extraordinarily broad investigative charge, the legislation gave the Commission only eighteen months to complete its task:

Section 610. Reports of Commission; Termination.

(a) INTERIM REPORTS.—The Commission may submit to the President and Congress interim reports containing such findings, conclusions, and recommendations for corrective measures as have been agreed to by a majority of Commission members.

(b) FINAL REPORT.—Not later than 18 months after the date of the enactment of this Act, the Commission shall submit to the President and Congress a final report containing such findings, conclusions, and recommendations for corrective measures as have been agreed to by a majority of Commission members.

(c) TERMINATION.—

(1) IN GENERAL.—The Commission, and all the authorities of this title, shall terminate 60 days after the date on which the final report is submitted under subsection (b).

(2) ADMINISTRATIVE ACTIVITIES BEFORE TERMINATION.—The Commission may use the 60-day period referred to in paragraph (1) for the purpose of concluding its activities, including providing testimony to committees of Congress concerning its reports and disseminating the final report.

These challenges were exacerbated by the fact that the legislation placed the commission in the legislative branch of government ("Sec. 601. Establishment of Commission. There is established in the legislative branch the National Commission on Terrorist Attacks Upon the United States ..."), while its investigative subject was primarily the executive branch, creating in effect a built-in separation of powers issue for the commission's work.

All of these factors, as well as the politically divided make-up of the commission prescribed by the statute, weighed heavily on the minds of the chair and vice chair of the 9/11 Commission as they began their work in the winter of 2002–03:

> We were set up to fail. The thought occurred to both of us as we prepared to meet for the first time on a cold day just before the Christmas season of 2002. The full 9/11 Commission would not meet for another month; this meeting would be just the two of us.
>
> A thicket of political controversy lay ahead. The legislation creating the commission had been signed into law by President George W. Bush, after extended wrangling between Congress and the White House through the heated and often bitter midterm elections of 2002. We were scheduled to issue our final report in May 2004, just as the presidential election would be approaching full boil.
>
> We had an exceedingly broad mandate. The legislation creating the commission instructed us to examine
>
> > (i) intelligence agencies; (ii) law enforcement agencies; (iii) diplomacy; (iv) immigration, nonimmigrant visas, and border control; (v) the flow of assets to terrorist organizations; (vi) commercial aviation; (vii) the role of congressional oversight and resources allocation; and (viii) other areas of the public and private sectors determined relevant by the Commission for its inquiry.
>
> In other words, our inquiry would stretch across the entire U.S. government, and even into the private sector, in an attempt to understand an event that was unprecedented in the destruction it had wrought on the American homeland, and appalling even within the catalogue of human brutality.

* * *

> Both of us were aware of grumbling around Washington that the 9/11 Commission was doomed—if not designed—to fail: the commission would splinter down partisan lines; lose its credibility by leaking classified information; be denied the necessary access to do its job; or alienate the 9/11 families who had fought on behalf of its creation. Indeed, the scenarios for failure far outnumbered the chances of success. What we could not have anticipated were the remarkable people and circumstances that would coalesce within and around the 9/11 Commission over the coming twenty months to enable our success.
>
> But on December 18, 2002, we were starting without any blueprint for how to go forward. The clock had started ticking almost a month earlier, when President Bush signed the bill creating a 9/11 Commission. So we were, in fact, already running behind.

KEAN & HAMILTON, *supra*, at 14–16.

Beyond funding, the broad investigative mandate, and the deadline for completion of the investigation, Kean and Hamilton also realized that "[t]he issue of subpoena power was hugely important."[26] The subpoena powers granted to the 9/11 Commission and the manner in which it used those powers is one of the most important legal issues presented by the 9/11 Commission investigation. The Commission's subpoena powers were set out in section 605(a) of its enabling legislation:

Sec. 605. Powers of Commission.

(a) In General.—

(1) Hearings and evidence.—The Commission or, on the authority of the Commission, any subcommittee or member thereof, may, for the purpose of carrying out this title—

(A) hold such hearings and sit and act at such times and places, take such testimony, receive such evidence, administer such oaths; and

(B) subject to paragraph (2)(A), require, by subpoena or otherwise, the attendance and testimony of such witnesses and the production of such books, records, correspondence, memoranda, papers, and documents, as the Commission or such designated subcommittee or designated member may determine advisable.

(2) Subpoenas.—

(A) Issuance.—

(i) In general.—A subpoena may be issued under this subsection only—

(I) by the agreement of the chairman and the vice chairman; or

(II) by the affirmative vote of 6 members of the Commission.

(ii) Signature.—Subject to clause (i), subpoenas issued under this subsection may be issued under the signature of the chairman or any member designated by a majority of the Commission, and may be served by any person designated by the chairman or by a member designated by a majority of the Commission.

(B) Enforcement.—

(i) In general.—In the case of contumacy or failure to obey a subpoena issued under subsection (a), the United States district court for the judicial district in which the subpoenaed person resides, is served, or may be found, or where the subpoena is returnable, may issue an order requiring such person to appear at any designated place to testify or to produce documentary or other evidence. Any failure to obey the order of the court may be punished by the court as a contempt of that court.

---

26. *Id.* at 19.

(ii) ADDITIONAL ENFORCEMENT.— In the case of any failure of any witness to comply with any subpoena or to testify when summoned under authority of this section, the Commission may, by majority vote, certify a statement of fact constituting such failure to the appropriate United States attorney, who may bring the matter before the grand jury for its action, under the same statutory authority and procedures as if the United States attorney had received a certification under sections 102 through 104 of the Revised Statutes of the United States (2 U.S.C. §192 through 194). [*Ed. Note: These statutes make failure to comply with a subpoena a misdemeanor offense punishable by up to one year in prison and a fine of up to $1,000.00.*]

Note the limitations on issuance of subpoenas in the statute above. The statute requires an affirmative vote of six of the ten commissioners, or approval by both the chair and vice chair, to issue a subpoena. With a commission comprised of five Democrats and five Republicans, headed by a Republican chairman and a Democratic vice chairman, this meant that any subpoena issued would require bipartisan support. One commentator has observed that the procedures for issuing subpoenas in the 9/11 Commission legislation had the effect of requiring bipartisan agreement or compromise before the Commission could act:

> These rules were intended to have an important braking effect: the Commission could not force an executive branch agency or current or former executive branch officer to provide information without the agreement of all the commissioners nominated by one of the political parties. The power-sharing scheme would either force bipartisan agreement and compromise or render the commission completely unable to act.[27]

While requiring bipartisan support for commission action may seem desirable in the abstract, as a practical matter it posed a significant limitation on the commission's ability to issue subpoenas.

The political issues raised by the statute's subpoena approval process had a greater effect on the commission's work than merely requiring bipartisan support for the issuance of a particular subpoena. One of the most divisive issues that confronted the

---

27. Mark Fenster, *Designing Transparency: The 9/11 Commission and Institutional Form*, 65 WASH. & LEE L. REV. 1239, 1277 (2008). Philip Shenon, a reporter for the *New York Times* who covered the Commission throughout its life and then wrote a book about it, has described the political stakes that were implicated by the Commission's subpoena powers:

There was a real political fear of an independent commission. Rove began rewriting the strategy for Bush's 2004 reelection campaign literally the day after 9/11. He knew that Bush's reelection effort centered on his performance on terrorism; almost nothing else would matter to voters. If the commission did anything to undermine Bush's antiterrorism credentials—worst of all, if it claimed that Bush had somehow bungled intelligence in 2001 that might have prevented the attacks—his reelection might well be sunk.

PHILIP SHENON, THE COMMISSION: THE UNCENSORED HISTORY OF THE 9/11 INVESTIGATION 25 (Hachette Book Group USA 2008).

Commission at the outset of its investigation was how aggressively it should use its subpoena powers. Kean and Hamilton, perhaps wary of the potential political divisions that might be exacerbated by frequent votes on whether or not to issue subpoenas, chose not to use the commission's subpoena power as a regular matter of course for the commission's requests for documents and testimony. In making this decision they rejected the views of two experienced investigators on the Commission, former Watergate prosecutor Richard Ben-Veniste and former Clinton administration Deputy Attorney General Jamie Gorelick.[28] This strategy of not utilizing the subpoena power that the Commission had been given by Congress arguably created problems for the commission later, when it became apparent that some government agencies had failed to comply with less formal letter requests for documents and had to be served with subpoenas.[29] The issue of commission use of subpoena powers is discussed further in the Notes below.

In addition to the issues surrounding the process for issuing subpoenas, the powers granted to the 9/11 Commission for enforcing subpoenas were subject to important limitations that are not readily apparent from a review of the statutory language. On its face, the statute that is set out above appears to include strong subpoena enforcement powers, providing for both civil contempt remedies for failure to comply with a commission subpoena and "additional" criminal enforcement powers sanctions if a majority of the commissioners votes in favor of a criminal referral. These powers are less efficacious than they might appear, however. First, and most important, the civil contempt process requires lengthy court proceedings, and likely an even longer appellate review process, to obtain an enforceable final order. Kean and Hamilton have described their thinking on the subpoena enforcement timing problem:

> If we had issued subpoenas, litigation could have ensued as the subpoenas were contested in the courts. After all, subpoenas are not self-enforcing. A court has to decide to issue an order to enforce one. In our case, federal agencies could have taken us to court and litigated the matter. Since we had a limited amount of time and staff, the last thing we needed was to get bogged down in a court case about whether or not we were entitled to certain documents—better to have those discussions in a cooperative negotiation.

KEAN & HAMILTON, *supra*, at 64.

Although the criminal contempt option provided under the statute might appear to provide a less time-consuming means of addressing a refusal to comply with a commis-

---

28. *See* KEAN & HAMILTON, *supra*, at 64 ("Jamie Gorelick argued that subpoenas should accompany every document request, and Richard Ben-Veniste concurred that it would not be unusual to issue blanket subpoenas in an investigation such as ours."). Kean and Hamilton reportedly rejected one candidate to serve as the Commission's general counsel, experienced federal prosecutor Carol Elder Bruce, because in an interview she told them that "the commission would be making a terrible mistake if it did not quickly issue subpoenas to the Bush administration" and that the use of subpoenas was a "no-brainer" for a veteran criminal investigator." *See* SHENON, *supra*, at 93–94.

29. *See* SHENON, *supra*, at 200–204 (describing the Commission's problems obtaining requested information from the FAA and NORAD).

sion subpoena, it likely would be ineffective in the most important cases of subpoena resistance—those involving subpoenas to obtain witness testimony or documents from the executive branch. The reason this is true is that the criminal enforcement process in the statute is not self-executing by the commission; it requires the cooperation and assistance of a federal prosecutor to bring the matter before a grand jury and initiate a criminal prosecution.[30] While the language of the relevant statute appears to *require* a U.S. Attorney to bring a criminal prosecution in such cases,[31] historical experience and applicable Department of Justice policies suggest that a U.S. Attorney will not do so in cases where the President directs executive branch subordinates not to comply.[32] (The problem of enforcing legislative branch subpoenas against executive branch officials is analyzed in greater detail in Chapter 4, on Separation of Powers and Disputes Between the Branches of Government.) For these reasons, the subpoena enforcement powers contained in the 9/11 Commission legislation in application would not have proved effective as means of compelling timely compliance with commission subpoenas.

One additional matter concerning the 9/11 Commission's investigative practices is worthy of special attention. The 9/11 Commission, like the Roberts Commission investigation of Pearl Harbor and the Warren Commission investigation of the Kennedy assassination, was at bottom an investigation of the conduct and performance of our national government. All three investigations involved extraordinarily calamitous events that perhaps could or even should have been prevented by the government agencies responsible for protecting against such events. In an investigation of government, most of the important information and many of the key witnesses will come from inside government. It is likely that present and former government officials, at all levels of authority and responsibility, will provide some of the most important investigative testimony, both as to what occurred and as to how well government performed—or how it failed to perform as it should have. It is also likely that the agencies that are the subject of investigation will have strong institutional interests in defending their performance and resisting any suggestions that they failed to perform adequately. The net result is strong institutional pressure by the government agencies involved to defend their performance, which creates an inherent conflict of interest when representatives of those agencies participate in the investigative process. Recognition of this

---

30. *See* 2 U.S.C §194 (the statute that is referenced in the 9/11 legislation as providing the procedure for criminal enforcement proceedings). Chapter 4 discusses the problems surrounding criminal enforcement of legislative branch subpoenas.

31. *See id.* (providing that the contempt certification is presented "to the appropriate United States attorney, *whose duty it shall be* to bring the matter before the grand jury for its action") (emphasis added).

32. *See* Prosecution for the Contempt of Congress of an Executive Branch Official Who Has Asserted a Claim of Executive Privilege, 8 U.S. Op. Off. Legal Counsel 101 (1984); Response to Congressional Requests for Information Regarding Decisions Made Under the Independent Counsel Act, 10 U.S. Op. Off. Legal Counsel 68 (1986). For additional information on congressional subpoena enforcement procedures, see Morton Rosenberg & Todd B. Tatelman, *Congress's Contempt Power: A Sketch*, Congressional Research Service Report for Congress, Aug. 1, 2007; Louis Fisher, *Congressional Investigations: Subpoenas and Contempt Power*, Congressional Research Service Report for Congress, April 2, 2003.

institutional pressure and inherent conflict of interest has important implications for an investigative commission's organization and procedures.

The most obvious "lesson learned" in this area can be taken from the Warren Commission's reliance on the FBI as its investigative organ—do not rely for investigative support on a government agency the conduct of which is within the scope of the commission's investigation. As discussed in the preceding section, the Warren Commission's reliance on the FBI left it vulnerable to criticisms that its investigation was compromised because in some investigative areas the FBI might have been more concerned with protecting its own interests than with supporting the commission's investigation. The 9/11 Commission sought to avoid this problem by assembling a staff of independent investigators and not relying on the FBI for investigative support.[33]

The potential problems in this area extend beyond investigative support and staff resources, however. The 9/11 Commission investigation highlights another manner in which agencies that are within a commission's investigative purview can influence the commission's investigative process. A major issue in the 9/11 Commission investigation was the presence of agency "minders" or observers at the commission's interviews of present and former government officials. The Bush White House initially took the position that an agency representative must be allowed to observe the interviews of all government witnesses, including both present and former employees. The 9/11 commissioners objected: "We wanted our witnesses to be candid and, when appropriate, critical about their agency's performance. A minder might cause somebody to think twice before speaking candidly."[34] Despite the obvious merits of this position, the 9/11 Commission compromised and permitted agency minders to attend the interviews of all current government employees, but not former employees. The wisdom of this compromise is open to question, as it is current employees who are most likely to fear reprisal if they provide information that might displease their superiors and adversely affect their employment and careers. This issue is discussed further in the Notes at the conclusion of this Chapter.

---

33. Even this precaution was not sufficient to entirely insulate the 9/11 Commission from criticism for its assessment of the FBI's role and performance. The 9/11 Commission has been criticized for succumbing to then-FBI Director Robert Mueller's aggressive lobbying of the Commission members not to recommend breaking up or dramatically reorganizing the FBI:

> Mueller's lobbying campaign with the 9/11 Commissioners could not have been more aggressive. He was in their faces, literally. The commissioners said later that it was a remarkable thing to have the director of the FBI announce that he was ready to open his schedule to them at a moment's notice. He would return phone calls within minutes. He would meet the commissioners whenever and wherever they wished—breakfast, lunch, dinner, at the FBI's expense, of course. If a commissioner wanted to meet with Mueller in Washington, he would volunteer to drive across town to do it....

SHENON, *supra*, at 365. The criticism on this point reflects the observation that Mueller's lobbying campaign appears to have been successful—the 9/11 Commission recommended that the FBI retain its role as the nation's lead domestic counterterrorism agency. *See id.* at 402–04.

34. *See* KEAN & HAMILTON, *supra*, at 104.

The 9/11 Commission ultimately obtained additional funding from Congress and a two-month extension to complete its report.[35] The Commission issued its unanimous final report in July 2004. The report was the subject of a great deal of public attention and interest. While most of that interest can be attributed to the importance of the report's subject matter, both the extremely public manner in which the Commission had conducted its work and the upcoming 2004 presidential election no doubt added to the public's interest in the report.[36] The novel way that the Commission chose to write and release its report also distinguished it from past Commissions.

The 9/11 Commission made a conscious decision to make its report as accessible and "user-friendly" as possible, in order to encourage ordinary citizens to read it and support the recommendations it contained. Rather than follow the practice of past commissions and rely on the Government Printing Office for distribution, the Commission arranged for a mass-market publishing company, W.W. Norton, to publish the report and make it immediately available in bookstores throughout the country at a price of $10 a copy. In addition to this innovative distribution strategy, the Commission chose to avoid the jargon-laden "bureaucrat-speak" that is more typical of government reports, and instead strive for crisp, clear prose that would appeal to readers outside of government. That strategy, and the clear, extremely readable prose style of the entire report, is apparent in the first two paragraphs of the report:

> Tuesday, September 11, 2001, dawned temperate and nearly cloudless in the eastern United States. Millions of men and women readied themselves for work. Some made their way to the Twin Towers, the signature structures of the World Trade Center complex in New York City. Others went to Arlington, Virginia, to the Pentagon. Across the Potomac River, the United States Congress was back in session. At the other end of Pennsylvania Avenue, people began to line up for a White House tour. In Sarasota, Florida, President George W. Bush went for an early morning run.

> For those heading to an airport, weather conditions could not have been better for a safe and pleasant journey. Among the travelers were Mohamed Atta and Abdul Aziz al Omari, who arrived at the airport in Portland Maine.[37]

This prose style was well-received by readers of the report from all walks of life and probably contributed significantly to the report becoming a national bestseller in bookstores around the country. The report's popularity and critical acclaim was reflected in

---

35. For a description of the extraordinary efforts that were required to obtain the extension for the 9/11 Commission, see KEAN & HAMILTON. *supra*, at143–149.

36. Commission chairs Kean and Hamilton later recognized the combination of factors that precipitated public interest in the report: "The Commission had generated its own perfect storm: by issuing a bipartisan report on the most urgent national security matter of the day in the midst of the most intense political season imaginable, we had put the onus on Congress and the president to come together across partisan lines, and to act." KEAN & HAMILTON, *supra*, at 308.

37. THE 9/11 COMMISSION REPORT: FINAL REPORT OF THE NATIONAL COMMISSION ON TERRORIST ATTACKS UPON THE UNITED STATES (W.W. Norton 2004) 1.

the report's selection as a finalist for the 2004 National Book Award for nonfiction—a noteworthy accomplishment for a government report.

Another point to note in assessing the effectiveness of the 9/11 Report is the calculated manner in which it uses footnotes to convey detailed information and preserve the clear, uncluttered prose style of the report itself. For example, the first footnote after the introductory paragraphs quoted above provides a great deal of additional information about the two hijackers who departed from Portland, Maine on the morning of September 11:

> 1. No physical, documentary, or analytical evidence provides a convincing explanation of why Atta and Omari drove to Portland, Maine, from Boston on the morning of September 10, only to return to Logan on Flight 5930 on the morning of September 11. However, Atta reacted negatively when informed in Portland that he would have to check in again in Boston. Michael Touhey interview (May 27, 2004). Whatever their reason, the Portland Jetport was the nearest airport to Boston with a 9/11 flight that would have arrived at Logan in time for the passengers to transfer to American Airlines Flight 11, which had a scheduled departure time of 7:45 a.m. See Tom Kinton interview (Nov. 6, 2003); Portland International Jetport site visit (Aug. 18, 2003).
>
> Like the other two airports used by the 9/11 hijackers (Newark Liberty International Airport and Washington Dulles International Airport), Boston's Logan International Airport was a "Category X" airport: i.e., among the largest facilities liable to highest threat, and generally subject to greater security requirements. See FAA report, "Civil Aviation Security Reference Handbook," May 1999, pp. 117–118. Though Logan was selected for two of the hijackings (as were both American and United Airlines), we found no evidence that the terrorists targeted particular airports or airlines. Nothing stands out about any of them with respect to the only security layer that was relevant to the actual hijackings: checkpoint screening. See FAA briefing materials, "Assessment and Testing Data for BOS, EWR, and IAD," Oct. 24, 2001. Despite security problems at Logan (see, e.g, two local Fox 25 television investigative reports in February and April 2001, and an email in August 2001 from a former FAA special agent to the agency's leadership regarding his concern about lax security at the airport), no evidence suggests that such issues entered into the terrorists' targeting: they simply booked heavily fueled east-to-west transcontinental flights of the large Boeing aircraft they trained to fly that were scheduled to take off at nearly the same time. See Matt Carroll, "Fighting Terror Sense of Alarm; Airlines Foiled Police Logan Probe," *Boston Globe*, Oct. 17, 2001, p. B1.

This combination of readable prose text and fact-intensive, detail-oriented footnotes proved successful and provides a model for future government reports that are intended for a broad national audience.

Although the Commission enjoyed tremendous success in terms of readership and public interest in its final report, the recommendations contained in the report did not fare quite as well. After the Commission's statutory life expired in August 2004, the members of the 9/11 Commission formed a nonprofit organization, the 9/11 Public Discourse Project, to continue to lobby Congress and the executive branch to adopt the recommendations in the final report. Among other activities, the Public Discourse Project issued a series of "report cards" detailing the extent to which the government had implemented the recommendations in the 9/11 Report. An in-depth analysis of the 9/11 Commission's recommendations and the government's response to those recommendations is beyond the scope of this Chapter, but the mixed record of success with respect to adoption of its recommendations—and the frustration of the 9/11 commissioners—is apparent in the excerpt below from the statement Kean and Hamilton released to accompany the final "report card" issued in December 2005:[38]

> We are safer—no terrorist attacks have occurred inside the United States since 9/11—but we are not as safe as we need to be.
>
> We see some positive changes. But there is so much more to be done. There are far too many C's, D's, and F's in the report card we will issue today. Many obvious steps that the American people assume have been completed, have not been. Our leadership is distracted.
>
> Some of these failures are shocking. Four years after 9/11:
>
> — It is scandalous that police and firefighters in large cities still cannot communicate reliably in a major crisis.
>
> — It is scandalous that airline passengers are still not screened against all names on the terrorist watchlist.
>
> — It is scandalous that we still allocate scarce homeland security dollars on the basis of pork barrel spending, not risk.
>
> We are frustrated by the lack of urgency about fixing these problems.
>
> Bin Ladin and al Qaeda believe it is their duty to kill as many Americans as possible. This very day they are plotting to do us harm.
>
> On 9/11 they killed nearly 3,000 of our fellow citizens. Many of the steps we recommend would help prevent such a disaster from happening again. We should not need another wake-up call.
>
> We believe that the terrorists will strike again. If they do, and these reforms have not been implemented, what will our excuses be?
>
> While the terrorists are learning and adapting, our government is still moving at a crawl.

---

38. 9/11 Public Discourse Project, Remarks by Chairman Thomas H. Kean and Vice Chair Lee H. Hamilton, Final Report of the 9/11 Public Discourse Project, December 5, 2005 (available at http://www.9-11pdp.org/press/2005-12-05_statement.pdf). A great deal of additional information about the 9/11 Commission's recommendations and the government's response can be found on the website of the public discourse project: www.9-11pdp.org.

Notes and Questions

1. **Congressional Investigations or Independent Commissions?** In two of the three of the commission investigations examined in this Chapter—the Pearl Harbor investigation and the Warren Commission investigation of the Kennedy assassination—initial investigations by presidential commissions proved inadequate to address public concerns and questions, and had to be supplemented by subsequent full-blown congressional investigations. Does this suggest that congressional investigations are a superior means of finding and publicizing the essential facts about events of great public importance? If so, should Congress hesitate to cede primary investigative authority for an event of great national importance to a presidential commission? Based upon what you have learned about congressional investigations and independent commissions from the materials in this book, what are the advantages and disadvantages of independent commission investigations compared to congressional investigations? Whatever your views on this question, it is likely that Congress will continue to create independent "blue ribbon" investigative commissions to address particularly large and complex matters. For example, in 2009 Congress created a special ten-member Financial Crisis Inquiry Commission to investigate the causes of the 2007–2008 economic crisis. *See* Fraud and Economic Recovery Act of 2009, Pub. L. No. 111-21 (May 20, 2009). For purposes of this book, it is noteworthy both that the Financial Crisis Inquiry Commission appears to have been largely modeled on the 9/11 Commission and that the legislative history suggests that many members of Congress hoped to create an independent commission that would perform in much the same manner as the Pecora congressional investigation that is discussed above in Chapter 1. For a contemporary account of the enormous continuing influence of the Pecora investigation, even more than seventy-five years later, see Kate Philips, *Financial Inquiries and the Pecora Legacy*, N.Y. TIMES (May 6, 2009).

2. **The Difficult Problem of Individual Accountability.** One of the most controversial aspects of the 9/11 Commission investigation was the refusal of the commission to impose individual accountability or find personal fault with the actions of responsible government officials and employees prior to the 9/11 attacks. Many close observers of the 9/11 Commission's work, particularly some members of the victims' families, had hoped that the 9/11 Commission would identify the individuals who bore some measure of personal responsibility for the government failures that allowed the attacks to succeed. *See* KEAN & HAMILTON *supra*, at 54 (quoting 9/11 family members advocate Steve Push as saying, "I think this Commission should point fingers. ... [T]here were people, people in responsible positions, who failed us on 9/11."). Similar issues arose during the Warren Commission investigation and thereafter with respect to the conduct of members of President Kennedy's Secret Service security detail (*see* HAROLD WEISBERG, WHITEWASH: THE REPORT ON THE WARREN REPORT 1 (1965) ("For the Secret Service escort, who dedicate themselves to the safety of the President, this day [November 22, 1963] began with nine of them engaged in a post-midnight diversion, including moderate drinking, in clear violation of regulations. Although discipline was

mandatory under the regulations, the Secret Service decided punishment would stigmatize these men for life. The men went unpunished, a decision with which the [Warren] Commission found no fault.")) and the FBI agents in Dallas who were monitoring the activities of Lee Harvey Oswald prior to the assassination (see GERALD McKNIGHT, BREACH OF TRUST: HOW THE WARREN COMMISSION FAILED THE NATION AND WHY 262–63 (University Press of Kansas 2005) (criticizing the failure of Dallas FBI officials to notify the Secret Service of Oswald's presence in Dallas)). The Roberts Commission, on the other hand, was ultimately criticized for placing too much personal blame on the military commanders in the field, as is discussed in more detail in the first section of this Chapter.

Although the 9/11 Commission followed the lead of co-chairs Kean and Hamilton in not seeking to assess personal responsibility in connection with the 9/11 attacks, one of the most dramatic moments of the Commission's entire investigation involved the issue of personal responsibility. Former Clinton and Bush White House national security official Richard Clarke galvanized the Commission's March 24, 2004 hearing when he accepted a measure of personal responsibility for the 9/11 attacks. Philip Shenon described the drama surrounding Clarke's testimony as follows:

> Clarke entered the hearing room and took his seat at the witness table. Tom Kean asked him to stand and be sworn in. As Clarke raised his right hand, scores of cameras began clicking, the flashes popping, as photographers maneuvered to find the one image that captured the best of all Washington dramas—the former White House insider turned whistle-blower. It was being compared by reporters to the sort of drama that John Dean's testimony provided in Watergate or Lieutenant Colonel Oliver North's testimony provided in the Iran-Contra affair.
>
> Clarke took his seat. Kean invited Clarke to give an opening statement, asking him to limit it to the preagreed ten minutes. The witness would not need nearly so much time.
>
> "Thank you, Mr. Chairman," Clarke began.
>
> "I have only a brief opening statement. I welcome these hearings because of the opportunity they provide to the American people to better understand why the tragedy of 9/11 happened and what we must do to prevent a reoccurrence. I also welcome the hearings because it is finally a forum where I can apologize to the loved ones of the victims of 9/11. For those of you who are here in the room, to those of you who are watching on television, your government failed you. And I failed you. We tried hard. But that doesn't matter. Because we failed. And for that failure, I would ask, once all the facts are out, for your understanding and your forgiveness. With that, Mr. Chairman, I'll be glad to take your questions."
>
> There was silence for a moment. Then it was replaced by gasps and then sobs from many of the family members in the audience. An apology? An ad-

mission of error? It was the first apology that the 9/11 Commission families had heard from anybody of importance in the Bush Administration. What Clarke had done seemed such a simple act, really. It was a request for forgiveness from someone who had reason to know what the government had done, and not done, to prevent something like 9/11. Even if Clarke's apology was rehearsed, even if the [Bush] White House was right and his motivations were entirely cynical, this was the moment of catharsis that many of the wives and husbands and children of the victims had been waiting for....

SHENON, *supra*, at 282–83.

As suggested by the accounts in the preceding chapters, personal responsibility also played a major role in the Pecora congressional hearings on the great depression, in which chief counsel Ferdinand Pecora captured the public's attention by skillfully assigning some measure of individual accountability to leaders of powerful Wall Street institutions, and the Iran-Contra congressional investigation, in which Oliver North successfully diverted attention from President Ronald Reagan by voluntarily assuming personal responsibility for much of the Iran-Contra scandal. In light of the important, yet very different, roles that the issue of personal responsibility and accountability has played in these investigations, how should future investigative commissions approach the issue of assigning individual responsibility and blame? Should only the most egregious instances of personal malfeasance or nonfeasance be highlighted, or should an investigation seek to identify and expose anyone who bears any measure of personal accountability? Is the proper balance somewhere between these two extremes, or did the 9/11 Commission follow the better approach in ruling out the issue from the outset of the investigation?

3. Institutional Accountability: Recurring FBI Failings? Individual responsibility and blameworthiness is not the only important accountability issue that arises in investigations of government failures—the issue of institutional accountability also may demand attention. For example, in both the Warren Commission investigation and the 9/11 Commission investigation, one of the most important questions facing the commissioners was whether the FBI had failed to perform adequately. Two specific incidents from those two investigations involving FBI failures to act have generated considerable controversy. In the Warren Commission investigation the failure of the FBI to alert the Secret Service of Lee Harvey Oswald's employment at the Texas School Book Depository on the Kennedy parade route has been criticized as a monumental dereliction of duty:

> It does not require special insight to appreciate how Dallas and the nation's history would have been dramatically different if the Secret Service had had Oswald's name on its "alert list." Although no analogy is perfect, a close parallel from modern U.S. history jumps to mind: the phone call that Watergate security guard Frank Wills made when he discovered tape holding a door unlocked within the complex that housed the Democratic National Committee headquarters. That call changed American history. It precipitated a cascade

of events that ended in the resignation of an American president. Had [Dallas FBI agent James P.] Hosty walked Oswald's file over to [Dallas Secret Service chief Forrest V.] Sorrels's office, this ordinary, and considering the circumstances, reasonable and expected action would also have changed history. With Oswald under surveillance, the Secret Service would have made certain that he never had [what Secret Service official Robert I. Bouck later characterized in Warren Commission testimony as] "unusual access," or any access at all, for that matter, to President Kennedy. It's a safe assumption that Secret Service agents and the Dallas police would have staked out the TSBD and possibly assigned more manpower in a visible show of force along the Houston-Elm Street stretch of the route to the Trade Mart. A show of force might have deterred any hidden gunmen in the vicinity of Dealey Plaza from carrying out plans to assassinate the president.

McKnight, *supra* at 263–64.

A similar issue concerning the performance of the FBI arose forty years later in the 9/11 Commission investigation. One of the most highly publicized matters within the 9/11 Commission's investigative purview was the failure of the FBI's headquarters to take any action in response to a July 10, 2001 electronic memorandum from the FBI's Phoenix field office[39] warning of suspicious activity involving young Muslim men enrolling in flight schools:

> Attorney General John Ashcroft and the F.B.I. director, Robert S. Mueller III, were told a few days after the Sept. 11 attacks that the F.B.I. had received a memorandum from its Phoenix office the previous July warning that Osama bin Laden's followers could be training at American flight schools, government officials said today.
>
> But senior Bush administration officials said neither Mr. Ashcroft nor Mr. Mueller briefed President Bush and his national security staff until recently about the Phoenix memorandum. Nor did they tell Congressional leaders.
>
> The disclosure is certain to magnify criticism of the F.B.I.'s performance, including its failure to act on the memorandum before the attacks on the World Trade Center and the Pentagon.
>
> The two men have not said publicly when they learned of the July 10 memorandum, but the officials said that within days of the attacks senior law enforcement officials grasped the document's significance as a potentially important missed signal.

---

39. For an in-depth account of the events leading up to the "Phoenix Memorandum" and the FBI's handling of it, see Senator Bob Graham with Jeff Nussbaum, Intelligence Matters: The CIA, the FBI, Saudi Arabia, and the Failure of America's War on Terror 42–49 (Random House 2004).

David Johnston & Don Van Natta Jr., *Traces of Terror: The F.B.I. Memo; Ashcroft Learned of Agent's Alert Just After 9/11*, N.Y. TIMES (May 21, 2002). In fact, the so-called "Phoenix memorandum" was only one in a number of "missed signals" involving the FBI in what the 9/11 Commission called "the summer of threat" that preceded the 9/11 attacks. 9/11 Commission member Richard Ben-Veniste summarized those missed signals as follows:

> Adding to the general awareness of such a terror tactic [using a hijacked airplane as a weapon] was the information during the late spring and summer of 2001 from all intelligence sources that al Qaeda was planning a spectacular attack. The CIA and FBI knew that at least two al Qaeda operatives were in the United States; the FBI knew in July 2001 from its alarmed Phoenix field office that an unusual number of foreign Muslim men were involved in commercial airliner training; the FBI and CIA knew in August that Zacarias Moussaoui, identified as a radical Muslim with jihadist ties, was apprehended in Minneapolis; the FBI agent who arrested Moussaoui had postulated a plot to fly a plane into the World Trade Center; the CIA, reporting to its director and top officials on the Moussaoui arrest, titled its briefing "Islamic Extremist Learns to Fly."

RICHARD BEN-VENISTE, THE EMPEROR'S NEW CLOTHES: EXPOSING TRUTH FROM WATERGATE TO 9/11 at 258–258 (St. Martin's Press 2009). (Allegations that the FBI did not take adequate actions in response to "red flags" before the January 6, 2021, attack on the U.S. Capitol are discussed further in the final section of this Chapter.)

Like the Warren Commission, however, the 9/11 Commission ultimately declined to target the FBI with institutional blame or harsh criticism and recommended that the FBI retain its role as the nation's lead domestic counterterrorism agency. That decision was not, however, without controversy within the Commission:

> For every insult hurled [CIA Director George] Tenet's way, there was a statement of effusive praise for FBI Director Mueller. For all of its astounding failures before 9/11, for all of the evidence that things had changed little at the FBI despite Mueller's promises, the commission would recommend that the FBI stay intact. Team 6, the commission's team of investigators that focused on the FBI, had felt strongly that the bureau needed to be overhauled, certainly when it came to combating terrorism. So they were appalled when they learned what changes the commission would recommend for the bureau—almost none. Several used the word *whitewash* when they saw a draft of the commission recommendations to be included in the final report. When it came to deciding what reforms were needed at the FBI, "we defer to Director Mueller," the draft said....
>
> The briefing [of the Commission by the staff objecting to the draft recommendations concerning the FBI] took place, and the final report's language on the FBI was toughened, if only slightly. The wording in the draft that most upset [staff member Caroline] Barnes and the others—the statement that the commission would "defer" to Mueller's judgment—was edited out of the report. But

the commission's larger recommendation, that the FBI remain intact, survived in the final draft, albeit with a call for the bureau to make new efforts to promote the work of agents and analysts who specialized in tracking down terrorists. The nation could no longer afford to have the FBI treat counterterrorism agents—like the ones in Minneapolis and Phoenix who might have stopped 9/11 if anyone in Washington had paid attention—as second class citizens.

SHENON, *supra*, at 403–04.

Although the 9/11 Commission did not recommend major reform at the FBI, and instead relied on FBI assurances that the agency could reform itself, the final public statement by the 9/11 Commission's chairs, Kean and Hamilton, in December 2005, suggests less than complete satisfaction with the FBI's progress:

> *Reforming the FBI*
>
> To protect ourselves at home, we need a strong domestic agency for both law enforcement and intelligence. Director Mueller has the right goals for FBI reform. There is progress—but there is not enough, and it is far too slow.
>
> There are still significant deficiencies in the FBI's analytic capabilities and in information sharing with other agencies and with local law enforcement. There is still too much turnover in management. There are shortfalls in human capital—in recruiting, hiring, training, and career development.
>
> The Bureau still struggles to make the intelligence mission the dominant mission of the agency.
>
> Reforms are at risk from inertia and complacency. Reforms must be accelerated, or they will fail. The President needs to lead. The Congress needs to provide careful oversight. Unless there is improvement in a reasonable period of time, Congress will have to look at alternatives.
>
> A strong and effective domestic intelligence function is not an option for the United States—it is an obligation. Our nation's security depends on its success.

9/11 Public Discourse Project, Remarks by Chairman Thomas H. Kean and Vice Chair Lee H. Hamilton, Final Report of the 9/11 Public Discourse Project, December 5, 2005.

Do the Warren Commission and 9/11 Commission experiences with the FBI provide any insights into how investigative commissions should approach the issue of institutional accountability? How deferential should commissions be to established agencies and authorities? How reluctant should commissions be to recommend changes that disturb the status quo and "shake up" official Washington? Do the long-term risks of being judged too timid offset to any degree the shorter-term risks of being accused of making recommendations that are too "radical" or too controversial?

4. Handling of "Sensitive" Witnesses. Another difficult investigative policy question in independent commission investigations such as those examined in this Chapter involves the handling of high-profile, "sensitive" witnesses. The handling of such witnesses may present dangerous political pitfalls, but the risks of being judged too deferential to key witnesses also are high. Examples from the Warren Commission and 9/11 Commission investigations illustrate the difficulty of the problems that can arise. The Warren Commission has been faulted for failing to take President Lyndon Johnson's testimony and for spending only a few minutes in a cursory interview of Mrs. Kennedy, as Senator and former Warren Commission staff member Arlen Specter has recounted:

> In the end Warren decided to take Mrs. Kennedy's deposition at her apartment. But he was not going to subject her to my detailed, protracted questioning, which he found so painful. I wound up questioning twenty-eight of the ninety-three witnesses who testified before the commission—but not Jacqueline Kennedy. The record on Mrs. Kennedy's deposition shows an abbreviated, nine-minute session. The interview omitted most of the lines of questioning I had proposed. It was almost worthless.

ARLEN SPECTER WITH CHARLES ROBBINS, PASSION FOR TRUTH 3 (William Morrow 2000).

The 9/11 Commission faced a similar issue in seeking the testimony of President George W. Bush and Vice President Richard Cheney. Ultimately, the White House and the Commission reached a compromise in which the Commission members were allowed to question the President and Vice President together, but were not allowed to question either of them alone. This compromise resulted in more than a little criticism of the Commission and of President Bush and Vice President Cheney.

What are the constitutional and separation of powers issues when a commission seeks to question a sitting president or vice president? What are the interests that support such questioning and what are the reasons for objecting, as a matter of policy or constitutional law, to such questioning? Are the considerations different for a former president or vice president? Both former President Clinton and former Vice President Gore voluntarily agreed to be questioned by the 9/11 Commission. Does the analysis change if it is a congressional committee, rather than an independent commission, that is seeking testimony from a sitting president? President Gerald Ford voluntarily appeared before Congress and provided testimony under oath to the House Judiciary Committee about his decision to pardon President Richard Nixon. Does Ford's congressional testimony and the joint Bush/Cheney testimony to the 9/11 Commission create a presumption that presidential testimony, when relevant, should be forthcoming in future investigations?

5. Best Practices and Procedures for Future Commissions. Do the three commission investigations that are examined in this Chapter suggest any "lessons learned" or "essential practices and procedures" applicable to future national independent investigative commissions? Consider in this regard the views of one of the authors in a 2009 law review article:[40]

---

40. Lance Cole, *Special National Investigative Commissions: Essential Powers and Procedures (Some Lessons from the Pearl Harbor, Warren Commission, and 9/11 Commission Investigations)*, 41 McGEORGE L. REV. 1 (2009) (edited for inclusion in this book and some footnotes omitted).

III. Recommended Practices and Procedures.

The experiences of the Roberts Commission, the Warren Commission, and the 9/11 Commission suggest some important common themes and noteworthy "lessons learned" regarding the conduct of special national investigative commissions. Although future such commissions will be as unique as the particular events and issues that precipitate their creation, some guiding principles can be identified and some essential practices and procedures can be recommended for future commissions. The following recommended practices and procedures are not intended as hard and fast rules for all commissions, but rather as starting points meriting careful consideration during the process of creating, organizing, and conducting national investigative commissions. Some of these recommended practices and procedures represent dramatic departures from past practice. Some would be expensive to implement and inconvenient to administer. And some would be strenuously opposed by "permanent" government departments and agencies. But expense, inconvenience, and institutional resistance are not sufficient reasons to compromise investigative practices and procedures when the subject of investigation is a failure of government the magnitude of the Pearl Harbor attack, the Kennedy assassination, or the 9/11 terrorist attacks. In such investigations the public interest in full accountability of government agencies and officials is paramount, and every possible effort should be made to create an historical record that is as complete and accurate as possible.

1. Commission Members: Roles, Time Commitments, and Conflicts of Interest.

An essential first step toward a successful independent commission investigation is to select commissioners who are able to devote the necessary time and effort to their commission's work. National investigative commission investigations are by their very nature extraordinarily challenging and time-consuming undertakings. They require leaders with relevant experience and as much in-depth knowledge of the matters under investigation as possible. But these requirements for sufficient time and relevant experience may conflict, as the commission candidates with the best qualifications also are likely to be those with the busiest and most demanding professional lives. A careful balance must be struck to avoid naming too many commissioners who have sterling credentials and impeccable public reputations but are unable to devote sufficient time to the commission's investigation. Arguably the Warren Commission failed to strike the right balance on this point and had too many members with ongoing competing responsibilities that detracted from their ability to devote substantial time to the commission investigation, most notably illustrated by Earl Warren's continued service as Chief Justice of the United States.[41]

---

41. [90] In addition to Warren's continued service on the Supreme Court, the seven-member Warren Commission included two U.S. Senators (John Sherman Cooper and Richard B. Russell) and two

Warren Commission critics have pointed to the lack of commissioner involvement in the actual investigation of the Kennedy assassination as one of the flaws of that commission's work. To avoid this criticism, and the potential corrosive effect on a commission's reputation, every possible effort should be made to select commissioners who do not have ongoing full-time commitments that are inconsistent with devoting the majority of their professional time to the commission's investigation. Although compromises may be necessary to obtain the services of the most able commissioners, commission candidates who cannot commit to making the commission's work their highest professional priority during the term of the commission's life probably should be rejected. At a minimum, the chair and the vice chair of the commission should be in a position to devote a substantial amount of their time to the commission's work and to appear as the "public face" of the commission.

In addition to being capable and available, it also is imperative that the members of a national investigative commission be free of any actual or perceived conflict of interest relating to the commission's work. Once again, the Warren Commission and the 9/11 Commission both provide cautionary examples of potential pitfalls. The prior service of Warren Commission member Allen Dulles as director of the Central Intelligence Agency has provided fodder for many Kennedy assassination conspiracy theorists' allegations of unexplored links between Lee Harvey Oswald and the CIA. The 9/11 Commission was initially derailed and valuable investigative time was lost when the first selections for its chair and vice chair, Henry Kissinger and George Mitchell, fell victim to conflict of interest concerns relating to Kissinger's consulting work and Mitchell's law firm clients.

Kissinger and Mitchell stepped down almost immediately, but conflict of interest issues continued to bedevil the 9/11 Commission. News reports focused on allegations of conflicts of interest surrounding 9/11 Commission members with connections to the airline industry. Although those allegations ultimately did not have a significant impact on the public's acceptance of the 9/11 Commission's report, they demonstrate how even vague and attenuated allegations of conflicts of interest can distract from and potentially undermine a commission's efforts. The backgrounds of all candidates for a national investigative commission should be carefully scrutinized for any client relation-

---

U.S. Representatives (Hale Boggs and Gerald R. Ford) who continued to serve in Congress during the Commission's investigation. A Warren Commission critic noted that "the attendance records of the Commission show that most of the Commissioners were present for only a minor portion of the hearings. Senator Russell, who attended the fewest, heard only 6 per cent of the testimony; whereas Allen Dulles, who attended the largest number of hearings, heard only about 71 per cent. Only three Commissioners heard more than half of the testimony, and the average Commissioner heard 45 per cent." EDWARD J. EPSTEIN, INQUEST: THE WARREN COMMISSION AND THE ESTABLISHMENT OF POLITICAL TRUTH 88–89 (Viking Press 1966). These statistics suggest that the Warren Commission model, with heavy membership of sitting members of Congress, is not optimal for an investigative commission, at least in terms of commissioner participation.

ships or other prior connections that could give rise to conflict of interest allegations. If possible, commissioners should be free of business or professional relationships that could reasonably be viewed as presenting a conflict of interest that might compromise a commissioner's independence and objectivity.

Some vague and unsubstantiated conflict of interest allegations can be dismissed as simply too attenuated to present problems in the minds of reasonable observers, such as allegations based upon routine consulting or law firm client matters in which the individual commission member played no personal role.[42] Other conflict of interest allegations are potentially more serious, particularly if they involve direct prior involvement in matters within a commission's investigative mandate. One of the more damaging allegations brought against the 9/11 Commission illustrates the perils that are present in this area. At a public hearing of the 9/11 Commission on April 13, 2004, then-Attorney General John Ashcroft took the remarkable step of asserting that one of the members of the 9/11 Commission itself, former Clinton administration Deputy Attorney General Jamie Gorelick, bore a measure of personal responsibility for shaping the policies inside the Justice Department that arguably had made it more difficult to discover and foil the 9/11 plot. The fact that Ashcroft was defending himself against charges that he had denied FBI requests for additional counterterrorism funding immediately prior to the 9/11 attacks, or the fact that Ashcroft's own Justice Department had continued the policies in question, did little to blunt the impact of his charges against Gorelick. Whatever conclusion one reaches on the merits of the Department of Justice policy issues being debated, it is undeniable that Ashcroft's attack on Gorelick diverted attention from the 9/11 Commission's investigation of the historical events preceding 9/11 and created an unwelcome sideshow in the midst of the commission's proceedings.

The service of former CIA Director Allen Dulles on the Warren Commission and the service of former Deputy Attorney General Jamie Gorelick on the 9/11 Commission are connected by a common prudential thread. Great caution should be exercised when naming to an investigatory commission a former high-ranking government official with any potential personal connection to the matters that the commission is investigating. While an unbiased reading

---

42. [92] Although even in those instances it may be prudent to take precautionary measures to counter any charges of bias or conflict of interest, such as having a commissioner agree to forgo any compensation derived directly or indirectly from the problem clients. In extreme cases a commissioner might agree not to participate in certain areas of a commission's investigation. This was the approach taken by the 9/11 Commission in response to allegations of conflicts of interest of the commission's executive director Philip Zelikow stemming from his prior work for the 2001 George W. Bush presidential transition team. Zelikow was required to agree to "recuse himself from all issues involving the transition from the Clinton to the Bush administration and that he be barred from participating in any interviews of senior Bush aides, including [Condoleeza] Rice." SHENON, *supra*, at 171. Whether or not such efforts to defuse conflict of interest allegations are ultimately effective is open to debate.

of history suggests that both Dulles and Gorelick made important contributions to the commissions they served, a strong case can be made that both commissions would have been better served by avoiding the controversies and criticisms that surrounded those particular commissioners.

This brief overview of issues relating to the qualifications and selection of commissioners to serve on national investigative commissions suggests a clear "bottom line" rule that should be departed from in only the most extraordinary circumstances: a national investigative commission should be comprised of members who are capable in terms of experience and qualifications, available with respect to other competing demands on their time, and free of any actual or perceived conflicts of interest that could reasonably be expected to undermine the Commission's work.

2. Commission Staffing and Investigative Resources.

Almost as important as the membership of a national investigative commission is the make-up and leadership of the commission's professional staff. As Philip Shenon observed in his book on the 9/11 Commission: "It is a polite fiction in Washington that the reports of blue-ribbon federal commissions are written by the commissioners themselves. In truth, most of the reports are written by a professional staff led by a full-time staff director."[43] The Warren Commission provides what may be the single most important example of investigative commission staff work in our national history.[44] Long before he became a United States Senator, Arlen Specter was the sole member of the Warren Commission staff with the responsibility for investigating the facts relating to President Kennedy's assassination.[45] In that staff capacity Specter

---

43. [102] SHENON, *supra*, at 38.

44. [103] A possible rival for the title of most important single investigative staff finding in our nation's history is the Senate Watergate Committee's discovery of the Nixon White House taping system. *See* [the previous discussion in this Chapter and in Chapter Three] (discussing the Senate committee's questioning of Alexander Butterfield). A good case can be made that the revelation of the Nixon tapes was the most important single piece of information revealed in all of the various Watergate investigations—and perhaps the greatest single evidentiary discovery in American legal history—because it was the contents of the tapes that ultimately forced Nixon to resign the presidency. Although that discovery was made in the context of a congressional investigation, not an investigation by a national investigative commission, it nonetheless demonstrates the importance and value of investigative staff work.

45. [104] *See* ARLEN SPECTER WITH CHARLES ROBBINS, PASSION FOR TRUTH 45–52 (William Morrow 2000) (recounting how Specter came to have sole responsibility for "Area 1" of the Warren Commission investigation, which covered President Kennedy's activities on the day of the assassination); *see also* EPSTEIN, *supra*, at 60–65 (noting at page 60 that "Instead of being handled by forty full-time lawyers, the entire task of ascertaining the basic facts of the investigation fell upon one lawyer—Arlen Specter."). Senator Specter supplements his account of his responsibility for "Area 1" with that of another Warren Commission staff member, David Belin:

One of the best-kept secrets inside the Commission was that Francis W.H. Adams, one of the two lawyers assigned to Area 1, performed virtually no work. He should have been asked to resign when it first became apparent that he was not going to undertake his responsibilities,

developed the "single-bullet theory" that is generally regarded as the Rosetta stone of the Kennedy assassination and as such has probably been subject to more scrutiny and after-the-fact attacks than any other investigative finding in world history. With the benefit of hindsight, few would dispute that the Warren Commission would have been better advised to devote more staff resources to that area of its investigation, not because more staff would have led to a different conclusion, but rather because more staff would have lessened the vulnerability of the commission's key finding to attacks and second-guessing based upon charges of inadequate investigation and alleged failures to reconcile competing evidence.

Although the Warren Commission experience with the single-bullet theory may be an extreme example, it illustrates dramatically the point that it is simply impossible to predict at the outset of an investigation which matters or issues will require the greatest staff investigative resources.[46] The only safe and prudent approach is to do everything possible to assemble an investigative staff that is adequate in both size and expertise to fulfill the investigative mandate of the commission.[47] As described above, both the Roberts Commission investigation of Pearl Harbor and the Warren Commission investigation of the

---

but because of some mistaken fear that this might in some way embarrass the Commission, Mr. Adams was kept on in name only and the entire burden of Area 1 fell upon Arlen Specter. Fortunately for the Commission, Arlen Specter was able to carry the entire weight of Area 1 on his own shoulders. Nevertheless, it is indicative of the nature of investigations by governmental Commissions that the need for a second lawyer in Area 1 was outweighed by a political decision. The ramifications of the fact that the decision was made by the Chief Justice of the United States are indeed chilling."

SPECTER, *supra*, at 52 (quoting DAVID W. BELIN, NOVEMBER 22, 1963: YOU ARE THE JURY (New York: Quadrangle/N.Y. Times 1973), p. 15). Epstein's account corroborates Belin's account. *See* EPSTEIN, *supra*, at 60. The recurring problem of national investigative commissions allowing political considerations to influence staffing and other key investigative decisions, particularly timing and funding, is discussed further *infra*.

46. [109] The Senate Watergate Committee staff's discovery of the Nixon White House taping system, *see* [Chapter 3 of this book], is another example of the unpredictability of the investigative process. The Watergate Committee staff members who questioned former Nixon aide Alexander Butterfield had no idea that they were about to discover a cache of crucial evidence that soon would lead directly to the political demise of the President of the United States. As a result, they conducted a relatively casual and informal interview of Butterfield, and the session was not transcribed or recorded. All parties involved would probably be happier today if a court reporter's transcript of the interview had been prepared, and history definitely would be the richer if that had taken place. The importance of transcribing witness statements is discussed in more detail *infra*.

47. [110] Fortunately, even high-profile national investigative commissions usually do not have investigative mandates that are as difficult and unpredictable as the three commissions that are the subject of this [Chapter]. *Cf.* KEAN & HAMILTON, *supra*, at 29 ("The only real examples of commissions with mandates of the same size and import as ours were the Warren Commission, in 1963–1964, and the Roberts Commission, in 1941–1942, which investigated the attack on Pearl Harbor."). Most commissions, at least if they have members with relevant investigative experience, should be able to make reliable judgments as to the amount of investigative staff resources they can reasonably be expected to require in order to complete their tasks in a timely fashion.

Kennedy assassination have suffered from charges that the commissions devoted insufficient investigative resources to crucial areas of their investigations. While there is no failsafe means of avoiding such criticisms, future commissions would be wise to err on the side of caution and assemble an investigative staff with ample "reserves" to pursue unanticipated investigative avenues and issues.

Quantity and depth of staff investigative resources is not the only important consideration. It also is important for an investigative commission, particularly one that is investigating a politically charged and divisive matter like the Kennedy assassination or the 9/11 attacks, to assemble an investigative staff with an extraordinary breadth of experience and widely diverse backgrounds. One of the strongest recurring criticisms of the Warren Commission investigation was that it relied too heavily on the FBI for investigative support. The obvious conflict of interest in having the FBI support any investigation of its own role in the events surrounding the Kennedy assassination is only the tip of a larger potential investigative conflict of interest iceberg, however. The greater, systemic problem is that in any investigation of a massive failure of government, which at bottom was the issue in the Pearl Harbor, Kennedy assassination, and 9/11 investigations, a staff that is weighted too heavily with investigators who came from government may be hesitant to challenge and question the actions of their former agencies or the government generally. For this reason alone, future national investigative commissions would be well advised to recruit a staff with a broad range of backgrounds and professional experiences to ensure a critical and independent staff perspective. Most important, a commission should not rely too heavily on investigative support of agencies or offices that are within the commission's investigative purview or have some actual or potential conflict of interest with respect to the commission's investigation, as was the case with the Warren Commission and the FBI.[48]

A final important consideration regarding commission staff resources is the organization of the staff and the staff's relations with the individual commission members. Both the Warren Commission and the 9/11 Commission have been criticized for having staff structures that insulated the commission members from the staff. While it may well be tempting for commissioners to adopt a formal "front office" structure that interposes senior staff administrators between the commission and its investigative staff—the staff structure that was

---

48. [112] Although the 9/11 Commission sought to avoid this problem by assembling its own investigative staff with a wide range of experience and expertise, *see* KEAN & HAMILTON, *supra* at 38–39, problems still arose in this area. Most notably, executive director Philip Zelikow's prior ties to the Bush administration transition team and Bush National Security Adviser Condoleeza Rice created serious problems in the public's perception of the commission's work. *See* SHENON, *supra*, at 262–63 (recounting Tim Russert's questioning of 9/11 Commission co-chairs Kean and Hamilton on *Meet the Press* about Zelikow's role in the investigation and conflicts of interest).

employed by both the Warren Commission and the 9/11 Commission—the costs of such a structure in terms of "bottom up" information sharing and commissioner involvement arguably outweigh any administrative benefits.[49] Here the bottom line is the same as in other areas of investigative tradecraft. Access to more information is almost always better than limitations on access to information. The more access the individual commission members have to the nuts and bolts of the staff's investigation, the more and better informed the commissioners are likely to be at the end of the investigative process. Moreover, commissioners who do not wish to be bogged down in the details of the staff's factual investigation will not be required to do so, as they always will have the authority to make their preferences known to the staff, while those who wish to get their hands dirty by digging into the factual details with the staff should be free to do so. Interposing a formal front office structure between the bulk of the staff and the commission members unavoidably interferes with information sharing. The wiser approach is to take pains to ensure that the commission's staff structure and organization will not unduly insulate commissioners from staff input and views.

3. Commission Funding, Timetables, and Deadlines.

Tom Kean and Lee Hamilton made the dramatic statement that the 9/11 Commission was "set up to fail" before the commission's work even began. The funding limitations and relatively short investigative timetable built into the 9/11 Commission's enabling statute created what Kean and Hamilton called "an impossible task" for the commission. The timing issue had been exacerbated by the commission's false start resulting from the Henry Kissinger and George Mitchell appointments and resignations. The Warren Commission faced similar problems arising from its tight investigative timetable, and critics of that commission have asserted that important investigative leads were not pursued because investigative time ran out. The Roberts Commission was also roundly criticized for conducting much too hurried an investigation of the Pearl Harbor attacks.

Obviously, these kinds of criticisms of an investigative commission's work should be avoided if at all possible. Whether a commission is established by executive order or by congressional legislation, every possible effort should be

---

49. [115] Some members of the 9/11 Commission opposed the implementation of a "front office" structure in that investigation, but their objections were overruled by co-chairs Kean and Hamilton. *See* KEAN & HAMILTON, *supra* at 37–38 (describing their decision to implement a "front-office triumvirate" of an executive director, deputy executive director, and general counsel who would manage the staff). Other commissioners feared that such a staff structure would create the same kind of information "stovepipes" that had plagued the FBI and CIA prior to 9/11 and made them unable to "connect the dots" prior to the attacks, *see* SHENON, *supra*, at 85 (describing concerns of commissioner and former Senator Max Cleland), and that a front office structure would unduly concentrate control of the investigation in the executive director, *see id.* at 69–70 (describing concerns of commissioner and former Watergate prosecutor Richard Ben-Veniste).

made to provide adequate funding and set a realistic timetable. This is not to say that reasonable and well-considered limitations on funding and the permitted duration of an investigation are not necessary and desirable. Large, complex investigations have a tendency to expand beyond their original objectives, and recent history of independent counsel investigations[50] suggests that both a deadline and a funding limit are essential for such investigations. What is required in this area is a careful balance between the need for adequate time and funds for a complete and thorough investigation, on the one hand, and the need for limits on costs and a timely completion of the investigation, on the other hand.

Unfortunately, not one of the three major investigations that are the subject of this [Chapter] managed to strike this balance properly. The Roberts Commission was conducted too hurriedly, and as a result it is widely perceived as a failure. The Warren Commission has suffered greatly from critics' claims that it did not devote enough time and investigative resources to the central events of the Kennedy assassination. The 9/11 Commission faced an uphill battle from the outset of its investigation, due to funding constraints and an unrealistic completion date in the original legislation. It then was forced to waste valuable time and commissioner attention to obtain additional funding and a two-month extension to complete its report.

These three significant failures to address properly the funding and timing issues in what were arguably the three most important national investigative commissions of the last century suggest that special attention should be focused on these issues when future commissions are created. Two guiding principles can be extracted from these unfortunate past missteps. First, it is clear that when a national investigative commission is established, funding for the commission's work should be adequate at the outset, to avoid necessitating distracting and demoralizing subsequent requests for additional funds. Accepting obviously inadequate funding as a political compromise to help get a commission established, as occurred with the 9/11 Commission, may appear to be a smart move at the time, but in the long run it is both unwise and extremely counterproductive. The same considerations apply to the initial timetable that is established for an investigation. While a reasonable reporting deadline is appropriate, the 9/11 Commission experience teaches that the timetable for completing the commission's work should not be unrealistically short in terms of the commission's investigative mandate. The Warren Commission experience suggests that future commissions should be wary of imposing internal deadlines that may unduly truncate staff investigations. The

---

50. [124] The length and cost of Independent Counsel Lawrence Walsh's investigation of the Iran-Contra affair and Independent Counsel Kenneth Starr's investigation of Whitewater and the Monica Lewinsky matter were the source of widespread criticism and public disapproval, and likely were the principal reasons Congress ultimately declined to renew the Independent Counsel Act. [*Ed. Note: Those investigations are discussed in Chapters 5 (Iran-Contra) and 7 (Clinton-Lewinsky).*]

Roberts Commission experience shows that the consequences of a rushed investigation can be calamitous in terms of history's final assessment of a commission's work. When history will be the final judge of an investigation's merit, a little extra money and time may ultimately prove to be well-spent.

A final timing and funding lesson that can be drawn from these three commission investigations is perhaps the most difficult to apply in the real world. In all three cases that are the subject of this [Chapter], the investigative process was trumped by political considerations. The Roberts Commission rushed to judgments in an ill-considered effort to appease an impatient president and an angry public. The Warren Commission strove mightily to act quickly to calm a nervous public. The 9/11 Commission declined to seek to extend its investigation into a presidential election season, even though the rush to conclude before the election campaign season began in earnest severely compromised the time available for deliberation and final drafting of its report. Although each of these decisions is understandable, and hindsight is always more clear than foresight, all three commissions probably would have been considerably less vulnerable to subsequent attack—and perhaps would have produced superior final products—if they had simply disregarded political considerations and refused to rush their investigations. For these reasons, the most important funding and timing lesson that can be drawn from these three commissions is that future commissions should not be subject to artificial deadlines dictated by political or other considerations that are irrelevant to the commission's investigative mission.

4. Subpoena Power—Use and Enforcement.

Once an investigative commission is constituted and staffed it must collect information if it is to fulfill its mandate. Experience suggests that for a commission to function effectively it must have, and should use, subpoena power to compel the production of documents and testimony. While the Roberts Commission and the Warren Commission for the most part enjoyed cooperation in collecting evidence, the 9/11 Commission had a different experience. After an early—and internally controversial—decision not to use subpoena power to collect evidence, the 9/11 Commission was ultimately forced to use its subpoena power to obtain necessary information from recalcitrant federal agencies.

While it is tempting to assess the 9/11 commission experience as simply an example of an unwise initial policy decision, and conclude that the commissioners who urged use of subpoenas at the outset of the investigation were correct,[51] that assessment would gloss over the complexity of the legal issues

---

51. [128] Commissioners Ben-Veniste and Gorelick reportedly advocated strongly in favor of such a policy. Representatives of the families of the victims of the 9/11 attacks also urged co-chairs Kean and Hamilton to conduct an aggressive investigation, stating "We want to see lots of subpoenas." *See* KEAN & HAMILTON, *supra*, at 54–55. Despite these admonitions Kean and Hamilton, who were not lawyers

involved. Although it is possible that a policy of uniformly issuing subpoenas and demonstrating a willingness to enforce those subpoenas by aggressively utilizing the available statutory enforcement measures would have avoided the problems the 9/11 Commission encountered, it is not clear that this approach necessarily would have ensured compliance with the commission's information requests. The reason for this uncertainty stems from two related practical limitations that significantly hampered the ability of the 9/11 Commission to effectively use its subpoena power—the limited life of the 9/11 Commission and the limited efficacy of the subpoena enforcement measures in the Commission's enabling statute.

The 9/11 Commission's relatively short lifespan made any delays spent litigating a subpoena enforcement action particularly unpalatable to the commissioners, especially co-chairs Kean and Hamilton. The short lifespan also increased the likelihood that in any subpoena confrontation a recalcitrant subpoena recipient could successfully adopt a "run out the clock" litigation strategy and simply outlast the commission. This timing problem applied to both of the subpoena enforcement methods available to the 9/11 Commission under its enabling statute. The first means of enforcing a 9/11 Commission subpoena, seeking a civil court order from a federal district court to enforce the subpoena, meant that enforcement of the subpoena would be subject to the scheduling vagaries and unpredictable appeals process of the federal courts. The second enforcement method, requesting a U.S. Attorney to bring the matter before a federal grand jury for prosecution, also provided no assurance of a prompt resolution of a subpoena dispute. Moreover, grand jury secrecy requirements would have precluded the commission and its staff counsel from participating fully in the efforts to enforce the subpoena. As a practical matter, therefore, neither of the subpoena enforcement powers granted to the 9/11 Commission were sufficient to ensure that it could obtain the information it needed within the short time frame available to it.

Even putting aside timing issues, the subpoena enforcement powers given to the 9/11 Commission, as discussed in more detail above, were not adequate

---

and therefore may have been somewhat wary of adopting a litigation-based approach to information collection, decided to employ a strategy of seeking voluntary cooperation rather than employing a more adversarial subpoena strategy:

> There was a political side as well. Subpoenas of the White House or executive branch agencies from the 9/11 Commission would have appeared adversarial. It was neither our charge nor our intention to be an adversary to the White House; to do so would have led half the country, and possibly several of our Republican commissioners, to question our motives. We were supposed to be independent, not necessarily confrontational. We were investigating a national catastrophe, not a White House transgression; this was 9/11, not Watergate.

Id. at 64–65. *See also* SHENON, *supra*, at 70–71 (describing Kean and Hamilton's initial policy decision that "[t]here would be no routine subpoenas, ... subpoenas would be seen as too confrontational, perhaps choking off cooperation from the Bush administration from the very outset of the investigation").

to ensure compliance from the most important sources of information sought by the commission—federal government agencies and offices, including the White House. Because the 9/11 Commission was a legislative branch entity, seeking a federal court order enforcing a subpoena and seeking contempt of court sanctions if the order was not obeyed, would have raised serious separation of powers issues if the party resisting the subpoena was an executive branch office or agency.[52] When congressional subpoenas have been resisted by federal agencies, the federal courts have been reluctant to intervene and have preferred to push the parties toward a political compromise that avoids judicial fiat as a means of resolving the conflict.[53] Although a federal district court recently upheld the power of Congress to seek a declaratory judgment enforcing its subpoenas to executive branch officials,[54] the case was settled before the appeals process was complete, and the decision of the district court left many of the most important issues unresolved.[55]

The criminal enforcement process available to the 9/11 Commission was even less likely to yield a satisfactory resolution of a subpoena dispute with an executive branch agency, as the applicable federal statute does not clearly require a U.S. Attorney—who is an executive branch official and can be expected to follow the President's directions—to prosecute another executive branch official who is acting at the direction of the President in defying a congressional subpoena.[56] Thus, in the event of a showdown with the Bush administra-

52. [137] Such a confrontation would have created "a perfect storm" from a separation of powers perspective, involving all three branches of government in an unprecedented legal confrontation (with regard to the unprecedented nature of such a potential confrontation, it is worth noting that the Watergate battle for the Nixon White House tapes involved a congressional committee, *see Senate Select Committee on Presidential Campaign Activities v. Nixon*, 498 F.2d 725 (D.C. Cir. 1974), and a Department of Justice Special Prosecutor, *see United States v. Nixon*, 418 U.S. 683 (1974), not an independent investigatory commission housed in the legislative branch such as the 9/11 Commission).

53. [138] *See, e.g., United States v. House of Representatives of the United States*, 556 F. Supp. 150 (D.D.C. 1983) (declining to intervene in a dispute between Congress and the Reagan administration); *Senate Select Committee on Presidential Campaign Activities v. Nixon*, 498 F.2d 725 (D.C. Cir. 1974) (concluding that the Senate Committee failed to demonstrate sufficient need to obtain Nixon White House tapes).

54. [139] *See Committee on the Judiciary, United States House of Representatives v. Miers*, 2008 WL 2923350 (D. D.C. July 31, 2008) (finding that the Bush administration position that senior White House aides enjoyed absolute immunity from congressional subpoenas was "entirely unsupported by existing case law" and affirming that "Congress has a right—derived from its Article I legislative function—to issue and enforce subpoenas [to executive branch officials]").

55. [140] The *Miers* opinion does not address the merits of the executive privilege claims at issue and does not decide whether the Congress's need for information about the U.S. Attorneys firings would outweigh a valid claim of executive privilege. *See id.* For additional background on the U.S. Attorneys firings matter that precipitated that case, and the constitutional issues at stake, see David M. Driesen, *Firing U.S. Attorneys, An Essay*, 60 ADMIN. L. REV. 707 (2008).

56. [143] *See generally* Todd D. Peterson, *Prosecuting Executive Branch Officials for Contempt of Congress*, 66 N.Y. UNIV. L. REV. 563 (1991). [As discussed in Chapter 4,] the Department of Justice Office of Legal Counsel has a policy of not prosecuting congressional contempt citations brought against executive branch officials who refuse to testify before Congress on the basis of instructions by

tion, neither of the enforcement mechanisms available to the 9/11 Commission could be relied upon as tools to compel the executive branch to produce information that the Commission might seek.[57] An appreciation of the weakness of the legal tools in their arsenal makes it more difficult to criticize Kean and Hamilton for adopting the conciliatory information collection approach that is described above.

So what is the solution to this problem—must national investigative commissions be left largely impotent in their efforts to obtain what may well be the most important information that they are charged with obtaining? Is there no good way to balance the needs of a properly constituted investigative commission against legitimate efforts by executive branch agencies and offices to withhold information that they believe the national interest requires withholding? As always in our constitutional system of divided government, the judicial branch must serve as the final arbiter of such disputes, even if it is reluctant to do so, and the legislation that created the 9/11 Commission did provide for judicial branch resolution of subpoena disputes. The problem with that legislation, as explained above, is that neither the civil nor the criminal enforcement options available to the 9/11 Commission provided workable solutions. A more effective and less time-consuming subpoena enforcement tool is needed to ensure that national investigative commissions can fulfill their responsibilities.

A possible solution to this problem is to provide national investigative commissions, particularly those like the 9/11 Commission that are investigating a

---

the President to assert executive privilege. For example, Attorney General Michael Mukasey instructed U.S. Attorney for the District of Columbia Jeffrey Taylor not to present to a grand jury for criminal prosecution the refusals of senior Bush administration officials Harriet Miers and Joshua Bolten to comply with congressional subpoenas in the U.S. Attorneys firing investigation. *See generally* John Dean, *Judge Bates Slams the Bush White House's Claims of Congressional Immunity: Why There May Be No Consequences for the White House, Despite the Clear Ruling*, FINDLAW (August 8, 2008) (available at http://writ.news.findlaw.com/dean/20080808.html).

57. [144] An example of an instance in which the 9/11 Commission was unable to obtain information from the Bush administration is the extensive efforts by the Commission to obtain first access to "war on terror" detainees and then, when that failed, to obtain documents containing information obtained from detainee interrogations. *See* JANE MAYER, THE DARK SIDE 278–281 (Anchor Books 2009). Mayer described the showdown that almost took place between the 9/ll Commission and the Bush administration as follows:

The fight over the Commission's access to the detainees built to a head on January 21, 2004. Kean and Hamilton faced off against Tenet, Rumsfeld, and Gonzales in a White House meeting. Tenet and Gonzales "took a very hard line" said [9/11 Commission executive director Philip] Zelikow. They were adamant. Afterward, Zelikow argued for the Commission to defy the CIA and issue a subpoena. "You can imagine how explosive this would have been," said Zelikow. "It would have been a dramatic and very, very difficult confrontation on all sides. But we thought the matter was important enough." The Commission took a vote, but the majority of members opposed getting into a public confrontation with the CIA.

Id. at 280.

complex matter and are subject to a fixed reporting deadline, with a means of obtaining expedited judicial review and enforcement of their subpoenas. For example, the enabling legislation that creates a commission (or, in the case of commissions created by Executive Order, such as the Roberts Commission and the Warren Commission, the Joint Resolution of Congress that provides a commission with subpoena power) could provide that civil subpoena enforcement actions shall be heard by a special federal three-judge district court panel, already available under existing law, and decided on an expedited schedule, with direct appeal to the Supreme Court, also already available under existing law, so as to resolve such disputes as expeditiously as is possible under our legal system.[58] This approach would be consistent with the national interest in prompt resolution of these important disputes and would place responsibility for making the final decision with the appropriate actor in our constitutional system, the Supreme Court.

Such a process would also have several important practical advantages that are particularly well-suited to resolving subpoena disputes involving national investigative commissions. The availability of an expedited judicial enforcement and appeals process makes it less likely that subpoena recipients would try to "run out the clock" on a commission's investigations, particularly if they were asserting legal arguments of dubious merit that would be unlikely to withstand judicial review. This is a significant step forward from the untenable position of the 9/11 Commission, which had no realistic means available to enforce its subpoenas within the time span of its investigation. It also is more consistent with what the public would expect of a national commission investigating a matter of great national importance. It is not likely that the public—or Congress when it created the 9/11 Commission—expected that a commission investigating a national catastrophe would be unable to obtain all the

---

58. [148] A similar approach has been proposed to end stalemates between Congress and the executive branch in disputes over enforcement of congressional subpoenas. *See* EMILY BERMAN, EXECUTIVE PRIVILEGE: A LEGISLATIVE REMEDY (Brennan Center for Justice, New York University Law School 2009). Berman proposes that Congress adopt a new "Executive Privilege Codification Act" that contains the following provisions:

Sec. 108 Three Judge Panel. "Any civil action brought pursuant to this statute shall be heard and adjudicated by three judges appointed in accordance with 28 U.S.C. §2284. Any party may appeal the decision of the panel directly to the Supreme Court in accordance with 28 U.S.C. §1253."

Sec. 109 Expedited Schedule. "The federal courts shall place an action filed pursuant to this statute on an expedited schedule and make its timely resolution a priority."

See id. at 48–49. Even if one questions whether these provisions tip the balance of power too much toward the Congress in "garden variety" political disputes between a Congress controlled by one party and an executive branch controlled by the other party, for the extraordinary circumstances of a national investigating commission such as those that are the subject of this [Chapter], a strong argument can be made that the balance should be tipped toward disclosure and away from obstruction of the investigation.

information it needed from the very federal government of which it was a part. Finally, in the event of an intractable dispute between a commission and a government agency, it is appropriate that the Supreme Court should be the final arbiter of what information should be provided to the commission, rather than having the matter decided by an executive branch that may be acting out of political self-preservation or a commission that may be overreaching or overzealous in pursuing its investigative mandate.

If an effective subpoena enforcement mechanism is put in place for a commission, then it is possible to avoid the problem that confronted 9/11 co-chairs Kean and Hamilton, and to set out some general principles guiding the use of subpoenas by national investigative commissions. First, every commission that is investigating a matter of broad public importance should be granted subpoena power to compel testimony and the production of documents and other evidence.[59] Second, and most important, the commission must be given expedited subpoena enforcement procedures so that subpoenas can be enforced against recalcitrant witnesses within the commission's investigative lifetime. With these procedures available, then the commission should make full use of its subpoena power, and all witnesses and documents should be compelled by subpoena from the outset of the commission's investigation. While these procedures do not guarantee that a commission will always obtain any evidence it may seek, they give a commission the most support and the strongest legal tools that are available under our constitutional system of government.

A final issue relating to subpoena power should be noted and considered carefully. As discussed above, the 9/11 Commission was constructed along partisan lines, with an equal number of Democrat and Republican members. Although the commission membership was equally divided by party, the issuance of a commission subpoena required either a bipartisan majority of six commissioners or bipartisan agreement of the chair and vice chair. The practical effect of this structure was to limit the Commission's subpoena power to subjects where a bipartisan consensus could be forged. While this requirement of bipartisanship may appear to have a desirable "braking effect" on a commission's ability to subpoena information, it imposes a high cost in terms of the scope and thoroughness of a commission's investigation. Arguably, if a commission has been properly constituted and its investigative authority has been carefully and appropriately defined in its enabling legislation or executive or-

---

59. [149] While this point may appear self-evident, not all commissions are given subpoena powers. For example, the Commission on Wartime Contracting in Iraq and Afghanistan, created by act of Congress in 2008, was not given subpoena powers. *See* Public Law 110181, Sec. 841 (National Defense Authorization Act (NDAA) for Fiscal Year 2009: Commission on Wartime Contracting in Iraq and Afghanistan (110th Con. 2008). The legislation creating that commission provides that "In the event the Commission is unable to obtain testimony or documents needed to conduct its work, the Commission shall notify the committees of Congress of jurisdiction and appropriate investigative authorities."

der, then any information within the commission's defined area of investigative jurisdiction should be subject to subpoena by the commission, without regard to whether a bipartisan majority of commission members supports the issuance of a particular subpoena. In addition, it is hard to see why gathering information alone should be perceived as a threat to a commission's operation, particularly if any final commission action regarding the information at issue will require majority support. In other words, in investigations of matters of enormous public importance more raw information should be better than less. If a commission has more information at its disposal it will be better informed in developing its conclusions and recommendations, and better able to inform the public fully as to the matters it has been charged with investigating.

For all of these reasons, a better approach to commission subpoena power would be to provide for issuance of a subpoena if a specified minimum number of commission members wish to subpoena information (for example, three members of an eight-member commission or four members of a ten-member commission). Such a requirement should be sufficient to ensure that only serious matters of investigative attention would be the subject of subpoenas, while also preventing a "rogue commissioner" or small minority of commissioners from abusing the commission's subpoena power. Most important, it would remove altogether the most likely source of contentious partisan divisions from a commission's investigative activity. Instead of being influenced by partisan considerations, the focus of subpoena deliberations would be on individual commissioner responsibility and appropriate use of a commission's scarce investigative resources. Finally, providing more liberal authority for issuance of subpoenas should result in greater initial attention to carefully defining a commission's investigative mandate, which is a more appropriate limit on a commission's subpoena power than *post hoc* reliance on the political affiliation of the commissioners who support issuing a particular subpoena.[60]

If one thinks of the Roberts Commission investigation of the Pearl Harbor attack or the Warren Commission investigation of the Kennedy assassination, rather than the more recent 9/11 Commission investigation,[61] the merits of a

---

60. [154] This approach would also further appropriate judicial review of commission subpoenas if a subpoena recipient sought to contest a commission subpoena. The reviewing court would simply assess whether the subject matter of the subpoena was within the defined scope of the commission's investigation, a task that courts routinely perform in all manner of government investigations, and rule accordingly. Subpoenas that went beyond the scope of the commission's investigative authority would not be enforced by the courts, ensuring that a minority of commissioners could not extend the commission's investigation beyond its defined investigative mandate.

61. [155] The 9/11 Commission may be a particularly poor example to use in considering this issue. The fact that the 9/11 attacks occurred shortly after the most closely contested presidential election contest [to that point] in modern history and the resulting transfer of executive branch control from one party to another created a particularly divisive political environment in which to conduct an independent, nonpartisan investigation of the attacks. In addition, it is likely that the political divides

broader commission subpoena power are more readily apparent. Today few would argue that relevant information sought by any three members of the Warren Commission (less than a majority of the seven-member commission) should have been off limits and unavailable to that commission, and most people would agree that more information collection and consideration, rather than less, would have been desirable in investigating the Kennedy assassination. Similarly, in light of the poor performance of the Roberts Commission, discussed above, and the extent to which its investigative work had to be replicated by subsequent investigations, it is difficult to argue that its investigation would have been undermined by allowing any two members of that five-member commission to issue a subpoena. With the benefit of hindsight and the greater analytical detachment that the passage of time provides, it is easier to see that the perceived dangers of a broader independent commission subpoena power are overstated, and that a better approach would be to avoid requiring a bipartisan majority to issue investigative subpoenas.[62]

5. Witness Testimony—Essential Powers and Procedures.

If there is one lesson that resonates most clearly from the three commission investigations that are examined in this [Chapter], it is that every effort should be made to create as complete and detailed an investigative record as possible. The Roberts Commission's failure to properly record and document its early witness interviews was later seen as a significant blunder, and the Warren Commission has suffered from all manner of conspiracy and cover-up allegations that have sought to exploit every conceivable flaw and gap in that com-

---

that surrounded that investigation are still fresh enough to make it difficult to give even the legal issues it presents the kind of dispassionate and nonpartisan analysis that they should receive. For those reasons, the analysis that follows focuses on the Roberts Commission and the Warren Commission, rather than the 9/11 Commission.

62. [156] Whatever the merits of this argument for more liberal subpoena powers for independent investigative commissions, recent history suggests that Congress, in the present political environment at least, is not likely to embrace it. As noted above, the Commission on Wartime Contracting in Iraq and Afghanistan, created by act of Congress in 2008, was not given subpoena power. More recently, in May 2009, Congress created a Financial Crisis Inquiry Commission to investigate "the causes, domestic and global, of the current financial and economic crisis in the United States." See Fraud Enforcement and Recovery Act of 2009, Pub. L. No. 111-21 (May 20, 2009). That Commission had ten members, six chosen by the House and Senate Democratic leaders and four chosen by the Republican leaders in Congress; the Democratic leadership will name the chair and the Republican leadership will name the vice chair. See id. Most interesting for purposes of the discussion of commission subpoena powers in this [Chapter], although the commission has a majority of members appointed by Democrats, the law requires the assent of at least one Republican member of the commission to issue a subpoena. See id. The effect of this provision is to require in effect a bipartisan supermajority to issue a subpoena, which is directly contrary to the more liberal subpoena power for independent commissions that this Article advocates. The wisdom of imposing this limitation on the Financial Crisis Inquiry Commission is questionable, as it significantly curtails the scope of the commission's subpoena power, but it does suggest that even in investigating a matter as important as the global financial crisis Congress unfortunately appears to be more concerned with partisan gamesmanship than with creating an independent commission that can obtain all of the relevant evidence and facts.

mission's investigative record. Even the 9/11 Commission, which was well aware of the perceived shortcomings of the Roberts Commission and Warren Commission investigations, was unable to avoid problems stemming from a failure to document adequately its investigative activities. One example from the 9/11 Commission experience illustrates the problems that can arise in this area.

After the 9/11 Commission report was published, a member of Congress made public allegations that a Department of Defense intelligence officer had told members of the 9/11 Commission staff that one of the most notorious 9/11 hijackers, Mohammed Atta, had been under U.S. government surveillance prior to the 9/11 attacks through a secret Pentagon intelligence program called "Able Danger." The staff interview of the intelligence officer had not been transcribed, because rather than conducting staff questioning of witnesses as formal depositions with a verbatim transcript of the questions and answers,[63] the 9/11 Commission practice was to have the responsible staff members prepare a "memorandum for the record" ("MFR") after each witness interview. Although a thorough and carefully prepared staff memorandum is certainly a good record of an investigative question and answer session,[64] it is not an adequate substitute for a verbatim transcript because it does not capture every word and therefore is subject to dispute after the fact as to its accuracy. This is exactly what happened in the Able Danger situation, where the Defense Department interviewee claimed that something was said in the interview and the 9/11 Commission staff denied that claim. The most that could finally be said about the matter by the commission's chair and vice chair was that "The MFR prepared shortly after the meeting makes no mention of Atta."[65] A verbatim transcript of the interview would have made it possible for the 9/11 Commission to "prove a negative" and demonstrate conclusively that the interviewee did not make the disputed statement. This example illustrates both the great value of verbatim transcripts of witness statements and the important point that it is impossible to predict in advance which witness interviews will yield the most important or the most controversial information.

There are other practical reasons why preparing verbatim transcripts of witness statements is advisable. Although it might appear initially that the

---

63. [159] This was the procedure followed by the Warren Commission and is the practice often followed in high-profile congressional investigations, *see, e.g.*, S. Hrg. 104-869, Vols. XIV–XVIII, Depositions before the Special Committee to Investigate Whitewater Development Corporation and Related Matters (GPO 1997) (multi-volume collection of staff depositions in the Senate Whitewater investigation), and of course is the normal procedure in both civil litigation depositions and grand jury criminal investigations, in which a court reporter will transcribe the proceedings.

64. [160] This is the procedure followed by the FBI, which requires agents to prepare a "302" memorandum to document an investigative interview. Whether FBI 302 reports are complete and accurate in all material respects is often an issue in subsequent criminal proceedings.

65. [161] KEAN & HAMILTON, *supra*, at 114.

costs and inconveniences (particularly when classified or highly confidential information is being discussed) outweigh the benefits of preparing verbatim transcripts, and that it is less costly and more efficient to instead rely on staff memoranda for an investigative record—the approach the 9/11 Commission followed—that is not necessarily the case. Enormous amounts of staff time and effort are required to draft complete and scrupulously accurate memoranda of witness interviews. If staff time was an unlimited resource, this would not be a concern, but the reality is that staff investigative time is always a scarce resource for investigative commissions. So the cost of not transcribing witness interviews is actually very high and the result of using a less precise method of documentation, as the Able Danger example discussed above demonstrates, may not satisfy a commission's needs if disputes subsequently arise about what a witness actually said to the commission's staff.

Cost, efficiency, and efficacy for resolving factual disputes are not the only reasons that preparing verbatim transcripts of all witness statements is the better practice for a national investigation commission to follow. As discussed above, availability of verbatim transcripts of witness interviews can be essential if issues subsequently arise as to whether or not a witness has knowingly and intentionally provided false information. A uniform practice of administering an oath to all witnesses is also advisable so as to make it clear that witnesses are under a strict legal obligation to provide complete and accurate testimony. For all of these reasons, despite the cost and inconvenience of doing so, the best practice is for investigative commissions to swear all witnesses and prepare verbatim transcripts of all witness statements [or maintain a digital audio or video recording of all witness statements].[66]

---

66. [167] This is the procedure that the Roberts Commission ultimately followed, after an initial false start taking unsworn and unrecorded statements from senior military officers. *See* Kitts, *supra*, at 24–25. It is also the procedure that the Warren Commission followed in most instances. The 9/11 Commission may have faced more obstacles than those commissions in following this approach, because significant portions of its investigation involved classified information. Without minimizing the difficulties presented by dealing with large amounts of classified information, there are ways to address the problem that will not compromise the accuracy and completeness of a commission's investigative record. Stenographers with security clearances can record witness statements. If witness information is too sensitive even to allow a stenographer with a security clearance to participate, then the session (or portions of the session, if the most sensitive issues can be addressed separately) can be tape recorded and the tape recording maintained under seal by the agency that controls the information. This practice would provide a means of resolving disputes like the "Able Danger" matter described above. It would also be desirable, in the interest of public disclosure and a complete historical record, to provide some mechanism for subsequent declassification review and eventual public release of all or most such commission records. This is similar to the procedures that Congress eventually adopted for dealing with the Kennedy assassination records, *see* President John F. Kennedy Assassination Records Collection Act of 1992, Pub. L. No. 102-526, 106 Stat. 3443, and the Nixon White House tape recordings, *see* Presidential Recordings and Materials Preservation Act of 1974, Pub. L. 93-526, 88 Stat. 1695. While such procedures might be overkill in a routine government investigation, for special investigative commissions pursuing matters as important as Pearl Harbor, the Kennedy assassination,

An investigative commission also should take precautions to ensure that its ability to obtain accurate and forthcoming testimony from witnesses is not compromised by external influences. As discussed above, the 9/11 Commission was concerned about government agency "minders" being present at staff interviews of government employees, but capitulated to the Bush administration's insistence that agency representatives be allowed to sit in on interviews. This is an area where the 9/11 Commission should not have compromised. The potential for mischief if government agency "minders" are allowed to "monitor" an employee's interview is obvious to anyone with any knowledge of how government bureaucracies work.[67] The problem is compounded when a major purpose of an investigation is to determine whether government agencies performed properly and whether there are management or policy problems within government that need to be addressed. It is simply unrealistic to believe that government agency employees will be forthright and candid in assessing the performance and possible shortcomings of the agency that employs them when they know that their statements will be reported back to their superiors at the agency. Future national investigative commissions should pay greater heed to the practical realities of investigative fact-finding and adopt procedures that will ensure as accurate and complete an investigative record as possible.

For the same reason, national investigative commissions investigating major historical events like Pearl Harbor, the Kennedy assassination, and the 9/11 attacks should be given the power to grant testimonial immunity to witnesses. The Warren Commission had immunity power, but did not use it. The 9/11 Commission did not have immunity power, but witness immunity issues did not arise during its investigation. More recently, concerns about granting immunity to witnesses have been a major point of contention in congressional consideration of the creation of some kind of commission to investigate the treatment of detainees and other actions of the Bush administration subsequent to the 9/11 terrorist attacks.[68]

An in-depth analysis of the immunity issue is beyond the scope of this [Chapter], but one central point merits emphasis—immunity power is often essential if an investigation is to discover the truth. This is the reason that immunity is routinely used in criminal investigations, and in many cases immunizing lower-level participants is the only way to obtain the true facts about

---

and the 9/11 attacks it is a mistake to shortchange history by adopting less rigorous measures on grounds of cost and convenience.

67. [170] The same concerns are present with witnesses from the private sector, but the problem is particularly acute in investigations focusing on the performance of government agencies, such as the three independent commission investigations that are the focus of this [Chapter].

68. [172] *See, e.g.*, Jack M. Balkin, *A Body of Inquiries*, N.Y. TIMES (Jan. 10, 2009) (arguing that "American commissions and hearings should have the power to bestow immunity to compel testimony").

criminal activity and hold responsible those who directed the activity. If it is appropriate to grant immunity in routine criminal prosecutions, allowing admitted criminals to escape punishment in return for providing essential information and testimony to prosecute others, the same tool should be available in an investigation into matters of enormous public importance such as those that are the subject of the commissions discussed in this [Chapter]. Two examples from recent history illustrate this point. Few today would argue that it was a mistake for the Senate Watergate Committee to grant John Dean immunity because society would have been better served by punishing Dean more harshly rather than having him share his dramatic story of Nixon White House misdeeds with a congressional committee and a riveted nation of television viewers. It is admittedly a closer case, but most would agree that the country was better served by having Oliver North and John Poindexter testify under immunity about the Reagan administration's Iran-Contra misconduct,[69] even though that televised congressional testimony ultimately caused their criminal convictions to be reversed and allowed them to escape punishment for the crimes they committed.[70]

These examples illustrate the principle that in some instances the public's need to know can outweigh the interests of the criminal justice system in pros-

---

69. [175] One reason the case is closer is that while subsequent events proved that John Dean was truthful in his Senate Watergate testimony, *see, e.g.*, BEN-VENISTE, *supra*, at 23 ("Everything that John Dean had testified to under oath before the Senate Watergate Committee, and more, was irrefutably corroborated by the tape-recorded words of the conspirators themselves."), there is reason to believe that North and Poindexter were less than truthful in their immunized testimony and probably shaded the truth to protect their superiors, *cf. Final Report of the Independent Counsel for Iran/Contra Matters*, Part XI, Concluding Observations (1993) ("Congress gave immunity to North and Poindexter, who incriminated only themselves and who largely exculpated those responsible for the initiation, supervision and support of their activities.").

70. [176] *See generally United States v. North ("North I")*, 910 F.2d 843 (D.C. Cir. 1990); *United States v. North ("North II")*, 920 F.2d 940, D.C. Cir. 1990 ("*North II*"), *cert. denied* 500 U.S. 941 (1991); United States v. Poindexter, 951 F.2d 369 (D.C. Cir. 1991), *cert. denied* 506 U.S. 1021 (1992). *But cf. Final Report of the Independent Counsel for Iran/Contra Matters*, Part XI, Concluding Observations (1993):

The disrespect for Congress by a popular and powerful President and his appointees was obscured when Congress accepted the tendered concept of a runaway conspiracy of subordinate officers and avoided the unpleasant confrontation with a powerful President and his Cabinet. In haste to display and conclude its investigation of this unwelcome issue, Congress destroyed the most effective lines of inquiry by giving immunity to Oliver L. North and John M. Poindexter so that they could exculpate and eliminate the need for the testimony of President Reagan and Vice President Bush.

Immunity is ordinarily given by a prosecutor to a witness who will incriminate someone more important than himself. Congress gave immunity to North and Poindexter, who incriminated only themselves and who largely exculpated those responsible for the initiation, supervision and support of their activities. This delayed and infinitely complicated the effort to prosecute North and Poindexter, and it largely destroyed the likelihood that their prompt conviction and appropriate sentence would induce meaningful cooperation.

ecuting particular individuals for their criminal actions.[71] As with consideration of the issue of appropriate subpoena power for a national investigative commission, consideration of the immunity issue is probably best examined not in the context of a controversial and politically charged current commission proposal, such as the proposed "truth commission" investigation of the Bush administration, but rather in the context of a commission that benefits from the clearer view of hindsight and subsequent experience, such as the Warren Commission investigation of the Kennedy assassination. One need only consider the damage to the reputation of our national government and the tremendous public resources that have been expended as a result of the failure of the Warren Commission's investigation to satisfy the public's concerns about the Kennedy assassination. If the facts of that investigation had been different, and definitive answers could have been obtained by granting immunity to a few individuals, doing so clearly would have been in the national interest. Future commissions investigating matters of great national importance should have the power to use every tool that our legal system provides in finding the truth about the matters they are charged with investigating, and immunity is perhaps the single most powerful truth-compelling tool in our legal arsenal.

6. Transparency and Public Access.

The final recommendations for independent investigative commission policies and procedures will be unsurprising in light of the arguments advanced

---

71. [177] Even the federal prosecutor who arguably suffered the greatest interference from immunity grants, Iran-Contra Independent Counsel Lawrence Walsh, has acknowledged that in cases of great public importance—and the independent commission investigations that are the subject of this [Chapter] undoubtedly are such cases—the public's right to know and Congress's need for information in order to legislate must prevail over the more narrow interests of the criminal justice system:

> [T]he competing roles of Congress and the Executive (here represented by Independent Counsel) must be borne in mind. As Independent Counsel recognized from the outset of his investigation, it is Congress (in the case of the Iran/contra affair, its Select Committees) that is primarily responsible for the accurate public disclosure of the facts concerning transactions such as the Iran/contra matters. Ultimately, it is Congress that is empowered to legislate in a manner that not only will preclude future similar transactions in a narrow sense, but that also will facilitate the effective management of foreign policy and that will discourage disregard for existing legal strictures.

> Although the Independent Counsel also has a reporting function, his first responsibility, in contrast, is the prosecution of criminal conduct. Accordingly, it is not primarily his duty to develop for the public a knowledge of what occurred.

> When a conflict between the oversight and prosecutorial roles develops—as plainly occurred in the Iran/contra affair—the law is clear that it is Congress that must prevail. This is no more than a recognition of the high political importance of Congress's responsibility. It also is the appropriate place to strike the balance, as resolution of this conflict calls for the exercise of a seasoned political judgment that must take a broad view of the national interest.

Final Report of the Independent Counsel for Iran/Contra Matters, Part XI, Concluding Observations (1993).

above. History shows that secrecy and lack of transparency are perhaps the greatest long-term threats to a commission investigation. Future commissions should avoid following procedures that may later enable critics to charge a "cover up" or a failure to vigorously pursue all appropriate and reasonable lines of investigative inquiry.[72] For that reason the operating policies and procedures of a national investigative commission should tilt strongly toward openness and transparency whenever and however possible. In general, commission hearings should be open to the public and the testimony of all significant witnesses should be presented in open public hearings.[73] If there are legitimate reasons why particular testimony cannot be made public, such as testimony involving classified information, then provision should be made for closed sessions, but with procedures in place to provide for eventual public release of the information. To further facilitate eventual public disclosure of commission activities and an accurate historical record, minutes of nonpublic commission meetings should be prepared and either made public with the commission's final report or made subject to procedures facilitating their eventual public release.[74] The end result of these policies and procedures should be a commission fact-finding and deliberation process that is open to contemporaneous

---

72. [181] The Warren Commission example alone is sufficient to demonstrate the validity of this assertion. *See generally* KEAN & HAMILTON, *supra*, at 25 ("For decades, the Warren Commission's findings have been poked and prodded by conspiracy theorists.").

73. [182] *Cf.* KEAN & HAMILTON, *supra*, at 29 ("We could not repeat those mistakes [of the Warren Commission and the Roberts Commission]. To avoid them we had to create a new model for how to conduct a high-profile commission. We would be nonpartisan and independent. *We would be public instead of secretive.*") (emphasis added). Notwithstanding Kean and Hamilton's after-the-fact embrace of a public approach to the 9/11 Commission's work, another commissioner has described how narrowly the commission avoided what he characterized as "a near-death experience" of adopting a closed hearing approach, voting by only a 6–4 margin (with Hamilton in the minority favoring closed hearings) to hold open hearings. *See* BEN-VENISTE, *supra*, at 219–20. Ben-Veniste speculates that perhaps Lee Hamilton's "bad experience with Oliver North in the Iran-Contra hearings over which he presided as chairman of the House Intelligence Committee—where North's media-savvy performance seemed to wrest control of the hearings from his congressional interrogators—had a scarring effect on Lee." *See id.*

74. [184] One of the members of the 9/11 Commission has subsequently provided a candid and enlightening account of the differing views of the members of that commission on the issue of how to treat the minutes of commission meetings:

I pushed early and continuously throughout the life of the commission for the most vigorous and independent examination of the facts and circumstances leading up to 9/11. I had no quarrel with those who were more interested in policy considerations and recommendations but I felt those recommendations would have to flow from a robust and credible investigation of the facts in order to be accepted by Congress and the public. And I believed we should operate in as open a manner as possible. I was therefore taken aback by the proposal voiced by our chairman at the February [2003] meeting that the minutes of our meetings reflect only decisions made by the commission and not include the comments of individual commissioners or record the way we might vote individually on issues before us. Eventually, after a few meetings, I was to prevail in my repeated requests for more "fulsome" minutes that reflected what we talked about and how we voted. And, when we were finishing our final report, I proposed that we include the minutes of our meetings in an appendix to the report. My proposal was soundly rejected;

public examination and that will create the most accurate and complete possible historical record.

Conclusion

These recommendations are based on one guiding principle, that when investigating matters of enormous national importance every possible effort should be made to conduct the investigation in a manner which will ensure that all relevant facts are discovered and made public. Although the special circumstances of particular future investigative commissions may require departures from some of these recommendations, past experience suggests that future commissions should be extremely wary of adopting any procedure that might later call into question the independence, thoroughness, and good faith of their investigation.

The Special Commission That Was Not Created: The January 6 Committee— A New Paradigm for Congressional Investigations?

In May 2021, after the January 6 attack on the U.S. Capitol, Representative Bennie Thompson, the chair of the House Homeland Security Committee, and Representative John Katko, the committee's ranking member, introduced legislation to create a bipartisan commission to investigate the attack. The proposed commission was modeled on the 9/11 Commission, with five members from each political party and subpoena power that required either a bipartisan majority vote of the members or agreement of the chair and vice chair. The House of Representatives passed the bill on May 19, 2021, by a bipartisan vote of 252–175, with 35 Republicans joining all Democrats to approve the legislation. The bill died in the Senate on May 28, 2021, where a vote of 54–35 (with eleven Senators not voting) fell short of the 60 votes required to invoke cloture and overcome a Republican filibuster.

On June 24, 2021, Speaker of the House Nancy Pelosi announced that she would create a House select committee to investigate the January 6 attack. On June 30, 2021, the House passed a resolution creating a 13-member select committee, with only two Republicans, Representative Liz Cheney of Wyoming and Representative Adam Kinzinger of Illinois, voting in favor of the resolution. Under the resolution, Pelosi was to appoint the thirteen members of the committee, five of whom were to be appointed in consultation with House Minority Leader Kevin McCarthy. Pelosi later rejected two of McCarthy's five selections for the committee, and McCarthy then withdrew all five of his selections. Pelosi then named Cheney and Kinzinger to the committee, with

---

the minutes were not to be publicly available until June 2009, five years from when we issued our report.

Ben-Veniste, *supra*, at 214.

Cheney to serve as the committee's vice chair. The result was a select committee that was technically bipartisan but was created without any members that were selected or approved by the House Republican leadership.

These unusual circumstances led to a House select committee, chaired by Bennie Thompson and co-chaired by Cheney, that had only two Republican members and no significant partisan discord between the committee's Democratic and Republican members. The resulting cooperation enabled the committee to employ some new techniques that departed from the traditional approach to congressional hearings. One commentator analyzed the ways in which the January 6 Committee used "TV tricks" in conducting its hearings:

> Skeptics call the Congressional hearings on the January 6th siege of the U.S. Capitol show business....
>
> Yet the House select committee investigating the attack is achieving something rare on Capitol Hill: Hearings that are surprisingly tangible, understandable, and substantive instead of the typical Congressional ping-pong match of clashes, arguments and even more arguments about whose turn it is to argue....
>
> To achieve that, the hearings relied on subtle television news techniques and choices, rather than sensationalism. And they did so in two ways.
>
> The first involves how the material is shaped.
>
> With each day's hearing, the Jan. 6 committee has committed to a single story with a narrative arc, consisting of main characters and dramatic conflicts. Each panel assembled fits in with the larger theme of the day, building to a larger point. And the investigative panel has drawn upon a raft of authenticating sources—audio, depositions, emails, memos, social media posts, texts, video, and more....
>
> These presentations relied on a second television news technique, which is to maintain a clear story told at a brisk pace and focused on the desired subjects. The committee hired former ABC News President James Goldston. Associates tell NPR he sees the job as a civic contribution rather than a partisan task.
>
> As a result, lawmakers on the committee dispensed with the usual five-minute opening statements that are often an opportunity for grandstanding for hometown coverage or viral moments. They did not engage in round-robin questioning, but designated a specific panel member for each session.
>
> In this way, the committee sidesteps confusion of whom to listen to. Excerpts of taped testimony or public speeches are rarely longer than a minute or two—often far shorter....
>
> When there are text exchanges or Twitter threads, each statement is unveiled on the screen individually, with pauses for the implications to seep in. To vary the voices, different committee investigators narrate what happened in specific elements, introducing video and audio clips....

The viewers absorb the importance of what is being talked about, not the prestige of who is speaking.

This represents an extraordinary demonstration of discipline for a congressional committee, with a minimum of showboating, yielding hearings put together like a Ted Koppel-vintage episode of *Nightline* or *Dateline NBC* or a taut investigative podcast....

More than 20 million people watched the first night of prime-time hearings; fewer have watched the daytime sessions since....

Yet those numbers best the audience for Trump's first impeachment. And the nation is hearing heartfelt testimony by people in difficult jobs trying as best they can to live up to their oaths. In many cases, they are Republicans. By and large, their accounts have forced the nation's news outlets to pay attention, distributing their message to a far wider audience on the air and online.

The vast majority of Americans, 70% according to a recent Quinnipiac University poll, say it's important for Congress to hold these hearings so the public can learn what led to the Jan. 6 attack.

The ancient Greeks left us with two big stories about how unheeded warnings are treated. Cassandra the prophet was invariably prescient. And she was equally invariably ignored. The people she sought to warn were time and again overtaken by violence and doom. There was a lot of that going around. It was the Trojan Wars, after all.

The other story is a fable, courtesy, we are told, of a storyteller named Aesop. There's a boy with ominous concerns of a wolf and hoax cries for help. The boy repeatedly makes the equivalent of classical Greek prank 911 calls. The wolf ultimately devours the town's flock of sheep as everyone tunes out the warnings.

The legacy of the House Select Committee investigating the Capitol attack will hinge on whether viewers and the voting public treat it as prophetic or hyperbolic. Thanks to careful adaptation of TV techniques, the committee has proved, so far, to have a strong and disturbing story to tell.

David Folkenflick, *Jan. 6 Hearings Use TV Tricks to Great Effect Even as Critics Call Them Show Biz*, NPR.ORG (June 23, 2022).[75]

As noted above, one reason the January 6 Committee has been able to depart from the typical approach to congressional hearings is the lack of partisan discord among the committee's members. This unity of purpose has made it possible to hold hearings that are more effective at communicating the committee's findings to the public:

---

75. ©2022 National Public Radio, Inc. Excerpts from news report titled "Jan. 6 hearings use TV tricks to great effect even as critics call them" by David Folkenflik was originally published on NPR. org on June 23, 2022, and is used with the permission of NPR. Any unauthorized duplication is strictly prohibited.

Too often, particularly in the past decade, the public has seen congressional hearings that either made little sense or resembled political food fights. With members often haranguing witnesses and denouncing their own colleagues, these proceedings suggested that the "investigation" was focused more on scoring political points than on exposing the facts. One of the core reasons for this, of course, is the extreme polarization that continues to grip Congress, but another is that with respect to highly partisan issues, the standard hearing protocol tends to obscure key issues, rather than reveal facts in a clear way so the public can understand them.

Congressional hearings commonly follow a format in which the chair and ranking member each give an opening statement followed by statements by other members of the committee. That is then followed by opening statements by the first panel of witnesses. Each member, then, is usually given five minutes to question the witnesses on the panel. The order of questioning rotates between the two parties, Republicans and Democrats, until all committee members who want to ask questions have been satisfied. Usually there are several such panels.

While the intention of that process is to give each member the opportunity to participate, when the issue is highly partisan the result for the listening audience is often confusion and diversion from the most important facts and the true purpose of the hearing. The Jan. 6 committee chose to break that mold and agree beforehand to have brief opening statements by the chair and vice chair, no opening statements by the other members or witnesses, and to limit questioning largely to one member. The result has been to dramatically improve the clarity and public understanding of the facts.

Complementing this new order is the committee's use of visuals—excerpts from the earlier depositions and visual displays of key texts and memoranda. Using this technology has enabled the public to see firsthand the evidence the committee members have seen and heard. The difference in the impact is dramatic.

Some critics complain that the committee had made up its mind on the facts before the hearings. Well, that's true in most congressional hearings. The job of the committee during its investigation is to dig deeply into the facts so that the committee knows what the documents reveal and what the witnesses have said and will say in their testimony. The purpose of the hearings is to show the public what the committee has learned—in particular, the key evidence and how the committee interprets it. And when the subject of the hearings is highly political, the key evidence can get lost in the political back and forth among the members or in questions being asked that are extraneous to the purpose of the hearing. See, for example, the Benghazi hearings.

But here, the Jan. 6 committee has shown us how a committee, with forethought, the judicious use of technology, and bipartisan cooperation, can provide to the public detailed information in a clear and convincing manner that focuses on the substance of the material being presented and not on the personalities or political aspirations of the committee members.

This requires, of course, the involvement and agreement of all committee members. Obviously, such unity of purpose is not always possible; in fact, it's all too rare. But it is possible, as evidenced by previous successful investigations, such as Watergate and the Joint Inquiry into the 9-11 Terrorist Attacks, where all participants agree that informing the public in an understandable way is the real goal of congressional hearings. Hopefully, future investigations of this nature will adopt the mindset and methods of the Jan. 6 committee for the benefit of the public and American democracy.

Jim Townsend, *The January 6 Committee Is Modeling a Better Way to Conduct Hearings*, THE HILL (July 12, 2022).

At the time of this writing, the work of the January 6 Committee was still underway, and the committee had not concluded its hearings or issued its final report and recommendations. Even before the committee had concluded its work, however, no less of an expert on investigative hearings than Lee Hamilton—co-chair of the Iran-Contra Committee and vice chair of the 9/11 Commission—recognized that the hearing techniques employed by the January 6 Committee had "demonstrated what congressional committees are capable of achieving":

> Most news stories, of course, have focused on the alarming revelations uncovered by the committee—in essence, the lengths to which a sitting president and his allies went in trying to short-circuit the clearly expressed will of the American people. But some coverage has instead focused on how the select committee has gone about its work: the technology it's using and its careful structuring of the hearings to create a clear narrative of the events leading up to and following the attack on the Capitol. . . .
>
> There is much about this that's new: the use of relevant footage, maps, and reconstructions that are available instantly when needed; interweaving videotaped and in-person testimony to deepen the narrative; production values that make the hearings seem up-to-the-minute, rather than a throwback to an earlier era. But there is also much about this that is, in fact, time-tested congressional process.
>
> What the hearings are doing is what congressional committees at their best have always done: focus on a complicated topic, present the facts about it to the American people, leave us all better informed than we were before, and possibly have an impact on how government operates. It's not hard to come up with a list of high-profile congressional hearings that have had this kind of effect, from the 1954 Army-McCarthy hearings to the Watergate hearings in 1973 to the 1987 Iran-Contra hearings and the 2019 hearings on special counsel Robert Mueller's investigation into Russian interference in the 2016 elections. But I would argue that even low-profile committee work—hearings

aimed at checking in on the operations of the executive branch or how well policy initiatives have performed—have held similar value for our democracy.

I've always believed that part of the job of a politician is to educate the public—about the facts and about their meaning for the US and for public policy. It is incredibly difficult these days for voters to sort out information—we're all bombarded with facts, opinion, information and misinformation and even disinformation. But if, as a country, we're to build consensus based on the real world, then you have to start with the facts. Ultimately, a democratic society depends on the ability of citizens to form good judgments based on the realities facing us; if they don't, the country suffers.

The same, of course, goes for policy-makers. In that case, the country depends not just on their ability to ground their work in the facts, but to explore an issue and then deliberate on what to do about it. The deliberative process—which in Congress was once rooted in the work of committees—produces better law: It forces members of Congress to understand an issue, accommodate different interests, and ultimately knock out bad ideas and bad proposals in favor of initiatives that can command a consensus. Overall, as congressional power has consolidated in the hands of a few strong leaders, committees have lost that kind of influence; Congress generally holds far fewer hearings than it did a few decades ago.

So I take the Jan. 6 committee's innovations as a good sign. It has updated the mechanics of the process to create a compelling lesson in the value of thorough research and leveling plainly with the American people about what the facts show. In short, it has demonstrated what Congress is capable of achieving. Here's hoping other committees are taking note.

Lee Hamilton, *The Jan. 6 Committee Reminds Us of What Congress Can Do*, Center on Representative Government, University of Indiana (July 27, 2022).

Notes and Questions

1. Fleeting Accolades or Lasting Impact? As the commentary above indicates, the initial reviews of the work of the January 6 Committee were favorable. How much impact has the January 6 Committee had on the conduct of congressional investigations? Have some of the "television-friendly" techniques described above been adopted by more typical partisan-divided congressional committees? Or will the January 6 Committee prove to be more of a "one-off" because of the unusual circumstances that resulted in Speaker Nancy Pelosi choosing all the members of the Committee?

2. The Power of Video Evidence—and Adequate Funding. Review the recommendations for independent investigative commissions at the end of the previous section of the Chapter. Did the January 6 Committee effectively implement some of those recommendations? For example, the January 6 Committee used video recordings of pre-hearing depositions, which could then be excerpted and played at its public hearings, to document witness testimony. Has that innovation been widely used in other congressional investigations since the January 6 Committee hearings? Will its demonstration of the power of video evidence prove to be one of the January 6 Committee's most significant and enduring influences on the conduct of congressional investigations? Consider also the recommendation at the end of the previous section of this Chapter for adequate funding and staff resources at the outset of an investigation. Was some of the success of the January 6 Committee due to the unusually generous funding and staffing it enjoyed? Commentators have noted that the January 6 Committee differed from most congressional committees in its funding and staff resources:

> Yet another reason for the committee's success so far is the resources allocated to it. Over the first four months of 2022, the committee spent an amount of money comparable to other permanent committees in the House—whose responsibilities extend far beyond completing a single investigation. (It's worth noting that the Jan. 6 committee should have filed reports on its spending for additional months but has yet to do so.) What's more, funding for regular committee operations in the House is generally divided across the majority and minority parties in a roughly two-thirds/one-third ratio. But given the unity of purpose of the Jan. 6 panel, we might think of its funding as somewhat more comparable to the majority staff of a committee—meaning that the Jan. 6 investigators effectively had a much larger budget for their narrower set of responsibilities than a typical set of congressional investigators.

> According to the most recent available quarterly data from the House of Representatives, as of late March [2022], the committee employed roughly 50 employees, including a former Republican member of Congress. Since then, they've also brought on, in some capacity, the former president of ABC News, who reportedly is helping the committee produce its hearings as gripping television. Some high-profile staffing decisions had made headlines for unfortunate reasons, especially early on: Two hires, a Department of Homeland Security attorney who had spent time overseeing the agency's intelligence operations and a former CIA inspector general, have previously been accused of retaliating against whistleblowers. But the staff's ranks are filled mostly with the kind of experienced Hill staff and former federal government lawyers one would want when trying to conduct a serious investigation. All this suggests that the importance of sufficiently resourcing Congress's work is one important lesson that the legislative branch should learn from the Jan. 6 committee's successes thus far.

> But even in acknowledging good work, we need also to be honest about the limits of the committee's model and approach. A great deal of what was so effective about the Jan. 6 committee will not apply so easily to much of what Congress does—nor should we want it to.

> The single-minded commitment of a group of bipartisan House members to delineate out-of-bounds conduct in a democracy is worth celebrating at this

moment, and we certainly want legislators to find common ground on the rule of law and reining in executive branch overreach. But bipartisanship should be seen as a means to an end, not an end in and of itself. . . .

Quinta Juricec & Molly E. Reynolds, *The Lessons—and Limits—of the Jan. 6 Committee*, LAWFARE (Aug. 5, 2022).

3. Allegations of FBI Failings—Yet Again. Note 3 following the section of this Chapter on the 9/11 Commission investigation discusses questions faced by both the 9/11 Commission and the Warren Commission about whether the FBI had failed to act on evidence in its possession prior to the 9/11 attacks and the assassination of President Kennedy. Similar questions arose after the January 6 attack on the U.S. Capitol:

> While the public may have been surprised by what happened on Jan. 6, the makings of the insurrection had been spotted at every level, from one side of the country to the other. The red flags were everywhere.
>
> One of the most striking flares came when a tipster called the FBI on the afternoon of Dec. 20: Trump supporters were discussing online how to sneak guns into Washington to "overrun" police and arrest members of Congress in January, according to internal bureau documents obtained by The Post. The tipster offered specifics: Those planning violence believed they had "orders from the President," used code words such as "pickaxe" to describe guns and posted the times and locations of four spots around the country for caravans to meet the day before the joint session. On one site, a poster specifically mentioned Sen. Mitt Romney (R-Utah) as a target.
>
> An FBI official who assessed the tip noted that its criminal division had received a "significant number" of alerts about threats to Congress and other government officials. The FBI passed the information to law enforcement agencies in D.C. but did not pursue the matter. "The individual or group identified during the Assessment does not warrant further FBI investigation at this time," the internal report concluded.
>
> The paralysis that led to one of the biggest security failures in the nation's history was driven by unique breakdowns inside each law enforcement agency and was exacerbated by the patchwork nature of security across a city where responsibilities are split between local and federal authorities.
>
> While the U.S. government has been consumed with heading off future terrorist plots since 9/11, its agencies failed to effectively harness the security and intelligence infrastructure built in the wake of that assault by Islamic extremists to look inward at domestic threats.

Red Flags, WASH. POST (Oct. 31, 2021) (special investigative report). Are criticisms of the FBI in connection with the Kennedy assassination, the 9/11 attacks, and the January 6 attack just "Monday morning quarterbacking" that fails to appreciate the challenges faced by hardworking law enforcement officials who do not have the same benefits of hindsight that their critics enjoy? Or are those criticisms indicators of a recurring failure to act on obvious red flags at a large and extremely bureaucratic institution? If you think it is the latter, what solution would you propose? How would you change the current federal law enforcement structure to improve threat assessment and provide for responsible proactive threat-prevention measures that do not undermine our civil liberties?

Chapter Nine

Concluding Observations

The Challenges of Representing Clients in Congressional Investigations and the Importance of Effective Congressional Oversight

While the conventional assumption is that the strength of legislative bodies lies in the power to legislate, a respectable tradition has long argued that it lies as much or more in the power to investigate. The investigative power may indeed be the sharpest legislative weapon against Executive aggrandizement.

Arthur M. Schlesinger, Jr., 1975

Representing Clients in Congressional Investigations

The congressional hearing, as demonstrated by the materials in the preceding chapters of this book, is a unique forum that can unnerve, test, and even destroy the most resolute, adept, and competent witnesses. With its virtually open-ended charter, lack of ground rules, and complete absence of predictable outcomes, the congressional investigative hearing becomes the ultimate Rorschach test in which the outcome is measured by witness survival and public perception. The unique nature of the congressional investigative forum creates special problems for both the witness who provides testimony and the counsel who represents the witness. Some of the essential considerations in preparing a witness for congressional testimony are outlined below.

A. Psychological and Attitudinal Preparation for Congressional Testimony

Like performance in any public forum, attitudinal conditioning and psychological preparation by counsel can play a key role in the ability of a witness to respond to the congressional inquiry. To perform competently in the congressional arena, counsel must consider carefully both the nature of the forum and the predicament of the witness who must appear in the forum. While the congressional inquiry is as old as the republic itself, and its methods more extensively chronicled than almost any other institution, it is less appreciated by most practicing attorneys than many of its rivals, such as the grand jury or the civil trial court. The preceding materials in this book have been selected to assist prospective counsel in congressional investigations better understand the unique characteristics of, and the special legal rules applicable to, the congressional investigative process.

In preparing a witness for congressional testimony, counsel must first focus attention on the extraordinary demands that are placed upon a client who is called as a witness in a congressional proceeding. The special predicament in which the witness confronting the modern investigative committee is placed has been recognized since the dawn of the modern, televised era of congressional investigative activity: "He may well be embarrassed and resentful at being summoned to appear before an investigative body at all. Nowhere is the spotlight of public attention focused more sharply than upon the witness called before a congressional committee. There, frequently heard, and since the advent of television, eyed by the American public, he faces the queries of the nation's law makers."[1] It is essential in this situation that counsel undertake to prepare the witness by providing a perspective that will allow them to understand the origins and common threads of congressional inquiries so as to induce a more informed, and therefore more comfortable and competent, testimonial performance. And, as is discussed in more detail below, the experience of testifying at a modern, televised congressional hearing is much more of a dramatic "performance" than that of a witness in any other legal proceeding—more so even than a defendant in a criminal trial who chooses to take the stand and testify in his or her own defense.

The first point that counsel should convey to the witness in beginning the process of preparation for congressional testimony is an appreciation of the long history and ancient origins of the congressional investigative committee. "A legislative committee of inquiry ... is an institution rivaling most legislative institutions in the antiquity of its origin."[2] And, in many respects, the institution has changed very little since the Parliamentary and colonial experiences that defined the history of the institution. From the House investigation of St. Clair's ill-fated Indian expedition in 1792, to the Credit Mobilier scandal of 1870, to the modern era that is the focus of this book and encompasses the Teapot Dome, HUAC/McCarthy, Watergate, Iran-Contra, Whitewater, and January 6 investigations, the congressional investigatory mode has become engrained as part of both the widely accepted legislative function and the national psyche. Although columnists, witnesses, and academic commentators all have on countless occasions chronicled its excesses, called for its reform, and excoriated the media for dissemination of its one-sided proceedings, the institution of the congressional "investigation" has not only survived, but flourished. If nothing else, the inevitability and predictability

---

1. Note, *Contumacy Before the Legislature*, 21 GEO. WASH. L. REV. 602, 603 (1952).

2. James Landis, *Constitutional Limitations on the Congressional Powers of Investigation*, 40 HARV. L. REV. 153, 159 (1926).

of the congressional investigative hearing should help to ease witness apprehension and temper any outrage over the "unfairness" of the predicament.

Because the witness faces a forum that he or she does not control, and which must be confronted on a procedurally imbalanced and mismatched (against the witness) basis, the equalizing factor must be the sheer mental acuity and perspicacity of the witness—facing the forum with an understanding of both the process that will be followed and the role of the witness in that process. The witness should understand that, unlike collateral fora, congressional committees do not render immediate verdicts or judgments, inflict punishments, or find parties liable. Indeed, the considered choice of the Framers of the Constitution was to deny the legislature these powers because of the abuses of "trial by legislature" they had witnessed in England.

Rather than the more widely understood power of judicial bodies to decide disputes and render judgments, the power of the congressional investigative committee derives from its ability to publicly expose wrongdoing and castigate the perpetrators, to roam freely in and out of subject areas, to use unauthenticated documents or other "evidence" that would not be admissible in a judicial proceeding, to extol virtues and condemn vices—in short to create an "atmosphere" in which to explore social issues and draw conclusions. This aspect of the congressional investigative process has been harshly condemned throughout the history of the republic, but those condemnations have not diminished to any significant degree the awesome investigatory powers that a congressional investigative committee can wield. In the nineteenth century, Justice Samuel Miller, the second of President Lincoln's five appointees to the Supreme Court, authored a decision that was highly critical of Congress' exercise of its investigative power[3] and indeed for years was viewed as casting grave doubt on the ability of Congress to investigate to assist itself in drafting legislation. In writing privately around the time of the case, the Justice expressed views aptly reflecting the sentiments of more contemporary critics of congressional excess:

> I think the public has been much abused, the time of legislative bodies uselessly consumed and rights of the citizens ruthlessly invaded under the now familiar pretext of legislative investigation and that it is time that it was understood that courts and grand juries are the only inquisitions into crime in this

---

3. In *Kilbourn v. Thompson*, 103 U.S. 168 (1880), a special House committee was formed to inquire into the nature of "a real estate pool" and transactions involved in the bankruptcy of Jay Cooke & Co. "The House resolution" authorized the committee "to compel testimony stressed the government's interest in the case as a result of 'improvement deposits' of public money having been made with the London branch of the bankrupt company." M. Nelson McGreary, *Congressional Investigations: Historical Developments*, 18 U. Chi. L. Rev. 425, 428 (1951). When the manager of the pool was asked by the committee to produce certain papers, he declined and was arrested by the House Sergeant-at-Arms. The Supreme Court, in an opinion by Justice Miller, ruled for the witness and held that the committee had exceeded its investigatory powers by inquiring "into the personal affairs of individuals ... [which] could result in no valid legislation on the subject to which the inquiry referred." *See* 103 U.S. at 195. Subsequent Supreme Court decisions arising out of the Teapot Dome (discussed in Chapter 1 above) and McCarthy era (discussed in Chapter 2 above) investigations adopted a more generous—though not unlimited—conception of the scope of the investigative powers of congressional committees.

country. I do not recognize the doctrine that Congress is the *grand inquest* of the nation, or has any such function to perform, nor that it can by the name of a report slander the citizen so as to protect the newspaper which publishes such slander. If the whole body cannot do this much less can one house do it....

As regards needed information on subjects purely legislative no doubt committees can be raised to inquire and report, money can be used to pay for such information and laws may be made to compel reluctant witnesses to give it under proper guaranty of their personal rights. This is sufficient, without subjecting a witness to the unlimited power of a legislative committee or a single branch of the legislative body.[4]

Much the same sentiments were expressed by critics of congressional excesses during the Teapot Dome investigations. Professor Wigmore excoriated the Teapot Dome committee proceedings as follows:

The senatorial debauch of investigation—poking into political garbage cans and dragging sewers of political intrigue—filled the winter with stench which has not yet passed away.... As a prosecutor, the Senate presented a spectacle ... [and] fell ... in the popular estimate to the level of professional searchers of the municipal dunghills.[5]

What is important about these remarkably consistent nineteenth and early-twentieth century criticisms of the congressional investigative process is not the obvious tone of disdain or even the pejorative cast placed on a recognized constitutional function of the Congress by so noted and respected a legal scholar as Wigmore, but the fact that they ultimately had no significant impact. As previous chapters document, the congressional investigative function continued to flourish throughout the first half of the twentieth century, survived the excesses of the McCarthy era, and then blossomed into national theatre under the bright television lights that accompanied the Watergate and Iran-Contra hearings.

In preparing a witness for a congressional appearance, fostering an appreciation of these historical antecedents is critical. The witness should accept the reality that his or her testimony, personally challenging and unpleasant though it may be, is another in a long line of exercises on a continuum extending back throughout American history. The hearing must be viewed, therefore, with perspective, and this alone can reduce the disabling effects associated with an appearance by a witness before an oversight committee.

A second essential step for counsel in a congressional investigation is to help the witness purge himself of any feelings of persecution, however justified or well founded, because it detracts from <u>performance</u> at the hearing and performance—the ability to

---

4. Charles Fairman, *Justice Samuel F. Miller: A Study of a Judicial Statesman*, 50 Pol. Sci. Q. 15, 35–36, n.72 (1935) *quoting* Letter from Samuel F. Miller to William Pitt Ballinger (Mar. 20, 1881).

5. John H. Wigmore, *Evidence—Legislative Power to Compel Testimonial Disclosure*, 19 Ill. L. Rev. 452, 453 (1925).

respond under fire—is the only gauge of success. A witness will be less likely to feel persecuted and unfairly treated if he or she appreciates the inherently political nature of the congressional investigative process that makes it unlike other legal proceedings:

> The other major differences between the grand jury and the legislative committee arise from the differing motivations and pressures on their members. The grand jurors are at least formally independent of political pressure. Their position presents an obvious contrast with that of the legislator whose sensitivity to political considerations <u>might</u> encourage him to undertake spectacular investigations and might give him a strong interest in uncovering unpopular conduct.[6]

The witness should be advised that blatantly political motives on the part of legislators in pursuing an investigation are not fruitful grounds for objection, because the courts have held that the "motives" of legislators may not be questioned by either the judicial or executive branch.[7] The witness should also be advised that the license given to legislators extends beyond motivation to conduct during a hearing. The Supreme Court has recognized that a legislator's special status in this regard "has enabled reckless men to slander [in committee hearings] and even destroy others with impunity, but that was the conscious choice of the Framers."[8] It is imperative that a witness understand and accept this constitutional "fact of life" in order to be prepared to remain stoic and unperturbed in the face of possibly abusive and insulting questioning by legislators.

Once the political nature of the process is understood, a well-prepared witness can take some solace from the fact that the legal risks presented by a congressional investigative hearing are almost exclusively collateral and indirect. Short of refusing to answer questions deemed beyond the scope of congressional ken and being held in contempt or being prosecuted for false or perjurious testimony, little direct legal exposure exists. What the witness does well to remember is the list of persons who have appeared before congressional committees and who have been "targeted" not for the substance of their actions, but for sometimes seemingly trivial inconsistencies constructed by the committee as obstruction or perjury. Such risks are discussed in more detail below.

In conclusion, to prepare for the ordeal of a congressional investigative hearing the witness must appreciate, and in some sense accept, the historical underpinnings of the exercise. Witnesses must recognize that the hearing is largely "staged" for the ulterior purposes of the committee (to create a particular legislative record or perhaps simply to use the witness to score political points), and not necessarily to elicit a complete and accurate picture. The role that is left for the witness in this often inhospitable environment is simply to strive to get his or her "story" (or that of his or her company) into "the

---

6. Note, *The Grand Jury as an Investigatory Body*, 74 Harv. L. Rev. 590, 602 (1961).

7. *United States v. Johnson*, 383 U.S. 169 (1966); *United States v. Brewster*, 408 U.S. 501, 516 (1972).

8. *Hutchinson v. Proxmire*, 443 U.S. 111, 131–32 (1979), *quoting United States v. Brewster*, 408 U.S. at 516.

record." The witness should envision the hearing as a dissertation for posterity and an opportunity to establish a record that can be cited in the future. Thoughts of "satisfying" the committee inquiries, ameliorating its biases, or shaking its basic assumptions should be abandoned in favor of simply making "the record" for your case. With these goals firmly in mind, the witness is mentally and psychologically prepared, and the hearing can be approached with less trepidation.

B. Avoiding False Statements, Perjury, and Obstruction of Justice Charges

Once the witness is mentally and psychologically prepared to face the rigors of providing congressional testimony, the attention of counsel must shift to the most serious legal risks that the witness faces when providing congressional testimony. For counsel advising a congressional witness, the prime directive is to avoid allowing the witness to commit a crime while providing testimony. A number of federal statutes apply to congressional testimony—whether sworn "on the record" testimony provided pursuant to subpoena at a formal hearing or unsworn statements provided voluntarily in an informal interview or deposition conducted by legislators or staff. The relevant statutory provisions were summarized in a law review article noting that successful prosecutions for lying to Congress are surprisingly rare (but not so rare as to remove the risk of criminal liability):

P.J. Meitl, *The Perjury Paradox: The Amazing Under-Enforcement of the Laws Regarding Lying to Congress*

25 QUINNIPIAC LAW REVIEW 547, 565–70 (2007)

[Ed. Note: Some footnotes omitted and some footnotes moved to text.]

In general, three federal statutes have been designed and utilized to safeguard Congress's right to obtain truthful information. First, 18 U.S.C. §1621, with roots dating to 1909, deals with perjury directly, making it a felony to lie to Congress under oath. Second, 18 U.S.C. §1505, a felony obstruction statute, makes it a crime to influence, obstruct, or impede congressional investigations. Lastly, 18 U.S.C. §1001, the basic federal false statements statute, has been used by prosecutors to reach untruthful statements made by witnesses. Although these statutes carry significant penalties for violations, each presents difficult problems in relation to enforcement. Thorny elements and high standards of proof, coupled with powerful defenses, often leave prosecutors and Congress with large obstacles to contend with in the contemplation of bringing a case against an individual for lying to Congress.

1. 18 U.S.C. §1621.

The general perjury statute, 18 U.S.C. §1621, makes it a crime for those who have taken an oath to lie before a competent tribunal. The statute states:

Whoever—(1) having taken an oath before a competent tribunal, officer, or person, in any case in which a law of the United States authorizes an oath to be administered, that he will testify, declare, depose, or certify truly, or that any written testimony, declaration, deposition, or certificate by him subscribed, is true, willfully and contrary to such oath states or subscribes any material matter which he does not believe to be true; is guilty of perjury ...

The government needs to prove that the witness took an oath authorized by a law of the United States, before a competent tribunal, and while under such oath, willfully or knowingly made a false statement as to material facts. The first two elements of the statute are rather straightforward. The oath requirement is easily satisfied and need not take any particular form. Courts have construed "competent tribunal" to include congressional committees so long as they are acting within proper legislative purposes.[9]

Section 1621, however, does present three difficult requirements. First, the prosecution must prove that the defendant testified with willfulness or knowledge that his statement was false beyond a reasonable doubt. Unless the defendant admits to his lies, this requirement must be proved through circumstantial evidence, which is often time-consuming and difficult.

Second, the prosecution must prove that the statement was actually false. In previous decades, this was only satisfied by direct evidence, but recently courts have allowed circumstantial evidence to be used to meet the threshold. Typically, this type of evidence cannot be accomplished solely upon the testimony of a single witness. Thus, courts have generally required two witnesses to corroborate a statement's untruthfulness before a conviction can be sustained. This requirement can be bypassed if other evidence is presented that can be used to corroborate the testimony of at least one witness regarding the truthfulness of the statement.

Third, the false statement must also be material under section 1621, meaning that it "is capable of influencing" the tribunal to which it is addressed with respect to "any proper matter of inquiry." In general, when evaluating materiality, "courts consider the venue in which the false testimony was made" and the "greater the tribunal's authority to investigate, a greater number of statements are considered material." Thus, given Congress's expansive powers to investigate, most statements will be deemed material.

There are some significant defenses to perjury under section 1621. A defendant who testifies falsely because of mistake, confusion, a bad memory, or in-

---

9. [92] *See United States v. Clarridge*, 811 F. Supp. 697, 708 (D.D.C. 1992) (finding congressional committee was a competent tribunal because Congress has broad investigatory powers as part of its law-making function); *see also United States v. Cross*, 170 F. Supp. 303, 309–10 (D.D.C. 1959) (holding that a congressional subcommittee was not competent where the purpose of the tribunal was outside its legislative purpose).

consequential inconsistencies cannot rightfully be found guilty under section 1621. Such claims are often refuted by the prosecution's use of circumstantial evidence but still provide an avenue to escape liability for many statements. Under section 1621, a witness is not offered the defense of recantation—the correction of previous false testimony. Some courts have allowed defendants to use a recantation as evidence that they lacked the willfulness or intent to commit perjury, thus obviating one of the elements.

As well, a defendant may claim that the government and Congress have laid a "perjury trap" that has ensnared the defendant. In the garden variety perjury trap case, the government calls a witness or defendant to testify numerous times, in an effort to produce conflicting statements or contradicting stories. Given the busy schedules of many witnesses before Congress and the detailed nature of many of the questions presented, it is not hard to imagine how a witness might make statements that could be deemed false. The defense is rarely successful, and the use of attorneys in congressional hearings and questioning, as opposed to the unavailability of a lawyer in a grand jury proceeding, usually safeguards the witness.

In sum, section 1621 is a difficult statute to use to garner a successful prosecution. The willfulness requirement, the need to prove actual falsity, and the requirement that the statement be material are considerable hurdles for the prosecution. Combined with the array of defenses that defendants can raise, section 1621 poses considerable obstacles.

2. 18 U.S.C. §1505.

In order to prove a violation of section 1505, the prosecution must show that: (1) the defendant was aware of, (2) a pending proceeding before a department or agency of the United States, and (3) intentionally and corruptly endeavored to influence, obstruct, or impede that proceeding.

The first element—awareness—is easily proved, as the statement is often made in the pending proceeding itself. The term "proceeding" is construed rather broadly by the courts as it includes both the investigative and adjudicative functions of a department or agency. Even activity performed before an investigation is formally commenced will be found to fall within the investigative aspect of the proceeding element.

The element of intentionality is rather straight-forward, as it is construed as acting purposefully. A defendant is culpable so long as his conduct has the natural and probable effect of obstructing justice. The term "corruptly" on the other hand has undergone significant revision in terms of definition. After the case involving John Poindexter's conviction for violating section 1505 and its eventual reversal on the grounds that the term "corruptly" was unconstitutionally vague, Congress reacted immediately by providing a definition of the term "corruptly" as used in section 1505. It is now defined as "acting with an improper purpose, personally or by influencing another, including making a false or misleading statement, or withholding, concealing, altering, or destroying a document or other information."[10]

Although section 1505's elements are easier to satisfy than section 1621, it is still troubling for prosecutors as they must show intentionality and an improper purpose—elements that require proving a certain state of mind of the defendant, a difficult task in many cases. [*Ed. Note: See Note 2 below for additional information on the state of mind requirement for section 1505.*]

3. 18 U.S.C. §1001.

One of the most widely utilized and broadly construed white-collar statutes resides in 18 U.S.C. §1001. Prosecutors are fond of section 1001 as it is a

> ... catch-all, reaching those false representations that might substantially impair the basic functions entrusted by law to [the particular] agency, but which are not prohibited by other statutes. It is intended to serve the vital public purpose of protecting governmental functions from frustration and distortion through deceptive practices, and to reach those false statements that might support fraudulent claims against the Government, or that might pervert or corrupt the authorized functions of those agencies to whom the statements were made.[11]

The government must prove that the defendant: (1) knowingly and willfully made or concealed a (2) materially (3) false, fictitious, or fraudulent statement or representation within (4) the jurisdiction of the executive, legislative, or judicial branch of the federal government.

The defendant must have a knowing or willful intent. This intent can include the intent to deceive, mislead, or induce belief of false information. Juries can find this element through circumstantial evidence of intent and knowledge. A reckless disregard of the truth satisfies the intent element—often described as willful blindness.

Courts have construed a statement or omission to be material if it either actually influences or has a natural tendency or capacity to influence a decision or function of a federal agency. There is no requirement that the agency actually believed in the truth of the statement.

In regard to falsity, prosecutors can establish the element by showing either an affirmative false representation or by proving that the defendant concealed a material fact. Section 1001 has usually been held to require literal falsity, but a statement that is literally true, yet still misleads federal agents, can be found sufficient. Unlike perjury, there is no requirement under section 1001 that the statement be made under oath.

---

10. [107] 18 U.S.C. §1515(b) (2006).

11. [108] *United States v. Olson*, 751 F.2d 1126, 1128 (9th Cir. 1985) (internal citations and quotations omitted).

The last element is rather easily met as well, as the jurisdictional element is satisfied whenever a false statement is submitted to any of three branches of government. Such a rule was only implemented in 1996. Prior to that, only false statements that were made to departments and agencies of the federal government were within the purview of section 1001. As amended, the scope of the term "department" in section 1001 now includes Congress and the federal judiciary.

Despite being a catch-all, section 1001, like section 1621, is difficult because of its requirement that willfulness or knowledge, actual falsity and materiality be proved. All three statutes designed to deter lies and misleading answers to congressional questioning carry high standards of proof and often dissuade successful prosecutions.

Notes and Questions

1. **Witness Psychology and Preparation.** What are the special challenges facing a witness in a high profile, televised congressional hearing? How would you go about preparing a witness for congressional testimony in such circumstances? How did Oliver North succeed so spectacularly in his extraordinarily high-profile Iran-Contra televised congressional testimony (see Chapter 5), when so many other witnesses have wilted under the hot television lights and the relentless questioning of legislators? How should a witness who is not fortunate enough to have been blessed with North's communication skills and telegenic talents approach preparation for televised congressional testimony? For additional insights on the process of preparing for a congressional hearing, see James F. Fitzpatrick, *Enduring a Congressional Investigation*, 18 LITIGATION 16 (Summer 1992). Fitzpatrick provides a colorful description of a legendary incident in the annals of congressional investigation lore:

> The value of seasoned lawyering was dramatically demonstrated in 1987 in successive hearings on Drexel Burnham Lambert and the conduct of Michael Milken and Drexel CEO Fred Joseph. The hearing was before the master of all congressional investigators, Rep. John Dingell, chairman of the House Energy and Commerce Subcommittee on Oversight and Investigation. Dingell has a well-developed reputation for toughness, but he is also deservedly considered to be fair. In the first hearing, Edward Bennett Williams, representing Milken, "gave a tour de force performance," in the words of the *Legal Times*. Having determined that his client would assert a Fifth Amendment privilege, Williams negotiated an agreement, confirmed in writing by the committee staff, that Milken would simply be required to file an affidavit asserting that he would rely on the Fifth Amendment. But at the last moment Chairman Dingell changed his mind and subpoenaed Milken. Williams was able to use that reversal to put the chairman on the defensive—where he rarely finds himself. Milken appeared, but before Milken asserted his privilege, Williams insisted that all the televisions, radios, and cameras be turned off, an arcane House rule

that a *subpoenaed* witness need not be subjected to the glare of intrusive publicity. [*Ed. Note: This rule of the House of Representatives is no longer in effect.*] The nation—and Chairman Dingell—was denied the media spectacle of Milken taking the Fifth.

In contrast, on the very next day, the consequences of a less experienced congressional advocate became apparent. Again before Chairman Dingell, Drexel CEO Joseph was accompanied by an esteemed securities specialist from a well-known Wall Street firm. After Joseph was introduced, his counsel volunteered to offer testimony on the securities laws. Chairman Dingell asked whether he wanted to be sworn in. Counsel agreed, unwittingly taking the bait. The chairman then told counsel that "if you are sworn, you do waive the attorney-client privilege." He said he was making a point of this so that counsel did "not blunder into thickets for which you were unprepared." Counsel beat a hearty, and embarrassing, retreat from that thicket.

Id. at 16.

Although the House of Representatives rule on radio and television broadcasts and still photography is no longer in effect, its invocation by legendary Washington superlawyer Edward Bennett Williams illustrates the importance of being well-prepared and well-informed when serving as counsel to a witness in a congressional investigation. Consider in this regard the experience of one of the authors of this book, who successfully invoked the same rule, several years before Williams did so, when acting as counsel to a witness before the Subcommittee on Asian and Pacific Affairs of the House of Representatives Committee on Foreign Affairs in a 1986 hearing on matters relating to former President of the Philippines Ferdinand Marcos (and note the less-receptive response to the efforts of counsel for a subsequent witness to invoke the same rule on a "me too" basis):

[Subcommittee Chair] MR. SOLARZ: At this point the committee will call as its next witness Mr. Barry Knox.

I understand, before Mr. Knox actually takes the witness stand—I would appreciate it if somebody on the staff could substitute Mr. Knox's name for Mr. Bullock's name in front of the witness table—that his attorneys would like to make a statement to the committee. For the purpose of the record, if Mr. Knox's attorneys could identify themselves, that would be appreciated.

MR. BRAND: Stanley Brand.

MR. LOWELL: Abbe Lowell.

MR. SOLARZ: Which of you two gentlemen would like to make a statement?

MR. BRAND: Mr. Chairman, pursuant to rule 11, clause 3(f)(2) of the House rules, rule 11, clause 3 and rule 21 of the committee rules, I hereby invoke on behalf of Mr. Knox the right afforded to him to require that all television and photographic lenses be covered and all microphones be covered or turned off during his testimony at this hearing.

MR. SOLARZ: In view of the fact, Mr. Brand, you are a former counsel to the House in which capacity you served with great distinction, I have no reason to doubt the accuracy of your citation, but I hope you won't hold it against me if I ask your successor, who I think is present, or his assistant, to inform the committee as to whether, in fact, this request is indeed covered by the rules of the House.

MR. BRAND: As long as he gives the same answer I have no objection.

MR. TIEFER: The answer given by the House rules, is that under the house rules, and I quote:

> No witness served with a subpoena by the committee shall be required against his or her will to be photographed at any hearing or to give evidence or testimony while the broadcasting of that hearing by radio or television is being conducted.
>
> The request of any such witness who does not wish to be subjected to radio, television, or still photograph coverage, all lenses shall be covered and all microphones used for coverage turned off.

MR. SOLARZ: In view of the fact we have consistently throughout these hearings bent over backward to accommodate concerns of several of the witnesses who have come forward and in view of the fact that this request is consistent with the rules of the House and indeed, seems to be in order, as chairman of the subcommittee, I will then ask television cameras to leave the room so that the witness, pursuant to his privilege under the House rules, can testify without television cameras being present or if they can remain, I gather I am told they can remain if you cover the lenses.

Also, all microphones of radio and other broadcast equipment used for coverage will have to be turned off. As soon as the Chair sees the cameras covered, I will ask the witness to take the witness stand.

The witness is within his rights to make this request and we have no alternative but to accede to it.

Mr. Brand, are you satisfied the request has been complied with?

MR. BRAND: Thank you, Mr. Chairman.

* * *

MR. SOLARZ: Mr. Knox, thank you very much for your cooperation.

   [Witness excused.]

MR. SOLARZ: Mr. Tantoco, do you want to come to the witness stand?

MR. MOORE: Mr. Chairman, I plan to invoke the same rule.

MR. SOLARZ: Do you want to sit down first and identify yourself?

MR. MOORE: I would be glad to.

MR. SOLARZ: Thank you.

Please identify yourself for the record.

MR. MOORE: I am William Moore, counsel for Mr. Tantoco.

MR. SOLARZ: What rule are you invoking?

MR. MOORE: I don't have the number before me. The same rule that was invoked by the previous counsel.

MR. SOLARZ: What do you understand the rule to be?

MR. MOORE: I understand it to be as it was read while I was in the room a few minutes ago.

MR. SOLARZ: What are you asking us to do?

MR. MOORE: I am asking that all cameras either be covered or taken out of the room, and that all radio devices or microphone devices be turned off, and that any tape of any kind be turned off.

MR. SOLARZ: Pursuant, then, to rule XI, clause 3(f)(2), et cetera, the witness has, pursuant to his rights under the Rules of the House, asked that the television cameras be closed off. And I would request the cameramen to please cover their cameras at this time.

MR. ENGLEBERG: I am Steve Engleberg, with the New York Times. As I understand what he just said, he is asking recording devices to be turned off.

Is that correct?

MR. SOLARZ: Let me read the rule to you and the other people from the press here.

The rule reads:

> No witness served with a subpoena by the committee shall be required against his will to be photographed at any hearing or to give evidence or testimony while the broadcasting of that hearing by radio or television is being conducted. At the request of any such witness who does not wish to be subjected to radio, television, or still photography coverage, all lenses shall be covered and all microphones used for coverage turned off.

MR. ENGLEBERG: It would not be used for broadcasting?

MR. SOLARZ: That is a very good question. I will ask that of Counsel of the House.

I am informed by Counsel to the House that if a tape recording is not going to be used for either radio or television broadcasting, then a tape recording can be made of the testimony.

Once again, I will now invoke the rule. I regret to have to do this, but it is the prerogative of the witness and it is his right under the rules of the House to have the cameras covered. And I would appreciate it, gentlemen, if you would do so or leave the room.

Mr. Tantoco, can you—

Mr. Tantoco, would you please raise your right hand? Do you swear to tell the truth, the whole truth, and nothing but the truth so help you God?

MR. TANTOCO: I do.

Hearings Before the Subcommittee on Asian and Pacific Affairs of the Committee on Foreign Affairs, House of Representatives, Ninety-Ninth Congress, 1st and 2nd Sessions, Jan. 23, 1986, at 375–76, 396.

2. Obstruction of Justice—Cases and Sarbanes-Oxley Act Expansion. The obstruction of justice statute that is discussed above, 18 U.S.C. §1505, is drafted to encompass obstruction of congressional proceedings:

> Whoever corruptly, or by threats or force, or by any threatening letter or communication influences, obstructs, or impedes or endeavors to influence, obstruct, or impede the due and proper administration of the law under which any pending proceeding is being had before any department or agency of the United States, *or the due and proper exercise of the power of inquiry under which any inquiry or investigation is being had by either House, or any committee of either House or any joint committee of the Congress—*

> Shall be fined under this title, imprisoned not more than 5 years or, if the offense involves international or domestic terrorism (as defined in section 2331), imprisoned not more than 8 years, or both.

18 U.S.C. §1505 (emphasis added). For an example of a case in which a high-level government official violated section 1505, see *United States v. Griles* (Crim. No. 07-CR-079 (ESH), D.D.C. 2007), in which the number-two official in the Department of the Interior entered a guilty plea to a one-count criminal information charging him with obstruction of proceedings before the United States Senate in an investigation arising out of the Jack Abramoff lobbying scandal. The criminal information charged the following conduct as a violation of the obstruction statute:

<u>Defendant's Obstruction of Proceedings</u>
<u>Before the United States Senate</u>

> 11. From on or about October 20, 2005, to on or about November 2, 2005, in the District of Columbia, the defendant, JAMES STEVEN GRILES, did knowingly and corruptly influence, obstruct, and impede, and endeavor to influence, obstruct, and impede the due and proper exercise of the power of inquiry under which an investigation and review was being had by the United States Senate and a Committee of the United States Senate. That is, during his October 20, 2005 interview with investigators working for the United States Senate Committee on Indian Affairs, and during his November 2, 2005 testimony at a public hearing held before members of the United States Senate Committee on Indian Affairs, the defendant, JAMES STEVEN GRILES, knowingly and intentionally made a series of materially false and fictitious declarations to, and withheld material information from, Senators and Senate

investigators in response to questions about the true nature and extent of defendant GRILES' relationship with Person A, the person who introduced Abramoff to the defendant; how and why the defendant's relationship with Abramoff thereafter developed; and the nature of Abramoff's access to the defendant.

All in violation of Title 18, United States Code, Section 1505.

Id. Note that the conduct that formed the basis of the obstruction of justice charge against Mr. Griles included false statements to investigators working for the Senate committee, as well as false statements he made during a formal committee hearing. (See Note 3 below for additional discussion of the possible criminal penalties that can be imposed for false statements to congressional staff members outside the formal hearing process.)

In 2002, as part of the Sarbanes-Oxley Act, Congress passed another obstruction of justice statute that is aimed at destruction or alteration of evidence in federal investigatory proceedings:

> Whoever knowingly alters, destroys, mutilates, conceals, covers up, falsifies, or makes a false entry in any record, document, or tangible object with the intent to impede, obstruct, or influence the investigation or proper administration of any matter within the jurisdiction of any department or agency of the United States or any case filed under title 11, or in relation to *or contemplation of* any such matter or case, shall be fined under this title, imprisoned not more than 20 years, or both.

18 U.S.C. §1519 (emphasis added). Note that, in addition to language that covers acts of obstruction in "contemplation of" a federal investigatory proceeding, the Sarbanes-Oxley obstruction provision is punishable by a prison term of up to twenty years, rather than the five-year term provided in §1505. *See id.; see also Arthur Andersen LLP v. United States,* 544 U.S. 696 (2005) (interpreting the criminal intent requirements of the federal witness-tampering statute, 18 U.S.C. §1512).

3. The Special Dangers Presented by the Federal False Statements Statute. Of all the criminal statutes discussed above, perhaps the one that presents the greatest danger for witnesses in congressional investigations—or any other federal proceeding or inquiry—is the federal false statements statute, 18 U.S.C. §1001. As noted above, a perjury prosecution under the general perjury statute, 18 U.S.C. §1621, requires proof that the defendant, while under an oath authorized by a law of the United States and before a competent tribunal, willfully or knowingly made a false statement as to material facts. The federal false statements statute, in contrast, does not require that the defendant be under oath or testifying before a tribunal—or even providing testimony in a formal legal proceeding—to be convicted of a felony false statements offense. Accordingly, this statute is frequently employed by federal prosecutors in cases involving informal statements to FBI agents, customs and border patrol agents, and all manner of other federal agents and officers. *See, e.g., United States v. Rodgers,* 466 U.S. 475, 480–82 (1984) (upholding prosecution for false statements to FBI and secret service agents, and collecting cases involving false statements to other federal officers and agents). The Supreme Court has interpreted the statute so broadly that a defendant can be convicted even if he makes a false statement without "actual knowledge of federal agency jurisdiction." *See United States v. Yermian,* 468 U.S. 63, 66 (1984) (upholding conviction of defense contractor employee who made false statements on a security questionnaire submitted to his employer but claimed "that he had no actual knowledge that his false statements would be transmitted to a federal agency").

The false statements statute is particularly dangerous for witnesses in congressional proceedings because of its application to unsworn statements to congressional staffers outside of hearings or other formal congressional proceedings. An example illustrating the risks involved in informal staff interviews involved Major League Baseball star player Miguel Tejada and the House of Representatives Committee on Oversight and Government Reform investigation of steroid use by Major League Baseball players. Tejada, who spoke English as a second language, was interviewed by committee staff members in a Baltimore hotel room, with the assistance of a translator, and "although defendant TEJADA was not placed under oath, the committee staff advised defendant of the importance of providing truthful answers." *See United States v. Tejada,* Magistrate No. 09-MJ-077 (D.D.C. 2009) (Statement of Offense at para. 11). Tejada made false statements about his discussions with other players about steroid use and his knowledge of steroid use by other players. *See id.* at para. 9–12. Tejada was able to avoid felony false statements charges by pleading guilty to a misdemeanor offense of Misrepresentations to Congress in violation of 18 U.S.C. §192, *see id.,* but the case presents a dramatic example of the risks of criminal prosecution for false statements to congressional staff members.

Finally, the broad interpretation that the courts have given to the federal false statements statute merits special attention:

> It is well established that this section encompasses within its proscription two distinct offenses, concealment of a material fact and false representation. The objective of both offenses may be the same, to create or foster on the part of a Government agency a misapprehension of the true state of affairs. What must be proved to establish each offense, however, differs significantly. False representations, like common law perjury, require proof of actual falsity; concealment requires proof of wilful nondisclosure by means of a 'trick, scheme or device.'

United States v. Diogo, 320 F.2d 898, 902 (2d Cir. 1963) (internal citations omitted). Consistent with this broad interpretation of the statute, in considering the appeals of lifestyle guru and media mogul Martha Stewart and her stockbroker Peter Bacanovic, the Second Circuit further explained the distinction discussed in *Diogo:*

> The several different types of fraudulent conduct proscribed by section 1001 are not separate offenses, as Bacanovic suggests; rather they describe different means by which the statute is violated. *See United States v. Crisci,* 273 F.3d 235, 238–39 (2d Cir. 2001) (no duplicity issue where indictment charges

several means of committing a single crime); *United States v. Murray*, 618 F.2d 892, 896 (2d Cir. 1980) (several offenses in one count is duplicitous, several means of committing an offense in a single count is not). The District Court did not err by failing to instruct the jurors that they must agree unanimously as to which theory of the offense—false statement or concealment—supported the verdict. *See Schad v. Arizona*, 501 U.S. 624, 631 (1991) (where a single count alleges that the defendant committed a charged offense by one or more specified means, "[w]e have never suggested that ... the jurors should be required to agree upon a single means of commission, any more than the indictments were required to specify one alone") (plurality opinion).

United States v. Diogo, 320 F.2d 898 (2d Cir. 1963), does not require a different conclusion. Despite the presence of language that might appear favorable to Bacanovic on this point, when this Court said in dictum that false representation and concealment are "two distinct offenses," *id.* at 902, we were not addressing the issue of duplicitous pleading. Rather, this Court was discussing the differences between the proof necessary to establish each of the theories. *See id.* at 901–02. *We noted that a conviction for false representation requires evidence of actual falsity, while concealment is proved by showing "wilful nondisclosure by means of a 'trick, scheme or device."* *Id.* at 902 (quoting 18 U.S.C. §1001).

United States v. Stewart, 433 F.3d 273 (2d. Cir. 2006) (emphasis supplied). The possibility of using the false statements statute in cases where statements to investigators were not actually false, but only used "trick, scheme or device" to mislead or withhold information, when coupled with the statute's application to unsworn statements outside the context of formal legal proceedings, makes the statute among the most dangerous weapons in the legal arsenal of aggressive federal prosecutors. *Cf. Bronston v. United States*, 409 U.S. 352 (1973) (reversing perjury conviction under the general perjury statute, 18 U.S.C. §1621, when the defendant's answers were literally true but intentionally misleading and incomplete).

The Importance of Effective Congressional Oversight

The materials in the preceding chapters of this book demonstrate how aggressive congressional oversight can be used to expose and remedy executive branch misconduct, as in the Teapot Dome and Watergate investigations, but also can be misused to violate the rights of innocent citizens, as in the HUAC and McCarthy era investigations. In light of this two-edged character of the congressional investigative sword, how much investigative power should Congress be allowed to wield? What is the appropriate balance between congressional oversight powers and executive branch autonomy? Consider the views of United States Senator Charles Schumer of New York, in a 2007 law review article presenting an impassioned call for "a robust and active Congress":

Charles E. Schumer, *Under Attack:*
Congressional Power in the Twenty-first Century

1 HARVARD LAW & POLICY REVIEW 3 (2007)

[*Ed. Note: Some footnotes omitted.*]

I. INTRODUCTION

Every basic civics text recites that our government is divided into three branches and that these three branches are co-equal partners. But as true as that once was, this system of exquisite checks and balances is at risk of being made anachronistic by recent legal and political developments. The traditional functions of Congress as lawmaker and a check on other branches have come under sustained and systematic assault from both the judicial and executive branches.

The assault from the Executive began as a gradual diminution of congressional power after a post-Nixon-era zenith, but has accelerated most dramatically under President George W. Bush. The threat to Congress from the Judiciary comes in the form of rulings invalidating congressional enactments at an alarming pace over the past fifteen years, largely in service of a cramped interpretation of congressional authority under both the Commerce Clause and Section 5 of the Fourteenth Amendment. Together, these twin trends have undermined Congress's role as lawmaker and its role as a bulwark against overreaching by the other branches.

Although the trends in the two other branches of American government have developed separately, they are born of the same philosophy. Commentators and political actors have traditionally focused on just one or the other trend, but in my view it is the unprecedented combination of these two threats that poses a real danger to our democracy. There is much more at stake here than institutional pride and the collective egos of 535 elected legislators. The costs of an anemic Congress over the long term are considerable.

First, continued erosion of Congress's lawmaking power undermines democracy. Preemption of the legislative function by the President increases the concentration of power and the risk of abuse. It also decreases the transparency that accompanies a legislative process marked by open debate and compromise. Preemption of the legislative function by the Judiciary similarly diminishes democracy.

Second, in the absence of a prompt reassertion of Congress's power, its powerlessness risks becoming institutionalized. Unflexed, congressional muscles atrophy. Handicaps created by the Executive may be difficult to dismantle. Federalism precedents espoused by the Judiciary may be impossible to undo. Even if one believes that the current President has not taken executive power too far (though I do), the next president, from whichever party, will likely continue the trend if unchecked. A compliant Congress risks permanently undermining its credibility and its relevance. When Congress needs to rein in a future president, it may find that it lacks the institutional capacity to do so.

In sum, Congress does have a role equal to the other branches and must have this equal role. It is a role envisioned by the Framers, enshrined in the Constitution, and ennobled by the historical examples of our greatest legislators. A responsible and responsive Congress can solve many of the problems America confronts, improve respect for government by providing oversight and demanding accountability, and decrease partisan gridlock in Washington.

Undoubtedly, Congress is at something of an institutional disadvantage against the Executive. It has no agencies and bureaucracy to rival the Secretary of Defense or the Attorney General. Rather, Congress consists of 535 individual lawmakers divided between two parties and dedicated to unique and varying agendas. However, members of both parties ought to agree that our representative system demands—and the American people deserve—a Congress that is not just a rubber stamp for the Executive, but an independent, co-equal, and assertive branch of government. A Congress grown weak and compliant imperils democracy.

This Article addresses recent executive and judicial branch encroachment upon congressional power. Part II argues that, consistent with the Founders' vision, Congress must be assertive and strong, particularly with respect to its two preeminent functions—making laws and checking the Executive. Part III analyzes the threat from the executive branch. It describes the current administration's calculated efforts to expand its power at the expense of Congress, focusing on its conduct of the war on terror and its resistance to oversight in this area and others. Part IV examines the threat from the judicial branch, explaining that the New Federalism, pursuant to which numerous acts of Congress have been struck down, is a dangerous usurpation of Congressional authority. Finally, Part V presents several ways Congress can re-assert its powers and take firmer control over the nation's future.

II. THE NEED FOR A ROBUST AND ACTIVE CONGRESS

Divided government is the hallmark of American constitutional democracy. As James Madison wrote in *The Federalist* No. 47: "The accumulation of all powers, legislative, executive and judiciary, in the same hands, whether of one, a few or many, and whether hereditary, self-appointed or elective, may justly be pronounced the very definition of tyranny." The Founders, acutely sensitive to British political history and the American revolutionary experience, struck a careful and delicate balance that would forge a more effective government than was possible under the Articles of Confederation, while guarding against a slip back to tyranny. At the heart of this balance was a strong legislature. A simultaneously strong President and Congress are not mutually exclusive; rather, they are fundamental to freedom, security, and effective governance.

The particular emphasis the Founders put on the vitality of Congress is evident in the structure of the Constitution itself, which sets forth the powers of Congress before turning to any other branch.[12] Indeed, as Professor Akhil Amar has explained,

---

12. [4] Indeed, the founding generation considered popularly elected representatives more closely connected to the populace than other officials. At the Constitutional Convention of 1787, George

Congress stands "as first among equals, with wide power to structure the second-mentioned executive and third-mentioned judicial branches." As the branch closest to the people, Congress has the responsibility to protect the general welfare by making laws and providing a check on the Executive.

Congress's chief mandate, of course, is the making of laws. The first clause of the first section of the first article of the Constitution provides: "All legislative Powers herein granted shall be vested in a Congress of the United States." That legislative authority includes, pursuant to Section 8 of Article I, the power to "lay and collect Taxes," to "provide for the common Defence and general Welfare of the United States," to "regulate Commerce with foreign Nations, and among the several States," to "constitute Tribunals inferior to the supreme Court," to "raise and support Armies," and a host of other powers. To affect all of this, moreover, the Constitution grants the legislature the authority to "make all Laws which shall be necessary and proper for carrying into Execution the foregoing Powers."

Congress's job of oversight—too often overlooked and underemphasized—is a critical element of its exercise of "necessary and proper" powers. Though the work of hearings and oversight is usually incremental, sometimes tedious, and occasionally conducive to political opportunism, it remains the backbone of a strong body politic. Indeed, in the context of America's system of checks and balances, congressional oversight of the executive branch is, in the view of some, equal in importance to the legislative function. In his 1885 work *Congressional Government*, Woodrow Wilson famously noted that "[q]uite as important as legislation is vigilant oversight of administration." More recently, one scholar has written: "[T]here is no substitute for congressional oversight in our democracy. Without it, our public life would be considerably impoverished."[13] The Supreme Court itself has recognized the necessary connection between Congress's power to legislate and its power to investigate and oversee: "This Court has often noted that the power to investigate is inherent in the power to make laws because '[a] legislative body cannot legislate wisely or effectively in the absence of information respecting the conditions which the legislation is intended to affect or change.'"[14] Thus, the Constitution's broad grant of power to the preeminent branch has as its indispensable and logical corollary vigorous and vigilant oversight.

Mason suggested that the House of Representatives "was to be the grand depository of the democratic principles of the government." THOMAS E. MANN & NORMAN J. ORNSTEIN, THE BROKEN BRANCH 19 (2006).

13. [8] Charles Tiefer, *Congressional Oversight of the Clinton Administration and Congressional Procedure*, 50 ADMIN. L. REV. 199, 216 (1998).

14. [9] *Eastland v. United States Servicemen's Fund*, 421 U.S. 491, 504 (1975) (quoting *McGrain v. Daugherty*, 273 U.S. 135, 175 (1927)); *see also Morrison v. Olson*, 487 U.S. 654, 694 (1988) (holding that some oversight is "incidental to the legislative function of Congress"); *Doe v. McMillan*, 412 U.S. 306, 313 (1973) (the "acts of authorizing an investigation pursuant to which ... materials were gathered" is a central part of the legislative process); *Barenblatt v. United States*, 360 U.S. 109, 111 (1959) (oversight authorized within the Constitution).

The oversight function, moreover, is the logical and necessary expression of the Founders' vision of checks and balances. As Madison wrote in *The Federalist* No. 51, the Republic would function well only within such a competitive and oppositional system: "[I]n all the subordinate distributions of power, ... the constant aim is to divide and arrange the several offices in such a manner as that each may be a check on the other." Finally, the tools for oversight have been strengthened by specific legislation, such as the Legislative Reorganization Act of 1946.

Notwithstanding recent congressional obeisance and abdication, the legislature has a long and grand tradition of checking power, spotlighting abuse, preventing fraud, and preserving liberty. Historical examples of vital congressional checking abound, even in wartime. Twelve days after Pearl Harbor, for example, conservative Senator Robert Taft—known as "Mr. Republican"—emphasized the importance of debate and deliberation in the United States Senate and said, "as a matter of general principle, I believe there can be no doubt that criticism in time of war is essential to the maintenance of any kind of democratic government."

Criticism meant not only speeches from the floor of the United States Congress, but also organized investigation. Thus, in the 1940s, Senator Harry Truman provided aggressive oversight over the military and uncovered billions of dollars of wasteful spending. In the 1970s, the bipartisan Church Committee uncovered abuses and held officials to account at the FBI and CIA. In the 1980s, Congress investigated Iran-Contra through public hearings, which led President Reagan to establish the independent Tower Commission.

It is clear, then, that responsible oversight is Congress's duty, and that it can effectively flex its muscles when it has the will.[15] Lately, that will has been lacking. When President Bush assumed office, "[t]he institutional rivalry designed by the framers gave way to a relationship in which Congress assumed a position subordinate to the executive. Party trumped institution."[16]

As the 110th Congress begins, both Congress's legislative and oversight abilities have atrophied. Although Congressional clout has historically ebbed and flowed as a function of shifting international threats, domestic circumstances, and party dominance, there appears no doubt that Congressional power is at its lowest ebb in memory.

First, Congress's sister branches have challenged, undermined, and usurped its legislative function to a significant degree. The Executive, for example, in recent years has relied unduly upon presidential signing statements to undercut and reinterpret

---

15. [13] Daryl Levinson and Richard Pildes have argued that the Madisonian conception of inter-branch competition has never accurately depicted American politics, and that inter-branch rivalry gave way to partisanship not long after the founding of the Republic. *See* Daryl J. Levinson & Richard H. Pildes, *Separation of Parties, Not Powers*, 119 Harv. L. Rev. 2312, 2313 (2006). Nonetheless, the Truman example—as well as the heavy oversight that existed from 1993 to 1994—demonstrates that single-party control of both branches has not always halted healthy inter-branch competition.

16. [14] Mann & Ornstein, *supra*, at 139.

congressional enactments.[17] Although signing statements have been used since early American history, and Presidents of both parties have issued them to articulate their interpretation of statutory provisions, President Bush has employed them far more aggressively than his predecessors. In the process, the President has dangerously infringed on the lawmaking role of Congress.

As a former Republican official has testified, "These [signing] statements, which have multiplied logarithmically under President George W. Bush, flout the Constitution's checks and balances and separation of powers. They usurp legislative prerogatives and evade accountability."[18] A former Clinton official had this to say: "The Bush administration's frequent and seemingly cavalier refusal to enforce laws, which is aggravated by its avoidance of judicial review and even public disclosure of its actions, places it at odds with these principles and with predecessors of both parties."[19] Critics also emphasize that, unlike earlier Presidents, President Bush has not balanced his use of signing statements with the presidential veto. During his six years in office, President Bush has vetoed only one law. In particular, the Administration's track record of using signing statements to do everything from restricting oversight to blocking congressional involvement in the war on terror has raised a number of alarms; indeed, the President has taken issue with an unprecedented number of congressional enactments: over 750.[20]

The Executive has also undermined the legislative prerogative in a more fundamental way by repeatedly insisting on unilateral action with respect to the war on terror rather than cooperating with Congress to modify laws that might be in need of changes or updates. As set forth below, this is true both of the Administration's secret implementation of a terrorist surveillance program (rather than working together with Congress to modify surveillance laws) and in its independent establishment of a military tribunal system (rather than working together with Congress to modify the Uniform Code of Military Justice). The Executive's approach to both matters has drawn judicial rebuke and potentially slowed progress in the war on terror.

The Judiciary, meanwhile, has undermined the lawmaking authority of Congress with the Supreme Court's New Federalism, reflecting a trend of diminishing judicial deference to Congress's ability to find facts and enact appropriate laws. Thus, as Judge John Noonan wrote, "[t]he Court's effort to give more power to the states has led at the same time to the accretion of power by the Court" and also to its striking down an unprecedented number of federal laws, as it substitutes its own judgment for that of Congress.

---

17. [15] The Use of Presidential Signing Statements: Hearing Before the S. Comm. on the Judiciary, 109th Cong. (2006) (statement of Charles J. Ogletree, Jr., Professor, Harvard Law School).

18. [16] The Use of Presidential Signing Statements: Hearing Before the S. Comm. on the Judiciary, 109th Cong. (2006) (statement of Bruce Fein, Partner, Fein & Fein).

19. [17] Walter Dellinger, *A Slip of the Pen*, N.Y. TIMES, July 31, 2006, at A17.

20. [18] Charlie Savage, *Bush Challenges Hundreds of Laws, President Cites Powers of His Office*, BOSTON GLOBE, Apr. 30, 2006, at A1.

Second, Congress's oversight function is also on the wane. To fulfill its oversight function, Congress requires access to information from the executive branch. As early as 1792, President George Washington furnished documents so Congress could investigate military losses during Major General Arthur St. Clair's 1791 campaign against Indian tribes in Ohio, and reserved only the right to withhold documents "the disclosure of which would injure the public." President Washington viewed executive privilege as a narrow tool to protect the national interest. In the years since, the executive branch has refused disclosure, preserving and expanding its own power. As a result, access to documents has provoked countless struggles between the executive and legislative branches throughout American history. Over the years, however, Congress has developed various forms of leverage to force compliance, including the power of the purse, the power to impeach, the use of congressional subpoenas, the holding of executive officials in contempt, GAO investigations, and the blockage of nominations. Unfortunately, Congress has demonstrated little interest in using any of these tools during the Bush era.

Two independent scholars have shown that Congress has quite dramatically fallen down on its job to act as a check on the executive branch during the Bush Administration, observing that after a notable decline following the Republican takeover of Congress under President Clinton "oversight has all but disappeared" under the Bush Administration.[21] Their observations are striking:

- In the House Government Reform Committee, there were 135 hearings described as "oversight" in the 1993–94 session of Congress; a decade later, there were only 37 such hearings.[22] By this objective measure, oversight in that committee fell 73%.

- The House Energy and Commerce Committee produced 117 pages of activity reports relating to oversight in the 1993–94 session; a decade later, it generated only 24 pages, a 79% drop.[23]

- While Congress heard 140 hours of testimony on the subject of President Clinton's alleged use of his Christmas mailing list to identify campaign donors in the mid-1990s, House Republicans heard only 12 hours of testimony on Abu Ghraib.[24]

- Notwithstanding the tradition of wartime oversight, the Senate Armed Services Committee held no hearings specifically on operations in Afghanistan in 2003 and 2004.

---

21. [23] *See* Norman J. Ornstein & Thomas E. Mann, *Congress Checks Out*, FOREIGN AFF., Nov.–Dec. 2006, at 67, 70 (citing Susan Milligan, *Congress Reduces Its Oversight Role; Since Clinton, A Change In Focus*, BOSTON GLOBE, Nov. 20, 2005, at A1).

22. [24] *Id.* at 71.

23. [25] *Id.*

24. [26] *Id.*

The data only reflect what is painfully apparent even to Republican members of Congress—oversight has fallen precipitously during the past six years. Recently, even some Republicans have bemoaned the sorry state of oversight in Congress. One Representative acknowledged, "I don't think we have been doing the job we should have been doing for several years on oversight."[25] Another simultaneously acknowledged the fact of decreased oversight and candidly supplied a principal reason for the falloff: "Our party controls the levers of government. We're not about to go out and look beneath a bunch of rocks to try to cause heartburn. Unless they really screw up, we're not going to go after them."[26]

What has given rise to this state of affairs? In no small measure, it has been caused by an unfortunate congressional acquiescence. At bottom, congressional power wanes at the peril of the people. The dangers of a weak Congress are discussed at greater length below.

* * *

[*Ed. Note: Senator Schumer then details what he describes as "The Executive Assault on Congressional Power" and "The Judicial Assault on Congressional Power."*]

V. A MUSCULAR CONGRESS

In November 2005, the Democratic leadership of the Senate invoked a parliamentary rule to force the body into closed session to discuss failures in oversight over the Iraq War, and the ineffectiveness of the Intelligence Committees concerning the run-up to war. The move succeeded in bringing attention to Congress's failure to hold the Administration to account, but it hardly solved the problem of Congress's weakened resolve. In the years ahead, Democratic and Republican members of Congress must join together, get tough, and fulfill their institutional responsibilities. Congress ought to start by providing more aggressive oversight over departments and agencies and taking a more assertive role in the war on terror. These are practical solutions, not partisan ones, and they are in the interests of all Americans, no matter which party controls the legislative branch.

A. Congressional Oversight

As described above, Congress has a rich tradition of oversight and meaningful involvement both in national security matters and in domestic affairs. To win the war on terror, America needs a strong President. As Commander-in-Chief, the President should have every tool necessary to fight and win the war on terror. While presidential power is vital, however, it is not infallible. As a result, Congress has an important role to play in providing oversight and demanding accountability. To fulfill that role, Congress must start by asserting its right to information and answers from the Executive branch more aggressively. The leadership of both parties ought to demand that the President

---

25. [27] David Nather, *Congress as Watchdog: Asleep on the Job?*, 61 CQ WKLY. 1190, 1191 (2004) (quoting Republican Rep. Jim Kolbe).

26. [28] *Id.* at 1190 (quoting Republican Rep. Ray LaHood).

fully brief members of the Intelligence Committees on its counterterrorism program and provide access to information about the Administration's war on terror.

Second, Congress needs to use that information to hold the Administration to account when it fails to conduct the war on terror effectively. Mistakes are inevitable in any war, but that does not mean we cannot learn from them and take actions to correct our course. When the President of the United States chooses to give Administration officials the Presidential Medal of Freedom for making mistakes rather than hold them accountable,[27] it is incumbent upon Congress to demand that missing accountability. America needs a smart, flexible, and effective war on terror—and Congress has a role to play in making that so.

Third, Congress should pass proposals already on the table to recreate the Truman Committee for the current wartime situation. The goal of this committee should be the same as Harry Truman's goal—to seek out corruption and waste for the betterment of the war effort as a whole. A bipartisan embrace of this committee's creation would go a long way toward restarting Congress's dormant oversight capacity.

Similarly, Congress must reassert its traditional domestic role. For example, the politicization of the Department of Justice and other agencies is not inevitable, and Congress has the power to step in. The Senate Judiciary Committee can start by conducting more frequent and meaningful oversight hearings. The Committee ought to be more vigilant in requiring Justice Department officials to answer its questions, and in demanding information. The Senate has a variety of tools to force compliance, and it should consider using them when appropriate and necessary. Congress needs to do more to ensure that the Justice Department once again becomes independent and responsive to the whole American public, not just one party.

These lessons are by no means limited to the Department of Justice. Every congressional committee should recommit itself to oversight. There should be a Congress-wide push for greater flow of information, and robust oversight hearings to ensure efficiency and hold officials accountable for their actions. Congress ought not to cede its power of oversight and allow itself to be marginalized.

Congress also ought to consider long-term, innovative solutions, such as adjusting its committee structure so it is more conducive to responsible, bipartisan oversight; working with other branches to create stronger institutions of checks and balances (such as inter-branch, bipartisan commissions that can provide a check through public reports when one branch exceeds its power); and making it easier to convene independent commissions in the vein of the 9/11 Commission and the Commission on Presidential Debates to transcend the partisan gridlock of Congress, identify problems, and propose solutions. My goal in advocating increased oversight and congressional power is not a political one. The objective of congressional oversight should not be used to embarrass or to score political points. Instead, my goal is to fix an imbalance

---

27. [154] President Bush awarded Gen. Tommy Franks, George Tenet, and Paul Bremer the Presidential Medal of Freedom on December 14, 2004.

I believe is detrimental to American government no matter which party is in power. The robust balance of powers envisioned by our founders leads to more successful outcomes regardless of political affiliation.

* * *

[Ed. Note: Senator Schumer then details what he views to be the proper role of the Senate in fulfilling its constitutional duty to "Advise and Consent" in the judicial confirmation process.]

C. Conclusion

For years, President Bush has repeated a simple point when challenged about the aggressiveness of his Administration's policies: "I came to Washington to solve problems." Like the President, every member of Congress came to Washington to solve problems, and to make America stronger and safer. However, the power of Congress to satisfy its constitutional responsibilities and provide for the general welfare of the American people has diminished in recent years. The strength and influence of Congress is not a partisan issue, and its power should not ebb and flow depending on which party controls which levers of government. The American people deserve active and aggressive lawmakers—not despite the troubled times we live in, but because of the troubled times we live in.

EPILOGUE

The momentous election of November 7, 2006, sent a clear message that voters were looking for a change. Although there are many areas of possible change that the new Democratic majority looks forward to addressing in the coming Congress, accountability in government is among the first to be addressed. Voters were fed up with a Congress that failed to ask questions, investigate or probe into a costly and deadly war. Voters want a Congress that stands up, instead of laying down and allowing the Executive and Judicial branches to roll right over it.

The preceding Article lays out why Congress must seize the initiative to reinstitute accountability in our federal government, and how it should begin to go about doing just that. By increasing oversight and working hard to reestablish the role of the Congress, we can transform the Congress from an obsequious follower into the strong, robust representative of the people that our founders envisioned ... and that our current citizenry has demanded.

Notes and Questions

1. Partisan Attack or Cause for Bipartisan Concern? Informed by the materials in the preceding chapters of this book, do you agree with Senator Schumer's assessment of the recent history of congressional oversight, or is he using the issue of congressional oversight as a vehicle for a partisan attack on the policies of the George W. Bush administration? For another article raising concerns about the current state of legislative oversight, published shortly after the 2008 presidential election, see Jonathan Mahler, *After the Imperial Presidency*, N.Y. TIMES (Nov. 9, 2008):

Ask a long-serving member of the United States Senate—like, say, Patrick Leahy of Vermont—to reflect on the Senate's role in our constitutional government, and he will almost invariably tell you a story from our nation's founding that may or may not be apocryphal. It concerns an exchange that supposedly took place between Thomas Jefferson and George Washington in 1787, the year of the constitutional convention in Philadelphia. Jefferson, who had been serving as America's ambassador to France during the convention, asked Washington over breakfast upon his return why he and the other framers created a Senate—in addition to the previously planned House of Representatives and presidency—in his absence.

"Why did you pour that coffee into your saucer?" Washington reportedly replied.

"To cool it," Jefferson answered.

"Even so," Washington said, "we pour our legislation into the senatorial saucer to cool it."

The United States Senate has been called the world's greatest deliberative body. By serving six-year terms—as opposed to the two-year terms in the more populist and considerably larger House of Representatives—senators are supposed to be able to stand above the ideological fray and engage in thoughtful and serious debate. What's more, the filibuster rule allows a single senator to halt the creep of political passions into the decision-making process by blocking a given vote.

Perhaps nowhere is the ethos of the Senate, this commitment to principle over politics, more memorably captured than in the classic 1939 film "Mr. Smith Goes to Washington," when Jimmy Stewart, who plays an idealistic freshman senator wrongfully accused of graft, refuses to yield the floor until he has cleared his name. (After almost 24 hours, he winds up passing out from exhaustion but is ultimately exonerated.)

"We're supposed to be the conscience of the nation," Senator Leahy told me recently in his Washington office, which is decorated with New England folk art, including a print of a dog and cat cuddling on a throw rug that looks as if it could be on loan from a bed-and-breakfast in his home state.

Leahy is one of Congress's so-called Watergate babies. He was elected to the Senate following Nixon's resignation in 1974, and his arrival on Capitol Hill coincided with the sweeping bipartisan effort to investigate the Nixon administration's abuses of executive power. "There was a sense inside the Senate among both Republicans and Democrats that the government had gotten off course and that we had a responsibility to find out what happened," Leahy recalled.

Weeks after the 34-year-old Leahy was sworn into the Senate, his Democratic colleague from Idaho, Frank Church, began his legendary probe into domestic spying during the cold war. Church's bipartisan Senate committee interviewed more than 800 officials and held 21 public hearings, uncovering widespread abuses by the C.I.A. and the F.B.I. "I had just come from eight years as a federal prosecutor," Leahy told me, "so I knew a little something about convening grand juries and issuing subpoenas. But this was on a scale magnified a thousand times anything I had ever seen."

If Leahy speaks about that era with a certain nostalgia, it's because he recognizes that the power of the Senate, which blossomed during his early years in Congress, has now withered. The story of the United States is in many ways the story of the push and pull between the executive and legislative branches. Consider just the last half-century or so. In the late 1940s, Congress moved aggressively to recoup some of the power it had lost to Franklin Delano Roosevelt, who took full advantage of his presidential prerogative during a 12-year tenure that spanned both the Depression and World War II. (Among other things, Congress passed the 22nd Amendment, which limited future presidents to two terms in office.) President Harry Truman and other cold warriors pushed back; the '50s and '60s were dominated by the high-stakes diplomacy and covert overseas operations of the Soviet Union-United States conflict, shifting the balance of power back to the executive—until the aforementioned Nixon reaction. Yet much of the authority that Congress recaptured during the post-Watergate and post-Vietnam administrations of Carter and Ford it gave back when Ronald Reagan assumed the presidency and flexed his presidential muscle to push through an ambitious agenda that included massive tax cuts and an escalation of America's global struggle against Communism.

During Bill Clinton's tenure, what was shaping up as a strong presidency was brought to heel by an independent counsel and impeachment hearings. By the time Clinton finished his second term, it looked to many experts as if the White House would be working with diminished authority for years to come: the presidential historian Michael Beschloss called George W. Bush "the first truly postimperial president."

As it turned out, the power of the president soared to new heights under Bush. Many of the administration's most aggressive moves came in the realm of national security and the war on terror in particular. The Bush administration claimed the authority to deny captured combatants—U.S. citizens and aliens alike—such basic due-process rights as access to a lawyer. It created a detention facility on Guantánamo Bay that it declared was outside the jurisdiction of the federal courts and built a new legal system—without any input from Congress—to try enemy combatants. And it argued that the president's commander-in-chief powers gave him the authority to violate America's laws and treaties, including the Geneva Conventions.

The assertion and expansion of presidential power is arguably the defining feature of the Bush years. Come January, the current administration will pass on to its successor a vast infrastructure for electronic surveillance, secret sites for detention and interrogation and a sheaf of legal opinions empowering the executive to do whatever he feels necessary to protect the country. The new administration will also be the beneficiary of Congress's recent history of complacency, which amounts to a tacit acceptance of the Bush administration's expansive views of executive authority. For that matter, thanks to the recent economic bailout, Bush's successor will inherit control over much of the banking industry. "The next president will enter office as the most powerful president who has ever sat in the White House," Jack Balkin, a constitutional law professor at Yale and an influential legal blogger, told me a few weeks ago.

* * *

As has now been widely noted, the chief architect of the Bush administration's expansive view of executive power was Vice President Dick Cheney, whose interest in pumping up the presidency dates to the mid-1970s, when, as President Ford's chief of staff, he had a front-row seat for Congress's post-Watergate crusade against the executive branch. Ten years later, as a member of the House of Representatives, Cheney dissented from the majority of his colleagues in the Iran-contra affair, arguing that President Reagan possessed the power to provide arms to the contras—even though Congress had expressly prohibited him from doing so.

Yet even absent a Cheney, it's very likely that any president, Republican or Democrat, would have accrued more authority in the aftermath of 9/11. The president needs the flexibility to move quickly and forcefully to protect the country during wartime, even if this entails concealing information from the public and encroaching on civil liberties. "It is of the nature of war," Alexander Hamilton wrote, "to increase the executive at the expense of the legislative authority." And Hamilton was speaking about conventional warfare—not the war on terror with all its novel challenges.

In a sense, it's hard to fault Congress for the historic surrender of its authority during the Bush years. Like the Iran-contras arms deals, many of the actions that the administration undertook after 9/11—like the rendition of suspected terrorists to "ghost prisons" in foreign countries and the warrantless wiretapping of American citizens—were kept secret, even from lawmakers, which made oversight impossible. The administration also did everything it could to block unwanted disclosures about its policies, routinely invoking the formerly obscure "state-secrets privilege" to avoid revealing details of its treatment of enemy combatants.

When the administration did choose to pass on information to Congress, it did so selectively, not always reliably, and with a very clear political goal in mind. In "Angler: The Cheney Vice Presidency," Barton Gellman, a reporter at The Washington Post, wrote that when Cheney was lining up support for the invasion of Iraq, he met with Representative Dick Armey, the Republican majority leader. Behind closed doors, he told Armey, who had been skeptical, that Saddam Hussein had made "substantial progress" toward building a miniature nuclear weapon. Armey duly voted for the invasion.

Still, Congress was hardly unaware of what was going on. Many of the most aggressive positions that the Bush administration staked out after 9/11—from the creation of Guantánamo to what amounted to the suspension of America's Geneva Conventions obligations governing the treatment of captured combatants—were a matter of public record. Not only did Congress not flinch at such unilateral actions, but it also helped enable the expansion of presidential authority by passing the USA Patriot Act, which gave the executive sweeping new law-enforcement powers.

* * *

It was the Clinton impeachment trial in 1999, though, that finally pushed the Senate into the trenches of political warfare and polarized the institution once and for all. Senators now saw themselves as members of their respective political parties first—and representatives of their constituencies second. After George W. Bush's election in 2000, many Republicans on Capitol Hill saw it as their duty to protect him from their Democratic colleagues. "The Republican leaders in both houses of Congress made the decision that they were going to be field soldiers in the president's army, rather than members of an independent branch of government," Ornstein says.

* * *

Senator Arlen Specter plays squash almost every day, usually before dawn in the basement of the Federal Reserve building, one of the few remaining courts in Washington designed for hardball, the largely outdated form of the game that he prefers. He keeps a record of the scores of all of his matches against a rotating group of opponents, including a 27-year-old staff member whom the senator has been known to call at 5:30 a.m. with directions to get dressed and meet him on the court in half an hour. Even now, at the age of 78 and having recently survived Hodgkin's disease, Specter is enormously competitive. During a recent match, when he suspected that I might be easing up a bit, he barked at me to play harder.

After our match, over breakfast in the Senate dining room, I asked Specter, who was chairman of the Judiciary Committee from 2005 to January 2007, how he thought Congress had fared vis-à-vis the executive branch during the Bush administration. "Decades from now," he answered, "historians will look back on the period from 9/11 to the present as an era of unbridled executive power and Congressional ineffectiveness."

Having risen to the Senate from the courtrooms of Philadelphia, Specter is a stickler for process. Even now, he becomes visibly angry when he recalls reading in the newspaper that the National Security Agency was illegally wiretapping United States citizens. "I was madder than hell," he told me. "It was a flat violation of the Foreign Intelligence Surveillance Act, and it violated the well-established custom of briefing the chairman and ranking member of the Judiciary Committee on matters like this."

When I asked Specter whether he thought he had done everything he could to prevent the executive branch from expanding its authority, he became a little indignant: "I fought it every step of the way—I'm still fighting it."

There is truth to this, though the story is more complicated. During the Bush years, Specter did write numerous pieces of legislation intended to bolster Congress's role in the war on terror. In February 2002, he introduced a bill that would have established a system of trials for suspected Al Qaeda detainees. It never made it out of the Senate Armed Services Committee, leaving the administration to devise the trial system itself. In 2006, Specter proposed the Presidential Signing Statements Act, which would have empowered Congress to file suit to have a signing statement declared illegal by a federal court. This, too, never went anywhere.

As Specter sees it, the very same rules that are intended to ensure thoughtful deliberation inside the Senate put it at a disadvantage with respect to the White House. "The executive branch requires the decision of one person, as opposed to the legislative branch, which requires 10 votes just to get my bill out of committee," he says.

But Specter also missed his share of opportunities to stand up for Congress in the battle over the president's wartime powers. When Attorney General Alberto Gonzales testified before the Judiciary Committee in early 2006 about the illegal wiretapping, Specter didn't require that he be sworn in, nor did he ask for any of the Justice Department's internal legal memorandums on the secret surveillance program. What's more, Specter's own legislative response to the warrantless-wiretapping scandal, which he proposed in 2006, was widely seen as a capitulation to the White House.

* * *

Nor has the Democratic Congress made much use of the rest of its tools against the executive branch. Take, for instance, the Senate's power to confirm appointments. When President Bush nominated Michael Mukasey to serve as attorney general in the fall of 2007, the Senate could have easily insisted on any number of conditions before confirming him, even something as simple as a public statement that the president is bound by the laws passed by Congress. There was a clear precedent for such deal making. In 1973, the Senate refused to confirm President Nixon's attorney general nominee, Elliot Richardson, until Richardson agreed to name a special prosecutor to investigate Watergate. The Senate even insisted that it be allowed to sign off on the name of the special prosecutor before moving ahead with Richardson's confirmation. The Senate made no such preconditions with respect to Mukasey. In fact, he was confirmed even after stating during his confirmation hearing that the administration's secret surveillance program was not illegal because the president has the right to ignore statutory law if he thinks it's necessary to defend the country.

* * *

For those concerned about the expansion of presidential power, Barack Obama's answers to the Boston Globe's 2007 questionnaire were encouraging. Among other things, he said the president can't conduct surveillance without warrants or detain United States citizens indefinitely as unlawful enemy combatants. He also said that it's illegal for the president to ignore international treaties like the Geneva Conventions and that if Congress prohibits a specific interrogation technique by law, the president cannot employ it. "The president is not above the law," Obama said.

It would be a mistake, though, to view presidential power as a left-right issue. Historically, Democratic presidents have been no less eager than their Republican counterparts to leverage the authority of their office. Recall that the last Democrat to occupy the White House, Bill Clinton, launched airstrikes on Kosovo in a war against Yugoslavia without Congressional authorization and liberally invoked executive privilege during the various investigations into his private life and financial dealings.

History has shown that where you stand on executive authority is largely a matter of where you sit. Before his election, Abraham Lincoln criticized President James Polk for provoking the Mexican War; as president, Lincoln unilaterally suspended habeas corpus and ordered a blockade of the ports of rebel states. As a senator, Richard Nixon—of all people—criticized President Truman's frequent invocations of executive privilege.

Bruce Fein, a Justice Department lawyer in the Reagan administration who is now a critic of presidential power, told me a few weeks ago that he expects the next president to "take everything Bush has given him and wield it with even greater confidence because Congress has given him a safe harbor to do so with impunity." This may be overstating the point, but it's worth keeping in mind that in the final year of Bush's presidency—while facing a Democratic Congress and historically low approval ratings—he was able to push through a federal bailout bill that vested almost complete control over the economy in the Treasury secretary (who reports to the president), not to mention a major rewriting of the 1978 Foreign Intelligence Surveillance Act that will make it easier for the White House to spy on American citizens.

At the president's urging, the new FISA bill, which Obama and McCain supported, also went a step further, granting immunity to telecom companies that cooperated with the government's secret surveillance program. As a result, we will probably never know how many people were spied on, what criteria were used to select them and what was done with the information gleaned from the wiretaps.

These are just a few of the many unanswered questions raised by the White House's policies in the war on terror. Presumably, as more detainee lawsuits make their way through the federal courts, we will learn additional details about the mistreatment of enemy combatants, particularly because the new administration's lawyers won't have the same incentive to suppress such information. But there has been no talk of the newly elected Congress undertaking a sweeping investigation of the Bush administration's activities along the lines of the Church Committee.

During my conversations with the senators, I sometimes had the impression that their irritation with the White House's arrogance toward Congress had overshadowed their concerns about the administration's policies themselves. I wondered if along the way they had lost sight of their duty to represent the interests of their constituents.

For all of the legislature's complaints about being excluded from the political process during the Bush years, it seems fair to question whether Congress really wants to be a full partner in America's government. Senators may not like being kept in the dark, but they seem to prefer to leave the big decisions—especially those concerning national security—to the executive. "There's a psychology of vassalage to the president," Fein says. "They don't want to be out there on a limb."

Given these diminished ambitions, even if the legislative branch does reassert itself in the next administration, what exactly will that mean? Will Congress simply insist on being asked for its blessing before empowering the president to do whatever he sees fit? And if so, what will it take for what the historian Arthur Schlesinger Jr. identified as democracy's greatest virtue—"its capacity for self-correction"—to kick in and restore the constitutional balance?

What do you think of Mahler's account? Are the sentiments expressed by the Senators that he interviewed based upon political partisanship, institutional myopia, individual political ambition, or altruistic constitutional concerns about the current state of congressional oversight and executive-legislative relations? Consider the responses of the Trump Administration to congressional oversight that are discussed in the preceding chapters of this book—were Congress's powers of oversight further diminished during the Trump Administration?

2. The Current State of Congress—What, If Anything, Should Be Done? Do these arguments for more aggressive congressional oversight have merit? Consider the discussion of the January 6 Committee in Chapter 8—will that investigation mark the beginning of a new approach to the investigative role of Congress? If Congress needs to reassert itself to restore the balance of power between the political branches that was intended by the Framers of the Constitution, what should be done to restore that balance? As you think about this question, consider the following purposes of congressional oversight, as identified and explained by the Congressional Research Service:

Congress has engaged in oversight throughout its history. Investigating how statutes, budgets, and policies are implemented by the executive branch enables Congress to assess whether federal agencies and departments are administering programs in an effective, efficient, and economical manner and to gather information that may inform legislation. The expansion of the national government and bureaucracy has only increased Congress's need for and use of available oversight tools to check on and check the executive. This "checking" function serves to protect Congress's policymaking role and its place under Article I in the U.S. constitutional system of checks and balances.

Congress's oversight role is also significant because it shines the spotlight of public attention on many critical issues, which enables lawmakers and the general public to make informed judgments about executive performance. Woodrow Wilson, in his classic 1885 study *Congressional Government*, emphasized that the "informing function should be preferred even to its [lawmaking] function." He added that unless Congress conducts oversight of administrative activities, the "country must remain in embarrassing, crippling ignorance of the very affairs which it is most important it should understand and direct."[28]

Oversight occurs in virtually any congressional activity and through a wide variety of channels, organizations, and structures. These range from formal committee hearings to informal Member contacts with executive officials, from staff studies to reviews by congressional support agencies, and from casework conducted by Member offices to studies prepared by non-congressional entities such as academic institutions, private commissions, or think tanks.

Congressional oversight of the executive branch is designed to fulfill a variety of purposes, such as those outlined below.

Ensure Executive Compliance with Statutory Requirements and Legislative Intent

Congress, of necessity, must delegate discretionary authority to federal administrators. To make certain that these officers faithfully execute laws according to the intent of Congress, committees and Members can review the actions taken and regulations formulated by departments and agencies. This purpose grows in importance as Congress delegates more rulemaking authority to agencies.

Improve the Efficiency, Effectiveness, and Economy of Governmental Operations

A large federal bureaucracy makes it imperative for Congress to encourage and secure efficient and effective program management and to make every

---

28. [15] Woodrow Wilson, *Congressional Government* (Boston: Houghton Mifflin, 1885) at 303. More recently, Professor Josh Chafetz, a scholar of Congress and its role in the federal government in the 21st century, has referred to this function as "congressional overspeech." Josh Chafetz, *Congressional Overspeech*. 89 FORDHAM L. REV. 596 (2020).

dollar count toward the achievement of program goals. A basic objective is strengthening federal programs through better managerial operations and service delivery. Such steps can improve the accountability of agency managers to Congress and enhance program performance.

Evaluate Program Performance

Systematic program performance evaluation remains an evolving technique of oversight. Modern program evaluation uses social science and management methodologies—such as surveys, cost-benefit analyses, and efficiency studies—to assess the effectiveness of ongoing programs. Information about program performance may be useful to Congress as it fulfills its roles as both legislator and appropriator and makes decisions about government programs and the amount of funding they will receive.

Prevent Executive Encroachment on Legislative Prerogatives and Powers

Many commentators, public policy analysts, and legislators state that Presidents and executive officials may overstep their authority in various areas, such as the impoundment of funds, executive privilege, and war powers. Increased oversight—as part of the constitutional checks and balances system—can redress what many in the public and Congress might view as executive arrogation of legislative prerogatives.

Investigate Alleged Instances of Poor Administration, Arbitrary and Capricious Behavior, Abuse, Waste, Dishonesty, and Fraud

Instances of fraud and other forms of corruption, wasteful expenditures, incompetent management, and the subversion of governmental processes can provoke legislative and public interest in oversight.

Assess Agency or Officials' Ability to Manage and Implement Program Objectives

Congress's ability to evaluate the capacity of agencies and managers to carry out program objectives can be accomplished in various ways. For example, numerous laws require agencies to submit reports to Congress. Some of these are regular, occurring annually or semi-annually, for instance, while others are activated by a specific event, development, or set of conditions. Reporting requirements may promote self-evaluation by the agency. Organizations outside of Congress—such as offices of inspector general, the Government Accountability Office (GAO), and study commissions—also advise Members and committees on how well federal agencies are working.

Review and Determine Federal Financial Priorities

Congress exercises some of its most effective oversight through the appropriations process, which provides the opportunity to assess agency and departmental expenditures in detail. In addition, most federal agencies and programs are under regular and frequent reauthorizations—on an annual, two-year, five-year, or other basis—giving authorizing committees the opportunity to review agency activities, operations, and procedures. As a consequence of these oversight efforts, Congress can abolish or curtail obsolete or ineffective programs by cutting off or reducing funds. Congress might also increase funding for effective programs.

Ensure that Executive Policies Reflect the Public Interest

Congressional oversight can appraise whether the needs and interests of the public are adequately served by federal programs. Such evaluations might prompt corrective action through legislation, administrative changes, or other means and methods. Legislative reviews might also prompt measures to consolidate or terminate duplicative and unnecessary programs or agencies.

Protect Individual Rights and Liberties

Congressional oversight can help safeguard the rights and liberties of citizens and others. By revealing abuses of authority, oversight hearings and other efforts can halt executive misconduct and help prevent its recurrence through, for example, new legislation or indirectly by heightening public awareness of the issue(s).

Draw Public Attention to Issues

Congressional oversight can provide Congress and its Members with the opportunity to highlight issues, activities of the government, and other events that they wish to bring to the attention of the public. In some instances, Congress may believe that it will be better able to achieve a goal if public pressure or energy is directed to a particular matter and that oversight activities may be one way to generate that attention.

Congressional Research Service, *Congressional Oversight Manual* (updated March 31, 2021). How many of these functions are currently being fulfilled by Congress? Which of these do you think merit more effort on the part of Congress? What should Congress do to improve in those areas?

3. Protection of Civil Liberties and the Rights of Witnesses. A recurring theme in the preceding chapters of this book has been the need to balance the rights of witnesses against the needs of Congress to collect information and to conduct oversight. Do you think the current state of the law, as set out in the preceding chapters, strikes an appropriate balance? Consider in this regard the following analysis and recommendations of a prominent scholar of congressional oversight and investigations in a 2015 law review article:

Andrew McCanse Wright, *Congressional Due Process*

85 Mississippi Law Journal 401 (2015)

[Ed. Note: Footnotes omitted except as indicated.]

Congress demonstrates institutional indifference to due process[29] for government officials, private citizens, and corporate entities subject to its oversight investigations. Those who find themselves in the cross-hairs of a committee investigation are often surprised to find out that a whole panoply of fundamental concepts of procedural fairness—right to counsel, regulation of discovery, neutrality of arbiters, safeguarding of confidential information, rights of confrontation, common law privileges, rights of privacy—are either disavowed or inadequately protected by Congress. In other instances in which Congress has adopted a policy to honor a witness's or target's due process interest, its enforcement mechanism often fails.

To date, Congress has failed to heed criticism of its investigative practices by witnesses, practitioners, academic journals, and courts. As discussed in this article, the House and Senate could significantly enhance congressional due process without sacrificing oversight effectiveness.

Congressional oversight is a constitutionally derived function of vital importance to effective governance, as well as an appropriately limited Executive.[30] As such, its processes should serve substance. While the limitation of due process rights in these oversight investigations slightly expands the amount of information available to Congress—by removing legal barriers and ignoring objections of those who may possess evidence—it also comes at functional and institutional costs, which ultimately outweigh any possible benefit.

Deficient procedural protections in congressional investigations have normative and practical consequences. Unregulated congressional investigative practices expose the subjects of oversight to unnecessary reputational harms. These practices can be self-defeating when they impede the fact-finding function. Worthwhile congressional oversight activity can be overshadowed by the perception that Congress is dismissive of witness rights. Indifference to witnesses' due process concerns undermines the legitimacy of investigations and ultimately impugns Congress itself. Congress could materially enhance its oversight legitimacy by embracing due process norms.

---

29. [3] For purposes of this article, "congressional due process" includes the formal substantive and procedural components of the Due Process Clause, but also extends to more diffuse, yet important, elements of procedural fairness grounded in other provisions of the Constitution, common law, rules of evidence, and rule of law principles.

30. [9] *See* Andrew McCanse Wright, *Constitutional Conflict and Congressional Oversight*, 98 Marq. L. Rev. 881, 900–07 (2014) (discussing the legally recognized, and functional, purposes of congressional oversight).

The Constitution applies to congressional action, including the civil liberties and due process provisions.[31] However, congressional and judicial proceedings differ in nature and purpose. As Congress notes in a recent litigation brief: "Congressional investigations are fact-finding inquiries convened to produce information upon which Congress can bring its legislative judgment to bear; they are not intended to resolve disputes between parties and are not subject to rules of evidence...."[32] Congress relies on *Hannah v. Larche*[33] for the proposition that "when governmental action does not partake of an adjudication, as for example, when a general fact-finding investigation is being conducted, it is not necessary that the full panoply of judicial procedures be used."[34] In addition, where a constitutional protection is strictly a trial right, it will not apply to congressional hearings or investigative processes even if the value undergirding it does.

Even when a constitutional provision applies to congressional processes, there is understandable judicial reticence to regulate the proceedings of a coordinate branch of government. The D.C. Circuit characterizes this view: "[T]he courts must presume that the committees of Congress will exercise their powers responsibly and with due regard for the rights of affected parties."[35] This limited legal precedent tends to give Congress wide latitude to manage its own proceedings. As such, legislative self-regulation, rather than constitutional law, is the primary mechanism for the establishment of congressional due process.

Congress should address these concerns and overhaul its investigative procedures. Applying due process rules to these investigations would have several important effects. First, these rules would enhance procedural rights in front of the investigative committee. Second, they would have an appreciable effect on the political context within which the investigative conflicts play out. Third, such rules would bolster the legitimacy of the process from the perspec-

---

31. [10] *Watkins v. United States*, 354 U.S. at 187–88 ("The Bill of Rights is applicable to investigations as to all forms of governmental action. Witnesses cannot be compelled to give evidence against themselves. They cannot be subjected to unreasonable search and seizure. Nor can the First Amendment freedoms of speech, press, religion, or political belief and association be abridged.").

32. [11] Memorandum of Points and Authorities in Support of Plaintiff's Motion for Summary Judgment at 28, *Comm. on Oversight & Gov't Reform v. Holder*, 979 F. Supp. 2d 1 (D.D.C. 2013) (No. 1:12-cv-01332-ABJ).

33. [12] 363 U.S. 420 (1960).

34. [13] *Id.* at 442. As an example of congressional reliance on this quotation, see Memorandum of Points and Authorities in Support of Plaintiff's Motion for Summary Judgment, at 29, *Holder*, 979 F. Supp. 2d 1 (D.D.C. 2013) (No. 1:12-cv-01332-ABJ).

35. [15] *Ashland Oil, Inc. v. FTC*, 548 F.2d 977, 979 (D.C. Cir. 1976) (quoting *Ashland Oil, Inc. v. FTC*, 409 F. Supp. 297, 308 (D.D.C. 1976)). *See also In re Provident Life & Accident Ins. Co.*, No. CIV-1-90-219, 1990 U.S. Dist. LEXIS 21067, at *6 (E.D. Tenn. June 13, 1990) ("Congress ... stands as a separate and co-equal branch of government which is capable of making its own determinations regarding privileges asserted by witnesses before it.").

tive of the courts when called upon by Congress to enforce subpoenas, contempt citations, and obstruction prosecutions.

* * *

A. Due Process in Congressional Rules

Congress should adopt rules that would honor due process. Congressional proceedings will always be inherently political because the goal of legislative inquiry is to form an informed policy judgment. Because that function is informative and not adjudicative, less process is due. However, Congress could do a lot more to provide due process and enhance investigative legitimacy without sacrificing oversight interests. While by no means exclusive, this section suggests a number of congressional due process rules for consideration.

1. Code of Oversight Decorum and Creditability

Congressional rules requiring decorum and creditability operate at a level of generality. They should be expanded to include specific obligations of Senators and Representatives, and their staffs, to treat witnesses with dignity, respect individuals' constitutional rights, treat confidential witness information appropriately, and maintain the integrity of the fact-finding process.

As an enforcement mechanism, the House and Senate Rules Committees should establish a process whereby aggrieved parties could present their concerns about oversight abuses. A decision to hold a public forum on a particular matter should operate like the Supreme Court's certiorari process, with a vote threshold to take up the matter that constituted the number of minority members on the committee. That would empower either the majority or minority party to create the forum independently so it could not be quashed as a matter of partisanship. Even if an aggrieved party finds procedural enforcement of such rules problematic, having specific congressional rules will empower private parties, their counsel, other committee members, and the media to more favorably shape the political environment of the investigation.

2. Formal Investigation Initiation

Congress should require formal initiations of investigation in advance of any formal process. At present, only one House committee's rules address formal authorization of a particular investigation, and that provision is limited to its subcommittees. While contempt resolutions require action by the entire chamber, at that point most of the investigative activity has already occurred in the absence of formal initiation.

Under such a system, a committee may seek information voluntarily by means of document request or informal briefing. However, a committee vote to initiate a formal investigation should be a condition precedent to issuance of a subpoena. This should happen during a separate committee business meeting during which the scope of the investigation can be debated and marked up.

Thereafter, the committee or chair could issue a subpoena pursuant to the resolution authorizing the investigation.

The initiation resolution would then provide notice to the party about the committee's jurisdiction, the committee's specific investigative authorization, and the scope of the investigation. Such resolution would also have beneficial effects on any subsequent court review, including pertinency analysis. In all, a formal initiation process would give investigations the imprimatur of a formal deliberative process, thereby enhancing Congress's investigations greater legitimacy of congressional investigations.

3. A Legislative *Gideon*

Congress needs to honor a robust right to counsel for oversight witnesses and targets. Some congressional rules recognize rights to legal representation before committees; however, the counsel role they allow is generally quite limited. The House Rules provide that "[w]itnesses at hearings may be accompanied by their own counsel for the purpose of advising them concerning their constitutional rights."[36] Under House Rules, counsel's role is limited to personal constitutional advice.

Like the Senate, most House committees that address counsel rights have language limiting the scope of advice to "constitutional rights" of the client. One House committee provides for institutional counsel to be present "if the scope of the deposition is expected to cover actions taken as part of the deponent's employment."[37] The Senate and House intelligence committees have rules that offer to help provide a witness with voluntary counsel. These committees also require counsel to have the requisite security clearances. Further, in the House, the lawyer is expressly prohibited from examining witnesses before the committee but is invited to propose questions or suggest additional witnesses.

The House and Senate should establish robust right-to-counsel rules. These rules should be institution-wide so that parties and the bar can establish stable expectations. They should expressly recognize the full scope of legal advice and abolish any provisions that could be read to limit advice to constitutional rights. There should also be some opportunity for counsel to speak on behalf of their client witnesses at public hearings. Further, Congress should address access to counsel through referral services and funding for indigent witnesses. There should also be a legislative *Miranda*: Congressional agents should have an obligation to inform witnesses and subjects of counsel and self-incrimination rights when invoking compulsory investigative processes.

---

36. [269] H.R. Rule XI(2)(k)(3), 114th Cong. (2015), available at http://clerk.house.gov/legislative/house-rules.pdf.

37. [272] H.R. Comm. on Educ. and the Workforce Rule 10(e), 114th Cong. (2015), available at http://www.gpo.gov/fdsys/pkg/CPRT-114HPRT93187/pdf/CPRT114HPRT93187.pdf.

4. Formal Recognition of Testimonial Privileges

Congress should adopt a policy recognizing testimonial privileges. Testimonial privileges protect intimate spousal relationships and promote candid advice from doctors, lawyers, and religious advisors. The rule could contain a standard for overcoming the privilege based on overwhelming need or other established exceptions. However, a presumption of testimonial privilege would honor important policy goals and enhance the procedural fairness of congressional investigations by limiting intrusions into the private sphere of life. The symbolism of privilege recognition would create legitimacy benefits that would likely far outstrip the information costs to Congress.

Congress should also honor work product doctrine, and should broaden the concept of preparation in anticipation of litigation to include preparation for congressional proceedings. While legislative inquiry is not an adversarial proceeding, congressional requests are often adversarial. Preparing to face Congress presents analogous fairness concerns and need for advice attendant to litigation work product.

When a testimonial or work product privilege has been raised as an objection to document production, the rules should require the objector to produce a privilege log and afford him an opportunity to appeal to the leadership an adverse ruling at the committee level.[38]

5. Protection of Confidential Information

Congress should comprehensively address treatment of confidential information. Congress regularly requests documents and testimony with important confidential business information, proprietary and trade secret information, national security information, law enforcement information, and private personal information that would be covered by the Privacy Act in other contexts. There has been a long and unfortunate history of leaking damaging information to the media to further investigative narratives. The Speech or Debate Clause serves as an effective and nearly absolute bar to judicial regulation of unwarranted congressional disclosures. However, House and Senate rules could provide for self-regulation through a requirement that committees identify confidential information and prohibit members and staff from unauthorized disclosures. Further, it could make violations of such rules grounds for discipline.

---

38. [279] For example, consider this scenario: a party objects to the provision of materials based on the attorney-client privilege and produces a privilege log. Based on the review of the log, the House committee chair overrules the objection and commands production. The party should have a procedural right to appeal to the Speaker and Minority Leader, including *in camera* review. In the face of an adverse ruling, perhaps the rules should authorize the party to seek a vote of the House or even court review if there is a concrete risk of collateral consequences in a parallel judicial proceeding.

6. Rebuttal to Hearsay, Defamation, and Allegations

Congressional investigations regularly include allegations of misconduct or material that could be defamatory. In addition, Congress has no prohibitions on the use of hearsay. A few congressional rules address these reputational and reliability concerns, but they are inadequate. Congress could address hearsay and defamation by providing meaningful rebuttal or confrontation rights. Such rights would ameliorate these concerns without turning congressional hearings into full-blown adversarial proceedings.

One Senate committee invites, by rule, any person who has been identified in a hearing in a manner that "tends to defame him or otherwise adversely affect his reputation" to file "a sworn statement of facts relevant to such testimony or evidence" for the committee's consideration.[39] One House committee merely notes that the "Committee is the sole judge of the pertinence of testimony and evidence" submitted by outside parties.[40] Two House committees make a more solid commitment by providing that the committee "shall afford a person an opportunity voluntarily to appear as a witness" and the Committee will "receive and shall dispose of requests from such person to subpoena additional witnesses."[41]

These provisions are steps in the right direction, but they need to be standardized across the House and Senate. In addition, there should be a presumption that a party with reputational interests at stake may supplement the record.

A private request for a committee subpoena against another party would move Congress much closer to an adversarial proceeding. Similarly, cross-examination rights would also make a fundamental turn toward adversarial model.[42] Reputational interests ought to be sufficiently protected by an affirmative ability to give evidence rather than a private right of subpoena in congressional proceedings.

7. Witness Notice and Disclosures

Oversight witnesses and targets should have settled expectations that Congress will provide a reasonable amount of time to comply with oversight requests. The one-week public hearing notice provisions in the House and Sen-

---

39. [280] S. Comm. on Energy & Natural Res. Rule 14, 114th Cong. (2015), available at http://www.energy.senate.gov/public/index.cfm/rules.

40. [281] H.R. Comm. on Sci., Space, and Tech. Rule III(f), 114th Cong. (2015), available at http://science.house.gov/sites/republicans.science.house.gov/files/documents/hearings/Committee%20on%20Science%2C%20Space%2C%20and%20Technology%20Rules%20114th%20Congress%20v2_0.pdf.

41. [282] H.R. Comm. on Agric. Rule VIII(j)(1), 114th Cong. (2015), available at http://agriculture.house.gov/about/rules-and-jurisdiction.htm; H.R. Comm. on Admin. Rule 9(f)(5), 114th Cong. (2015), available at http://cha.house.gov/about/rulescommittee-house-administration.

42. [283] Perhaps there could be a provision, much like some voir dire models, in which the aggrieved party could submit a limited number of questions for an accuser to be asked by the congressional committee.

ate imply that voluntary witnesses will have at least one week of notice, as well. When a witness is compelled to testify at a hearing or deposition, however, congressional rules do not provide guidance as to how much notice must be given.

In addition, only a handful of Senate committee rules provide any standard of the substance of the subpoena that would provide notice to the subpoena recipient. Other Senate committees have rules that assume a subpoena power but do not establish any process or standards. In contrast, the rules rarely require proof of service or provide a minimum threshold of time to comply.

Three House committees' subpoena provisions address notice to the recipient, while the rest remain silent. Where committee rules specify a deposition power at all, rules tend to require the barest notice to the deponent. These provisions merely require the subpoena to "specify the date, time, and place of the deposition" without any minimum length before its return date.

Congress should enhance and standardize notice provisions for witnesses by establishing reasonable return date minimums for subpoenas and deposition notices. For example, one week seems like a reasonable baseline standard for a purely testimonial subpoena. However, a subpoena duces tecum should have something more like a standard one-month return date. Of course both standards would be subject to negotiated extensions and the rules could provide for a formal committee finding of exigency that would allow a shorter return date.

Witnesses should also be provided with an opportunity to review documents they will be questioned about in advance of their testimony. Members of Congress can question witnesses in public hearings about documents they have not had a chance to review, including those of which the witness was not an author or recipient. As recommended by former congressional impeachment counsel Abbe Lowell, Congress could provide provisions for document disclosures to witnesses in advance of depositions and hearings.[43]

8. Discovery Management and Objections

Informal discovery—including transcribed interviews, briefings, and document requests—are the bread-and-butter of oversight, yet they are wholly unregulated by language of Senate and House rules. Rather, they operate in the shadow of the rules and are defined by the relative leverage provided by the availability of subpoenas and depositions. Without a credible objection process or neutral arbiter, there is almost no check on the reasonableness of the congressional request.

---

43. [291] Abbe D. Lowell, *Overseeing Oversight*, NAT'L LAW JOURNAL (Nov. 20, 2006), available at http://www.chadbourne.com/files/Publication/4848dbb3-6880-4de1-84c7-14f800cb9158/Presentation/PublicationAttachment/f63ae119-b2d4-4742-9c2f19cee4954ff6/AbbeLowell_NLJoped112006. pdf (arguing for committee document productions to witnesses in advance of congressional hearings).

At the chamber level, neither House nor Senate Rules regulate subpoena scope or provide a mechanism for the recipient to object. Congressional committees, too, have almost no rule language designed to regulate or limit the scope or substance of a subpoena beyond the basic recitations about witnesses, documents, memoranda, and records. Nor do almost any committee rules provide a platform for the recipient to raise objections. One Senate committee's deposition rules note that the chair of the committee has sole power to rule on any objection by a witness during a deposition, and another allows a ruling by any committee member. The House Committee on Oversight and Government Reform has the most robust rules related to deposition objections, and its rules leave rulings to the discretion of the Chair with a committee appeal right.

A subpoena often merely recites an earlier document request sent under the committee chair's name. In turn, that prior letter usually received almost no member-level vetting other than the committee chair's normal internal letter writing process. When drafting a subpoena, the enforcement of the prior request undermines the incentive to narrow the scope of the congressional command.

The House and Senate should establish discovery management provisions. Further, as noted above, Congress should create a credible objection process as well as erect formal processes and standards for bipartisan consideration of appeals of chair rulings.

* * *

Conclusion

As one practitioner put it: "As difficult as the courtroom can be, there is a place today that is far worse, a place where many of the rules so fundamental to our western legal system do not seem to apply."[44] Congress could significantly enhance its due process without hindering its fact-finding function. In turn, courts could incentivize much needed reforms by casting a more skeptical eye at congressional requests for judicial enforcement. Legislative institutions should embrace the constitutional norms of procedural fairness so that the concept of congressional due process is not oxymoronic.

---

44. [304] Paul M. Thompson, *A Fate Worse than Litigation: The Congressional Investigation*, Executive Counsel, vol. 6, no. 1 (Feb./Mar. 2009), available at http://www.mwe.com/info/pubs/afateworsethanlitigation.pdf.

About the Authors

Lance Cole is Professor of Law and Director of the Center for Government Law and Public Policy Studies at Penn State University's Dickinson School of Law. Professor Cole's research and scholarship focuses on legal issues relating to government investigations of business entities and individuals, including the congressional investigation and oversight process. Prior to joining the Penn State Dickinson faculty Professor Cole served as Deputy Special Counsel (Minority) to the Senate Special Committee on Whitewater. While a member of the Penn State Dickinson faculty Professor Cole served as a legal consultant on the staff of the National Commission on Terrorist Attacks Upon the United States (the "9/11 Commission").

Stanley Brand is the Distinguished Fellow in Law and Government at the Penn State Dickinson Law where he teaches Election Law, Federal Regulation and Legislative Practice Seminar, Sports and Entertainment Law, Independent Counsel Seminar, and Criminal Law. From 1976–1983, he served as general counsel to the U.S. House of Representatives under Speaker Thomas P. "Tip" O'Neill where he litigated major cases involving separation of powers and the constitutional powers of the House, including before the Supreme Court. In private practice since 1984, he has represented individuals, business entities, and public officials in grand jury, Department of Justice, Inspectors General, and congressional investigations, trials and appeals. From 1992–2020, he was Vice President of the National Association of Professional Baseball Leagues ("MiLB"), the governing body of Minor League Baseball.

Michael R. Dimino is Professor of Law at Widener University Commonwealth Law School, where he teaches and writes in a wide variety of subjects, including constitutional law and election law. Professor Dimino graduated from the State University of New York at Buffalo and Harvard Law School, and served as Articles Editor of the Harvard Journal of Law & Public Policy. Following law school, Professor Dimino clerked for Associate Judge Albert Rosenblatt of the New York State Court of Appeals, Senior Circuit Judge Laurence Silberman of the United States Court of Appeals for the District of Columbia Circuit, and Judge Paul Friedman of the United States District Court for the District of Columbia. Professor Dimino is a two-time recipient of Widener's Faculty Scholarship Award, a two-time recipient of Widener's Outstanding Professor Award, and a Fulbright scholar.

Index

Note: Page number followed by 'n' refer to notes.